Clinical Negligence
A Practical Guide

To Victoria and Livy

Clinical Negligence
A Practical Guide

Seventh Edition

General Editor of the Seventh Edition

Andrew Buchan, LLB (Hons)
Barrister, Cloisters

Contributors

Andrew Buchan, LLB (Hons)
Barrister, Cloisters

Dr Thomas Boyd
General Practitioner

Simon Dyer
Barrister, Cloisters

Sarah Fraser Butlin
Barrister, Cloisters

Hannah Godfrey
Barrister, Cloisters

Caron Heyes
Solicitor, Blake Lapthorne

Patricia Hitchcock QC
Barrister, Cloisters

Catherine Hopkins
Solicitor and Legal Director of AvMA

Linda Jacobs
Barrister, Cloisters

Nick Knowles
Solicitor, Stewarts Solicitors

William Latimer-Sayer, LLB (Hons), MA
Barrister, Cloisters

His Honour Judge Denzil Lush
Senior Judge of the Court of Protection

Martyn McLeish
Barrister, Cloisters

Ravi Nayer
Employed Barrister, Kennedys LLP

Catriona Stirling
Barrister, Cloisters

Lisa Sullivan
Barrister, Cloisters

The First to the Sixth Editions were written by Charles Lewis, of the Middle Temple, Barrister, former open classical scholar of Oriel College, Oxford.

Bloomsbury Professional

Bloomsbury Professional Limited, Maxwelton House, 41–43 Boltro Road, Haywards Heath, West Sussex, RH16 1BJ

© Bloomsbury Professional Limited 2012

Bloomsbury Professional is an imprint of Bloomsbury Publishing Plc

A CIP Catalogue record for this book is available from the British Library.

ISBN   978 1 84766 673 4

Typeset by Phoenix Photosetting, Chatham, Kent
Printed and bound in Great Britain by CPI Group (UK) Ltd, Croydon, CR0 4YY

Foreword

Clinical negligence litigation poses unique challenges for all those who work in this field. For claimants and defendants alike, the process which governs the judicial determination of allegations of negligent medical treatment is complex, time-consuming and often traumatic.

Litigation in this area has, however, come a long way since the very first edition of this excellent book arrived on the scene. Judges who are called upon to try these cases are now invariably assisted by highly experienced practitioners who have mastered the principles, understand the issues and, through meticulous preparation, ensure that the disputes are explored and resolved thoroughly and efficiently.

The fact that there is now such a high level of skill and experience amongst clinical negligence practitioners is due, in no small part, to the availability of knowledge, practical guidance and wise advice of the kind to be found in this, the seventh edition of the text, from well-respected experts in the field.

The reader has access to comprehensive guidance on almost every aspect of this litigation, including a full analysis of the relevant legal principles governing breach of duty, causation, consent and the calculation of compensation, the thorny issues of funding and costs, the way in which clinical services are delivered in this country, complaints procedures, and procedures in the Court of Protection. The way in which human rights are engaged and protected in this area is also considered, together with an insightful analysis of the important role played by expert witnesses in this litigation.

The authors are to be commended for delivering such an informative, readable and comprehensive account of the current state of play in relation to every aspect of clinical litigation. This book merits a place on the bookshelf of anyone who works in this area, or who is interested in understanding more about the way in which disputes concerning medical treatment are presently conducted and resolved in this country.

Laura Cox
Royal Courts of Justice
February 2012

Acknowledgements

First, I would like to thank Charles Lewis for writing the first six editions of this excellent work and for choosing me to carry on the editorship.

Secondly I would like to thank Jemma Lee for her research. I first met Jemma when she was an intern at Cloisters. She is very keen to practice in clinical negligence and having achieved a First Class LLB from the University of Warwick and a Wolfson, Denning and Hardwicke scholarship from Lincoln's Inn, I am sure it won't be long before she does.

Caron Heyes is grateful to John White, clinical negligence team leader and Partner at Blake Lapthorn Solicitors, for his support and commenting upon Chapter 2.

Patricia Hitchcock would like to acknowledge the research that Catherine Collins did.

Nick Knowles would also like to thank his colleague Julian Chamberlayne, for his kind advice and support.

Lastly I would like to thank my fellow authors (particularly Martyn McLeish) and the staff at Bloomsbury Professional (particularly Kiran Goss) who were very supportive and showed great patience after the hiccups caused by my road traffic accident in 2007. Thankfully, I have recovered.

Andrew Buchan
Cloisters
February 2012

Contents

PART FIVE

The authors

ANDREW BUCHAN – GENERAL EDITOR

Author of Chapters 1 Introduction, 9 The proof of negligence, 10 Consent, 13 Psychiatric injury, co-author of Chapter 16 Procedure from issue to trial ('Multi-party actions' section) and all the Appendices

Practitioner publications

1   General Editor and co-author of *Clinical Negligence* (Bloomsbury Professional, 7th edition 2012).
2   He conceived and wrote the first draft of *Personal Injury Schedules – Calculating Damages* (Bloomsbury Professional, 3rd edition 2010), the leading practitioner textbook on schedules of loss.
3   General Editor and co-author of *Personal Injury Practice* (Bloomsbury Professional, 5th edition 2008).

He has written numerous articles on clinical negligence and personal injury. He has lectured widely on both subjects. For the last four years he has spoken on webinars for personal injury and schedules of special damage.

Directory references

In *1996 Chambers* rated him as a *leading junior* in clinical negligence. He is recommended in both *Chambers UK* and *Legal 500* for personal injury. The *Legal 500 (2012)* describes him as 'incredibly knowledgeable'. *Chambers UK (2012)* describes him as 'utterly fearless' and 'driven and wholehearted in his approach'.

Experience in clinical negligence

Andrew was called to the Bar in 1981. In 1987 he specialised in clinical negligence after he was put on the AvMA expert database for counsel. This resulted in him advising upon a wide variety of cases with many reported in Clinical Risk. He has tried not to specialise in particular types of clinical negligence and has therefore accumulated a wide experience of different types of clinical negligence cases. These include multi-party actions at a generic and case counsel level.

He brought the first successful case for the negligent sterilization of a woman with no children. He probably brought the first successful case for damages caused by a twisting masonoeuve fracture during childbirth; negligent stillbirth; failure to diagnose a subarachnoid haemorrhage; cervical cancer treatment causing infected tissue and fistula formation; failed sterilization due to failure of the filshie clip. His limitation cases included cases on knowledge and s 33 discretion. The appropriate test for a compulsory patient detailed under the Mental Health Act 1983. Whether knowledge that an operation had been unsuccessful was the same as knowledge of injury caused by negligence. Section 33 discretion exercised for misleading medical advice.

He acted for a US Air Force Sergeant who had received negligent medical treatment in a UK hospital whilst on service in the UK. International law questions of jurisdiction and the Status of Forces Act. He has had several successful claims for the negligence treatment by orthopaedic surgeons. He has conducted successful cases against ambulance services for delay. He has conducted many cases concerning consent to treatment involving from posterior cruciate ligament repair to consent to stereotactic radiosurgery.

Andrew has been generic and case counsel in several multi-party actions, from Myodil to Volclay.

More recently he has succeeded in several cases involving the failure to diagnose and/or treat malignant melanoma, meningitis, and non-Hodgkin's lymphoma.

Andrew has been a CEDR accredited mediator since 2000.

He is a member of PIBA, AvMA, Inquest Lawyer's Group, PNBA, ELBA, and BIICL. He was on the Bar Council from 1995–2003.

CARON HEYES

Author of Chapter 2 The structure of the National Health Service, and contributed to Chapter 17 The inquest ('Funding and the recoverability of costs' section)

Caron is a claimant clinical negligence specialist and heads the Blake Lapthorn Clinical Negligence London team. She is a member of the Law Society Clinical Negligence Accreditation Panel and APIL.

The majority of her practice is in clinical negligence claims across a broad spectrum of claim types, including claims for injuries arising out of participation in drugs trials (including contract issues), negligent IVF treatment, negligent treatment at birth and/or during the neonatal period, substandard cardiothoracic surgery, orthopaedic surgery, and oncological treatment. She is experienced in supporting clients through the complaints process and with any referrals to the GMC or NMC.

As well as working for Blake Lapthorn, Caron works on a voluntary basis with Action against Medical Accidents (AvMA) (since May 2009) and has provided input into various campaigns and policy issues, consultations, and conferences, and helped set up their Inquest Project. Between November 2010 and December 2011 AvMA were a core participant at the Mid Staffordshire NHS Foundation Trust Public Inquiry, and Caron worked with AvMA's CEO on that Inquiry.

Caron regularly speaks at legal courses provided by AvMA and CLT, provides in-house training for charities, and has had various articles published in specialist press on a range of issues.

CATHERINE HOPKINS

Author of Chapter 3 Non legal remedies
Catherine Hopkins is a solicitor who specialises in clinical negligence. She is currently Legal Director of Action against Medical Accidents (AvMA) a charity that provides advice and assistance to clients who have complaints or claims relating to medical treatment and campaigns for patient safety and justice.

She qualified as a solicitor in 1997 and worked in private practice for 11 years specialising in clinical negligence and is accredited to AvMA's specialist clinical negligence panel.

As Legal Director of AvMA she heads up the Legal Services Department and is responsible for devising and implementing legal policy and strategy for the charity. She is also a qualified general nurse, midwife and health visitor. Catherine has worked previously with Penningtons and Darbys solicitors.

CATRIONA STIRLING

Author of Chapter 4 Legal remedies
Catriona is a tenant at Cloisters, having joined chambers in 2010 following successful completion of her pupillage. She advises and acts across the whole range of personal injury and clinical negligence cases.

Catriona's personal injury practice encompasses drafting, advisory work and court appearances and she has appeared in a number of fast track trials and interim hearings in the county courts. Her growing clinical negligence practice includes drafting pleadings and advising in low value claims.

Catriona has recently spent two legal terms working as Judicial Assistant to Lord Justice Mummery and Lord Justice Pill in the Court of Appeal.

MARTYN MCLEISH

Author of Chapters 5 The duty of care, 6 Breach of duty and strict liability, and 25 Costs
Martyn practises at Cloisters. He is recommended in the *Legal 500* for clinical negligence and noted to have 'a very reassuring clear structure to his approach'. His practice covers a wide variety of claims. Recent cases include claims for wrongful birth arising from the failure to diagnose spine abnormality, a claim against a private hospital for failure to consent to plastic surgery, and several ongoing claims for negligently performed spinal surgery. Martyn has particular experience of high value quantum cases arising from brain injury at birth. He is a member of the Bar Council

CFA Panel and the Executive Committee of PIBA and lectures regularly on clinical negligence practice and costs.

SIMON DYER

Author of Chapters 7 Causation and damage and 8 Foreseeability and remoteness

Simon Dyer was called to the Bar in 1987 and is a tenant at Cloisters. He has specialised in personal injury claims since 1990 and clinical negligence since 2000. He acts mostly for claimants and is instructed largely by specialist clinical negligence and personal injury firms.

Simon is usually instructed as sole counsel and conducts hearings, conferences and roundtable meetings, as well as drafting complex pleadings, including large schedules and written advice.

He is currently recommended in *Chambers and Partners 2011* for both clinical negligence and personal injury. *Chambers and Partners 2012* says that Simon is 'a "good all-rounder," who is both "good with clients" and in court. He regularly acts as sole counsel in high-value claims'.

He is also recommended for personal injury and clinical negligence in the *Legal 500 (2011)*.

Simon's publications include *Gross negligence manslaughter*, Clinical Risk, January 2004 and *Claims for psychiatric injury, caused by hospital misinformation* Clinical Risk, May 2002.

Recent highlights include *K* v *Powys*, a £5 million claim for a claimant who suffered brain damage due to misprescription of an anti-epileptic drug in hospital and *C* v *Kettering Hospital*, a £7 million claim for quadriplegia caused by hypoxia during child birth.

SARAH FRASER BUTLIN

Author of Chapters 11 Wrongful birth and 12 The Congenital Disabilities Act 1976

Sarah Fraser Butlin is a tenant at Cloisters and is a clinical negligence practitioner. She is experienced in high value cerebral palsy cases, as well as matters such as negligent laparoscopic cholecystectomy, failed vasectomy and alopecia. Sarah has a particular interest in matters involving unusual and ground-breaking legal points. She has recently settled an unlawful killing claim involving Arts 2 and 8 issues. She is currently instructed on another case arguing negligent misstatement and intended beneficiary points.

Sarah also has a strong academic profile, including as an Affiliated Lecturer in Labour Law at the University of Cambridge and acting as an external examiner for SOAS University of London.

She uses this to excellent effect, particularly in her appellate work.

Sarah has also authored the following:

- *Clinical negligence and Article 8 – pushing the boundaries?* Clinical Risk, May 2011.
- *Reverse indemnities: friend or foe?* Clinical Risk, January 2008 .
- The Personal Injury section of the 17th edition of *Bullen and Leake*.

Highlight cases include:

- *Ketley* v *Hull and East Yorks NHS Trust* – unlawful killing claim following extubation, successful settlement.
- *Dakin* v *Doncaster Central NHS PCT* – successful settlement of very substantial stress at work claim; junior to Simon Taylor QC.

WILLIAM LATIMER-SAYER

Author of Chapter 14 Economic loss

William specialises in catastrophic personal injury and clinical negligence. He has a special interest in quantum and the majority of his work is related to contested assessment of damages hearings. He is consistently highly-rated by the independent legal directories, being named as one of only two 'star' individuals in London for personal injury work by *Chambers and Partners* and a Band 1 junior by both *Chambers and Partners* and the *Legal 500* for clinical negligence.

Although he accepts work on behalf of claimants and defendants, his practice is predominantly claimant based. William is the General Editor of *Schedules of Loss: Calculating Damages* (Bloomsbury Professional, 3rd edition 2010), the leading practitioner textbook on schedules of loss. In 2011 following an invitation from the Chairman, he became a member of the Ogden Working party, which is responsible for drafting the Ogden Tables, used by all practitioners and judges to assess damages in personal injury and clinical negligence cases.

William was nominated for the Chambers and Partners' Personal Injury Junior of the Year in 2008, 2009 and 2010, winning in 2008 and 2010.

RAVI NAYER

Author of Chapters 15 Procedure pre-issue and 16 Procedure from issue to trial

Ravi Nayer is an employed barrister at Kennedys LLP. He is a specialist in cases which have an insurance or international element, and whilst at the Bar and in employed practice has represented patients, dentists, GPs, surgeons, and insurers. He has experience of product liability and multi-party claims, especially the unique evidential and procedural challenges arising from these cases. Ravi recently served as the Judicial Assistant to the President of the Queen's Bench Division in the Court of Appeal. He has an LLM in Advanced Civil Procedure, and has written widely on procedural and substantive legal issues for, amongst others, the NLJ, JPIL and BPIN, including most recently on the issue of hospitals' non-delegable duties in the context of the outsourcing of genetic testing. Ravi is a trustee and former chair of City and Hackney Mind.

LINDA JACOBS

Author of Chapters 17 The inquest and 23 Wales
Linda Jacobs is a tenant at Cloisters who specialises in clinical negligence, personal injury, and healthcare law; inquest and professional regulatory law; and Criminal Injury Compensation Authority Appeal Panel claims. Linda has extensive advisory and advocacy experience in a broad range of clinical negligence cases, including failure to diagnose and incorrect treatment (for example, failure to investigate and refer a baby with urinary symptoms resulting in renal failure; and negligent hip replacement surgery resulting in permanent disability); delayed diagnosis of cancer; fatal accidents claims (for example, failure to diagnose and treat a myocardial infarction; and failure to ensure adequate artificial ventilation); failure to obtain consent, including a successful claim for aggravated damages; high value catastrophic injury claims, including birth-related brain injury and neurological injury; claims involving negligent nursing care; and dental negligence claims. Her personal injury practice incorporates work-related injuries; occupational illness and disease; road traffic accidents; product liability; dangerous animal claims; and civil claims under the Protection from Harassment Act 1997. Linda has particular expertise in representing families and hospitals/care homes at inquests often preceding successful civil litigation claims. In addition, Linda has experience of appellate advisory work following inquests. Linda has been instructed by healthcare practitioners in cases before the General Medical Council and the Nursing and Midwifery Council.
Prior to being called to the Bar, Linda was a Sister in intensive care in one of London's leading teaching hospitals. Her specialist medical knowledge and experience means that she is comfortable dealing with complex medical facts and issues, expert evidence, and complex quantum cases.

LISA SULLIVAN

Author of Chapter 18 Limitation
Lisa Sullivan is a tenant at Cloisters and is a specialist in clinical negligence and personal injury.
Lisa has experience of a wide range of clinical negligence claims, from high-value cerebral palsy and spinal injury cases including cauda equina, to claims involving wrongful birth, delayed diagnosis of cancer, negligent colorectal surgery, negligent hip and knee replacement, laser eye surgery, treatment affecting fertility and miscarriage and dental negligence claims.
Her experience in personal injury covers road traffic claims, including severe spinal injury, and work-related injuries. Workplace claims have included disease claims; fatal accident claims; secondary victim claims; injuries following exposure to moving parts of machinery; manual handling claims; work equipment claims and occupational stress.
Lisa also has experience of a full range of quantum issues and in particular local authority care issues.

She has lectured on a variety of subjects including causation, limitation, capacity, Ogden 6, Workplace Regulations and fraudulent/exaggerated claims. Lisa is an advocacy trainer for PIBA and Inner Temple and has trained on the South Eastern Circuit Advanced Advocacy Course.

Lisa is recommended in both *Chambers UK* and *Legal 500* for clinical negligence. In *Chambers 2010* Lisa was described as 'exceptionally bright' and impressed with her 'down to earth manner with clients'.

Some of her highlight cases include *Crofton* v *NHSLA* regarding the impact of local authority provision of care or direct payments on a tortfeasor's liability for care costs; and on whether damages and the income arising from them should be taken into account by the local authority in assessing the need for care and in the assessment of means, *Collins* v *Plymouth City Council* [2009] EWHC 3279 (Admin), a judicial review on similar issues and *B* v *Hospital Foundation Trust* regarding an incomplete tetraplegia following missed spinal fracture in a 69-year-old which settled for £1.1 million.

DOCTOR THOMAS BOYD

Co-author of Chapter 19 The medical records

Dr Boyd is a general practitioner in Bushey, Hertfordshire. He trained in Cambridge and at University College Hospital. He has over 30 years of clinical experience and has been extensively involved in educating and examining general practitioners, which gives him an insight into the standard of care expected of a minimally competent doctor. He was Associate Dean of Postgraduate General Practice and is a senior examiner for the Royal College of General Practitioners. He is an experienced expert, having provided reports in over 1000 cases for claimants' solicitors, medical defence organisations, the General Medical Council, the Crown Prosecution Service and the Treasury Solicitor. He has given evidence in Court in civil and criminal proceedings and to the General Medical Council. He has addressed AvMA's annual clinical negligence conference, contributed to the AvMA Medical and Legal Journal and to another textbook. He has delivered seminars on medical negligence issues to many groups of doctors and lawyers.

PATRICIA HITCHCOCK QC

Author of Chapter 20 Experts

Patricia is one of the three silks heading the Cloisters clinical negligence and personal injury team. She is a specialist in catastrophic injury, clinical negligence and related administrative and regulatory matters, and a mediator (CEDR accredited 2003). Regularly instructed for many years in major seven-figure cases, she is especially interested in brain and spinal injuries, oncology and mental health, and cases involving children and adolescents.

Before coming to the Bar, Patricia worked as a non-fiction book editor, and was elected Mother of the NUJ Chapel at Hutchinson Books. She was called to the Bar in 1988 and embarked initially on a broad-based common law practice – personal injury, employment, discrimination, education –

dominated by criminal defence, with around 100 Crown Court trials. She specialised in medical law in 1996 and took silk in 2011. She has chaired three AvMA medico-legal conferences; is an editorial committee member and contributor to the AvMA Medical and Legal Journal; and is also co-author of Division VI: Limitation in *Butterworths Personal Injury Litigation Service*. She is married to a sculptor, with two adult children.

HANNAH GODFREY

Author of Chapter 21 Human rights
Hannah is a barrister at Cloisters. Called to the bar in 2002 she has been a clinical negligence specialist since 2008 and is recommended by the *Legal 500 (2011)* as an 'analytical' up-and-comer.

Hannah is regularly instructed as sole counsel in a wide range of complex clinical negligence claims; she is particularly interested in colorectal and other abdominal surgery, the diagnosis and treatment of orthopaedic injuries and conditions (including spinal) and ophthalmology.

Hannah has an unusual breadth of advocacy experience for a junior in her field, drawing on a busy immigration and employment tribunal practice in her early years at the bar. She is developing considerable expertise in specialised quantum issues as a junior in maximum value cerebral palsy and spinal cases, drafting detailed excel schedules claiming up to and over £10 million.

Hannah predominantly represents claimants. She has a special interest and expertise in fatal accident claims and inquests. She is a member of PIBA, AvMA and the Inquest Lawyers' group.

HIS HONOUR JUDGE DENZIL LUSH (SENIOR JUDGE OF THE COURT OF PROTECTION)

Author of Chapter 22 Capacity and the Court of Protection
Denzil Lush read history at University College London, and law at Corpus Christi College Cambridge. He was admitted as a solicitor in England & Wales in 1978, and is also qualified to practise as a solicitor and notary public in Scotland. He was formerly a partner in Anstey & Thompson (now known as Foot Anstey), Solicitors, Exeter, and was a part-time Chairman of the Social Security Appeals Tribunal from 1994 to 1996, before being appointed Master of the Court of Protection on 24 April 1996.

He became the Senior Judge of the Court of Protection when the Mental Capacity Act 2005 came into force on 1 October 2007. Article 4 of the Mental Capacity Act 2005 (Transitional and Consequential Provisions) Order 2007 provides that he is to be treated as a circuit judge.

He is the author of *Elderly Clients: A Precedent Manual* (Jordan Publishing, 1996; 3rd edition 2010), *Cohabitation: Law Practice and Precedents* (Jordan Publishing, 1993; 4th edition 2009) and *Cretney & Lush on Lasting and Enduring Powers of Attorney* (Jordan Publishing, 6th edition, 2009), and has contributed chapters to various medical and legal reference books. He is one of the consulting editors of Court of Protection Law Reports.

Judge Lush was formerly a member of the Law Society's Mental Health and Disability Sub-Committee. He was a member of the British Medical Association's working party that drew up the Code of Practice on Advance Statements about Medical Treatment, and contributed to *Assessing Mental Capacity: Guidance for Doctors and Lawyers*, published jointly by the British Medical Association and the Law Society in 1995 (3rd edition 2009). He was also a member of the working party on structured settlements, which reported to the Master of the Rolls in August 2002.

He is a judicial member of STEP (the Society of Trust and Estate Practitioners), and was presented with the Geoffrey Shindler Award for Outstanding Contribution to the Profession at the STEP Private Client Awards 2009/10. He is a patron of SFE (Solicitors for the Elderly); was formerly a trustee of the PEOPIL Foundation (Pan-European Organisation of Personal Injuries Lawyers); and was a member of the international team of lawyers who drafted the Yokohama Declaration on Adult Guardianship Law in 2010.

NICK KNOWLES

Author of Chapter 24 Funding

Nick Knowles had 20 years' experience in all aspects of civil litigation, much of it high profile, before joining Stewarts Law LLP as a partner in 1999. Since then he has specialised in claimant clinical negligence cases. In 2000 he became a member of the AvMA specialist clinical negligence panel. He is a Fellow of the Royal Society of Medicine and a Fellow of APIL.

He specialises in catastrophic brain and spinal cord injury cases. He was recommended in *Chambers 2009* as a solicitor 'who thinks deeply about his cases and really knows what he's doing'. He was mentioned in 2010 as 'a highly experienced practitioner with a clear vision of what he wants – he will go the extra mile for his clients'. In *Chambers 2011* he 'impresses with his sound judgement'.

He acted for the claimant in the important case of *Masterman-Lister*. He has had numerous substantial settlements and last year he achieved total compensation on behalf of clients in the region of £20 million.

Acronyms

BMLR   Butterworths' *Medico-Legal Reports*, published from June 1992.

JPIL   *Journal of Personal Injury Litigation.*

Med LR The *Medical Law Reports*. From the beginning of 1998 the series has been published by Lloyds of London Press (the citation has been changed to [2001] Lloyd's Rep Med).

ML   *Medical Litigation*: this is the journal that since the beginning of 1998 kept practitioners up to date with all the latest developments in the medical negligence field – judgments with commentaries, writs, settlements, appeals set down, news and views, articles, etc. It ceased hard copy publication at the end of 2004. Its management continues to run two websites: www.medneg.com for practitioners, and www.medicalclaims.co.uk for the public.

MLC   *Medical Litigation Cases*: this is the invaluable database of full transcripts on the Internet at *www.medneg.com*, originally conceived by *Medical Litigation* and now run by *Medical Litigation Online*. Access is by subscription and every UK judgment relevant to medical claims since the end of 1997, as well as many overseas judgments, is posted in full transcript. Also, significant older medical cases are currently being posted all the while. In addition, every other UK medical negligence decision from every available hard copy source appears in summary form in the medical negligence index section. In line with the switch to electronic publishing and citation, MLC will be dropping the citation of the year and will only read, eg, *A* v *B* MLC 00999, rather than *A* v *B* [2001] MLC 00999. For that reason some MLC cases in the text are given a year reference and others are not. Where I have given only a MLC reference for a case I have in any event added the year as I think that information is helpful. The website also contains many articles, news items, and indexed lists of lawyers and experts. The site has an excellent search engine. Anyone practising in the field of medical claims needs to subscribe to this website.

Table of statutes

References at the right-hand side of the column are to page numbers.

Table of statutory instruments

References at the right-hand side of the column are to page numbers.

Table of cases

References at the right-hand side of the column are to page numbers.

A

B

M

N

P

R

S

W

Z

Quotations

On law

In law, what plea so tainted and corrupt,
But, being seasoned with a gracious voice,
Obscures the show of evil?

The Merchant of Venice (Bassanio)

I must say that, as a litigant, I should dread a lawsuit beyond almost
anything else, short of sickness and death.

Judge Learned Hand

The definition of the duty of care is a matter for the law and the courts.
They cannot stand idly by if the profession, by an excess of paternalism,
denies their patients a real choice. In a word, the law will not permit the
medical profession to play God.

Sir John Donaldson MR

The problem with Bolam *is that it inhibited the courts exercising a*
restraining influence. The courts must recognise that theirs is essentially a
regulatory role and they should not interfere unless interference is justified.
But when interference is justified they must not be deterred from doing so
by any principle such as the fact that what has been done is in accord with
a practice approved of by a respectable body of medical opinion.

Lord Woolf (January 2001)

On medicine

Physicians of all men are most happy. What good success soever they have,
the world proclaimeth, and what faults they commit, the earth covereth.

Francis Quarles (1592-1644)

In the practice of surgery particularly, the public are exposed to great
risks from the number of ignorant persons professing a knowledge of the
art, without the least pretensions to the necessary qualifications, and they
often inflict very serious injury on those who are so unfortunate as to fall
into their hands.

Baron Garrow (1822)

The doctor is often more to be feared than the disease.

Old French proverb

Doctors are men who prescribe medicine of which they know little to human beings of whom they know nothing.

Voltaire

The primary function of the doctor is to entertain the patient while he gets better on his own.

Voltaire

Proper treatment will cure a cold in not more than seven days, but left to itself it will hang on for a week.

HG Felsen

It is unwise to place any profession or other body providing services to the public on a pedestal where their actions cannot be subject to close scrutiny. The greater the power the body has, the more important is this need.

Lord Woolf (January 2001)

Chapter 1

Introduction

Andrew Buchan

Is this the 1980s all over again?

As the French would say, 'Plus ça change, plus c'est la même chose'. As of 22 January 2012 the fate of the National Health Service appears to stand in the balance. The funding of clinical negligence litigation is, once again, under major review. Claimant's lawyers are being accused of being greedy and milking the system.

It is not the job of this textbook to attempt to answer why this is happening. Just to say that the scholar who has studied and relied upon the last six editions of this book will realise how the emphasis has changed from a necessarily litigious approach (where the claimant's lawyers were truly on the back foot against well organised and experienced defendant's lawyers) to the current state of affairs where there is greater equality of arms as a large number of claimant's legal battles have been won and claimant's lawyers are also more experienced. As a result, the emphasis has to be on recognising and dealing with complaints as soon as practicable and avoiding litigation if at all possible. The advice and principles set out in this book apply for conciliation as well as litigation.

This Seventh Edition reflects this modern approach. I have deliberately chosen a large selection of experienced clinical negligence practitioners to update and supplement the chapters of the Sixth Edition. The respective authors have been left to decide whether to amend Charles Lewis's Chapters or to re-write them from scratch. Some have chosen the latter, some have not.

A FASCINATING SUBJECT

> There is arguably no area of law that provokes such public interest, and so immediately, from the non-lawyer as clinical negligence.

Within the legal profession, the work has a cachet that ordinary personal injury does not. This is bemusing because some personal injury cases can be extremely complicated with respect to liability. Some clinical negligence cases less so. Lawyers, particularly counsel, are quick to say that they specialise in the field, even if their involvement is modest.

Many of the solicitors who are qualified to do the work form a tight-knit group, striving to outdo their rivals with some striking victory, and ever on the look-out for new ways of extending the boundaries of the clinical negligence claim.

Why does this branch of the law attract such interest and evoke so keen, often so emotional, a response from the lay person? It is partly because it is almost everyone's experience to have at one time or another been in the hands of the doctors, but, more importantly, it stems above all from the nature of the doctor's role. The patient looks to the physician on the one hand as the comforter and healer who will make him well and happy; he has the learning and the magic that will bring relief from fear and pain. The patient, whether consciously acknowledging it or not, longs to be relieved or comforted. All this gives the physician a hierophantic status. On the other hand, the patient resents his dependence and is not averse to debunking the myth; a myth, be it noted, that he has himself created. This relationship is not entirely dissimilar to the emotional duality that a child feels towards his parents. In an age where the child has learnt that obedience to parents is not necessarily the norm, parental control is less and less effective, and for today's children anything is permissible, it is not surprising that the divine aspect of the medical profession has taken a beating (aided enormously by their own well-publicised malpractices). There is perhaps something of a temptation when specialising in cases against the medical profession to regard it as a sort of crusade, as do many of those who specialise in actions against the police, as if not only policemen but also doctors represent some sort of authority figures with which one has not within oneself completely come to terms; and when that happens one forgets too easily the marvellous skills and devoted care that generally characterise the practice of medicine. But this is not a textbook on psychology; the issues raised here are merely by way of explanation for the fascination that lawsuits against the medical profession have for the ordinary member of the public and for the almost emotional response that they can arouse in lawyer and non-lawyer alike.

A similar attitude, based on archetypes, is found in respect of judges, where the archetype invests ordinary people with a patina of awful superiority. Because the unconscious mind is affected by the archetype of judge as stern dispenser of both wisdom and punishment the reality of the average judge is not perceived. While proper respect is due to every person, of whatever station in life, the holder of judicial office is not by reason of his appointment alone imbued with any special qualities. All that one might conclude is that the judge, as indeed the lawyer, is likely to be more in his head than the average person, who has not spent most of their life arguing, as Swift said of lawyers in 1726, 'in words multiplied for the purpose and in a language no other mortal understands, that black is white and white is black, according as he is paid'.

The above, largely philosophical, first paragraph was written in 1987 for the first edition of this work. It remains valid comment today, nearly three centuries later, even though the practical picture of clinical negligence, at ground level as it were, and the workings of the courts and the lawyers involved, as well as the attitude of the public to suing for compensation, has radically altered.

THE GROWTH OF LITIGATION

There is no doubt that clinical negligence litigation has grown enormously over the last 30 years. In earlier times such a claim was unusual and stood little chance of success. That was partly because it was not within the current ethos to accuse the god-like doctors of incompetent treatment: patients shrank from such a course and judges did not approve of it. Lord Denning used to say that to prove a doctor guilty of negligence required a higher standard of proof than if the accusation was levelled against a non-professional.[1] In 1953 Finnemore J said:

> It is the duty of a doctor to exercise reasonable skill and care, but a simple mistake in diagnosis or treatment is not of itself negligence. The court is not bound to shut its eyes to the fact that there are quite a few cases at the present time in which doctors are sued for negligence. That may arise from the changing relationship between doctor and patient, but *it* matters not. There is a considerable onus on the court to see that persons do not easily obtain damages simply because there is some medical or surgical mistake made. But the court will not shrink from facing the issue if it finds that the doctor has failed to give to a case the proper skill and care which patients have a right to expect.[2]

That represented the traditional view: insistence that medical mistakes did not necessarily involve negligence, regardless of the consequences, and a friendly nod in the direction of the patient.

Practicalities, both social and legal, were also against the patient. Few doctors were prepared to give evidence for the patient. It took years to create lists of fair-minded specialists who would give an impartial opinion on the standard of care. Even now, if the patient goes to the wrong expert, he will get a whitewash (whitewashes are still the forte of a fair number of oft-appearing defence experts, regardless of their parroting their impartial duty owed to the court). In earlier years statements of witnesses and the evidence of experts were not disclosed until they came to the witness box. It was trial by ambush. Gradually the scene changed, thanks to the persistent efforts of those, like Action for Victims of Medical Accidents (now known as Action against Medical Accidents – AvMA) and the lawyers who supported it, who fought unrelentingly for the rights of the patient. Now, due particularly to the Woolf reforms, a cards-on-the-table approach is a living and mandatory reality. But there are still one or two judges, usually appointed from a successful defence practice at the Bar, who are unreasonably slow to find for the patient and who will always, if at all possible, 'prefer' the evidence of the defence expert to that of the claimant's expert.

What is more difficult to pinpoint is the growth of medical negligence litigation, if any, over the last few years. Governments will produce statistics purporting to prove whatever they want to prove, for example

---

1   In *Hucks* v *Cole* [1993] 4 Med LR 393, CA, Lord Denning said that a charge of negligence against a professional man was serious. It stood on a different footing to a charge of negligence against the driver of a motor car. The consequences were far more serious. It affected his professional status and reputation. The burden of proof was correspondingly greater. As the charge was so grave, so should the proof be clear.

2   *Edler* v *Greenwich and Deptford Hospital Management Committee* (1953) Times, 7 March.

exponential growth in NHS liability for medical claims; but usually their statistics are biased, often demonstrably so, because they are politicians and their statistics are therefore unreliable. It is unlikely, with substantial reductions in the eligibility of legal aid for medical claims and the reluctance of the Legal Services Commission to give the green light to any claim, that there has been any growth in this litigation over the last few years or that there will be any in the future. What has pushed up substantially the amount of total NHS outlay on claims (so that awards of well over £4 million no longer occasion surprise) is the general increase in the calculation of future loss (due to judicial acceptance of what is known as the 2.5% multiplier), and increased life expectancy for injured persons thanks to progress in medical care. Beside the effect of this change, the parsimonious increase in general damages authorised not long ago by the Court of Appeal pales into insignificance.

Such evidence as there is strongly suggests that the actual number of claims has been falling over the last few years. This is hardly surprising given the aforesaid reluctance of the legal aid authority to fund these claims and the grudging way they authorise any increase in the scope of a legal aid certificate. More positively, the availability of mediation for small claims where money is not the main objective, the expert handling of most claims by certificated solicitors and the early clarification of claims and defences under the clinical negligence protocol have all helped to reduce the number of claims commenced, and, even more so, the number of claims actually brought to trial.[3]

A note on aggravated and exemplary damages

In some legal claims, substantial further amounts can be awarded on top of general damages for aggravated or exemplary damages, though well short of the huge jury awards for punitive damages that are made from time to time in USA jurisdictions.[4] The suggestion is not infrequently made in medical claims that aggravated or exemplary damages should be claimed, usually on the basis that, as perceived by the patient, the negligence has been gross or the behaviour of the medical personnel highly offensive. As explained below, such claims will rarely be successful.

The distinction between the two sorts of damages is that aggravated damages are given to compensate the claimant when the harm done to him by a wrongful act has been aggravated by the manner in which the act was done. Exemplary damages, on the other hand, are intended (within defined limits – see below) to punish the defendant for opprobrious conduct, ie a form of punitive damages.

It has been said more than once that neither aggravated nor exemplary damages have any place in medical negligence actions in this country (see *Barbara* v *Home Office* (1984) 134 NLJ 888; *G* v *North Tees Health Authority* [1989] FCR 53; *Kralj* v *McGrath* [1986] 1 All ER 54). In *H* v

---

3   There is an interesting editorial on this topic by Peter Walsh in *Clinical Risk*, Vol 9, Issue 3, p 108.
4   Punitive damages in the USA are of a different order. In October 1997 a South Carolina jury awarded $262.5m against the Chrysler Corporation in favour of the parents of a six year old boy who was thrown to his death out of a Dodge Caravan when the lock failed. £250 million of this award was punitive damages.

Ministry of Defence [1991] 2 QB 103 the Court of Appeal did suggest that exemplary damages might be awarded if the defendants had abused their authority. The ambit of exemplary damages as laid down by the House of Lords in the two leading cases of *Rookes v Barnard* [1964] AC 1129 and *Cassell Co Ltd v Broome* [1972] AC 1027 is narrow (only available where there had been oppressive conduct by the executive or similar body, or the defendant had sought to make a profit from his wrongdoing).[5] In *Kuddus v Chief Constable of Leicestershire Constabulary* [2001] 2 WLR 1789 the House of Lords extended the catchment area for exemplary damages somewhat by holding that their relevance was not limited to torts where the claim had already been recognised before 1964 as one to which exemplary damages could be applicable. However, the judges were clearly unhappy about the general confusion over exemplary damages, and certainly there is nothing in their speeches to benefit the claimant in a medical negligence action. Nevertheless we may usefully note that Dyson J awarded aggravated damages (15% of his award of general damages) against a dentist who, callously and simply for his own profit, recommended and carried out all manner of unnecessary treatments on a variety of patients (*Appleton v Garrett* [1997] 8 Med LR 75).

In *Hunter Area Health Service v Marchewski* [2001] MLC 0296 the New South Wales Court of Appeal considered the question whether aggravated damages were ever appropriate to a negligence claim. The judge had awarded a further 20% on top of general damages on the ground that the hospital's decision not to resuscitate a doomed child without telling the parents (who would not have consented to such a course) callously increased their suffering (it was otherwise a reasonable medical decision). In the event, the appeal court did not decide the broad issue (though it signified its agreement with the English authorities), but set aside the award on the narrower ground that to admit aggravated damages where the claim was being brought for pure psychiatric injury would be inconsistent with the current parameters prescribed for claims for psychiatric injury.[6]

The common law in New Zealand is different. There they are not, as we are, 'still toiling in the chains of *Rookes v Barnard*', to borrow the expression used in the judgment in September 2002 of the Privy Council in the medical case of *A v Bottrill* MLC 0854, [2000] UKPC 44. Free from such constraints, the court decided in that case that even intentional misconduct or conscious recklessness was not in principle an essential prerequisite of the court's discretionary jurisdiction to award exemplary damages, for it extended to all cases of tortious wrongdoing where the defendant's conduct satisfied a criterion of outrageousness. In this case the doctor, whose false reporting rate on pap smears in relation to cervical cancer was 50% or higher, had clearly been outrageously negligent, but the New Zealand Court of Appeal had wrongly held that the claim must fail as he had not been shown to have been consciously reckless. So the

---

5   The court said in *Kralj v McGrath* (supra) that there was no precedent for awarding damages for anger and indignation aroused by a defendant's high-handed way of dealing with the relevant incident (in this case the obstetric negligence at the delivery of a child had been horrific and the defendant's response thereafter highly unsatisfactory).

6   The Law Commission produced a report on exemplary and aggravated damages in 1997 (Cmnd No. 247).

issue fell to be re-determined by that Court. It is clear, however, that without intentional misconduct or conscious recklessness the conduct would have to be, by objective standards, quite appalling to justify an award and so such cases will be very rare. If ever English law escapes the trammels of *Rookes* v *Barnard*, this Privy Council judgment is likely to be much in point.

In *Richardson* v *Howie* [2004] All ER (D) 74 (Aug), Ms Richardson and Mr Howie had a volatile relationship. Whilst on holiday in June 2000, they had an argument which escalated violently, culminating in Mr Howie hitting Ms Richardson several times around the head and neck with a bottle. He continued to do so after the bottle had broken with the force. He also slammed her head against the floor when she would not obey his instruction to 'shut the fuck up'. Ms Richardson suffered multiple lacerations and bruises. She subsequently brought a claim against Mr Howie for assault and battery. The Court of Appeal decided that the correct approach was to factor these aggravating elements suffered by the claimant into her compensatory award for general damages. Save possibly in a wholly exceptional case, there should be no additional award beyond that required to compensate the claimant.

THE EXPENSE OF LITIGATION

Whoever wins a medical negligence action the taxpayer, and/or other patients, are the losers. The lawyers always get something out of it, but who would begrudge them that? If the patient achieves compensation the NHS has to pay the costs of both sides as well as the compensation.

All the recent changes to funding and to the NHS generally, as well as to legal procedures, are dealt with in more detail in the next few chapters. But however clinical negligence litigation is funded and whatever the rules of procedure, it will always be expensive because every medical claim with apparent potential requires from the outset that the medical records be obtained, sorted and carefully investigated, that at least one and probably more than one expert report be obtained from carefully selected independent experts, and that then, unless liability is admitted, the claim be subjected to protracted and complex argument over the content, acceptability and consequences of the medical care afforded to the patient.

ON THE OTHER HAND

The cry is often heard from certain quarters to the effect that greedy patients, over-indulgent judges and, worst of all, unprincipled lawyers, are bringing the NHS to its knees, to the general detriment of the public, and that something has to be done about the growth of clinical negligence claims and the huge rise in the number and the quantum of compensation awards. Yet some of the foremost authorities on the subject offer a different view. In January 2001 at University College, London, Lord Woolf said that in the past courts had been excessively deferential to the medical profession but that this automatic assumption of beneficence had been dented. He said it was unwise to place any profession or other body providing services to the public on a pedestal where their actions could not be subject to close scrutiny. The courts should take a more robust view of negligence by the medical profession and not be deterred by the accepted test for negligence that asked whether what had been done was in accord with a respectable body of medical opinion. He said he could not help believing that the behaviour of the medical personnel involved in recent scandals betrayed a lack of appreciation of the limits of their responsibility. Though not motivated by personal gain, they had lost sight of their power and authority, and had acted as though they were able to take any action they thought desirable, irrespective of the views of others. That over-deferential approach was captured by the phrase 'doctor knows best'. The contemporary approach was a more critical one. It could be said that doctor knows best if he acted reasonably and logically and got his facts right. Lord Woolf also pointed out the increase of more than 30% over the previous year in the number of complaints to the General Medical Council and said this had called the very future of that body into question. He said other factors had made judges less deferential: the difficulties people had in bringing successful claims; increasing awareness of patients' rights; the closer scrutiny of doctors by courts in places such as Canada and Australia, and the scale of medical negligence litigation, which was a 'disaster area'. Lord Woolf said all this indicated that the health service was not giving sufficient priority to avoiding medical mishap and treating patients justly when mishaps occurred (for the full text, see (2001) 9 *Medical Law Review*).

At about the same time, Sir Donald Irving, chairman of the GMC, accused doctors of 'deep-seated flaws', including excessive paternalism, secrecy and lack of respect for patients. Dr Michael Wilkes, chairman of the BMA's medical committee, responded, saying that no one in the medical profession expected the public – or the courts – to put doctors on a pedestal, and that the medical profession was working very hard to improve the quality of practice and to ensure that cases of incompetence were dealt with swiftly and fairly.

Over the last few years the element of hostility between lawyers and doctors has reduced to an appreciable extent owing to better liaison, communication and association. In other words, the two professions talk to each other more, rather than just waving their assegais. There is now a greater understanding that the litigation war arises principally from medical mistakes rather than greedy lawyers or ungrateful patients and that therefore eradicating mistakes by a combination of risk assessment, clinical governance and proper training (and not overworking the staff) is the way to turn a war into an alliance, which would benefit not only the public coffers but also the patients.

So the truth lies somewhere between the opposing views. The medical profession is largely good, often marvellous, but sometimes less than satisfactory. The lawyers, on both sides, are largely fair-minded and responsible, but sometimes too quick and too keen to sue or to defend. The judges are on the whole astute and impartial, but sometimes neither one nor the other. However, the practice of the courts in assigning medical trials to whomever is available, rather than to a judge with at least some experience of medical claims, is not conducive to an informed judgment, but only to a guaranteed lottery. But at least the inexperienced judges usually demonstrate a degree of humility in the face of the wide experience of the lawyers appearing before them. Some experienced judges, on the other hand, are overweening in their arrogance, acting the great panjandrum. This gentle criticism does not apply, I hasten to add, to any of the High Court judges, but rather to one or two big fish in little ponds out in the provinces.

Part One

Chapter 2

The structure of the National Health Service

Caron Heyes

Understanding the chain of command in the NHS can often be essential to extract the correct disclosure to build a case. This will apply not just in civil negligence claims against the NHS and private health care practitioners, but also in rationing cases, Human Rights Act claims and Disability Discrimination Act 1995 claims.

The purpose of this chapter is to describe the structure of the NHS, the government bodies that exist to regulate and support it, and how to identify the correct defendant in amidst of those organisations. It is also an aide to identifying which organisation may hold information that will help build the claim.

Much of the information in this chapter is drawn from the NHS Handbook 2010/11,[1] an annual publication produced by the NHS Confederation and strongly recommended as a purchase for any clinical negligence department. The NHS Confederation is an independent membership body for the full range of organisations that make up the modern NHS. These include Ambulance Trusts, Acute and Foundation Trusts, Mental Health Trusts, Primary Care Trusts and a number of independent sector organisations that deliver services within the NHS as more responsibility for cases is being delivered to local authorities; the Confederation is seeing them join as well. The Confederation seeks to influence the development of healthcare policy aiming to ensure that new and existing initiatives lead to improvements in the system and advancements in patient care.

Firstly some statistics: the NHS employs 1.75 million staff, and estimates are that on average people use the NHS 2,153 times during their lifetime – the equivalent of once a fortnight. It is a massive organisation with a heavy burden of care. It is also a constantly evolving, dynamic organisation, of limited resources. This chapter is written at a time when significant changes are proposed to the NHS structure, to effect significant financial savings and improve accessibility. The thrust

---

1   *The NHS Handbook 2010/11* by Peter Davies, published by the NHS Confederation. Available at £18.95 from the NHS Confederation, www.nhsconfed.org.uk.

of those proposals were first proposed in the NHS White Paper, *Equity and excellence: liberating the NHS*. Published in July 2010, this paper set out the 2010 Coalition Government's long-term vision for the future of the NHS. Their vision builds on the core values and principles of the NHS – a comprehensive service, available to all, free at the point of use, and based on need, not ability to pay.[2] Following the White Paper's publication, over 6,000 responses were received by the Government. This led to changes to some of the proposals, which are set out in the document *Liberating the NHS: legislative framework and the next steps* and the Health and Social Welfare Bill currently progressing through Parliament. The changes proposed are radical and far ranging.

The timescale for changes is spread over the next four years, to 2014. Where changes are currently proposed we have outlined the likely changes. However be alert to the possibility that an institution that exists at the time of writing this book may no longer be in existence by 2014, and its functions may have been subsumed in another organisation.

THE NHS: ACCOUNTABILITY

The NHS is essentially the responsibility of Parliament and the Department of Health. The Department of Health is assisted nationally by a range of 'arm's length bodies', and regionally by the Strategic Health Authorities (SHAs). SHAs will be wholly abolished under current proposals.

Currently Primary Care Trusts (PCTs) act as local commissioning agents, and providers of direct care services, while NHS Trusts, Foundation Trusts and independent healthcare organisations provide the services. A chain of accountability runs from local bodies up through the regions to government, ending with parliament. Commissioning responsibility is proposed to shift in the main to GPs over the next two years, and a new National Commissioning Board (NCB) will be created to take on the overall control of commissioning, with GPs and PCT clusters having some commissioning powers. However the chain of accountability will not change.

Parliamentary oversight of the NHS

The NHS is funded by the taxpayer, and Parliament scrutinises the service through the medium of parliamentary debates, and a range of Select Committees, in particular the Health Committee and the Public Accounts Committee.

The Department of Health

There are currently six health ministers in the Department of Health, responsible for health and social care. They provide political leadership

---

2   *Liberating the NHS* is the Coalition Government's proposals for change, including abolishing Strategic Heath Authorities by 2013. A copy can be found at www.dh.gov.uk/en/Publicationsandstatistics/Publications/PublicationsPolicyAndGuidance/DH_11735 and was published on 12 July 2010 by the Department of Health. Also published is a key review of arm's length bodies.

and are responsible for making the main executive decisions on strategy, policy framework priorities, and provision of overall resources. However they do not become involved in local decisions and it is going to be a very rare case where the Department of Health will be named as a party in any litigation arising out of medical treatment provided to an individual by a particular trust or health care provider.

Until now, the Department of Health has been the national headquarters of the NHS, negotiating funding with the Treasury and allocating resources to the health service at large. However the new Coalition Government is setting up an independent NCB. This will allocate resources and provide commissioning guidelines, and will also take in-house certain responsibilities currently borne by other arm's length bodies. As well as overseeing the commissioning process, it will take on the role of improving public health. It is also intended that the commissioning of local services will pass to GPs in the main, with significantly slimmed down Primary Care Trusts commissioning only those residual services best commissioned at a wider level. The NCB will oversee the whole process.

THE NHS: HOW CLINICAL SERVICES ARE DELIVERED

Strategic Health Authorities (SHAs)

In England, Strategic Health Authorities act as the local headquarters of the NHS. They were created in 2002 and total ten in number. They provide leadership, coordination and support across a defined geographical area, rather than commissioning services. At the current time, any questions of recruitment and retention, and development of NHS staff policies, should be addressed to these organisations to look for facts and figures, particularly given one of their three main tasks is to build capacity and capability in terms of people, facilities and buildings within and across organisations. For instance much has been made of shortages of staff in A&E and in midwifery maternity services. Information pertaining to a particular region's supply of such personnel might conceivably be found within the Strategic Health Authority for that region. However they will be all abolished by early 2013 and we anticipate that that information will be held by the NCB and local commissioners of services.

Primary Care Trusts (PCTs)

The Primary Care Trust is the cornerstone of the NHS locally. PCTs exist in England, Wales and Scotland. In Northern Ireland they have five commissioning groups driven by GPs. They are all to be abolished by April 2013 with functions for commissioning transferring to GP consortia and the NCB from early 2012 in a staged process.

PCTs currently have two functions, as a commissioner of medical services, and as a direct provider by employing staff such as, for instance, midwives. In terms of the commissioning role, they commission a range of services, including mental health services, GP practices, screening programmes, patient transport, dentistry, pharmacies and opticians. So, for instance, if information is required about a failure in a cervical smear screening process, one should seek disclosure from the local PCT as to the process of the screening, auditing, what happens when patients do not attend, and local protocols.

In terms of direct provision of services, they may provide a wide range of out-of-hospital services such as district nursing, health visiting, therapy, and disease prevention services (such as smoking cessation support). They are to separate their commissioning and provider functions by early 2012, with GP consortia taking over commissioning (Clinical Commissioning Groups (CCGs)), whilst PCTs will retain some direct provision of some services, with the centralised NCB commissioning services that need to be commissioned on a National basis rather than to meet local needs.

More information about PCTs can be found through the NHS confederation PCT network.[3]

NHS Trusts

There are currently around 200 NHS Trusts overseeing around 1,600 hospitals and specialist care centres. In addition there are 11 Ambulance Trusts. Additionally there are the Foundation Trusts. NHS Trusts were abolished in Scotland in 2004 and in Wales in 2009, where they have specialist service Trusts. In Northern Ireland there are five Trusts. They earn income through providing healthcare services, commissioned by PCTs.

Currently, a tariff derived from nationally referenced costs has removed prices from local negotiations, so that Commissioners focus instead on gains in patient choice, quality, and shorter waiting times. However, tariffs will represent the maximum price of the service from 2011 with the intended aim of this change being to create the ability to negotiate prices down.

Trusts are largely self-governing organisations with boards comprising a chair, five non-executive directors and five executives and usually the medical nursing and finance directors running them.

Foundation Trusts

The Health and Social Care (Community Health and Standards) Act 2003 enabled some NHS Trusts to end government control of them by turning them into competing independent corporations called Foundation Trusts. The Act allows both NHS and non-NHS bodies, including private companies, to apply to become Foundation Trusts. Although their principal purpose is to provide goods and services to the NHS, they are able to carry out any type of business. With guaranteed independence from direct government control, their sole statutory general duty is to operate 'effectively, efficiently, and economically'. They do not have shareholders but are expected to make and retain surpluses for new investment or for servicing loans raised on the financial markets. The scale of such borrowing will depend on their ability to make surpluses. The Government has given them several powers to generate surpluses, including buying and selling land and assets, and retaining the proceeds,

---

3   www.nhs.confed.org/pctn.

creating commercial arms or joining existing commercial ventures, and subcontracting clinical services to commercial companies.

It must be emphasised that Foundation Trusts are free from central government control. The intention behind establishing Foundation Trusts had been to establish a new NHS service with local delivery and accountability, yet working to national standards. They do not exist anywhere other than in England. They are independent public benefit corporations, and remain part of the NHS. Therefore they remain subject to NHS standards, performance ratings, and inspection systems. They are accountable to Parliament, to their regulator, Monitor, (on economic matters) and the CQC (on equality) and to their governors who are elected by local Foundation Trust members.

Recently the Francis Enquiry into failings at the Mid Staffordshire Hospitals Foundation NHS Trust has highlighted that though Foundation Trusts are able to access capital from the private and public sectors, and in theory can make decisions more responsive to needs identified by their local communities and local stakeholders, the fact that they can operate without transparency and are driven by financial targets can allow terrible failings in care to occur. A public enquiry, led by Robert Francis QC, running from November 2010 through to December 2011 has examined, amongst other matters, the effectiveness of the Foundation Trust regulator, Monitor.

Care Trusts

Care Trusts are designed to allow close integration of health and social care commissioning, and provide both within a single NHS organisation. Sometimes the local authority will partner with an NHS Trust to establish a Care Trust. These types of Trusts usually focus on specialist Mental Health in Older People services. Hence, where concerns arise over inpatient mental health treatment, quite often the client, although referred by a GP operating under one PCT, and treated within a hospital falling within a particular NHS Trust, has actually had his care directly provided by a separate Care Trust. This is down to shared management arrangements and it is worth noting that there are ten Care Trusts among the total of 151 PCTs at the current time.

Children's Trusts

There has been a long standing intention (since 2004) to integrate key children's services within a single organisational focus. Children's Trusts were intended to be partnerships between organisations that provide, commission or are involved in services to children and young people and are normally led by local authorities. The scheme is in its infancy, and it is not clear how Children's Trusts will move forwards.

Independent providers

The term 'independent providers' means private sector companies, voluntary organisations and social enterprises. The aim is to increase the offering of choice to NHS patients by using such providers. Since 2008, health service patients have freedom of choice of any hospital treatment centre in England that meets NHS standards and costs, including those in the independent sector. The NHS increasingly subcontracts care out to private providers. For instance hip replacements and cataract surgery are commonly outsourced.

Concerns have arisen, however, as to who is responsible for the care provided by independent providers. Is the Trust who referred the patient then responsible in a civil claim or is it always the independent provider? Identifying responsibility will depend in part upon obtaining the contract between the parties to assist in identifying whether the independent providers provided a blanket indemnity to the NHS. Reference may need to be had to regulatory frameworks as well. Notwithstanding who bears responsibility for the treatment, it is expected the independent providers will adopt the same NHS standards; therefore protocols that are applied within the NHS should also apply to the independent provider. It is also worth investigating the ownership structure of the private provider in case the Trust has any investment or ownership role in it (eg in the provision of laboratory services).

Private sector companies have begun to carry out elective surgery and diagnostic tests of NHS patients under five-year contracts. They are gradually playing an increasing role, and the volume of services they provide the NHS have risen rapidly over the last five years.

Independent sector treatment centres, units that carry out planned surgery and treatment in areas that have traditionally had the longest waiting times, have provided more than 1.7 million operations, diagnostic assessments and primary care consultations to NHS patients according to the NHS Confederation.[4] The type of work they do falls into three categories: short stay inpatient work; day cases; and community-based diagnostic work, eg endoscopy and ultrasound.

The third sector

This term encompasses a range of institutions that fit neither the public nor private organisation definition. They include small local community and voluntary groups, large and small charities, cooperatives and social enterprises. They usually provide inpatient and outpatient mental health services, sexual health services, drug rehabilitation and palliative care. There would appear to be an intention by the Department of Health to increase participation by third sector partners in the provision of care. In practical terms it is therefore essential to identify who has actually provided care to the client, who funds it, and who makes the decisions about who was entitled to treatment and what they're entitled to.

Further information about how the NHS commissions services, sets priorities and the rules on competition can be found in the NHS Handbook, which in turn will provide the reader with further references.

PRIMARY CARE PROVIDERS

Primary care is usually provided by GPs, community nurses, health visitors and health professionals, pharmacists, dentists and opticians.

---

4   *The NHS Handbook 2010/11*, Ch 1 'The Structure of the NHS in England', p 31, by Peter Davies, published by the NHS Confederation.

One of the key issues with primary care is that continuity of care is maintained. 90% of NHS patients receive their treatment in primary care.

GPs

Most GP practices are independent contractors, and formed in partnerships, although they also employ salaried GPs. They are required to provide essential services which include advising people who are ill, making referrals, managing the terminally ill and those with chronic diseases. They have the option of also providing additional services such as contraception or childhood immunisations. Some surgeries also provide enhanced services such as minor surgery units. This is part of a general intention to broaden the range of services GPs offer. If commissioning is to go into the hands of GPs, this will promote an increase in the range of services GPs can offer. It will also require GPs to create commissioning consortia, and to embrace new skills and obligations. It would appear however that many GPs welcome the opportunity to commission services, whilst others fear the consequences if the proposed changes should fail.

GP out of hours services

GP out of hours services have provided a rich source of cases for claimant lawyers, GMC regulators and patient action groups in recent years. By 'out of hours' it is meant from 6:30 pm Monday to Thursday until 8 am the following day, and from 6:30 pm on Friday until 8 am on the following Monday, as well as public holidays. About 75% of out of hours provision is currently carried out by GP cooperatives and the balance is provided by commercial providers. In addition, these services are supported by Ambulance Trusts with the NHS Direct supplying initial call handling services.

From 1 January 2005, all providers of out of hours services have been required to comply with the national out of hours quality requirements. These were first published in October 2004 and clarifications were issued in 2006. Those guidelines can be found in the *National quality requirements in the delivery of out of hours care.*[5]

The Department of Health carried out an extensive review of out of hours services provided by GPs following the death of David Jones, after treatment by a locum GP from Germany. That report established that there is currently an unacceptable variation in how PCTs commission and monitor out of hours services, and made 24 recommendations for change. The GMC also examined the practice of the individual locum involved and currently many questions are being posed as to how GP out of hours services can be made more efficient and safe.

To investigate treatment by out of hours services, one needs to establish ownership of the company, the employment status of the GP administering care, protocols worked under and standards adhered to. Often the GP who attended on the patient through the out of hours service will be self-

---

5   www.dh.gov.uk/en/Publicationsandstatistics/Publications/PublicationsPolicyAnd
    Guidance/DH_4137271.

employed and they should be sued in their own right, rather than the out of hours service owners.

Walk-in centres

Also known as minor injury units or urgent care centres, they are open seven days a week from 7 am to 10 pm. They may offer assessment by an experienced NHS nurse as well as information, out of hours GP, dental and local pharmacy services. There are around 90 walk-in centres throughout England. Concerns have been raised about whether reasonable standards of care can be met in these walk-in centres, which might be based in a local hospital unit yet operate entirely separately from the hospital, being staffed by GPs and locums. Often a walk-in centre, though located in the hospital grounds, will be managed by the PCT not the hospital trust. It is argued this can lead to assessment by the wrong level of practitioner, and delay access to the correct expert. It also increases the risk of errors and delays in diagnosis, referral and communication.

Dentistry services

Dental services in primary care are provided through contracts with individual, self-employed dentists. There is currently a pilot project going on considering whether linking dentists' income to the number of NHS patients registered with them, rather than simply the number of treatments they provide, would increase access to dental care in the community. If there is an issue with dental care provided, the PCT will be the institution with primary responsibility for commissioning that dentist's services, and will be involved in any complaint process. However, usually liability for the treatment will rest with the individual dentist because he is providing services under a contract.

Community pharmacies

Over recent years there has been a significant increase in the use of community pharmacies to provide medicine and some essential treatment without the intervention of the GP. Dispensing and providing medication support is deemed part of essential services, but a number of advanced services may also be provided, such as smoking cessation services. The intention is that pharmacists will take on provision of vaccinations, screening for vascular disease and certain sexually transmitted diseases, as well as being able to prescribe medicines, so saving significant GP time.

Where investigating a potential pharmaceutical error, it may be the pharmacy that is liable. To identify the correct defendant, discover whether the pharmacy operates under contract to the local PCT/NCB. If so, the defendant is most likely also the owner of that pharmacy. Pharmacies in the UK are predominantly owned by large groups, eg Boots or Lloyds pharmacies. A company search will be necessary to identify the owner of the pharmacy. An additional complication may be that, quite often, private chemists will hire locum pharmacists, or a pharmacist on a self-employed basis. This means they are working as a self-employed contractor, in which case they offer an indemnity to the contracting pharmacy, and therefore they should be sued in person.

When suing the pharmacy, the pharmacy may be represented by the National Pharmaceutical Association. This is a trade body. Full membership includes legal defence costs and it may be their legal department that has to be dealt with for the majority of independent pharmacists.

Opticians

Optometrists carry out eye tests, prescribe glasses and contact lenses, and identify the presence of eye disease. They are independent contractors and can treat patients who would otherwise have to be seen in hospital. Where they work under contract for local PCTs, they work to an agreed protocol, and undertake specified clinical procedures designed to relieve GPs and hospital eye services, as well as providing patient care in the community. They have to be registered with the General Optical Council. The PCT is responsible for managing their contracts.

In addition, there are dispensing opticians who fit and sell glasses, interpret prescriptions but do not test eyes. They may be qualified to provide contact lenses under instruction from an optometrist. If operating privately rather than under contract to the NHS, it will be necessary to identify their insurer.

Ophthalmic medical practitioners are doctors specialising in eyes and eye care and offer the same terms of service as optometrists do.

Finally, ophthalmologists are doctors specialising in eye diseases and who perform eye surgery, working in hospital eye departments.

Community health services

Community health services can provide more personalised care, closer to patients' homes. Community health services are a major part of the NHS, and encompass a diverse range of statutory registered practitioners, including art therapists, drama therapists, occupational therapists, prosthetists, paramedics, physiotherapists, speech and language therapists, community nurses, district nurses with a post-graduate qualification, registered nurses and nursing assistants, and health visitors.

Services offered predominantly include care to the elderly and new mothers, as well as district nursing. There is also provision of specialist nursing care, for instance with expertise in stoma care, continence services and midwifery services.

Midwifery services are principally provided under contract to a local Trust provider or through a particular GPs surgery. Careful consideration needs to be had as to who employs those midwives and who sets the protocols and procedures by which they carry out their work. Although they may be technically employed by their midwifery practice, it may be that the Healthcare Trust they are attached to, for instance, has a say in the appointment of new midwives and provides greater control than is immediately apparent. This may create a vicarious responsibility on the part of the contracting Trust for the actions of the midwifery practice.[6]

---

6   Cf *Farraj* v *King's Healthcare NHS Trust* (2009) EWCA Civ 1203.

Community health services also provide continuing care. Continuing care is care provided over an extended period to someone, aged 18 or over, to meet physical and mental health needs that have arisen as a result of disability, accident or illness. These services may be provided by a combination of NHS and local authorities. If the patient lives in a care home, the NHS will contribute to the cost of registered nursing care. Financial issues are not taken into account when deciding eligibility for NHS continuing care, though they are for non-medical care.

In such cases it would be worth investigating and seeking disclosure from the health and social care organisations and local authorities involved in the case to ascertain their protocols and the partners they work with.

It is of note that clinical psychology services are often provided by specialist Mental Health Trusts with more than 40% of referrals coming from general practice. These services are more likely to be attached to hospitals, though working in community settings. Community rehabilitation may be delivered by specialist teams drawn from both intermediate care and community hospital care. Where the case arises out of the standard of community care, ascertain who held final responsibility for the actions and care provided by a community care provider, and who set up the care plans.

DELIVERY OF URGENT AND EMERGENCY CARE

The system for delivering urgent and emergency care includes NHS Direct, community pharmacies and self-care, GP services, walk-in centres and minor injuries units, ambulance services, hospital A&E departments and critical care services. New critical care indicators to measure performance are being developed by the Department of Health, with indicators for emergency departments and ambulance services having been introduced in April 2011.

Urgent care is defined as care for patients who have an injury that requires immediate attention but it is not serious enough to go to an A&E department.

NHS Direct

NHS Direct is a 24-hour telephone health advice and information service staffed by nurses. Staff use a computer-based decision support system to suggest the best course of action and can pass calls directly to emergency services.

Ambulance services

Ambulance services have changed significantly in the last ten years and the intention is to transform ambulance services further to provide more diagnosis, treatment and care in people's homes. There is an argument that in some cases survival rates are better in specialist centres than in A&E departments. Hence by increasing the amount of paramedical care provided in people's homes or in specialist centres, it is hoped unnecessary A&E admissions will be reduced. For instance there is a cardiology initiative ongoing where certain paramedics are trained specifically in the resuscitation and testing of people with heart pain so that those patients, instead of being taken to emergency departments, are taken directly to a cardiac unit. In other words, ambulance services are improving their ability to assess, diagnose and treat patients. However it is intended that by increasing the availability of immediate treatment by emergency services, less patients will need to attend A&E. This may have the benefit of reducing delays in treatment. Furthermore, crews now use satellite navigation systems and emergency ambulances carry ECG machines and telemetry, which lets the crew send information about a patient's condition directly to the receiving hospital.

Until April 2011, standards for ambulance services included the following:

- 75% of Category A (immediately life threatening) calls should receive a response within eight minutes. This initial response can be by traditional ambulance or a range of other options including car, motorbike or volunteer community responder.
- If a Category A patient requires transport, this should arrive within 19 minutes of the request for transport being made, 95% of the time.
- 95% of Category B calls are to be responded to within 19 minutes.

Response times are measured from the moment the call is connected to the control room rather than from when details are taken from the caller.[7]

However from April 2011 the introduction of a set of clinical quality indicators for ambulance services is intended to measure the performance of the ambulance service by quality and patient outcomes. 11 indicators replaced the Category B, 19-minute response time target, which is perceived by government as having no clinical justification. The indicators apply to all ambulance calls. The indicators have been written and were introduced alongside new indicators for A&E (see below).

Timeliness of care is still an important factor and so ambulance services are still required to respond to Category A (immediately life-threatening) patients within eight minutes, and provide transport (where needed) to these calls within 19 minutes, as set out in the NHS 2010/11 Operating Framework as existing commitments.

Response time targets are reported annually to the Information Centre (IC) by all NHS Ambulance Trusts, which the IC then publish in the KA34 Annual Statistical Bulletin.[8]

A&E departments

Accident and emergency departments account for around 20% of all admissions to hospital. It is well recognised that A&E departments often suffer from long delays because of the lengthy chain of tests, decisions and treatment that may be invoked in trying to diagnose what is wrong with the patient. As a result, the accident and emergency department will often work from a significant number of protocols which will need to be referred to if intending to pursue a claim arising out of any treatment in A&E.

---

7   Information about standards to be met and individual trust response rates can be found at www.ic.nhs.uk/pubs/ambserv0809. Furthermore, this information will be accessible under a FOI information request from individual Trusts.

8   www.ic.nhs.uk/statistics-and-data-collections/audits-and-performance/ambulance.

April 2011 saw the introduction of a set of clinical quality indicators for A&E services, replacing the standard set by the previous Government that no patient would spend more than four hours in A&E departments from arrival to admission, transfer or discharge. They were developed for the Department of Health by Professor Matthew Cooke, National Clinical Director for Urgent and Emergency Care working with the College of Emergency Medicine, the Royal College of Nursing and lay representatives.

The purpose of the clinical quality indicators is to provide a more balanced and comprehensive view of the quality of care. This includes outcomes, clinical effectiveness, safety and service experience, as well as timeliness. Each A&E department will be required to present data on performance against the indicators on their website, as well as some narrative text to explain what their performance means and how they plan to continuously improve their service.

A&E departments can use the results of the indicators, benchmarking their own site against other sites with similar profiles, to gauge performance and identify improvements. Commissioners will be able to use the indicators to set goals for improvements in the quality of the care they are commissioning. In addition, in the transition year of 2011/12, the Department of Health has included the indicators in its approach to performance management under the Operating Framework for the NHS in England. The new A&E indicators, in summary are:

1   percentage of patients with certain ambulatory care conditions admitted;
2   unplanned re-attendance rate;
3   total time spent in the A&E department;
4   left without being seen rate;
5   service experience;
6   time to initial assessment;
7   time to treatment; and
8   consultant sign-off.

More details of the indicators, their definitions and how they will be used by clinicians to determine which patients should be treated first and in what manner, can be found in the document *A&E clinical quality indicators: implementation guidance and data definitions*.[9] A&E statistics[10] on current performance can also be reviewed on the DH website.

OTHER CARE PROVIDERS

Mental health

Statistics suggest that mental illness accounts for over 50% of all referred illnesses, and 40% of all disability in Britain. The National Mental Health Development Unit is a small central team that provides support in implementing mental health policy by advising on best practice. Mental

9   www.dh.gov.uk/en/Publicationsandstatistics/Publications/PublicationsPolicyAnd Guidance/DH_122868.
10   www.dh.gov.uk/en/Publicationsandstatistics/Statistics/Performancedataandstatistics/ AccidentandEmergency/index.htm.

health services are provided as part of primary and secondary care with responsibility split between the NHS social care and the independent and voluntary sectors. However the PCT is currently responsible for the commissioning of mental health services, sometimes jointly, with local authorities. The 59 specialist Mental Health Trusts and 14 PCT providers provide acute inpatient care, community rehabilitation services, residential care centres, day hospitals and drop-in centres. The carers are governed by the Mental Health Act 2008. Records are likely to be extensive and are far more detailed than might be seen in another hospital treatment setting.

Prison healthcare

People in prison have poorer health generally than the population at large. Historically there have often been some great failings in the care provided to prisoners but since 2006 changes have been made to try and eradicate those failings.

Local PCTs are responsible now for commissioning healthcare for their regional prisons, with the aim being to provide prisoners with the same quality and range of healthcare services as the public receives from the NHS. There is a national partnership agreement between the Department of Health and the Home Office on behalf of the prison service and that underpins local partnership arrangements. Prison services usually now employ a GP and provide in-prison primary care, and specialist care will be provided to the prisoners through their local Trusts and other specialist services by contract.

Defence medical services

The defence medical services comprise the Surgeon General's department, the Joint Medical Commands, including the defence departments' dental services and medical services in the Royal Navy, the Army and the Royal Air Force. The defence medical services are headed by the Surgeon General. Over 7,000 regular uniformed medical personnel from all three services belong to them. They generally work alongside civilian medical and dental staff employed by the Ministry of Defence.

There are six Ministry of Defence hospital units based in the NHS. There are also 15 rehabilitation units located across the UK, and in Germany. In addition there are 15 departments in the UK providing military community mental health services. The defence medical services also provide primary care to serving personnel and their dependents, both in the UK and in stations overseas.

Often problems arise when serving personnel have left the Army and there hasn't been proper transfer of their medical records or indeed a proper continuity of care between that received in the forces and that received as a civilian. The intention is to improve this transfer and continuity of process for personnel.

Healthcare for asylum seekers

Refugees and asylum seekers with an outstanding application for refuge in the UK are entitled to free NHS services. However if their application should be refused, they are no longer entitled to free NHS treatment.

This can lead to a situation where failed asylum seekers, who cannot return home, can no longer access free healthcare that may be essential to their survival. They may have complex healthcare requirements yet they will not have the money to pay for private care.

The Department of Health Asylum Seeker Coordination Team coordinates the healthcare policy of asylum seekers and refugees. Asylum seekers usually stay in a network of induction centres on their arrival where they undergo an initial health assessment, normally by a nursing sister and/or GP. They are then issued with a national handheld health record. PCTs and local councils are the bodies responsible for ensuring adequate access to interpreters within their own area.

GOVERNANCE AND REGULATION

Tools of governance for Trusts

Good governance is the framework used to make all NHS staff accountable for quality improvement and safeguarding standards. The Chief Medical Officer's definition of clinical governance is:

> A system through which NHS organisations are accountable, continuously improving the quality of their services and safeguarding high standards of care by creating an environment in which clinical excellence will flourish ... its main features are a coherent approach to quality improvement, clear lines of accountability clinical quality systems and effective processes of identifying and managing risk in addressing poor performance.

Clinical audit is another important instrument of clinical governance, both carrying out audit and making public the outcomes of the audit. The National Clinical Audit Advisory Group aims to guide and improve the process of audit and acts as a steering group of the National Clinical Audit and Patient Outcomes programmes, which commission national audits. These in turn are administered by the Healthcare Quality Improvement Partnership. One of their actions was to publish a Trust's survival rates for common cardiothoracic procedures on the web.

Under the Health Act 2009, all providers of NHS care have to publish annual quality accounts indicating the quality of the care they provide. These require Trust Boards to review the quality of the services, the priorities for improvement and how they intend to achieve those changes. These accounts are not a comprehensive assessment of every service, more an overview.

Trusts also have Ethics Committees. These review new procedures to be embarked on within the Trust and keep minutes that may be disclosable in a case. They can provide key information as to the standards the Trust sets for procedures, particularly where a Trust has not yet put in place a formalised protocol for a particular procedure.

Finally, the use of a central alerting system ensures that patient safety alerts and related guidance are distributed to the NHS and other health and social care providers. These include emergency alerts, drug alerts and medical device alerts issued on behalf of the Medicines and Healthcare Products Regulatory Agency, the National Patient Safety Agency, and the Department of Health. The public can access this computerised alerting system at www.cas.dh.gov.uk.

Trust Boards

As discussed above, PCTs and NHS Trusts are accountable to local communities and up through the Strategic Health Authorities to the Department of Health. Foundation Trusts are accountable to the independent regulator, Monitor. However all Trusts are immediately accountable to their independently appointed boards. The roles and responsibilities of NHS boards are broadly the same throughout the UK. They take corporate responsibility of their organisation's strategies and actions. With the current policy emphasis on decentralisation and local leadership, their role is more important than ever.

Quite often NHS boards will delegate their powers to informally constituted committees such as a clinical governance committee or a risk management committee. Obtaining the minutes of those committees can be very helpful and are available under a Freedom of Information Act request, if not posted on the Trust's website. However, Foundation Trust Board meetings do not have to publish their board minutes. They have distinctive governance arrangements which reflect their independence from central government control.

Currently appointments to boards are managed by the NHS Appointments Commission but this is an arm's length body that the current Government intends abolishing, with responsibility for recruitment possibly passing to the National Commissioning Board.

Patient advice and liaison services (PALS)

Every NHS Trust should have a PALS office providing on the spot help and information about health services. They don't hold any core information and their efficiency varies from Trust to Trust. Their role in the complaints system is dealt with in Chapter 3.

Care Quality Commission (CQC)

Operating since April 2009 as the successor body to the Healthcare Commission, the CQC regulates health and adult social care services, whether provided by the NHS, local authorities, private companies or voluntary organisations. It registers health and adult social care providers and monitors and inspects all health and adult social care. It is empowered to use enforcement powers such as fines, public warnings or closures if standards are not met. It can assess commissioners' and providers' performances, and may carry out special reviews of particular services, where concerns about quality exist. Changes are proposed to their structure, with the Government intending that the current risk-based regulatory regime will remain largely unchanged. However, the Health and Social Care Bill does set out a number of important changes for the CQC:

- HealthWatch England will be established as a new independent consumer champion within the CQC.
- Providers will have a joint licence overseen by both Monitor and the CQC.
- The NCB will take over the assessment of commissioning.

It is intended that HealthWatch should be a separate arm of the regulator, close enough to the CQC to influence regulation and share information, but able to retain enough independence to be a strong voice for patients, constantly challenging on behalf of local people. There will also be local Healthwatch Groups. Interaction between local and national groupings is not yet confirmed, but the intention is that Healthwatch will give voice to the patient perspective.

The CQC is also in discussions with Monitor over the proposed new joint licensing system, and once the NCB is in place, assessment of commissioning will become the responsibility of the NCB. Thus, the intention is for the CQC's role to be clearly focused on getting standards of quality and safety in place across the whole sector.

The CQC is required to report the outcomes of its work to the public and professionals. Any report that may be published by the CQC about individual institutions may be of great use in understanding how a healthcare provider may have failed a particular client.

Monitor

Monitor was set up in 2004 under the Health and Social Care (Community Health and Standards) Act 2003 to authorise and regulate Foundation Trusts. Its role includes:

- controls over the use and sale of public (former NHS) assets;
- decisions about what NHS health services are required for the local population and whether they will be provided by the public or private sector;
- control of the scale, nature, location, and duration of local health services delivered by Foundation Trusts;
- control of the scale of public and private provision;
- control of trust dissolution and merger;
- control of foundation trust's borrowing levels; and
- control over private patient's income.

Monitor has the power to intervene in the running of the Foundation Trusts in the event of failings in healthcare governance, financial performance or other aspects of its activities. Ultimately it can de-authorise a Foundation Trust, though it is notable that that sanction has never yet been applied. It is independent of government, though accountable to Parliament. The intention of the current Government is to develop it into an economic regulator so that it also oversees aspects of access competition and price setting in the NHS.

National Institute of Health and Clinical Excellence (NICE)

Set up in 1999, NICE is best known for providing guidelines about clinical practice and making decisions about what medication may be prescribed. Without a doubt, NICE's guidelines are important and its website should always be consulted to identify what guidance they may have issued about a particular medical treatment or practice that is being investigated. The fact is that guidelines are just that, ie not providing mandatory procedures. That does not underplay the importance of these guidelines in setting benchmarks for treatment standards and guidance as to prevailing acceptable practices.

It is also worth noting that NICE guidelines come into being after a period of consultation. During the consultation period all affected treatment centres should be aware of the proposed changes and actively involved in contributing to the changes being drafted. Therefore a Trust may not be able to defend failure to take account of guidelines because they came into play after the index event, if it can be shown that they participated in any part of the consultation process. Often the Ethics Committees of NHS Trusts and PCTs will have responsibility for dealing with consultations.

NICE, of course, has particular responsibility for authorising NHS use and prescriptions of new drugs. Key challenges to the validity of those guidances have been run in recent years, and recent litigation established that in deciding which drug should be provided to a patient, the PCT has to take careful consideration of, and be guided by, the views of the treating consultant.[11]

Thus NICE guidelines on a range of medical treatment, that it develops in consultation with healthcare providers and clinicians, are essential in considering whether care has been provided in accordance with recognised practice.

Parliamentary Health Service Ombudsman

The Health Service Commissioner (also known as the Parliamentary and Health Service Ombudsman) undertakes independent investigations into complaints about the NHS in England, as well as government departments and other public bodies. It is completely independent of the NHS and government.

It will only look into complaints against private health providers if the treatment was funded by the NHS.

It publishes detailed reports of investigations that identify common themes in complaints. These are intended as training tools and all clinical directors and complaints managers are supposed to be made aware of them. However they do not identify individual patients. If there was a HSC investigation, the report must be obtained. Usually the HSC will obtain a clinical opinion before reaching their conclusion and that is invaluable in assessing the claim. However only a minute number of matters are investigated by the HCC and there are significant delays in investigating matters at the moment.

Audit Commission

This is an independent public body, responsible for ensuring that public money is spent economically, efficiently and effectively. It covers local government, housing, criminal justice, fire and rescue services as well as the NHS. It is of note here simply because it publishes reports that will produce information that may be of relevance to a case arising in a particular Trust, for instance MRSA infection.

---

11 *Eisai Ltd* v *NICE* [2008] EWCA Civ 438.

The Audit Commission sits alongside the National Audit Office, which works closely with a Commons public accounts committee. At the time of writing the Audit Commission is to be abolished.

Council for Healthcare Regulatory Excellence (CHRE)

The CHRE promotes best practice and consistency in professional self-regulation. It covers nine bodies: the General Medical Council, General Dental Council, General Optical Council, General Osteopathic Council, General Chiropractic Council, Health Professions Council, Nursing and Midwifery Council, General Pharmaceutical Council and the Pharmaceutical Society of Northern Ireland. With Parliamentary approval it can force regulatory changes and it also has the power to refer on decisions about a professional's fitness to practice to the High Court for review. More detail about its functions and likely changes to come are set out below.

Information technology

The NHS is operating a national programme for IT, the aim being to ensure that all doctors, nurses and other healthcare professionals working in the NHS will be interconnected. Access to these records is restricted. For instance, an NHS employee, in order to access records, has to log in using their NHS card. This means that it is possible to track how often and when records of a particular patient were reviewed, and who by.

The intention is that a single electronic records system to which all care providers have access will eventually come into being, with every patient having a two-part care record. The detailed care record will be held locally and will be formed from the detailed notes made by every healthcare professional who treats the patient. The summary care record will be held nationally and will contain essential information selected from the detailed records, such as allergies or medication. Patients will be able to access their own summary care record and they can choose not to have a record created or for it not to be shared.

THE NHS: ITS ARM'S LENGTH BODIES AND PROPOSED CHANGES TO THEIR STRUCTURE

The Department of Health (DH) is currently responsible for 21 arm's length bodies (ALBs) employing 17,500 staff. Each is a stand-alone national organisation with executive functions. Significant changes are proposed to the current structures. These proposals follow a review of 18 of the DH's arm's length bodies, and wider system reforms outlined in the White Paper *Equity and excellence: liberating the NHS*. On 26 July 2010, the DH published its report of the review, setting out the future configuration of the ALB sector. It intends:

> .... radically simplifying the architecture of the health and care system. The Government's plans for decentralisation ... will bring major savings. PCTs ... and practice-based commissioners will together be replaced by GP consortia. The Department will radically reduce its own NHS functions. Strategic Health Authorities will be abolished.

... Subject to Parliamentary approval, we will abolish organisations that do not need to exist. We will streamline those functions that need to remain, to cut cost and remove duplication and burdens on the NHS. In future, the Department will impose tight governance over the costs and scope of all its arm's-length bodies. For example, to prevent duplication and aid transparency, the Secretary of State will consider, for any particular arm's-length body, setting out an explicit list of functions that it is not to undertake, to complement the positive list of what it is expected to do. In future, quangos' independence will be about how they perform clear and agreed functions, not the freedom to assume new roles.

Changes will be implemented through regulatory and legislative changes, and the first bills are already being put through Parliament. The key Bill under consideration to effect the proposed changes is the Health and Social Care Bill, which was introduced into Parliament in early 2011. By this piece of legislation, the NHS Commissioning Board and GP consortia will have their functions conferred directly upon them, and the powers of the Secretary of State over the NHS will be constrained and made more transparent, while retaining overall political accountability to Parliament. The overall aim remains to cut costs, simplify the national landscape in the NHS, remove duplication and better align the ALBs sector with the rest of the health and social care system. There is an intention to create a more coherent and resilient regulatory system thus creating new bodies – the NHS Commissioning Board, the Public Health Department and a new research body.

To this end the DH proposes to have:

- one quality regulator (NHS Commissioning Board);
- one economic regulator (Monitor);
- one medicines and devices regulator (MHRA, NICE); and
- one research regulator (TBC).

In terms of plans for specific ALBs, the plans are that:

- Monitor, the Care Quality Commission, the National Institute for Health and Clinical Excellence, the Medicines and Healthcare products Regulatory Agency, the Health and Social Care Information Centre and the NHS Blood and Transplant ALBs will remain in existence, most likely taking on additional responsibilities;
- the functions of the Human Fertilization and Embryology Authority and the Human Tissue Authority will be transferred to other bodies;
- the Health Protection Agency and the National Treatment Agency will be abolished as statutory organisations and their functions transferred to the Secretary of State as part of the new Public Health Service;
- the Alcohol Education Research Council, the Appointments Commissions, the National Patient Safety Agency and NHS Institute for Innovation and Improvement will be abolished;
- the Council for Healthcare Regulatory Excellence will be moved out of the sector to operate on a full-cost recovery basis – in other words, they will be expected to fund themselves through industry levies;
- the General Social Care Council will be abolished and its functions transferred to the Health Professions Council; and
- the Litigation Authority and NHS Business Services Authority are currently subject to a commercial review by industry experts with a view to considering if their functions could be commercially provided.

ALBS AND THEIR FUNCTIONS, NOW AND AFTER THE WHITE PAPER

Care Quality Commission (CQC)

The CQC's function is primarily to deliver the registration of NHS organisations, bringing together the Mental Health Act Commission, the Health Care Commission, and the Commission for Social Care Inspection.

In the future the NHS Commissioning Board will take over the CQC's current responsibility of assessing NHS commissioners (although the CQC will continue to conduct period reviews of adult social care and retain its responsibilities under the Mental Health Act). The CQC will operate a joint licensing regime with Monitor.

HealthWatch England, a new independent consumer champion to be formed, concerned with patient's rights and concerns, will be located within the CQC, with a distinct identity.

Monitor

Monitor was set up to oversee Foundation Trusts, to audit them and to subject them to remedial action if they did not meet standards. Subject to legislation, Monitor will be transformed into a new economic regulator. More has been set out about this ALB under the section 'Foundation Trusts' above.

Medicines and Healthcare products Regulatory Agency (MHRA)

The Medicines and Healthcare products Regulatory Agency (MHRA) was set up in April 2003 from a merger of the Medicines Control Agency and the Medical Devices Agency. The MHRA is the government agency which is responsible for ensuring that medicines and medical devices work, and are acceptably safe. The MHRA regulates a wide range of materials from medicines and medical devices to blood and therapeutic products/services that are derived from tissue engineering.[12] Its functions include:

- assessing the safety, quality and efficacy of medicines, and authorising their sale or supply in the UK for human use;
- overseeing the UK Notified Bodies that audit medical device manufacturers;
- operating post-marketing surveillance and other systems for reporting, investigating and monitoring adverse reactions to medicines and adverse incidents involving medical devices and taking any necessary action to safeguard public health, for example through safety warnings, removing or restricting the availability of products or improving designs;
- operating a proactive compliance programme for medical devices;
- operating a quality surveillance system to sample and test medicines and to address quality defects, monitoring the safety and quality of imported unlicensed medicines and investigating Internet sales and potential counterfeiting of medicines;
- regulating clinical trials of medicines and medical devices;

---

12   www.mhra.gov.uk/Aboutus/index.htm.

- monitoring and ensuring compliance with statutory obligations relating to medicines and medical devices through inspection, taking enforcement action where necessary;
- promoting good practice in the safe use of medicines and medical devices;
- managing the General Practice Research Database (GPRD) and the British Pharmacopoeia (BP) and contributing to the development of performance standards for medical devices;
- offering scientific, technical and regulatory advice on medicines and medical devices; and
- providing the public and professions with authoritative information to enable informed dialogue on treatment choices.

Alerts

Key to the lawyer researching a case where there has been a failure of equipment, or an adverse drug reaction, is to know if an alert may have been issued about risks associated with that product. The MHRA website lists all alerts issued. They distribute their alerts to the NHS through the CAS system (see above). There is a duty upon Trusts to report an adverse event involving a medicine or product. Thus in a case where the defendant relies on a defence of product failure rather than operator error, there should also be a report by them to the MHRA, which should be disclosed. The reports do not simply identify product errors, they also identify common operator errors that, if avoided, will avoid injury to patients.

They also manage the General Practice Research Database (GPRD), which contains information used to detect healthcare trends and monitor the safety and risk benefits of market licensed medicines.

New research regulator

The DH commissioned the Academy of Medical Sciences to carry out an independent review of the regulation and governance of medical research involving human participants, their tissue and/or data. *A new pathway for the regulation and governance of health research* was published in January 2011. The report was prepared by a working group, chaired by Professor Sir Michael Rawlins FMedSci. In response to the review, the Government announced steps to streamline the regulation and governance of health research as part of its Plan for Growth, which was published alongside the budget in March 2010. Key actions announced include:

- The creation of a new Health Research Regulatory Agency to streamline regulation and improve the cost effectiveness of clinical trials.
- The introduction of new incentives for efficiency in research initiation and delivery.
- A commitment to increasing the proportionality of the EU Clinical Trials Directive and its implementation.

The report itself was commissioned against a backdrop of increasing concern about the way in which medical research is managed. There is insufficient space here to do justice to the complex regulatory framework around research programmes obtaining authority to carry out a drug trial and reporting and monitoring them. If a client is injured following participation in a drug programme, obtain a copy of the application for authority to carry out the trial, the reports of adverse outcomes, all trial documentation and a copy of any policy that may exist to insure the participants. Investigate whether the drug trial involved treatment administered by the NHS or privately. If administered by NHS staff, it may then fall outside the insurance scheme and have to be pursued as a normal clinical negligence claim.

The new research regulator may make this process easier and more transparent making it therefore simpler to understand whether a participant in a drug trial has suffered an unexpected adverse outcome.

Generally, if dealing with a claim arising out of injury following participation in medical research, consideration should be given to whether the cause of action is in contract, because it arises out of agreement to participate in the trial, and where consideration for an indemnity from the drug trial provider is the participant's participation in the trial. This impacts when assessing limitation, as where a claim includes elements of personal injury, the limitation period is not six years but three years as it comes within s 11 of the Limitation Act.

Human Tissue Authority (HTA)

The Human Tissue Authority (HTA) is a watchdog that supports public confidence by licensing organisations that store and use human tissue for purposes such as research, patient treatment, post-mortem examination, teaching, and public exhibitions. It also gives approval for organ and bone marrow donations from living people.

The HTA was established on 1 April 2005 under the Human Tissue Act 2004 (HT Act) which extends to England, Wales and Northern Ireland. The HTA is an Executive Non-Departmental Public Body (ENDPB) sponsored by the Department of Health.

The Authority's chair and 14 members were appointed by the Secretary of State for Health. The Chair and eight of the members are lay and the remaining six are professionals drawn from some of the groups with a direct interest in the application of the HT Act. The Authority is supported by an Executive of 42 staff. This number has been achieved by outsourcing the corporate support function.

The HTA's aim is to create a regulatory system for the removal, use and disposal of human tissue and organs that is clear, consistent and proportionate and in which professionals, patients, families and members of the public have confidence. The strategic objectives that support this aim and information on how the HTA plans to achieve them are included in the Strategic Plan and the Annual Business Plans.

Many of its functions will be merged into other agencies after the reform process.

Human Fertilisation and Embryology Authority (HFEA)

The HFEA has three roles:

- as a regulator of fertility treatment procedures and clinics, and research involving human embryos. They set standards for, and issue licences to centres;

- as an information regulator/collector; and
- as an information provider to the public.

The HFEA provides information for the public, in particular for people seeking treatment, donor-conceived people and donors. They also determine the policy framework for fertility issues, which are sometimes ethically and clinically complex.

Their responsibilities in providing guidance and advice are to:

- investigate serious adverse incidents and reactions and to keep a register of serious adverse incidents and serious adverse reactions;
- produce and maintain a Code of Practice, providing guidelines to clinics and research establishments about the proper conduct of licensed activities;
- maintain a formal register of information about donors, licensed treatments and children born as a result of those treatments;
- publicise the HFEA's role and provide relevant advice and information to donor-conceived people, donors, clinics, research establishments and patients, including servicing the statutory right of access to register information;
- review information about –
  - human embryos and developments in research involving human embryos,
  - the provision of treatment services and activities governed by the Human Fertilisation and Embryology (HFE) Acts 1990 and 2008; and
- advise the Secretary of State for Health on developments in the above fields where appropriate.

Relevant statutes are the HFEA Code of Practice, and the HFE Act 2008.

Changes are proposed to close the HFEA, and transfer its functions to other bodies. For instance, regulatory function regarding research could be transferred to a new research regulator. At the time of writing the DH proposes that the HFEA should remain as a separate ALB in the short term with the aim that its functions will be transferred by the end of the current Parliament. During this period the DH will examine the practicalities of how to divide the HFEA functions between the new research regulator and the CQC. A move of such functions to a new research regulator is intended to make it possible for the remaining functions of the HFEA relating to the regulation of fertility clinics to be transferred to the CQC, with information collection and retention functions to pass to the Health and Social Care Information Centre.

Council for Healthcare Regulatory Excellence (CHRE)

The Council for Healthcare Regulatory Excellence promotes the health and well-being of patients and the public in the regulation of health professionals. They scrutinise and oversee the work of the nine regulatory bodies that set standards for training and conduct of health professionals, bodies including the GMC and NMC.

They share good practice and knowledge with the regulatory bodies, conduct research, and introduce new ideas about regulation to the sector. They monitor policy in the UK and Europe and advise the four UK government health departments on issues relating to the regulation of health professionals. They are an independent body accountable to the UK Parliament and funded by Government.

The relevant legislation governing them and their functions are the NHS Reform and Health Care Professions Act 2002 and the Health and Social Care Act 2008. Under these Acts, they have the powers to carry out the following activities:

- **Monitor how the health professions regulators carry out their functions**
  Every year they carry out a performance review with each regulator. The review looks at how the regulators carry out their functions against agreed standards. It highlights good practice and identifies issues that might benefit from a co-ordinated approach.

- **Referring cases to Court where decisions are considered too lenient**
  When concerns about the conduct or performance of a health professional are referred to a regulatory body, the regulator carries out an investigation to determine whether the concerns are valid and whether the professional should continue to practise. Final stage decisions made by the regulators on professionals' fitness to practise are reviewed and if a decision is considered by the CHRE to be unduly lenient and fails to protect the public interest, they can refer the case to the High Court, the Court of Sessions for Scotland or the High Court of Justice for Northern Ireland.

- **Promoting good practice**
  They work with the regulatory bodies to improve quality and share good practice. For example, sharing learning points arising from the scrutiny of fitness to practise cases and organising seminars to explore regulation issues.

- **Advising Health Ministers**
  The Secretary of State and Health Ministers in Scotland, Wales and Northern Ireland request advice from the CHRE about the regulation of health professions.

- **Influencing national and international policy on health professions regulation**
  They consult with the UK Government and governments in Wales, Scotland and Northern Ireland on the development of guidelines for the sector. In addition, they keep abreast of international policies that may affect health regulation in the UK, particularly in Europe. They work with colleagues in the UK and abroad, ensuring that they are aware of these developments.

- **Involving patients and the public in their work**
  One function is to promote the health and well-being of patients and the public in regulation through working with patients and the public who are members of the Public Stakeholder Network and through research, consultations and meetings with other groups of patients and patient representative organisations.

It is proposed to make CHRE a self-funding body through a levy on those it regulates. The DH also proposes to extend CHRE's remit to set standards for and to quality assure voluntary registers held by existing statutory health and care professions regulators, and other professional bodies.

General Social Care Council (GSCC)

The GSCC is the only professional regulator answerable to the Secretary of State and it regulates social workers. It is proposed to abolish the GSCC and transfer the regulation of social workers out of the ALB sector, and to the Health Professions Council (HPC) so as to make it financially independent of the Government.

The abolition of the GSCC and the transfer of its functions to the HPC will require primary legislation. The timing of such changes is dependent on discussion with the HPC and the GSCC.

Health Protection Agency

The Health Protection Agency is an independent UK organisation that was set up by the Government in 2003 to protect the public from threats to health from infectious diseases and environmental hazards. It does this by providing advice and information to the general public, to health professionals such as doctors and nurses, and to national and local government.

The Health Protection Agency and the National Treatment Agency for Substance Misuse are to be abolished and their functions are to be transferred to the Secretary of State as part of the Public Health Service. This would include the functions which support the local delivery of drug treatment services.

Alcohol Education and Research Council (AERC)

The AERC has charitable status and administers a fund of approximately £8 million to support research into the prevention of alcohol-related harm. The DH does not provide funding for this body. The DH intends to remove the organisation.

NHS Blood and Transplant (NHSBT)

The NHSBT is a Special Health Authority in the NHS with responsibility for optimising the supply of blood, organs, plasma and tissues and raising the quality, effectiveness and efficiency of blood and transplant services. NHSBT is responsible for:

- encouraging people to donate organs, blood and tissues;
- optimising the safety and supply of blood, organs and tissues;
- helping to raise the quality, effectiveness and clinical outcomes of blood and transplant services;
- providing expert advice to other NHS organisations, the Department of Health and devolved administrations;
- providing advice and support to health services in other countries;
- commissioning and conducting research and development; and
- implementing relevant EU statutory frameworks and guidance.

It operates the Bio Products Laboratory and the Plasma Supply Chain. Proposals are to transfer these two groups into a DH owned limited company. The Bio Products Laboratory (BPL) manufactures a wide range of plasma products and is part of the NHSBT. BPL, whose manufacturing facility is located at Elstree, near London, UK, is committed to research and development.

BPL has been involved in the processing of human plasma since 1950 when it was first established as part of the Lister Institute by the Medical Research Council (MRC), and started manufacturing specific immunoglobulins in 1972. In 1987, BPL opened its new £60 million manufacturing facility, designed to provide self-sufficiency of plasma products for England and Wales.

They operate as a business with commercial objectives and disciplines and compete in both the UK and over 45 international markets. They are committed to provide a continuous supply of reliable, high quality plasma-derived products worldwide.

BPL manufactures a wide range of products from blood plasma. These products fall broadly into three main groups:

- human coagulation factors;
- human immunoglobulins;
- human albumin solutions.

BPL also produces a small volume of products (on request) for niche markets.

Health and Social Care Information Centre (IC)

The IC supervises and organises the collection, analysis and dissemination of information. For instance it holds aggregate data not currently widely available to patients, the public, researchers and other organisations in a standard format. With this in mind, the DH proposes that the IC will become the national repository for data across healthcare, public health and adult social care with lead responsibility for data collection and assuring the quality of those returns. The IC will need to meet the needs of a multiplicity of customers. This proposal would result in other ALBs relinquishing their data collection roles to the IC. The DH also recognises that the relationship between the NHS Commissioning Board and the IC will be critical to ensure the NHS Commissioning Board can exercise its management function.

The Health Bill will contain provisions to put the IC on a firmer statutory footing, with clearer powers across organisations in the health and care system.

Appointments Commission (AC)

The AC is a central recruiting organisation for all higher level national posts. The future of PCTs, as set out in the White Paper, and the ending of PCT public appointments means that the Commission's NHS work would come to an end. The future model across government involves what is described as 'a sizeable reduction' in the number of national public appointments. Accountability for these appointments would rest with ministers and the process will remain subject to scrutiny by the Commissioner for Public

Appointments. The Government has also signaled that key appointments may also be subject to Select Committee scrutiny.

Given the changing landscape in respect of NHS and public appointments, the DH is of the view that there will be no need for an ongoing central public body to carry out the functions that the commission currently provides beyond 2012. Therefore it proposes the abolition of the AC during 2012 and intends to engage with the Commission on managing the transition period to abolition.

National Patient Safety Agency (NPSA)

The NPSA exists to support wider quality and safety improvement. For instance, the patient safety division, relating to reporting and learning from serious patient safety incidents, is part of the NPSA. The NPSA has three main functions:

- **National Reporting and Learning Service**
  The NRLS aims to identify and reduce risks to patients receiving NHS care and leads on national initiatives to improve patient safety. Through its national reporting system, the NRLS collects confidential reports of patient safety incidents from healthcare staff across England and Wales. Clinicians and safety experts help analyse these reports to identify common risks and opportunities to improve patient safety.

  Feedback and guidance are provided to healthcare organisations to improve patient safety. These include alerts to address specific safety risks, tools to build a strong safety culture and national initiatives in specific areas such as hand hygiene, design, nutrition and cleaning.

  The NRLS works closely with the Royal Colleges, frontline staff and organisations, patient groups, strategic health authorities, other NHS bodies, academic centres and sectors beyond healthcare to promote patient safety.

  In particular, the NPSA commissions and monitors three core ongoing enquiries:
  1   National Confidential Inquiry into Suicide and Homicide by People with Mental Illness;
  2   Confidential Enquiry into Maternal and Child Health;
  3   National Confidential Enquiry into Patient Outcome and Death.
  Through its funding and monitoring of these three independent National Confidential Enquiries, the NRLS can maximise the benefits of their in-depth research to better improve patient care.

- **National Clinical Assessment Service**
  NCAS supports the resolution of concerns about the performance of individual clinical practitioners to help ensure their practice is safe and valued. NCAS does this through two closely collaborating aspects of its service. Its case management service gives expert advice and support to local healthcare organisations and their staff. Where necessary, this is amplified with specialist assessment of performance and support of local action planning to restore and assure safe practice.

  NCAS also works with healthcare organisations to share its experience, with the aim of helping healthcare services deal effectively with performance concerns. This is done through the publication of themes, trends and results emerging from its work, and educational events.

NCAS currently provides a service to healthcare organisations throughout the UK and its associated administrations, crossing both public and private sectors. It covers doctors and dentists, and will also cover pharmacists from April 2009.

- **National Research Ethics Service**
  The National Research Ethics Service (NRES) protects the rights, safety, dignity and well-being of research participants that are part of clinical trials and other research within the NHS. NRES also facilitates and promotes ethical research.

  NRES protects research participants by maintaining a UK-wide system of ethical review via NHS Research Ethics Committees (RECs). RECs review research applications and give an ethical opinion regarding their proposed participant involvement. Applicants include pharmaceutical and medical device companies, healthcare professionals in the NHS, academic researchers including students, and prison health researchers. RECs are entirely independent of research funders and hosts. This enables them to put participants at the centre of their decision making.

It is likely that many of its functions in the future will be subsumed in the NHS Commissioning Board.

NHS Institute for Innovation and Improvement (NHS III)

The NHS III is currently funded largely through grant in aid from the DH. The NHS Commissioning Board will assume a leadership role in commissioning for quality improvement and the responsibility for improving outcome that will occur at every level of the NHS. In assessing the NHS III, the DH is not satisfied that it meets the criteria for the ALB sector and therefore the NHS III will be abolished as an ALB, transferring to the NHS Commissioning Board those functions that will support the Board in leading on quality, improvement and building capacity within the wider system.

NHS Litigation Authority (NHSLA)

The NHSLA is the ALB that claimant clinical negligence lawyers will deal with most. The NHSLA handles negligence claims made against NHS bodies through five schemes. Three of these relate to clinical negligence claims (CNST, ELS and the ex-RHAs scheme), while two cover non-clinical risks, such as liability for injury to staff and visitors along with property damage (LTPS and PES, known collectively as RPST). While only NHS bodies are eligible for membership of these schemes, Independent Sector Treatment Centres, treating NHS patients, may benefit from CNST cover via their referring Primary Care Trust. As well as handling negligence claims, it works to improve risk management practices in the NHS. It is also responsible for resolving disputes between practitioners and Primary Care Trusts, giving advice to the NHS on human rights case law and handling equal pay claims on behalf of the NHS.

A highly influential organisation in any negotiations with bodies such as the Civil Justice Council, MOJ and the judiciary, and with strong media support, the NHSLA is able to influence the whole manner in which clinical negligence litigation is undertaken. Prior to its inception some ten years ago, nearly 80 firms acted for the various NHS trusts in the UK. Now there are only ten panel firms able to represent the Trusts. Freedom of choice of solicitors is only allowed for inquest work. All Trusts are part of the Clinical Negligence ST scheme and this means claims are managed centrally. The aim is to improve risk management and reduce adverse incidents.

Under NHS indemnity, NHS employers are ordinarily responsible for the negligent acts of their employees where these occur in the course of the NHS employment. The NHSLA is therefore representing the Trusts, not the individual doctors who are indemnified by their employers. An individual may also be separately represented through their defence organisation. This is likely where there is, for instance an inquest where a question is raised regarding their fitness to practice. In terms of its approach to claims handling, the NHSLA adopts a somewhat commercial insurance based approach. They have a clear remit, as set out in the Framework Document 13, to ensure that claims made against the NHS are handled fairly and consistently, with due regard to the interests of both patients and the NHS. As mentioned above, they operate a legal panel of ten firms. The panel is dynamic, and subject to change. At the last panel tender, one of the 11 incumbents lost its position. In addition to the legal panel for clinical cases, there are NHS procurement hubs that appoint law firms for a variety of roles particularly in commercial, real estate and PFI finance work.

The NHSLA website is an excellent source of information about risk management and guidelines. AvMA keep its lawyer members up to date with relevant announcements but it is always worthwhile reviewing the website to see their guidance on particular risk management issues.

For instance, they publish on their website copies of all materials used at all workshops in support of the NHSLA standards and assessments under risk management presentations. They release annually CNST Maternity Standards. They also produce and publish template policy documents. Trusts do not have to adopt these policies but they are useful guidance for assessing whether a practice in a hospital may be in breach of guidelines.

There are also NHSLA Risk Management Standards and associated documents regularly produced, as follows:

- NHSLA Risk Management Standards for Acute Trusts, Primary Care Trusts and Independent Sector Providers of NHS Care;
- NHSLA Risk Management Standards for Mental Health & Learning Disability Trusts;
- NHSLA Risk Management Standards for Ambulance Trusts.

There is also an updated handbook to support the standards which includes guidelines for completing the evidence templates. This can be very helpful when trying to identify what documents to request in order to properly investigate the claim. It cannot be emphasised enough that requesting key documents will short cut the litigation process. Investigating a claim no longer requires simply obtaining medical records, it is also important to look at their complaints process, the SUI, relevant protocols, multi-disciplinary team notes, and the standards applied by the CNST scheme.

NHS Business Services Authority (NHSBSA)

The NHS Business Services Authority is a Special Health Authority, an arm's length body of the Department of Health which provides a range of central services to NHS organisations, NHS contractors, patients and the public. The work they do includes:

- management of the NHS Pension Scheme in England and Wales which has over two million members and receives contributions of over £7 billion per annum;
- administration of the European Health Insurance Card (EHIC) scheme in the UK;
- provision of NHS Counter Fraud and Security Management services in England and Wales;
- management of a ten-year outsourced contract for the delivery of supply chain services to the NHS in England and Wales;
- payments to pharmacists in England for prescriptions dispensed in primary care settings;
- payments to dentists for work undertaken on NHS contracts in England and Wales;
- provision of management information to over 25,000 registered NHS and DH users on costs and trends in prescribing and dental care in England and Wales;
- administering a range of health benefit schemes across the UK, including a low income scheme, medical and maternity exemption schemes, tax credit NHS exemption cards (in the UK) and prescription pre-payment certificates (in England). In total they process over six million claims per annum;
- management of schemes for NHS Student Bursaries and NHS Social Work Bursaries in England;
- management of the NHS Injury Benefit Scheme in England and Wales; and
- provision of a range of hosted employment, human resources and financial services, employing around 2,000 staff and administering payments of over £100 million on behalf of various DH teams and programmes.

NHS Evidence

NHS Evidence provides free access to clinical and non-clinical information – local, regional, national and international. Information includes evidence, guidance and government policy. NHS Evidence accreditation recognises organisations who achieve high standards in producing health or social care guidance. Successful organisations are identified on search results by a seal of approval called an Accreditation Mark.

SUMMARY

The NHS is an enormous and complex institution made up of a diverse range of institutions, practitioners and systems. It continues to evolve, as it has from the first day of its creation. Key proposed changes to be passed through Parliament, if passed into legislation, will alter both management and the regulation of the NHS. Those changes will also shift the power to commission services to local GP consortia and hand over control of Trusts entirely to Foundations. Only time can judge the validity and effectiveness of those changes. In the meantime, as a clinical negligence lawyer, awareness of what service provided your client's care, and under which protocols and guidelines, remains important. In any case you undertake involving NHS services, it is important to recognise where information can be found and whether it might be held as part of the patient's personal records (in which case you access it under the Data Protection or Access to Records Acts) or public statistics, in which case you will have to use the Freedom of Information Act.

Chapter 3

Non legal remedies

Catherine Hopkins

THE INITIAL COMPLAINT

When a patient experiences an adverse outcome following medical treatment, the first step in almost all circumstances should be to make a formal complaint. Where the treatment complained of was delivered by the NHS, the NHS complaints procedure will apply. This procedure governs all complaints about NHS treatment in the UK, with some small differences in the devolved jurisdictions. The private patient will need to complain directly to the consultant, hospital or clinic and if the complaint is about the conduct of a specific member of staff the complaint may be made to the relevant professional organisation.

While only legal action offers proper financial compensation, there are good reasons why the patient should make a complaint first. Issues, such as staff rudeness, long waiting lists or lack of communication, are more properly dealt with by making a complaint. While a patient is advised to make a complaint as soon as possible after the event when memories are still fresh, it may be too early immediately after treatment to assess the merits of a civil claim. Often the full extent of an injury is not known in the immediate aftermath of treatment; meanwhile the patient can use this time to make a complaint. In addition, the Legal Services Commission (LSC) requires applicants to have first made a complaint before applying for funding, except in certain exceptional circumstances. There are a number of organisations that can help with making a complaint.

WHEN A COMPLAINT ARISES

Where a patient has received treatment at the hands of the medical profession (including non-treatment such as refusal to visit, give an appointment, treat, prescribe, etc) with which he is not satisfied, he has a number of courses of action.

Where once the litigation route and the non-litigation route were thought to be a matter of either/or, this is no longer so. The patient does not have to decide whether he is looking for financial compensation or for satisfaction of another sort, eg an explanation, reassurance or apology. Whether or not he is going to consider a civil claim for compensation, a patient is also entitled to an explanation from the healthcare provider as to what went wrong and, if possible, why.

When making a complaint there are a number of routes the patient can follow, depending on the type of complaint he wishes to make, ie against whom and in relation to what (NHS or private treatment or the conduct of an individual health care professional). Although in exceptional circumstances a small payment may be made, the aim of pursuing a complaint is not to obtain compensation. Complaints procedures are investigations into the conduct of the healthcare provider (or a member of its staff) with a view to correcting any mistake, maladministration or misconduct for the future. This correction may also involve offering the patient further treatment as well as explanations and, where appropriate, apologies. Any patient contemplating applying for Legal Aid to fund an investigation into a civil claim must first make a complaint.

A patient who wishes to claim compensation, or to take advice on whether he has a claim for compensation, should go to an accredited solicitor – see the section 'Accredited solicitors' below.

COMPLAINTS ABOUT NHS TREATMENT

New regulations making some changes to the NHS complaints procedure came into force in April 2009. If a patient is unhappy with the treatment or service received from the NHS, he is entitled to make his complaint, have it considered, and receive a response from the NHS organisation or primary care practitioner concerned.

The NHS complaints procedure covers complaints made by a person about any matter connected to the provision of NHS services by NHS organisations or primary care practitioners (GPs, dentists, opticians and pharmacists). The procedure also covers services provided overseas or by the private sector where the NHS has paid for them. The patient should normally complain within 12 months of the event(s) concerned or within 12 months of becoming aware that there is something to complain about. Primary care practitioners and complaints managers in NHS organisations have discretion to waive this time limit if there are good reasons for not complaining earlier and the complaint can still be investigated effectively and fairly.

The first stage of the NHS complaints procedure is 'local resolution'. The patient should ask the hospital or trust concerned for a copy of its complaints procedure, which will explain how to proceed. The first step will normally be to raise the matter (in writing or orally) with the practitioner, eg the nurse or doctor concerned, or with their organisation, which will have a complaints manager. This is called local resolution. Local resolution aims to resolve complaints quickly and as close to the source of the complaint as possible using the most appropriate means; for example, use of conciliation. Most cases are resolved at this stage.

Previously there was a different regime for Foundation Trusts. Under the new regulations anyone wishing to complain about an NHS Foundation Trust should, in the first instance, follow the NHS complaints procedure outlined above.

The second stage of the NHS complaints procedure, if the patient is still unhappy, is to refer the matter to the Parliamentary and Health Service Ombudsman.

Prior to the 2009 regulations coming into force, if a patient was unhappy with the response to his complaint after the local resolution stage, he would ask the Healthcare Commission for an 'independent review' of the case. Experience under the old scheme suggested that there were fundamental flaws in the procedure that resulted in less than wholly impartial analysis of the complaint at the independent review stage.

DATA PROTECTION ACT REQUESTS

At the same time as making a complaint, the patient may make a Data Protection Act request for copies of his medical records. It is established that such a request includes all documents, including (but not exclusively) notes from every discipline, internal enquiries concerning the patient's treatment, test results, radiology and medical photographs. Charges prescribed in the Data Protection Act apply.

SERIOUS UNTOWARD INCIDENT

In some circumstances there will already have been an internal enquiry into the circumstances of the complaint and possibly a Serious Untoward Incident (SUI) investigation. The principle definition of a SUI (as defined by NHS London) is 'something out of the ordinary or unexpected, with the potential to cause serious harm, and/or likely to attract public and media interest that occurs on NHS premises or in the provision of an NHS or a commissioned service'. Trusts must report SUIs to their Strategic Health Authority (SHA). The SHA will need full details of the incident (all person identifiable information must be anonymised), including when and how it happened, and information about how it is being managed, including media handling arrangements, if appropriate. When making a Data Protection Act request for his records, the patient should also ask the Trust if there has been an internal investigation into the incident (including a SUI investigation) and request all documents in connection with the investigation.

At the time of writing, the Government proposes abolishing SHAs. It is not known what will happen about SUIs and their reporting. It is hoped that the Care Quality Commission will receive notice of these inquiries.

CARE QUALITY COMMISSION (CQC)

On 1 April 2009, the CQC took over health and social care regulation in England from the Healthcare Commission. It is an independent body established to promote improvements in healthcare. The CQC is not involved in the NHS complaints process and cannot consider individual complaints about the NHS. It does, however, encourage patients to let it know about their complaints, in the hope that this will help it to improve services for everyone. If an event is sufficiently serious, the CQC can investigate on its own behalf separately from the investigation of the patient's complaint.

The Commission's address is:

Care Quality Commission,
Finsbury Tower,
103–105 Bunhill Row,
London
EC1Y 8TG
Tel: 03000 616161
Email: mailto:enquiries@cqc.org.uk
Website: www.cqc.org.uk

COMPLAINTS WHEN LITIGATION IS CONTEMPLATED

At one time, a hospital would not investigate a patient's complaint if he appeared to be contemplating litigation. Trusts were entitled to refuse to respond to a complaint if litigation was contemplated. The mere act of receiving a request for disclosure of medical records was often sufficient to cause a Trust to refuse to correspond. In *R v Canterbury and Thanet District Health Authority* [1994] 5 Med LR 132, the Divisional Court upheld the discontinuance by the defendants of an independent review when it became clear that the complainants were contemplating legal proceedings (the complaints were against a psychiatrist for negligent diagnoses of sexual abuse). The court said that the procedure depended upon the co-operation of the consultant whose actions were the subject of the inquiry and that his co-operation would clearly not now be forthcoming. The primary purpose of the procedure was either to get a second opinion and thereby a change of diagnosis or treatment, or to enable the health authority to change its procedures in the light of what transpired at the inquiry. Further, if the matter was likely to go to court, that would provide a far more searching inquiry than the independent review procedure. The new regulations that came into force in April 2009 permitted the investigation of a complaint to continue even when a civil claim for compensation was contemplated or indeed underway (with some variation for the devolved jurisdictions, see below). With the advent of the revised procedure in 2006, Trusts cannot unreasonably refuse to investigate a complaint unless they can demonstrate that the investigation and response will prejudice future litigation.

CURRENT LEGISLATION AND PROCEDURE

On 1 April 2009, the National Health Service (Complaints) Regulations 2004 were repealed and the majority of the Local Authority Social Services and National Health Services Complaints (England) Regulations 2009 came into force (with the remainder coming into force on 1 October 2010). These Regulations derive from powers given to the Secretary of State for Health in the Health and Social Care (Community Health and Standards) Act 2003 to make provision for the handling and consideration of complaints by NHS bodies in England (or a cross-border Special Health Authority).

The Regulations make provision for 'responsible bodies' (which include NHS bodies and certain other providers who provide services under arrangements with NHS bodies) to make arrangements for the handling and consideration of complaints. They must designate a person to be responsible for ensuring compliance with the arrangements, and a complaints manager to be responsible for managing the complaints procedure. Regulation 13 provides for how complaints are to be made and processed initially. The responsible body must acknowledge the complaint not less than three working days after the day on which it is received. The acknowledgement may be made orally or in writing. At the time the acknowledgement is made, the responsible body must offer to discuss with the claimant the manner in which the complaint is to be handled and the period within which the investigation of the complaint is likely to be completed and the response sent to the complainant. If the complainant does not accept the offer of a discussion, the responsible body must determine the response period and notify the complainant of that period in writing.

Regulation 14 provides for the investigation of the complaint and the response to the complainant. The responsible body must investigate the complaint in a manner appropriate to resolving it speedily and efficiently. During the investigation the responsible body must keep the complainant informed, as far as reasonably practicable, as to progress. As soon as reasonably practicable after completing the investigation, the responsible body must send the complainant a response which includes a report which gives an explanation of how the complaint has been considered and the conclusions reached in relation to the complaint. The response must also confirm whether the responsible body is satisfied that any action needed in consequence of the complaint has been taken or is proposed to be taken; as well as details of the complainant's right to take his complaint to the Health Service Commissioner. If no such response is sent within six months of the complaint being received, the responsible body must write to the complainant explaining why, and send a full response as soon as reasonably practicable.

In addition, each responsible body is required to ensure that its complaints arrangements are made available to the public (reg 16) and to prepare and make available an annual report regarding complaints received (reg 18).

PRIMARY CARE PRACTITIONERS AND PERSONAL MEDICAL SERVICES

The regulations listed below set out the statutory framework for the handling of complaints at a local level by primary care practitioners and about personal medical services. They provide that services they cover must have in place a complaints procedure which meets the requirements of the Local Authority and National Health Service Complaints (England) Regulations 2009 (as set out above):

- SI 2005/641 – National Health Service (Pharmaceutical Services) Regulations 2005;

- SI 2006/552 – National Health Service (Local Pharmaceutical Services etc) Regulations 2006;
- SI 2005/3361 – National Health Service (General Dental Services Contracts) Regulations 2005;
- SI 2005/3373 – National Health Service (Personal Dental Services Agreements) Regulations 2005;
- SI 2008/1185 – General Ophthalmic Services Contracts Regulations 2008;
- SI 2004/291 – National Health Service (General Medical Services Contracts) Regulations 2004;
- SI 2004/627 – National Health Service (Personal Medical Services Agreements) Regulations 2004.

As well as complaining to his primary care practitioner, the patient may also complain to his Primary Care Trust.

NHS SCOTLAND

Although under separate legislation, the NHS complaints procedure in Scotland proceeds in the same way as in England with referral to the Scottish Public Services Ombudsman if the patient is not satisfied with local resolution.

NHS NORTHERN IRELAND

Northern Ireland has an integrated complaints process for health and social care, also implemented in April 2009 with the issue of *Standards and Guidelines for Resolution and Learning*. The procedure is broadly similar to that of England and more details can be obtained from Health and Social Care Northern Ireland at www.hscni.net. The criteria for refusing to investigate in the event litigation is indicated varies slightly from the rest of the UK. Guidelines to NHS bodies in Northern Ireland state that they 'should not take the initial communication, even if from a solicitor as an indication that the patient intends to take legal action but if proceedings are issued or the patient advises of his intention to litigate then investigation of the complaint should cease'.

NHS IN WALES

Putting Things Right (NHS redress in Wales)

Redress in Wales ('*Putting Things Right*') came into force on 1 April 2011. Claims up to £25,000 can be dealt with under the scheme. *Putting Things Right* is not simply focused on claims but also encompasses the complaints process, how adverse incidents are investigated, risk management and patient safety. Potentially, the proposals could provide significant improvements on past arrangements. Patient organisations have welcomed the broader aims of the scheme but remain concerned about how the scheme will be implemented in practice. Further information can be found in Chapter 23 and at www.puttingthingsright.wales.nhs.uk.

THE OMBUDSMAN

The Office of the Parliamentary and Health Service Ombudsman (or Health Service Commissioner as it is also known) was established by the National Health Service Reorganisation Act of 1973. The relevant statutory provisions are now found in the Health Service Commissioners Act 1993 (as amended). The Ombudsman will investigate and report, making recommendations following complaints about NHS treatment. Previously, there were separate offices for England, Wales and Scotland but the same person could, and previously did, fill all three posts. Since devolution, separate legislation has been enacted for complaints about the National Health Service in Scotland and Wales, and there are some differences in the complaints procedure that operates in Northern Ireland. The Scottish Public Services Ombudsman now has jurisdiction over complaints about the NHS in Scotland, under the Scottish Public Services Ombudsman Act 2002. In Wales, the Public Services Ombudsman has jurisdiction over complaints about the NHS in Wales, under the Public Services Ombudsman (Wales) Act 2005 and there is a separate ombudsman for Northern Ireland. The 1993 Act has been amended such that it now deals only with the Health Service Ombudsman for England.

If a patient is not satisfied with the response he receives to his complaint from local resolution, he can contact the Parliamentary and Health Service Ombudsman (or the equivalent in Scotland, Wales and Northern Ireland) for further consideration of his complaint. The organisation complained to should have directed the patient to the ombudsman in the letter responding to the initial complaint, in the event that he was not satisfied with the explanation given. The patient can telephone the ombudsman for initial advice or submit a written complaint on the form available on the ombudsman's website.

When the ombudsman receives a complaint, there is a two stage process. The first stage is Assessment. The complaint is acknowledged within two days and then checked to ensure the Ombudsman has the legal power to investigate and whether local resolution is complete. Then, provided there has been administrative fault leading to some injustice or hardship and reasonable prospects of a satisfactory resolution, the complaint is passed to the next stage, investigation.

At this stage, if the issues cannot be settled by intervention then a full investigation takes place. After investigation a number of actions can be taken. In her annual report, the Ombudsman provides details of complaints she has dealt with and their outcomes. In the past, the Ombudsman has ordered a Trust to apologise, and review its policy for dealing with certain emergencies and ordered another Trust to set out an action plan giving details of lessons learnt and what it plans to do to prevent recurrence. The Ombudsman can, in rare circumstances, order the healthcare provider to make a payment to the patient in recognition of distress or inconvenience but it will not be of the same order as if a patient litigated and should not be seen as comparable. The ombudsman will investigate all areas of NHS healthcare provision including hospitals, GPs, dentists, opticians, pharmacists and the ambulance service.

The Ombudsman cannot investigate clinical complaints arising before April 1996, ie complaints about treatment afforded or withheld, or complaints against family health service providers. The wide extensions to her catchment area created by the 1996 amendments apply only to complaints arising after March 1996.

The Ombudsman will not investigate personnel matters, such as staff appointments or removals, pay, discipline and superannuation or contractual or other commercial transactions. Discretionary decisions which an authority has a right to take are also not part of the Ombudsman's remit (but she can look at whether the authority has followed proper procedures and considered all relevant aspects in reaching its decision). The Ombudsman will also not investigate if there is to be a public enquiry into an event such as a serious incident or major breakdown in service. The ombudsman's representative will speak to the patient as part of her investigation and at the end of the investigation both the patient and the healthcare provider complained of will receive a written report.

There is a time limit for complaints to be made to the Ombudsman. Complaints should be made within one year of the date on which the matter first came to the notice of the complainant (though the Ombudsman may, if she thinks fit, waive this requirement).

Contact details

England

The Parliamentary and Health Service Ombudsman,
Millbank Tower,
Millbank,
London
SW1 4QP
Helpline: 0345 015 4033
Email: phso.enquiries@ombudsman.org.uk
Website: www.ombudsman.org.uk

Scotland

Scottish Public Services Ombudsman,
4 Melville Street,
Edinburgh
EH3 7NS
Helpline: 0800 377 7330
Email: ask@spso.org.uk
Website: www.spso.org.uk

Wales

Public Service Ombudsman for Wales,
1 Ffordd yr Hen Gae,
Pencoed
CF35 5LJ
Tel: 01656 641 150
Email: ask@ombudsman-wales.org.uk
Website: www.ombudsman-wales.org.uk

Northern Ireland

The Ombudsman
Freepost
BEL1 6BR
Helpline: 0800 34 34 24
Email: ombudsman@ni-ombudsman.org.uk
Website: www.ni-ombudsman.org.uk

THE STATUTORY INQUIRY

In exceptional circumstances, the Secretary of State may decide that the issues complained of merit a Public Enquiry. The Secretary of State's powers arise under s 1 of the Inquiries Act 2005. An enquiry may be held where it appears to the minister that particular events have caused, or are capable of causing, public concern, or there is public concern that particular events may have occurred. If the Minister thinks that any health body has failed to carry out any of its functions under the relevant legislation, he can declare it to be in default and replace its members. The Shipman inquiry was held under the predecessor legislation to the Inquiries Act 2005.

PROCEDURE FOR PRIVATE PATIENTS

The complaints procedures as described above are applicable in respect of NHS treatment; they do not apply to private patients. Private patients should complain directly to their medical practitioner and or the private hospital or clinic where they received their treatment. The Independent Healthcare Advisory Services (IHAS) (www.independenthealthcare.org.uk) may also be able to help. Their guide, *Making complaints: a guide for patients*, supported by the Patients Association, provides details on how to complain and applies to all organisations that have signed up to the IHAS code. The code is voluntary. NHS patients receiving care within an independent hospital are entitled to use the IHAS procedure although they may also use the NHS procedure to complain to their PCT or other commissioning authority.

COMPLAINTS AND PUBLIC FUNDING

In Vol 3 of the Funding Code Guidance 18.2, the Legal Services Commission set out the requirement for the applicant to make a complaint to the healthcare provider before funding is granted. The requirement is to pursue local resolution through to the letter of response. The LSC will not usually expect the applicant to pursue a complaint further than that, but failure to complete local resolution will result in automatic refusal in all but exceptional circumstances. The exceptions are: urgency (limitation imminent), severe injury or prejudice and where the Trust refuses to investigate.

NHS REDRESS

The NHS Redress Act 2006 envisaged an alternative to litigation for lower value claims. It was recognised that conventional litigation with its attendant costs of expert evidence, court fees etc is not always appropriate for claims of lower value. NHS redress would allow the Trust to investigate, obtain expert evidence and if appropriate make an offer of compensation. The only legal fees paid would be those in getting advice on the offer made, the standard civil burden of proof would apply. Despite pilots and much discussion, NHS redress has not yet come into force in England and there are no immediate plans to do so.

However in Wales, *Putting Things Right*, which came into force in April 2011, aims to integrate complaints and claims. The procedure removes the independent review stage of the complaint (to bring it in line with England) and links the investigation of complaints and settlement of claims with improvements in patient safety. Trusts have to provide details of how to put in place procedures to prevent repeat incidents. Where there is a claim it is proposed to rely on joint expert advice and for legal advice to be provided by panel solicitors only at a fixed fee. The scheme does not apply to higher value claims, ie those valued at above £25,000.

COMPLAINTS ABOUT INDIVIDUAL PROFESSIONALS

The General Medical Council (GMC)

Complaints about serious professional misconduct by a GP or hospital doctor may be addressed to the GMC. Complaints may be submitted online using the form provided on the GMC website or by post using the printable form that can be downloaded from the website. After an initial screening exercise to ensure that the complaint meets the GMC criteria, a decision is made whether to investigate or take no further action. Even if no further action is taken, the GMC will still inform the doctor's employer that a complaint has been made. If the employer is the NHS, any further action is left up to the Trust. If the doctor is in private practice or works as a locum, the GMC expect the employer to relay any concerns back and will reconsider whether to investigate in the light of any new information. If the GMC decides to investigate, it will ask the doctor to comment on the allegations and give the patient a chance to respond. Following the investigation, the decision may be to take no further action, issue a warning or impose conditions on practice or refer to a full hearing. A doctor may be subjected to an interim order suspending him pending the full hearing.

The hearing is governed by the formal rules of evidence. Sanctions where the complaint is upheld range from issuing a warning to a requirement to work under supervision to striking off. The doctor has a right of appeal to the High Court, which he must lodge within 28 days of the panel decision. Any sanctions imposed by the panel will not take effect until either the time for appeal has elapsed or the result of the appeal known. However, if the panel is sufficiently concerned that public safety is at risk, they can suspend a doctor pending the outcome of the appeal.

In the Patients' Help section of its website, the GMC provides details on how to make a complaint and how it investigates. Currently a complaint must be made within five years of the conduct in question, but this has recently been challenged. There are also case studies and links to agencies that can help. Only allegations of serious professional misconduct are investigated at a full hearing. Examples of serious professional misconduct include neglect or disregard of responsibilities to patients for their care and treatment, abuse of professional privileges in prescribing drugs or issuing medical certificates, abuse of professional confidence, abuse of the financial opportunities of medical practice, abuse of the doctor/patient relationship, and personal behaviour that could bring the profession into disrepute.

Recent publicity surrounding deficiencies in hospital management and individual doctors has caused the GMC to review its monitoring of performance standards. Public criticism has been particularly strong because in some cases the poor performances have been of long standing. New procedures are being implemented to improve monitoring and be compatible with the Human Rights Act. Included in the new procedures is a plan for ongoing revalidation of all doctors. This will include providing continuing evidence of fitness to practice. The GMC is giving consideration to the appropriate standard of proof in complaints against individual doctors, which at the moment requires proof beyond reasonable doubt.

The address for the GMC is:

General Medical Council Fitness to Practice,
St James Buildings,
79 Oxford Street,
Manchester
M1 6FQ
Tel: 0845 357 0022
Email: practise@gmc-uk.org
Website: www.gmc-uk.org

The Nurses and Midwives Council (NMC)

The NMC regulates qualified nurses and midwives only. The procedure for making a complaint is set out on the Council's website including the provision of a form to report the complaint to the Fitness to Practice.

When complaints are first received, they are checked to ensure all the information necessary to make an initial decision is provided for consideration. Some allegations of fitness to practice are dismissed at the first screening stage. The rest and all allegations of fraud and incorrect entry (on the register) are referred to the NMC Investigation Committee. The panel decides on the paperwork if there is a case to answer.

If it is decided there is a case to answer and in all fraudulent or incorrect entry cases, the Investigating Committee refers the case to a differently constituted Investigating Committee panel for adjudication. Where the allegations relate to fitness to practice and where there is a case to answer, the case is referred to the Conduct and Competence Committee or the Health Committee for adjudication.

A panel can adjudicate either on the paperwork or can hold a hearing where evidence is given by all the people concerned. Panels consist of a nurse or midwife and lay members. Hearings can take place in Edinburgh, Cardiff, Belfast and London. If a complaint is upheld, the committee panel's orders vary from no further action to striking an individual off the register. The nurse or midwife can appeal a decision to the High Court; the appeal must be lodged within 28 days of the individual receiving the letter containing the panel committee's decision. Nurses and midwifes who have been struck off the register can apply to be reinstated after five years.

Complainants are encouraged to make complaints to the NMC as soon after the events complained of as possible, although the NMC has no time limit for considering complaints and will look at each case of complaint on its individual merits. Similarly there is not a strict timetable for investigating the complaint, just the assumption that the investigation will be conducted in a reasonable time. Complainants should use the form designated for the purpose available on the NMC website.

There has been debate over who regulates non-qualified healthcare assistants (HCAs) and student nurses, but at the time of writing they are not regulated by the NMC and complaints about the conduct of an individual student or HCA should be made directly to their employer. The NMC do however regulate the training and examination of nurses pursuing the Registered Nurse or Registered Midwife qualification and as such a complaint about an individual during training may have an effect on first registration.

The provision for regulation of HCAs is less straightforward. If the HCA works for an NHS Trust, complaints should be dealt with in accordance with the general provisions in the NHS complaints procedure as outlined above. If working for local authority social services, a similar complaints procedure operates. However some HCAs work via agencies and if directly employed by a patient to work in the home, the only course of action may not be effective. The reason for this is that the complaint may have to be made to an agency and by the time the complaint is received the HCA may have moved on. Work is currently underway to consider what organisation will regulate HCAs and how they might, in the light of no nationally recognised qualification, be regulated.

The address for the NMC is:

Fitness to Practise Department,
Nursing and Midwifery Council,
61 Aldwych,
London
WC2B 4AE
Tel: 020 7462 580
Email: fitness.to.practise@nmc-uk.org
Website: www.nmc-uk.org

Other professionals

The Health Professionals Council (HPC) registers and regulates 15 healthcare-related professions including physiotherapists, occupational therapists, speech and language therapists and paramedics. Registration means that a health professional meets national standards for their profession in training, performance and conduct. The regulated professionals must meet the standards set by the council (usually by qualifying with a nationally recognised qualification and complying with the CPD requirements) and are then permitted to use a legally protected title (such as physiotherapist).

The HPC can take action if there is a complaint; they will investigate and may hold a fitness to practice hearing which could lead to an order preventing the individual from practicing. Full details of how to make a complaint and the fitness to practice process as well as a list of all the healthcare professionals that the HPC regulate can be found on their website.

The address for the HPC is:

Health Professionals Council,
Park House,
184 Kennington Park Road,
London
SE11 4BU
Tel: 0800 328 4218
Email: flp@hpc-uk.org
Website: www.hpc-uk.org

ASSISTANCE WITH MAKING A COMPLAINT

A number of organisations can help with complaints. The patient's choice will depend on the nature of the complaint and what result the patient wants to achieve.

Patient Advice and Liaison Services (PALS)

PALS is the Patient Advice and Liaison Service, set up by the Government when Community Health Councils were abolished. PALS offices are situated in hospital buildings and are part of the Trust but are not part of the complaints procedure. PALS officers will assist patients with issues such as environmental (waiting rooms or wards), relationships with members of staff or in obtaining a clearer explanation of treatment options.

Because they are on the spot and can act as an advocate directly with the healthcare provider, PALS officers are well placed to help with issues as soon as they arise. In some instances, such as obtaining a clear explanation of treatment options, this help may prevent a complaint escalating.

Although PALS officers can assist in making a formal complaint, many patients may wish to have assistance from an entirely independent organisation. As PALS offices are situated on the hospital premises and are part of the Trust, PALS can be seen as not being independent.

Citizens Advice Bureau and ICAS

Citizens' Advice Bureaux (CABs) will provide the patient with general advice on how to complain. They can also refer on to other agencies which can provide more practical assistance such as the local Independent Complaints Advocacy Service (ICAS), set up after Community Health

Councils were abolished, or AvMA (see below). The CAB address can be found under various local listings including yellow pages (or yell.com) and local websites or at www.citizensadvice.org.uk.

ICAS

Information regarding ICAS can be found online at www.pohwer.net/how_we_can_help/how_icas_can.html. This website offers a self-help pack, which includes tips in a number of areas, including writing a complaint letter, but this has not been updated since the NHS complaints procedure changed on 1 April 2009, so it is currently out of date in some respects.

Community Health Councils which formerly provided assistance were abolished in England in 2004 but remain in Wales and will help.

Action Against Medical Accidents (AvMA)

AvMA is a charity that exists to campaign for patient safety and justice and to help anyone who has experienced an adverse outcome following healthcare. Its website has information on making a complaint and sample letters. The helpline for patients is open from 10 am to 5 pm Monday to Friday. Helpline operators may refer callers on to case workers. AvMA's case workers will help clients make a complaint. The help will include analysis of medical records, letter writing and advising on questions to ask at face to face meetings. AvMA case workers will occasionally accompany clients to face to face meetings with healthcare providers. Advice and assistance is also provided in connection with inquests into deaths following medical care. Assistance includes providing questions for family members to ask at the inquest, a McKenzie Friend or in some circumstances an advocate pro bono. If appropriate, and at the client's request, AvMA will refer clients to one of its panel solicitors (accredited solicitors – see below). Panel members will advise on and take instructions to pursue a civil claim on behalf of the patient if it appears that there has been damage caused by the medical care. AvMA case workers will, with the client's permission, receive regular reports from the panel solicitor and maintain a client relationship until the end of the case.

AvMA's address is:

AvMA,
44 High St,
Croydon
CR0 1YB
Tel: 020 8686 9555 (solicitors only, clients should phone the helpline)
Helpline: 0845 123 23 52
Email: advice@avma.org.uk
Website: www.avma.org.uk

The Patients' Association

This body also represents the interests of the consumer patient. Its website contains information on making a complaint and sample letters. General advice can be obtained from its helpline but the organisation does not provide individual assistance to complainants.

The Patients' Association's address is:

The Patients' Association,
PO Box 935,
Harrow,
Middlesex
HA1 3YJ
Helpline: 0845 608 4455,
Website: www.patients-association.com

Member of Parliament

This can be a useful avenue of complaint, particularly where the patient is getting no response to inquiries or letters. A letter from an MP can often speed up the process of providing a response.

Accredited solicitors

Both the Law Society and AvMA maintain a system of accreditation called panel membership. The criteria for membership of the two panels are similar but not identical. Membership of either panel is a quality mark and indicates that the individual solicitor has a certain level of experience and expertise measured against an objective standard.

Only firms who have at least one panel member (of either panel) in their clinical negligence department may offer its clients funding by Legal Aid. The only specialist panels recognised by the LSC are those accredited by AvMA and the Law Society.

If patients contact AvMA for help and advice and wish to consult a solicitor with a view to bringing a civil claim, AvMA will only refer them to one of its panel solicitors.

Details of AvMA panel members are available at www.avma.org.uk/pages/clinical_negligence_specialist_solicitors.html and of Law Society panel members at www.lawsociety.org.uk/choosingandusing/findasolicitor.law. Information on Firms which offer Legal Aid for clinical negligence claims can be found at www.communitylegaladvice.org.uk/en/directory/directorysearch.jsp. All of these websites have search functions that enable searches by region and/or specialism.

Although only Law Society and AvMA panel memberships are recognised by the LSC as able to offer legal aid funding, other organisations will refer to panel membership or accreditation schemes. When legal expense insurers refer to panel solicitors, this refers to the relationship between the insurer and the solicitor or solicitor's firm. The solicitor may be a specialist clinical negligence practitioner (although more usually a solicitor who undertakes personal injury and clinical negligence work) and he will not necessarily have AvMA or Law Society panel membership.

While also not being recognised by the LSC and careful not to style itself as panel membership, APIL accreditation is a scheme that has four levels according to experience and expertise and includes corporate accreditation. In common with AvMA and Law Society panel membership, the application process requires that the applicant provides information on individual practice and firms practice as well as referees. Some publicly available information can be found on the website www.apil.org.uk. Full details of the application process and criteria for the different levels of accreditation are in the members only section of the website.

Becoming accredited

Applicants to both panels must have at least three years post-qualification experience in clinical negligence litigation (usually more). Applicants must provide evidence of experience by way of case studies and of the resources, support and supervision procedures in their firm. The application process and the forms themselves differ between AvMA and the Law Society. Both panels charge an administration fee as part of the application process. Details of requirements and application forms for AvMA panel membership can be found at www.avma.org.uk/pages/avma_specialist_clinical_negligence_panel.html. For the Law Society see www.lawsociety.org.uk/productsandservices/accreditation/accreditationclinicalnegligence.page.

Chapter 4

Legal remedies

Catriona Stirling

VICARIOUS LIABILITY

An employer is vicariously responsible for the negligent acts or omissions of his servant committed within the scope of the employment, but, as a general rule, not for the negligence of an independent contractor, provided he showed due care in selecting the contractor.

The correct defendant in respect of allegations of negligence at a hospital is the body in charge at the time of the negligence (ie the health authority for older claims and the NHS trust for more recent ones). The trust or health authority is liable for the negligence of any of its staff, including all medical personnel it engages to carry out the necessary treatment upon the patients, because it is under a primary non-delegable duty of care to see that the patient receives proper treatment. It is therefore unnecessary to pray in aid the principle of vicarious liability. A health authority is not responsible for the negligence of a doctor who has been selected and employed by a private patient (or his GP).

A private clinic is probably responsible only for the negligence of its resident staff, though where it selects and engages the surgeon itself a court is these days likely to find a primary duty of care, just as with an NHS hospital.

The majority of GPs are self-employed, thus, in the normal case, a GP is alone liable for his own negligent acts. He is also liable for the acts of anyone he employs, and may possibly be liable for outside services he engages to look after patients in his absence. A number of salaried GPs, however, are employed and some GPs who work for out-of-hours services to supplement their income are also employed.

General principles

The general principles of vicarious liability, that is the liability of one person for the negligence of another, are as follows (they are stated in summary form as the topic is too complex to be discussed here in detail, and our concern is with the clinical negligence context so I give merely the outline of the law and one or two useful references). The House of Lords has said that vicarious liability means that, with regard to third parties, the employer, although personally blameless, stands in the shoes of the wrongdoer employee for the purpose of liability to the claimant. [1] Vicarious liability is substitutional, not personal.

The claimant must usually show first that the negligence complained of was due to the act or omission of an employee of the defendant. An employee is one who is engaged upon a contract of service. The test of employment has varied through the years. Basically, a man is not an employee if the person who engaged him has no say in how he does his work, but only in what work he is to do. If the person engaged is subject to the control and directions of the other in respect of the manner in which the work is to be done, he will be an employee (the leading case is *Mersey Docks and Harbour Board* v *Coggins and Griffith (Liverpool) Ltd* [1947] AC 1, HL). It is often not easy to decide on applying this test whether there is a situation of employment. A good reference point is the judgment of MacKenna J in *Ready Mixed Concrete (South East) Ltd* v *Minister of Pensions and National Insurance* [1968] 2 QB 497.[2]

In *Kapfunde* v *Abbey National plc* [1999] ICR 1, CA, a GP had a contract with Abbey National whereby she assessed the health of any prospective employee. She had, upon written material, not an examination, declared that the claimant was unsuitable to be employed as she had sickle cell disease and so was at risk of having a lot of time off work for illness. Having unsuccessfully sued for racial discrimination, the claimant went on to allege in this action that the GP owed her a duty of care, which she had breached. The Court of Appeal upheld, *inter alia*, the judge's findings that the GP was on a contract for services and not a contract of service and therefore Abbey National would not in any event be vicariously liable for any breach of duty by her.[3] In *North Essex Health Authority* v *Dr David-John* [2003] Lloyds Rep Med 586, the Employment Appeal Tribunal held that the GP was not in any contractual relationship with the health authority, but that, if he was, it was as an independent contractor. This is the normal position for self-employed GPs.

The claimant must then show that the negligence complained of was committed within the course or scope of the employee's employment. The traditional method of looking at this was to determine whether the unauthorised and wrongful act of the employee was one way, albeit an improper way, of discharging his obligations under the contract of employment, or whether it was an independent act unconnected with his employment. An employee may be acting within the scope of his employment even if he acted in express disregard of instructions or prohibitions from his employer or if he acted purely for his own benefit, rather than that of the employer, if he had apparent authority to do so.

The leading case in this area is now *Lister* v *Hesley Hall Ltd* [2002] 1 AC 15, HL. The claimants in *Lister*, who had been resident some years earlier at the defendant's school for boys with emotional and behavioural difficulties, sued for personal injury in respect of sexual abuse by the warden employed by the defendants. The House of Lords said that it was important to avoid becoming involved in the simplistic and erroneous

---

1   *Dubai Aluminium Co Ltd* v *Salaam* [2002] UKHL 48, [2003] 2 AC 366.
2   Reference may also be made in this context to the House of Lords' judgment in *McDermid* v *Nash Dredging and Reclamation Co* [1987] AC 906.
3   For another analysis of the distinction between a contract for services and a contract of service, see *Thames Water Utilities* v *King* (23 July 1998, unreported), CA.

task of trying to determine whether the acts for which an employer was sought to be held vicariously liable were modes of doing authorised acts. The proper approach was to adopt a broad assessment of the nature of the employee's employment. The defendant had undertaken to care for the boys in its charge through the services of the warden. The warden's torts were sufficiently closely connected with his employment that it would be fair, just and reasonable (that ubiquitous phrase again!) to hold the defendant vicariously liable.

In *Mattis* v *Pollock* [2003] EWCA Civ 887, [2003] 1 WLR 2158, CA, a nightclub was held vicariously responsible for the stabbing of a customer by its doorman, where the fight began in the club but the stabbing took place later after the doorman had gone home, armed himself with a knife and found his enemy on the street. The Court of Appeal said that the doorman was employed to keep order and to act in an aggressive and intimidatory manner, and it would be fair and just to hold the club vicariously responsible for the assault. It is in fact hardly surprising the club was held liable, given that the doorman had not been registered for doorman work by the licensing authority. Still in the salubrious realm of nightclubs, in *Naylor* v *Payling* [2004] EWCA Civ 560, [2004] PIQR P36, CA, a customer was assaulted by a doorman. The doorman was employed by a security agent who had a contract with the club to provide security. The agent had failed to take out any public liability insurance, so the customer sued the club instead of the agent. The customer did not seek to argue that the agent was an employee rather than an independent contractor, but that the club owed customers a duty to ensure that the agent was properly insured. The Court of Appeal rejected his claim, saying that the agent had reasonably appeared competent to the club, both originally and over the period of some 18 months prior to the assault, and it was not incumbent on the club to ensure that he was properly insured. This situation has arisen in the medical context also, for example, where a culpable locum GP has no insurance. He is not employed by anyone; he is an independent contractor, and it seems that the resident GP need do no more than book his locum (there is much more scope for that now that GPs do not need to be on night duty themselves!) through a reputable agency.

In *Attorney-General* v *Hartwell* [2004] UKPC 12, [2004] 1 WLR 1273, PC, the Privy Council considered a claim against the Government of the British Virgin Islands as being vicariously liable for the injuries accidentally received by the claimant, a British holiday-maker, who was unfortunately in the line of fire when a policeman employed by the Government discharged a loaded firearm in a bar in pursuance of a personal vendetta against his wife and her suspected lover. The claimant succeeded in that the court said that the defendants were in breach of a duty of care in issuing the policeman with a firearm when they had failed to investigate two complaints that had earlier been made against him of violent behaviour. However, the point here is that they held the Government *not* to be vicariously liable for the assault, saying that the acts of the employee (he had travelled to a neighbouring island, not on duty, but with the express intent of seeking his wife out) were not sufficiently closely connected with those acts which he was authorised to do.

Hartwell was applied in *N* v *Chief Constable of Merseyside Police* [2006] EWHC 3041 (QB), [2006] All ER (D) 421 (Nov), where the Chief Constable was not vicariously liable where a police officer who was wearing his uniform and held himself out as a police officer took an intoxicated woman to his home and raped her. The judgment made it clear, however, that the circumstances as a whole must be looked at, and that the result may have been different if the policeman had been exercising a police function, such as making an arrest.

In *Gravill* v *Carroll* [2008] EWCA Civ 689, [2008] ICR 1222, CA, the Court of Appeal held that a rugby club was vicariously liable when one of its players assaulted another player. The assault was so closely connected to the player's employment that it would be fair and just to hold the club liable.

In *Maga* v *Birmingham Roman Catholic Archdiocese Trustees* [2010] EWCA Civ 256, CA, the claimant, a minor, had been sexually abused by an assistant priest. The Court of Appeal held that it was fair and just to impose vicarious liability on the church trustees, considering a number of factors in reaching the conclusion that there was a sufficiently close connection between the assistant priest's employment at the church and the abuse inflicted on the claimant. One of the most important factors considered was the fact that the priest's role gave him the status, authority and opportunity to draw the claimant into a position where he could abuse him.

The 'scope of employment' principle could assume significance in a clinical negligence context. This doctrine means that negligence by medical personnel falling outside the scope of their employment would not render the health authority or trust vicariously liable (for example, staff playing a game of cricket on the lawns and carelessly hitting the ball at a patient sitting in the sun, or an off-duty nurse running down a patient as she drives out of the grounds). However, as we shall see, there is a primary non-delegable duty of care imposed upon a trust or health authority.

In *Rosen* v *Edgar* (1986) 293 BMJ 552, the claimant, acting in person, sued a consultant for acts done by his senior registrar. It was held, as one would expect, that a senior employee was not answerable for the fault of a junior employee, for he did not employ him, albeit he had overall supervision of him.

An interesting case is *Godden* v *Kent and Medway Strategic Health Authority* [2004] EWHC 1629 (QB), [2004] Lloyds Rep Med P521, where patients of a GP who had been convicted of assaulting them sued the health authority for breach of a duty of care at common law and deriving from s 29 of the National Health Service Act 1977, and as vicariously liable for the GP's torts. On an application by the defendant to strike out the claim, Gray J held that the contention of a duty of care failed (the health authority was not responsible under the Act for the provision of the relevant medical services – GPs were) except in so far as it was arguable that the defendant had a duty to act upon information it had earlier received about the GP's conduct. Oddly, he was unwilling to strike out what would seem to be an impossible allegation that the health authority was liable vicariously for the GP's torts. It does not employ GPs. They are on contracts for services: in other words they are independent contractors. The case does not appear to have been cited or followed in subsequent cases and there is no reported judgment of a full liability trial.

Whether an act falls within the course of employment is a question of fact in each case, and a broad view must be taken of all the surrounding circumstances.

The common law tests outlined above do not apply where a statute makes express provision in relation to vicarious liability. The Equality Act 2010 provides in s 109 that an employer will be vicariously liable for acts of unlawful discrimination covered by the Act, which are done by employees or agents. However, it will be necessary to show that the worker was acting as an employee or agent within the meaning of s 109 of the Equality Act 2010 (see *Mahood* v *Irish Centre Housing Limited*, (22 March 2011, unreported), EAT) and even if a sufficient degree of control could be established over a worker to render an employer liable at common law in tort for his actions, in the context of torts based on anti-discrimination legislation, it may be necessary to take account of statutory defences.

If an employee contravenes a statute which does not make express provision regarding vicarious liability, the common law tests are relevant to determining whether the employer may be vicariously liable. In the leading case of *Majrowski* v *Guys and St Thomas' NHS Hospital Trust* [2006] UKHL 34, [2007] 1 AC 224, HL, the House of Lords held that an employer could be vicariously liable for harassment committed by an employee in contravention of the Protection from Harassment Act 1997. However, note the decision of the Court of Appeal in *Fecitt* v *NHS Manchester* [2011] EWCA Civ 1190, where it was held that the doctrine of vicarious liability could not operate to make an employer liable under s 47B of the Employment Rights Act 1996. The doctrine required a legal wrong on an individual employee's part, and an employee could not be personally liable for acts of victimisation against whistleblowers (in contrast to discrimination cases, where employees could be personally liable for acts of victimisation).

It is, of course, necessary to establish who is the employer. This used to be fairly easy in the medical field. The GP was responsible for the surgery and GP visits, the health authority for everything else. Then NHS Trusts arose. They now proliferate, so that all sorts of medical care are in the control of different types of Trust, whether a Hospital Trust or a Community Trust, or, now, Primary Care Trusts. A health visitor, for example, may be employed by a GP, by a Community Trust, by a Primary Care Trust or by a health authority. A GP may even be employed by a Trust. Clinics may be run as part of a GP practice, or by a Trust or a health authority. Who will be responsible for walk-in centres? Who is responsible for telephonic advice given by NHS Direct or other out of hours services? The possibilities are legion. A claimant has to be careful, far more than before, to identify the source of the alleged negligence and ascertain who, if anyone, is the relevant employer. See below under 'Suing the wrong defendant'.

Independent contractors

As we have seen, there is in general no liability for the acts of an independent contractor, ie one who is free to perform the work contracted for in his own way. The general principle was confirmed by the Court of Appeal in *Biffa Waste Services Ltd* v *Maschinenefabrik Ernst Hese GMBH* [2008] EWCA Civ 1257, [2009] BLR 1, CA.

Sometimes, the factual matrix within which the question of 'independence' and control arises is complex. In *P* v *Harrow London Borough Council* [1993] 2 FCR 341, QBD, a local education authority which, in furtherance of its duty under the Education Act 1981 to make provision for children with special educational needs, sent boys with emotional behavioural difficulties to an independent school approved by the Secretary of State for Education and Science, was held by Potter J not liable in negligence for sexual abuse committed on the boys by the headmaster of the school while the boys were in his charge. The contact between the local authority and the boys was said by the court to have been wholly in the context of assessment and place provision and not in the context of physical control or direction, which was at all times in the charge of the parents and the staff of the school. Compare *Lister* v *Hesley Hall Ltd* (above).

Sometimes, employees are loaned or hired to other employers temporarily for the purposes of carrying out a particular task or transaction. The employee remains under a contract of employment with his original employer, but in some circumstances a principle of deemed employment can apply such that vicarious liability can be attributed to the third party.

Viasystems v *Thermal Transfer* [2005] EWCA Civ 1151, [2006] 2 WLR 428 concerned work on an air conditioning system in a factory. The first defendants had been engaged to do the work. They subcontracted the work to the second defendants, who contracted with the third defendants for the provision of a fitters' mate. The fitters' mate negligently damaged the ducting system, causing the factory to flood. At the time of his negligence, he was under the supervision of both a fitter who was employed by the third defendants, and the second defendants' supervisor. The Court of Appeal held that both the employer, and the third party exercising day-to-day control over the employee could be vicariously liable for the employee's negligence. The question was: 'Who was entitled, and in theory obliged, to control the employee's relevant negligent act so as to prevent it?' Entire and absolute control was not a necessary precondition of vicarious liability and dual vicarious liability was legally possible. However, the court noted that such situations would be rare.

In *Hawley* v *Luminar Leisure Ltd* [2006] EWCA Civ 18, [2006] IRLR 816, a doorman had been supplied to the defendant nightclub by a third party, under a contract for the supply of security services. He assaulted a member of the public. The Court of Appeal held that the owners of the nightclub were vicariously liable for the assault. Although the doorman was not directly employed by the nightclub, he could properly be deemed to be an employee of the nightclub for vicarious liability principles. On the facts, only the nightclub and not the doorman's employer should be held liable for the assault, on the basis that there had been a total transfer of control to the nightclub.

In *Various Claimants* v *Institute of the Brothers of the Christian Schools* [2010] EWCA Civ 1106, the Court of Appeal held that the Institute, an unincorporated association of lay brothers, were not vicariously liable for alleged abuse perpetrated by brothers who were supplied by the Institute as some of the teaching staff of a particular school. The alleged abusers included non-Institute members of staff. The Institute had not been responsible for running the school and did not exercise effective control over a brother's doing of his teaching job. The discipline exercised by the Institute, however strict, was not sufficient to render it liable. In order to determine whether vicarious liability existed in any particular case, firstly the relationship between the defendants had to be examined, and then the connection between the second defendant and the act or omission of the first defendant had to be examined. Vicarious liability could exist as between one member of an unincorporated association and another. The second stage of the enquiry into the existence of vicarious liability was often more difficult and fact-sensitive than the first stage. A consideration which would often be highly relevant to whether there was the necessary close connection between the tort and the relationship between the parties was whether the second defendant had put the first defendant, for his own purposes, into a position in which the risk of a tort of the kind committed was inherent. The judge had been right to conclude that the Institute was not running the school and did not exercise effective control over a brother-teacher's doing of his teaching job. Accordingly the judge had been right to hold that the Institute did not carry vicarious liability for torts committed by its brothers arising from their teaching occupations at the school.

Agency workers

There has been much litigation regarding the employment status of agency workers. Agency workers have, in recent years, been much used by the NHS, thus the question of vicarious liability in relation to agency workers is an important one for the clinical negligence practitioner. The traditional position if a worker is supplied by an agency to its client on a temporary basis is that the client is regarded as a user of the worker's services and not his employer. Most agency workers are not employed by the agency, but have a mere 'contract for services'. The agency undertakes only to look for work for the worker and facilitate any engagement. Thus, it has often been found that an agency worker does not have an employer.

Even if there is no express contract between a worker and an agency client, if the worker works consistently for, and under the direction of, the client, ie the client controls what the worker does and how he does it, it may be possible to imply a contract between the worker and the client. However, following *James* v *London Borough of Greenwich* [2008] EWCA Civ 35, [2008] ICR 545, CA, such a contract will only be implied where necessary to do so. This requires some words or conduct which indicate that the true nature of the relationship is no longer one of agency, as it originally was. Even once the existence of a contract is established, it is still necessary to establish that its nature is that of employment. The court approved observations made by the EAT to the effect that in the usual agency relationship there were no mutual obligations between the worker and the client. In addition, mere length of service could not justify the implication of a contract.

Following *Hawley,* if it is possible to imply a contract of employment between the agency worker and the client, the client should be vicariously liable for the worker's actions.

What is the situation if no such contract of employment can be implied? If the agency worker is self-employed, but subject to the day-to-day direction and control of the end-user, is there vicarious liability for the agency worker? *Hawley* and *Viasystems* are examples of the imposition of vicarious liability on a non-employer to whom a worker is provided by his employer. The Court of Appeal in these cases clearly regarded the determining factor in relation to vicarious liability as being control of the employee. It would seem that these decisions should be followed in agency cases.

PRIMARY LIABILITY

If the employer has a primary duty to perform an act, he will be liable if his agent in the performance of that act, whether independent contractor or not, performs the act negligently.[4] It is not generally clear to what extent a person has, apart from a contractual or statutory duty, a primary duty of care in respect of an activity,[5] although fortunately it is now beyond argument that under English law a health authority is under a primary non-delegable duty of care in respect of the treatment that is afforded the patient under its auspices.

It may be that the scope of the primary duty in law cannot as a general rule be extended beyond acts which create a source of danger. In respect of hazardous activities, the employer is liable for the negligence of an independent contractor. Liability is, however, restricted in all cases to acts which fall within the duty of care of the employer: he is not liable for the collateral negligence of the independent contractor, ie for acts which are not in fulfilment of the activity in respect of which the primary duty of care is imposed on the employer (a leading case is *Padbury* v *Holliday and Greenwood Ltd* (1912) 28 TLR 494, CA). The liability of the employer for the acts of the independent contractor should not be seen as an example of vicarious liability, that is to say liability assumed by one person on behalf of another, but rather as an example of the situation where a person is himself under a primary duty of care which he cannot delegate to another (see below under 'The primary duty of care').

Health authority or Trust as defendant

The appropriate defendant when the action arises out of NHS treatment in hospital is the health authority or NHS Trust (whichever was in charge of the hospital at the time of the alleged negligence).[6] A few hospitals have for years had special constitutions, so that the hospital itself or its board

---

4   A primary duty can often be construed in a contractual context (see eg *Wong Mee Wan* v *Kwan Kin Travel Services Ltd* [1996] 1 WLR 38, PC, the case of the negligently driven speedboat on a Chinese package holiday).

5   A claim for a non-delegable duty of care as between a Lloyd's Name and his members' agent failed in *Aiken* v *Stewart Wrightson Members' Agency* [1995] 1 WLR 1281, Potter J.

6   The National Health Service Act 2006 provides by Sch 3, para 16: 'Any rights acquired, or liabilities (including liabilities in tort) incurred, in respect of the exercise by a Primary Care Trust of any function exercisable by it by virtue of section 7, 9 or 15 [which relate to the general functions of primary care trusts] are enforceable by or against that Primary Care Trust (and no other body).' Similar provisions apply with regard to Strategic Health Authorities.

of governors is the appropriate defendant, but usually in the past a NHS hospital came within the jurisdiction of a health authority at district level, and it was that authority which had to be made the defendant. Now that virtually all hospitals have opted out of health authority control under the National Health Service and Community Care Act 1990 (though remaining, of course, within the NHS), the appropriate defendant if one is suing in respect of treatment at a hospital will be the new body. The hospital administrator will always provide the correct name of the body that runs the hospital.

However, it should always be borne in mind that the body responsible for any negligent conduct in NHS treatment is the body in charge of the hospital at the time of the alleged negligence. This body may have changed its name or even disappeared as a separate body. It may have merged or it may have been subsumed into an existing body or into a new body entirely. Although the legislature will always have provided for another body to have taken over the pre-existing liabilities of the old body (the NHS Litigation Authority if all else fails), it will *not* be the NHS Trust that may now be running the hospital (a Trust would not exactly be delighted to hear that its limited funds are going to be targeted to settle the health authority's liabilities!). Again, it is not difficult to find out the name of the body running the hospital at the time of the alleged negligence, and it is just as easy to find out, if that body is no longer extant under the same name, what body is now responsible for the pre-existing liabilities of the original body.

Action may be brought for an act or omission that is directly the responsibility of the authority, such as a failure to provide appropriate medical facilities (see, for example, *Bull and Wakeham* v *Devon Health Authority* [1993] 4 Med LR 117, CA, where the court found that the system of obstetric cover provided was not acceptable in that it gave rise to a real inherent risk that an obstetrician might not attend reasonably promptly); or for an act or omission that is directly the responsibility of the hospital, such as a failure to take appropriate general anti-infection measures (*Lindsey County Council* v *Marshall* [1937] AC 97, HL and see *Miller* v *Glasgow Health Board* [2010] CSIH 40, 2010 GWD 20-402, CS); or for specific acts of negligence by its staff.[7] By and large, all medical personnel working at the hospital may be regarded as employed by the health authority or Trust. Obviously, the nursing staff are and the resident doctors and technicians, but, even though, strictly speaking, senior staff and consultants are probably not 'employed', the point is, rightly, not taken (except in the case of private hospitals).

There is no point in adding the particular doctor as defendant where the health authority or trust is in any event clearly liable for any negligence on the doctor's part. It increases costs, delays the trial, and it may be unfair on a young doctor unnecessarily to turn the spotlight and put the pressure on him when he may have been doing his overworked best, perhaps also when he had been, for lack of better qualified staff, required to discharge a responsibility for which he was not yet properly trained.

---

7   See *Robertson* v *Nottingham Health Authority* [1997] 8 Med LR 1 at 13, CA, *per* Brooke LJ.

Suing two defendants

The situation often arises that there appear to be two different parties potentially liable, for example GP and hospital, or two different hospitals run by different health authorities. Liability may be in the alternative or both may be severally liable. One is then anxious about costs in the event of succeeding against one only. This topic is considered in Chapter 25.

Suing the wrong defendant

It is, of course, better to sue the correct defendant from the outset. In appropriate cases, the correct defendant may properly raise a plea of limitation where the claimant seeks to add or substitute him at a later stage. The rules on adding a new defendant in the context of limitation are not easy to understand (see Chapter 18 under 'Amending a claim'). However, it may not be necessary to enter the treacherous waters of limitation simply because you seek to change the name of the defendant. For example, a health authority is not going to object if you get the wrong title when you are clearly intending to sue that body. Perhaps that body now has a new name or has been subsumed into another already existing or newly created body. If, however, you have named a completely different health authority instead of the body that was in charge of the hospital at the relevant time, there may be a little more difficulty. On the other hand, it would be surprising if a health authority raised a plea of limitation where the mistake was to have sued the NHS Trust in respect of negligence occurring at a time when the health authority was still in charge of the hospital.

If the wrong defendant has been sued, the mistake could probably be corrected pursuant to CPR 19.2, 19.5 or 17.4. In *Gregson* v *Channel Four Television Corporation* [2000] CP Rep 60, (2000) Times, 11 August, CA, the court said, echoing the previous law, that CPR 19.5 applied where the application was to substitute a new party for a party who was named in the claim form in mistake for the new party, and CPR 17.4(3) applied where the intended party was named in the claim form but there was a genuine mistake as to the name of the party and no-one was misled. The court said there was no significant conflict between the two rules. In this case CPR 17.4 applied: it was not a question of substituting a new party, and the judge's discretion in favour of the claimant had been correctly exercised.

In *Adelson* v *Associated Newspapers Ltd* [2007] EWCA Civ 701, [2008] 1 WLR 585, the Court of Appeal clarified the law. The court said that mistakes as to the name of a party divide into two categories: errors of identification (where the wrong party is erroneously identified as the proper party) and errors of nomenclature (where the correct party is identified, but erroneously called by the wrong name). CPR 17.4 and 19.5 cover mistakes of nomenclature rather than identification.

The court considered the problems which arise where a claimant knows the attributes of the person he wishes to sue (for example his landlord), but does not know the actual identity of that person:

> If on inquiry he is incorrectly informed that a named third party has those attributes and he commences an action naming that third party as defendant but describing in the pleading the attributes of the person intended to be sued, is the case one of misnomer of the person intending to be sued or error of identification?

Such a situation could arise where a patient had seen a GP at the relevant time, but did not know which GP in the practice had seen the patient. The Court of Appeal considered that such a mistake would be remediable under CPR 17.4 and 19.5, but that the court may not exercise its discretion to allow such a change if the correct defendant was unaware of the claim until the limitation period had expired. In such a situation, therefore, it would be best to sue the practice as a whole, or to plead liability on the ordinary principles of partnership.

In *Lockheed Martin Corp* v *Willis Group Ltd* [2010] EWCA Civ 927, the Court of Appeal held that where a claimant had sued the wrong defendant by mistake and applied under CPR 19.5 to substitute a new party as defendant, the claimant did not have to show that the mistake had not misled the other party or had not caused reasonable doubt as to the identity of the party it intended to sue.

Cases under the old rules (RSC)

In *Adelson,* the Court of Appeal said that, when interpreting the provisions of the CPR in respect of the substitution of parties, it is necessary to have regard to the jurisprudence under RSC, Ord 20, r 5. The old rule which permitted an amendment to correct the name of the party when there had been a mistake, provided the mistake did not cause any reasonable doubt as to the identity of the person intending to sue, was RSC, Ord 20, r 3 and the courts will presumably continue to have regard to the jurisprudence under this rule as well. Thus, amendments will continue to be permitted where there is a simple mistake in the identification of a party, for example, an error in spelling, or a correct surname but wrong first name. The seminal case in recent years regarding RSC, Ord 20, r 3 was *Evans Construction Co Ltd* v *Charrington & Co Ltd* [1983] QB 810, CA. In *Ritz Casino Ltd* v *Khashoggi* ([1996] CLY 890), an amendment was permitted where the claimant had sued in the wrong company name upon two dishonoured cheques. In *Hibernian Dance Club* v *Murray* [1997] PIQR P46, CA, the court held that a mistake in suing the members and/or proprietors of the club under a collective title apt to describe them but devoid of personality at English law, as opposed to suing individually named defendants, was not such as to cause any reasonable doubt that the claim was being asserted against the membership as a whole. The provisions of RSC, Ord 20, r 5 were apt to cover such a case where the action had been hitherto a nullity because the claimant had sued an entity which did not exist in law.[8]

The private patient

The private claimant has to be careful. Though a private clinic is responsible for its resident staff, on the basis that they are employed by the clinic, a consultant may be an independent contractor, engaged on a contract for services rather than a contract of service. If he is not

---

8   See also *Signet Group plc* v *Hammerson UK Properties Ltd* [1998] 03 LS Gaz R 25, CA.

employed by the clinic, the clinic will generally not be vicariously liable for his actions; and, furthermore, it is doubtful if a court would accept the argument that he was engaged to perform hazardous activities and for that reason the clinic must be held vicariously responsible if he is negligent in the course of performing them (one of the exceptions to the rule that a person who engages an independent contractor is generally not liable for his negligence, provided that due care was taken in the selection of the contractor). So the private patient will probably have to sue the consultant concerned if it is his acts or omissions that are alleged to be negligent. It is, however, arguable that, provided it was the clinic and not the patient that engaged the surgeon, albeit upon a contract for services, the clinic is under the same primary duty of care as an NHS hospital (there seems no reason to limit Lord Denning's words (see below) as to the primary duty of care to NHS institutions). Where a clinic, specialising in a particular form of treatment, eg liposuction or ophthalmic laser treatment, contracts with a patient to provide medical treatment, it is highly likely that the court would find that the clinic had a primary non-delegable duty of care in tort, or a similar duty on a proper construction of the contract.

In *Ellis* v *Wallsend District Hospital* [1990] 2 Med LR 103, the New South Wales Court of Appeal held that a public hospital was not vicariously liable for the acts of an 'honorary medical officer', a neuro-surgeon, who was treating a patient pursuant to a direct engagement between him and the patient. This case needs to be studied by anyone seeking to impose liability outside the NHS framework on a health authority or hospital for a doctor's negligence.

The Queen's Bench case of *Loft* v *Gilliat* [2003] MLC 1084 is of interest. A couple claimed damages for negligent advice given to the wife when she was awaiting implantation of her eggs (to be fertilised by a donor) with a view to conceiving a second child (the same way as her first had been conceived), her medical charge being in the hands of a private unit, the Infertility Advisory Centre. She was undergoing this treatment because her husband's sperm could transfer to the child his disease of Huntington's chorea. Mrs Loft claimed that prior to implantation of the eggs, someone at the clinic (but not the defendant) advised her, amazingly, to have intercourse with her husband as that would make the uterus more receptive to the eggs. She then conceived a second daughter, but by her husband's sperm, not through the IVF treatment. The child was sadly suffering from the disease (her birth was in 1989 but the diagnosis was not made for some nine years, so there was no limitation problem for the mother's claim). Mrs Loft claimed financial compensation for her daughter's disability, but she did not claim against the company that owned the centre at the relevant time because it was in liquidation. She sought to hold the medical director, Dr Gilliat, liable, on the basis that he was in charge of the clinic and that she had made the contract with him (he having represented the centre at the contractual stages). At the relevant time, he was not an employee of the company. He was an independent contractor and he was not personally treating Mrs Loft at the time. The case was difficult. Dr Gilliat denied that he was liable to Mrs Loft by reason of his being in charge of the centre and he denied that he was vicariously liable for acts of the staff at the centre. His case was that the company was trading as the advisory centre. The contract was between the company and Mr and Mrs Loft. His contentions were accepted by the judge.

Contract

The private patient's relationship with her doctors and hospitals will depend on the contracts she makes with them.

An attempt to establish a general principle that an NHS patient has a contract with her GP failed in *Reynolds* v *Health First Medical Group* [2000] Lloyd's Rep Med 240 (this ploy was an endeavour in an unplanned pregnancy case to avoid being caught by the *McFarlane* decision – as to which see Chapter 11). Another such attempt was made in *Dow* v *Tayside University Hospitals* [2006] SLT (Sh Ct) 141, where the claimant attempted to establish that she had contracted with the defendant through the agency of the doctor who was charged with terminating her pregnancy, who had not warned of any risk of failure and had warranted that her pregnancy would be terminated. The Sheriff Court appeared open to the argument that such a contractual relationship was possible. Although it dismissed the claim, it held that, proceeding on the basis that the procedure was 'treatment' provided under the National Health Service (Scotland) Act 1978, there could possibly be a contractual relationship in addition to the one imposed by statute, but only where it was clear that the doctor concerned was exceptionally entering into a contract and was not relying on the statutory relationship alone. However, in *Wylie* v *Grosset* [2011] CSOH 89, the Outer House of the Court of Session accepted that the relationship between a doctor and a patient in terms of a clinical drugs trial was contractual where the patient information sheet constituted an offer and the consent form signed by the patient was the acceptance. The patient information leaflet had made reference to the terms on which compensation would be provided in the event of the patient sustaining an injury. Giving those words their ordinary meaning, however, they did not amount to any sort of guarantee that compensation would actually be paid, but meant that the issue would be governed by the guidelines referred to in that context in the leaflet. There may be an expectation of compensation in appropriate circumstances, but the terms of the information sheet did not go so far as to impose a legally enforceable obligation. No clear obligation arose in this case.

Charlesworth on Negligence (7th edition) at p 542 stated:

> The duty in contract is only owed to the parties to the contract, but it would seem that there is in most cases a contract between patient and medical practitioner, even if the patient himself is not liable for payment of the services rendered, such payment being made by someone else;

but no authority was given for that proposition. In *Emeh* v *Kensington and Chelsea and Westminster Area Health Authority* [1985] QB 1012, CA, Slade LJ spoke of the claimant 'contracting' with the health authority (though he was not concerned with this particular point). On the other hand, it appears to have been assumed in *Hotson* v *East Berkshire Health Authority* [1987] AC 750, HL, *obiter*, that an NHS patient is not in a contractual relationship with the NHS or its staff. It appears that the better view is that the NHS patient has no contract.

It is in any event clear that, given a contract, the duty of care is owed both in contract and in tort (see *Midland Bank Trust Co v Hett Stubbs & Kemp* [1979] Ch 384), and that the claimant can elect which remedy to pursue.[9]

The GP

If negligence is alleged against a GP or anyone employed by him (eg nurses, receptionists, secretaries), including any locum he engages, it is the GP who is the appropriate defendant (a physician was held liable for his apprentice's negligence in *Hancke v Hooper* (1835) 7 C & P 81).[10] It has to date seemed unlikely that he would be held to have a primary non-delegable duty towards the patient to ensure that any alternative care he arranges for when he is 'off' comes up to appropriate professional standards.[11] But with the development of primary care groups and Primary Care Trusts and the transfer to them of so many of the previous functions of the health authority, it would make sense, logical as well as practical, if the concept of non-delegable duty of care was extended to cover primary care (see below). The locum or doctor concerned in the alternative service is, of course, liable for any negligent act or omission on his part. But at the moment it is not easy to take the GP's liability for an independent locum further than to say that he must be reasonably satisfied of the competence of the deputising service he engages. Most GPs are engaged, on contracts for services, by Primary Care Trusts.[12] While the duty to provide GP care is in the hands of the local health authority, it may be possible to contend that the health authority is under a primary non-delegable duty to provide GP care, similar to its duty in respect of hospital care, and that therefore the health authority is liable for the GP's negligence (see below under 'The primary duty of care'). But this is the argument, it would seem, that was not accepted by Gray J in *Godden v Kent and Medway Strategic Health Authority*, at any rate as to a primary duty of care (see above). Probably, the GP does not

---

9   In *Lancashire and Cheshire Association of Baptist Churches Inc v Howard & Seddon Partnership* [1993] 3 All ER 467, it was held that there was no reason in principle why a duty of care in tort should not exist, and be sued upon, in the context of a contractual professional relationship. In *Henderson v Merrett Syndicates Ltd* (and associated cases) [1995] 2 AC 145, the House of Lords held that Lloyd's underwriting agents owed to various Lloyd's Names a concurrent duty of care in contract and in tort to carry out their underwriting functions with reasonable care and skill, and that the claimants could elect which remedy to pursue. In *Holt v Payne Skillington* [1996] 02 LS Gaz R 29, 77 BLR 51, CA, it was said that a duty in tort could in appropriate circumstances be wider than the concurrent duty in contract.

10 As mentioned above, there may be cases where the GP was at the relevant time employed by an NHS trust (pursuant to the National Health Service (Primary Care) Act 1997).

11 In *Lobley v Going* [1985] N–J & B 431, it was stated that if it was brought to a GP receptionist's attention that a small child had been brought to the surgery in an ill condition, with respiratory difficulties about which the parents were concerned, it was her duty to inform the doctor immediately and if she did not do so she would be guilty of negligence. It would follow that the employer GP, or GP practice, would be vicariously answerable for that negligence (on the facts it was held that she had not been negligent).

12 See *Roy v Kensington and Chelsea and Westminster Family Practitioner Committee* [1992] 1 AC 624, HL.

have a contract with his patient, unless the patient is a private patient (see above under 'Contract'). A GP is not permitted to act privately for a patient who is on his NHS list (as one knows, the GP may refer the patient to a consultant who may treat privately). It might occasionally be the case that certain services carried out upon the premises of a general practice are performed by agents of the health authority or of some trust, rather than employees of the doctor, for example, immunisation services. Care always needs to be taken in identifying the employer. For example, the health visitor, the community nurse and the community midwife, though working closely with the GP, are usually employed by the health authority or nowadays by some Trust or other, and although they may be acting at times under the direction of the GP, it is the health authority (or Trust) in such cases and not the GP who will be responsible for any mistakes they personally make. However, as stated above, the situation may well be getting more complex with the changes currently under way in primary care (see Chapter 2). Where the practice is a Primary Care Trust, as opposed to a primary care group, the Trust should be recognised as having legal personality, like any other NHS Trust.

GPs are not obliged to insure, although it is likely to be a condition of any partnership agreement that participating doctors do insure. There is apparently no obligation on a consultant in private practice to insure, either, though he would be wise to![13]

The primary duty of care

The most important point about NHS hospital treatment is that it is not necessary to prove the facts that would give rise to vicarious liability, because the hospital has a primary non-delegable duty of care to provide proper treatment.

While the courts were still applying the distinction between employer and independent contractor for the purpose of establishing liability on the part of a hospital for the negligence of medical personnel, the nice distinctions of the common law mentioned above (eg as to whether the employer could control the manner in which the work was done) were important. So in *Hillyer* v *St Bartholomew's Hospital* [1909] 2 KB 820, CA, Kennedy LJ expressed the view that a hospital, though responsible for the exercise of due care in selecting its professional staff, whether surgeons, doctors or nurses, was not responsible if they or any of them acted negligently in matters of professional care or skill:

> I see no ground for holding it to be a right legal inference from the circumstances of the relation of hospital and patient that the hospital authority makes itself liable in damages if members of the professional staff, of whose competence there is no question, act negligently towards the patient in some matter of professional care or skill, or neglect to use or use negligently in his treatment the apparatus or appliances which are at their disposal.

It was even said that as soon as the nurses enter the operating theatre, the health authority was no longer liable for any errors they may make

13   An employee held out as a partner was held liable with the partners for negligence by any of them (*Nationwide Building Society* v *Lewis* [1998] Ch 482, CA).

because they were then under the control of the surgeon, for whose errors the health authority was not responsible.

In *Davis* v *LCC* (1914) 30 TLR 275, a local education authority could not be held liable for a medical practitioner's negligence in carrying out an operation upon a school pupil if he had engaged a competent practitioner and if that practitioner was not in his employment.

In *Gold* v *Essex County Council* [1942] 2 KB 293, the Court of Appeal was concerned to distinguish between different types of staff: the hospital would not be responsible for the acts of a consulting surgeon or physician, but the position of a house physician or surgeon was left open. Goddard LJ said that responsibility for the position of doctors on the permanent staff would depend on whether the doctor was engaged on a contract for services or a contract of service. On the facts, the defendants were responsible for the negligence of a radiographer who was a full-time employee.

In *Collins* v *Hertfordshire County Council* [1947] KB 598, Hilbery J considered that a hospital was responsible for the acts of a house surgeon but not for the acts of a part-time surgeon.

In *Cassidy* v *Ministry of Health* [1951] 2 KB 343, MLC 0001, CA, it was left to Lord Denning, as ever, to direct the law onto a path more appropriate to modern social needs. In that case, Somervell LJ was prepared to hold a hospital liable for the acts of permanent medical staff, those who were employed to provide the patient with nursing and medical treatment, but not for the acts of a visiting or consulting surgeon or physician. Both he and Singleton LJ decided for the claimant on the basis that, even though the claimant could not pinpoint the employee who had been negligent, there had clearly been negligence by one or more employees of the hospital.

Denning LJ said that the hospital was under a duty to take reasonable care of all patients, whether private or not. They would be discharging that duty through their staff, and it was no answer for the hospital to say that the staff concerned were professionals who would not tolerate any interference with the way they did their work. When hospitals undertook to treat a patient, and themselves selected, appointed and employed the professionals who were to give the treatment (as opposed to the patient himself selecting and employing the staff – which he would be doing if he were to ask a consultant to operate on him privately), the hospital was responsible for any negligence, no matter whether of doctors, surgeons, nurses or anyone else; and 'it does not depend on the fine distinction whether the medical man was engaged under a contract of service or a contract for services'.

> I take it to be clear law as well as good sense that where a person is himself under a duty to use care, he cannot get rid of his responsibility by delegating the performance of it to someone else, no matter whether the delegation be to a servant under a contract of service or to an independent contractor under a contract for services.

In *Roe* v *Minister of Health* [1954] 2 QB 66, McNair J at first instance held himself bound by the majority in *Cassidy*'s case to find that a specialist anaesthetist who carried on a private anaesthetic practice but was under an obligation to provide a regular service to the hospital concerned, and on the occasion in question had been assisting the theatre staff of the hospital, was not a person for whose acts the hospital could be held liable. On appeal, Somervell LJ said that he regarded the anaesthetist as on the permanent staff of the hospital and therefore it would be liable for his errors. Morris LJ said that the hospital had undertaken to provide all the necessary facilities and equipment for the operation and the obligations of nursing and anaesthetising. This was going some way towards Denning LJ's concept of a primary non-delegable duty of care, but Morris LJ was still basing himself on the maxim of vicarious liability, *respondent superior*.

Once again, it was Denning LJ who brushed aside nice distinctions with a robust and lucid exposition:

> I think that the hospital authorities are responsible for the whole of their staff, not only for the nurses and doctors, but also for the anaesthetists and surgeons. It does not matter whether they are permanent or temporary, resident or visiting, whole-time or part-time. The hospital authorities are responsible for all of them. The reason is because, even if they are not servants, they are the agents of the hospital to give the treatment. The only exception is the case of consultants or anaesthetists selected and employed by the patient himself.

Early cases, before the acceptance of the primary duty of care, are worth a glance:

- *Evans* v *Liverpool Corpn* [1906] 1 KB 160, where a hospital was not liable for the negligent discharge by a physician of a boy still infectious from scarlet fever;
- *Hillyer*'s case (above), where the hospital was not liable for the burning of a patient's arms in the operating theatre;
- *Strangways-Lesmere* v *Clayton* [1936] 2 KB 11, no liability for the negligence of nurses in administering the wrong dosage (overruled by *Gold*'s case (above));
- *Dryden* v *Surrey County Council and Stewart* [1936] 2 All ER 535, no liability for the discharge home after an operation of a patient with a wad of surgical gauze still inside her;
- *Junor* v *McNicol* (1959) Times, 26 March, HL, where a house surgeon was declared not liable for the negligent treatment of a child because he was acting under the instructions of the consultant;
- *Perionowsky* v *Freeman* (1866) 4 F & F 977, where surgeons were not liable for negligent bathing of a patient by nurses;
- *Morris* v *Winsbury-White* [1937] 4 All ER 494, where a surgeon was not liable when a tube was found in the patient's body three months after surgery as it could have been put or left there by the nurses and house doctors any time after the operation.

These cases were important in the context of vicarious liability, when it mattered on whom the claimant could fix liability. Vicarious liability in the context of clinical negligence may well still assume significance for the private patient, eg in the case of a private clinic, where the clinic may be able to avoid liability for the mistakes of a visiting consultant, though probably only where the patient has chosen and privately contracted with him, or, if the consultant is being sued himself, he may be able to avoid responsibility for the mistakes of others not under his direct control at the time.

The interaction between vicarious responsibility and the non-delegable duty of care, and the significance of the distinction between these two

bases of liability, was considered by the Court of Appeal in the case of
Wilsher v *Essex Area Health Authority* [1987] QB 730 (reversed on
another ground by the House of Lords).[14]

In *X (minors)* v *Bedfordshire County Council* [1995] 2 AC 633, HL, Lord
Browne-Wilkinson said:

> This allegation of a direct duty of care owed by the authority to the plaintiff is
> to be contrasted with those claims which are based on the vicarious liability of
> the local authority for the negligence of its servants, ie for the breach of a duty
> of care owed by the servant to the plaintiff, the authority itself not being under
> any relevant duty of care to the plaintiff ...
>
> This distinction between direct and vicarious liability can be important since
> the authority may not be under a direct duty of care at all or the extent of the
> duty of care owed directly by the authority to the plaintiff may well differ from
> that owed by a professional to the patient. However, it is important not to lose
> sight of the fact that, even in the absence of a claim based on vicarious liability,
> an authority under a direct duty of care to the plaintiff will be liable for the
> negligent acts or omissions of its servant which constitute a breach of that
> direct duty. The authority can only act through its servants.
>
> The position can be illustrated by reference to the hospital cases. It is
> established that those conducting a hospital are under a direct duty of care to
> those admitted as patients to the hospital (I express no view as to the extent
> of that duty). They are liable for the negligent acts of a member of the hospital
> staff which constitute a breach of that duty, whether or not the member of
> the staff is himself in breach of a separate duty of care owed by him to the
> plaintiff.[15]

However, the boundaries and extent of the primary non-delegable duty of
care to provide proper care remain unclear.

M v *Calderdale and Kirklees Health Authority* [1998] Lloyd's Rep Med
157, CC, was, before being overruled, a case of great interest. A girl of 17,
an NHS patient, was sent by her NHS consultant to a private clinic for
a termination. She did not choose the clinic. She simply went where she
was told to go. She remained pregnant, gave birth to a child, and obtained
judgment for the negligence of clinic and surgeon. The surgeon was not
insured and the clinic was being wound up. Naturally, she looked to the
NHS for her damages. The defendants claimed that they had no liability
for the errors of the private clinic and surgeon as they were independent
contractors who had been chosen with all due care. The judge rejected
their argument, holding that, both by virtue of s 1 of the National Health
Service Act 1977 and at common law, they had a continuing primary non-
delegable duty of care to the patient which was not discharged by their
selection of a private clinic to perform the operation (he also found that
they had not used due care in their selection of a clinic). He approved of

---

14 Sir Nicholas Browne-Wilkinson V-C said: '... a health authority which so conducts its
    hospital that it fails to provide doctors of sufficient skill and experience to give the
    treatment offered at the hospital may be directly liable in negligence to the patient.'

15 The Ontario Court of Appeal has reviewed the concept of the non-delegable duty of
    care and by a majority declined to follow the English cases (*Yepremian* v *Scarborough
    General Hospital* (1980) 110 DLR (3d) 513). Arnup JA said that great care had to be
    taken when considering the English cases as the interrelationship of the state, the
    medical profession, the hospitals and their patients had developed in England along
    different lines from those it had followed in Ontario.

the passage in *Clerk and Lindsell on Torts* (17th edn, 1995) para 5.16, to the effect that the hospital authority itself is under a duty to its patients which it does not discharge simply by delegating its performance to someone else, no matter whether the delegation be to an employee or an independent contractor.

However, the Court of Appeal expressly disapproved of *Calderdale* in *A v Ministry of Defence* [2004] EWCA Civ 641, [2005] QB 183, CA. Negligence in a German hospital caused brain injury at birth to the child of a serving British soldier. Guy's and St Thomas' Hospital had undertaken to the MOD in 1996 to procure secondary medical care for servicemen in Germany and their dependants. The German medical units were called Designated German Providers (DGPs). The Court of Appeal held that there was no basis in law for imposing on the MOD a non-delegable duty of care in this context, ie a duty to ensure proper skill and care by the German hospital. The duty, as with the engagement of any independent contractor, was confined to an obligation to provide access to an appropriate system of hospital care provided by another, which duty was fulfilled by the exercise of reasonable care by the MOD in its selection of an agent (here Guy's and St Thomas') to procure DGPs.

In *Farraj v King's Healthcare NHS Trust* [2008] EWHC 2468, QBD and [2009] EWCA Civ 1203, [2010] PTSR 1176, CA, the Court of Appeal overturned a decision by the High Court that a hospital was partially liable to the claimants in respect of the genetic testing of a tissue sample which was sent to be cultured by a reputable independent cytogenetics laboratory. The mother's obstetrician had taken the trust's report as confirming that maternal contamination had been completely excluded. However, the report recognised that there was a very small background risk of maternal contamination. The person who had carried out the culturing process had expressed doubts about whether she was setting up a culture of foetal cells. The High Court held that the laboratory should have informed the trust of those doubts and were accordingly liable for a breach of duty of care owed to the claimants. However, the trust should have proactively asked for information about the sample. In the circumstances, liability was established against both defendants.

The Court of Appeal held that the hospital and the laboratory had a clearly understood arrangement by which the hospital was entitled to assume that the sample was satisfactory unless the laboratory informed it to the contrary. The hospital and trust had therefore not been negligent. The general rule was that where a person under a duty of care entrusted the performance of the duty to an apparently competent contractor, he was not under a duty to check the contractor's work, being entitled to rely on its proper performance. Even assuming (without deciding) that the concept of a non-delegable duty extended to hospital cases, that did not justify the conclusion that, on the facts of this case, the hospital owed a non-delegable duty to the parents in respect of genetic testing. There was a significant difference between treating a patient who was admitted to hospital for that purpose and carrying out tests on samples. The special duty that existed between a hospital and a patient arose because the hospital undertook the care, supervision and control of persons who, as patients, were in special need of care. The parents in this case were not admitted to the hospital for treatment. There was no need to depart from the general rule and find that any special duty was owed.

Independent providers

The NHS increasingly subcontracts care out to independent providers, which can be private sector companies, voluntary organisations or social enterprises. Such programmes aim to create additional capacity within the NHS, to reduce waiting times and to increase patient choice. There are three key types of waiting list initiatives which provide for the role of the independent sector in NHS provided care: Independent Sector Treatment Centres (ISTCs), Extended Choice Networks (ECNs) and Free Choice Networks (FCNs).

Who is the correct defendant if something goes wrong when a patient is treated by an independent provider? Is it the body who referred the patient or will it be the independent provider? There is no clear legal authority on this point. The referring body will only be liable if it owes a non-delegable duty of care that extends to treatment in another hospital. While there was held to be no non-delegable duty in *Farraj*, that case concerned independent testing of samples by a laboratory, which is a quite different situation. However, as we have seen, there was also held to be no non-delegable duty in *A v Ministry of Defence,* where medical treatment in Germany was arranged.

The courts may consider that these existing authorities should not be followed in a case where, for example, a patient has been referred to another organisation in an effort by the NHS to reduce waiting lists. There would be a strong policy argument for imposing a primary non-delegable duty upon the NHS in such cases. However, this issue does not appear to have been tested in the courts.

The question of who is the correct defendant may not be quite as significant as might otherwise be thought, however. The NHSLA's Clinical Negligence Scheme for Trusts (CNST) provides indemnity cover for NHS bodies in England who are members of the scheme against clinical negligence claims made in relation to NHS patients who are treated by or on behalf of those NHS bodies. ISTCs cannot (yet) join the scheme in their own right. However, they can benefit from cover when treating NHS patients via the membership of their referring PCT. It appears that any clinical negligence liability that is incurred when an NHS patient receives care at an ISTC, an ECN or an FCN is probably covered by CNST.[16.]

The contract between the parties should, however, always be carefully examined, as the independent provider may have provided an indemnity to the NHS. Furthermore, different arrangements may apply to one-off waiting list initiatives, where the indemnity terms of the relevant contract are likely to be paramount.

When a claim is made against a member of CNST, the NHS body remains the legal defendant. However, the NHSLA takes over full responsibility for handling the claim and meeting the associated costs.

SUING OVER POLICY DECISIONS

The following sections look at claims that are not rooted in alleged clinical negligence but relate more to policy decisions or alleged system or

---

16   See, for example the NHSLA's website at www.nhsla.com/FinanceIT/FAQs/. Accessed 7 January 2012.

administration failures, whether by government, the NHS or a particular health body. In this context fall claims over the allocation of resources, over closures of units, over inadequacies of infrastructure, over refusals to authorise a particular treatment, and so forth. The grounds for any such claim may now be more extensive thanks to the human rights aspect, though lawyers need to handle this aspect of any proposed claim with caution (see Chapter 21, Human Rights).

In *R* v *Secretary of State for Social Services, ex p Hincks* (1979) 123 Sol Jo 436, affd (1980) 1 BMLR 93, CA, four orthopaedic patients at a Birmingham hospital, who were being obliged to wait longer than was medically advisable for treatment because of a shortage of facilities due in part to a policy decision not to build a new hospital block for economic reasons, applied for declarations against the Minister and Regional and Area Health Authorities that the statutory duties imposed by ss 1 and 3 of the National Health Service Act 1977 had not been discharged. The patients needed to establish in the first place that they had a *locus standi* to bring the action; if they had, they asked for a declaration that the authorities were in breach of their statutory duties, and they sought both an order requiring them to perform their duties, and also damages for the pain and suffering caused to them by the delay in treatment. They failed. Wien J said that the Minister's duty was to provide such services as he considered necessary and that such a wording gave him a discretion as to how financial resources were to be used. If there was not enough money then all needs could not be met. In those circumstances, it was impossible to say that the Minister, or any other body, was in breach of statutory duty. The court would only interfere where the Minister had acted as no reasonable Minister could possibly act, or had acted so as to frustrate the policy of the Act. Nor did he take the view that the Act gave any right of action to the individual patient to sue in respect of an alleged breach of the Minister's general duties.

The Court of Appeal agreed with the trial judge; Bridge LJ pointed out that the Minister must be entitled to make policy decisions about the allocation of financial resources in the light of overall long-term planning or he would be called upon to disburse funds that were not in fact available.

In *Department of Health and Social Security* v *Kinnear* (1984) 134 NLJ 886, QBD, sufferers from the whooping cough vaccine brought an action against the Department in relation to the manner of promoting the vaccine. Stuart-Smith LJ struck out their claim in so far as it involved an attack on the exercise by the Department under s 26 of the National Health Service Act 1946 of their discretion as to whether arrangements should be made for immunisation against such a disease. The judge said that it was in the bona fide exercise of that discretion that the Department had adopted a policy of promoting immunisation against whooping cough. That policy, being within the limits of the discretion and the result of its bona fide exercise, could not give rise to a cause of action (though one may note that that part of the claim that regarded actions of an operational rather than a policy nature, allegations *inter alia* that negligent or misleading advice had been given by the Department as to the manner and circumstances in which immunisations were to be performed, was not struck out).

The *Kinnear* decision was followed in part in the Scottish Court of Session in *Ross* v *Secretary of State for Scotland* [1990] 1 Med LR 235, where a pursuer's direct case against the Scottish Home and Health Department alleging that she suffered brain damage as a result of being vaccinated against smallpox was dismissed because it was based on considerations of ministerial policy and matters of discretion and was, therefore, irrelevant in the absence of averments of bad faith. The *Kinnear* decision was distinguished in part in that the judge, Lord Milligan, said that that part of the *Kinnear* claim that was permitted to proceed appeared to be of an 'operational' nature and so not of assistance in his case. A similar decision on the main issue had been reached by Lord Grive in the Scottish case of *Bonthrone* v *Secretary of State for Scotland* 1987 SLT 34, where the pursuer's claim for injury allegedly sustained as a result of vaccination against whooping cough, diphtheria and tetanus without there having been given adequate warning of the risk of encephalopathy or other side effects had been struck out as attacking the ambit of exercise of a discretion rather than action taken to implement a discretionary decision.

In *Re HIV Haemophiliac Litigation* (1990) 41 BMLR 171, [1990] NLJR 1349, CA, Ralph Gibson LJ said that in appropriate circumstances a duty of care might be imposed in regard to the discharge of functions under the Act of 1977.

In *Danns* v *Department of Health* [1996] PIQR P69, QBD, a claim that owed more to the creative imagination of the claimant's advisers than to any realistic assessment of the prospect of success was brought, following a late recanalisation after a vasectomy and the consequent birth of a child to the claimant's wife, against the Department on the ground that it should have publicised the risk of failure of such a procedure by the time of the vasectomy in 1983. The claim was based in part on s 2 of the Ministry of Health Act 1919 which provides:

> It shall be the duty of the Minister ... to take all such steps as may be desirable to secure the preparation, effective carrying out and co-ordination of measures conducive to the health of the people, including measures for the prevention and cure of diseases ... the treatment of physical and mental defects ... the initiation and direction of research, the collection, preparation, publication and dissemination of information and statistics relating thereto, and the training of persons for health services.

The usual action where it is alleged that the patient should have been told of the risk of late recanalisation is an action against the doctor or hospital responsible for the procedure (see above). Presumably in this case the claimant's advisers had concluded that the facts did not permit such a claim, and therefore they chanced their arm on an action against the Department of Health, *faute de mieux* one might say.

Not surprisingly, Wright J held that a breach of this section would not give rise to a private law right of action, that it clearly conferred upon the Minister a discretion to decide what steps he should or should not take in discharge of his ministerial function, and that in the present context any decisions by the Minister as to what materials were to be disseminated under the provisions of the section were entirely a question of policy in respect of which he was entitled to exercise his discretion. In any event, he was fully entitled to leave it to the medical profession to decide what advice or counselling it should give to those coming forward for a vasectomy. The Court of Appeal, agreeing with the judge and stating that the Department did not owe the claimant a duty of care as there was no sufficient relationship of proximity, dismissed the appeal, saying that the prospects of success on appeal had been slight ([1998] PIQR P226).

In *R* v *Central Birmingham Health Authority, ex p Walker* (1987) 3 BMLR 32, CA, an unsuccessful application was made for judicial review of the health authority's decision that, although it was agreed that baby Walker needed a certain operation, it could not carry it out at that time for resource reasons. The Master of the Rolls said:

> It is not for this court, or indeed any court, to substitute its own judgment for the judgment of those who are responsible for the allocation of resources. This court could only intervene where it was satisfied that there was a *prima facie* case, not only of failing to allocate resources in the way in which others think that resources should be allocated, but of a failure to allocate resources to an extent which was '*Wednesbury* unreasonable', to use the lawyers' jargon, or, in simpler words, which involves a breach of a public law duty. Even then, of course, the court has to exercise a judicial discretion. It has to take account of all the circumstances of the particular case with which it is concerned.[17]

In another case against the same health authority less than two months later, the father of four year old Matthew Collier failed to persuade the Court of Appeal to intervene where desperately needed open-heart surgery was delayed for months, even though Matthew had been placed at the top of the waiting list, due to shortage of intensive care beds and nurses. The court said that there was no evidence that the health authority had acted unreasonably or in breach of any public duty (*R* v *Central Birmingham Health Authority, ex p Collier* [1988] CA, transcript, 6 January).[18]

In *R* v *North West Thames Regional Health Authority, ex p Daniels* [1993] 4 Med LR 364 the Divisional Court, despite sympathising with the predicament of the boy, Rhys Daniels, and actually finding that the District Health Authority had failed, contrary to reg 19(1) of the Community Health Councils Regulations, SI 1985/304, to consult the community health council before closing the bone marrow unit at Westminster Children's Hospital, was, predictably, unwilling to order the reopening of the unit because making an order would not benefit the boy. The court said it was sure that the unit at Bristol would do all it could. Although one understands that the proceedings had the useful effect of getting the NHS to ensure that appropriate treatment was speedily made available, the parents, most sadly, had to decide in September 1997

---

17   Under the well-established *Wednesbury* principle, the court will only intervene if it is shown that the decision taken was one which no reasonable body could have arrived at if it had been taking into account all relevant matters – in other words, the decision must be shown to be irrational (see *Associated Provincial Picture Houses* v *Wednesbury Corpn* [1948] 1 KB 223, CA).

18   Reference may also be made to *Wyatt* v *Hillingdon London Borough Council* (1978) 76 LGR 727, CA, where it was held that provisions in the Chronically Sick and Disabled Persons Act 1970 gave default powers over the health authority to the Minister that precluded the remedy sought from the courts. In *R* v *Inner London Education Authority, ex p F* (1988) Times, 28 November, the Divisional Court declined to review a consultant psychiatrist's decision to transfer a patient. In *R* v *Ealing District Health Authority, ex p F* (1992) 11 BMLR 59, the court made it clear that it would not compel psychiatric supervision of a patient. In *X* v *A, B and C* (1991) 9 BMLR 91, the court declined to order treatment requested by a paedophile, stating that wrongful acts within the context of public law afforded no remedy to the individual.

that no further treatment should be attempted and Rhys died just before Christmas 1998, aged nearly eight.

In *R* v *Sheffield Health Authority, ex p Seale* (1994) 25 BMLR 1, Auld J held that it was not unreasonable for the health authority to limit IVF treatment to women between the ages of 25 and 35 in view of their limited budget. He said that although they had undertaken to provide such treatment for patients within their area, that did not mean they were bound to provide the service on demand and regardless of financial and other concerns.[19]

In *R* v *Cambridge District Health Authority, ex p B* [1995] 1 WLR 898, CA, the father of a ten year old girl, who had already been treated with two courses of chemotherapy, applied for an order compelling the health authority to fund a third course and a second bone marrow transplant when she suffered a relapse of her acute myeloid leukaemia. The health authority had declined to treat, principally on the basis that the proposed treatment, being of an experimental nature, was not in the child's best interests, and also on the ground that the huge expense involved would not be an appropriate use of their limited resources. The trial judge, Laws J, while not being prepared to order the health authority to treat, required them to reconsider their decision on the ground that their reasoning had been flawed because the treatment was not experimental and because they had not properly explained their funding priorities. The Court of Appeal reversed his decision. The Master of the Rolls provided what at that time might have been thought to be the last word on the attitude of the courts to decisions on funding by health authorities:

> I have no doubt that in a perfect world any treatment which a patient, or a patient's family, sought would be provided if doctors were willing to give it, no matter how much it cost, particularly when a life was potentially at stake. It would however, in my view, be shutting one's eyes to the real world if the court were to proceed on the basis that we do live in such a world. It is common knowledge that health authorities of all kinds are constantly pressed to make ends meet. They cannot pay their nurses as much as they would like; they cannot provide all the treatments they would like; they cannot purchase all the extremely expensive medical equipment they would like; they cannot carry out all the research they would like; they cannot build all the hospitals and specialist units they would like. Difficult and agonising judgments have to be made as to how a limited budget is best allocated to the maximum advantage of the maximum number of patients. That is not a judgment which the court can make. In my judgment, it is not something that a health authority such as this authority can be fairly criticised for not advancing before the court.

And Sir Stephen Brown said:

> After the most critical, anxious consideration, I feel bound to say that I am unable to say that the authority in this case acted in a way that exceeded its powers or which was unreasonable in the legal sense. The powers of this court are not such as to enable it to substitute its own decision in a matter of

---

19 On the fringe of this 'resource' question we can note *R* v *Secretary of State for Health, ex p Keen* [1990] 1 Med LR 455, where Professor Keen, Director of the Unit for Metabolic Medicine and Director of Clinical Services/Medicine at Guy's Hospital, failed in an application for judicial review of the expenditure of resources on the preparation, before the National Health Care and Community Service Bill became law, for a change of the hospital's status to that of self-governing NHS Trust.

this kind for that of the authority which is legally charged with making the decision.

It is understood that in the event money was provided by a benefactor for the necessary treatment, but that, most sadly, the child did not survive.

However, perhaps presaging the current greater willingness of the courts to intervene, Dyson J held in *R* v *North Derbyshire Health Authority, ex p Fisher* [1997] 8 Med LR 327 that the policy of the health authority relating to the administration to patients suffering from multiple sclerosis of the drug beta interferon was unlawful because it failed to give serious consideration to the advice offered in the relevant NHS circular. That circular requested purchasing authorities and providers within the NHS to develop and manage the entry of such drugs into the NHS and in particular to initiate and continue prescribing beta interferon to hospitals. Insofar as the health authority had any policy at all, the judge was satisfied that it amounted in effect to a blanket ban on the prescription of the drug. It is clear that the judge found the evidence produced by the health authority to be wholly unsatisfactory. He was understandably unimpressed by a weasel-speak minute from the health authority which, having accepted that in the light of a speech by the Secretary of State for Health a blanket ban was not acceptable, noted: 'However it might be possible to have creative constraints'. The judge granted a declaration that the policy of the health authority was unlawful, quashed its decision to decline to prescribe the drug to Mr Fisher, and ordered it to form and implement a policy which took into account the policy of the circular. He did not, of course, order the health authority to treat the patient.[20]

In *R* v *Brent and Harrow Health Authority, ex p London Borough of Harrow* [1997] 3 FCR 765, 34 BMLR 9, the local education authority, who were being sued by a pupil in an attempt to compel them to provide speech, occupational and physiotherapy, as required by s 16 of the Education Act 1993, brought a similar action against the health authority requiring them to allocate resources for that purpose. Turner J said that allocation of resources must be done according to a number of competing priorities, of which the provision of services under the Education Act was only one. The health authority could not reasonably be expected to recalculate and reallocate resources according to a particular demand which arose at any particular moment. They were entitled to ration their scarce resources as they had done in the present case.

However if funds are used for a clearly unauthorised purpose, the court will take appropriate action. In *R* v *Secretary of State for Health, ex p Manchester Local Medical Committee* (1995) 25 BMLR 77, Collins J acceded to an application for judicial review of the refusal of the Secretary of State to take action when he was informed that the surplus funds allocated to a family health services authority for the provision of general medical services and the reimbursement of claims by GPs for practice

---

20 In *R (on application of Longstaff)* v *Newcastle PCT* [2003] EWHC 3252 (Admin), [2004] Lloyds Rep Med 400, Charles J held in December 2003 that the defendant NHS trust, who had refused to provide funding for the applicant haemophiliac to be treated with the recombinant Factor VIII, had not been under a duty to seek further information as to the reasons for his decision to refuse to accept treatment with plasma derived Factor VIII products.

staff costs, rent and premises improvement grants had in fact been used by the authority for the (unlawful) appointment of facilitators to arrange or assist in the provision of general medical services in the region.

On the question of allocation of resources, we may also note *Wilsher* v *Essex Area Health Authority* [1987] QB 730, CA, which is authority for the proposition that the employment through lack of funds of relatively inexperienced young doctors in responsible positions does not reduce the level of the standard of care which the patient has a right to expect. And even though the Secretary of State would not himself be responsible, it appears from the judgments of Glidewell LJ and Sir Nicolas Browne-Wilkinson VC that in an appropriate case a hospital management committee might be itself directly liable in negligence for failing to provide sufficient qualified and competent medical staff, it being said that there was no reason in principle why a health authority should not be liable if its organisation were at fault in that way.

Consider also *Bull and Wakeham* v *Devon Health Authority* [1993] 4 Med LR 117, MLC 0022 where the Court of Appeal, upholding the judge's decision in favour of the claimant, said that the system of obstetric cover provided by the hospital had given rise to a real inherent risk that an obstetrician might not attend reasonably promptly. But what if the hospital had alleged that its budget could not cover any better system?

The question of defective systems also arose in *Robertson* v *Nottingham Health Authority* [1997] 8 Med LR 1, CA, where significant breakdowns in the defendants' systems of communication in respect of obstetric care were proved and shown to constitute breaches of proper practice. Brooke LJ said that a health authority had a non-delegable duty to establish a proper system of care just as much as it had a duty to engage competent staff and a duty to provide proper and safe equipment, safe premises and a reasonable regime of care, ie a regime of a standard that could reasonably be expected of a hospital of the size and type in question – in the present case a large teaching centre of excellence. It mattered not whether those at fault could be individually identified. If they could, the hospital would be vicariously liable for their negligence, but, if not, the hospital would be in breach of its own duty of care for failing to provide a proper system.[21] But what the judge did not say is that those obligations were regardless of whether sufficient funds had been made available.[22]

---

21 One would like to think that successful claims could be brought against hospitals based on unacceptable standards of hygiene (and that the defence would not have the chutzpah to plead lack of funds); but such claims are hard to prove in terms of causation, not so much in the sense of showing that the patient contracted a specific infection while in hospital but in the sense of showing that it was contracted from a hospital source that would not have been infective given proper management. Hence the lack of success so far for MRSA claims.

22 In *Mercer* v *Royal Surrey County and St Luke's Hospitals NHS Trust* [2000] MLC 0289, the system for contacting an obstetric anaesthetist when needed was held to be defective. In *Ocloo* v *Royal Brompton and Harefield Hospital NHS Trust* [2001] MLC 0539, there was admitted system negligence in failing to arrange a follow-up appointment for a heart patient (however the claim failed on causation). In *Loraine* v *Wirral University Teaching Hospital NHS Trust* [2008] EWHC 1565 (QB),[2008] LS Law Medical 573, a system in place at a hospital whereby records of earlier pregnancies were not, in general, retrieved when treating a woman in a subsequent pregnancy, was held to be flawed and to have exposed the claimant's mother to an avoidable risk.

More recently

Latterly the courts have shown themselves even more ready to oversee and, where considered appropriate, invalidate administrative decisions, including decisions as to the allocation of resources, and on various grounds to set them aside. However, it is still difficult to succeed in such actions and whether the courts would ever be willing to make a direct order for allocation to a particular purpose, on human rights grounds or any other, remains doubtful.

In *R* v *North and East Devon Health Authority, ex p Coughlan* [2000] 2 WLR 622, [1999] MLC 0105, CA, the Court of Appeal set aside a decision by the health authority to close a home for disabled residents on the ground that, having told the residents at an earlier date that it would be a permanent home for them, there was no sufficient 'over-reaching public interest' which would justify the health authority breaking that 'home for life promise'. A further ground, involving highly complex argument, was that the health authority had misinterpreted its responsibilities under the National Health Service Act 1977. The judge below, Hidden J, had also been satisfied that the necessary elements for consultation had not been satisfied. He had said that he accepted entirely that the respondent authority was master of its own resources, but the decisions it made as to its own resources had to be made reasonably. A reasonable resolution of the problem would have to include a conclusion on all relevant arguments and the exclusion of all irrelevant ones. He had said the approach of the authority was flawed from the outset as it treated a promise of a permanent home merely as a promise to provide care. The assessments the authority carried out were not proper multi-disciplinary assessments, as required by the relevant guidance, and no regard was paid to the Social Services assessment that the home 'ideally suited' the applicant. In relation to the process of decision-making, the judge had said that the procedures were 'far from the stuff of which true consultation is made'.

Jackson J followed the lead of the Court of Appeal when he declared unlawful a decision by a health authority to close a long-stay hospital for patients with profound learning disabilities. He said that the health authority had failed to have regard to promises previously made that the patients would have a home for life at the hospital or to the specific needs of those patients in relation to their relocation (*R* v *Merton, Sutton and Wandsworth Health Authority, ex p Perry* [2001] Lloyd's Rep Med 73).

However, in *Cowl* v *Plymouth City Council* [2001] EWCA Civ 1935, the Court of Appeal, perhaps tiring of the many appeals against closure of homes and the like, now as a matter of course padding out the claim with a human rights plea, refusing an application for judicial review of a council's decision to close one of their residential homes for the elderly, said that, where the lawfulness of a decision to close such a home was in question, the lawyers on both sides were under a heavy obligation to resort to litigation only if it was really unavoidable. They should strive to resolve the issues, or a significant part of them, outside the litigation process. A decision to similar negative effect was *R (on application of Haggerty)* v *St Helen's Council* [2003] EWHC 803 (Admin), Silber J. The Court of Appeal referred with approval to the comments made in *Cowl* in *R (on the application of C)* v *Nottingham City Council* [2010] EWCA Civ 790, a case concerning the provision of local authority accommodation to children.

R v Brent, Kensington & Chelsea & Westminster Mental NHS Trust, ex p C [2002] EWHC 181 was an unsuccessful application for judicial review of the mental health trust's decision to close a residential lodge. *R (on the application of Dudley) v East Sussex County Council* [2003] EWHC 1093 (Admin) was an unsuccessful application for judicial review of the council's decision to close a long-term residential care home for the elderly. Maurice Kay J said there was no breach of any human rights in the process.

In *R (on the application of Bishop) v Bromley LBC* [2006] EWHC 2148 (Admin), (2006) 9 CCL Rep 635, the claimant applied for judicial review of the decision of the respondent local authority to close a day-care facility. Parker J held that where the circumstances were not exceptional, a complete multi-disciplinary assessment would not be required before a decision to close a local authority care home was taken. The effects of transferring its day-care services to another centre, although significant, were not sufficient to engage Sch 1, Part I, Art 8(1) of the Human Rights Act 1998, and even if they were, the putative interference would be justified under Sch 1, Part I, Art 8(2) on the ground that it was required for the economic well-being of the local authority and those in need of its services.

In *R v Lindley* [2006] EWHC 2296 (Admin), (2006) 103(39) LSG 35, the claimant disabled person applied for judicial review of the defendant local authority's decision not to send him to a particular care facility. He had resided for 20 years in a care home run by the local authority. He suffered from cerebral palsy, arthritis, dysarthria, was doubly incontinent and had restricted movement. When the local authority proposed to close the care home, it communicated its intentions to the residents and assured them that they would be able to move to a new facility and have their care needs met there. The claimant had initially begun judicial review proceedings to prevent closure of the home, but upon his nursing assessment being changed such that he would be unable to move to the new facility, he contended that the local authority had created a legitimate expectation that he would be moved to the new care home and have his assessed needs met there whatever the level of need. Hodge J dismissed the application, holding that on the facts it was clear that for the bulk of the period since the assurances had been given, the claimant had not relied upon them and they had not created a legitimate expectation that was enforceable. The assurances given had to be considered in context. Moreover, the local authority's knowledge of the claimant's needs had developed since it made the assurances and it was right for it to have changed its conclusions as to how his needs were to be met.

In *R (on the application of Hide) v Staffordshire CC* [2007] EWCA Civ 860, (2008) 11 CCL Rep 38, the Court of Appeal held on an application for permission to appeal that, where a local authority had given public assurances that it would abide by the law and comply with the legal requirements of consultation, following a decision in principle to close a number of care homes and day centres, it was hopeless to seek to move by way of judicial review on the basis that those assurances would not be complied with.

In *R (on the application of Wilson) v Coventry City Council* [2008] EWHC 2300 (Admin), (2009) 12 CCL Rep 7, Judge Pelling QC held that decisions by two local authorities to close certain care homes had been neither unreasonable nor contrary to Art 2 of the European Convention on Human Rights 1950, where the totality of the medical evidence, which the local authorities' decision-makers had taken account of, had not established a statistically demonstrable rise in mortality following geriatric relocation, and the local authorities had undertaken to provide individual assessments of every resident before their transfer. Where a decision to close care homes had been taken, there was no legal requirement to undertake individual assessments before that decision was made, as opposed to after it was made but before the transfer of residents took place. While Art 2 of the Convention was capable of applying to a local authority closing a care home, for a claimant to establish a breach under that article, a real and imminent risk to life had to be shown as a result of that closure and a failure by the local authority to take all steps within its power to avoid that.

In *R (on the application of Watts)* v *Wolverhampton City Council* [2009] EWCA Civ 1168, the Court of Appeal refused permission to appeal against a refusal of permission to apply for judicial review of a decision to close a care home and transfer its residents to other homes. The claimant went to the European Court of Human Rights, which held in *Watts* v *United Kingdom* (2010) 51 EHRR SE5 that her complaints of, *inter alia,* violation of Arts 2, 3 and 8 of the European Convention on Human Rights were inadmissible. She had not established that there was a particular and quantified risk to her life in the transfer, which had been carefully planned by the defendant to minimise the impact of the move upon her. Any stress and distress caused to her did not meet the threshold to found a claim under Art 3. While there was some interference with her Art 8 rights, that interference was proportionate, for reasons including the council's need to manage its resources effectively.

The High Court in *R (R P)* v *London Borough of Brent* [2011] EWHC 3251 (Admin) refused to quash a decision made by the defendant to close one of its residential units providing short-term respite care for disabled children earlier than had previously been decided. The decision made was not irrational, nor contrary to the defendant's public sector equality duty under s 149 of the Equality Act 2010.

Turning to the funding of particular treatments, in *R* v *Secretary of State for Health, ex p Pfizer Ltd* [1999] MLC 0103, 51 BMLR 189, Collins J held that Department of Health Circular 1998/158 advising that doctors should not prescribe Viagra was unlawful both as seeking to override a doctor's professional judgment as to what treatment would best benefit his patient, and also as being in breach of the European Directive 89/105/EEC (which required that publicity be given to the criteria applied in measures to restrict or exclude from the public domain medicinal products for human use).

In *R* v *North West Lancashire Health Authority, ex p Miss A, D and G* [2000] 1 WLR 977, [1999] MLC 0111, CA, the Court of Appeal upheld a decision of Hidden J, invalidating a decision by the health authority in relation to the treatment it was or was not prepared to provide to transsexuals, ie a decision on the allocation of its limited resources. The health authority had refused the applicants gender reassignment surgery, from male to female. Suffering as they did from an inability to accept the gender they were born with, they were in principle entitled to be considered for treatment under the NHS. However the health authority had decided upon a policy that such surgery would be refused unless there were exceptional circumstances over and above the clinical need.

The court said that the allocation and weighting of priorities in funding different treatments from finite resources was a matter of judgment for the health authority; that it was proper for an authority to adopt a general policy; that a policy to allocate a low priority to gender reassignment surgery was not in principle irrational; but that in this case the policy was undermined and invalidated by evidence which showed that the health authority did not in fact regard gender dysphoria as a genuine illness requiring more than psychiatric reassurance, an approach that did not reflect its own medical judgment. The court therefore quashed the relevant resource allocation policies and all decisions based on them and required the health authority to give proper weight to its acknowledgement that gender dysphoria was an illness, to address the clinical evidence as to the need for and effectiveness of gender reassignment procedures, to indicate reasons in broad terms for the priority to be given to providing such treatment, and to make effective provision for exceptions in individual cases from any general policy restricting funding for such treatment.[23]

Hidden J's approach at first instance is worth studying. He accepted that it was for the health authority and not the court to allocate limited budgets to the maximum advantage for the number of patients. Nevertheless, he said, in formulating or applying policy to any particular case before it, the authority had to consider whether there was a demonstrable medical need for the treatment in question. Although the court would not seek to allocate scarce resources in a tight budget, it would ensure that the health authority had asked the right questions and had addressed the right issues before arriving at its policy. In this case the authority was unable to define or exemplify what it meant by the proviso of 'overriding clinical need'. The judge said that it was not entitled to limit its treatment to counselling and so to exclude hormone treatment and surgery. Therefore its decision was unlawful and irrational, arrived at without consideration of relevant matters such as the question of what was the proper treatment or what was actually recognised as the illness of gender identity dysphoria. Relevant considerations were not taken into account and irrelevant ones were. The policy unlawfully fettered the discretion of the health authority in its duty towards each particular patient of providing treatment and facilities for the prevention of illness and the cure of persons suffering from gender identity dysphoria.

In *R (on the application of Rogers)* v *Swindon NHS Primary Care Trust* [2006] EWCA Civ 392, [2006] 1 WLR 2649, the Court of Appeal allowed an appeal against the decision of Bean J that the defendant trust's policy not to provide Herceptin to early stage breast cancer sufferers who were HER2 positive, save in exceptional circumstances, was not unlawful. It held that the policy to refuse funding for treatment with an unlicensed drug, save where exceptional personal or clinical circumstances could be shown, was irrational, as the policy could not be rationally explained.

The defendant had funds available to provide the drug for all patients who fulfilled the clinical requirements and whose clinician had prescribed it, but its policy was to refuse funding save where exceptional personal

---

23 For the human rights aspect of these cases, see Chapter 21.

or clinical circumstances could be shown. It was held that a policy of withholding assistance save in unstated exceptional circumstances would be rational in the legal sense provided that it was possible to envisage, and the decision maker did envisage, what such exceptional circumstances might be. If it was not possible to envisage any such circumstances, the policy would be in practice a complete refusal of assistance and as such would be irrational because it was sought to be justified not as a complete refusal but as a policy of exceptionality. In deciding whether the defendant's policy was rational or not, the court had to consider whether there were any relevant exceptional circumstances that could justify it granting treatment to one patient but refusing it to another within the eligible group. There was no rational basis for distinguishing between patients within the eligible group on the basis of exceptional clinical circumstances any more than there was on the basis of personal circumstances. Once the defendant had decided, as it had, that it would fund Herceptin for some patients and that cost was irrelevant, the only reasonable approach was to focus on the patient's clinical needs and to fund patients within the eligible group who had been properly prescribed Herceptin by their physicians. The defendant's policy was irrational and therefore unlawful and was quashed. However, it is notable that this was not a case about the allocation of scarce resources. The defendant had funding available to treat all eligible patients.

The decision of the PCT to refuse to fund the treatment of the claimant with Herceptin was quashed. The Court of Appeal was going to hear further submissions, which were not reported, but at the stage of giving the judgment was of the view that it could not and should not order the PCT to fund the treatment, but that the PCT should reconsider its policy and formulate a lawful policy upon which to base decisions in particular cases, including that of the claimant, in the future.

In *R (on the application of Otley)* v *Barking and Dagenham NHS Primary Care Trust* [2007] EWHC 1927 (Admin), (2007) 10 CCL Rep, Mitting J held that it was unlawful for the defendant NHS trust to refuse to fund a treatment for cancer, which included the use of an anti-cancer drug not available for normal prescription, where the treatment produced beneficial results and the patient's case was exceptional.

The claimant had been privately prescribed a combination of three anticancer drugs that included Avastin, which was not available from the NHS. The funds available to the claimant allowed for five courses of treatment. The response to treatment was positive and a further prescription of Avastin was applied for. A panel of the defendant trust held that sanctioning the use of Avastin would not significantly prolong the claimant's life or be cost effective. Upon being asked to reconsider its decision, a critical analysis of the drug was subsequently prepared, which held that Avastin should be authorised in exceptional circumstances, and set out the exceptionality criteria. One member of the panel queried the precise ratio of Avastin to the other drugs in the treatment. He found that the claimant had not received Avastin for several months and that her disease did not appear to have significantly progressed in that time. The panel held that the claimant did not fit the exceptionality criteria and refused to fund the treatment.

Mitting J held that the reasoning and decision of the panel was irrational and unlawful. The query about the ratio of the drugs in the treatment was irrelevant. It was a simple fact that the treatment that had been prescribed, including Avastin, produced beneficial results and there were no other treatments available to the claimant that could be prescribed within normal NHS standards that were likely to have any benefit to her. Further, the panel had not taken into account the slim but important chance that treatment including Avastin could prolong the claimant's life for more than a few months. What the panel had in mind was the short-term effect on the claimant's life of the prescription of Avastin. It was held that, on any fair-minded view of the exceptionality criteria, the claimant's case was exceptional. The case was not one in which the availability of scarce resources was a decisive factor. The panel's decision was quashed and the defendant gave an undertaking that funding of a further five cycles of treatment would be provided to the claimant, after which her situation would be reviewed.

In *R (on the application of Ross)* v *West Sussex Primary Care Trust* [2008] EWHC 2252 (Admin), (2008) 11 CCL Rep. 787, Grenfell J held that the refusal of the defendant NHS Trust to provide funding to a cancer sufferer for a potentially life-extending drug was a decision that no reasonable trust could have made having regard to the exceptional circumstances of the patient's case, in particular his intolerance to other forms of treatment and the clinical efficacy and cost effectiveness of allowing him access to that treatment. The trust had refused to fund the treatment on the basis that it was neither clinically efficacious nor cost effective and that the claimant's need was not exceptional within the meaning of that term as contained in the trust's in-house policy. It was held that the trust had, in attempting to formulate fair guidelines as to what would amount to an exceptional case, introduced an unnecessary element of confusion. The trust's policy was unlawful because it contained a contradiction in terms. It was not, as it purported to be, a policy for exceptional cases because a person was automatically disqualified if he was likened to another. In reality, in order to qualify, the patient had to demonstrate uniqueness rather than exceptionality. Once a patient had established himself as falling within a category of exceptionality, a trust still had to have regard to principles of clinical efficacy and cost effectiveness before sanctioning funding for treatment, but, once an exceptional case was made out, particularly where matters of extending life were concerned, a trust should take a less restrictive approach to cost effectiveness when considering the case for funding.

In *R (on the application of Eisai Limited)* v *National Institute for Health and Clinical Negligence* [2008] EWCA Civ 438, (2008) 11 CCL Rep 385, the Court of Appeal held that NICE acted unfairly during a consultation process by making available to consultees only a read-only version of an economic model used to assess the cost-effectiveness of drugs and refusing to make available a fully executable version of the model. The model was central to the appraisal committee's determination of a drug's cost-effectiveness. The robustness or reliability of the model was therefore a key question.

In *R (on the application of St Helens BC)* v *Manchester Primary Care Trust* [2008] EWCA Civ 931, [2009] PTSR 105, a local authority appealed against a decision that it was responsible for paying for the care at home of a woman whose mental and psychological conditions required constant care. The respondent Primary Care Trust decided that the woman's need was not primarily for healthcare and that, except for physiotherapy and other specific healthcare matters, the trust should not fund her care. The Court of Appeal held that a Primary Care Trust, as the delegate of the Secretary of State, was a primary decision maker. In the circumstances, its decision that it was not responsible for paying for the care in her home of a woman requiring constant care was amenable to orthodox judicial review, but not to a fully-fledged substantive challenge which the court itself must decide.

The question of what reliance can be placed upon ministerial statements made in the legislature arose in the Scottish case of *Fargie, Petitioner* [2008] CSOH 117, 2008 SLT 949. A widow applied to the supervisory jurisdiction of the Court of Session, seeking to challenge the eligibility criteria of a non-statutory fund set up to provide compensation for persons who had contracted hepatitis C after being supplied blood products by the NHS. The fund had been adopted as a scheme by the Scottish Ministers on 24 April 2007, under s 28 of the Smoking, Health and Social Care (Scotland) Act 2005. A provision that no payments would be made in respect of persons who had died prior to 29 August 2003 prevented her claiming compensation following the death of her husband on 7 March 2003. The claimant argued, *inter alia*, that she had a legitimate expectation to receive payment as a ministerial statement of 29 January 2003 had created a legitimate expectation in intimating that all persons alive at that date would receive payment. Lord Uist held that the Scottish ministers were entitled to select the cut-off date having regard to the allocation of limited financial resources within the health budget and the fact that the setting up of the fund was publicly announced on that date. It could not properly be said that the deceased had a legitimate expectation to payment based on the ministerial statement of 29 January 2003; it had to be read in its context which was the wish to help victims who were still alive, but that no details had been worked out, and when regard was had to its entirety, the subsequent fixing of the said cut-off date was entirely consistent with it. It would be dangerous if courts held ministerial statements made in the legislature as amounting to something which could found a legitimate expectation.

In *R (on the application of F)* v *Wirral BC* [2009] EWHC 1626 (Admin), [2009] BLGR 905, the claimants applied for judicial review of the respondent local authority's assessment of their social services and care needs. McCombe J held that while the Administrative Court was astute to correct any illegality of approach on a public authority's part, it was not the proper forum in which to probe into the adequacy of community care assessments, and the remedy of judicial review would not be granted where there was an alternative remedy in the form of the statutory complaints procedure under the Local Authority Social Services Complaints (England) Regulations 2006. However, note *Smith* v *North Eastern Derbyshire Primary Care Trust* [2006] EWCA Civ 1291, in which the Court of Appeal held that a PCT could not avoid or mitigate the performance of its statutory duty to consult patients, pursuant to s 11 of the Health and Social Care Act 2001, by suggesting an approach to a patients' forum. The engagement of a patients' forum did not amount to an alternative remedy such as to deny a claimant relief in judicial review proceedings.

In *R (on the application of Bristol-Myers Squibb Pharmaceuticals Ltd)* v *National Institute for Health and Clinical Excellence* [2009] EWHC

2722 (Admin), [2010] 1 CMLR 31, Blake J held that there had not been a breach of Directive 89/105 where NICE had refused to recommend using a drug in the NHS, in accordance with criteria notified to the European Commission, as the drug was not cost-effective when there was a high demand for it and resources were scarce.

In *R (on the application of AC)* v *Berkshire West Primary Care Trust* [2010] EWHC 1162 (Admin), Bean J held that a policy adopted by the defendant, under which breast augmentation was classified as a 'non-core' procedure in terms of treatment for gender identity disorder and was not therefore routinely funded by the NHS, was not irrational and nor did it discriminate against transsexual patients. The trust had due regard to the need to eliminate discrimination against transsexual patients and to the need to promote equality of opportunity between transsexual and non-transsexual patients, and its gender identity disorder policy had been drafted with great care and after extensive consultation.

While breast augmentation had been funded in the case of a natal woman who had a congenital absence of breast tissue, in that case the psychological distress suffered had been far more significant, making that situation exceptional. It was well known that NHS budgets were under severe pressure from the increasing longevity of the population and the development of expensive new drugs and surgical procedures. It was therefore lawful for the trust to have policies about which treatments would, and which would not, be routinely funded. It was equally proper for the trust to adopt a general policy for the exercise of its discretion, and to allow for exceptions to it in exceptional circumstances.

In *R (on the application of McDonald)* v *Kensington and Chelsea RLBC* [2011] UKSC 33, the Supreme Court held that the local authority, which provided home-based community care to a person with limited mobility who suffered from bladder problems requiring her to urinate several times during the night, was entitled to withdraw the provision of an overnight carer who helped her access a commode where it had assessed that her needs could equally be met by the provision of incontinence pads or absorbent sheets. Such a decision did not violate her rights under Art 8 of the ECHR. The local authority had respected her personal feelings as well as taking account of her safety, her independence and its own responsibilities towards other care recipients. Its proposal regarding the use of pads was proportionate and in the interests of other service users.

In *R (on the application of Condliff)* v *North Staffordshire Primary Care Trust* [2011] EWCA Civ 910, the claimant was morbidly obese and wished to have gastric by-pass surgery funded by the NHS. He did not qualify for the surgery under the relevant policy of the defendant but he made an individual funding request on the ground of exceptionality. The defendant's individual funding request policy stated that, when determining exceptionality, 'social factors', which were non-clinical factors, would not be taken into account. The request was refused. The claimant contended that the policy breached his rights under Art 8 of the European Convention on Human Rights by excluding social or non-clinical factors from consideration. The Court of Appeal held that the policy did not breach Art 8. The defendant was entitled to refuse funding for the gastric by-pass. The claimant's state of health was having a seriously adverse effect on his private and family life in the most basic way which, without surgery, would continue. However, the application of the policy did not involve a lack of respect for the claimant's private and family life. The policy of allocating scarce medical resources on a basis of the comparative assessment of clinical needs was intentionally non-discriminatory. Performing the function of allocating limited resources strictly according to the defendant's assessment of medical need was to do no more than to apply the resource for the purpose for which they were provided without giving preferential treatment on non-medical ground. Attempts made to impose a positive obligation on the state to provide support for an individual under Art 8 had been unsuccessful. Article 8 could not be relied on as giving rise to a positive duty to take into account welfare considerations wider than the comparative medical conditions and medical needs of different patients. The trust was entitled to set an individual funding request policy which reflected what it reasonably considered to be the fairest way of treating patients. There was nothing in the authorities leading to the conclusion that the defendant's policy was to be regarded as showing a lack of respect for the claimant's private and family life so as to bring Art 8 into play. However, even if Art 8 were applicable, there were legitimate equality reasons for the trust to adopt the policy and its decision was well within the area of discretion or margin of appreciation open to it.

Finally, the courts have also considered on several occasions recently what impact alternative sources of funding that are available to patients have on the obligation to provide funding to those patients. In *Crofton* v *NHS Litigation Authority* [2007] EWCA Civ 71, the Court of Appeal held that a local authority was obliged to disregard any award of damages for personal injury when determining whether it was necessary for it to meet a claimant's care needs. In *Peters* v *East Midlands HA* [2008] EWHC 778 (QB), a patient had been left gravely handicapped as a result of the negligence of a health authority, but the local authority also had a statutory obligation under the National Assistance Act 1948 to provide for the costs of her care in a private care home. Butterfield J held that the claimant was entitled to opt for self-funding future care and accommodation and was not required to rely on statutory provision by the local authority. There was no reason why she should not be able to claim for the cost of future care and accommodation from the defendants. There was no reason, in policy or principle, for requiring that a claimant who wishes to opt for self-funding and damages in preference to reliance on the statutory obligations of a public authority should not be entitled to do so as a matter of right. (The risk of double recovery, however, had to be dealt with.) The extent of the disregard of damages for personal injury claims included the whole of the damages and not just general damages. In *R (on the application of Booker)* v *NHS Oldham* [2010] EWHC 2593 (Admin), it was held that it was unlawful and irrational for the defendant to withdraw nursing care from an eligible patient on the basis that she had the means to fund a privately provided care package by reason of damages received from an insurance company.

Part Two

Chapter 5

The duty of care

Martyn McLeish

INTRODUCTION

In everyday life the word 'negligence' is used in different ways. 'Negligence' is commonly associated with carelessness but lack of care alone will not found a cause of action. The jurisprudence that determines the limit and extent of legal liability ('legal negligence') is the product of an historical evolution with inevitable anomalies, contradictions, and complexities that require explanation.

In broad terms 'legal negligence' has three constituent parts:

1   duty – a situation or relationship in which one party has an obligation to another;
2   breach – the failure of the defendant to discharge the standard expected of someone exercising reasonable skill and care in fulfilling his obligation; and
3   damage – loss or injury to a party caused by breach.[1]

In terms of liability the doctor and patient relationship has to be understood within the general concept of legal negligence. When we ask 'Has the doctor been negligent?' we are asking a much more specific question: whether he has been in breach of a duty to take reasonable care of the patient that has resulted in a foreseeable loss. Many cases will fail because the claimant cannot show that the alleged failure of the medical practitioner 'caused' her injury. In others the court will find that the duty has not been breached because the treatment given was reasonable. In some cases the court may find that the injury sustained was not foreseeable and, therefore, there was no breach of duty. In most cases the existence of a duty of care itself is not in issue.

The discussion of the duty of care in a clinical negligence context is not of academic interest alone. First, it is important to understand what we mean when we say that a duty of care is owed by a doctor to a patient. Second, the organisation and nature of medical practice changes over time and the law of negligence must develop accordingly. Third, as the

---

1   Of course the link between the breach and the damage has to be proved: legal causation. This is the subject of Chapter 7.

law of negligence itself develops in other areas, the application of the law to medical practice will also change.

THE DOCTOR'S DUTY TO THE PATIENT

Most readers will consider it obvious that a doctor owes a duty of care to a patient, but what is the legal basis for that duty? Since *Donoghue v Stevenson* [1932] AC 562 the highest courts have sought to give clarity and definition to those circumstances when a duty of care arises. In broad terms the courts have developed a tripartite test:

1   the foreseeability of harm;
2   the closeness or proximity of the relationship between the parties; and
3   the imposition of a duty of care in the circumstances is consistent with public policy, what is fair, just, and reasonable, as set out by the House of Lords in *Caparo Industries plc v Dickman* [1990] 2 AC 605.

A GP owes a duty of care to examine, diagnose, and treat his patient with reasonable skill and care. Physical or psychiatric injury caused by negligent treatment or a failure to treat will be actionable. However, the issues become more complicated when we consider the extent of the duty and the possible limitations of legal liability. What is the extent of a doctor's liability? Is it limited to physical injury and consequential losses, or does it include financial loss suffered as a result of the patient's reliance on advice or treatment in the absence of physical or psychiatric injury? While we accept a duty is owed to the patient, what about other parties – friends, family, employers or others – who may 'rely' on the doctor's recommendations or suffer damage as a result of the failure to take certain steps? In treating a patient when will a wider duty be owed to members of the public whose safety is put at risk as a result of a medical practitioner's actions? Will a duty only be owed when there is a foreseeable risk to particular, known individuals? Some tentative answers can be made to these questions if we first consider some generic characteristics of the doctor's duty of care.

The doctor-patient relationship

Because the existence of such a duty is historic it is not easily analysed within the context of the modern tripartite test discussed above. The existence of the duty is not based on the 'foreseeability' of harm but on the relationship between doctor and patient. The duty is to be understood within the context of that relationship and the 'status' of the parties: a doctor exercises reasonable skill and care in the treatment of another who becomes his 'patient' as a result of the doctor's assumption of responsibility for his well-being. The relationship is integral to the existence of the duty of care: the relationship would not exist but for the doctor's assumption of responsibility.

The duty of care is a duty to take all reasonable steps, including the duty to commence activity, where appropriate, for the proper medical care of the patient. Where there is existing doctor-patient relationship negligent omissions, as well as the failure to take appropriate steps, will found a cause of action. In *Barnett* v *Chelsea and Kensington Hospital Management Committee* [1969] 1 QB 428 Nield J held that a hospital owed a duty to a person who presented himself at the casualty department, notwithstanding that he had not yet been received into the hospital. Similarly, once a 999 call requesting the dispatch of an ambulance was accepted the ambulance crew owed a duty to take reasonable care to the injured party (*Kent* v *Griffiths, Roberts and London Ambulance Service* [2000] 2 WLR 1158, CA).

Medical treatment of non-patients

The rescuer cases

In order for the duty to arise there must be a doctor-patient relationship. A doctor does not owe a duty to intervene when a medical emergency is encountered outside his professional life. If a bleeding man comes to one's door for help, one is not legally obliged to lend assistance. Likewise a doctor is not legally obliged to assist in the aftermath of a car accident or if medical care is required on an aeroplane (*Capital and Counties plc v Hampshire CC* [1997] QB 1004, CA).

Of course in many situations both doctors and non-medical bystanders will help. In lending assistance an ordinary member of the public owes a duty to act reasonably (cf *Harrison* v *British Railways Board* [1981] 3 All ER 679). If the actions taken injure the victim or make his or her condition worse, the rescuer may be liable in damages (*Capital and Counties plc* v *Hampshire*). But the man or woman in the street cannot be taken to have any specialised knowledge and his or her actions cannot be measured by the standard of a professional rescuer. A first aider owes a duty to assist in giving first aid, but the standard of care provided is that of a first aider and not a doctor (cf *Cattley* v *St John's Ambulance Brigade* (1988, unreported).

Confronted with an emergency situation a doctor who decides to act assumes a duty of care to the victim. The duty of care arises from the decision of the doctor to act. At this point the relationship of rescuer to victim is analogous to that between doctor and patient. In assuming such a duty the doctor must consider and if necessary embark upon some form of treatment, as in the absence of the doctor-patient relationship an omission to act will not found a cause of action. A doctor may assist in a way that falls short of providing medical treatment. So a doctor who tells relatives that a patient has died does not assume a doctor-patient relationship (*Powell* v *Boldaz* [1998] Lloyd's Rep Med 116, CA). However, once a decision is taken to act, the doctor will be in breach of duty if he fails to take reasonable care in treating the victim. Circumstances may place a limit on what a doctor can practically do in such circumstances and there are judicial statements to the effect that the duty is limited not to make the victim's condition worse, see *Capital and Counties plc v Hampshire*. A doctor may make the victim's condition worse either by activity or the failure to take reasonable steps. In either event if he or she fails to take reasonable care the victim will have a cause of action.

THE DOCTOR'S DUTY TO OTHERS

Insurers and employers

It may seem contradictory that if the basis for the duty of care is the relationship between doctor and patient, the scope of the duty should encompass the rights of others to bring an action against a doctor. However, in practice it does. If negligent medical treatment results in the death of a patient the estate of the deceased and dependents have a right of action against the doctor. This is a claim brought under statute – the Fatal Accidents Act 1976 and the Law Reform (Miscellaneous Provisions) Act 1934 – but the common law has also developed a more expansive approach to the doctor-patient duty. For example, a doctor may be liable for psychological shock provoked by the sight of a family member's injuries caused by the doctor's negligence notwithstanding the absence of any relationship between the doctor and the victim.[2]

A doctor's duty of care goes beyond causing or failing to prevent physical injury. Just as a doctor assumes a responsibility in his clinical treatment of the patient, he assumes further responsibility in providing other forms of professional service, in particular conducting health examinations and preparing reports for employers, prospective employers, insurance companies, and for the purposes of legal proceedings.

No simple statement of general application can be made in relation to these cases, in part because the factual circumstances and obligations with which they are concerned vary from case to case. For example, non-treating medical practitioners may examine an employee's medical records and prepare a report without any physical examination of the actual employee. The failure to observe a serious health problem may result in a condition going untreated that should have been detected. The failure to record such a condition may result in financial loss to both employee and employer but the failure to treat may also result in physical injury. What happens if the opposite occurs: a serious health condition is wrongly diagnosed as a result of which a job applicant is denied the position? What remedy would unsuccessful applicants have against the doctor whose negligent advice effectively cost them the job? Does it make a difference if the doctor conducts an examination as well as writing a report? Does the 'purpose' of the report, to whom it is made and what it is to contain, determine the extent of any liability?

In *Roy* v *Croydon Health Authority* [1997] PIQR P444 the defendant required the claimant to undergo a medical examination as a prospective employee. The defendants' radiologist failed to note that an X-ray disclosed a serious pathology. In this case the defendant admitted that it owed a duty of care in these circumstances. In *Baker* v *Kaye* [1997] IRLR 219 Robert Owen QC (as he then was) held that a doctor retained by a company for the purpose of examining a potential employee's medical fitness owed him a duty of care in carrying out his examination and in interpreting the results when reporting to the company.

There is a significant distinction between *Roy* v *Croydon* and *Baker* v *Kaye*. In *Roy* the failure to detect the condition caused physical injury

---

2   This is the 'aftermath' principle as set out by the House of Lords in *McLauglin* v *O'Brian* [1983] 1 AC 410.

to the claimant, in *Baker* the claimant's loss was economic, the financial consequence of not securing prospective employment. The importance of this distinction between physical injury and economic loss is made clear in *Kapfunde* v *Abbey National PLC* [1999] Lloyd's Rep Med 48, when the Court of Appeal held that *Baker* v *Kaye* was wrongly decided. In *Kapfunde* a GP had a contract with Abbey National whereby she assessed the health of a prospective employee on the basis of written materials, not an examination. She considered that the claimant was unsuitable to be employed as she had sickle cell disease so was at risk of having a lot of time off work for illness. The Court of Appeal held that the doctor did not owe a duty of care to the claimant. The GP was working under a contract with Abbey National. The purpose of her recommendation related to selecting potential employees. She had never seen the claimant and there was no close relationship between them. The claim was one for economic loss not physical injury.

The crucial consideration in these cases is not the doctor-patient relationship. These are not clinical situations when an examination is carried out and recommendations made as part of on-going treatment. In these cases the medical practitioner reports upon the patient in a particular situation: what responsibilities the doctor assumes and to whom the resultant duties are owed vary according to the circumstances. So in *Kapfunde* the GP had a duty to Abbey National to give advice applying reasonable skill and care, but owed no duty to the claimant in providing her advice to Abbey National. Doctors carrying out examination for insurance companies owe a duty of care in making appropriate recommendations to the insurance company not to the patient. The doctor is contracted to make recommendations to the insurance company, not to treat the patient.[3]

Other remedies may be available to an employee if loss arises out of the employee-employer relationship. Cases such as *Kapfunde* may now fall foul of the Equality Act 2010. Paragraph 5.5 of the Code issued alongside the Disability Discrimination Act states that an employer can stipulate essential health requirements. But the employer may need to justify doing so, and to show that it would not be reasonable for him to have to waive them in an individual case. This means that an employer should always consider whether suitable adjustments can be made to facilitate the individual's employment.

The duty of care owed to patients in these situations may be limited only to conducting the examination itself with reasonable skill and care and not causing any injury to the patient in carrying it out (*Re N* [1999] Lloyd's Rep. Med 257, CA).

The narrow interpretation of the role of medical practitioners in these circumstances is neither compelling nor satisfactory. The legal analysis belies the human reality of the situation which arises. Michael Jones has observed that it is difficult to accept that a doctor carrying out such an examination would ignore the fact of a serious medical condition and not report it the examinee.[4] He is surely right.

---

3 The point has been made *obiter*: see *M (A Minor)* v *Newham LBC* [1995] 2 AC 633 and *E (a minor)* v *Dorset CC* [1995] 2 AC 633.
4 Michael A Jones, *Medical Negligence* (4th edition, 2008) at 2-079.

Advice given in legal proceedings

Two particular issues arise in relation to medical practitioners providing advice in relation to legal proceedings. The first is when a party relies upon such advice to undertake activity or treatment that may result in injury or loss. In *Landall* v *Dennis Faulkner & Alsop* [1994] 5 Med LR 268 an orthopaedic surgeon giving advice in a personal injury claim advised the claimant to have spinal fusion surgery. The claimant alleged that this advice was negligent and that he suffered serious injury as a result. At trial it was held that there was no liability. The advice given by the orthopaedic surgeon was given for the purposes of legal proceedings and not as part of the claimant's treatment.

Landall is also an example of the second issue. Because the orthopaedic surgeon was also acting in contemplation of litigation his advice was also covered by expert witness immunity. Historically the immunity extends to witness statements and experts reports made in contemplation of both civil and criminal proceedings. So in *Evans* v *The London Hospital's Medical College (University of London)* [1981] 1 WLR 184 Drake J. struck out a claim against a pathologist for negligent preparation of a report that led to criminal proceedings. In *M* v *Newham London Borough Council* [1995] 2 AC 633 Lord Browne-Wilkinson said that a psychiatrist would have witness immunity where, having been instructed by the local authority to examine a child by way of an inquiry into sexual abuse and its possible perpetrators, she would naturally know that her report might found proceedings. In *Jones* v *Kaney* [2010] EWHC 61 (QB) Blake J struck out a claim against a psychologist who radically and allegedly negligently changed her opinion after joint discussion with the defendant's expert. However, he certified that the issue of expert witness immunity was a suitable subject for consideration by the Supreme Court. The Supreme Court decided that the immunity could not be justified and allowed the appeal (*Jones (appellant)* v *Kaney (respondent)* [2011] UKSC 13). Although the law of expert immunity has been transformed by this decision existing case law gives some indication of how it may impact upon practice.

A medical practitioner's liability in negligence for pre-litigation acts is clearly established. In *Hughes* v *Lloyds Bank plc* [1998] PIQR P98, CA a claimant settled her personal injury claim based upon letters she obtained from her GP about her condition. Although these letters had been used in connection with legal proceedings the GP was not immune from suit. Proceedings had not been issued. The letters had been provided for the purposes of negotiation not as part of disclosure. The claim for negligence against the GP would not be struck out.

Hughes is a strike-out case and it is important to consider that claims against medical practitioners providing advice in connection with legal proceedings are likely to be beset with difficulty. In *N* v *Agrawal* [1999] Lloyd's Rep Med. 257, CA the claimant alleged that the defendant, who examined her following her complaint of sexual assault and made a report upon this examination, owed her a duty to attend court and give evidence at the trial of her alleged assailant. The failure to give evidence had resulted in an exacerbation of psychological trauma. The Court of Appeal struck out the claim on the ground that a witness was not under a duty to any person to give evidence.

Immunity has been waived in other circumstances. In *Meadow* v *General Medical Council* [2007] QB 462 the Court of Appeal held that expert witnesses had no immunity against disciplinary proceedings before professional tribunals where fitness to practice was in issue. In *Phillips* v *Symes (No 2)* [2004] EWHC 2330 (Ch), [2005] 1 WLR 2043 Peter Smith J held that expert witnesses were not immune from being held liable to wasted costs orders.

A treating doctor does not have to foresee the consequences of his advice on legal proceedings. In *Stevens* v *Bermondsey and Southwark Group Hospital Management Committee* (1963) 107 Sol Jo 478, a casualty officer negligently diagnosed the claimant as having suffered a minor injury. She was not liable to the claimant for the financial loss sustained as a result of undersettling her claim for damages for personal injury.

THE DUTY OF DOCTORS EXERCISING STATUTORY POWERS

The notion that a doctor owes a duty of care to his patient is uncontroversial. Doctors will also owe a duty of care when, in certain situations, they assume responsibility for the care of others who are not their patients. In providing reports to employers, insurers, and lawyers, the scope of the doctor's duty of care is limited by the circumstances of the case. Many doctors or other health care professionals are employed by or contracted to public authorities in the provision of social and education services. The liability of public bodies for injury and loss caused by failures in the exercise of statutory powers is one of the most complex and controversial issues in contemporary jurisprudence. The central issues involved can only be briefly outlined for the purposes of this chapter.

The distinctive feature of these cases is that the duty of care arises from the statutory function itself and is not based on the relationship between the claimant and defendant, unless a duty is also owed as a result of some other relationship such as that between employer and employee (see *Connor* v *Surrey County Council* [2010] EWCA Civ 286, CA).

In *X (minors)* v *Bedfordshire County Council* [1995] 2 AC 633 the House of Lords was concerned with test cases where a local authority, exercising its statutory powers, took children into care. Lord Browne-Wilkinson held a common law duty of care might arise in the performance of such functions, however, a distinction had to be drawn between those situations when a public body's decision was based on the exercise of a discretion or judgment or there were administrative failings leading to injury or damage. For example, the decision to close a school might not give rise to a private law cause of action, but the failure to keep a school reasonably safe would found a claim for damages for injury arising as a result of the neglected conditions of the building.

A clear distinction between operational and 'policy' decisions may become more difficult when we are concerned with the judgment of professionals not only exercising their judgment but also balancing competing considerations and risks, including limited public resources. In *X* v *Bedfordshire* the House of Lords held that a psychiatrist or social worker examining or investigating evidence of sexual abuse on behalf of the local authority in the exercise of statutory child care functions does not owe a duty of care to a child or her mother. However, the possibility that professionals exercising such judgment could have a practical immunity from suit was not accepted by the European Court of Human Rights (*Z* v *United Kingdom* (2001) 34 EHRR 97).

The House of Lords had to reconsider the issues in *X* v *Bedfordshire* through the lens of the Strasbourg jurisprudence in *Barrett* v *Enfield* [2001] 2 AC 550. In this case the claimant alleged the local authority had failed in its duty of care while he was in care. Their Lordships drew a distinction between decisions taken for policy reasons and those taken as part of the local authority's 'operational' function. The court was not equipped to adjudicate on the policy decisions of statutory bodies which had to be allowed a wide discretion in allocating resources and prioritising care. However, where decisions did not involve issues of policy the traditional common law of negligence could apply. The courts could consider the circumstances of the case, weigh the evidence, and determine whether a decision fell within the policy or operational functions of the local authority. In this way the development of the common law has avoided 'blanket' immunity defeating valid claims against public authorities. However, the existence of a duty of care will be determined according to the three stage test of foreseeability, proximity, and what is fair, just and reasonable.

The most important example of the three stage test being applied is *JD (FC)* v *East Berkshire Community Health NHS Trust* [2005] 2 WLR 993. The claimants were parents who were wrongly suspected of child abuse as a result of the misdiagnosis of their children by doctors. Their claims were struck out by the House of Lords. This decision was not based on the foreseeability of injury or the 'proximity' or closeness of the relationship between the parties involved. Both of these limbs of the test were satisfied. The claims were struck out on public and legal policy grounds. First, if a doctor investigating the question of abuse should be liable to parents if he acted without due care, there was no reason why a negligent surgeon should not be liable for psychiatric harm suffered by parents in all cases when negligence results in the injury or death of a child. Second, the floodgates would be open to parents if a doctor with the medical charge of a child also owed a duty of care to the parents. Third, the doctor was charged with the protection of the child, not the parent. Fourth, the interests of the child in these situations were not identical with those of the parent. Fifth, in these particular cases the interest of the child and parent were in conflict: indeed there could only ever be a conflict of interest in such cases as in carrying out their duty of investigation the doctors had regard only to the interests of the children.

The education cases

The European Court of Human Rights has been the midwife to a more liberal approach to the liability of statutory bodies. In *Phelps* v *Hillingdon London Borough Council* [2001] 2 AC 619 the House of Lords considered the liability of professionals employed by education authorities exercising statutory duties under the Education Acts. Lord Slynn held that in these cases the court had to consider (a) why that person should *not* owe a duty of care, and (b) why, if the duty is breached by that person, the authority should *not* be liable.

An educational psychologist employed by a local education authority will, or is likely to, owe a duty of care to a pupil, and the local education authority owes a general duty through its teachers to provide a suitable education for its pupils. In *E* v *Dorset County Council* [1995] 2 AC 633 the House of Lords refused to strike out claims against a local education authority for the failure of its psychologists, teachers and officials to identify the special educational needs of the claimant. In *D N* v *Greenwich London Borough Council* [2004] EWCA Civ 1659 the Court of Appeal held that a local education authority was liable for the negligence of an educational psychologist who had failed, among other things, to identify the claimant's complex social and communication needs.

The interests of professionals have to be considered as well as the right of a child to claim damages in negligence. In *Devon County Council* v *Clarke* [2005] EWCA Civ 266 the Court of Appeal held that it was wrong to characterise all educational negligence cases as being single claims for a failed education over a period of time as if special rules applied to them. The jurisdiction to award damages in cases of this sort was not to be seen as a charter for claimants to make allegations against all the professionals who had been involved in a child's education, secure in the knowledge that, provided they succeeded in one allegation against one professional, they would recover all their costs from the local education authority. In *Carty* v *Croydon London Borough Council* [2005] EWCA Civ 19 the court said there were two areas of potential enquiry in such a case. The first was whether the issue was justiciable at all, the second was the application of the three-stage *Caparo* test – foreseeability of damage, proximity, and whether it was fair, just and reasonable that the law should impose a duty of care. In *Nuttall* v *Mayor & Burgesses of Sutton London Borough Council* [2009] EWHC 294 (QB) an educational psychologist owed a duty to a child with special educational needs to assess the needs of the child with the care and skill to be expected of a reasonably competent educational psychologist. However, in practical terms, it would only be if an educational psychologist conducted an assessment negligently or formulated a recommendation negligently, or both, that any liability would arise. In order to recover damages for negligence, the claimant had also to prove that he had suffered loss as a result of the matters of which he complained.

THE DUTY OWED TO MEMBERS OF THE PUBLIC

The notion that a doctor owes a duty of care to his patient is uncontroversial. A doctor who reacts to an emergency to assist members of the public in an emergency will also owe those treated a duty to take reasonable care. In some cases the treatment a doctor recommends for a patient will involve wider considerations of the patient's well-being and the safety of others. Legal liability in such situations will depend on the circumstances of the case and, in particular, whether or not injury to a specific individual or a particular group of individuals was foreseeable. For example, in *Goodwill* v *British Pregnancy Advisory Service* [1996] 1 WLR 1397 the Court of Appeal found that a doctor carrying out a vasectomy does not owe a duty of care to all women with whom the patient will have sexual intercourse in the future.

Different considerations may arise when the risk of injury to members of the public is imminent and not merely theoretical. Earlier cases suggest that a doctor was under a duty of care to potential victims of a dangerous patient who was not properly contained: see *Holgate* v *Lancashire Mental Hospitals Board* [1937] 4 All ER 19 and *Ellis* v *Home Office* [1953] 2 All ER 149, CA. However these older authorities have to be approached with a degree of caution. They predate the three-stage test for breach of duty with which we are now so familiar. Moreover, they sit uncomfortably with the decisions reached by the House of Lords in relation to the duty owed by the police to the victims of crime. In *Hill* v *Chief Constable of West Yorkshire* [1988] 1 WLR 1049 the House of Lords held that no claim could be brought by the victim's estate against the police for its failure to apprehend her murderer. The Court of Appeal applied *Hill* in *Palmer* v *Tees Health Authority* [1999] Lloyd's Rep Med 351. In this case the mother of a murdered child was unable to bring a claim against the health authority alleging negligence in failing to diagnose the perpetrator of the crime as a risk to children. A health authority owed no duty of care to the public generally in respect of its care of such patients. There was no relationship between the defendant and the victim. Neither the claimant nor her daughter could have been identified as potential victims before the crime was committed.

In *Palmer* the Court of Appeal applied the three stage test following *Caparo* and found that there no 'proximity'. In that case, as we have seen, there was no relationship between the defendant and the victims of the crime. The facts were different in *Osman* v *Ferguson* [1993] 4 All ER 344 although the Court of Appeal came to the same result. In this case a teacher developed an obsession with one of his pupils. The police were aware of the teacher's increasingly menacing behaviour towards the pupil and his family. Despite an escalation in the teacher's erratic behaviour, the police did not prosecute, and eventually he killed the boy's father and injured his brother. Applying *Hill* the Court of Appeal struck out the claim, although in this instance the proximity test was satisfied. The European Court of Human Rights held that the striking out of the claim was a restriction on the claimant's right of access to a court under Art 6(1) of the European Convention on Human Rights.[5]

A complicating factor in these cases is that in most situations the act of violence causing injury or death is a crime. Two issues arise. The first is whether or not the illegal act itself can found a cause of action. The second is whether a doctor or health authority can be liable for an illegal act perpetrated by a patient who may or may not commit such acts while under their control.

In *Clunis* v *Camden and Islington Health Authority* [1998] QB 978, CA the plaintiff had been detained in hospital for treatment of a mental disorder. The hospital discharged him and he stabbed a man to death. The plaintiff sued the health authority, alleging that it had been negligent in discharging him. The health authority applied to strike out the action on the ground that damages could not be recovered for the consequences of the plaintiff's own unlawful act. The court accepted this submission. The plaintiff has been convicted of a serious criminal offence. The court ought not to allow itself to be made an instrument to enforce obligations alleged to arise out of the plaintiff's own criminal act.

---

5   *Osman* v *UK* [2000] 29 EHRR 245.

The House of Lords considered the issues further in *Gray* v *Thames Trains Ltd* [2009] UKHL 33. In this case the claimant was a passenger on a train involved in a major railway accident. He suffered post-traumatic stress disorder which he alleged had been caused by the accident. Whilst suffering from that disorder he killed a man. His plea of guilty to manslaughter on the ground of diminished responsibility was accepted by the Crown and he was ordered to be detained in a hospital under the Mental Health Act. The claimant brought an action in negligence against the defendants, including damages for loss of earnings, loss of liberty and post-traumatic stress disorder. The House of Lords ruled that in order to avoid inconsistency in the justice system a civil court would not award damages to compensate a claimant for an injury or disadvantage which the criminal courts had imposed for a criminal act for which he was responsible; the criminal court by its sentence had found the claimant to have had personal responsibility even if he had acted with diminished responsibility.

Cases involving detention

Earlier cases seem to establish a duty of care on a doctor when recommending the admission of a patient to hospital for mental disorder (*Everett* v *Griffiths* [1920] 3 KB 163, CA; *de Freville* v *Dill* (1927) 96 LJKB 1056). In cases involving detention under s 3 of the Mental Health Act the state, through the health authority, owes an operational duty to patients (*Savage* v *South Essex NHS Trust* [2008] UKHL 74). A health authority was under a duty to take steps to prevent a detained mental patient from committing suicide if it knew or ought to have known that there was a real and immediate risk of suicide. The situation, however, may be different if the patient was voluntarily and not compulsorily detained (*Rabone* v *Pennine Care NHS Trust* [2010] EWCA 698). The Supreme Court is due to hear the claimant's appeal in this case.

Chapter 6

Breach of duty and strict liability

Martyn McLeish

INTRODUCTION

A doctor has a duty to take reasonable care of his patient. This duty will be breached if the doctor fails to provide care which conforms to the standard reasonably expected of a competent doctor. The inability of a doctor to treat a patient successfully is not by itself enough to found a claim in negligence. A doctor in general practice cannot be expected to have the skill and expertise of a surgeon. Nevertheless, an inexperienced doctor will be judged by the standards of an experienced doctor. The standard is that which is reasonable in the circumstances of the case. Two questions arise: what is the standard of care in a particular case, and how is the claimant to prove that the defendant has failed to come up to that standard?

Determining the standard of care expected of a doctor depends upon a legal analysis of the facts of the case and is highly dependent upon expert medical evidence. As with all professionals, the law has to accord medical practitioners a degree of respect. In many cases evidence of good practice will provide sufficient evidence of reasonable care. However, in all branches of science and learning there will be differences of opinion as to what is or is not reasonable practice. A doctor may hold a minority view, but so long as this view is held by a respectable body of medical opinion, it is reasonably held, and his treatment of a patient in line with such opinion will not give rise to liability.

THE *BOLAM* TEST

The standard of care that is required of a person undertaking an activity is that which is reasonable. Every person who enters into a learned profession undertakes to bring to the exercise of it a reasonable degree of care and skill. The seminal statement of this approach to clinical negligence is that of McNair J in *Bolam* v *Friern Hospital Management Committee* [1957] 1 WLR 582 at 586:

Where you get a situation which involves the use of some special skill or competence, then the test as to whether there has been negligence or not is not the test of the man on the top of a Clapham omnibus, because he has not got this special skill. The test is the standard of the ordinary skilled man exercising and professing to have that special skill. A man need not possess the highest expert skill ... it is sufficient if he exercises the ordinary skill of an ordinary competent man exercising that particular art.

Following *Bolam*, it is possible to set out some simple propositions about the standard of care:

1   A doctor's duty is to exercise skill and care according to the ordinary and reasonable standards of those who practice in the relevant field of medicine. So the standard of care expected of a specialist is that of a specialist.

2   In ordinary circumstances a doctor following a generally approved practice will not be held to be negligent (*Marshall* v *Lindsey County Council* [1935] 1 KB 516, CA at 540 *per* Maugham LJ).

3   A court cannot choose between two approved practices, ie between two schools of thought (*Maynard* v *West Midlands Regional Health Authority* [1984] 1 WLR 634, HL).

4   If a respectable body of medical opinion, albeit a minority one, would at the time of the alleged negligence have approved of the course taken by the defendant, there will be no negligence.

5   In determining whether a body of doctors constituted a responsible body for the purposes of the *Bolam* test it is not simply a matter of counting heads: in appropriate circumstances the judge could find that a small number constituted the necessary defence (*Defreitas* v *O'Brien* [1995] 6 Med LR 108, CA).

6   The test for establishing negligence is whether or not the failure of the doctor would have occurred had he been acting with reasonable skill and care (*per* Lord President Clyde in *Hunter* v *Hanley* 1955 SLT 213 at 217).

7   The *Bolam* test is comprehensive, covering questions of treatment, diagnosis, and assessment and disclosure of risk.

The relationship between the legal analysis, the facts and the expert evidence has been neatly summarised by Lord Scarman:

In short, the law imposes the duty of care: but the standard of care is a matter of medical judgment.

(*Sidaway* v *Board of Governors of the Bethlem Royal Hospital and the Maudsley Hospital* [1985] AC 871 (HL) at 881.)

Examples

Pargeter v *Kensington and Chelsea and Westminster Health Authority* [1979] 2 Lancet 1030. The defendants avoided liability by showing that there was a respectable body of medical opinion that took the view that papaveretum should be administered after an open eye operation, even though there was an opposing school of thought.

Hughes v *Waltham Forest Health Authority* [1991] 2 Med LR 155, CA). The fact that two distinguished surgeons in a particular speciality were critical of the decision of two of their colleagues did not prove that the action of the latter was negligent, even if it had turned out to be a mistake. The proper test of negligence was whether the surgeons, in reaching their decision, had displayed such a lack of clinical judgment that no surgeon exercising proper care and skill could have made the same decision.

Taylor v *Worcester and District Health Authority* [1991] 2 Med LR 215. The claimant's claim for damages for awareness during a Caesarean section failed because the judge concluded that the anaesthetist had followed a procedure that was acceptable at the time of the operation (ie in 1985) despite the fact that procedures had changed since.

Adderley v *North Manchester Health Authority* (1995) 25 BMLR 42, CA. It was held that a diagnosis of schizophrenia, though wrong, was not negligent on the *Bolam* principle. The appeal court being bound by the judge's finding that it was a 'two schools of thought' case. No pun intended.

Ashcroft v *Mersey Regional Health Authority* [1983] 2 All ER 245. Kilner Brown J said that the question was whether it had been established on a balance of probabilities that the doctor had failed to exercise the care required of a man possessing and professing special skill in circumstances which required the exercise of that special skill. No added burden of proof rested on the claimant.

Burgess v *Newcastle Health Authority* [1992] 3 Med LR 224. A neuro-surgeon avoided liability in respect of his management of a right frontal craniotomy by showing that a 'widely respected body of neuro-surgeons' would have acted in the same way.

Defreitas v *O'Brien* [1993] 4 Med LR 281 (QBD). Both orthopaedic surgeon and neuro-surgeon avoided liability by showing that their management was acceptable to a responsible body of medical opinion.

Bolam does not apply to the facts

The *Bolam* test applies to the issue of whether or not a doctor's actions were in accordance with reasonable practice. It is not concerned with the actual facts of the case which have to be established in the ordinary way on the balance of probabilities. The judge will simply have to decide whose evidence he accepts, giving the reasons for his decision. Where there is an issue of causation, such as whether treatment which was not given would have cured the patient or otherwise reduced or avoided injury, a dispute between the experts does not involve the *Bolam* test. In *Fallows* v *Randle* [1997] 8 Med LR 160, CA Stuart-Smith LJ said:

> In my judgment that principle has really no application where what the judge has to decide is, on balance, which of two explanations – for something which has undoubtedly occurred which shows that the operation has been unsuccessful – is to be preferred. That is a question of fact which the judge has to determine on the ordinary basis on a balance of probability. It is not a question of saying whether there was a respectable body of medical opinion here which says that this can happen by chance without any evidence, it is a question for the judge to weigh up the evidence on both sides, and he is, in my judgment, entitled in a situation like this, to prefer the evidence of one expert witness to that of the other.

Situations where the court has considered not applying a simple *Bolam* analysis

There are cases where the court has been concerned that common practice itself may not be reasonable. In *Clarke* v *Adams* (1950) 94 Sol Jo 599, the judge found that the standard warning given by radiologists before giving heat treatment was negligent because it did not give the patient a clear indication as to when the danger point in the treatment might be reached.

In other cases the court has been concerned with the reasons given for a particular practice. In *Hucks* v *Cole*, a 1968 case reported at [1993] 4 Med LR 393, CA, a doctor who failed to treat a patient with penicillin was held negligent even though responsible doctors testified that they would have acted as the defendant had. Sachs LJ said that if the court was satisfied that there was a gap in professional practice whereby the patient was exposed to unnecessary risks, the court would expect the professional practice to be altered accordingly. It was not conclusive of proper practice that other practitioners would have acted as the defendant did. The judge was not satisfied that their reasons for so doing stood up to analysis.

In *Knight* v *Home Office* [1990] 3 All ER 237 Pill J rejected a claim that a mentally disordered prisoner who committed suicide had not been properly looked after by the prison hospital staff on the ground that the decision to observe him at 15-minute intervals had been a decision that ordinary skilled medical staff in their position could have made. However, in the course of his judgment he said that the reasons given by the doctors for their decision should, however, be examined by the court to see if they stood up to analysis.

The courts have also been willing to impose their own view of what is reasonable and what is not upon professions other than the medical profession. In *Nye Saunders & Partners* v *Bristow* (1987) 37 BLR 92, CA the trial judge found on the evidence that at the relevant time there was no body of responsible professional opinion among architects that would have failed to give a warning as to inflation when estimating building costs, but that, even if he was wrong there, he was prepared to hold that no prudent architect would have omitted such a warning. The Court of Appeal refused to interfere with either of those findings. In *Edward Wong Finance Co Ltd* v *Johnson Stokes & Master* [1984] AC 296 the Privy Council found an established conveyancing practice among Hong Kong solicitors to be unacceptable. In *Deeny* v *Gooda Walker Ltd* [1996] LRLR 183 Phillips J (as he then was) considered that if 'a profession collectively adopted extremely lax standards in some aspect of its work' the court 'would not acquit practitioners of negligence simply because they had complied with those standards.' The application of these authorities to medical negligence is not straightforward.

One consequence of the operation of the *Bolam* test is the implausibility of a judge holding that a respected body of medical opinion is flawed. However, another crucial aspect of the test is how it applies to the facts. The court will find on the balance of probabilities what steps a doctor took in treating a patient. The court will then have to decide whether or not those actions were in accordance with the exercise of ordinary skill and care. In clinical practice a patient may present with a variety of symptoms and a number of potential diagnoses, there may be a range of possible treatments, giving rise to a genuine divergence of view about how to proceed. Not every doctor is House. Applying *Bolam* no claim can succeed where the treatment option selected is considered reasonable by a recognised body of medical opinion, even a minority one. However, in every case evidence given about what a doctor should have done is counter-factual: it is an exposition of what a practitioner may have done in the same circumstances as the defendant.

BOLITHO AND THE MODERN APPROACH TO *BOLAM*

Respect for medical practitioners and appropriate deference to their skill and expertise cannot determine liability in every case. In *Bolitho* v *City and Hackney Health Authority* [1998] AC 232 the House of Lords considered the *Bolam* test within the context of the court's objective of doing justice in the case by the application of its own logical analysis of the expert evidence.

In *Bolitho* the defendant admitted negligence on the basis that a doctor failed to attend the claimant while he was in hospital with an obstruction in his bronchial air passage. Had the doctor attended she said she would not have intubated the claimant. There were two schools of thought about whether or not the doctor should have intubated. The defendant called evidence from one expert who would not have intubated; the claimant called evidence from five experts saying that they would have done.

Such evidence gives cause for concern for several reasons. The first is the patient's fear that medical practitioners may 'close ranks': that the simple marshalling of supportive evidence from doctors will be enough to defeat the claim. However, the courts have always been sensitive to this possibility. In *Chapman* v *Rix*, a 1960 decision reported in [1994] 5 Med LR 239, the House of Lords indicated that a doctor could not necessarily escape liability merely by calling colleagues to say they would have done the same as he had done. The same point was made by Lord Browne-Wilkinson in *Bolitho*:

> The court is not bound to hold that a defendant doctor escapes liability for negligent treatment or diagnosis just because he leads evidence from a number of medical experts who are genuinely of opinion that the defendant's treatment or diagnosis accorded with sound medical practice.

The judge may take the view that, whatever the defence experts say about what they would have done at the time, they are wrong, ie faced with the actual situation, they would not have acted as the impugned doctor did. An example of this can be found in the dissenting judgment of Simon Brown LJ in *Bolitho* in the Court of Appeal. However, if the defendant's case were accepted it would still need to satisfy the judge that the practice involved was responsible.

A second concern is that cases are decided by judges, applying the law to the facts, and not by medical experts' opinion of good practice. For this reason there must be some basis for scrutinising clinical treatment. The decision reached has to withstand analysis. However, a practical difficulty lies in determining the basis for such analysis. The court may have heard from careful and thoughtful witnesses who give their evidence honestly, based on considerable experience. A judge usually has no medical knowledge or clinical experience with which to judge that evidence. Although the evidence of unreasonableness will usually be argued by the claimant's experts, judges are understandably reluctant to say that one body of opinion was 'unreasonable'.

The third issue, therefore, is the basis upon which the court can hold a medical opinion to scrutiny. In *Bolitho* Lord Browne-Wilkinson held that the task of the judge was to be satisfied that the experts had directed their minds to the question of comparative risks and benefits and reached a reasonable, logical, and defensible conclusion. Having considered *Hucks* v *Cole* and *Edward Wong Finance Co Ltd* v *Johnson Stokes & Master* Lord Browne-Wilkinson concluded:

> These decisions demonstrate that in cases of diagnosis and treatment there are cases where, despite a body of professional opinion sanctioning the defendant's conduct, the defendant can properly be held liable for negligence ... In my judgment that is because, in some cases, it cannot be demonstrated to the judge's satisfaction that the body of opinion relied upon is reasonable or responsible. In the vast majority of cases the fact that distinguished experts in the field are of a particular opinion will demonstrate the reasonableness of that opinion. In particular, where there are questions of assessment of the relative risks and benefits of adopting a particular medical practice, a reasonable view necessarily discloses that the relative risks and benefits have been weighed by the experts in forming their opinions. But if, in a rare case, it can be demonstrated that the professional opinion is not capable of withstanding logical analysis, the judge is entitled to hold that the body of opinion is not reasonable or responsible.

He continued:

> I emphasise that in my view it will very seldom be right for a judge to reach the conclusion that views genuinely held by a competent medical expert are unreasonable. The assessment of medical risks and benefits is a matter of clinical judgment which a judge would not normally be able to make without expert evidence ... it would be wrong to allow such assessment to deteriorate into seeking to persuade the judge to prefer one of two views both of which are capable of being logically supported. It is only where a judge can be satisfied that the body of expert opinion cannot be logically supported at all that such opinion will not provide the bench mark by reference to which the defendant's conduct falls to be assessed.

AFTER *BOLITHO*

From a practical perspective cases are more likely to be won by undermining the credibility of the defendant expert witnesses than on the application of the law following *Bolitho*. The judge is permitted to take the view that the defence expert is simply wrong, perhaps because not all the relevant factors have been considered, or the opinion expressed does not represent a responsible body of medical opinion. (See also Chapter 20, Experts) In *Midland Bank Trust Co Ltd* v *Hett Stubbs & Kemp* [1979] Ch 384 Oliver J said at 402:

> Clearly, if there is some practice in a particular profession, some accepted standard of conduct which is laid down by a professional institute or sanctioned by common usage, evidence of that can and ought to be received. But evidence which really amounts to no more than an expression of opinion of a particular practitioner of what he thinks he would have done had he been placed, hypothetically and without the benefit of hindsight, in the position of the defendants, is of little assistance to the court.

Where a judge finds in favour of one expert rather than other he must give proper reasons for the decision. In *Ratty* v *Haringey Health Authority*

[1994] 5 Med LR 413 the Court of Appeal reversed the judge's finding in favour of the plaintiff on the ground that, given that he accepted the evidence and the standing of the defendants' experts, he was not entitled to hold that no responsible practitioner would have acted as the accused surgeon did without giving proper reasons.

A finding that an expert's opinion represents the view of an acceptable body of opinion is not enough (*Smith v Southampton University Hospitals NHS Trust* [2007] EWCA Civ 387). The judge must subject the opinion expressed to proper analysis.

In *Marriott* v *West Midlands Regional Health Authority* [1999] Lloyd's Rep Med 23, CA the trial judge found that, if the GP expert's evidence did in fact establish that there was a body of GPs who would not have referred the patient to hospital, 'then such approach is not reasonably prudent'. The Court of Appeal said that the judge was entitled, following *Bolitho,* to subject a body of opinion to analysis to see whether it could properly be regarded as reasonable, and she had been entitled to conclude that it could not be reasonable to fail to refer the patient in such a condition.

In *Penney, Palmer and Cannon* v *East Kent Health Authority* [1999] Lloyd's Rep Med 123 (QBD), [2000] Lloyd's Rep Med 41, CA the judge found that the *Bolam* principle did not apply because there was no dispute about acceptable or unacceptable practice, only a factual dispute about whether screeners had given the wrong classification to smears. Even if the principle had applied he was satisfied that the evidence of the three experts called by the defence did not stand up to logical analysis because the screeners did not have the ability to draw a distinction between benign and pre-cancerous cells, and so should have classified the smears as borderline. On appeal the court said that the *Bolam* test did apply as the screeners were exercising skill and judgment in determining what report they should make, but they agreed with the judge that the logical analysis test was applicable, and that it led to the conclusion that the exonerating opinion of the defence experts did not stand up to analysis.

In *Walsh* v *Gwynedd Health Authority* ML 5/98 p 9, the County Court judge at Llangefni rejected a consultant psychiatrist's expert evidence about lack of suicidal intention on the part of a patient when seen by a registrar and his exoneration of the registrar's management, on the ground that his expert opinion did not stand up to analysis.

In *Calver* v *Westwood Veterinary Group* [2001] PIQR P168, MLC 0350 the Court of Appeal held that there had been no justification for the judge condemning as illogical the defence expert's exoneration of the defendant vet's management of a sick mare.

In *Reynolds* v *North Tyneside Health Authority* [2002] Lloyds Rep Med 459 Gross J said that, even if there was a body of opinion which would support not performing a vaginal examination immediately upon the admission of a pregnant woman following spontaneous rupture of the membranes. The only justification offered for that view, which was the increased risk of infection, could not withstand scrutiny, because it was illogical and indefensible.

In *AB v Leeds Teaching Hospital NHS Trust* [2005] QB 506 (QBD) Gage J held that the practice of not informing the parents of deceased children that their child's organs had been removed and retained by the hospital was not acceptable.

FACTORS AFFECTING THE STANDARD OF CARE

Error of judgments

Modern professionals are subject to continuing professional education and are obliged to keep up to date with advances in understanding. The professions learn from their mistakes. The admission of a mistake or an error of judgment on its own will not found a claim in negligence. Unless the mistake is one which does not require the exercise of skill and judgment such as where the doctor mistakenly provides the wrong medicine (see, for example, *Penny* above). The treatment a doctor gives must be considered in the light of *Bolam* and the test to be applied is whether or not in the circumstances of the case the care provided fell below the standard to be expected of a competent practitioner exercising reasonable skill and care. So in *Ashton v Alexander and Trent Regional Health Authority* (1988, unreported) the Court of Appeal held that the admission of a mistake by a surgeon did not equate to negligence and the trial judge had to apply the appropriate test: whether or not the error was one a reasonably competent professional would have made exercising proper care.

There are many aspects of invasive medical treatment that result in recognised complications even though all proper care has been taken. The fact that a patient does not recover as anticipated does not of itself indicate negligence. However, a distinction has to be drawn between a clinical judgment which proves to be erroneous and one which was mistaken at the time it was made. Both may be negligent. If the doctor failed to foresee potential consequences he should reasonably have foreseen his assessment may have been at fault, the treatment chosen may have been mistaken, and the advice given to the patient may have been wrong. If, however, this was a clinical judgment when there were a number of factors that had to be weighed, and a reasonable body of medical opinion would have proceeded in the same way, there is no negligence subject to the treatment prescribed withstanding logical scrutiny. If in retrospect a doctor recognises that a mistake was made at the time as there was a failure to take into account various observable facts, the *Bolam* test will still apply, and if a reasonable body of medical opinion would have acted in the same way the defence may succeed subject to the application of *Bolitho*.

The disclosure of risk

The exercise of judgment, balancing various factors, and assessing risks is part of the care a doctor provides. The disclosure of the risks to the patient, therefore, must also comply with the *Bolam/Bolitho* tests. The doctor has a duty to disclose the risks of treatment in accordance with an acceptable body of medical opinion: *Sidaway* v *Bethlem Royal Hospital* [1985] AC 871, HL and *Gold* v *Haringey Health Authority* [1988] QB 481, CA. This situation is considered below in Chapter 10, under 'Duty of disclosure: general'.

Departing from usual practice

A doctor is entitled to use his common sense, experience and judgment in the way he decides to treat any patient. A slight departure from the textbook does not establish negligence (*per* Streatfeild J in *Holland* v *Devitt & Moore Nautical College* (1960) Times, 4 March). It has to be shown that the defendant took a course which no physician of ordinary skill would have taken if acting with reasonable care. However, where a doctor departs from standard methods of treatment there must be good reasons for doing so.

It was alleged in *Slater* v *Baker and Stapleton* (1767) 2 Wils 359 that the defendant, an apothecary and chief surgeon at St Bartholomew's, had been negligent in treating a broken leg. He had re-broken it and then attempted to straighten it through extension rather than compression, using a machine. The jury found for the claimant, and, affirming the verdict, the court said the defendants had 'acted ignorantly and unskilfully, contrary to the known rule and usage of surgeons'.

In *Cooper* v *Nevill* (1961) Times, 24 March, where a surgeon had left an abdominal pack in the patient's body, the Privy Council said there was no justification for any departure from the normal routine.

Where there was a departure from normal practice in performing a colporrhaphy operation (to remedy stress incontinence) within three months of birth, which proved to be unsuccessful, it was held that such a departure had not been shown to have been justified and therefore constituted a breach of the duty of care owed to the patient (*Clark* v *MacLennan* [1983] 1 All ER 416).

However, there will be situations where the variety of symptoms with which a patient appears and the need for the development of new techniques mean that novel approaches are justified. In *Wilsher* v *Essex Area Health Authority* [1987] QB 730, CA Mustill LJ said that:

> Where the doctor embarks on a form of treatment which is still comparatively untried, with techniques and safeguards which are still in the course of development, or where the treatment is of particular technical difficulty ... if the decision to embark on the treatment at all was justifiable and was taken with the informed consent of the patient, the court should ... be particularly careful not to impute negligence simply because something has gone wrong.

In *Hepworth* v *Kerr* [1995] 6 Med LR 139 the judge was satisfied that the defendant anaesthetist had been negligent in adopting a new anaesthetic technique which, as he knew, had never been attempted routinely before by anyone else. Although he had practised the technique previously on some 1,500 patients to a greater or lesser extent, he had never attempted to make any proper scientific validation of it, and without that validation he was not justified in involving the patient in such a fundamental departure from conventional practice.

State of knowledge

It is a doctor's duty to keep reasonably abreast of medical knowledge, and for that purpose he needs to be aware of recent developments published in the medical press. Where a medical practitioner continues to use an obsolete procedure, he may well be negligent in continuing to employ it (cf *Roe* v *Minister of Health* [1954] 2 QB 66).

However, new techniques do not necessarily prove old methods are negligent unless it can be shown that they are wrong or carry an unacceptable risk to the patient that is no longer justified. In *Newbury* v *Bath District Health Authority* (1998) 47 BMLR 138 the patient unsuccessfully claimed damages for a lumbar fusion. Ebsworth J said that neither the claimant's nor the defendant's expert witnesses would have performed the surgery using the technique employed by the surgeon. His choice of technique was unwise, but that was not the correct legal basis for the assessment of liability. The question was whether, on a logical analysis of the decision, it was one a reasonably competent consultant could have made at the time. A competent consultant would keep abreast of the field and adjust procedures appropriately in the light of information received, but would be entitled to keep an old, tried method for use where properly judged to be suitable. That other surgeons might use different methods with success did not render the use of well-tried methods negligent. The surgeon was entitled to make the judgment which he had made and was not negligent in so doing, nor had the surgery been carried out negligently.

The length to which a doctor must go to keep abreast of the latest knowledge will depend on the level of speciality. A doctor is not expected to read and ingest every available item. In *Crawford* v *Charing Cross Hospital* (1953) Times, 8 December, CA a surgeon was not expected to know that a particular placing of a patient's arm during a blood transfusion was dangerous, as the only evidence of that fact had been one article in a recent medical journal. In the first case on industrial deafness, *Thompson* v *Smiths Shiprepairers (North Shields)* [1984] QB 405, CA, Mustill J said:

> One must be careful when considering documents culled for the purpose of a trial, and studied by reference to a single isolated issue, not to forget that they once formed part of a flood of print on numerous aspects of industrial life, in which many items were bound to be overlooked. However conscientious the employer, he cannot read every textbook and periodical, attend every exhibition and conference, on every technical issue which might arise in the course of his business; nor can he necessarily be expected to grasp the importance of every single item which he comes across.

A gynaecologist had to keep himself aware of general developments in the mainstream literature. He did not need to be familiar with the content of more obscure journals (*Gascoine v Ian Sheridan & Co.* [1994] 5 Med L R 437).

Practices adopted in another country were not necessarily evidence of the appropriate standard in the UK. In *Robb and Unitt* v *East London and City Health Authority* [1999] MLC 0102 Ebsworth J considered evidence of US research and international practice. It did not follow that a particular technique was negligent simply because it could be shown that things were done differently elsewhere. It was a matter of degree and common sense. However, in some cases the field of expertise may be so narrow that it will be necessary to obtain expert opinion from abroad.

(In)Experience

The same standard of care is expected from the learner driver as from any other driver on the road (*Nettleship* v *Weston* [1971] 2 QB 691, CA). However, a learner driver chooses to drive on the highway; it is not a matter of necessity. Learner doctors are an essential part of the health service. They will treat patients, though they should be supervised. Following *Nettleship* the courts expect them to show the same level of care and skill as their experienced colleagues. The patient does not choose an inexperienced doctor.

The issue was considered in the medical context at the Court of Appeal stage in *Wilsher* v *Essex Area Health Authority* [1987] QB 730. Mustill LJ said that he did not accept the notion of a duty tailored to the actor rather than the act which he elects to perform. If hospitals abstained from using inexperienced personnel they could not staff their wards and theatres and the junior staff could never learn, but:

> ... it would be a false step to subordinate the legitimate expectation of the patient that he will receive from each person concerned with his care a degree of skill appropriate to the task which he undertakes, to an understandable wish to minimise the psychological and financial pressures on hard-pressed young doctors ... In a case such as the present the standard is not just that of the averagely competent and well-informed junior houseman (or whatever the position of the doctor), but of such a person who fills a post in a unit offering a highly specialised service.

Glidewell LJ said that the law required the trainee or learner to be judged by the same standard as his more experienced colleagues. If it did not, inexperience would frequently be urged as a defence to an action for professional negligence.

Direct liability – system failure

In *Bull and Wakeham* v *Devon Area Health Authority* [1993] 4 Med LR 117, CA there was a medically unacceptable delay of one hour in securing the attendance of a suitably qualified doctor to deal with an emergency arising in the delivery of a second twin, as a result of which he suffered brain damage. On the question whether the defendants should have had in place a system which guaranteed prompt attendance, Slade LJ said the evidence pointed strongly either to inefficiency in the system for summoning the assistance of the registrar or consultant or to negligence by some individual in the working of that system. Dillon LJ said that any hospital which provided a maternity service for expectant mothers ought to be able to cope properly with premature delivery of twins, and there should have been at the hospital a staff reasonably sufficient for the foreseeable requirements of the patient. He described the hospital's system for providing senior attendance where the need arose as 'unreliable and essentially unsatisfactory'. Mustill LJ said that the system fell short of the required standard, which demanded at the least that a doctor of suitable experience be available within 20 minutes to handle any emergency. It was not a question of an 'ideal' solution appropriate to 'centres of excellence', nor a question of highly specialist techniques or advanced new instrumentation which it would be unrealistic to expect in provincial hospitals, but just a question of getting the right people together in the right place at the right time.

In *Robertson* v *Nottingham Health Authority* [1997] 8 Med LR 1, CA there were significant breakdowns in the defendant's systems of communication in respect of obstetric care which were proved to constitute breaches of proper practice. Brooke LJ said that a health authority had a non-delegable duty to establish a proper system of care just as much as it had a duty to engage competent staff and a duty to provide proper and safe equipment, safe premises and a reasonable regime of care, ie a regime of a standard that could reasonably be expected of a hospital of the size and type in question – in the present case a large teaching centre of excellence. It mattered not whether those at fault could be individually identified. If they could, the hospital would be vicariously liable for their negligence, but, if not, the hospital would be in breach of its own duty of care for failing to provide a proper system.

Lack of funds

A hospital may be unable to deliver as high a standard of care as it would wish or as normal standards would dictate because it does not have the equipment, doctors, and the staff. If there is a failure in care is it any defence for the hospital to say that the staff worked as hard and as long, and with as much expertise, as they could, but economies prevented further care or more experienced doctors from being provided?

In *Ball* v *Wirral Health Authority* [2003] Lloyds Rep Med 165, where the claim (in part) was that the health authority failed to have adequate facilities for the care of babies suffering from respiratory distress syndrome, Simon J said that the fact that an area of medicine might be underfunded or that a particular hospital might not have the same facilities as another might give rise to public concern but did not necessarily provide the basis for a successful claim in negligence, as English public and private law in general left decisions on funding and facilities to those who had legal responsibility for making them.

In *Hardaker* v *Newcastle Health Authority* [2001] Lloyds Rep Med 512, where a diver claimant contended that he had suffered injury because the hospital had failed to keep its decompression chamber manned adequately and at all proper times, Burnton J said that the court was not competent to adjudicate upon a health authority's system for dealing with such a rare medical event as decompression illness, where the issue was one of allocation of resources; and it was not, in any event, enough for the claimant to criticise the system without suggesting a more suitable alternative.

Emergencies

The standard of care to be expected may vary with the specific circumstances prevailing at the time. One can hardly expect the same meticulous attention in a hospital that is coping with a rail disaster or an epidemic as at normal times. In *Wilsher* v *Essex Area Health Authority* [1987] QB 730 at 749 Mustill LJ said:

> ... in what may be called 'battle conditions' ... an emergency may overburden the available resources, and if an individual is forced by circumstances to do too many things at once, the fact that he does one of them incorrectly should not lightly be taken as negligence.

Alternative therapies

Claims against alternative practitioners create a difficulty when it comes to assessing the standard of care given. Is it the standard that others practising in the same field consider to be appropriate, or is it to be judged by a more orthodox standard? If the management is to be judged by others practising in the field, the level of care acceptable to those practitioners might outrage orthodox practitioners. If it is to be judged by orthodox practitioners, there would be no scope for alternative practitioners.

Cases have been brought against physiotherapists, osteopaths, chiropractors and other practitioners of robust massage and manipulation. Some of these disciplines have regulatory bodies, and it may be possible to prepare a claim based on the opinion of an expert well-versed in that field with the support also of an orthodox expert, such as an orthopaedic consultant.

In *Shakoor* v *Situ* [2000] 1 WLR 410, CA the defendant was a properly trained, well-qualified and experienced practitioner of Chinese herbal medicine. He prescribed a remedy to a patient who then suffered a fatal idiosyncratic reaction by way of acute liver failure. It was alleged that the defendant had been negligent because papers in orthodox medical journals warned of such a risk. The widow did not adduce any evidence from an expert in Chinese herbal medicine, but relied only on the published matter and on evidence from orthodox consultants that they had no reason to believe that the treatment was effective. The defendant himself had a supportive opinion from a fellow practitioner. The judge (Bernard Livesey QC) said that, even if practitioners in the relevant art agreed that the care was proper, a claimant could still succeed by showing that the prevailing standard of skill in that art was deficient in the UK, having regard to risks which were not (but should have been) taken into account. It was not enough that orthodox practitioners might condemn the management. It was an important consideration that the patient had chosen to go to an alternative practitioner. 'Why should the patient later be able to complain that the alternative practitioner has not provided him with skill and care in accordance with the standards of those orthodox practitioners whom he has rejected?' Neither assessment was conclusive – neither that afforded by orthodox practitioners, nor that from practitioners in the impugned art. The judge said that an alternative practitioner practising his art alongside that of orthodox medicine must take account of the implications of that fact. The defendant had a duty to ensure that the remedy prescribed was not merely believed to be beneficial, but he had also a duty to ensure that it was not harmful. He had to keep abreast of relevant publications in the orthodox field as well, to the extent that a similar practitioner in the orthodox field would be expected to keep abreast. A similar practitioner would be a GP. The judge went on to conclude that the published material relied on by the claimant was not sufficiently unambiguous to have deterred a competent GP from prescribing such a remedy. The defendant was found to have acted in accordance with the standard of care appropriate to traditional Chinese herbal medicine as properly practised in accordance with the standards required in the UK.

Self-inflicted injury

Leaving a suicide-risk patient unobserved and with an open window behind his bed was held to constitute a lack of proper care, so that the hospital was liable when the patient got out of the window and threw himself off a roof. A high degree of surveillance was required in the care of patients with suicidal tendencies. The duty of care extended to a duty to protect the patient from the risk of self-inflicted injuries: *Selfe* v *Ilford and District Hospital Management Committee* (1970) 114 Sol Jo 935. In *Lepine* v *University Hospital Board* (1964) 50 DLR (2d) 225; affd (1965) 54 DLR (2d) 340, a hospital was held negligent for not having a constant watch on a patient suffering from a dangerous condition of post-epileptic automatism, who jumped from a window. However, when a patient of suspected suicidal tendencies managed to elude the nurses, went home and killed herself, the hospital was found not to have been negligent: *Thorne* v *Northern Group Hospital Management Committee* (1964) 108 Sol Jo 484. In *Mahmood* v *Siggins* [1996] 7 Med LR 76, a GP was held to have been negligent for not referring a manic depressive to the local community mental health team. The patient later jumped from a third floor balcony. In *D* v *South Tyneside Healthcare NHS Trust* [2004] PIQR P150 the Court of Appeal dismissed a claimant's appeal where a patient, put on hourly observation, had left the hospital, swallowed medication and suffered brain injury. The court said that there was a reasonable body of professional opinion that supported the contention that hourly observation was sufficient and that observation every 15 minutes was not called for.

Children

Children require a watchful eye. Where a seven-year-old boy was left without supervision near an open window and fell out, the hospital was liable (*Newnham* v *Rochester and Chatham Joint Hospital Board* (1936) Times, 28 February). But where the injury occurs in a non-medical context, ie it does not give rise to considerations about care and treatment, the conclusion may be different. Thus a hospital was not negligent where a girl of nine injured herself when she ran into glass swing doors in the hospital, at a time when the orderly was momentarily absent. The hospital's duty in the non-medical context was said to be that of an ordinary prudent parent (*Gravestock* v *Lewisham Group Hospital Management Committee* (1955) Times, 27 May). It was not negligent to leave a partially disabled child to manage a jug of hot inhalant in bed on her own (*Cox* v *Carshalton Hospital Management Committee* (1955) Times, 29 March).

A CONTEMPORARY RE-STATEMENT OF THE LAW

In *Ministry of Justice* v *Cheryl Carter* [2010] EWCA 694 the Court of Appeal restated the essential principles of *Bolam* and *Bolitho*. The claimant was serving a term of imprisonment and was a regular visitor to the healthcare clinic. She complained of a lump in her right breast to three doctors. The judge found no negligence in relation to two doctors, he also found that the third doctor had conducted a clinical examination with reasonable care, finding no abnormality. However, the judge held that on the basis of the previous history of complaint and although it was not mandatory the GP should have referred the claimant. In reaching this conclusion the judge relied upon the potential seriousness of a breast lump and the relative ease with which a referral could have been made.

The Court of Appeal allowed the defendant's appeal. The judge should have applied *Bolam* and *Bolitho*. The GP was not in breach of duty in not referring the claimant. The defendant's expert agreed that referral was not mandatory. It was not open for the judge to take a middle course between the expert evidence of the claimant and the defendant. The expert evidence of both sides had to be subjected to logical analysis. If the defendant's expert's opinion withstood such analysis there was no breach of duty.

THE BURDEN OF PROOF

In negligence generally the existence of a duty of care is closely associated with the foreseeability of injury. Where an employee suffers asbestosis as a result of his employer's breach of statutory duty, there may be a presumption that damages will be recovered. Otherwise the non-liability of the employer will 'empty the duty of its content'.[1]

The relationship between breach of duty of care and the foreseeability of harm is more difficult in a clinical negligence context as there may well be 'injury' in the absence of negligence: as a result, for example, of well recognised complications associated with a certain medical procedure. Medicine is also a science, developing and changing over time. There will always be limitations on what can be known and, therefore, on what can be 'proved'.

The ordinary case: the claimant's burden

In the ordinary case the burden of proving negligence rests with the claimant. The circumstances in which that burden may shift to the defendant in clinical negligence cases are very limited. In *Clark* v *MacLennan* [1983] 1 All ER 416 Pain J said that where there had been a failure to take a generally recognised precaution which had been followed by damage of the kind that that precaution was designed to prevent, the burden of proof shifted to the defendant to show either that he was not in breach of duty or that the damage was not caused by the breach. In that case there had been a departure from the usual practice of not performing an operation for stress incontinence within three months of delivery. That departure was found to have been unjustified and therefore constituted a breach of the duty of care. It was followed by a consequence that that precaution was designed to prevent: a breakdown of the repair effected in the operation. The judge held that in such circumstances the defendants had to satisfy the court that damage had not flowed from their breach of duty to the patient.

The approach is most probably wrong. In *Wilsher* v *Essex Area Health Authority* [1988] AC1074 the House of Lords expressly denied that the burden shifted in such circumstances. In *Gregory* v *Pembrokeshire Health Authority* [1989] 1 Med LR 81 at 85 Rougier J rejected the suggestion that whenever the fault complained of was a fault in omission the burden

---

1   See the comments of Lord Bingham in *Fairchild* v *Glenhaven Funeral Services Ltd* [2002] UKHL 22.

of proving causation shifted to the defendants: 'the burden of proof on the balance of probabilities remains on the plaintiff throughout'. In *Defreitas* v *O'Brien* [1995] 6 Med LR 108, CA Otton LJ said the *Bolam* test did not impose any burden of proof on the defendant to establish that his diagnosis or treatment would be acceptable to a responsible body of medical opinion. The burden of proof was on the claimant.

Shifting the burden of proof

Res ipsa loquitur

[The facts speak for themselves]

In the ordinary case a judge will hear the lay and expert evidence, decide the facts, and apply his analysis of the expert evidence and the law to them. However, there may also be cases in which the facts themselves are indicative of a failure to take reasonable care. If a bag of flour falls on my head it is reasonable to infer that whoever was responsible for the flour has failed to take proper care.

The legal formulation of such a simple proposition is nonetheless somewhat cumbersome: if an accident is such as in the ordinary course of things does not happen if those who have the management use proper care, it affords reasonable evidence, in the absence of explanation by the defendant, that the accident arose from want of care (*per* Erle CJ in *Scott* v *London and St Katherine Docks Co* (1865) 3 H & C 596, Ex Ch). This is the classic formulation of the maxim *res ipsa loquitur* in the context of the law of negligence.

Res ipsa loquitur has a role to play in clinical negligence cases but the circumstances are limited, and the maxim is often invoked incorrectly and inappropriately. In *Cassidy* v *Ministry of Health* [1951] 2 KB 343 Denning LJ explained the possible application of the maxim by the example of the patient who arrives in hospital to be cured of two stiff fingers and leaves with four. In such circumstances the hospital would have to show how the deterioration in the claimant's condition was not caused by any want of care on its part. He considered that in such a situation the patient had a *prima facie* case against the hospital authorities. He applied this analysis in *Roe* v *Minister of Health* [1954] 2 QB 66. Where patients in hospital for minor operations were paralysed by the spinal anaesthetic each was given the defendant had to explain how this could have come to pass.

When we consider this legal formulation it is important to draw out several strands that limit its application. First, there must be an adverse outcome. Second, the principle only applies where the precise cause of the accident cannot be specified, whether upon direct evidence or by inference: I do not know why a bag of flour fell on my head, but I do not need to show why it happened: the fact of the accident is enough to satisfy the law that I have cause for complaint. Third, the facts of the accident must be such that it would be fair and reasonable for the court to make an inference: 'the circumstances are more consistent, reasonably interpreted without further explanation, with ... negligence than with any other cause of the accident happening' (*per* Kennedy LJ in *Russell* v *London and South-western Rly Co* (1908) 24 TLR 548, CA at 551). These are accidents that 'in ordinary circumstances' do not happen. Fourth, even where the principle applies the defendant is able to defend the claim successfully if it can show that the injury could have occurred without negligence; see for example the comments of Otton LJ in *Hooper* v *Young* [1998] 2 Lloyd's Rep Med 61, CA. Sometimes the court will say that the inference gives rise to a *prima facie* case: a case that the defendant not only has to meet but has the burden of proving.

Proving an adverse outcome

The claimant has to establish the facts upon which to base a plea of *res ipsa loquitur*. So in *Ludlow* v *Swindon Health Authority* [1989] 1 Med LR 104, when the claimant alleged she had been awake during a Caesarean section as a result of what must have been the negligent administration of the anaesthetic, the judge said that for the doctrine of *res ipsa loquitur* to apply, the claimant had first to establish that she had indeed been awake during the operation. As the judge was not satisfied of these facts the doctrine could not help her.

The facts proven will not give rise to a proper plea of *res ipsa loquitur* if such injury could have occurred with the exercise of reasonable care. A surgeon performing a laminectomy may penetrate too far and injure the nerve or the spinal cord. One cannot say that 'the matter speaks for itself'. The question is whether or not a surgeon exercising due care would make that mistake. However, the situation may be different if the risk of such injury was so small as to indicate want of care. In *Betts* v *Berkshire Health Authority* [1997] 8 Med L Rep 87 the fact that the risk of damage to the testicle during the procedure was less than 0.03% was indicative that the surgery had been negligent on the balance of probabilities.

The absence of non-negligent explanation

A distinction has to be made between cases in which the facts are known and the courts are able to infer negligence from the circumstances, and those cases where the court applies the maxim when there is no other non-negligent explanation for the injury. If the facts are sufficiently established the question may be whether negligence is to be inferred or not (*per* Lord Porter in *Barkway* v *South Wales Transport Co Ltd* [1950] 1 All ER 392, HL at 395). For example, where there is evidence of habitual careless behaviour which could have caused it, the court may infer that to be the cause in the absence of any other explanation (*Clowes* v *National Coal Board* (1987) Times, 23 April).

One must draw a distinction between the situation where there is more than one possible cause for the injury and the situation where the precise cause is unknown. In the second situation one may be able to take advantage of the maxim. In the first situation it is simply a matter for the judge to decide what was the operative cause, and, in doing this, he is entitled to prefer the evidence of one expert to another. He may also draw inferences from the evidence. In *Skelton* v *Lewisham and North Southwark Health Authority* [1998] Lloyd's Rep Med 324 Kay J decided that the only possible explanation on the facts for the administration of certain drugs preoperatively was an episode of hypotension causing brain injury. In *Bull* v *Devon Area Health Authority* [1993] 4 Med LR 117, CA Slade LJ said that the trial judge had gone further than he needed when he found that the claimant had excluded all possible causes of his injury other than that for which he contended, because it would have been sufficient to make the less unqualified finding that the cause for which he contended was established on the balance of probabilities.

Examples

In *Mahon* v *Osborne* [1939] 2 KB 14, where the surgeon was sued when a swab was left inside the patient, the majority of the Court of Appeal was of the view that the principle did not apply in the case of a complex operation where a number of medical staff took part, but it is now clear that the correct view was that taken by Goddard LJ when he said if a swab is found in the patient's body the surgeon is called upon for an explanation 'not necessarily why he missed it but that he exercised due care to prevent its being left there'; see also *Urry* v *Bierer* (1955) Times, 15 July.

In *Clarke* v *Worboys* (1952) Times, 18 March, the patient's buttock was burnt in electro-coagulation treatment; the Court of Appeal reversed the judge's finding and held that the evidence showed that such an accident would not happen if reasonable care were used.

The maxim was successfully invoked by the widow of a man who was asphyxiated when he swallowed a dental throat pack in *Garner* v *Morrell* (1953) Times, 31 October.

In *Leckie* v *Brent and Harrow Area Health Authority* [1982] 1 Lancet 634, it was held that a 1.5 cm cut on the cheek of a baby delivered by Caesarian section would not happen without some lack of care.

In *Woodhouse* v *Yorkshire Regional Health Authority* [1984] 1 Lancet 1306 the patient's ulnar nerves were severely damaged in an operation for a subphrenic abscess. The judge said that the evidence established that this sort of injury would not occur if the standard precautions to avoid this recognised hazard had been taken. The Court of Appeal upheld his decision.

In *Coyne* v *Wigan Health Authority* [1991] 2 Med LR 301 the defendants agreed that *res ipsa* applied when hypoxia leading to brain damage occurred during recovery from a routine operation.

In *Saunders* v *Leeds Western Health Authority and Robinson* [1993] 4 Med LR 355 the heart of a four-year-old girl stopped for some 30 minutes during an operation under anaesthetic to remedy a congenitally deformed hip. The defendants agreed that did not normally happen without want of care.

Rebuttal

It is always open to a defendant to rebut a case of *res ipsa* either by giving an explanation of what happened which was inconsistent with negligence or by showing that all reasonable care had been taken. So, for example in *Roe* v *Minister of Health* the hospital gave an explanation of the accident which was accepted by the court as absolving them from any negligence.

In *Jacobs* v *Great Yarmouth and Waverney Health Authority* [1995] 6 Med LR 192 the Court of Appeal said that *res ipsa loquitur* meant no more than that on the facts that a claimant was able to prove, although he might not be able to point to a particular negligent act or omission on the part of the defendants, the fair inference to draw was that there had been negligence of some sort on the part of the defendants. If there were further evidence presented by the defendants, those facts might be shown in an entirely different light so that it would not be possible to draw the inference of negligence.

It is not entirely clear on the authorities how far the defendant must go to shift the onus of proof back to the claimant, in particular, whether he has to show a possible or a likely cause of the accident that would not involve negligence. In *Moore* v *R Fox & Sons* [1956] 1 QB 596, CA it was not sufficient for the defendants to show several hypothetical causes consistent with the absence of negligence and that the accident might have occurred without negligence on their part; to discharge the onus they had to go further and either show that they had not been negligent or give a reasonable explanation of the cause of the accident which did not connote negligence.

Examples

In *Howard* v *Wessex Regional Health Authority* [1994] 5 Med LR 57, Morland J said that *res ipsa* could not help the patient where she had sustained tetraplegia following maxillo-facial surgery by way of a sagittal split osteotomy, because her injury was most likely due to a fibro-cartilaginous embolism, which would not connote negligence.

In *Moore* v *Worthing District Health Authority* [1992] 3 Med LR 431, Owen J rejected a plea of *res ipsa* where a patient was left with bilateral ulnar nerve palsy following a mastoidectomy. He absolved the defendants from failing to protect the arms properly while the patient was under anaesthetic by accepting their contention that the patient had been abnormally vulnerable to such an injury.

In *O'Malley-Williams* v *Governors of National Hospital for Nervous Diseases* (1975) 1 BMJ 635 it was held that the maxim did not apply where partial paralysis was sustained by the claimant because the injury sustained was recognised as an inherent risk of the treatment undergone.

Reasonable traction could have caused the claimant's lesion of the musculocutaneous nerve, as could also excessive traction, and so the maxim could not help him, in the case of *Levenkind* v *Churchill-Davidson* [1983] 1 Lancet 1452.

In *Brazier* v *Ministry of Defence* [1965] 1 Lloyd's Rep 26 the defendants satisfied the judge that he should not infer negligence on the part of a person giving an injection to the claimant as the cause of the needle breaking, because the actual cause could properly be inferred to be a latent defect in the shaft of the needle (similarly in *Corner* v *Murray* [1954] 2 BMJ 1555).

STRICT LIABILITY

The Consumer Protection Act 1987

Strict liability for injury is imposed on the producers and certain suppliers of any product falling within the Consumer Protection Act 1987 supplied after 1 March 1988. The definition of 'product' covers medical products, equipment and drugs. It may also cover blood and blood-based materials.

Section 2 of the Act provides that where any damage is caused wholly or partly by a defect in a product to any person 'the relevant party' shall be liable for the damage. The relevant party may be the producer of the product, an importer, or the supplier. If he can identify the producer he will not be liable even if the producer cannot satisfy a judgment.

Section 3(1) of the Act defines the meaning of 'defect':

> Subject to the following provisions of this section, there is a defect in a product for the purposes of this Part if the safety of the product is not such as persons generally are entitled to expect; and for those purposes 'safety', in relation to a product, shall include safety with respect to products comprised in that product and safety in the context of risks after damage to property, as well as in the context of risks of death or personal injury.

What persons are generally entitled to expect is considered in s 3(2):

> In determining for the purposes of sub-section (1) above what persons generally are entitled to expect in relation to a product all the circumstances shall be taken into account, including—
> (a)　the manner in which, and purposes for which, the product has been marketed, its get-up, the use of any mark in relation to the product and any instructions for, or warnings with respect to, doing or refraining from doing anything with or in relation to the product;
> (b)　what might reasonably be expected to be done with or in relation to the product; and
> (c)　the time when the product was supplied by its producer to another; and nothing in this section shall require a defect to be inferred from the fact alone that the safety of a product which is supplied after that time is greater than the safety of the product in question.

Liability depends upon what members of the public are likely to expect; what warnings should be given; and what the scale and nature of any potential risks are. So a user's expectation is that a condom will not fail. However, where there were no claims made by the manufacturer that a condom will never fail and no-one has ever supposed that any method of contraception will be 100% effective, a fracture in a condom was not proof of a defect (*Richardson* v *LRC Products* [2000] Lloyd's Rep Med 280). However, the transfusion of infected blood was evidence of a product defect (*A* v *The National Blood Authority* [2001] Lloyds Rep Med 187). The public had a right to expect that such products would be 100% safe. As the product in *A* v *The National Blood Authority* was defective, the claimants did not have to prove any fault on the part of the defendant.

Another example of a successful claim brought under the Consumer Protection Act is *Abouzaid* v *Mothercare (UK) Ltd* (2001) Times, 20 February, CA. The claimant injured his eye when attempting to fasten a sleeping bag to his young brother's pushchair by means of elasticated straps. The strap slipped from his grasp and the buckle hit him in the eye. The judge said that the product was unsafe due to failure to provide proper instructions, particularly in the case of younger children, and the manufacturer should have appreciated the risk. Expert evidence was to the effect that the hazard had not been recognised by anyone in the business in 1990, but ten years later such a product could be said to have a safety defect. The judge said that if it had one now, it had one then. The public's expectation had not changed since 1990. The Court of Appeal was not satisfied that there was liability at common law, but endorsed the finding of liability under the Act. The defence under s 4(1)(e) (that the state of scientific and technical knowledge at the time was not such that the defect could be discovered), relying as it did on the absence of any record of similar accident, was not valid, as such evidence did not fall within the meaning of scientific and technical knowledge.

Vaccine Damage Payments Act 1979

The Act was passed as a result of anxiety arising in the early 1970s over the possibility that the whooping cough vaccine could cause brain damage. A DWP publication on the operation of the scheme is available at www.direct. gov.uk/en/MoneyTaxAndBenefits/BenefitsTaxCreditsAndOtherSupport/ Disabledpeople/DG_10018714.

In *Loveday* v *Renton* [1990] 1 Med LR 117, the claimant sought to establish that the whooping cough vaccine could cause brain damage. Stuart-Smith LJ found, after a long and complex trial, that it had not been established that the whooping cough vaccine was capable of causing permanent brain damage in young children. He said that all four of the suggested mechanisms for the nexus between the vaccine and the damage were improbable. He also added, *obiter*, that even if that nexus had been established, the claimant would surely find it impossible to show that the GP had been negligent in vaccinating. *Loveday* also attempted to pursue compensation through the Vaccine Damage Tribunal (*R* v *Vaccine Damage Tribunal, ex p Loveday* [1985] 2 Lancet 1137).

Few claims are made to the scheme and even fewer succeed. The number of claims received and successful payments made under the Act, in each financial year from April 2000 to 7 June 2006 was as follows:

1 April to 31 March	*Number of claims received*	*Number of claims successful*
2000/01	205	0
2001/02	146	2
2002/03	417	5
2003/04	165	4
2004/05	111	4
2005/06	106	4
2006/07 (to 7 June 2006)	14	2
Total	1,164	21

Source: Vaccine Damage Payments Unit Database.[2]

2   HC Deb, 16 June 2006, c1482W; www.theyworkforyou.com/wrans/?id=2006-06-16c.76172.h.

Chapter 7

Causation and damage

Simon Dyer

INTRODUCTION

The claimant in a negligence action has to show that as a result of the defendant's negligence, ie breach of a duty of care owed to him, he has suffered damage. The damage may be physical (to person or property), mental or financial, but it must be:

- caused by the breach of duty – a patient who cannot show that an admitted act of negligence contributed to his present condition has not proved a causative link between the negligence and his injury;[1]
- a type of damage which is recognised by the law – certain types of damage are not recognised by the law, at any rate if they stand alone, eg distress and disappointment, mental strain or nervous shock not amounting to a psychiatric disorder or illness. Mere financial loss is not recoverable if it stands alone, ie not accompanied by any physical injury to person or property and did not arise in the context of a fiduciary or proximate relationship between the parties; and
- it must come within the foreseeable area of risk created by the breach of duty. The damage will not be the subject of compensation, even if directly caused by the breach of duty, if it is of a completely different type or caused in a completely different way than that which was foreseeable. The injury suffered must come within the scope of the duty to avoid the injury. This is best explained by example. In *Thompson* v *Bradford* [2006] Lloyd's Rep Med 95, an eight year old boy attended his GP for his polio vaccination. He also had a suppurating perianal abscess. The GP advised that the vaccination should go ahead. This was found to be appropriate advice by the trial judge. The parents were not advised, however, that the abscess might require surgery and that there might be an adverse reaction to the vaccination occurring at the same time as the need for surgery. This was held by the trial judge to be negligent. Had the parents been told

---

1   That is why some defendants in medical negligence actions concentrate, often *faute de mieux*, on causation, casting around with increasing desperation for any argument they, or, more often, the expert they instruct can find, to support a contention that the result would not have been improved even with proper care.

this, they would have delayed the vaccination and probably avoided the polio. This was held to be an unforeseeable consequence of the combination of the vaccine and the lancing of the abscess three days later. The trial judge found the GP liable because had he given the correct advice, ie that there may be an adverse reaction at the same time as the need for surgery, the parents would have delayed the vaccination until after the surgery. The polio would then not have developed. The Court of Appeal overturned the trial judge's decision on the ground that the polio did not flow from any relevant breach of duty. In other words, because the increased risk of polio when combined with an operation was not reasonably foreseeable it is not a relevant breach of duty for the GP to have failed to warn of another risk (ie discomfort due to an adverse reaction at the time of the requirement for other surgery) which might have caused as a matter of fact the parents to delay and therefore avoid the polio. The injury to be avoided must therefore be within the scope of a relevant duty to be imposed on the doctor. In *Lorraine* v *Wirral University Teaching Hospital* [2008] LS Med 573, it was held that the defendant was liable for brain damage caused by hypoxia since such damage was a foreseeable consequence of the negligence, even though the precise mechanism of injury was not foreseeable.

All these matters are considered in detail below.

The different factors in negligence are not clearly separate from one another, they shade off into and overlap each other. A woman who loses wages looking after a lover who has gone to bed because the doctor wrongly and negligently told him he was ill and needed bed-rest may be told by the court that her claim cannot succeed because the doctor owed her no duty of care, or that she cannot recover for mere economic loss, or that the damage she suffered was too remote, or not foreseeable, or that it was not caused by the breach of duty because her decision to look after her friend broke the chain of causation; or the court may even, as a last resort, pray in aid public policy.[2] In the final analysis, a claim that does not clearly come within the body of case law created by the courts in the past, ie a claim that presents a novel quality, will be accepted or rejected by the courts according to the judge's overall view as to whether it is appropriate that it should succeed or not (what has been called 'the judicial hunch'); and if the judge feels that the claim should not succeed, he will hang his decision on one or other of the legal pegs that are available. Judicial hunches are influenced by social considerations which vary with the era; they are currently being influenced by awareness of human rights. In *Savage* v *South East Essex NHS Trust* [2008] UKHL 74, the House of Lords considered whether a claim for damages under Art 2 of the ECHR against a hospital for failing to prevent suicide by a patient in a psychiatric facility. The House of Lords held that there could be a duty to such a compulsorily detained patient under Art 2 where there was real and immediate risk to life. In *Rabone* v *Pennine Care NHS Trust* [2010] EWCA Civ 698, the Court of Appeal clearly stated that Art 2 does not impose upon the state an operational obligation towards all

---

2   A current buzzword that means much the same thing, used by Lord Steyn in *McFarlane* v *Tayside Health Board* [2000] 2 AC 59, HL, is 'distributive justice'.

persons who are at 'real and immediate' risk of death unless there is some additional element, such as detention by the state. Health trusts therefore do not have Art 2 operational obligations towards voluntary patients in hospital. It is noteworthy that an appeal against the Court of Appeal decision was recently heard by the Supreme Court although at the time of writing judgment has not been handed down.

The claimant has, of course, to show that he has suffered some damage (negligence is not actionable without proof of damage). What amounts to injury in the context of the personal injury action was considered in *Church v Ministry of Defence* (1984) 134 NLJ 623, where a worker in the Chatham docks sustained from the inhalation of asbestos dust symptomless pleural plaques in his lungs together with symptomless incipient fibrosis that could possibly develop into asbestosis and consequent anxiety when he realised what had happened. Pain J said that there was a small risk that the claimant might go on to suffer further incapacity and it would be wrong in the light of current knowledge about the disease to disregard the plaques as not amounting to an injury in law.[3]

In *Sykes* v *Ministry of Defence* (1984) Times, 23 March, Otton J found that such plaques, involving definite structural changes, even without the incipient fibrosis that Mr Church suffered, plus the risk of the onset of separate lung complaints amounted to actionable damage. (In any event, increased vulnerability must surely amount to damage, for it gives rise to the chance of injury developing.)

Asymptomatic pleural changes in the form of pleural plaques and thickening, plus anxiety about his condition falling short of nervous shock were 'actionable damage' for the purposes of an award to a claimant of provisional damages under s 32A of the Supreme Court Act 1981 (*Patterson* v *Ministry of Defence* [1987] CLY 1194, *per* Simon Brown J).

Sykes and *Patterson* were overturned by the House of Lords in the *Rothwell* v *Chemical and Insulating Co Ltd* [2008] 1 AC 281. The House of Lords held that asymptomatic pleural plaques were not actionable physical damage. Furthermore, the argument that psychiatric damage caused by the anxiety provoked by knowing that a clamant might go on to develop mesothelioma or other asbestos-related disease was not actionable either. It was held that such damage was not a reasonably foreseeable consequence of having asymptomatic pleural plaques in a person of normal fortitude. A limited scheme making plural plaques compensatable was introduced in August 2010. However, the scheme closed a year later and, at present, pleural plaques are not compensatable in England and Wales – although it is perhaps worth noting that the Northern Ireland Assembly and the Scottish Parliament have both passed bills restoring the right to claim compensation for pleural plaques.

A worsened prognosis, eg where there is a delay in diagnosing cancer, can constitute compensatable injury (see, for example, *Judge* v *Huntingdon Health Authority* [1995] 6 Med LR 223). But see below, *Gregg* v *Scott*, under 'Loss of a chance'.

---

3   He also said that anxiety alone was an actionable injury, but this must be wrong in view of the clear authority that mental states not amounting to psychiatric disorder and not accompanied by other actionable injury give no cause of action (see Chapter 13).

PROOF OF CAUSATION

The claimant has to prove that the breach of duty caused his injury. In clinical negligence cases, this very often entails the claimant proving what would have happened (and that whatever that was, he would be better as a result) had there been no negligence. Proving hypothetical past events is therefore an essential part of proving factual causation. It should be remembered that the test is what probably would have happened were it not for the negligence. The *Bolam* test is usually irrelevant to this enquiry, except if, as in *Bolitho* for example, it is said that the impugned doctor would not have done the thing (in that case intubated the claimant) that would have made a difference in any event, ie regardless of her negligence in failing to attend, because that was not her practice. Then and only then does the question arise: 'Would the hypothetical conduct of the doctor concerned in the absence of negligence have been negligent itself?' If it would, the defendant cannot rely upon it. An example is *Gouldsmith* v *Midstaffordshire General Hospitals NHS Trust* [2007] EWCA 397. In that case, the claimant suffered occlusions in the blood vessels in her left hand. She went to hospital but was not referred as she should have been to a specialist centre. She was treated with anticoagulants. Her fingers were amputated. It was her case that had she been referred on she would have had an operation to repair the lesion and she would not have lost her fingers. The defence argued that surgery was not the correct treatment and that anticoagulation was appropriate. The trial judge found that she should have been referred and that had she had the operation her fingers would have been saved. But he found that causation had not been made out by the claimant because she had not proved either that the operation would have been carried out if referred or that every specialist exercising proper care would have operated on her. The Court of Appeal rejected this reasoning and allowed the claimant's appeal (Maurice Kay LJ dissenting) stating that the relevant question was simply what would have happened on referral to the specialist hospital. The question of whether it would have been negligent to fail to operate does not then arise.

Commonly the question of what would have happened is dealt with by the experts based on their experience of similar situations in their own hospitals and practices. This evidence can of course be displaced by direct evidence of the particular circumstances and practices of the doctors who treated the claimant. A close eye has to be kept on this issue.

An interesting and useful case involving the proof of a series of hypothetical past events is *Bright* v *Barnsley District Hospital* [2005] Lloyd's Law Reports 449. Mr Recorder Burrell QC sitting as a High Court Judge found for the claimant on the following facts. (Incidentally this case was decided before the HL decision in *Gregg* v *Scott*.) The child claimant (Billy-Joe) was born with cerebral palsy. She had suffered profound hypoxia lasting between ten and 25 minutes at sometime after the 36th week of pregnancy. There had been a negligent omission to carry out ultrasound monitoring to check foetal growth at 32 weeks. It was agreed between the experts that this scan would probably (60% chance) have shown foetal growth at the fifth centile. This result would have triggered a second scan that would have confirmed growth retardation (60% chance) which would have led to a controlled delivery at 37 weeks with an 80% chance of birth without brain damage.

The defendants argued that the cumulative chance of delivering an undamaged child was 60 × 60 × 80 = 38.4%. The claimant had therefore failed to prove on the balance of probability that she would have been born without brain damage. The Judge rejected this approach, he said (see p 460):

> After establishing breach, in the absence of a known person about whom there is evidence to indicate what he or she might actually have done, the question is what would a reasonable radiographer at the hospital have found at the first 32 week scan which should have been carried out? In my judgment it is settled and conventional law that this has to be answered on the balance of probabilities and it is agreed that on balance that such a scan would probably have revealed a foetus at the 5th centile. This is a question of (hypothetical) fact to be decided on the balance of probability. Thereafter for the purpose of deciding what would then have happened, this finding (i.e. 32 weeks' scanning revealing 5th centile baby) is something which is to be treated as though it would have occurred in fact.

Further at p 460:

> It seems to me that there should be no difference in approach where the court is deciding a hypothetical fact i.e. deciding on what would have happened as opposed to deciding whether something had or had not actually happened ...

The commentary to the case makes the point as follows:

> When enquiring in to past hypothetical facts it is logical and consistent for the court to adopt the same approach as enquiries in to past actual events. Either the hypothetical event would or would not have happened. If on the balance of probability an event would have happened, then that event has been proved and is to be treated as though a certainty. Each hypothetical event after a negligent omission to act is taken in turn. The chances of each event happening merely inform the decision as to whether it is proved that particular event probably would have occurred. If it is proved, the chances are then irrelevant to causation and are not to be taken cumulatively.

The issue of causation can raise notoriously difficult intellectual issues, eg as to what was the cause or an operative or significant cause of an accident, and in what circumstances the chain is broken, but on the whole the courts give pragmatic answers depending on their assessment of the factual situation.

> Causation is to be understood as the man in the street, and not as either the scientist or the metaphysician would understand it. Cause here means what a ... man would take to be the cause without too microscopic analysis but on a broad view (*per* Lord Wright in *Yorkshire Dale Steamship Co* v *Minister of War Transport* [1942] AC 691 at 706, HL).

And Lord Denning once said:

> ... it is not every consequence of a wrongful act which is the subject of compensation. The law has to draw a line somewhere. Sometimes it is done by limiting the range of persons to whom duty is owed, sometimes it is done by saying there is break in the chain of causation. At other times it is done by saying that the consequence is too remote to be a head of damages. All these devices are useful in their way. But ultimately it is a question of policy for the judges to decide ...

However, what is the common sense answer in any situation often admits of divergent views (see, for example, the varying views of the Law Lords about the cause of an accident when an unsafe roof fell on a miner in *Stapley* v *Gypsum Mines Ltd* [1953] AC 663, HL).

MEDICAL CASES

Causation is tremendously important in medical cases, and always needs careful consideration. This is because the aetiology of medical conditions is often unclear and because the situation will often be complicated by the presence of an underlying illness or other pre-existing vulnerabilities.

In every case, the chain of causation, whether only one link long or more, must be carefully considered. For example, it is all very well to prove that a GP should have visited, but one is likely also to need to consider what he would have found, what action he would or should have taken, and what result that would probably have had. One probably needs to ask a specialist what the GP would have found if he had conducted such examination as the GP expert says he should. One then has to ask the GP expert whether finding what the specialist says would have been found at that time required immediate hospital referral or whether a review in a few hours or advice to the patient or parents to call if the situation deteriorated would do. One then asks the specialist whether, assuming the GP had taken the least urgent action which would have remained within the bounds of reasonable management, the outcome would probably have been different. This may involve further links in the chain of causation by way of analysing what the hospital or specialist to which the patient should have been referred would probably have done and when. In a cancer case, one may find the expert unable to say whether earlier diagnosis and treatment would have produced a better outcome. If that is so, one cannot establish causation. In an obstetric case it is not infrequently possible without too much difficulty to establish a failure of care. But it is a quite different matter to prove that proper care, usually involving earlier delivery (often by Caesarean section), would have avoided the injury. The expert evidence on that issue may well be extremely technical and speculative. One may be unable to show that the injury was not sustained considerably earlier in the pregnancy, or, at the other end of the spectrum, one may be unable to show that the period of perinatal hypoxia would have been sufficiently curtailed by earlier delivery to avoid damage.[4]

The possible scenarios on causation in medical negligence claims are legion, as the cases show. All one can do is make a careful analysis of what probably would have happened, step by step, if proper management, as certified by the appropriate experts, had taken place. Many and varied are the possible defences on causation. It is an unusual case that does not offer some opportunity for such a defence. Hence the fascination of the subject for defendants. The reports are full of cases where the defence

---

4   An unfortunate example is *De Martell* v *Merton and Sutton Health Authority,* where the patient had already won an important preliminary hearing establishing the right at common law to sue for pre-natal injury ([1993] QB 204, CA).

has succeeded on some causation argument or other. One surprising example is *Pearman* v *North Essex Health Authority* [2000] Lloyd's Rep Med 174, where the defence expert convinced the judge, contrary to common sense (as the judge admitted), that the claimant could not prove that earlier treatment of cauda equina syndrome would have produced a better outcome. And there are plenty of cerebral palsy claims that have failed on causation (an example is *Matthews* v *East Suffolk Health Authority* [1999] MLC 0170 – and a further defendant in that case succeeded in a different causation defence in respect of a failure to administer antibiotics). The same goes for most orthopaedic claims (along the lines of proper treatment would not have made any difference to the outcome). Where damage appears post-operatively, other causes can often be postulated (for example *Gray* v *Southampton and South West Hampshire Health Authority* [2000] MLC 0209). But perhaps the most distressing – one could say objectionable – causation argument was the successful defence in the *Bolitho* case, which is discussed below.

Further examples of cases on causation

The significance of causation in medical negligence cases is indicated by the number of times it has been an issue in reported cases every year, and the manifold ways in which medical claims can be contested by causation defences, whether valid or trumped up. A glance through the headnotes for any of the series of medical reports online or in hard copy will demonstrate this.

If failure to treat a patient made no difference because he would have died anyway, his death is not caused by the negligence. Thus in *Barnett* v *Chelsea and Kensington Hospital Management Committee* [1969] 1 QB 428, MLC 0005, a casualty officer was negligent in not treating a night watchman who complained of vomiting after drinking tea. He later died of arsenic poisoning. His widow's claim failed on the ground that the workman would have died even if he had received all due care, because the judge concluded on the evidence that there was no chance that the only effective antidote could have been administered in time.

In *Robinson* v *Post Office* [1974] 1 WLR 1176, CA, a doctor was found to be negligent in not administering a test dose of an anti-tetanus serum before injecting it in a patient who had cut his leg. The patient was allergic and developed encephalitis which led to brain damage and paralysis. The Court of Appeal said that the question (on this issue) was whether the negligence of the doctor had 'caused or materially contributed' to the claimant's injury, and that the onus was on the claimant of proving on the balance of probabilities that it had. The Court of Appeal said that the judge had been right to conclude on the evidence before him that even if the test dose had been administered there would have been no observable reaction in the patient and that therefore the doctor would in any event have gone on to administer the injection. So the injury would have happened anyway.[5]

---

5   The old case of *Rich* v *Pierpoint* (1862) 3 F & F 35 was to similar effect: the wrongful administration of tartaric acid made no difference to the outcome – it 'turned out to be of no consequence'.

In *Vernon* v *Bloomsbury Health Authority* [1995] 6 Med LR 297, the court held that, even if the defendants had been negligent in failing to monitor the patient while on Gentamicin, further assays would probably not have revealed any danger signals.

In *Hotson* v *East Berkshire Area Health Authority* [1987] AC 750, the House of Lords denied compensation to an infant claimant on the basis that his injury would not on the balance of probabilities have benefited by the treatment which the defendants negligently failed to afford him (see below for a full discussion of that case and 'loss of a chance').

In *Gregory* v *Pembrokeshire Health Authority* [1989] 1 Med LR 81, the claimant was delivered of a child suffering from Down's syndrome. She alleged, correctly, that the consultant had been negligent in not telling her that the sample from her amniocentesis had not produced sufficient cultures to determine whether her child would suffer from Down's syndrome. She contended that, had she been so informed, she would have had the test repeated, the result would have been positive and she would have arranged for an abortion. The judge accepted that she could have obtained a legal abortion, but he concluded that she would have discussed the matter first with the consultant and would as a result have accepted what would have been his advice, namely not to undergo a second amniocentesis (amniocentesis always carries a risk to the foetus; there was no reason to suspect at that time that something was actually amiss, and the statistical chance of chromosomal abnormality was 1 in 800). So the outcome would have been the same even had the defendants not been negligent; therefore the claim for the cost of raising the child failed. And the Court of Appeal saw no reason to criticise the judge's conclusion, arrived at on the evidence and his assessment of the witnesses, that the claimant would not have proceeded to a second amniocentesis. A claim similarly failed in *Deriche* v *Ealing Hospital NHS Trust* (2003) MLC 1083 where Buckley J held that, even if a pregnant woman had been properly counselled about the risk of fetal damage from her chicken pox, she would not have decided to terminate the pregnancy.

Compare *Rance* v *Mid-Downs Health Authority* [1991] 1 QB 587, [1990] 2 Med LR 27: here a mother of a child born suffering from spina bifida alleged that the defendants should have discovered the defect in the foetus and she would then have had an abortion. Brooke J said that, even if he were satisfied that negligence had been made out, any abortion would have had to take place when the gestational age was more than 27 weeks; this would have been a crime by virtue of the Infant Life (Preservation) Act 1929 because the child would then have been capable of being born alive; and a claim for damages which depended for its success on establishing a chain of causation which included the commission of a criminal offence could not be accepted by the court. The situation was as if the mother had failed to prove that she would have proceeded to an abortion, so the outcome would have been the same. If the facts of this case were repeated at the present time, the judge would not find that the proposed abortion would be a crime, thanks to s 37(1)(d) of the Human Fertilisation and Embryology Act 1990, which permits the termination of a pregnancy at any stage where there is a substantial risk that if the child were born it would be seriously handicapped. Similarly in *Briody* v *St Helens and Knowsley Area Health Authority* [2002] QB 856, the Court of Appeal held that a claim for the costs of surrogacy (where a claimant had been made infertile through medical negligence) which would involve breach of the Surrogacy Arrangements Act 1985 are not recoverable.

In *Smith* v *Barking, Havering and Brentwood Health Authority* [1994] 5 Med LR 285, the claimant proved that the defendants had been negligent in not warning her of the risks of a difficult operation on the cervical canal but failed in her claim for damages for serious injury suffered in the operation because the judge was satisfied that, even if warned, she would still have agreed to the operation as it was her only chance of avoiding the onset of tetraplegia.

However, in *Chester* v *Afshar* [2004] UKHL 41, the defendant, a neurosurgeon, failed to inform the claimant of the small risk of cauda equine syndrome developing during the operation. The operation was performed non-negligently. Cauda equine syndrome developed. The trial judge found that it was not possible to say whether the claimant would have gone ahead with the surgery although she would probably have sought a second opinion first and the operation which was not urgent may therefore have taken place on a later date. The House of Lords held by a majority (Lords Bingham and Hoffman dissenting) that the claimant could not prove that the failure to warn of the small risk was the cause of the cauda equine syndrome because she could not say that she would not have gone ahead with the surgery if she had been told of the risk. For policy reasons, ie for the duty to obtain consent before operating to have any meaning, the usual rules of causation had to be altered to allow the claimant to recover damages. At [2005] 1 AC 134, para 87 Lord Hope of Craighead said that 'The function of the law is to enable rights to be vindicated and to provide remedies when duties have been breached' and that unless that was done the right to be consented before an operation would be 'a hollow one, stripped of all practical force and devoid of all content'. It will be interesting to see whether, in the face of evidence that a claimant would have gone ahead with an operation on the same day and with the same surgeon even if he had been told of a risk which then eventuated, the right to be properly consented will be allowed to trump the normal rules of causation.

In *Birch* v *University College London Hospital NHS Foundation Trust* [2008] EWHC 2237, the failure to obtain consent to the risk of angiogram (ie the risk of stroke which eventuated) as opposed to other alternative tests was held to be causative of injury as the claimant would probably not have consented had he been warned.

Then there was the House of Lords decision in the *Wilsher* case, considered in detail below, where it was held that the claimant had failed to prove that his injury was due to negligence rather than to one or another of various other possible causes which did not involve negligence.[6]

---

6   In *Pickford* v *Imperial Chemical Industries* [1997] 8 Med LR 270, the Court of Appeal said that where there were two alternative explanations of the cause of an injury advanced by the medical experts, the judge had simply to decide upon the evidence which was the most likely. However, it is not clear to what extent this proposition was invalidated by the House of Lords decision (which restored the decision of the trial judge in favour of the defendants on the basis that it had been for the claimant to establish the cause of her injury, not for the defendants to prove some other cause ([1998] 1 WLR 1189)).

Causation also proved the stumbling block for the claimants who sought to allege that the pertussis vaccine caused brain damage to their children (see *Loveday* v *Renton* [1990] 1 Med LR 117).

In the Australian case of *H* v *Royal Alexandra Hospital for Children (NSW)* [1990] 1 Med LR 297, the claimant, a boy born in May 1973, established negligence by the hospital in not warning his parents of the risk of AIDS infection from the blood product that was used to treat his hemophilia in September 1983, but the court found that he had failed to establish that, given the appropriate warning, his parents would have refused the treatment. Similarly, even if the manufacturers of the product had been negligent in not giving such a warning to the doctors and hospitals to whom they supplied it, the judge's conclusion was that such a warning would not have affected the attitude of the doctors to the use of the product on this patient (a conclusion which was reinforced by, if not solely due to, the fact that the treating doctors were aware of the risks in any event). It was for causation considerations of this type that the hugely expensive benzodiazepine group litigation in this country eventually fizzled out.[7]

Sellers v *Cooke and East Dorset Health Authority* [1990] 2 Med LR 13 and 16, CA is interesting: although the claimant succeeded in persuading the Court of Appeal that certain fresh evidence suggesting a negligent termination of her pregnancy could not reasonably have been obtained by her for the trial (which she had lost), the court went on to hold that, even if that evidence were to establish that her pregnancy had been negligently terminated, that would not have affected the outcome, because the judge had found that the foetus would probably not in any event have survived.

In *Marsden* v *Bateman* [1993] 4 Med LR 181, the claimant failed to establish that her brain damage was due to untreated neonatal hypoglycaemia rather than a congenital condition.

In *Stockdale* v *Nicholls* [1993] 4 Med LR 190, the claim failed because the judge held that earlier admission to hospital would not have affected the outcome, in that the claimant would still have been admitted for observation only, and the unavoidable and unpredictable onset of septicaemia resulting in fitting and brain damage would have occurred in hospital at the same time and with the same results.

In *Robertson* v *Nottingham Health Authority* [1996] 7 Med LR 421, the trial judge held that the period of culpable delay during labour had made no difference to the outcome because the foetal brain injury had been sustained before the mother had been admitted to hospital. The Court of Appeal held that the judge should have found a more extended period of delay, but, despite that and the fact that he had not dealt in his judgment with the significance of an apparently normal first CTG trace, his conclusion on causation would probably have been the same ([1997] 8 Med LR 1).

In *Brown* v *Lewisham and North Southwark Health Authority* [1999] Lloyd's Rep Med 110, [2000] MLC 0081, the trip a patient was obliged to undertake by train and taxi from Guy's Hospital in London back to his

---

7   See also *CJD Litigation Straddlers A and C* v *Secretary of State for Health* (22 May 1998), Morland J. (The test was: 'If the hypothetical warning letter had been sent, would the clinicians probably have stopped the treatment?')

Blackpool hospital following his negligent discharge with a chest infection was not a cause of later vascular gangrene leading to amputation of a leg. An idiosyncratic reaction to Heparin at the Blackpool hospital was the cause; it would have happened in any event.

In *Brock* v *Frenchay Healthcare Trust* [1999] MLC 0101, there had been a negligent delay in administering Mannitol, but earlier administration would not have helped.

In *Windyk* v *Wigan Health Authority* [1999] MLC 0088, a claim for a negligently-advised operation on a man with little sight (he then lost what little he had), the defendants failed to show that he would in any event have progressed to complete loss of vision.

In *Hossack* v *Ministry of Defence* [2000] MLC 00185, CA, no causal connection was found between a negligent failure to downgrade a soldier for training status and the development of chronic medial tibial syndrome. The court imported into the tortious context the well-known contractual principle that an event which simply provides the opportunity for something else to happen is not thereby the cause of it (the 'Galoo' principle – see [1994] 1 WLR 1360, CA).

In *C* v *A Health Authority* (3 November 1998, ML 12/98 p 7), a negligent failure to offer a booking appointment was not causative of the birth of a congenitally handicapped child because the consultant, reasonably, would not in any event have recommended the sort of scan which might have shown the defect.

In *Coffey-Martin* v *Royal Free Hampstead NHS Trust* (15 December 2000, unreported), QBD, Foskett QC, the mother proved breach of duty in that the defendants did not examine her anal sphincter following the birth of her child, but failed on causation as the court concluded that examination would probably not have detected the damage, and, even if it had, repair procedures would probably not have avoided much of the injury.

Where a solicitor fails to serve a writ in a medical claim but the claim is adjudged hopeless, there will be no causation and the claim against the solicitor will be struck out (*Harris* v *Bolt Burdon* (2 February 2000, unreported), CA.

Recently it was held that where a GP negligently failed to make a referral, a presumption exists in favour of the claimant that they would have received the correct treatment in the event that the referral had been made. It is for the GP to demonstrate, where appropriate, that the hospital's subsequent treatment would have been negligent in any event (*Wright* v *Cambridge Medical Group* [2011] EWCA Civ 669).

The Bolitho *case*

In *Bolitho* v *City and Hackney Health Authority* [1993] 4 Med LR 381, CA, affd [1997] 4 All ER 771, HL, the facts can be summarised in this way: a child was ill in hospital; it was agreed that it was negligent that during the night no doctor had responded to a call made by the night sister; it was agreed that, if a doctor had come and had intubated the child, the cardiac arrest and brain damage that he went on to suffer would have been avoided. One might think that the defendants would have paid up on these facts, but no. They chose to argue (successfully) that the claimant could not prove that, if a doctor had come, she would probably have intubated. The claimant's expert said that it would have been mandatory to intubate; the defendants' expert said that he would not have intubated. The doctor (Dr Horn) who should have responded to the call from the sister said that she would not have intubated. Faced with this conflict of medical opinion, the judge held that the claimant had not proved that the outcome would probably have been different if the doctor had responded to the nurse's call. By a majority, the Court of Appeal upheld this decision.

Pending appeal to the House of Lords in *Bolitho,* the Court of Appeal considered a not dissimilar situation in *Joyce v Merton, Sutton and Wandsworth Health Authority* [1996] 7 Med LR 1. It was agreed that if a vascular surgeon had been called to the ward to review the patient following the initial operation on his arm and had operated within 48 hours, the injury (by way of thrombosis leading to brain stem infarction) would probably have been avoided. But the defendants argued successfully that, even if a vascular surgeon had been called in, the findings of the judge on causation could not be overturned. Those findings were that there was no relevant deterioration in the condition of Mr Joyce during the 48 hours following the procedure; that it was not mandatory to call for a vascular surgeon; and, most significantly, even if a vascular surgeon had monitored the condition of the patient, no vascular surgeon at that hospital would or should have seen a need to operate. In other words:

1   the course that would have ensued would in any event have been conservative treatment; and
2   it could not be said that such a conservative course was unacceptable.

In the *Bolitho* case, the claimant could not show that the doctor would have intubated, nor that it would have been mandatory to intubate. In the *Joyce* case, the claimant could not show that a vascular surgeon would have operated within the crucial 48-hour period, nor that it would have been mandatory for him to have done so.

The House of Lords upheld the decision of the Court of Appeal and for the same reasons ([1998] AC 232, [1997] 4 All ER 771). Lord Browne-Wilkinson gave the only speech (although Lord Slynn expressed a degree of anxiety at the actual result). Their conclusions can be shortly expressed. The judge had asked the right two questions:

1   Would Dr Horn (or her junior) have intubated? Answer: the judge's acceptance of her evidence that she would not have intubated could not be interfered with.
2   Would it have been negligent if she had not intubated? Answer: the judge was impressed with the expert evidence called for the defence. He had no grounds for rejecting it as illogical or unreasonable, nor, said the House of Lords on reviewing the evidence and pointing out that the condition of the child at the relevant time did not appear on the evidence to have deteriorated to the point where intubation would have been necessary, had they.

The trouble with this sad story is not that the approach of the courts was at any time unsatisfactory in law, but that one cannot help feeling that the defendants, in creating their defence, were just too clever by half.

'Material contribution'

It is trite law that any contribution to the injury which is not negligible (ie does not fall within the *de minimis* principle) may be taken to have 'materially contributed' to the injury (see *Bonnington Castings Ltd v Wardlaw* [1956] AC 613, MLC 0003, *per* Lord Reid, and *Clarkson v Modern Foundries Ltd* [1958] 1 All ER 33). It is, or should be, also hornbook law that if you prove that a cause made a material contribution to your injury, you can recover for the whole of the injury, leaving the tortfeasors (if more than one) to sue each other for contribution. The first of these principles is dealt with in this section, the second (though they overlap, of course) in the later section, under 'Divisible injury'. So if an injury is caused by negligent cause A or non-negligent cause B and the claimant is unable to establish on the balance of probability that cause A rather than B is the effective cause of the injury, then he will fail to establish causation. However, if the claimant can establish that the cause of the injury is a combination of causes, ie A *and* B and that it is not possible to say to what extent each cause has contributed to injury, then the claimant has established causation and should recover in full. The rationale for full recovery is presumably that it would not be just to an injured claimant to simply guess the extent of the contribution made by the negligent cause. In practice, the potential effects of negligent and non-negligent causes in clinical negligence cases are often argued about and the subject of compromise in the form of apportionment of damages between respective causes. Experts are often asked to say how much better would the claimant have been for example without the negligence. Very often there is little or no scientific basis for the answers that are given. Cases proceed on informed guesswork as to what might have been without the negligence.

In *Hotson* v *East Berkshire Area Health Authority* [1987] AC 750, HL, Lord Bridge said that the claimant had to prove that the delay in treatment was 'at least a material contributory cause' of his injury.

In *Murray* v *Kensington and Chelsea and Westminster Area Health Authority* (11 May 1981, unreported), CA, a baby's sight was lost due to excessive oxygen. The trial judge had found one incident only of negligence on the part of the doctors, namely in administering extra oxygen in the first 36 hours of life, but had found for the defendants nevertheless on the basis that it was not proved that it was that particular quantity of oxygen that had caused the injury, for it could have been caused by later doses, in respect of which no negligence was found. The Court of Appeal upheld his decision. It seems hard on the claimant that the judges were not prepared to conclude on the evidence that the initial excess had probably made a material contribution to the injury.

In the Scottish case of *Kay* v *Ayrshire and Arran Health Board* [1987] 2 All ER 417, HL, a child suffering from pneumococcal meningitis was negligently given three times the proper dose of penicillin. Liability was admitted for the short-term effects of convulsion and temporary paralysis, but denied in respect of the permanent deafness that later occurred. The House of Lords, confirming the appeal court's reversal of the trial judge's award of damages for the deafness, said that there was no evidence which would support a finding that the overdose caused the deafness or even materially increased the risk of its occurring. On the evidence, the probability was that it was the original meningitis that caused the deafness.

In *Hutchinson* v *Epsom and St Hellier's NHS Trust* [2002] MLC 1072 the defendants' failure to carry out liver function tests on the deceased and their consequent failure to advise him to stop drinking made a material contribution to his death. The deputy High Court judge held that the widow was entitled to recover in full.

In *King* v *Samsung Heavy Industries Ltd* (10 April 2002, unreported), the Court of Appeal said that, where the finding had been that an employer's breach of duty, though not necessarily the main or sole cause of the claimant's carpal tunnel syndrome, had been a material cause contributing to the injury, that was sufficient for a finding of liability against the employeIn *Wilsher* v *Essex Area Health Authority* [1988] AC 1074, HL, where it was alleged that administration of excessive oxygen had caused neonatal blindness, the House of Lords was unanimously of the view that there had to be a retrial for the simple enough reason that on the evidence there were a number of possible causes for the injury to the child and the judge had not at any time made any finding that excess oxygen was the actual cause, the effective cause or even the most likely cause (that omission seems to have been due to the judge's misunderstanding of part of the expert evidence). Had he made that finding, his conclusion would have been unassailable. But he did not and so a retrial before another judge on the issue of causation was unavoidable (the attempt by the majority of the Court of Appeal to shore up the trial judgment was unacceptable to the House of Lords).[8]

In *Simmons* v *British Steel plc 2002* [2004] PIQR P33, the House of Lords held that the defendant employer was liable for the claimant's psychiatric illness where one of the causes had been the claimant's anger following an accident at work for which the employer was liable.

In *Bailey* v *Ministry of Defence* [2008] LS Med 481, the claimant was admitted to hospital for an operation to remove a gallstone. After the operation, the claimant became very weak and developed pancreatitis. She was sent to the intensive care unit. The claimant's condition stabilised and she was transferred to the ward. There she was given a drink, vomited and was unable to clear her throat. She aspirated the vomit causing a cardiac arrest which led her to suffer hypoxic brain damage. The judge found that the cardiac arrest had been caused by the claimant's weakness which had two cumulative causes, ie the first defendant's lack of care and the claimant's pancreatitis, which was not the result of the first defendant's negligence. He held that since the negligent lack of care had contributed materially to the claimant's overall weakness, causation had been established. The Court of Appeal dismissed the defendant's appeal, Lord Justice Waller at paragraph 46 held:

> I would summarise the position in relation to cumulative cause cases as follows. If the evidence demonstrates on a balance of probabilities that the injury would have occurred as a result of the non-tortious cause or causes in any event, the claimant will have failed to establish that the tortious

---

8   There was in fact no retrial as an amicable settlement was reached about the end of 1990, under which a proportion of the total damages claimed was paid to the claimant.

cause contributed. *Hotson's* case exemplifies such a situation. If the evidence demonstrates that 'but for' the contribution of the tortious cause the injury would probably not have occurred, the claimant will (obviously) have discharged the burden. In a case where medical science cannot establish the probability that 'but for' an act of negligence the injury would not have happened but can establish that the contribution of the negligent cause was more than negligible, the 'but for' test is modified, and the claimant will succeed.

Bailey was also followed by Walker J in his *obiter* judgment in the case of *Ingram* v *Dr Williams* [2010] EWHC 758, QB. The judge held that the claimant would have established the causation of all his losses and recovered damages in full where it had been agreed between the experts that the alleged negligence had made 'a material but unquantifiable reduction in the degree of disability suffered'. The apportionment approach (the *Holtby* approach) between causes argued for by the defendants was specifically rejected. Much in reality depends upon the type of evidence adduced. If there can be a logical and reasoned apportionment, then the *Holtby* approach may still be adopted.

Another recent example of the robust application of the material contribution exception to the 'but for' test in clinical negligence cases is *Boustead* v *North West Strategic Health Authority* [2008] LS Law Med 471. In that case there were a number of potential causes of brain damage in a new born infant. One was the delay in delivery by caesarean section. Others included his prematurity. Mr Justice Mackay held that the negligent delay was one of current cumulative causes and since it had materially contributed to the hypoxia but to an unknown and unknowable extent, the claimant was entitled to recover.

The distinctions of interest are therefore between competing causes and cumulative causes – between material contribution to the risk of injury as in the *Fairchild* exception and material contribution to injury itself. Where, on the balance of probability, therefore, the negligently caused hypoxia had materially contributed to the brain damage, but to an unknown or unknowable extent, liability is established. If, on the other hand, the hypoxia was one of a number of potential causes and it was impossible to say on the balance of probability whether it had caused or materially contributed to the injury, then liability would not be established.

Incidentally it should be remembered that 'material contribution' has been defined as something more than de minimis: see *Bonnington Castings* v *Wardlaw* [1956] AC 613. It is not necessary for the claimant to prove that the negligent cause was the sole cause or even the main cause of injury.

Materially increasing the risk

Pursuant to the *McGhee* case (below), it had been thought that even if the claimant could not show that what was done materially contributed to his injury (because the state of medical knowledge at the time was not sufficiently advanced to demonstrate the connection), it was nevertheless enough if he showed that what was done materially increased the risk of injury. In those circumstances, the court would be entitled to infer, as a matter of fact, that what was done did play a part in the causing of the injury:

It has often been said that the legal concept of causation is not based on logic or philosophy. It is based on the practical way in which the ordinary man's mind works in the everyday affairs of life. From a broad and practical viewpoint I can see no substantial difference between saying that what the defendant did materially increased the risk of injury to the plaintiff and saying that what the defendant did made a material contribution to his injury (*per* Lord Reid in *McGhee* v *National Coal Board* [1973] 1 WLR 1 at 5, MLC 0007, HL).

This principle was extended by a majority of the Court of Appeal in *Wilsher* v *Essex Area Health Authority* [1987] QB 730, where the fact that the administering of an excess of oxygen was only one of the possible causes of loss of sight in a neonate did not preclude the court from attributing the injury to that cause. The principle was also applied in *Bryce* v *Swan Hunter Group plc* [1988] 1 All ER 659 and *Fitzgerald* v *Lane* [1987] QB 781, CA. But we then learnt from the judgment of the House of Lords in the *Wilsher* case that the interpretation put upon Lord Reid's words in the *McGhee* case was misconceived, and that that case added nothing to the traditional rules on causation: it was up to the claimant to show on the balance of probabilities that the act or omission complained of caused or materially contributed to his injury (see below for further discussion of *Wilsher*). So the matter stood until the very important House of Lords decision in *Fairchild* v *Glenhaven Funeral Services Ltd* (see the section below for a discussion about that case).

The 'but for' test

It is not always easy to be confident about applying the 'material contribution' test. It may feel more logical to ask the question: would the injury have been sustained if the alleged negligence had not taken place? In some circumstances, the tests may give different answers. That is because injury may be caused by more than one factor. Where a patient suffers brain damage from an underlying illness and also as a result of wrong medication, the 'but for' test might yield the result that the patient had not shown causation because the underlying illness would probably have resulted in the injury in any event, while the 'material contribution' test would establish causation. In other cases, the inability to satisfy the 'but for' test might also lead to the conclusion that the other factor did not play a material part in the injury. The 'but for' test could obviously not be applied in the case of joint tortfeasors, because each defendant could escape liability by pleading that even if he had not been negligent the injury would nevertheless have been sustained. It is also important to bear in mind the rule that joint tortfeasors are individually liable for the whole of the relevant damages in the context where there is a negligent late referral to hospital or to a specialist, and the hospital or specialist is also negligent in the management of the patient. In those circumstances, it should not be open to the first defendant to plead that the injury was caused only by the second failure of management (but see below under 'Divisible injury' and 'Breaking the chain of causation').

In *Page* v *Smith (No 2)* [1996] 1 WLR 855, CA, the Master of the Rolls said:

> Secondly, it was argued that the judge had erred in asking whether on the balance of probabilities the defendants' negligence had materially contributed to the recrudescence of the plaintiffs' symptoms. He should, it was said, have

asked himself whether on the balance of probabilities the plaintiff would have suffered the injury for which he was claiming compensation but for the defendant's negligence. I do not for my part accept these criticisms. In a case in which other causes could have played a part in the causation of the defendant's exacerbated symptoms, it was in my view entirely appropriate for the judge to direct himself in the way that he did, reminding himself that a cause was only to be regarded as material if it was more than minimal or trivial or insignificant. I cannot in any event see that in a case such as this the outcome would be different whichever test is formulated. The judge had already accepted the view expressed by one of the medical experts that the plaintiffs' recovery would probably have continued but for the accident. The judge adopted a straightforward, pragmatic approach which was in my judgment entirely appropriate in the circumstances.

This was a claim for the exacerbation of a psychiatric injury (chronic fatigue syndrome) caused by a road traffic accident. The issue whether a psychiatric injury had to be foreseeable in the context of a road traffic accident had already gone to the House of Lords, where it had received a negative response ([1996] AC 155).

In *Vernon* v *Bosley* [1997] 1 All ER 577, CA, the issue was to what extent, if any, the claimant, who had suffered the unimaginably traumatic experience of watching his two daughters drown when the car driven by their nanny crashed into a river, could recover for nervous shock, seeing that (a) bereavement had in itself been a cause of his illness, and (b) damages for bereavement and the consequent grief reaction were not recoverable beyond the bereavement award. The 'but for' test would probably have yielded the result that his illness would have been suffered in any event as a result of 'mere' bereavement, ie even if he had not been present at the tragedy. Nevertheless, he recovered in full. The Court of Appeal, in long and complex judgments, refused to discount the injury and the relevant compensation merely because some part of it was referable to and caused by grief and the consequences of bereavement. As Evans LJ said:

> I would hold that damages are recoverable for mental illness caused or at least contributed to by actionable negligence of the defendant ie in breach of a duty of care, notwithstanding that the illness may also be regarded as a pathological consequence of the bereavement which the plaintiff, where the primary victim was killed, must inevitably have suffered.[9]

The 'but for' test gives a wrong answer also in the context of a loss-causing event where the negligent act had no more synergistic connection with the event than that it afforded it an opportunity to occur (see *Hossack* v *Ministry of Defence* (above)).[10]

---

9   In a minority judgment, Stuart-Smith LJ came to the 'clear conclusion that the claimant did not discharge the onus that was upon him of proving that the shock of witnessing the accident caused or substantially contributed to the illness from which he was suffering'. He said that to reach a contrary conclusion was speculation and guesswork.

10   The Court of Appeal case of *Chapman* v *Tangmere Airfield Nurseries Ltd* (4 December 1998; see JPIL (1999) p 65) provides useful matter on 'material contribution', the 'but for' test, and contributory negligence. Evans LJ said that for liability it was sufficient for the defendant's negligence to have been, put colloquially, *a* cause. It did not have to be *the* cause. He also deprecated the judge's resort to a 'but for' test.

There is a discussion of the interplay between 'material contribution', 'material increase in risk' and the 'but for' test in the interesting case of *Donachie* v *Chief Constable of the Greater Manchester Police* [2004] EWCA Civ 405.

The *Fairchild* case

The decision of the House of Lords in *Fairchild* v *Glenhaven Funeral Services Ltd* [2002] 3 WLR 89, MLC 0786 may be summarised in this way. Where two (or more) employers have been similarly negligent in failing to protect an employee from the risk of contracting a disease (mesothelioma in this instance) and the employee contracts that disease but it is not possible in the current state of medical and scientific knowledge to show during which employment the disease was probably contracted, both employers are to be held to have caused the disease and so both are liable to the employee. The disease in this case is apparently not cumulative and is contracted once for all at a single moment when a fibre enters the respiratory system. It was not possible to tell under whose employment that fibre was ingested.

An analogy may posit two independent hunters each negligently discharging identical bullets in the direction of a jogger with the result that one only of the bullets cripples the jogger. It is impossible to show whose bullet caused the damage. No sensible person, I venture to think, would deny the jogger his claim, but would say that, as both the hunters had negligently created the identical risk of an injury which in fact materialised, they should both be liable. That is the effect of the House of Lords judgments. Incidentally, it is worth noting on the side that neither counsel nor the court suggested that each individual employer should only be liable for part of the compensation due to the injured employee; in other words the doctrine of material contribution was given its proper effect in this case.

To explain the function of the new rule on causation we need first to look more closely at the House of Lords judgment in the case of *McGhee* v *National Coal Board* [1973] 1 WLR 1 MLC 0007, HL. One recalls that all that the claimant could prove in that case by his expert medical evidence was that the employer's failure to provide showers had increased the risk of his contracting dermatitis; he could not prove that the provision of showers would probably have prevented the disease, ie that he probably would not have contracted it if there had been no negligence. The speeches of the House of Lords giving judgment in his favour were understood at the time to be pronouncing a rule of causation to the effect that there was 'no substantial difference between saying that what the defendant did materially increased the risk of injury to the claimant and saying that what the defendant did made a material contribution to his injury' (*per* Lord Reid at p 5). However, Lord Bridge said in *Wilsher* v *Essex Area Health Authority* [1988] AC 1074 that *McGhee* did not introduce any new principle of causation because the conclusion of the House of Lords was merely based on a factual inference that they drew in the circumstances of the case to the effect that the evidence established to their satisfaction that the failure to provide showers had in fact made a material contribution to the claimant contracting the dermatitis. However, a large part of the speeches of the House in *Fairchild* was devoted to a minute analysis of what the judges in *McGhee* had and what they had not said. Their conclusion (by a clear majority of four to one) was that the *McGhee* decision was not based on any inference from the evidence but did indeed propose a new principle of causation, albeit in the limited circumstances that the House was now prepared to endorse.

What then are those limited circumstances?

Lord Bingham said that such injustice as there might be in imposing liability on a duty-breaking employer, who might not in fact have been the one responsible for injuring the claimant, was heavily outweighed by the injustice of denying redress to a victim (and all his brethren went on to agree with him). However, this attribution of liability to a defendant where he had not on traditional legal principles been proved to have caused the claimant's injury was limited, for the present time at any rate, to a scenario where certain conditions were satisfied. The conditions specified by Lord Bingham are tightly based around the facts of the instant case, and require that an employee should have contracted mesothelioma from inhaling asbestos dust at some time while working for one or other of a number of different employers, all of whom had been negligent in relation to the risk of contracting such an injury, and that because of the current limits of human science the claimant should be unable to prove within whose employment he had in fact contracted the injury. Clearly the rule as so defined is of no use in medical negligence claims. However, Lord Bingham said that it would be unrealistic to suppose that the principle that he was affirming would not over time be the subject of incremental and analogical development, but he did not suggest more specific possibilities.

Lord Nicholls, agreeing in effect with the full tenor of Lord Bingham's judgment, said that the principle must be closely confined in its application or it could become a source of injustice to defendants. There must be good reason for departing from the normal threshold 'but for' test, and the reason must be sufficiently weighty to justify depriving the defendant of the protection that test normally and rightly afforded him. Policy questions would loom large. It was not possible to be more specific.

Lord Hoffman said that it was open to the House to formulate a special rule of causal relationship in the type of case with which they were dealing. Otherwise guilty employers would escape all liability and negligently injured claimants would never achieve compensation. He, too, made it clear that this exceptional rule was being limited to the salient facts of the instant case. But he, like the House of Lords in *Wilsher,* rejected the reasoning of the Court of Appeal in that case, which was based on their belief that *McGhee* established a general principle that, where a defendant had materially increased the risk of a claimant sustaining a particular injury, that was enough to prove that he had made a material contribution to the injury. He said that, unlike the instant case, it could not be said that the duty to take reasonable care in treating patients would be virtually drained of content unless the creation of a material risk of injury were accepted as sufficient to satisfy the causal requirements for liability. The political and economic arguments involved in the massive increase in liability of the NHS which would have been a consequence of the broad rule favoured by the Court of Appeal in *Wilsher*'s case were far more complicated than the reasons given in *McGhee* for imposing liability upon an employer who failed to take simple precautions. Nevertheless he too indicated that the rule might well be capable of development and application in new situations.

Lord Rodger concluded that the claimants should be taken in law to have proved a material contribution to their injury by defendants who had been shown to have by their negligence materially increased the risk of them contracting mesothelioma. Then he, alone of the judges, went on to suggest the more general conditions within which the new principle should apply. This is useful because the new rule obviously has to be definable in terms not restricted to an employee developing mesothelioma from being exposed to asbestos while in more than one employment. There must be a more general rule underlying that specific instance of it.

Lord Rodgers suggested that:

- the necessary causation must be unprovable by current science;
- the defendant's conduct must have materially increased the risk of injury to the claimant and must have been capable of causing the injury;
- significantly, the claimant must prove that his injury was in fact caused by the sort of risk that the defendant had negligently created. So if other risks of a different nature could have caused the injury the principle would not apply. *Wilsher* is an example of this. The agencies implicated in creating the risks must operate in substantially the same way. He said that the principle applied where the other source(s) of the injury involved lawful conduct by the same defendant but *quaere* if the conduct was that of another person or a natural occurrence.

The reason the principle would not apply in a case like *Wilsher* is that there were a number of different agents that could have caused the RLF (retrolental fibroplasia, an ophthalmic disease) and excess oxygen was only one of them. The other possible causes were of a completely different nature. The defendants were only implicated in respect of the excess oxygen risk. Had the trial judge made a finding of fact that excess oxygen was the most likely cause, the claimant would have succeeded. But he did not – probably because there was no evidence on which such a finding could properly be based. He merely applied the *McGhee* principle, as did the Court of Appeal. The House of Lords said, as they have also done in the *Fairchild* case, that such an application is not permissible. As Lord Rodger said:

> The principle does not apply where the claimant has merely proved that his injury could have been caused by a number of different events, only one of which is the eventuation of the risk created by the defendant's wrongful act or omission. This will usually mean that the claimant must prove that his injury was caused, if not by exactly the same agency as was involved in the defendant's wrongdoing, at least by an agent that operated in substantially the same way.

In speaking to the Personal Injury Bar Association in 2002, Lord Hope said:

> It is clear that the law will not soften its demands without a clear and compelling reason. So it must be demonstrated by evidence that there was only

one possible cause, that in subjecting the claimant to that cause the defendant was in breach of its duty of care and that by doing so it materially increased the risk of injury. But it must also be demonstrated that it is not possible to go further and establish the causal link which the law normally requires. If that is the case, a material increase in the risk will be sufficient to satisfy the causal requirements for liability.

Despite the clearly limited boundaries of this new rule of causation, it appears that the courts may be regarding the rule as of more general application. For example, in *Brown* v *Corus (UK) Ltd* [2004] PIQR P476, the Court of Appeal held an employer liable for causing a vibration syndrome where it had materially increased the risk of the claimant contracting the disease, even though the precise reduction in the exposure that proper management would have brought about could not be known. Note that there was no question of more than one possible cause here. There was only the proof that the employer was in breach for not having taken steps to reduce the exposure.

The application of the *Fairchild* principle to clinical negligence cases may be limited (see below). The House of Lords have been at pains to point out that the principle is applicable only to mesothelioma cases or to those that are closely analogous (see *Novartis Grimsby* v *Cookson* [2007] EWCA Civ 1261 where exposure to amines doubled the risk of bladder cancer).

The House of Lords considered another mesothelioma case in *Barker* v *Corus* [2006] 2 AC 572. The main issue in this case was apportionment, an issue not raised in *Fairchild*. It was held (reversing the decision of the Court of Appeal) that a defendant should only be liable to the extent that it had materially increased the risk of injury. This decision has been reversed as far as mesothelioma cases is concerned by s 3 of the Compensation Act 2006, so that in effect, as against the claimant, all defendants who have materially increased the risk of the claimant developing mesothelioma are jointly and severally liable to compensate him for his entire loss. However, all other cases that fall within the *Fairchild* exception are governed by *Barker* and therefore subject to apportionment. This leads to the potentially anomalous position that a tortfeasor who materially contributes to an injury is liable for the whole injury (assuming it is not possible to prove the extent of the contribution), whereas a tortfeasor who materially increases the risk of injury is only liable for the extent to which he has increased the risk (in practice the percentage of total duration of exposure to the noxious agent for which the defendant is responsible).

In *Hull* v *Sanderson* [2009] PIQR P114, the Court of Appeal made it clear that the *Fairchild* exception would only operate in a personal injury case where it was impossible to show which of two or more causes had resulted in injury. In this case, an infection contracted in a turkey factory by a claimant could have occurred in several different ways, any of which was capable of proof on the balance of probabilities.

The Supreme Court recently revisited the *Fairchild* exception when considering the issue of whether the rule can apply in cases where only one defendant is proved to have exposed the victims to asbestos, but where the victims themselves were also at risk of developing the disease from environmental exposure. In *Sienkiewicz* v *Greif (UK) Ltd*; *Knowsley MBC* v *Willmore* [2011] UKSC 10, it was held that the exception applies to cases of mesothelioma involving a single defendant so long as it can be demonstrated that the single defendant 'materially increased the risk' of the victim contracting mesothelioma. Lord Phillips stated that:

> I doubt whether it is ever possible to define, in quantitative terms, what for the purposes of the application of any principle of law, is de minimis. This must be a question for the judge on the facts of the particular case. In the case of mesothelioma, a stage must be reached at which, even allowing for the possibility that exposure to asbestos can have a cumulative effect, a particular exposure is too insignificant to be taken into account, having regard to the overall exposure that has taken place.

He further went on to state:

> The reality is that, in the current state of knowledge about the disease, the only circumstances in which a court will be able to conclude that wrongful exposure of a mesothelioma victim to asbestos dust did not materially increase the victim's risk of contracting the disease will be where that exposure was insignificant compared to the exposure from other sources.

One additional aspect of the decision worth noting is that the Supreme Court rejected the epidemiological argument that in a single exposure case there was a requirement to demonstrate that the defendant's breach of duty doubled the risk of developing the disease. Lord Phillips addressed when it was appropriate to use epidemiological evidence and stated:

> ... I see no scope for the application of the 'doubles the risk' test in cases where two agents have operated cumulatively and simultaneously in causing the onset of a disease. In such a case the rule in *Bonnington* applies. Where the disease is indivisible, such as lung cancer, a defendant who has tortiously contributed to the cause of the disease will be liable in full. Where the disease is divisible, such as asbestosis, the tortfeasor will be liable in respect of the share of the disease for which he is responsible.

> Where the initiation of the disease is dose related, and there have been consecutive exposures to an agent or agents that cause the disease, one innocent and one tortious, the position will depend upon which exposure came first in time. Where it was the tortious exposure, it is axiomatic that this will have contributed to causing the disease, even if it is not the sole cause. Where the innocent exposure came first, there may be an issue as to whether this was sufficient to trigger the disease or whether the subsequent, tortious, exposure contributed to the cause. I can see no reason in principle why the 'doubles the risk' test should not be applied in such circumstances, but the court must be astute to see that the epidemiological evidence provides a really sound basis for determining the statistical probability of the cause or causes of the disease.

> ... Where there are competing alternatives, rather than cumulative, potential causes of a disease or injury, such as in *Hotson,* I can see no reason in principle why epidemiological evidence should not be used to show that one of the causes was more than twice as likely as all the others put together to have caused the disease or injury.'

Relevance to medical cases

There are many scenarios where proof that proper management would have avoided the injury is lacking. Up till now such a claim has been lost for failure to prove causation. Strictly interpreted, it seems to me that for a *Fairchild* argument to succeed, there would have to be more than one possible cause, proof that the defendant materially increased the risk of the injury, and that the limits of science made it impossible to establish causation in the normal way. However, if we allow ourselves a broader base for the new rule, it does not take much imagination to envisage how the more usual claim where, simply, causation is weak could have a chance now of succeeding with the aid of a cleverly formulated argument based on 'material increase in risk'. One awaits such an event with eager anticipation.

An example: in *Gray* v *Southampton Health Authority* (2001) MLC 0209, CA, severe post-operative brain damage occurred in a context of hypotension or hypoxia. None of the experts was able to say with confidence what the cause of the brain damage was. Could a *Fairchild* cum *McGhee* argument have now won the case for the claimant?

Divisible injury

Old law overturned?

The Court of Appeal decision in *Holtby* v *Brigham & Cowan (Hull) Ltd* [2000] Lloyd's Rep Med 254, [2000] PIQR Q293 is not easy to reconcile with the established law on material contribution in causation (ie that if you prove a material contribution to your injury as against one tortfeasor, he is liable to compensate you for the whole of the injury). It might be taken to mean that where two separate agencies (hospitals, doctors, etc) are responsible for a patient's injury, he can only recover a percentage of his damages from each, the total still to be 100% but the contribution to be made by each defendant to be decided by the judge.

However, the case need not and should not be interpreted so widely. The key to its proper interpretation (if there is one) lies in the concept of a *divisible injury*, ie one where it is clear that the defendant could not have been responsible for more than a part of the injury *and* it is just that he should not pay for the whole of the injury. The facts were that in this claim for injury from exposure to asbestos dust, the claimant had only spent half the period of exposure at the defendant's site. It appeared from the medical evidence that the claimant's condition would have been better if he had only been exposed while working for the defendant. It was therefore successfully argued that a part of the injury had not been caused by the defendant. Obviously, apportioning the injury could only be a matter of impression (the trial judge was said to have been generous when he applied a discount of only 25%). But this concept of apportionment of injury (and hence of compensation) is ripe for abuse. If applied at all, it should only be applied in cases where (a) it is reasonable to discern different injuries or at any rate different levels of injury as having been caused by different tortfeasors (or a tortfeasor and a non-tortfeasor), and (b) it is reasonable to deny the injured party full compensation from a particular defendant.

The limits of the *Holtby* principle were described by the Court of Appeal in the personal injury case of *Environment Agency v Ellis* [2009] PIQR P5. In that case the claimant suffered a back injury at work. Liability was established without contribution. He was also diagnosed with symptomless degenerative change in his back which would have developed in any event regardless of injury. Subsequently the claimant fell at home and suffered further injury. The defendant submitted that there should be an apportionment between the various causes (70% pre-existing condition, 20% to the accident at work, and 10% to the fall at home). The trial judge awarded the claimant 90% of his damages. The defendant appealed and the claimant cross appealed. The Court of Appeal dismissed the appeal and allowed the cross appeal, awarding the claimant 100% of his damages. It was held that the asymptomatic back condition had not been proven to be a cause at all on the evidence and that the 10% reduction for the fall at home was not a truly divisible injury. The *Holtby* principle was usually to be confined to cases where there is successive harm caused by a number of different agencies where the harm is divisible.

In *AB v Ministry of Defence* [2009] EWHC 1225, Foskett J pointed out at para 227 that 'whether damage is divisible or indivisible is a matter of fact and that there may be debatable borderline cases where that which is divisible or indivisible may not be immediately recognisable'.

Settled law

The settled law of cases such as *Bonnington* [1956] AC 613, MLC 0003, HL and *Wilsher* [1988] AC 1074, MLC 0016, HL cannot be, and has not been, disturbed by this decision of the Court of Appeal. The issue of divisibility of the injury was not raised in those cases. It looks as if it could have been raised in *Bonnington*, but it was not. The inference from this is that no one ever thought of it before. The bare pronouncement by Stuart-Smith LJ in the *Holtby* case that, although a material contribution to an injury entitles the claimant to succeed, 'strictly speaking, the defendant is liable only to the extent of that contribution', appears to be unsupported by authority and at variance with established law.

In *Thompson* v *Smiths Shiprepairers (North Shields Ltd)* [1984] QB 405, Mustill J was faced with a situation where the claimant had *already* contracted the disease when the period of negligent exposure began. That is why he allowed recovery only in respect of an extra slice of injury. But that should not lead to piecemeal awards simply because different employers have each contributed to the injury. Sometimes a workman will have worked for a number of employers, perhaps some of them negligent and others not. Is his injury to be parcelled up into small lots?

Longmore J, in the asbestosis case of *Milner* v *Humphreys and Glasgow Ltd* (24 November 1998, unreported), said:

> ... the principle [is] that where an injury is indivisible, any tortfeasor whose act has been a proximate cause must compensate for the whole injury, leaving the tortfeasor to sort out with other possible tortfeasors any other appropriate claim for contribution ... Where there are causes concurrent in time, the likelihood is that a resulting injury will be indivisible; but where causes are sequential in time, it is not likely that an injury will be truly indivisible especially if the injury is a disease which can get worse with cumulative exposure.

> ... the principle is that where it is proved that a wrongful act has made a material contribution to the plaintiff's injury, the law regards this as sufficient discharge of the plaintiff's burden of proof on causation to render the defendant liable for the injury in full. That does not mean that no question of apportionment can ever arise, but it does, in my judgment, meant that, unless the defendant pleads and proves facts which *justify* [my emphasis] apportionment, the plaintiff can recover in full.

However, it is essential that the application of the divisibility concept be restricted to appropriate cases. Even where divisibility is discernible, it must be up to the good sense of the judge whether or not to apply the concept.

In *Simmons* v *British Steel plc 2002* [2004] PIQR P33, the House of Lords held that the defendant employer was liable for the claimant's psychiatric illness where one of the causes had been the claimant's anger following an accident at work for which the employer was liable. Lord Rodger said that the usual rule, to be found in *Wardlaw* v *Bonnington Castings* (above) applied and that, in the absence of any basis for identifying and apportioning the respective roles played by the various factors in the development of the pursuer's condition, the pursuer was entitled to recover damages for all of his injuries.

This seems to be the opposite of the view the Court of Appeal took in *Allen* v *British Rail Engineering* [2001] PIQR Q101, a vibration white finger case. There they are saying that indivisibility will be the exception and apportionment will be the general rule ('in principle the amount of the employer's liability will be limited to the extent of the contribution which his tortious conduct made to the employee's disability'). The traditional rules seem to have been bent to accommodate these multiple industrial claims, and divisibility is interpreted impossibly widely, meaning no more than 'apportionability'. Any judge's guess or stab at apportioning will do.

The Rahman *case*

There was an even less convincing application of the concept of divisibility in *Rahman* v *Arearose Ltd and University College London NHS Trust* [2000] 3 WLR 1184, [2000] MLC 0223, CA (note that no reference is made in the judgment to the *Holtby* case).

The importance of the *Rahman* case is that the Court of Appeal was asked to decide on apportionment of liability in the unfortunately far too common situation where a non-medical negligent act causes a patient to present at hospital and then negligent medical treatment adds to the hitherto foreseeable adverse consequences of the original injury. Perhaps the original injury was sustained at work, or in a road traffic accident. It should have been minor, but negligent medical treatment, whether of commission or omission, has made it much worse. This scenario also raises the issue of 'breaking the chain of causation'. The two issues overlap; breaking the chain has a section to itself below. The facts can be simply stated: a manager at Burger King was viciously assaulted as a result of his employer not taking proper measures to protect him. Among his injuries was serious damage to one eye. However (this is not explicitly stated in the judgment but it must be so), he would probably not have lost the sight of that eye if he had not received admittedly negligent treatment at the hospital.

This is a type of situation that arises time and again in medico-legal practices. Is the answer to any suggestion for division of responsibility and compensation that the employer is not responsible in law for loss of the eye, as negligent medical treatment should not be deemed by the law (even though a common enough occurrence these days!) to be a foreseeable consequence, and is therefore a *novus actus*? (See below under 'Breaking the chain of causation'.) If that is the correct answer, one has to apportion both general and special damage, so that the employer pays only for the foreseeable consequences of the injury, just as, if the initial injury had been a non-negligent accident, the hospital would only be liable for the extra slice of injury that it had caused (and the consequences of that extra slice).

Or should one hold both defendants liable in full, on the doctrine of material contribution, leaving apportionment to be defined as between the defendants?

No previous authority

Although this sort of situation is common, it seems never to have been the subject of litigation before (maybe such claims are virtually always settled by amicable division of responsibility). The nearest one can get to it are the many old cases under the Workmen's Compensation Act 1925, where the injured workman had to prove that his disability had been caused by the accident rather than by the hospital's negligent treatment. Those cases are not particularly helpful as the social and policy considerations of the time would have been very different and because they were not straightforward tort cases, but involved decisions from arbitrators as to whether a disability fell within the words of the Act or not ('... results from the injury'). Nevertheless, it is worth looking briefly at one of them, faute de mieux, where the House of Lords by a majority concluded that negligent medical treatment broke the chain of causation so that the disability did not 'result from' the injury at work (*Hogan* v *West Hartley Bentinck Collieries (Owners) Ltd* [1949] 1 All ER 588, HL).

Hogan's *case*

In *Rothwell* v *Caverswall Stone Co Ltd* [1944] 2 All ER 350, CA, du Parcq LJ had said at 365 that negligent medical treatment, whether of commission or omission, 'may amount to a new cause'. In *Hogan*, Lord Simonds agreed, and said that the question whether the incapacity was due to the original accident or the intervention of a *novus actus* 'can only be answered on a consideration of all the circumstances and, in particular, of the quality of that later act or event'. Lord Normand said that it was axiomatic that additional injury caused by medical negligence should not be attributed to the original injury (though additional injury resulting from non-negligent medical treatment should).

Lord MacDermott disagreed. He saw no reason why the workman should lose the right to compensation under the Act just because he had been unfortunate enough to suffer from negligent medical treatment. Lord Reid agreed with him, saying that it was within the contemplation of the Act that the negligent treatment necessitated by the original injury might be inefficient (but he seems to have been meaning inefficiency of a lesser degree than actual negligence). More significantly, he was the only judge to ask why there should not be dual causes for the incapacity.

The Rahman *case (continued)*

In the *Rahman* case, the parties appear to have expected the court to divide up the injury, or perhaps only as between the defendants. The psychiatrists had been asked to prepare a joint report which attempted in particular the extraordinary task of attributing different *aspects* of the very substantial psychiatric injury to the different torts (the assault and the medical treatment). I do not know if they expected the court to attribute different aspects of the injury to the different defendants, *vis-à-vis* the claimant, both in respect of the claim for general damages and in respect of the allied manifold claims for special damages.

The salient issue in such a situation must be whether the doctrine of 'material contribution' is displaced by the doctrine of *novus actus*. However, at no point in the *Rahman* judgment (given only by Laws LJ) is there any reference to the doctrine of material contribution. In *Rahman*, the court, having declared for the purposes of apportionment under the Civil Liability (Contribution) Act 1978 that the two defendants were not concurrent tortfeasors, was then concerned to fix the proportion of liability which each defendant should bear *vis-à-vis* the claimant, there being no question of each being liable for the whole of the injury subject to apportionment among themselves.

Laws LJ said more than once that it would be wrong for a defendant to pay for any part of the injury or its consequences which, on the evidence, he clearly was not responsible for. That may sound fair on the face of it, but it ignores the principle of material contribution, and, if his approach is to be adopted, will allow for this sort of complex and highly speculative divisibility exercise, by experts and judges, in many more cases than hitherto.

In *Rahman*, the court went to infinite pains to divide up responsibility down to the last small head of special damage. This complexity could have been avoided by applying the test of material contribution, as was done in the cases (not mentioned in the judgment) of *Vernon* v *Bosley* [1997] 1 All ER 577, CA, and *Page* v *Smith (No 2)* [1996] 1 WLR 855, CA. It would still have been necessary to clarify what proportion of the total damages each defendant should bear as between themselves, but their insurers could probably have come to an agreement on that.

After complex analysis of the different aspects of what was really an indivisible injury, the Court of Appeal upheld the judge's original apportionment of 25% to the employer and 75% to the hospital. As between the two defendants, it might have been helpful to seek to divide up responsibility in this way (in the absence of agreement), but this was not a truly divisible injury, neither in its physical nor its psychiatric consequences, nor in its special damages claims. Each defendant should have been wholly liable as against the claimant.

For a sensible treatment of the divisibility question, see *Athey* v *Leonati* [1999] Lloyd's Rep Med 458: some of our judges might do well to heed the approach of the British Columbia Court of Appeal. The trial judge had awarded 25% damages on the basis that the claimant's disc herniation had been caused 25% by the negligence of the defendant drivers and 75% due to pre-existing disease. The court said there was no room to divide up the causes where one was non-tortious, and in any event 25% was a 'material contribution' and therefore rendered the defendants liable for the whole of the injury.

Negligence that increases injury

In many cases, the most that the patient is given by his causation expert is that proper treatment would probably have reduced the injury. It is then important to achieve some sort of definition of the extra slice of injury, partly in order to be able to assess general damages, and partly (and usually more significantly) in order to define what special damage (whether in the form of care, transport needs, accommodation or whatever) can be attributed to the extra slice of injury. In that particular context, it is surely necessary to establish that the aids, equipment and care claimed for would not have been necessary without the extra slice of injury. In *Tahir* v *Haringey Health Authority* [1998] Lloyd's Rep Med 104, CA, Otton LJ said that in such a context it is not sufficient to show that delay materially increased the risk of injury or that delay could cause injury, because the claimant had to go further and prove that damage was actually caused, and, more significantly, it was not sufficient to show a general increment of injury from the delay because 'some measurable damage' had to be proved. The Lord Justice went on to say that in the absence of any evidence before the trial judge which either identified or qualified additional deficit, it was not possible to assess damages. However, Sir Ralph Gibson said that:

> If it was common ground, or if the judge held upon evidence which she accepted, that in probability each hour of delay caused significant aggravation of, or addition to, the residual disability suffered by the plaintiff, then I would agree that the judge could properly assess damages as she did. The fact that the doctors could not identify any particular form of residual disability resulting from such delay, or precisely quantify any worsening of any form of residual disability as a result of that delay would not, in my judgment, deprive the plaintiff of the right to appropriate damages. I cannot accept, however, that any such common ground existed.

Leggatt LJ said that neither expert had identified any respect in which the plaintiff was actually worse off on account of the delay, and in the absence of any identification of any individual disability that occurred or was increased, and of any attempt to define the extent of any increase, the plaintiff's claim failed because there was no evidence before the judge that any damage caused by the defendants' negligence was more than minimal. He added the interesting observation that:

> When a doctor has been at fault no court wishes to send his patient away empty-handed. But where the fault is not shown to have resulted in any particular loss of amenity, there is nothing which the court can legitimately translate into money by way of compensation.

It is understandable that the claimant in this case found himself in difficulty because the case was presented on the basis that the negligence had been responsible for the whole of a substantial injury and it only became apparent during the trial that it was not going to be possible to prove more than a relatively minor increment.[11]

Breaking the chain of causation

As we have seen, an intervening act or event occurring after the original act of negligence may operate to break the chain of causation, with the

---

11   In *Taylor* v *West Kent Health Authority* [1997] 8 Med LR 251, Kay J found that delay in diagnosing breast cancer did not substantially alter the outcome, but that there was a degree of injury in that the claimant would probably have lived 18 months longer. Damages were left to the parties to agree.

result that the wrongdoer is not liable for loss caused by that event. There is no clear test or formula for deciding whether an act, which may be of a third party or of the claimant himself, and may be lawful or unlawful, voluntary or involuntary, will break the chain of causation. The most useful test is to ask whether the act was reasonably foreseeable at the time of the original negligence, but that is not conclusive of the issue. The court will in any event judge each case on its own facts and decide the question according to its own view of whether justice requires the tortfeasor to compensate the claimant for the additional damage suffered from the intervening act.

We have already seen that the court will adjudge an effect too remote where it regards it as inappropriate that the wrongdoer should be made liable in respect of it. In such cases it may be said that the effect is not to be regarded in law as having been caused by the original negligence. This may be so even though the effect appears to be both directly and foreseeably caused by the negligence, without any intervening act that could be said to have broken the chain of causation. Where, however, there is such an intervening act, whether of human agency, lawful or unlawful, voluntary or involuntary, or whether of a third party or of the claimant himself, or whether it be an event which is not of human origination, the court is free, if it chooses, to say that the intervening act, which in the case of a third party's act and sometimes in the case of the claimant is described by the Latin tag of *novus actus interveniens* (an independent supervening act), breaks the chain of causation, so that the damage flowing from it cannot be regarded in law as having been caused by the original negligence.

However, it is by no means easy to predict when such an intervening act will be regarded as breaking the chain of causation. At times, the test applied seems to have been whether the intervening act was reasonable in the circumstances, but currently the question seems to turn on foreseeability, though that is not necessarily conclusive of the issue. Was it reasonably foreseeable that the intervening act would occur? On that basis, the courts have several times ruled on a wrongdoer's liability for the criminal acts of third parties (*Stansbie* v *Troman* [1948] 2 KB 48, CA; *Lamb* v *Camden London Borough Council* [1981] QB 625, CA; *Ward* v *Cannock Chase District Council* [1985] 3 All ER 537; *P Perl (Exporters) Ltd* v *Camden London Borough Council* [1984] QB 342, CA; *King* v *Liverpool City Council* [1986] 1 WLR 890, CA; *Smith* v *Littlewoods Organisation Ltd* [1987] AC 241, HL). Compare also *Topp* v *London Country Bus (South West) Ltd* [1993] 1 WLR 976, CA, with *Grand Metropolitan plc* v *Closed Circuit Cooling Ltd* [1997] JPIL 191 (vehicles left with keys in ignition: was an unlawful taking a *novus actus?*).

Lord Reid said in *Home Office* v *Dorset Yacht Co* [1970] AC 1004, HL that for a *novus actus* not to break the chain of causation, it would have to be an act which was likely or probable to happen; but Lord Denning and Watkins LJ took a contrary view in *Lamb*'s case (above), where a judicious mix of 'reasonable foreseeability' and 'policy' was applied to deny recovery. Watkins LJ said that a robust and sensible approach to the question of remoteness would often produce an instinctive feeling that the event or act being weighed in the balance was too remote to sound in damages (this is the 'judicial hunch' or 'gut reaction' referred to, from time to time, above). Lord Denning said:

> ... it is not every consequence of a wrongful act which is the subject of compensation. The law has to draw a line somewhere. Sometimes it is done by limiting the range of persons to whom duty is owed. Sometimes it is done by saying that there is a break in the chain of causation. At other times it is done by saying that the consequence is too remote to be a head of damage. All these devices are useful in their way. But ultimately it is a question of policy for the judges to decide ...
>
> It seems to me that it is a question of policy which we, as judges, have to decide. The time has come when, in cases of new import, we should decide them according to the reason of the thing. In previous times, when faced with a new problem, the judges have not openly asked themselves the question: what is the best policy for the law to adopt? But the question has always been there in the background. It has been concealed behind such questions as: Was the defendant under any duty to the plaintiff? Was the relationship between them sufficiently proximate? Was the injury direct or indirect? Was it foreseeable or not? Was it too remote? And so forth. Nowadays we direct ourselves to considerations of policy.

But the guidelines of foreseeability, remoteness etc, must still serve a purpose. Policy is an unruly and unpredictable steed. It may tip the balance in many cases, but if it is the only criterion the law becomes fearfully uncertain, and depends only on the view of the particular tribunal. It is still necessary and appropriate for cases to be argued on the lines of the law as set out in the precedents, as far as the legal principles can be gleaned therefrom, and even if that is not very far it is better than nothing.

Where an injury is subsumed into a later injury (eg a broken leg is then severed in a later accident), the original tortfeasor remains liable for the damage he did, and cannot take advantage of the later event to reduce his liability (*Baker* v *Willoughby* [1970] AC 467, HL); but a supervening serious illness which was unconnected with the accident and which was already dormant within the claimant at the time of the accident will go to reduce the damages payable (*Jobling* v *Associated Dairies Ltd* [1982] AC 794, HL). If a car is already damaged so that a wing needs respraying, a defendant who crashes into that wing cannot be held liable for the cost of the respraying, only for any extra cost he puts the owner to (*Performance Cars Ltd* v *Abraham* [1962] 1 QB 33, CA).

This issue of supervening cause, like all aspects of causation, is a fruitful source of academic disputation, and for the practitioner admits of no easy formula. Lord Wilberforce said in *Jobling's* case (above) that no general, logical, or universally fair rules could be stated, which would cover, in a manner consistent with justice, cases of supervening events, whether due to tortious, partially tortious, non-culpable or wholly accidental events. The courts could only deal with each case as best they could to provide just but not excessive compensation.

In a case we looked at above, *Hogan* v *West Bentinck Hartley Collieries (Owners) Ltd* [1949] 1 All ER 588, where an injury at work to a workman's thumb was followed by an ill-advised amputation of the thumb, it was held by a bare majority in the House of Lords that that unreasonable operation broke the chain of causation (Lord Simonds said that the question of *novus actus* could only be answered on a consideration of all the circumstances and, in particular, the quality of the later act or event). In *Roberts* v *Bettany* (22 January 2001, unreported), CA, the court said it was a question of whether the intervening act was of so powerful a nature that the conduct of the defendants was not a cause at all but merely part of the surrounding circumstances.

In the Australian case of *Martin* v *Isbard* (1946) 48 WALR 52, where after being involved in an accident, the claimant contracted an anxiety and litigation neurosis because she was wrongly told by her doctor that she had suffered a fracture of the skull, it was held that the advice given by the doctor broke the chain of causation as it was a *novus actus.*

It was held in *Robinson* v *Post Office* [1974] 1 WLR 1176, CA, that where the Post Office had through their original negligence caused the minor leg injury of their employee, the claimant, the doctor's negligence in failing to administer a test dose before injecting with an anti-tetanus serum did not break the chain of causation. They had to take the claimant as they found him, which included his allergy to the anti-tetanus serum.

Where the act is that of the claimant himself, a number of other factors come into play. If that act is so unreasonable as to eclipse the defendant's wrongdoing, then it will have broken the chain of causation and the defendant will not be liable for the ensuing damage. An odd example of this is the South African case of *Alston* v *Marine and Trade Insurance Co Ltd* 1964 (4) SA 112, where the fact that the claimant, who had suffered brain injury in a motor accident, ate cheese while on a certain drug and as a result suffered a stroke, was held to break the chain of causation even though the claimant could not have known it was dangerous to do that.

An example of a case where the conduct of the claimant did not break the chain of causation is *Emeh* v *Kensington and Chelsea and Westminster Area Health Authority* [1985] QB 1012, where the Court of Appeal in no uncertain terms reversed the trial judge's finding that the refusal of an abortion by a woman who had become pregnant after a negligently performed sterilisation was so unreasonable an act that it eclipsed the original negligence.

There is considerable material on *novus actus* in *Reeves* v *Metropolitan Police Comr* [1998] QB 169, CA, revsd [2000] 1 AC 360, HL, where the police were found to be negligent in closing the flap on the door of a cell where they were holding a prisoner who was known to be a suicide risk (despite being sane). By a majority, the Court of Appeal held that the voluntary act of the deceased in committing suicide was not a *novus actus.* The House of Lords agreed, stating that a deliberate and informed act intended to exploit a situation created by a defendant did not negative causation where the defendant was in breach of a specific duty imposed by law to guard against that very act. Neither the defence of *novus actus* nor that of *volenti non fit iniuria* (meaning that the claimant took upon himself by his deliberate and conscious act the risk of harm) could succeed. But a defence of contributory negligence did succeed to the tune of 50% of the compensation otherwise due (see the section below on contributory negligence).[12]

---

12 In *Sabri-Tabrizi* v *Lothian Health Board* 1998 SC 373, Lord Nimmo-Smith held at first instance that a woman's decision to continue intercourse with the protection of a condom after she knew that her sterilisation had failed was a *novus actus,* so that the defendants were not liable for a pregnancy that occurred despite the condom. This seems unreasonable. In *Gill* v *Home Office* (6 July 2000, unreported), CA, there was held to be no *novus actus* where an inadequately detained prisoner with a history of violence assaulted a prison officer when allowed to go to slop out unaccompanied. The court said that the injury sustained was the very kind of injury that was foreseeable if he were let out.

We may here add to our treatment of the 'divisible injury' in this way: given that a fairly common scenario in the medical context where a defendant seeks to take advantage of a plea of *novus actus* is where both GP and hospital have been negligent, the former for not making earlier referral and the latter for not treating the injury or disease competently, it is clear that the GP should not be heard to say that he can escape liability because the hospital should have cured the problem. That is tantamount to resurrecting the ancient doctrine of 'last opportunity' (under which only the person who had the last opportunity to avoid the accident was liable). The correct answer is that they are both tortfeasors and both responsible, in such proportion as the court directs, for the relevant compensation. A more subtle argument on the part of the GP would be to contend that it would have made no difference if he had referred earlier because the patient would have received the same incompetent and ineffective treatment from the hospital. One answer to that contention would be to satisfy the court that the patient would probably have received competent treatment (ie competent and curative treatment). Even if the GP proved that, although the patient could have been cured by competent treatment, the hospital would on earlier referral probably still have provided incompetent treatment, one would hope that the court would nevertheless find that both GP and hospital played a material part in causing the injury for which compensation is claimed, rather than finding that in the circumstances the GP's negligence was not causative of injury.

In the common dual liability situation for a patient's claim, where the original accident, whether road traffic, or employment or whatever, is mistreated at hospital, it appears from the material we have considered above under 'Divisible injury' that a court would not simply hold that the medical negligence broke the chain of causation. More likely, it would apportion the damages as between the two defendants in such proportion as it considered was merited by their respective fault.[13]

In *Webb* v *Barclays Bank plc and Portsmouth Hospitals NHS Trust* [2001] MLC 0400, [2002] PIQR P61 the claimant fell and injured herself through the negligence of the first defendant, an injury which led to amputation through the negligence of the second defendant. The Court of Appeal said that, on the point of contribution as between the defendants, the question was whether, when an employee was injured in the service and by the negligence of her employer, his liability to her is terminated by the intervening negligence of a doctor brought in to treat the original injury, but who in fact made it worse. The answer was that the chain of causation in such a case would only be broken where the medical treatment was of such a degree of negligence as to be an entirely inappropriate response to the injury. Such was not the instant case. Perhaps then it can be said that only gross clinical negligence will break the chain of causation from the original negligent event. Responsibility was assessed at 25% for the first and 75% for the second

---

13 The widow of the actor and comedian, Roy Kinnear, obtained £650,000 from the film company that was responsible for the fatal injury he sustained when he fell from a horse while filming in Spain. Some time later, Hidden J ordered the Spanish hospital to pay 60% of the damages for failing to treat the injury properly (1994) Times, 22 December.

defendant. In *Panther* v *Wharton* [2001] MLC 0358, the deputy High Court judge came to a similar conclusion where the chain was from GP to hospital ('Dr Wharton's negligence [at the hospital] was not a *novus actus interveniens*: it did not cause the need for the amputations, he failed to act so as to prevent them. That omission did not constitute an event of such impact that it obliterated the wrongdoing of Dr Adegoko [the GP]').

In *Spencer* v *Wincanton Holdings* [2009] EWCA 1404, a claimant who had suffered a road accident leading to amputation of his leg who then tripped and suffered further injury some three years later was held by the Court of Appeal not to have broken the chain of causation from the original accident by his own act. The finding of 33% contributory negligence was not appealed.

Duty to mitigate

Another principle that falls to be considered in this context is the rule that a claimant is under a duty to take reasonable steps to minimise his loss; if those steps include submitting to medical examination and accepting medical treatment, then failure so to do will go to reduce the award (*Selvanayagam* v *University of West Indies* [1983] 1 WLR 585, PC). In *Geest plc* v *Lansiquot* [2002] Lloyds Rep Med 482, the Privy Council said that if a defendant intends to contend that a claimant has failed to act reasonably to mitigate his loss, notice of such contention should be clearly given long enough before the hearing to enable the claimant properly to prepare to meet it, and the onus of proving unreasonable refusal of medical treatment is on the defendant.

CONTRIBUTORY NEGLIGENCE

Where some blameworthiness attaches to the claimant's conduct, in that he has shown a failure to take proper care for his own safety, the matter can be dealt with by a proportionate reduction in the award on the principle of contributory negligence. That is not very likely to arise in medical negligence cases, but an example is *Brushett* v *Cowan* [1991] 2 Med LR 271, where the Newfoundland Court of Appeal held that the claimant, who was a registered nursing assistant with some experience in orthopaedics, was 50% to blame for her injury when she fell while using crutches and broke her leg, because she had failed to seek instructions regarding the proper use of the crutches. Or a patient may be held negligent for failing to report to his GP when the hospital had advised him to do so or for failing to attend review appointments. In the end, it is simply a matter of common sense whether the patient has been irresponsible in regard to his own health and safety.

We noted above a case where the House of Lords found contributory negligence by virtue of a deliberate act of self-harm by a rational prisoner in police custody (*Reeves* v *Metropolitan Police Comr*).

In *Fraser* v *Winchester Health Authority* (1999) 55 BMLR 122, CA, a young support worker who was injured in an explosion when she changed a gas cooker cylinder in a tent lit by candle was held to have been one-third contributorily negligent for her own safety (the defendants had given no instructions on the manoeuvre, but the claimant agreed that she should have known better).

In *Jebson* v *Ministry of Defence* [2000] PIQR P201, the Court of Appeal, reversing the judge, found that where an intoxicated off-duty soldier, travelling with his mates in the back of an inadequately supervised army lorry, had injured himself by foolishly attempting to climb on to the canvas roof of the vehicle from the tailgate, the way in the which the injury had been caused fell within the area of foreseeability for which the failure of the defendants to provide proper supervision was referable. The court then upheld the judge's finding of 75% contributory negligence.

In *Marshall* v *Lincolnshire Roadcar Co* (7 December 2000, unreported), CA, a woman aged 20 was injured when she stepped off a bus before it had completely stopped at the bus stop. The driver was at fault in opening the doors early, but, strangely, the court upheld, only by a majority, the judges finding that this was not a case of contributory negligence because the claimant was 100% to blame for her accident. For good measure, the majority added that her action was also a *novus actus*.

In *Pidgeon* v *Doncaster Health Authority* [2002] Lloyds Rep Med 130, the County Court judge at Sheffield held that the health authority was liable for the negligent evaluation of a cervical smear test which failed to reveal a pre-cancerous condition, but the claimant was two-thirds responsible (contributorily negligent) for the development of cervical cancer as she had failed to attend screenings in the following nine years. The case of *Sabri-Tabrizi* (see footnote 13) was distinguished as the claimant's failure in *Pidgeon* was not so utterly unreasonable as to break the chain of causation entirely.

Where a claim is pursued for professional negligence for loss of the chance of suing, any contributory negligence likely to have been found at the original trial must be factored in when assessing the percentage of total damages to be awarded (*Sharpe* v *Addison* [2003] EWCA Civ 1189, CA). See the following section for further explanation.

In *Badger* v *Ministry of Defence* [2006] 3 All ER 173, Mr Justice Stanley Burton reduced the claimant's damages for lung cancer by 20% because he had continued to smoke despite warnings since 1971 on cigarette packets. Whether such reductions could be applied for similar conduct in clinical negligence cases is perhaps open to doubt particularly if the purpose of treatment is to cure cancer and that treatment has been negligently delayed for example.

In *St George* v *Home Office* [2008] EWCA Civ 1068, the trial judge awarded a 15% reduction to the damages of a claimant whose drink and drug addiction had contributed to his fall from a prison bunk bed. However, the Court of Appeal reversed this and held that although he was at fault for becoming addicted to drugs and alcohol as a teenager, adopting a common sense approach it was not a potent cause of the injury suffered. In any event, it would not be just and equitable to reduce the claimant's damages given that he had presented himself as a person suffering from addiction.

In *Horsley* v *Cascade Insulation Services Ltd* [2009] EWHC 2945, a mesothelioma case with a lifetime smoker claimant, it was held by Eady J that the question of smoking reduced the overall damages by 20% for contributory negligence.

LOSS OF A CHANCE

This section considers what a patient has to prove where the admitted breach of duty involves a failure to treat. This limited aspect of causation deserves special consideration because the complaint arises time and again: 'I was denied the proper treatment for my condition. They admit negligence. I might have been cured.' (Or, in the appropriate case, 'My wife/husband/child might have lived'.)

What is the problem?

The problem is that, according to traditional jurisprudence, one has to prove that, on the balance of probabilities – ie more likely than not or at least a 51% chance, the outcome would have been better. Why should it not be enough, it is often asked (especially by the patient or his family), given that proper treatment was neglected, to show a chance (let us say, a more than minimal chance) that the treatment would have been successful, and so to award a proportion of total damages dependent upon the percentage chance of the treatment being successful?

What is the modern origin of the rule that the likelihood of a successful outcome must be shown to have been more than evens? For that we turn to the seminal case of *Hotson* v *Fitzgerald* [1987] AC 750, CA, MLC 0012, HL.

Hotson v Fitzgerald

The facts can be simply stated. The defendants' doctor failed to treat the young claimant at the proper time and so he developed a permanent disability of the hip. The evidence established that, even if he had been properly treated, he would still probably (a 75% chance) have contracted the disability. The defendant said that therefore the claimant had not proved on the balance of probabilities that he had suffered an injury. The claimant argued that he had been deprived of the chance of recovery and should therefore receive one-quarter of full compensation for his injury. The defendants' argument was in accord with traditional jurisprudence, but both at first instance and in the Court of Appeal the claimant's contention was accepted. The Master of the Rolls said:

> ... it is unjust that there should be no liability for failure to treat a patient, simply because the chances of a successful cure by that treatment were less than 50%. Nor by the same token can it be just that if the chances of a successful cure only marginally exceed 50%, the doctor or his employer should be liable to the same extent as if the treatment could be guaranteed to cure. If this is the law, it is high time that it was changed, assuming that this court has power to do so ... the essence of the plaintiff's claim is that he has lost any benefit which he would have derived from timely treatment.

The court said that this benefit sounded in damages, subject to proper evaluation. The categories of loss were never closed, and it was not only financial or physical injury that were fit subjects for compensation.

In the House of Lords

But the House of Lords unanimously decided that the finding by the trial judge that there had been only a 25% chance that any treatment would have been beneficial, ie would have prevented the necrosis, was equivalent to a finding that the claimant had not proved on the balance of probabilities that the admitted negligence had caused the necrosis, and so the claim could not succeed. The correct approach was to decide first as a matter of fact and in the usual way what was the condition of the claimant when he arrived at the hospital. In this particular case, the question could be framed as: 'Had the blood vessels running along the claimant's leg been injured to such an extent that necrosis was in any event inevitable?' The court said that the finding of only a one in four chance of benefit meant that the claimant would not have benefited from treatment, ie they applied the traditional rule that a court can only conclude that something would have happened if it is more likely than not that it would have happened.

Lord Bridge said that unless the claimant proved on the balance of probabilities that the delayed treatment was at least a material contributory cause of the avascular necrosis, he failed on the issue of causation and no question of quantification could arise.

Lord Ackner said that to follow the principle of proportionate deduction for the chance of benefit was 'a wholly new doctrine which has no support in principle or authority and would give rise to many complications in the search for mathematical or statistical exactitude'.

In this way the House of Lords affirmed the traditional jurisprudence.

Let us assume that we can prove that treatment should have been given at a certain (earlier) time. As we have seen, we are constrained by the *Hotson* decision to prove that, more likely than not, treatment would have produced a substantially better outcome (we use the word 'substantially' in order to give the claim sufficient financial expectations to justify proceedings).

Do not confuse

We should not confuse the question of showing a percentage chance of there having been a better outcome with the question of by what percentage an assuredly better outcome would have been better. If one can show that the outcome would probably have been better, it does not matter that the degree of betterment can only be expressed as a percentage and that that percentage may itself be less than 50%. In many cases involving a failure to give timely treatment for cancer, the most the experts can do is suggest statistics for survival, ie as it would have been and as it now is, given the delay in diagnosis and treatment. Provided one can achieve some clarity on the degree of worsened outcome, given that the experts are satisfied that on the balance of probability the prognosis would have been better, the case on causation is proved, and all one has to do (although this may not be easy) is to evaluate for the purposes of quantum the difference between the two prognoses.

In *Judge* v *Huntingdon Health Authority* [1995] 6 Med LR 223, a breast cancer case, Titheridge QC, sitting as a High Court judge, found that on the balance of probability breast nodes had not been involved in the cancer at the time when diagnosis and treatment should have taken place, and that therefore there had been, on the statistics, an 80% chance of a cure at that time. However, he went on, wrongly in my view, to indicate that the claimant was entitled to 80% of full damages. An 80% probability of survival should have been taken as proof of survival and therefore full damages awarded.

This section needs to be read now in the light of the House of Lords decision in *Gregg* v *Scott* [2005] MLC 1202.

Gregg v *Scott* and the loss of a prognosis

Introduction

The basic facts of this case are capable of fairly short summary, though also capable of well nigh endless legal argument. The judges of the House of Lords took months to reflect and research and finalise their views. Even then, the result in this extremely important case comes to us only by a bare majority.

Diagnosis of cancer (lymphoma in the left axilla) was delayed by GP negligence for nine months. In that time, it made further progress (invading the pectoral muscles) causing the patient additional pain and suffering, requiring more intensive treatment, and possibly affecting the prognosis.

Two things need to be made clear at this point. The first is that the original claim was based on the assertion that the patient would probably have survived (ie survived ten years, which is taken by the medical profession, and accepted by the lawyers, to equate with a cure) but now, as a result of the negligent delay, would not. This had to be changed as it was discovered shortly before trial that his cancer was particularly malignant so that, instead of the hitherto claimed probability of survival he had in fact had from the outset, even if treated timeously, a less than even chance of survival. Undeterred, his advisers amended his claim to what was in effect loss of a chance, or – more precisely – injury by way of a diminished chance of survival. Note that each time the case was tried the outlook for the patient, by reason of his survival up to the respective time, had grown better, so that by the time the matter came before the Lords one had to wonder if he would have done any better anyway!

The second point, commented upon by their Lordships, is that, although there was clearly a (relatively small) claim for the additional physical suffering caused by the spread of the cancer during the period of delay, that was not a head of claim being pursued by the claimant. He put all his eggs in the basket of loss of prognosis, ie reduced chance of survival.

One further preliminary note: the whole case was done on statistics, by way of evidence from medical experts. By the time of the trial at first instance, the original statistic (above 50%) for likely cure if treated timeously had fallen to 42%, whereas the actual prospect of cure, given the delay in diagnosis, was only 25%. Bear in mind again that it does not necessarily follow that the chances of survival would have suffered that reduction if there had been no delay. *Post hoc* is not the same as *propter hoc*.[14]

Approaches

If one accepts this statistical basis for judging a claim (artificial in so many ways), there are two possible approaches. The first is the traditional

---

14 Let the dumbers-down put that into a neat English translation, if they can!

one: to succeed the claimant need prove that he would have been cured but now will not be, issues which are to be decided on the balance of probabilities. The 45% statistic means that probably he would not have survived ten years (would not have been cured) anyway; so he has suffered no injury. This was the basis of the *Hotson* decision in the Lords. However, as we have seen, that decision, that the child's leg would not have been 'cured' in any event, was based on a finding of fact by the trial judge that so many blood vessels had been lost by the time he came to hospital that the failure to treat him properly at the hospital caused no loss as the leg was doomed in any event. The statistics offered a 25% chance of survival for the leg if properly treated, but the judge did not base his finding that the leg would have been lost on that (at any rate not on that alone). He had this physical fact on which to base his finding, ie the physical fact that the condition of the leg, which was vitally relevant to its prospect of survival, was such that there could be no prospect of survival. In the case of *Gregg* the evidence of statistical chance was paramount, making it more purely a claim for loss of a chance. There was no evidence to allow the sort of physical finding that was possible in *Hotson*. The only relevant evidence was what the experts gave by way of statistics culled from this or that series in the literature. Very unsatisfactory, but *faute de mieux*!

On the traditional approach (and ignoring the unreliability of statistics when applied to a specific case) the only response could be that the claimant had lost nothing as he would not on the balance of probability have been cured in any event.

The second approach would be to admit in circumstances of this sort an exception to the traditional legal test, as was done twice in recent years: in the *Fairchild* case (see the section so titled earlier in this chapter) and in *Chester* v *Afshar* [2005] 1 AC 134, MLC 1170. Two of the judges supported this approach, but three were not prepared to modify the traditional approach. (The trial judge had dismissed the claim; so had the Court of Appeal but only by a majority.)

So the House, which had showed such imagination in carving out new paths to yield the just result in *Fairchild* and in *Chester* v *Afshar*, baulked at the final fence in this third recent test of their judicial creativity.

Lord Nicholls

Lord Nicholls, for allowing the claimant's appeal, said that a remedy for a claimant in this situation was essential. The loss of a 45% prospect of recovery was just as much a real loss for the patient as the loss of a 55% prospect of recovery. In both cases, the patient was worse off. He lost something of importance and value. I would interpose here to say that formulation seems to me to beg the question whether a diminished prospect is in fact an 'injury'. This gets perilously close to the clearly inadmissible claim of persons who, living in the neighbourhood of a factory when a noxious emission negligently occurs, claim for their reduced prospects of survival, at a time when there is no reason to believe they have suffered anything at all apart from now being at risk where they were not at risk before.

So the question is not whether a chance has been lost – clearly it has – but whether such a 'loss' is cognisable by the law as a claimable head of damages. In some circumstances, of course, loss of a chance is recognised as a claimable loss. Loss of a chance to try for a job or role or whatever, loss of a chance of bringing a successful claim, loss of a chance where the loss would hinge on what a third party might have done; but note that these claims are all for loss of a chance involving financial loss, not physical injury. As already remarked, the law has for years recognised a consequential or parasitic loss of chance of physical integrity, as when something is added to general damages for the chance of osteo-arthritis or epilepsy developing. But none of these scenarios are much similar to an isolated (stand alone) medical claim for loss of a chance of surviving (wholly or in relation to a part of the body). Nevertheless, Lord Nicholls said that, where there is substantial uncertainty about whether the desired outcome would have been achieved (and there surely is uncertainty, I would add, where the whole question turns on what statistic the experts manage to derive from a study of what reports are available about what may have happened to a limited number of other patients whose situation may have been in some respects similar to that of the claimant), the law would do better to define the claimant's actionable damage more narrowly by reference to the opportunity the claimant lost. The judge said that medical science would often be uncertain what the outcome would have been, and so loss of a chance of favourable outcome should be the basis for damages. The doctor's duty, here breached, was to promote the patient's prospects of recovery (not to reduce them, I would add). He went on to point to the inherently limited usefulness of statistics (about other patients) when used to predict what would have happened to a particular patient. But 'in the present context use of statistics for the purpose of evaluating a lost chance makes good sense'. Lord Nicholls also emphasised the difference between a *Hotson* case, where a finding of fact about the physical condition of the patient at the time of the negligence determined in itself a certain enough conclusion about the likely outcome, and a *Gregg* case where there was no such prior finding of fact possible. It is interesting to note that as long ago as 1987 (in *Hotson*) Lord Bridge had recognised the distinction between these two sorts of cases.

Lord Nicholls argued strongly for the recognition of a lost chance as a head of damage in cases where medical opinion could only assess the patient's original prospects of recovery on a statistical basis ('fraught with a significant degree of medical uncertainty').

Clearly there is much force in this argument. A law which permits recovery when the chance of survival has gone from 60% to 45% but not when it has gone from 45% to virtually nil does not command respect. The problem, of course, lies in the introduction into these cases of statistics. That is what gives the whole argument of the majority such an unrealistic flavour. Once you say that the statistics show that this particular patient had only a less than 50% chance of recovery, the case is lost, as the traditional approach moves to dominate the debate. But if you allow that the statistics cannot reasonably be used in that way and that they only show various possibilities, it becomes easier to accept that the traditional approach should not be followed.

Lord Hope

Lord Hope agreed that the claimant's appeal should be allowed. He was not the only judge to comment in some surprise on the fact that the claimant was not pursuing any injury claim except the loss of a chance of recovery. But he used the fact of the unclaimed physical injury to support his view that the significant reduction in the prospects of recovery which the claimant had suffered could and should be claimable in damages. He said that the physical injury, in addition to pain and suffering, caused a reduction in the prospects of a successful outcome and this loss of prospects was consequential on the physical injury and so was a proper subject for damages. Not quite the way Lord Nicholls put it, but yielding the same overall conclusion.

Clearly, the question of recognising loss of prospects as a stand-alone claim is one of policy. In *Fairchild* and in *Chester* v *Afshar*, the House was prepared on policy grounds to declare for the patient. Here they were not.

The majority

Lord Phillips

Lord Phillips, in a detailed study, argued that the statistics had been misinterpreted by all except him. He said the position had been complicated by the better than expected progress of the patient during the long course of the litigation. Nor was he convinced that the progress of the cancer during the nine months' delay was due to the negligence of the defendant doctor. He said, surely rightly, that the expert's model was a very inadequate tool for assessing the effect of delay in treatment on the claimant's progress and that his subsequent clinical progress was of critical significance in re-assessing the issue. He said that the closer the claimant became with the passage of time to being a survivor (ie surviving ten years) the smaller the likelihood that the delay in commencing his treatment had had any effect on his expectation of life. Analysis of statistics was very difficult in medical cases. That was a reason for adopting the easier and more robust method of traditional valuation. (But that was being based on 'unreliable' statistics too!). Lord Phillips said he was well aware of the need for justice but he was not persuaded that justice demanded that this sort of statistical loss should sound in damages. As he had already explained, the difficulties in evaluating such a case on the chance basis rather than the traditional probability basis ('the complications of this case') had persuaded him that the traditional basis should not be abandoned for any sort of special rule. 'Awarding damages for the reduction in the prospect of a cure where the result of treatment is still uncertain is not a satisfactory exercise.'

Lord Hoffman

Lord Hoffman did not see any clear way in which a new rule for cases of this sort could be formulated. He did not favour the 'consequential' hook proposed by Lord Hope. He said that the various control mechanisms proposed to confine liability for loss of a chance within artificial limits were not attractive. A wholesale adoption of possible rather than probable causation as the criterion of liability would be so radical a change in our law as to amount to a legislative act, which would have enormous consequences for insurance companies and the NHS.

Baroness Hale

Baroness Hale said that she was for a long time attracted by the principal argument submitted for the claimant, namely that the loss of prognosis was simply consequential on the physical damage, ie the spread of the cancer during the period of delay. But, she said, on a proper interpretation of what the trial judge had written, he did not find that the delay caused the spread. She agreed that the instant case was not covered by *Hotson* as the outcome in *Hotson* was determined inevitably by the poor condition of the leg on arrival at hospital, whereas the outcome for the cancer could not be so determined but remained uncertain, capable of expression only on a statistical basis. It was, as accepted by the claimant, a question of policy whether the traditional approach should be modified in cases of this sort by allowing a claim for loss of or reduction in the chance of a successful outcome. There were attractions in allowing an award of damages for loss of such a chance where physiological changes were provable, but such an approach would be difficult to apply, particularly in showing that the delay had caused the loss of chance.

I think that we have to see the strongest objections of Baroness Hale in the following passages. She was particularly affected by the prospect that any claim for personal injury could be drafted as a claim for loss of chance of a better outcome, and she did not see how the two bases for a claim – loss of chance and balance of probability – could co-exist. It would not make sense if the claimant could at more than 50% go for probability and so get 100% damages and at 49% go for loss of a chance and so get substantial damages. Defendants would lose out either way. But if loss of a chance was adopted and probability had to be dropped, claimants who would now get 100% damages would in future be limited to a proportion unless they showed 100% probability (ie certainty). Expert evidence and trials would be far more complex and costly, and recovery far less predictable. Further, there would be no reason to limit the change in the basis of recovery to medical claims.

Baroness Hale summarised her view by saying that 'the complexities of attempting to introduce liability for the loss of a chance of a more favourable outcome in personal injury claims have driven me, not without regret, to conclude that it should not be done'.

Comment

I can see no reason why loss of chance, in appropriate cases, should not go to swell general damages where it is shown that it arises from physiological changes which are due to the negligence. In other words it is a consequential loss, consequential on negligence causing physical injury. The courts, as we well know, have no problem in saying in effect to a claimant: 'You have suffered a physical injury which has meant (*inter alia*) that you are now at a 15% risk of developing epilepsy whereas before the negligence the risk was minute or non-existent. Your chance of remaining free of epilepsy has therefore been reduced from close to 100% to 85%. You may never contract epilepsy but there is that risk now due to the negligence. We will take that factor into account when assessing general damages.' Why then should a court not say in the appropriate case: 'It is proved that if your cancer had been treated timeously you would have had a 45% chance of no relapse and so of keeping your breast/womb (or whatever). It is also proved that the negligent delay has impaired that prospect, to the extent that now there is virtually no chance (or only a 20% chance). The risk of your suffering that injury has been appreciably increased, [just as the risk of possible epilepsy is increased in the earlier example]. We will take that factor into account in assessing general damages.'

The court might find it hard to assess quantum, particularly in cases where potential loss of working years is involved, but plenty of quantum assessments are difficult without causing the court to throw up its hands in despair (or the towel in). I cannot see anything in the *Gregg* speeches which could outlaw that approach, which is consistent with the traditional law. Indeed Baroness Hale, given proper causation, would seem to accept it.

Further examples

Many further examples could be given of a patient failing on causation because he could not prove on the balance of probabilities that proper treatment would have resulted, in one way or another, in a better outcome. In *Gregory* v *Pembrokeshire Health Authority* [1989] 1 Med LR 81, the judge said there was no question of assessing the chances that the claimant, had she been properly advised, would have proceeded via a second amniocentesis to an abortion – he had simply to decide on the evidence whether on the balance of probabilities she would or would not.

In *Hardaker* v *Newcastle Health Authority* MLC 0395, [2001] Lloyds Rep Med 512, Burnton J held that the claimant failed on causation as the expert evidence as to whether immediate decompression would have produced a better outcome for the claimant diver proved only an unquantified chance of a better but unidentified outcome. Therefore the claimant had failed to prove he had suffered any damage, as a chance of a better recovery below 50% did not sound in damages. It is interesting to note that Burnton J (rightly) viewed the observations of Andrew Smith J in *Smith* v *NHS Litigation Authority* [2001] Lloyds Rep Med 90, as made *per incuriam*. Andrew Smith J had said that, even if the congenital displacement of the hip, which was the subject of the action he was trying, would probably not have been discovered by a competent examination, the claimant would have been able to claim percentage damages.

However, the situation is different in Australia. The Court of Appeal of Victoria allowed damages for loss of a chance of a better outcome on earlier diagnosis in the case of *Gavalas* v *Singh* [2001] MLC 0388, saying that the precise boundaries of such a claim awaited future determination. A similar view had been taken the year before by the New South Wales Court of Appeal in *Rufo* v *Hoskin* [2004] MLC 1119, where the court said the judge did not err in not being satisfied, on the balance of probabilities, that the breaches of duty by the respondent, which he found to have occurred, caused the fractures suffered by the appellant and it was open to the judge not to be satisfied that:

(a) but for the negligence, the injury (by way of fractures) would not have occurred;

(b) that the negligence materially contributed to the occurrence of the fractures; or

(c) that the fractures were the realisation of a risk created by the negligence.

However, the evidence strongly supported a conclusion that the negligence materially increased a risk, which was otherwise very substantial, that fractures would occur; and that the occurrence of the fractures was a realisation of that total risk – as distinct from the increment to the risk created by the negligence. The appellant was entitled to be compensated for the loss of the chance that, but for the negligence, the fractures would not have occurred (or would not have occurred at the time or with the severity of their actual occurrence). Accordingly, it was an error for the judge to hold that the increased risk was too speculative to justify an award of damages: so long as such an increase was material, the court was required to do its best to assess it. Well!

Where chance is assessed

However, there are many situations where the courts assess the chance of an event and award proportionate damages. On one occasion proportionate damages were awarded in a medical case (though in reverse, as it were, and so to the patient's disadvantage). In *Clark* v *MacLennan* [1983] 1 All ER 416, Pain J found that the defendants were in breach of their duty in performing a certain operation prematurely and that if it had been performed at the right time the patient would have stood a two in three chance of avoiding the injury. But instead of saying that she had proved on the balance of probabilities that her injury was caused by the breach of duty, he awarded her two-thirds of full damages. However, this acceptance of the 'chance' approach in a personal injury action is very much a one-off phenomenon.

One further medical case that appears on the face of it to be an illustration of the percentage approach is *Bagley* v *North Herts Health Authority* [1986] NLJ Rep 1014, where Simon Brown J, true to his reasoning in the Court of Appeal in the *Hotson* case, having found that a hospital had been negligent in not carrying out blood tests on a mother, as a result of which she gave birth to a stillborn child, knocked 5% off the damages awarded because, even had the hospital acted properly, there would still have been a 5% chance that the child would not have lived. However, it is understood that the parties had already agreed a 5% discount, so that the judge was merely implementing their agreement rather than endorsing of his own accord a percentage approach.[15]

Scenarios involving 'chance'

The question arises whether there is any reasonable distinction between the scenarios where the 'chance' approach has been accepted and the medical negligence context. Claims, in contract or in tort, for being prevented from auditioning for a role have long involved compensation for the loss of the ability to compete and so, expressly or implicitly, of the chance of competing successfully.

---

15   In *Ata-Amonoo* v *Grant* (26 January 2001, unreported), CA, the court said that in assessing damages for loss of a chance it was legitimate for the judge to deal with the sums involved in general terms and not to specify the actual percentage discounts.

The most obvious 'chance' scenario for our purposes is where a solicitor is sued for not having properly processed a claim. It is clear law that in such a context the court will award damages in proportion to the chance of success of the original action (the right to sue is regarded, quaintly, as a chose in action and it is that asset which falls to be valued). The seminal case is *Kitchen* v *Royal Air Forces Association* [1958] 1 WLR 563, CA; and a medical example is *Gascoigne* v *Ian Sheridan & Co and Latham* [1994] 5 Med LR 437, where 60% of the total damages relevant to the original medical claim was awarded.

In *Harrison* v *Bloom Camillin* [1999] 45 LS Gaz R 32, a claim against solicitors for failing to process an action against accountants for negligent advice, Neuberger J carefully assessed every aspect of the mooted claim against the accountants to arrive at an estimate of the chances of success and the likely damages. He ended with a deduction of 35% for the risk of losing on negligence and a further 20% for the risk of losing on causation.[16]

In *O'Shea* v *Weedon & Co* ML 8/98, p 8, Alliott J found that the original claim for a failed sterilisation that the defendant solicitor had failed to progress had not stood a 'real and substantial rather than merely a negligible prospect of success', and so the claim against the solicitor failed. In *Hatswell* v *Goldsbergs (a firm of solicitors)* [2001] EWCA Civ 2084, the Court of Appeal endorsed the judge's conclusion that the claimant's chances of success in his original medical negligence claim were nil. He would have been seeking to prove by his own recollection some 14 years after the event that he had made complaints to his GP which were completely inconsistent with the contemporaneous medical notes.

In *Sharpe* v *Addison* [2003] EWCA Civ 1189, the Court of Appeal, holding that the claim of a victim of a road traffic accident would not have been 'of no real value', said the test as to whether a claim was worthless was very similar to the test for striking out.

Another example is that a widow in a Fatal Accidents Act claim will be awarded compensation in proportion to the chances she had of financial support from the deceased.

It is also relevant that in a normal personal injury action a percentage chance (often as little as 10%) of some further injury arising in the future (eg osteo-arthritis developing in an injured joint) will be assessed and a suitable addition made to the award.

But, as mentioned above, the traditional jurisprudence is that a probability has to be shown. In *Sykes* v *Midland Bank Executor and Trustee Co Ltd* [1971] 1 QB 113, the Court of Appeal would not accept that clients who entered into an underlease after negligent advice from their solicitors could recover damages in proportion to the chance, as assessed by the court, that they would not have signed the underlease had they been properly advised. The court's task was to decide whether or not on the balance of probabilities the claimants had shown that they would not have signed if properly advised. Salmon LJ said that the argument for damages proportionate to the chance the claimants would have executed the underlease if properly advised would lead to the strange result that,

---

16   In *Hanif* v *Middleweeks* (19 July 2000, unreported), CA, the court said that a purely mathematical approach to assessing an overall loss of the chance to pursue proceedings was not appropriate.

unless the defendants could prove with certainty that they had not caused damage, they would be liable for the remote chance that they had done so. This is unconvincing, because the same argument could be applied to all the contexts where loss of a chance is accepted as the basis for compensation.

The insurance cases

In *Dunbar* v *A and B Painters Ltd* [1986] 2 Lloyd's Rep 38, the insured party sued his brokers, whose negligent misrepresentation to the insurers had voided the policy. On a quite different ground (because the employee had fallen from a height above the 40-foot maximum covered by the policy) the insurers would have been entitled to refuse to indemnify the insured in any event. The employee recovered against the employer (the insured party). The question was whether the negligent brokers should reimburse the employer in full. The brokers argued that if there was, say, a 30% chance that the insurers would have repudiated the policy in any event, they should be relieved of liability *pro tanto*. The employers said that the correct approach was to ascertain whether on the balance of probabilities the insurers would have repudiated the contract and, if the answer was in the negative, the brokers should reimburse them, the employers, in full. The Court of Appeal disagreed: the correct approach was not to ask if on the balance of probabilities the insurers would in fact have refused to indemnify on the 'height' ground, but to assess the chance that they would have refused and award proportionate damages. They said the judge had wrongly adopted the 'probability' test, but in the event it did not make any difference because he had in any case effectively assessed that chance at nil. Therefore, his decision to award full damages against the brokers, whether on a 'probability' basis or an 'assessment of chance' basis was appropriate. The court cited the similar earlier case of *Fraser* v *B N Furman (Productions) Ltd* [1967] 1 WLR 898, CA, though on a careful reading of that case it does not offer support for a 'chance' approach in this context. Further, it is not easy to reconcile the *Dunbar* decision with the *Sykes* case referred to above.

Further cases

In *Spring* v *Guardian Assurance plc* [1995] 2 AC 296, the House of Lords held that an employer who negligently gave a bad reference for the claimant, their ex-employee, might be liable to him in damages. Lord Lowry said that the claimant did not have to prove that the prospective employer would probably have employed him, merely that he had lost a reasonable chance of employment (which would have to be evaluated).

In *Allied Maples Group* v *Simmons & Simmons* [1995] 1 WLR 1602, the Court of Appeal held that, where the claimant purchasers had shown that the defendants, their solicitors, should have given them further information about the proposed sale which would *on the balance of probability* have caused them to seek to renegotiate the terms of the sale, they did not have to prove that they would probably have achieved a renegotiation; it was enough that they could *establish a more than minimal chance* of that (and it was that chance which fell to be assessed for damages). The basis for this distinction between proof on a balance of probability and proof of a chance appears from the judgments to depend upon whether the necessary inquiry concerns what the claimants themselves would have done or what an independent third party would have done. However, in that event it is not easy to see why the 'loss of a chance' approach should not apply in a *Bolitho* situation (*Bolitho* v *City and Hackney Health Authority* (above)). The chain of causation in that case depended on what the defendants' doctor would have done if she had responded to the nurse's nocturnal call to come to the ward. The fact that she happened to be an agent of the defendants is neither here nor there. It might have been, for example, a negligent failure to refer to a different hospital that constituted the proven allegation of negligence. Are we to conclude that in such a context the question what the doctors at that other hospital would have done should be resolved on a 'chance' basis, whereas in the fortuitous event of the hospitals being managed by the same health authority the question of causation should be resolved on a probability basis? That would be absurd.

The Court of Appeal followed the reasoning of the *Allied Maples* case in *First Interstate Bank of California* v *Cohen Arnold & Co* [1996] 5 Bank LR 150, CA.

In *Rosling King* v *Shaw* (7 December 1995, unreported), QBD, the defendant proved upon his counter-claim that the negligence of the claimants had deprived his Danish lawyer of the opportunity of levying execution against a debtor of the defendant while that debtor was still in funds. Nicholas Strauss QC assessed the chances of the Danish lawyer acting successfully in that way at 30%.

In *Stovold* v *Barlows* [1996] PNLR 91, CA, Stuart-Smith LJ (who seems to have been responsible for the genesis of this 'third party' rule in his judgment in the *Allied Maples* case) affirmed this approach to causation where the question was what an independent third party might have done. In that case the negligence of the defence solicitors was alleged to have cost the claimant vendor the completion of the sale of his home. The Court of Appeal said that the approach of the trial judge was wrong when he took the view that the claimant had to satisfy the court on the balance of probabilities that the prospective purchaser would have completed the sale. The proper approach was to evaluate the loss of the claimants' chance that, if the documents that should have arrived had arrived, the sale would have gone ahead. The court themselves assessed that chance at 50%, thus reducing the judge's award of total damages by half.

In *Doyle* v *Wallace* [1998] PIQR Q146, the Court of Appeal assessed the chance that the claimant would have become a teacher, not the probability, as it depended on what a third party might have done. The defendant had argued that the chances of the claimant becoming a teacher would have been less than 50% and therefore she could not recover any damages for loss of earnings as a teacher.[17]

There is an interesting gloss on the subject in an informative article on the Human Growth Hormone litigation by Mark Mildred at [1998] JPIL 262. The defendants argued that the question whether treatment would have been stopped if the clinicians had been given certain information fell to be evaluated on percentage terms. Morland J rejected that argument

---

17   See also *Anderson* v *Davis* [1993] PIQR Q87.

(judgment 22 May 1998), saying that once a claimant had proved on the balance of probabilities that treatment would have been stopped, he was entitled to succeed. A discount was appropriate only in relation to quantification of uncertain damages, for example the likelihood of promotion to a higher paid job or the like. However, it might be thought that, as the clinicians were not the defendants, the issue involved what a third party would have done, and therefore, if there is any principle at all flowing from the *Allied Maples* case, loss of a chance would apply in this context.[18]

In *Normans Bay Ltd* v *Coudert Brothers* [2003] EWCA Civ 215, a complex commercial case, solicitors were sued for negligent advice in relation to a bid for shares in a Russian company. Though the bid appeared to be successful, it was later declared invalid by the Moscow Arbitration Court. The claimant contended that proper advice would have meant that the bid would have been made in a form that would have been safe from invalidation. The court below and on appeal declared that the prospect that the bid would not have been invalidated must be assessed on chance, not probability. In the event the Court of Appeal reviewed the chance and reduced it from 70% to 40%.

The most recent case in this context of chance generally (not 'third party' chance) is *Gregg* v *Scott*, which has its own section above.

Conclusion

The short fact of the matter is that there is no logical explanation, at least as far as the 'third party' rule is concerned, for the distinction drawn by the courts between situations where damages are assessed on a percentage basis and those where damages are assessed on a probability basis. In the first place it cannot be of any intrinsic significance whether the chance of an action being taken had the situation been different relates to an action to be taken by the claimant, by a party to the action, or by a third party. Further, as indicated above, there will be situations where it is simply fortuitous whether or not the hypothetical action under investigation is an action that would have been taken by an agent of the defendants or of some other body, and therefore it makes little sense to have two different tests of causation depending on that meaningless distinction.

The solution?

Given the House of Lords decision in *Gregg* v *Scott,* loss of a chance of a better outcome is dead in the water for the normal medical claims, unless

---

18 In *Smith* v *National Health Service Litigation Authority* [2001] Lloyd's Rep Med 90, [2001] MLC 0286, Andrew Smith J rejected the claim that, as a baby in 1973, the claimant had not been properly examined for signs of congenital displacement of the hip, but added, *obiter,* that, had he found that she had not been properly examined, he would have assessed the *chance* that examination would have led to detection and successful treatment of the condition. However, it is not possible to understand his reasons for distinguishing the issue before him from the similar issue before the House of Lords in the *Hotson* case and for stating that the 'chance' principle of the *Allied Maples* case applied rather than the 'balance of probabilities' principle of the *Hotson* case.

it can be joined as parasitic or consequential damage to another head of claim, probably general damages, in which case there is still hope it might succeed. As to the 'third party' rule, that is unlikely to become any clearer, as it is a flimsy construct.

Chapter 8

Foreseeability and remoteness

Simon Dyer

Damages are recoverable only in respect of injury of a type that was foreseeable (though no definition of 'type' is available). But this must be read subject to the important rule that the wrongdoer must take the claimant as he finds him, so that the fact that the injury develops unexpected complications or, through hypersensitivity, more harm is suffered than was to be expected is no bar to recovery. Nor is the fact that the injury did not arise in the precisely foreseeable manner.

Strictly, injuries which are of an unforeseeable type and do not come within the rule that the wrongdoer must take the claimant as he finds him are not subjects for compensation (an example would be where a brick is thrown from a window and there is a foreseeable risk from it striking someone, but in fact it hits an electricity cable and in a manner not to be foreseen causes a person in the vicinity to be electrocuted – injury from impact would seem of a different kind from injury by electrocution). A judge would be entitled to hold the wrongdoer not liable for the injury suffered, but in practice he might well find a way to implement his 'gut reaction' to the situation and award compensation, eg by 'finding' that there was in fact some slight degree of foreseeability of electrocution.

TOO REMOTE

Even if the claimant has established a duty of care, a breach of that duty, and loss of a type recognised by the law and caused by the breach, the defendants will only be liable to compensate for that loss if it was reasonably foreseeable at the time of the breach that it could arise. In other words, the basic principle (though subject, as we shall see, to substantial exceptions) is that you cannot recover for an injury that was not foreseeable.

This is sometimes expressed as a statement that the loss must not be too remote. But that catch-all expression is also used to mean that no duty was owed to the particular claimant (the claimant was too remote, not being within the area of foreseeable risk created by the defendant's actions, and therefore so was the damage he suffered); or that no duty was owed to take care not to inflict the particular sort of harm suffered, or not to inflict it in that particular way; or that the chain of causation was broken; or that policy militates against recovery. Thus a mother who suffers nervous shock on being told of the death of her son and is denied damages on the basis that she does not come within the 'aftermath' principle (see Chapter 13) may be told that the damage she suffered was too remote. This may mean that no duty was owed to her by the tortfeasor, or that the intervening act of her informant broke the chain of causation, or that the law or policy forbids recovery in the particular circumstances.

To assist clarity of thought on this issue, it is better therefore to avoid the expression 'too remote' (it is in fact unhelpful in any context), and say simply that the loss must be reasonably foreseeable. As we have seen, foreseeability of harm, though a prerequisite for a duty of care, does not of itself prove the existence of a duty. It is a prerequisite for a duty of care because, if there is no reasonable foreseeability of harm arising from an act there can be no duty of care in relation to it. Here, however, we consider the essential requirement of foreseeability in the context of recoverability of loss. We assume therefore in the discussion that follows that duty and breach have been proved.

The basic principle is that a tortfeasor is liable only for the natural and probable consequences of his actions, those that he, as a reasonable man, could have foreseen as likely to occur, and which should therefore have caused him to hold his hand. Damage which occurs directly from the breach is not the subject of compensation, as a general rule, unless it was also foreseeable. This is the result of the Privy Council decision in *Overseas Tankship (UK) Ltd* v *Morts Dock and Engineering Co Ltd* (also known as *The Wagon Mound*) [1961] AC 388, which overruled the long-standing decision to the contrary of the Court of Appeal in *Re Polemis* [1921] 3 KB 560.

A fairly recent medical case provides a good example of the operation of the principles of remoteness and foreseeability. In *R* v *Croydon Health Authority* MLC 0019, [1998] Lloyd's Rep Med 44, CA, the claimant, a trained nurse, married and of child-bearing age, had to undergo a medical check with a view to taking employment with the defendants. The defendants' radiologist who interpreted her X-rays was admittedly negligent in not referring her for specialist opinion. It was admitted that, had that been done, the serious pathology of primary pulmonary hypertension would have been diagnosed, she would have been warned of the serious risk to her health if she were to become pregnant, and she would have chosen not to become pregnant, particularly as pregnancy might shorten her life and therefore leave her child without a mother. As it was, the negligence of the radiologist deprived her of that warning and therefore a few months later she became pregnant, giving birth in due course to a healthy child. It was understandable that she claimed compensation for, among other things, the trauma of the pregnancy and the cost of upkeep of her daughter. She succeeded at first instance ([1997] PIQR P444), but on appeal the court held that, as far as the radiologist was concerned, a decision to become pregnant fell outside the area of foreseeability. In other words, it was too remote. The court said that the radiologist never actually saw the claimant and knew very little about her except her age (this in itself is unconvincing, as the defendants would have had detailed knowledge of her and they should be taken in this context to stand in the shoes of their radiologist). Kennedy LJ said that the claimant's domestic life fell outside the scope of the radiologist's duty. The damage was too remote.

'The express obligations assumed by the radiologist did not, as it seems to me, extend to the plaintiff's private life'. Chadwick LJ said:

> ... a proper examination of the facts in the present case leads to the conclusion that, whatever duty of care was owed to the plaintiff by the health authority as a prospective employer, the scope and extent of that duty stopped short of responsibility for the consequences of the decision by the plaintiff and her husband that she should become pregnant. I think it essential to keep in mind that the relationship between the plaintiff and the health authority was that of prospective employee and employer. There was nothing in the evidence before the trial judge to suggest the relationship between the plaintiff and her prospective employer had anything to do with whatever plans the plaintiff and her husband may have had for starting a family.

Whatever semantic analysis one likes to construct, the reality of the matter is that the trial judge thought the employers should pay for the child because without their negligence the child would not have been born, whereas the Court of Appeal thought otherwise. However one dresses one's reasons up in the terminology of remoteness or foreseeability, this sort of decision turns on a question of policy, or, less elegantly, gut reaction.[1] (The issue of liability for the cost of upkeep of a child born in such circumstances is dealt with in Chapter 11.)

DEGREE OF FORESEEABILITY

It is not clear how foreseeable a consequence has to be, ie what chance of its happening is sufficient. In *The Wagon Mound (No 2)* [1967] 1 AC 617, the Privy Council's view was that once *some* foreseeability of fire was proved that was sufficient, however remote that possibility. It was said in the Australian case of *Commonwealth of Australia* v *Introvigne* (1982) 150 CLR 258, that 'a risk of injury is foreseeable so long as it is not far-fetched or fanciful, notwithstanding that it is more probable than not that it will not occur'. These propositions, however, are hardly consistent with what is generally understood to be the law, that the loss has to be reasonably foreseeable – unless we are being told that reasonable foreseeability of harm is appropriate for establishing a duty of care but any degree of foreseeability short of the far-fetched is enough in the context of compensation. We can well do without yet another subtle refinement in the law of negligence!

EXCEPTIONS

Policy

To the basic rule that the wrongdoer is liable for the natural and probable consequences of his wrongful act, and for no other consequences, there are

---

1   It is of interest to note the principle applicable in contract, that it is not enough for a claimant to show that 'but for' the breach something would not have happened; he must go further and show that the breach did not merely give the occasion for the further events (see eg *Galoo Ltd* v *Bright, Grahame, Murray* [1994] 1 WLR 1360, CA). In other words, he must satisfy the court of a sufficient connection between the breach and the later events for which compensation is claimed for the court to be satisfied that the defendants should pay.

a number of very substantial exceptions. In the first place, the law will draw a line at some point as a matter of policy to prevent over-extensive recovery.

> The law cannot take account of everything that follows a wrongful act; it regards some subsequent matters as outside the scope of its selection, because 'it were infinite for the law to judge the cause of causes' or consequence of consequences ... In the varied web of affairs the law must abstract some consequences as relevant, not perhaps on grounds of pure logic but simply for practical reasons (*per* Lord Wright in *Liesbosch, Dredger (Owners)* v *SS Edison (Owners)* [1933] AC 449 at 460, HL).

It is always difficult to predict and impossible to define the line where liability stops. It is left to the good sense of the judge in each particular case to decide where practical convenience and policy dictate that it be drawn.

> It is something like having to draw a line between night and day; there is a great duration of twilight when it is neither night nor day; but ... though you cannot draw the precise line, you can say on which side of the line the case is (*per* Blackburn J in *Hobbs* v *London and South Western Rly Co* (1875) LR 10 QB 111 at 121).

The legal basis for drawing the line is variously expressed:

> In order to limit liability ... the courts sometimes say either that the damage claimed was 'too remote' or that it was not 'caused' by the defendant's carelessness or that the defendant did not 'owe a duty of care' to the plaintiff (*per* Thesiger J in *SCM (UK)* v *Whittall* [1970] 1 WLR 1017 at 1031).

Or it may simply be said that justice or social convenience demands that a limit be placed upon the defendant's liability. For a good example of policy invalidating a claim where logic would allow it, see *McFarlane* v *Tayside Health Board* [2000] 2 AC 59, HL, which is treated in detail in Chapter 11.

'You must take the claimant as you find him': the 'egg shell skull' principle

The most comprehensive exception to the foreseeability principle that goes to extend a defendant's liability is the rule that a tortfeasor must take the claimant as he finds him, in relation both to his physical condition and to his financial circumstances. If you carelessly knock a man over in circumstances where you could reasonably expect a slight injury and a claim for average earnings lost over a relatively short period, you will nevertheless be liable for full damages if he turns out, through an inherently weak physical condition, to suffer far greater damage and for a longer period, and also to be a very high earner, perhaps with several extremely lucrative contracts lined up which he cannot now fulfil.

> One who is guilty of negligence to another must put up with idiosyncrasies of his victim that increase the likelihood or extent of damage to him; it is no answer to a claim for a fractured skull that its owner had an unusually fragile one (*per* Mackinnon LJ in *Owens* v *Liverpool Corpn* [1939] 1 KB 394 at 400–1, CA).

It is not only if the foreseeable injury proves more serious than could have been anticipated that the tortfeasor must pay, but also if a different type of injury arises out of the foreseeable injury. Thus, in *Robinson* v *Post Office* [1974] 1 WLR 1176, CA, where a claimant developed encephalitis as a result of an allergic reaction to an anti-tetanus injection, the defendants, whose negligence was responsible for the original slight injury that led to the need for an injection, were held liable to compensate him for the full extent of his injury.[2]

There have been very many cases where unforeseeable complications involving a different type of physical injury from that which could have been foreseen have been the subject of compensation. For example, in *Warren* v *Scruttons* [1962] 1 Lloyd's Rep 497, a defendant had to compensate for the unforeseeable aggravation of an existing eye condition that developed after the claimant had hurt his finger on a frayed rope. A cancer which unforeseeably developed from a foreseeable burn on the lip was held to be a proper subject for compensation in *Smith* v *Leech Brain* [1962] 2 QB 405. Where a woman had to wear a surgical collar as a result of a foreseeable physical injury she was able also to recover compensation for injury suffered when she fell down stairs due to the fact that she could not see so well with the collar on (*Wieland* v *Cyril Lord Carpets Ltd* [1969] 3 All ER 1006). Eveleigh J said:

> ... in determining liability for ... possible consequences of personal injury, it is not necessary to show that each was within the foreseeable extent or foreseeable scope of the original injury in the same way that the possibility of injury must be foreseen when determining whether or not the defendant's conduct gives a claim in negligence.[3]

In the road traffic case of *Giblett* v *P & NE Murray Ltd* [1999] 22 LS Gaz R 34, CA, the court said that the claimant did not have to prove that her psychiatric injury in the form that it took or its sequelae were reasonably foreseeable by the defendants. Even in the context of nervous shock, or any other attributable psychiatric condition, the defendant had to take the primary victim as he found him: it would avail the defendant nothing that the victim had a psychologically vulnerable 'egg shell' personality.

In *Simmons* v *British Steel* [2004] UKHL 20, the House of Lords held that a claimant who suffered a minor head injury at work was entitled to recover damages for the psychiatric harm partly caused by his anger at the treatment he had received by his employers following the accident. Since he had sustained physical injury which was foreseeable it was unnecessary for him to prove that his psychiatric injury was foreseeable. It was held that the defenders had to take their victim as they found him.

The House of Lords in *Ladger* v *O'Connor* [2004] 1 AC 1067 held that the previous rule preventing recovery of losses caused by a claimant's impecuniosity (see *Liesbosch Dredger* v *SS Edison* [1933] AC 449) was no longer good law. A defendant must now take his victim as he finds him physically, mentally and financially.

---

2 See also *Brice* v *Brown* [1984] 1 All ER 997 where the nervous shock sustained was particularly severe due to a basic mental instability. There is also relevant material in the judgments of the Court of Appeal in *Vernon* v *Bosley* [1997] 1 All ER 577.

3 Where a second injurious condition does *not* flow from the original injury, causation has to be established on the balance of the probabilities in respect of the second condition (see Lord Bridge's judgment in *Hotson* v *East Berkshire Area Health Authority* [1987] AC 750, HL).

'TYPE' OF INJURY SUFFERED

Of course, if no injury could be foreseen then the fact that an abnormally susceptible claimant suffered some injury does not give rise to a claim; there would probably be neither a duty nor a breach in those circumstances, but even if there were, there would be no liability where no injury could reasonably be foreseen from the acts in question. For an injury to be claimable, it must, if it does not accompany a foreseeable injury, at least be of the same type as the foreseeable injury (although, as we see below, it is quite unclear what is meant by 'type'). Thus, in *Bradford* v *Robinson Rentals Ltd* [1967] 1 WLR 337, a driver was negligently exposed to freezing conditions in an unheated vehicle as a result of which he developed the unforeseeable injury of frostbite. Rees J made it clear that recovery was permissible in respect of the frostbite as the foreseeable injury, ie common cold, pneumonia, chilblains, was of the same type as that which was in fact suffered. In *Ogwo* v *Taylor* [1988] AC 431, the House of Lords held that injury caused to a firefighter from the steam that arose when he sprayed water on to a fire was not different in kind from injury caused directly by the flames.

The apparent necessity for a connection between the type of damage that was foreseeable and the type of damage that was suffered arises from the decision of the Privy Council in *The Wagon Mound* (above). That case arose out of the careless spillage of oil on the waters of Sydney harbour. Damage to slipways by pollution was foreseeable, but the damage by fire that occurred was not. The Privy Council said that as the damage that occurred was of a different type from what was foreseeable (ie damage by fire and not damage by pollution), recovery was not permitted. Ironically, in *The Wagon Mound (No 2)* [1967] 1 AC 617, which concerned the same facts, a contrary decision was reached as to liability, but that was because the evidence given in that trial established, as we saw above, that there was a slight possibility to be foreseen of damage by fire.

What is completely unclear is what is meant by 'type' of damage in the context of physical injury. A claimant is assisted by the rules that the defendant must take him as he finds him, and that neither the extent of the damage has to be foreseeable nor the precise manner in which it arose, and it is hard to see what practical scope is left for a rule that restricts liability by providing that the injury suffered has to be of a type that was foreseeable. In *Thurogood* v *Van den Berghs and Jurgens* [1951] 2 KB 537, the Court of Appeal permitted recovery by an injured workman when he caught his fingers in a fan even though the foreseeable injury was by catching his necktie in it (a decision that seems good sense); but that was upon an application of the principle derived from *Re Polemis* [1921] 3 KB 560, CA, that all damage directly caused was claimable for, and that principle was rejected by the Privy Council in *The Wagon Mound* (above). In *Tremain* v *Pike* [1969] 1 WLR 1556, Payne J refused relief to a herdsman who contracted a rare disease from rats' urine because the only foreseeable consequence from exposure to rats was rat-bite or food-poisoning, which was said to be 'entirely different in kind'. This decision must surely have been wrong (see, to an apparently contrary intent, *H Parsons Livestock Ltd* v *Uttley Ingham & Co Ltd* [1978] QB 791, CA).

In *Woodhouse* v *Yorkshire Regional Authority* [1984] 1 The Lancet 1306, the claimant suffered foreseeable digital contracture deformity from a carelessly performed operation. The defendants were held liable also for a hysterical condition that developed because they had damaged a claimant with a hysterical personality and they had to take her as they found her. In *H* v *Royal Alexandra Hospital* [1990] 1 Med LR 297, the fact that a haemophiliac given AIDS-contaminated blood products was infected with a retro-virus and not with a virus (which alone was foreseeable when the negligent act took place) was of no assistance to the defendants as the damage was of the same kind as what was foreseeable.

In *Doe* v *USA* [1990] 2 Med LR 131, the US Rhode Island District Court held that it was foreseeable in 1983 that if a patient required through negligence an extensive blood transfusion he might contract AIDS from it.

In *Aswan Engineering Establishment Co* v *Lupdine Ltd* [1987] 1 WLR 1, the Court of Appeal held that, where material packed in pails was exposed for hours to the Arabian sun so that the pails collapsed, the manufacturers of the pails were not liable to the users because the damage suffered was of an unforeseeable type. However, it would seem better to say that the manufacturers had not been negligent in the way they manufactured and marketed the pails because no loss was reasonably foreseeable from their use. It does not seem an appropriate situation to bring in the rule as to type of damage, which only applies when there has been a breach of duty resulting in some loss.

In *Wood* v *Bentall Simplex Ltd* [1992] PIQR P332, a farmer was held not to have contributed to his own death by building a grid of a non-approved pattern across the entrance to his slurry tank because the consequence of death by asphyxiation after he entered the tank to clear a blockage resulting from the unorthodox construction was not foreseeable. All that was foreseeable was that a person entering the tank to cure the (foreseeable) blockage might slip and fall. The Court of Appeal said that the test of liability for injury by asphyxiation was foreseeability of injury by asphyxiation.

In *Page* v *Smith* [1996] AC 155, the House of Lords was principally concerned with the question of whether a claimant involved in a road traffic accident could recover damages for psychiatric injury where only physical injury was foreseeable. The Court of Appeal had held that possibility of psychiatric injury was essential and that in the instant case it had not been foreseeable. The House of Lords by a bare majority restored the decision of the trial judge. Lord Lloyd held that psychiatric injury in a road traffic accident was foreseeable. But he went further than that. He said that, whereas possibility of psychiatric injury was a crucial ingredient where the claimant was the secondary victim (for discussion of primary and secondary victims see Chapter 13), it would not be sensible in the case of a primary victim, in an age when medical knowledge is expanding fast and psychiatric knowledge with it, to commit the law to a distinction between physical and psychiatric injury which might already seem somewhat artificial, and might soon be altogether outmoded. 'Nothing will be gained by treating them as different "kinds" of personal injury, so as to require the application of different tests in law.' Lord Browne-Wilkinson held that in the instant circumstances psychiatric injury was foreseeable, and, further, expressly endorsed Lord Lloyd's remarks about the dangers of seeking to draw hard and fast lines between physical and psychiatric illness. He said that for the courts to impose different criteria for liability depending on whether the injury was physical or psychiatric was likely to lead to a growing complication in straightforward personal injury cases. The law would be more effective if it accepted that the results of being involved in a collision might include both physical and psychiatric damage. Lord Ackner was for allowing the appeal on the basis that psychiatric injury was foreseeable. He did not go further than that. On the other hand, Lord Jauncey, in a long and carefully reasoned judgment, concluded that for recovery for psychiatric injury foreseeability of psychiatric injury was essential, and he was not satisfied that in the circumstances of this accident there was such foreseeability. Lord Keith supported that view. It therefore appears that not only were the *dicta* to the effect that foreseeability of personal injury would suffice for a claim for 'mere' psychiatric injury arising out of a road traffic accident *obiter* but, further, such a view was endorsed by only two of the judges. Two were of a contrary view and one was silent on the issue.[4] Nevertheless it is now accepted law that this decision established the following principles (*per* the Court of Appeal in *Donachie* v *Chief Constable of the Greater Manchester Police* [2004] EWCA Civ 405):

- A defendant owes a duty of care to a person where he can reasonably foresee that his conduct will expose that person to a risk of personal injury.
- For this purpose, the test of reasonable foreseeability is the same whether the foreseeable injury is physical or psychiatric or both.
- However, its application to the facts differs according to whether the foreseeable injury is physical or psychiatric; in the latter case, if the claimant is not involved in some sort of 'event' caused by the negligence, he is a 'secondary' victim and liability is more difficult to establish.
- If the reasonably foreseeable injury is of a physical nature but such injury in fact causes psychiatric injury, it is immaterial whether the psychiatric injury was itself reasonably foreseeable. Equally if, as in the instant case, the breach of duty causes psychiatric injury causing in turn physical injury, it is immaterial that neither the psychiatric injury nor the particular form of the physical injury caused was reasonably foreseeable.[5]

In *Hepworth* v *Kerr* [1995] 6 Med LR 139, the judge was satisfied that, although the specific risk of anterior spinal artery syndrome from the deliberately induced anaesthetic hypotension was not one which could reasonably have been foreseen, it was enough that risk of major organ

---

4   We may note here that it was held in *Walker* v *Northumberland County Council* [1995] ICR 702, that psychiatric damage was foreseeable where employees were put under excessive strain by their workload. In *Schofield* v *Chief Constable of West Yorkshire* [1999] ICR 193, where a policewoman suffered psychiatric injury, but not physical, when a sergeant negligently discharged a firearm, the Court of Appeal said that the case was similar to *Page* v *Smith*: it was enough that there was a foreseeable risk of physical injury.
5   For an interesting slant on how the appeal judges are currently viewing the distinction, if any, between physical and mental injury, see the aviation case of *King* v *British Helicopters* [2002] 2 WLR 578, HL, and in the Court of Appeal *sub nomine Morris* v *KLM* [2001] 3 WLR 351, where the correct interpretation of 'bodily injury' in the Carriage by Air Act 1981 was under review.

under-perfusion was reasonably foreseeable and it mattered not that that source of danger acted in an unpredictable way. The mechanism and the source of danger were the same, and the defendant had run the unnecessary and foreseeable risk of causing injury to the claimant by under-perfusion of major organs of the body. What happened was 'but a variant of the foreseeable' and 'within the risk created by the negligence'.

THE 'PRECISE MANNER'

We have already adverted to the rule that it does not help a defendant to argue that, although the type of damage could be foreseen, the precise manner in which it arose could not. In *Hughes* v *Lord Advocate* [1963] AC 837, where a child picked up a lighted Post Office paraffin lamp and entered an unguarded manhole, damage by burning was foreseeable, so that although the manner in which that damage arose was not foreseeable (the child was burned not by the oversetting of the lamp but by an explosion), that did not prevent recovery. In *Stewart* v *West African Terminals* (1964) 108 Sol Jo 838, the Court of Appeal said that as long as a result is within the general sphere of contemplation, and not of an entirely different kind, the precise chain of events need not be foreseeable.

> It is not necessary that the precise concatenation of circumstances should be envisaged. If the consequence was one which was within the general range which any reasonable person might foresee (and was not of an entirely different kind which no-one would anticipate) then it is within the rule that a person who has been guilty of negligence, is liable for its consequences (*per* Lord Denning).

> ... the precise mechanics of the way in which the negligent act results in the original injury do not have to be foreseen (*per* Eveleigh J in *Wieland* v *Cyril Lord Carpets* [1969] 3 All ER 1006).

The question of the manner in which the damage arose overlaps with the question whether the damage was of a type that was foreseeable. The difficulties that can arise over these subtle distinctions when injury occurs in an unforeseen manner and one has then to ask whether it still remains within the type of injury foreseeable is illustrated by *Doughty* v *Turner Manufacturing Co Ltd* [1964] 1 QB 518, CA, where it appears that the fact that there was a foreseeable risk only of damage from splashing when a cover was carelessly let slip from a height of a few inches into molten liquid prevented recovery for injury caused when the liquid erupted due to an unforeseeable chemical reaction a few moments later. Such subtle distinctions were eschewed in *H Parsons Livestock Ltd* v *Uttley Ingham & Co Ltd* [1978] QB 791, where the Court of Appeal said that as long as some illness to the claimant's pigs was foreseeable as a result of the defendant's negligence, they were liable for the unforeseen illness that did in fact develop, the consequence being of the same type as that which was foreseeable (this was a claim in contract but the court said that the law as to the amount of damages recoverable was the same in contract as in tort).

In *Jolley* v *Sutton London Borough Council* [2000] 1 WLR 1082, the House of Lords reversed the wholly unreasonable conclusion of the Court of Appeal. A boat was left abandoned on land by the defendants. Children played with it. They propped it up; it fell off the prop; the claimant was injured. The defendants admitted they should not have left it there and that some injury was foreseeable from children playing on it and falling through rotten planking. The Court of Appeal decided that injury from the boat falling over after having being propped up was not foreseeable and was of a different type and kind from an injury caused by simply falling through rotten planking. The House of Lords, pointing out that the wider risk could have been eliminated without any more expense than that involved in eliminating the narrower risk (ie by removing the boat), restored the judgment of the trial judge in favour of the claimant.

In *Jebson* v *Ministry of Defence* [2000] PIQR 201, the Court of Appeal, reversing the judge, found that where an intoxicated off-duty soldier, travelling with his mates in the back of an inadequately supervised army lorry, had injured himself by foolishly attempting to climb on to the canvas roof of the vehicle from the tailgate, the way in the which the injury had been caused fell within the area of foreseeability for which the failure of the defendants to provide proper supervision was referable. The court then upheld the judge's finding of 75% contributory negligence.

In *London Borough of Islington* v *UCL Hospital NHS Trust* [2005] EWCA Civ 596, MLC 1254, where the local authority who had to provide care for a patient negligently injured by the hospital sought to recover the cost of that care from the hospital, the Court of Appeal said that the defendant must be taken to have known that the range of patients whom it treated would have a range of care requirements and financial needs. Care by a local authority in a case in which it could not recover the cost of the care could not be seen as so unusual as to fall outside that range. The precise manner in which the injury would occur did not have to be foreseeable, so the defendant did not have to know that Mrs J would require local authority care and would not be able to pay for it; but only to have institutional knowledge that some patients with Mrs J's disability would fall into that category.

CONCLUSION

For the purposes of the medical negligence action, we may sum up (remembering that we are here only dealing with the question what damage may be compensated for, given a breach of duty, and also bearing in mind that the law is far from clear in this area) as follows.

If there was no foreseeability of harm on the facts that the defendants knew or ought to have known, then recovery for any injury occasioned will not be permitted.

If there was foreseeability of physical damage, however slight the chance and however slight the injury to be foreseen, then compensation may be got for all physical injury resulting from the breach of duty that is of the same type as the injury to be foreseen, plus any injury, however unforeseeable, that is consequent upon the foreseeable injury. Unforeseeable injury not consequent upon a foreseeable injury is not compensatable, but this is subject to the rule that the tortfeasor must take the claimant as he finds him.

Subject to that rule, some injury must actually be suffered that falls within the type of injury to be foreseen, ie within the area of risk created (in *The Wagon Mound* (above), the Privy Council said that foreseeability must be of 'the damage that happened – the damage in suit'). Whether a court these days is likely in practice to say that the injury suffered was of a different type or kind from the injury that could have been foreseen and thus deny recovery to a person injured through another's admitted negligence may be doubted. If a man carelessly tosses a brick out of an upper window and it falls on to an electric cable which causes a passer-by to be electrocuted through an unforeseeable chemical reaction, it may well go against the judicial grain to hold that the injured party cannot recover because the only foreseeable injury was from being struck by the brick and electrocution was a different type of damage. Probably in such a case the court would 'find' that there was a slight degree of foreseeability of electrocution.

When all is said and done, on this aspect of negligence as on every other, the determining factor will be the judge's view as to whether justice dictates recovery. He will then find a legal peg on which to hang his decision. That is particularly easy in the field of negligence, where so much is uncertain and lacks precision. As Lord Wright said in *Hay (or Bourhill)* v *Young* [1943] AC 92 at 107, HL, '... negligence is a fluid principle, which has to be applied to the most diverse conditions and problems of human life.' It may well be that, as RWM Dias has said, 'the principles of the future will be that a negligent person shall be liable according as the court thinks reasonable in the circumstances'. The progress of law within a society is always from formalism to flexibility, albeit that in the common law tradition judicial activism is usually disguised by an artfully contrived appearance of deference to authority.[6]

---

6   'In previous times, when faced with a new problem, the judges have not openly asked themselves the question: What is the best policy for the law to adopt? But the question has always been there in the background. It has been concealed behind such questions as: Was the defendant under any duty to the plaintiff? Was the relationship between them sufficiently proximate? Was the injury direct or indirect? Was it foreseeable or not? Was it too remote? and so forth' (*per* Lord Denning).

Chapter 9

The proof of negligence

Andrew Buchan

INTRODUCTION

There are a number of difficulties a claimant faces in proving negligence. They include the problem of ascertaining exactly what was done in the course of treatment, of securing expert evidence which will allege and substantiate a want of due care, of proving a causative link between the treatment and the injury, and of overcoming any possible pro-doctor prejudice in the mind of the judge, and, if the matter goes further, the appeal court.

The burden of proving negligent conduct resulting in injury is upon the claimant. Where there is no direct or circumstantial evidence which permits a conclusion to be drawn as to how the accident happened, the claimant may pray in aid the maxim *res ipsa loquitur* (the matter speaks for itself). This applies where what happened is not the sort of thing that would normally happen in the absence of negligence in some form or another. The court may then find that there was negligence even though it is not known what form that negligence took. If the defendants give a reasonable explanation as to how the accident might have happened without negligence, or show that they had in fact taken every possible care of the patient, the court will not be entitled to rely on the maxim.

DIFFICULTIES IN CAUSATION

Another obstacle to proving a claim for compensation is that, even if one knows what specific acts or omissions were alleged to have been negligent, one has to prove that not only did they constitute a less than reasonable standard of care, but also that they were the cause of injury or loss to the patient. Negligence is not actionable without proof of loss or injury arising from the negligent acts or omissions. But the aetiology of medical conditions is notoriously complex and obscure. Would the correct or timely treatment have prevented death or resulted in the patient being better off than he actually is? How to prove that a particular act or omission caused any part of the claimant's present condition? Can one give, and is it relevant to give, an estimation of the chances of proper treatment having saved or helped him? The problem of causation, of showing that what was done or omitted was not only negligent by professional standards but also caused or may have caused a deterioration in the condition of the patient that would not otherwise have occurred, is considered above in Chapter 7.

BURDEN OF PROOF

The burden of proving what needs to be proved to establish a case rests on the claimant. It has been said that there are no special rules about the burden or standard of proof in cases involving professional negligence, but that it must necessarily be harder to prove negligence where a case concerns the 'complicated and sophisticated professional activities of a doctor, lawyer or architect' (*Dwyer* v *Roderick* (1983) 80 LS Gaz R 3003, 127 Sol Jo 805, CA).

In *Hucks* v *Cole* MLC 0604, [1993] 4 Med LR 393, CA, Lord Denning had said that:

> A charge of negligence against a professional man was serious. It stood on a different footing to a charge of negligence against the driver of a motor car. The consequences were far more serious. It affected his professional status and reputation. The burden of proof was correspondingly greater. As the charge was so grave, so should the proof be clear.

It is clear that that does not represent the modern law.[1]

In *Ashcroft* v *Mersey Regional Health Authority* MLC 0337, [1983] 2 All ER 245 the judge said that the question was whether it had been established on a balance of probabilities that the physician had failed to exercise the care required of a man possessing and professing special skill in circumstances which required the exercise of that special skill. No added burden of proof rested on the claimant. The more skilled a person was the more care which was expected of him. That test should be applied without gloss either way (Kilner Brown J).

The claimant has to persuade the court that the only explanation for the injury that can reasonably be accepted is one that involves negligence. If the court cannot select between two explanations for complications following treatment, only one of which involves negligence, then the claimant has not proved his case (*per* Beldam J in *Harrington* v *Essex Area Health Authority* (1984) Times, 14 November).[2]

In *Clark* v *MacLennan* [1983] 1 All ER 416, Pain J said that where in the context of a general duty of care there had been a failure to take a generally recognised precaution which had been followed by damage of the kind that that precaution was designed to prevent, the burden of proof shifted to the defendant to show either that he was not in breach of

1   The same thing may be said for the odd pronouncement from Lord Denning in *Bater* v *Bater* [1950] 2 All ER 458, CA (approved by the Court of Appeal in *Hornal* v *Neuberger Products Ltd* [1956] 3 All ER 970, Lord Denning being a party thereto) to the effect that the degree of probability required to establish proof could vary with the gravity of the allegation. Are we supposed to think, for example, that 51% probability is enough to prove negligence against a shopkeeper or builder, but 75% is required against a doctor? Hardly!

2   A judge is entitled to conclude that he simply does not know what happened, in which case, if *res ipsa loquitur* does not apply, the claim fails (*Ratcliffe* v *Plymouth and Torbay Health Authority* [1998] Lloyd's Rep Med 162, CA).

duty or that the damage was not caused by the breach. In that case there had been a departure from the usual practice of not performing a certain operation for stress incontinence within three months of delivery; that departure was found to have been unjustified and therefore constituted a breach of the duty of care. It was followed by a consequence that that precaution was designed to prevent, ie breakdown of the repair effected in the operation, and it was therefore up to the defendants to satisfy the court that that damage had not flowed from their breach of duty to the patient. However, it was expressly denied by the House of Lords in *Wilsher* v *Essex Area Health Authority* MLC 0016, [1988] AC 1074 that the burden shifted in such circumstances. In *Gregory* v *Pembrokeshire Health Authority* MLC 0596, [1989] 1 Med LR 81 at 85, Rougier J rejected the suggestion that whenever the fault complained of was a fault in omission the burden of proving causation shifted to the defendants:

> 'the burden of proof on the balance of probabilities remains on the plaintiff throughout'.

In *Defreitas* v *O'Brien* [1995] 6 Med LR 108, CA Otton LJ said the *Bolam* test did not impose any burden of proof on the defendant to establish that his diagnosis or treatment would be acceptable to a responsible body of medical opinion. The burden of proof was on the claimant.

Lost records

It is a sad fact of life that if, as not uncommonly transpires, vital records are 'missing' a claim that could otherwise be proved may fail. However, Latin may help here. In *Malhotra* v *Dhawan* [1997] 8 Med LR 319, the Court of Appeal, considering the maxim *omnia praesumuntur contra spoliatorem*, indicated that inferences could be drawn against a party who had destroyed relevant evidence (although the court said the maxim only applied where that had been done to stop the other party showing how much of his property had been taken).[3] In *Le Page* v *Kingston and Richmond Health Authority* MLC 0610, [1997] 8 Med LR 229, John Samuels QC, sitting as a deputy judge of the Queen's Bench Division, said that the defendants could not properly complain if he drew inferences from surviving documentation which might have been contradicted by other records which they had improperly destroyed.

In *Skelton* v *Lewisham and North Southwark Health Authority* MLC 0662, [1998] Lloyd's Rep Med 324, the inadequacy of the anaesthetic notes (brief, unsigned, without a record of key events and pressures), although not causative of the damage, was said by the judge to be indicative of an unexplained carelessness. In *Rhodes* v *Spokes and Farbridge* MLC 0640, [1996] 7 Med LR 135, Smith J said:

> A doctor's contemporaneous record of a consultation should form a reliable evidential base in a case such as this. I regret to say that Dr Farbridge's notes of the plaintiff's attendances do not provide any such firm foundation. They are scanty in the extreme. He rarely recorded her complaints or symptoms; he rarely recorded any observations; usually he noted only the drug he prescribed ... The failure to take a proper note is not evidence of a doctor's negligence or of

---

3   In *Dobson* v *North Tyneside Health Authority* [1997] 1 WLR 596, the Court of Appeal said that for the maxim to apply it had to be shown that the spoliator was a 'wrongdoer'.

the inadequacy of treatment. But a doctor who fails to keep an adequate note of a consultation lays himself open to a finding that his recollection is faulty and someone else's is correct. After all, a patient has only to remember his or her own case, whereas the doctor has to remember one case out of hundreds which occupied his mind at the material time.

RES IPSA LOQUITUR

What we consider here is a situation that often arises, where not merely is it unclear why the patient's condition has deteriorated or what the cause must have been of the injury he suffered, but where he cannot even point to any act or omission and say that that was wrong, and in all probability caused his present condition, because the only acts or omissions he knows to have taken place are unimpugnable. Therefore, all he can say is that something must have been done which should not have been done, because his injury could not have arisen without something having been done wrong. This is the principle of evidence known as *res ipsa loquitur*, 'the matter speaks for itself'.

There must be reasonable evidence of negligence. But where the thing is shown to be under the management of the defendant or his servants, and the accident is such as in the ordinary course of things does not happen if those who have the management use proper care, it affords reasonable evidence, in the absence of explanation by the defendant, that the accident arose from want of care (*per* Erle CJ in *Scott* v *London and St Katherine Docks Co* (1865) 3 H & C 596, Ex Ch).

The maxim applies where 'the circumstances are more consistent, reasonably interpreted without further explanation, with ... negligence than with any other cause of the accident happening' (*per* Kennedy LJ in *Russell* v *London and South-western Rly Co* (1908) 24 TLR 548 at 551, CA).

The court is in any event entitled to make an inference as to how an accident happened upon the evidence before it. It may be that no one can give direct evidence of how it happened, but, if the evidence that is given permits a reasonable inference to be drawn as to the cause, the court in drawing such an inference is not applying the principle of *res ipsa loquitur*, for that principle only applies where the cause cannot be specified, whether upon direct evidence or by inference.

> If the facts are sufficiently known the question ceases to be one where the facts speak for themselves, and the solution is to be found by determining whether on the facts as established negligence is to be inferred or not (*per* Lord Porter in *Barkway* v *South Wales Transport Co Ltd* [1950] 1 All ER 392 at 395, HL).

An example of this type of inference is found in the case *Clowes* v *National Coal Board* (1987) Times, 23 April, in which the Court of Appeal said that, where there is no clear evidence of an accident but the court knows of habitual careless behaviour which could have caused it, the court may assume that to be the cause in the absence of any other explanation.

The maxim is also misapplied if it is sought to be used where it is known what the doctor did and the dispute is as to whether that constituted negligence. A surgeon performing a laminectomy may penetrate too far and injure the nerve or the spinal cord. One cannot say indignantly: 'Of course it was negligent; the matter speaks for itself.' That is simply a misunderstanding of what the maxim means in law. It would be up to expert evidence to establish whether or not any surgeon exercising due care could make that mistake.

The statement of claim usually pleads that the claimant will pray in aid the principle of *res ipsa loquitur,* but that would appear to be unnecessary if the pleading is otherwise complete as to the facts alleged (see *Bennett* v *Chemical Construction (GB) Ltd* [1971] 3 All ER 822, CA).

The maxim has often been applied where a defendant is carrying out lifting or building operations and the claimant is injured by a falling article. It is not known what made it fall, but the court declares that it would be unlikely to have happened without negligence.

In *Howard* v *Wessex Regional Health Authority* MLC 0603, [1994] 5 Med LR 57 Morland J said that *res ipsa* could not help the patient where she had sustained tetraplegia following maxillo-facial surgery by way of a sagittal split osteotomy, because her injury was most likely due to a fibro-cartilaginous embolism, which would not connote negligence. As the helpful note by Margaret Puxon QC at the end of the report of *Howard* shows, it appears that the defendants, as not infrequently happens in medical cases, advanced their explanation for the injury very late in the day. It seems surprising that the judge accepted it.

In *Delaney* v *Southmead Health Authority* MLC 0582, [1995] 6 Med LR 355 the patient alleged that she had sustained damage to her arm as a result of negligent placing during surgery. The Court of Appeal upheld the finding of the judge in favour of the defendants. They said that, even if *res ipsa* applied, it was always open to a defendant to rebut a case of *res ipsa* either by giving an explanation of what happened which was inconsistent with negligence or by showing that he had exercised all reasonable care. Stuart-Smith LJ doubted that the principle was useful in medical negligence actions, at least not where 'all the evidence in the case has been adduced',[4] and Dillon LJ said:

> I cannot for my part accept that medical science is such a precise science that there cannot in any particular field be any room for the wholly unexpected result occurring in the human body from the carrying out of a well-recognised procedure.[5]

In *Jacobs* v *Great Yarmouth and Waverney Health Authority* MLC 0710, [1995] 6 Med LR 192, a case of anaesthetic awareness, the Court of Appeal said (in 1984) that *res ipsa loquitur* meant no more than that on the facts that a claimant was able to prove, although he might not be able to point to a particular negligent act or omission on the part of the defendants, the fair inference to draw was that there had been negligence of some sort on the part of the defendants; but if there were further evidence presented by the defendants, those facts might be shown in an entirely different light so that it would not be possible to draw the inference of negligence.

---

4   Judge Thompson QC commented on this observation in *Ritchie* v *Chichester Health Authority* [1994] 5 Med LR 187 at 206.

5   Stuart-Smith LJ offered further thoughts on the principle of *res ipsa* in *Fallows* v *Randle* [1997] 8 Med LR 160 at 163, CA where he cited a passage from Megaw LJ in *Lloyde* v *West Midlands Gas Board* [1971] 1 WLR 749 at 755, CA. The Court of Appeal decision in *Ratcliffe* v *Plymouth and Torbay Health Authority* [1998] Lloyd's Rep Med 162 repays study. It shows that a judge is entitled to conclude that he simply does not know what happened, and that in such circumstances there is no presumption that *res ipsa* applies.

In *Hooper* v *Young* MLC 0602, [1998] 2 Lloyd's Rep Med 61, CA Otton LJ said that it was a pity *res ipsa* had ever entered the case because it had no place where the event that caused the injury (damage to a ureter by kinking of the suture) could have happened without negligence.

In *Girard* v *Royal Columbian Hospital* (1976) 66 DLR (3d) 676, where the patient had suffered permanent paralysis of both legs after a spinal anaesthetic, the Canadian judge, Andrews J, exonerating the anaesthetist, used words similar to Dillon LJ in the *Delaney* case (above):

> The human body is not a container filled with a material whose performance can be predictably charted and analysed. It cannot be equated with a box of chewing tobacco or a soft drink. Thus, while permissible inferences may be drawn as to the normal behaviour of these types of commodities, the same type of reasoning does not necessarily apply to a human being. Because of this, medical science has not yet reached the stage where the law ought to presume that a patient must come out of an operation as well as or better than he went into it.

In *Bull and Wakeham* v *Devon Area Health Authority* MLC 0022, [1993] 4 Med LR 117, CA two of the judges differed on the question whether *res ipsa* applied to the failure of the hospital to have an obstetrician attend the mother at the vital time, Mustill LJ taking the view (at 142) that as the facts of the 'accident' were largely known the principle did not apply.

Despite the sporadic judicial observations disapproving of a plea of *res ipsa*,[6] the maxim serves a purpose when properly used. How did an eight-year-old mentally retarded child come to be on a main road when she should have been in the care of her school? No one knew. But the application of *res ipsa* led to the conclusion that in some way or another there must have been a want of care on the part of the school staff (*J* v *North Lincolnshire County Council* [2000] PIQR P84, CA).

Rebuttal

The defendant may rebut the presumption of negligence, but not merely by showing the general precautions he had taken. It is not entirely clear on the authorities how far the defendant must go to shift the onus of proof back to the claimant, in particular, whether he has to show a possible or a likely cause of the accident that would not involve negligence. It was said in *Moore* v *R Fox & Sons* [1956] 1 QB 596, CA that it was not sufficient for the defendants to show several hypothetical causes consistent with the absence of negligence and that the accident might have occurred without negligence on their part; to discharge the onus they had to go further and either show that they had not been negligent (it would seem to be enough in this connection if the defendants satisfied the court that all possible precautions had been taken) or give a reasonable explanation of the cause of the accident which did not connote negligence.

It was said in *Ng Chun Pui* v *Lee Chuen Tat* [1988] RTR 298, PC, that the burden of proving negligence remains upon the claimant, despite the applicability of the doctrine of *res ipsa loquitur*.

---

6   'There is substantial doubt whether *res ipsa loquitur* is ever susceptible to refined arguments and detailed analysis of authority', *per* Judge LJ (*Carroll* v *Fearon, Bent and Dunlop Ltd* [1998] PIQR P416, CA – a claim for injury caused by a defective tyre).

The cases make it clear that one must draw a distinction between the situation where there is more than one possible cause for the injury and the situation where the precise cause is unknown. In the second situation one may be able to take advantage of the maxim. In the first situation it is simply a matter for the judge to decide what was the operative cause, and, in doing this, he is entitled to prefer the evidence of one expert to another (*Fallows* v *Randle* [1996] MLC 0591 is an example of this; reference may also be made to *Betts* v *Berkshire Health Authority* [1997] 8 Med LR 87). He may also draw inferences from the evidence. In *Skelton* v *Lewisham and North Southwark Health Authority* MLC 0662, [1998] Lloyd's Rep Med 324, Kay J decided that the only possible explanation on the facts for the administration of certain drugs preoperatively was an episode of hypotension causing brain injury. In *Bull* v *Devon Area Health Authority* MLC 0022, [1993] 4 Med LR 117, CA Slade LJ said that the trial judge had gone further than he needed when he found that the claimant had excluded all possible causes of his injury other than that for which he contended, because it would have been sufficient to make the less unqualified finding that the cause for which he contended was established on the balance of probabilities.

Whose negligence?

In some of the older cases, the issue has been whether it can be shown that the negligence the court is asked to infer must have been that of the defendant himself or one of his agents and not that of someone for whom the defendant was not responsible. One would, therefore, encounter the problem as to who was the servant or agent of the surgeon and who was the servant or agent of the hospital (see Chapter 4). Now that most cases are brought against the NHS Trust or health authority, which is responsible for all the medical personnel involved in the treatment of the patient, this particular issue is not likely often to arise (it could still be relevant in the field of private practice and in cases against a GP). Suffice it to say that the claimant must show that the accident could not reasonably have happened without some want of care on the part of the defendant himself or his agents.

Examples

When one considers the number of times the maxim has been accepted by a court as an aid to its decision, one can only wonder why it has come in for such bad press recently. Probably the answer is that it is due to unnecessary and inapposite recourse to it by claimant's lawyers in many cases.

Whether or not the accident is one which the court will find would not usually happen without some negligence somewhere will depend on expert evidence. Things can go wrong in operations without there being any negligence. Denning LJ had this to say in *Cassidy* v *Ministry of Health* [1951] 2 KB 343 at 365, MLC 0001:

> If the plaintiff had to prove that some particular doctor or nurse was negligent he would not be able to do it. But he was not put to that impossible task: he says, 'I went into the hospital to be cured of two stiff fingers. I have come out with four stiff fingers, and my hand is useless. That should not have happened if due

care had been used. Explain it if you can.' I am quite clearly of the opinion that that raises a *prima facie* case against the hospital authorities: see *per* Goddard LJ in *Mahon* v *Osborne* [1939] 2 KB 14, 50. They have nowhere explained how it could happen without negligence. They have busied themselves in saying that this or that member of their staff was not negligent. But they have not called a single person to say that the injuries were consistent with due care on the part of all the members of their staff. They called some of the people who actually treated the man ... but they did not call any expert at all to say that this might happen despite all care. They have not therefore displaced the *prima facie* case against them ...

Both Somervell LJ and Singleton LJ agreed that the facts disclosed a *prima facie* case of negligence on the basis of *res ipsa loquitur* ([1951] 2 KB 343 at 348, 353).

In *Roe* v *Minister of Health* [1954] 2 QB 66, patients in hospital for minor operations were paralysed by the spinal anaesthetic each was given:

The judge has said that those facts do not speak for themselves, but I think that they do. They certainly call for an explanation. Each of these men is entitled to say to the hospital: 'While I was in your hands something has been done to me which has wrecked my life. Please explain how it has come to pass' (*per* Denning LJ at 81).

Morris LJ said:

When [the claimants] proved all that they were in a position to prove they then said *res ipsa loquitur*. But this convenient and succinct formula possesses no magic qualities: nor has it any added virtue, other than that of brevity, merely because it is expressed in Latin. There are certain happenings that do not normally occur in the absence of negligence, and upon proof of these a court will probably hold that there is a case to answer.

However, in this case, the hospital gave an explanation of the accident which was accepted by the court as absolving them from any negligence (the ampoules of anaesthetic had been kept in a solution of phenol, which seeped into the anaesthetic after the ampoules had developed in some way or another tiny, undetectable cracks or molecular flaws. At that time such a possibility and the danger arising therefrom were totally unknown).

In this case Lord Denning also referred to the position where both hospital and private doctor deny negligence but give no explanation for the patient's injury. He said:

I do not think that the hospital authorities and [the doctor] can both avoid giving an explanation by the simple expedient of throwing responsibility on to the other. If an injured person shows that one or other or both of two persons injured him, but cannot say which of them it was, then he is not defeated altogether. He can call on each of them for an explanation.

In *Saunders* v *Leeds Western Health Authority and Robinson* MLC 0657, [1993] 4 Med LR 355 the heart of a four-year-old girl stopped for some 30 minutes during an operation under anaesthetic to remedy a congenitally deformed hip. The defendants agreed that did not normally happen without a want of care somewhere but they offered an explanation as to how the accident might have happened. Mann J rejected their explanation and said:

The plaintiff's reliance on *res ipsa loquitur* makes it unnecessary for her to suggest a specific cause for the cardiac arrest. It is plain from evidence called on her behalf that the heart of a fit child does not arrest under anaesthesia if proper care is taken in the anaesthetic and surgical processes.

This decision has been thought to constitute a helpful departure for claimants in the court's willingness to infer negligence, at any rate in the context of injury under or from anaesthetic; but, though the case is certainly not without significance as a precedent, it is important to note that the defendants admitted here that the principle of *res ipsa* applied to the facts. See also *Glass* v *Cambridge Health Authority* [1995] 6 Med LR 91.

In *Moore* v *Worthing District Health Authority* MLC 0981, [1992] 3 Med LR 431, Owen J rejected a plea of *res ipsa* where a patient was left with bilateral ulnar nerve palsy following a mastoidectomy. He absolved the defendants from failing to protect the arms properly while the patient was under anaesthetic by accepting their contention that the patient had been abnormally vulnerable to such an injury, despite the absence of any real evidence of such a condition. One wonders if this is an example of a contrived explanation of an injury by the defence being accepted by a judge who is reluctant to find doctors guilty of mismanagement.

Other examples

In *Mahon* v *Osborne* [1939] 2 KB 14, where the surgeon was sued when a swab was left inside the patient, the majority of the Court of Appeal was of the view that the principle did not apply in the case of a complex operation where a number of medical staff took part, but it is now clear that the correct view was that taken by Goddard LJ when he said:

> There can be no possible question but that neither swabs nor instruments are ordinarily left in the patient's body ... If therefore a swab is left in the patient's body, it seems clear that the surgeon is called upon for an explanation. That is, he is called upon to show, not necessarily why he missed it but that he exercised due care to prevent its being left there.

This view was endorsed by the Court of Appeal in *Urry* v *Bierer* (1955) Times, 15 July, where there was a dispute as to which of the two, surgeon or nurse, had the responsibility for seeing all the swabs were removed after an abdominal operation. As mentioned above, now that the hospital will be liable in almost all cases for the negligence of any of those who treat the patient, this sort of tedious analysis of who had what responsibility and who was whose agent is unlikely to arise.

Reference may also be made to *Cavan* v *Wilcox* (1973) 44 DLR (3d) 42, where the maxim was applied to the situation of a patient who developed gangrene after he had been given an injection in his arm; and to *Fish* v *Kapur* [1948] 2 All ER 176, where it was held that the maxim did not apply where a dentist's patient's jaw was broken during an extraction.

In *Clarke* v *Worboys* (1952) Times, 18 March, where the patient's buttock was burnt in electro-coagulation treatment, the Court of Appeal reversed the judge's finding and held that the evidence showed that such an accident would not happen if reasonable care were used.

The maxim was successfully invoked by the widow of a man who was asphyxiated when he swallowed a dental throat pack (*Garner* v *Morrell* (1953) Times, 31 October).

In *Ludlow* v *Swindon Health Authority* MLC 0611, [1989] 1 Med LR 104, where the claimant alleged she had been awake during a Caesarean section as a result of what must have been the negligent administration of the anaesthetic, the judge said that for the doctrine of *res ipsa loquitur* to apply, the claimant had first to establish that she had indeed been awake during the operation. As he was not satisfied of that the doctrine could not help her.

In *Leckie* v *Brent and Harrow Area Health Authority* [1982] 1 Lancet 634, it was held that a 1.5 cm cut on the cheek of a baby delivered by Caesarean section would not happen without some lack of care. The matter spoke for itself.

Reasonable traction could have caused the claimant's lesion of the musculocutaneous nerve, as could also excessive traction, and so the maxim could not help him, in the case of *Levenkind* v *Churchill-Davidson* [1983] 1 Lancet 1452.

The claimant was successful in *Woodhouse* v *Yorkshire Regional Health Authority* [1984] 1 Lancet 1306. She was a pianist whose ulnar nerves were severely damaged in an operation for a subphrenic abscess. The judge said that the evidence established that this sort of injury would not occur if the standard precautions to avoid this recognised hazard had been taken. The Court of Appeal upheld his decision. *Contra O'Malley-Williams* v *Governors of National Hospital for Nervous Diseases* (1975) 1 BMJ 635, where it was held that the maxim did not apply where partial paralysis was sustained by the claimant (who was also an accomplished pianist) because the injury sustained was recognised as an inherent risk of the treatment undergone, namely an aortagram for recurrent episodes of loss of vision in the right eye.

In *Brazier* v *Ministry of Defence* [1965] 1 Lloyd's Rep 26 the defendants satisfied the judge that he should not infer negligence on the part of a person giving an injection to the claimant as the cause of the needle breaking, because the actual cause could properly be inferred to be a latent defect in the shaft of the needle (similarly in *Corner* v *Murray* [1954] 2 BMJ 1555).

In the Scottish case of *Fowler* v *Greater Glasgow Health Board* 1990 SLT 303n a court of first instance was unable to infer negligence in treatment from the fact that the doctors had failed later to give the parents of a dead child an explanation of what had happened.

In *Coyne* v *Wigan Health Authority* MLC 0573, [1991] 2 Med LR 301 the defendants agreed that *res ipsa* applied when hypoxia leading to brain damage occurred during recovery from a routine operation, but they failed to satisfy the judge that it was due to the (non-negligent) cause of silent regurgitation of gastric content. Therefore the matter did 'speak for itself' and the claimant succeeded.

For another application of the maxim, see the final part of the judgment of Waterhouse J in *Bentley* v *Bristol and Weston Health Authority (No 2)* MLC 0339, [1991] 3 Med LR 1 (damage to the sciatic nerve during a total hip replacement).

APPEALS AND THE BURDEN OF PROOF

The principles of appeal

The two most significant principles of law affecting appeals are:

(a)   the trial judge had the great advantage of seeing and hearing the witnesses, whether lay or expert, and so the appeal tribunal must be

very slow to interfere with those findings (as opposed to the *inferences* which the judge drew from his findings or from facts not in dispute); and
(b)   the exercise of a discretion by the judge should not be invalidated merely because the appeal tribunal would have exercised their discretion differently.

The second principle comes to the fore in medical negligence claims upon the issue of discretion under s 33 of the Limitation Act 1980, which is treated at length in Chapter 18. What we consider here is the extent to which the Court of Appeal has on occasions interfered with the findings and conclusions of the trial judge and how it has justified such interference. In *Pickford* v *ICI* [1997] 8 Med LR 270, CA Stuart-Smith LJ said:[7]

> I am well aware of the inhibitions laid upon this court in interfering with and reversing the trial judge's findings of fact, especially primary findings. The law is succinctly summarised in the Annual Practice at paragraph 59/1/55 and is very familiar to any member of this court. I do not propose to set it out *in extenso*. We were also referred by Mr Hytner to a passage in the speech of Lord Bridge of Harwich in *Wilsher* v *Essex Area Health Authority* [1988] AC 1074 where he reminded the court that similar principles apply in relation to the evaluation of disputed medical evidence. But it is our duty to reconsider the matter, paying great weight to the opinion of the trial judge, especially where there is a conflict of evidence and the demeanour and bearing of the witness plays a significant part in the judge's decision.

And Ward LJ said in *Briody* v *St Helens and Knowsley Health Authority* MLC 0099, [1999] Lloyd's Rep Med 185:

> Although this court is well able to consider the medical records as they stand, the case depended on more than drawing inevitable inferences from those statements and the judge had the unenviable task of assessing the witnesses and deciding, if there were a conflict, which evidence he preferred. Although I do not shrink from overruling him if, on full consideration, I come to the conclusion that he was wrong, nonetheless, due weight is to be given to the decision of the judge at first instance and I need to be satisfied that his overall conclusion was *plainly* wrong. That requires a close look at the whole of the evidence.

The advantage enjoyed by the trial judge extends to the hearing of expert witnesses. In *Wilsher* v *Essex Area Health Authority* MLC 0016, [1988] AC 1074, HL, Lord Bridge said (at 1091):

> Where expert witnesses are radically at issue about complex technical questions within their own field and are examined and cross-examined at length about their conflicting theories, I believe that the judge's advantage in seeing them and hearing them is scarcely less important than when he has to resolve some conflict of primary fact between lay witnesses in purely mundane matters.

In *Wardlaw* v *Farrar* MLC 1079, [2004] Lloyds Rep Med 98, a fatal accident claim over the death of the defendant GP's patient arising out of

---

7   The actual decision of the Court of Appeal in this claim for repetitive strain injury was reversed by the House of Lords ([1998] 1 WLR 1189), but not so as to invalidate the above cited remarks of Stuart-Smith LJ.

a failure to consider a diagnosis of pulmonary embolism and so arrange hospital admission, the Court of Appeal said that the judge had evidently been much more impressed by the expert cardiological evidence called for the defendant and there was clear authority that an appellate court should be very slow to interfere with a trial judge's views on the quality of the evidence of expert witnesses whom he had had the advantage of seeing and hearing; so the court would not interfere with the judge's assessment and the appeal was dismissed.

In *Gray* v *Southampton & South West Hampshire Health Authority* [2001] MLC 0662, a claim for brain damage sustained in or around a surgical procedure, the Court of Appeal said that where the trial judge had not rejected the evidence of the attending anaesthetist it was not open to them to reach conclusions of primary fact the effect of which would be to reject such evidence.

Must a judge give reasons for his conclusions?

A judge does not always have to spell out his reasons for every conclusion to which he comes (*Abada* v *Gray* (1997) 40 BMLR 116, CA, a personal injury claim where the trial judge was held to have been entitled to prefer the defendant's medical evidence, even though he had made no express findings of fact). But where no inference as to the judge's reasoning can reasonably be drawn from a judgment that did not make express findings on relevant issues, a retrial will be ordered (*Sewell* v *Electrolux Ltd* (1997) Times, 7 November, CA).

In *Eckersley* v *Binnie* (1988) 18 Con LR 1 at 77, CA Bingham LJ said:

> In resolving conflicts of expert evidence the judge remains the judge; he is not obliged to accept evidence simply because it comes from an illustrious source; he can take account of demonstrated partisanship and lack of objectivity. But, save where an expert is guilty of a deliberate attempt to mislead (as happens only very rarely), a coherent reasoned opinion expressed by a suitably qualified expert should be the subject of a coherent reasoned rebuttal, unless it can be discounted for other good reason.

Many, if not most, medical negligence trials are decided by the judge's preference for the evidence of one expert rather than another. So important is the quality of expert and the evidence he gives, and the manner in which he gives it, that judicial comments on experts in all medical negligence cases are now collected on the database of *Medical Litigation* (at www.medneg.com). Of course, it does not follow that an expert is not a good expert simply because a judge does not accept his evidence. He may have failed to impress the judge for any number of peripheral reasons. But if he is explicitly criticised by the judge, as is not uncommon, perhaps for being partial or lacking independence, or 'going too far', or it is said that he vacillated or changed his tune, there is usually a good reason for such criticism.

In *Stefan* v *General Medical Council* (1999) 49 BMLR 161 the Privy Council said that, although at common law there was no general duty to give reasons universally imposed on all decision-makers, the trend of the law had been towards an increased recognition of the duty upon decision-makers of many kinds (the case involved a challenge to a decision of the health committee of the GMC that the appellant's fitness to practice was seriously impaired due to mental condition and the consequent indefinite suspension of his registration).

In *English* v *Emery Reimbold & Strick* [2002] 1 WLR 2409, a personal injury claim where the critical issue was whether a disabling dislocation of the claimant's spine was attributable to an injury for which the defendant was responsible, the Court of Appeal gave guidelines on how and when to appeal on the ground that the trial judge's reasons for his decision were inadequate. The court said:

1   It was the judge's duty to produce a judgment that gave a clear explanation for his order.
2   An unsuccessful party should not seek to upset a judgment on the ground of inadequacy of reasons unless, despite the advantage of considering the judgment with knowledge of the evidence given and submissions made at trial, that party was unable to understand why it was that the judge had reached an adverse decision.
3   The effect of the human rights legislation and Strasbourg jurisprudence [yes, it crept in here, too] was that a decision should be reasoned; however the extent of the reasoning did not go further than that required under domestic law.
4   The practice of giving no reasons for a decision as to costs could only comply with Article 6 of the European Convention on Human Rights if the reason for the decision was implicit from the circumstances in which the award was made.
5   The following course was recommended to deal with cases where inadequacy of reasons was at issue.

When an application for permission to appeal on the ground of lack of reasons was made to the trial judge, the judge should consider whether his judgment was defective. If he concluded that it was, he should set out to remedy the defect by the provision of additional reasons, refusing permission to appeal on the basis that he has adopted that course. If he concluded that the reasons were adequate he should refuse permission to appeal. If an appellate court found an application for permission to appeal well founded, it should consider adjourning the application and remitting the case to the trial judge with an invitation to provide additional reasons for his decision or, where appropriate, his reasons for a specific finding. Where the appellate court was doubtful as to the adequacy of the reasons it was appropriate to adjourn to an oral hearing on notice. Where permission to appeal was granted the appellate court should review the judgment in the context of the evidence and submissions at trial in order to determine whether it was apparent why the judge reached his decision. If satisfied that the reason was apparent then the appeal should be dismissed. If the reason for the decision was not apparent then the appeal court should decide whether itself to proceed to a new hearing or to direct a new trial.

Examples

In the professional negligence (surveyors, not medical) case of *Flannery* v *Halifax Estate Agencies* [2000] 1 WLR 377, CA Henry LJ said that the professional judge today owed a duty to give reasons, although there were some exceptions (not relevant for our purposes). He said it was not a useful task to attempt to make absolute rules as to the requirement for the judge to give reasons, because issues were so infinitely various. But with expert evidence it should usually be possible to be more explicit in giving reasons (he cited *Eckersley* v *Binnie* (above)). The parties should be left in no doubt why they had won or lost. Further, a requirement to give reasons concentrated the mind of the judge, so that his deliberations would probably be more soundly based on the evidence. The extent of the duty depended on the subject matter. Where the dispute involves something in the nature of an intellectual exchange, with reasons and analysis advanced on either side, the judge must enter into the issues canvassed before him and explain why he preferred one case over the other. This was likely to apply particularly in litigation where, as in the instant case, there was disputed expert evidence. The court said that in the instant case the judge's preference for the defendants' expert, which was decisive, should have enabled him to give his reasons in the form of the 'coherent reasoned rebuttal' referred to by Bingham LJ in the *Eckersley* case. So the judge had been under a duty to give reasons but had not done so. The court could not know whether he had had adequate or inadequate reasons for his conclusion. In the circumstances the appeal by the claimants was allowed.

On the other hand, consider the medical case of *Polson* v *de Silva* [1999] MLC 0076, CA. This had been a successful claim against a GP for failing to respond to a mother's request to visit her sick child at home, with the result that the child sustained hearing loss from meningitis. The court said that the judge had carefully considered the evidence and had been fully entitled to prefer the expert evidence of the two consultant physicians for the claimant over that of the defendant's expert witness. There was an ample basis for the judge to conclude that earlier treatment would have avoided the deafness. Clearly, in this case the court was satisfied that the judge had properly considered the evidence and had had valid reasons for preferring the evidence of the claimants' experts.

In *Lakey* v *Merton, Sutton and Wandsworth Health Authority* [1999] MLC 0075, the patient appealed against a finding that a decision by the hospital not to X-ray the patient's leg had not been negligent. The argument was that the judge had failed to evaluate the evidence of the two experts and to make clear findings as to what part of the evidence of each he accepted and what part he rejected. The Court of Appeal gave this issue careful consideration, stating that in order to weigh the submissions *it was necessary to analyse the manner in which the judge expressed his conclusions* (my emphasis). The court concluded that in fact the judge had explained his reasoning very fully and had 'explained himself at considerable length', relying on at least six specific reasons. It is interesting to note that towards the end of his judgment, Thorpe LJ said:

> I suspect that in this field of litigation it is not uncommon for the forensic experts to take relatively extreme positions in the hope of securing an outcome for the party by whom each is instructed. I suspect also that in this case the judge found that each was guilty of some error in presentation.

It is also important to note that the learned Lord Justice said:

> So it seems to me that it is not incumbent on a judge to explain at great length why he has found the expert contribution perhaps partisan and perhaps

unhelpful. His function is to explain clearly the conclusions which he has reached, and Mr Justice Holland certainly did that in this case with exemplary clarity and logic.

In the cervical smears case (*Penney, Palmer and Cannon* v *East Kent Health Authority* MLC 0068, [1999] Lloyd's Rep Med 123; affd MLC 0126, [2000] Lloyd's Rep Med 41, CA) the claimants had two histopathologists, the defendants three. The two sides were in total disagreement over what the smears disclosed (the evidence about interpreting smears was immensely technical), but even more significantly over what the average screener, exercising due care, should have written in his report. By and large, the claimants' experts said the warning of 'borderline' changes should have been signalled. The defendants' experts said that writing up the reports as 'negative' was not unreasonable (the claimants had gone on to suffer invasive cancer).

The judge concluded that a proper standard of care had not been shown. He based his conclusion on the fact that at almost every point he *preferred the evidence of the claimants' experts*. Using the words of *Bolitho* (see Chapter 6), he said he did not consider the evidence of the defendants' experts stood up to logical analysis.

The Court of Appeal dismissed the defendants' appeal.

In *Ludlow* v *National Power plc* (17 July 2000, unreported), CA the court said that a judge was required to give reasons for a decision so that a party was in no doubt as to why he had lost and could assess whether the decision was properly appealable. However, the particular judgment left no doubt as to why the claimant had failed to satisfy the judge that an accident at work had caused psychiatric illness. The judge had preferred the evidence of the defence psychiatrist on the issue, and this he had been entitled to do as he had taken the view that that expert had had a wider range of relevant experience than the claimant's expert.

Compare *Coleman* v *Dunlop Ltd* [1998] PIQR P398, CA, in which a new trial was ordered where, in a claim for repetitive strain injury sustained at work, the judge had simply stated a preference for the defence consultant on the basis of wider relevant experience without making appropriate findings of primary fact and explaining her inferences therefrom. Henry LJ said:

> In my opinion, on trial of the action it is the duty of the judge first to resolve the issues before him and to give reasons. It is true that, in relation to matters in these courts, there is no statutory duty on the judge to give reasons. It is also true that for a long time it has been contended that the common law imposed no such duty. But the common law is a living thing, and it seems to me that the point has now come where the common law has evolved to the point that the judge, on trial of the action must give sufficient reasons to make clear his findings of primary fact and the inferences that he draws from those primary facts sufficient to resolve the live issues before him, explaining why he has drawn those inferences.

In an industrial liability case it was said that the judge should have given intellectual reasons for his preference (*Dyson* v *Leeds City Council* (22 November 1999, unreported)). In *Smyth* v *Greenhouse Stirton & Co* (4 October 1999, unreported) it was said that explicit reasons for preferences were not necessary where they could be inferred from the judgment. In *Matthews* v *East Sussex Health Authority* [1999] MLC 0170, the judge had been entitled to give particular weight to the evidence of the defence pathologist. In *Carr* v *Stockport Health Authority* [1999] MLC 0082, the judge had been entitled to prefer the evidence of one lay witness to another without referring specifically to their demeanour.

In *SmithKline Beecham Biologics SA* v *Connaught Laboratories Inc* (1999) 51 BMLR 91, the Court of Appeal said that in all cases the judge's judgment ought to provide a coherent summary of the issues, the evidence and the reasons for the decision, whether the judgment is delivered orally in open court, or handed down in open court in written form with copies available for the press and public.

In *Temple* v *South Manchester Health Authority* [2002] MLC 0846, a claim for alleged mismanagement in the treatment in hospital of a child's diabetic ketoacidosis, the Court of Appeal, dismissing the claimant's appeal, said that although the reasons the judge gave for accepting the views of an expert paediatrician called for the defence were open to some criticism, such criticisms could not by themselves outweigh or undermine the positive impression made by her oral testimony, supported in substantial measure by the published material. Similarly, in *Clifford* v *Grimley* [2001] EWCA Civ 1658 (not a medical case) the Court of Appeal said that the extent of the trial judge's duty to give sufficient reasons for his conclusions was dependent on the subject matter in each individual case. A short analysis of the evidence in this case was held to be sufficient.

In *Montanaro* v *Home Office* [2002] MLC 0777 Sedley LJ said the giving of reasons was a key judicial function and there was little use in giving reasons if a full and accurate record of them was not made (see below for further details).

In *Gow* v *Harker* [2003] MLC 1035, a claim for injury caused through mismanagement of a blood test, the Court of Appeal said that, when on the evidence there were so many improbabilities and at least one apparent impossibility, and the judge did not address the issues in his judgment adequately or at all, his judgment could not be upheld, the defendant's appeal succeeded and a new trial was ordered in front of a different judge. Similarly, in *Glicksman* v *Redbridge Health Care NHS Trust* [2001] MLC 0219, a claim for alleged negligent performance of the repair of a suspected incisional hernia, the Court of Appeal, discerning in the judgment below no reasoned rebuttal of any expert's view in circumstances which called out for definition of the issues, marshalling of the evidence and for reasons to be stated, ordered a new trial in front of a judge experienced in medical negligence.

See also *Baird* v *Thurrock Borough Council* (7 November 2005, unreported), CA where the court invalidated a finding of liability by the judge as he had given no reasons for preferring the claimant's evidence to the contrary evidence of two other lay witnesses

Practice Direction

A relevant Practice Direction ([1999] 1 WLR 2) tells us that the court which has just reached a decision is often in the best position to judge whether the case is or is not one where there should be an appeal. The appeal court will rarely interfere with a decision based on the judge's evaluation of oral evidence as to the primary facts or if an appeal would involve examining the fine detail of the judge's factual investigation.

Leave is more likely to be appropriate where what is being challenged is the inference which the judge has drawn from the primary facts, or where the judge has not received any particular benefit from having actually seen the witnesses, and it is properly arguable that materially different inferences should be drawn from the evidence. The appeal court will not interfere with the exercise of discretion of a judge unless the court is satisfied the judge was wrong. The burden on an appellant is a heavy one.

Recent appeals

The following brief survey of appeals and their outcome may help to give some further indication of the approach of the Court of Appeal in medical cases and, most significantly, their treatment of a judge's findings of fact. Appeals turning on points of substantive law are not considered here as they feature in other parts of the book.

Successful appeals by the defendant

Marwan Nawaf Nayef Raji-Abu-Shkara v *Hillingdon Health Authority* MLC 0617, [1997] 8 Med LR 114 (Waite, Roch, Auld LJJ): the court allowed the defendants' appeal from the judge's finding that the respiratory arrest that had caused the claimant's brain damage had been due to a failure of medical and nursing care. This is a good example of the court's willingness to make its own assessment of the evidence given below, form its own conclusions about its effect, and reverse the judge on the ground that he had no reason to reject the defence evidence and no good reason to reach the conclusions that he did.

Robertson v *Nottingham Health Authority* MLC 0644, [1997] 8 Med LR 1 (Sir Stephen Brown P, Roch, Brooke LJJ): this claim alleged perinatal brain damage due to hypoxia that should have been avoided. The judge found negligence but no causation. On appeal by both parties the court was prepared on the evidence to enlarge the period of culpable delay in delivering the child, but said that, even given the longer period, the judge would still have found that the injury had been sustained before the period of culpable delay began.

Tahir v *Haringey Health Authority* MLC 0632, [1998] Lloyd's Rep Med 104, CA (Leggatt, Otton LJJ, Sir Ralph Gibson): the trial judge found negligent delay in attending to the claimant's symptoms but rejected the claimant's case that the delay had caused his serious neurological injury, and she awarded modest compensation for a small increment in the extent of the injury. The defendants succeeded on appeal on the ground that there had been no evidence before the judge on which she could properly find that the delay had caused any additional injury.

Hooper v *Young* MLC 0602, [1998] Lloyd's Rep Med 61, CA (Stuart-Smith, Waite, Otton LJJ): the defendants succeeded on appeal on the ground that the evidence did not permit the judge to conclude that preoperative injury to a ureter by kinking of the suture had happened through negligence, seeing that it could equally have happened without negligence and there was nothing in the evidence making the former more likely. Stuart-Smith LJ offered the observation that it was important that the court did not make facile findings of negligence against doctors.

Ratty v *Haringey Health Authority* MLC 0638, [1994] 5 Med LR 413 (Balcombe, Kennedy, Evans LJJ): the court, having made yet another careful analysis of medical evidence adduced at first instance, found themselves persuaded to set aside a finding by the judge of negligence in undertaking and performing colorectal surgery consequent upon a diagnosis of cancer. The court upheld only a minor aspect of the claim, and so reduced the award from nearly £130,000 to £5,000.

Hughes v *Waltham Forest Health Authority* MLC 0605, [1991] 2 Med LR 155, CA (Fox, Butler-Sloss, Beldam LJJ): the court reversed the judge's finding that there had been negligence in the management of the deceased's gastric pathology, on the basis that the evidence called by the defendants established that a body of responsible opinion would find the management to have been acceptable. And the court (*obiter*) reversed the judge's finding on causation, saying that the evidence did not establish that the management, whether negligent or not, had been an effective cause of death.

Knight v *West Kent Health Authority* MLC 0057, [1998] Lloyd's Rep Med 18 (Kennedy, Morritt, Chadwick LJJ): this is a good example of how carefully the Court of Appeal will scrutinise the evidence to see whether the judge's findings of negligence can be supported. In this case a critical issue was whether the baby's head was higher in the vaginal canal at the time when it was admitted and whether the consultant should have intervened. This was important because two hours later the mother suffered substantial injury from a strenuous forceps delivery, and it was alleged that at the earlier time the head would have been higher and so a Caesarean section and not a forceps delivery would have been indicated. The court concluded that there was insufficient evidence for the judge's finding that the baby's head would have been too high for a forceps delivery. They also said that the judge's other determinative finding, that the forceps delivery was not performed to a proper standard of care, depended upon her conclusion that the obstetrician had encountered resistance when starting to pull, which was not supported by the evidence.

Dunn v *Bradford Hospital NHS Trust* [1999] MLC 0084 (Beldam, Chadwick LJJ): there was no proper evidence on which the judge could base his conclusion that it was through negligence that the claimant had fallen from a hospital trolley. The Court of Appeal also strongly criticised the judge for his disparaging remarks about the defence lawyers, which it said were quite without foundation.

Burke v *Leeds Health Authority* [2001] MLC 0314, CA: where the judge had found that the oncologists recommending treatment by intense chemotherapy for a child's leukaemia were negligent not to have told the parents that it would be possible, though not optimum, to delay treatment for a while, the defendant's appeal succeeded on the basis that the judge's finding of breach of duty could not be sustained in the absence of any expert evidence supporting such a conclusion. The treatment had led to spastic quadriplegia.

Unsuccessful appeals by the claimant

Scott v *Wakefield Area Health Authority* MLC 0659, [1997] 8 Med LR 341, CA (Beldam, Ward, Schiemann LJJ): the claimant unsuccessfully contended that the judge's conclusion that the defendants had not negligently managed his visual disability was not supported by the evidence.

Jacobs v *Great Yarmouth and Waverney Health Authority* MLC 0710, [1995] 6 Med LR 192 (Stephenson, O'Connor, Griffiths LJJ – judgment given in 1984): the claimant unsuccessfully contended that the judge had not been entitled to find on the evidence that her 'anaesthetic awareness' had been post-operative, not preoperative.

Delaney v *Southmead Health Authority* MLC 0582, [1995] 6 Med LR 355 (Dillon, Butler-Sloss, Stuart-Smith LJJ – judgment given in 1992): the claimant unsuccessfully argued that the finding of the trial judge was against the weight of the evidence when he concluded that her brachial plexus lesion had not been caused by improper placing of her arm during her cholecystectomy.

Sellers v *Cooke* MLC 0660, [1990] 2 Med LR 16, CA (Slade, Balcombe, Butler-Sloss LJJ): the trial judge found that neither negligence nor causation had been established in this claim for negligent obstetric attention resulting in the death of the foetus. The Court of Appeal dealt only with causation (because there had been a successful application to admit fresh evidence on appeal relating to negligence), and concluded that in any event, ie regardless of whether the fresh evidence might have persuaded them that the judge's finding on negligence could not stand, his negative conclusion on causation (that the child would have died anyway) could not be successfully challenged.

Gregory v *Pembrokeshire Health Authority* MLC 0596, [1989] 1 Med LR 81 (O'Connor, Nicholls, Taylor LJJ): the judge found that the claimant mother should have been told that the amniocentesis sample had been inadequate, but that she would have accepted what would have been the consultant's advice, namely not to risk another amniocentesis; so she failed on causation because her Down's syndrome child would have been born in any event. The Court of Appeal felt unable to interfere with this negative finding on causation, emphasising, as it always does except where it wants a different result, that the judge, who had heard and seen the witnesses, was in the best position to assess the evidence, and to draw inferences from and reach conclusions upon it.

Sherlock v *North Birmingham Health Authority* (1997) 40 BMLR 103, [1998] JPIL 230 (Pill, Henry, Chadwick LJJ): the Court of Appeal refused to interfere with the judge's findings that, even though the advice of the paediatric senior registrar should have been sought, he would not have advised transfer to the intensive care unit (the procedure that would probably have avoided respiratory collapse of the patient) and that it would not have been mandatory to effect such transfer.

Lavelle v *Hammersmith and Queen Charlotte's Special Health Authority* (16 January 1998, unreported) (Hirst, Henry, Auld LJJ): where the new-born claimant was disastrously injured during a balloon atrial sepostomy (to correct his congenital heart condition) and there were two possible ways the injury could have been caused, only one of which involved negligence, the trial judge was held to have been entitled to conclude on the evidence that it had not been proved that the injury had been caused in the negligent manner.

Brock v *Frenchay Healthcare Trust* MLC 0101, [1999] MLC 0101 (Simon Brown, Auld, Thorpe LJJ): the judge's finding could not be faulted where he concluded that the delay in administering Mannitol after a head injury had not affected the outcome.

Brown v *Lewisham and North Southwark Health Authority* MLC 0081, [1999] Lloyd's Rep Med 110 (Beldam, Morritt, Mantell LJJ): the judge had been entitled to conclude that there was no evidence to support the claimant's contention that the journey by way of transfer between a London and a Blackpool hospital had been an effective cause of the deep vein thrombosis that led to loss of a leg.

Hallatt v *North West Anglia Health Authority* MLC 0055, [1998] Lloyd's Rep Med 197 (Hobhouse, Swinton Thomas, Buxton LJJ): the judge had been entitled to find that a single and isolated observation of mild glycosuria during pregnancy at 29 to 30 weeks did not mandate a glucose tolerance test.

Matthews v *East Suffolk Health Authority* [1999] MLC 0170 (Henry, Robert Walker LJJ, Alliott J): the finding by the judge that prompt treatment with antibiotics would not have lessened the brain damage sustained by the appellant, because it had already occurred, was upheld.

Carew v *Bexley and Greenwich District Health Authority* [1999] MLC 0125 (Peter Gibson, Pill, Chadwick LJJ): the judge had fairly concluded that there were no warning signs of a mother's pre-eclampsia and that the single failure to take a urine sample was not causative of the child's brain damage as it would probably not have yielded a significant result.

Lakey v *Merton, Sutton and Wandsworth Health Authority* [1999] MLC 0075 (Nourse, Thorpe, Potter LLJ): the judge had been entitled to conclude that the A & E decision not to X-ray a patient presenting with gross pain in the right hip was reasonable.

Vadera v *Shaw* [1998] MLC 0335 (Henry, Otton, Buxton LJJ): the judge had been entitled to find on the evidence that a single high reading was not a basis for a finding of hypertension, and that there was no substantive history of headaches in this patient, who alleged that the contraceptive pill, Logynon, had caused her to have a stroke.

Morris v *Blackpool Victoria Hospital NHS Trust* [2004] MLC 1169, CA: this was an obstetric case where it was agreed all round that a further scan would have revealed IUGR (inter-uterine growth retardation) and the child would then have been delivered promptly so as to avoid his brain injury. The judge's finding that the child had not been suffering from IUGR went wholly against the weight of the evidence and the Court of Appeal were bemused by it. But the appeal by the claimant failed notwithstanding, because the judge's other important finding that there had been no mandatory indication to perform another scan, and therefore no breach of duty (and so, of course, no causation), was reasonable, said the appeal court, and was not affected by his substandard performance on the wholly distinct IUGR issue.

Successful appeals by the claimant

Arkless v *Leicestershire Health Authority* (22 October 1998), Medical Litigation 11/98 p 6 (Stuart-Smith, Otton, Tuckey LJJ): given the findings of fact of the Recorder as to the presence of clinical signs of congenital displacement of the hip at the six to nine months check and the view of the defence expert that examination should have detected such signs, the only conclusion open to the judge should have been that the health visitor had not conducted a competent examination.

Montantaro v *Home Office* [2002] MLC 0777: in a claim by a prisoner that a prison doctor had negligently failed to diagnose his scaphoid fracture, the court allowed his appeal on the ground that the trial judge's interventions had been made largely against the claimant and the judge had had no warrant for finding that no fracture had been sustained by the time the doctor saw the prisoner and the claimant had therefore not had a fair trial (human rights featured prominently).

Starcevic v *West Hertfordshire Health Authority* [2001] MLC 0428: this is an interesting case. The main issue in this appeal from Kennedy J was whether the deceased had complained of pain and swelling in his calf and on that issue whether the widow's account or the medical staff's account should be preferred. On consideration of all the evidence, the appeal court concluded that the only possible conclusion was that the widow's evidence should have been accepted by the judge, her appeal was allowed and agreed damages awarded.

Webb v *Barclays Bank plc and Portsmouth Hospitals NHS Trust* MLC 0400, [2002] PIQR P61: this was not strictly a successful appeal by claimant though it resembled one. It occurred in the following circumstances. Mrs Webb sustained a fall while employed by Barclays. Upon advice from a doctor at the hospital she underwent an amputation. She sued both employer and hospital, the former for failing to provide a safe environment for work, and the latter for negligent advice causing her to have an amputation which she did not need. The bank settled the totality of her claim and served a contribution notice on the hospital alleging that the advice to accept an amputation had been negligent and that Mrs Webb would have declined an amputation had she been given proper advice. Mrs Webb did not give evidence at the trial of the contribution issue. The judge was not satisfied that causation was proved. But the Court of Appeal said that there was ample evidence to show that if she had been given proper advice she would have declined the amputation. Therefore the contribution notice was valid and the appeal was allowed.

Unsuccessful appeals by the defendant

Fallows v *Randle* MLC 0591, [1997] 8 Med LR 160 (Stuart-Smith, Peter Gibson, Ward LJJ): a failed sterilisation case, where the court dismissed the defendants' appeal, saying that it had been open to the judge to prefer the evidence of the claimant's expert as to the probable reason why the clip was found not to be on the Fallopian tube.

Lybert v *Warrington Health Authority* MLC 0712, [1996] 7 Med LR 71 (Nourse, Millett, Otton LJJ): the court refused to interfere with the judge's finding that no proper warning of the failure rate had been given before a sterilisation, or that in the particular circumstances of the case where the couple were awaiting the claimant's hysterectomy they would have taken the added (and admittedly unusual) precaution of using a condom while waiting for the hysterectomy. Comment: it was certainly open to the appeal court on the evidence to have come to directly contrary conclusions, so this has to be seen as a sympathetic decision (see further Chapter 11).

Bull and Wakeham v *Devon Area Health Authority* MLC 0022, [1993] 4 Med LR 117, CA (Slade, Dillon, Mustill LJJ): the defendants failed to persuade the court to reverse the judge's findings that they did not have in place an adequate system of obstetric care and that that had caused or contributed to perinatal injury. This case offers useful material on the (theoretically) limited scope for the appeal court to interfere with findings based on a judge's assessment of the oral evidence.

O'Keefe v *Harvey-Kemble* (1998) 45 BMLR 74 (Swinton Thomas, Potter LJJ): the Recorder had been entitled to find that insufficient information had been given to the patient before a breast reduction operation and that she would have declined the procedure if properly informed of the risks. Reading between the lines of the judgments, one gets the impression that the judges were a little surprised at the Recorder's dismissal of the defence evidence, but nevertheless felt unable to interfere with his conclusions.

Briody v *St Helens and Knowsley Health Authority* MLC 0099, [1999] Lloyd's Rep Med 185 (Simon Brown, Ward, Walker LJJ): the court would not interfere with the vital finding that the obstetrician had failed to satisfy himself that the head was likely to be a good fit for the pelvis.

Burrows v *Forest Healthcare NHS Trust* [1999] MLC 00149: the judge had been entitled to find that it had been negligent not to open a third port when performing a laparoscopy and that, had that been done, the small bowel would probably not have been cut.

Penney, Palmer and Cannon v *East Kent Health Authority* [2000] Lloyd's Rep Med 41, [1999] MLC 0126 (Lord Woolf and Hale LJJ) the Canterbury cervical smears case: the judge found that the *Bolam* principle did not apply because there was no dispute about acceptable or unacceptable practice, only a factual dispute about whether the cytoscreeners had given the wrong classification to smears; but, even if the principle had applied, he was satisfied that the evidence of the three experts called by the defence did not stand up to logical analysis because the cytoscreeners did not have the ability to draw a distinction between benign and pre-cancerous cells, and so should have classified the smears as borderline. On the defendants' unsuccessful appeal the court said that the *Bolam* test did apply as the cytoscreeners were exercising skill and judgment in determining what report they should make, but they agreed with the judge that the logical analysis test was applicable and that it led to the conclusion that the exonerating opinion of the defence experts did not stand up to such analysis.

Polson v *de Silva* [1999] MLC 0076 (Simon Brown, Waller LLJ): the defendants failed in their attempt to invalidate the judge's conclusion that treatment some 48 hours after the symptoms of bacterial meningitis had appeared would probably have avoided deafness.

Note that other examples can be found in the various preceding sections dealing with appeals, particularly the section headed 'Must a judge give reasons for his conclusions?'.

Chapter 10

Consent

Andrew Buchan

INTRODUCTION

The law on consent has evolved significantly over recent years. There has been legislation relating to obtaining valid consent – the Human Tissue Act 2004, the Mental Capacity Act 2005 and several important cases. As is well known, the Human Rights Act 1998 came into force in October 2000. All public authorities are required to act in accordance with the rights set out in the Human Rights Act, and all other statutes have to be interpreted by the courts so far as possible in accordance with those rights. (See further Chapter 21 and the British Medical Association (BMA) Handbook of Ethics and Law[1] that gives advice on how the Human Rights Act relates to a range of relevant issues).

The General Medical Council (GMC) has produced a new guide, *Consent: patients and doctors making decisions together* (2008). The guide emphasises the need to work in partnership with the patient or, if the patient lacks capacity, with those working close to the patient and with other members of the healthcare team. It develops the guidance given in the GMC's *Good Medical Practice* (2006). This chapter explains this guidance.

It is a general legal and ethical principle that valid consent must be obtained before starting treatment or physical investigation, or providing personal care, for a person. This principle reflects the right of patients to determine what happens to their own bodies, and is a fundamental part of good practice. A healthcare professional who does not respect this principle may be liable both to legal action by the patient and to action by their professional body. The phrase 'healthcare professional' will be used in this chapter to include physicians, doctors, nurses and other healthcare staff.

While there is no English statute setting out the general principles of consent, the common law has established that touching a patient without valid consent may constitute a criminal offence of assault and/or battery and be a trespass to the person. The failure to obtain proper consent,

---

1   BMA (2004) *Medical Ethics Today: The BMA's Handbook of Ethics and Law* (2nd edition) London BMI Group.

resulting in harm may be a factor in a claim of negligence against the healthcare professional involved. Poor handling of the consent process may also result in complaints from patients through the NHS complaints procedure or to professional bodies (see Chapter 3).

Thus without consent the procedure is a battery, and damages can be recovered without proof of fault, although if the patient would have consented if asked, and the operation has benefited him, damages are likely to be nominal.

RECENT DEVELOPMENTS

The Human Tissue Act 2004 came fully into force on 1 September 2006. It sets out the legal framework for the storage and use of tissue from the living and for the removal, storage and use of tissue and organs from the dead, including 'residual' tissue following clinical and diagnostic procedures. The Human Tissue Act makes consent a legal requirement for the removal, storage and use of human tissue or organs and sets out whose consent is needed in which circumstances. The Act also established the Human Tissue Authority (HTA). The HTA is responsible for approving the transplantation of organs from living donors and bone marrow and peripheral blood stem cells from adults who lack the capacity to consent and children who lack the competence to consent. Further guidance on consent and codes of practice are available below and on the HTA's website.[2]

The Mental Capacity Act 2005 came fully into force on 1 October 2007. It sets out a statutory framework for making treatment decisions for people who lack the capacity to make such decisions themselves (see also Chapter 22). The Act establishes statutory principles governing these decisions, setting out who can make them and when. It sets out the legal requirements for assessing whether or not a person lacks the capacity to make a decision.

Where a person lacks the capacity to make a decision for themselves, any decision must be made in that person's best interests. The Mental Capacity Act introduced a duty on NHS bodies to instruct an independent mental capacity advocate (IMCA) in serious medical treatment decisions when a person who lacks the capacity to make a decision has no one who can speak for them, other than paid staff. The Act allows people to plan ahead for a time when they may not have the capacity to make their own decisions: it allows them to appoint a personal welfare attorney to make health and social care decisions, including medical treatment, on their behalf or to make an advance decision to refuse medical treatment.

Further guidance is available below and in the Mental Capacity Act (2005) Code of Practice.[3]

There have been a number of recent legal cases. These include:

- *Ms B* v *An NHS Hospital Trust*.[4] Following an illness, Ms B became tetraplegic and reliant on an artificial ventilator. She asked that the

---

2   www.hta.gov.uk.
3   www.publicguardian.gov.uk/mca/code-of-practice.htm.
4   *Ms B* v *An NHS Hospital Trust* [2002] 2 All ER 449.

ventilator that was keeping her alive be switched off, and claimed that the continued provision of artificial ventilation against her wishes was an unlawful trespass. The court was asked to decide whether Ms B had the capacity to make the decision about whether the ventilator should be removed. The Court held that Ms B did have capacity to refuse treatment and had therefore been treated unlawfully. Where a patient has the capacity to make decisions about treatment, they have the right to refuse treatment – even when the consequences of such decisions could lead to their death. If a doctor feels unable to carry out the wishes of the patient, their duty is to find another doctor who will do so.

- *Glass* v *United Kingdom*.[5] The European Court of Human Rights held that a decision of health professionals to override the wishes of the mother of a seriously ill child gave rise to a breach of Art 8 of the European Convention on Human Rights (ECHR). The court was critical of the fact that the courts were not involved at an earlier stage, and held that, in the event of a continued disagreement between parents and doctors about a child's treatment, the courts should be consulted, and particularly before the matter reaches an emergency situation.
- *Chester* v *Afshar*.[6] The House of Lords held that a failure to warn a patient of a risk of injury inherent in surgery, however small the probability of the risk occurring, denies the patient the chance to make a fully informed decision. The judgment held that it is advisable that health practitioners give information about all significant possible adverse outcomes and make a record of the information given.
- *Burke* v *The General Medical Council*.[7] The Court of Appeal held that the General Medical Council (GMC) guidance on withholding and withdrawing life-prolonging treatment was lawful. A patient cannot demand a particular treatment, but health professionals must take account of a patient's wishes when making treatment decisions. Where a patient with capacity indicates his wish to be kept alive by the provision of Artificial Nutrition and Hydration (ANH), doctors are required to provide ANH for as long as such treatment continues to prolong life. Where life depends upon the continued provision of ANH, ANH will be clinically indicated. A health professional who deliberately brought that patient's life to an end by withdrawing ANH would be in breach of their duty and guilty of murder. If the patient lacks capacity, all reasonable steps that are in the person's best interests should be taken to prolong his life. Although there is a strong presumption in favour of providing life-sustaining treatment, there are circumstances when continuing or providing life-sustaining treatment stops providing a benefit to a patient and is not clinically indicated.
- In *Janet Birch* v *University College London Hospital NHS Foundation Trust* [2008] EWHC 237 (QB), (2008) 104 BMLR 168, the claimant (B) claimed damages against the defendant NHS trust for injuries that she sustained as a result of the performance of invasive surgery.

5   *Glass* v *United Kingdom* (61827/00) [2004] 1 FLR 1019, ECtHR.
6   *Chester* v *Afshar* [2004] UKHL 41.
7   *Burke* v *The General Medical Council* [2005] 3 WLR 1132.

B had been admitted to hospital displaying atypical symptoms of vascular third nerve palsy. The consultant doctor recommended that she undergo an MRI scan in order to exclude the possibility that she was suffering from either a posterior communicating artery aneurysm or cavernous sinus pathology. There were no available MRI slots available to B at that hospital so her consultant requested that she be transferred to a neurology ward in a specialist hospital operated by the Trust; later, she was transferred to a neurosurgical ward at that hospital. The Trust's neurosurgeons decided to perform a catheter angiography; a mildly invasive procedure that had increased risks for people in B's position. The associated risks of angiography were explained to B, who then signed the relevant consent form. Subsequently, there were complications with surgery that resulted in a stroke. The court held that there was no valid consent.[8]

ASSAULT AND BATTERY

As stated above any contact by the physician with the patient's body, whether by laying hands on it, eg for an operation, for an injection, for massage or, less directly, by the use of a machine directing electromagnetic or other waves at the body, eg radiotherapy, chemotherapy, X-rays, sound or heat treatment, is potentially a trespass to the person, as involving an invasion of the patient's bodily integrity.[9]

It is not significant whether the conduct complained of is termed a trespass, an assault or a battery. The nub of it is the unlawful, intentional application of force to the person of another.

> If a man intentionally applies force direct to another, the plaintiff has a cause of action in assault and battery, or, if you so please to describe it, in trespass to the person ... (*per* Lord Denning, in *Letang* v *Cooper* [1965] 1 QB 232, CA).

It is generally thought that the interference with the claimant's bodily integrity has to be by way of an intentional act; otherwise the cause of action lies in negligence (see *Fowler* v *Lanning* [1959] 1 QB 426). An intention to injure is not essential, but the act that violates the bodily integrity of the claimant, ie the contact, must be intentional. In *Wilson* v *Pringle* [1987] QB 237, the Court of Appeal said, in the context of the horseplay that goes on between schoolboys, that the contact must be proved to be a hostile contact. Hostility was not to be equated with ill-will or malevolence, and would be a question of fact. Clearly, one cannot require any sort of hostility to be proved when a surgeon operates without consent. Yet it is a battery. The 'hostility' factor must surely be limited to situations where the contact could otherwise be one of the incidents of friendly intercourse (eg slapping a batsman on the back after a good innings or part of accepted horseplay among friends). One would do best to adopt the formulation of

---

8   *Janet Birch* v *University College London Hospital NHS Foundation Trust* [2008] EWHC 2237 (QB), (2008) 104 BMLR 168.

9   Every human being of adult years and sound mind has a right to determine what shall be done with his own body; and a surgeon who performs an operation without the patient's consent commits an assault (*per* Cardozo J in *Schloendorff* v *Society of New York Hospital* 105 NE 92 (NY, 1914)).

Goff LJ in *Collins* v *Wilcock* [1984] 1 WLR 1172, when he said that there was a general exception to the illegality of intentional physical contact which embraced all physical contact generally acceptable in the ordinary conduct of daily life. Goff LJ expressly disassociated himself from the antic notion that a battery is only committed where the action is 'angry, revengeful, rude or insolent' (Hawkins *Pleas of the Crown* (8th edition, 1824) Vol 1, Ch 15, section 2) – words hardly apt to describe a surgical intervention! Wood J took this view in *T* v *T* [1988] Fam 52, when he said that, as the law stood, a surgeon who performed a termination of pregnancy on a 'mentally handicapped' adult would be liable for trespass (assuming it was not a medical emergency) despite the absence of hostile intent (see below under 'Mentally disordered persons').

Another example of a 'friendly' (non-hostile) assault is the hairdresser who, without getting proper consent, applies a 'tone rinse' to a customer's hair (*Nash* v *Sheen* [1953] CLY 3726).

In *Allan* v *New Mount Sinai Hospital* (1980) 109 DLR (3d) 634, an anaesthetist who acted without negligence was held liable in battery for unforeseeable injury suffered by the patient because he administered the injection that led to the injury into the patient's left arm, the patient having expressly told him not to inject into that limb. The defendant acted in accordance with normal medical procedure, but he had ignored the claimant's instructions. He was accordingly liable for trespass to the person, and for all the damage that flowed directly from that trespass.

In *Appleton* v *Garrett* MLC 0045, [1997] 8 Med LR 75, Dyson J awarded aggravated damages for trespass where the defendant had prescribed and carried out unnecessary dental treatment for the sole purpose of getting himself more work.[10]

Different causes of action: the merits of assault v negligence

A number of factors distinguish the action for assault from that for negligence:

1   Fault, as we have seen, is irrelevant. If the patient can show he did not consent to the treatment he will be able to recover damages without proof of negligence.
2   Whereas in the action for negligence the defendant is only liable for loss and injury which was foreseeable at the time of the negligent act (see Chapter 8), the tortfeasor in trespass is liable for all damage flowing directly from the assault, whether foreseeable or not. The wrongful act consists of a trespass, and for that the defendant is liable in respect of all loss and injury flowing directly from the assault, however unforeseeable (see *Allan* v *New Mount Sinai Hospital*

---

10   In *R* v *Richardson* (1998) 43 BMLR 21, a criminal conviction was overturned on appeal where a dentist who had been struck off continued to treat her patients with their apparent consent but without telling them of her disqualification. The Court of Appeal said that only a mistake about the nature of the act alleged to constitute an assault or the identity of the assailant vitiated consent in criminal law, and for this purpose a person's professional status or qualifications did not constitute part of their identity. Consequently, the appeal would be allowed. The court said the civil law concept of informed consent had no place in the criminal law.

(above) *per* Linden J). Nevertheless, the injury or loss must be of a type which the law recognises, and within the rules as to remoteness of damage in the sense that it must be directly caused by the assault (see Chapter 8).

3   Whereas negligence is not actionable without proof of actual damage or loss, trespass has no such requirement. Even if no injury is suffered, damages may be awarded to compensate for the fact of the assault (these are likely to be nominal in such a case, though one can envisage an award for, for example, the indignity suffered). The limitation period will therefore start to run, in the absence of special factors (see Chapter 18), when the assault takes place and not when injury is suffered, as the cause of action is complete at the time of the assault. In negligence the cause of action is not complete until damage has been suffered and the limitation period only starts to run when the claimant appreciates that or ought to have.

4   The limitation period for a claim for assault is six years, not three, as it has been held, oddly enough, that the provisions of s 11 (and consequently s 14) do not apply to such a claim (*Stubbings* v *Webb* [1993] AC 498, HL).

5   The fact that the patient would have consented to an assault if asked does not absolve the defendant from liability, but it would seem sensible to take that fact into account in reducing damages, for otherwise a person might recover damages for an operation, carried out without consent, but which benefited him and which he would have agreed to if asked. If the cause of action is in negligence, the defendant is entitled to contend that the patient has suffered no injury because, even if he had not been negligent, eg even if he had explained the nature of the operation properly, the patient would still have agreed to it.

What about emergency treatment?

It may be that no action will lie for assault in respect of emergency treatment reasonably and carefully carried out upon a patient without his consent, based on public policy and the principle thatthe patient would have consented if it had been possible to ask him.

There is no English reported case directly on the right or duty of a doctor to carry out emergency treatment on a patient when consent cannot be obtained, but commentators generally agree that, where such treatment is necessary to preserve the life or the health of the patient, no action lies for assault. Another possible basis for this immunity, beside that of implied consent, is the duty of the physician, albeit a moral rather than a legal one, to take all reasonable steps to preserve life. (See the Hypocratic oath in Appendix VI.)

In *Wilson* v *Pringle* [1987] QB 237, the Court of Appeal, speaking of the 'legal rule [that] allows a casualty surgeon to perform an urgent operation on an unconscious patient who is brought into hospital' said:

> The patient cannot consent, and there may be no next-of-kin available. Hitherto it has been customary to say in such cases that consent is to be implied for what would otherwise be a battery on the unconscious body. It is better simply to say that the surgeon's action is acceptable in the ordinary conduct of everyday life, and not a battery.

In *Re MB* [1997] 8 Med LR 217, the Court of Appeal said, *obiter*, that emergency medical treatment could be given, provided it was a necessity and did no more than was necessary in the best interests of the patient. This is known as the necessity principle. The Court of Appeal outlined the basic principles at common law when dealing with capacity to consent.

In *Marshall* v *Curry* [1933] 3 DLR 260, a case decided in the Supreme Court of Nova Scotia, a surgeon who found and removed a grossly diseased testicle during an operation for a hernia was found when sued for trespass to have acted properly.

> Where a great emergency which could not be anticipated arises [a doctor is justified in acting] in order to save the life or preserve the health of the patient (*per* Chisholm CJ).

But the fact that it is convenient to perform the operation at the time is not sufficient to give the doctor immunity from an action for trespass; it must actually be necessary. In *Murray* v *McMurchy* [1949] 2 DLR 442, the Supreme Court of British Columbia imposed liability on a surgeon who, while performing a Caesarean section, discovered fibroid tumours on the uterus of the patient and, concerned for the hazards of any future pregnancy, tied her tubes. Here the action of the doctor, though undertaken from the best of motives, was not a necessity at that particular time (for a suitably academic treatment of this topic, see PDG Skegg *A justification for medical procedures performed without consent* (1974) 90 LQR 512).

In *R* v *Bournewood Community and Mental Health NHS Trust, ex p L* [1999] 1 AC 458, HL, the court held that the common law doctrine of necessity allowed informal detention of mental patients, ie without actual consent or formal detention under the Mental Health Act. The general principle of necessity was said to apply where there was a necessity to act when it was not practicable to communicate with the assisted person, and the action taken must be such as a reasonable person would in all the circumstances take, acting in the best interests of the assisted person (as *per* Lord Goff in *Re F* [1990] 2 AC 1, HL).

OBTAINING CONSENT

As stated above, the GMC has produced a new guide, *Consent: patients and doctors making decisions together* (2008). It develops the guidance given in the GMC's *Good Medical Practice* (2006). This guide warns that whilst not being a statutory code 'serious or persistent failure to follow this guidance will put your registration at risk'.

The standards expected of healthcare professionals by their regulatory bodies may at times be higher than the minimum required at common law. Although this chapter focuses primarily on the legal position, it will also indicate relevant guidance from regulatory bodies. It should be noted that the common law has historically been based on the standards set by the professions for their members (see further Chapter 9); therefore where the standards required by professional bodies are rising, it is likely that the legal standards will rise accordingly.

Valid consent

For consent to be valid, it must be given voluntarily by an appropriately informed person who has the capacity to consent to the intervention in question. (This will normally be the patient but not necessarily so. It can be someone with parental responsibility for a patient under the age of 18, someone authorised to do so under a Lasting Power of Attorney (LPA) or someone who has the authority to make treatment decisions as a court appointed deputy.) Acquiescence where the person does not know what the intervention entails is not 'consent'.

The primary question – does the person have capacity to give consent?

Under the Mental Capacity Act 2005, a person must be assumed to have capacity unless it is established that they lack capacity. If there is any doubt, then the healthcare professional should assess the capacity of the patient to take the decision in question. This assessment and the conclusions drawn from it should be recorded in the patient's notes. Guidance on assessing capacity is given in Chapter 4 of the Mental Capacity Act (2005) Code of Practice.

The Mental Capacity Act 2005 defines a person who lacks capacity as a person who is unable to make a decision for themselves because of an impairment or disturbance in the functioning of their mind or brain. It does not matter if the impairment or disturbance is permanent or temporary. A person lacks capacity if:

- they have an impairment or disturbance (for example a disability, condition or trauma or the effect of drugs or alcohol) that affects the way their mind or brain works; and
- that impairment or disturbance means that they are unable to make a specific decision at the time it needs to be made.

An assessment of a person's capacity must be based on their ability to make a specific decision at the time it needs to be made, and not their ability to make decisions in general. A person is unable to make a decision if they cannot do one or more of the following things:

- understand the information given to them that is relevant to the decision;
- retain that information long enough to be able to make the decision;
- use or weigh up the information as part of the decision-making process;
- communicate their decision – this could be by talking or using sign language and includes simple muscle movements such as blinking an eye or squeezing a hand.

People may have capacity to consent to some interventions but not to others, or may have capacity at some times but not others.

A person's capacity to consent may be temporarily affected by factors such as confusion, panic, shock, fatigue, pain or medication. However, the existence of such factors should not lead to an automatic assumption that the person does not have the capacity to consent.

Capacity should not be confused with a healthcare professional's assessment of the reasonableness of the person's decision. Under the

Mental Capacity Act and the common law, a person is not to be treated as unable to make a decision merely because they make an unwise decision. A person is entitled to make a decision which may be perceived by others to be unwise or irrational, as long as they have the capacity to do so.

However, if the decision that appears irrational is based on a misperception of reality, as opposed to a different value system to that of the health practitioner – for example a patient who, despite the obvious evidence, denies that his foot is gangrenous, or a patient with anorexia nervosa who is unable to comprehend their failing physical condition – then it might be reasonable (ie objectively justifiable) to think that the patient cannot comprehend, weigh or make use of the relevant information and hence may lack the capacity to make the decision in question.

The Mental Capacity Act also requires that all practical and appropriate steps are taken to enable a person to make the decision themselves. These steps include the following:

- Providing relevant information. For example, if there is a choice, has information been given on all the alternatives?
- Communicating in an appropriate way. For example, could the information be explained or presented in a way that is easier for the patient to understand?
- Making the patient feel at ease. For example, are there particular times of the day when the person's understanding is better?
- Supporting the patient. For example, can anyone else help or support the person to understand information and to make a choice?

Guidance on how people should be helped to make their own decisions is given in Chapter 3 of the Mental Capacity Act (2005) Code of Practice.

Is any consent given voluntarily?

To be valid, consent must be given voluntarily and freely, without pressure or undue influence being exerted on the person either to accept or refuse treatment. Such pressure can come from partners or family members, as well as health or care practitioners. The healthcare professional should be alert to this possibility and where appropriate should arrange to see the person on his own in order to attempt to verify that the decision is truly his own.

When people are seen and treated in environments where involuntary detention may be an issue, such as prisons[11] and mental hospitals[12] (see

---

11   For example, in *Re T* [1992] and *Freeman* v *the Home Office (No 2)* [1984] QB 524. The Court of Appeal said in *Freeman* v *Home Office (No 2)* that a prisoner was able to give a valid consent to the administering of drugs, and whether he had actually done so was a question of fact for the trial judge, and a court had to be alive to the risk that in a prison setting an apparent consent might not be a real one. A prisoner who has not given consent to treatment may, of course, maintain an action for assault (*Barbara* v *Home Office* (1984) 134 NLJ 888). In *Secretary of State for the Home Department* v *Robb* [1995] Fam 127, Thorpe J authorised prison staff to accept the decision of an adult prisoner of sound mind to refuse all nutrition. The judge said that a prisoner of sound mind, just like any other adult, had a specific right of self-determination. It was not absolute, requiring to be balanced against potentially countervailing state interests in preserving life, preventing suicide and protecting innocent third parties, but in this case there were no such countervailing considerations.

12   For example, care should be taken that a so called 'voluntary' patient who consents to treatment, is not doing so knowing that if he refuses he will be sectioned under the Mental Health Act 1983 as amended and become 'involuntary'.

below), there is a potential for treatment offers to be perceived coercively, whether or not this is the case. Coercion invalidates consent, and care must be taken to ensure that the person makes decisions freely. Coercion should be distinguished from providing the person with appropriate reassurance concerning their treatment, or pointing out the potential benefits of treatment for the person's health. However, threats such as withdrawal of any privileges, loss of remission of sentence for refusing consent or using such matters to induce consent may well invalidate the consent given, and are not acceptable.

Consent requires knowledge as well as understanding – has the person received sufficient information about the proposed treatment?

The duty of disclosure: general

What if the patient knows something, but not everything, about the treatment proposed? How much does the doctor have to reveal? And does a failure to reveal mean that no valid consent can be given, so that the healthcare professional is liable in trespass, or should it be seen as an aspect of negligence, so that the action will lie only in negligence, with the consequent limiting factors applicable to such an action (as set out above)?

In *Chatterton* v *Gerson* [1981] QB 432, Bristow J considered a claim by a woman that an operation to relieve pain in a post-operative scar area in the right groin had been carried out without consent and negligently. The operation had proved unsuccessful, and she claimed for assault, on the basis that her consent was vitiated for lack of proper explanation as to the nature of the procedure to be undertaken, and for negligence, on the basis that the defendant was in breach of his duty of care towards her because his failure to give a proper explanation of the nature and the implications of the proposed operation made it impossible for her to give an informed consent.

On the question whether there was a real consent so as to free the physician from liability for assault, and on the distinction between a claim for assault and one based on negligence, the judge said:

> It is clear law that in any context in which consent of the injured party is a defence to what would otherwise be a crime or a civil wrong, the consent must be real. Where, for example, a woman's consent to sexual intercourse is obtained by fraud, her apparent consent is no defence to a charge of rape. It is not difficult to state the principle or appreciate its good sense. As so often, the problem lies in its application ...

> In my judgment what the court has to do in each case is to look at all the circumstances and say 'Was there a real consent?' I think justice requires that in order to vitiate the reality of consent there must be a greater failure of communication between doctor and patient than that involved in a breach of duty if the claim is based on negligence. When the claim is based on negligence the plaintiff must prove not only the breach of duty to inform, but that had the duty not been broken she would not have chosen to have the operation. Where the claim is based on trespass to the person, once it is shown that the consent is unreal, then what the plaintiff would have decided if she had been given the information which would have prevented vitiation of the reality of her consent is irrelevant.

> In my judgment once the patient is informed in broad terms of the nature of the procedure which is intended, and gives her consent, that consent is real, and the cause of the action on which to base a claim for failure to go into risks and implications is negligence, not trespass ... in my judgment it would be very much against the interests of justice if actions which are really based on a failure by the doctor to perform his duty adequately to inform were pleaded in trespass.

That remains the best statement of the English law on the question when an apparent consent is invalid for lack of information, so as to afford a claim for assault.

In *Abbas* v *Kenney* [1996] 7 Med LR 47, where the patient claimed that she had not been told clearly enough that a pelvic clearance might be undertaken, Gage J said that a doctor has a duty to explain what he intends to do and the implications of what he is going to do. It must be explained in such a way that the patient can understand. The precise terms, however, and precise emphasis on what he intends to do is a matter for the individual doctor, based on his clinical judgment.

Only if the healthcare professional fails to 'inform in broad terms of the nature of the procedure which is intended' will the apparent consent be vitiated and an action for assault lie. In *Slater* v *Baker and Stapleton* (1767) 2 Wils 359, it was said that 'a patient should be told what is about to be done to him, that he may take courage and put himself in such a situation as to enable him to undergo the operation' – courage is what was needed in those days, one may be sure!

Any lesser failure in giving information can give rise only to an action in negligence for breach of duty. What then is the surgeon's duty of disclosure?

The risks of the operation

Every operation is attended by its risks. So is most treatment. Every drug can produce unwanted side effects. No treatment can be guaranteed to succeed. When something goes wrong the patient first asks whether the doctor has been negligent in his treatment. Has he made a negligent diagnosis, or prescribed the wrong drugs when he should have known better? Or has he performed the operation without due care? When it appears that, in the strictly medical context, the doctor's performance has been unimpugnable, the patient's complaint is likely to be: 'You never told me this might happen. If you had I would have declined the treatment.' The English courts have had to consider which of two tests to adopt for assessing the duty upon a doctor to disclose the risks inherent in a particular treatment. The tests may be termed 'the medical standard' and 'informed consent'.

(A) THE MEDICAL STANDARD OF DISCLOSURE

Under the medical standard, the medical profession is permitted to set its own standards of disclosure without supervision by the court. The profession itself decides what disclosure is to be made in any particular case. It is enough for a defendant to avoid liability if he shows that at the time of the treatment there was a body of responsible medical opinion, albeit a minority one, that would have done what he did. This enables a defendant to succeed simply by producing one or two physicians who endorse his conduct, and it is of no avail for the claimant to produce evidence to a contrary effect. If the court accepts that there was such a body of medical opinion it will not be entitled to choose between the differing schools of thought. This is a unique advantage for the professionals. The court is forever choosing between differing expert testimonies in other fields and making up its own mind as to what constitutes negligence.

This medical standard had for a long time been accepted as the test for assessing negligence in treatment and diagnosis (see Chapters 6 and 9 above for a full discussion), but it was not clear before the decision of the House of Lords in the *Sidaway* case (see below) that it would be applicable to the question of disclosure of risks.

(B) THE DOCTRINE OF INFORMED CONSENT

There had grown up across the Atlantic, in some US jurisdictions and also in Canada, a different test, whereby the court had the right to assess and delineate the extent of the duty of disclosure in any particular case. This was the test of 'informed consent'. If the patient was not given sufficient information upon which he could reach an informed decision whether to accept the treatment proposed or not, then he was not able to give a valid consent. It was for the court to decide whether he had been given that information, not for the doctors. The leading cases illustrating this doctrine are, in the US, *Canterbury* v *Spence* 464 F 2d 772, MLC 0006 (1972); *Scaria* v *St Paul Fire and Marine Insurance* 227 NW 2d 647; *Zelesnik* v *Jewish Chronic Disease Hospital* 336 NYS 2d 163 (1975); and in the Supreme Court of Canada, *Hopp* v *Lepp* (1980) 112 DLR (3d) 67 and *Reibl* v *Hughes* (1980) 114 DLR (3d) 1.

The courts have variously said:

> To bind the disclosure obligation to medical usage is to arrogate the decision on revelation to the physician alone. Respect for the patient's right of self-determination on particular therapy demands a standard set by law for physicians rather than one which physicians may or may not impose upon themselves.

> The duty to disclose or inform cannot be summarily limited to a self-created custom of the profession, to a professional standard that may be non-existent or inadequate to meet the informational needs of a patient.

> Risk disclosure is based on the patient's right to determine what shall be done with his body. Such right should not be at the disposal of the medical community.

According to the doctrine of informed consent, a risk is required to be disclosed when a reasonable person, in what the physician knows or should know to be the patient's position, would be likely to attach significance to the risk or cluster of risks in deciding whether or not to forgo the proposed therapy. The physician can plead therapeutic privilege, and show that there was a good clinical reason why a particular disclosure should not have been made.

Expert evidence of current medical practice remains cogent and persuasive evidence of the appropriate standard, but it is not conclusive. As it was neatly put in a Canadian case:

> No longer does the medical profession alone collectively determine, by its own practices, the amount of information a patient should have in order to decide whether to undergo an operation (*White* v *Turner* (1981) 120 DLR (3d) 269).

Anyone interested in applications of the doctrine of informed consent might wish to read some of the cases in which the Canadian reports abound: *Videto* v *Kennedy* (1981) 125 DLR (3d) 127; *Bucknam* v *Kostuik* (1983) 3 DLR (4th) 99; *Considine* v *Camp Hill Hospital* (1982) 133 DLR (3d) 11; *Ferguson* v *Hamilton Civil Hospitals* (1983) 144 DLR (3d) 214; *Casey* v *Provan* (1984) 11 DLR (4th) 708; *Grey* v *Webster* (1984) 14 DLR (4th) 706.

The Saskatchewan Court of Appeal's decision in *Haughian* v *Paine* (1987) 37 DLR (4th) 624, is interesting. Although based on the doctrine of informed consent, it makes the generally valid point that a patient is entitled to be told of non-surgical alternatives to the treatment proposed.

Kitchen v *McMullen* [1990] 1 Med LR 352, New Brunswick Court of Appeal, can be used to illuminate the difference in the law on the doctor's duty to disclose the risks of an operation or treatment between Canadian law, where the patient's rights are respected, and here, where they are not. In short, the claimant was given an anti-coagulant (Hemofil) to control bleeding after a tooth extraction. Like all blood products, Hemofil carries a small risk of hepatitis, which materialised. The claimant sued for damages on the ground that he should have been warned of the risk, claiming that, if he had been warned, he would not have accepted the treatment.

Now, under the Canadian doctrine of informed consent, the doctor has a duty to disclose all 'material' or 'unusual or special' risks. Those risks are (more or less) such risks as the court feels would affect the mind of a patient when deciding whether or not to accept the treatment proposed. What is important here is that it is for the court to decide the status of the risk, not for the doctors. So if the court decides the risk was 'material', then it matters not that no doctor ever discloses it. A doctor is in breach of his duty in not doing so. In this way, the Canadian court protects the right of a patient to be properly informed about the treatment proposed. But under English law, as explained below, there is no duty to disclose any risk unless there is no body of responsible medical opinion, not even a minority one, that would follow the course of not disclosing it. So it was left to the medical profession to decide what the patient may or may not know about the treatment he is being offered. So much for patients' rights.

The second aspect of the Canadian test is to decide if a reasonable patient in the claimant's position would have declined or accepted the treatment if warned. This issue is similarly relevant under our law: if the court decides that the risk should have been disclosed (for example, it is likely to find that the risk of failure of a sterilisation should these days be disclosed to the woman), it still has to decide if the patient would have nevertheless accepted the operation or the treatment (thus it might well find that the woman would have taken the 1 in 500 risk of the sterilisation failing, rather than try some other, probably even less secure, method). Canadian law has a rather complex test of whether a reasonable patient would have refused the treatment: our test is simply to ask whether the claimant has satisfied the court on the balance of probabilities that he would have refused it.

The actual decision in the *Kitchen* case was that all three judges found that the risk was one that should have been disclosed to the patient, but two of them then decided that he would have accepted the risk (the third said he would have waited to see if the bleeding got worse). So his action failed.

In *Ellis* v *Wallsend District Hospital* [1990] 2 Med LR 103, the New South Wales Court of Appeal held that, where the patient's evidence was that if warned of the risks of an operation she would have declined it, the trial judge was not at liberty to reject that evidence unless there was contrary evidence showing the claimant's contention to be 'inherently incredible' or 'inherently improbable'.

(C) THE ENGLISH TEST

The English test for establishing negligence in matters of treatment and diagnosis was clear. The medical standard test had been clearly set out in the direction to the jury given by McNair J in *Bolam* v *Friern Hospital Management Committee* [1957] 1 WLR 582. This direction had become a *locus classicus* and was expressly endorsed by the House of Lords in *Whitehouse* v *Jordan* [1981] 1 WLR 246 and *Maynard* v *West Midlands Regional Health Authority* [1984] 1 WLR 634. But did it apply to the duty to disclose material risks? In fact, the *Bolam* case included an allegation of failure to disclose the risks inherent in the treatment undertaken, but it was generally thought that it was still arguable that the test for the duty of disclosure was not necessarily the same as the test for diagnosis and treatment. In the seminal case of *Hunter* v *Hanley* 1955 SLT 213, MLC 0002, a Scottish case upon which McNair J relied, Lord President Clyde had spoken only of diagnosis and treatment:

> In the realm of diagnosis and treatment there is ample scope for difference of opinion and one man clearly is not negligent merely because his conclusion differs from that of other professional men ... The true test for establishing negligence in diagnosis or treatment on the part of a doctor is whether he has been proved to be guilty of such failure as no doctor of ordinary skill would be guilty of if acting with ordinary care ...

In *Hills* v *Potter* [1984] 1 WLR 641n, Hirst J rejected any form of the doctrine of informed consent as having no place in English law and adopted the medical test (though he made it clear that the claimant would have failed in either event).

(D) THE *SIDAWAY* CASE

The leading case on this issue is *Sidaway* v *Board of Governors of the Bethlem Royal Hospital and the Maudsley Hospital* [1985] AC 871, MLC 0010, HL. The facts were that the claimant suffered paralysis following an operation upon her cervical vertebrae. The operation carried a small risk of untoward damage, about a 2% risk of damage to nerve root or spinal cord. Damage to the cord would produce a far more serious result, and the risk of that happening was less than 1%. The surgeon warned of the risk of damage to the nerve root but not of the risk to the spinal cord. The trial judge found that the patient had not been told of all material risks so as to be able to give a fully informed consent to the operation, but, as he was satisfied that the surgeon, in giving the limited disclosure that he did, was following a practice that had the backing of a body of responsible medical opinion at the time of the operation, the claimant must fail, because the test in English law was the medical standard, not informed consent.

The Court of Appeal by a majority endorsed this view ([1984] QB 493). Dunn LJ said a contrary result would damage the doctor/patient relationship and might well have an adverse effect on the practice of medicine. Sir Nicolas Browne-Wilkinson said that the particular quality of that relationship meant that the duty of disclosure in that context should be approached on a different basis from that applicable to ordinary professional men, that the patient must have all the information he reasonably should, but that to test the reasonableness of the disclosure made one look to the standards of the profession. However, the Master of the Rolls said that, although evidence of the medical practice was important, the definition of the duty of care was not to be handed over to the medical profession. It was a matter for the law and the courts, which could not stand idly by if the profession, by an excess of paternalism, denied their patient a real choice. In other words, he said, the law will not permit the medical profession to play God.[13]

Although the House of Lords' judgments reveal different bases for their conclusions, it is tolerably clear that they, albeit by a bare majority, endorsed the medical test, though adding a proviso. Lord Diplock said that the *Bolam* test should be applied to the context of disclosure as to that of treatment and diagnosis. He pointed out that there might at any one time be a number of practices that satisfied the test, and he said:

> To decide what risks the existence of which a patient should be voluntarily warned [about] and the terms in which such warning, if any, should be given, having regard to the effect the warning may have, is as much an exercise of professional skill and judgment as any other part of the doctor's comprehensive duty of care to the individual patient, and expert medical evidence on this matter should be tested in just the same way.

On the question of informed consent, Lord Diplock said that the doctrine was jurisprudentially unsound as it sought to transfer to the sphere of negligence considerations as to consent that were only meaningful in the context of assault and battery (it is indeed true that the US courts had had difficulty in reconciling the absence of 'consent' with a cause of action not in battery but in negligence).

Lord Bridge, with whom Lord Keith agreed, rejecting the informed consent approach, said that a decision as to what degree of disclosure of risks is best calculated to assist a particular patient to make a rational choice as to whether or not to undergo a particular treatment must primarily be a matter of clinical judgment, and so the issue was to be decided primarily on the basis of expert medical evidence, applying the *Bolam* test; but he added (this is the proviso I mentioned above) that the judge might in certain circumstances come to the conclusion that disclosure of a particular risk was so obviously necessary to an informed choice on the part of a patient that no reasonably prudent medical man would fail to make it. He instanced a 10% risk of a stroke from an operation, though he pointed out that there might even there be some cogent clinical reason militating against disclosure.

---

13   Only the lawyers can do that!

Lord Templeman's approach was different: he said that neither was the patient entitled to know everything nor the doctor to decide everything. The doctor was under an obligation to provide information adequate to enable the patient to reach a balanced judgment, subject always to the doctor's own obligation to say and do nothing which he was satisfied would be harmful to the patient: the court would award damages if satisfied that the doctor blundered and that the patient was deprived of information which was necessary for that purpose. Although Lord Templeman makes it clear that in his view the patient is not entitled to know everything, particularly if he does not ask, there is in his judgment no suggestion that the court is bound by medical evidence. He says more than once that it is for the court to decide whether sufficient information was given. This puts him on the same side of the conceptual fence as Lord Scarman, who effectively adopted the doctrine of informed consent, though holding against the claimant on the facts.

In *Moyes* v *Lothian Health Board* [1990] 1 Med LR 463, a Scottish court of first instance rejected a claim that certain risks alleged to be inherent in an angiography procedure should have been disclosed to the patient, principally because it was shown that at the time of the procedure, in 1981, it was consistent with responsible medical practice to give no warning at all. This may not be the same today.

In *Heath* v *West Berkshire Health Authority* [1992] 3 Med LR 57, the claimant failed in her allegation that she should have been warned of the risk of lingual nerve damage arising from an operation to extract a wisdom tooth because the evidence accepted by the judge was that at the time of the operation there was a responsible body of medical opinion that gave no such warning.

In *Smith* v *Tunbridge Wells Health Authority* [1994] 5 Med LR 334, a surgeon failed to inform a man of 28 sufficiently clearly before a rectopexy of the risk, sadly fulfilled, that the procedure could make him impotent. The judge held that, as his condition was not particularly serious, he would probably have declined the operation. Similarly, in *McAllister* v *Lewisham and North Southwark Health Authority* [1994] 5 Med LR 343, a neurosurgeon had failed properly to warn his female patient of the relevant risks before surgery to correct arteriovascular malformation in her leg. What is particularly of note is that the judge held that she would probably have declined the operation if she had been warned, even though her evidence was to the effect that she really could not answer such a hypothetical question.

In *Smith* v *Salford Health Authority* [1994] 5 Med LR 321, the patient failed on causation, ie he proved that the warnings given before surgery on his neck were inadequate but the judge concluded that proper warnings would not have put him off the operation. However, he still won the case as he succeeded in proving operative negligence.

In *Williamson* v *East London and City Health Authority* [1998] Lloyd's Rep Med 6, Butterfield J held a plastic surgeon liable for not giving sufficient information about the extent of the breast operation she intended to perform.

In *Webb* v *Barclays Bank and Portsmouth Hospitals NHS Trust* [2001] Lloyds Rep Med 500, the Court of Appeal said that, where a doctor through ignorance brought about by his negligent failure to inform himself fully about the pathology of the patient's knee, that did not absolve him from the consequences of his negligent advice which resulted from such ignorance. Had he conducted a proper investigation and given the patient the appropriate advice, she would not then have consented to the amputation. In *Enright* v *Kwun* [2003] MLC 1017, Morland J held that the medical attendants of a 37-year-old pregnant woman had failed to tell her of the one in 250 risk of Down's syndrome and the option of an amniocentesis. If they had, she would have had the amniocentesis which would have shown the defect and she would then have opted for a termination.

(E) THE LORD BRIDGE PROVISO

Little has so far been made of the proviso Lord Bridge offered in the *Sidaway* case (above). Would a court be willing to hold that a doctor could be liable for not disclosing a risk despite it being shown that it was not the practice of the profession at the time to do so? The relaxation of the strict *Bolam* principle afforded by the *Bolitho* decision (as explained in Chapters 6 and 9) might suggest that the court would be willing to be the ultimate arbiter of what should be disclosed, similarly to the Canadian principle (Lord Browne-Wilkinson expressly said in *Bolitho* that he was not considering the issue of disclosure of risks). Lord Woolf offered some support to this suggestion in the case of *Pearce* v *United Bristol Healthcare NHS Trust* [1998] PIQR P53, [1999] MLC 0086, CA.

(F) *PEARCE* V *UNITED BRISTOL HEALTHCARE NHS TRUST*

The claimant mother maintained an unusual contention. She had tragically given birth to a dead child in December 1991. The consultant had advised her a few days before the birth, some two weeks after the estimated date of delivery, to wait yet longer, rather than be induced. It was not suggested that his advice that induction would be dangerous was negligent. But it was alleged that he should have disclosed the small additional risk involved in waiting, and, if he had done so, the mother would have sought and obtained a Caesarean section. Lord Woolf, who gave the only reasoned judgment, gave detailed consideration to the *prudent doctor* proviso. Lord Woolf described these words in the speech of Lord Bridge (in *Sidaway*) as 'particularly apposite':

> ... even in a case where, as here, no expert witness in the relevant medical field condemns the non-disclosure as being in conflict with accepted and responsible medical practice, I am of opinion that the judge might in certain circumstances come to the conclusion that disclosure of a particular risk was so obviously necessary to an informed choice on the part of the patient that no reasonably prudent medical man would fail to make it. The kind of case I have in mind would be an operation involving a substantial risk of grave adverse consequences, as, for example, the 10 per cent risk of a stroke from the operation which was the subject of the Canadian case of *Reibl* v *Hughes*. In such a case, in the absence of some cogent technical reason why the patient should not be informed, a doctor, recognising and respecting his patient's right of decision, could hardly fail to appreciate the necessity for an appropriate warning.

Lord Woolf expressed himself in terms much more consistent with the Canadian, American and Australian law of disclosure of material risks (ie where, put loosely, the court is the arbiter of what needs to be disclosed and not the medical profession), rather than the far more doctor-oriented English law. He said:

> In a case where it is the alleged that a plaintiff has been deprived of the opportunity to make a proper decision as to what course he or she should take in relation to treatment, it seems to me to be the law, as indicated in the cases to which I have just referred, that if there is a significant risk which would affect the judgment of a reasonable patient, then in the normal course it is the responsibility of a doctor to inform the patient of that significant risk, if the information is needed so that the patient can determine for him or herself as to what course he or she should adopt.

And he said that when one refers to a 'significant risk' it is not possible to talk in precise percentages. And:

> ... where there is what can realistically be called a 'significant risk', then in the ordinary event, as I have already indicated, the patient is entitled to be informed of that risk.

The way in which Lord Woolf expressed himself offers opportunities in the future for the effective use of the prudent doctor proviso, in the sense that a patient should find it easier to argue in appropriate circumstances that a risk should have been disclosed, and the court should declare such, even though the defendants show that there is a body of medical opinion that approves of non-disclosure in the relevant circumstances.[14]

Practical difficulties – of consent

In practice, claims for failure to warn of risks are difficult. In the first place, they are usually an after-thought, by solicitor or patient, where the obvious allegation, ie negligence in advising or carrying out treatment or medical care, has proved unfounded upon receipt of expert medical advice. Thoughts then turn to the possibility of claiming that information should have been given before the treatment, which would have – so it has to be presumed – led to a substantially better outcome. A number of hurdles need to be overcome. First, one has to establish a duty to give specific information, ie one has to show that at the relevant time there would be no responsible body of medical opinion, not even a minority one, that would have found it acceptable not to give that information. Then one has to prove that such information was not given. The defendant may say that it was, in which case it is a matter of his word against the patient's. The patient may be helped if there is no record of such information being given. Then, usually the most difficult hurdle of all, the patient has to show that, if the information had been given, he would have avoided substantive injury. This usually means that he would have declined the procedure. Or sometimes it may mean that, having received all proper information, he would have elected for another procedure. In either event, he will have to prove that one or other of those courses would have been followed. If there was no substantially better alternative, he will have to show that he would have declined the treatment. But in most

---

14   See also in the Introduction (see Chapter 1) Lord Woolf's observations in his recent address to University College, London.

cases it will be clear that he needed the treatment and unlikely that he would have continued to endure his pathology merely because he was told of a small risk of adverse effects.

Even if he can show that he would have declined the operation, he still has to show that his current condition is substantially worse than it would have been. Proof of these various matters is not impossible, as the successful cases show, but causation, in this sort as in all sorts of medical claims, needs strict analysis. Parents who claim that they would have let their child die if they had known that an essential heart operation carried a small risk of brain damage are likely to have difficulty in establishing that contention. For the highly significant case of *Chester* v *Afshar*, see the section so headed below.

The Australian approach

The High Court of Australia has explicitly refused to follow *Sidaway*. In *Rogers* v *Whittaker* [1993] 4 Med LR 79, the evidence showed that a responsible body of medical practitioners would not have disclosed to the claimant the risk to her good left eye from sympathetic ophthalmitis if her defective right eye were removed. This would have been enough to lose her the case if *Sidaway* had been applied. However, it was held that it was for the courts to adjudicate on what was the appropriate standard of care after giving weight to 'the paramount consideration that a person is entitled to make his own decision about his life', that breach of duty of care was not to be concluded on the basis of the expert medical evidence alone, that evidence of accepted medical practice was a useful (but not a conclusive) guide for the courts, and that the factors according to which a court determined whether a medical practitioner was in breach of the standard of care would vary according to whether it was a case involving diagnosis, treatment, or the provision of information and advice: the different cases raised varying difficulties which required consideration of different factors. The finding of the courts below that the defendant had been negligent in not disclosing the risk was upheld.

It is arguably time now that the English courts reviewed their rejection of the doctrine of informed consent and their consequent refusal to acknowledge any right in the patient to be given any information beyond what the medical profession sees fit to disclose. Lord Woolf has given a lead. Let it be followed.

The duty to answer questions

The judgments of the Law Lords in the *Sidaway* case make it clear that, when questioned specifically by a patient of apparently sound mind about risks involved in a proposed treatment, the doctor must answer as truthfully and as fully as the questioner requires. This duty to answer has been said, though *obiter*, by Lord Donaldson MR to apply to questions asked *after* treatment, ie in an effort to find out exactly what was done and what, if anything, went wrong. This was said in the context of an application for pre-trial disclosure (*Lee* v *South West Thames Regional Health Authority* [1985] 1 WLR 845, CA).

Before absolving a doctor, therefore, who has made only a limited disclosure, the court should at the very least be satisfied that there was a responsible body of medical opinion that would at that time have made only such limited disclosure, that the patient did not (expressly or impliedly) ask for further information, and that it could not be said that any prudent doctor would have made further disclosure.

It was said at first instance in *Blyth* v *Bloomsbury Health Authority* [1993] 4 Med LR 151, that a health authority that receives a reasonable request from a patient as to the possible side effects of a drug that is prescribed for her (Depo-Provera in this case), but administers the drug without warning of possible dangers, will be liable to pay damages if it is proved that the patient would not have taken the drug had she been given the relevant information. However, allowing the authority's appeal, the Court of Appeal said that there was no evidence on which the judge could properly have found that insufficient information was given in answer to the claimant's request so as to constitute a breach of duty. The court also said, *obiter*, that even where a patient asks for information, the duty to inform him is governed by the *Bolam* principle, so that in this context, too (the context of a patient actively seeking information before deciding whether or not to accept the proposed treatment), the medical standard must be applied. This reading of the observations of the Law Lords in the *Sidaway* case is, it is submitted, not only a misreading but is in itself quite unacceptable. It turns over to the medical profession the decision as to what to reveal when they are specifically asked for information, thus totally negating the right of a patient to be properly informed before deciding whether to submit to treatment.[15]

In *Wyatt* v *Dr Curtis and Central Nottingham Health Authority* [2003] MLC 1080, the GP (first defendant) admitted negligence in not warning a pregnant mother of the risk to her baby of her chicken pox. She then sought to hold the health authority at least equally liable for not ascertaining that the GP had not warned the mother, on the basis that the mother had impliedly asked the doctor at the hospital for the relevant information. But this attempt at establishing a 'constructive' request for information did not succeed. The Court of Appeal held that the hospital was entitled to assume that competent advice had already been given to the mother by her GP.

Chester *v* Afshar

The facts in this important case (MLC 1170, [2004] UKHL 41) are easy enough to summarise. The neurosurgeon, Mr Afshar, was found by the trial judge to be in breach of duty in not warning the patient of the small risk of paralysis resulting from cauda equina compression during the lumbar operation. The risk materialised through no fault of the surgeon and the unfortunate patient suffered serious permanent injury. The judge, Sir Denis Henry, did not find for a fact that she would never have had the operation if warned (that would have been an open and shut case for the patient, just as it would have been a hopeless case if the finding was that the warning would not have deterred the patient). He found that she would have declined to have it at that time, but would have sought a

---

15   On the duty to disclose risks if asked, see also *Smith* v *Auckland Hospital Board* [1965] NZLR 191; *Hatcher* v *Black* (1954) Times, 2 July.

second or even a third opinion. He made no finding one way or another as to whether she would have had it somewhere at someone's hands at some future date. The judge concluded that that was good enough to show that the surgeon was liable for the injury. The Court of Appeal agreed. One may think it was perfectly logical and sensible to state that, even if she did at some future time undergo the operation, the chances of the injury arising were the same as originally, ie a very great deal less than 50%, and therefore the appropriate conclusion was that the injury would not have occurred. Of course, if the fact that the patient suffered this injury was good evidence that she probably would have suffered it also in any later operation, which is sometimes the case, then she could not succeed. But that was not the case here.

Their Lordships, with the possible exception of Lord Walker, took the view that, as the surgeon's breach of duty had not increased the risk of the injury happening (ie the very fact that the chance of injury, though still very low, would remain precisely the same at any future operation), he had not caused the injury. As indicated above, I would prefer to argue that the chance of her suffering the injury at any future date was 1% and therefore, on the balance of probabilities, she would not have suffered it. But, with the possible exception of Lord Walker, who alone made the point that the scenario might well be different at a later date (in terms of surgeon, environment and maybe other more subtle factors), the House agreed that to permit the claimant to succeed in this case there would have to be an extension to the normal rules of causation (just as there was in their decision in the mesothelioma case of *Fairchild*.

The claimant nevertheless succeeded, albeit by a bare majority (just as in the similar Australian case of *Chappell* v *Hart* [1999] MLC 0067). Three of the judges were for making such an extension on policy grounds, two were not. The policy is that patients' rights to disclosure have to be protected. If the surgeon fails to recognise those rights and the very injury against which he was required to give a warning materialises, it is only right and proper that he should be held liable, even if that amounts to putting him in the position of insurer.

The simplest expression of the minority view was put by Lord Hoffman, who said that the claimant had failed to prove her loss as the risk would have been the same whenever or wherever the operation might have been carried out. In other words, the purpose of warning was to enable the patient, if she so wished, to take steps to remove or minimise the risk – which it had not been proved she would or could have done. Therefore the surgeon's failure to warn had not been the cause of her injury. Nor did he see any good reason for a policy extension. Lord Bingham took a similar view on both conclusions, stating that he saw no reason to provide for potentially very large damages to be paid by a defendant whose breach of duty had not been shown to have worsened the physical condition of the claimant.

Those in favour of the claimant's case were Lords Steyn, Hope and Walker. They agreed with the minority (at any rate the first two clearly did) that the application of normal principles of causation would not permit the claimant to succeed, and then went on to allow the policy extension, saying that, just as in *Fairchild*, there was in this case too, no causation proved on ordinary legal principles, but that there was a special case for making an exception and declaring that in these particular circumstances there would be a special rule for deeming causation to have been proved, or at any rate – and this is of course the important issue shorn of legal casuistry – for imposing liability on the surgeon.

What does this decision mean in practical terms to the medical negligence practitioner? In the first place it means that if the patient would have declined an operation if given a necessary but omitted warning of a risk and the risk materialised and the relevant injury occurred, her claim is not defeated by the fact that, though declining the operation at that time, she would probably have decided thereafter to have it anyway. But are there any limits to this? What if she would have decided, after taking a second opinion, to have it a few days later with the same surgeon in the same hospital? Perhaps the court would conclude that the chance of the risk materialising in those circumstances did not remain the same, but, as it had already been seen to have happened in virtually identical circumstances, it could be inferred that it would probably happen again. On the other hand, the risk in this *Chester* case was one that materialises totally at random, and one remembers that the chances of the tossing of a coin producing, say, a sixth consecutive tails is still 50%.

In the second place, this decision, by the very manner in which it is based on policy, indicates (a) that patients' claims may in other contexts be able to initiate new rules of law, and (b) that some members of the House of Lords clearly have empathy – with the position of the patient *vis-à-vis* the doctor.

To give valid consent, the person needs to understand the nature and purpose of the procedure. Any misrepresentation of these elements will invalidate consent. Where relevant, information about anaesthesia should be given alongside information about the procedure itself.

It is particularly important that a person is aware of the situation when students or trainees carry out procedures to further their own education. Where the procedure will further the person's care – for example taking a blood sample for testing – then, assuming the student is appropriately trained in the procedure, the fact that it is carried out by a student does not alter the nature and purpose of the procedure. It is therefore not a legal requirement to tell the person that the clinician is a student, although it would always be good practice to do so. In contrast, where a student proposes to conduct a physical examination that is not part of the person's care then it is essential to explain that the purpose of the examination is to further the student's training, and to seek consent for that to take place.

Although informing people of the nature and purpose of procedures enables valid consent to be given as far as any claim of battery is concerned, this is not sufficient to fulfil the legal duty of care to the person. Failure to provide other relevant information may render the practitioner liable.

In considering what information to provide, the health practitioner should try to ensure that the person is able to make an informed judgement on whether to give or withhold consent. Case law on this issue is evolving. Therefore practitioners ought to err on the side of caution by informing the person of any 'material' or 'significant' risks or unavoidable risks, even if small, in the proposed treatment, any alternatives to it, and the risks incurred by doing nothing. A Court of Appeal judgment stated that it will normally be the responsibility of the doctor to inform a patient of 'a significant risk which would affect the judgment of a reasonable patient'.[16] Following *Chester* v *Afshar*,[17] healthcare professionals should give information about all significant possible adverse outcomes and make a record of the information given.

The GMC provides guidance on the type of information that patients may need to know before making a decision, and recommends that doctors should do their best to find out about patients' individual needs and priorities when providing information about treatment options. It advises that discussions should focus on the patient's 'individual situation and risk to them' and sets out the importance of providing the information about the procedure and associated risks in a balanced way and checking that patients have understood the information given.[18] BMA guidance advises that if in doubt about the amount of information to give a patient, doctors 'should contact their hospital lawyers or their medical defence organisation'.[19]

In the very rare event that the healthcare professional believes that to follow the GMC guidance set out above in full will cause the patient serious harm, the GMC guidance states that this view, and the reasons for it, should be recorded in the patient's notes. When such concerns arise it is advisable to discuss the issue within the team caring for the patient. In individual cases the courts will examine such justification with great care. The mere fact that the patient might become upset by hearing the information, or might refuse treatment, is not sufficient to act as a justification.

Some people may wish to know very little about the treatment that is being proposed. If information is offered and declined, it is good practice to record this fact in the notes. However, it is possible that individuals' wishes may change over time, and it is important to provide opportunities for them to express this. GMC and BMA guidance encourages doctors to explain to patients the importance of knowing the options open to them while respecting a person's wish not to know, and states that basic information should always be provided about what the treatment aims to achieve and what it will involve.

In *Newbury* v *Bath District Health Authority* (1998) 47 BMLR 138, the patient unsuccessfully claimed injury for an improperly performed lumbar decompression and fusion. The issue of consent was whether the patient was entitled to more information than she was given. Ebsworth J said that there might be circumstances in which a patient would be entitled to be told that a proposed operation was not in the mainstream of treatment. That would obviously be so if the treatment involved a method which was either entirely new, or relatively untried, or if it was one that had fallen out of use because it had been shown to be defective and was no longer accepted by a responsible body of medical opinion. The evidence in this case did not reach that state, there being no evidence that the technique used had been condemned at the date it was employed. Whilst it would have been preferable for the claimant to have been told that the

16 *Pearce* v *United Bristol Healthcare NHS Trust* (1999) 48 BMLR 118.
17 [2004] UKHL 41.
18 GMC (2008) *Consent: patients and doctors making decisions together*, London: GMC.
19 BMA (2004) *Medical Ethics Today: The BMA's Handbook of Ethics and Law* (2nd edition). Update to Chapter 2, London: BMJ Group, www.bma.org.uk/ethics/MET2007updates.jsp.

proposed use of Harrington rods was unusual and for her to be given the alternative, there was no duty on the consultant to tell her. There had been no negligence in obtaining consent.

The duty to inform of less risky treatment

There can be circumstances where a duty to inform a patient of the significant risks of a medical procedure are not discharged unless the patient was made aware that fewer or no risks were associated with another procedure.

In *Janet Birch* v *University College London Hospital NHS Foundation Trust* [2008] EWHC 2237 (QB), (2008) 104 BMLR 168, the claimant (B) claimed damages against the defendant NHS trust for injuries that she sustained as a result of alleged clinical negligence in the performance of invasive surgery. B had been admitted to hospital displaying atypical symptoms of vascular third nerve palsy. The consultant doctor recommended that she undergo an MRI scan in order to exclude the possibility that she was suffering from either a posterior communicating artery aneurysm or cavernous sinus pathology. There were no available MRI slots available to B at that hospital so her consultant requested that she be transferred to a neurology ward in a specialist hospital operated by the Trust; later, she was transferred to a neurosurgical ward at that hospital. The Trust's neurosurgeons decided to perform a catheter angiography; a mildly invasive procedure that had increased risks for people in B's position. The associated risks of angiography were explained to B, who then signed the relevant consent form. Subsequently, there were complications with surgery that resulted in a stroke. B submitted that:

1   the decision to perform the catheter angiogram that led to her stroke was negligent; there had been no proper assessment of her history and condition and no proper risk benefit analysis of how her condition should be investigated; no reasonable body of doctors would have proceeded to perform a catheter angiography rather than an MRI scan;
2   the trust negligently failed to disclose the comparative risks of MRI scanning to her.

Cranston J held:

1   There was at the time no consensus within the medical profession as to whether MRI or angiography was the better imaging method for diagnosing aneurysms of the type B might have had. There were certainly other large and responsible medical units that would have performed angiography in the same circumstances. Furthermore, the relevant neurosurgeon had undertaken the relevant risk benefit analysis before concluding that the urgency of the case required angiography. That was a decision that could, in the circumstances, withstand logical scrutiny as a practice accepted by reasonable medical professionals, *Bolam* v *Friern Hospital Management Committee* (1957) 1 WLR 582 QBD and *Bolitho (Deceased)* v *City and Hackney HA* (1998) AC 232 HL applied. The decision not to use MRI was not negligent.

2   If there was a significant risk that would affect the judgment of a
     reasonable patient then, in the normal circumstances, it was the
     responsibility of a doctor to inform that patient of that risk so as to
     enable him to determine for himself which course he should adopt,
     Pearce v United Bristol Healthcare NHS Trust (1999) ECC 167 CA
     (Civ Div), *Chester* v *Afshar* (2004) UKHL 41, (2005) 1 AC 134, *Bolam*
     and *Bolitho* applied, *Sidaway* v *Board of Governors of the Bethlem
     Royal Hospital* (1984) QB 493 CA (Civ Div) considered. By logical
     extension of that principle, the duty to inform a patient of significant
     risks would not be discharged unless and until a patient was made
     aware that fewer or no risks were associated with another available
     and alternative treatment. In the instant case, B had been informed of
     the risks involved with catheter angiography *but not the comparative
     risks of MRI*. Although there was no requirement that a doctor should
     disclose comparative risks of alternative treatments in every case
     there were special circumstances in the instant case that justified the
     imposition of such a duty. B had entered a neurosurgical rather than
     a neurology ward under a recommendation that she undergo MRI
     and would have selected the option of undergoing the less invasive
     procedure had she been properly apprised of the comparative risks.
     Accordingly, B had been subjected to an unnecessary procedure that
     had caused a stroke; the trust's failure to discuss the implications of
     the various imaging methods and the comparative risks rendered
     the trust liable to B for breach of duty.

In *Burke* v *Leeds Health Authority* [2001] MLC 0314, CA, where the
judge had found that the oncologists recommending treatment by intense
chemotherapy for a child's leukaemia were negligent not to have told the
parents that it would be possible, though not optimum, to delay treatment
for a while, the defendant's appeal succeeded on the basis that the judge's
finding of breach of duty could not be sustained in the absence of any
expert evidence supporting such a conclusion. The treatment had led to
spastic quadriplegia.

Additional operative procedures

During an operation it may become evident that the person could benefit
from an additional procedure that was not within the scope of the original
consent. If it would be unreasonable to delay the procedure until the
person regains consciousness (for example because there is a threat to
the person's life), it may be justified to perform the procedure on the
grounds that it is in the person's best interests. However, the procedure
should not be performed merely because it is convenient. For example,
a hysterectomy should never be performed during an operation without
explicit consent, unless it is necessary to do so to save life.

In *Davis* v *Barking, Havering and Brentwood Health Authority* [1993]
4 Med LR 85, McCullough J said that a separate consent was not required
where, within proper medical practice, a caudal anaesthetic (about which
the patient had not been told) was added to her general anaesthetic
during an operation for marsupialisation of a Bartholian cyst. He said
that sectionalising consent for every step in a procedure would lead to
the 'deplorable' prospect of this type of action being brought in trespass

rather than in negligence ('deplored' to a greater or lesser extent by Bristow J in *Chatterton* v *Gerson* [1981] QB 432; Hirst J in *Hills* v *Potter* [1984] 1 WLR 641n at 653; and Lord Scarman in the *Sidaway* case [1985] AC 871 at 883, MLC 0010, HL).

If a person has refused certain additional procedures before the anaesthetic (for example, specifying that a mastectomy should not be carried out after a frozen section biopsy result), then this must be respected if the refusal is applicable to the circumstances (see below for more details on advance decisions). The GMC guidance states that it is good practice to seek the views of the patient on possible additional procedures when seeking consent for the original intervention.

WHAT HAPPENS IN NON-THERAPEUTIC CONTEXTS?

There are various references in the argument and judgments in the *Sidaway* case to the 'healing' or 'therapeutic' context in which that case was set. Is this rule, whereby the medical profession sets its own standards for disclosure, limited to such a context? It is perhaps understandable that the decision as to what should be disclosed to the patient about the risks of the operation should be viewed as a clinical decision and part and parcel of the delicate relationship between the physician and a sick patient – there may well be therapeutic considerations. But what if there are none, or none of any great substance? What if the patient needs advice about an elective procedure and the options involved in, for example, cosmetic surgery, or birth control or diet? This question arose in *Gold* v *Haringey Health Authority* [1986] 1 FLR 125.

The facts were that when, in 1979, Mrs Gold entered her third pregnancy, she and her husband decided to have no further children after that one. They reached a provisional decision that Mr Gold would be vasectomised. But when she informed the consultant at the ante-natal clinic that she wanted no more children, she was told that a sterilisation would be arranged for her. Nothing was said about the other contraceptive options and nothing was said about the failure rate of sterilisation. There was evidence to the effect that, in 1979, there was a responsible body of medical opinion that would not have spoken of the options or the failure rate. The judge said that the *Sidaway* case was decided in a therapeutic context, and that he was concerned with a different situation, where a woman asks for advice as to methods of contraception and is told that sterilisation is right for her without being told of other options and without being given the information that there is a risk of failure. He said that in that context the adequacy of what she is told was to be determined not exclusively by reference to the prevailing medical practice but by the court's view as to whether the person giving advice – who might be a hospital doctor, a GP, a counsellor at a family planning clinic or a health visitor – acted negligently. He saw no reason to extend the exceptional test in respect of negligent advice given by a doctor to the context of contraceptive counselling. And he found that there was a duty upon the doctors concerned to have mentioned the options and the failure rate, a duty which they had not discharged.

However, the Court of Appeal took a different view ([1988] QB 481). They said that the distinction the judge drew between therapeutic contexts, where the *Bolam* principle applied, and non-therapeutic contexts, such as contraceptive counselling, was artificial and contrived, and ran counter to the intent of the *Sidaway* decision. The fact that medical practice as to warning was divided at the time of Mrs Gold's sterilisation meant *ipso facto* that a doctor who did not warn could not be held in breach of his duty. The result of this decision is that, even in the context of an adult and healthy woman wanting to know the best way to avoid having any more children, her right to information to help her decide is governed solely by what the profession is willing to tell her, and the court will not assert any other right to information on her behalf. As long as there are some doctors, sufficient to constitute a responsible body of opinion, who give only a limited or no disclosure (in this or any other context), such disclosure will be declared by the court to be consistent with the patient's rights.[20] However, this decision was given some 17 years ago, before *Bolitho* and before *Pearce*. It would be nice to think that it no longer represented the law.

Research and innovative treatment

The same legal principles apply when seeking consent from a person for research purposes as when seeking consent for investigations or treatment. GMC guidance advises that patients 'should be told how the proposed treatment differs from the usual methods, why it is being offered, and if there are any additional risks or uncertainties'. Clinical trials are covered by the Medicines for Human Use (Clinical Trial Regulations) 2004.[21]

If the treatment being offered is of an experimental nature, but not actually part of a research trial, this fact must be clearly explained to a person with capacity before their consent is sought, along with information about standard alternatives. It is good practice to give a person information about the evidence to date of the effectiveness of the new treatment, both at national/international levels and in the practitioner's own experience, including information about known possible side-effects.

There is a more stringent need for disclosure of risks where the treatment is to any extent experimental. In *Chadwick* v *Parsons* [1971] 2 Lloyd's Rep 49, affd [1971] 2 Lloyd's Rep 322, CA, the defendant admitted liability on the basis that in his desire to find patients in need of a particular treatment, he was so enthusiastic about the prospects of success that he failed to disclose the serious risks which the operation carried.

The fact that English law allows the doctor's duty to be judged by the doctors themselves created particular difficulties in the context of the keyhole (minimally invasive) endoscopic procedures. Laparascopic

---

20   The various factors which go to decide what should be revealed before any particular treatment, whether the professional standard prevails or the court has an overall jurisdiction to decide whether the medical practice is appropriate, were considered in detail by Woodhouse J in the New Zealand case of *Smith* v *Auckland Hospital Board* [1964] NZLR 241 (overruled on other grounds [1965] NZLR 191, but Woodhouse J's views were specifically endorsed by the Ontario courts in *Male* v *Hopmans* (1965) 54 DLR (2d) 592, and on appeal (1967) 64 DLR (2d) 105).

21   *Medicines for Human Use (Clinical Trials) Regulations 2004*, SI 2004/1031, www.legislation.gov.uk/ si/si2004/20041031.htm.

sterilisation had been around for a long time, but in recent years more and more surgical procedures are carried out by keyhole techniques. Because neither the medical profession nor their disciplinary bodies took care to ensure that no practitioner jumped on to the bandwagon without proper training, many procedures were carried out by inadequately trained surgeons. The lack of accredited training made it hard to prove that a particular doctor was acting outside acceptable limits as viewed by the profession; and even more difficult to define satisfactorily, ie in a manner that would constitute legal proof pursuant to the *Sidaway* test, that more information, whether about the proposed treatment or other options, should have been given. Even now, some years down the line, it is difficult to establish that the profession has formed any consensus about what information should be given to the patient. Different practitioners, all eagerly accepting patients for the brave new forms of surgical technique, give various bits of information to their patients, no doubt according to their own lights, but in those circumstances it is not possible for the patient to prove that all responsible practitioners would give some specific information. Unless the courts adopt in that context the only sensible approach, namely to make up their own minds, upon the evidence given as to the nature and novelty of the procedure and the experience of the defendant, what he reasonably should have said to the patient, there is little chance of a successful claim, and, in the wider scene, little chance of getting the profession to get its act in order.

Where the person is an adult who lacks capacity or a child, then the experimental treatment cannot be given, unless it would be in their best interests. In the case of *Simms* v *Simms*[22], the court found that where a responsible body of relevant professional opinion supported innovative treatment, that treatment would meet the *'Bolam* test' (see above). Where there is no alternative treatment available and the disease is progressive and fatal, it will be reasonable to consider experimental treatment with unknown benefits and risks but without significant risks of increased suffering to the patient, and where there is some chance of benefit to the patient. In this case, the court held that the treatment was in the best interests of both a child and an adult lacking capacity.

Consent to visual and audio recordings

Consent should be obtained for any visual or audio recording, including photographs or other visual images. The purpose and possible future use of the recording must be clearly explained to the person before their consent is sought for the recording to be made. If it is to be used for teaching, audit or research, people must be aware that they can refuse without their care being compromised and that when required or appropriate it can be anonymised. GMC guidance gives more detailed advice, including situations when permission is not required and about obtaining consent to use recordings as part of the assessment or treatment of patients and for training or research.[23]

---

22 *Simms* v *Simms* [2003] Fam 83.
23 GMC (2002) *Making and Using Visual and Audio Recordings of Patients,* London: GMC, www.gmc-uk.org/guidance/current/library/making_audiovisual.asp.

WHO SHOULD SEEK CONSENT?

The clinician providing the treatment or investigation is responsible for ensuring that the person has given valid consent before treatment begins, although the consultant responsible for the person's care will remain ultimately responsible for the quality of medical care provided. The GMC guidance states that the task of seeking consent may be delegated to another person, as long as they are suitably trained and qualified. In particular, they must have sufficient knowledge of the proposed investigation or treatment, and understand the risks involved, in order to be able to provide any information the patient may require. The practitioner who eventually carries out the investigation or treatment must also be able to determine whether the person has the capacity to make the decision in question and what steps need to be taken if the person lacks the capacity to make that decision (see below and Chapter 22). Inappropriate delegation (for example where the clinician seeking consent has inadequate knowledge of the procedure) may mean that the 'consent' obtained is not valid. Clinicians are responsible for knowing the limits of their own competence, and should seek the advice of appropriate colleagues when necessary.

WHEN SHOULD CONSENT BE SOUGHT?

The seeking and giving of consent is usually a process, rather than a one-off event. For major interventions, it is good practice where possible to seek the person's consent to the proposed procedure well in advance, when there is time to respond to the person's questions and provide adequate information (see above). Clinicians should then check, before the procedure starts, that the person still consents. If a person is not asked to signify their consent until just before the procedure is due to start, at a time when they may be feeling particularly vulnerable, there may be real doubt as to its validity. In no circumstances should a person be given routine pre-operative medication before being asked for their consent to proceed with the treatment.

THE FORM OF CONSENT

The validity of consent does not depend on the form in which it is given. Written consent merely serves as evidence of consent: if the elements of voluntariness, appropriate information and capacity have not been satisfied, a signature on a form will not make the consent valid. For surgical procedures, a written consent is usually taken. This will refer in short form to the operation to be undertaken, and is likely to authorise 'such further or alternative operative measures as may be found to be necessary during the course of the operation' (see 'Additional operative procedures', above).

For treatment involving little risk, the consent may be oral; in appropriate cases it may be implied from the fact that the patient has consulted the doctor. It has been said that consent to such surgical and medical treatment as the doctors might think necessary is not to be implied simply from the fact of entering hospital (*Stoffberg* v *Elliott* (1923) CPD 148). An apparent consent, oral or written, will not be valid if the physician should have seen that the patient did not realise the significance of what he was giving his consent to (*Chatterton* v *Gerson* [1981] QB 432; *Kelly* v *Hazlett* (1976) 75 DLR (3d) 536).

Although completion of a consent form is in most cases not a legal requirement (exceptions include certain requirements of the Mental Health Act 1983 and of the Human Fertilisation and Embryology Act 1990 as amended) the use of such forms is good practice where an intervention such as surgery is to be undertaken. Where there is any doubt about the person's capacity, it is important, before the person is asked to sign the form, to establish both that they have the capacity to consent to the intervention and that they have received enough information to enable valid consent to be given. Details of the assessment of capacity, and the conclusion reached, should be recorded in the case notes.

In *Re C* [1994] 1 WLR 290, Thorpe J held that a 68-year-old schizophrenic was entitled to an injunction preventing the hospital from amputating his leg because it had not been established that the patient's general capacity was so impaired by his illness as to render him incapable of understanding the nature, purpose and effects of the treatment advised and so his right of self-determination had not been displaced.

If the person has capacity, but is unable to read or write, they may be able to make their mark on the form to indicate consent. It would be good practice for the mark to be witnessed by a person other than the clinician seeking consent, and for the fact that the person has chosen to make their mark in this way to be recorded in the case notes. Similarly, if the person has capacity, and wishes to give consent, but is physically unable to mark the form, this fact should be recorded in the notes. Or, the person can direct someone to sign the form on their behalf, but there is no legal requirement for them to do so. If consent has been given validly, the lack of a completed form is no bar to treatment, but a form can be important evidence of such consent.

Consent may be expressed verbally or non-verbally: an example of non-verbal consent would be where a person, after receiving appropriate information, holds out an arm for their blood pressure to be taken. However, the person must have understood what examination or treatment is intended, and why, for such consent to be valid. It is good practice to obtain written consent for any significant procedure, such as a surgical operation or when the person participates in a research project or a video recording (even if only minor procedures are involved).

Special circumstances – form of consent

Requirements concerning gametes

It is a legal requirement under the Human Fertilisation and Embryology Act 1990 as amended that consent must be obtained in writing before a person's gametes can be used for the treatment of others, or to create an embryo *in vitro*. Consent in writing is also required for the storage of gametes. Information and an opportunity to receive counselling must be provided before the consent is given. Where these requirements are not satisfied, it is unlawful to store or use the person's gametes for these purposes. Clinicians should ensure that written consent to storage exists before retrieving gametes.

Outside specialist infertility practice, these requirements may be relevant to health practitioners whose patients are about to undergo treatment that might render them sterile (such as chemotherapy or radiotherapy), where a patient may wish to have gametes, or ovarian or testicular tissue, stored prior to the procedure. Healthcare practitioners may also receive requests to remove gametes from a person who is unable to give consent.

Requirements for living donation

The Human Tissue Authority is responsible for the regulation, through a system of approvals, of the donation from living people of solid organs, bone marrow and peripheral blood stem cells for transplantation into others. Information on the legal requirements and how to proceed is available from the HTA.[24]

THE DURATION OF CONSENT

When a person gives valid consent to an intervention, in general that consent remains valid for an indefinite duration, unless it is withdrawn by the person. However, if new information becomes available regarding the proposed intervention (for example new evidence of risks or new treatment options) between the time when consent was sought and when the intervention is undertaken, the GMC guidance states that a doctor or member of the healthcare team should inform the patient and reconfirm their consent. The clinician should consider whether the new information should be drawn to the attention of the patient and the process of seeking consent repeated on the basis of this information. Similarly, if the patient's condition has changed significantly in the intervening time, it may be necessary to seek consent again, on the basis that the likely benefits and/ or risks of the intervention may also have changed.

If consent has been obtained a significant time before undertaking the intervention, it is good practice to confirm that the person who has given consent (assuming that they retain capacity) still wishes the intervention to proceed, even if no new information needs to be provided or further questions answered. The position of those who lack capacity is covered below and in Chapter 22.

WHEN CONSENT IS REFUSED OR WITHDRAWN

If an adult with capacity makes a voluntary and appropriately informed decision to refuse treatment (whether contemporaneously or in advance), this decision must be respected, except in certain circumstances as defined by the Mental Health Act 1983 (see below). This is the case even where this may result in the death of the person (and/or the death of an unborn

---

24   www.hta.gov.uk.

child, whatever the stage of the pregnancy).[25] Refusal of treatment by those under the age of 18 is covered below.

In *St George's Healthcare NHS Trust* v *S* [1999] Fam 26, [1998] 3 All ER 673, CA, a 36-year-old mother, suffering from pre-eclampsia, refused medical advice to have a Caesarean section, despite being told of the risk to her and her child from natural birth. She was then consigned to a mental hospital against her will. Transferred to a labour ward, she continued to refuse consent to a section. A judge at first instance authorised the section dispensing with her consent. A baby girl was duly born. The mother then appealed to the Court of Appeal. The court upheld her complaints. It declared that, even when his own life depended on receiving medical treatment, an adult of sound mind was entitled to refuse; that, although pregnancy increased the personal responsibilities of the woman, it did not diminish her entitlement to decide whether to undergo medical treatment; and an unborn child was not a separate person from his mother and its need for medical assistance did not prevail over her right not to be forced to submit to an invasion of her body against her will, whether her own life or that of her unborn child depended on it, and that right was not reduced or diminished merely because her decision to exercise it might appear morally repugnant; and that, unless lawfully justified, the removal of the baby from within the mother's body under physical compulsion constituted an infringement of her autonomy and amounted to a trespass, and the perceived needs of the foetus did not provide the necessary justification. Further, the detention under the Mental Health Act 1983 was declared unlawful because detention against the will of the party was not justified merely because his thinking process was unusual and contrary to the use of the overwhelming majority of the community at large. In any event, a patient detained pursuant to the Act could not be forced into medical procedures unconnected with his mental condition unless his capacity to consent to such treatment was diminished.

A few weeks after giving their May 1998 judgment, the court formulated guidelines for all medical practitioners applying to any case involving capacity when surgical or invasive treatment might be needed. These guidelines have been adopted by the BMA but are still sufficiently important and comprehensive to require setting out in full at this point:

The guidelines depend on basic legal principles which are summarised:

1. They have no application where the patient is competent to accept or refuse treatment. In principle a patient may remain competent notwithstanding detention under the Mental Health Act 1983.
2. If the patient is competent and refuses consent to the treatment, an application to the High Court for a declaration would be pointless. In this situation the advice given to the patient should be recorded. For their own protection, hospital authorities should seek unequivocal assurances from the patient (to be recorded in writing) that the refusal represents an informed decision, that is, that she understands the nature of and reasons for the proposed treatment, and the risks and likely prognosis involved in the decision to refuse or accept it. If the patient is unwilling to sign a written indication of this refusal, this too should be noted in writing. Such a written indication is merely a record for evidential purposes. It should not be confused with or regarded as a disclaimer.

---

25 *Re B* [2002] 1 FLR 1090.

3.   If the patient is incapable of giving or refusing consent, either in the long term or temporarily (eg due to unconsciousness), the patient must be cared for according to the authority's judgment of the patient's best interests. Where the patient has given an advance directive, before becoming incapable, treatment and care should normally be subject to the advance directive. However, if there is reason to doubt the reliability of the advance directive (for example, it may sensibly be thought not to apply to the circumstances which have arisen), then an application for a declaration may be made.

Concern over capacity
4.   The authority should identify as soon as possible whether there is concern about a patient's competence to consent to or refuse treatment.
5.   If the capacity of the patient is seriously in doubt, it should be assessed as a matter of priority. In many such cases the patient's GP or other responsible doctor may be sufficiently qualified to make the necessary assessment, but in serious or complex cases involving difficult issues about the future health and well being or even the life of the patient, the issue of capacity should be examined by an independent psychiatrist, ideally one approved under s 12(2) of the Mental Health Act 1983. If following this assessment there remains a serious doubt about the patient's competence, and the seriousness or complexity of the issues in the particular case may require the involvement of the court, the psychiatrist should further consider whether the patient is incapable by reason of mental disorder of managing her property or affairs.

[The court then goes on to set out guidance which, since 1 October 2007, has been superseded by the jurisdiction of the Court of Protection (see further below and Chapter 22). It then concludes with a reference to the necessity principle.]

Conclusion

There may be occasions when, assuming a serious question arises about the competence of the patient, the situation facing the authority may be so urgent and the consequences so desperate that it is impracticable to attempt to comply with these guidelines. The guidelines should be approached for what they are, that is, guidelines. Where delay may itself cause serious damage to the patient's health or put her life at risk then formulaic compliance with these guidelines would be inappropriate.

In *Ms B* v *An NHS Hospital Trust* [2002] EWHC 429 (Fam), Dame Elizabeth Butler-Sloss held that a seriously physically disabled patient, but one with the mental capacity to make decisions about treatment even when a consequence of such decisions could be death, had the right to decide to refuse treatment. Autonomy was a fundamental principle in English law, as was the sanctity of life.

On the other hand, in *R* v *Feggetter, ex p Wooder* [2002] EWCA Civ 554, the Court of Appeal sanctioned treatment against the will of a competent patient. It said that decisions to give a psychiatric patient treatment against his will (in this case a decision made by a second opinion appointed doctor) had, by virtue of the Human Rights Act, and by virtue of the fact that medical treatment was to be given which would violate the autonomy of a competent non-consenting adult, to be accompanied by reasons given. Moreover, this decision has been followed in the case of *R (on the application of O)* v *West London Mental Health Trust* [2005] EWHC 604 (Admin) whereby it was considered that there is a duty to give reasons when a decision is made to deprive a patient of their personal liberty.

Caesarean section cases

In a number of cases at first instance, emergency orders were made at short notice authorising Caesarean sections upon women who had not consented. The mother was not always represented and the medical evidence was often scanty. In one case, the woman refused only because she had a needle phobia (*Re L* [1997] 2 FLR 837). The issues arising in this context have now been extensively considered and ruled upon twice by the Court of Appeal.

In *Re MB* (1997) 38 BMLR 175, the court held an emergency hearing in February 1997 that was not completed until the early hours of the morning.[26] The mother was 23. The child was presenting by the breech. Caesarean section was obviously desirable; otherwise there was a 50% risk to the child (though none to the mother). The mother wanted a Caesarean section and consented to it, but each time she saw the anaesthetic needle, or the mask, she changed her mind. So the problem was purely one of needle phobia. Her mental state was that she was a naive, not very bright, frightened young woman, but was not exhibiting any psychiatric disorder. At first instance the judge authorised the use of reasonable force for the purpose of performing a Caesarean section.

The Court of Appeal first set out basic principles:

1   In general, it was a criminal and tortuous assault to perform physically invasive medical treatment, however minimal the invasion might be, without the patient's consent.
2   A mentally competent patient had an absolute right to refuse to consent to medical treatment for any reason, rational or irrational, or for no reason at all, even where that decision might lead to his or her own death.
3   Emergency medical treatment could be given, provided the treatment was a necessity and did no more than was reasonably required in the best interests of the patient.

The court reviewed the various Caesarean section cases at first instance, and said that, with the exception of *Re S (adult: surgical treatment)* [1993] 1 FLR 26, the court had expressly decided that the mother did not have the capacity to make the decision. The Court of Appeal was alive to the objections that had been made to these orders, principally that no woman should be compelled to undergo such an invasive surgical procedure against her will, not even if it was necessary to save the life of her child.

On the issue of capacity to consent, the court offered the following guidelines:

1   Every person is presumed to have the capacity to consent to or to refuse medical treatment unless and until the presumption is reported.
2   A competent woman who has the capacity to decide may for religious reasons, other reasons, for rational or irrational reasons or for no reason at all, choose not to have medical intervention, even though the consequence may be the death or serious handicap of the child

---

26   In view of the comprehensive and authoritative judgment in this case, the earlier cases at first instance are not detailed here. They can be found within the judgment.

she bears, or her own death. In that event, the courts do not have the jurisdiction to declare medical intervention lawful and the question of her own best interests objectively considered does not arise.

3   Panic, indecisiveness and irrationality in themselves do not as such amount to incompetence, but they may be symptoms or evidence of incompetence.

4   A person lacks capacity if some impairment or disturbance of mental functioning renders him unable to make a decision whether to consent to or to refuse treatment. A patient will be unable to make a decision on consent when he cannot understand and retain the relevant information, or cannot assess it properly, or through confusion, shock, fatigue, pain or drugs may temporarily lose the capacity. Panic and fear may also destroy capacity.

In the particular case, the court concluded that the mother's needle phobia rendered her incapable at the relevant time of making a decision at all.

The court then decided that the *best interests* of the mother required the Caesarean section to be carried out. There was medical evidence that she was likely to suffer significant long-term damage if her child sustained injury or died, but, on the other hand, would suffer no lasting harm if the anaesthetic were given.[27]

The court went on to consider the important issue of whether the interests of the unborn child were relevant. The court firmly stated that there was no jurisdiction to consider the unborn child as a person whose interests needed protecting. That would need the intervention of Parliament. Finally, the court advised on the procedure to be adopted where the capacity of the patient to consent to or refuse the medical intervention was in issue.

The other case is *St George's Healthcare NHS Trust* v *S* (below). The guidelines formulated by the court in that case have been set out below.

Despite the Human Rights Act, it is open to the court to hold, if the circumstances are appropriate and the court so desires, that the mother is (ie must be) suffering from some impairment or disturbance of mental functioning and so unable to understand and assess the information given to her by the doctors.

The timing of the withdrawal of consent

A person with capacity is entitled to withdraw consent at any time, including during the performance of a procedure. Where a person does object during treatment, it is good practice for the practitioner, if at all possible, to stop the procedure, establish the person's concerns and explain the consequences of not completing the procedure. At times, an apparent objection may in fact be a cry of pain rather than withdrawal of consent, and appropriate reassurance may enable the practitioner to

---

27   Consideration of what is in the patient's best interests is appropriate to the context of withdrawal of treatment, but it should not be used to give a doctor a licence to proceed in the absence of consent other than in an emergency. In *Frenchay Healthcare NHS Trust* v *S* [1994] 1 WLR 601, CA, Lord Donaldson MR said: 'It is, I think, important that there should not be a belief that what the doctor says is the patient's best interest *is* the patient's best interest. For my part I would certainly reserve to the court the ultimate power and duty to review the doctor's decision in the light of all the facts.'

continue with the person's consent. If stopping the procedure at that point would genuinely put the life of the person at risk, the practitioner may be entitled to continue until that risk no longer applies.

Assessing capacity during a procedure may be difficult and, as noted above, factors such as pain, panic and shock may diminish capacity to consent. The practitioner should try to establish whether at that time the person has capacity to withdraw a previously given consent. If capacity is lacking, it may sometimes be justified to continue in the person's best interests (see below), but this should not be used as an excuse to ignore distress.

Advance decisions to refuse treatment

A person may have made an advance decision to refuse particular treatment in anticipation of future incapacity (sometimes previously referred to as a 'living will' or 'advance directive'). A valid and applicable advance decision to refuse treatment has the same force as a contemporaneous decision to refuse treatment. This is a well-established rule of common law, and the Mental Capacity Act 2005 now puts advance decisions on a statutory basis. The Act sets out the requirements that such a decision must meet to be valid and applicable. Further details are available below and in Chapter 9 of the Mental Capacity Act (2005) Code of Practice, but in summary these are:[28]

- the person must be 18 or over;
- the person must have the capacity to make such a decision;
- the person must make clear which treatments they are refusing;
- if the advance decision refuses life-sustaining treatment, it must be in writing (it can be written by someone else or recorded in healthcare notes), it must be signed and witnessed and it must state clearly that the decision applies even if life is at risk;
- a person with capacity can withdraw their advance decision at any time.

Healthcare professionals must follow an advance decision if it is valid and applicable, even if it may result in the person's death. If they do not, they could face criminal prosecution or civil liability. The Mental Capacity Act 2005 protects a health professional from liability for treating or continuing to treat a person in the person's best interests if they are not satisfied that an advance decision exists which is valid and applicable. The Act also protects healthcare professionals from liability for the consequences of withholding or withdrawing a treatment if at the time they reasonably believe that there is a valid and applicable advance decision. If there is genuine doubt or disagreement about an advance decision's existence, validity or applicability, the case should be referred to the Court of Protection (see Chapter 22). The courts do not have the power to overturn a valid and applicable advance decision. While a decision is awaited from the courts, healthcare professionals can provide life-sustaining treatment or treatment to stop a serious deterioration in the patient's condition.

---

28 www.publicguardian.gov.uk/mca/code-of-practice.htm.

If an advance decision is not valid or applicable to current circumstances, healthcare professionals must consider the advance decision as part of their assessment of the person's best interests (see below). Advance decisions made before the Mental Capacity Act came into force may still be valid if they meet the provisions of the Act. There are transitional arrangements for advance decisions to refuse life-sustaining treatment made before 1 October 2007. Further information is available on the Department of Health website.[29]

Some healthcare professionals may disagree in principle with a person's right to refuse life-sustaining treatment. The Mental Capacity Act does not change the current legal position. Healthcare professionals do not have to act in a way that goes against their beliefs; however, they must not simply abandon patients or cause their care to suffer. A patient should have the option of transferring their care to another healthcare professional or, if the patient lacks capacity, arrangements should be made for the management of the patient's care to be transferred to another healthcare professional.[30]

Patients should always be offered measures that are essential to keeping them comfortable.[31] This is sometimes referred to as 'basic' or 'essential' care, and includes warmth, shelter, actions to keep a person clean and free from distress and the offer of food and water by mouth. The BMA's guidance advises that basic care should always be provided unless it is actively resisted by a patient, and that 'refusals of basic care by patients with capacity should be respected, although it should be continued to be offered'. Advance decisions made under the Mental Capacity Act cannot refuse actions that are needed to keep a person comfortable. The Act allows healthcare professionals to carry out these actions in the best interests of a person who lacks capacity. An advance decision can refuse artificial nutrition and hydration.

However, although basic/essential care would include the offer of oral nutrition and hydration, it would not cover force feeding an individual or the use of artificial nutrition and hydration. The courts have recognised that an individual with capacity has the right to choose to refuse food and drink, although this may be qualified if the person has a mental disorder. Towards the end of such a period an individual is likely to lose capacity, and the courts have stated that if the individual has, while they have capacity, expressed the desire to refuse food until death supervenes, the person cannot be force fed or fed artificially when they lack capacity. If the person is refusing food as a result of mental disorder, then detention and treatment without consent may be a possibility under the Mental Health Act 1983, different considerations may apply and more specialist guidance should be consulted.[32]

---

29   www.dh.gov.uk/en/Publichealth/Scientificdevelopmentgeneticsandbioethics/Consent/ DH_076863.

30   *Re B (adult: refusal of medical treatment)* [2002] EWHC 429 (Fam) at paragraph 100(viii); paragraph 9.61 of the Mental Capacity Act (2005) Code of Practice.

31   BMA (2007) *Withholding and Withdrawing Life-prolonging Medical Treatment: Guidance for decision making* (3rd edition) Part 2.11, London: BMJ Group.

32   Mental Health Act Commission (1979) *Guidance Note 3: Guidance on the treatment of anorexia nervosa under the Mental Health Act 1983* (updated March 1999).

DIFFICULT CASES

Self-harm

Cases of self-harm present a particular difficulty. Where the person is able to communicate, an assessment of their mental capacity should be made as a matter of urgency. If the person is judged not to have capacity, then they may be treated on the basis of temporary incapacity (see below and Chapter 22). Similarly, patients who have attempted suicide and are unconscious should be given emergency treatment if any doubt exists as to either their intentions or their capacity when they took the decision to attempt suicide.

However, as noted above, patients with capacity do have the right to refuse life-sustaining treatment (other than treatment for mental disorder under the Mental Health Act 1983) – both at the time it is offered and in the future. Making a decision which, if followed, may result in death does not necessarily mean that a person is or feels suicidal. Nor does it necessarily mean that the person lacks the capacity to make the decision now or in advance. If the person is clearly suicidal, this may raise questions about their capacity to make the decision. If a patient with capacity has harmed themselves, a prompt psychosocial assessment of their needs should be offered. However, if the person refuses treatment and use of the Mental Health Act 1983 is not appropriate, then their refusal must be respected.[33] Similarly, if practitioners have good reason to believe that a patient genuinely intended to end their life and had capacity when they took that decision, and are satisfied that the Mental Health Act is not applicable, then treatment should not be forced upon the person, although reasonable attempts made to encourage them to accept help cannot be criticised.

Post operation – use of removed tissue

The Human Tissue Act 2004[34] makes consent the fundamental principle underpinning the lawful retention and use of body parts, organs and tissue from the living or the deceased for specified health-related purposes and public display. It also covers the removal of such material from the deceased. (It does not cover removal of such material from living patients – this continues to be dealt with under the common law and the Mental Capacity Act 2005.)

The 2004 Act regulates removal, storage and use of human tissue. This is referred to in the Act as 'relevant material' and is defined as material that has come from a human body and consists of, or includes, human cells. Cell lines are excluded, as are hair and nail from living people. Live

---

33 National Collaborating Centre for Mental Health, commissioned by the National Institute for Clinical Excellence (2004) *National Clinical Practice Guideline 16: Self-harm*, www.nice.org.uk/nicemedia/pdf/CG16FullGuideline.pdf.

34 The Human Tissue Act 2004 repeals and replaces the Human Tissue Act 1961, the Anatomy Act 1984 and the Human Organ Transplants Act 1989 as they relate to England and Wales. It also repeals and replaces the Human Tissue Act (Northern Ireland) 1962, the Human Organ Transplants (Northern Ireland) Order 1989 and the Anatomy (Northern Ireland) Order 1992.

gametes and embryos are excluded as they are already regulated under the Human Fertilisation and Embryology Act 1990. [35]

The Human Tissue Act 2004 lists the purposes for which consent is required in Sch 1, and they are referred to as 'scheduled purposes'. The consent required under the Act is called 'appropriate consent', which means consent from the appropriate person, as identified in the Act. Where there has been a failure to obtain or misuse of consent, penalties of up to three years imprisonment or a fine, or both, are provided for in the Act.

Full details on the requirements of the Human Tissue Act 2004 and the HTA's codes of practice are on the Human Tissue Authority's (HTA) website.[36] These should be consulted to ensure compliance.

ADULTS WITHOUT CAPACITY

General principles

The Mental Capacity Act 2005 came fully into force in October 2007 and applies in England and Wales to everyone who works in health and social care and is involved in the care, treatment or support of people over 16 years of age who may lack capacity to make decisions for themselves. It is largely based on previous common law and creates a single, coherent framework for decision-making, including decisions about treatment. This part and Chapter 22 summarises the main provisions of the Mental Capacity Act. Detailed guidance is provided in the Code of Practice,[37] which has statutory force. The Act imposes a duty on health professionals (and other healthcare staff) to have regard to the Code of Practice.

Under English law, no one is able to give consent to the examination or treatment of an adult who lacks the capacity to give consent for himself, unless they have been authorised to do so under a Lasting Power of Attorney or they have the authority to make treatment decisions as a court appointed deputy (see Chapter 22) Therefore, in most cases, parents, relatives or members of the healthcare team cannot consent on behalf of such an adult. However, the Mental Capacity Act sets out the circumstances in which it will be lawful to carry out such examinations or treatment.

In general, the refusal to an intervention made by a person when they had capacity cannot be overridden if the advance decision is valid and applicable to the situation (see above). There are certain statutory exceptions to this principle, including treatment for mental disorder under the Mental Health Act 1983, which are set out briefly below.

The legal requirements in the Mental Capacity Act are underpinned by five statutory principles. One of these key principles is that any act done for, or any decision made on behalf of, a person who lacks capacity must be done, or made, in that person's best interests. This principle applies to health professionals as it does to anyone working with and caring for a person who lacks capacity. The Act also creates a new offence of ill

---

35   www.opsi.gov.uk/acts/acts1990/ukpga_19900037_en_1; as amended by the Human Fertilisation and Embryology Act 2008 – see www.opsi.gov.uk/acts/acts2008/ukpga_20080022_en_1.
36   www.hta.gov.uk.
37   www.publicguardian.gov.uk/mca/code-of-practice.htm.

treatment or wilful neglect of someone who lacks capacity by someone with responsibility for their care or with decision-making powers.

Information on assessing capacity is given above. A person's capacity (or lack of capacity) refers specifically to their capacity to make a particular decision at the time it needs to be made.

The Mental Capacity Act provides healthcare professionals with protection from civil and criminal legal liability for acts or decisions made in the best interests of the person who lacks capacity. The Act makes it clear that when determining what is in a person's best interests a healthcare professional must not make assumptions about someone's best interests merely on the basis of the person's age or appearance, condition or any aspect of their behaviour.

The Act requires that a healthcare professional must consider all the relevant circumstances relating to the decision in question. These are described as factors that the healthcare professional is aware of and which are reasonable to take into account.

In considering the relevant circumstances, the Act rules that the healthcare professionals must take the following steps:

- Consider whether the person is likely to regain capacity and if so whether the decision can wait.
- Involve the person as fully as possible in the decision that is being made on their behalf.
- As far as possible, consider:
    - the person's past and present wishes and feelings (in particular if they have been written down);
    - any beliefs and values (eg religious, cultural or moral) that would be likely to influence the decision in question, and any other relevant factors; and
    - the other factors that the person would be likely to consider if they were able to do so.
- As far as possible, consult other people if it is appropriate to do so and take into account their views as to what would be in the best interests of the person lacking capacity, especially:
    - anyone previously named by the person lacking capacity as someone to be consulted;
    - anyone engaging in caring for or interested in the person's welfare;
    - any attorney appointed under a Lasting Power of Attorney (see below and Chapter 22);
    - any deputy appointed by the Court of Protection to make decisions for the person (see below and Chapter 22).
- For decisions about serious medical treatment, where there is no one appropriate other than paid staff, healthcare professionals have to instruct an IMCA (see below).
- If the decision concerns the provision or withdrawal of life-sustaining treatment, the person making the best interests decision must not be motivated by a desire to bring about the person's death.

The Mental Capacity Act (2005) Code of Practice makes it clear that the steps set out in the Act should form the starting point for considering all the relevant circumstances of each case, and often other factors will be important. Further guidance on interpreting best interests is provided in Chapter 5 of the Code of Practice.

In *Cheshire West & Chester Council* v *P (by his litigation friend the Official Solicitor)* [2011] EWCA Civ 1257 P had cerebral palsy and Down's syndrome and needed a high level of care due to his significant physical and learning disabilities. He lacked the mental capacity to make decisions about his care and residence. He resided in a care home and had a long history of exhibiting challenging behaviour by being uncooperative and harming himself and others. The judge below found that P had been completely deprived of his liberty, first because he could not go anywhere or do anything without the support and assistance of care home staff and secondly because his behaviour required a range of measures, including physical restraint and the intrusive procedure of inserting fingers into his mouth whilst he was being restrained, to prevent him from eating his continence pads. The Court of Appeal, after reviewing the relevant authorities, identified the following factors which were likely to be significant in the type of deprivation of liberty cases coming before the Court of Protection:

(a) the starting point was the 'concrete situation', taking account of a range of criteria such as the type, duration, effects and manner of implementation of the measure in question;

(b) deprivation of liberty had to be distinguished from restraint because restraint alone was not deprivation of liberty;

(c) account had to be taken of the individual's whole situation and context was crucial, *Guzzardi* v *Italy* (A/39) (1981) 3 EHRR 333 and *Engel* v *Netherlands* (A/22) (1979-80) 1 EHRR 647 applied, *Secretary of State for the Home Department* v *JJ* [2007] UKHL 45, [2008] 1 AC 385 followed;

(d) mere lack of capacity to consent to living arrangements could not in itself create a deprivation of liberty and the fact that a domestic setting could involve a deprivation of liberty did not mean that it often would, *Surrey CC* v *CA* [2010] EWHC 785 (Fam), [2011] MHLR 108 approved;

(e) it was legitimate to have regard both to the objective 'reason' for a placement and treatment and also the objective 'purpose', *Austin* v *Commissioner of Police of the Metropolis* [2009] UKHL 5, [2009] 1 AC 564 followed;

(f) subjective motives or intentions had only limited relevance since an improper motive or intention might have the effect that what would otherwise not be a deprivation of liberty was, for that very reason, a deprivation whilst a good motive or intention could not render innocuous what would otherwise be a deprivation of liberty;

(g) it was always relevant to evaluate and assess the 'relative normality' of the situation, *Secretary of State for the Home Department* v *JJ* followed;

(h) the assessment had to take account of the particular capabilities of the person concerned since what might be a deprivation of liberty for one person may not be for another;

(i) in most contexts the relevant comparator was the ordinary able bodied adult but not in the kind of cases that came before the Family Division and the Court of Protection, concerning children and adults with disabilities whose lives were dictated by their own cognitive and other limitations;

(j)   in such cases, the comparator was an adult of similar age with the same capabilities as the adult concerned, affected by the same condition or suffering the same inherent mental and physical disabilities and limitations.

In the case of a child, the comparator was a child of the same age and development, *Surrey CC* v *CA* [2011] EWCA Civ 190, [2011] 2 FLR 583 applied. In the instant case, the judge had not compared P's situation with the kind of life he would have been leading as someone with his disabilities and difficulties in a normal family setting. There was nothing to show that the life he was living there was significantly different from the kind of life that anyone with those difficulties could normally expect to lead, whatever kind of setting they were living in. On the contrary, there was a strong degree of normality in his life, assessed by reference to the relevant comparator. The judge's reasoning in relation to the measures applied to P from time to time was equally problematic. The measures involved the kind of occasional restraint that anyone caring for P in any setting would have to adopt from time to time. The finger sweep was obviously intrusive but had to be looked at in context. It was little different from what any properly attentive parent would do if a young child was chewing something unpleasant or potentially harmful. It involved a degree of restraint but that was far removed from anything approaching a deprivation of liberty. P's care plan did not involve a deprivation of his liberty.

In the case of *Local Authority* v *H* [2012] EWHC 49 (COP) Hedley J made an order declaring that H lacked capacity to consent to sexual relations and a consequential order to protect her best interests which was very restrictive amounted to the deprivation of her liberty. He stated:

> The question of capacity to consent to sexual relations is clearly both sensitive and difficult. Such a finding may have wide ranging implications not only for H and those responsible for her care but for any who have dealings and, in particular, sexual relations with her as any expressed consent may be void and the person concerned be at risk of conviction for a serious offence under the Sexual Offences Act 2003.

He referred to five reported cases[38] and stated:

> ... First, since all cases save (iii) involve first instance decisions and since Baroness Hale's observations in C are obiter, then notwithstanding the distinction of each judge, no decision is binding on a High Court Judge sitting as a nominated judge of the Court of Protection. Secondly the judgments are as between themselves not capable of reconciliation. This is clearly an unsatisfactory state of affairs given the importance of the concept under consideration. It is, however, a real problem as in so many cases (like this one) the actual outcome is one with which all parties can live and there is accordingly no appeal. There is no procedure for bringing this issue before an appellate court save by appeal in a specific case. What then is this court to do? Clearly I cannot avoid expressing a view with the attendant risk of yet further confusion. Yet it cannot be any part of my role, nor would I regard myself as equipped to attempt it, simply to subject those five judgments to critical

---

38   (i) *XCC* v *M B, N B & MAB* [2006] 2 FLR 968 (Munby J); (ii) *Local Authority X* v *M M* [2007] EWHC 2003 Fam (Munby J); (iii) *R* v *C* [2009] UKHL 42 (per Baroness Hale); (iv) *DCC* v *L S* [2010] EWHC 1544 Fam (Roderick Wood J). (v) *DBC* v *A B* [2011] EWHC 101, COP (Mostyn J).

analysis and then solemnly pronounce as between them. I propose in fact to approach the task in this way: having acknowledged those decisions, I propose to attempt an analysis of my own from first principles, guided by the Statute, and then (and only then) to compare (and no doubt contrast) my conclusions with those reached in the five cases.

It is of course important to remember that possession of capacity is quite distinct from the exercise of it by the giving or withholding of consent. Experience in the family courts tend to suggest that in the exercise of capacity humanity is all too often capable of misguided decision making and even downright folly. That of itself tells one nothing of capacity itself which requires a quite separate consideration.

Healthcare professionals should keep sufficient records to demonstrate that the decision has been based on all available evidence and has taken into account any conflicting views. What is in a person's best interests may well change over time. This means that even where similar actions need to be taken repeatedly in connection with the person's care or treatment, the person's best interests should be reviewed regularly.

In cases of serious doubt or dispute about an individual's mental capacity or best interests, an application can be made to the Court of Protection for a ruling (see Chapter 22). The duty officer of the Official Solicitor can advise on the appropriate procedure if necessary.[39] See also Chapter 8 of the Mental Capacity Act (2005) Code of Practice for further information. Details of the circumstances in which a referral should be made to the court are given below.

Duration of lack of capacity

It is possible for capacity to fluctuate. In such cases, it is good practice to establish, while the person has capacity, their views about any clinical intervention that may be necessary during a period of anticipated incapacity, and to record these views. The person may wish to make an advance decision to refuse treatment (see above) or a statement of their preferences and wishes (see above). If the person does not make a relevant advance decision, decisions about that person's treatment if they lack capacity must be made in accordance with the Mental Capacity Act (see above). This would include considering whether the person is likely to regain capacity and, if so, whether the decision can wait, as well as the statutory principle that all practical steps must be taken to enable the person to make their own decision.

Statements of preferences and wishes

A healthcare professional must take all statements of a person's preferences and wishes into consideration as part of a best interests assessment. Written statements which request specific treatments made by a person before losing capacity should be given the same consideration as those made by people who currently have capacity to make treatment

---

39   Further details about the Official Solicitor can be found at www.officialsolicitor.gov.uk/ os/offsol.htm (contact would usually be made through the legal department of the NHS body involved).

decisions. However, a healthcare professional would not have to follow a written request if they thought that the specific treatment would be clinically unnecessary or not appropriate for the person's condition, and therefore not in the person's best interests. If the decision is different to a written statement, a healthcare professional should keep a record of this and be prepared to justify the decision if challenged. There is an important legal distinction between a written statement expressing treatment preferences, which a healthcare professional must take into account when making a best interests decision, and a valid and applicable advance decision to refuse treatment , which healthcare professionals must follow. Healthcare professionals cannot ignore a written statement that is a valid and applicable advance decision to refuse treatment.

Lasting power of attorney (LPA)

The Mental Capacity Act enables a person aged 18 or over to appoint an attorney to look after his health and welfare decisions if he should lack the capacity to make such decisions in the future. Under a personal welfare LPA, the attorney – if he has the authority to do so – can make decisions that are as valid as those made by the person himself. The LPA must be made in the form, and meet the criteria, set out in the regulations,[40] and it must be registered with the Office of the Public Guardian before it can be used.

The LPA may specify limits to the attorney's authority, and the LPA must specify whether or not the attorney has the authority to make decisions about life-sustaining treatment. Healthcare practitioners directly involved in the care or treatment of a person who lacks capacity should not agree to act as that person's attorney other than in exceptional circumstances (for example if they are the only close relative of the person). If the person lacks capacity and has created a personal welfare LPA, the attorney will have the authority to make decisions and consent to or refuse treatment as set out in the LPA. Healthcare practitioners should read the LPA if it is available, in order to understand the extent of the attorney's power.

The attorney must follow the statutory principles under the Mental Capacity Act and make decisions in the best interests of the person lacking capacity. If the decision is about life-sustaining treatment, the attorney must not be motivated by a desire to bring about the person's death. Attorneys also have a legal duty to have regard to the guidance in the Mental Capacity Act (2005) Code of Practice. If there is a dispute that cannot be resolved, eg between the attorney and a doctor, it may have to be referred to the Court of Protection. More information about LPAs is given in Chapter 7 of the Code of Practice.[41]

Court appointed deputies

If a person lacks capacity to make a decision relating to their personal welfare, then the Court of Protection can make an order making a decision

---

40   www.publicguardian.gov.uk/mca/code-of-practice.htm.
41   *Mental Capacity Act 2005 (Lasting Powers of Attorney, Enduring Powers of Attorney and Public Guardian) Regulations 2007*, SI 2007/2161 and www.publicguardian.gov.uk/forms/Making-an-LPA.htm.

on their behalf. Alternatively, the Court of Protection can appoint a deputy to make decisions on behalf of the person who lacks capacity. The Mental Capacity Act makes it clear that in such situations it is preferable for the Court of Protection to make the decision if at all possible, and that if a deputy is appointed, then their powers should be limited in scope to what is absolutely necessary.

The court must ensure that any deputy appointed has the necessary skills and abilities and is prepared to take on the duty and responsibility of the role. Both the court and any deputy must follow the statutory principles of the Act and make decisions in the person's best interests.

Deputies for personal welfare decisions will only be required in the most difficult cases, where important and necessary actions cannot be carried out without the court's authority or where there is no other way of settling the matter in the best interests of the person who lacks capacity. For example, a deputy could be appointed to make ongoing decisions, having consulted all relevant parties. This could be useful where there is a history of family disputes.

If a deputy has been appointed to make treatment decisions on behalf of a person who lacks capacity then it is the deputy rather than the healthcare professional who makes the treatment decision. A deputy cannot go against a decision of an attorney under an LPA made before the person lacks capacity. Deputies must follow the Mental Capacity Act's statutory principles and must make decisions in the person's best interests. A deputy cannot refuse consent to the provision of life-sustaining treatment. More information about the powers of the Court of Protection and the role of deputies is given in Chapter 8 of the Code of Practice.

Independent mental capacity advocates (IMCAs)

The Mental Capacity Act has, since April 2007 in England and since October 2007 in Wales (See Chapter 23), introduced a duty on NHS bodies to instruct an IMCA in serious medical treatment decisions when a person who lacks capacity to make a decision has no one who can speak for them, other than paid staff. In matters that meet the definition of serious medical treatment,[42] IMCAs are only able to represent and support people whose treatment is arranged by the NHS. They have the right to information about an individual and can see relevant healthcare records.

The duties of an IMCA are to:

- support the person who lacks capacity and represent their views and interests to the decision-maker;
- obtain and evaluate information, both through interviewing the person and through examining relevant records and documents;
- obtain the views of professionals providing treatment for the person who lacks capacity;
- identify alternative courses of action;
- obtain a further medical opinion, if required; and
- prepare a report (that the decision-maker must consider).

---

42 See Mental Capacity Act (2005) Code of Practice, Chapter 10, paragraph 10.42 et seq for further information on what is regarded as 'serious medical treatment'. www. publicguardian. gov.uk/mca/code-of-practice.htm.

IMCAs are not decision-makers for the person who lacks capacity. They are there to support and represent that person and to ensure that decision-making for people who lack capacity is done appropriately and in accordance with the Mental Capacity Act. More information is given at www.dh.gov.uk/imca and in Chapter 10 of the Mental Capacity Act (2005) Code of Practice.

Consent forms

Where treatment is provided to a person who lacks capacity following a best interests decision, any consent form should not be signed by someone else unless they have a personal welfare LPA that authorises them to make the decision in question, or they are a court appointed deputy with similar authority. It is good practice to note either in the records or on a 'patient unable to consent' form why the treatment was decided to be in the patient's best interests.

Referral to the Court of Protection

The Mental Capacity Act established the Court of Protection to deal with decision-making for adults (and children in a few cases) who may lack the capacity to make specific decisions for themselves. The Court of Protection deals with serious decisions affecting personal welfare matters, including healthcare, which were previously dealt with by the High Court. In cases of serious dispute, where there is no other way of finding a solution or when the authority of the court is needed in order to make a particular decision or take a particular action, the court can be asked to make a decision.

The courts have identified certain circumstances when referral should be made to them for a ruling on lawfulness before a procedure is undertaken. These are:

- decisions about the proposed withholding or withdrawal of ANH from patients in a permanent vegetative state;
- cases involving organ, bone marrow or peripheral blood stem cell donation by an adult who lacks the capacity to consent (see below for information on children);
- cases involving the proposed non-therapeutic sterilisation of a person who lacks the capacity to consent to this (eg for contraceptive purposes); and
- all other cases where there is a doubt or dispute about whether a particular treatment will be in a person's best interests.

Other cases likely to be referred to the court include those involving ethical dilemmas in untested areas (such as innovative treatments for variant CJD[43]), or where there are otherwise irresolvable conflicts between healthcare staff, or between staff and family members. More information about the powers of the Court of Protection and the cases that should be referred to the court is given in the Mental Capacity Act (2005) Code of Practice and in a Court of Protection Practice Direction.[44]

---

43 *Simms v An NHS Trust* [2002] EWHC 2734 (Fam).
44 www.publicguardian.gov.uk/docs/09E_-_Serious_Medical_Treatment_PD.pdf.

The courts have stated that neither sterilisation which is incidental to the management of the detrimental effects of menstruation nor abortion need automatically be referred to court if there is no doubt that this is the most appropriate therapeutic response. However, these procedures can give rise to special concern about the best interests and rights of a person who lacks capacity. The need for such procedures occasionally arises in relation to women with a severe learning disability. It is good practice to involve as part of the decision-making process a consultant in the psychiatry of learning disability, the multidisciplinary team and the patient's family, and to document their involvement. Less invasive or reversible options should always be considered before permanent sterilisation. Where there is disagreement as to the patient's best interests, a reference to court may be appropriate.

In *V C* v *Slovakia* (2011) ECtHR (N Bratza P) 8/11/2011 there had been breaches of Arts 3 and 8 of the ECHR where a Roma woman had undergone sterilisation after being asked to provide her consent to the procedure without being fully informed about it and at a time when she was in labour.

Case law may extend the list of procedures concerning which referral to the court is good practice.

Although some procedures may not require court approval, their appropriateness may give rise to concern. For example, some patients with learning disability may exhibit challenging behaviour, such as biting or self-injury. If such behaviour is severe, interventions such as applying a temporary soft splint to the teeth or using arm splints to prevent self-injury are exceptionally considered, within a wider therapeutic context. As with hysterectomies undertaken for menstrual management purposes, great care must be taken in determining the best interests of such patients as distinct from dealing with the needs of carers and others who are concerned with the individual's treatment.

The rules for seeking a declaration that a sterilisation procedure upon a minor (or a mentally disordered person) might lawfully be carried out were set out at [1993] 3 All ER 222, dated May 1993. It has been held that a declaration is not required for a medically indicated hysterectomy on a minor (*Re E (a minor)* [1991] 2 FLR 585). These principles must be read subject to the recent guidance from the Court of Appeal in *St George's Healthcare NHS Trust* v *S* (above).

Research

The Mental Capacity Act sets out a legal framework for involving people who lack the capacity to consent to taking part in research. The Act provides for when such research can be carried out and for safeguards to protect people involved in the research who lack capacity, for example ensuring that the wishes and feelings of the person who lacks capacity are respected. Anyone setting up or carrying out such research will need to make sure that the research complies with the provisions set out in the Act and will need to follow the guidance given in Chapter 11 of the Mental Capacity Act (2005) Code of Practice. The Act does not include clinical trials, which are covered by the Medicines for Human Use (Clinical Trials) Regulations 2004.

The Act requires that a family member or unpaid carer must be consulted about any proposal and agree that the person who lacks capacity can be part of the research. If such a person cannot be identified, then the researcher must nominate a person who is independent of the research project to provide advice on the participation of the person who lacks capacity in the research. The person consulted should be asked for advice about whether the person who lacks capacity should participate in the research project and what, in his opinion, the person's wishes and feelings about taking part would be likely to be if he had capacity. The person's past or present wishes, feelings and values are most important in deciding whether he should take part in research or not. If the person without capacity shows any sign that he is not happy to be involved in the research, then the research will not be allowed to continue.

Healthcare professionals may be providing care or treatment for a person who is taking part in a research project, and may be asked for their views about what the person's feelings are or need to advise the researchers if the person seems upset about any aspect of the research.

CHILDREN AND YOUNG PEOPLE – WITHOUT CAPACITY

The legal position concerning consent and refusal of treatment by those under the age of 18 is different from the position for adults. For the purposes of this guidance 'children' refers to people aged below 16 and 'young people' refers to people aged 16–17.

Young people aged 16–17

For children over 16, the Family Law Reform Act 1969 provides, by s 8:

> 8(1) The consent of a minor who has attained the age of sixteen years to any surgical, medical or dental treatment which, in the absence of consent, would constitute a trespass to his person, shall be as effective as it would be if he were of full age; and where a minor has by virtue of this section given an effective consent to any treatment it shall not be necessary to obtain any consent for it from his parent or guardian.
>
> (2) In this section 'surgical, medical or dental treatment' includes any procedures undertaken for the purposes of diagnosis, and this section applies to any procedure (including, in particular, the administration of an anaesthetic) which is ancillary to any treatment as it applies to that treatment.
>
> (3) Nothing in this section shall be construed as making ineffective any consent which would have been effective if this section had not been enacted.

It will be seen that by virtue of s 8 of the Family Law Reform Act 1969, people aged 16 or 17 are presumed to be capable of consenting to their own medical treatment, and any ancillary procedures involved in that treatment, such as an anaesthetic. As for adults, consent will be valid only if it is given voluntarily by an appropriately informed young person capable of consenting to the particular intervention. However, unlike adults, the refusal of a competent person aged 16–17 may in certain circumstances be overridden by either a person with parental responsibility or a court (see below).

Section 8 of the Family Law Reform Act 1969 applies only to the young person's own treatment. It does not apply to an intervention that is not potentially of direct health benefit to the young person, such as blood donation or non-therapeutic research on the causes of a disorder. However, a young person may be able to consent to such an intervention under the standard of *Gillick*[45] competence, considered below.

In order to establish whether a young person aged 16 or 17 has the requisite capacity to consent to the proposed intervention, the same criteria as for adults should be used (see above). If a young person lacks capacity to consent because of an impairment of, or a disturbance in the functioning of, the mind or brain then the Mental Capacity Act 2005 will apply in the same way as it does to those who are 18 and over. If however they are unable to make the decision for some other reason, for example because they are overwhelmed by the implications of the decision, then the Act will not apply to them and the legality of any treatment should be assessed under common law principles. It may be unclear whether a young person lacks capacity within the meaning of the Act. In those circumstances, it would be prudent to seek a declaration from the court. More information on how the Act applies to young people is given in Chapter 12 of the Mental Capacity Act (2005) Code of Practice.

If the 16/17-year-old is capable of giving valid consent then it is not legally necessary to obtain consent from a person with parental responsibility for the young person in addition to the consent of the young person. It is, however, good practice to involve the young person's family in the decision-making process – unless the young person specifically wishes to exclude them – if the young person consents to their information being shared.

Children under 16 – the concept of *Gillick* competence

In *Gillick* v *West Norfolk and Wisbech Area Health Authority* [1986] AC 112, HL, an action by a parent to get declared unlawful DHSS advice permitting a doctor to prescribe the pill to children without telling their parents, the court said that the parental right to determine whether or not a child should receive medical treatment terminated when the child achieved a significant understanding and intelligence to enable him to understand fully what was proposed; but it was also said that parental rights clearly existed and did not wholly disappear until majority. Lord Scarman said:

> ... the parental right yields to the child's right to make his own decisions when he reaches a sufficient understanding and intelligence to be capable of making up his own mind on the matters requiring decision.

This is sometimes described as being '*Gillick* competent'. A child of under 16 may be *Gillick* competent to consent to medical treatment, research, donation or any other activity that requires their consent.

The concept of *Gillick* competence is said to reflect a child's increasing development to maturity. The understanding required for different interventions will vary considerably. Thus a child under 16 may have the capacity to consent to some interventions but not to others. The child's capacity to consent should be assessed carefully in relation to each decision that needs to be made.

---

45   *Gillick* v *West Norfolk and Wisbech AHA* [1986] AC 112. For a useful article on *Consent and Children: A Practical Summary* see Tim Wright in Clinical Risk (September 2011).

In some cases, for example because of a mental disorder, a child's mental state may fluctuate significantly, so that on some occasions the child appears *Gillick* competent in respect of a particular decision and on other occasions does not. In cases such as these, careful consideration should be given as to whether the child is truly *Gillick* competent at the time that they need to take a relevant decision.

If the child is *Gillick* competent and is able to give voluntary consent after receiving appropriate information, that consent will be valid and additional consent by a person with parental responsibility will not be required. It is, however, good practice to involve the child's family in the decision-making process, if the child consents to their information being shared.

Where advice or treatment relates to contraception, or the child's sexual or reproductive health, the healthcare professional should try to persuade the child to inform his parent(s), or allow the medical professional to do so. If however the child cannot be persuaded, advice and/or treatment should still be given if the healthcare professional considers that the child is very likely to begin or continue to have sexual intercourse with or without advice or treatment, and that unless they receive the advice or treatment then the child's physical or mental health is likely to suffer.

In *W v Official Solicitor* [1972] AC 24, HL, the court was prepared to countenance the ordering of a blood test upon a minor to determine paternity if it was in the public interest that it should be so ordered. And, on the other side of the coin, a judge authorised an abortion upon a 15-year-old girl against the wishes of her parents because the court was satisfied that the girl both wanted and understood the implications of the operation (*Re P (a minor)* (1982) 80 LGR 301).

In *Re R (a minor) (wardship: consent to treatment)* [1992] Fam 11, CA, the issue was whether a psychiatrically disturbed girl of 15 in the care of the local authority could effectively refuse consent to the administration of the anti-psychotic drugs that the treating doctors thought were essential to her condition. Waite J had taken the view, which had been the generally understood view, that the *Gillick* decision meant that neither parent nor court could override the decision of a *Gillick*-competent child to accept or refuse treatment. However he also concluded that in fact the child was not *Gillick* competent and so could not give a valid refusal.

In the Court of Appeal, Lord Donaldson took a much wider view of the court's powers and a much narrower view of the child's. He said that the court in the exercise of its wardship jurisdiction, which was wider than, independent of, and not derived from the parental powers (and had, of course, not been in issue in the *Gillick* case), was entitled to override the wishes of a ward, and indeed also of the parents, whether consenting to or refusing treatment, and whether the child was *Gillick* competent or not. He also said that parents could give a valid consent to treatment in the face of the child's refusal, and that if Lord Scarman in *Gillick* had meant otherwise his words were *obiter*. The farthest Lord Donaldson went was to accord the child a right to insist on such treatment as the doctors advised even if the parents objected. However, these far-reaching observations were in themselves *obiter* as the court held that this particular patient, even though she had lucid intervals when according to the medical evidence she was in her rational mind, could not be regarded in the context of her fluctuating disease as being generally of sufficient understanding to meet the criteria for *Gillick* competence.

There is certainly ground for concern at the assumption by the court of overriding powers in the case of a *Gillick*-competent child; it can be strongly argued that the court's powers in this context should be no greater than that of a natural parent. Furthermore, what power has the court to deprive the competent child over 16 years of age of the right to consent that he has been given by Parliament?

A year later, Lord Donaldson had occasion to repeat his assertion that, although a minor over the age of 16 has a right to consent to medical treatment in defiance of his parents' wishes, that does not include an absolute right to refuse treatment. In *Re W (a minor) (medical treatment)* [1993] Fam 64, the Court of Appeal, in the exercise of its inherent jurisdiction to protect minors, overrode the refusal of a girl aged 16 to consent to necessary treatment for anorexia nervosa. Thorpe J had held that the child was *Gillick* competent but that the court would exercise an overriding right to order the treatment necessary to save her life. In the Court of Appeal, Lord Donaldson said that the court's inherent powers under the *parens patriae* jurisdiction were theoretically limitless and certainly extended beyond the powers of a natural parent, and it was clear beyond doubt that the court could override the wishes of a *Gillick*-competent minor, not by ordering the doctors to treat, but by authorising them to treat according to their clinical judgment of what was in the best interests of the patient.

However, in this case, too, the court doubted that the minor was able to give a valid or informed refusal because the nature of her disease would impair her judgment, in that it created a compulsion to refuse treatment or to accept only treatment that was unlikely to be effective.

Note here the decision reached by Douglas Brown J in *South Glamorgan County Council* v *W and B* (1992) 11 BMLR 162: the court authorised psychiatric treatment against the wishes of a competent 15-year-old girl.

Reference may also be made to *Re K, W and H (minors) (consent to treatment)* [1993] 1 FCR 240, where Thorpe J said that parents' wishes could override refusal of *Gillick*-competent minors (though all three minors in the case were in fact held not to be competent).

In *Re M (child: refusal of medical treatment)* (1999) 52 BMLR 124, Johnson J authorised a heart transplant operation on a 15-year-old girl against her wishes but in accordance with her mother's wishes. He said that, although there were risks attached to the surgery and thereafter, including the risk that she would carry resentment for the rest of her life at what would be done to her, those risks had to be matched against the certainty of death if the transplant was not carried out. M's refusal to consent was important but not decisive and, while there was great gravity in the decision to override M's wishes, it was necessary to do so in order to achieve what was, on balance, best for her.

In *R* v *Portsmouth Hospitals NHS Trust, ex p Glass* (1999) 50 BMLR 269, CA, a child, considered to be in a terminal state by the hospital, was treated with diamorphine contrary to his mother's wishes. Violent scenes ensued at the hospital. After the child had been discharged from the hospital, the Trust suggested to the parents that it would be better if any further treatment took place elsewhere. A misconceived claim for judicial review of the hospital's actions was then commenced. Obviously the court was not going to give directions on clinical management, particularly when the critical period was long over. However, for present purpose it is worth noting what Scott Baker J said at first instance (the Court of Appeal agreed):

> Life and death cases, like the present one, often raise incredibly difficult issues to which there is no right answer. Anyone who doubts the potential difficulties of the issues in this case should read three documents which have been exhibited with the applicant's bundle of authorities and literature. They are: *Seeking Patients' Consent: The Ethical Considerations* by the General Medical Council; *Withdrawing and Withholding Treatment*: A consultation paper from the BMA's Medical Ethics Committee; and *Withholding and Withdrawing Life Saving Treatment in Children – a Framework for Practice* from the Royal College of Paediatric and Child Health, September 1987.

And Lord Woolf said:

> There are questions of judgment involved. There can be no doubt that the best course is for a parent of a child to agree on the course which the doctors are proposing to take, having fully consulted the parent and for the parent to fully understand what is involved. That is the course which should always be adopted in a case of this nature. If that is not possible and there is a conflict, and if the conflict is of a grave nature, the matter must then be brought before the court so the court can decide what is in the best interests of the child concerned. Faced with a particular problem, the courts will answer that problem.

> In my judgment that is the desirable way forward. Of course it does involve expense; it involves coming to the courts to obtain a ruling. The courts will do their best to reduce that expense. But the answer which will be given in relation to a particular problem dealing with a particular set of circumstances, is a much better answer than an answer given in advance. The difficulty in this area is that there are conflicting principles involved. The principles of law are clearly established, but how you apply those principles to particular facts is often very difficult to anticipate. It is only when the court is faced with that task that it gives an answer which reflects the view of the court as to what is in the best interests of the child. In doing so it takes into account the natural concerns and the responsibilities of the parent. It also takes into account the views of the doctors, and it considers what is the most desirable answer taking the best advice it can obtain from, among others, the Official Solicitor. That is the way, in my judgment, that the courts must react in this very sensitive and difficult area.

Most recently, in *R (on the application of Axon)* v *Secretary of State for Health* [2006] QB 539, a mother sought judicial review of guidance issued by the Department of Health in 2004 which outlined the advice and treatment a health professional was to give a young person under 16 in respect of various sexual matters including contraception, sexually transmitted infections and abortion. The guidance stated that confidential advice and treatment could be given to young people who could understand the advice and its implications without their parents being notified or consulted in the event that the young person could not be persuaded to consult their parents, given that it was in the best interests of the young person to offer confidential advice and treatment. The claim for a declaration that the guidance was unlawful was dismissed and *Gillick* was followed. In doing so, Silber J offered the following guidelines in respect of such cases:

(1) That the young person, although under 16 years of age, understands *all* aspects of the advice. (In the light of Lord Scarman's comments in the *Gillick* case, at p 189c, set out in para 13(v) above, he or she must 'have sufficient maturity to understand what is involved'. That understanding includes all relevant matters and it is not limited to family and moral aspects as well as all possible adverse consequences which might follow from the advice.)

(2) That the medical professional cannot persuade the young person to inform his or her parents or to allow the medical professional to inform the parents that their child is seeking advice and/or treatment on sexual matters. (As stated in the 2004 Guidance, where the young person cannot be persuaded to involve a parent, every effort should be made to persuade the young person to help find another adult, such as another family member or a specialist youth worker, to provide support to the young person.)

(3) That (in any case in which the issue is whether the medical professional should advise on or treat in respect of contraception and sexually transmissible illnesses) the young person is very likely to begin or to continue having sexual intercourse with or without contraceptive treatment or treatment for a sexually transmissible illness.

(4) That unless the young person receives advice and treatment on the relevant sexual matters, his or her physical or mental health or both are likely to suffer. (In considering this requirement, the medical professional must take into account all aspects of the young person's health.)

(5) That the best interests of the young person require him or her to receive advice and treatment on sexual matters without parental consent or notification.

The requirement of voluntariness

Although a child or young person may have the capacity to give consent, this is only valid if it is given voluntarily. This requirement must be considered carefully. Children and young people may be subject to undue influence by their parent(s), other carers or a sexual partner (current or potential), and it is important to establish that the decision is that of the individual himself.

Child or young person with capacity refusing treatment

Where a young person of 16 or 17 who could consent to treatment in accordance with s 8 of the Family Law Reform Act 1969, or a child under 16 but *Gillick* competent, refuses treatment, it is possible that such a refusal could be overruled if it would in all probability lead to the death of the child/young person or to severe permanent injury.

In the case of *Re W (a minor) (medical treatment)*,[46] the court stated that it has jurisdiction to override a refusal of a child/young person, at least where they seek to refuse treatment in circumstances that will, in all probability, lead to the death of the child/young person or to severe permanent injury; or where there is a serious and imminent risk that the child/young person will suffer grave and irreversible mental or physical harm.

---

46   *Re W (a minor) (medical treatment)* [1992] 4 All ER 627.

The courts have, in the past, also found that parents can consent to their competent child being treated even where the child/young person is refusing treatment.[47] However, there is no post-Human Rights Act 1998 authority for this proposition, and it would therefore be prudent for healthcare professionals to obtain a court declaration or decision if faced with a competent child or young person who is refusing to consent to treatment, to determine whether it is lawful to treat the child.

Where the treatment involved is for mental disorder, consideration should be given to using mental health legislation.

The changes made to s 131 of the Mental Health Act 1983 by s 43 of the Mental Health Act 2007 mean that when a young person of 16 or 17 has capacity (as defined in the Mental Capacity Act 2005) and does not consent to admission for treatment for mental disorder (either because they are overwhelmed, do not want to consent or refuse to consent), they cannot then be admitted informally on the basis of the consent of a person with parental responsibility (see Chapter 36 of the Code of Practice to the Mental Health Act 1983, as amended 2008[48]).

A life-threatening emergency may arise when consultation with either a person with parental responsibility or the court is impossible, or the person with parental responsibility refuses consent despite such emergency treatment appearing to be in the best interests of the child. In such cases the courts have stated that doubt should be resolved in favour of the preservation of life, and it will be acceptable to undertake treatment to preserve life or prevent serious damage to health.

Child lacking capacity

Where a child under the age of 16 lacks capacity to consent (ie is not *Gillick* competent), consent can be given on their behalf by any one person with parental responsibility (if the matter is within the 'zone of parental control'[49]) or by the court. As is the case where patients are giving consent for themselves, those giving consent on behalf of child patients must have the capacity to consent to the intervention in question, be acting voluntarily and be appropriately informed. The power to consent must be exercised according to the 'welfare principle': that the child's 'welfare' or 'best interests' must be paramount. Even where a child lacks capacity to consent on their own behalf, it is good practice to involve the child as much as possible in the decision-making process.

Where necessary, the courts can overrule a refusal by a person with parental responsibility. It is recommended by the Department of Health and BMA that certain important decisions, such as sterilisation for contraceptive purposes, should be referred to the courts for guidance, even if those with parental responsibility consent to the operation going ahead.

---

47 *Re R (a minor) (wardship: medical treatment)* [1991] 4 All ER 177.
48 www.dh.gov.uk/en/Publicationsandstatistics/Publications/
    PublicationsPolicyAndGuidance/DH_084597.
49 The concept of the 'zone of parental control' derives largely from case law from the European Court of Human Rights in Strasbourg. Chapter 36 of the Code of Practice to the Mental Health Act 1983, as amended, gives guidelines about what may fall in the zone, which will depend on the particular facts of each case.

In *Glass* v *The United Kingdom* 61827-00 [2004] ECHR 103[50] the European Court of Human Rights in a case where doctors treated a child contrary to his mother's wishes, without a court order, made clear that the failure to refer such cases to the court is not only a breach of professional guidance but also potentially a breach of the European Convention on Human Rights. In situations where there is continuing disagreement or conflict between those with parental responsibility and doctors, and where the child is not competent to provide consent, the court should be involved to clarify whether a proposed treatment, or withholding of treatment, is in the child's best interests. Parental refusal can only be overridden in an emergency.

The Children Act 1989 sets out persons who may have parental responsibility. These include:

- the child's mother;
- the child's father, if he was married to the mother at the time of birth;
- unmarried fathers, who can acquire parental responsibility in several different ways:
  - for children born before 1 December 2003, unmarried fathers will have parental responsibility if they:
    - marry the mother of their child or obtain a parental responsibility order from the court,
    - register a parental responsibility agreement with the court or by an application to court,
  - for children born after 1 December 2003, unmarried fathers will have parental responsibility if they:
    - register the child's birth jointly with the mother at the time of birth,
    - re-register the birth if they are the natural father,
    - marry the mother of their child or obtain a parental responsibility order from the court,
    - register with the court for parental responsibility;
- the child's legally appointed guardian;
- a person in whose favour the court has made a residence order concerning the child;
- a local authority designated in a care order in respect of the child;
- a local authority or other authorised person who holds an emergency protection order in respect of the child. Section 2(9) of the Children Act 1989 states that a person who has parental responsibility for a child 'may arrange for some or all of it to be met by one or more persons acting on his or her behalf'. Such a person might choose to do this, for example, if a childminder or the staff of a boarding school have regular care of their child. As only a person exercising parental responsibility can give valid consent, in the event of any doubt then specific enquiry should be made. Foster parents do not automatically have parental responsibility.

Consent given by one person with parental responsibility is valid, even if another person with parental responsibility withholds consent. However,

---

50   This is the same case as: *R* v *Portsmouth Hospitals NHS Trust, ex p Glass* (1999) 50 BMLR 269, CA.

the courts have stated that a 'small group of important decisions' should not be taken by one person with parental responsibility against the wishes of another, citing in particular non-therapeutic male circumcision and immunisation.

The Court of Appeal upheld an order of Wall J refusing permission for circumcision to be carried out on a child where the Muslim father wanted it and the mother did not (*Re J (child's religious upbringing and circumcision)* (1999) 52 BMLR 82.[51]

In *Re O (a minor) (medical treatment)* [1993] 4 Med LR 272, Johnson J authorised a blood transfusion for a two-month-old girl born 12 weeks prematurely, despite the objections of her Jehovah's Witness parents. Booth J acted similarly to overrule the wishes of the parents of a ten-month-old girl suffering from leukaemia in the case of *Camden London Borough Council v R (a minor) (blood transfusion)* (1993) 15 BMLR 72, stating that the court could grant a specific order to permit a transfusion under s 8 of the Children Act 1989, and that it was not necessary to invoke the inherent jurisdiction of the court.

Similarly, in *Devon County Council v S* (1992) 11 BMLR 105, Thorpe J authorised a non-urgent transfusion to enable chemotherapy upon a boy aged four-and-a-half where there was only an even chance of success and his Jehovah's Witness parents objected.

Reference may also be made to in *Re E* [1993] 1 FLR 386, in which Ward J authorised a life-saving blood transfusion for a leukaemic boy of 15 from a family of Jehovah's Witnesses.[52]

In *Re L (a minor)* (1998) 51 BMLR 137, the President authorised blood transfusions for a Jehovah's Witness, a girl of 16, who had sustained severe burns, on the basis that her sheltered lifestyle as a Witness limited her understanding of her condition and the need for treatment, and that the treatment sought was in her best interests.

See also *Re T (a minor) (wardship: medical treatment)* [1997] 1 WLR 242, CA, discussed below under 'The quality of life and terminally ill patients'.

In *Re B (a child)* [2003] EWCA Civ 1148, the Court of Appeal upheld the judge's decision when he granted the father's applications under s 8 of the Children Act 1989 that, contrary to the mother's wishes, the children's best interests required that they receive the full MMR vaccination.

Where persons with parental responsibility disagree as to whether these procedures are in the child's best interests, it is advisable to refer the decision to the courts. It is possible that major experimental treatment, where opinion is divided as to the benefits it may bring the child, might also fall into this category of important decisions, although such a case has not yet been considered in the English courts.

---

51 Female circumcision is always prohibited, under the Prohibition of Female Circumcision Act 1985; *Re J* [2000] 1 FLR 571 at 577; *Re B (a child) sub nom in Re vaccination / MMR litigation; A v B; D v E sub nom in Re C (a child) (immunisation: parental rights); in Re F (a child) (immunisation: parental rights)* (2003).

52 In *Re W (a minor) (HIV test)* [1995] 2 FCR 184, Kirkwood J authorised a blood test on a child whose mother had died of an Aids-related illness as being in the best interests of the child. Wilson J authorised a blood test on a baby for HIV detection despite the parents' opposition (*Re C (a child)* also *sub nom Camden London Borough Council v A, B and C*) (1999) 50 BMLR 283).

Where there is doubt about whether a parent is acting in the interest of the child or young person, then the healthcare practitioner would be unwise to rely on the parent's consent, for example if a child alleges abuse and the parent supports psychiatric treatment for the child. The Government's guidance *Working Together to Safeguard Children* covers situations involving parental consent where abuse or neglect is suspected.[53]

In order to consent on behalf of a child, the person with parental responsibility must themselves have capacity. Where the person with parental responsibility for a child is themself under 18, they will only be able to give valid consent for the child's treatment if they themselves are *Gillick* competent (see above). Whether or not they have capacity may vary, depending on the seriousness of the decision to be taken.

Where a child is a ward of court, no important step may be taken in the life of the child without the prior consent of the court. This is likely to include more significant medical interventions but not treatment for minor injuries or common diseases of childhood.

In an emergency, it is justifiable to treat a child who lacks capacity without the consent of a person with parental responsibility, if it is impossible to obtain consent in time and if the treatment is vital to the survival or health of the child.

Research on children or young people

Where children lack capacity to consent for themselves, parents may give consent for their child to be entered into a trial where the evidence is that the trial therapy may be at least as beneficial to the patient as the standard therapy. It may also be compatible with the welfare principle for a person with parental responsibility to give consent to a research intervention that is not strictly in the best interests of the child, but is not against the interests of the child either. Such an intervention must involve only minimal burden to the child.

Decisions about experimental treatment must be made in the child's best interests (see above).

Using children as bone marrow donors

This is covered by the Human Tissue Authority's code of practice on donation of allogeneic bone marrow and peripheral blood stem cells for transplantation, and healthcare professionals should consult this for detailed information on the legal requirements and how to proceed.[54]

---

53 HM Government (2006) *Working Together to Safeguard Children: A guide to inter-agency working to safeguard and promote the welfare of children,* London: HM Government, www.dh.gov.uk/en/PublicationsandStatistics/Publications/PublicationsPolicyAndGuidance/ DH_4007781.

54 Human Tissue Authority (2006) *Code of Practice – Donation of allogeneic bone marrow and peripheral blood stem cells for transplantation,* Code 6, London: Human Tissue Authority, www.hta.gov.uk/legislationpoliciesandcodesofpractice/codesofpractice.cfm.

LIFE-SUSTAINING TREATMENT – WITHDRAWING AND WITHHOLDING

The general principles

A healthcare professional's legal duty is to care for a patient and to take reasonable steps to prolong his life. Although there is a strong presumption in favour of providing life-sustaining treatment, there are circumstances when continuing or providing life-sustaining treatment stops providing a benefit to a patient and is not clinically indicated. There is no legal distinction between withdrawing and withholding life-sustaining treatment. A person with capacity may decide either contemporaneously or by a valid and applicable advance decision that he has reached a stage where he no longer wishes treatment to continue. If a person lacks capacity, this decision must be taken in their best interests and in a way that reflects his wishes (if these are known).

The legal principles around consent are the same for all medical interventions, including decisions to withdraw or withhold life-sustaining treatment, but the issues surrounding seriously ill or dying patients are necessarily more grave and sensitive. Persons with the capacity to do so can make such decisions for themselves. If the person is an adult who lacks capacity to make such decisions then the provisions of the Mental Capacity Act 2005 will apply to these, as to other decisions. When making a best-interests decision in relation to life-sustaining treatment, healthcare professionals should be aware that the Mental Capacity Act requires that the healthcare professional must not be motivated by a desire to bring about the person's death.

Sometimes decisions will need to be made immediately – for example whether it is appropriate to attempt resuscitation after severe trauma.[55] In an emergency situation, where there is doubt as to the appropriateness of treatment, there should be a presumption in favour of providing life-sustaining treatment. When more time is available and the patient is an adult or child without capacity, all those concerned with the care of the patient – relatives, partners, friends, carers and the multidisciplinary team – can potentially make a contribution to the assessment. The discussions and the basis for decisions should be recorded in the patient's notes.

Legally, the use of artificial nutrition and hydration (ANH) constitutes medical treatment. Thus the legal principles that apply to the use of ANH are the same as those that apply to all other medical treatments, such as medication or ventilation. Decisions about the proposed withholding or withdrawal of ANH from a patient in a permanent vegetative state should be referred to court (see above). The case of *NHS Trust A* v *M, NHS Trust B* v *H* [2002] Fam 348, Fam Div confirmed that this is compatible with the Human Rights Act 1998.

There is an important distinction between withdrawing or withholding treatment that is of no clinical benefit to the patient or is not in the patient's

---

55   See Health Service Circular 2000/28 for further guidance on resuscitation decisions. It advises that NHS trusts should have appropriate resuscitation policies in place. www. dh.gov.uk/en/Publicationsandstatistics/Lettersandcirculars/Healthservicecirculars/DH _4004244.

best interests, and taking a deliberate action to end the patient's life. A deliberate action that is intended to cause death is unlawful. Although there is a strong presumption in favour of providing life-sustaining treatment, there are circumstances when continuing or providing life-sustaining treatment stops providing a benefit to a patient and is not clinically indicated. Healthcare professionals should discuss the situation with a patient with capacity and agree if and when the patient no longer wishes treatment to continue. If the patient lacks capacity, this decision must be taken in their best interests and in a way that reflects their wishes, beliefs and values (if these are known). Suitable care should be provided to ensure that both the comfort and dignity of the patient are maintained.

Adults and children with capacity

Except in circumstances governed by the Mental Health Act 1983, if an adult with the capacity to make the decision refuses life-sustaining treatment, or requests that it be withdrawn, practitioners must comply with the person's decision, even if it may result in the person's death.

In *Re B (adult: refusal of medical treatment)* [2002] 2 All ER 449 the court decided that if a refusal is ignored, they will be treating the person unlawfully.

The case of *Burke* v *GMC* established that an adult patient with capacity does not have the legal right to demand treatment that is not clinically indicated. Where a patient with capacity indicates his wish to be kept alive by the provision of ANH, the doctor's duty of care will require them to provide ANH while such treatment continues to prolong life. A patient cannot demand that a healthcare professional does something unlawful such as assisting them to commit suicide.

If a child with capacity makes such a request or refusal it is possible that such a refusal could be overruled if it would in all probability lead to the death of the child or to severe permanent injury (see above). Moreover, a decision which may result in the individual's death requires a very high level of understanding, so that many young people who would have the capacity to take other decisions about their medical care would lack the capacity to make such a grave decision.

Refusal of treatment by a child with capacity must always be taken very seriously, even though legally it is possible to override their objections. It is not a legal requirement to continue a child's life-sustaining treatment in all circumstances. For example, where the child is suffering an illness where the likelihood of survival even with treatment is extremely poor, and treatment will pose a significant burden to the child, it may not be in the best interests of the child to continue treatment.

Adults and children lacking capacity

If a child lacks capacity, it is still good practice to involve the child as far as is possible and appropriate in the decision. The decision to withdraw or withhold life-sustaining treatment must be made in the best interests of the child. The best interests of a child in the context of the withholding of medical treatment should be interpreted more broadly than medical interests, and should include emotional and other factors. There is a strong presumption in favour of preserving life, but not where treatment would be futile, and there is no obligation on healthcare professionals to give treatment that would be futile. If there is disagreement between those with parental responsibility for the child and the clinical team concerning the appropriate course of action, a ruling should be sought from the court as early as possible. This requirement was emphasised in the *Glass* judgment (see above).

A person with parental responsibility for a child or young person is legally entitled to give or withhold consent to treatment. A person with parental responsibility cannot demand a particular treatment to be continued where the burdens of the treatment clearly outweigh the benefits for the child. If agreement cannot be reached between the parent(s) and the healthcare professionals, a court should be asked to make a declaration about whether the provision of life-sustaining treatment would benefit the child. In exceptional cases, the court has been willing to authorise the withdrawal of life-sustaining treatment against the parents' wishes.[56] However, the views of the parents are given great weight by the courts and are usually determinative unless they conflict with the child's best interests.

THE QUALITY OF LIFE AND TERMINALLY ILL PATIENTS

Perhaps the most difficult and anxious decision the courts have ever been asked to take in this context arose in the conjoined twins case (*Re A (children) (conjoined twins: surgical separation)* [2000] 4 All ER 961, CA). For a variety of reasons, the court authorised the operation that would terminate the life of one twin (a child that was in any event dependent for her vital organs on her sister) but would give the other twin a fair chance of a reasonable life. The issues raised in that unique case were more a matter of medical, and general, ethics than of medical negligence, and the lengthy judgments at least as philosophical as jurisprudential, and for that reason they are not treated in detail here. Suffice it to say that there was an issue of consent, in that the parents were not consenting to the operation and the doomed twin had no say in the matter. The 'quality of life' of the two twins was a vital element in the court's decision.

Human rights considerations figure prominently in the context of 'quality of life' cases (such as fall to be decided after the Act came into force). The factor of 'quality of life' arises most commonly where a patient is terminally ill or in a vegetative state.

In *Re B (a minor) (wardship: medical treatment)* [1981] 1 WLR 1421, heard in the Court of Appeal in August 1981, a child born suffering from Down's syndrome needed an operation to clear an intestinal blockage if she was to live. If it was carried out, she stood a good chance of living 15 to 20 years. The parents refused their consent to the operation, believing that it was in the child's best interests that she be allowed to die, rather than face a short life of severe handicap. The local authority had her made a ward of court, and, when the surgeon in charge accepted the parents' decision, applied to the court. At first instance, Ewbank J refused to order the operation to be performed by another willing surgeon.

---

56   *Re C (a minor) (medical treatment)* [1998] 1 FLR 384.

On appeal, Templeman LJ said that it was a very poignantly sad case. The child would probably not be a 'cabbage' but would certainly be very severely mentally and physically handicapped. He said it was the duty of the court to decide whether it was in the interests of the child that the operation should take place and, while the view of the parents should be given substantial weight, it was wrong to approach the matter on the basis simply that the parents' wishes should be respected. The question was: 'Was the child's life demonstrably going to be so awful that in effect she must be condemned to die?' The trial judge was clearly of the view that it was not. He said that, although there might be cases of severe proved damage where the future was so uncertain and where the life of the child was so bound to be full of pain and suffering that the court might be driven to a different conclusion (so to allow the child to die), the evidence in the instant case only went to show that if the operation took place and was successful, then the child might live the normal span of a Down's syndrome child with the handicaps and defects and life of a Down's syndrome child, and it was not for the court to say that life of that description ought to be extinguished. Dunn LJ agreed. He said that there was no evidence that the child's short life was likely to be an intolerable one. The child should be put into the same position as any other Down's syndrome child and she must be given the chance to live an existence.

These judgments show that the parents will not be granted by the courts the right to decide whether or not their baby should live in such circumstances; that the courts are willing to consider the quality of life as a valid factor influencing their decision (they may well take the view that there is no rule that life is to be preserved at all costs); and that life would need to be proved to be utterly dreadful, to the point of being intolerable, one might say unliveable, before it should be considered not worth preserving.

In *Re C (a minor) (wardship: medical treatment)* [1990] Fam 26, the Court of Appeal was concerned with a 16-week-old baby suffering from congenital hydrocephalus (she had already been made a ward of court for non-medical reasons). A paediatrician had reported on behalf of the Official Solicitor that she was irreversibly brain-damaged, that her condition was hopeless and that the objective of treatment should be to ease her suffering and not to prolong her life. The court accepted that she should be treated within the parameters of the report but declined to give specific instructions as to that treatment.

In *Re J (a minor) (wardship: medical treatment)* [1991] Fam 33, [1990] 2 Med LR 67, the Court of Appeal said that a court, acting solely on behalf of and in the best interests of a ward who was profoundly, but not terminally, ill, might in appropriate circumstances approve a medical course of action which failed to prevent death. The correct approach in determining the child's best interests was to assess the quality of life if life-prolonging treatment were given and to decide whether, in all the circumstances, such a life, judged from the child's viewpoint, would be intolerable to him. There was therefore no absolute rule that, save where a ward was terminally ill, the court should never withhold consent to treatment to prolong life regardless of its quality and of any additional suffering which the treatment itself might cause. In this case the court approved the consultant's advice that if further resuscitation by way of ventilation was required, it would not be in the child's best interests unless his doctors thought so at the time.

In *Re J (a minor) (child in care: medical treatment)* [1993] Fam 15, an infant, who was born in January 1991, had suffered severe brain injury in a fall a year later. The local authority, acting under s 100 of the Children Act 1989, applied to the court to determine whether the consultants' decision was appropriate, namely that, if the baby suffered a life-threatening event, only ordinary resuscitative measures should be employed, not intensive therapeutic measures such as artificial ventilation. Waite J made an order that if a life-threatening event occurred full resuscitative measures should be employed. The Court of Appeal said that that order was inconsistent with established law. It was up to the treating doctors in the exercise of their clinical judgment to decide at any relevant time what treatment was appropriate. Leggatt LJ said the court was not depriving the doctors of the right to give life support, but was merely declining to deprive them of the power that they had always had of deciding themselves what was the appropriate treatment. Balcombe LJ said that it would put the doctors in an impossible position to order them to treat in a certain way, because if they did they might be acting contrary to what they believed was best for their patient and if they did not they would be in contempt of court. Lord Donaldson also made the distressing but valid point that doctors had to have regard day in, day out to the limitation of resources when deciding what treatment to give to what patient (as we know from the decided cases, the court will not dictate the allocation of resources).

In *An NHS Trust v MB* [2006] 2 FLR 319, an 18-month-old infant was diagnosed with the severest form of spinal muscular atrophy and had been in hospital since he was seven weeks old. The claimant NHS Trust sought a declaration that it should be lawful and within the child's best interests to withdraw ventilation whilst the parents sought a declaration that a tracheostomy be performed in order to allow for long-term ventilation.

In *Airedale NHS Trust v Bland* [1993] AC 789, the House of Lords approved an order authorising discontinuance of life-sustaining treatment in the case of a patient who had been in a persistent vegetative state for some three years since the Hillsborough stadium tragedy. It was said that the principle of the sanctity of life, which was not absolute, was not violated by ceasing to give medical treatment and care involving invasive manipulation of the patient's body, to which he had not consented and which conferred no benefit upon him.

In *Frenchay Healthcare NHS Trust v S* [1994] 1 WLR 601, a young adult had been admitted to hospital following an overdose of drugs. It was clear that his condition had developed into a persistent vegetative state, with no cognitive function and no chance of recovery. His nasogastric feeding tube had become dislodged and the consultant considered that it was not in his best interests to replace it. The Court of Appeal said that, although ultimate power was reserved to the court to review a doctor's decision as to what was in the patient's best interests, there was no reason to question the consultant's conclusion, albeit the context of acute emergency did not permit leisurely investigation, and so the court endorsed the judge's decision to grant a declaration to the defendants that they might lawfully refrain from intervention. The then Master of the Rolls said in the course of his judgment:

It is, I think, important that there should not be a belief that what the doctor says is the patient's best interest *is* the patient's best interest. For my part I would certainly reserve to the court the ultimate power and duty to review the doctor's decision in the light of all the facts.

In *Re A* [1992] 3 Med LR 303, Johnson J made a declaration that a child, who was brain-stem dead, was dead for all legal and medical purposes and that disconnecting the ventilator would not be unlawful.

In *Swindon and Marlborough NHS Trust* v *S* [1995] 3 Med LR 84, Ward J declared that it was lawful for a patient in a persistent vegetative state, who was being cared for at home by her family, to be allowed to die by the discontinuance of all life-sustaining treatment.

In *Re T (a minor) (wardship: medical treatment)* [1997] 1 WLR 242, the Court of Appeal refused to authorise a liver transplant upon an 18-month-old boy against the wishes of his parents. The medical evidence was unanimous that he would otherwise die before he was three and that it was in his best interests to have the operation. Mother and child had gone to live abroad (the mother gave evidence at first instance by video link). The court said that the paramount consideration in such cases was the best interests of the child. The court stated that the judge, who had authorised the procedure, had concentrated on the clinical issues instead of taking a wider view and considering the further implications of such an order. Care of the child post-operatively would devolve upon the mother and would require her complete co-operation with the medical regime. Forcing her to play this crucial and irreplaceable part in the aftermath of major invasive surgery throughout the childhood of her son was a consideration that could not be ignored. The judge had failed to put into the balance these broader considerations. The court was not prepared to overrule the decision of the parents, and to order mother and child to return to the UK to accept the proposed surgery, and in that way to require the mother to undertake all the necessary care. The paediatrician was clearly of the view that, even assuming that the operation proved wholly successful in surgical terms, the child's subsequent development could be injuriously affected if his day-to-day care depended upon the commitment of a mother who had suffered the turmoil of having her child compelled against her will to undergo, as a result of a coercive order from the court, a major operation against which her own medical and maternal judgment wholeheartedly rebelled. To prolong life was not always the sole objective of the court and to require it at the expense of other considerations might not be in a child's best interests. The judge had wrongly regarded the parents' decision as unreasonable.

The Scottish courts have held that, where a hospital patient was permanently unconscious and insensate and it was no longer possible to suggest that the continuance of medical treatment was of any benefit to him, there were no longer any best interests to be served by continuing such treatment, and accordingly the court, pursuant to its authority as *parens patriae* would authorise the relevant medical practitioners to discontinue life-sustaining treatment (*Law Hospital NHS Trust* v *Lord Advocate* [1996] 2 FLR 407, 1996 SLT 869). In *South Buckinghamshire NHS Trust* v *R (a patient)* [1996] 7 Med LR 401, Sir Stephen Brown P validated a Do Not Resuscitate (DNR) notice in respect of a 23-year-old man who had been born with a serious malformation of the brain and cerebral palsy and was existing in a low awareness state at an NHS Trust residential home. It was proposed to perform a gastrostomy. The judge said that the principle of law to be applied was that of the best interests of the patient, and the correct approach was for the court to judge the quality of life the patient would have to endure if given the treatment and to decide whether, in all the circumstances, such a life would be so afflicted as to be intolerable to that patient. In the particular case, the judge concluded that it would not be in the best interests of the patient to subject him to cardio-pulmonary resuscitation in the event of his suffering a cardiac arrest. In *Re C* [1996] 2 FCR 569, 32 BMLR 44, the same judge authorised the switching off of the life-support machines in the case of a three-month-old baby who was enduring 'an almost living death' and for whom the future was 'quite hopeless'. Although the child was neither braindead nor in a coma, she could not see, hear, move or communicate, and was expected to live no more than a further two years during which time her condition would deteriorate causing further pain and distress.

In *Re C (a minor)* [1998] Lloyd's Rep Med 1, where a child of some 16 months was suffering from spinal muscular atrophy, had a life expectancy of not more than a year, and was enduring increasing distress from the procedures being taken to keep her alive, and where the parents for religious reasons could not consent to any measures which would shorten her life, Sir Stephen Brown P made an order permitting withdrawal of ventilation and non-resuscitation in the event of respiratory arrest.

The Royal College of Paediatrics and Child Health produced guidelines in September 1997 for situations in which doctors should consider withdrawing medical treatment from children and allowing them to die. The guidelines say such a decision is warranted where the child is braindead or in a permanent vegetative state; where care delays death without easing suffering; where the child survives so physically or mentally impaired that it is unreasonable to expect him to suffer further; or where the illness is so progressive and irreversible that further treatment is intolerable (the procedure for obtaining leave to withdraw resuscitative treatment in cases of vegetative state can be found at [1994] PIQR P312).[57]

In *A National Health Service Trust* v *D* [2000] Lloyd's Rep Med 411, Cazalet J held that a declaration, contrary to the wishes of the parents, permitting doctors to non-resuscitate in the event of cardiac or respiratory arrest of a 19-month-old boy with irreversible brain damage was not in breach of the right to life under the Human Rights Act as the treatment advised was in the child's best interests, and it also protected his rights under Art 3 not to be subjected to inhuman and degrading treatment, which included the right to die with dignity.

In *A NHS Trust* v *M* [2000] MLC 0272, Butler-Sloss P held that, if artificial nutrition and hydration were withdrawn from two patients who had been for years in a permanent vegetative state, there would not be a breach of the right to life. She said that the article did not impose an absolute obligation to treat if such treatment would be futile. The article only imposed a positive obligation to give life-sustaining treatment in

---

57 Reference may be made to *R* v *Portsmouth Hospitals NHS Trust, ex p Glass* MLC 0114, (1999) 50 BMLR 269, CA, which is considered in the section headed 'Children under 16 – the concept of Gillick competence'.

circumstances where, according to responsible medical opinion, such treatment was in the best interests of the patient (see Chapter 21). In *NHS Trust A* v *H* (2001) 2 FLR 501, the President said that the state of the law as represented by the judgment in the *Bland* case (above) was compatible with Art 2 of the Convention and that in the instant case of a permanent vegetative state it would be lawful to discontinue all life-sustaining treatment. (In view of recent miraculous recoveries, the court may perhaps in due course amend the *Bland* directions.)

In *B* v *An NHS Hospital Trust* [2002] MLC 0737, the President awarded nominal damages for trespass to a competent patient whose clearly expressed wishes not to be artificially ventilated were ignored for a number of months.

Contrast *R (on the application of Burke)* v *GMC* [2004] EWHC 1879 (Admin), where Munby J said that under the Convention, as at common law, if a patient was competent or, although incompetent, had made an advance directive which was valid and relevant to the treatment in question, his decision to require the provision of artificial nutrition and hydration in his dying days was determinative of the issue. The judgment of the Court of Appeal reversing the decision of the judge is dealt with in Chapter 21.

In *Re LM (a child)* [2004] EWHC 2713, Butler-Sloss P decided that it was in the best interests of a baby suffering from a life-limited genetic disorder, who had only a few weeks or months to live, not to undergo further aggressive treatment in the form of mechanical ventilation. And in *Wyatt* v *Portsmouth NHS Trust* [2005] EWHC 693 (Fam), Hedley J held that it would not be in the best interests of a child suffering from chronic respiratory disease to die in the course of futile aggressive treatment. In the event of respiratory collapse, all treatment up to but not including incubation and ventilation would be in her best interests.

The Court of Appeal recently reviewed the whole issue of 'best interests' in the case of *Wyatt and Wyatt* v *Portsmouth Hospitals NHS Trust* [2005] 1 WLR 3995, a case involving a seriously disabled two-year-old girl with a complex medical history who had never left hospital. The court said the welfare of the child was paramount and the judge must look at the question from the assumed viewpoint of the patient. There was a strong presumption in favour of a course of action which would prolong life but that presumption was not irrebuttable. The term 'best interests' encompassed medical, emotional and all other welfare issues.

And in *NHS Trust* v *A* (1 September 2005, unreported), MLC 1283, CA, a case which concerned the withdrawal of support, which was naturally intrusive, for the heart, lungs and kidneys of an 86-year-old man, the court said the correct question should be formulated as: 'Was it in the best interests of the patient that the treatment which was prolonging his life should be continued; that there was no absolute rule to prevent a court declaring that doctors might no longer need to give treatment where the result of not giving the treatment would be to result in the earlier death of the patient; that it was for the court and not for a doctor to decide what was in the best interests of the patient; and that in this case the court would declare that the doctors treating the patient in the intensive care unit were not bound to continue to give invasive and uncomfortable treatment to the patient where there was no benefit to him?'

Where a patient lacks capacity to consent it is for the court ultimately to determine whether it is in the best interests of a patient to withdraw intrusive life sustaining treatment on the basis of an assessment of the medical evidence before it. (See *An NHS Trust* v *(1) A (an adult, represented by The Official Solicitor as Litigation Friend) (2) SA* (2006) Lloyd's Rep Med 29.)

In *Re OT* [2009] EWHC 633 (Fam), it was held, against the wishes of the parents, that withdrawal of life sustaining treatment, which was no longer in the child's best interests was not a breach of Art 2 or 8 of the ECHR. Where there was uncontroverted medical evidence that a seriously unwell nine-month-old child was experiencing distress and long-term paediatric care was not in his best interests, a hospital trust was granted a declaration allowing ventilation to be withdrawn and offering the child palliative care to allow him to die with the least distress.

If an adult lacks capacity, and has not made a valid and applicable advance decision to refuse life-sustaining treatment, the provisions of the Mental Capacity Act will apply and the decision must be based on the best interests of the adult, again involving the person as far as this is possible.

As with all decisions made under the Mental Capacity Act, before deciding to withdraw or withhold life-sustaining treatment, the healthcare professional must consider the range of treatment options available in order to work out what would be in the person's best interests. All of the factors set out in the Mental Capacity Act (2005) Code of Practice should be considered, and in particular the healthcare professional should consider any statements that the person has previously made about their wishes and feelings about life-sustaining treatment. Healthcare professionals should also refer to relevant professional guidance when making decisions regarding life-sustaining treatment.

Where a patient had indicated, while he had capacity, his wish to be kept alive by the provision of ANH, the doctor's duty of care will require the doctors to provide ANH while such treatment continues to prolong life. Where life depends upon the continued provision of ANH, ANH will be clinically indicated. If the patient lacks capacity, all reasonable steps that are in the person's best interests should be taken to prolong their life. Although there is a strong presumption in favour of providing life-sustaining treatment, there are circumstances when continuing or providing life-sustaining treatment stops providing a benefit to a patient and is not clinically indicated.[58]

OTHER EXCEPTIONS TO THE GENERAL PRINCIPLES

Certain statutes set out specific exceptions to the principles noted above. These are briefly noted below. Those concerned with the operation of such statutes should consult more detailed guidance.

Mentally disordered persons

Part IV of the Mental Health Act 1983 as amended by the Mental Health Act 2007 sets out circumstances in which persons liable to be detained

---

58 *Burke* v *the General Medical Council* [2005] 3 WLR 1132.

under the Act may be treated without consent for their mental disorder. The Mental Health Act 1983 has no application to treatment for physical disorders unrelated to the mental disorder, which remains subject to the common law principles described in previous chapters, even where the person concerned is detained under the Act. The Mental Health Act Code of Practice offers guidance on consent and medical treatment in this context.[59]

The Mental Health Act 1983, besides providing by s 62 that urgent treatment may be given to a patient without his consent, permits treatments for the mental disorder from which the patient is suffering (other than the more serious treatments) to be given without his consent.[60] The Mental Health Act 1983, as amended, divides treatment for mental disorder into seven categories. It is not proposed to go into the scope of these provisions within this book. The Mental Health Act 1983 only applies to treatment of detained patients for mental disorder. For all other forms of treatment, the patient is in the same position as a non-detained patient (*NHS Trust* v *C (adult patient: medical treatment)* [2004] All ER (D) 175).

What if the patient is incapable of giving consent for routine medical treatment unconnected with mental disorder? A mentally handicapped person who is not mentally disordered within the meaning of the Act may also be in this position. In *R* v *Dr M, ex p N* [2002] EWCA Civ 1789, the Court of Appeal said that a court could be properly satisfied that it was appropriate to give permission for treatment to be given to a patient who did not consent to it only if it had been convincingly shown that the treatment was a medical necessity.

In *Re D (a minor)* [1976] Fam 185, the court was required to decide if it should authorise the sterilisation of a 'mentally handicapped' 11-year-old girl. On the evidence, Heilbron J concluded that that was not an appropriate course, the court proceeding on the assumption that a parent could give consent for such an operation on a child, and that, where the child was a ward of court, the court could give that consent in place of the parent.

In *Re B (a minor)* [1988] AC 199, the House of Lords upheld the order of the courts below, who had authorised a sterilisation upon a severely mentally handicapped girl of 17. It was said that sterilisation of a minor would always need the court's approval. The court expressly left undecided the question whether (apart from the limited context afforded by the Mental Health Act 1983, as set out above) any person or court could authorise or give consent to medical treatment upon an adult who was not capable of giving consent himself.

The House of Lords considered the relevant issues in *Re F* [1990] 2 AC 1. This 33-year-old patient was born in 1953 and as a result of a respiratory

---

59   Department of Health (2008) *Code of Practice: Mental Health Act 1983,* London: DH, www. dh.gov.uk/en/Publicationsandstatistics/Publications/PublicationsPolicyAndGuidance/ DH_084597.
60   In *B* v *Croydon Health Authority* [1995] Fam 133, a declaration was obtained from the Court of Appeal that tube-feeding a mental patient who was refusing to eat did not require her consent as it constituted 'medical treatment given for the mental disorder' from which she was suffering within the meaning of s 63 of the Mental Health Act 1983.

infection as a baby had the general mental capacity of a four- or five-year-old. She had recently formed an attachment to another patient within her hospital and ran the risk of becoming pregnant (the pill and an IUD were contra-indicated). All her carers, the judge at first instance and the Court of Appeal concluded that it was in her best interests to be sterilised. The court decided that there was a rule at common law, hitherto unknown, that a doctor was entitled, where the patient was unable to give consent, to carry out any treatment which was in the best interests of the patient; and the best interests of the patient were to be measured according to the classic *Bolam* test, namely that if there was a responsible body of medical opinion that would have supported what the doctor did, then he cannot be criticised. This is a very dangerous rule (for the patient), and a novel one – fortunately it is probably *obiter*, in that it was not necessary to the actual decision. What it would mean is that not only is a doctor exonerated in an emergency situation as long as he acts in accordance with some accepted practice or another, which is understandable, and not only can he carry out upon a mental patient any treatment that would have the approval of any minority body of medical opinion but also, during an operation, he can perform other procedures that take his fancy as long as a minority opinion would support him. It is a pity that the words of Lord Donaldson when the case was in the Court of Appeal were not heeded:

> [Consent] is a crucial factor in relation to all medical treatment. If it is necessarily absent, whether temporarily in an emergency situation or permanently in a case of mental disability, other things being equal, there must be greater caution in deciding whether to treat and, if so, how to treat.

> As far as the actual decision is concerned, the court said that it followed that there was no legal obligation on the doctors to seek the approval of the court before sterilising a patient whose mental condition made consent impossible to obtain, but the court strongly urged the medical profession to seek that approval first (Lord Griffiths was alone in saying that the court should insist that its approval be sought first).

In *Re LC (medical treatment: sterilisation)* [1997] 2 FLR 258, Thorpe J declined an application by the local authority, supported by the mother, for the sterilisation of a girl in her 20s with a mental age of three. She had been indecently assaulted while in the care of a specialist residential home. The judge concluded that, on balance, her current level of care and supervision was of such a high standard that it would not be in the girl's best interests to impose on her a surgical procedure which was not without its risks nor without painful consequences.

In *Re S (adult patient) (sterilisation)* [2001] Fam 15, the Court of Appeal, reversing the order of the judge below, said that it was not in the best interests of a mentally handicapped 29-year-old woman to be sterilised: a coil was a better option. It reached a similar conclusion (*mutatis mutandis*) in respect of proposed male sterilisation in *Re A (medical treatment: male sterilisation)* (1999) 53 BMLR 66, CA, saying that the concept of best interests related to the mentally incapacitated person and were not limited to best medical interests, but encompassed medical, emotional and all other welfare issues. In this case a vasectomy operation at the present time was not essential to A's future well-being.

The rules for seeking a declaration that a sterilisation procedure upon a mentally handicapped person may lawfully be carried out were set out at [1993] 3 All ER 222 in a Practice Note dated May 1993. They must be read subject to the Court of Appeal guidance in *St George's Healthcare NHS Trust* v *S* (above). It has been held that a declaration is not required for a medically indicated hysterectomy on a mentally handicapped adult (*Re GF* [1993] 4 Med LR 77), nor for a termination (*Re SG* [1993] 4 Med LR 75). In *Re H (a mental patient)* [1993] 4 Med LR 91, Wilson QC held that there was no call for a declaration to be given to legitimate investigations for a brain tumour in a mentally handicapped 25-year-old. The judge was clearly concerned that the medical profession should not think it must be forever seeking authorisation from the court for its procedures.

In *R* v *Kirklees Metropolitan Borough Council, ex p C (a minor)* [1993] 2 FLR 187, the Court of Appeal held that a local authority could give valid consent for a psychiatric admission in respect of a child in its care.

In *R* v *Mental Health Act Commission, ex p W* (1988) Times, 27 May, the Divisional Court reversed the refusal of the mental health commissioners to issue a certificate to a patient under s 57 of the Mental Health Act 1983 to the effect that he was capable of understanding the nature, purpose and likely effects of the treatment for paedophilia that he desired to undergo.

In *Re Y (mental patient: bone marrow donation)* [1997] Fam 110, Connell J authorised a bone marrow transplant from a mentally disordered adult to her sister, who was suffering from pre-leukaemic bone marrow disorder. The donor lived in a community home, and was regularly visited by her sister and her mother. The judge said that there was evidence that the mother's life also would be prolonged by a successful transplant between her daughters, and he concluded that the donor would receive an emotional, psychological and social benefit from the operation and suffer minimal detriment. Accordingly, the blood tests and the bone marrow harvesting operation would be in her best interests.

In *Re Z (medical treatment: hysterectomy)* (1999) 53 BMLR 53, Bennett J authorised a laparoscopic sub-total hysterectomy on a mentally disordered woman of 19, saying that, since her periods brought her nothing but misery, pain and discomfort and served no useful purpose either reproductively or emotionally, it was in her best interests that her periods should cease altogether. Were she to become pregnant she would be incapable of raising a child and the trauma of pregnancy, childbirth and the inevitable removal of her child would be a catastrophe for her. Furthermore, if she had to undergo an abortion the psychological and emotional fallout would be disastrous. Therefore, the risk of pregnancy had to be removed completely. The subtotal hysterectomy would not only dramatically improve her quality of life by eliminating her menstrual periods, but also give her total protection from pregnancy. Accordingly, it was in her best interests that she undergo a laparoscopic subtotal hysterectomy and so her mother's application would be granted.

In a number of recent cases, the President of the Family Division, Dame Elizabeth Butler-Sloss, has authorised an innovative form of treatment for patients lacking capacity who were suffering from variant CJD, a rare and fatal neuro-degenerative condition: see, for example, *EP* v *Trusts A, B, and C* [2004] Lloyds Rep Med 211. The court said that the treatment, though innovative, was in the best interests of the patients. The concept of best interests encompassed medical, emotional, and all other welfare issues.

In *An NHS Trust* v *D* [2004] Lloyds Rep Med 107, Coleridge J authorised the termination of pregnancy of a mental patient on the ground that the procedure was in her best interests, and he gave guidance as to when it was necessary in such a situation to apply to the court for a declaration.

In *(1) Trust A (2) Trust B* v *H (an adult patient by her litigation friend, the Official Solicitor)* (2006) 2 FLR 958, a patient detained under the Mental Health Act 1983 lacked capacity to make decisions about her medical treatment for her ovarian cyst and gynaecological condition, and it was in her best interests to undergo treatment that would include a total hysterectomy. A patient such as H had the right not to be subjected to degrading treatment under Art 3 of the ECHR. If H's position was to be alleviated, the Court found that there was no feasible alternative to surgery. Without it her symptoms would become worse. The surgery would improve her quality of life and mental health, and her life expectancy would be increased. Forcible administration of post-operative chemotherapy was not covered by the declarations granted.

Neither the existence of mental disorder nor the fact of detention under the 1983 Act should give rise to an assumption of incapacity. The person's capacity must be assessed in every case in relation to the particular decision being made. The capacity of a person with a mental disorder may fluctuate.

Significant amendments to the Mental Health Act 1983 have been made by the Mental Health Act 2007. The Mental Health Act 1983 will continue to provide legal authority, within certain limits and subject to certain safeguards, to treat detained patients for mental disorder without consent. Except in emergencies, however, it will no longer be permissible to use the Mental Health Act 1983 to administer electro-convulsive therapy (ECT) to a patient who has capacity to consent to it, but who does not. Additionally, if a person made an advanced decision when they had capacity, saying that they never wished to receive ECT and the hospital knows about this, then the treatment cannot be given. The only exception would be in an emergency if it was immediately necessary to save a patient's life or to prevent a serious deterioration of the patient's condition.

In addition, except in emergencies it will not be permissible to administer ECT as a treatment for mental disorder in any circumstances to any child or young person under the age 18 (whether or not they are otherwise subject to the Mental Health Act 1983) unless it has been independently approved in accordance with the Mental Health Act 1983. Further guidance is given in the Mental Health Act Code of Practice.[61]

There will also be a new procedure by which certain patients discharged from detention under the Mental Health Act 1983 can be made subject to community treatment orders (CTOs), making them liable to recall to hospital for further treatment if necessary. While patients are subject to CTOs they may only be treated for mental disorder in accordance with the Mental Health Act 1983. Unless they have been recalled to hospital, it will not be permissible to treat such patients without their consent if

---

61 Department of Health (2008) *Code of Practice: Mental Health Act 1983*, London: DH, www. dh.gov.uk/en/Publicationsandstatistics/Publications/PublicationsPolicyAndGuidance/ DH_084597.

they have the capacity to consent to the treatment in question but do not do so. Treatment for mental disorder of patients subject to CTOs who lack capacity to consent will be permitted, subject to the rules set out in the new Part 4A of the Mental Health Act 1983.

It will remain the case that no-one (whether or not detained under the Mental Health Act 1983) may be given neurosurgery for mental disorder ('psychosurgery') or have hormones surgically implanted in order to reduce male sex drive, unless they consent to the procedure and it has been independently approved in accordance with s 57 of the Mental Health Act 1983.

None of these changes will affect the principle that treatment for physical disorders, unrelated to the mental disorder for which the patient is receiving compulsory treatment, does not come within the scope of mental health legislation.

The Public Health (Control of Disease) Act 1984 provided that, on an order made by a magistrate, persons suffering from certain notifiable infectious diseases could be medically examined, removed to and detained in a hospital without their consent. A magistrate when ordering the detention of a person in a hospital could not order that a person undergo medical treatment. The treatment of such persons must be based on the common law principles previously described. The 1984 Act is now amended by the Health and Social Care Act 2008. Under Part 2A there is express provision prohibiting regulations under new s 45B or 45C from legislating for the administering of medical treatment by force. Nor will there be power for a magistrate to order compulsory treatment under new s 45G, which gives powers to magistrates to make orders in relation to persons who pose a threat to the health of others.

Chapter 11

Wrongful birth

Sarah Fraser Butlin

THE FAILED STERILISATION AND SIMILAR MISHAPS

An unplanned pregnancy can arise as a result of a failed sterilisation, male or female. The claim is that the woman has had to endure a pregnancy. In addition, if the pregnancy is not terminated, a child, whether disabled or not, has been born who would not have been born if there had been no negligence in or around the sterilisation. A similar claim is made where a pregnancy should have been terminated but, due to negligence, was not. For example, the termination was incompetently performed or ante-natal screening negligently failed to detect foetal defects which would have resulted in a lawful termination.

There are effectively five scenarios to consider:

1   wrongful pregnancy with a healthy child due to a negligently performed sterilisation operation;
2   wrongful pregnancy with a disabled child;
3   a disabled woman's wrongful pregnancy with a healthy child;
4   wrongful birth claims, that the woman would have terminated the pregnancy if she had known that she was carrying a disabled child;
5   wrongful life claims brought by a child claiming that they would not have been born but for the negligence.

Because wrongful life claims are disallowed as being contrary to public policy (Scenario 5, and dealt with further below), it is important to remember for the purposes of limitation that the claims will be by the parents, not the child.

STERILISATION

The failure rate of sterilisation

The lifetime risk of failure for tubal occlusion is generally accepted to be one in 200. Where Filshie clips are used, on the data available, it is two to three per thousand.[1] Separate figures for operator failure and natural

---

[1]   Royal College of Obstetricians and Gynaecologists, *Male and Female Sterilisation*, Evidence-based Clinical Guideline Number 4.

recanalisation are not available. The failure rate for vasectomy has usually been considered to be substantially lower, though some experts say that is not proven. The failure rate for vasectomy, once the initial period for testing the semen for sperm has been successfully concluded, is generally thought to be no more than one in 2000. Failure of vasectomy discovered during the post-operative testing period is referred to as 'early recanalisation', thereafter 'late recanalisation'.

Lines of attack

In failed sterilisation claims, there are generally two separate lines of attack: firstly, an incompetently performed operation and secondly, the failure to warn the patient of potential failure of the operation.

Expert evidence will be required to establish that the operation was incompetently performed. Generally, where conception has taken place within a few months of a sterilisation by Filshie clips most, but not all, experts would say that the most likely inference is that one of the clips was not properly applied to the tube (different considerations may apply where the sterilisation was not by clips or rings). A few experts, particularly if instructed by the defence, would argue that a fistula could have formed soon after the procedure or the tube recanalised unusually quickly.

The situation is much more difficult where pregnancy takes place a considerable time after the sterilisation. If the patient may be about to undergo a Caesarean section or a further sterilisation, one should ensure that a reliable observer (this may be the treating doctor) reports on the state of the tubes.

If a clip is found on the wrong structure, such as a neighbouring ligament, there can be no proper defence. The defence expert occasionally maintains that misplacing the clip can happen in the best of hands. This is untrue. The clip should properly occlude the lumen of the tube. The doctor should be able to see this. If he is in any doubt, it is his duty to advise the woman to have a hysterosalpingogram (see *McLennan* v *Newcastle Health Authority* MLC 0615, [1992] 3 Med LR 215). Therefore it follows that if the clip is found on the tube but not properly occluding the lumen, there is no proper defence.

There may also be further evidence about the position of the clip after the relevant parts of the tubes have been sent for histological examination.

If the clip is found not to be on any structure but lying loose in the peritoneal cavity, this will indicate negligence, as, whatever defence might be offered, properly applied clips do not fall off, at least not until sufficient time has elapsed for the tube to atrophy substantially. This sort of defence was unsuccessfully maintained in *Fallows* v *Randle* MLC 0591, [1997] 8 Med LR 160, CA. [2]

The *second* line of attack is to allege that the woman was not warned of the failure rate and the proper consenting process was not undertaken. It may be helpful to refer to the guidelines produced by the Royal College of Obstetricians and Gynaecologists.[3] However this line of attack is unlikely

---

2   For the medical and evidential complexities that can arise in a case that alleges misplacement, see Popplewell J in *Taylor* v *Shropshire Health Authority* MLC 0048, [1998] Lloyd's Rep Med 395.

3   As at footnote 1 above, read together with their *Obtaining Valid Consent*, Clinical Governance Advice 6.

to succeed these days as the standard consent form for sterilisation gives such a warning, and in most cases it is not reasonably open to the woman to say that she did not have time to read it. Also, most doctors will put a note in the records at some time pre-operatively to the effect that they have warned. A further difficulty will be in proving that no warning was given. This may simply be a dispute of fact between doctor and patient. However, usually a specialised form of consent for a sterilisation will be used which will warn of the risk. Assuming the patient signed the form well before the operation, it will not avail to say she did not read it.

Even where there has been a failure to warn, causation is a major hurdle. In the context of sterilisation it has virtually never been known for a woman to refuse the procedure on being told of the small failure rate.[4] Occasionally for medical reasons a further pregnancy would pose such a threat to the health of mother or child that it can be alleged that her partner would also have been sterilised, or other additional contraceptive precautions would have been taken, if she/they had been told of the failure rate.[5] Alternatively one can allege that, although a warning would not have deterred the woman from accepting the operation, she would have realised she was pregnant soon enough to enable a simple termination rather than having to undergo the more complex and, to her, unacceptable option of a late termination.[6]

Vasectomy

It is almost always impossible to show that a vasectomy has been performed incompetently. The anatomy does not usually permit that argument. Therefore any allegation has to be that the semen was improperly declared to be sperm-free. It may be that the patient was told that he was sterile when there had only been one sperm test, or perhaps the laboratory reports were misinterpreted by the doctor. However in such cases, one would expect a pregnancy to follow fairly soon after the sterilisation operation, otherwise natural recanalisation is the more likely explanation.

A claim for omission to warn of the risk of late recanalisation (ie after the successful conclusion of the post-operative testing period) is subject to the same difficulties as a similar claim in respect of female sterilisation.[7] Interestingly in *Goodwill* v *British Pregnancy Advisory Service* [1996] 1 WLR 1397, the Court of Appeal rejected a claim by a woman who sued the doctor who carried out the vasectomy for not warning his patient at the time of the failure rate. She had started a relationship with a man three years after his vasectomy. The vasectomy spontaneously reversed and the claimant gave birth to a healthy daughter. The Court of Appeal

---

4 In *Ellis* v *Wallsend District Hospital* [1990] 2 Med LR 103, the New South Wales Court of Appeal said that a patient's evidence that she would have declined surgery if properly warned should not be rejected unless it was inherently incredible or inherently improbable.

5 Although see *Gowton* v *Wolverhampton Health Authority* MLC 0959, [1994] 5 Med LR 432 and *Lybert* v *Warrington Health Authority* MLC 0712, [1996] 7 Med LR 71, CA.

6 See *Thake* v *Maurice* [1986] QB 644, MLC 0011, CA, affirming [1984] 2 All ER 513.

7 For example, see *Stobie* v *Central Birmingham Health Authority* (1994) 22 BMLR 135. An attempt to sue the Department of Health for failing to disseminate information about failure rates to the public generally unsurprisingly failed in *Danns* v *Department of Health* [1996] PIQR P69.

said that the claim, involving as it did the allegation that the doctor had owed a duty of care to an indeterminately large class of females who might have sexual relations with his patient during the patient's lifetime, was manifestly unsustainable and frivolous, vexatious and an abuse of process. However, it should be noted that the claimant faced insurmountable difficulties on her own case: she had only removed her contraceptive coil after taking advice from her GP, who had alerted her to the possibility, albeit small, of the vasectomy failing.

Occasionally it is disputed that it was the claimant who impregnated the mother of the child, at which point paternity must be established.

SCENARIO 1: WRONGFUL PREGNANCY WITH A HEALTHY CHILD

Prior to *McFarlane* the courts had generally held that damages could be recovered for the expense of bringing up a healthy child who would not have been born had it not been for some sort of negligent mismanagement (*Emeh* v *Kensington, Chelsea and Westminster Area Health Authority* [1985] QB 1012). The claims were for economic damage and most settled for about £50,000 to £80,000. The principle was that the new child had the right to be brought up in the same standard of living as the previous children.

However, the decision by the House of Lords in *McFarlane v Tayside Health Board* [2000] 2 AC 59 turned this on its head. Despite the criticism it received, it was expressly approved by the House in the *Rees* case (see below).

The position in relation to the birth of a healthy child following a negligent failed sterilisation, is that any *personal injury* to the mother caused by the negligence, for example the pregnancy and any stress or psychological damage as a result, will be recoverable. However such injury is unlikely to attract more than about £10,000. Special damages flowing directly from the fact of pregnancy could increase the award. However no damages are recoverable for the cost of bringing up the child.

This has been supplemented by the decision in *Rees* v *Darlington Memorial Hospital NHS Trust* [2003] MLC 1053 where it was held that a further award of £15,000 could be made for the loss of the woman's right to control the extent of her family (see below at Scenario 3).

It is important to note that one point in the decision in *Emeh* is still good law: namely that, 'save in exceptional circumstances' a woman's decision not to have an abortion was not an act that broke the chain of causation. The Court of Appeal did not explain what those exceptional circumstances might be and it is difficult to see what would be accepted as exceptional enough to effectively require a woman to have an abortion.

The *McFarlane* case

The facts in the *McFarlane* case were simple. A couple decided to have a vasectomy having had four children. They were given the all clear on the semen samples, which was admitted to have been incorrect information, though negligence was not admitted. The mother later became pregnant and gave birth to a healthy child. They brought a claim for personal injury based on the pregnancy and the economic cost of bringing up the child.

The claim for the pregnancy

The defendants argued, astonishingly, that even the claim for the unwanted pregnancy should be disallowed on the basis that a pregnancy should not be regarded as a personal injury, not even an unwanted one. Even more surprisingly, that contention had been accepted in the Scottish court of first instance. However, on both appeals the judges had no difficulty in allowing that part of the claim (damages for that aspect of the claim had been agreed at £10,000; the economic claim was put at £100,000, a fairly usual figure for such a claim). Lord Millett suggested that about £5,000 should be allowed for the frustration of the couple's desire to restrict their family (it is not clear if this would be in addition to compensation for the pregnancy itself).

Two different approaches

As can be seen from the summary below, some of the judges favoured a policy-type approach (based on general moral and societal considerations) over a legalistic one (based on standard legal principles such as foreseeability, proximity, causation and reasonable restitution), while others vice versa. But they all agreed that the economic claim could not stand.

However, whatever the grounds they gave for their conclusions, one cannot help seeing in the outcome further evidence of a general policy decision taken at the highest level, to the effect that the amount and incidence of personal injury damages over the whole spectrum must be kept as low as possible, no doubt on the basis that that is best for society as a whole.

The judges' reasoning

Lord Slynn based his view on the standard *Caparo* rule (*Caparo Industries plc* v *Dickman* [1990] 2 AC 605, HL) that economic loss is only recoverable where there was a sufficient relationship of proximity to be able to say that the defendants had assumed responsibility for the consequences in respect of which recovery was being claimed and that it was fair, just and reasonable to impose such a duty. As one knows, this 'test' gives the court an unfettered right to impose its own view of policy. Apart from 'policy', it is not easy to see why Lord Slynn decided this question in the negative. He could just as easily have decided it in the 'logical' (his word) fashion, namely that the cost of upbringing was an obviously foreseeable consequence of the negligence and impossible to dissociate from it.

Lord Steyn decided the question as a moral issue and on the grounds of 'distributive justice', which means the just distribution of burdens and losses among members of a society. Lord Steyn said that was what lay behind the negative decisions in the various jurisdictions to which the court had been referred,[8] and said this was not a matter of public policy. He said the real reasons for the court's conclusions should not be masked by unreal and formalistic propositions along the lines of no loss,

---

8   Their Lordships conducted an exhaustive investigation into decisions in other jurisdictions. Although the English authorities were virtually all one way (positive), there have been a substantial amount of negative decisions elsewhere.

no foreseeable loss, no causative link, only reasonable restitution, etc. Judges should give real reasons for their decisions.

> The truth is that tort law is a mosaic in which the principles of corrective justice and distributive justice are interwoven. And in situations of uncertainty and difficulty a choice sometimes has to be made between the two approaches. In my view it is legitimate in the present case to take into account considerations of distributive justice. That does not mean that I would decide the case on grounds of public policy. On the contrary, I would avoid those quick sands. Relying on principles of distributive justice I am persuaded that our tort law does not permit parents of a healthy unwanted child to claim the costs of bringing up the child from a health authority or a doctor. If it were necessary to do so, I would say that the claim does not satisfy the requirement of being fair, just and reasonable.

Like Lord Slynn, Lord Steyn did not wish to base his conclusion on the 'set-off' argument (ie allow for the 'joys' of parenthood as against the economic demands).

More reasons

However, Lord Hope took the view that the benefits or set-off principle was relevant, but then said that as it was impossible to value them as against the damage by way of the cost of upkeep and therefore the logical (*sic*) conclusion was that such recovery was not permissible. Otherwise the parents would be getting more than they had lost!

He also adopted, perhaps less unreasonably, the *Caparo* test of proximity which also led him to a negative conclusion.

Lord Clyde agreed with this approach. He said that policy considerations could be found to point either way, eg sanctity of human life as against the right of parents and benefit to society of limiting families. Therefore, the decision should not be founded on policy considerations. For him the principal relevant consideration was the legal rule of reasonable restitution.

> In such a context I would consider it appropriate to have regard to the extent of the liability which the defenders could reasonably have thought they were undertaking. It seems to me that even if a sufficient causal connection exists the cost of maintaining a child goes far beyond any liability which in the circumstances of the present case the defenders could reasonably have thought they were undertaking.

But why? Why should not a defendant understand that if a child is born through his negligence he will have to shoulder the financial burden rather than the parents?

Lord Clyde also considered that the extent of these economic claims was out of proportion to the wrongdoing. Again, the rationale for this is unclear given the vast changes that will be brought to bear on the individuals impacted by the birth of a child.

Lord Millett was, strangely, not prepared to assume that the reason for the couple not wanting a fifth child was financial. He then made it clear that he did not accept the set-off/benefits argument, nor the strictly legalistic ones. He took what one might term the 'moral high ground':

> There is something distasteful, if not morally offensive, in treating the birth of a normal, healthy child as a matter for compensation ... I accept the thrust of

both the main arguments in favour of dismissing such a claim. In my opinion the law must take the birth of a normal, healthy baby to be a blessing, not a detriment. In truth it is a mixed blessing. It brings joy and sorrow, blessing and responsibility. The advantages and the disadvantages are inseparable. Individuals may choose to regard the balance as unfavourable and take steps to forego the pleasures as well as the responsibilities of parenthood. They are entitled to decide for themselves where their own interests lie. But society itself must regard the balance as beneficial. It would be repugnant to its own sense of values to do otherwise. It is morally offensive to regard a normal, healthy baby as more trouble and expense than it is worth.

There are many arguments for and against such moralising. It may also be argued that 'distributive justice' does not necessarily suggest a negative decision to this claim: there is nothing unjust about allowing these claims (they will not bankrupt the NHS) and a deal of injustice to the parents in denying it. What would have happened if Mrs McFarlane had given birth to octuplets?

Post-*McFarlane*

It is worth nothing that since *McFarlane* the High Court of Australia has decided a similar case along the same lines. This was by a majority of four to three, after both courts below had found in favour of the claimant! (*Cattanach* v *Melchior* [2003] MLC 0722.)

The issue of a second pregnancy after a failed sterilisation is difficult. In *Sabri-Tabrizi v Lothian Health Board* (1998) 43 BMLR 190, it was held that where a woman knew she was still fertile (because she had already had one pregnancy terminated following the failed sterilisation) and had sexual intercourse with her husband, using only condoms, this broke the chain of causation between the negligent sterilisation procedure and the birth of the child. Consequently her claim was struck out. This seems a rather strange result as the defendants, through their negligence, made it impossible for the couple to have any safer intercourse than that provided by condoms. Therefore it appears to be a very harsh decision of the court to hold that she was unreasonable in having sexual intercourse.

A contractual claim in the county court, attempting to get round the limiting effect of *McFarlane* was unsurprisingly unsuccessful (*Reynolds* v *Health First Medical Group* [2000] Lloyd's Rep Med 240). The claim alleged a contract between patient and GP and sought to maintain that a claim for upbringing was based on a contractual, not tortious relationship. The judge rejected the existence of a contract between an NHS patient and her GP. Although he did not need to go further, it is clear that the contention that *McFarlane* would not apply to a contractual relationship is quite hopeless, except in the highly unlikely event of the contract specifically providing that the defendant undertook responsibility for the extended economic losses.

Another novel claim was brought in *Marian Richardson v LRC Products Ltd* [2000] Lloyds Rep Med 280. The couple brought a claim pursuant to the Consumer Protection Act for the birth of a child, after a condom split during use (the teat parting from the body of the condom at about shoulder level). The claim was put in two ways: first, the condom had been exposed to the detrimental and weakening influence of ozone during the course of manufacture, and secondly that it must have been defective in some way or another because otherwise it would not have fractured. Most of the case related to scientific evidence. The judge rejected the claim in relation to ozone exposure. He also held that he was satisfied by evidence given by a defence expert that condoms occasionally failed for no known reason. This is perhaps a little harder to understand. Just because it has not been possible on occasions in the past to discover why a condom has split, that does not mean one has to conclude that it was not inherently defective.

However, the judge went on (*obiter*) to disallow the claim on quite another ground. He said that there had been a duty to mitigate the damage, and that Mrs Richardson should have sought out the 'morning-after' pill, whether by telling her GP what had happened or in some other way, which would probably have avoided the pregnancy. Failure to do this invalidated the claim. Mrs Richardson's explanation was that it was a Saturday afternoon and she did not think it was such an emergency to need to call on the out of hours service. However the judge held that she should have telephoned them. This is an extremely harsh decision, particularly given that in other circumstances, a woman is not obliged to accept a termination. In addition, the judge stated summarily that he saw no reason why *McFarlane* should not apply to a consumer product case. This actually needs a little more thought. If the rationale of the House of Lords judgment can properly be said, on the majority view, to be a matter of distributive justice, ie that the NHS or the medical profession should not have to bear the cost of raising the unplanned child, then this argument would not apply to the profit-making manufacturer. If the true rationale is that it is odious to award damages for a healthy child (or impossible to calculate them given the need to deduct the benefit of a child), then it could be conceded that it would be just as odious (or impossible) where a manufacturer would be footing the bill.

Value of the claim

In general damages, an uncomplicated, unplanned pregnancy going to term has always been worth about £6,500. If there are complications, the award of general damages can be increased. If the pregnancy was terminated, whether by abortion or miscarriage (there is, of course, no obligation to terminate – *Emeh* v *Kensington and Westminster and Chelsea Health Authority* [1985] QB 1012, CA), there may be psychological injury for which additional general damages can be sought.[9]

In terms of special damages, there may be a claim for the wasted expenses involved in preparing for the birth. This will include loss of earnings while pregnant and in the initial recovery period. However, following *McFarlane* a claim for loss of earnings when a mother had to give up work to look after her healthy, unplanned child was rejected by the Court of Appeal in *Greenfield* v *Irwin (aka Greenfield* v *Flather)* (2001) MLC 0341, CA.

In addition, there is the *Rees* claim of around £15,000 for the loss to the woman of her right to limit her family (see below).

---

9   See for example *Taylor* v *Shropshire Health Authority* [2000] MLC 0226, where the judge awarded £15,000.

SCENARIO 2: WRONGFUL PREGNANCY WITH A DISABLED CHILD

In *McFarlane*, the House implicitly left open the question of whether the cost of care and allied expenses could be claimed where the child was born disabled. This was considered by the Court of Appeal in *Parkinson* v *St James and Seacroft University Hospital NHS Trust* [2001] MLC 0360. While it was approved by two judges in the House of Lords in *Rees*, one cannot be certain that should the issue be expressly considered by the House of Lords the same outcome would result.

Nevertheless the position at present is that a mother can recover the additional cost of care and additional expenses in raising an unplanned disabled child than an unplanned healthy child. She may also recover a slightly higher award for general damages for her shock on discovering that she has given birth to a disabled child (see *Hardman v Amin* (below)).

The *Parkinson* case

Parkinson v *St James and Seacroft University Hospital NHS Trust* [2001] MLC 0360, was an important case. It was the first time, post-*McFarlane*, that the Court of Appeal had considered the question of what compensation could be obtained for the unplanned birth of a disabled child.

The facts can be simply stated: a disabled child had been born due to an admittedly negligently performed sterilisation. The birth of a fifth child had been 'catastrophic' for the family and the marriage (Brooke LJ). At first instance, Longmore J had allowed only the additional costs flowing from the disability. Both sides appealed; both appeals were dismissed.

Somewhat surprisingly the court did not think it relevant to consider the earlier cases at first instance, Brooke LJ stating that the policy issues were different where the allegation was that there should have been a termination (rather than that there should never have been a conception). The logic of this is difficult to follow, but at least it had the effect of relieving the court from entering into an analysis of the complex and inconsistent arguments deployed in those judgments.

First, how disabled does the child have to be to make a claim? Hale LJ adopted the test of disability found in s 17(11) of the Children Act 1989: a child is disabled if he is blind, deaf or dumb or suffers from mental disorder of any kind or is substantially and permanently handicapped by illness, injury or congenital deformity or such other disability as may be prescribed. Brooke LJ said that 'significant disability' (the phrase used in the *McFarlane* case) would cover disabilities of the mind, including severe behavioural disabilities, but not minor defects or inconveniences. Each case would be judged on its own facts.

Next, the response to the main issue. The effect of the decision is to allow 'the extra costs of caring for and bringing up a disabled child' in that 'a disabled child needs extra care and expenditure' (*per* Hale LJ). The award should be limited to 'the extra expenses associated with the child's disability', 'the special upbringing costs associated with rearing a child with a serious disability' (*per* Brooke LJ).

What we are not told, however, is what heads of expense or loss can properly be brought within these formulae. Does it, for example, include compensation for parental care? Does it include all the heads of claim for professional care, aids and equipment, accommodation etc that are relevant where the child's injury is caused by medical mismanagement? Also unclear is whether this court was of the view that the claim went beyond majority.

Brooke LJ offered an impressive cerebral analysis of the numerous bases currently available for admitting or rejecting a claim for compensation based on the tort of negligence (the three-fold test, proximity, assumption of responsibility, fair-just-reasonable, corrective or distributive justice, public policy, what the man on the Clapham tube train might think, and so on). He analysed the judgments in the House of Lords, saying that the task was made more difficult by the fact that the Law Lords had spoken 'with five different voices'. He concluded that there was no valid argument against parents being recompensed for the costs of extraordinary care in raising a deformed child.

Hale LJ's judgment demands careful study. The judge brought into clear and inescapable focus the very substantial changes that pregnancy brings to the physical, psychological, and social life of a woman. Along with these physical and psychological consequences goes a severe curtailment of personal autonomy. Through this part of her judgment, it appears that Hale LJ indicates that she would have expected claims for any unplanned birth to have included a claim by way of valuation of parental care.

On *McFarlane* Hale LJ said:

> Their Lordships' reasons for denying what would on normal legal principles be recoverable [ie that losses flowing directly from negligence should be compensated] were variously and elegantly expressed ... In truth they all gave different reasons for arriving at ... the same result.

Like many of us, Hale LJ found it difficult to understand why, once it is agreed that the doctor assumes some responsibility for preventing conception, he is nevertheless liable for only some of the clearly foreseeable, indeed highly probable, resulting losses. At one point, she suggested that a mother might be driven to have an abortion as a result of the *McFarlane* decision, presumably if she knew or learnt in time enough about the law to realise that she would have no claim for financial help in respect of all the 'dis-benefits' the child would bring her.

Note also that Hale LJ said that many would challenge the assumption that the benefits of having a new child outweighed the disadvantages so as to 'cancel out' the claim. She said that many would argue that the true costs to the primary carer of bringing up a child are so enormous that they easily outstripped any benefits. And the notion of a child bringing benefit to the parents is deeply suspect, smacking of commodification [*sic*] of the child, regarding the child as an asset to the parents. She suggested that a conventional sum could be deducted from a claim to allow for the so-called 'benefit' of having a child.

SCENARIO 3: A DISABLED WOMAN'S WRONGFUL PREGNANCY WITH A HEALTHY CHILD

The *Rees* case

In *Rees* v *Darlington Memorial Hospital NHS Trust* [2003] MLC 1053, seven judges heard the appeal in the House of Lords. The decision went by a bare majority against the claimant. The unusual fact of this case is that the unplanned child was healthy; it was the mother who was disabled. She had very little vision and for that reason expressly had asked for a sterilisation, which was negligently performed.

Counsel for the claimant sought in the first place to convince the court to reverse *McFarlane*. The court was not convinced. They declared that it had been a good decision (it had been the unanimous decision of five Lords of Appeal in extra-ordinary including Hope, Millett and Steyn who also featured in this *Rees* case), and, further, that, even if they now harboured any doubts, which was not admitted, they would not go back on it for reasons of security (of the law).

As to simple compensation under *McFarlane* for a healthy child, this was a little surprising. In *McFarlane* Lord Millett had been the lone voice that proposed that all a *McFarlane* mother should recover should be a nominal sum of £5,000 for the loss of her right to control the extent of her family. He had not even been willing to allow what the others had been willing to allow, namely something for the pregnancy itself. In the *Rees* case, the judges, four of them – Bingham, Nicholls, Millett, Scott – who considered that the *Rees* scenario fell within the *McFarlane* rule, adopted, and adapted, the Millet suggestion. They allowed the pregnancy damages, *plus* the Millett award, which they increased (Millett agreed) to £15,000. This 'gloss' on *McFarlane*, as they called it, was heavily criticised by Lord Steyn. He said that such a gloss ran counter to the views of the majority in *McFarlane*, had not been considered in the court, was a radical and most important development which should only be embarked upon after rigorous examination of competing argument, was a solution of a heterodox nature which had neither English nor foreign juridical support, was contrary to principle, that it was a novel procedure for judges to undertake the creation of such a remedy and was beyond the permissible limits of judicial creativity, that his brethren had strayed into forbidden territory, that it was a backdoor evasion of the legal policy enunciated in *McFarlane*, and could only be effected by Parliament! Lord Hope also disliked such a 'gloss'!

Legal policy

All the judges were prepared to declare, insofar as they were supporting *McFarlane* and any of its derivatives, that (a) an orthodox application of familiar and conventional principles of the law of tort would have permitted the claimant in *McFarlane* to recover damages for the costs of bringing up her healthy child. Indeed Lord Bingham said that he did not find it surprising that that had been the law here before *McFarlane*. And (b) the denial to a *McFarlane* claimant of such otherwise clearly recoverable damages was not due to the court's view of public policy but to the court's view of legal policy.

Ratio of the McFarlane *rule*

As we have seen, this was not clear in the *McFarlane* speeches themselves, as the judges gave a variety of reasons. In *Rees*, although Lord Steyn remarked amusingly that he was not proposing 'to undertake the gruesome task of discussing the judgments in *McFarlane*', the *McFarlane* ratio was reasonably summarised down to two principles. The first is that a child is a God-given gift and, in respect of a healthy child at any rate, its birth should not be the subject of a claim; the second is that the benefit principle requires that the benefit a claimant receives from having a child must be set against the economic loss claimed and as that benefit is incalculable, no damages can be awarded for the economic loss. Of course, these two points can be challenged and argued over.

Does the McFarlane *rule apply to all negligent birth claims or is there an exception for the disabled child / mother? (Ie the* Parkinson *and* Rees *aspects) –* per *Lords Bingham, Nicholls, Millett, Scott*

Lord Bingham said he would apply the rule, without differentiation, to *all* claims. He said it was anomalous that the defendant's liability should relate to a disability which the defendant had not caused. He also said it was undesirable that parents, in order to recover compensation, should be encouraged to portray their children or themselves as disabled. And he used the argument that it would be difficult to quantify the additional costs attributable to the disability. Lord Nicholls took a similar view. He thought it was disproportionate for the NHS to bear all the costs of bringing up the child, and he said the birth of a child should not be treated as comparable to a parent suffering a personal injury. Lord Millett stuck by the nominal award in 'healthy' cases that he had advocated in *McFarlane,* but it is interesting, and important, to note that he explicitly kept an open mind about disabled child cases. He said that he would not find it morally offensive if additional costs could be recovered in a *Parkinson* case, but that did not have to be decided in the instant appeal. As to the disabled mother scenario, he stated, rightly surely, that it is a mistake to assume that, because the costs attributable to the disability are 'extras' whether the disabled party is the child or the parent, there is any symmetry between the two 'disabled' scenarios. He then said that just as there would be a range of varying circumstances for a non-disabled mother, so would there be for the disabled mother.

Lord Scott stressed the 'incalculable benefit' rule, and said that the mother's visual disability did not take the case out of the normal principle established by the *McFarlane* rule. All the features that justified creating an exception under the *McFarlane* rule were present, too, in the disabled mother scenario. On the *Parkinson* scenario, he, too, kept an open mind, but he did make the interesting suggestion that a disabled child claim should only succeed if the reasons for the original sterilisation or other procedure had included a fear that any child could be born disabled. In relation to a sterilisation where there had been no such fear, apart from the normal chance of that happening (one in a few hundred), he appears to be telling us that the birth of a disabled child would not be sufficiently foreseeable to justify a claim. Then he says that on the facts existing in *Parkinson*, the decision of the Court of Appeal was not justified.

So the *obiter* tally so far in relation to a *Parkinson* claim from the majority of four judges who rejected the *Rees* claim, is two against, one somewhat supportive (Millett), and one supportive provided there had been an actual fear of any child born being disabled.

The Parkinson *and the* Rees *aspects (per Lords Steyn, Hope and Hutton)*

These were the three judges, the minority, who accepted Mrs Rees' claim. Lord Steyn said he agreed with the decision in *Parkinson*. The policy on which the *McFarlane* principle was based simply did not apply to the seriously disabled child. However, in the case of the disabled mother, it was not possible to regard her as unaffected by the *McFarlane* principle. An exception would have to be made if she was to recover. He would favour such an exception.

Lord Hope agreed with the decision in *Parkinson* even though he had been a strong advocate of the 'incalculable benefit' argument in *McFarlane*. Presumably the additional costs of upbringing in the context of disability are for some reason not caught by that argument. And he saw no reason not to allow the exception to apply in the case of a disabled parent, too. He agreed that in all these cases care would need to be taken in calculating the additional costs, but to describe the task as one of acute difficulty seemed to him to be an over-statement. By allowing the seriously disabled parent to recover the extra costs of child-rearing which were due to her disability, the law would be doing its best to enable her to perform the task of child-rearing on equal terms with those who did not have any such disability.

Lord Hutton said (a) that it was fair, just and reasonable to award damages for the extra costs of bringing up a disabled child, and (b) that the difficulties hypothesized by Waller LJ in the Court of Appeal should not deter the court from accepting a *Rees* claim. There was a clear distinction between a healthy mother and a disabled mother. Pointing to hard cases on the boundary of recoverability did not invalidate the principle of recovery by a disabled mother.

So in respect of a *Parkinson* scenario (the disabled child), the tally among the judges who favoured Mrs Rees' claim, three of them (as against four who did not), was, as one would expect, all in favour. Overall it was three in favour, two against, a fourth probably in favour (Millett) and one in favour, it appears, only if there had been a real fear that any further child could suffer from a congenital handicap.

Final outcome

Ultimately Mrs Rees' claim failed with four judges against the claim and three for it.

SCENARIO 4: WRONGFUL BIRTH CLAIMS

The Courts have not distinguished between wrongful pregnancy cases where a disabled child is born, and wrongful birth claims. However there is a very great difference between a wrongful birth claim (where the *parents* bring a claim for the additional costs of a disabled child that they would have terminated but for the negligence) and a wrongful life claim (brought by the *child* arguing that but for the negligence they would not have been born).

A wrongful birth claim therefore operates in the same way as a claim in Scenario 2 above. By way of example, in *Hardman* v *Amin* MLC 0369,

[2000] Lloyd's Rep Med 498, the mother argued that she would have terminated her pregnancy because of rubella infection. Liability was admitted for the birth of a disabled child. Henriques J, in a judgment carefully considering all available authorities, felt unconstrained by *McFarlane*. He allowed general damages for the pregnancy and specifically for the shock of the mother realising that she had given birth to a disabled child. He held that the continuation of a pregnancy resulting in the birth of a disabled child was a personal injury; that the claim for upkeep was a claim for pure economic loss, but that there was sufficient proximity between the defendant GP and the patient for the birth of a disabled child to be a consequence in law of the original negligence, and that awarding compensation for that consequence would not go beyond reasonable restitution. He held that a claim for the past and future care given by the mother as a result of the disability was permissible (either on the ordinary principles of a personal injury claim including a 25% discount for non-commercial care or by way of claim for loss of amenity – as per Newman J).

In *Groom* v *Selby* [2001] MLC 0483, CA (at first instance MLC 0294), a GP admitted negligence in not diagnosing a pregnancy in time for the mother to have found a termination to be acceptable, which she otherwise would have done. The additional factor in this claim was that the child, Megan, was born apparently healthy but, because of an infection contracted from the maternal vagina perinatally, went on to develop septicaemia and brain damage. Nevertheless, the judge at trial treated her as a child born 'unhealthy' rather than healthy. The Court of Appeal dismissed the defendant's appeal, saying that their decision recently given in *Parkinson* disposed of the instant appeal. They saw no distinction between wrongful conception and wrongful birth cases; contracting the disease was a foreseeable consequence of birth, the defendant was deemed to have accepted responsibility for the foreseeable and disastrous consequences of her negligence, and an award of compensation limited to the special upbringing associated with rearing a child with a serious disability was fair, just and reasonable. The child was apparently to be viewed as 'born disabled' (within the meaning of expression in *McFarlane*) because, it was said, her exposure to the bacterium occurred during the process of birth. All the causes of her meningitis were in place when the umbilical cord was severed: all that remained was for the bacterium to penetrate a weak point in the child's skin or mucous membranes and the damage was done.

In *Enright* v *Kwun* [2003] MLC 1017, Morland J, a mother aged 37 succeeded in establishing liability for a failure by her medical attendants to offer her the option of an amniocentesis. If she had been given the option, she would have accepted the procedure, the Downs syndrome defect would have been discovered and she would have opted for a termination.

LIMITATION IN SCENARIOS 1 TO 4

The limitation period cannot begin before the woman knows she is pregnant. Even then one can reasonably argue, in cases of operator failure, that she cannot know what the relevant act or omission is (to which her pregnancy is due) until she receives some explanatory medical input (usually in the form of an expert medical report). But it is clearly safer to work from the date she knew she was pregnant.

In *Walkin* v *South Manchester Health Authority* [1995] 1 WLR 1543, CA, the mother issued within the three-year period a writ claiming damages for personal injuries and economic loss arising from a failed sterilisation followed by the birth of a child. That writ was never served. Some two years later she issued a second writ outside the three-year limitation period, but claimed only for economic loss in an attempt to take advantage of the normal six-year period of limitation. The Court of Appeal, not surprisingly, did not endorse this ploy. They said that, whether or not she was claiming damages for the unwanted pregnancy, her claim was for 'damages in respect of personal injuries' within the meaning of s 11(1) of the Limitation Act 1980. However, Roch LJ reserved the question of the proper limitation period in the case of a failed vasectomy where the woman did not know of the vasectomy and actually wanted a child. The judge said that in those circumstances a pregnancy that was not 'unwanted' by the woman would not be a personal injury to her or anyone else and the man's loss would be purely financial.

In *Godfrey* v *Gloucestershire Royal Infirmary NHS Trust* [2003] MLC 1010, a wrongful birth claim for failure to give the mother proper advice about termination was held to be a personal injury action, following *Walkin*, and therefore out of time, but Leveson J exercised s 33 discretion to permit the claim to proceed nevertheless.

SCENARIO 5: WRONGFUL LIFE CLAIMS

An action on behalf of a child, whether born normal or handicapped, alleging that his birth (not his injuries though) only came about because the doctors were negligent, is a non-starter.

The action for wrongful life, as it has been called in the US (in contra-distinction to the action for wrongful birth), is an action by the child himself, claiming that through the doctor's negligence he has been born, where if the doctor had not been negligent he would not have been born.

The metaphysical issues raised by this contention are impossible to resolve satisfactorily in a court of law, or elsewhere for that matter. The child does not complain that the doctor's negligence has caused him to be born disabled because the doctor did not cause or contribute to the disability. But, he says, if you had sterilised or aborted my mother properly (or however the claim might arise), I would not now be living. Theoretically, a healthy child could make the same contention. But if there is any claim at all to be countenanced here, obviously it is even more difficult, perhaps even ludicrous, for a healthy child to contend that he has been injured by the mere fact of being born, whereas, in the case of a severely disabled child, there is at least some superficial attraction in the contention that his quality of life is so wretched as to amount to a continuous state of suffering, and that he should be compensated for having to endure that. The logical fallacy is, of course, as already indicated, that the negligence, assuming there to have been negligence, is not responsible for the difference between a life of suffering and a reasonable life (this can often be compensated under the Congenital Disabilities (Civil Liability) Act

1976 (see below)), but between a life of suffering and a state of non-life; and how can the court possibly evaluate the state of non-being?

Transatlantic cases

The US courts have almost invariably rejected this claim. The Illinois Court of Appeal said in 1963: 'Recognition of the plaintiff's claim means the creation of a new tort, a cause of action for wrongful life. The legal implications of such a tort are vast, the social impact could be staggering ...' (*Zepeda* v *Zepeda* 41 Ill App 2d 240 (1963)). In a 1977 case (394 NYS 2d 933), a New York court, while permitting the parents of a deformed child to recover for pain and suffering over the birth, rejected the child's claim. It has been said by the Supreme Court: 'Thus, the threshold question here is not whether life with deformities, however severe, is less preferable than death, but rather whether it is less preferable than the "utter void of non-existence".'

In the Canadian case of *Cataford* v *Moreau* (above), the judge, rejecting the child's claim, said:

> La naissance d'un enfant sain ne constitue pas pour cet infant un dommage, et encore moins un dommage compensable en argent. Il est bien impossible de comparer la situation de l'enfant après sa naissance avec la situation dans laquelle il se serait trouvé s'il n'était pas né. Le seul énoncé du problème montre déjà l'illogisme qui l'habite. D'ailleurs par quelle perversion de l'esprit pourrait-on arriver à qualifier comme un dommage l'inestimable don de la vie?

> [The birth of a healthy baby does not constitute a loss for that child, let alone a loss that can be compensated for by money. One cannot compare the child's position after being born with what it would have been had he not been born. Merely to state the problem demonstrates its inherently illogical nature. Moreover, by what sort of warped outlook could one put under the head of loss or damage the priceless gift of life?]

There was, however, one occasion when a New York court refused to strike out the claim of a deceased child born with a fatal kidney disease after his parents had been told that the disease would not be transmitted to the foetus. It was said by the court to be 'tortious to the fundamental right of a child to be born as a whole, functional human being'. That decision was not upheld on appeal – the reasoning of the lower court seems to have fallen into the fallacy referred to above, where the defendant is illogically held responsible for the suffering of the child.

The *McKay* case

The first and, probably, the only action in which the claim for wrongful life has been considered in the English courts came before the Court of Appeal in February 1982. The facts in *McKay* v *Essex Area Health Authority* [1982] QB 1166, CA, were that a child was born disabled as a result of her mother having contracted German measles during the pregnancy. It was alleged, *inter alia*, that the medical staff were negligent in not giving the mother proper advice and information which, had it been forthcoming, would have led to an abortion. So the mother claimed on her own account. But there was also a claim on behalf of the child for her having 'suffered entry into a life in which her injuries are highly debilitating'. In other words she claimed for having been born, or at any rate, for having been born into a life of handicap and suffering.

On a preliminary hearing, the Master struck out the child's claim as disclosing no reasonable cause of action; Lawson J restored it on the ground that it was really a claim for injuries suffered and was highly arguable; the Court of Appeal was unanimously of the view that the Master's decision was right (although, as a matter of procedure, Griffiths LJ was not prepared to interfere with the judge's exercise of his discretion).

Stephenson LJ pointed out the lack of success such a claim had met with in the US, and that the Law Commission report on injuries to unborn children (Cmnd 5709), which was followed by the Congenital Disabilities (Civil Liability) Act 1976, counselled against admitting such a claim. He said that the claim must be viewed as an allegation that the defendants were negligent in allowing the child to be born at all. For the medical advisers to owe a duty to the child, over and above that which they owed the mother to give her the opportunity to terminate the child's existence, would constitute a further inroad on the sanctity of human life, which would be contrary to public policy. In addition, the judge noted the impossibility of evaluating the difference between the child's disabled existence and the non-negligent consequence, namely her non-existence.

Ackner LJ said that he could not accept that the common law duty of care to a person could involve the legal obligation to them, whether or not *in utero*, being to terminate their existence. Such a proposition ran wholly contrary to the concept of the sanctity of human life. On the question of damage, he said that what the doctor was blamed for was causing or permitting the child to be born at all, not for causing or contributing to her injuries. He also asked how a court could begin to evaluate non-existence. 'No comparison is possible and therefore no damage can be established which a court could recognise. This goes to the root of the whole cause of action.'

Griffiths LJ, while of the view that, procedurally, the application should fail and the matter be argued at the trial, had no doubt that the claim did not lie. 'The most compelling reason to reject this cause of action is the intolerable and insoluble problem it would create in the assessment of damages.'

All the judges expressed the view that s 4(5) of the Congenital Disabilities (Civil Liability) Act 1976, while not applying to the instant birth, because it took place prior to the Act coming into force, had the effect of abolishing this cause of action for births after that date. This, with respect, is clearly wrong, in the sense that it puts an interpretation upon the section which Parliament did not intend, and which the words cannot bear, however desirable the result may be thought to be. The Act gave a child the right to sue a tortfeasor for injuries sustained in the womb; one would therefore expect that the Act would seek to abolish any common law cause of action that might possibly exist corresponding to the new statutory cause of action, and this is exactly what it does. The action for wrongful life is not an action in respect of the child's disabilities at birth; as the court itself said in this case (as noted above) it is a claim for having been born at all. The section is simply concerned with actions for personal injury suffered before or possibly at birth. That the section does not apply to the action for wrongful life is demonstrated not only by the context of the Act and the obvious intended scope of the subsection, but also by the reflection that this action would in theory, if it existed, be open to a healthy child. The fact that the claimant may be disabled rather than healthy is not of the essence of the claim (see below for a discussion of the 1976 Act).

The New South Wales Court of Appeal has upheld the judgments dismissing three cases where a disabled child claimed damages for 'wrongful life', declaring the claims unjusticiable (*Waller* v *James, Harriton* v *Stephens, Waller* v *Hoolahan* [2004] MLC 1104). Surprisingly, one of the three judges dissented.

In 2001, the French Parliament passed a law reversing the success that such a claim had enjoyed in the highest court (the *Perruche* case).

LOSS OF FERTILITY

This is the reverse side of the coin and the value of any claim will depend significantly on whether there is consequent psychiatric damage and whether the person already has a family or not. The Judicial Studies Board Guidelines (9th Edition), Ch 5 provides the following:

(E) Reproductive System: Male		
(b)	Cases of sterility usually fall into one of two categories: surgical, chemical and disease cases (which involve no traumatic injury or scarring) and traumatic injuries (frequently caused by assaults) which are often aggravated by scarring	£90,000 £12,000
	(i) The most serious cases merit awards approaching	
	(ii) The bottom of the range is the case of the much older man and merits an award of about	
(c)	An uncomplicated case of sterility without impotence and without any aggravating features for a young man without children	£36,000 to £45,500
(d)	A similar case but involving a family man who might have intended to have more children	£15,250 to £20,000
(e)	Cases where the sterility amounts to little more than an 'insult'	In the region of £4,250

(F) Reproductive System: Female		
The level of awards in this area will typically depend on:		
	(i) whether or not the affected woman already has children and/or whether the intended family was complete;	
	(ii) scarring;	
	(iii) depression or psychological scarring;	
	(iv) whether a foetus was aborted.	
(a)	Infertility whether by reason of injury or disease, with severe depression and anxiety, pain and scarring	£73,500 to £108,000
(b)	Infertility without any medical complication and where the injured person already has children. The upper end of the bracket is appropriate in cases where there is significant psychological damage	£11,500 to £23,500
(c)	Infertility where the injured person would not have had children in any event (for example, because of age)	£4,250 to £8,000

As can be seen, the amount awarded for loss of fertility will depend on the age of the woman and whether she already had the size of family she wanted. There are numerous quantum reports available throughout the spectrum of awards. However, when assessing the claim it will be important to ensure that there is expert evidence available if the claimant has suffered psychological sequelae. The claimant's intentions as to having children or having further children will need to be explored and evidenced.

In *Briody* v *St Helens and Knowsley Health Authority* [2000] PIQR Q165, Ebsworth J awarded £66,000, to include compensation for substantial psychiatric consequences, where a 19-year-old woman lost her first child and her womb. The costs of surrogacy were not allowed, on the basis that the chances of success were slim and the arrangement would in any event be unlawful. The Court of Appeal agreed ([2001] MLC 0165).

Chapter 12

The Congenital Disabilities Act 1976

Sarah Fraser Butlin

The Act enables a child who was injured while they were a foetus to recover damages for his disabilities from the person responsible, provided that person is in breach of duty to the parent. This applies to breaches at pre-conception and post-conception.

THE PROBLEM

What if negligent treatment harms the foetus, so that the child is born handicapped? Perhaps drugs for the pregnant woman have been manufactured, marketed or prescribed without proper care. Or perhaps her antenatal care has been deficient. And what if, before conception took place, the mother's (or the father's) reproductive capacity was, unknown to her (or to him), harmed by treatment or drugs so that later she conceived a handicapped child? Or there may have been a transmission to the mother (or father) of tainted blood, years before, or tainted semen in an artificial insemination. Or a Rhesus negative mother was not given, after the birth of a Rhesus positive child, the anti-D gamma globulin injections that would immunise her, so that in her next pregnancy her blood contaminated the foetus, with the result that her second child suffered Rhesus disease.[1] Or perhaps fertility treatment was pursued to prevent a child being born with a particular known genetic condition, but an embryo was selected which had that condition.

These are just a few of the possibilities where negligence towards a parent can result in the birth of a handicapped child.

---

1   Liability was admitted in the case of *Roberts* v *Johnstone* [1989] QB 878, CA, where the defendants, although knowing that a mother had in 1975 mistakenly been given a blood transfusion of Rhesus positive blood, failed, her husband being Rhesus negative, to protect her child when she later, in 1981, became pregnant, so that the claimant was born severely handicapped from hemolytic disease (she recovered some £400,000 damages (see also *Lazenvnick* v *General Hospital of Munro City Inc,* Civ Act 78-1259, Cmnd Pa, 13 August 1980)).

In the post-conception case, the argument is that the child was injured, albeit when they were a foetus and without legal status, with the result that they were born disabled. In the pre-conception case, the argument is that but for the negligent treatment of father or mother, the child would not have been disabled.

THE COMMON LAW

Under English law, it is the case that a child has no rights and no standing as a litigant until birth (*Paton* v *British Pregnancy Advisory Service Trustees* [1979] QB 276). In *C* v *S* [1988] QB 135, the Court of Appeal ruled that an 18-week foetus was not a 'child capable of being born alive' within the meaning of the Infant Life (Preservation) Act 1929, so that an otherwise lawful termination of pregnancy at that stage under the Abortion Act 1967 was not a crime. The Appeal Committee of the House of Lords later that day rejected all the arguments of the young father who sought an injunction to stop his girlfriend from having the abortion. Therefore their Lordships, as well as agreeing with the issue decided by the Court of Appeal, must have been of the view that the father had no standing to interfere with the mother's proposed abortion and that the foetus was not a legal person for the purposes of bringing an action through his father, or indeed anyone, to restrain the act which would destroy it.

Before 1990, there was no English authority which decided whether the common law recognised the right of a child injured while a foetus to sue once they were born (although the Irish case of *Walker* v *Great Northern Rly Co of Ireland* (1890) 28 LR Ir 69 gave a negative answer). The thalidomide litigation did not provide an answer, as a settlement was reached, and in any event it appears that the defendants did not deny the right of the children to recover if, which they denied, there had been negligence (see *S* v *Distillers Co* [1970] 1 WLR 114).

In the Canadian case of *Montreal Tramways* v *Léveillé* [1933] 4 DLR 337, the court was prepared to recognise the right of a child to recover for damages negligently inflicted upon it when in the womb. At the same time they pointed out:

> The great weight of judicial opinion in the common law courts denies the right of a child when born to maintain an action for pre-natal injuries (*per* Lamont J).

Such a claim was later recognised in the South African case of *Pinchin* v *Santam Insurance Co* 1963 (2) SA 254 (Supreme Court, Witwatersrand Local Division), in the Australian case of *Watt* v *Rama* [1972] VR 353, in the Canadian case of *Duval* v *Seguin* (1972) 26 DLR (3d) 418, and in the Australian case of *X and Y* v *Pal* [1992] 3 Med LR 195.

Then in the cases of *Burton* v *Islington Health Authority* and *De Martell* v *Merton and Sutton Health Authority* [1993] QB 204, MLC 0927, the Court of Appeal held that children damaged *in utero* before the Act came into operation were nevertheless entitled to sue for damages at common law.[2] The defendants argued that at the time of the damage

---

2   The *de Martell* case later failed on causation ([1995] 6 Med LR 234).

being suffered, the claimant was still in the womb and therefore not a legal person. The Court of Appeal rejected this and held that damage to a foetus was foreseeable from the negligence. Importantly, they held that the cause of action accrued when the foetus was born injured, and, at the same time, they had the necessary legal personality to sue. The court held, approving *Montreal Tramways* v *Léveillé* (above), that at that point the child has all the rights of action which it would have had if the child had actually been in existence at the date of the accident. The Court of Appeal approved the reasoning of the two judges at first instance. Potts J had said in *B* v *Islington Health Authority* [1991] 1 QB 638, that there was a potential duty on the defendants towards the child who might later be born and that the cause of action was complete when the birth took place. Phillips J had said in *De Martell* v *Merton and Sutton Health Authority* [1991] 2 Med LR 209:

(a)   that the claimant's case accorded with the legislative policy and that the Act of 1976 recognised the possibility that the claimant had a valid claim at common law; and
(b)   that the damage was suffered by the claimant at the moment he achieved personality and inherited the damaged body for which the defendants, on the assumed facts, were responsible.

He held that the events prior to the birth in February 1967 were mere links in the chain of causation between the defendants' assumed lack of skill and care and the consequential damage to the claimant. The decision of the English Court of Appeal was followed by the Scottish appeal court in *Hamilton* v *Fife Health Board* [1993] 4 Med LR 201.

THE ACT

The Congenital Disabilities (Civil Liability) Act 1976 was based on the recommendations of the Law Commission contained in their *Report on Injuries to Unborn Children* (Cmnd 5709, August 1974). (The text of the Act is set out below in Appendix I.) The statute applies to births after 22 July 1976 (s 4(5)).

It is obvious, but crucial to remember, that the right of the child to claim compensation depends on its injuries having been caused by a tortious act ('occurrence'). There is still the usual requirement to establish fault. The statute simply resolves the disjunction between the person to whom the duty was owed, and which was breached, and the person (ie the child) who was injured. In the words of the statute, the 'child's disabilities are to be regarded as damage resulting from the wrongful act of that person and actionable accordingly at the suit of the child' (s 1(1)).

Liability may occur in two ways. First, pre-conception. Where medical treatment negligently impairs the reproductive capabilities of a woman or a man, the medical professional can be liable to any child that is born disabled as a result of that treatment, provided that neither parent knew the risk they were taking when having intercourse. Secondly, post-conception. Where negligent medical treatment affects the mother during her pregnancy, or the mother or the child during birth, and causes injury to the child, the medical professional can be liable to that injured child.

Put simply, the tortfeasor would be liable to the mother or father if they had suffered any damage. However it is the child that has suffered the damage. The Act allows the child to sue the tortfeasor for the damage caused by the tortfeasor's breach of duty, even though the tortfeasor did not owe them a duty and the child may not even have existed at the time of breach (s 1). It is irrelevant that the mother or father suffered no damage from the breach (s 1(3)).

However the child is not entitled to sue the tortfeasor if either parent knew 'at that time' (which presumably means when having intercourse) of the risk created by the tortious act that any child they conceived might be disabled (s 1(4)). Although where the father is the tortfeasor, this does not exclude liability where the mother was not aware of the risk (s 1(4)).

A child will have an action against any tortfeasor, except (usually) his mother.[3] This may be a 'pre-conception' tortfeasor where the tortious act has affected the ability of either parent to have a healthy child (s 1(2)(a)). Alternatively it may be a 'post-conception' tortfeasor where the tortious act has affected the mother during pregnancy, or her or the child in the course of its birth (s 1(2)(b)). While the child cannot sue his mother, save in relation to road traffic accidents (s 2), the child can sue his father for injuring his mother, for example by infecting her with a sexually transmitted disease (s 1(4)).

The Act was amended by the Human Fertilisation and Embryology Act 1990 to extend its scope to children born following fertility treatment. The provisions are effectively the same as for children born naturally but they ensure that tortious acts during the fertility treatment itself which results in the child's disabilities are actionable (s 1A). The tortfeasor is not liable to the child if at the time of insemination or placing of the embryos, either parent was aware of the risk of the child being born disabled (s 1(3)). Importantly s 1(4) provides that references to 'parent' in this context, refer to the parent concerned and s 4A confirms that it includes a person who would be a parent but for ss 27 to 29 of the Human Fertilisation and Embryology Act 1990. This is specifically in order to deal with the complexities of the meaning of 'parent' in fertility treatment, particularly where gamete donation has taken place.

The child must be born alive in order to bring the claim (s 4(2)(a)). (Section 4(4) provides that for the purpose of recovering damages for loss of expectation of life, the child must live for at least 48 hours; but for deaths after 1982, the provisions of the Administration of Justice Act 1982 have now in any event abolished the right to claim under that head.)

The child must also show that he was born disabled. The Act defines this as being born with any deformity, disease or abnormality, including a predisposition (whether or not it is susceptible of immediate prognosis) to physical or mental defect in the future (ss 1(1) and 4(1)).

Liability to the child may be reduced or extinguished where, if the claim was brought by the parent, the defendant could take advantage of a term in a contract he made with the parent (s 4(6)). However this should now be read with s 2 of the Unfair Contract Terms Act 1977 which precludes

---

3   A child would have no civil claim against its mother for having injured it in the womb, for example through drug-taking. However when a mother is driving, she is under the same duty to take care of her unborn child as the law imposes on her with respect to the safety of other people (s 2).

a person, whether by contract or notice, from excluding or restricting his liability for death or personal injury resulting from negligence.

Liability may also be reduced to the extent the court thinks just and equitable where it is shown that the parent shared the responsibility for the child being born disabled (this must refer to contributory negligence or some fault on the part of the parent) (s 6(7)).

CAUSATION

As in all medical negligence claims, the 'occurrence' (tortious act) must be shown to have caused the disabilities. Causation is particularly difficult in the context of pre-natal injury and strong clear expert evidence will be required. This is likely to be the key battleground in any claim.

THE DAMAGE

The child sues in respect of the disabilities caused by the original tortious act, the 'occurrence'. This has nothing to do with the non justiciable action for wrongful life (see Chapter 11). In other words, the Act does *not* allow a child to argue that they would not have been born at all, only that they would have been born without the disability.

The Act 'replaces any law in force before its passing, whereby a person could be liable to a child in respect of disabilities with which it might be born' (s 4(5)).

LIMITATION

It is clear from s 4(3) that the limitation period will be the same as if the injuries had been suffered at birth. It will not begin while the child is still a minor (see Chapter 18). An action could therefore be brought as of right by a claimant aged 20 years in respect of an incident that injured his mother many years before he was born. However evidence, particularly in relation to causation, will become much harder to gather the longer the time period.

EXTENSIONS AND RESTRICTIONS

By s 6(3) of the Consumer Protection Act 1987, that Act applies to the provisions of the Congenital Disabilities (Civil Liability) Act 1976, thus affording its protection to the unborn child (see Chapter 11).

Chapter 13

Psychiatric injury[1]

Andrew Buchan

Shock, anxiety, depression, disappointment or grief, not amounting to psychiatric disorder, is not compensatable when it stands alone, but it may be taken into account to increase the award when it accompanies other, recognised injuries. Nervous shock amounting to psychiatric disorder is as much a head of damage as physical injury. To recover, the claimant has to be within the range of persons likely to be harmed by nervous shock; but even then the law permits recovery in the case of one who suffers nervous shock as a result of a person's death only where the shock is suffered by a close relative who either witnesses the death or its immediate aftermath.

PRIMARY AND SECONDARY VICTIMS

It is important first to distinguish between primary and secondary victims. This was made abundantly clear by the House of Lords in *Page* v *Smith* [1996] AC 155. Lord Keith pointed out that the cases divided broadly into two categories, those in which the claimant was involved as a participant in the incident which gave rise to the action, and those in which the claimant was a witness to injury caused to others, or to the immediate aftermath of an accident to others. Lord Lloyd said that in the instant case the claimant was not in the secondary position of a spectator or bystander (he was alleging psychiatric, but not personal, injury as a result of a minor traffic accident), but was a participant, directly involved in the accident and well within the range of foreseeable physical injury, and so a primary victim. The judge pointed out that the factual distinction

---

1 Nervous shock claims can be worth a great deal of money, at any rate where the injury precludes employment. Mr Tredget, who could not return to work as a result of nervous injury sustained when he was present at the stillbirth of his child, received in the region of £300,000 by way of settlement (his case on liability is considered in detail below). Mr Peter Vernon, a successful businessman who could no longer work after seeing his daughters drown in a car accident, was awarded £1m by Sedley J for loss of earnings (plus £37,500 for general damages and £152,000 for future care): (1995) 28 BMLR 1 (liability had been admitted) – see below.

between primary and secondary victims of an accident was obvious and of long-standing. He said that none of the control mechanisms, by way of tests of proximity and ties of affection (as to which, see below), were required in the case of a primary victim. Although foreseeability of psychiatric injury remained a crucial ingredient when the claimant was the secondary victim, for the very reason that the secondary victim was almost always outside the area of physical impact and therefore outside the range of foreseeable physical injury, foreseeability of physical injury was sufficient to found a claim based solely upon psychiatric injury.

This chapter is concerned principally with the claim by a secondary victim.[2]

WHAT IS PSYCHIATRIC INJURY CAUSED BY SHOCK?

Nervous shock is more than the normal emotions of distress, disappointment, unhappiness, grief, anxiety or depression: these do not constitute a head of damages in themselves but can serve to increase an award for a recognised loss, whether physical or financial (eg the 'spoilt holiday' cases where disappointment over a spoilt holiday can increase the award beyond the mere financial cost of the holiday). Nervous shock means an actual mental disorder, a 'positive psychiatric illness' (*per* Lord Bridge in *McLoughlin* v *O'Brian* [1983] 1 AC 410, HL).

In *Nicholls* v *Rushton* (1992) Times, 19 June, the Court of Appeal restated in the clearest terms the rule that nervous reaction falling short of actual psychological illness cannot be the subject of compensation unless it is parasitic to physical injury. And in *Hicks* v *Chief Constable of South Yorkshire Police* [1992] PIQR P433, the House of Lords said that horror and fear for one's own safety (as the Hillsborough stadium collapsed), not amounting to recognisable psychiatric damage, do not sound in damages.

In *Reilly* v *Merseyside Health Authority* [1995] 6 Med LR 246, an unsuccessful claim for damages for extreme claustrophobia suffered by an elderly couple trapped in a lift for over an hour, the Court of Appeal said that that was not a nervous disorder but nothing more than 'excitement of normal human emotion'. Presumably the medical report failed to identify an actual psychiatric disorder consequent upon the frightening experience.

In *Page* v *Smith* [1996] AC 155, HL, Lord Keith said that the decided cases indicated that 'nervous shock' meant a reaction to an immediate and horrifying impact, resulting in some recognisable psychiatric illness. There had to be some serious mental disturbance outside the range of normal human experience, not merely the ordinary emotions of anxiety, grief or fear. And Lord Jauncey said that the ordinary emotions of anxiety, fear, grief or transient shock were not conditions for which the law gave compensation.

---

2   For further enlightenment on the distinction between primary and secondary victims, see *Schofield* v *Chief Constable of West Yorkshire Police* (1998) 43 BMLR 28 CA, in which post traumatic stress disorder was sustained by a woman police officer when her sergeant discharged a loaded firearm in the confines of a bedroom where they were making inquiries of the family.

Contra, in *M (a minor)* v *Newham London Borough Council* [1995] 2 AC 633, CA, the Master of the Rolls rejected the claim that the psychiatric damage said to have been suffered by a child as a result of allegedly incompetent diagnosis of sexual abuse was not damage which the law recognised as compensatable injury.[3] He pointed to Lord Ackner's words in the Hillsborough stadium case (*Alcock* v *Chief Constable of South Yorkshire Police* [1992] 1 AC 310), where the Law Lord had acknowledged that future development of the law was to be expected, and to the warning given by Lord Bridge in *McLoughlin* v *O'Brian* (above) against the temptation of seeking to freeze the law in a rigid posture.

At first instance in *RK and MK* v *Oldham NHS Trust* [2003] Lloyds Rep Med 1, Simon J said that emotional responses of even the most serious type did not found a claim in damages and the court should not infer an injury where experts in the field did not.

In *Grieves* v *F T Everard & Sons* [2007] UKHL 39, the appellant (G) had been negligently exposed to asbestos dust by the respondent employers, and had developed pleural plaques. The presence of such plaques did not usually occasion any symptoms. The plaques did not cause asbestos-related diseases, but they signalled the presence in the lungs and pleura of asbestos fibres that might independently cause life-threatening or fatal diseases. G had developed not merely anxiety but clinical depression, a recognised psychiatric illness, in consequence of being told that his pleural plaques indicated a significant exposure to asbestos and the risk of future disease. It was held that (1) The symptomless plaques were not damage that could found a cause of action. It was not merely that the plaques caused no immediate symptoms. The important point was that, save in the most exceptional case, the plaques would never cause any symptoms, did not increase the susceptibility of G to other diseases or shorten his expectation of life. They had no effect upon his health at all. Neither the risk of future disease nor anxiety about the possibility of that risk materialising amounted to damage for the purpose of creating a cause of action, *Gregg* v *Scott* [2005] UKHL 2, [2005] 2 AC 176 and *Hicks* v *Chief Constable of South Yorkshire* [1992] 2 All ER 65 were applied. Although the law allowed the risk of future disease and consequent anxiety to be taken into account in computing the loss suffered by someone who had actually suffered some compensatable physical injury, in the absence of such compensatable injury, there was no cause of action under which damages could be claimed and, therefore, there could be no computation of loss in which the risk and anxiety could be taken into account, *Brunsden* v *Humphrey* (1884–85) LR 14 QBD 141 considered. Also, the pleural plaques did not amount to damage when aggregated with the risk of future disease or anxiety. It was not possible, by adding together two or more components, none of which in itself was actionable, to arrive at something that was actionable. Further, s 32A of the Supreme Court Act 1981, which allowed a claimant to obtain provisional damages where there was a chance that a serious disease would develop in the future, did not support the aggregation theory. The provision made it clear that it applied only where the claimant had a cause of action. (2)

---

3   This aspect of the case does not seem to have been relevant to the appeal to the House of Lords ([1995] 2 AC 633, HL).

G's psychiatric illness was not a reasonably foreseeable consequence of his employers' breach of duty. It was not reasonably foreseeable that the creation of a risk of an asbestos-related disease would cause psychiatric illness to a person of reasonable fortitude, *Page* v *Smith* [1996] AC 155 was distinguished.

This case would have been decided differently if the House of Lords had found that the psychiatric illness was reasonably foreseeable. But where does that leave the eggshell personality? Having succeeded on breach of duty and causation, G should have been able to recover damages upon the principle that the tortfeasor takes his victim as he finds him.

In *Eileen Corr (administratrix of the estate of Thomas Corr, deceased)* v *IBC Vehicles Ltd* [2006] EWCA Civ 331, the claimant succeeded because she was able to prove that her late husband's suicide was reasonably foreseeable following upon his injury. See further below.

The older cases

Where the nervous shock is allied to a more apparent physical injury, there has been no problem with recovery. But where it stands alone, the courts have been reluctant to permit recovery, both, in the older cases, because knowledge of mental trauma was scanty, and also because of a feeling that public policy should draw the line at recovery for mental shock.

Thus, where a level crossing attendant negligently allowed a pregnant woman to cross the railway lines in her carriage in front of an oncoming train and she suffered nervous shock and a miscarriage, the Privy Council would not permit her to succeed. But that was in 1888 (*Victorian Railways Comrs* v *Coultas* (1888) 13 App Cas 222). A pregnant barmaid suffered nervous shock when a negligently driven van crashed into the pub. She succeeded, but only because her shock arose 'from a reasonable fear of immediate personal injury to [herself]' (*Dulieu* v *White & Sons* [1901] 2 KB 669). The scope of the claim was extended by the majority decision in *Hambrook* v *Stokes Bros* [1925] 1 KB 141, CA: a mother suffered shock through fear that her children had been injured when she saw a runaway lorry careering down a hill from the bend round which her children had just gone out of sight (her apprehension was unhappily justified). The significance of this decision was twofold: first, it severed the link between nervous shock and fear of impact to oneself; second, it suggested extension of the claim to cases where the disaster had already occurred and the fear of what might be about to occur was no longer relevant.

The only case in which the House of Lords had considered the matter before *McLoughlin* v *O'Brian* (above) was *Hay (or Bourhill)* v *Young* [1943] AC 92. The claimant heard the noise of a road accident as she alighted from a bus, went of her own volition to the scene and, seeing upon the road the blood of the dead motorcyclist (who was not known to her), suffered shock. Understandably, her claim was rejected. It could be said she as passer-by was owed no duty by the negligent driver, at least no duty as far as the infliction of injury by shock was concerned, or that the actual injury suffered was too remote, or unforeseeable.

In *Hinz* v *Berry* [1970] 2 QB 40, CA, it was agreed without dispute that a mother could recover for psychiatric illness caused by her witnessing a ghastly accident to her family on the other side of the road. Lord Denning MR said that it was settled law that 'damages can be given for nervous shock caused by the sight of an accident, at any rate to a close relative'.

But recovery had not always been limited to a 'close relative'. In *Chadwick* v *British Railways Board* [1967] 1 WLR 912, the estate of a rescuer at the Lewisham rail disaster recovered in respect of a psychiatric disorder caused by his work amid the dead and dying that night. (See also *Galt* v *British Railways Board* (1983) 133 NLJ 870, where a train driver recovered for nervous shock occasioned by his seeing in front of him two men on the track whom he then thought he went on to strike and kill.) In *Wigg* v *British Railways Board* [1986] NLJ Rep 446n, (1986) Times, 4 February, Tucker J held that it was reasonably foreseeable that a train driver who stopped the train and got down to help a passenger, who had in fact been killed due to the negligence of the guard in giving the starting signal, might suffer nervous shock thereby.[4]

Recovery for nervous shock was extended by the House of Lords in *McLoughlin* v *O'Brian* [1983] 1 AC 410, where a mother was told at home by a witness that her family had just been involved in a serious road accident. She rushed to the hospital to find one child dead, two others seriously injured, and her husband in a state of shock. She herself suffered nervous shock, organic depression and a change of personality. She lost her claim at first instance and in the Court of Appeal, on the ground that her injury was not foreseeable and she herself was owed no duty of care, but the House of Lords reversed the decision. Lord Wilberforce promulgated the 'aftermath' principle. Recovery was permitted, but only where the shock came through sight or hearing of the event or its immediate aftermath. This is an example of judicial law-making – but none the worse for that. If therefore a relative visits the hospital to find a patient dying because of negligent treatment and suffers himself some psychiatric disorder as a result of nervous shock, he could recover damages. Probably also if he sees the corpse soon after, provided the relationship is sufficiently close; but not if the shock is occasioned merely by being told of the death and its circumstances, however horrible, and however close the relationship. In *Schneider* v *Eisovitch* [1960] 2 QB 430, recovery for shock on being so informed was permitted as an additional item of damages, where a wife, injured along with her husband in a road accident, learned that he had died. (It is of interest to note that the New South Wales legislature intervened as early as 1944 to permit recovery for this sort of injury suffered by a close relative of a person 'killed, injured or put in peril', irrespective of any spatial or temporal nexus with the accident.)

So we can summarise by saying that claims for nervous shock by witnesses, or secondary victims as they are now called, have had only slow and restricted acceptance in English law. The claim was first recognised

---

4   For an example of an unsuccessful claim for shock suffered by a rescuer, see the Piper Alpha case of *McFarlane* v *EE Caledonia Ltd* [1994] PIQR P154, where the Court of Appeal held that there had been insufficient involvement or risk of involvement by the claimant in the tragedy (the fire-fighting vessel he was in was never in danger). Similarly, *Hegarty* v *EE Caledonia Ltd* (1997) Times, 13 February, CA.

where the claimant had been put in fear of imminent physical harm (this context should really be seen as one of primary victim, just as if the harm had materialised), then extended to shock caused by fear that imminent harm was about to befall others, to the witnessing of a shocking event (also to shock caused to a rescuer by actually participating in a horrific event), then, by the House of Lords decision in *McLoughlin* v *O'Brian* (above) to shock caused by coming upon the aftermath of a horrific event. Recent developments have done nothing to extend the ambit of the claim for the secondary victim.

Further developments

In the Hillsborough stadium case (*Alcock* v *Chief Constable of South Yorkshire* [1992] 1 AC 310), the House of Lords held that a claimant claiming for nervous shock over the death or injury of another must satisfy the test of proximity, in that it must have been foreseeable that this particular claimant might suffer nervous shock over the death of that particular relative or friend. The law would not define a class of qualifying relationships. The required proximity (to be based upon close ties of love and affection) was to be proved by evidence; it could in the case of obviously close familial ties be presumed (a presumption that could, however, be rebutted by appropriate evidence). The court was prepared to make the presumption in the case of claimants who had lost a son or a fiancé but not, in the absence of evidence of closeness, in the case of a brother, brother-in-law or grandson. Second, the court reaffirmed Lord Wilberforce's limited extension of the right of recovery to the 'aftermath' principle, ie the witnessing of the traumatic event or its immediate aftermath. It was not possible to bring within that principle the viewing of the distressing scenes on television, emphasis being laid on the fact that the television code of ethics meant that the suffering of recognisable individuals was not broadcast. Although it was not impossible that a television viewer might be sufficiently proximate in appropriate circumstances (probably where the telecast was horrifyingly graphic), the viewing of the television scenes in this case did not create the necessary degree of proximity and could not be 'equiparated' with the position of a claimant at the ground. Thus, there are two tests of proximity for the claimant to satisfy, the first relating to the victim, the second to the event – the second can be further divided into the proximity of the claimant to the accident and the means by which the shock has been caused. Lord Ackner said that 'shock' involved the sudden appreciation by sight or sound of a horrifying event which violently agitated the mind; as the law presently stood, it did not include psychiatric illness caused by the accumulation over a period of time of more gradual assaults on the nervous system. So illness caused by the stress of caring for an injured relative over a period of time would not be compensatable.

The court's decision was that none of the claimants could succeed – those at the ground failed the test of proximity of relationship, those elsewhere failed the test of proximity in time and space (those who came to the hospital or mortuary later were said not to be within the 'immediate' aftermath as they did not get there for some eight hours –

the mother in *McLoughlin* v *O'Brian* (above) had arrived at the hospital within one hour).[5]

A harsh example of the restrictions that the Court of Appeal has placed on the ambit of the nervous shock claim can be seen in *Taylorson* v *Shieldness Produce Ltd* [1994] PIQR P329, CA. Parents went immediately one morning to the hospital to which their 14-year-old son, their only child, had been admitted after being crushed under a reversing vehicle. They did not see him at the hospital, but they followed the ambulance that transferred him to another hospital, the father glimpsing him in the ambulance, the mother seeing him briefly as he was being rushed into the intensive care unit on a trolley. They did not see him then for a few hours while he was being treated. The father saw him that evening, when he had black eyes, blood on his face and a tube attached to the top of his head to relieve pressure on the brain. The mother saw him the next day in a similar state. The boy remained unconscious for two days. Then the life support machine was switched off. The parents were with him throughout that time.

The court said that the shocking events were not sufficiently proximate and that the involvement of the parents did not come within the aftermath principle. It seems that the first conclusion was based on the lack of close contact in the first few hours and the second on the refusal of the court to adopt the reasoning in the Australian case of *Jaensch* v *Coffey* (1984) 155 CLR 549 and extend the aftermath period to include the two days waiting at the bedside of the dying child.

It is also to be noted that the court found that causation was not proved, in that it took the view that the real cause of the psychiatric injury was the loss of their child and that the injury would have been sustained even if there had been no question of any participation in any aftermath.[6]

In *Page* v *Smith* [1996] AC 155, where a claimant who had been involved in a minor traffic accident and had suffered no physical injury alleged that he had suffered a psychiatric injury, in that his pre-existing pathology of chronic fatigue syndrome had become chronic and permanent, the House of Lords held by a bare majority that, as the claimant was the primary victim and not a mere witness or bystander, the rules of proximity did not apply, and therefore, as some injury, albeit physical if not actually psychiatric, was foreseeable from the accident, he was entitled to recover damages.[7]

---

5 *Contra, McCarthy* v *Chief Constable of South Yorkshire* (11 December 1996, unreported), QBD Toulson J, where a claimant had had a good view from his stand of the horrific events of the day in which his half-brother died.

6 In the Canadian case of *Beecham* v *Hughes* [1988] 6 WWR 33, the husband of a woman brain-damaged in a car crash was unable to recover damages for his own nervous shock as the evidence indicated that it had been caused not by his presence at the accident and its immediate aftermath but by his ongoing distress at the condition of his wife.

7 Followed by Garland J in *Zammit* v *Stena Offshore Ltd* [1997] CLY 1857, where a diver suffered psychiatric but not physical injury in a diving accident (which left him suspended and helpless at the end of an umbilical for half an hour) caused by his employer's negligence. However, the Court of Appeal held, surprisingly, in *Gifford* v *Halifax Building Society* [1995] JPIL 323 that psychiatric injury was not reasonably foreseeable upon the giving of negligent financial advice that led to the loss of the claimant's home. Why not? (The fact that judgment was given a few days before the decision of the House of Lords in *Page* v *Smith* was published is irrelevant.) We may also briefly note *Abada* v *Gray* (1997) 40 BMLR 116, CA, where the rejection by the trial judge of a claim that a traffic accident had led to schizophrenia and epilepsy was upheld.

In *Vernon* v *Bosley* [1997] 1 All ER 577, CA where the claimant had witnessed the drowning of his two children (than which a more dreadful experience could hardly be imagined),[8] the Court of Appeal held that the legal test determining recoverability was whether the claimant had suffered mental injury caused by the negligence of the defendant and not whether he had suffered post-traumatic stress disorder rather than pathological grief disorder. Accordingly, the secondary victim could recover damages for mental illness caused or at least contributed to by the actionable negligence of the defendant, notwithstanding that the illness could also be regarded as a pathological consequence of the bereavement which the claimant had inevitably suffered. It followed that damages payable to a claimant who was a secondary victim of a breach of a duty of care owed by the defendants and who suffered mental illness, which was properly regarded as a consequence both of his experience as a bystander and of an intense and abnormal grief reaction to the bereavement which he suffered, should not be discounted for his grief and the consequences of bereavement, even though his illness was partly so caused. This decision appears to be inconsistent with the judgment of the Court of Appeal in *Calascione* v *Dixon* (1993) 19 BMLR 97, where they held that the trial judge had been right to distinguish between post-traumatic stress disorder suffered by a mother on seeing the corpse of her son mangled after a road traffic accident and pathological grief reaction which was not due to the accident or its aftermath.

In *Frost* v *Chief Constable of South Yorkshire Police* [1998] QB 254, CA, revsd [1999] 2 AC 455, HL, the House of Lords, reversing the decision of the Court of Appeal, held that police officers, who had suffered psychiatric injury when performing rescue duties in the aftermath of the Hillsborough football stadium disaster, could not recover damages. They were secondary victims and had to satisfy the tests for secondary victims. The fact that they were employed by the defendant did not affect that requirement. Noting that many relatives who were secondary victims had failed in earlier claims, the court said it would be unfair if police officers could recover in similar circumstances. Lord Steyn said that the law in this field was 'a patchwork quilt of distinctions which are hard to justify'; and Lord Hoffmann said that the search for principle had been called off in the *Alcock* case, that it was too late to go back on the control mechanisms stated in *Alcock*, and until there was legislative change the courts must live with them and judicial developments must take them into account.

In *Young* v *Charles Church (Southern) Ltd* (1997) 33 BMLR 146, [1997] JPIL 291, the Court of Appeal permitted recovery for psychiatric illness sustained through witnessing the electrocution of a workmate as a result of the defendants' negligence (the Scottish Court of Session had reached a contrary conclusion in *Robertson* v *Forth Road Bridge Joint Board* [1995] IRLR 251, but that was before the House of Lords decision in *Page* v *Smith* [1996] AC 155, HL).

---

8   The judgment of Sedley J at first instance can be found at (1995) 28 BMLR 1. The initial huge award, including £1m for loss of earnings, £37,500 for general damages and £152,000 for future care, was reduced on a separate appeal upon the admission of fresh evidence indicating a better prognosis (*Vernon* v *Bosley (No 2)* [1997] 1 All ER 614, CA).

In *Hunter* v *British Coal Corpn* [1999] QB 140, CA, the claimant had suffered psychiatric injury by way of 'surviving guilt' after a pit explosion which killed his mate. As he had left the actual scene of the accident some minutes before to look for equipment (though he was still fairly close, heard the explosion and saw the cloud of dust rising), and as he was not in any danger himself, the court said his claim could not succeed. He could not be treated as a secondary victim because he had not witnessed the accident; he had (merely) suffered an abnormal grief reaction on hearing of the death, triggered by an irrational feeling of responsibility; his 'survivor's guilt' was too remote an injury. This case is an excellent illustration of how artificial and generally unsatisfactory is the current state of the law in relation to nervous shock claims.

In *Monk* v *PC Harrington Ltd* [2008] EWHC 1879, a claimant who heard of an accident at work via portable radio immediately as it occurred and then went to the site of the accident in order to lend assistance was neither a rescuer who reasonably feared for his own safety nor was he an unwilling participant in the accident. As such the claimant did not satisfy the requirements of being a primary victim, and he was also unable to recover as a secondary victim as he did not meet the requirements laid out in *Alcock*.

In the highly distressing case of *Galli-Atkinson* v *Seghal* [2003] Lloyds Rep Med 285, the Court of Appeal held that the immediate aftermath of a fatal road accident in which the claimant's daughter was killed extended from the moment of the accident until the moment the claimant left the mortuary. The visit to the mortuary, not long after the claimant had arrived at the police cordon at the site of the accident, was not merely to identify the body, which still bore the horrifying marks of the fatal injury, but also to complete the story as far as the claimant was concerned. An 'event' for the purposes of establishing a claim by a secondary victim might be made up from a number of components, as had been said in *North Glamorgan NHS Trust* v *Walters* (see below).

Comparatively, the Supreme Court of Canada has departed from House of Lords precedent in the context of nervous shock in the case of *Mustapha* v *Culligan of Canada Ltd* (2008) 293 DLR (4th) 29 SCC. In facts similar to *Donoghue* v *Stevenson*, Mr and Mrs Mustapha unsuccessfully sued for damages alleged to have arisen from nervous shock in both contract and tort upon finding a fly in a bottle of water which had been delivered by the defendant. The Supreme Court rejected Mr Mustapha's claim and set out four requirements for succeeding in a claim for negligence:

1   a duty of care;
2   breach of the standard of care;
3   damage; and
4   causation of that damage in fact and in law by that breach.

There was, therefore, no distinction made between primary and secondary victims for nervous shock. During the course of her judgment, McLachlin CJC distinguished between 'psychological injury' which constitutes personal injury and 'psychological upset'. She also distinguished compensable injury as an injury that is serious and prolonged and goes above that which is no more than an ordinary annoyance. In respect of the fourth criteria, a traditional tort approach of whether or not the injury was reasonably foreseeable was adopted so as to establish a causal link in law. Moreover, it was considered that there needed to be a real risk that the injury could occur and an objective assessment of whether a person of ordinary fortitude would have suffered the same injury was adopted over the subjective test. Once the claimant met this test, then damages would be assessed following the reasoning in *White* on an egg-shell skull basis.

In a medical context, judgment was given by the House of Lords based on the allegedly negligent decisions made by medical professionals during clinical investigation, diagnosis and reporting of a child's condition which resulted in psychiatric injury to the child's parents. In *D v East Berkshire Community Health NHS Trust* [2005] 2 All ER 443, doctors believed children to have been the subject of non-accidental injury by a parent or suspected that false reporting had been given which gave rise to a risk of future non-accidental injury. It later transpired that such accusations had been unfounded and that the parents themselves had suffered psychiatric injury as a direct consequence of those accusations. The House of Lords held, by a 4:1 majority, that where the relationship between the doctor and the parents was confined to the fact that they were the parents of the doctors' patient, then the appropriate level of protection for the parents was that clinical and other investigations had to be conducted in good faith. Carelessness was not enough to create a duty of care.

Nervous shock caused by damage to property – an unusual case

In *Attia* v *British Gas plc* [1988] QB 304, a woman had allegedly suffered positive psychiatric illness (as opposed to 'normal' grief and distress) through seeing her home burnt down before her eyes as a result of the defendants' negligence. The Court of Appeal refused to strike out the claim for nervous shock (the claim for damage to property had been settled), saying that there was in principle no reason to preclude recovery if the injury and foreseeability were proved in the usual way. In other words, nervous shock arising out of damage to property rather than damage to the person is not for that reason alone to be irrecoverable. Scott J has doubted whether shock caused by the disclosure of confidential medical information could properly be reflected in an award of damages (*W v Egdell* [1990] Ch 359). See also the sharp rejection by the Court of Appeal in *Powell* v *Boldaz* [1998] Lloyd's Rep Med 116 of the claim for nervous shock sustained as a result of getting certain upsetting written information in A4 rather than A5 form.

Also unusual, not so much for the law as for the facts, is *Donachie* v *Chief Constable of Greater London Police* [2004] EWCA Civ 405. The claimant police officer was, without proper thought for his safety, given a task by his superior officer of placing a tracking device under a suspect's car while the suspect was in the pub. Due to the defective nature of the device, he had to try nine times before succeeding. All the while his fear for his own safety grew in case the suspect and friends should emerge from their drinking. As a result he developed a clinical psychiatric state, leading to an acute rise in blood pressure, which caused a stroke. The Court of Appeal, summarising the principles to be derived from *Page* v *Smith* [1996] 1 AC 155, HL (these are set out in Chapter 8), said that there was a reasonable foreseeability that the employer's breach of duty would cause physical injury to the officer, though not of the kind he actually suffered and via the unforeseeable psychiatric injury actually caused by the employer's negligence. So he was a primary victim in respect of whom there was a reasonable foreseeability of physical injury and, in consequence, in respect of whom it was not necessary to prove involvement in an 'event' in the form of an assault or otherwise. If A put B in a position, said the court, whereby A can reasonably foresee that B would fear physical injury, and B, as a result, suffers psychiatric injury and/or physical injury, B was then a primary victim.

Still within the realm of the unusual, we find *Froggatt* v *Chesterfield and North Derbyshire Royal Hospital NHS Trust* [2002] MLC 0887, Forbes J. A young wife had undergone a mastectomy followed by radiotherapy and chemotherapy, only to be told the following month that the diagnosis of cancer had been an error. She then underwent extensive reconstruction surgery, which left her cosmetically and physically impaired and with substantial psychiatric symptoms, for which she obtained appropriate damages. What was unusual is that her husband succeeded in obtaining damages as a secondary victim having suffered psychiatric injury by way of sudden shock and horror on seeing his wife undressed for the first time, and her son obtained a small amount of damages as a secondary victim for psychiatric damage suffered when he overheard a telephone conversation in which his mother discussed the fact that she had cancer and was likely to die. This is surely the far boundary of the nervous shock claim. Could the defendants have foreseen the telephone conversation or injury arising therefrom? Or the arising of the husband's psychiatric illness? The claims of husband and son were dealt with in very short measure at the end of an extensive judgment on the patient's claim. It is doubtful that these claims would stand up to a lengthier analysis.

THE MEDICAL ACCIDENT

What if a close relative suffers psychiatric damage through being present at and around the death and/or terminal illness in hospital (or elsewhere) of a loved one, the injury being due to medical negligence? There is no reason in principle why the tests of proximity (or the 'aftermath' test) should not be satisfied in this context. Until recently, there was no English authority on the point, but several settlements of such claims had been achieved. In the Australian case of *Jaensch* v *Coffey* (1984) 155 CLR 549 (not a medical accident case), Deane J permitted recovery for nervous shock where a wife came to her injured husband's bedside in hospital, and through her constant attendance upon him and her fear that he was going to die suffered severe anxiety and depression.[9] The judge said:

> The aftermath of the accident extended to the hospital to which the injured person was taken and persisted for so long as he remained in the state produced by the accident up to and including immediate post-accident treatment ... Her

---

9   Note, incidentally, that the claimant's predisposition to such injury was no defence; similarly in *Brice* v *Brown* [1984] 1 All ER 997, Stuart-Smith LJ held that, once nervous shock was a foreseeable consequence of a breach of duty, it made no difference that the precise nature and extent of the injury were not foreseeable (the claimant had suffered particularly severely due to a basic mental instability) – see Chapter 8 under 'You must take the claimant as you find him'.

psychiatric injuries were the result of the impact upon her of the facts of the accident itself and its aftermath while she was present at the aftermath of the accident at the hospital.

In principle, there is no difference between claims for shock due to horrific scenes at the hospital after a road accident and the same after a medical accident, so the case of *Taylorson* (above) is also in point. However, the difficulty with the medical accident context is that horrific scenes are less likely, and so the question that immediately springs to mind is how the element of shock can be satisfied in such a case (assuming that there is no such shocking element as the relative finding the loved one dying or dead at home). In the Hillsborough case, Lord Ackner said:

> 'Shock', in the context of this cause of action, involves the sudden appreciation by sight or sound of a horrifying event, which violently agitates the mind. It has yet to include psychiatric illness caused by the accumulation over a period of time or more gradual assaults on the nervous system.

In *Jaensch* v *Coffey* (above), Brennan J said:

> I understand 'shock' in this context to mean the sudden sensory perception – that is, by seeing, hearing or touching – of a person, thing or event, which is so distressing that the perception of the phenomenon affronts or insults the claimant's mind and causes a recognizable psychiatric illness.

There are now, besides the judgment in *Taylorson* (set out above), recent decisions in medical negligence actions, including one from the Court of Appeal, which make it more difficult for a claim of this sort to succeed.

In *Taylor* v *Somerset Health Authority* [1993] 4 Med LR 34, MLC 0025, Auld J rejected a claim by a widow who had come to the hospital after her husband had suffered a fatal heart attack at work (due to earlier medical mismanagement). She had not believed that he had died, not even when she was so informed by a doctor. She then saw him lying peacefully behind curtains in the basement of the hospital. The judge said that this did not fulfil the test of temporal proximity (in other words, she was too late on the scene). He also said that there had to be an external traumatic event; however, in the *Sion* case (see below) Peter Gibson LJ made it clear that an external horrific event was not a prerequisite as the crucial element in this sort of claim was a sudden awareness, violently agitating the mind, of what was occurring or what had occurred. It could, nevertheless, be argued that in the *Taylor* case what was absent was the necessary element of horror or sudden shock. One has to remember that one cannot claim merely for psychiatric injury caused by the death of a loved one. The claim is a claim for *shock*.

In *Sion* v *Hampstead Health Authority* [1994] 5 Med LR 170, MLC 0027, the Court of Appeal struck out as doomed to fail a claim by a father who suffered psychiatric injury through attending for some two weeks by the bedside of his 23-year-old son who had been injured in a traffic accident and fatally deteriorated in hospital due, allegedly, to negligent medical treatment. The court took the view on the pleadings, having regard principally to the psychiatric report that was served with the particulars of claim, that there was no evidence of 'shock', no sudden appreciation by sight or sound of a horrifying event, but rather a continuous process that ran from the father's first arrival at the hospital to a death two weeks later that was by then not unexpected – and on then to his realisation after the inquest of the possibility of medical negligence.

This seems odd. In the first place, does it make any sort of sense that there would probably have been a good claim if the father had still been hoping for recovery when death occurred and had therefore been 'shocked' when there was a sudden fatal deterioration? Secondly, there do in fact appear to have been discrete 'shocking' events during the two-week period, such as a sudden (though not immediately fatal) deterioration, sudden respiratory difficulties, cardiac arrest and transfer to the intensive care unit.

A more imaginative judgment (in the best sense) was given in the Central London County Court by Judge White on 4 February 1994 in the case of *Tredget and Tredget* v *Bexley Health Authority* [1994] 5 Med LR 178, MLC 0024. Although this was before the Court of Appeal judgment, it was after Brooke J had struck out Mr Sion's claim at first instance, and nothing that was said in the Court of Appeal invalidates Judge White's approach.

In the first place, this case concerned claims for nervous shock sustained by both parents as a result of a traumatic and frightening delivery of their fatally injured child, following negligent failure to go for an earlier Caesarean section, and as a result of attending upon their son during his short life of some two days. So the case was rather different from the usual 'attending by the bedside' case.

Judge White accepted, as did the Court of Appeal in the *Sion* case, the following requisites for a successful claim:

> The plaintiff must show he has suffered an actual psychiatric illness caused by shock (ie the sudden and direct appreciation by sight or sound of a horrifying event or events, rather than from stress, strain, grief or sorrow or from gradual or retrospective realisation of events); that there was propinquity in time or space for the causative event or its immediate aftermath; that such injury was reasonably foreseeable; and that the relationship between plaintiff and defendant was sufficiently proximate.

It is surprising that the health authority sought to argue that there had been no element of shock in the events that the parents had experienced, and disappointing that they should have chosen to contest the mother's claim on that basis. Fortunately, the judge sensibly declined to see the two-day period as lacking the element of shock. He saw the traumatic birth (in which the husband had been involved, and which had been complicated by shoulder dystocia – an obstetric emergency) and the delivery of a clearly traumatised baby and the ensuing harrowing hours as a single event ('frightening and harrowing') which satisfied the requisite of a sudden shock to the nervous system. He said:

> Of course, it was not in the nature of an immediate catastrophe which lasts only a few seconds – panic in a stadium or a motor accident – but one just as traumatic, for those immediately involved as participants, as each of the parents was ...

> In my judgment, if this is a new step in the development of the law, it is not only ... within the principles that have been set out, but has its own in-built limits, being founded on the special relationship, with all that follows, of the parent with the child at the unique human moment of birth.[10]

---

10 We may note here that in *Allin* v *City and Hackney Health Authority* [1996] 7 Med LR 167, a mother recovered damages for psychiatric injury sustained on being informed wrongly (and negligently) that her new-born child had died.

In *Palmer* v *Tees Health Authority* [1998] Lloyd's Rep Med 447, the mother of a child murdered by a released psychiatric patient could not recover damages for nervous shock when she saw the child's body three days later, a decision upheld by the Court of Appeal ([1999] Lloyd's Rep Med 351, [2000] PIQR P1).[11] In *Farrell* v *Merton Sutton and Wandsworth Health Authority* [2000] MLC 0236, ML 8/00, Steel J held that where a mother sustained psychiatric damage through being aware during a Cesarian section under inadequate anaesthetic and also through learning of her child's brain damage when she saw him for the first time the next day, throughout all those events she remained a primary victim.[12]

In *North Glamorgan NHS Trust* v *Walters* [2002] MLC 0876, [2003] PIQR P316, the mother attended the last two days of her infant son's life after he had suffered a fatal injury due to the defendant's negligence. She was first told that brain damage was unlikely, later that he had in fact suffered severe brain injury and needed life support. The child later died in his mother's arms when the support was withdrawn. *Sunt lacrimae rerum*. The Court of Appeal, dismissing the defendant's appeal, and declaring that the only issue in the case was whether the mother's illness 'arose from the sudden appreciation by sight or sound of a horrifying event or its immediate aftermath', said that the law permitted a realistic view to be taken of what constituted an 'event'. 'Event' was for secondary victims a convenient description for the series of events which made up the entire event beginning with the negligent infliction of damage to the conclusion of the immediate aftermath, whenever that might be. Its identification was a matter of judgment from case to case depending on the facts and circumstances of each case. On the facts of this case, the court said that there was an inexorable progression from the moment when the fit causing the brain damage occurred which shortly thereafter made the child's death inevitable and the dreadful climax when he died in his mother's arms. It was a seamless tale lasting for a period of 36 hours which, for the mother, was undoubtedly one drawn-out experience. The entire event was undoubtedly a 'horrifying' event. The assault on the mother's nervous system began when she was woken by her child's convulsion and she reeled under successive blows as each was delivered.

---

11 In *Tranmore* v *T E Scudder Ltd* [1998] JPIL 336, visiting the mortuary 24 hours after his son had been killed by falling rubble took the father outside the 'aftermath' principle, even though he had visited the accident site at the time (he had not seen his son there, though).

12 In *Toth* v *Ledger* [2000] MLC 0521, CA, a father claimed damages from an allegedly negligent GP for nervous shock sustained through attending his five-year-old son's terminal hours in hospital following untreated hypoglycemia (due to glycogen storage disease). Despite having earlier settled his claim for bereavement, the father was allowed to pursue a second action for damages for nervous shock, the court taking the view that the well-known principle of *Henderson* v *Henderson* did not operate to make the second action an abuse of court. The question of abuse had to be decided on a broad merits-based assessment. The claim for nervous shock had been delayed by legal aid problems. Had there been none, it would have been included in the first action. The defendants had not been led to believe at the time of settlement that it would not be pursued. It was not an abuse of court. (Readers interested in this litigation could go to the GMC issue reported as *R* v *General Medical Council, ex p Toth* MLC 0270, [2000] Lloyd's Rep Med 368, wherein Mr Toth successfully obtained an order from Lightman J requiring the GMC, who were not in fact opposing the claimant on any substantive issue, to continue to investigate his complaint against the GP.)

In other words, the blows were each of them a sudden assault; the picture was not of a gradual assault (some distinction!). Clarke LJ said that although the court's decision did not actually involve taking the step forward of allowing a claim for a secondary victim for psychiatric illness caused by the accumulation over a period of time of more gradual assaults on the nervous system (as opposed to a sudden assault on same), he for his part would have been willing to take that step forward on the facts of the instant case if that had been necessary.

A lamentable step backward, however, was taken by a deputy High Court judge in *Ward* v *Leeds Teaching Hospital NHS Trust* MLC 1265, [2004] Lloyds Rep Med 530, CA where the defendants succeeded in their wretched argument that the psychiatric injury suffered by a mother at the death of her daughter due to a negligently handled anaesthetic was not due to the events in hospital but due to the bereavement *simpliciter*. The judge took the view that there was no shock or horrifying event for the mother as she sat by her daughter's bedside (on and off) for two days awaiting her death. The death of a loved one in hospital, he said, did not meet that description unless also accompanied by circumstances that were wholly exceptional in some way so as to shock and horrify. No wonder the law in this field, and the odd judge, is so often considered an ass.

At this point we may glance at *Farrell* v *Avon Health Authority* [2001] Lloyds Rep Med 458 where a father who, arriving at hospital, was told his newborn child had died but then that that had been a mistake and he lived, obtained damages as a primary victim for foreseeable psychiatric damage. One might have thought he would have been overjoyed to learn of the hospital's mistake, but apparently not.

WHAT NEEDS TO BE PROVED?

What, then, does the claimant need to establish to succeed in this sort of claim (assuming he cannot show himself to have been a primary victim)?

- In the first place, the psychiatric report must certify clearly that the claimant has suffered an actual psychiatric injury, ie going beyond the normal ambit of a bereavement reaction, grief, fear or distress.
- Next, one has to show that the circumstances were such that nervous shock was foreseeable.
- Next, the claimant needs to satisfy the test of familial proximity, ie to show that nervous shock to this relative or close friend was foreseeable. Note the arbitrary treatment of this requirement by the House of Lords in the Hillsborough case.
- Next, the claimant needs to satisfy the test of temporal and spatial proximity, ie show that the claimant was sufficiently close in time and space to the events that are alleged to have caused the injury.
- Next the report must identify a discrete shocking event (or events) that constituted a sudden assault upon the nervous system of the claimant and was responsible wholly or at any rate materially for the injury. It may be unwise to rely on any protracted period of time as being the horrifying event unless the sights and sounds during that period were more or less continuously horrifying, although recent

cases (see above) indicate that the courts are applying a less severe test in this context.

- The psychiatric report should make it clear that the injury would probably not have been sustained simply through the loss of the loved one, ie in the absence of the identified shocking event(s).

How far these stringent conditions can be satisfied in a claim arising out of medical mismanagement remains unclear. It must depend on the precise events. If the claimant was present when a shocking emergency or a shocking deterioration in the patient occurred, or comes to the hospital and finds the patient in a state that reasonably shocks, or perhaps is present at an unexpected, and therefore in itself shocking, death, the claim might well be successful. But if there is a slow process of decline leading to a death that was not really unexpected at the time, or at any rate was on the cards, and the death did not involve any particularly shocking factors beyond the actual dying, the claim may fail. It would have failed a little while ago, but now, as I have said, a more generous judicial interpretation of the factors necessary for such a claim to succeed may prevail. In the PIBA lecture (see above), Lord Phillips said that 'the aftermath principle is one of considerable elasticity'.[13]

A knee-jerk reaction?

Generally speaking, the oft heard criticism that the patient body has now become a group of acquisitive compensation seekers, ready, with ever helpful lawyers, to spring into litigious action (in both senses) at the drop of a scalpel is misconceived. However, in the context of proposed nervous shock claims there may be some truth in it. One can easily enough get the impression that as soon as any health body makes any insensitive move or fails to treat patients with consideration, the cry for compensation is heard, a lawyer arises to represent the aggrieved, and other members of the family (for good measure), and litigation is proposed, often with apparently little regard to the legal basis for a claim. The body organs 'scandal' is an example of this. However regrettable the hospitals' behaviour may have been, it was very difficult to see how a court would hold that, in disposing of a child's (or an adult's) remains, a hospital owed a common law duty to the family not to treat the body in such a way as to cause foreseeable and proven psychiatric illness to them if and when their actions were discovered.[14] For the way Gage J dealt with the issue, see *AB v Leeds Teaching Hospital NHS Trust* [2004] MLC 1101.

---

13   It is worth noting that the Australian High Court has rejected our control mechanisms. In *Annetts v Australian Stations Pty Ltd* [2002] HCA 35, a 16-year-old died of exhaustion alone in the outback when working as a jackaroo. His parents joined the unsuccessful search for him, finding only his blood-stained hat. Three months later his body was found. The parents recovered for psychiatric damage sustained over this period. In *Gifford v Strang Patrick Stevedoring Pty Ltd* [2003] HCA 33, children who suffered psychiatric injury on being told of their father's death recovered damages. Now there is a move afoot to introduce some sort of control mechanism. Some states have already done this by legislation.

14   See *Dobson v North Tyneside Health Authority* [1997] 1 WLR 596, CA. Maybe recourse can be had to the 'human right' to family life (though in such circumstances 'life' would not appear to be the right word).

FATAL ACCIDENT AND BEREAVEMENT

On behalf of the deceased himself, that is to say the estate of the deceased, a claim lies only for funeral expenses. The claim for loss of expectation of life, which used to be set at a formal figure of about £1,250, was abolished by the Administration of Justice Act 1982. The deceased also has no claim for loss of earnings during the lost years, ie the years when he would have earned had he been alive. There may be a small claim for his suffering in the interval, if there was one, between the injury and his death. Apart from that, nothing. So one can see how truer than ever is the common law saying 'It is cheaper to kill than to maim'. Had he been maimed, the deceased could have claimed a substantial sum for pain and suffering and loss of amenity, all his lost earnings and the cost of all necessary care for the rest of his life.

The tortfeasor, or his insurance company, will not, however, escape scot-free if the deceased had dependants (by virtue of the Fatal Accidents Act 1976, as amended). For full details of the fatal accidents legislation, the reader is referred to the standard textbooks. The important points to note here are as follows.

First, by virtue of the amendment made to the Act by the Administration of Justice Act 1982, the spouse of the deceased or a parent of an unmarried minor deceased (note: a child cannot claim for loss of a parent) killed by negligence can claim from the tortfeasor (regardless of any dependency) the statutory bereavement award of £11,800 in respect of causes of action arising on or after 1 January 2008.[15] This is, of course, a minimal amount and is no sort of compensation for the loss of a loved one. But it has to be remembered that at common law, the general rule is that no person has a financial or indeed a legal interest in the life of another person, so that no duty of care is owed by A to B not to kill B's relative (or employee, for that matter) by negligence. So the statutory award represents a legislative exception to the common law rule in a context where no duty of care was owed to the claimant. The 'aftermath' principle represents, as we have seen, another limited exception to the rule.

Second, the general effect of the long-standing and important statutory exception to the common law rule effected by the fatal accidents legislation is that those who were or had an expectation of being financially supported by the deceased may claim their loss from the tortfeasor over the whole of the period during which they could have expected to be supported by him. Again, for the details of this legislation, the reader is referred to the standard textbooks.

In *Eileen Corr (administratrix of the estate of Thomas Corr, deceased)* v *IBC Vehicles Ltd* [2006] EWCA Civ 331, the appellant (C) appealed against the decision that she was not entitled to damages following the suicide of her husband (D) in a claim against his employer (V). D had been badly injured in a factory accident that V admitted had been caused by its negligence or breach of statutory duty. D subsequently suffered post-traumatic stress disorder and was later treated in hospital for depression. Some six years after the accident he committed suicide. C

---

15 A deceased child must have died, not merely sustained the lethal injury, before his 18th birthday for the parents' entitlement to arise (*Doleman* v *Deakin* (1990) Times, 30 January, CA).

brought a claim against V on behalf of his estate and under the Fatal Accidents Act 1976. The judge held that V had been in breach of its duty of care but that that duty did not extend to a duty to take care to prevent D's suicide and that his suicide was not reasonably foreseeable. C contended that the only requirement was the foreseeability of some injury and that depression and consequent suicide lay within the scope of the employer's duty. V contended that the duty did not extend to a duty to protect D from self-harm and that the suicide broke the chain of causation between the negligence and its consequences. It was held (1) On the evidence D's suicide did not break the chain of causation between V's negligence and the consequences of the suicide, *Holdlen Pty Ltd* v *Walsh* (2000) 19 NSWCCR 629 considered. (2) C did not need to establish that at the time of the accident D's suicide was reasonably foreseeable as a kind of damage separate from psychiatric and personal injury. Responsibility for the effects of suicide depended on whether it flowed from a condition for which, by reference to appropriate foreseeability criteria, the defendant was responsible. In the instant case C founded her claim on depression, which was admitted to have been a foreseeable consequence of V's negligence, and the uncontroverted evidence was that suicide was a not uncommon consequence of severe depression. The compensable consequences of the depression included D's eventual suicide.

DEATH OF AN INFANT AND NERVOUS SHOCK

It is not easy to know how to assess damages for a stillbirth or a miscarriage. They will, of course, vary according to the time at which the miscarriage takes place and according to the degree of nervous shock (ie actual psychiatric injury) suffered by the mother. But there is little in the way of precedent.

One must first bear in mind that mental trauma unaccompanied by physical injury will not found a claim in negligence unless the mental trauma amounts to actual psychiatric damage (to be proved by a medical report). It should be possible in most cases of miscarriage or stillbirth to identify a physical injury, eg the pain of the abortion or the prolongation of labour beyond the appropriate point.[16] It may well be that damaging the child *en ventre*[17] constitutes in itself a physical injury to the mother.

For an early miscarriage, up to a few weeks, say, the award is likely to be about £2,500 – of course, if any sequelae are proved, eg substantive psychiatric injury, or difficulty or impossibility of conception, gestation or parturition in the future, damages will be substantially increased. The estimate above applies to a miscarriage that leaves no substantive sequelae.

After the early days, the award will increase as the pregnancy advances until you have the stillbirth. The real question on assessing for a stillbirth (again, assume no substantive nervous shock, only the normal sorrow,

---

16   In some other contexts, it will be essential to prove nervous shock, eg where cancer is negligently diagnosed and, although the patient does not accept treatment and is therefore not physically harmed by the misdiagnosis, they suffer very great anxiety for a period of time until the diagnosis is corrected.

17   The medics prefer us to say '*in utero*'.

distress and disappointment, with some identifiable physical injury on which to hang that) is whether one takes the bereavement award as a guide. However, as explained above, that is an award under the fatal accident legislation and presupposes no common law duty of care owed to the relative (the spouse or parent). So it can be viewed as a bonus added by the legislation. In the case of the stillbirth, there is of course a duty of care owed to the mother. Nevertheless, the old principle of the common law that no person has an interest in the life of another means that traditional learning would say that the mother cannot be compensated for the death of her child as such (apart from the bereavement award, which presumably cannot apply where the child is not born alive and so is never a 'person' within the meaning of the legislation).

Cases

There are a few reported cases on damages for stillbirth. In *Bagley* v *North Herts Health Authority* [1986] NLJ Rep 1014, Simon Brown J acknowledged that damages could not be awarded to the mother for grief and distress as such (Lord Wilberforce had made that clear in *McLoughlin* v *O'Brian* (above)) or for loss of society, or for the statutory bereavement award, but he found other means of compensating her. He awarded damages for loss of satisfaction in bringing the pregnancy to a successful end, for disappointment at the shattering of her plans for a family and for being deprived of the joy of bringing up an ordinary healthy child, and he said that those damages would amount to not less than the statutory sum. In fact, the mother received some £18,000, but a lot of that was for other heads of claim such as actual physical sequelae (she suffered a substantial nervous illness as a result). Counsel in the case has said that one could probably think in terms of about £6,000 for the actual stillbirth.

In *Kralj* v *McGrath and St Theresa's Hospital* [1986] 1 All ER 54, where £10,000 general damages were awarded after a horrendous and agonising piece of obstetric mismanagement had caused the stillbirth of one of a pair of twins, Woolf J said that not only was the mother entitled to damages for shock at what had happened, but, if her injury was aggravated by the grief she was suffering, that could be reflected in the award. Having stated that it would be wholly inappropriate to introduce into the medical context the concept of aggravated damages, the judge awarded compensation also for the financial loss that would arise if the parents went on to implement their desire for a larger family; if they decided not to, then that award would be appropriate nevertheless to cover disappointment over the loss of their objective; £10,000 was awarded for pain and suffering, and £18,000 for loss of the mother's earnings. It is not possible to know how much of the total award was for the stillbirth pure and simple (if one may use that expression) – indeed it is probable that the judge did not assess that aspect separately in his own mind.

In *Grieve* v *Salford Health Authority* [1991] 2 Med LR 295, Rose J awarded a woman with a pre-existing vulnerable personality £12,500 in respect of initial prolongation of labour, some additional pain, loss of her stillborn child and of the satisfaction of a successful conclusion to the pregnancy, plus psychological damage likely to endure for some four years from the date of the stillbirth. This could possibly be seen as about £6,000 for the stillbirth in itself and about £6,000 for the four-year nervous illness.

In *Kerby* v *Redbridge Health Authority* [1993] 4 Med LR 178, a twin was fatally injured before birth in 1988 by admitted negligence, and survived only three days. Ognall J said, with reference to the dicta in *Bagley* (above), that damages for 'dashed hopes' would duplicate the bereavement award, but he awarded, nevertheless, in addition to the bereavement award, £10,000 for the Cesarian section and consequent scar, a depressive illness of moderate severity lasting some six months, and the constant reminder of what might have been by the presence of the surviving twin.

If the matter were put to the test, it is likely that a court would award close to the bereavement award for a stillbirth pure and simple. One line of argument that might suggest that damages should not greatly exceed the bereavement award is as follows: what if the child dies shortly after birth, let us say through poor neonatal care? How does one justify any award other than the bereavement award in that case? In which event, why should the situation be radically different if the child died just before birth? No duty of care is owed by the pediatricians to the mother in respect of their care of the neonate. Probably the only way of increasing the award substantively beyond the bereavement level of £7,500 in such a context is to show that the mother suffered substantial nervous shock – ie an actual psychiatric injury – that comes within the 'aftermath' principle of *McLoughlin* v *O'Brian* (above).

A final note: In earlier editions of this book it was suggested that, regardless of whether 'normal' grief and distress at loss of a loved one will attract the bereavement award or no compensation at all in a given situation, the award for nervous shock should only reflect that element of suffering which is additional to 'normal' grief and distress (see the report on the Zeebrugge Ferry awards in Kemp & Kemp *Quantum of Damages*, C4-350). However, the Court of Appeal judgments in *Vernon* v *Bosley* [1997] 1 All ER 577 (see the section above on 'Further developments') may have given the lie to that observation.

Chapter 14

Economic loss

William Latimer-Sayer

INTRODUCTION

Mere economic loss, ie economic loss that is not consequent upon physical damage to person or property or the threat of it, is as a general rule not recoverable in tort, as opposed to contract. It is, however, recoverable when it arises from careless statements, provided there is a duty in the circumstances on the person making the statement to take care; that duty will arise in the context of a fiduciary relationship. Recent years have seen the formulation by the courts that recovery is also permitted where there is a sufficient relationship of proximity between the parties to permit the court to infer that the defendant voluntarily assumed a duty of care in respect of the alleged negligent activity; but it is hard to know in any particular case whether or not the court will discern such a relationship. Apart from these contexts, a line will be drawn by the court as a matter of policy to prevent recovery for economic loss that does not flow from, ie is not consequent upon, some physical damage or the threat of it.

There has never been any problem in compensating for financial loss where it accompanies injury to person or property. If your car is damaged, you can hire another pending repair; if you are injured, you can recover lost earnings. Nor has there been any difficulty in permitting recovery for economic loss consequent upon breach of contract. But, as regards liability in tort, carelessness, whether in act or word, which gives rise to foreseeable economic loss only is a different matter. 'The reluctance to grant a remedy for the careless invasion of financial or pecuniary interests is long-standing, deep-rooted and not unreasonable' (*per* Professor Heuston). The court might declare that there was no duty of care, as where a large supermarket setting up next door to a small competitor puts the latter out of business, or that the damage was too remote, or that public policy drew the line at recovery in respect of the loss claimed, or simply that mere economic loss was not recoverable.

As with so many aspects of the law of negligence, the question of recovering economic loss is one of policy. Whenever the courts draw a line to mark out the bounds of 'duty', they do it as a matter of policy so as to limit the responsibility of the defendant. Whenever the courts set bounds to the 'damages' recoverable – saying that they are, or are not, too remote – they do it as a matter of policy so as to limit the liability of the defendants (*per* Lord Denning MR in *Spartan Steel and Alloys Ltd* v *Martin & Co (Contractors) Ltd* [1973] QB 27, CA at 36).

The 'electricity' cases

Where economic loss is consequent upon physical injury, it is usually recoverable. Thus, in *SCM (United Kingdom) Ltd* v *W J Whittall & Son Ltd* [1971] 1 QB 337, defendants who negligently cut off the electricity supply to the claimants' factory were held liable by the Court of Appeal for the loss of profit which resulted from the solidifying in the furnaces of molten metals, because it stemmed from the damage to furnace and metal, but not for further economic loss which was said to be too remote. Lord Denning said that recovery for mere economic loss was not usually permitted by the law, on the ground of public policy, rather than by the operation of any logical principle; and Winn LJ said that, apart from the special case of liability for negligently uttered false statements, there was no liability for negligent unintentional infliction of any form of economic loss which was not itself consequential upon foreseeable physical injury or damage to property.

In the similar *Spartan Steels* case (above), the defendants negligently damaged the electric cable supplying the claimants' factory, who had therefore to pour molten metal out of their furnaces, for otherwise it would have solidified and damaged the furnaces. They lost part of the value of the metal and their profit on its resale. In addition, they claimed for loss of profit on the four further melts they could have performed in the time the power was off. Though they succeeded at first instance, the Court of Appeal would not permit recovery in respect of the four melts, on the basis that whereas loss of profit on the metal that was poured out was consequential on the physical damage to that metal and the risk of damage to the furnaces, loss of profit on the four hypothetical melts was mere economic damage not consequent upon the physical damage or the risk of physical damage. Lord Denning said that the more he thought about the subject of recovery for economic loss, the more difficult he found it to put each case into its proper pigeonhole:

> Sometimes I say: 'There was no duty.' In others I say: 'The damage was too remote.' So much so that I think the time has come to discard those tests which have proved so elusive. It seems to me better to consider the particular relationship in hand, and see whether or not, as a matter of policy, economic loss should be recoverable or not.

In truth, as Edmund Davies LJ pointed out in a strong dissenting judgment, there was no logical distinction between the two losses. It must simply be seen as a matter of policy that the court insisted on drawing a line to the defendants' liability.[1]

---

1   Economic loss can be recovered where it is claimed as part of a claim which originates in a claim for physical damage: *SCM (United Kingdom) Ltd* v *W J Whittall & Son Ltd* [1971] 1 QB 337; *Spartan Steel and Alloys Ltd v Martin & Co (Contractors) Ltd* [1973] QB 27, CA; *Muirhead* v *Industrial Tank Specialities* [1986] QB 507; *Ehmler* v *Hall* [1993] 1 EGLR 137, CA.

Development

For a time, beginning with the decision of the House of Lords in *Anns* v *Merton London Borough Council* [1978] AC 728, it seemed that economic loss which was foreseeable should be recoverable, as any other loss, unless there were policy considerations in the particular case militating against such recovery. This general formulation was later whittled down by the courts; the context in which it was proposed, the liability of local authority inspectors for certifying defective foundations, was itself reduced to the situation where physical damage was created or threatened; and then the very decision itself, imposing liability for economic loss in these circumstances, was declared misconceived because the court in 1978 had failed to recognise that the damage for which it was permitting compensation was mere economic loss and to do that was to introduce a wholly new and unsuitable extension to the law (see further below on this).

In *Junior Books* v *Veitchi* [1983] 1 AC 520, the House of Lords held that, assuming the facts pleaded were true, subcontractors who laid a defective floor would be liable to the claimant occupiers of the building for the cost of repair and certain financial loss flowing therefrom. This was despite the fact that there was neither a contractual nexus between the parties nor any physical damage or threat of it to the building. It was said that where there was a sufficient relationship of proximity between the parties, the duty of care extended to the duty not to inflict carelessly economic loss (Lord Roskill said that the defendants, as subcontractors, were in almost as close a commercial relationship with the plaintiff as it was possible to envisage, short of privity of contract).

Lord Brandon dissented, saying that to impose liability would be to create obligations appropriate only to a contractual relationship, and that the authorities made it clear that in the absence of physical damage or the threat of it mere economic loss was not recoverable.

Retrenchment

Recovery for mere economic loss was denied in shipping contexts – by the Court of Appeal in *Leigh and Sillavan Ltd* v *Aliakmon Shipping Co* [1985] QB 350, where buyers sued shipowners in contract and tort for damage to goods caused by bad stowage; and by the House of Lords in *Candlewood Navigation Corpn* v *Mitsui OSK Lines Ltd* [1986] AC 1, involving a time charterer's claim for financial loss. In *Muirhead* v *Industrial Tank Specialities* [1986] QB 507, the Court of Appeal rejected a claim for mere economic loss by the user against the manufacturer of lobster tanks. It was said that there was not a sufficiently close relationship between the two for such a duty to arise; there had to be such a very close proximity of relationship between the parties and reliance by the claimant on the defendant that the defendant was to be taken voluntarily to have assumed direct responsibility to the claimant.[2]

Then came the highly significant House of Lords' decision in *Caparo Industries plc* v *Dickman* [1990] 2 AC 605, where it was held that auditors of a company owed no duty of care not to inflict economic loss on

---

2   See also *Virgo Steamship Co* v *Skaarup Shipping Corpn* [1988] 1 Lloyd's Rep 352.

shareholders or potential investors who relied on the audit in deciding whether to invest (further) in the company. The court said that liability for economic loss due to negligent misstatement was confined to cases where the statement or advice had been given to a known recipient for a specific purpose of which the maker was aware, and on which the recipient had relied and on which he had acted to his detriment. As the auditors had no reason to think that their report would go to the claimant, let alone that it would be relied on by them in deciding whether to invest (further) in the company, there was no sufficient proximity between them and the claimants to found a duty of care (see also Chapter 5 for further cases).

The decisions of the House of Lords in July 1990 in *Murphy* v *Brentwood District Council* [1991] 1 AC 398, and *Department of the Environment* v *Thomas Bates & Son* [1991] 1 AC 499 concerned liability for economic loss caused not by misstatement but by negligent conduct. The House of Lords made it clear that, as presently constituted, they shared the disquiet that had been voiced increasingly in the last five years or so about the wholesale extension of the law of negligence, in cases where no physical injury had been sustained, that was inherent in and threatening to develop as a logical outcome from the 1978 decision of the House of Lords (as then constituted) in *Anns* v *Merton London Borough Council* [1978] AC 728. In our present context, the point to note is that the court made it clear that there can be no general formula for establishing when mere economic loss is recoverable – one can only look to decided cases and see if one's own case falls more or less within the factual matrix of any case where liability has been imposed.

There is, of course, scope for the court to admit a new situation, for the categories of negligence are never closed, but it would need careful argument and the court would need to be convinced that policy and justice required that liability be imposed. One such example of the court being so convinced is *Spring* v *Guardian Assurance plc* [1995] 2 AC 296, where the House of Lords held that an insurance company owed a duty of care to a former representative when providing him or prospective employers with a reference (the breach of duty was by way of careless statement and the damage purely economic). Another is *Welton* v *North Cornwall District Council* [1997] 1 WLR 570, where the Court of Appeal permitted recovery for economic loss in respect of building works required, quite wrongly, to be done to a restaurant by an incompetent environmental health officer. The court said:

- that the officer had 'assumed a responsibility' to take care in respect of what he said to or required of the restaurant owner; and
- that it was fair, just and reasonable, and in accordance with public policy, that a duty of care should be imposed.

In *Hamble Fisheries Ltd* v *L Gardner & Sons Ltd* [1999] 2 Lloyd's Rep 1, where damages for economic loss occasioned by the failure of marine engines was claimed in tort against the manufacturer (for not warning of that possibility), the Court of Appeal, dismissing the purchaser's appeal, said that the general rule was as set out in the *Murphy* case (above): there was no duty on a manufacturer towards a consumer for economic loss. The pertinent question was whether in a given situation there was a special relationship of proximity on the manufacturer to safeguard the consumer from economic loss. *Contra*, in *Bailey* v *HSS Alarms* (2000) Times, 20 June, the Court of Appeal discerned the requisite special relationship between a property owner and a company who provided security services to the property (the two parties not being in direct contractual relationship). The company was held liable to the owner for economic loss when thieves broke in and stole a substantial amount of property.

In *Commissioner of Police of the Metropolis* v *Lennon* [2004] 1 WLR 2594, the claimant police officer had asked for advice from an employee of the Commissioner who had held herself out as familiar with the ins and outs pertaining to the claimant's transfer to a new force, in particular in connection with the preservation of his housing allowance. That advice was wrong and caused the claimant economic loss. The Court of Appeal dismissed the Commissioner's appeal, saying it was irrelevant that the employee was not a professional adviser as she had expressly assumed responsibility for giving the claimant the advice in relation to possible loss of housing allowance. She had led the claimant to believe that he could leave it to her and could rely on her, and had not told him to seek advice elsewhere. No new category of duty situation had been created by the judge. It was well established that liability in tort for pure economic loss could arise from the negligent carrying out of a task undertaken pursuant to an express voluntary assumption of responsibility, given appropriate reliance by the relevant party.

The 'wrongful birth' cases (dealt with in detail in Chapter 11) have usually raised issues about the right to claim for economic loss, and the decisions of the courts have been influenced strongly by policy considerations, of which the case of *McFarlane* v *Tayside Health Board* MLC 0127, [2000] 2 AC 59, HL is the most egregious example.

COMMENT

In the absence of a special relationship of proximity and/or a voluntary assumption of risk (it is not clear what terminology to use – see eg *Reid* v *Rush & Tompkins Group* [1990] 1 WLR 212, CA), there is no duty of care not to inflict mere economic loss. It remains very difficult to predict if in a given situation the court will or will not discern the requisite special relationship. The position is, of course, clear enough if a product causes *physical* injury, as the ginger beer with the decomposing snail in it taught us many years ago (*Donoghue* v *Stevenson* [1932] AC 562).

Junior Books v *Veitchi* [1983] 1 AC 520 must be seen now as a flash in the pan: if that case recurred today, Lord Brandon's dissenting judgment would be followed – no court is going now to hold that a subcontractor is under a duty of care in his work not to inflict mere economic loss on the building owner with whom he is not in a contractual relationship.[3] That said, the liability of subcontractors for economic loss is still a developing area of jurisprudence and therefore it may be difficult to strike out such a claim.[4]

---

3 The House of Lords made it clear enough in *D & F Estates* v *Church Comrs for England* [1989] AC 177 what they thought of the *Junior Books* decision.
4 *Linklaters Business Services* v *Sir Robert McAlpine* [2010] EWHC 1145 (TCC), 130 Con LR 111, (2010) NPC 61.

MEDICAL CONTEXT

Most, but not all, medical negligence actions are in respect of personal injury. This may take the form of physical injury or a recognisable psychiatric disorder. Within the doctor-patient relationship there is normally a sufficient proximity and reliance by the patient on the doctor to give rise to a duty not to inflict mere economic loss, so that, for example, a careless diagnosis that leads to the patient taking time off work will give rise to compensation for lost wages.[5] Where a negligently premature discharge from hospital of an infected child causes his siblings to contract the infection, resulting in financial loss to the parents, a court would probably hold the hospital liable (see on these facts *Evans* v *Liverpool Corpn* [1906] 1 KB 160, where the father failed in his action against the hospital, but on the basis that, as the law then, stood the hospital was not liable for the negligence of the discharging physician). However, it is important that the alleged breach of duty is a 'relevant breach' of duty such that it renders the defendant liable for the state of affairs that arose (see *Brown* v *Lewisham and North Southwark Health Authority* [1999] Lloyd's Rep Med 110). In other words, the resulting damage or type of damage must have been foreseeable from the alleged breach of duty. For example, in the case of *Thompson* v *Bradford* [2005] EWCA Civ 1439, the defendant GP was held not to be liable for failing to give advice as to whether he should postpone a polio vaccination due to an unusual abscess on the claimant's buttock. A competent GP should have provided information to the claimant's parents that the abscess was unusual and might require surgery, and that it might be uncomfortable to undergo such surgery a short time after the vaccination. However, it was common ground that the GP could not have foreseen the increased risk in the claimant contracting polio. Therefore the breach of duty was not a relevant breach of duty and the Court of Appeal overturned the finding of liability against the GP.

Claims for the cost of upkeep of an unplanned child may be for economic loss only, ie where there is no claim made for any personal injury (see Chapter 11, where it is explained that, although such claims are no longer possible in the case of a healthy child, they appear to be possible to a limited extent if the unplanned child is born handicapped).

Outside the special doctor-patient relationship, the courts have generally been reluctant to impose liability for pure economic loss and recent examples of failed cases include:

- A local authority that provided care to a person injured by the negligence of an NHS trust was not able to recover the cost of care from the trust in negligence.[6]
- A local authority that had organised a horse fair was not liable to a member of the public who was seriously injured whilst at the fair for failing to take out public liability insurance.[7]

---

5   The time limit for such claims is six years: see *Younger* v *Dorset Strategic Health Authority* [2006] Lloyd's Rep Med 489.
6   *Islington LBC* v *University College London Hospital NHS Trust* [2005] EWCA Civ 556.
7   *Glaister* v *Appleby-in-Westmorland Town Council* [2009] EWCA Civ 1325.

- An orthopaedic surgeon providing treatment to a football player under the terms of a medical insurance policy owed no duty of care in tort in respect of any foreseeable economic loss caused to the football club resulting from his negligent treatment.[8]
- Health authorities do not owe a duty of care in tort to proprietors of nursing homes when making applications without notice for cancellation of their registration under the Registered Homes Act 1984.[9]
- A local authority not liable for failing to make an application for compensation to the Criminal Injuries Compensation Board in relation to a child in their care.[10]
- A bookmaker was not liable for failing to implement a telephone betting exclusion agreement preventing a compulsive gambler from continuing to place bets.[11]
- A hospital was held not to owe a non-delegable duty of care in respect of genetic testing of a tissue sample which was sent to be cultured by a reputable independent cytogenetics labatory.[12]
- A mother was held not to owe her son a duty of care to take reasonable steps to keep him safe from injury from the hands of his father, where the discharge of the duty would have involved the break-up of the family.[13]

---

8   *West Bromwich Albion Football Club Ltd* v *Medhat El-Safty* [2006] EWCA Civ 1299.
9   *Ashok Jain* v *Trent Strategic Health Authority* [2009] 1 AC 853.
10 *VL* v *Oxfordshire CC* [2010] EWHC 2091 (QB).
11 *Calvert* v *William Hill Credit Ltd* [2008] EWCA Civ 1427.
12 *Farraj* v *King's Healthcare NHS Trust* [2009] EWCA Civ 1203.
13 *XA* v *YA* [2010] EWHC 1983 (QB).

Part Three

Chapter 15

Procedure to service of proceedings

Ravi Nayer

PRIOR TO ISSUE

The Pre-Action Protocol

The Pre-Action Protocol for the Resolution of Clinical Disputes, which came into force on 26 April 1999, was the first major initiative of the Clinical Disputes Forum, one of whose aims is to find less adversarial and more cost-effective ways of resolving disputes about healthcare and medical treatment. The protocol, the full text of which is set out at Appendix II, states that it is intended to encourage a climate of openness when something has 'gone wrong' with a patient's treatment, or the patient is dissatisfied with the treatment or its outcome. It is expressly said to reflect the once new, but now familiar, emphasis upon 'clinical governance' within 'healthcare'.

The protocol is intended to be sufficiently broadly based, and flexible, to apply to all aspects of the health service: primary and secondary, public and private sectors. The introductory sections to the protocol should be read in full at least once. They explain why the protocol has been produced and what its aims are. The protocol is not intended to be a comprehensive code governing all the steps in clinical disputes, but rather a code of good practice which parties should follow when litigation might be a possibility.[1] The courts are expected to treat the standards set in the protocol as the normal reasonable approach to pre-action conduct. Any decision about sanctions is left to the courts and, in this regard, practitioners would be wise to also read the more wide-ranging Practice Direction on Pre-Action Conduct.

Within the protocol itself, one finds a 'commitments' section, summarising the guiding principles which both sides are invited to endorse in the context of patient dissatisfaction, complaints and claims; and a 'steps' section which sets out in a more prescriptive form a recommended sequence of actions to be followed if litigation is a prospect. Here, it is enough to note that, together with implementing a number of

---

1   The court may take into account (non)-compliance with a protocol when giving directions (CPR 3.1(4), (5), 3.9(1)(e)), and when making orders for costs (CPR 44.3(5)(a)).

governmental systems, the healthcare provider's principal commitment is to advise patients of any adverse outcome and to provide on request an explanation and, if appropriate, an offer of remedial treatment, an apology and/or compensation. The patient's commitments include a consideration of the full range of options available following an adverse outcome, including a request for information, a meeting, a complaint, mediation and negotiation. The protocol explicitly abjures any intention to be prescriptive about alternative approaches to settling disputes (or about issues in relation to expert evidence).

The prescribed steps include obtaining the medical records, writing a Letter of Claim, and the response to it (known as a Letter of Response). A useful flow chart setting out the steps for patients is appended to the Pre-Action Protocol and set out at Appendix II.

Obtaining the medical records

Standard forms for the request should be used (as in Annex B to the protocol). The request should contain sufficient information to alert the healthcare provider where the adverse outcome has been serious. Copy records should be provided within 40 days for a cost within the limits provided by the Data Protection Act 1998 (in respect of applications for access to health records where the patient has died, these are still to be found in the largely repealed Access to Health Records Act 1990). The healthcare provider is not expected to investigate every case where records are requested, but it is expected to have a policy on what cases will be investigated. In the rare event of failure to provide the records within the stipulated 40 days, an application to the court can be made. Third-party record holders are expected to co-operate. For further details see Chapter 19.

Letters of Claim

Following receipt of medical records, and usually after seeking expert advice, the next step is for patients' advisors to send a Letter of Claim to the health care provider. Plainly, therefore, such notifications are case-specific and intended to be more than just a generic intimation of a claim.

The following is a useful summary of what should be included in the Letter of Claim:

(a) the patient's name, address, and date of birth;
(b) the dates of allegedly negligent treatment;
(c) the events giving rise to the claim;
(d) the allegations of negligence and their causal link with injuries (which can be as complex as the circumstances require);
(e) the patient's injuries, condition and future prognosis;
(f) a request for clinical records if not previously sought or provided; and
(g) the likely value of the claim and/or the mains heads of loss.

As with the Pre-Action Protocol for Personal Injury Claims and the Pre-Action Protocol for Professional Negligence, claimants are expected to wait three months from the sending of their Letter of Claim before issuing proceedings (upon the basis that there is no issue of impending limitation and/or the patient does not require immediate protection). Of course, even if limitation is in issue, a claimant will still have four months from issue to *serve* their claim form (as to which, see below) and engage in meaningful dialogue. In simple terms, the aim is to give the healthcare provider the facts necessary to begin and, even on an initial basis, conclude investigations so that both parties can assess the relative merits of their cases, what further evidence is needed and, ultimately, whether settlement can be reached. Even where settlement is not possible, the Pre-Action Protocol intends that the litigation process can proceed with increased focus and efficiency – the rewards for both parties' effort in the pre-action period.

AFTER ISSUE

Serving proceedings

Claim form and particulars of claim

The claim form must be served within four months of issue (CPR 7.5).[2] The particulars of claim, if not served with or in the claim form, must be served within 14 days of service of the claim form, but in any event no later than the last day permitted for service of the claim form (CPR 7.4). Under the CPR, a party's pleadings, as well as any further information given in relation to them voluntarily or by court order under Part 18, are collectively referred to as its 'statement of case' (see the glossary at CPR 2.3). These are documents intended to set out a party's stall (whether by way of claim or defence), and, to that end, must always be verified by a statement of truth.

Rules 16.2 and 16.3 state that the claim form must contain a concise statement of the nature of the claim, the remedy sought, and anything else required by any relevant practice direction. Rule 16.4 states what the particulars of claim must contain (principally, a concise statement of the facts on which the claimant relies).[3] For personal injury and fatal accident cases, Practice Direction 16, paras 4 and 5, contain important additional requirements – including the need, where the claimant is relying on the evidence of a medical practitioner, for a medical report 'about the personal injuries which he alleges in his claim', and 'a schedule of details of any past and future expenses and losses which he claims'.[4]

---

2   Note that by virtue of r 6.5(4)(d) where a party has specified an address for service, eg his solicitors, serving the claim form on the party will not be proper service (*Nanglegan* v *Royal Free Hampstead NHS Trust* (2001) Times, 14 February, CA). See also *Elmes* v *Hygrade Food Products* (24 January, 2001, unreported), CA.

3   In *IBC Vehicles* v *Durr Ltd* (12 January 2000, unreported), Tugendhat QC said that there was a tendency for the court to accept that a case might be adequately notified to the other party in an expert's report or witness statement, even if it had not been adequately pleaded in the statement of case. However, it must be doubted whether the Court of Appeal would agree, even allowing for a degree of flexibility in the present climate.

4   It is not mandatory to serve a medical report or a schedule, though without them it will not be possible to claim special damages, and any injury alleged may well be hard to prove without medical support (see *Saunders* v *Gwent Community NHS Trust* [2000] MLC 0251, CA – this was an application for permission to appeal; so one needs to bear in mind that Lord Woolf has said that judgments on such applications should not be relied on as authorities (*Clark* v *University of Lincolnshire and Humberside* [2000] 1 WLR 1988, CA)).

Some practitioners will note that the words of these two requirements are not the same as those appearing in the Rules of the Supreme Court, for example the medical report is not required specifically to 'substantiate' the injuries alleged, and the schedule requirement does not speak of an 'estimate' of future losses. The omission of the word 'substantiate', in particular, indicates that it will no longer be possible for defendants to argue, as some have unconvincingly done in the past, that the report has to confirm causation as well as clarifying current condition and prognosis. (The now defunct draft Clinical Negligence Practice Direction provided that a schedule of loss would not be required unless the court so ordered on the application of the defendant, which was a very sensible provision as it is pointless and uneconomical to require a schedule of loss at the outset in a high value clinical negligence claim).

Venue

If the claim includes a claim for damages for personal injury (as most, but not all, clinical negligence claims do), it can only be started in the High Court if its value, as assessed under the High Court and County Courts Jurisdiction Order 1991, is over £50,000. Practitioners will calculate what the claimant seeks to recover in accordance with the list of relevant factors at CPR 16.3(6). Furthermore, there are provisions (see Practice Direction 7A, para 2.4) for starting a low value claim in the High Court if (a) the value of the claim is in dispute; (b) it is particularly complex; and/ or (c) the outcome of the claim has importance to the public *and* needs a High Court judge. However, as a matter of practical strategy, all claims *outside* London might do well to be heard in the County Court as the High Court listing is usually fraught with administrative difficulties and the circuit judge allocated the case will as a matter of course be accredited to try High Court actions anyway. Nevertheless, an experienced High Court Master in charge of clinical negligence claims has privately indicated that he would find it acceptable for a multi-track medical claim to be started in the High Court even if worth less than £50,000.

Extending time

The court has a general discretion to extend the time for serving a claim form, provided that the application is made before the last date for service (ie four months after issue). After that time, the claimant has to show that he has acted promptly in applying and that, despite taking all reasonable steps, has been unable to serve the form (or that the court has been unable to serve it).

The court has no power to extend time for service of a claim form where the period prescribed for service in CPR 7.6(2) has expired and the claimant cannot bring himself within the provisions of CPR 7.6(3) (a) to (c) (*Vinos* v *Marks and Spencer plc* [2000] MLC 0243, CA, where the claimant's solicitors had not taken all reasonable steps to serve the form). Conversely, the court may allow an application to extend time prospectively, even where it is not satisfied that the claimant has taken all reasonable steps to serve the Claim Form (*Marshall* v *Maggs* reported under *Collier* v *Williams* [2006] EWCA Civ 20, CA). The general discretion given by CPR 3.1(2)(a) (the court's general powers of case management) to extend time limits do not apply (as the provisions of CPR 7.6 must be deemed 'provided otherwise' within the meaning of CPR 3.1(2));[5] nor did the general power to correct 'an error of procedure such as a failure to comply with a rule or practice direction' under CPR 3.10.

In *Kaur* v *CTP Coil Ltd* (9 July 2000, unreported), CA (where, in addition, the form was served outside the limitation period), it had not been reasonable for the claimant's solicitors to have left the preparation of the schedule of loss until the last minute. The claimant was not entitled to rely on the general powers given to the court by CPR 3.10 (as per the *Vinos* case). Nor, for the same reasons, could he rely on CPR 3.9 (which gives the court another general power, namely the power to give relief from sanctions imposed for a failure to comply with any rule, practice direction or court order). Note that the time within which a *defence* must be filed (14 days after service of the particulars of claim, or 28 days if an acknowledgment of service has been filed (CPR 15.4), can be extended by agreement between the parties for a further period up to 28 days (CPR 15.5)).

The court has power to dispense with service, although the Court of Appeal has shown reluctance to dispense where service out of time has been due to the claimant's fault (*Anderton* v *Clwyd* [2002] EWCA Civ 933).[6] This issue of extending time remains uncertain as one decision succeeds another and a body of case law on the new rules is laboriously constructed. As yet, the situation remains somewhat confused. For further reading, enjoy *Cranfield* v *Bridgerove Ltd* [2003] EWCA Civ 656; *Lakah Group* v *Al Jazeera Satellite Channel* [2003] EWHC 1297 (and the associated hearing at 1231); and *Mersey Docks Property Holdings* v *Kilgour* [2004] EWHC 1638. In *Hashtroodi* v *Hancock* [2004] EWCA Civ 652, the Court of Appeal said that the power to extend time retrospectively must be exercised in accordance with the overriding objective (which necessarily imports Article 6 rights, which the reader will note are qualified – access to courts not being an unlimited or unregulated right) and the extension should not have been granted below, where the delay was due to the solicitor's incompetence. To summarise the rule so far as it is possible: the weaker the reason for an extension the less likely it is to be granted.

More recently, *FG Hawkes (Western) Ltd* v *Beli Shipping Co Ltd* [2010] 1 Lloyd's Rep 449, Comm, was a case where the claimant, having benefited from two extensions of time to issue its claim form (it being issued on the last date possible), then having received an extension of time, failed

---

5   Note that, provided the rules do not 'provide otherwise', an application for an extension of time can be granted under the general power given to the court by CPR 3.1(2)(a) even after the time for compliance has expired. In *Keith* v *CPM Field Marketing Ltd* (2000) Times, 29 August, the Court of Appeal said that, where an application for an extension was made under CPR 3.1(2)(a), an application for relief from any relevant sanction under CPR 3.9 should be inferred and the court should therefore systematically consider all the factors set out in CPR 3.9 before reaching its decision.

6   For a slight relaxation of this principle see *Wilkey* v *BBC* [2002] EWCA Civ 1561. The group of separate cases at [2002] EWCA Civ 933 raise various other points on service, including deemed day of service under CPR 6.7, non-exclusion of Saturdays and Sundays from the calculation of deemed day of service, the suggestion that CPR 6.7 could need amendment, and the distinction between a case where no service had even been attempted (so an extension of time would have to be sought) and one where a reasonable but unsuccessful attempt to serve had been made (here an order dispensing with service could be sought).

to serve the claim form out of the jurisdiction within the specified six months. Three weeks before the end of the period for service, the claimant sought to confirm the defendant's address or whether the claim form could be served on the managers in Croatia. An *ex parte* extension was granted, but it was overturned on application to the High Court. Gross J held that where there was no reason for the failure to serve the claim form within the time allowed other than incompetence, neglect or oversight on the part of the claimant or its legal representative, that would be a powerful reason for refusing to grant an extension of time, though not an absolute bar. It was incumbent on a claimant to take reasonable steps to ascertain a defendant's address for service and the fact that a claimant was giving priority to another claim was not a good reason for the grant of an extension. Where the claimant's solicitors did nothing for five months, that was a strong reason for not extending time (even where the defendant knew of the proceedings, would suffer no prejudice by an extension and where the extension was applied for before the end of the expiry of the service period).

The most recent case on this issue is one that will have particular resonance with claimant solicitors. In *Cecil* v *Bayat* [2011] EWCA Civ 135, the High Court granted an extension of six months for service out of the jurisdiction in a commercial claim for USD400m on the basis that the claimant needed time to secure funding. Thereafter, a further extension of six months was granted, during which time limitation expired. Ultimately, the claim form was served 11 months after it was first issued only once a CFA and ATE insurance were in place. Both extensions, having been granted without notice, were challenged by the defendants. Overturning the decision below, the Court of Appeal held that the jurisprudence of CPR 7.6(2) would not, on those facts, allow for the pursuit of funding to be a good reason to extend time under CPR 7.5(2). The Court of Appeal reminded us that 'the starting-point is that a defendant has a right to be sued, if at all, by means of a writ issued within the statutory period of limitation and served within the period of its initial validity' (at [100]).

On balance, it is advisable to avoid applying for an extension of time for servicenot least because the defendant can apply to have the extension removed *ex post facto*.

The contents of the particulars of claim

It is now permissible, but of course not obligatory, for any party to refer in his pleading to any relevant point of law, to the name of any of his witnesses, and to attach any document he deems necessary to his case (Practice Direction 16, para 14.3).

But the rules for good pleading remain the same; they are even confirmed by the requirement in CPR 16.4 for including 'a concise statement of the facts on which the claimant relies'. Long, inflated pleadings are not more impressive than short ones. A pleader who is thinking clearly and has confidence in his ability to express that thinking clearly will not omit anything that needs to be included. This writer would advise pleaders, and those who instruct them, as follows: do not believe that the more prolix you are, the more effective or impressive your pleading becomes. For example, it is not necessary to set out the whole medical history.

The pleader should have analysed the case and be totally focussed on the events he is relying on in support of the allegation(s) of negligence – pleading only them.

On the other hand, the pleader should be precise, not vague. He should not leave the field open for the defendant(s) to serve a long and tedious request for further information, which wastes time and money as the questions are sent to the expert, before his answers are sent back to be included in the draft. It is much better to tell the defendant in the statement of case exactly what action or omission the claimant alleges to have been negligent; when it occurred; why it is alleged to have been negligent; what the claimant contends should have been done instead; and, finally, what the claimant says was the result to him of that negligent act or omission. The extra work aside, lawyers will find that performing this task as early as possible will help to bring the crux of the claim (or any obstacles in its running) into focus.

Though sometimes hard to do as one says, it is good practice to *not* put under your Particulars of Negligence sweeping allegations in the hope that you will in that way cover all possibilities, eg 'The defendants failed properly or at all to monitor the progress of the claimant's labour', or 'The defendants failed to provide an adequate system of anaesthetic/obstetric cover', or 'The defendants failed properly to train and/or instruct their staff/trainees in such and such', or 'The defendants failed to observe and/or heed and/or act upon the signs of foetal distress'. These are all much too general and are just asking for the said tedious request for particulars. Be specific: eg 'The defendants failed properly to monitor the progress of the claimant's labour, in that at such and such a time they did such and such whereas they should have done such and such'. Sometimes the error lies simply in not adding to the general allegation words to the effect 'The facts and matters to be relied on in connection with this allegation are set out above at paras ... '. Of course, to get this sort of clarity and particularity, the claimant's advisors must ensure that their expert has answered the appropriate questions with sufficient precision (and that they actually understand what the claimant's positive case is). Finally, the pleading must be compelling to the reader.

Staughton LJ wrote in *Counsel:*

> A good rule for drafting documents is to sit back at the end and ask of every phrase that one has written, whether it was necessary to write it at all.

He also said:

> Unthinking copy of precedents, when nothing is ever left out as antiquated or obsolete, produces many documents which are too long, too old-fashioned and too obscure.

In *Ashmore* v *Corpn of Lloyd's* [1992] 1 WLR 446, HL, Lord Templeman said that pleadings should define the issues, be brief, chronological and consistent, and that counsel should not advance a multitude of ingenious arguments in the hope that out of ten bad points, the judge would be able to fashion a winner. He was expressly critical of the tendency in some cases for legal advisers to make every point, conceivable and inconceivable, without judgement or discrimination. We would do well to bear in mind the words of Rose LJ In *Re Freudiana Holdings Ltd* (1995) Times, 4 December, CA:

The legal profession must re-learn, or re-apply, the skill which was the historic hallmark of the profession but which appears to be fast vanishing: to present to the court the few crucial determinative points and to discard as immaterial dross the minor points and excessive detail.

Despite the new rules for pleading described above, this former guidance remains a useful point of reference, as does the judgment in *Hockaday* v *South West Durham Health Authority* [1994] PIQR P275, where the Court of Appeal offered a highly technical analysis of the requirements for pleading a defence:

(1)   The fundamental rule of pleading is that both a statement of claim and a defence must set out the material facts upon which the party pleading intends to rely.

(2)   As to a bare traverse: a denial or a refusal to admit is a perfectly good plea, provided that all that is thereby intended is to put the plaintiff to proof of his case, but it may be that concealed in a traverse is an affirmative case, and that may well be so where the traverse is of a negative averment.

(3)   If it is clear, either from the nature of the case or from the admission of counsel or otherwise, that it is intended to set up an affirmative case, particulars of the affirmative case ought to be delivered; otherwise the other party and the court will be in doubt as to what the issues are to be determined at the trial.

We should bear in mind that pleadings are not a game to be played at the expense of litigants, nor an end in themselves, but a means to an end, and that end is to give each party a fair hearing (*Trust Security Holdings* v *Sir Robert McAlpine & Sons* (1994) Times, 21 December, CA, *per* Saville LJ). Indeed, such an approach is central to the preservation of time and other resources, so critical to modern civil procedure.

Finally, the experts must vet the draft before it is served. It is they who will have to support the allegations of negligence (and the other medical aspects of the claim) in court.

Late service of particulars of claim

It is worth noting that here the court is far more relaxed about the matter than it is in respect of late service of the claim form.[7] In *Price* v *Price* [2003] 3 All ER 911, the conduct of the claimant's case had been disgraceful in a number of respects; yet the Court of Appeal said that it would be a disproportionate response to stop the case by refusing an extension altogether, and so it granted an extension on conditions.

The medical report

Now that cases are being progressed by expert solicitors, it is unlikely that anyone will make the fundamental, and previously not uncommon, mistake of serving a report on liability or causation with the pleading. Sometimes however the report on condition refers to other documents, provoking a knee-jerk reaction in the defendants by way of demanding to

---

7   This was explicitly explained by the Court of Appeal in *Totty* v *Snowden* [2002] PIQR P189 and *Hewitt* v *Wirral and West Cheshire Community NHS Trust* (above).

see those other documents, whatever they might be and however clearly they might be privileged. On this, see 'Disclosure' in Chapter 20.

The medical report does not always have to be a full report from an independent expert to comply with the rule. In the personal injury case of *Edwards* v *Peter Black Healthcare (Southern) Ltd* [2000] ICR 120, CA, a letter from the hospital was held to be sufficient in the circumstances; and in *Knight* v *Sage Group plc* (28 April 1999, unreported), CA, where a claimant in person served only a GP report, the court said that, although it did not satisfy the rules requirement, it was sufficient 'for the initial period of proceedings'.

The medical report should not be treated as if it were a pleading. In *Sion* v *Hampstead Health Authority* [1994] 5 Med LR 170, CA, Staughton LJ said that the claimant was not wholly and rigidly confined to what was said in the medical report; it should be treated only as a general outline of the claimant's case.[8]

The defence

A defence must be served within 14 days of receipt of the particulars of claim, or 28 days if an acknowledgment of service has been filed (CPR 15.4). The parties can agree to an extra 28 days (in which case the defendant must inform the court in writing).

By CPR 16.5 the defence must state which of the claimant's allegations he admits or denies, and which he requires the claimant to prove. Where he denies an allegation, he must give his reasons for so doing and, if he intends to put forward a different version of the events from the claimant, he must set it out. A specific denial may be implied from the nature of the defence case. But if an allegation is not dealt with explicitly or implicitly, an admission will be inferred. These provisions thankfully put an end to the blanket denials favoured by many clinical negligence defendants in the past, which, today, would in all likelihood constitute an abuse of process liable for strike out (CPR 3.4(2)(a)).

Practice Direction 16, para 13 adds that the defendant must state in the defence whether he agrees, disputes or has no knowledge of the matters contained in the claimant's medical report; and if the defendant disputes any part of the report, he must give his reasons. If he has already obtained his own report on which he intends to rely, he must attach it to the defence (this is presumably limited to any report on condition and prognosis). He must be similarly explicit in respect of any schedule served (however he is only likely to be able to serve a useful counter-schedule) in the simpler cases.

---

8   In *Woods* v *West Dorset General Hospital NHS Trust* (17 February 1998, unreported), the Court of Appeal, not surprisingly, confirmed the striking out of a medical negligence claim where the only report served with the pleading was one that exonerated the defendants!

Chapter 16

Procedure from service to trial

Ravi Nayer
Assisted by Andrew Buchan for Multi-party actions

JUDICIAL DIRECTIONS

Following service by the court on the parties of the allocation questionnaire (after a defence has been filed and pursuant to CPR, Part 26) and its filing at court, a clinical negligence claim will be assigned to the multi-track. The court is then directed by CPR 29.2 to fix a case management conference for the purpose of giving relevant directions (otherwise known as 'case management directions') on every aspect of the future progress of the case. This, of course, is the hypothetical route-map for case progression, and it is only the rarest of clinical negligence cases in which extensions and alterations to directions made at the outset will not be required. Nevertheless, under the CPR, the emphasis on 'active' case management (as fully defined in CPR 1.4(2), but essentially aimed at whittling down the issues which parties disagree about and ensuring they are cost-effectively and speedily determined) requires this approach. Such directions, when properly drafted, also serve the useful practical purpose of focusing parties' minds from the beginning to a known end point. The court may approve directions agreed by the parties without requiring them to attend, but that does not happen often, especially in larger value or complex clinical negligence actions.

The case management directions are likely to lay down a detailed timetable for every report, every exchange, every agenda, every meeting, between which experts, and every joint report, as well as for the service of schedules and counter-schedules, chronologies, summaries and skeleton arguments – in fact everything the parties and the court can reasonably contemplate at the time of making the directions. This is known as case management, albeit under the CPR it is a responsibility considered to be far broader than mere timetabling, extending to compelling litigants to achieve certain procedural milestones for the sake of wider procedural justice.

The Masters of the High Court, who are assigned to clinical negligence claims, have developed a useful set of standard directions (see Appendix IV). This is not binding on other courts, but courts outside London often use them. In at least one respect, the direction relating to relevant medical texts and articles, the Court of Appeal has said it is the exemplar that should be followed (see *Wardlaw* v *Farrar* [2003] EWCA Civ 1719, at [24]).

HHJ Grenfell has been tasked to construct uniform Model Directions. Master Yoxall and Master Roberts expect to agree new Model Directions for use in the RCJ in about February or March 2012.

Whatever form directions take, it is essential that exchange of witness statements takes place two or three months before exchange of expert reports in order to allow sufficient time for the experts to consider the witness statements.[1] The Court of Appeal has said more than once that the expert report must take on board the witness statements served by the other party (see, for example, *Johnson* v *John and Waltham Forest Health Authority* [1998] MLC 0224, CA).

Under the CPR, with its emphasis on economy and proportionality, the scope of parties to vary case management directions/dates fixed by the court is far more limited. Although CPR 2.11 allows for parties to agree (in writing) to vary time limits, save where expressly precluded, in practice this is more limited. For example, on the multi-track, the parties may not change the date for compliance with any requirement if it would necessitate varying the date of a case management conference, a pre-trial review, the return of the listing questionnaire, the trial or the trial period (r 29.5(2)). Note also the manner in which the parties' autonomy to agree the variation of unless orders is curtailed by CPR 3.8(3). Where the time limits are likely to be exceeded, even where all parties consent to that state of affairs, it is advisable to apply to the Court with an explanation and a request for an extension rather than just to let the time lapse without compliance; indeed, such agreement will often be a helpful and cost-effective precursor before seeking the court's approval by way of a consent order pursuant to CPR 3.1(2)(a).

This chapter considers those case management orders which are illustrative of those available to the Court, the varieties of which are, in truth, boundless.

MULTI-PARTY ACTIONS

Every clinical negligence practitioner should have some knowledge of the mechanisms of a multi-party action if not but to recognise that one's client may be a party and what best advice to give. Multi-party actions are important to those who specialise in the bringing or defending of claims for injuries caused by defective medical products or drugs.[2] Although the jurisprudence of multi-party claims has been developing for some time,[3]

---

1   In *Rayment* v *Ministry of Defence* (1998) 47 BMLR 92, Harrison J, drawing a clear distinction between reports on liability and causation and reports on quantum, held that the Master's order for sequential disclosure of the latter was appropriate. He said there was the significant potentiality for duplication and waste of costs if there were simultaneous exchange of experts' reports on quantum.

2   Pre and post the introduction of the CPR, notable claims have arisen from treatments using the MMR/MR vaccine; Eraldin (a beta-blocker); Opren (an anti-arthritic drug); Myodil (a contrast dye used to read x-rays); Norplan (a contraceptive implant); Lariam (an anti-malarial); Zyban (an anti-smoking drug); Gammagard (a blood product used to treat immune disorders); Seroxat (an SSRI anti-despressant drug) and tainted blood (see Hepatitis C litigation).

3   From the early 1980s.

formal procedures for multi-party actions are still relatively new to the common law; their genesis can be found in the experience that has been forged out of many multi-party cases. It is not for this book to go into the detail of those cases but, where relevant, some are mentioned below. The need for formal procedures was recognised in Lord Woolf's Final Access to Justice Report and thereafter Part 19 (rr 19.10 to 19.15) of the CPR.

Each multi-party action is different but the principles of group party litigation are not difficult to fathom. These are:

(a) Keep the costs down to a minimum so that instead of many lawyers working on the same generic problem a generic team does so and provides guidance to individual case counsel and solicitors.

(b) The generic team must be able to make sometimes speedy tactical decisions on behalf of the group.

(c) Identify a system for identifying and managing cases. Solicitors need to know whether they need to refer their client to generic solicitors. This might require extensive advertising and may be important when deciding upon an individual client's date of knowledge.

(d) Ensure, at the beginning, that all claimants agree to a common system for resolving their claims. Failure to do so can lead to unnecessary infighting within the group and leaves the cohort vulnerable to attack by clever defendants trying to divide and rule by offering to settle the strongest cases. The usual method is for each client to agree to abide by advice on the terms of settlement from generic counsel.

(e) Identify client cohorts that have generic issues in common.

(f) Once the cohort(s) of clients have been identified, work out all the common problems that need to be dealt with at either a generic and/ or case specific level.

(g) Work out the important issues that need to have a decision, eg duty, breach, causation, limitation.

(h) Ensure that good communication exists between the generic team and the case teams throughout the case.

(i) Ensure that the most cost effective issues are dealt with first. For example, where causation is reasonably obvious, try issues of liability before obtaining medical reports and schedules of special damages for all the claimants. Otherwise these costs will be wasted if the case fails on liability. But make sure that the defendant agrees or that the court has made a specific direction on this point. Also get a direction that if the defendant wants to settle that case by making a lump sum offer, sufficient time be permitted for the claimants' claims to be quantified. This might involve using a recognised and agreed statistical analysis of each cohort.

(j) Ensure that a scheme is set up for the distribution of any damages so that it properly and fairly reflects the loss suffered and the strengths and weaknesses in each cohort or case. This is mandatory where claimants lack capacity. (See Chapters 10 and 22.)

The most innovative developments of Part 19 (see Appendix VIII) are the introduction of the Group Litigation Order (often known by its abbreviation, GLO[4]), and the management court.

---

4   A list of all current GLOs is kept by the Queen's Bench Division and can be accessed online. At the time of writing, 75 GLOs are in place spanning a full spectrum of cases.

The management court is the court specified to deal with the litigation in the GLO (Part 19, para 6.7).

The Group Litigation Order is defined by CPR 19.10 as an order that provides for 'the case management of claims which give rise to common or related issues of fact or law'. It should be noted that this definition preserves much of the pre-CPR discretion open to the court in its management of multi-party actions. The notes to the CPR expressly state that, unlike with Representative Proceedings (see CPR 19.6), the interests of the individuals do not have to be the 'same' (which stems from Lord Woolf's intention that GLOs should take much of the strain then being placed on Representative Proceedings). The aim is to ensure that in respect of common issues any judgment of the court is binding on all those who belong to the Group Register (see CPR 19.12), which is mandatorily set up and kept up-to-date pursuant to a GLO. They are intended to promote an awareness of the existence of potential multi-party actions as early as possible and ensure that the court addresses the issues necessary to avoid cost and delay, for example by ordering the trial of a preliminary issue (for example, as was ordered in *A v National Blood Authority* [2001] 3 All ER 289).

In addition to identifying the existence of common or related issues, the court must consider whether a GLO is appropriate. The Group Litigation Practice Direction (19BPD.5) specifically places this duty on the applicants' solicitors before applying for a GLO, which will have to be dealt with in a supporting witness statement. For example, orders would be refused where actions would be better resolved by being consolidated or by representative actions or lead cases being ordered to be heard (as to which see *Hobson v Ashton Morton Slack Solicitors* [2006] EWHC 1134).

Additionally, it will be problematic if there are funding issues or if it is not clear that a sufficient number of claimants who seriously intend to pursue their claims exist (see the recent case of *Austin v Miller Argent (South Wales) Ltd* [2011] EWCA Civ 928, in refusing the GLO the first instance judge did note that the application could be brought again at a later stage). Certainly, the overriding objective is relevant to the exercise of discretion – not least because such orders are case management orders – and the court will be keen to ensure that those cases which would be valuable enough to proceed on their own (in contrast to those where the low quantum would make it uneconomical to proceed but for a GLO) will, by the making of a GLO, proceed *more* quickly and *more* cost-effectively for the parties and the court. In this regard, management of the Group Register is critical. Despite this, however, Part 19 lays down virtually no criteria about whether, when, by whom or how specific criteria should be chosen and applied to control entry onto the Register (in this sense, the old ad hoc discretionary approach is preserved).[5]

---

5   In the Myodil litigation the defendants obtained two cut-off dates – one for claimants to notify them of potential claims and a second for putative claimants to serve individual statements of case. However, note that because of the long latency period of vCJD in the Creutzfeldt-Jakob Disease litigation the cut off dates to join the litigation are likely to be long. The effective date for breach probably ends in 1996. See www.telegraph.co.uk/health/healthnews/7168326/Does-vCJD-still-pose-a-major-public-health-threat.html and Clinical Risk (September 2011) Vol 17, No 5, pp 192–194; *Latrogenic Creutzfeldt-Jakob Disease: litigation in the UK and elsewhere* Clinical Risk (January 2005) Vol 11, No 1, pp 4–13, David Body and Jonathan Glasson.

Three issues, besides liability and causation which, in practice, often arise where GLOs are in place are (a) calculating damages, (b) distribution of damages, and (c) costs.[6]

Most multi-party actions settle. However, it will often be prohibitively expensive to calculate the true value of all of those claims on the Group Register. Two approaches are regularly used.

In the first approach, damages calculations can be based on the hypothetical average group member's damage, rather than a specific assessment of each individual claimant. That is then multiplied by the number of claimants on the Group Register and a global sum calculated. The criticism of this approach is that it will tend to overcompensate those claimants with vastly weaker claims and undercompensate those claimants with very strong claims. This approach will tend to depend on the disparity in individual merits across the population of the Group.

The second approach is for aggregate damage awards, where the management court or defendants consider what injury has been done to the Group without having to resolve matters per individual claim. So long as the evidence is reliable and a reasonable degree of accuracy can be achieved, this method has found favour in a number of jurisdictions, not least because it avoids a multiplicity of hearings on damages. It seems clear that each method gives rise to conflicts of interest between group members – both in calculation of the central pot and in its distribution – but these must be balanced against the cost (time and money) of not reaching a swift conclusion.

The costs of multi-party litigation will undoubtedly be large, which is indicative from the courts' willingness today to make costs capping orders placing ceilings on Group costs. The approach adopted by the courts to the apportionment of costs tends to be the same for both legally aided and privately funded claimants in that costs of lead actions are borne equally (on a several basis) by all members of the Group Register at the time the order is made. More specifically, in most cases, the court will separate those costs which are 'common costs' (ie costs which are incurred (a) in relation to the GLO issues; (b) in a claim while it is proceeding as a test claim; or (c) by the lead solicitor in administering the group litigation) and those which are individual costs (ie those costs incurred in relation to an individual claim on the group register); see CPR 48.6A, 'Costs where the court has made a group litigation order'. In practical terms, it will be difficult for claimants to obtain legal aid funding for claims involving medical products, unless there has been an earlier declaration by the relevant regulator that such a product is dangerous in its normal conditions of use.[7] Such cases will instead proceed by way of CFA if the merits are deemed strong enough.

FURTHER INFORMATION

A preliminary request for further information or clarification is governed by Part 18. Practice Direction 18 provides that, before any application

---

6   See SMC Gibbons, *Group litigation, class actions and Lord Woolf's three objectives – a critical analysis* (2008) 27(2) CJQ 208, for a comprehensive academic treatment of these issues.
7   LSC Manual, Volume 3 ('Funding Code').

is made to the court, the party desiring the information must first write to the other side asking for it. A request should be concise and strictly confined to matters which are 'reasonably necessary and proportionate to enable him to prepare his own case or to understand the case he has to meet' (the guidance that supplements CPR 18.1 further providing that such requests should only be in relation to a 'matter which is in dispute in the proceedings'). However, requests may be made in a letter rather than a separate document if they are brief. They should not be made piecemeal if they can be made in a single comprehensive document.

What information will pass as being 'reasonably necessary' for a party to prepare their own case is not totally clear in practical terms. The recipient of such a request will of course be reluctant to assist fishing expeditions, whilst, at the same time, having no wish to earn the court's rebuke and incur an adverse costs order by ignoring a reasonable and reasoned request. There is a fine line. In the clinical negligence context, one practical issue that this author has seen become the subject of a request is detailed information in relation to a party's insurance cover (and, indeed the policy itself). Speaking practically, if the recipient of a request is confident in their position, there is relatively little to lose in disclosing insurance details (especially, if that knowledge might push the requesting party toward settlement or softens their stance generally). What, however, is the position where the insurance position is ambiguous or unhelpful? Can a defendant (as will usually be the case) refuse disclosure? There is competing authority on the point. In *Harcourt* v *Griffin* [2007] EWHC 1500 (QB), a high value personal injury case, the request was allowed in circumstances that there was some real basis for concern that a realistic award might not be satisfied, albeit that such jurisdiction would be exercised cautiously. On the other hand, albeit in the commercial context, in *West London Pipeline & Storage Ltd* v *Total UK Ltd* [2008] EWHC 1296, Comm, Steel J refused a similar application, noting that insurance policies were not disclosable under Part 31 whether as part of standard disclosure or otherwise; that they did not support or adversely affect any party's case; and that they were not relevant to the issues nor did they constitute documents which might lead to a train of inquiry enabling a party to advance his own case or damage his opponent's. As a matter of legal reasoning, the judgment in *Total* is the more persuasive. Nevertheless, the lengths the courts are willing to go in pursuit of 'effective case management' – even at the expense of stretching the meaning of 'dispute' in CPR 18.1 and overriding the rule (of law and practice) that certain information should be kept from other parties – remain to be seen.

Parties, however, should note that the position in respect of seeking insurance details will be different where a claimant seeks to avail itself of indemnity by way of the (presumably) soon to be enacted Third Parties (Rights against Insurers) Act 2010. Providing claimants fulfil the criteria in Sch 1 of the Act, they will be entitled to certain information, including:

1   whether there is a contract of insurance that covers the supposed liability or might reasonably be regarded as covering it; and, if so,
2   who the insurer is;
3   what the terms of the contract are; and
4   whether the insured has been informed that the insurer has claimed not to be liable under the contract in respect of the supposed liability.

STRIKING OUT

A decision to strike out a party's statement of case is the most serious step in any proceedings, depriving that party of the opportunity to run some or all of his arguments at trial. Despite this, the power of the court to strike out a party's statement of case is broad and a key weapon in the court's case management armoury. This is borne out by the number and widely framed terms of the CPR 3.4 gateways governing the strike out discretion. Interpretation of the scope of these gateways, and when and how the court should exercise its immense discretion has, unsurprisingly, given rise to a great deal of satellite litigation in recent years, not all of which is consistent. What, however, the busy practitioner should bear in mind is, when faced with arguing for or against strike out of a party's case, (a) the court will have foremost in its mind the overriding objective; and (b) the probable merits of the arguments under consideration will therefore be a key determinant in which way the decision will go, courts naturally being reluctant to strike out arguments that may bear fruit at some future date.

Pre-1999

Before the introduction of the CPR, there was a mass of complex and indigestible authority on striking out (whether for want of prosecution, abuse of process or any other reason) garnered over many years. These cases showed off the subtle distinctions relied upon by lawyers and judges to excuse party default at almost every turn, which so characterised pre-CPR civil litigation and seriously clogged up the court system. Now, decisions on whether to strike out all or part of a party's statement of case are simply to be made in accordance with the 'justice' of the case (helpfully fleshed out in CPR 1.1(2) and, more generally defined as the balancing act between avoiding the wasting of time and financial resources, and ensuring a correct[8] outcome).

The Rules

CPR 3.4 provides that the court may strike out a 'statement of case' (see Chapter 15 for the definition of this term) if it discloses no reasonable ground for bringing or defending the claim, or is an abuse of the court's process or is otherwise likely to obstruct the just disposal of the proceedings (obstruction in this context means 'impede to a high extent'), or there has been a failure to comply with a rule, practice direction or court order. The instances in the rule are not exhaustive; thus, there is still power to strike out in respect of a vexatious litigant or for want of prosecution.

CPR 3.8 provides that any sanction (including striking out all or parts of statements of case) specified to come into effect by the rules on a certain event (referred to as 'unless' or, sometimes, 'peremptory' orders) shall do

---

8   The 'correct' outcome will often be the 'right' outcome. However, the modern emphasis upon proportionality and justness necessarily entails that the correctness of every decision under the CPR is only in as much as it is fair and proportionate in all the circumstances.

so unless the party affected makes an application for relief supported by evidence – CPR 3.9(2). This means that parties cannot any longer, between themselves, agree to waive such a sanction. Rule 3.9 provides that the court must on any such application have regard to 'all the circumstances', including the parties' conduct; whether there is a good explanation for the default; prejudice caused by the default and that which might be caused by the proposed relief; the defaulting party's history of complying with other rules, orders, practice directions and the relevant (if there is one) pre-action protocol; the administration of justice; whether the errors have been those of the party or his lawyer; and whether any trial date can still be met. The court must, at least, consider all of those considerations listed in CPR 3.9;[9] a failure to expressly do so leaving the decision on relief open to reconsideration by the appeal court (see *Azeez* v *Momson* [2008] EWHC 623, where CPR 3.9 was not expressly referred to; see also the discussion in *Woodhouse* v *Consignia Plc* [2002] EWCA Civ 275). Ultimately, however, the court must stand back and look at all of these factors in the round. The non-exhaustive list of considerations the court may have regard to means that, most typically where a statement of case has been struck out, the appeal court can also have regard to the likely merits of the defaulting party's statement of case. Where CPR 3.9 is engaged (usually by application, proceeding in accordance with Part 23[10]), the court will also have regard to the overriding objective of CPR 1.1, which includes ensuring that the case is dealt with expeditiously and fairly and allotting to it only an appropriate share of the court's resources, while taking into account the need to allot resources to other cases.

Situations analogous to strike outs

It is clear that where a party is, for example, denied the opportunity to present evidence, instruct an expert witness, or serve witness statements (which in civil proceedings stand as evidence in chief), it may be impossible to continue with their claim or defence. In this way, such sanctions are analogous to strike outs. Hence, in *Bheroo* v *Camden and Islington NHS Trust* (29 June 2000, unreported), CA, the Court of Appeal reversed a difficult to fathom decision whereby the judge had refused to allow a short extension for the service of the schedule of loss. The appeal court said there had been no irregularity in issuing the claim (as opposed to serving it) without a schedule, or a medical report for that matter, but that, even if there had been, there was no reason to refuse a short extension, particularly as that would have the effect of dismissing the claim.

The search for consistency

Previous editions of this text focused on the seemingly quixotic attitude of the courts to pre-CPR case law concerning sanctions (ie whether or

---

9   The reader will note that where a party applies to the court before the date on which any sanction is due to come into force, the court will not apply the 'relief from sanctions' provisions of the CPR, but consider the prejudice caused by the alteration of the relevant order (*Robert* v *Momentum Services Ltd* [2003] EWCA Civ 299, CA).

10   Whilst strike out decisions will often follow the application of one or more parties to the litigation, this will not always be the case, since the court has the discretion to exercise most of its powers, under the CPR, on its own initiative: see CPR 3.3.

not it is relevant). The interest was largely sparked on the one hand by an acknowledgment by judges and practitioners alike that the previous case law and practice surrounding sanctions had become irrational, disproportionate and unworkable – with huge numbers of sub-rules growing up around relief applications. However, this interest also stemmed from a growing realisation amongst many that the primary purpose of avoiding backward glances to old decisions – to save time and resources and improve the justness and consistency of decision-making (a key aspiration of modern civil procedure) – was being undermined by an increasing trend to develop more and more rules to deal with party non-compliance, and countenance satellite litigation. To put it another way, sanctions under the CPR – the aim of which are to further the overriding objective of civil justice – were having an effect completely opposite to that intended.

Nevertheless, the CPR's approach to sanctions, of which strike out is its most draconian tool, was intended to be a move away from the kind of judicial indulgence, readily seen in the old cases. For a true appreciation of the previous culture see, for example, Millet J's comments in *Logicrose Ltd* v *Southend United Football Club Ltd* (5 February 1988, unreported) where, considering an application to strike out a claimant's action in the middle of the substantive hearing on the ground that the responsible director of the claimant had 'deliberately suppressed [a crucial document] and, for a time, successfully concealed its existence from the Court', he held:

> In my view a litigant is not to be deprived of his right to proper trial as a penalty for his contempt or his defiance of the Court, but only if his conduct has amounted to an abuse of the process of the Court which would render any further proceedings unsatisfactory and prevent the Court from doing justice. Before the Court takes that serious step it needs to be satisfied that there is a real risk of this happening.

This was symptomatic of past problems, where the emphasis was on prejudice. If there was none, matters would more often than not carry on as before. More than being a history lesson, however, it is instructive to today's practitioners. We should not be surprised to find that the judicial attitude displayed in cases like *Logicrose* will not (or at least *should* not) be readily found today; court indulgence should be the exception rather than the rule. Below is a review of the key strike out cases under CPR 3.4(2)(a), (b) and (c), both where the courts have been strict and more accommodating.

Temperance

In the important case of *Biguzzi* v *Rank Leisure plc* [1999] 1 WLR 1926, the Court of Appeal, Lord Woolf presiding, recognised for the first time that draconian sanctions were not the automatic response to infringements of the new rules. One cannot in this instance do better than quote the summary in the headnote:

> Held, dismissing the appeal, that under the Civil Procedure Rules 1998 the keeping of time limits was very important and the court had an unqualified discretion under rule 3.4(2)(c) to strike out a case where a litigant failed to comply with the Rules or an order of the court; but that under the Rules the

court had broad powers and, in many cases, there would be alternatives to the draconian step of striking out the claim that would make clear that the court would not tolerate delay but would also, in accord with the overriding objective in Part 1 of the Rules, enable the case to be dealt with justly; that judges had to be trusted to exercise their wide discretion fairly and justly in all the circumstances, while recognising their responsibility to litigants in general not to allow the same defaults to occur as had occurred in the past, and the Court of Appeal would not interfere unless relevant principles had been contravened; and that, accordingly, since the judge had applied the relevant principles in exercising his discretion, the court would not interfere with his decision.

On an application by the defendant to extend the time for service of witness statements, in *Mealey Horgan plc* v *Horgan* (1999) Times, 6 July, Buckley J said it would be unjust to exclude a party from giving evidence at trial save in very rare circumstances, eg where there had been deliberate flouting of court orders, or inexcusable delay such that the only way the court could fairly entertain the evidence would be by adjourning the trial. *Mealey* is also a good illustration of the courts' reliance upon the concept of proportionality to allow appeals from refusals to grant relief from sanctions (see also *Whittaker* v *Soper* [2001] EWCA Civ 1462, CA, at [37]–[38]).

Note also the reluctance of the appeal courts to interfere with a judge's discretion to strike out a statement of case, and sanctions more generally. By way of example, see *Woodward* v *Finch* (8 December 1999, unreported), CA, where the Court of Appeal, Lord Woolf again presiding, refused to interfere with the judge's exercise of his discretion in favour of the claimant, saying that it had not been shown that he had contravened any recognised principle. The key points to have in mind where a sanction has been imposed (the consequences of which the first instance judge has refused to waive) are that (a) the lower courts are trusted to consider the full suite of sanctions available to them when imposing any sanction; and (b) when considering relief applications, courts are expected to go through the CPR 3.9 considerations. If the courts adopt this guidance, appellate interference will be restrained (*Bansal* v *Cheema* [2000] MLC 0380, CA, below).

In *AXA Insurance Co* v *Swire Fraser* (2000) Times, 19 January, CA, the Court of Appeal held that CPR 3.4(2)(c) gave the court a wide discretion which did not require proof of prejudice to a party if the action were to proceed, though the question of prejudice would still be relevant to the court's decision (although compare the marked difference in emphasis here with that of *Logicrose*, above). The new rules simply enabled the court to adopt a more flexible approach. Further, the discretion enabled the court to strike out actions where there had been deliberate default or a failure to comply with a court order without resort to the court's inherent jurisdiction to strike out actions for abuse of process.

In *McLoughlin* v *Grovers* [2001] EWCA Civ 1743, the Court of Appeal said that a claim for damages for psychiatric illness caused by solicitors' negligent preparation of the claimant's criminal defence should not have been struck out as not being reasonably foreseeable in tort or too remote in contract. Preliminary issues should usually be questions of law decided on the basis of a schedule of agreed or assumed facts.

In *Walsh* v *Misseldine* (29 February 2000, unreported), CA, the court, exercising its own discretion by consent of the parties, emphasised that a flexible approach should be taken in every case suited to the instant facts, and demonstrated how an order could be framed to meet the justice of the particular case (no strike out, but no enlargement of claimant's pleading or schedule allowed).

In *Godden* v *Kent and Medway Strategic Health Authority* [2004] EWHC 1629, Gray J declined to strike out an action by patients against their GP where, he said, it was arguable that a health authority could be held liable vicariously for the acts of a GP who had indecently assaulted and possibly negligently treated his patients (this kind of case, where claimants seek to push at the edges of the common law, is further discussed below).

In *Cank* v *Broadyard Associates Ltd* [2000] MLC 0382, CA, the court criticised the decisions of two County Court judges in making and confirming a strike out of the defence for failure to comply with an order made in the proceedings. The judges had relied on a technical breach (the claimant received the required material only two or three days late); there was no merit in striking out an adequately particularised defence; and the second judge had failed to go through the checklist of matters in CPR 3.9, especially paras (g), (h), and (i).

A hard line

In contrast, strike out remains the appropriate remedy in the more serious case (*UCB Corporate Services Ltd* v *Halifax (SW) Ltd* (1999) Times, 23 December, CA). *Biguzzi* was not intended to give greater leniency to a claimant than he would have had under the old regime.

Wholesale disregard of an order for setting down led the court to uphold the striking out order in *Shikari* v *Malik* (1999) Times, 20 May, CA. It was said that litigants cannot rely on the court tolerating what had been tolerated previously under the old rules. The court also said that the exercise of discretion was not limited by the decision in *Hytec Information Systems* v *Coventry City Council* [1997] 1 WLR 1666, where the Court of Appeal, presided over by Lord Woolf, had said that a party was generally bound by the conduct, ie the errors, of his legal representative. *Hytec,* though a pre-CPR case, also provides enduring and noteworthy guidance about intentional bad behaviour. The Court of Appeal noted that:

> If a party intentionally or deliberately flouts the order he can expect no mercy. He has to persuade the court that in all the circumstances, the injustice to him outweighs the interest of the administration of justice and the injury to the other party (per Ward LJ, at p 1674).

In *Cheltenham Laminating Co* v *Polyfibre Ltd* (12 October 1999, unreported), CA, with both parties in substantial default, the court nevertheless upheld the refusal to extend the time for service of statements and the consequent striking out of the claim, stating that under the new regime, fairness did not depend solely on the basis of fairness to the parties themselves, but also to other litigants and any delay would affect other proceedings.

Simon J declined to strike out a claim arising out of the well known report of the British Geological Survey assessing the hydrochemical charter of the main aquifer units of central and north-eastern Bangladesh and possible toxicity of groundwater to fish and humans in *Sutradhar* v *Natural Environment Research Council* (8 May 2003), QBD. He stated that the concept of proximity in the context of duty of care could not be determined in isolation from the concepts of foreseeability of harm and fairness (the oft-relied upon justification for judicial leniency at this stage of proceedings). However the Court of Appeal ([2004] EWCA Civ 175) allowed the defendant's appeal by a majority and struck the claim out, saying that there was clearly insufficient proximity between the parties for a duty of care to arise.

For a particularly unattractive decision from the Court of Appeal, refusing to interfere with a strike out ordered by the district judge and confirmed by the Recorder, see *Nascimento* v *Kerrigan* (1999) Times, 23 June. In this personal injury claim, there had been a mere failure to provide a translation of the Portuguese medical report. The court emphasised that after one appeal the test for success in a further appeal was more stringent. See also *Collins* v *CPS Fuels Ltd* [2001] EWCA Civ 1597, where the Court of Appeal upheld a strike-out for procedural non-compliance notwithstanding that:

(a) the defendant had conceded the issue of liability;
(b) the claimant's delay had not resulted in any prejudice to the defendant, and in fact was necessary to allow the extent of the claimant's injuries to emerge; and
(c) the failure was that of the claimant's solicitor, and not of the claimant herself.

A case with extreme facts, (thankfully) not likely to be often replicated, is that of *Raja* v *Van Hoogstraten* [2006] EWHC 1315, Ch. There, Lightman J struck out the defence and counterclaim of a convicted murderer on grounds that, by murdering an opposing party (whose evidence would have been prominent in any trial), the defendant had rendered a fair trial impossible, the said conduct amounting to an abuse of process.

Another bite of the cherry[11]

In *Securum Finance Ltd* v *Ashton* [2000] 3 WLR 1400, CA, the court said that there was no longer a principle that a second action begun within the limitation period after the first action had been struck out for inordinate and inexcusable delay should *not* be struck out, save in exceptional circumstances. The pursuit of the new action will be weighed against the overriding objective of dealing with cases justly and, in particular, the court's need to allot its limited resources to other cases (r 1.1(2)(e) is in point in such cases). Essentially, the question will be asked whether the right to bring a second claim disproportionately interferes with the rights of other litigants to use the court's resources. In *Ashton*, the court echoed the words of the earlier case of *Arbuthnot Latham Bank Ltd* v *Trafalgar Holdings Ltd* [1998] 1 WLR 1426 (one of the earliest and most striking proclamations of the new procedural approach under the CPR), to the effect that wholesale disregard of the rules would now be regarded as an abuse of process justifying a striking out order.

---

11 See further Chapter 18 on Limitation.

Where, however, the limitation period for issuing a claim form has expired in-between a court striking out a party's statement of case as an abuse and that party re-serving a new claim form in the same matter, the court's approach was recently detailed in the clinical negligence case of *Leeson* v *Marsden and United Bristol Healthcare NHS Trust* [2008] EWHC 1011 (QB). Cox J made clear that what the court is *not* being asked to do is weigh, separately, whether the second claim involves an appropriate use of court resources and whether what has occurred amounts to an abuse, quite separately from considering all the other factors in the case, which otherwise fall properly to be considered under the Limitation Act 1980, s 33. The correct approach, therefore, is not to fetter judicial discretion by considering abuse arguments separately – an argument dismissed by Cox J – but to consider matters in the round, weighing up the balance of prejudice as required in s 33 applications to disapply the primary limitation period (the abuse issue being just one factor).[12] Until recently, there was some doubt about how to resolve *Leeson* with other cases on this issue. In *Dixie* v *British Polythene Industries Ltd* [2010] EWCA Civ 1170, the Court of Appeal attempted to lay the matter to rest. There it was noted that a mere negligent failure to serve a claim form in time was not, without more, an abuse of process (something more is required being, for example, inordinate and excusable delay, or wholesale disregard of the rules, or contumelious default). Interestingly, in contrast to Cox J's comments, Rix LJ did note that:

1   a second set of proceedings could be struck out for abuse in the first set of proceedings, whether or not the second was started in time, without recourse to s 33 considerations – since the courts are the ultimate arbiters of access to them; but

2   that even if the first action is struck out as abusive, if the second action cannot be determined 'in the abstract' it might be necessary to consider the question of abuse as part of the s 33 considerations (which though presented as the same approach taken in *Leeson*, strikes the author as more qualified).

SUMMARY JUDGMENT

CPR, Part 24 deals with summary judgment, which, if it is the defendant who is asking for it, is in effect a striking out application. This coinciding was expressly recognised in *Taylor* v *Midland Bank Trust Co Ltd (No 2)* [2002] WTLR 95 (although note *Moroney* v *Anglo-European College of Chiropractice* [2009] EWCA Civ 1560, see below). The court can give summary judgment against a party on the claim or on a particular issue if it considers that a party has no real prospect of succeeding on the claim/the defence or on the particular issue, and that there is no other compelling reason why the case or issue should be disposed of at a trial.

---

12   It remains to be seen, however, whether Cox J's approach can be resolved with authorities, such as *Aldi Stores Ltd* v *WSP Group Plc* [2007] EWCA Civ 1260, which make plain that, in considering whether pleadings etc are an abuse of process, it is not a question of the exercise of discretion, but rather there is only one correct answer. In this regard, also see the recent county court decision in *Dixie* v *British Polythene Ltd* (8 July 2009, unreported) CC (London).

Meanwhile, Practice Direction 3A, para 1.6 states that a defence may fall within CPR 3.4(2)(a) if it consists of a bare denial or otherwise sets out no coherent statement of facts, or the facts it sets out, while coherent, would not, even if true, amount in law to a defence to the claim. The court, therefore, has the discretion of dealing with cases on either a striking out or summary judgment basis, asking itself (in relation to either mechanism) whether the relevant argument has a realistic prospect of success. The starting point for any summary judgment application is *Swain* v *Hillman* [2000] PIQR P51, CA. On an appeal by the defendant from the refusal of summary judgment under CPR 24.2, the court, Lord Woolf presiding, said that 'no real prospect of succeeding' meant no realistic, as opposed to fanciful, prospect of success. Where there were issues which should be considered at trial, it would not be appropriate to – in effect – strike out the claim or, for that matter, the defence.

Despite the cross-over, practitioners would do well to note two points: first, that recourse to Part 24 *on top* of a strike out application will not infrequently be unhelpful (as was recently confirmed by the Court of Appeal in *Moroney* (above), with reference to *Independents Advantage Insurance Co v Personal Representatives of Cook (Deceased)* [2003] EWCA Civ 1103, at [19]). Second, the overlap between CPR 3.4 and Part 24 is by no means total. For example:

(i) CPR 3.4 (unlike Part 24) will apply to non-compliance with a rule, practice direction or court order;
(ii) Part 24 (unlike CPR 3.4) can apply to the summary disposal of specific issues, such as preliminary issues; and
(iii) a number of procedural hurdles present in Part 24 applications are absent from those proceeding under CPR 3.4.

FACTORS LIMITING DISMISSAL

Even on those occasions where the courts favour strike out, there are two factors in particular which strongly militate against the use of the court's power of strike out (whether by summarily determining a party's case or by upholding the effects of a particularly draconian unless order). The first is the human rights issue of a fair trial. The second is that the House of Lords is taking an innovative approach to negligence. Today, the two factors frequently overlap: human rights can lead to a developing jurisprudence as well as demanding that any interim or final decision in litigation be consistent with the Article 6 fair trial requirement of the Convention.

Article 6[13]

The courts must be aware of the possibility, even the likelihood, of a challenge on human rights grounds. In *S* v *Gloucestershire County Council* [2001] 2 WLR 909, CA, the court said that a summary trial could be a fair hearing within the meaning of Article 6(2) (it added that a claim for damages for sexual abuse by foster parents would only be

---

13 See further Chapter 21 on Human Rights.

struck out in the clearest case). Generally, the court would have to be satisfied, before it struck out a claim, that all substantial facts relevant to the allegations of negligence were before the court and that there was no real prospect of their being disputed or of oral evidence affecting the court's assessment of them (often, in fact, it will go one step further and, for the sake of argument, accept that the disputed facts founding the action will be proved). Accordingly, in *Swain* v *Hillman*, above, Lord Woolf presiding, said that 'no real prospect of succeeding' meant no realistic, as opposed to fanciful, prospect of success. Where there were issues which should be considered at trial, it would not be appropriate to – in effect – strike out the claim or, for that matter, the defence. He said the court was not to conduct a mini-trial at this stage. One might further question whether recent cases have, as a matter of practice, tightened the 'fanciful' test to one that requires cases to be 'doomed to fail' before they will be ripe to be struck out pursuant to either CPR 3.4(2)(a) or CPR 24.2(a)(i). See for example, the approach of the High Court in the personal injury action brought by victims and their families in respect of exposure to radiation of nuclear weapon testing in *AB* v *Ministry of Defence* [2009] EWHC 1225, QB.

Fifteen years ago (before the introduction of the Human Rights Act 1998), the House of Lords delivered a unanimous and fully reasoned decision in the two cases of *X (minors)* v *Bedfordshire County Council* and *M (a minor)* v *Newham London Borough Council* [1995] 2 AC 633 to the effect that professionals involved in investigating suspected abuse cases in exercise of a statutory duty did not also owe a duty of care at common law to the children concerned, let alone to the parents. However, several years later the ECtHR in Strasbourg decided that the five children in the *Bedfordshire* case had been neglected to such an extent by the local authority that it amounted to a violation of Article 3 of the Convention (inhuman and degrading treatment), and they awarded the very large (for Strasbourg) sum of compensation of £320,000 (*Z* v *United Kingdom* (2001) 34 EHRR 97). Further, both child and mother succeeded in Strasbourg in the *Newham* case in establishing a violation of Article 8 (respect for family life) (*TP and KM* v *United Kingdom* (2001) 34 EHRR 42). The negligence in this latter case lay in the failure of the health professional to listen to the child's account with proper attention, as a result of which the mother's partner was suspected of abuse and the child was removed from the mother's care for almost a year. The Strasbourg decision was based not on the decision to remove the child but on the failure to disclose the authority's 'evidence' to the mother immediately after the removal, an action which would apparently have led to them revising their decision. Since then, it has been generally accepted that, given the view of Strasbourg, a duty to act with appropriate care is in fact owed to the child in these cases, for otherwise English law would be in contravention of human rights. This change in the law was declared by the Court of Appeal in the case heard on appeal in the House of Lords (judgment was given by their Lordships in *JD (FC)* v *East Berkshire Community Health NHS Trust* [2005] UKHL 23).

It is unsurprising then that this combination of developing jurisprudence and human rights has, generally speaking, made our courts wary about striking out claims at an early stage of proceedings. Nevertheless, strike out is what the House of Lords did in the *East*

Berkshire case. The claimants were parents who were wrongly suspected of child abuse through the misdiagnosis of their children by doctors. Each in consequence suffered psychiatric disorder. In each case the true explanation for the child's condition was not discovered until regrettably late. The question was whether the doctors investigating the possibility of abuse against a child owed a duty not merely to the child but also to the parents. Only Lord Bingham considered the matter to be arguable and that therefore the claim should not be struck out. The other judges considered the arguments for the claimants to be clearly unsustainable and so the actions were struck out.

More recently, the issue of Article 6 in relief from sanctions cases has been reconsidered. In *Momson* v *Azeez* [2009] EWCA Civ 202, CA (a co-ownership case), the Court of Appeal considered, having been debarred from defending himself from and counterclaiming in an action brought by his former partner for breaching an unless order, whether on the morning of the scheduled trial it was just to relieve the appellant from the bar. The appellant had fallen foul of an unless order in respect of disclosure for conveyancing records (in his control) critical to the respondent's claim, so much so that it was found he had 'prevaricated and dragged his heels to try to delay, hinder and avoid [the respondent's] claim' (per Briggs J). In accordance with Arden LJ's guidance in *Stolzenburg* v *CIBC Mellon Trust Co Ltd* [2004] EWCA Civ 827, CA (at [161]), Rimer LJ held that the refusal of a court to grant relief against a debarring sanction will not contravene Article 6 provided that such refusal is proportionate and is for a legitimate purpose. As was confirmed in the more recent case of *Al Dawood Shipping Lines Ltd* v *Dynastic Maritime Incorporated* [2010] EWCA Civ 104, CA, it is clear therefore that what a court must now do is ask, first, whether the judge's decision to maintain the sanction, with or without conditions, constitutes a legitimate aim (namely, in *Azeez*, requiring the appellant to comply with an order of the court that had been made with a view to achieving a fair trial), is proportionate in the circumstances (generally the case if the outcome satisfies the overriding objective), and does not destroy the very right; and, secondly, whether it is tolerably clear from the judge's reasoning that this is so.

Development of the common law

As to the second factor, as a recent example, one may have in mind the Court of Appeal's decision in *Smith* v *Chief Constable of Sussex Police* [2008] EWCA Civ 39 where the injured victim of an attack brought a claim in negligence against the police, who allegedly had been informed of previous attacks and death threats against him but, despite having ample evidence to make an arrest, failed to take the necessary steps. The Court of Appeal considered that though 'fraught with difficulty', his negligence action against the police should not be struck out as disclosing no reasonable cause of action. It was deemed not 'doomed to failure' as it was arguable that the police owed the victim a duty of care. Although there was no claim for breach of the claimant's Convention rights, the one-year limitation period having expired, Pill LJ commented, at [53], that 'there is a strong case for developing the common law action for negligence in the light of Convention rights'. Moreover, it was 'unacceptable that a court, bound by section 6 of the 1998 Act, should judge a case such as the present by different standards depending on whether or not the claim is specifically brought under the Convention. The decision whether a duty of care exists in a particular situation should in a common law claim require a consideration of Article 2 rights' (at [57]). Although, ultimately, the House of Lords favoured conservative/public policy reasons in the field of police operations (despite a powerful dissenting opinion (again) from Lord Bingham, see *Van Colle* v *Chief Constable of the Hertfordshire Police* [2008] UKHL 50), the approach of the courts below the House of Lords remains rightly generous.

The development of the jurisprudence in education law (see *Phelps* v *Hillingdon London Borough Council* [2000] 3 WLR 776, one of four contemporaneous appeals that went to the House of Lords) illustrates the need not to stifle developing areas of law before they have taken root. The wide-ranging effect of the decision of the House of Lords is that an educational psychologist employed by a local education authority will, or is likely to, owe a duty to a pupil on whom she reports for her employer, and that a local education authority owes a general duty through its teachers to provide a suitable education for its pupils, particularly if they have special needs. In only one of the four cases under consideration had the Court of Appeal favoured the pupil.

Barrett v *Enfield London Borough Council* [1999] 3 WLR 79, HL, was a claim, struck out by the Court of Appeal and restored by the House of Lords, for negligent care of a child who had been placed in their charge under a care order (all aspects of their care were impugned, including general, domestic, educational, emotional and medical), and severe psychological and psychiatric problems were alleged to have resulted. Although the House acknowledged the likely difficulty of succeeding on such a claim, it was not willing to decide the issue of whether a duty was owed in law on the basis of assumed hypothetical facts. That should be decided on the facts as actually proved at trial. It has been said that an application to strike out should not be granted unless the court is sure the claim is bound to fail (*Hughes* v *Colin Richards and Co* [2004] EWCA Civ 266). The court cannot be sure of this in an area of developing jurisprudence since in such cases decisions as to novel points of law should be based on actual findings of fact (*Farrah* v *British Airways* (2000) Times, January 26, CA).

CIVIL RESTRAINT ORDERS

Wherever a statement of case is struck out for one of the reasons in CPR 3.4(2), the court may have recourse to its jurisdiction to make a civil restraint order (CRO). It *must* consider whether it is appropriate to make a CRO (in accordance with CPR 3.4(6)) when it strikes out a statement of case and, at the same time, considers it to be 'totally without merit'. A statement of case (and, by parity of reasoning, application notice, or application for permission to appeal) will be totally without merit where it is hopeless and bound to fail and essentially 'vexatious' (for an exposition of this term in the context of CROs, see *Bhamjee* v *Forsdick and Others Practice Note* [2003] EWCA Civ 1113, CA, at [7]).

In the experience of this author, a CRO is more often considered by the court, in the clinical negligence context, in low value claims against medical professionals (which may simply be a consequence of higher value claims having the benefit of legal advice and therefore being less likely to be totally without merit).

The making, varieties and consequences of CROs are governed by CPR 3.11, which makes provision for Practice Direction 3C. There it is made clear that there are three varieties:

- Limited CROs, where a party has made two or more applications which are totally without merit.
- Extended CROs, on the other hand, are deemed appropriate where a party has persistently issued claims or made applications which are totally without merit.
- General CROs, however, are for where a party persists in issuing claims or making applications which are totally without merit, in circumstances where an extended civil restraint order would not be sufficient or appropriate.

Most practitioners will more regularly come across limited CROs, ie those limited to the particular proceedings which prevent that party from making further applications in those proceedings, subject to further orders by the court. On the other hand, the vice at which the extended civil restraint order is directed is the party who issues and makes applications in more than one set of proceedings (see *Connah* v *Plymouth Hospitals NHS Trust* [2006] EWCA Civ 1616, CA). Interestingly, where a series of claims have been instituted, a CRO may even be made notwithstanding the fact that some of the claims apparently have merit, see *Thakerar* v *Lynch Hall & Hornby* [2005] EWHC 2751, Ch.

MEDICAL REPORTS[14]

The starting point in relation to experts (including medical experts) is that such evidence shall be restricted to that which is reasonably required to resolve proceedings (r 35.1).

Reports on the claimant's present medical condition, and his prognosis for the future, will be exchanged in the usual way, and agreed if possible. A claimant who unreasonably refuses to allow an examination by a defendant's expert is likely to have his action stayed (*Edmeades* v *Thames Board Mills Ltd* [1969] 2 QB 67, CA); but the onus of showing unreasonableness is on the defendant, who needs to show, if a stay is to be granted, that their case cannot properly be prepared without such an examination (*Lane* v *Willis* [1972] 1 WLR 326, CA). The court is unlikely to require the claimant to submit to an examination which is unpleasant, painful or risky, unless the interests of justice demand it (cf *Aspinall* v *Sterling Mansell Ltd* [1981] 3 All ER 866 with *Prescott* v *Bulldog Tools Ltd* [1981] 3 All ER 869).

In *Smith* v *Ealing, Hammersmith and Hounslow Health Authority* [1997] 8 Med LR 290 (a pre-CPR case, as with most in this area), the Court of Appeal refused an application to stay the action until the

---

14 For a more detailed discussion on the use of experts in the clinical negligence context see Chapter 20.

claimant submitted to a psychiatric examination, where he was claiming damages for a failed cosmetic operation on his face but was not claiming psychiatric injury. Conflict over a request for a medical examination of the claimant is not uncommon in claims for birth asphyxia leading to brain damage and cerebral palsy. Defendants will ask for a magnetic resonance (MR) scan because the result can sometimes demonstrate, by locating the site of the injury, that it must have occurred much earlier in the pregnancy, thus exonerating them from liability. Objection may be taken by the parents on the ground that a general anaesthetic would be required for the procedure and that that carries a small risk of serious harm. In *Hill* v *West Lancashire Health Authority* [1997] 8 Med LR 196, Gage J held that in such circumstances it was a question of carrying out the exercise of balancing the reasonableness of the request against the reasonableness of the refusal, and he found that the balance in the end came down in favour of the claimant because of the risk of harm. In *Laycock* v *Lagoe* [1997] PIQR 518, the Court of Appeal streamlined the test applied in *Hill* where the defendant was applying for an action for damages following a whiplash injury to be stayed until the claimant underwent an MR scan (there was an issue about the cause of cerebral atrophy, which the defendant said might be resolved by such a procedure). There, Kennedy LJ stated the test as follows:

> First, do the interests of justice require the test which the defendant proposes? If the answer to that is in the negative, that is the end of the matter. If the answer is yes, then the court should go on to consider whether the party who opposes the test has put forward a substantial reason for that test not being undertaken; a substantial reason being one that is not imaginary or illusory.

In exceptional cases, where, for example, the liability of the *defendant* depends largely upon his medical condition, the court has power to stay proceedings if he does not submit to a medical examination (see *Lacey* v *Harrison* [1993] PIQR P10, where the issue was whether the defendant was capable of remembering the accident to which he was the only witness).

As a matter of practice, the claimant may be allowed a friend to be present at the examination if he is nervous or if the doctor has a reputation for roughness, but he does not have a legal right to insist in every case that his own doctor be present when he is examined by the defendants' doctor unless there is a good and substantial reason (*Hall* v *Avon Area Health Authority (Teaching)* [1980] 1 WLR 481, CA; and see *Whitehead* v *Avon County Council* (1995) 29 BMLR 152, where the Court of Appeal refused an application by a nervous patient to have a friend present at a psychiatric examination). However, it is hard to see why a claimant, obviously nervous and possibly unwell, should be made to go through the trauma (as some claimants will no doubt consider it) of seeing the defendants' doctor alone, especially when the impartiality of defendants' doctors is not sufficiently universal to warrant the judge's confidence.

If the claimant shows good reason for objecting to a particular doctor, the court is likely to be sympathetic (*Starr* v *National Coal Board* [1977] 1 WLR 63, CA).

Then there arises the question whether a claimant who submits to an examination by the defendants' doctor is entitled to see the report. The short answer is no. Of course, if the claimant's solicitors made it a condition of their agreeing to the examination that the report should be disclosed, the court will order disclosure, and if the defendants want to rely in court on this report as to condition and prognosis, they will have to disclose it in good time, but it is a privileged document and they cannot be obliged to disclose it if they do not intend to rely on it. The court will not be quick to spell out an implied agreement to disclose even where the claimant has submitted to a medical examination by the defendants' doctor and shown his own doctor's reports to the defendants and they have been agreed (see *Causton* v *Mann Egerton (Johnsons) Ltd* [1974] 1 WLR 162, CA). In *Megarity* v *D J Ryan & Sons Ltd* [1980] 2 All ER 832, the Court of Appeal refused to endorse the practice that had from time to time been followed previously of requiring the claimant to submit to medical examination only upon the condition that the ensuing report be disclosed to him. The Court of Appeal reached a similar conclusion in *Hookham* v *Wiggins Teape Fine Papers Ltd* [1995] PIQR P392. Although it appears that at one time Lord Woolf was suggesting that every report obtained by a party should be disclosed, this has not become law (in the author's view, a good thing given the negative implications it would have in the serious clinical negligence context in particular).

In *Beck* v *Ministry of Defence* [2004] PIQR P1, CA, the defendant at a late stage in the case wanted to change its psychiatric expert as it had, it said, lost all confidence in its original expert as having proper knowledge of the relevant psychiatric issues in the case. Naturally the claimant's solicitors refused access for a new psychiatric examination. In the Court of Appeal, Simon Brown LJ had some sympathy with the defendant's position, in that this was a high value case, involving allegations against their psychiatric personnel, and without a further report they would be proceeding with an expert in whom they had no confidence. He said that, although it would be unfair to require a defendant upon such an application to argue in detail as to why the original report and the original expert were now deemed to be unsatisfactory because that would give the claimant unfair ammunition for cross-examination of their expert if the application were refused, nevertheless, once it had been decided that the defendant should be permitted to instruct another expert, there were very good reasons why the original report should be disclosed. One reason was that otherwise the claimant would be left wondering if the original expert had decided the claim was a good one. He added that there might be a case where such a condition of disclosure should not be attached to the permission, but it was not easy to envisage one. Ward LJ agreed, saying that expert shopping was to be discouraged and requiring the report to be disclosed was a check against possible abuse. The Master of the Rolls, agreeing, said that a claimant can properly object in any personal injury case to submitting to a second examination without good reason being shown for it. No second examination should be permitted if it appears to be 'a possibility' that the reason a defendant wants a fresh expert is that the first expert has reached a conclusion more favourable to the claimant than the defendant expected. Expert shopping was to be discouraged.

However, following *Beck*, in *Hajigeorgiou* v *Vasiliou* [2005] EWCA Civ 236, CA, the Court of Appeal held that the defendant would be entitled to appoint a second expert in his property litigation without disclosing the first expert's report (as was ordered at first instance), since the order granting permission for each party to appoint one expert, which had been settled by counsel, had not specified a named expert, even though the defendant's solicitors had made it clear in applying for that order that they intended to appoint a Mr Watson, having adduced evidence of his suitability. Interestingly, Dyson LJ took the opportunity to note (*obiter*) that where permission is needed, as in *Beck*, it was not only 'final' expert reports that were required to be disclosed but also any expert's report(s) containing the 'substance' of his opinion (ie privilege would be waived in respect of all of those issues to which that expert opined during the course of his instruction).

In *Allen* v *Dr S R Burne* [2007] EWHC 1639, QB, the issue of 'expert shopping' was once again considered. The protected party, having initially succeeded in a clinical negligence claim against his GP, subsequently overturned on appeal, sought to change his medical expert before the retrial ordered by the Court of Appeal. The case is interesting because the claimant had actually *heard* the evidence his expert would give first time round (albeit he was dissatisfied with it), rather than predicting it, meaning that any order disclosing evidence would have been of little concern to the claimant if permission to rely on another's expert report was granted. In any case, the High Court considered the same principles referred to above would still apply. Moreover, it held that the order for a 'retrial' in the Court of Appeal did not mean a complete procedural reboot, absent any 'special reason' to substitute his evidence, and permission to adduce new expert evidence was denied.

Most recently, in *Edwards-Tubb* v *J D Weatherspoon Plc* [2011] EWCA Civ 136, the *Beck-Vasiliou* debate was re-opened. The question in issue was when a claimant has obtained a medical report from expert A, but chose not to rely on it, instead seeking leave to rely on the evidence of expert B in the same field, ought it to be a condition of reliance on expert B that the report of expert A be disclosed? Hughes LJ, giving judgment for the Court of Appeal, answered by noting that there was no difference of principle between a change of expert instructed for the purpose of proceedings pre-issue and a change of expert only instructed, for the same purpose, post-issue – most of all because litigation privilege could be claimed in either scenario and so the rationale for disclosure in one and not the other was unsupportable. 'The claimant [is presented] with a price which must be paid for the leave of the court to rely on expert B; that price is waiver of privilege in relation to expert A', Hughes LJ noted, at [11]. However, he concluded that, whilst such an order is a matter of discretion, it is a power which 'should usually be exercised where the change comes after the parties have embarked upon the protocol and thus engaged with each other in the process of the claim', at [31]. His Lordship was less certain that the justification for disclosure was as strong where the first report was obtained pre-issue, albeit such discretion still exists.

Nevertheless, an important question arises from the jurisprudence on this issue: Does it, therefore, follow that where:

(a)   no order has yet been made for a specific, named expert;

and, in respect of defendants, where:

(b)   it is not necessary to have the claimant (re)examined,

disclosure of the first report might be avoided?

As the law presently stands, the answer must be that it does not have to be, although unlike disputes concerning the valuation of businesses

(*Vasiliou*), it will not often be the case that an examination can be foregone by the second expert. A rare occurrence, in the clinical negligence context, might be where a defendant, having appointed a medical expert for both condition and prognosis and, separately, breach and causation, wishes to obtain a second opinion on breach and causation. A second expert may well be able to be instructed, whilst relying, if necessary, upon the condition and prognosis report of the first expert. Although it will generally be obvious to other parties (and the court) that the first expert was asked to opine on both issues, that appears nothing to the point, as privilege will not need to be waived.

WITNESS STATEMENTS

The witness statement served from a witness called to give evidence stands as his evidence unless the court orders otherwise (CPR 32.2). With the permission of the court, he may amplify his statement at the trial and give evidence of new matters which have arisen since his statement was served on the other side. But permission will only be given where the judge considers that there is good reason not to confine his evidence to the contents of his statement (CPR 32.5). Note that if a party does not call a witness in respect of whom a statement has been served and does not put in the statement as hearsay evidence, the other party may put it in as hearsay evidence (CPR 32.5).[15] This clarifies the conflict between earlier authorities. In *Youell* v *Bland Welch & Co Ltd (No 3)* [1991] 1 WLR 122, Phillips J decided that not only did a statement of a witness lose its privileged status when served, but also that the court had a discretion to admit it in evidence on the application of the party on whom it had been served if its maker was not called to give evidence by the serving party (see also *Black & Decker Inc* v *Flymo Ltd* [1991] 1 WLR 753 (Hoffmann J). But in *Balkanbank* v *Taher* (1994) Times, 19 February, Clarke J, as well as holding that service of witness statements did not waive privilege in respect of connected documents, said that the party serving the statement retained an absolute right whether or not to call the witness or to put in as evidence all or part of the statement (see also *Booth* v *Warrington Health Authority* [1992] PIQR P137). A witness statement may be used only for the purpose for which it is served (CPR 32.12). If a witness statement is not served within the time specified by the court, the permission of the court is required if the witness is to be called (repeated party delays will, under the CPR, often be the subject of unless orders and other sanctions). Practice Direction 32 sets out detailed rules for the preparation of witness statements.

SUBMISSION OF NO CASE TO ANSWER

This is a useful (but very rarely used) tool for the defence and may properly be employed at the trial at the end of the claimant's evidence,

---

15 A party who has served a witness statement cannot be compelled to call that witness (*Society of Lloyd's* v *Jaffray* (2000) Times, 3 August).

usually in order to save costs, where the defendant genuinely believes that the claimant's evidence has not got over the initial evidential hurdle of making out a *prima facie* case. In any event, defendants will generally find judges relatively unenthusiastic about upholding a submission of no case to answer. In the first instance, the judge will be prevented from hearing evidence (even if adduced by the defendant) which may improve his view of the claimant's evidence. Second, judges are all too aware that such decisions carry an inherent risk of wasting further court resources in satellite litigation and rehearings, for the (usually) limited saving of determining the action without hearing the defendant's evidence. Given this, it is clear it should not be used, as it is so often by defendants in criminal trials, to have a go at the end of the prosecution case on the basis that they have nothing to lose by trying it on, but rather in a highly focused and considered way.

Submissions of no case to answer used not to be a good idea in civil cases as the defendant could then be put to his election, ie he would not be allowed to call any evidence if his submission failed. However, in two cases at first instance it has been held that under the CPR a defendant need not be put to his election. Following *Mullan* v *Birmingham City Council* (1999) Times, 29 July, Ebsworth J held in *Worsley* v *Tambrands Ltd (No 2)* [2000] MLC 0280, without putting the defence to their election, that a submission of no case succeeded because the claimant had not made out even a *prima facie* case that the defendants had failed to give proper warnings regarding the possible connection between their product and toxic shock syndrome and what to do in the event of certain symptoms arising.

In *Saed* v *Ealing Hospital NHS Trust* MLC 0511, [2002] Lloyds Rep Med 121, a claim for failure to diagnose tuberculous meningitis and consequent severe injury, the defendant made a submission of no case to answer at the close of the claimant's case. Mackay J said that normally a defendant should be put to his election as to calling evidence, following *Boyce* v *Wyatt Engineering* Ltd [2001] ECWA Civ 692, but where it was clear that the claimant had no chance of proving negligence, then, consistently with the overriding objective of litigation and CPR 3.1(2)(m), it was neither right nor necessary to put the defendant to its election.

Practitioners may sensibly ask, nevertheless, what relationship (the seemingly alien) tool that is a submission of no case to answer has with the civil courts' more customary interim powers, namely summary judgment (see above). The simple answer is that summary judgment is used before trial, whilst a submission of no case to answer is only deployed after closure of the claimant's evidence during trial. As to the critical issue of the standard of proof the court should adopt in either, the reality is that they vary little: in this regard the claimant gets something of the benefit of the doubt, with the courts adopting the 'real prospect of success' threshold from Part 24, and not assessing whether the claimant's evidence has established his case on the balance of probabilities (widely accepted to be a higher threshold). However, in *Benham Ltd* v *Kythira Investments Ltd* [2003] EWCA Civ 1794, CA, the Court of Appeal went further, suggesting that so long as a claimant provides a scintilla of evidence to support the inference for which they contend, unlike in summary judgment applications, judges should clearly recognise the real possibility that the defendant, if his submission failed, might choose to call no evidence (or, indeed, call evidence which in the event proved helpful to the claimant), thereby entitling the court to draw adverse inferences which strengthened the claimant's case. It is clear then that dismissing a claimant's claim at the half-way stage is not a jurisdiction to be exercised lightly.

Part Four

Chapter 17

The inquest

Linda Jacobs
Caron Heyes – Funding and the recoverability of costs

INTRODUCTION

If there is going to be an inquest, efforts should be made to make the most of the opportunity to find out what the hospital and/or GP says about the circumstances surrounding the death. Hospital staff and GPs should also use the opportunity to provide an explanation, and to allay any rumour or suspicion the family or wider community may have.

Coronial law is currently governed in England and Wales by the Coroners Act 1988 and the Coroners Rules 1984.[1] There are approximately 110 different Coroners' districts in England and Wales. Each jurisdiction is funded and resourced by a local authority or authorities; and the facilities and resources available to different Coroners vary. Coroners are independent judicial officers and are barristers, solicitors, or medical practitioners of at least five years' experience.[2] There are only 32 full-time Coroners in England and Wales; the remainder are employed on a part-time basis and are paid according to the number of cases that are referred to them.[3] A criticism expressed by the Shipman Inquiry was that Coroners differ significantly in their practices and there is a lack of uniformity in the interpretation of the statutory provisions.[4]

Coroners are assisted by Coroner's Officers whom are often retired police officers or police officers on secondment. There is recognition that Coroner's Offices should be employed from backgrounds that are more diverse as part of a change in emphasis from a coronial service focussed on crime towards a wider medical and social function.[5] The functions of Coroner's Officers vary from district to district, and include a wide range of non-standardised duties and practices. Coroner's Officers are often the first point of contact for representatives of those who are involved

---

1   SI 1984/552.
2   Coroners Act 1988, s 2.
3   www.judiciary.gov.uk/about-the-judiciary/introduction-to-justice-system/coroners.
4   *The Shipman Inquiry Third Report: Death Certification and the Investigation of Death by Coroners* (14 July 2003: Chairman Dame Janet Smith DBE), CM 5854, Chapter 7.
5   *The Shipman Inquiry Third Report: Death Certification and the Investigation of Death by Coroners* (14 July 2003: Chairman Dame Janet Smith DBE), CM 5854, Chapter 8.

in the investigation and inquest process, and many are exceptionally helpful.

The number of inquests held annually is significantly smaller that the number of deaths referred to Coroners. In 2010, approximately 230,600 deaths were reported to Coroners; representing 47% of all registered deaths.[6] However, inquests were opened in only 13% of all cases reported to Coroners.[7] The percentage of cases involving post-mortem examination, as a percentage of all deaths reported to Coroners in 2010, was approximately 44 %, representing a year-on-year decrease.[8] This chapter focuses on healthcare related deaths; and such deaths do not automatically give rise to an inquest.

REPORTING DEATHS TO THE CORONER

Coroners can only investigate deaths that are reported to them. At present, there is no statutory duty on doctors or other heath service personnel to report a death to the Coroner. Medical practitioners are often uncertain when they are required to report a death. However, in the healthcare environment, doctors report deaths to the Coroner where the cause of death is unknown; or where the deceased was not attended by a doctor during his last illness, or was neither seen within the 14 days preceding death or viewed after death by a doctor. In such circumstances, the doctor is unable to complete the Medical Certificate of Cause of Death.

Some Coroners provide guidelines to doctors working within their jurisdiction about deaths that should be reported,[9] and the Medical Protection Society has produced a non-exhaustive list as a guide for its members, including reporting to a Coroner a death that has occurred as a result of 'medical mishap'.[10] The General Medical Council states:

> You must assist the coroner ... in an inquest or inquiry into a patient's death by responding to their enquiries and by offering all relevant information. You are entitled to remain silent only when your evidence may lead to criminal proceedings being taken against you.[11]

Even if a doctor does not report a death to the Coroner, the Registrar of Births, Deaths, and Marriages must report certain deaths to the Coroner where the circumstances include a death occurring during an operation or before recovery from an anaesthetic; and a death that appears to be unnatural, or to have been caused by violence, neglect, by abortion, or occurred in suspicious circumstances.[12]

---

6   Ministry of Justice (Statistics Bulletin), *Statistics on deaths reported to coroners in England and Wales, 2010* (published May 2011): www.justice.gov.uk/coroners-deaths-reported-2011.pdf.

7   Ministry of Justice (Statistics Bulletin), *Statistics on deaths reported to coroners in England and Wales, 2009* (published May 2010): www.justice.gov.uk/coroners-deaths-reported-2010.pdf.

8   Ministry of Justice (Statistics Bulletin), *Statistics on deaths reported to coroners in England and Wales, 2009* (published May 2010): www.justice.gov.uk/coroners-deaths-reported-2010.pdf.

9   See Dorries, C, *Coroners' Courts: A Guide to Law and Practice* (2nd edition) Oxford University Press (2004) pp 62–68.

10   www.medicalprotection.org/uk/factsheets/coroner (correct as of March 2010).

11   General Medical Council, *Good Medical Practice 2006* at para 69.

12   Registration of Births and Deaths Regulations 1987, reg 41(2)(d)–(e).

There is a common law duty to report a death to the Coroner in circumstances that might require an inquest.[13] Consequently, anyone can report a death to the Coroner, including the family of a patient who dies in hospital. If a report is to be made, it is preferable to do so at the earliest opportunity so that the Coroner can collate all the essential evidence before it is no longer available. If the family have specific concerns about the treatment or care of the deceased, it is advisable to write to the Coroner at an early stage setting out their concerns. Such information often assists the Coroner in the investigation and helps identify witnesses that may be asked to provide evidence. These issues can always be developed and refined as the investigation progresses.

JURISDICTION

Once a death is reported, and the Coroner is satisfied that the body of the person is lying within his district,[14] the Coroner must consider whether he has jurisdiction to hold an inquest. The evidence considered by Coroners is not limited to admissible evidence.[15] The Coroner acquires jurisdiction to hold a mandatory inquest if there is reasonable cause to suspect that the deceased died:

(a)   a violent or unnatural death;
(b)   a sudden death of which the cause is unknown; or
(c)   in prison or in such a place or in such circumstances as to require an inquest under any other Act.[16]

An inquest can only be held where the case falls within s 8(1). There is no discretion for a Coroner to hold an inquest on the ground that he considers it to be in the public interest.[17]

Violent death

A violent death involves an injury, caused by a traumatic event that is accidental or deliberate, and with or without human intervention. The traumatic event might be self-inflicted, such as suicide.

Natural death/unnatural death

There is no statutory definition of natural or unnatural death. The Court of Appeal stated that the word 'unnatural' should be given its ordinary meaning, and that the question of natural or unnatural depends upon the cause of death, which was essentially a practical question of fact.[18] Therefore, a death that appears to be ostensibly from natural causes

---

13   *R* v *Clerk* (1702) 1 Salk 377.
14   Coroners Act 1988, s 8(1).
15   *R* v *South London Coroner, ex p Weeks* CO595 (6 December 1996, unreported), per Scott Baker J.
16   Coroners Act 1988, s 8(1).
17   *R* v *HM Coroner for Inner London North District, ex p Thomas* [1993] QB 610.
18   *R* v *HM Coroner for Inner London North District, ex p Thomas* [1993] QB 610 (also referred to as *R* v *Poplar Coroner, ex p Thomas*), per Simon Brown LJ.

may be an unnatural death for the purposes of coronial law. In *R on the application of Touche* v *Inner North London Coroner*,[19] the Court of Appeal considered whether the failure to monitor a mother's blood pressure after giving birth to twins delivered by Caesarean section that resulted in her death from a cerebral haemorrhage was an unnatural death. An experienced anaesthetist with an interest in obstetric anaesthesia gave expert evidence, and opined that the failure of the hospital staff to monitor Mrs Touche's blood pressure whilst she was receiving post-operative analgesics was 'astonishing' and described the level of neglect as 'starkly apparent'.

The Court of Appeal held that an unnatural death could be the result of neglect. The requirements are the need for basic medical attention to be obvious at the time; the patient to be dependent on others to provide that attention; and a gross failure to provide or procure the attention. Alternatively, for cases that fall outside the 'neglect' category, an unnatural death is a 'wholly unexpected death from natural causes which would not have occurred but for some culpable human failure'. It is the combination of the unexpectedness of the death and the culpable human failing that allows the death to occur which renders such deaths unnatural.[20] It is not necessary to prove a causative link between the death and the improper behaviour or treatment as this exceeds the requirement of a reasonable cause to suspect that the deceased died an unnatural death, as required by s 8(1) of the Coroners Act 1988.[21]

If a Coroner refuses to hold an inquest on the ground that it was a natural death, the family of the deceased are likely to need expert evidence of the circumstances that renders a death an unnatural death. This was the approach taken in *Canning* v *HM Coroner for the County of Northampton*.[22] In *Canning* the expert evidence failed to persuade the Coroner to hold an inquest; a decision that was upheld by the Court of Appeal.[23]

Sudden death of which the cause of death is unknown

If the cause of death is unknown and the death is reported to the Coroner, s 19(1) of the Coroners Act 1988 permits a Coroner to order a post-mortem examination where there is reasonable cause to suspect that the deceased died a sudden death of an unknown cause and the Coroner is of the opinion that a post-mortem examination may prove that an inquest is unnecessary. In such circumstances, the Coroner does not have the power to order a special examination. If the post-mortem examination reveals a natural cause of death and a mandatory inquest is not required for any reason under s 8(1) of the Coroners Act 1988, the death can be registered.[24]

From a legal perspective, a sudden death of which the cause of death is unknown appears to have two requirements. However, in *R (on the*

---

19   [2001] EWCA Civ 383, [2001] 3 WLR 148, [2001] 2 All ER 752.
20   *R* v *Inner London North Coroners, ex p Touche* [2001] EWCA Civ 383.
21   *Bicknell* v *HM Coroner for Birmingham / Solihull* [2007] EWHC 2547 (Admin).
22   [2006] EWCA Civ 1225, [2006] All ER (D) 187 (Nov).
23   See also *Bickness* v *HM Coroner for Birmingham / Solihull* [2007] EWHC 2547 (Admin), [2007] All ER (D) 166 (Nov) for a decision that went the other way.
24   Coroners Act 1988, s 19(3).

application of Kasperowicz) v *HM Coroner for Plymouth*, the Court of Appeal stated that the reason that the word 'sudden' was included in the legislation was obscure. The court stated that the purpose of the section was directed towards ensuring 'a proper ascertainment of the cause of every uncertified death'.[25] In the case of Mrs Kasperowicz, the doctor was unable to certify the cause of death and the deceased had not seen a doctor for 25 days prior to her death, although before that time she had been an inpatient. The family objected to a post-mortem examination on the basis of strong religious and personal beliefs. The Court of Appeal refused to grant permission for judicial review proceedings, stating that there was 'no question of the court halting or interrupting the process. It is a process required by law and, in so far as the coroner has exercised a judgement in requiring a post-mortem, he was plainly entitled to do so'.[26]

POST-MORTEM EXAMINATION

If the Coroner has jurisdiction to investigate a death and has decided to hold an inquest, it is likely that he will order a post-mortem examination to ascertain the cause of death;[27] although Coroners should consider whether the cause of death could be established without a post-mortem examination. Any post-mortem examination should take place as soon as practicable.[28] It may be possible to talk to the Coroners' pathologist about the results of the post-mortem examination before the inquest, but the permission of the Coroner must be sought in advance.

The post-mortem examination

There is no statutory definition of 'post-mortem examination', and it is generally understood to mean a detailed medical examination after death carried out by a pathologist. A post-mortem examination normally involves an external examination of the body, followed by dissection and removal of the major internal organs, including the heart, lungs, liver, kidneys, spleen and lungs; and may include the brain. The Coroners Act 1988 makes a distinction between a post-mortem examination and special examination. A special examination is a specific kind of post-mortem examination, and includes toxicology tests, and examination of the brain by a neuropathologist. A Coroner may order a special examination in addition to a post-mortem examination,[29] but only if he has already decided to hold an inquest.[30]

The extent of the post-mortem examination and any further special investigations depend upon the circumstances of each case. In September 2002, the Royal College of Pathologists issued its *Guidelines on autopsy practice* to address 'the wide variation in autopsy performance and

---

25 *R (on the application of Kasperowicz)* v *HM Coroner for Plymouth* [2005] EWCA Civ 44 at para 10.
26 *R (on the application of Kasperowicz)* v *HM Coroner for Plymouth* [2005] EWCA Civ 44 at para 12.
27 Coroners Act 1988, s 20.
28 Coroners Rules 1984, r 5.
29 Coroners Act 1988, s 20(1)(b).
30 Coroners Act 1988, s 20.

reporting practices, relating to inconsistent operation of the Coronial system across England and Wales'.[31] The guidelines have been supplemented with 'autopsy practice scenarios', including *Scenario 1: Sudden death with likely cardiac pathology* (Jan 2005) and *Scenario 5: Maternal death* (May 2010).[32] The guidelines may assist on reviewing the post-mortem report and questioning the pathologist at the inquest; and it is a breach of the procedural limb of Art 2 of the European Convention on Human Rights for a post-mortem examination to be ineffective.[33]

Wishes of the family

Some relatives strongly oppose a post-mortem examination on religious or ethnic grounds; and/or if deeply distressed by the thought of an invasive procedure being carried out on the body of the deceased. However, a Coroner does not require the consent of the family to order a post-mortem examination. Arguably, Art 8(1) of the European Convention on Human Rights (right to respect for private and family life) imposes a duty on Coroners to consider whether a post-mortem examination is necessary and proportionate to ascertain how a person came by his death; and this requires Coroners to make reasonable efforts to contact the family and inquire about their views on a post-mortem examination.[34] A decision by a Coroner to order a post-mortem examination where the family oppose such an examination will only be lawful if it is proportionate to the aims in Art 8(2), including, public safety; the protection of health; or to investigate a potential crime.

If the death is not suspicious, the Coroner should consider evidence from the family and medical practitioners that might enable him lawfully to avoid ordering a post-mortem examination.[35] Alternatively, it might be possible to use less invasive techniques, such as MRI scanning, to ascertain the cause of death;[36] although the Coroner, with advice from the pathologist and radiologist, will need to consider the efficacy of alternative investigations considering the particular circumstances of the death.[37] In *Kasperowicz,* the Court of Appeal stated that if the cause of death could be ascertained by less invasive means, then that was a matter of common decency and good practice as opposed to a matter of law.[38] However, there

---

31 The Royal College of Pathologists, *Guidelines on Autopsy Practice* (Report of a Working Group of The Royal College of Pathologists) September 2002, Executive Summary.

32 The guidelines and scenarios are available on the Royal College of Pathologist's website: www.rcpath.org.

33 *Kakouli v Turkey* (App No 38595/97) (Fourth Section ECHR) 22 November 2005, at 122–128.

34 *Death Certification and Investigation in England, Wales and Northern Ireland: A Report of a Fundamental Review 2003* (28 April 2003: Chairman Tom Luce), Cm 5831, Chapter 13.

35 See also *R (on the application of Kasperowicz) v HM Coroner for Plymouth* [2005] EWCA Civ 44 at para 13.

36 *R (on the application of Kasperowicz) v HM Coroner for Plymouth* [2005] EWCA Civ 44 at paras 14–15.

37 An MRI scan may not provide as much detail as a dissection post-mortem examination and there are a number of research studies examining the efficacy of MRI scanning versus a conventional post-mortem examination in identifying the cause of death.

38 *R (on the application of Kasperowicz) v HM Coroner for Plymouth* [2005] EWCA Civ 44 at para 15.

was no consideration of the fact that the Coroners Rules 1984 do not address the possibility of MRI scanning; which is an examination by a radiologist as opposed to a pathologist.

Pathologist

The Coroner appoints a pathologist to conduct the post-mortem examination, and most are carried out by pathologists working in the NHS. Some pathologists specialise in particular fields, and in appropriate cases, Coroners may choose to appoint a specialist pathologist, for example, a cardiac pathologist where death is the result of a sudden cardiac event in a young person without apparent heart disease. A Coroner's post-mortem examination is separate to the pathologist's NHS work, and the Coroner pays a fee for each examination.

If the deceased died in hospital, Coroners may request pathologists employed by, or associated with, the hospital staff to conduct the post-mortem examination, unless the pathologist declines to conduct the examination.[39] However, if the conduct of any member of the hospital staff is likely to be called into question, or the relatives of the deceased make a request, a pathologist based at another hospital or area should be appointed, provided this would not cause undue delay.[40] The Coroner should provide the pathologist with detailed information prior to the post-mortem examination. In healthcare related deaths, this should include the deceased's GP and/or hospital records; and any information from the deceased's family. The pathologist must inform the Coroner if he has formed the view on review of the initial information that the Coroner does not have jurisdiction over the body, or if a post-mortem examination will add nothing of significance to the Coroner's investigation.[41]

The Coroner must notify certain people and organisations of the date, hour, and place at which the post-mortem examination will take place.[42] This includes relatives of the deceased whom have notified the Coroner of a desire to attend, or be represented, at the post-mortem examination;[43] the deceased's regular medical attendant;[44] and the hospital if the deceased died in hospital.[45] These interested persons have right to be represented at the post-mortem examination by a legally qualified medical practitioner.[46] Any person whose alleged negligence or improper conduct partly or entirely caused the death is also entitled to be represented at the post-mortem examination.[47] Therefore, the hospital may nominate a representative to attend the post-mortem examination,[48] but the representative should not be the person whose conduct may be

---

39 Coroners Rules 1984, r 6(1)(c)(i).
40 Coroners Rules 1984, r 6(1)(c)(ii)–(iii).
41 The Royal College of Pathologists, *Guidelines on Autopsy Practice* (Report of a Working Group of The Royal College of Pathologists) September 2002 at paras 3.9 and 3.10.
42 Coroners Rules 1984, r 7(1).
43 Coroners Rules 1984, r 7(2)(a).
44 Coroners Rules 1984, r 7(2)(b).
45 Coroners Rules 1984, r 7(2)(c).
46 Coroners Rules 1984, r 7(3).
47 Coroners Act 1988, s 20(3)(b).
48 Coroners Rules 1984, r 7(3).

called into question. A person attending a post-mortem examination is an observer, and must not interfere with the examination.[49]

Standards of post-mortem examination

Standards of post-mortem examinations have been criticised by the courts;[50] the Shipman Inquiry;[51] and the *Report of a Fundamental Review* (Luce Report).[52] In the Report of the National Confidential Enquiry into Patient Outcome and Death (2006), *The Coroners' autopsy: do we deserve better?*, the quality of post-mortem reports was considered to be unacceptable in 26% of cases, where unacceptable meant that the post-mortem report did not sufficiently explain the cause of death, or was evidently wrong.[53] Some of the particular issues that the advisors to the study considered important were:

- that there was poor communication between Coroners and pathologists;
- that there were apparent gaps in the information provided to the pathologists by the Coroners;
- that in almost 20% of cases the cause of death stated seemed questionable;
- that in 6.25% of cases it was determined that samples for histology should have been taken to determine or further elucidate the cause of death; and
- that the very elderly may not have been examined as carefully as younger subjects.

The Royal College of Pathologists has written a Code of Practice of Performance Standards for Forensic Pathologists.[54] The Code states that the internal examination must follow the Royal College of Pathologists' Guidelines on Autopsy Practice, and includes a helpful guide as to the matters that must be included in the post-mortem report. Although written primarily from the standpoint of Home Office pathologists, policies and procedures covering all aspects of the post-mortem process should reflect guidelines from professional bodies[55] such as the Royal College of Pathologists.

The post-mortem report

The pathologist will complete a post-mortem report in the format set out in Sch 2 of the Coroners Rules 1984,[56] and concludes the post-mortem

---

49   Coroners Rules 1984, r 8.
50   *R v Clark* [2003] EWCA Crim 1020, at paras 169–170.
51   *The Shipman Inquiry Third Report: Death Certification and the Investigation of Death by Coroners* (14 July 2003: Chairman Dame Janet Smith DBE), CM 5854, Chapter 10.
52   *Death Certification and Investigation in England, Wales and Northern Ireland: A Report of a Fundamental Review 2003* (28 April 2003: Chairman Tom Luce), Cm 5831, Chapter 13.
53   *National confidential enquiry into patient outcome and death, the coroner's autopsy: do we deserve better?* (2006), Chapter 4 (the study group was 1,691 in size with a median age of 74 years).
54   www.rcpath.org/resources/pdf/CodeofPracForensicPath1104.pdf.
55   Human Tissue Authority, Code of Practice 3: Post-mortem Examination (September 2009) at para 137.
56   Coroners Rules 1984, r 10(1).

report with his opinion of the cause of death. The format of the conclusion follows guidelines issued by the World Health Organisation (WHO). Part I sets out the chain of causation resulting in death. Part II lists other significant conditions or diseases contributing to death, but not causally related.

In my opinion the cause of death was:

I

1(a): Disease or condition directly causing death

1(b): Disease or condition that led to the immediate cause of death (antecedent causes)

1(c): Morbid conditions (if any)

II

Other significant conditions contributing to the death, but not related to the disease or condition causing it

---

The pathologist must only provide the Coroner with the post-mortem report and the special examination report, although a copy can be disclosed to a third party with the Coroner's consent.[57] Coroners are not under a duty to disclose a post-mortem report to interested persons before the inquest without an application, and there is no duty on the Coroner to disclose the post-mortem report if there is good reason not to do so.[58] However, Coroners should provide an interested person with a copy of the post-mortem report and/or special examination reports following an application and on payment of the prescribed fee, if any.[59] Most Coroners provide copies of these documents to the family before the inquest is held. The post-mortem report may be 'provisional' in that the pathologist may alter his conclusions having heard the evidence at the inquest.

Second post-mortem examination

If the deceased's family are dissatisfied with the result of the Coroners' post mortem examination, they are entitled to a second post-mortem examination,[60] at their expense. If the Coroner is still in possession of the deceased's body, his permission will be required; and such permission should be given unless there are reasonable grounds to refuse.[61] Otherwise, a second post-mortem examination can be carried out once the Coroner has released the body, although that might not be until the inquest has concluded and therefore is of little practical assistance. In the alternative, the family may instruct their own pathologist to review the post-mortem examination results or any specimens that may have been collected. The pathologist instructed by the family can be called as a witness to give evidence at the inquest to rebut the findings and conclusions of the Coroner's pathologist.

---

57 Coroners Rules 1984, rr 10(2) and 13.
58 *R (on the application of McLeish)* v *HM Coroner for the Northern District of Greater London* [2010] EWHC 3624 (Admin), CO/4224/2009.
59 Coroners Rules 1984, r 57(1).
60 *R* v *HM Coroner for Greater London (Southern District), ex p Ridley* [1985] 1 WLR 1347.
61 *R* v *HM Coroner for Greater London (Southern District), ex p Ridley* [1985] 1 WLR 1347.

After the post-mortem examination

The Coroner has the right and duty to take possession of the deceased's body once he has acquired jurisdiction, and retain possession until completion of the inquest.[62] However, most Coroners will release the body to the family so that the funeral can be organised as soon as possible after the conclusion of the post-mortem examination. Some families may wish to delay the funeral until all the specimens are returned to the body. This decision may depend upon whether complete organs or small specimens, such as blood or tissue samples, have been retained; or whether further investigations on the body may be necessary. Where small specimens have been taken, relatives are often reassured by the fact that the specimens are miniscule.

Removal and retention of organs and tissue

In most cases, small samples of tissues and organs will be taken by the pathologist, although on occasions an entire organ is removed and retained. The retention of any material should be recorded on the post-mortem report. In some circumstances, the family may want tissues or blood samples retained by the pathologist in case further testing becomes necessary, particularly if they instruct their own pathologist. The rules relating to the retention of materials removed during post-mortem examination were updated by the Coroners (Amendment) Rules 2005, which took effect from 1 June 2005.[63]

Pursuant to these rules, the pathologist must preserve material that in his opinion is relevant to the cause of death or identification of the deceased,[64] and must notify the Coroner in writing that material has been retained.[65] The Coroner responds to the notification, specifying the time for which the material must be preserved,[66] although this cannot extend beyond the time when the Coroner's functions cease.[67] The Coroner must notify one of the deceased's relatives (spouse; civil partner; parent; child and any personal representative of the deceased) and any other relative who notified the Coroner of his intention to attend the post-mortem examination, that material has been retained; the time of retention; and the prescribed options for disposal when the material is no longer required.[68] The options for disposal are burial, cremation, or other lawful disposal by the pathologist.[69] There is no requirement for the pathologist to seek the family's view about the method of disposal, but it is likely that the Coroner will ask the family for an indication. Alternatively, the material can be returned to a relative upon their request,[70] or can be retained for research or other purposes, but only with the consent of one

---

62   *R* v *Bristol Coroner, ex p Kerr* [1974] QB 652.
63   SI 2005/1032. The amendment rules create four new rules, rr 9, 9A, 12 and 12A, which together replace Coroners Rules 1984, rr 9 and 12.
64   Coroners Rules 1984, r 9(1).
65   Coroners Rules 1984, r 9(2).
66   Coroners Rules 1984, r 9(5).
67   Coroners Rules 1984, r 9(9).
68   Coroners Rules 1984, r 6.
69   Coroners Rules 1984, r 9(8)(a).
70   Coroners Rules 1984, r 9(8)(b).

of the deceased's relatives.[71] Once the date for preserving the material has passed, the pathologist must record the method of disposal, that the material has been delivered to the specific person, or that the material has been retained on behalf of a specified person.[72]

PREPARING FOR THE INQUEST

Statutory questions

The function of an inquest is to seek out and record as many of the facts concerning the death as the public interest requires.[73] The proceedings and evidence at an inquest are directed towards ascertaining the statutory matters set out in s 11(5)(b) of the Coroners Act 1988 and r 36 of the Coroners Rules 1984:

- who the deceased was;
- where the deceased came by his death;
- when the deceased came by his death; and
- how the deceased came by his death.

Opening an inquest

The inquest is generally opened within a few days of death. It is a brief hearing and the primary purpose is to identify formally the deceased, although preliminary evidence of the cause of death might also be given. Many Coroners do not require the family to attend (although they may if they wish) and the identification of the deceased is provided by the Coroner's Officer. The Coroner usually signs copies of an interim death certificate, confirming the fact of death and indicating that an inquest has been opened and adjourned. The inquest is then adjourned to a date to be fixed. During this time, the Coroner will conduct his investigations and organise the full hearing. Alternatively, criminal investigations may be carried out and the inquest will be adjourned until those investigations and any proceedings have finished.

Interested persons

There are no parties to an inquest, only 'interested persons'. Section 47, one of the few sections of the Coroners and Justice Act 2009 that is in force, introduced a statutory definition of an 'interested person' that expands slightly the list of interested persons set out in r 20(2) of the Coroners Rules 1984. The list includes a spouse, civil partner, partner, parent, child, siblings, a personal representative of the deceased, and a person who may by an act or omission have caused or contributed to the death of the deceased, or whose employee or agent may have done so. There is a 'catchall' category to include any person the Coroner thinks has 'sufficient interest'.[74]

---

71 Coroners Rules 1984, r 9(8)(c).
72 Coroners Rules 1984, r 9A(7).
73 *R v South London Coroner, ex p Thompson* (1982) 126 Sol Jo 625.
74 Coroners and Justice Act 2009, s 47(2)(m).

Evidence

The Coroner will collate documentary evidence and any other evidence that is considered relevant to the particular case. In the healthcare context, this is likely to include the hospital and/or GP notes. Coroners cannot order disclosure. However, they can apply to the High Court under CPR 34.4 for a witness summons to compel the disclosure of documents for the purpose of the inquest.[75] Documents and statements provided to the Coroner should not be provided on the assumption that they are confidential, as the Coroner may disclose the documents to the other interested persons. Different Coroners have different practices on the documents that they will disclose. It is usually helpful for the legal representative of the family to write to the Coroner and the hospital/GP setting out the issues of concern. On occasions, Coroners will disclose the letter from the family to the hospital or GP. However, these letters often include information that is not relevant to the inquest, and the Coroner may write to the hospital or GP with a summary of the concerns of the family.

The hospital or GP surgery should consider whether all the documents that may have been generated as a result of the death of the deceased should be disclosed to the Coroner. Such documents include an adverse incident report, a serious untoward incident report, an internal investigation report, or a report prepared as a result of a complaint by the family following the death of the deceased. Only documents that are relevant to the inquest should be disclosed. It is advisable to disclose such documents early in the investigation, as disclosure on the day of the inquest might result in an adjournment.

There is no legal obligation for a potential witness to provide a witness statement or report for the Coroner. However, it is often advantageous to provide a carefully prepared statement, which may save time during the inquest. A prepared statement also ensures that the Coroner receives all the relevant evidence, as most witnesses are nervous giving oral testimony. Representatives for the family may wish to provide a statement; particularly if there may be factual disputes in relation to the deceased's mental or physical health prior to death, or the care received in hospital.

Representatives of the hospital and GP will usually prepare statements at the request of the Coroner's Officer. It is helpful if the witness includes his qualifications and experience in working within a particular speciality (if relevant) and at the hospital where the deceased died. The statement should be chronological, setting out the professionals' involvement with treating and caring for the deceased, including references (where appropriate) to the healthcare notes and an explanation of any medical treatments and terminology; and focused on the issues that are relevant to the inquest. If the hospital or GP surgery has made any changes to practice as a result of the death of the deceased, evidence of such changes should be included. The legal advisor for the hospital or GP should consider whether any of the information in the statement is subject to

---

75 *Inner West London Assistant Deputy Coroner* v *Channel 4 Television Corporation* [2007] EWHC 2513 (QB), [2008] 1 WLR 945.

the privilege from self-incrimination or legal professional privilege that should not be waived.

If representatives believe that all the relevant evidence has not been requested by the Coroner or disclosed to the Coroner, the Coroner can be asked to seek disclosure. A Coroner who refuses to request disclosure of relevant evidence and thereby fails to investigate a death fully may be subjected to judicial review proceedings.

Expert evidence

Healthcare deaths usually involve consideration of the practices of a doctor, nurse, midwife, or other healthcare professional, systems of healthcare, and the safety of buildings where patients are detained under mental health legislation. An important consideration for the Coroner is whether independent medical evidence should be obtained, and this should be considered at an early stage in the investigation.

Many Coroners call and rely upon the evidence of the consultant, senior nurse/midwife, other healthcare professional, and/or hospital manager so that he may express a view on the adequacy of the treatment provided by their hospital and/or system of healthcare. Understandably, families often find this approach objectionable for a number of reasons: the expert is not independent; the professional giving evidence may have caused or contributed to the death; they may not have had any in involvement in the patient's care; or the issues maybe outside their area of expertise.

In some cases, a Coroner may instruct an independent expert, either on his own initiative or at the request of an interested party, which is usually the family of the deceased. However, there is no principle that independent expert evidence is always required to render an inquest an effective investigation; it depends upon the circumstances of the case, including the expertise of the Coroner and the issues and evidence before him.[76] The reality is that independent experts are retained in only a small proportion of healthcare deaths,[77] and this is often attributed to the underfunding of the coronial service.

A failure to call expert evidence is reviewable by judicial review proceedings, illustrated by the case of *Jones v HM Coroner for the Southern District of Greater London*. In *Jones*, the Administrative Court held that there had been insufficient inquiry into the means by which the deceased died from Fentanyl toxicity (an opiod analgesic) that had been prescribed by an out of hours doctor's service.[78] The Coroner had been satisfied that the question of how the deceased came by his death was discharged by establishing that it was due to a fatal dose of Fentanyl. The Administrative Court stated that the scope of the inquest was too

---

76 *R (on the application of Goodson) v Bedfordshire and Luton Coroner (Luton and Dunstable Hospital NHS Trust, interested party)* [2004] EWHC 2931 (Admin), [2006] 1 WLR 432, [2005] 2 All ER 792 at para 71.

77 In *R (on the application of Goodson) v Bedfordshire and Luton Coroner (Luton and Dunstable Hospital NHS Trust, interested party)* [2004] EWHC 2931 (Admin), [2006] 1 WLR 432, [2005] 2 All ER 792 the Coroner assessed this to be in the region of 5–6% of inquests, although it was accepted that practice varied across the coronial districts (at para 36).

78 [2010] EWHC 931 (Admin).

narrow, relying on *R* v *HM Coroner for Inner West District, ex p Dallagio*,[79] where it was held that an investigation into the means by which the deceased came by his death would not necessarily be limited to the last link in the chain of causation. The court did not make any specific findings about expert evidence; although it is likely that such evidence would be required.

If there are available funds, the family of the deceased may obtain independent expert evidence. Communications with an expert for the purpose of obtaining information or advice in connection with existing or contemplated litigation are privileged, but only when the following conditions are satisfied:

(a) the litigation must be in progress or in contemplation;
(b) the communications must have been made for the sole or dominant purpose of conducting that litigation; and
(c) the litigation must be adversarial, not investigative or inquisitorial.[80]

If the report plainly indicates substandard treatment and care, it may be advisable to disclose it to the Coroner. However, the interested party and the expert must agree to this course of action. If the evidence assists the investigation, the Coroner can adopt the expert witness and call him to give evidence at the inquest.[81] In such circumstances, the defendant will have advance notice of the expert evidence for the claimant in any subsequent civil claim.

Alternatively, the family may instruct an expert to provide a report to identify the issues and areas of concern should be explored by the advocate for the family at the inquest. Such information often includes NICE standards or guidance of one of the medical colleges.

Advance disclosure

In healthcare deaths, the deceased's medical notes and x-rays, internal investigation reports, adverse incident reports, serious untoward incident reports, hospital policy and procedure documents and the witness statements of the hospital staff and GP are likely to be required by the family of the deceased. Medical records can be obtained under the Access to Health Records Act 1990.[82] However, advanced disclosure of other documents can be contentious. The Coroners Rules 1984 do not provide for pre-inquest disclosure,[83] although Coroners have discretion to disclose documentation to interested persons. There is a presumption in favour of as full disclosure as possible to interested persons and of all relevant

---

79 [1994] 4 All ER 139.
80 *Three Rivers District Council* v *Governor and Company of the Bank of England (No 6)* [2004] UKHL 48 at 102.
81 *R (on the application of Nicholls)* v *Coroner for the City of Liverpool* [2001] EWHC Admin 922.
82 Access to Health Records Act 1990, s 3(f): where the patient has died, the patient's personal representative and any person who may have a claim arising out of the patient's death.
83 Coroners Rules 1984, r 57 provides for post-inquest disclosure to interested persons of the post-mortem report, special examination report, notes of evidence, and any documents put into evidence at the inquest.

material, and in enhanced *Middleton* inquests[84] it is difficult to justify a refusal to disclose relevant material.[85] However, what is a 'relevant' document is within the discretion of the Coroner.[86]

In *Jamieson* inquests, many Coroners do not provide disclosure on their own initiative and on occasions refuse to disclose documents to interested persons when asked. Disclosure has been the subject of recent decisions of the Administrative Court. If advanced disclosure is refused, the solicitor representing the interested party should ask the Coroner to set out the reasons for refusal, as the decision may be amenable to judicial review. The following cases may help with disclosure.

- In *R (on the application of Bentley) v Avon Coroner,*[87] the Administrative Court considered disclosure where the deceased was a heroin addict who died in a bail hostel. The Coroner refused the advanced disclosure of the witness list, the post-mortem report, the witness statements, and other documents relevant to the inquest. The court held that the Coroner had discretion to permit advanced disclosure. The request for disclosure was reasonable. The fact that rules did not require disclosure and that it was an inquisitorial procedure were insufficient reasons to refuse the request. The claimant was entitled to participate in the inquest, but the court said that it was difficult to see how this right could be effectively exercised if he was kept in ignorance of the most basic facts until the inquest had commenced. There was an overriding obligation on the Coroner to conduct the inquest fairly.

- *R (on the application of Ahmed) v Coroner South East Cumbria*[88] was a traditional *Jamieson* inquest. The solicitor for the family of the deceased wrote to the Coroner asking for disclosure of copies of all the information and documents in the Coroner's possession prior to the inquest ('a blanket request'). The Coroner refused to comply with the request and asked the solicitor to be more specific about the documents that were required. The Administrative Court held that the Coroner should disclose the 'material central to the inquest', which included the witness statements of those called to give evidence.

- *R (on the application of Butler) v Coroner Black Country*[89] was another traditional *Jamieson* inquest. The deceased died at work, and a Health and Safety Executive Report was prepared. The Coroner refused to disclose the HSE Report and accompanying documents/statements on the ground that an embargo preventing disclosure had been agreed between the HSE and the Coroners' Society. It was held that the Coroner must consider whether fairness required him to exercise his discretion and make disclosure or to contact the

---

84 See below for a discussion of enhanced *Middleton* inquests and traditional *Jamieson* inquests.
85 *R (on the application of Catherine Smith) v Oxfordshire Assistant Deputy Coroner and Secretary of State for Defence* [2008] EWHC 694.
86 Some documents will be disclosed under various protocols, but none applies to healthcare deaths.
87 [2001] EWHC Admin 170, [2002] ACD 1.
88 [2009] EWHC 1653 (Admin).
89 [2010] EWHC 43 (Admin).

HSE to obtain its consent to disclosure. The Administrative Court stated that Coroner had failed to approach disclosure in line with the principles enunciated in *R (Bentley)* v *HM Coroner for Avon*.[90]

Scope of the inquiry including Art 2 of the ECHR

Human rights law has profoundly influenced coronial law, and there has been much discussion over the last decade of the scope of Art 2 of the ECHR and the function of the inquest in discharging the United Kingdom's obligations under it. The majority of the jurisprudence has focussed on violent deaths, and deaths of detainees in police or prison custody as opposed to healthcare deaths. Article 2 is one of the most fundamental provisions in the Convention. Article 2, which by virtue of s 6 of the Human Rights Act 1998 binds all public authorities in the United Kingdom, provides that:

> Everyone's right to life shall be protected by law. No one shall be deprived of his life intentionally save in the execution of a sentence of a court following his conviction of a crime for which the penalty is provided by law.

The European Court of Human Rights and domestic courts have interpreted Art 2 of the ECHR as imposing the following obligations:

1 not to take life without justification;
2 to establish a framework of laws, precautions, procedures and means of enforcement which will, to the greatest extent reasonably practicable, protect life; and
3 a procedural obligation to initiate an effective independent public investigation into any death occurring in circumstances in which it appears that one of the foregoing substantive obligations have been, or may have been, violated and it appears that agents of the State are, or may have been, in some way implicated.[91]

In the recent Court of Appeal case of *R (on the application of Humberstone)* v *Legal Services Commission (The Lord Chancellor intervening)*, Lady Justice Smith explained the obligations under Art 2, as follows:

> Article 2(1) provides that: 'Everyone's right to life shall be protected by law'. That primary duty imposes on the state a duty not to take life and also a duty to take appropriate legislative and administrative steps to protect life, for example by the provision of a police force and criminal justice system. It imposes on state authorities such as the police and prison authorities the duty to protect those in their immediate care from violence either at the hands of others or at their own hands: see *LCB v United Kingdom* [1998] 27 EHRR 212; *Osman v United Kingdom* [1998] 27 EHRR; *Edwards v United Kingdom* [2002] 35 EHRR 487 and *R (Amin) v Secretary of State for the Home Department* [2004] 1 AC 653, [2003] UKHL 51. The duty also extends to organs of the state, such as hospital authorities, to make appropriate provision and to adopt systems of work to protect the lives of patients in their care: see *Savage v South Essex Trust* [2009] 1 AC 681.[92]

---

90 *R (on the application of Bentley)* v *HM Coroner for the District of Avon* [2001] EWHC Admin 170, [2002] ACD 1.
91 *R (Middleton)* v *West Somerset Coroner* [2004] UKHL 10, [2004] 2 AC 182 at paras 2–3.
92 [2010] EWCA Civ 1479 at para 21.

When considering the scope of the inquiry, the Coroner must consider Art 2. Representatives of all interested persons should also consider the scope of the inquest and make representations to the Coroner as appropriate. Healthcare staff may wish to narrow the scope of the investigation to avoid criticism, to deter subsequent civil claims, and to prevent any adverse publicity. However, it has been held that 'an inquiry which leaves too many questions unanswered and too many issues unresolved is not a sufficient inquiry',[93] and may be the subject of a successful judicial review.

One difficulty in considering the potential scope of the inquiry is that imprecise language has been used in relation to the engagement of Art 2 leading to failure to consider the correct issues. In the recent Court of Appeal case of *Humberstone*, Lady Justice Smith, giving the judgment of the Court, provided welcome clarity to the State's duties to investigate deaths under the ECHR. Essentially, all inquests are Art 2 inquests. Article 2 of the ECHR may be engaged in two senses.[94]

Traditional (*Jamison*) inquests

First, Art 2 imposes an obligation on the State to provide a legal system by which the citizen may access an open and independent investigation of the circumstances of the death (ie a general investigative obligation). The Coroner's inquest, the availability of criminal and civil proceedings, and disciplinary proceedings will satisfy the general obligation.[95] These inquests are often described as traditional, ordinary, domestic, or *Jamieson* type inquests after the Court of Appeal decision in *R v North Humberside and Scunthorpe Coroner, ex parte Jamieson*.[96]

The inquest is directed towards ascertaining the statutory questions. However, in traditional *Jamieson* inquests, 'how' the deceased came by his death (Coroners Act 1988, s 11(5)(b)(ii) and Coroners Rules 1984, r 36(1) (b)) is narrowly interpreted as meaning 'by what means' the deceased came by his death.[97] The scope of the inquest will be determined by the Coroner, and in *Jamieson*, it was explained that:

> 'It is the duty of the coroner ... whether he is sitting with a jury or without, to ensure that the relevant facts are fully, fairly and fearlessly investigated ... He must ensure that the relevant facts are exposed to public scrutiny ... He fails in his duty if his investigation is superficial, slipshod or perfunctory. But the responsibility is his. He must set the bounds of the inquiry ...'[98]

The investigation and inquest should not be 'limited to the last link in the chain of causation' as this would 'defeat the purpose of holding an inquest at all if the inquiry were to be circumscribed'.[99] In addition, the

---

93   *R (Reilly) v HM Coroner for Coventry* [1996] 35 BMLR 48 at para 53.
94   *R (on the application of Humberstone)* v *Legal Services Commission* [2011] EWCA Civ 1479; [2010] All ER (D) 225 (Dec) at para 58.
95   *R (on the application of Humberstone)* v *Legal Services Commission* [2011] EWCA Civ 1479, [2010] All ER (D) 225 (Dec) at para 58.
96   *R v North Humberside and Scunthorpe Coroner, ex parte Jamieson* [1994] 3 All ER 972.
97   *R v North Humberside and Scunthorpe Coroner, ex parte Jamieson* [1994] 3 All ER 972.
98   *R v North Humberside and Scunthorpe Coroner, ex parte Jamieson* [1994] 3 All ER 972 at para 14 of the conclusions. Adopted in *Dallaglio*, at 154–155 by Simon Brown LJ.
99   *R v Inner West London Coroner, ex p Dallaglio and Lockwood Croft* [1994] 4 All ER 139 at 164.

investigation should not be limited to matters that caused the death, but should include the relevant systems at the hospital and the safeguards that were in place; and how the system operated on the day in question.[100] If, during the course of an inquest, it becomes apparent that a systemic defect may be to blame for the death of the deceased, the Coroner should convert the traditional *Jamieson* inquest into an enhanced *Middleton* inquest in order to discharge the States' obligations under the ECHR.

Enhanced (*Middleton*) inquests

Second, Art 2 imposes a procedural obligation on the State to conduct an effective investigation 'where there was ground for suspicion that the state might have breached a substantive obligation under article 2'[101] (ie the enhanced obligation). Inquests that arise out of the procedural obligation are often described as Art 2,[102] enhanced, or *Middleton* inquests, after the leading case of *R (Middleton) v West Somerset Coroner.*[103] The enhanced *Middleton* inquest, criminal proceedings, and public inquiries satisfy the procedural obligation.[104] In such cases, the obligation is proactively to initiate a thorough investigation into all the circumstances of the death.[105]

The enhanced *Middleton* inquest is directed at ascertaining the same statutory questions. However, 'how' the deceased came by his death (Coroners Act 1988, s 11(5)(b)(ii) and Coroners Rules 1984, r 36(1)(b)) is broadly interpreted to mean 'by what means and in what circumstances' the deceased came by his death.[106] This ensures that the inquest considers the circumstances alleged to have caused the breach of Art 2. The scope of the verdict is also wider compared to the traditional *Jamieson* inquest, as indicated in *R (on the application of Hurst) v London Northern District Coroner:*[107]

> Of course, the scope of the inquiry is ultimately a matter for the coroner. The 'verdict' and findings, however, are not. The Jamieson construction of 'how' severely circumscribes these. But where the Middleton construction applies, the verdict and findings are not merely permitted, but *required* to be wider: section 11 dictates that the inquisition 'shall set out, so far as such particulars have been proved … how … the deceased came by his death'. If in every case that means 'in what circumstances' as well as 'by what means', the coroner will inevitably in many cases have to widen the scope of the inquiry beyond that which, under the Jamieson approach, he would otherwise regard to be appropriate.

---

100 *R (on the application of Takoushis) v Inner North London Coroner* [2005] EWCA Civ 1440, [2006] 1 WLR 461 at paras 49–51.
101 *R (on the application of Smith) v Oxfordshire Assistant Deputy Coroner (Equality and Human Rights Commission Intervening)* [2010] UKSC 20, [2010] 3 WLR 223.
102 The use of Art 2 in this context is misleading.
103 [2004] 2 AC 182.
104 *R (on the application of Middleton) v West Somerset Coroner* [2004] UKHL 10, [2004] 2 AC 182 at para 20.
105 *R (on the application of Humberstone) v Legal Services Commission* [2011] EWCA Civ 1479, [2010] All ER (D) 225 (Dec) at para 67.
106 *R (on the application of Middleton) v West Somerset Coroner* [2004] UKHL 10; [2004] 2 AC 182 at para 35.
107 [2007] UKHL 13, [2007] 2 WLR 726 at para 51.

In *R (on the application of Amin)* v *Secretary of State for the Home Department*, Lord Bingham explained the purposes of the procedural duty:

> The purposes of such an investigation are clear: to ensure so far as possible that the full facts are brought to light; that culpable and discreditable conduct is exposed and brought to public notice; that suspicion of deliberate wrongdoing (if unjustified) is allayed; that dangerous practices and procedures are rectified; and that those who have lost their relative may at least have the satisfaction of knowing that lessons learned from his death may save the lives of others.[108]

To comply with the Art 2 procedural duty, the investigation must be:

(i)   independent;
(ii) effective;
(iii) reasonably prompt;
(iv) involve a sufficient element of public scrutiny; and
(v) the next-of-kin must be involved to an appropriate extent.[109]

As all inquests engage Art 2, the proper approach is to indentify the obligations that arise because Art 2 is engaged and consider whether there an arguable case that the State has been in breach of its substantive duty to protect life. This is a developing area of law. However, the procedural duty in healthcare deaths arises where death arguably results in the following circumstances:

1   Where there may have been a failure to provide systems, rules and procedures to protect life, for example, a systemic failure in the provision of medical care,[110] failure to provide suitable faculties, adequate staff, or appropriate systems of operation.[111]

2   Where the deceased was detained in hospital under the Mental Health Act 1983 and there was a real and immediate risk of suicide, of which the authorities knew or ought to have been aware. In such circumstances there is an operational obligation and the staff are required to do all that could reasonably be expected of them to prevent the patient committing suicide (*Savage* v *South Essex Partnership NHS Foundation Trust*).[112]

3   Where the deceased arguably died as a result of grossly negligent medical care.[113] By gross negligence, the Court of Appeal in *Takoushis*

---

108 [2003] UKHL 51; [2004] 1 AC 653 at para 31.
109 *Jordan* v *UK* [2001] 37 EHRR 52, at 106–107 adopted in *R* v *Home Secretary, ex p Amin* [2004] 1 AC 653 at para 25.
110 *R (on the application of Takoushis)* v *Inner London North Coroner* [2005] EWCA Civ 1440.
111 *R (on the application of Humberstone)* v *Legal Services Commission* [2011] EWCA Civ 1479, [2010] All ER (D) 225 (Dec) at para 58.
112 *Savage* v *South Essex Partnership NHS Foundation Trust* [2008] UKHL 74, [2009] 1 AC 681, at para 49; and see *R (on the application of Smith)* v *Oxfordshire Assistant Deputy Coroner (Equality and Human Rights Commission Intervening)* [2009] EWCA Civ 441; [2009] 3 WLR 1099 at paras 102–103.
113 This issue was mentioned in *R (on the application of Takoushis)* v *Inner London North Coroner* [2005] EWCA Civ 1440, [2005] All ER (D) 461 (Nov) at para 96 and *R (on the application of Humberstone)* v *Legal Services Commission* [2011] EWCA Civ 1479, [2010] All ER (D) 225 (Dec) at para 71, but no decisions were made on this point. Both Courts referred to the decision in *R (on the application of Khan)* v *Secretary of State for Health* [2003] EWCA Civ 1129, [2004] 1 WLR 971. Also see on this point *R (on the application of Moss)* v *HM Coroner for the North and South Districts of Durham and Darlington* [2008] EWHC 2940 (Admin), [2008] All ER (D) 292 (Nov) at paras 24–25.

stated (*obiter*) that it meant the kind of negligence that would be sufficient to sustain a charge of manslaughter.[114]

Simple or ordinary negligence in the care and treatment of a patient in hospital is insufficient to amount to a breach of the State's positive obligation to protect life.[115] In *Humberstone*, Lady Justice Smith cautioned against dressing up allegations of individual negligence as systemic failures.[116] However, she acknowledged that it is not always easy to distinguish between individual negligence and systemic failures.[117] For example, in *Takoushis* the allegations related to the nature of the triage system in the Accident and Emergency Department at St Thomas' Hospital,[118] and in *Humberstone* the allegations related to the resources and operational services of the Yorkshire Ambulance Service.[119] It is advisable to consider and collate evidence of systemic failings as early as possible, and to raise this issue at a pre-inquest hearing.

In *Rabone* v *Pennine Care NHS Trust*, the Court of Appeal held that Art 2 does not impose on the State an operational obligation to voluntary patients in hospital, who are suffering from physical or mental illness, even where there is a 'real and immediate' risk of death.[120] The Court said that it was clear that Art 2 does not impose upon the state an operational obligation towards all persons who are at 'real and immediate risk' of death; and that there had to be some additional element, for example, detention by the state, before the state authorities came under the operational obligation. *Rabone* has been appealed to the Supreme Court. One of the issues on appeal is whether Art 2 imposes an obligation on the state to take preventative operational measures to protect a voluntary mental health patient against a 'real and immediate' risk of suicide. At the time of writing, the decision of the Court is awaited.

Jury

Once the Coroner has determined the scope of the inquest, he must decide whether a jury is required.[121] The Coroner will consider whether a mandatory jury is required under s 8(3) of the Coroners Act 1988; or whether to exercise his discretion to summon a jury by virtue of s 8(4) of

---

114 *R (on the application of Takoushis)* v *Inner London North Coroner* [2005] EWCA Civ 1440; [2005] All ER (D) 461 (Nov) at para 96.
115 *R (on the application of Goodson)* v *Bedfordshire and Luton Coroner* [2004] EWHC 2931 Admin, [2005] All ER (D) 122 (Oct), at para 5; approved in *R (on the application of Humberstone)* v *Legal Services Commission* [2011] EWCA Civ 1479, [2010] All ER (D) 225 (Dec) at para 58.
116 *R (on the application of Humberstone)* v *Legal Services Commission* [2011] EWCA Civ 1479, [2010] All ER (D) 225 (Dec) at para 71.
117 See also *R (on the application of JL)* v *Secretary of State for Justice* [2008] UKHL 68, [2009] 2 All ER 521 at para 88 for a helpful discussion on systemic negligence and operational negligence.
118 *R (on the application of Takoushis)* v *Inner London North Coroner* [2005] EWCA Civ 1440, [2005] All ER (D) 461 (Nov).
119 *R (on the application of Humberstone)* v *Legal Services Commission* [2011] EWCA Civ 1479, [2010] All ER (D) 225 (Dec).
120 *Rabone* v *Pennine Care NHS Trust* [2010] EWCA Civ 698, [2010] All ER (D) 160 (Jun).
121 *R (on the application of Paul)* v *Deputy Coroner of the Queens's Households and the Assistant Deputy Coroner for Surrey* [2007] EWHC 408 (Admin), [2008] QB 172 at para 42.

the Coroners Act 1988. The Coroner also has the power to reconsider the decision not to call a jury at any time during the inquest.[122] The Coroner must carry out sufficient investigations before deciding whether a jury is required; and any relevant documentary and witness evidence should be provided before the decision to call or not to call a jury is made.[123] If a jury is summoned, it will consist of between seven and 11 people.[124] Section 9 of the Coroners Act 1988 sets out the qualifications of the jurors.

A jury must be summoned in certain circumstances as set out in s 8(3) of the Coroners Act 1988. This includes deaths that occur in prison and police custody; and deaths 'caused by an accident, poisoning or disease notice of which is required to be given under any Act to a government department, to any inspector or other officer of a government department or to an inspector appointed under Section 19 of the Health and Safety at Work etc Act 1974'.[125] Deaths are reportable by employers or a person in control of premises to the Health and Safety Executive by virtue of the Reporting of Injuries Diseases and Dangerous Occurrences Regulations 1995[126] (RIDDOR 1995). Regulation 10 of RIDDOR 1995, excludes deaths that occur out of an examination, treatment or operation carried out or supervised by a registered medical practitioner or registered dentist. However, other deaths may be reportable.

Section 8(3)(d) of the Coroners Act 1988 requires a Coroner to sit with a jury if it appears that there is reason to suspect that the death occurred in circumstances the continuance or possible recurrence of which is prejudicial to the health or safety of the public or any section of the public.[127] It is this provision that is most likely to be invoked in healthcare deaths.

Section 8(3)(d) was considered in *R (on the application of Paul) v Deputy Coroner of the Queens Household and the Assistant Deputy Coroner for Surrey*.[128] The Administrative Court held that the prospect of recurrence required for the section to be applicable is low: 'it is the possibility of recurrence and not any higher chance'.[129] Further, the circumstances of the accident need not have caused the death, and only a section of the public needed to be at risk from recurrence.[130] When considering s 8(3)(d), the Coroner should look into the future as at the time of the inquest.[131] Therefore, if the Coroner is satisfied that because of steps taken since the events surrounding the death there is no risk that the death occurred in circumstances the continuation or possible recurrence of which is

---

122 Coroners Act 1988, s 8(4).
123 *R (on the application of Takoushis)* v *Inner London North Coroner* [2005] EWCA Civ 1440, [2005] All ER (D) 461 (Nov) at para 55.
124 Coroners Act 1988, s 8(2)(a).
125 Coroners Act 1988, s 8(3)(c).
126 SI 1995/3163.
127 Coroners Act 1988, s 8(3)(b)–(d).
128 [2007] EWHC 408 (Admin), [2008] QB 172.
129 *R (on the application of Paul)* v *Deputy Coroner of the Queens Household and the Assistant Deputy Coroner for Surrey* [2007] EWHC 408 (Admin), [2008] QB 172 at para 32.
130 *R (on the application of Paul)* v *Deputy Coroner of the Queens Household and the Assistant Deputy Coroner for Surrey* [2007] EWHC 408 (Admin), [2008] QB 172 at paras 32 and 34.
131 *R (on the application of Takoushis)* v *Inner London North Coroner* [2005] EWCA Civ 1440, [2005] All ER (D) 461 (Nov) at para 64.

prejudicial to the health or safety of the public, there is no reason to empanel a mandatory jury under s 8(3)(d).[132]

Coroners may also summon a jury by exercising their discretion under s 8(4) of the Coroners Act 1988 if it appears to a Coroner that there is 'any reason for summoning a jury'. In making a decision, the Coroner will take into consideration the view of the deceased's family, whether the facts of the case resemble the type of situation covered by the mandatory jury provisions, including the policy considerations underpinning the provisions, and the benefit of a reasoned explanation for his conclusions (a jury is only able to give brief answers to a limited number of questions).[133] Therefore, it is vital for representatives to take instructions in relation to summoning a jury. The factors that may be relevant include the increased length of the inquest if a jury is summoned, that a jury may be more willing to return a verdict that criticise the hospital/GP; and the fact that a Coroner can provide a reasoned explanation for the conclusion.

Pre-inquest hearing

Coroners are increasingly holding pre-inquest hearings, particularly in complex cases, although such a hearing is held at the discretion of the Coroner. A pre-inquest hearing is a case management conference primarily to review procedural matters that should result in a more focussed inquiry. The issues will be considered including:

- the scope of the inquest, including arguments or concessions on the obligations engaged under Art 2 of the ECHR;
- whether a jury is required;
- the witnesses that will be called to give evidence and witness statements that can be read under r 37 of the Coroners Rules 1984;
- whether any further evidence is required;
- whether any expert evidence is necessary;
- whether disclosure is complete and the preparation of bundles (if required);
- confirmation that the original medical notes – nursing notes, observation charts, x-rays, and other documents will be available at the inquest;
- whether exhibits are required or facilities for viewing digital evidence; and
- the length and location of the hearing.

The pre-inquest hearing also provides an opportunity to explain and clarify with the Coroner and the other representatives the family's concerns and the relevant issues that they would like explored at the inquest. If detailed submissions are to be made the Coroner is likely to be assisted by a skeleton argument lodged with authorities in advance of the pre-inquest hearing. A pre-inquest hearing is usually held in public unless there are 'cogent reasons' for holding it in private (see *R (on the application of Coker)* v *HM Coroners for South London* [2006] EWHC 614 (Admin) at paras 18–19).

---

132 *R (on the application of Takoushis)* v *Inner London North Coroner* [2005] EWCA Civ 1440, [2005] All ER (D) 461 (Nov) at para 64.

133 *R (on the application of Paul)* v *Deputy Coroner of the Queens Household and the Assistant Deputy Coroner for Surrey* [2007] EWHC 408 (Admin), [2008] QB 172 at paras 42–45.

If the Coroner does not hold a pre-inquest hearing, the issues will need to be raised in correspondence or telephone discussions with the Coroners' Officer in sufficient time prior to the inquest. It is unhelpful to raise issues on the day of the inquest that should have been raised earlier.

THE INQUEST HEARING

The resumed hearing

The Coroner will list the inquest for a full hearing once the investigations are complete and criminal proceedings (if any) are finished. However, given the delays in the inquest system, this may not take place for a least a year, or often several years after the deceased died. This creates difficulties for all involved in the inquest process. The inquest is an inquisitorial process. However, inquests are often not entirely inquisitorial as representatives of the interested persons try to advance particular cases or agendas. The inquest will be heard in public; although the Coroner has the power to direct that the public be excluded from an inquest or part of an inquest if he considers it is the interests of national security to do so.[134] This is unlikely to arise in the healthcare context.

The relatives of the deceased will usually expect the inquest to reveal and explain all the circumstances surrounding the death and to apportion blame. However, the inquiry is limited to the four statutory questions, and r 42 of the Coroners Rules 1984 prohibits apportioning liability. Therefore, the expectations of the family and friends must be managed at an early stage in the process. Healthcare staff are often anxious about giving evidence and the practical effect of a critical verdict in relation to their employment and professional standing.

Witnesses called to give evidence

The Coroner is the sole arbiter of evidence heard at an inquest. The Coroner will decide which lay and expert witnesses are to be called to give oral evidence and he should be asked to provide a list of witnesses that will be called in advance of the inquest. However, the Coroner can be invited to call any witness who might assist, and representatives should alert the Coroner if they believe a witness will be able to assist, or whose conduct will be called into question.

The case of *R (Mack) v HM Coroner for Birmingham and Solihull*[135] is illustrative of the importance of calling appropriate witnesses. In *Mack*, the inquest was quashed because the Coroner failed to call the consultant gastro-enterologist who had been responsible for the patient over the nine days before his death. During these last days, there were a number of criticisms of the quality of the care and treatment, for example, defects in recording fluid balance, and tests which had been requested had not been carried out. Instead, the Coroner called the consultant who had been responsible for the deceased immediately before the consultant gastro-enterologist, and did not work on the ward about which the family

---

134 Coroners Rules 1984, r 17.
135 [2011] EWCA Civ 712.

raised most of their concerns. Therefore, whilst the witness could say, for example, that the patient's drug charts where unsatisfactory, he could not say if it was a one-off problem or a systematic problem on the ward. The practical point is that the Coroner had accepted the witness nominated by the hospital. Therefore, hospitals must ensure that it nominates witnesses who have cared for and/or treated the patient. The Administrative Court accepted that it is not possible to call every doctor or nurse who could give material evidence. However, the effect of the judgment may be that Coroners call more witnesses from hospitals to ensure that the investigation is sufficient.

Another example is *R (Bentley) v Coroner's District of Avon*, in which Sullivan J accepted the applicant's submissions that an inquest which does not hear evidence from the actual witness whose behaviour was said to lack competence could not be described as a sufficient inquest.[136] Consequently, the verdict of an inquest in which a Coroner made a number of criticisms about the GP, but where the GP was not called to give evidence, did not attend the inquest, was not notified of the inquest, and was not represented at the inquest, was quashed.[137]

The Coroner will decide the order that the witnesses will give evidence, but if a family member is giving evidence, they will usually be called first. In an inquest that will be heard over several days or longer, the Coroner usually provides a list of the order that the witnesses will be called. In healthcare deaths, Coroners usually hear the factual evidence first before the medical evidence, and the evidence of the pathologist is often heard last. This enables the pathologist to revise his opinion when the facts and circumstances of death are known. However, some Coroners call the pathologist to give evidence first, and the remainder of the evidence is directed to ascertaining how the deceased came by his death. If the pathologist is the first witness, the Coroner can be invited to recall the pathologist should any new evidence or issue arise that might alter his opinion. On occasions, the pathologist is not called to give evidence and the post-mortem report is admitted under r 37 of the Coroners Rules 1984 (see below); although this is unlikely to occur in healthcare deaths. Family members may not wish to hear the evidence of the post-mortem examination and may prefer to sit outside Court whilst the pathologist gives evidence. Instructions should be taken on this issue before the hearing, and it is often helpful to inform the Coroner's Officer that the family wish to sit outside Court for that part of the hearing.

Witnesses are examined under oath.[138] The Coroner will ask question of the witnesses first, and if the witness is represented, his advocate will ask questions of that witness last.[139] Coroners usually use the written statement or report prepared by the witness in advance of the hearing as a basis of asking questions to elicit the relevant evidence in open Court. The Coroner must examine any inconsistencies in a witness statement and seek an explanation.[140]

---

136 [2001] EWHC Admin 170, [2002] ACD 1.
137 *R (on the application of Dowler)* v *Coroner for North London* [2009] EWHC 3300 (Admin), [2010] 11 BMLR 124.
138 Coroners Act 1988, s 11(2).
139 Coroners Rules 1988, r 21.
140 *R v Inner North London Coroner, ex p Cohen* (1994) 158 JP at 650–651.

Interested persons (through their advocate or in person) are entitled to question the witnesses at an inquest.[141] Questions must be relevant to the particular issues that are raised by the inquest and within the scope of the inquiry. Coroners will disallow any question that is not relevant or any improper question.[142] Although some Coroners allow the advocate for the family a degree of latitude, it is preferable for advocates to identify any issues that are important to the family but are not relevant to the inquest before the hearing and liaise with the representative for the hospital or General Practitioner to obtain the required information. Leading questions can be asked as an inquest is not a trial, but such questions are usually only suitable where the issue is not contentious. There is no right to re-examine a witness, although Coroners often exercise discretion to allow follow up questions.

In an inquest into a healthcare death, it is usual for all the witnesses to sit in Court to hear the evidence of the other witnesses before they are called. However, Coroners have discretion to exclude witnesses from the Court (as in criminal proceedings) if there is a risk that a witness may alter his evidence as a result of the evidence that has already been heard.

Self-incrimination

Witnesses must answer questions, and a failure to answer constitutes an offence, which is publishable by a fine,[143] although the reason for the failure should be explained and considered. However, a witness is not obliged to answer any question that tends to incriminate himself. Rule 22(1) of the Coroners Rules 1984 provides:

(1) No witness at an inquest shall be obliged to answer any question tending to incriminate himself.

(2) Where it appears to the coroner that a witness has been asked such a question, the coroner shall inform the witness that he may refuse to answer.

The risk of self-incrimination is in relation to criminal proceedings, not civil proceedings.[144] The Coroner does not have the power to impose a blanket prohibition against relevant questions on behalf of the family, particularly when the witness has already waived privilege on factual matters in answering the Coroners questions.[145] Witnesses are also not obliged to answer questions that are covered by legal professional privilege, although privilege may be waived by the witness.

Evidential points

Notes of evidence

Coroners are required to take notes of the evidence,[146] although that obligation may be satisfied by the evidence being tape-recorded.[147] It is

---

141 Coroners Rules 1984, r 20(1).
142 Coroners Rules 1984, r 20(1)(b).
143 Coroners Act 1988, s 10(2)(b).
144 Civil Evidence Act 1968, s 14(1)(a).
145 *R* v *Lincolnshire Coroner, ex p Hay* [1999] All ER (D) 173 at para 57.
146 Coroners Rules 1984, r 39.
147 *R (on the application of Cash)* v *County of Northamptonshire Coroner* [2007] EWHC 1354 (Admin), [2007] 4 All ER 903.

advisable to check with the Coroner's Officer before the hearing whether proceedings will be recorded.

Uncontested documentary evidence

Under r 37(1) of the Coroners Rules 1984, a Coroner has discretion to admit documentary evidence in the absence of the person who made the statement if it is relevant to the inquest and in the Coroner's opinion is unlikely to be disputed.[148] However, interested persons may object to the admission of documentary evidence.[149] This usually results in the witness being called to give evidence, unless the maker of the document is unable to give oral evidence within a reasonable period.[150] Rule 37 of the Coroners Rules 1984 is a complete code dealing with all documentary evidence.[151]

Documentary evidence admitted under r 37 is read out by the Coroner in Court, unless the Coroner directs otherwise.[152] Rule 37(3) of the Coroners Rules 1984 provides the procedure that Coroners must follow to admit documentary evidence without the witnesses attending to given evidence at the inquest:

(3)   Subject to paragraph (4), before admitting such documentary evidence the coroner shall at the beginning of the inquest announce publicly—
    (a)   that the documentary evidence may be admitted, and
    (b)
        (i)   the full name of the maker of the document to be admitted in evidence, and
        (ii)   a brief account of such document, and
    (c)   that any person who in the opinion of the coroner is within Rule 20(2)[153] may object to the admission of any such documentary evidence, and
    (d)   that any person who in the opinion of the coroner is within Rule 20(2) is entitled to see a copy of any such documentary evidence if he so wishes.
(4)   If during the course of an inquest it appears that there is available at the inquest documentary evidence which in the opinion of the coroner is relevant to the purposes of the inquest but the maker of the document is not present and in the opinion of the coroner the content of the documentary evidence is unlikely to be disputed, the coroner shall at the earliest opportunity during the course of the inquest comply with the provisions of paragraph (3).

Most Coroners disclose the documentary evidence (or a brief summary of the evidence) that he believes is uncontested and can be admitted under r 37 in advance of the inquest, asking for the views of the interested persons. However, if a Coroner refuses the advanced disclosure of statements and documents, r 37 ensures that the document should be provided to all interested persons immediately before the hearing. This

---

148 Coroners Rules 1984, r 37(1).
149 Coroners Rules 1984, r 37(1).
150 Coroners Rules 1984, r 37(2).
151 *R (on the application of Paul)* v *Inner West London Assistant Deputy Coroner* [2007] EWCA Civ 1259, [2008] 1 All ER 981.
152 Coroners Rules 1984, r 37(6).
153 Coroners Rules 1984, r 20(2) refers to the interested persons.

is because an offer to provide a copy of the document after it has been admitted into evidence does not amount to compliance with r 37(3)(d) of the Coroners Rules 1984.[154]

Coroners have the power to admit into evidence a document made by a deceased person if the contents of the document are relevant to the purpose of the inquest,[155] and the Coroners Rules 1984 do not provide for any objection by the interested persons. This rule covers suicide notes that may be helpful in assessing the deceased's mental disposition before death. Where such notes exist, Coroners may elect not read out the full note, but confirm that a suicide note was written and summarise the deceased's state of mind.

Hearsay

A Coroner's inquest is not bound by the strict laws of evidence.[156] There is no rule preventing the admission of hearsay evidence (oral or written) at an inquest.[157] If admitted and the evidence is material, the Coroner should warn the jury about the weight and reliability of such evidence.[158]

Closing speeches

An advocate should advise the interested party that he represents on the possible verdicts before the start of the inquest. Some families and healthcare staff express the hope that the Coroner or jury will reach a particular verdict at the end of the evidence. However, it is inadvisable for an interested party to focus on the verdict alone. An approach that is verdict driven potentially restricts the evidence. An inquest is an opportunity for the family to ask questions and for an explanation of the events that resulted in the death of the deceased. It is also an opportunity for healthcare staff to provide an explanation, and to allay any rumour or suspicion the family or wider community may have.

Representatives of the interested persons may make legal submissions to the Coroner. If a jury has been empanelled, the submissions are made in the absence of the jury and before the Coroner sums up the evidence. The submissions must be directed to the law, and not to the facts as r 40 of the Coroners Rules 1984 states that 'no person shall address the coroner or jury as to the facts'. Consequently, an advocate cannot ask the Coroner to prefer one person's evidence to another where there is a dispute.

However, in *R on the application of Lin* v *Secretary of State for Transport*, the Administrative Court stated that an advocate was entitled to make submissions of law, in particular:

(i)   how the Coroner should direct the jury;
(ii) the form of the questionnaire; and
(iii) recommendations pursuant to r 43.

---

154 *R (on the application of Bentley)* v *HM Coroner for the District of Avon* [2001] EWHC Admin 170; [2002] ACD 1 at para 76.
155 Coroners Rules 1984, r 37(5).
156 *R* v *Divine, ex p Walton* [1930] 2 KB 29 at 36.
157 *R* v *Greater Manchester Coroner, ex p Tal* [1985] QB 67.
158 *R* v *Greater Manchester Coroner, ex p Tal* [1985] QB 67.

The Court stated *obiter* that such submissions 'would merely be beating in the wind unless they were founded on the facts of the instant inquiry'.[159] It is difficult to make submissions on the sufficiency of the evidence and appropriate verdicts, and in particular on a narrative verdict, without referring to the facts. However, some Coroners will accept skeleton arguments that include the relevant facts.

Summing up to the jury

The Coroner will sum up the evidence to the jury and direct them as to the law before they consider their verdict.[160] This includes drawing the attention of the jury to r 36(2) of the Coroners Rules 1984 (matters to be ascertained at an inquest); and r 42 of the Coroners Rules 1984 (no verdict shall be framed in such a way as to appear to determine any question of criminal liability on the part of a named person or civil liability).[161]

The rules are not prescriptive about the issues that must be covered in summing up, and Coroners typically include the following issues:

- a reminder of the purpose of the inquest;
- an explanation of rr 36(2) and 42 of the Coroners Rules 1984;
- an explanation of the questions to be answered on the inquisition form, the conclusions which the jury is to consider and any relevant law, and the necessary standard of proof;
- a summary of the salient points of evidence;
- instruction on how the jury might approach assessing the evidence;
- a direction on causation;
- a direction that the verdict must be unanimous (initially); and
- advice as to how the task should be approached.[162]

The summing up, particularly on the law, must be clear;[163] and there are numerous examples where the inquisition has been quashed because of misdirection on the law. Today, Coroners often use specimen directions in relation to potential verdicts, but the content should be agreed first with the advocates for the interested persons.

Bias

Coroners must be fair and impartial. An apparent bias by a Coroner is sometimes used as a reason for a Coroner to recuse himself, or to quash an inquisition. In *R v Inner West London Coroner P Dallaglio and Lockwood Croft*, Sir Thomas Bingham, MR stated that the Coroners' 'central and dominant role in the conduct of an inquest might be said to call for a higher standard since those interested in the proceedings are, to an unusual extent, dependent on his sense of fairness'.[164]

When considering the issue of apparent bias, the Court must first ascertain the circumstances that had a bearing on the suggestion that

159 [2006] EWHC 2575 (Admin), [2006] All ER D 472 (Jul) at para 56.
160 Coroners Rules 1984, r 41.
161 Coroners Rules 1984, r 41.
162 See Dorries, C, *Coroners' Courts: A Guide to Law and Practice* (2nd edition) Oxford University Press (2004) p 249.
163 *R v Inner South London Coroner, ex p Douglas-Williams* [1999] 1 All ER 344.
164 [1994] 4 All ER 139 at 163.

the Coroner was biased. The Court must then apply an objective question, 'whether the fair-minded and informed observer, having considered the facts, would conclude that there was a real possibility that the tribunal was biased.'[165] An example of bias that has been successful is a case in which a Coroner committed himself to the outcome on a particular issue that remained to be adjudicated on.[166]

VERDICTS AND RECOMMENDATIONS

At the end of the evidence, the Coroner or jury must set out their findings on the disputed facts and give a verdict, which are certified in an inquisition.[167] This is the answer to the four statutory questions: who the deceased was, and how, when and where the deceased came by his death.[168] A suggested inquisition is contained in Form 22, in Sch 4 of the Coroners Rules 1984, which sets out the following requirements:

1   The name of the deceased (if known).
2   Injury or disease causing death.
3   Time, place and circumstances at or in which injury was sustained.
4   Conclusion of the jury/Coroner as to the death.
5   Particulars required by the Registration Act–
     (i)   date and place of death;
     (ii)   name and surname of deceased;
     (iii) sex;
     (iv)   maiden surname of woman who has married;
     (v)   date and place of birth; and
     (vi)   occupation and unusual address.

The 'injury or disease causing death' is the medical cause of death set out in the World Health Organisation (WHO) format. Coroners usually following the medical cause of death given by the pathologist, unless there is other evidence to take into account. The 'time, place and circumstances at or in which injury was sustained' is analogous to when, where and how the decreased came by his death.

Verdict: adequacy of the evidence

At the conclusion of the evidence, the Coroner must decide what verdicts are open to himself or the jury. In determining whether a particular verdict is open to reach on the evidence, the test is similar to that laid down in the criminal case of *R* v *Galbraith*: whether taking the evidence at its highest a jury, properly directed, could reach that particular verdict.[169]

In *R* v *Inner South London Coroner, ex p Douglas-Williams*, the Court of Appeal endorsed the use of the *Galbraith* test at inquests. However, the Court qualified its application and indicated that the Coroner had a broad discretion:

---

165 *Porter* v *Magill* [2001] UKHL 67, [2002] 2 AC 357 at para 103.
166 *Hemsworth Application (Collette), An Application for Judicial Review by Collette Hemsworth* [2009] NIQB 33.
167 Coroners Act 1988, s 11(3)(a), (4)(a).
168 Coroners Act 1988, s 11 and Coroners Rules 1984, r 36(1)(a), (b).
169 [1981] 1 WLR 1039.

... in deciding whether to leave a possible verdict to the jury, the coroner had a broad discretion, and he did not need to leave all possible verdicts just because there was technically evidence to support them, since to do so could in some situations merely confuse and overburden the jury; it was sufficient if he left those verdicts which realistically reflected the thrust of the evidence as a whole.[170]

Coronial discretion in relation to verdicts was reconsidered in *R (on the application of Sharman)* v *HM Coroner for Inner North London.* The Administrative Court clarified the position:

that the coroner should, within the spectrum of verdicts open to the jury, decided which 'realistically reflected the thrust of the evidence' rather than be required to indulge in an analysis of each and every conceivable permutation.[171]

Therefore, where there are two almost identical verdicts, one can be discarded if leaving both verdicts would confuse and over burden the jury.[172] Verdicts that incorporate the adjective 'gross', such as neglect and gross negligence manslaughter, import a value judgment, to be assessed by a jury.[173]

Limits to verdicts: Coroners Rules 1984, rr 36 and 42

Coroners are entitled to give a verdict and judgment relevant to matters falling within his jurisdiction, but must not infringe rr 36 and 42 of the Coroners Rules 1984.

Rule 36 provides that:

(1)   The proceedings and evidence at an inquest shall be directed solely to ascertaining the following matters, namely–
    (a)   who the deceased was;
    (b)   how, when and where the deceased came by his death;
    (c)   the particulars for the time being required by the Registration Acts to be registered concerning the death.
(2)   Neither the coroner nor the jury shall express any opinion on any other matters.

In *R (on the application of Farah)* v *HM Coroner for Southampton and New Forest District of Hampshire,* the Administrative Court held that comments made by the Coroner that:

(i)   do not relate to any of the matters falling within his or her jurisdiction;
(ii)   are matters of opinion; and
(iii)   are sufficiently critical and offensive of any party, were unlawful.[174]

In *Farah*, the Coroner not only criticised the deceased's behaviour before his death, he criticised the solicitors representing the deceased's family

---

170 [1999] 1 All ER 344.
171 [2005] EWHC 857 (Admin) CO/6017/2004 at para 9; and see *R (on the application of Cash)* v *County of Northamptonshire Coroner* [2007] EWHC 1354 (Admin), [2007] 4 All ER 903 at paras 22–27.
172 See the case of *R* v *Inner South London Coroner, ex p Douglas-Williams* [1999] 1 All ER 344 for a discussion between the verdict of neglect and gross negligence manslaughter.
173 In the case of neglect see *R (on the application of Commissioner of Police for the Metropolis)* v *HM Coroner for Southern District of Greater London* [2003] EWHC 1892 (Admin), CO/222/2003 at para 60. In the case of gross negligence manslaughter see *R* v *Adomako* [1995] 1 AC 171 at 197 D/E.
174 [2009] EWHC 1605 (Admin), [2009] Inquest Law Reports 220.

for pursuing an allegation of racism. The Administrative Court granted declarations that some comments made by the Coroner were unlawful.

Rule 42 provides that:

> No verdict shall be framed in such a way as to appear to determine any question of–
>
> (a) criminal liability on the part of a named person, or
> (b) civil liability.

In *R v North Humberside Coroner, ex p Jamieson*, Sir Thomas Bingham, MR considered the potential conflict between the statutory duty to establish how the deceased came by his death and the prohibition in r 42:

> It may be accepted that in case of conflict the statutory duty to ascertain how the deceased came by his death must prevail over the prohibition in rule 42. But the scope for conflict is small. Rule 42 applies, and applies only, to the verdict. Plainly the coroner and the jury may explore facts bearing on criminal and civil liability. But the verdict may not appear to determine any question of criminal liability on the part of a named person nor any question of civil liability.[175]

Therefore, it is essential that r 42 is not interpreted in a way that is overextensive, particularly when directing a jury. Verdicts can be judgmental and imply blame without breaching r 42, otherwise there is the risk that there will be omissions in the findings regarding the circumstances of death. A finding by a Coroner or jury that there was a failure to carry out a task, or that precautions were inadequate or inappropriate, or that the illness causing death was treatable are not prohibited by r 42 as such findings do not determine any criminal or civil liability.

However, in the recent application for judicial review in the case of *My Care (UK) Limited* v *HM Coroner for Coventry,* Mr Justice Langstaff stated that the narrative verdict could name My Care (UK) Limited without breaching r 42.[176] My Care (UK) Limited had provided care to Mrs Pearson. At the end of the inquest, the Coroner reached a verdict that neglect had been causative of her death, and stated in a narrative verdict:

> The deceased died from sepsis caused by sacral pressure ulcer. The ulcer developed as a result of neglect in that, notwithstanding 4 visits 7 days per week, including dressing and undressing and toiletry needs, it had not been recognised by her carers that she had a developing pressure sore. The discovery of the pressure sore was made by her friend Iris Payne rather than her carers on or about the 15th December 2007. The matter was reported to her GP and district nurses attended on 17 December 2008. At that stage it was noted to be a grade 4 pressure sore.

My Care (UK) Limited complained that the verdict was a breach of r 42 as it identified the company as being responsible for the death. Mr Justice Langstaff disagreed, and stated that even if My Care (UK) Limited had been named, it was not a breach of r 42, and the application for judicial review was refused. Consequently, a submission can be made to the Coroner about naming the individual or company/organisation

---

175 [1995] QB 1 at 24 E.
176 *My Care (UK) Ltd* v *HM Coroner for Coventry* [2009] EWHC 3630 (Admin); CO/11963/2009 at paras 5 and 6.

responsible for neglect in a narrative verdict, and arguably any verdict, except a verdict of unlawful killing. Whether Coroners will actually name anyone in the verdict remains to be seen.

Rule 42 and a verdict of unlawful killing was the subject of an application for judicial review in 2010. In *R (on the application of Evans) v HM Coroner for Cardiff and the Vale of Glamorgan*, the Coroner returned a verdict of unlawful killing (gross negligence).[177] The verdict contained in the inquisition did not name the nurse who accidentally administered an overdose of insulin causing death, but a document prepared by the Coroner entitled 'Summing up and Verdict' referred to the nurse by name on numerous occasions. The Administrative Court gave permission for a hearing on whether r 42 was breached,[178] but at the time of writing it is not known if this is being pursued.

Verdicts and causation

In the recent case of *R (Lewis) v HM Coroner for the Mid and North Division of the County of Shropshire*, the Court of Appeal considered the extent to which causation is relevant to the verdict.[179] This is a significant issue because inquests usually investigate issues that are not subsequently included in the verdict. The issue in *Lewis* was whether a Coroner is obliged to leave to the jury a fact or circumstance that could have caused or contributed to the death, but it cannot be shown on the balance of probability to have done so.

Karl Lewis, who had a history of self-harm, was serving a prison sentence in a young offenders institution. One night, Lewis hanged himself from a light fitting; and was found by Officer Support Grade Knowles during a routine check. OSG Knowles had not received any suicide prevention or first aid training, and was not equipped with a 'fishknife', which is a special tool designed to enable suicide victims to be cut down promptly without further injury. OSG Knowles summoned assistance, but used the incorrect procedure so that the assistance took longer than it should have done to arrive. By the time Lewis was cut down, he was dead. It could not be determined on the balance of probability that more appropriate and swifter intervention by OSG Knowles would have saved Lewis; although it might have done. The Coroner prepared a questionnaire to elicit the jury's findings on the central matters. However, the jury was not asked to make any findings of fact about the actions of the prison staff that occurred after the body was discovered.

The Court of Appeal held that there was a power but not a duty to allow a jury to make findings of fact on non-causative matters. If non-causative matters are not left to the jury, this may hamper the Coroner's ability to make recommendations to prevent future fatalities at the end of the inquest (a Rule 43 Report[180]). This is because Rule 43 Reports are based on factual findings, and in a jury inquest, the jury makes the findings of fact.[181] In *Lewis*, the Rule 43 Report was based on uncontested evidence

177 [2010] EWHC 3478 (Admin).
178 [2010] EWHC 3478 (Admin), [2010] Inquest LR 217.
179 [2009] EWCA Civ 1403, [2010] All ER 858.
180 Coroners Rules 1984, r 43.
181 Coroners Act 1988, s 11(3).

that OSG Knowles did not have the required training or equipment. Therefore, the fact that the Coroner did not ask the jury to make findings of fact on these issues was irrelevant; the Coroner was able to submit a Rule 43 Report on the uncontested evidence. However, where the evidence is disputed and a Rule 43 Report is required to discharge the state's obligations under Art 2, the Coroner will need to put a non-causative issue to the jury or alternatively make findings on whether the state failed to comply with it obligation to protect life, irrespective of whether the failure resulted in death in order to exercise the r 43 power.

Verdicts: standard of proof

The facts to support most verdicts at an inquest must be proved to the civil standard of proof. However, the verdicts of suicide and unlawful killing require the facts to be found to the criminal standard. Breaches of Art 2 of the European Convention of Human Rights must also be established to the criminal standard of proof.[182] An open verdict reflects the fact that the evidence has not met the requirements for any other verdicts, and arguably does not require any standard of proof.

Verdicts in healthcare deaths

There are short-form verdicts and a narrative verdict. Short-form verdicts are viewed as traditional verdicts. They are set out in Form 22, in Sch 4 of the Coroners Rules 1984. The Form 22 list of potential verdicts is non-exhaustive, as Sch 4 is merely guidance.[183] In addition to announcing a short-form verdict, the Coroner must record the facts that he or she has found on the relevant issues. The relevant short-form verdicts in relation to healthcare deaths are natural causes, suicide/suicide whilst the balance of the deceased's mind was disturbed; accidental death/misadventure; want of attention at birth; unlawful killing and an open verdict. The alternative to the short-form verdict is a narrative verdict, where the Coroner explains what happened, although a short-form verdict may have a narrative verdict appended to it.[184]

Natural causes

A verdict of 'natural causes' is given were a suspected 'unnatural' death is found at the inquest to be the result of a natural disease process without significant human intervention. At the inquest, other potentially causative matters will be investigated, such as whether a delay in ordering a CT scan had caused or materially contributed to the death of a child.[185] In 2010, a

---

182 *Ireland* v *UK* (1879–1980) 2 EHRR 25 at 161.
183 *R* v *HM Coroner for Inner London North District, ex p Thomas* [1993] QB 610 (also referred to as *R* v *Poplar Coroner, ex p Thomas*).
184 *R (on the application of P)* v *HM Coroner for the District of Avon* [2009] EWCA Civ 1367, 112 BMLR 77 at 28.
185 *R* v *HM Coroner for Avon, ex p Smith* [1998] EWHC 174, (1998) 162 JP 403. This case actually arose out of the refusal of a Coroner to hold an inquest on the basis that the death was the result of natural causes (a cerebella haematoma).

verdict of natural causes was the most common verdict at inquests (29%), increasing from 12% in 1994.[186]

Suicide/suicide whilst the balance of the deceased's mind was disturbed

> Suicide is voluntarily doing an act for the purpose of destroying one's life whilst one is conscious of what one is doing, in order to arrive at a verdict of suicide there must be evidence that the deceased intended the consequence of the act.[187]

Suicide can never be presumed,[188] and evidence that the deceased intended to take his own life is required. In the absence of a letter left by the deceased, circumstantial evidence can be used to draw an inference of an intention to end life. For example, whether the deceased may have anticipated being found before death occurred, or whether survival was unlikely, such a jumping from a high building. Therefore, before reaching a verdict of suicide, a question that must be considered is 'whether other possible explanations were totally ruled out'.[189]

A verdict of suicide requires evidence to the criminal standard of beyond reasonable doubt.[190] If the evidence does not establish the cause of death to be suicide to the required criminal standard, it has been held that the appropriate verdict is an open verdict,[191] although it is arguable that a narrative verdict might better explain the circumstances of death. Coroners rarely record a death as 'suicide', preferring 'the deceased took his or her own life, or killed him/herself'. A verdict of suicide was found in 11% of all inquests in 2010; representing a downward trend.[192]

Suicide whilst the balance of the deceased's mind was disturbed

Form 22 provides for the addition of 'whilst the balance of his or mind was disturbed' to the verdict of suicide. For some families, this addition to the verdict tends to ameliorate the distress caused by a verdict of suicide. A disturbance of the mind verdict will only be available at an inquest if there is evidence in support, and only needs to be established on the balance of probabilities.

Accidental death/misadventure

There is some debate as to whether 'accidental death' and 'misadventure' are the same verdicts, although the majority of opinion is that it is a distinction 'without purpose or effect'.[193] 'Accidental' death is often

---

186 Ministry of Justice (Statistics Bulletin), *Statistics on deaths reported to coroners in England and Wales, 2010* (published May 2011): www.justice.gov.uk/coroners-deaths-reported-2011.pdf.
187 *R* v *Cardiff Coroner, ex p Thomas* (1970) 3 All ER 469 at 472.
188 *R* v *Cardiff Coroner, ex p Thomas* (1970) 3 All ER 469.
189 *R* v *HM Coroner for the County of Essex ex p Hopper* [1988] Crown Office Digest 7.
190 *R* v *Cardiff Coroner, ex p Thomas* (1970) 3 All ER 469.
191 *R* v *City of London Coroner, ex p Barber* [1975] 1 WLR 1310 at 1313.
192 Ministry of Justice (Statistics Bulletin), *Statistics on deaths reported to coroners in England and Wales, 2010* (published May 2011): www.justice.gov.uk/coroners-deaths-reported-2011.pdf.
193 *R* v *Portsmouth Coroners Court, ex p Anderson* [1987] 1 WLR 1640 as 1646 (*obiter*).

used when the death results from an unintended act with unintended consequences. A verdict of 'misadventure' is often used where a deliberate act has unintended consequences, for example, a patient who dies following an operation. Verdicts of death by accident or misadventure have been declining, from 47% of all verdicts returned in 1994 to 28% in 2010.[194]

A more important distinction is between accidental death/misadventure and death from natural causes in the medical context. This was considered in *R v HM Coroner for Birmingham and Solihull, ex p Benton*,[195] a case in which a child died in hospital following a bronchoscopy. The Court made the following distinction in relation to healthcare deaths:

Natural causes

> The first is where a person is suffering from a potentially fatal condition and medical intervention does no more than fail to prevent that death. In such circumstances the underlying cause of death is the condition that proved fatal and in such a case, the correct verdict would be death from natural causes. This would be the case even if the medical treatment that had been given was viewed generally by the medical profession as the wrong treatment. All the more so is the case where such a person is not treated at all, even if the failure to give the treatment was negligent.

Accident / misadventure

> Where a person is suffering from a condition which does not in any way threaten his life and such person undergoes treatment which for whatever reason causes death, then, assuming that there is no question of unlawful killing, the verdict should be death by accident, misadventure.

Want of attention at birth

This is an ancient verdict, which is a form of neglect. It is unlikely that such a verdict would be given today.

Unlawful killing

A verdict of unlawful killing includes murder and manslaughter, including:

1   wrongful act/constructive involuntary manslaughter, and
2   gross negligence manslaughter.

The standard of proof in unlawful killing is the criminal standard.[196] Unlawful killing is an infrequent verdict in the Coroners' Court. However, the fact that the Crown Prosecution Service has decided not to prosecute,[197]

---

194 Ministry of Justice (Statistics Bulletin), *Statistics on deaths reported to coroners in England and Wales, 2010* (published May 2011): www.justice.gov.uk/coroners-deaths-reported-2011.pdf.
195 (1997) 8 Med LR 362 at 366.
196 *R v West London Coroner, ex p Gray* [1998] 1 QB 467.
197 See the recent inquest before the HM Coroner for Cardiff and the Vale of Glamorgan. A nurse administered an overdose of insulin causing death. The verdict of the Coroner was that it was an unlawful killing, and the CPS indicated that it would review its decision not to prosecute. See news.bbc.co.uk/1/hi/wales/south_east/7967862.stm.

or that the prosecution resulted in an acquittal, does not bar the possibility of such a verdict in the Coroners' Court. A practitioner considering addressing a Coroner on such a verdict is advised to refer to a specialist criminal practitioner textbook.

Unlawful act manslaughter

The requirements for unlawful act manslaughter were set out by the Court of Appeal in *R* v *Inner South London Coroner, ex p Douglas-Williams*:

(i)   there must be an unlawful act (in this case an assault);
(ii)   that act must be dangerous in the sense that any reasonable and sober person would recognise that the assault exposed the victim to risk of some harm, albeit not necessarily serious harm; and
(iii) that the unlawful act caused death in the sense that it more than minimally, negligibly or trivially contributed to the death.[198]

Gross negligence manslaughter

The requirements for gross negligence manslaughter were set out by the House of Lords in the criminal case of *R* v *Adomako*.[199] In *Adomako*, the defendant anaesthetist failed to notice that a tube supplying oxygen to the patient (who had been paralysed for the operation) had become disconnected from a ventilator during an eye operation. The disconnection lasted some six minutes, and the patient suffered a cardiac arrest from which he subsequently died. Two expert witnesses gave evidence for the prosecution. One described the standard of care by the defendant as 'abysmal'. The other stated that a competent anaesthetist should have recognised the signs of disconnection within 15 seconds, and that the defendant's conduct amounted to 'a gross dereliction of care'.

The House of Lords held that the requirements for gross negligence manslaughter are:

1   the existence of a duty of care;
2   a breach of that duty of care;
3   the breach caused the death of the deceased; and
4   a finding by the jury that the breach was 'gross' and consequently criminal.

Lord Mackay stated that a finding of gross negligence would depend upon the seriousness of the breach of duty committed by the defendant in all the circumstances in which the defendant was placed when it occurred. The jury needs to consider whether, having regard to the risk of death involved, the conduct of the defendant was so bad in all the circumstances as to amount to a criminal act or omission.[200]

Gross negligence manslaughter was considered by the Court of Appeal in the context of the Coroners' Court in *R* v *Inner South London Coroner, ex p Douglas-Williams*.[201] The Court of Appeal set out the requirements for a verdict of killing by gross negligence manslaughter:

---

198 [1999] 1 All ER 344 at 350.
199 [1995] 1 AC 171.
200 *R* v *Adomako* [1995] 1 AC 171 at 187.
201 [1999] 1 All ER 344 at 350.

(i)   negligence consisting of an act or failure to act;
(ii) that negligence must have caused the death in the sense that it more than minimally, negligibly or trivially contributed to the death; and
(iii) the degree of negligence has to be such that it can be characterised as gross in the sense that it was of an order that merits criminal sanctions rather than a duty merely to compensate the victim.

Open verdict

An open verdict is a decision by the Coroner or the jury that there is insufficient evidence to reach any of the short-form verdicts, or the evidence does not meet the required standard of proof for a short-form verdict. Although an open verdict reflects the fact that the exact circumstances of how the deceased came by his death remain unknown, it is preferable for a narrative verdict to be given, setting out the facts that have been determined.

Neglect

A rider of 'contributed to by neglect' may be attached to verdicts of natural causes, want of attention at birth, suicide and accident /misadventure,[202] or could be included in a narrative verdict. Many families want neglect to be considered during the inquest where the deceased died in contentious circumstances. On the other hand, some families want reassurance that nothing more could have been done by the healthcare team to prevent the deceased from dying. Neglect is not a common verdict in inquests concerned with healthcare deaths. However, where a narrative verdict is given, Coroners can include failings that contributed to the death.

The leading case on neglect is *R* v *North Humberside Coroner, ex p Jamieson.*[203] Michael Jamieson was serving a long sentence of imprisonment. During his incarceration, Jamieson attempted suicide, and had received hospital treatment for depression. Whilst detained in the hospital wing, Jamieson exhibited worrying behaviour for some days and then committed suicide by hanging. The question for the Court of Appeal was whether the Coroner had wrongly directed the jury not to consider whether his death has been caused or contributed to by a lack of care by the prison authorities who had placed Jamieson in a single cell in a prison hospital without special supervision.

The Court of Appeal held that, at its highest, the applicant's case suggested that the doctors and the prison authorities gave the deceased an opportunity to take his life. The court provided guidelines for the conduct of cases involving the possibility of neglect:

> Neglect in this context means a gross failure to provide adequate nourishment or liquid, or provide or procure basic medical attention or shelter or warmth for someone in a dependent position (because of youth, age, illness or incarceration) who cannot provide it for himself. Failure to provide medical attention for a

---

202 Neglect is included in Form 22, in Sch 4 of the Coroners Rules 1984; which states that neglect can only be attached to verdicts of natural cases and want of attention at birth. However, Sch 4 is not binding: *R* v *HM Coroner for Inner London North District ex p Thomas* [1993] QB 610 (also referred to as *R* v *Poplar Coroner, ex p Thomas*).
203 [1995] QB 1.

dependent person whose physical condition is such as to show that he obviously needs it may amount to neglect. So it may be if it is the dependent person's mental condition which obviously calls for medical attention (as it would, for example, if a mental nurse observed that a patient had a propensity to swallow razor blades and failed to report this propensity to a doctor, in a case where the patient had no intention to cause himself injury but did thereafter swallow razor blades with fatal results). In both cases the crucial consideration will be what the dependent person's condition, whether physical or mental, appeared to be.[204]

Initially, the *Jamieson* test was interpreted as requiring a complete absence of care, or the failure to take an obviously necessary step. The requirements were the need for basic medical attention to be obvious, the patient to be dependent on others to provide that attention, and a gross failure to provide or procure that attention. In two cases following *Jamieson*, poor medical treatment and care was held not to satisfy these requirements. In *R v HM Coroner for Birmingham, ex p Cotton*, the court held that where death resulted from a clinical judgment (wrong medical treatment), which might or might not be negligent, a verdict of neglect could not be left to the jury.[205] The issue arose again in *R v HM Coroner for Surrey, ex p Wright*,[206] which was an application for judicial review where an anaesthetist failed to maintain the deceased's airway during minor dental surgery. Tucker J held that a verdict of neglect was not open to the Coroner, despite the Coroner's finding of fact that death resulted from a lack of care. Further, he held that neglect must be 'continuous or at least non-transient', and that was not an appropriate description of the negligent lack of care in this case.

Recent decisions indicate a widening of the *Jamieson* test, and that errors in diagnosis and treatment are capable of amounting to neglect. In *R (Davies) v Birmingham Deputy Coroner* the court held that an error by a nurse in deciding that an inmate's condition did not require further assistance until the following day could amount to neglect.[207] In *R (Nicholls) v Coroner for City of Liverpool*,[208] the court considered the alleged failure of a police medical examiner to properly recognise the fact that the deceased had swallowed drugs, believed to be heroin. Sullivan J said:

> Notwithstanding [Counsel's] submission that neglect and negligence are two different 'animals', there is, in reality, no precise dividing line between 'a gross failure to provide ... basic medical attention' and a 'failure to provide ... medical attention'. The difference is bound to be one of degree, highly dependent on the facts of the particular case.[209]

Neglect does not need to be confined to the acts or omissions of one person; and acts of omissions by different individuals and systemic failures may combine to form a 'total picture that amounts to neglect'.[210] Neglect may

---

204 *R v North Humberside and Scunthorpe Coroner, ex p Jamieson* [1994] 3 All ER 972 at 990–991.

205 [1995] 160 JP 123.

206 [1997] QB 786.

207 [2003] EWCA Civ 1739.

208 [2001] EWHC Admin 992.

209 *R (Nicholls) v Coroner for City of Liverpool* [2001] EWHC Admin 992 at para 52, Sullivan J and Rose LJ agreed.

210 *R (on the application of S) v Inner West London Coroner* [2001] EWHC Admin 105 at paras 13 and 29; 61 BMLR 222.

also be a 'continuous sequence of shortcomings'.[211] Not every failure in treatment or care will amount to neglect and it will depend upon the facts and circumstances of the case. Matters that may amount neglect in healthcare settings include:

1   the failure to monitor a patient's condition;[212]
2   the failure to provide effective medical treatment;[213]
3   the failure to properly recognise the deceased's medical condition;[214] and
4   the failure to take into account relevant and reasonably obtainable information in care and treatment.[215]

Neglect and causation

The causal test for neglect is somewhat uncertain. The original test set out in *Jamieson* was for a 'clear and direct' causal connection between the neglect and the death.[216] However, this is a difficult test to satisfy and on occasions the test has been modified by the courts.[217] In *R (on the application of Khan)* v *HM Coroner for West Herefordshire*, Richards J reviewed recent authorities on neglect and causation.[218] He concluded that it was sufficient to establish on the balance of probabilities that the conduct made a material contribution to death.[219] Neglect does not need to be the sole or predominant cause of death.[220]

Narrative verdict

A narrative verdict is the conclusions by a Coroner or a jury on the main issues arising out of the circumstances by which the deceased came by his death and is often associated with enhanced *Middleton* inquests. There is no guidance for Coroners on the form and content of a narrative verdict, but the main issues arguably include the matters that caused or contributed to death, any systemic failings, and any relevant circumstantial matters in enhanced *Middleton* inquests.[221] A narrative verdict is not required if a short-form verdict encapsulates the jury's

---

211 *R* v *HM Coroner for Wiltshire, ex p Clegg* (1997) 161 JP 521.
212 *R* v *Inner London North Coroner, ex p, Touche* [20001] EWCA Civ 383, [2001] 2 All ER 752.
213 *R* v *HM Coroner for Wiltshire, ex p Clegg* (1997) 161 JP 521.
214 *R* v *HM Coroner for Greater London (Inner West), ex p Scott* [2001] EWHC Admin 105, 165 JP 417.
215 *R* v *HM Coroner for Greater London (Inner West), ex p Scott* [2001] EWHC Admin 105, 165 JP 417.
216 *R* v *North Humberside and Scunthorpe Coroner, ex p Jamieson* [1994] 3 All ER 972 at 991.
217 See *R* v *HM Coroner for Coventry, ex p Chiefly Constable of Staffordshire* (2000) 164 JP 655; and *R (Nicholls)* v *HM Coroner for the City of Liverpool* [2001] EWHC Admin 922.
218 [2002] EWHC (Admin) 302, [2002] All ER (D) 68 (Mar).
219 *R (on the application of Khan)* v *HM Coroner for West Herefordshire* [2002] All ER (D) 68 (Mar) at 43(i).
220 *R (on the application of Commissioner of Police for the Metropolis)* v *HM Coroner for Southern District of Greater London* [2003] EWHC 1892 (Admin), CO/222/2003 at 57.
221 *R (on the application of Middleton)* v *HM Coroner for West Somerset* [2004] 2 AC.

conclusions on all the main issues.[222] Narrative verdicts may also be (and often are) used in traditional *Jamieson* inquests,[223] although the type of narrative findings that may be made is uncertain.[224]

It is for the Coroner to determine how best to elicit the jury's conclusion on the central issues in the inquest,[225] and in healthcare deaths it is likely that the jury will require assistance with complex medical evidence to ascertain the issues that must be decided. Some Coroners use questionnaires prepared by the Coroner and the advocates to elicit the conclusions of the jury, although care must be taken to ensure that the jury are not restricted in their answers. It is helpful if advocates prepare a draft questionnaire in advance of the hearing that can be refined as the inquest progresses.

Recommendations: Coroners Rules 1984, r 43

Rule 43 of the Coroners Rules 1984 provides Coroners with the power to make reports to a person or organisation where the Coroner believes that action should be taken to prevent the recurrence of fatalities. Rule 43 has been strengthened by the enactment of the Coroners (Amendment) Rules 2008, with effect from 17 July 2008.[226] However, delays in the coronial service result in a corresponding delay in the implementation of improvements, and this is of concern in light of the fact that a purpose of the inquest is to prevent future fatalities.

Rule 43 provides:

(1)   Where—
   (a)   a coroner is holding an inquest into a person's death;
   (b)   the evidence gives rise to a concern that circumstances creating a risk of other deaths will occur, or will continue to exist, in the future; and
   (c)   in the coroner's opinion, action should be taken to prevent the occurrence or continuation of such circumstances, or to eliminate or reduce the risk of death created by such circumstances,
   the coroner may report the circumstances to a person who the coroner believes may have power to take such action.[227]

Although it is a permissive power, Coroners are under a duty to make a Rule 43 Report in an enhanced *Middleton* inquest if the requirements of r 43 of the Coroners Rules 1984 are satisfied.[228] In the case of *R (Lewis)* v *HM Coroner for the Mid and North Division of the County of Shropshire* the

---

222 For example, in *Middleton* a short-form verdict of suicide was insufficient as the jury were unable to express its conclusion on the central issues of whether the deceased should have been recognised as a suicide risk and whether appropriate precautions should have been taken to prevent him taking his own life: *R (on the application of Middleton)* v *HM Coroner for West Somerset* [2004] UKHL 10, [2004] 2 AC 182.
223 *R (on the application of Longfield Care Homes)* v *HM Coroner for Blackburn* [2004] EWHC 2467 (Admin).
224 *R (on the application of Hurst)* v *Commissioner of Police for the Metropolis* [2007] UKHL 13, [2007] 2 AC 189.
225 *R (on the application of Middleton)* v *HM Coroner for West Somerset* [2004] 2 AC 182 at para 36.
226 SI 2008/1652.
227 Coroners Rules 1984, r 43, as amended by the Coroners (Amendment) Rules 2008.
228 *R (Lewis)* v *HM Coroner for the Mid and North Division of the County of Shropshire* [2009] EWCA Civ 1403, [2010] All ER 858 paras 16 and 38.

Court of Appeal held that evidence that there was inadequate equipment, training, and effective procedures required action to be taken to prevent similar fatalities. The power is reserved to the Coroner, but 'may well be influenced by the factual conclusions of the jury'.[229] A report cannot be made until the end of the evidence, except where an inquest is adjourned under s 16 or 17A of the Coroners Act 1988 and is not resumed.[230] The Coroner must announce his intention to make a report before the end of the inquest.[231]

The person or organisation that receives a report is under a duty to provide the Coroner with a written response within 56 days,[232] although an extension of time may be granted.[233] The response must contain details of any actions that have been, or will be, taken, or an explanation as to why no action is proposed.[234] If a person or organisation fails to respond, the Coroner should make reasonable attempts to follow the matter up.[235] However, there is no sanction for a failure to respond. In such circumstances, Coroners may retain this information and should a death occur in similar circumstances, there is evidence of a failure to take action.

The Coroner must send a copy of the report to the Lord Chancellor, any interested person,[236] and any person who the Coroner believes may find it useful or of interest,[237] which arguably includes the media. The Ministry of Justice collates the reports and produces a bi-annual summary report available on its website: *Summary of reports and responses under Rule 43 of the Coroners Rules*. So far, five summary reports have been published.

In all five summary reports, Rule 43 Reports were most commonly issued in connection with hospital deaths (average of 26–31%). The major issues are concerns about communication, lack of awareness by staff of procedures and protocols, or a failure to follow procedures and protocols, and staff training. An emerging trend in September 2010 was concern about the procedures on discharge from hospital and ensuring appropriate medical support and/or instructions for patients. In September 2011, the second most commonly issued reports were in relation to community healthcare and emergency service deaths. The summary report is a synopsis of the reports and responses but copies of a particular report can be obtained from the Lord Chancellor.[238]

Closure of the inquest, media, and publicity

At the conclusion of the inquest, the Coroner must send to the Registrar of Deaths a certificate of all the relevant information concerning the

---

229 *R (on the application of Middleton)* v *HM Coroner for West Somerset* [2004] UKHL 10, [2004] 2 AC 182 at para 38.
230 Coroners Rules 1984, r 43(2).
231 Coroners Rules 1984, r 43(3).
232 Coroners Rules 1984, r 43A(1)(b).
233 Coroners Rules 1984, r 43B.
234 Coroners Rules 1984, r 43A(1)(a).
235 Ministry of Justice, *Guidance for coroners in changes to rule 43: coroners reports to prevent future deaths*, para 4.8.
236 Coroners Rules 1984, r 43(1), (4)(a).
237 Coroners Rules 1984, r 43(1), (4)(b).
238 The details to be included in the letter and the contact information are included in each summary report.

death[239] for the death to be registered. The Coroner's Officer will often assist with information in relation to collecting the final death certificate.

Representatives of the media frequently attend inquests, often the initial and final days. At the conclusion of the inquest, they will usually ask whether the family or the hospital/GP would like to make a statement for publication. It is advisable to have discussed this with the client before the conclusion of the inquest so that a decision can be made whether a statement will be given by the family/hospital staff/GP or their legal representatives, and the latter is usually preferable. A statement can be prepared for the final day, or the media can be asked to contact the solicitor's office the following day. If relevant, the hospital or GP should consider whether to make an apology (and often this is done at the start of an inquest); and outline any changes in practice to prevent deaths in similar circumstances.

FUNDING AND THE RECOVERABILITY OF COSTS

When it comes to obtaining legal representation, the family will have to consider carefully how they will meet the costs. As the hearing is an inquisitorial process and there is no notion of winning or losing, public funding is only available in very restricted circumstances. Occasionally, inquest costs are met by the deceased or his family having legal expenses insurance that will cover the costs of the inquest. Generally, where there is also a civil claim, and where at the conclusion of the civil claim it can be shown that preparing for and attending the inquest progressed the civil claim, those inquest costs can be recovered from the paying party.[240] However, that may be some way down the line. Deciding how to meet the costs of an inquest is a difficult issue for the family; likewise for the solicitor representing them in a civil claim. Inquests are costly hearings to prepare for and run, and are very time consuming, often over a very short space of time. The following gives some guidance on how to obtain funding.

Although we deal with obtaining public funding first, we would emphasise that public funding for inquests is generally only obtainable where you can demonstrate at least an arguable case that the state has been in breach of its substantive duty to protect life, following on from the secretary of state's guidance on providing exceptional funding and the recent Court of Appeal decision in *Humberstone* (cited above). Furthermore, public funding is extremely limited and often only provides cover for very limited preparation and representation at the hearing itself. Obtaining that funding is an uphill struggle and is rarely granted. Once granted you are vulnerable to it being withdrawn at any time and it is unlikely to cover even core costs of attending the inquest. The current rates and what is paid are set out below.

---

239 Coroners Act 1988, s 11(7).
240 Costs of representing relatives are recoverable from a tortfeasor as costs of a subsequent successful civil action: *King* v *Milton Keynes General NHS Trust* (13 May 2004) Gage J; *Stewart* v *Medway NHS Trust* 2004 EWHC 901; *Roach* v *Home Office, Matthews* v *Home Office* [2009] EWHC 312 (QB).

Because of the difficulties in obtaining exceptional funding, and the low rates payable, solicitors may find it preferable to enter into a CFA with the family in cases where a successful civil claim is envisaged, and rely on the cases of *King* and *Roach* for recovery of costs at the conclusion of the civil claim.[241] CFAs involve risk on the part of the solicitor and often their counsel, but allow you to claim costs at the end of a successful civil claim at commercial inter-partes rates. Alternatively you can ask the family to privately fund the inquest. Where there is no civil claim to be pursued and no body that may be willing to finance the inquest, then privately financing legal services is the family's only option, unless they can persuade a charitable organisation to provide *pro bono* inquest services; for example, the British Legion has an inquest service that assists with providing representation and assistance at inquests, as does AvMA.

Public funding

Generally

If you have obtained an investigative certificate for a civil claim and there is also to be an inquest it will not cover representation at the inquest itself but will cover all the usual investigative stages that must be gone through to prepare for an inquest. Funding for representation at the inquest itself is only available under exceptional funding. Exceptional funding is only available if you can show that the inquest is to be the way in which the state complies with its Art 2 obligation to investigate cases where the state has been in breach of its substantive duty to protect life. This obligation does *not* arise routinely in clinical negligence cases (see *Takoushis* above).

The exceptional funding scheme is currently administered for the Ministry of Justice (MOJ) by the Legal Services Commission (LSC). The LSC Funding Code, Chapter 27 deals with the application process and familiarity with the code is essential when making the application. It contains the current payment rates.[242] This funding is available even if the traditional legal aid funding eligibility tests are not satisfied.[243] It is very important that public funding for Art 2 inquests is available. Often there is no prospect of a civil claim to cover the costs and the family cannot afford the minimum cost of £5,000 to prepare for and provide representation at, say, a two-day hearing. For example, the 7/7 inquest ongoing in 2010/11 was never going to lead to a civil claim for any family but the importance to the families, and the public importance of that hearing meant funding was made available. The Gosport Memorial Hospitals two-week inquest in 2009 likewise was funded by the LSC because of the wider general importance, and the concern that there had been systemic errors that had to be investigated. No family involved in these hearings realistically could afford the very high costs of having legal representation without the assistance of legal aid.

---

241 *King v Milton Keynes General NHS Trust* (13 May 2004) *SCCO AGS 04000350.*
242 www.legalservices.gov.uk/docs/cls_main/Funding_Code_Chapter_27_Exceptional_ Funding_Oct_11.pdf.
243 Access to Justice Act 1999, s 6(8)(b); Community Legal Service (Financial) (Amendment No 2) Regulations 2003 (SI 2003/2838).

The discretion to waive the financial eligibility criteria involves a consideration of:

- whether it is reasonable to expect the bereaved family to bear the full costs of representation;
- the nature and seriousness of the issues under investigation; and
- the view of the Coroner.

Obtaining exceptional funding

The application for exceptional funding should be made on a CLSAPP1 and appropriate means forms for every interested relative to the LSC Special Cases Unit. Means of the relatives has no relevancy for this type of funding. The application should make a sound and clear case as to why this case fits the MOJ requirements.

> An effective Article 2 inquiry must ensure that dangerous practices and procedures are identified and rectified and the risk of future like deaths minimised.

Funding should be granted to ensure the bereaved relatives 'may at least have the satisfaction of knowing that lessons learnt from the death .... may save the lives of others' (Keith J in *R* v *Minister for Legal Aid, ex p Main* [2007] EWHC 742).

Cases most likely to obtain exceptional funding will involve:

- allegations of gross negligence, criminal conduct or attempts to conceal facts;
- issues of medical, legal or factual complexity (arguably all clinical negligence matters so you will most likely have to show why the available witnesses such as the pathologist and treating doctors are unable to explain the issues without the input of legal representation);
- no family involvement in other investigations;
- doubts whether the family could effectively participate without representation;
- other represented agencies who might be able to present the same point of view as that of the relatives;
- a reason why the family or a family member may be at risk of prosecution if they do not have representation, as was the case in *Humberstone*.

Furthermore, following on from *Humberstone* it is advisable to obtain the Coroner's backing and support for legal aid. Without that support, it may be impossible to obtain exceptional funding.

Refusal of public funding

You may ask for reconsideration of the refusal by a LSC Senior Policy Adviser. If they still refuse your application, even with coronial support, the only option is to challenge by judicial review.

Extent of funding

Funding is for inquest advocacy against a budget submitted by the legal advisor. The legal advisor's budget should cover advocacy and immediate inquest preparation only. Other investigative work has to be financed separately, possibly under the Legal Help Scheme if there is no civil claim.

Unlike legal aid for normal case work, no funding certificate is issued and payment is made on submission in a letter setting out the finalised details of the claim. The legal advisor is paid as a one-off grant less a contribution assessed from relatives. That contribution is for the solicitor to collect from the family.

Payment rates

Current LSC exceptional funding payment rates (which no longer include a 50% uplift) are:

Solicitor Rates		Amount / hour (£)	
Item	Grade	Inside London	Outside London
Preparation (inc 50% uplift)	Senior solicitor	75.27	71.55
	Other solicitor	63.80	60.75
	Trainee solicitor	45.90	40.17
Conference with counsel (inc 50% uplift)	Senior solicitor	75.27	71.55
	Other solicitor	63.80	60.75
	Trainee solicitor	45.90	40.17
Attendance at hearing (inc 50% uplift)	Senior solicitor	57.05	57.05
	Other solicitor	45.90	45.90
	Trainee solicitor	27.68	27.68
Advocacy (by solicitor)	Senior solicitor	87.08	87.08
	Other solicitor	75.60	75.60
Travel and waiting	Senior solicitor	22.28	22.28
	Other solicitor	22.28	22.28
	Trainee solicitor	11.25	11.25
Counsel Rates			
Brief Fee	Junior counsel	£900.00	
	Leading counsel	£1800.00	
Refresher Fee (inc 100% uplift)	Junior counsel	£450.00	
	Leading counsel	£630.00	

In some cases the length and complexity of the inquest may justify payment of counsel at a higher rate. The Commission will consider any representations made on this point at the time of the application.

Contribution

The LSC is required by the Legal Aid Regulations to obtain a contribution towards representation costs from relatives. The contribution requirement can be waived by the LSC depending on the facts of the case. Thus, although the grant of exceptional funding is not means tested, the applicant's financial circumstances are taken into account. It is therefore important to set out:

- expenses already incurred;
- applicant's financial circumstances;
- the level of the proposed contribution;
- what hardship that contribution may cause to the applicant;
- the identity of the relatives; and
- the interests of the relatives in participating in and being represented at the inquest.

Contribution is collected by the interested party's solicitor and deducted from the payment to that solicitor made by the LSC.

Legal expenses insurance (LEI)

The availability of legal expenses insurance has increased hugely over the last few years. Most policies do not specifically include inquest representation. However where they will cover the investigations for a civil claim, if it can be demonstrated that participation in and attendance at the inquest is required to fully investigate the claim (and even save the insurer money), then cover for the inquest may be obtained by negotiation with the LEI provider. It will generally not be available for inquests where no civil claim is intended. The policy needs to be reviewed in each case.

Conditional fee agreements (CFAs)

There are cases where it would appear that there may be a civil claim arising out of the wrongful death of the deceased. In those circumstances, solicitors can take on the case under a conditional fee agreement. No special CFA is required for a civil claim including an inquest. Take into account that the case law as to recoverability of inquest costs assumes that only costs incurred to progress the civil claim are recoverable. Therefore be very clear when advising your client that if there are aspects of the inquest that do not progress the claim (for example, the family seeking answers to questions that are about conduct of clinicians and that have no bearing on the alleged negligence, or expert evidence is obtained for the inquest not later relied on for the civil claim) the costs of those aspects will remain payable by the family.

Recovering costs of the inquest after the conclusion of the civil claim

Roach v *Home Office* [2009] EWHC 312 (QB) (25 February 2009), decided in the Senior Courts Costs Office deals with the recoverability of costs. This case followed on from the case of *King* v *Milton Keynes General NHS Trust* (13 May 2004) SCCO AGS 04000350 which had accepted the approach to costs applied in *Bowbelle* (1997) 2 Lloyds Rep 196.

The case law has established that the costs of attendance at inquests are capable of being recovered as costs incidental to subsequent civil proceedings. In the case of Roach, the Home Office had sought to overturn earlier decisions and to argue that costs incurred in a prior proceeding (in this case the Inquest) could not be recovered in later proceedings. However the Court held that the position is governed by section 51 of the Supreme Court Act 1981 (as amended):

51 Costs in civil division of Court of Appeal, High Court and county courts

(1) Subject to the provisions of this or any other enactment and to rules of court, the costs of and incidental to all proceedings in:
    (a) the civil division of the Court of Appeal;
    (b) the High Court; and
    (c) any county court,
    shall be in the discretion of the court.

(2) Without prejudice to any general power to make rules of court, such rules may make provision for regulating matters relating to the costs of those proceedings including, in particular, prescribing scales of costs to be paid to legal or other representatives [or for securing that the amount awarded to a party in respect of the costs to be paid by him to such representatives is not limited to what would have been payable by him to them if he had not been awarded costs].

(3) The court shall have full power to determine by whom and to what extent the costs are to be paid.

...

The court also held that CPR 44.4(1) applied to inquest costs and therefore costs will not be allowed 'which have been unreasonably incurred or are unreasonable in amount' and dismissed the Home Office's submission that the costs of the inquest were not recoverable.

When claiming costs at the end of the civil claim, the role of lawyers in attending an inquest will be considered to fall into two equal parts: assisting the Coroner and obtaining evidence necessary to pursue the civil claim. Costs arising out of obtaining evidence to pursue the claim are recoverable inter-partes. So for example, you may attend an inquest where the family instruct you to ask questions on an issue that it is clear will not advance a civil claim. Those costs will most likely not be recoverable. Solicitors for the claimant(s) will need to demonstrate what aspect of their work for the inquest advanced the civil claim. Thus during the course of conduct of a civil claim that includes attendance at an inquest, it is advisable to firstly indicate as you go along why you think the work being carried out is relevant to the claim. It is also advisable to provide instructions to experts and/or counsel that make clear whether you are instructing them for the purposes of the civil claim or the inquest. The family should be clearly advised from the outset that all of the costs of the inquest may not be recovered and whether they will be expected to meet those costs ultimately.

Some additional points to note: proportionality applies to inquest costs. Also, there is always a risk that the defendant may admit liability prior to the inquest hearing. If that happens the justification for attending the hearing will need to be carefully considered; can it be argued that attendance goes to issues of say life expectancy? If attendance does not advance the case then the costs will not be recoverable inter-partes. However, in the presence of an admission there is always the option of asking the defendant to fund some of the family's costs of attending the hearing; they did not chose to have that hearing and whilst the civil claim meets their Art 2 rights, equally an early admission may mean the family's chance to ask questions about why and how their loved one died comes to an abrupt halt. The inquest then is the last and only chance to ask those questions, whether liability has been admitted or not.

POST-INQUEST REMEDIES

Decisions of Coroners can be challenged by way of judicial review and under s 13 of the Coroners Act 1988. Both procedures can be used, provided the qualifying criteria for each procedure are satisfied.

Judicial review

The Coroner's powers are set out in statute and secondary legislation, and the Office of the Coroner performs public duties. Therefore, coronial decisions and proceedings are amenable to judicial review. The people that are likely to have sufficient standing to bring judicial review proceedings are the 'interested persons', and any individual/organisation whose conduct is called into question at the inquest. In the healthcare context, this will include the family of the deceased, the hospital and/or GP, and healthcare staff.

In order to bring judicial review proceedings, there must be a public law error or failing by the Coroner. The grounds for challenging include:

1   A decision that was unlawful because the Coroner did not have the power to make the decision (*ultra vires*). The starting point is to consider the Coroners Act 1988 and the Coroners Rules 1984 to identify the provision under which the purported decision was made.
2   A decision that was irrational (Wednesbury unreasonable[244]). This is a decision that is so perverse that no reasonable Coroner properly directing himself to the law to be applied could have reached.
3   An error of law. Errors of law include misinterpreting a statute or secondary legislation, taking irrelevant considerations into account, failing to take relevant considerations into account, and failing to follow the proper procedures required by law.
4   An act was incompatible with a Convention right.[245] In coronial law, this is likely to include Art 2 and Art 8.
5   The proceedings were conducted in breach of procedural fairness or natural justice. These principles include the right to an unbiased decision maker and a right to a fair hearing.

The types of decisions by Coroners that have been the subject of judicial review proceedings include refusing to hold an inquest, failing to order a post-mortem examination, wrongfully limiting the scope of the inquest, failing to leave a particular verdict to the jury or an error of law in directing the jury on a verdict, failing to obtain expert evidence, failing to hear legal submissions on behalf of interested persons, and insufficiency of investigation.

---

244 *Associated Provincial Picture House Limited* v *Wednesbury Corporation* [1948] 1 KB 223.
245 Human Rights Act 1998, s 6(1).

Judicial review is a discretionary remedy. Therefore, even if there is an error in the decision-making process, the Administrative Court retains discretion as to whether it should grant the relief sought. Following a successful judicial review, the Administrative Court can quash the decision of the Coroner (Quashing Order) and order a new inquest, possibly before another Coroner. Alternatively, the court may impose a Prohibiting Order, preventing a Coroner from acting unlawfully or issue a Mandatory Order, to compel the Coroner to act in a particular way. In addition, or instead of the above orders, the Administrative Court might make a declaration.

Procedural points

Judicial review proceedings are subject to CPR 54. A claim should normally comply with the pre-action protocol for judicial review, must be made promptly, and in any event within three months of the date when the grounds of the claim first arose.[246] Early consideration must be given to the cost of such proceedings, including the costs of any intervening party.

A key decision in coronial proceedings is whether to make the application before the inquest has concluded. The Administrative Court is able to consider urgent applications, and Form N463 'Application for urgent consideration of judicial review claim' must be completed. The Coroner or Administrative Court may grant a stay of the inquest for the application to be heard in the Administrative Court.[247] A decision to bring judicial review proceedings whilst the inquest is ongoing is likely to be finely balanced: should the inquest continue, although potentially defective in some way with a risk of a re-hearing; or should proceedings be interrupted, causing a delay and possible difficulties for all the persons involved?

In *R (Khan)* v *HM Coroner for West Hertfordshire*, the Coroner rejected a submission to leave verdicts of unlawful killing and death contributed to by neglect to the jury. The Coroner adjourned the inquest to enable the deceased's wife to challenge that ruling. Richards J dismissed the application for judicial review and opined:

> In adjourning the inquest to enable his ruling to be challenged, the coroner acted with great fairness and with a view to avoid the unsatisfactory position which can arise where an inquest verdict is challenged after the event, on the grounds that the coroner [sic] erred in the verdicts he left or did not leave to the jury. The course adopted, however, has disadvantages, since four months will have elapsed since the jury will have heard the evidence. It is highly undesirable for there to be a long break at such a stage in proceedings. A further disadvantage is that the court did not have the benefit of the coroners' summing up as a means of putting the evidence in perspective. That suggests that the court ought to entertain considerable caution about entertaining a challenge to an interlocutory ruling of this kind.[248]

Coroners Act 1988, s 13

Section 13 of the Coroners Act 1988 provides a second route to challenging inquest proceedings. Unlike judicial review proceedings, there is no time

---

246 CPR 54.5.
247 CPR 54.10.
248 [2002] All ER (D) 68 (Mar).

limit for bringing proceedings. It is therefore particularly suitable if fresh evidence is discovered at a later time. Early consideration must be given to costs, as the court has a power to award costs on appeal.[249]

An application under s 13 requires the permission (fiat) of the Attorney-General. The application for a fiat should be addressed to the Attorney-Generals' Office.[250] If permission is granted, an application can be made by way of a Part 8 Claim Form to Administrative Court. The grounds of challenge[251] are that:

1   the Coroner refused to hold an inquest (s 13(1)(a));
2   an inquest was held, but by reason of fraud, rejection of evidence, irregularity of proceedings, insufficiency of inquiry, the discovery of new evidence or otherwise, it is necessary or desirable in the interests of justice that another inquest should be held (s 13(1)(b)).

If one of the grounds is made out, the Attorney-General and the Administrative Court will consider whether it is necessary or desirable in the interests of justice that the inquest verdict should be quashed and another inquest ordered. The 'interests of justice' is a broad concept, demonstrated by *R (on the application of Sutovic)* v *Northern District of Greater London Coroner*:

> Notwithstanding the width of the statutory words, its exercise by courts shows that the factors of central importance are an assessment of the *possibility* (as opposed to the probability) of a different verdict, the number of shortcomings in the original inquest, and the need to investigate matters raised by new evidence which had not been investigated at the inquest.

However, the possibility of a different verdict is not necessarily conclusive.[252] Other matters that the Administrative Court will take into account when considering whether to order a new inquest is the interest of the people who will be affected by the decision. Although the Administrative Court will consider the possibility of a different verdict at a new inquest, it must not usurp the functions of the Coroner and/or jury by reaching its own verdict.[253] If there is a problem with the verdict, for example, a potential verdict should not have been left to the jury, or the jury direction on the verdict were incorrect, the Administrative Court may quash part of the verdict.

Civil proceedings

A civil claim can arise out of a wrongful death, although proceedings may need to be issued and stayed before the inquest as a result of the delays inherent in the inquest system. The evidence given at an inquest should assist both parties in assessing the strength of their respective cases. Even if the family are not represented at the inquest, a representative of their legal team should attend and take notes of the evidence, particularly

---

249 Supreme Court Act 1981, s 51 and CPR 54.10(2)(e).
250 Attorney-General's Chambers, 20 Victoria Street, London, SW1H 0NF; tel: 0207 271 2492; website: www.atorneygeneral.gov.uk.
251 Coroners Act 1988, s 13(1).
252 See *Sutovic* at para 94 and 98 and *R (on the application of Aineto)* v *Brighton and Hove Coroner* [2003] EWHC 1896 (Admin) at para 12.
253 *R (Khan)* v *HM Coroner for West Hertfordshire* [2002] EWHC Admin 302 at para 45.

the evidence given by the witnesses for the hospital or GP surgery. If the Coroner has recorded the inquest, a copy of the recording or written transcript can be obtained upon payment of a fee.[254]

The Coroners Court is inquisitorial. Therefore, the parties to a civil claim are not bound by the findings of the Coroner, and a finding that death was due to natural causes does not preclude a civil claim. The Coroner's verdict is not admissible within civil proceedings. Consequently, if the verdict was death by natural causes contributed to by neglect, this cannot be pleaded as proof of the fact that there was neglect. However, the transcript is a record of the evidence given by the witnesses at the inquest, and can be put in cross-examination if a witness gives inconsistent evidence during a subsequent civil trial.

Coroners must provide interested persons with any document put into evidence at the inquest,[255] which includes statements read into evidence under r 37 of the Coroners Rules 1984, and any document referred to during the inquest. Coroners must retain documents in connection with an inquest or post-mortem examination for at least 15 years, unless a court directs otherwise,[256] and exhibits must be retained until, in the Coroner's opinion, they are no longer needed for criminal or civil proceedings.[257]

Criminal proceedings

Consideration of whether to prosecute an individual for a criminal offence arising out of the death usually occurs before the inquest. This is because s 16(1) of the Coroners Act 1988 provides that if a Coroner is informed that a person has been charged with certain offences, including the murder, manslaughter, corporate manslaughter of the deceased, or with encouraging or assisting suicide in connection with the death of the deceased,[258] he must adjourn the inquest.

The possibility of criminal proceedings may need to be reconsidered after the inquest if the Coroner or jury return a verdict of unlawful killing, and in such circumstance's Coroners refer the matter to the Director of Public Prosecutions. In *R* v *DPP, ex p Manning and Melbourne*, the Administrative Court considered the case of a person who died in prison custody whilst restrained by prison officers. The inquest jury returned a verdict of unlawful killing but a prosecution did not follow the inquest. The court held that where 'an inquest following a proper direction to the jury culminates in a lawful verdict of unlawful killing implicating a person who, although not named in the verdict, is clearly identified, who is living and whose whereabouts are known, the ordinary expectation would naturally be that a prosecution would follow.'[259] The court further held that it would expect the Director of Public Prosecutions to given reasons if a prosecution did not taken place in such circumstances.[260]

---

254 Coroners' Records (Fees for Copies) Rules 2002 (SI 2002/2401). Rule 2 sets out the charges.
255 Coroners Rules 1984, r 57(1).
256 Coroners Rules 1984, r 56.
257 Coroners Rules 1984, r 55.
258 Suicide Act 1961, s 2(1).
259 [2001] QB 330 at para 30.
260 *R* v *DPP, ex p Manning and Melbourne* [2001] QB 330 at para 30. Also see *R (on the application of Da Silva)* v *DPP* [2006] EWHC 3204 (Admin), CO/8477/2006 for a discussion about giving reasons in relation to the death of Jean Charles de Menezes.

Disciplinary/professional misconduct proceedings

The evidence given at an inquest may result in internal disciplinary proceedings initiated by the hospital or GP surgery. Although internal disciplinary proceedings may take place before the inquest, the employer may wish to hear all the evidence, including any expert evidence before proceedings are fully considered.

Professional disciplinary proceedings may take place before the inquest. However, after an inquest, Coroners and members of the public may make a complaint about an individual to any of the professional bodies, including the General Medical Council, the General Dental Council and the Nursing and Midwifery Council. If disciplinary proceedings take place after the inquest, the professional bodies may take evidence given at an inquest into account when considering whether the healthcare professional is guilty of misconduct. An inquest may also lead to an investigation by the Care Quality Commission. An example is the death of David Gray, who died when a locum doctor from Germany supplied by Take Care Now providing out-of-hours cover for GPs, administered a dose of morphine that was ten times the normal therapeutic dose.[261]

REFORM OF THE CORONIAL SERVICE AND DEATH CERTIFICATION SYSTEM

The last decade has seen two major reviews of the coronial service and system of death certification. One review was carried out by the Fundamental Review of Death Certification and Investigation Committee (Luce Committee 2003) which declared that:

> neither the certification system nor the investigation system is 'fit for purpose' in modern society. Both need substantial reform.[262]

The Shipman Inquiry: Death Certification and the Investigation of Death by Coroners, chaired by Dame Janet Smith reported in July 2003, declaring:

> there must be radical reform and a complete break with the past, as to organisation, philosophy, sense of purpose and mode of operation. The new Coroner Service that I shall recommend will be barely recognisable as the offspring of its parent.[263]

Critically, the Shipman Inquiry concluded that the systems for death registration, cremation certification, and coronial investigation failed to deter Dr Shipman from committing multiple murders and failed to detect his crimes.[264]

---

261 Care Quality Commission, *Investigation into the out-of-hours service provided by Take Care Now* (July 2010). www.cqc.org.uk/_db/_documents/20100714_TCN_Summary. pdf.
262 *Death Certification and Investigation in England, Wales and Northern Ireland: A Report of a Fundamental Review 2003* (28 April 2003: Chairman Tom Luce), Cm 5831.
263 *The Shipman Inquiry Third Report: Death Certification and the Investigation of Death by Coroners* (14 July 2003: Chairman Dame Janet Smith DBE), CM 5854, p 489.
264 *The Shipman Inquiry Third Report: Death Certification and the Investigation of Death by Coroners* (14 July 2003: Chairman Dame Janet Smith DBE), CM 5854.

These reviews identified a plethora of deficiencies and inadequacies in the coronial system. The draft Coroners Bill, seeking to address these shortcomings, was prefaced by a scathing description of the then current coronial service:

> The coroners' system at present is fragmented, non-accountable, variable in its processes and its quality, ineffective in part, archaic in its statutory basis, and very much dependant on the good people working in, or resourcing it, at present to its continued ability to respond to the demands we place on it.[265]

The Coroners and Justice Act 2009 received Royal Assent on 12 November 2009, and was due to be brought into force in April 2012. However, the new Coalition Government has indicated that the coronial provisions within the Act would not be implemented in their entirety, preferring a smaller number of amendments to the current system. Following a proposal by the Coalition Government to abolish the Officer of Chief Coroner, the position has been retained albeit without the power to hear appeals.

The Coroners and Justice Act 2009 represents a long overdue reform of the coronial system and death certification systems in England and Wales. The current legislation is based on the Coroners Act 1887, and the Coroners and Justice Act 2009 represents the first substantial reform of the law and procedure since that time. Many of the provisions in the new Act re-enact provisions in the Coroners Act 1988. However, new provisions address the weaknesses identified by the Luce Committee and the Shipman Inquiry. The following is an overview of the main changes to the current coronial and death certification systems. At the time of writing, no secondary legislation has been enacted. However, the previous Labour Government consulted on the procedural rules.[266]

Chief Coroner

The Coroners and Justice Act 2009 establishes a national framework and system of governance for the coronial service, and fewer coronial jurisdictions (estimated to be about 60 'Coronial Areas') staffed by full-time judicially qualified Coroners (it is envisaged that there will be a reduction in the overall number of Coroners to about 60–65). For the first time, a Chief Coroner and Deputy Chief Coroners will be appointed to lead the coronial service and will exercise judicial, managerial, and administrative powers.[267] The Chief Coroner will be responsible for setting standards; and issuing guidance and protocols on working practices. The system should therefore ensure unified practices and procedures. Unfortunately, the responsibility for providing facilities, staff remuneration, and other operational costs such as post-mortem examination fees incurred by each coronial district remain the responsibility of local authorities.[268]

---

265 Department for Constitutional Affairs, *Coroner Reform: The Governments Draft Bill – Improving death investigation in England and Wales* (June 2006) Cm 6849, p 4.
266 Ministry of Justice, *Reform of the Coroner System Next Stage: Preparing for implementation*, Consultation Paper CO06/10 (2010). The Consultation was opened on 11 March 2010 and the response report dated 14 October 2010. Both reports are available at www.justice.gov.uk/consultations/docs/coroner-reform.pdf.
267 Coroners and Justice Act 2009, s 35 and Sch 8.
268 Coroners and Justice Act 2009, ss 23, 35 and Sch 3, Pt 4.

Consequently, some of the regional inequalities between the different Coronial Areas will probably remain. The Chief Coroner must prepare an annual report, and any investigation that exceeds a year must be reported by a Coroner to the Chief Coroner[269] and be included in the annual report.

Certification and registration of death

The Coroners and Justice Act 2009 introduces a system of secondary certification of deaths not referred to the Coroner, and a new statutory duty to report deaths.[270] The intention is to move away from a system that allows a single doctor to issue a Medical Certificate of Cause of Death (MCCD). It was this weakness in the system that Dr Shipman exploited. The key change is the introduction of the post of Medical Examiner (ME) appointed by Primary Care Trusts in England and Local Health Boards in Wales.[271]

The ME will scrutinise the MCCD that was completed by the medical practitioner. Once informed about the death, the ME will make 'whatever enquires appear to be necessary in order to confirm or establish the cause of death'.[272] The ME will be entitled to have full access to medical notes and patient records.[273] The ME will also be empowered to discuss the circumstances of the death with the attending medical practitioner and the family,[274] but cannot insist that an individual or a specific organisation provides any information.[275] The ME will not be able to order a post-mortem examination, but can make such recommendations to the Coroner. Following enquires to establish or confirm the cause of death, the ME will issue a Medical Examiners Certificate stating the cause of death to the best of the examiners' knowledge and belief, or refer the case back to the Coroner if the cause of death remains undetermined.[276]

Coronial investigations

The Coroners jurisdiction to investigate death remains virtually unchanged. The Coroners and Justice Act 2009 distinguishes between a Coroners' duty to investigate a death and the duty to hold an inquest, thereby heralding the arrival of a new investigative ethos in the coronial service. Under this new approach, an inquest is viewed as the last and most formal stage in the overall investigative process. The previous Labour Government stated that the change of emphasis was intended to reflect the reality that an inquest was only required in a small proportion of cases.[277]

---

269 Coroners and Justice Act 2009, s 16.
270 Coroners and Justice Act 2009, s 18(1).
271 Coroners and Justice Act 2009, s 19(1).
272 Coroners and Justice Act 2009, s 20(1)(e).
273 Access to Health Records Act, s 3, as amended by the Coroners and Justice Act 2009, Sch 21, para 29.
274 Coroners and Justice Act 2009, s 20(1)(k)(i).
275 Coroners and Justice Act 2009, Explanatory Notes, para 176.
276 Coroners and Justice Act 2009, s 20(1)(h)(i), (ii).
277 Department for Constitutional Affairs, *Coroner Reform: The Governments Draft Bill – Improving death investigation in England and Wales* (June 2006) Cm 6849, p 8.

Following the implementation of the Coroners and Justice Act 2009, Coroners will be invested with new evidence gathering powers. Coroners will be empowered to summon witnesses and compel the adduction of evidence, including documents or witness statements for the purposes of the investigation, although the power is limited to England and Wales.[278] Further, Coroners will be empowered to enter and search land and seize items that are relevant to the investigation, although the Chief Coroner must give prior authorisation.[279] The rules governing these new procedures will mirror the relevant rules within the Police and Criminal Evidence Act 1984.[280]

There are virtually no changes to the procedures at an inquest (subject to the development of protocols and guidance). However, there is increased provision for disclosure. The difference in the interpretation of 'how' the deceased came by his death between inquests that engage the ordinary obligations (*Jamieson* inquests) and those that engage the enhanced obligations (*Middleton* inquests) are given statutory force.[281] The jury system remains virtually unchanged. At the end of an inquest, Coroners will be under a mandatory duty to report matters to individuals, organisations etc, with a view to preventing similar fatalities.[282]

Appeals

The Coroners and Justice Act 2009 introduced a radical change to the appeals system in coronial law. Under s 40 of the Act, interested persons would have been able to appeal to the Chief Coroner on a limited range of 'relevant decisions' made by Coroners. However, the Coalition Government has indicted that it intends to repeal s 40.

Charter for the bereaved

The previous Labour Government stated that one of its aims was for the 'coronial system to provide a better service for bereaved people'.[283] As part of the reforms, a *Charter for bereaved people who come into contact with a reformed Coroner system* was developed. The new Coalition Government issued a Consultation Paper entitled *The draft Charter for the current coroner service*. The consultation ended in September 2011 and the *Response to the consultation was* published on 15 December 2011. The new Charter is not restricted to bereaved people, and applies to all witness and properly interested persons. The Coalition Government has indicted that the final version of the Charter will be published in early 2012.

---

278 Coroners and Justice Act 2009, s 32 and Sch 5.
279 Coroners and Justice Act 2009, s 32 and Sch 5.
280 Ministry of Justice, *Reform of the Coroner System Next Stage: Preparing for implementation*, Consultation Paper CO06/10 (2010) pp 39–43.
281 Coroners and Justice Act 2009, s 5(2).
282 Coroners and Justice Act 2009, Sch 5.
283 Department for Constitutional Affairs, *Coroner Reform: The Governments Draft Bill – Improving death investigation in England and Wales* (June 2006) Cm 6849, p 3.

Chapter 18

Limitation

Lisa Sullivan

INTRODUCTION

Limitation is entirely a creature of statute. It has existed since 1623. Its purpose is to prevent prejudice to the defendant in having to face stale claims. The majority of clinical negligence actions will fall under the Limitation Act 1980. The relevant provisions have been the subject of much judicial consideration at appellate level in recent years; resulting in changes to and clarification of the application of the relevant provisions.

The importance of understanding limitation in clinical negligence cases cannot be underestimated. Issues of limitation arise in clinical negligence cases more frequently than in other areas of personal injury. There are many reasons why a claimant might not initially realise that they have a claim, ranging from not realising that the outcome of treatment was worse than it should have been because the injury is not apparent for a number of years, to trust in the medical profession that what happened was just one of those things.

THE PERIOD OF LIMITATION

Most clinical negligence actions are actions for negligence or breach of duty where the damages claimed consist of or include damages for personal injuries and are therefore subject to a three-year limitation period, by virtue of s 11 of the Limitation Act 1980. The limitation period starts to run from the date the cause of action accrues, or the date of knowledge of the claimant (as defined in s 14 of the Act) if later.

The limitation period provided under s 11 of the Limitation Act does not extinguish the claimant's claim. It provides a defence to it. That has two consequences. The first is that a defendant can agree to waive that defence in advance and the second is that they can chose not to rely on it. In the case of waiver, the defendant must expressly declare that the limitation period will not be relied upon in order for the waiver to be effective. If a claim form has been issued very shortly after the limitation period has expired, a defendant will sometimes decide not to pursue the defence, based on the likely success of an application to extend time, or argument about date of knowledge.

Although most will involve a personal injury, a clinical negligence action is not necessarily an action for personal injuries. It may be that the only claim is for financial loss, as where a patient is negligently told not to work any longer. If that was the case, the limitation period would not be three years under s 11, but would be a six-year period under s 2 (if the claim was brought in tort) or s 5 if brought in contract. In either case, the limitation period starts to run when the cause of action accrues. Where the damage is latent, the period may be extended to three years after the relevant knowledge is acquired under s 14A of the 1980 Act, subject to a 15-year longstop from the date of negligence. The provisions as to knowledge for latent damage are essentially the same as under s 14.

WHAT AMOUNTS TO A PERSONAL INJURY ACTION?

'Personal injuries' are defined by the interpretation section of the 1980 Act, s 38, as including 'any disease and any impairment of a person's physical or mental condition'.

A claim in which the negligence does not cause personal injury, even if it involves consideration of injuries, is not a personal injury action for these purposes. So the following situations have been found not to be claims for personal injury:

In *Ackbar* v *C F Green & Co* [1975] QB 582, it was held that a claim against an insurance broker for failing to obtain cover for the claimant was not a claim for damages for personal injuries, although the claim in fact arose out of the claimant's having suffered personal injuries.

Where an injured party claimed under the Third Parties (Rights against Insurers) Act 1930 against the insurers of his employers, who had been wound up, this was held by the Court of Appeal in the context of pre-action disclosure not to be a claim in respect of personal injuries (*Burns* v *Shuttlehurst Ltd* [1999] 1 WLR 1449).

A claim against a solicitor for not pursuing a clinical negligence action would not be a claim in respect of personal injuries. In *Broadley* v *Guy Clapham & Co* [1994] 4 All ER 439, CA, it appears to have been accepted without argument that a six-year period applied.

In *Pattison* v *Hobbs* (1985) Times, 11 November, the Court of Appeal held that where, following an allegedly negligently performed vasectomy, damages were claimed only for the cost of raising a healthy child, the action was not one which included a claim for personal injuries.

A claim against employers for failing to advise of the possibility of getting benefits for injury suffered during employment was not a personal injury action (*Gaud* v *Leeds Health Authority* (1999) 49 BMLR 105, CA).

But where the negligence is a cause of the personal injury, even if it is not the direct cause, it is a personal injury action. In *Norman* v *Aziz* [2000] PIQR P72, the Court of Appeal held that an action against the owner of a motor vehicle for permitting someone to drive it uninsured, the driver then injuring the claimant, was an action in respect of personal injuries and so subject to a three-year limitation period.

Sometimes it may not be clear if an undisputed consequence is to be regarded as an injury or not; for example, there is judicial authority to support the proposition that an unwanted pregnancy is an 'injury', whereas, if the pregnancy was welcome, it is not an injury.

In *Walkin* v *South Manchester Health Authority* MLC 0731, [1995] 1 WLR 1543, the Court of Appeal held that a claim for an unwanted pregnancy following a failed sterilisation and for the consequent costs involved in raising the unplanned child was a claim for 'damages in respect of personal injuries', and it was not possible for the claimant to abandon a claim for personal injury, ie the claim for compensation for the unwanted pregnancy, and in that way to assert a six-year period of limitation as for a claim simply for economic loss. In the circumstances of this particular case the decision can be readily understood because the claimant had already issued, but not served, a writ in the usual form before the expiry of the three-year period. It was only when she realised that a second writ would be outside that period (but within the six-year period) that the claim was reduced to one for economic loss only. However, it is to be noted that Roch LJ said that he had some difficulty in perceiving a normal conception, pregnancy and the birth of a healthy child as 'any disease or any impairment of a person's physical or mental condition' in cases where the only reasons for the pregnancy and subsequent birth being unwanted were financial. He also reserved the question of the proper limitation period in cases of failed male sterilisation because in those circumstances there would be no personal injury to the claimant. Neill LJ also reserved the question whether any personal injury at all would be suffered where a woman who desired to have a child became pregnant as a result of a failed vasectomy. This decision was followed in *Godfrey* v *Gloucestershire Royal Infirmary NHS Trust* [2003] MLC 1010.

In the dyslexia case of *Phelps* v *Hillingdon London Borough Council* MLC 0228, [1999] 1 WLR 500, CA, on appeal [2000] 3 WLR 776, HL, held that the prolongation of a congenital defect (here dyslexia) could amount to a personal injury.

Assault

A quick note on claims for assault: this may arise in the clinical negligence context as the result of a procedure being undertaken without proper consent from the patient or inappropriate examination amounting to an assault.

Before 2008, a distinction was drawn between actions for personal injury arising out of assault and those arising out of negligence.[1] Since the House of Lords decision in *A* v *Hoare* [2008] UKHL 6, this distinction is no longer relevant. Actions for personal injury arising out of assault also fall within s 11 of the Act and are subject to a three-year (extendable) limitation period. When does the limitation period begin?

---

1 The leading case prior to 2008 was *Stubbings* v *Webb* [1993] AC 498, HL. That was a claim brought by a woman who was abused by her family before she was 15. She suffered psychological damage but did not bring a claim until she was 30. It was held that assault claims were subject to the non-extendable six-year limitation period in s 2 of the Act rather than s 11 and therefore her claim was statute barred. The difficulty of this distinction was demonstrated in *Seymour* v *Williams* [1995] PIQR P470, CA, where a claim against an abusive father was statute barred under s 2 of the Act, but claims against the mother, who had not been abusive, but had known of the abuse and done nothing to protect her child, was allowed to continue under s 11.

Normally, the limitation period begins when the cause of action accrues (ie when negligent conduct gives rise to injury) subject to the claimant's date of knowledge.

Capacity

The exception to this is that the limitation period will not begin if, at the time the cause of action arises (when the negligent conduct has given rise to injury), the claimant is under a disability (s 28 of the Act). Section 38 of the Act defines persons under a disability as a child (not yet 18) or a person who lacks capacity to litigate within the meaning of the Mental Capacity Act 2005. For a detailed discussion of whether a person lacks capacity see Chapters 10 and 22.

The limitation period does not start to run until the claimant ceases to be under a disability, when a claimant turns 18, or regains capacity. Once that occurs, the limitation period starts to run from the date of gaining capacity as if that was the date on which the cause of action arose.

If a claimant loses capacity after the cause of action arises (a supervening disability), the limitation period is not stopped from running, but the disability should be taken into account on a s 33 application. See *Kirby* v *Leather* (1965) 2 QB 367 and *Rogers* v *Finemodern Ltd* [1999] All ER (D) 1193.

Deliberate concealment

Under s 32(1)(b) of the Act, deliberate concealment of relevant facts by a defendant may operate to delay the commencement of the limitation period; see *Williams* v *Fanshaw Porter Williams* [2004] EWCA Civ 157. By s 32(2), a *deliberate* commission of a breach of duty in circumstances in which it is unlikely to be discovered for some time equates with deliberate concealment (see *Cave* v *Robinson Jarvis and Rolf* [2003] 1 AC 384, HL).

KNOWLEDGE

Section 14 of the Limitation Act defines the necessary knowledge:

(1) Subject to subsection (1A) below, in section 11 and 12 of this Act references to a person's date of knowledge are references to the date on which he first had knowledge of the following facts –
(a)   That the injury in question was significant;
(b)   That the injury was attributable in whole or in part to the act or omission which is alleged to constitute negligence, nuisance or breach of duty; and
(c)   The identity of the defendant; and
(d)   If it is alleged that the act or omission was that of a person other than the defendant, the identity of that person and the additional facts supporting the bringing of an action against the defendant;
and knowledge that any acts or omissions did or did not, as a matter of law, involve negligence, nuisance or breach of duty is irrelevant.

Knowledge can be actual knowledge of the claimant or it can be constructive knowledge. Section 14(3) sets out the test for constructive knowledge:

(3) For the purposes of this section a person's knowledge includes knowledge which he might reasonable have been expected to acquire –

(a)   From facts observable or ascertainable by him; or

(b)   From facts ascertainable by him with the help of medical or other appropriate expert advice which it is reasonable for him to seek;

but a person shall not be fixed under this subsection with knowledge of a fact ascertainable only with the help of expert advice so long as he has taken all reasonable steps to obtain (and where appropriate, to act on) that advice.

Difficulty with knowledge of the identity of the defendant is unlikely to arise in a medical claim, though it is conceivable that it might prove difficult, for example, to identify the GP who treated.[2] If the wrong GP has been sued, the mistake could probably be corrected pursuant to CPR 19.2, 19.5 or 17.4. In *Gregson* v *Channel Four Television Corpn* (2000) Times, 11 August, CA, the court said, echoing the previous law, that CPR 19.5 applied where the application was to substitute a new party for a party who was named in the claim form in mistake for the new party, and CPR 17.4(3) applied where the intended party was named in the claim form, but there was a genuine mistake as to the name of the party and no-one was misled. The court said there was no significant conflict between the two rules. In this case CPR 17.4 applied: it was not a question of substituting a new party, and the judge's discretion in favour of the claimant had been correctly exercised.

Actual knowledge

The claimant has to *know* that he has suffered a *significant* injury that is *attributable* to the alleged negligent act or omission. It is expressly provided that knowledge of *fault*, ie that the relevant act or omission was negligent, is irrelevant (s 14(1)).[3]

'Know'

What amounts to 'knowledge' of the facts? Must a claimant know for certain, or is a lesser level of knowledge enough? It is clear that certainty is not required and mere suspicion is not enough, but is a belief enough?

In *Davies* v *Ministry of Defence* (26 July 1985, unreported), CA (Civil Division) Transcript No 413 of 1985, May LJ held that:

'knowledge' is an ordinary English word with a clear meaning to which one must give full effect: 'reasonable belief' or 'suspicion' is not enough.

In *Halford* v *Brookes* [1991] 1 WLR 428 at 443, Donaldson LJ distinguished *Davies* as an exceptional case where, despite the claimant's initial belief that his dermatitis was attributable to the act or omission of an employee, he received medical and legal advice, which he accepted, that it

---

2   It is usually a good idea to sue the practice as a whole on ordinary partnership principles. Where the practice is a Primary Care Trust, as opposed to a Primary Care Group, the Trust should be recognised as having legal personality, like any other NHS Trust.

3   This means, among other things, that where one expert reports that there is no cause of action and later another says the opposite, that does not mean that the limitation period begins only with the second report (*Jones* v *Liverpool Health Authority* [1996] PIQR P251, CA).

was not attributable to the act or omission of the employer. He held that 'knowledge' means 'know with sufficient confidence to justify embarking on the preliminaries to the issue of a writ, such as submitting a claim to the proposed Defendant, taking legal and other advice and collecting evidence'. On that basis, he held that 'suspicion, particulate if it is vague and unsupported, will indeed not be enough, but reasonable belief will normally suffice.'

These two approaches were considered in *Nash v Eli Lilly & Co* [1993] 1 WLR 782, MLC 0021. The Court of Appeal said that there was in fact no conflict between the two approaches and that:

> Knowledge is a condition of mind which imports a degree of certainty and ... the degree of certainty which is appropriate for these purposes is that which, for the particular claimant, may reasonably be regarded as sufficient to justify embarking upon the preliminaries to the making of a claim for compensation such as the taking of legal or other advice.
>
> Whether or not a state of mind for these purposes is properly to be treated by the court as knowledge seems to us to depend, in the first place, upon the nature of the information which the claimant has received, the extent to which he pays attention to the information as affecting him, and his capacity to understand it. There is a second stage at which the information, when received and understood, is evaluated. It may be rejected as unbelievable. It may be regarded as unreliable or uncertain. The court must assess the intelligence of the claimant; consider and assess his assertions as to how he regarded such information as he had; and determine whether he had knowledge of the facts by reason of his understanding of the information.

On the one hand, it is not easy to see why embarking on the preliminaries to the making of the claim for compensation, ie going to see a solicitor, implies knowledge on the part of the claimant. He may go to see a solicitor – in fact he often does – for the very reason that he does not know where he stands or where the truth lies. He may be asking the solicitor to seek clarification of his lack of understanding of what happened.[4] On the other hand, the court did envisage the possibility that a particular claimant might have been taking the view that, although she had received information on which knowledge could be based, she needed expert confirmation before her belief could attain that degree of firmness to amount to knowledge.

It will be a matter for decision upon the facts of the individual case whether expert confirmation was required for knowledge to be had. *Spargo v North Essex District Health Authority* MLC 0651, [1997] 8 Med LR 125 is an example of a case where the Court of Appeal held, not unreasonably, that the judge's finding that expert confirmation had been needed could not be supported.[5] In *Spargo*, the claimant was wrongly committed to a mental hospital with a mistaken diagnosis of permanent brain damage. She had always taken the view that she had been wrongly committed. That was her view without the benefit of medical evidence, despite her

---

4   At another point in the judgment, the court said a claimant would have knowledge where he had sought advice *and taken proceedings* [emphasis added]. This case should not be taken as authority for the proposition that merely going to a solicitor for advice about a possible claim constitutes knowledge (and see below the commentary on the case of *Sniezek*).

5   So, too, *Skitt v Khan and Wakefield Health Authority* [1997] 8 Med LR 105.

treating doctors maintaining their diagnosis was correct. That was her clear view when she attended her solicitors. The following is said, in the context of knowledge of attributability (for which see below) about the level of knowledge needed:

> A plaintiff has the requisite knowledge when she knows enough to make it reasonable for her to begin to investigate whether or not she has a case against the defendant. Another way of putting this is to say that she will have such knowledge if she so firmly believes that her condition is capable of being attributed to an act or omission which she can identify (in broad terms) that she goes to a solicitor to seek advice about making a claim for compensation.

> On the other hand, she will not have the requisite knowledge if she thinks she knows the acts or omissions she should investigate but in fact is 'barking up the wrong tree': or if her knowledge of what the defendant did or did not do is so vague or general that she cannot fairly be expected to know what she should investigate, or if her state of mind is such that she thinks her condition is capable of being attributed to the act or omission alleged to constitute negligence, but she is not sure about this, and would need to check with an expert before she could be properly be said to know that it was.

On the other hand, in *Ali* v *Courtaulds Textiles Ltd* [1999] Lloyd's Rep Med 301, the Court of Appeal, reversing the trial judge, held that the claimant, who had taken all reasonable steps to obtain expert knowledge, could not have known that his deafness was attributable to noise rather than age until he got his expert report.

In *Rowbottom* v *Royal Masonic Hospital* MLC 0553, [2002] Lloyds Rep Med 173, the Court of Appeal held, by a majority, that a claimant who was alleging that he had suffered injury from a failure to administer antibiotics could only have had the relevant knowledge when he received his second expert report. That report told him that lack of antibiotics was responsible for his injury; up till then he had thought it was failure to install a drain. Two other cases at first instance on this issue of no knowledge until expert report received are *Mirza* v *Birmingham Health Authority* [2001] MLC 0412 and *Burton* v *St Albans and Hemel Hempstead NHS Trust* [2002] MLC 0856.

In *Sniezek* v *Bundy (Letchworth) Ltd* [2000] PIQR P213, [2000] MLC 0225 (Simon Brown, Judge LJJ, Bell J), another case that focused on the meaning of the word 'know', the court equated with knowledge a firm, consistent and convinced belief on the part of the claimant, despite repeated contrary medical advice, that his respiratory problems were caused by his work conditions. On the one hand, the court put much emphasis on the third of Brooke LJ's principles in *Spargo* ([1997] PIQR P235), the first paragraph set out above, to the effect that a claimant with a firm belief who goes to a solicitor to seek advice about making a claim for compensation has knowledge (unless – principle four – she is in fact barking up the wrong tree; or her knowledge remains vague, so that she cannot be fairly expected to know what should be investigated; or she believes but is not sure and needs to check with an expert). On the other hand, all three judges deprecated the mountain of past authority analysing and re-analysing the ordinary word 'know'. Simon Brown LJ suggested a simple distinction between a claimant who was a mere believer and one who was a firm believer, whilst recognising that the decision as to which side of the line the claimant fell would be a difficult one. Bell J similarly distinguished between a firm belief, which a claimant retained whatever expert advice he received, and a claimant who believed that he may have or even probably had a significant injury attributable to his working conditions but was not sure and felt it necessary to have expert advice on those questions. Judge LJ clearly supported a simple test. He said that the question was one of fact in each case. He doubted whether any considerable legal refinement was necessary or appropriate. He thought that five or ten minutes of argument should enable the judge to make up his mind rather than a long trawl through the authorities, treating a question of fact as a question of law.

Once knowledge has been obtained, it cannot be lost. In *Young* v *Catholic Care (diocese of Leeds)* [2008] UKHL 6, the claimant was sexually abused as a child and had subsequently blocked out the memory. He made a claim for psychiatric injury and it was held that he must have known that he suffered injury whilst the abuse was happening and therefore his date of knowledge was whilst the abuse was occurring – his understandable psychological reaction was something to take into account under s 33 of the Act.

So what is the requisite level of knowledge?

Firm belief can amount to knowledge in appropriate circumstances. It can even amount to knowledge despite contrary negative expert advice in appropriate circumstances. But it needs to be firm enough to amount more or less to an enduring conviction, and although going to a solicitor would normally suggest the necessary knowledge, the inference does not inexorably follow (note that in *Sniezek*, Judge LJ explicitly said that nothing in the authorities or in the Act supported a conclusion that time automatically started to run against a claimant who had taken legal advice). The circumstances in which firm belief will amount to knowledge depend on the particular facts of the case and do not call for further defining. It is however worth bearing in mind that once a claimant has been to see a solicitor, it will be more difficult to deny actual knowledge.

Adult claimants with capacity in birth injury cases

In *Appleby* v *Walsall Health Authority* [1999] Lloyd's Rep Med 154, MLC 0020, Popplewell J found that a claimant born in 1971 with cerebral palsy affecting only motor control did not acquire actual knowledge until 1996. Even if his mother had actual knowledge years earlier, that knowledge could not be imputed to him.[6] A similar issue arose more recently in *Whiston* v *London Strategic Health Authority* [2010] EWCA Civ 195. The claimant was born in 1974 and again suffered with cerebral palsy affecting only motor control. The claimant was 21 in 1995. He issued proceedings in 2006. It was argued by the defendant that the claimant had actual knowledge as he knew that the disability was linked to the circumstances of his birth; his parents had told him his disability was due to forceps delivery, but had said nothing about the competence of the obstetrician using them (which was one of the allegations of negligence). The claimant,

---

6 Note that the reasoning in this case on constructive knowledge is no longer good law following *Adams* v *Bracknell BC*.

on the other hand, said that he had got on with life and never thought of himself as disabled, he had gone to school on a scholarship and to Cambridge University, where he got his undergraduate degree and a PhD in mathematics. He had only investigated further when his condition deteriorated, within three years of issue. The claimant was found not to have actual knowledge.

'Significant' injury

Section 14(2) of the Act defines what 'significant injury' is:

> For the purposes of this section, an injury is significant if the person whose date of knowledge is in question would reasonably have considered it sufficiently serious to justify his instituting proceedings for damages against a defendant who did not dispute liability and was able to satisfy a judgment

The wording of the section raises the question of whether this is a subjective test, an objective test or a combination of the two; the consideration is whether the actual claimant (with their knowledge) would reasonably have considered it sufficiently serious.

If it is partly subjective, is account taken of the claimant's personal characteristics (his intelligence, his character etc) and if so, how much? The House of Lords in *A v Hoare* [2008] UKHL 6 considered the issue and (although doubted by Baroness Hale) held that it was a purely objective test. The test is applied to what the claimant knows of their injury, probably including their constructive knowledge, but the test is whether a reasonable person with that knowledge would have considered the injury sufficiently serious to justify instituting proceedings. The personal characteristics of a claimant, including their injury, are irrelevant to that question.[7]

So when, objectively, is an injury significant? Sometimes there may be argument about what constitutes an injury. In *Dobbie v Medway Health Authority* MLC 0038, [1994] 1 WLR 1234, MLC 0038, where the claimant, expecting to have a lump removed from her breast, underwent removal of the whole breast upon a mistaken diagnosis of cancer, the Court of Appeal took the view that loss of the breast constituted an injury as it had not in fact been diseased.

Although even minor injuries are usually enough to be considered serious, *Harding v People's Dispensary for Sick Animals* [1994] PIQR P270, CA is an example of a claimant reasonably believing for a considerable time after an accident (some 18 months) that her back and leg pain were not significant, because she reasonably thought it was a temporary sprain of the back. In *Field v British Coal Corporation* [2008] EWCA Civ 912, the claimant suffered from slight hearing loss which he believed was due to a build-up of wax and infection – essentially an intermittent condition which was temporary in nature. It was held that given that knowledge (no further knowledge was to be imported to him), a reasonable person would not have considered the injury sufficiently serious. In fact, Mr Field had noise-induced hearing loss for about five years before he knew he had such hearing loss.

---

7   See Lord Hoffman at para 34.

A patient is unlikely to succeed in an argument that, although she knew of a minor (but still significant) injury, time did not run in respect of a deterioration of, or more serious consequence of, that same original injury of which she did not know (*Roberts* v *Winbow* MLC 0074, [1999] Lloyd's Rep Med 31, CA). If the claim is not for an original injury but for an exacerbation of that injury, the question then is: When did the claimant first have knowledge that the exacerbation was significant? (*McManus* v *Mannings Marine Ltd* [2001] EWCA Civ 1668.)

Where a patient knows that he is suffering adverse effects from a drug prescribed by his doctor, he cannot argue that that is not a significant injury because the benefit he is getting from it balances out the equation (*Briggs* v *Pitt-Payne and Lias* MLC 0073, [1999] Lloyd's Rep Med 1, CA).

Attributability

What is it that the claimant has to *know*? He has to know that the significant injury is reasonably *attributable* to the act or omission alleged to constitute negligence. So, in addition to the requirement that he should *know* that he has suffered a *significant injury,* he must also be able to identify a particular act or omission, on which he will later rely as being negligent, as a reasonably possible cause of his injury. This question of attributability has often been the central issue in the reported cases. With what degree of precision must he be able to identify the relevant act or omission?

Knowledge of 'negligence' not necessary

The Act provides in s 14(1) that the claimant's knowledge of whether or not the relevant act or omission constituted a breach of duty is not relevant; in other words he does not need to know that the defendant has been negligent (see *Fennon* v *Anthony Hodari & Co* [2000] All ER (D) 1917).

Omission cases

In the case of an *omission* to treat, it is clear that he needs to know not merely that treatment did not take place, but that there was or may well have been a missed opportunity for him to benefit from treatment.

Smith v *West Lancashire Health Authority* [1995] PIQR P514, CA, was a case where the allegation was one of omission rather than commission (ie that the doctors had failed to do something they should have done, rather than had done something they should not have done). The patient was treated conservatively at A&E in 1981 for a simple fracture at the base of a ring finger. After two months he was told they would have to operate. He ended up with a disability and lost his job in 1989. Having consulted a solicitor, he obtained a positive medical report in 1991. The court applied the principle of specificity: the question was when did the patient know, or when should he have found out, that he had suffered a significant injury from the act or omission alleged to constitute negligence? Clearly the omission consisted in not operating immediately. The Court of Appeal, reversing the trial judge, said that the patient did not know that was the relevant omission until he got the expert report, nor was there any reason for him to have found it out earlier. He knew he had not had an operation at the outset, but 'he did not know that his problem was in any way associated with the absence of an operation at that time'. The important point is that, although this patient ended up with a disability, there was no reason for him to suspect it was attributable to anything done or not done by the doctors (remember that knowledge of fault is irrelevant). This reasoning was endorsed in *Forbes* v *Wandsworth Health Authority* [1997] QB 402, MLC 0671, [1996] 7 Med LR 177, CA, where a delay of less than 24 hours in operating (therefore an omission rather than a positive act) caused the claimant's leg to be amputated. The claimant could not be expected to know that the injury was attributable to the omission without medical advice as it was a matter of medical science of which he was unaware. Also relevant is *Hayward* v *Sharrard* MLC 0061, [1998] JPIL 326 (patient unaware that an X-ray had been misinterpreted as showing no fracture), and *James* v *East Dorset Health Authority* [1999] MLC 0129, where Sedley LJ said:

> I do not believe that in enacting section 14 Parliament intended to reward those alert to assume that every misfortune is someone else's fault and to place at a disadvantage those who do not assume the worst when there is nothing to alert them to it.

In *Oakes* v *Hopcroft* [2000] Lloyd's Rep Med 394, CA, the claimant, having suffered an accident at work, settled her claim on the basis of a report from the defendant doctor. Years later, after continuing disability and then a further report from a different specialist, she sued the first expert for negligent diagnosis. The court, reversing the judgment below, said that she had not known of the essence of her complaint, nor could have been expected to discover it, until she received the second report.[8]

How precisely must the act or omission be known? With what degree of precision must the claimant be able to identify the act or omission? Is it enough to know that the operation or treatment has resulted in an injury, or must the patient know more precisely how it happened?

Two cases which raised concerns that claimants would be fixed with knowledge of attributability when in fact they did not actually have knowledge were *Broadley* v *Guy Clapham & Co* [1994] 4 All ER 439, MLC 0043, [1993] 4 Med LR 328, CA and *Dobbie* v *Medway Health Authority* [1994] 1 WLR 1234, MLC 0038, [1994] 5 Med LR 160. In fact, they did not pose such problems for the patient as some people thought at the time. In *Broadley*, the claimant knew she had come out of an operation on her knee with an unlooked-for result, namely a foot-drop.

Legatt LJ said it was not necessary that the claimant should have knowledge of the *mechanics* of damage; it was enough that soon after the operation she knew something was wrong with her foot which was not an inevitable consequence of it, and therefore she should reasonably have made inquiry.

In *Dobbie*, the claimant went into hospital to have a lump removed from her breast. The surgeon, wrongly believing the lump to be cancerous,

---

8   In *Smith* v *National Health Service Litigation Authority* [2001] Lloyd's Rep Med 90, [2001] MLC 0286, Andrew Smith J held that a claimant born in 1973 with a congenitally displaced hip had not known that her disability might be reasonably attributable to an omission in her medical treatment (failure to examine her properly as a baby) until 1994 (however the claim failed on the facts).

removed the whole breast. The claimant had not given her consent for the breast to be removed. Soon after the operation she knew that her breast had been removed and that the breast they had removed had turned out to be non-cancerous. She was led to believe that the practice was usual and proper. She argued that she didn't have the requisite knowledge of attributability because she did not know that excision of the lump for microscopic examination could and should have preceded removal of the breast (which was the essential allegation of negligence). The judge in fact found that she knew that she had been admitted for excision of the lump, that the breast had been removed, that the lump was not malignant and that the decision to remove the breast had been taken before microscopic examination had been carried out. It was held that she knew of her injury and that it was attributable to the removal of her breast. The fact that she did not know that the removal of the breast before the microscopic examination had been undertaken was blameworthy was irrelevant. The difficulty seen with this decision is that Mrs Dobbie acquired knowledge before she found out that the treatment was unjustified – she believed that it had been proper treatment. But she did have a significantly worse outcome than she had expected and one can hardly quarrel with the argument that she should have investigated the matter given the disparity in outcome to what was expected. It would be different if she had consented to the possibility of the removal of her breast in advance of the operation. Then she would not have known that the outcome was worse than anticipated.

In *Spargo* v *North Essex District Health Authority* [1997] MLC 0651, the Court of Appeal reversed the trial judge's finding that the plaintiff did not have actual knowledge more than three years before the commencement of proceedings. The brief facts were that at the age of four in 1975 the plaintiff was confined to a psychiatric hospital on a mistaken diagnosis of permanent brain damage. Her difficulty on limitation was that, when cross-examined, she said that she knew that she had suffered in hospital for a long time and that she firmly believed that that was because of the mistaken diagnosis. In her mind, all her suffering was attributable to the mistaken diagnosis of organic brain damage, and that was her clear view when she first saw her solicitor in October 1986. The trial judge held that this was one of those cases, foreseen by the Court of Appeal in *Nash* v *Eli Lilly* [1993] 1 WLR 782, MLC 0021, where the patient's belief about the attributability of her problem cannot amount to knowledge until an expert report confirms her view. The Court of Appeal disagreed: this plaintiff on her own evidence was convinced that the diagnosis of brain damage had caused her injury (through being confined as a result for a substantial period of time to a mental hospital). She had that conviction as early as 1986 at which time she also had a report on an intelligence test she had taken which indicated that the original diagnosis had been mistaken. The trial judge had actually found that 'she was clear in her mind that the connection was there between the disturbances and what she had suffered'. In those circumstances, the decision of the Court of Appeal which held that she had actual knowledge no later than 1986 is readily understandable.

In coming to the decision, Brooke LJ reviewed the preceding case law, including *Dobbie* and set out the following principles, which have been followed in subsequent cases:

(1)   The knowledge required to satisfy section 14(1)(b) is a broad knowledge of the casually relevant act or omission to which the injury is attributable;

(2)   'Attributable' in this context means 'capable of being attributed to', in the sense of being a real possibility;

(3)   A plaintiff has the requisite knowledge when she knows enough to make it reasonable for her to begin to investigate whether or not she has a case against the defendant. Another way of putting this is to say that she will have such knowledge if she so firmly believes that her condition is capable of being attributed to an act or omission which she can identify (in broad terms) that she goes to a solicitor to seek advice about making a claim for compensation;

(4)   On the other hand she will not have the requisite knowledge if she thinks she knows the acts or omissions she should investigate but in fact is barking up the wrong tree; or if her knowledge of what the defendant did or did not do is so vague or general that she cannot fairly be expected to know what she should investigate; or if her state of mind is such that she thinks her condition is capable of being attributed to the act or omission alleged to constitute negligence, but she is not sure about this, and would need to check with an expert before she could properly be said to know that it was."

This was followed in the non-medical case of *Hallam-Eames* v *Merrett Syndicates* MLC 0703, [1996] 7 Med LR 122, which was a decision upon one of the economic claims in the Lloyd's Names saga. The limitation provisions of s 14A of the Limitation Act 1980, inserted by the Latent Damage Act 1986, are to all intents and purposes identical with the personal injury provisions of s 14. In short form, the allegation was that the defendants had negligently written contracts for the claimants which involved them in substantial liabilities without having the material on which to assess the potential liabilities. The act was identified as the act that was 'causally relevant' for the purpose of an allegation of negligence so that the claimant 'must have known the facts which can fairly be described as constituting the negligence of which he complains'.

It was therefore held that it was not enough for the claimants to have known that the contracts had been written, because they also needed to know that they had been written at a time when the potential liabilities of the parties were impossible to assess. *Dobbie* was analysed on the same principle, the act which would constitute negligence was not that the breast had been removed but that a *healthy* breast had been removed. That was the essence of her complaint, and she had knowledge of those broad facts.

Rowbottom v *Royal Masonic Hospital* MLC 0553, [2002] Lloyds Rep Med 173, is an example of a claimant who is 'barking up the wrong tree'. There will be no knowledge of attributability if the claimant has not identified the facts which would constitute negligence. The relevant act constituting negligence was a failure to administer antibiotics. The Court of Appeal held he could only have had the relevant knowledge when he received his second expert report. That report told him that lack of antibiotics was responsible for his injury; up till then he had thought it was failure to install a drain. He had been 'barking up the wrong tree'.

Constructive knowledge

If the claimant does not have actual knowledge, they may still be fixed with constructive knowledge. The burden of proof is on the defendant to prove the date of constructive knowledge. Section 14(3) provides:

For the purposes of this section a person's knowledge includes knowledge which he might reasonably have been expected to acquire—
(a) from facts observable or ascertainable by him; or
(b) from facts ascertainable by him with the help of medical or other appropriate expert advice which it is reasonable for him to seek;
But a person shall not be fixed under this sub-section with knowledge of a fact ascertainable only with the help of expert advice so long as he has taken all reasonable steps to obtain (and, where appropriate, to act on) that advice.[9]

For a number of years, there were two lines of cases coming to different conclusions as to what, if any, individual characteristics of the claimant can be taken into account in deciding what knowledge a person might reasonably be expected to acquire. In other words, is this an objective or subjective test of reasonableness?

The first line of cases followed *Nash* v *Eli Lilly & Co* [1993] 1 WLR 782. The test was said to be to enquire what the particular claimant should have observed or ascertained, asking of him no more than is reasonable. In deciding what is reasonable, the particular position, circumstances, character and intelligence of the individual claimant should be taken into account.

The second followed *Forbes* v *Wandsworth Health Authority* [1997] 1 QB 402, CA. The test was said to be an objective one, and the character and intelligence of the claimant were therefore irrelevant.

The House of Lords has now clarified the issue and the test is an objective one.

In *Adams* v *Bracknell Forest Borough Council* [2004] UKHL 29, the claimant brought a claim against his local education authority for negligently failing to help him with dyslexia between 1981 and 1988. He was born in March 1972. He issued the claim in June 2002, aged 30. There were no useful medical notes extant, nor, it appears, much in the way of useful evidence any teacher could give so long after the event. The claimant said he first knew he probably was dyslexic when he was speaking to a friend at a dancing class in November 1999, who happened to be an educational psychologist. She said she thought he was dyslexic and, as a result, he went to see a solicitor in January 2000. An expert confirmed severe dyslexia and severe psychological symptoms including panic attacks and social phobia, consequent upon undiagnosed and untreated learning difficulties. Mr Adams, an intelligent man, had not sought any advice about his literacy problems because he wanted to hide them. He did not want people to think he was stupid. He spoke to his doctor about the psychological problems but not about his inability to read and write. Yet, said Lord Hoffman, 'on a social occasion on 19th November 1999 he spilled out the entire story to Ms Harding, a lady nearly 20 years his senior whom he says he hardly knew and had no reason to believe had any expertise in the matter. After talking to her the first thing he did was to consult a solicitor'. The trial judge had found that Mr Adams had

---

9   In *Henderson* v *Temple Pier Co* [1998] 1 WLR 1540, the Court of Appeal held that the claimant was fixed with the knowledge that her solicitors should have acquired earlier about the identity of the defendants. This, incidentally, was the case the absence of knowledge of which by counsel led the Court of Appeal to utter harsh admonitions in *Copeland* v *Smith* [2000] 1 WLR 1371, about the need for counsel to be aware of the relevant authorities!

known since childhood that he had psychological problems and that they were 'linked in some way to his problems with reading and writing'. But he did not know that the education authority could have helped him. It was this finding that led both courts below to find that he did not have actual earlier knowledge (accepted by the defendants) but which also led them to conclude that there was no reason why he should have got it (before speaking to his lady friend) – which was the issue on which the defendants were to appeal successfully to the House of Lords.

The issue was: is the question as to what the claimant should reasonably be expected to have done in the line of making enquiries or seeking expert help to be answered on a subjective or an objective basis; that is, do you factor in all the personal characteristics of the particular claimant or do you ask what would your average sufferer reasonably have done? Their Lordships concluded (by a majority) that the test was an objective one, but there were different formulations as to the objective test.

Lord Hoffman said that the claimant must be assumed to be the person who has suffered the injury in question, but that the particular character or intelligence of the particular claimant was not relevant. The normal expectation is that a person suffering from a significant injury will be curious about its origins. But, if the injury itself would reasonably inhibit a claimant from seeking advice, that would be a relevant factor to be taken into account, but no other personal characteristic would be relevant. In the case of dyslexia, in order for it to be taken into account he would expect medical evidence to show that the dyslexia itself would have caused such inhibition; such evidence was not present in *Adams*. Lord Phillips agreed with Lord Hoffman. Lord Scott also agreed with Lord Hoffman's conclusions but added that the test should be 'mainly objective'; 'what would a reasonable person placed in the situation in which the claimant was placed have said or done?'.[10] However, it is not clear what the person's 'situation' would cover. It would cover a brain injury in issue in the case, but what about a pre-existing learning disability short of a lack of capacity?

Baroness Hale pointed out that it had rarely, if ever, been necessary to resolve the difference between the two tests to decide the case and she wondered if there was in practice much difference between the two approaches. She did not want to rule out that personal characteristics might be relevant to knowledge, and in particular that the qualifications, training and experience would probably be relevant whilst intelligence may not. But she agreed that strictly personal characteristics such as shyness or embarrassment were not relevant.

Lord Walker thought that Baroness Hale's distinction between personal characteristics which affect a person's ability to acquire information and personal characteristics which affect a person's reaction to the information once acquired would be useful in some cases, but that characteristics such as shyness, embarrassment and lack of assertiveness might fall under both categories.

The test for s 14(3) was considered again by the House of Lords in *A v Hoare* [2008] UKHL 6. The argument in *A v Hoare* was around s 14(2), what the test for the significance of an injury is; that section was compared to

---

10   Para 73.

s 14(3). Lord Hoffman described s 14(3) as a test for imputing knowledge by reference to what a claimant ought to have done, as opposed to s 14(2) which is a standard of seriousness applied to what the claimant knew or must be treated to have known. He said that because s 14(3) turns on what the claimant ought reasonably to have done, it must take into account the injury which the claimant has suffered. 'You do not assume that a person which has been blinded could have reasonably acquired knowledge by seeing things'.

It is notable that this more restrictive approach to s 14 knowledge is contrasted with the s 33 discretion. Lord Carswell said:

> If, as I think to be the case, section 14 should be construed in that manner, which is less favourable to the claimant, there requires to be a more liberal approach to the exercise of discretion than has always been the case. For the reason which my noble and learned friends and I have set out, that less favourable construction of section 14 is correct in principle, but it must follow that the favourable factors which have hitherto been taken into account in reaching a conclusion under section 14 should form a part, and in appropriate cases a very significant part, of the judge's determination in exercising his desertion under section 33.[11]

The courts have, since *Adams* and *Hoare*, construed s 14(3) as a strictly objective test (save for the claimant's injuries) and have considered the factors which used to be considered in this section under s 33. For example, in *Whiston* v *London Strategic Health Authority* [2010] EWCA Civ 195, the test applied at first instance was 'when would a reasonable person in the circumstances of the Claimant, suffering from cerebral palsy and with the same level of disability have the curiosity to begin investigating with expert help whether his injury could be considered capable of being attributed to something the hospital staff did or didn't do at the time of his birth?'[12]

A dispute arose about whether it was relevant, when looking at the circumstances of the claimant, to take into account the difference between a claimant who is injured at birth, and therefore has known nothing else, and a claimant who is injured as an adult. It was argued that the latter would be much more likely to be curious about the cause of his injuries than the former.

In the Court of Appeal, Lord Justice Dyson said 'In my judgement, the ratio of *Adams* is that section 14(3) requires an objective test to be applied ...The importance of *Adams* is that it settled the difference between the objective (or mainly objective) test applied in *Forbes* and the subjective test enunciated in the earlier cases to which I have referred in favour of the former'.[13] He agreed that the fact that a claimant has been suffering the injury since he was born is a relevant circumstance of the case when assessing the extent to which someone is reasonably to be expected to be curious about the cause of his disability.

It is now therefore settled that it is an objective test: when would a reasonable person in the circumstances of the claimant, suffering from the same injury as the claimant, have the curiosity to begin investigating,

---

11   Para 70.
12   Paras 32–33.
13   Para 54.

with expert help, whether their injury could be considered as capable of being attributed to something the defendant did or didn't do?

SECTION 33 DISCRETION

Section 33 of the Limitation Act 1980 provides:

33.—(1) If it appears to the court that it would be equitable to allow an action to proceed having regard to the degree to which—

(a)   the provisions of section 11 or 11A or 12 of this Act prejudice the plaintiff or any person whom he represents; and

(b)   any decision of the court under this subsection would prejudice the defendant or any person who he represents;

the court may direct that those provisions shall not apply to the action, or shall not apply to any specified cause of action to which the action relates.

...

(3) In acting under this section the court shall have regard to all the circumstances of the case and in particular to—

(a)   the length of, and the reasons for, the delay on the part of the plaintiff;

(b)   the extent to which, having regard to the delay, the evidence adduced or likely to be adduced by the plaintiff or the defendant is or is likely to be less cogent than if the action had been brought within the time allowed by section 11;

(c)   the conduct of the defendant after the cause of action arose, including the extent (if any) to which he responded to requests reasonably made by the plaintiff for information or inspection for the purpose of ascertaining facts which were or might be relevant to the plaintiff's cause of action against the defendant;

(d)   the duration of any disability of the plaintiff arising after the date of the accrual of the cause of action;

(e)   the extent to which the plaintiff acted promptly and reasonably once he knew whether or not the act or omission of the defendant, to which the injury was attributable, might be capable at that time of giving rise to an action for damages;

(f)   the steps, if any, taken by the plaintiff to obtain medical, legal or other expert advice and the nature of any such advice he may have received.

These are not the only factors to which the court must pay attention. The overall consideration is where the balance of prejudice lies and whether a fair trial is still possible.[14]

There are a plethora of cases on this section, but as each case is dependent on the circumstances of that particular case, they are often helpful more as examples than strict precedent. It is often possible to find two cases with similar facts and differing outcomes. However, since the tightening of the requirements for knowledge in s 14, some consideration has been given to the purpose of s 33 which does provide useful general guidance as to the proper approach to the s 33 discretion.

In *Cain* v *Francis* [2008] EWCA Civ 1451, the Court of Appeal had to consider the issue of whether any weight should be given in the balancing exercise to the defendant's loss of a 'windfall defence'. That is to say, when a defendant suffers no other prejudice as a result of the claim being issued

---

14   *Cain* v *Francis* [2008] EWCA Civ 1451.

outside the limitation period (should the claim be allowed to proceed) save for the loss of the limitation defence. In a case where, for example, the defendant has admitted liability prior to the expiry of limitation, this defence has been described as a windfall. In order to decide whether that should be a consideration to be put in the balance, the court considered the history and purpose of the discretion. The leading judgement was given by Lady Justice Smith. Her Ladyship said:

> It is a fundamental precept of the common law that a tortfeasor should compensate the victim of the tort. At common law, the victim, now the claimant, could sue the tortfeasor at any time, without limitation. It is also a fundamental precept that any person who is sued in respect of a tort should have a fair opportunity to defend himself. In 1623, a uniform limitation period of six years was introduced for all actions. The rationale behind the limit was to protect defendants from stale claims. It was not fair and just to impose liability on a defendant who had not had a proper opportunity to investigate the allegations against him and to assemble the evidence necessary to defend himself. There may have been other policy reasons for the provision, such as the desirability of finality but, as between the parties, the reason was to protect the defendant form a stale claim.[15]

> ...Any limitation bar is arbitrary...The imposition of an arbitrary limit could only ever hope to do rough justice...Parliament introduced...section 33...The only rationale which would have underlain the introduction of this provision was a desire to refine the rough justice of the old arbitrary provision. Instead of a limitation rule of thumb, the courts would be required to consider what was fair and just in all the circumstances of the individual case. In my view the words of section 33 must be construed against that background. The operation of section 11 has given him a complete procedural defence which removes the obligation to pay. In fairness and justice, he only deserves to have that obligation removed if the passage of time has significantly diminished his opportunity to defend himself (on liability and/or quantum). So the making of a direction, which would restore the Defendant's obligation to pay damages, is only prejudicial to him if his right to a fair opportunity to defend himself has been compromised.[16]

> ...It seems to me that, in the exercise of discretion, the basic question to be asked is whether it is fair and just in all the circumstances to expect the Defendant to meet the claim on the merits, notwithstanding the delay in commencement. The length of delay will be important, not so much for itself, as to the effect it has had. To what extent has the Defendant been disadvantaged in his investigation of the claim and/or assembly of the evidence, in respect of the issues of both liability and quantum? But it will also be important to consider the reasons for the delay. Thus there may be some unfairness to the defendant due to the delay in issue but the delay may have arisen for so excusable a reason that, looking at the matter in the round, on balance it is fair and just that the action should proceed. On the other hand, the balance may go in the opposite direction, partly because the delay has caused procedural disadvantage and unfairness to the defendant and partly because the reasons for the delay (or its length) are not good ones.[17]

In summary, the purpose of s 33 is to do fairness between the parties, balancing the *effects* of the delay on the defendant and the *reasons* for the delay on the part of the claimant.

---

15 Para 64.
16 Paras 67–68.
17 Para 73.

The section sets out specific factors which must be considered in each case (if only to see if they apply). Again there are a plethora of cases demonstrating each. It is useful however to consider the issues that might arise in the clinical negligence context.

(A) THE LENGTH OF AND REASONS FOR THE DELAY

The period of delay in question is that after the expiry of the limitation period, however any delay before the expiry of the limitation period is a relevant factor to be taken into account in all the circumstances of the case.[18] In looking at whether the reasons are 'good' ones or not, the test is subjective.[19]

In *Whiston* v *London Strategic Health Authority*,[20] the fact that a claimant who was injured at birth, suffering cerebral palsy affecting mobility only, had got on with his life, obtaining a PhD in mathematics from the University of Cambridge and employment as a qualitative analyst and who didn't consider himself disabled, was given permission to proceed with his claim, despite, in considering his knowledge, a finding that he had not displayed the curiosity of a reasonable person in his position. His approach to his disability was a good reason for not bringing a claim.[21]

In *Berry* v *Calderdale Health Authority* [1998] Lloyd's Rep Med 179, CA, the court refused to exercise the discretion because no reason was given for the delay. The delay was about a year.

(B) THE EFFECT OF DELAY ON COGENCY OF EVIDENCE

In *Farthing* v *North East Essex Health Authority* [1998] Lloyd's Rep Med 37, MLC 0053, Simon Brown LJ and Hale J said, in respect of an allegation of negligence around a hysterectomy in 1981, that the case did not turn on the recollection of witnesses as to precisely what was done, but upon the contemporaneous records. The delay was 15 years from the damage but the discretion was exercised. In *Smith* v *Leicestershire Health Authority* [1998] Lloyd's Rep Med 77, the Court of Appeal (Roch, Mantell LJJ, Sir Patrick Russell) reversed a decision of May J whereby he held that a spina bifida patient, born in 1943, who claimed in respect of clinical negligence going back some 40 years, had constructive knowledge in 1983 and that it would not be equitable to exercise discretion in her favour. The appeal court held that there was no proper ground for a finding of constructive knowledge and, further, that the judge's exercise of discretion was flawed as he had given too much weight to the mere passage of time and insufficient weight to the fact that a defendant's evidential disadvantage was not great where a case will turn on the extant medical records, and so it pales into insignificance beside the prejudice to the claimant if not permitted to proceed. In such a situation, the experts could still make proper analyses. However, in *Skitt* v *Khan*

---

18   *Donovan* v *Gwetoys* [1990] 2 All ER 1018.
19   *Coad* v *Cornwall and Scilly Isles Health Authority* [1997] 1 WLR 189.
20   [2010] EWCA Civ 195.
21   Similarly in *Coad* v *Cornwall and Scilly Isles Health Authority* [1997] 1 WLR 189, genuine ignorance of legal rights was found to be a good reason for the delay.

and Wakefield Health Authority [1997] 8 Med LR 105, where a relevant witness had died and the defendant doctor's health was such he would be unable to give evidence, there was prejudice to the defendant due to the non-availability of the witnesses. The delay was four years. The discretion was not exercised.

In *Conry* v *Simpson* [1983] 3 All ER 369, the defendant had properly destroyed relevant documents, which meant the evidence was less cogent.

(C) THE CONDUCT OF THE DEFENDANT

In *Hammond* v *West Lancashire Health Authority* [1998] Lloyds Rep Med 146, x-rays were destroyed despite the defendant having been notified of the claim and medical records had been requested. The prejudice to the defendant in not having those x-rays was discounted significantly as a result.

(D) DISABILITY

This refers to disability arising after the cause of action. Section 28, which suspends time running whilst a claimant lacks capacity, only applies where the lack of capacity is present at the time the cause of action arises. The disability being referred to is capacity rather than physical disability.[22]

(E) THE EXTENT TO WHICH THE CLAIMANT ACTED REASONABLY ONCE THEY KNEW OF A POTENTIAL CLAIM

This is an objective test.[23] In *Buckler* v *J F Finnegan Ltd* [2004] EWCA Civ 920, the Court of Appeal reversed the judge who disapplied the limitation period where a workman who had decided originally not to sue for so slight an injury as pleural thickening to one lung, changed his mind years later when he mistakenly thought his condition had deteriorated. This can be compared to *Doughty* v *North Staffordshire Health Authority* [1999] PIQR P260 where, unrelated to the claim, the claimant had a severely handicapped daughter. Her husband blamed her for their daughter's handicap and had left leaving her bringing her daughter up alone and going through a divorce. She had been injured 28 years before issue, as a child, and the delay was 11 years. The discretion was exercised to disapply the limitation period.

(F) THE STEPS TAKEN TO OBTAIN ADVICE

In *Roberts* v *Winbow* [1997] PIQR P77, where the claimant instructed solicitors prior to the limitation period, but the expert reported after expiry of the primary limitation period (18 months after instructions were sent), the discretion to extend was exercised. The solicitor had not

---

22   *Yates* v *Thakenham Tiles Ltd* [1995] PIQR P135 CA; but an impairment of the claimant's health short of 'disability' may be given due weight by the court: *Davis* v *Jacobs and Camden and Islington Health Authority* MLC 0071, [1999] Lloyd's Rep Med 72, CA at 86.

23   *Coad* v *Cornwall and Scilly Isles Health Authority* [1997] 1 WLR 189.

issued as the claimant was funded by legal aid and it was thought not appropriate to issue in the circumstances of the case with no causation report.

In addition, the court must consider the whole of the circumstances. Relevant factors include the apparent merits of the claim,[24] whether it would be proportionate for the claim to proceed,[25] whether the issues depend on recollection[26] or extant medical records, whether the claimant has a claim against his solicitors,[27] whether the defendant had reasonably early notice of a possible claim,[28] and the personal situation of the claimant in having to cope with the injuries sustained.[29] Factors which have found not to be relevant include the fact that a defendant is insured (*Kelly* v *Bastible* [1997] 8 Med LR 15, CA) and any other financial prejudice to the defendant.[30] The discretion must be exercised reasonably: refusing to allow a case to proceed where it is one day out of time is not reasonable (*Hartley* v *Birmingham City District Council* [1992] 1 WLR 968, CA).

Other cases on discretion

The discretion is an unfettered one, and the Court of Appeal should be loath to interfere with its exercise by the judge (see *Conry* v *Simpson* [1983] 3 All ER 369; *Firman* v *Ellis* [1978] QB 886; *Bradley* v *Hanseatic Shipping* [1986] 2 Lloyd's Rep 34).

In *Mold* v *Hayton and Newson* (17 April 2000, unreported), [2000] MLC 0207, CA, the court reversed the exercise of the judge's discretion whereby he permitted an action for failure to examine timeously for vaginal cancer to proceed 18 years out of time, on the ground that it was not appropriate to grant such a huge extension without giving clear reasons for doing so, and the judge had not given clear reasons.

The rule in *Walkley* v *Precision Forgings* and the effect of *Horton* v *Sadler*

The rule in *Walkley* v *Precision Forgings* that if a claim form was issued within time, and not validly served, or was struck out or the claim otherwise discontinued, an application could not be made under *section* 33 to disapply the limitation period in respect of a second claim form issued outside the limitation period was overruled in *Horton* v *Sadler* [2006] UKHL 27. A second claim form can therefore be issued. In *McDonnell* v *David Walker (Executor of the Estate of Richard Walker, deceased)* [2009] EWCA Civ 1257, Waller LJ held that the tension between the (stringent)

---

24   But a cast iron case is not a passport to proceed: an untruthful claimant should not be given discretion (*Long* v *Tolchard & Sons Ltd* (2000) Times, 5 January, CA).
25   *Adams* v *Bracknell Forest Borough Council* [2004] UKHL 29.
26   The court can infer impairment of recollection from the lapse of time – *Price* v *United Engineering Steels Ltd* [1998] PIQR P407, CA – specific evidence of impairment is not required.
27   *Thomson* v *Brown Construction (Ebbw Vale) Ltd* [1981] 1 WLR 744, HL; *Ramsden* v *Lee* [1992] 2 All ER 204, CA; *Das* v *Ganju* [1999] PIQR P260, CA
28   See *Long* v *Tolchard & Sons Ltd* [2001] PIQR P18, CA.
29   See *Godfrey* v *Gloucestershire Royal Infirmary* [2003] EWHC 549, QB and *Khairule* v *North West Strategic Health Authority* [2008] EWHC 1537.
30   *Cain* v *Francis* [2008] EWCA Civ 1451.

terms of CPR 7.6, which only allows an extension of time for service of a claim form if the claimant has taken all reasonable steps to do so within the limitation period, even if no prejudice has been suffered by a defendant and the broad discretion under s 33 is a relevant factor to be taken into account in the s 33 discretion.

It was argued in *Atkas* v *Adepta* [2010] EWCA Civ 1170 that to issue a second claim form when the first had not been served through the claimant's solicitor's negligence was an abuse of process and such a claim form should be struck out. That argument was rejected. Whilst issuing a second claim form can be an abuse of process (in the same way as it can be if done within the limitation period), the mere act of doing so is not an abuse of process. The relevance of the 'tension' referred to by Lord Justice Waller is also doubted.

Preliminary trial

Although a preliminary trial on limitation is frequently desirable, it should not be ordered where the limitation issues are intricately bound up in the substantive issues (*Fletcher* v *Sheffield Health Authority* [1994] 5 Med LR 156, MLC 0035; see also *Roberts* v *Winbow* MLC 0074, [1999] Lloyd's Rep Med 31, CA at 39 and *Worsley* v *Tambrands* [2000] MLC 0186, CA). If limitation is not dealt with as a preliminary issue but at the conclusion of the evidence, the decision on whether to allow the s 33 applications should be made before consideration of the merits of the claim itself.[31]

FATAL ACCIDENT CLAIMS

The limitation period provided by s 12 of the 1980 Act for actions under the Fatal Accidents Act 1976 (amended by s 3 of the Administration of Justice Act 1982) is three years from the date of death, or the date of 'knowledge' of the dependant for whose benefit the action is brought, whichever is the later. If, at the date of death, the deceased's right of action was already time-barred by s 11, then the dependants' action is also barred, no account being taken of the possibility that the deceased might have got leave to proceed under s 33; but provided the limitation period had not expired at the date of death, the dependants can on their own account ask for their action to be permitted to proceed under s 33 (by virtue of s 12(1) and (3)).

Although only one action can be brought on behalf of all dependants,[32] dependants are to be considered separately for the purpose of limitation. Therefore one dependant may be barred where another is within the limitation period because his knowledge arose later, or because he is under a disability (s 13(1)). The court has power to exclude a dependant from participating in the action if their claim would be outside the limitation period (s 13(2)). That power is limited by s 13(3), which provides that no direction to exclude shall be given if it is shown that if the action were

---

31   *KR* v *Bryn Alyn Community (Holdings)* Ltd (in liquidation) [2003] EWCA Civ 85.
32   Fatal Accidents Act 1976, s 2(3).

brought exclusively for the benefit of that dependant, it would not be defeated by a defence of limitation.

A fatal accident claim may often include a claim for, for example, terminal suffering or care given to the deceased while he was still alive. That is not a fatal accident head of claim, but is a claim pursuant to the Law Reform (Miscellaneous Provisions) Act 1934, and the limitation period in respect of that claim is not necessarily the same. The relevant provision is s 11(5) of the Limitation Act 1980, which provides that the three-year period runs from the date of death or the date of the personal representative's 'knowledge'. In many cases, the distinction will not be important, but it could be. For example, the personal representative may have acquired the relevant 'knowledge' years before, which will prevent him claiming on behalf of the estate or as a dependent (subject to any application for s 33 discretion), whereas the claim by any dependent children will not be affected.

AMENDING A CLAIM

Amending the statement of claim

The issue sometimes arises that a claimant needs to add a new party after proceedings have been begun. Perhaps the culprit appears to be a different GP from the current defendant, or perhaps a GP or health authority needs to be added to the frame. Alternatively, a new allegation of negligence may need to be made against the existing defendants following, for example, an expert seeing new records. The legislative provisions are not particularly easy to understand, but can usefully be summarised by saying that the judge has no general power to add a defendant (or a new cause of action) out of time, except by exercising discretion under s 33 (see s 35(3)). Section 35(4) and (5) lays down guidelines for the enaction of rules of court to permit new claims to be added, but provides that the rules can be more restrictive than the guidelines. Therefore, it is to the rules of court that one has to look upon any such application.

CPR 17.4 (amendments to statements of case after the end of a relevant limitation period) enables amendments to be made where the effect will be to add or substitute a new claim, provided the new claim arises out of the same facts or substantially the same facts as a claim in respect of which the party applying for permission has already claimed a remedy in the proceedings. Genuine mistakes over identity may be corrected under this rule provided the mistake was genuine and not one which would cause reasonable doubt as to the identity of the party in question.[33]

CPR 19.5 provides that for the addition or substitution of a party, the relevant limitation period must have been current at the start of the proceedings and the amendment must be necessary, which means that the court must be satisfied that the substitution arises out of a mistake, or the change must be made to enable the claim to be properly carried on. There is, of course, power to amend where the court directs, under

---

33   See *International Distillers* v *J F Hillebrand (UK) Ltd* (2000) Times, 25 January. See also the commentary above (under 'Knowledge') on *Gregson* v *Channel Four Television Corpn* (2000) Times, 11 August, CA.

s 33, that the time limits under s 11 or 12 shall be disapplied (and it is specifically provided that the issue whether those sections apply is to be determined at trial). These powers arise from s 35 of the Limitation Act.

The mistake under CPR 19.5 must be a mistake as to the name of the party rather than the identity of the party, so the sort of mistake where the claimant gives the right description of the defendant (in the body of the pleading) but the wrong name.[34]

In *Sayer* v *Kingston and Esher Health Authority* (1989) Independent, 27 March, CA, the Court of Appeal endorsed the judge's decision to permit an amendment of the claim on the eve of the trial whereby the previous case alleging mishandling of the Caesarean section was replaced by allegations of mismanagement earlier in the labour and after delivery. The court said that as the new claims arose out of substantially the same facts as those already pleaded, the judge had discretion to allow the amendment under s 35(5) of the Limitation Act 1980.[35]

In *Welsh Development Agency* v *Redpath Dorman Long Ltd* [1994] 1 WLR 1409, the Court of Appeal held that leave could not be given to add a new claim after the expiry of the limitation period unless it fell within one of the stated exceptions in the Act and the then current rules of court, and that the relevant date for when a new claim should be taken to be made was not the date when the application for leave to amend was issued, but when the amendment was actually made. Reference may also be made to *Howe* v *David Brown Tractors (Retail) Ltd* [1991] 4 All ER 30, CA.

In *Sion* v *Hampstead Health Authority* MLC 0027, [1994] 5 Med LR 170, CA, the defendants' counsel took an obviously bad point on adding a claim after the expiry of the limitation period. It was agreed that the rules permitted a new claim to be added where it arose out of substantially the same facts as a cause of action in respect of which relief had already been claimed in the action, but he said that as the statement of claim in fact disclosed no cause of action, the rule did not apply. The court gave the obvious response, namely that if the pleading could be amended to disclose a cause of action substantially on the facts as pleaded, the pre-condition to adding a new cause of action was satisfied.

The patient seeking to add a party should try to show that the relevant knowledge was not acquired more than three years before such date as the amendment is likely to be made if it is granted; failing which, she may be able to show a genuine mistake (on this, see *Evans Construction Co Ltd* v *Charrington & Co Ltd and Bass Holdings Ltd* [1983] QB 810, CA, approved in *Signet Group plc* v *Hammerson UK Properties plc* [1998] 03 LS Gaz R 25, CA); failing that possibility, discretion must be sought under s 33. See also *SmithKline Beecham plc* v *Horne-Roberts* [2001] MLC 0667, where an application within the MMR litigation to substitute Smithkline as defendants in place of Merck was permitted because there had been a 'mistake' within the meaning of s 35 of the Limitation Act 1980 and the ten-year time limit applicable to the claim was a 'period of limitation'

---

34 See *Adelson* v *Associated Newspapers Ltd* [2007] EWCA Civ 701 and *Lockheed Martin Corporation* v *Willis Group Limited* [2010] EWCA Civ 927.

35 It is useful to note that the Court of Appeal have said that there is no need to amend the pleading every time the medical condition changes, provided that notice in the form of appropriate medical evidence is given to the defendants (*Oksuzoglu* v *Kay* [1998] Lloyd's Rep Med 129).

within CPR 19.5(3). See also *Parsons* v *George* [2004] EWCA Civ 1912, where the mistake related to the identity of the claimants' landlord.

In *Senior* v *Pearsons and Ward* (26 January 2001, unreported), CA, the court said that the question whether or not the new claim arose out of the same facts as the existing claim was a matter of impression. The Act and the CPR both focused on the particular facts in each case as being relevant. See also *Savings and Investment Bank* v *Fincken* (2001) Times, 2 March. In the RTA claim of *Goode* v *Martin* [2002] PIQR P333, the Court of Appeal allowed an amendment of the claim out of time whereby the claimant was permitted to plead the different facts alleged in the defence. Although this new claim was, on a strict interpretation of the rule (CPR 17.4), impermissible as not arising out of the same facts as the original claim, the court said that, the Human Rights Act having come into operation since the Master's original order disallowing the application, to prevent the claimant from now putting her case on the basis of the facts as pleaded in the defence would constitute an impediment on her access to the court.

Striking a claim out during the currency of the period of limitation

There used to be a rule of practice that a claim would not be struck out during the limitation period, as the claimant could simply start another action. There was an exception where an abuse of court could be discerned.[36] However, all that law seems now to be history. In *Securum Finance Ltd* v *Ashton* [2001] Ch 291, CA, the court said that there was no longer a principle that a second action begun within the limitation period after the first action had been struck out for inordinate and inexcusable delay should not be struck out, save in exceptional circumstances. The pursuit of the new action had to be weighed against the overriding objective of dealing with cases justly and, in particular, the court's need to allot its limited resources to other cases (CPR 1.1(2)(e) is in point here).

---

36 Relevant cases were: *Birkett* v *James* [1978] AC 297, HL; *Tolley* v *Morris* [1979] 2 All ER 561, HL; *Janov* v *Morris* [1981] 1 WLR 1389, CA; *Hogg* v *Hamilton and Northumberland Health Authority* [1993] 4 Med LR 369, CA; *Headford* v *Bristol and District Health Authority* MLC 0033, [1994] 5 Med LR 406.

Chapter 19

The medical records

Andrew Buchan and Dr Thomas Boyd

THE RECORDS OF TREATMENT

The patient's medical records are the backbone of almost all clinical negligence claims. They must be obtained, intelligently sorted and read. After that, they will be submitted to an expert, who will make his report based on them and any other relevant information, such as witness statements from patient and family. The pre-action protocol sets out pro formas for requesting records and for responding to such a request. It is not mandatory to use the pro forma, but it would be unwise not to (see Appendix II). The box that asks the patient to give grounds for his claim need not be taken too seriously. It is not a legal requirement, and is in any event unlikely to be able to be clearly answered at such a preliminary stage.

All relevant records should be obtained. Records of treatment at other hospitals earlier or later than the impugned treatment may well illuminate aspects of the claim. On the other hand, they may relate to conditions not pertinent to the claim, in which case one would expect the expert solicitor not to spend money getting them. GP records are almost always relevant.

Copy records should be checked against the originals. Originals will often yield a better insight into the medical events by revealing more clearly the appearance of the entries (eg colours, writing pressures). Often the photocopying will not extend to the dates in the left margin of the nursing notes, or will show only the last of the two digits for the day of the month – which creates confusion. In one case, the parties were misled in that way when the hole-puncher had obliterated the first digit (*Johnson* v *John and Waltham Forest Health Authority* (1998) MLC 0244, CA).

Often certain records will be missing. If relevant, they should be chased up with vigour. It is amazing what turns up eventually. The law on getting such documents is explained below. But what if records have been lost for good or destroyed?

Records lost or destroyed

HC(80)7 advises a minimum retention period of 25 years for obstetrics records; until the 25th birthday or eight years after the last entry for children and young people; for mentally disordered persons 20 years from the date of cure; and in any other case eight years.

In *Malhotra* v *Dhawan* [1997] 8 Med LR 319, the Court of Appeal, considering the maxim *omnia praesumuntur contra spoliatorem*, indicated that inferences could be drawn against a party who had destroyed relevant evidence (although the court said the maxim only applied where that had been done to stop the other party showing how much of his property had been taken).[1] In *Le Page* v *Kingston and Richmond Health Authority* MLC 0610, [1997] 8 Med LR 229, John Samuels QC, sitting as a Deputy Judge of the Queen's Bench Division, said that the defendants could not properly complain if he drew inferences from surviving documentation which might have been contradicted by other records which they had improperly destroyed.

In *Skelton* v *Lewisham and North Southwark Health Authority* [1999] MLC 0662, [1998] Lloyd's Rep Med 324, the inadequacy of the anaesthetic notes (brief, unsigned, without a record of key events and pressures), although not causative of the damage, was said by the judge to be indicative of an unexplained carelessness. In *Rhodes* v *Spokes and Farbridge* MLC 0640, [1996] 7 Med LR 135, Smith J said:

> A doctor's contemporaneous record of a consultation should form a reliable evidential base in a case such as this. I regret to say that Dr Farbridge's notes of the plaintiff's attendances do not provide any such firm foundation. They are scanty in the extreme. He rarely recorded her complaints or symptoms; he rarely recorded any observations; usually he noted only the drug he prescribed ... The failure to take a proper note is not evidence of a doctor's negligence or of the inadequacy of treatment. But a doctor who fails to keep an adequate note of a consultation lays himself open to a finding that his recollection is faulty and someone else's is correct. After all, a patient has only to remember his or her own case, whereas the doctor has to remember one case out of hundreds which occupied his mind at the material time.

Do the records prove themselves?

The answer is no, strictly. But normally in a trial it is tacitly accepted that they are not going to be challenged, unless one party has put the other side on notice that the timing or content or authoring of a particular note is not accepted. In *Arrowsmith* v *Beeston* (18 June 1998, unreported), CA, it was said that GP records are not evidence of the correctness of the diagnosis made unless the maker of the record is called to give evidence. In *Steele* v *Millbrook Proving Ground Ltd* (6 May 1999, unreported), CA, the relevant issue was whether the rotator cuff syndrome from which the claimant in an employment accident case was suffering was due to the accident or not. In concluding that it was, the judge had relied to an extent on GP records which tended to confirm the claimant's account. Upon objection by the defendants, the Court of Appeal said that there was no doubt that medical records were evidence of the facts recorded in them, and the weight to be attached to the records in this case, given that neither party called the GP to give evidence, was a matter for the judge.

---

1   In *Dobson* v *North Tyneside Health Authority* [1997] 1 WLR 596, the Court of Appeal said that for the maxim to apply it had to be shown that the spoliator was a 'wrongdoer'.

Occasionally a party to a clinical negligence action will serve a notice to admit medical records (the Treasury Solicitor has been known to do this). As I have indicated, that is probably the correct procedure, strictly speaking.

The Data Protection Act 1998 and the Freedom of Information Act 2000

The Act of 1998, intended to implement Directive 95/46/EC,[2] repealed the Data Protection Act 1984 and the Access to Health Records Act 1990 with effect from 1 March 2000, except to the extent that it applied to deceased patients. So the new Act is the route for access to medical records. It has its own jargon. A patient is a 'data subject', the holder of the records is a 'data controller', and the records are 'information constituting data'. Clinical records include 'all paper and computer records whenever created'.[3] A health record means any record which consists of information relating to the physical or mental health or condition of an individual and which has been made by or on behalf of a health professional in connection with the care of that individual (s 68). A health professional includes, by s 69, all forms of medical practitioners (eg doctors, dentists, opticians, nurses, midwives, osteopaths, chiropractors, speech therapists, physiotherapists) and anyone registered as a member of a profession supplementary to medicine (within the catchment of the Professions Supplementary to Medicine Act 1960). Under s 7, an individual or his representative has a right to access and get a copy of his clinical records on making a request in writing with the prescribed fee. Copies are to be supplied within 40 days unless such supply would involve disproportionate effort. An explanation must be supplied where the records contain terms otherwise unintelligible. There are provisions for an application to the court by either party.

The Act is drafted in general terms. The Data Protection (Subject Access Modification) (Health) Order 2000, SI 2000/413 sets out specific rules concerning health records. Disclosure may be refused where serious harm might be caused to the physical or mental health of the patient. Medical records that have been created in the expectation that they would not be disclosed to the person making the request are exempt from the Act. In *Hubble* v *Peterborough Hospital NHS Trust* (2001) MLC 0347, a Recorder held that X-rays fell within the Act and so no extra charge for copying them could be levied. Although not expressly decided, the same reasoning would seem to apply to the CTG traces, in respect of which an additional charge had already been paid.

The Freedom of Information Act 2000 applies, by and large, to non-personal data. Although most documents which might be helpful to a clinical negligence claim can be obtained under normal disclosure rules, it is not difficult to see that some might fall outside the ambit of those rules in the more complex or wide-ranging claim, and the Act of

---

2   Note that the human rights aspect of accessing medical records is considered in Chapter 21.
3   The Data Protection Act 1984 did not apply to paper records; one had to turn to the Access to Health Records Act 1990 for them. (See the Court of Appeal's judgment in *R* v *Mid-Glamorgan Family Health Services Authority, ex p Martin* [1994] 5 Med LR 383.) The 1984 Act was also limited to records created after October 1991.

2000 could be particularly useful in accessing information previously undivulged relating (for example) to Trust or health authority systems and data or Department of Health and government management, thus assisting in the investigation and formulation of a claim. This might well be particularly helpful to group claims, where the budget for such an investigation is so much greater than for the single claim. Though on the surface exceptionally wide-ranging, the Act is complex and hedged about with exceptions. This is not the place to offer more than a brief summary.

Individuals already have the right to access information about themselves (personal data) which is held on computer and in some paper files under the Data Protection Act 1998. The Act of 2000 extends this right of access (as far as public authorities are concerned) to allow access to all the types of information held, whether personal or non-personal. This may include information about third parties, although the public authority will have to take account of the Data Protection Act 1998 before releasing any personal information. The Act gives two related rights:

- the right to be told whether the information exists; and
- the right to receive that information.

The right to access the information held by public authorities can be exercised by anyone, worldwide. The Act is also retrospective. This right to access information came into effect on 1 January 2005.

The Act is 'challenged with the task of reversing the working premise that everything is secret, unless otherwise stated, to a position where everything is public unless it falls into specified excepted cases' (Lord Chancellor's first Annual Report on the implementation of the Act, November 2001). As indicated, it gives a general right of access to all types of recorded information held by public authorities, sets out exemptions from that right and places a number of obligations on public authorities (health bodies are, of course, included in the term 'public authority'). The Act also makes appropriate amendments to the Data Protection Act 1998 and the Public Records Act 1958. Subject to the exemptions, any person who makes a request to a public authority for information must be informed whether the public authority holds that information. If it does, that information must be supplied, subject to certain conditions.

Every public authority is required to adopt and maintain a publication scheme setting out how it intends to publish the different classes of information it holds, and whether there is a charge for the information. Some trusts have already put their publication schemes online. Two codes of practice issued under the Act provide guidance to public authorities about responding to requests for information and records management. The Act is enforced by the Information Commissioner and was brought into force in two parts, with full implementation on 1 January 2005. The requirement to publish and maintain a publication scheme was phased in during 2003 and 2004. Individual rights of access to information came into force across all public authorities in January 2005.

Before 2005, there were Codes that gave the public access to some information held by government departments. These were little used and were considered to be exclusive rather than inclusive. The Freedom of Information Act covers over 100,000 public bodies. It is proclaimed that the Act will ensure that much more information will be routinely and freely available about the way in which we are governed and the way decisions that affect all our lives are reached, at both national and local levels. With the introduction of publication schemes in 2003/04, a vast amount of information not previously accessible became available as a matter of routine. Publication schemes mean that public bodies have to ensure that information which they say is available through their publication scheme is truly and easily available, and they will have to indicate in their schemes how they will achieve this. The legislation allows for public bodies to charge for access subject to certain restrictions but this too should be notified in the publication scheme.

The main features of the individual right of access are:

1   Every written request for information, including emails, will be considered to be an access request under the Freedom of Information Act. There is no set format, nor is there any requirement to justify the request. There are no citizenship or residency restrictions and the only requirement is that applicants provide a name and address.
2   Access requests must be dealt with within 20 working days.
3   If the information is not available or the information is not supplied, the applicant must be told why.
4   In cases where either the precise information covered by the request is unclear or where the scope is so wide as to make it likely that the request would be refused on the grounds of cost, public bodies are encouraged to discuss with the applicant the nature of their request to see whether it can be redefined to lead to a positive outcome.
5   The Act requires public bodies to set up an appeals procedure to review refusals at the request of the applicants and, if the applicant remains unhappy at the refusal, there is an avenue of recourse to the Information Commissioner.

The modest hope has been offered to the effect that the Act will encourage transparency in decision-making, leading to a re-establishment of the trust between national and local public bodies and the people they serve.

THE RIGHT TO PRE-ACTION DISCLOSURE

The Access to Health Records Act 1990 did not apply to records created before November 1991, as to which the old law remained in force. Given that the 1998 Act applies to all clinical records whenever created, the old law has assumed considerably less significance in clinical negligence claims. However, there may from time to time be documents the patient wants to see which do not comprise data caught by the Act. For example, in *Hewlett-Parker* v *St George's Healthcare NHS Trust* [1998] MLC 0072, Owen J ordered disclosure of an NHS complaints file (pursuant to the then current RSC Ord 24, r 8). It is therefore useful to summarise the old law.

Pre-action disclosure is provided for by s 33 of the Supreme Court Act 1981, s 52 of the County Courts Act 1984, and CPR 31.16. Note that this facility is only available against a likely party to future proceedings. Disclosure against a non-party can only be obtained after action is commenced[4] –

---

4   It is not permissible to join a party simply to get disclosure (*Douihech* v *Findlay* [1990] 1 WLR 269).

apart of course from any rights under the 1998 Act. Disclosure against a non-party is governed by s 34 of the Supreme Court Act 1981, s 53 of the County Courts Act 1984, and CPR 31.17.

Pre-action disclosure is no longer limited to personal injury cases. In *Burrells Wharf Freeholds Ltd* v *Galliards Homes Ltd* [1999] 33 EG 82, the court rejected the submission that Art 5 of the Civil Procedure (Modification of Enactments) Order 1998, which removed the former restriction to personal injury cases, was *ultra vires*.

Any application must be supported by evidence. The applicant must show that he and the respondent are likely to be parties to proceedings, that the documents he seeks fall within the ambit of disclosable documents under the general provisions of CPR 31.6, and that early disclosure is desirable in order to dispose fairly of the anticipated proceedings or to assist the dispute to be resolved without proceedings or to save costs.

On an application for disclosure against a non-party, it must be shown that the documents sought are likely to support the case of the applicant or adversely affect *another* [my emphasis] party's case, and that disclosure is necessary in order to dispose fairly of the claim or to save costs.[5]

The Court of Appeal considered the ambit of the Act of 1981 and the new rules in the case of *American Home Products Corpn and Professor Sir Roy Calne* v *Novartis Pharma AG* (2001) IPD 24021. This was an action for alleged infringement of a patent for the use of rapamycin in the preparation of a drug for inhibiting organ or tissue transplant rejection. The court found a similar limitation to the Act's 'any documents which are relevant to an issue' in the words of CPR 31.17, enabling the court to make an order 'only where the documents ... are likely to support the case for the applicant or adversely affect the case of one of the other parties to the proceedings'.

Confidentiality of medical records

It goes without saying that a person's medical records are confidential and normally not to be disclosed to anyone but his doctors. The main exception to this is that in a personal injury action or a clinical negligence action he is taken to have waived his right to confidentiality so that the defendants are entitled to see all relevant records (and in most cases that will embrace all his records). Any unacceptable disclosure is likely also to be a contravention of the right to privacy under Art 8 of the Convention.

In *R* v *Plymouth City Council, ex p Stevens* [2002] EWCA Civ 388, where a mother sought to see the medical records of her adult son who was in the guardianship of the respondent council, the court said that, although there was a legitimate interest in protecting the confidentiality of personal information about a person in the guardianship of his local authority, his nearest relative was entitled to have direct access to that information when she needed it in order to determine whether she should oppose the renewal of the guardianship. This reasoning was followed by Sumner J in *Re R (a child)* [2004] EWHC 2085 (Fam), where the judge made an order for pre-action disclosure under CPR 31.16, subject to conditions, in

---

5   The House of Lords considered the relevant principles in *O'Sullivan* v *Herdmans Ltd* [1987] 1 WLR 1047.

respect of a potential claim by a child against the respondent Trust for failing to diagnose his condition. The judge said that the balance came down in favour of full disclosure even though the Trust's notes contained sensitive material about the applicant's mother.[6]

In *A Health Authority* v *X* [2001] EWCA Civ 2014, the Court of Appeal said that a judge who had ordered the disclosure to a health authority of case material used in care proceedings and GP patient records had correctly balanced the public interest in effective disciplinary procedures for the investigation and eradication of medical malpractice against the confidentiality of the documents, and had correctly used his power to attach conditions to the disclosure. In the absence of exceptional circumstances, an application for the release of papers in care proceedings should be determined by the trial judge.

In *A* v *X* & *B* (*non-party*) [2004] EWHC 447 (QB), a defendant who had admitted causing injury by his negligent driving sought to reduce the victim's damages by proving, by way of disclosure of the medical records of the victim's brother, that the victim's brain disability was familial (genetic) and would have arisen in any event. Morland J, refusing the application, said that only in a very exceptional factual situation would a court be justified in civil proceedings in ordering disclosure of a non-party's confidential medical data and that this was not such a case. In *Bennett* v *Compass Group UK* [2002] EWCA Civ 642, defendants to a claim in respect of an accident at work had sought, reasonably enough one would have thought, to obtain disclosure of the employee's medical records. The records had been referred to in an expert medical orthopaedic report served on behalf of the claimant. The Court of Appeal said that the judge had had jurisdiction to make his order that the claimant provide the defendant with a signed form of authority for release of her GP and hospital records direct to the defendant, although care was to be taken in the exercise of that jurisdiction. The defendant had a right to inspect the records under CPR 31.3, and also as records relied on by the claimant's expert in his report, under CPR 31.14(e).[7]

In *Ashworth Security Hospital* v *MGN Ltd* (2002) MLC 0800, the House of Lords agreed with the Court of Appeal in upholding the judge's order that a journalist's employer at the *Daily Mirror* should disclose the identity of an intermediary as a means of identifying the source of information on a patient detained under the Mental Health Act 1983. The court said that the disclosure of confidential medical records to the press was misconduct which was not merely of concern to the individual establishment in which it occurred; it was an attack on an area of confidentiality which should be safeguarded in any democratic society and the protection of patient information was of vital concern to the National Health Service. However, when the hospital sought to compel the intermediary journalist who had originally obtained the information from hospital sources, ie information

---

6 It is also worth noting the costs point: the judge said that ordinarily a party required to provide pre-action disclosure would be awarded his costs but in the circumstances each side should pay its own costs. It is not the practice in my experience that a party who successfully challenges the refusal of a likely party to proceedings bears the costs of the application.

7 Note that in care proceedings it will generally be the case that the court should be provided with medical records of parents (see *Re B (disclosure to other parties)* (2001) 2 FLR 1017 and *Re B, R and C (Children)* 12 November 2002, CA).

derived from the patient's records, to disclose the identity of those sources, the Court of Appeal, managing to distinguish the House of Lords decision, declined to make the order sought, saying that protection of journalistic sources was one of the basic conditions of press freedom and there was no overriding requirement in the case to allow what would otherwise be a breach of Art 10 of the European Convention on Human Rights (*Ackroyd v Mersey Care NHS Trust* [2003] Lloyds Rep Med 379).[8]

For guidance concerning the disclosure of medical records of patients detained under the Mental Health Act 1983 in Mental Health Review Tribunal proceedings, see *Dorset Healthcare NHS Trust v MH* (2010) BMLR 1.

Misleading disclosure

Where a health authority had grossly misled the claimant's medical and legal advisers in their disclosure of X-rays, the Court of Appeal ordered a new trial (*Cunningham v North Manchester Health Authority* [1997] 8 Med LR 135).

OTHER PRE-ACTION FACILITIES

By s 33(1) of the Act of 1981, the court may make orders for:

- the inspection, photographing, preservation, custody and detention of property which by s 35(5) includes any land chattel or other corporeal property of any description [possibilities of inspection of hospital premises and machines here] that appears to the court to be property which may become the subject matter of subsequent proceedings or as to which any question may arise in any such proceedings; and
- taking samples of any such property and carrying out any experiment on or with it.

In *Ash v Buxted Poultry Ltd* (1989) Times, 29 November, Brooke J held that the court had power to order one party to a personal injury action to permit the other to make a video recording of a relevant industrial process so as to facilitate the judge's understanding of the case. This power could be of use in the odd clinical negligence case, eg to film the process of a machine in hospital.

In *Dobson v North Tyneside Health Authority* [1997] 1 WLR 596, the Court of Appeal held that there was no right of property in the brain of a deceased and that there was no duty to preserve the brain after *post mortem* and after the rest of the body had been buried. The claim was therefore struck out.[9] In *AB v Leeds Teaching Hospital NHS Trust*

---

8   There is some fear for confidentiality as the Government proposes at huge expense to put all health records on a central database. But such fear is unwarranted. If the Government's track record on IT is taken into account, in the civil service and defence, for example, as well as in health, it won't work.

9   In *R v Kelly* (1998) 51 BMLR 142, it was held that parts of a dead body can be property within s 4 of the Theft Act 1968 if they have acquired different attributes as a result of the application of skill, such as dissection or preservation techniques, for exhibition or teaching purposes.

and Cardiff and Vale NHS Trust (2004) MLC 1101, an imaginative group action by parents of deceased children whose organs had been removed at post-mortem, the claim was for psychiatric injury caused on discovery of the removal of the organs. Gage J held that the parents had no possessory rights in the organs (although a duty of care could exist in such circumstances – see Chapter 5).[10]

The reverse side of the coin

Subject to any conflict with human rights (see Chapter 21), we may note *Dunn* v *British Coal Corpn* [1993] PIQR P275, in which the Court of Appeal held that where a claim for damages for an industrial accident included a substantial claim for loss of earnings, the claimant was obliged to disclose all his medical records and not just those relating to the accident (the Court of Appeal has confirmed that the duty to disclose medical records in this type of situation was a duty to disclose not only to the medical advisers for the other party but also to the legal advisers – *Hipwood* v *Gloucester Health Authority* MLC 0708, [1995] 6 Med LR 187).

In the Irish case of *Irvin* v *Donaghy* [1996] PIQR P207, where the application by the defendants for the claimant's medical records was made direct to the GP and hospital, it was said that a sensible practice had grown up of providing that the documents were in the first instance to be inspected by the claimant who could object to the production on grounds of privilege. The court had to seek to ensure that only the relevant parts of confidential documents were made available to the applicant. There was no objection in principle to the claimant having a right to object to the production of irrelevant material and he should have the opportunity to cover up entries in the medical records which were irrelevant, just as the claimant could in the traditional context of discovery between parties.

Section 35(1) provides that the court is not to make an order for disclosure if it considers that compliance with the order would be likely to be injurious to the public interest. As the court has a general discretion whether to exercise its power to order disclosure or not, this provision seems otiose.

Disclosure should not be refused on the ground that the claim is time-barred unless that is clear beyond reasonable argument, particularly as discovery might reveal material which would affect the position (*Harris* v *Newcastle upon Tyne Health Authority* [1989] 1 WLR 96, CA).

PRIVILEGE

Privileged documents must be disclosed but can be withheld from inspection. Rule 31(3) acknowledges this, but, if challenged, the existence of privilege has to be proved. The two classes of privilege that are likely to be relevant to disclosure of medical records are legal professional privilege and public interest.

---

10 A breach of the human right to family life under Art 8 was included in the plea, of course.

Legal professional privilege

Correspondence and other communications between a solicitor and his client are privileged from production even though no litigation was contemplated or pending at the time, provided that they are of a confidential nature and the solicitor was acting in his professional capacity for the purpose of giving legal advice or getting it on behalf of the client, as from counsel. If a document to which legal professional privilege attaches does find its way into the hands of the defendant, he may use it as desired, regardless of the privilege, but if he has not yet made use of it, he can be restrained from so doing (*Goddard* v *Nationwide Building Society* [1987] QB 670, CA; *English and American Insurance Co* v *Herbert Smith & Co* [1988] FSR 232; and see also *Guinness Peat Properties* v *Fitzroy Robinson Partnership* [1987] 1 WLR 1027, CA – and see below the section on documents obtained by mistake).

But it is in the class of documents that are only privileged if made when litigation was contemplated or pending that any problems on disclosure of medical records are likely to arise. The general principle is that communications between a solicitor and third party, whether directly or through an agent, which come into existence after litigation is contemplated or commenced and are made with a view to such litigation, either for the purpose of giving or obtaining advice in regard to that litigation, or of obtaining or collecting evidence to be used in it, or obtaining information which may lead to the obtaining of such evidence, are privileged. This privilege includes documents which are obtained by a solicitor with a view to enabling him to prosecute or defend an action, or to give advice with reference to existing or contemplated litigation, but does not include copies he obtains of documents that are not themselves privileged. It is with reference to reports of accidents and similar documents which are made before litigation is commenced and generally have the purpose of putting the senior personnel or the solicitors of the potential defendants fully in the picture that problems have arisen. Such reports have a dual purpose at least, that of producing as clear an account of the incident as possible and as soon as possible so that the facts may be ascertained and any necessary action taken, and that of providing a basis on which solicitors may be instructed if necessary and proceedings defended (or settled) if they are instituted. It is not easy to discern in the shifting sands of the law what the legal rules are for defining the test of 'made with a view to litigation'. Similarly, it is not clear at what point litigation may be said to have begun to be 'contemplated'.[11]

Dominant purpose

In *Waugh* v *British Railways Board* [1980] AC 521, the defendants sought privilege for an internal report that was made in accordance with their

---

11   Privilege does not attach to pre-existing documents obtained, but not created, for the purposes of litigation (*Ventouris* v *Mountain* [1991] 1 WLR 607, CA). Note also that the Court of Appeal stated that just because a document had to be disclosed, it did not automatically follow that production or inspection would be ordered. Privilege, as opposed to admissibility, becomes irrelevant once a document has in fact been disclosed (*Black & Decker Inc* v *Flymo Ltd* [1991] 1 WLR 753).

usual practice after an accident. It contained contemporary accounts from witnesses. The defendants deposed that one of the principal purposes in preparing it had been so that it could be passed to their chief solicitor to enable him to advise the Board on their legal liability and defend any proceedings if so advised. After considerable dissension below, the House of Lords, agreeing with Lord Denning MR's judgment in the Court of Appeal, said that the due administration of justice strongly required that a contemporary report such as this, which would almost certainly be the best evidence as to the cause of the accident, should be disclosed, and that for that important public interest to be overridden by a claim of privilege the purpose of submission to the party's legal advisers in anticipation of litigation must be at least the dominant purpose for which it had been prepared; that in that particular case that purpose had been of no more than equal weight with the purpose of facilitating proper railway operation and safety. Therefore, the claim to privilege failed. The court added that the fact that the report stated on its face that it had finally to be sent to the solicitor for advice could not be conclusive as to what in fact the dominant purpose of its creation was.[12]

This principle was applied to a health authority report in *Lask* v *Gloucester Health Authority* [1991] 2 Med LR 379. The Court of Appeal held that a confidential accident report, which NHS circulars required to be completed by health authorities, both for the use of solicitors in case litigation arose in respect of the accident and also to enable action to be taken to avoid a repetition of the accident, was not privileged since the dominant purpose of its preparation had not been for submission to solicitors in anticipation of litigation, and this was so decided even though both health authority and solicitor had deposed that that had in fact been its dominant purpose and the report itself referred only to that purpose (the court saw in the wording of the relevant Health Circular material which enabled it to reject the sworn statements in the affidavits). This may be contrasted with *McAvan* v *London Transport Executive* (1983) 133 NLJ 1101, CA in which reports that had been prepared by a bus crew and an inspector after an accident had occurred were held by the court to be privileged as the dominant purpose in their preparation was to ascertain blame in the event of a claim being made.

In *Green* v *Post Office* (15 June 1987, unreported), the Court of Appeal ordered disclosure of an accident report brought into existence by an employer for the dual purpose of providing information not only on which legal advice could be obtained if a claim for personal injuries was made by the employee but also on which the employer could consider whether any remedial action was required to avoid a repetition of the accident at work.

Medical reports

Although Lord Woolf wanted all communications between patients' solicitors and medical experts to be disclosed, that has fortunately not

---

12 In *Secretary of State for Trade and Industry* v *Baker* [1998] Ch 356, the Vice-Chancellor said that it would not be enough to establish 'dominant purpose' if production of the document did not involve a risk of impinging upon the inviolability of lawyer/client communications.

become the law.[13] Medical reports, whether on liability or prognosis, and indeed any expert report that a party has commissioned, are privileged and he cannot be required to produce them (*Worrall* v *Reich* [1955] 1 QB 296, CA; *Causton* v *Mann Egerton (Johnsons) Ltd* [1974] 1 WLR 162, CA). If you want a sight of the defendants' doctor's report when you show them yours or agree to send the client to a medical examination, you must get their agreement first. It is not safe to rely on an implied agreement, even though Lord Denning MR said in the *Causton* case in a strong dissenting judgment:

> I hope that in future the solicitors for every plaintiff will refuse to allow any defendants to have any medical examination of the plaintiff except on the terms that the defendants will disclose the medical reports following the examination. This has become so usual in practice that I think it may be said to have become the 'usual terms'. This is most desirable. We know that the medical men of this country give their reports honestly and impartially by whichever side they are instructed, and it is only fair that if one side shows his the other should reciprocate.

The usual order for disclosure of medical reports on the claimant's condition and prognosis means only that if a party does in fact intend to produce such evidence in court, he must disclose it first.

If the reports are not prepared in anticipation of litigation, eg where they have been made by an employer in order to establish whether an employee is able to return to work, the court may order disclosure if that is necessary for the fair disposal of the case (*Ford Motor Co* v *X Nawaz* [1987] ICR 434, EAT).

In *Jackson* v *Marley Davenport Ltd* [2004] 1 WLR 2926, the Court of Appeal said that CPR 35.13 did not provide the courts with the power to order disclosure of earlier reports made by experts in preparation of a final report. Where an expert made a report for legal advisers for the purposes of a conference, such a report was subject to litigation privilege at the time it was made. It was not intended that the CPR should abrogate privilege, and references to the disclosure of experts' reports in CPR 35.10(2) had to be references to the expert's actual evidence and not to earlier draft reports (*Carlson* v *Townsend* [2001] PIQR P346 applied). A bold attempt had already been made in *Linstead* v *East Sussex, Brighton and Hove Health Authority* [2001] PIQR P356 to consign legal professional privilege to the waste bin using the ubiquitous human rights plea, here under Art 6, the right to a fair trial. The claimant sought to force disclosure of an earlier statement made by a midwife to the defendants at a time when clearly proceedings were pending. Forbes J refused the application, saying that the privilege was paramount and absolute when not waived or abrogated. The right to a fair trial did not entitle interference with the right to legal confidentiality. The Human Rights Act did not alter the nature and effect of legal privilege, which was not subject to any balancing exercise of weighing competing public interests.

The House of Lords has three times recently had occasion to consider legal professional privilege. In *B* v *Auckland District Law Society* [2003] 2 AC 736, a case on appeal from New Zealand, they held that privilege had

---

13   Note, however, that in certain circumstances the court can order disclosure of an expert's instructions under r 35(10)4 (see Chapter 20).

not been waived where documents had voluntarily been made available expressly for limited purposes. In *Medcalf* v *Weatherill* [2002] 3 WLR 172, they held that it was unfair to make wasted costs orders against counsel for pursuing allegations of fraud where legal professional privilege prevented counsel from adducing evidence as to whether they had any reasonably credible material before them to prove those allegations. Reference may also be made to *Dempsey* v *Johnstone* [2003] EWCA Civ 1134, where the Court of Appeal held that the question whether counsel had been negligent in pursuing a claim could only be resolved by a sight of counsel's written advice and that was not permitted as the document was privileged.

The third House of Lords decision is *Three Rivers Council* v *Bank of Credit and Commerce International* [2004] 3 WLR 1274. The court said that legal advice privilege attached to advice given by solicitors about the preparation and presentation of evidence to be submitted to an inquiry since legal advice for the purposes of privilege included advice as to what should prudently and sensibly be done in the relevant legal context. Legal professional privilege was not an extension of litigation privilege, but a single integral privilege whose sub-heads were legal advice privilege and litigation privilege; it was litigation privilege that was restricted to proceedings or anticipated proceedings in a court of law.

Proceedings contemplated

The other question – at what point can one say that proceedings are contemplated? – can also give rise to difficulties. It can be said that as soon as any accident has occurred, there is a prospect of litigation. Some cases have endorsed that approach, principally *Seabrook* v *British Transport Commission* [1959] 1 WLR 509 ('I think that, whenever a man is fatally injured in the course of his work on the railway line, there is at least a possibility that litigation will ensue', *per* Havers J); but it is doubtful if that case is authority for anything anymore in view of *Waugh* v *British Railways Board* (above) and *Alfred Crompton Amusement Machines Ltd* v *Customs and Excise Comrs (No 2)* [1974] AC 405, HL, which would appear to be authority for the proposition that, where a decision needs to be taken by a potential defendant before solicitors are instructed, documents coming into existence before that decision is taken cannot be said to have been made when litigation was in contemplation and are therefore not privileged. There would appear to be scope for arguing on that basis for the disclosure of a great many accident reports (the documents in the *Alfred Crompton* case comprised material collected for the purpose of preparing a valuation of the claimant's goods for an assessment to purchase tax, but the principle is equally applicable to accident or medical reports).

Whose privilege?

The general rule is that the privilege is that of the client and of no-one else; only the client can waive the privilege (though the privilege is not lost by reason of the death of the client). The somewhat complex facts of *Lee* v *South West Thames Regional Health Authority* [1985] 1 WLR 845, CA, illustrate what appears to be an exception to the principle that privilege may be claimed only by the party for whose benefit the document was prepared, or at any rate a limit upon that principle.

> Pre-action disclosure was sought on behalf of a small boy who suffered brain damage, probably through lack of oxygen when he was on a respirator either in hospital or in the ambulance. The health authority for the hospital had, after litigation was contemplated against them, required from the defendants, who were responsible for the ambulance service, a report on what had or might have happened. That report was agreed by the parties to be privileged as far as the hospital health authority was concerned; but its disclosure was sought against the defendants, it being argued that the privilege was not theirs to assert. The Court of Appeal refused to order disclosure, saying that, although the defendants appeared to be advancing the other authority's claim to privilege, the cause of action being asserted against the defendants was not a wholly independent cause of action, but arose out of the same incident as that which rendered the hospital authority a likely defendant. However, that conclusion was 'reached with undisguised reluctance because we think that there is something seriously wrong with the law if Marlon's mother cannot find out exactly what caused this brain damage'.

Public interest privilege

It is all too easy for a public body that wishes to avoid embarrassing disclosures, or to create or preserve a sense of mystique, to claim that disclosure of certain important documents would be damaging to the public interest. Where the claim is based on the ground of national security, it may well succeed as that is an argument which our courts take very seriously. So, too, where the interests of children are involved. But in all cases, such a claim must be carefully scrutinised so that public bodies that are seeking to take the easy way out should not be encouraged to expect to succeed.

Strictly, this is not a claim for privilege that a party may advance, but rather an immunity from production that the court should invoke of its own accord if the party does not, on the basis that such production would be injurious to the public interest, ie that withholding the documents is necessary to the proper functioning of the public service. It features most frequently in the area of governmental decisions or policy, and police or similar investigations, but it could be found occasionally in the clinical negligence action. Every potential claim to immunity will be considered on its own facts, but a decision as to a particular type of document is likely to be of persuasive authority when a similar situation occurs later. There are many reported cases on public interest privilege. One example, in the medical field, must suffice here.

> In September 1990 haemophiliacs seeking compensation for having been infected with the HIV virus from contaminated clotting agents secured in the Court of Appeal the release of many important documents that the government were unjustly trying to withhold from them on the factitious ground, so dear to government, that the public interest demanded that they remain secret (see *Re HIV Haemophiliac Litigation* (1990) 41 BMLR 171, [1990] NLJR 1349).

Documents obtained by mistake

It is not unusual to find privileged documents among the medical records, such as memos or letters from the 'accused' doctor to the hospital administrator, health authority solicitor or MDU, which have clearly been included through oversight – someone has simply copied everything in the file without properly scrutinising the documents. In such a case, the general rule is that you cannot take advantage of their oversight and must send back the documents and any copies, though that rule seems to admit of the strange exception that if you did not realise when you saw the document that it had been supplied by mistake, you need not give it back (see *Guinness Peat Properties Ltd* v *Fitzroy Robinson Partnership* [1987] 1 WLR 1027, CA and *Derby & Co* v *Weldon (No 8)* [1991] 1 WLR 73). In *Kenning* v *Eve Construction Ltd* [1989] 1 WLR 1189, Michael Wright J refused to order the return of a clearly privileged covering letter from an expert which had been inadvertently disclosed along with his report, on the ground that if the defendants were going to call that expert, they were in any event obliged to disclose all his evidence, warts and all. Where defendants had no reason to suspect a mistake when certain documents had been included by the claimants in the trial bundle, they were entitled to assume that they were documents on which the claimants intended to rely, whether privileged or not, and that any privilege had been waived (*Derby & Co* v *Weldon (No 10)* [1991] 1 WLR 660).

Where the defendant's solicitor in a claim for industrial injury reasonably believed that the claimant's advisers had waived privilege in sending him a copy of a medical report, the claimant was entitled to make use of it at the trial (*Pizzey* v *Ford Motor Co Ltd* [1994] PIQR P15, CA).

In *IBM Corpn* v *Phoenix International* [1995] 1 All ER 413, Aldous J held that the question whether the disclosure was understood by the solicitor for the other party to be a mistake should be adjudged according to the likely reaction of the reasonable solicitor.

The rules remain the same despite the new CPR: *Breeze* v *John Stacey & Sons* (1999) Times, 8 July, CA (where the mistake was not obvious there was no duty on the receiving party to inquire further).[14]

In *Fayed* v *Commissioner of Police for the Metropolis* [2002] EWCA Civ 780, the Court of Appeal, reviewing the principles involved, said that an injunction to prevent the use of documents that were subject to legal professional privilege or public interest immunity but had been voluntarily, though mistakenly, sent to the other side for inspection, should only be granted where the mistake would have been obvious to a reasonable solicitor.

CONTENTS OF THE RECORDS[15]

The medical records are likely to contain some or all of the following:

* accident and emergency department record card;
* GP's referral letter;
* admitting doctor's notes on examination;

---

14 Where a *prima facie* case of fraud against a party has been made out, the court may overrule an otherwise properly made claim to privilege (*Derby & Co* v *Weldon (No 7)* [1990] 1 WLR 1156).

15 The sections that follow were written by Dr David Kirby. They explain content for non-computerised records, still by far the majority of records.

- ward doctor's clinical notes;
- operating record;
- anaesthetic record;
- daily nursing notes;
- laboratory reports on blood and other bodily samples;
- radiographs and reports on radiographs;
- electrocardiograms (ECG) and reports;
- electroencephalograms (EEG) and reports;
- temperature, pulse and respiration charts;
- fluid balance charts;
- head injury charts;
- partogram (midwifery only);
- foetal heart trace (maternity only);
- correspondence to and from other hospitals involved in treatment and with the GP.

A GP's notes will include medical record cards, correspondence from hospitals and the results of tests.

NHS records belong to the Secretary of State. Records maintained by private hospitals do not include doctors' notes, which are their own property, and may often be kept separately by the treating doctor. Unlike NHS hospitals, private hospitals may not be responsible for the default of consultants, as opposed to nursing staff (see Chapter 4).

GP RECORDS

The primary purpose of a general practice record is to aid in the continuity of care of the patient. Ideally it should allow a GP to reconstruct previous consultations without recourse to memory or questioning of the patient and to take over care seamlessly from a colleague. Unfortunately few GP records live up to this ideal. The doctors' regulatory body, the General Medical Council (GMC), specifies[16] a basic standard:

> In providing care you must:
>
> > keep clear, accurate and legible records, reporting the relevant clinical findings, the decisions made, the information given to patients, and any drugs prescribed or other investigation or treatment;
> >
> > make records at the same time as the events you are recording or as soon as possible afterwards.

General practice records have several secondary functions, including the defence of the doctor should he later be the subject of criticism. The medical defence organisations repeatedly remind their members of the importance of good records and give examples in their case reports of poor records which have made the defence of a claim impossible and good records which have enabled criticism to be dispelled. There is a loose correlation between the standard of the notes and quality of care: it is extremely rare to encounter a GP who practices excellent medicine and makes poor notes and, conversely, to come across a GP with a poor standard of clinical practice and good record-keeping.

---

16   General Medical Council *Good Medical Practice* (London: GMC, 2006).

Many GPs who are the subject of a claim will, when their notes are inadequate, rely in their defence on statements of their usual practice. Claimant lawyers may assert that what has not been noted has not been done. Defences based on usual (or even invariable) practice are inevitably flawed. A paper[17] from the Netherlands (which has a rather similar system of general practice to that in the UK) elegantly demonstrated that performance, what doctors actually do, is very poorly correlated with competence, what they are capable of doing. It also showed that doctors performed significantly below standard in actual practice. A good clinical record remains the best defence against an allegation of substandard practice.

The electronic patient record (EPR)

Most general practices started to keep computer records in the 1990s and computer records have become universal since the introduction of the new GP contract in 2004. The contract introduced the Quality and Outcomes Framework (QOF see further, www.nice.org.uk/aboutnice/qof/qof.jsp), which included financial incentives for GPs to make and maintain up-to-date clinical summaries of their patients' medical histories, which should now be present in the majority of records. There are also incentives to record items such as blood pressure, smoking status and ethnicity.

The enthusiasm for computer records has been very variable both between and within practices, leading to a situation where paper and computer records have operated in tandem. Many doctors have embraced the new technology so wholeheartedly that there is a widespread perception amongst patients that their GP is more interested in his computer than he is in them. The undesirable practice of using both computer and paper records, with obvious potential deleterious effects on clinical care, operated in many practices during the 1990s and persists in some practices today. Dual systems of record-keeping also complicate the task of lawyers and experts in ensuring that they have gathered all the available evidence and in constructing chronologies.

General practitioners use one of the computer systems approved by the Department of Health, from one of the suppliers in the 'GP Systems of Choice' (GPSoC) scheme (details are available at www. connectingforhealth.nhs.uk). Currently there are six suppliers, some of whom supply more than one system. The systems use different and incompatible software, are different in operation and generate different records. This creates difficulties for doctors working in more than one practice, when records are transferred between practices and for lawyers and experts who may lack any knowledge of the system being used by a doctor who is the subject of a claim against him.

The Department of Health issued detailed guidelines[18] to general practitioners on the use of computer systems. The guidance specifies in detail how GPs should use, maintain and transfer electronic records. GP computer systems all include an 'audit trail', separate from the electronic

---

17 Rethans J et al *Does competence of general practitioners predict their performance? Comparison between examination setting and actual practice* (BMJ 1991; 303:1377–80).
18 www.dh.gov.uk *Good practice guidelines for general practice electronic patient records* (v 3.1, June 2005).

patient record (EPR), which enables one to establish who made a record, when that record was made and whether there have been any changes to the record. The guidance states:

> It is the audit trail that enables a record to be taken back to any date and viewed as it was on that date. Audit trails are of great medico-legal importance in determining the true state of entries in the EPR at any time in the past.

The audit trail of the computer of the notorious mass-murderer Harold Shipman showed that many of his records were fabricated and was one of the factors which led to his detection.[19] Proving that an entry is false or has been made non-contemporaneously in a negligence action is likely to involve the employment of considerable information technology expertise.

A GP computer record will typically include registration details, a summary of the medical history, basic data relating to prevention such as smoking status, blood pressure, a record of consultations, a list of all prescriptions issued, a record of drugs available on repeat prescription and the records of investigations performed. Many practices now scan correspondence into the electronic record, where it should be visible as an attachment. When requesting records from practices it is important to specify that complete disclosure is required: it is not uncommon, for example, for the printout generated by a practice to include only the latest issue of a drug on repeat prescription rather than all prescriptions or to fail to include attachments. Sometimes a case may generate the need for a record whose existence is not obvious: the crucial evidence relating to an abnormal test result which has negligently not been acted upon may be lurking within an undisclosed part of the electronic mailbox in which such results are sent from the local hospital laboratory to the GP.

The fact that different parts of the record appear on different screens is a potential source of error in general practice medicine because important information may not be easily visible or may be difficult to access. Important information from a recent hospital attendance, for example, might only be accessible if an attachment is opened in a new screen.

If a patient has moved practices after a medical error, the details transferred to the new practice might be an incomplete record. It may therefore be necessary to approach the original practice to obtain complete disclosure.

The record of each consultation will include at least one Read code, a coded term used in clinical practice. The codes are arranged in hierarchical structure and allow clinical entries to be searched for the purposes of audit or reporting. Read codes are arranged in chapters for items such as symptoms, examination findings, diagnostic and therapeutic procedures and diagnoses. A doctor who wished to record the fact that a patient had a heart attack might use the Read code 'G30 Acute myocardial infarction' or might explore the hierarchy to be more specific and enter 'G301 Anterior myocardial infarction'. Many GPs find Read codes difficult to use and inappropriate or incorrect Read codes are frequently encountered. Alternatively, doctors may resort to the use of a small repertoire of easily remembered codes for every consultation, such as 'had a chat to patient' or 'patient reviewed'. The codes are regularly updated to include, for example, new drugs, diseases or procedures.

---

19   www.the-shipman-inquiry.org.uk.

In addition to the Read code, each clinical entry should identify the date of the consultation, the author of the record and it should contain a free text narrative. This will typically include the symptoms of which the patient complained (sometimes preceded by 'S' for subjective), examination findings (sometimes preceded by 'O' for objective), a diagnosis (often Read coded), any treatment prescribed and details of other management, such as a referral. The poor keyboard skills of many general practitioners cause some of them to write shorter records than when writing, even though the written notes of general practitioners were frequently criticised for their brevity.

GPs should also routinely record their telephone consultations with patients, although there is evidence[20] that documentation of telephone advice is particularly poor. If a patient's telephone records show a telephone call of significant length to a GP practice then an explanation may be required if there is no corresponding record.

Computer records may enhance patient safety. Prescribing systems flag up warnings of potential drug interactions or contraindications, though some GPs find that these appear so frequently when they are clinically irrelevant that they routinely override them. The systems can incorporate reminders and prompts to tell the GP that the patient needs, for example, to have his blood pressure checked, his medication reviewed or his thyroid function measured.

Many GPs use computerised appointment systems linked to the EPR. In theory, these might allow one to determine the precise length of a consultation. However, the complexity of the systems and the varying ways in which doctors use them mean that this is frequently not possible. Nonetheless, asking for disclosure of computer appointment system records might allow one to establish that a patient did in fact attend on a specific day at a particular time.

GPs are increasingly making electronic referrals through 'Choose and Book', a national service which allows patients to book their own appointments from a choice of 'providers' either over the internet or by telephone. These referrals are allocated a unique reference number, which will appear in the record with the prefix 'UBRN'. Referral letters are sent and may be retrieved electronically.

Telephone recordings

Many GP out of hours services record the telephone conversations between call-handlers, triage nurses or doctors and patients. The recordings of such calls may be invaluable evidence, for either the doctor or the patient, in a clinical negligence case. The following is a verbatim transcript of the essential part of the history given to an out of hours doctor by a 23-year-old man:

> Yesterday, I mean I've been bad anyway, I've had like a cold and that, but yesterday I went out for a walk with my dog and like one minute I was all right and suddenly I had a pain at the back of my neck and the back of my head... And my hearing went funny, I couldn't hear properly...like I was kneeling on the floor and throwing up and everything and like all night, I've been, my head's been hurting, like nausea and I've been throwing up all night.

---

20   Car J, Sheikh A *Telephone consultations* (BMJ 2003; 326:966-9).

This young man clearly gave a history of the sudden onset of a severe headache accompanied by vomiting and other symptoms. This constitutes a subarachnoid haemorrhage (bleeding into the subarachnoid space around the brain) until proved otherwise and requires that the patient be admitted immediately to hospital. This young man was not admitted to hospital and died five weeks later when he suffered a more severe haemorrhage. The second haemorrhage would have been prevented by competent management. The existence of the telephone recording made a claim against the doctor impossible to defend.

Paper records: the Lloyd George record

Most patients born before 2004, and some born after 2004, will have an envelope of Lloyd George records containing continuation cards, correspondence and results of investigations. There might in addition be a summary card, a card detailing repeat prescriptions, a record of immunisations and a new patient questionnaire, completed by the patient on registering. It was not uncommon for GP records to be a chaotic jumble of cards and paper, making effective use of the information contained impossible. An effective doctor will have ordered records with a summary. Once this summary has been incorporated into a computer record the Lloyd George envelope may remain unused.

Doctors have notoriously bad handwriting and entries on the Lloyd George continuation cards may be very difficult to read. However, a written record allows doctors to incorporate items like diagrams of the abdomen and highlight parts of the record, which is usually not possible with current GP computer software. There is abundant anecdotal evidence that it is easier to overlook important data on a computer screen than on a paper record.

Many GPs use idiosyncratic abbreviations and shorthand. A list of the more common abbreviations appears at Appendix V. The idiosyncratic nature of GP records means that there is no infallible method for interpreting an entry such as 'O/E SOB++' (on examination short of breath ++). How short of breath is '++'? Most doctors would use '++' to signify 'very' but it would be difficult to challenge a GP who claimed otherwise.

Written records should be contemporaneous and non-contemporaneous entries should be clearly identified as such. It may be difficult to identify an amendment to a written record or a non-contemporaneous entry. However, more than one doctor has been trapped by not knowing that Lloyd George continuation cards bear the date of printing in the bottom right-hand corner. Making an entry for a consultation that took place before the printing of the card is quite likely to lead to investigation by the GMC.

Other records

There may be other sources of evidence relevant to a clinical negligence claim whose existence is not obvious but whose disclosure would assist the claim. General practitioners and their staff usually keep a daybook and/or a telephone log and a book or electronic record of requests for visits, which usually contain some details of the symptoms or condition underlying the request. There may also be separate records of two-week wait referrals (for suspected cancer). Records of complaints and complaints correspondence should be kept separate from the patient record. There may also be minutes of a significant event analysis or other meetings relating to a medical error. No two general practices operate identical information systems, so it is desirable to make requests for disclosure as open and broad as possible.

The future

The National Programme for Information Technology was established in 2005 and introduced the summary care record. This is intended to make a structured summary of medical data available on a national database and accessible to staff in the NHS over a secure internet connection. By May 2010, 29.8 million people in England had been sent a letter telling them that a summary care record (SCR) would be created for them if they did not opt out. Concerns have been expressed about the accuracy of the data and about the security and confidentiality of the system. Recent research[21] on pilot sites concluded that 'the benefits of centrally stored electronic summary records seem more subtle and contingent than many stakeholders anticipated, and clinicians may not access them.' So far, few clinicians or patients have benefited from the project.

HOSPITAL RECORDS

National Health Service hospital records are more ordered and more consistent in their quality than are the records kept by GPs. They are usually in A4 size folders and are divided into sections. There is some variation in the nature of these sections and their order, but the usual principles are as follows.

The folder contains records kept by nurses as well as those kept by doctors, but these are usually arranged in separate bundles, each in chronological order. In the medical notes, each admission to hospital is filed as a complete unit, which usually opens with an 'admission sheet' on which various particulars are recorded by a clerk as soon as possible after the patient enters the hospital. These include name, address, date of birth, next of kin and consultant responsible.

There should follow a thorough record of the patient's complaints and an appraisal of their current clinical state made by the FY1 (Foundation Year 1) doctor (formerly called a house officer), the most junior of the team of doctors that is to care for the patient during his admission. This is called the 'clerking' and it constitutes a most important and valuable record, both because it is done at a most crucial time in a patient's care, especially in the case of emergency admissions, and because custom dictates that it is carried out with a great degree of thoroughness and in a certain order. Thus, this record should allow readers, if it has been done properly, to have a full understanding of the patient's clinical state at that time, if they can 'read' the traditional system of layout and abbreviation which medical students are taught to use.

---

21 Greenhalgh T et al *Adoption and non-adoption of a shared electronic summary record in England: a mixed-method study* (BMJ 2010; 340:c3111).

In the next section, an example with a glossary is presented to help 'translate' records. It is possible to attempt this because doctors throughout the UK are taught to use much the same system – the clarity and thoroughness of their clerkings of patients is one of the chief ways in which a consultant, who is responsible for their training, will assess the competence of the junior doctor, so the junior will wish to make his records comprehensible and useful to the consultant. Therefore, the adequacy of the hospital records is some indication of the quality of care patients have received. A junior doctor who is neglectful or overworked will keep less thorough and comprehensible records, and if his seniors, the specialist registrar or consultant, are also neglectful, this failure will not be corrected.

After the FY1 doctor has thus recorded the admission of the patient to the hospital, the doctor who is immediately responsible for supervising his work may write in the notes, usually using the same format, but more briefly. Thus, frequently in hospital records the same clinical findings are recorded again under the same date, in a different handwriting, which may be that of an FY2 (Foundation Year 2) doctor or a specialist registrar.

There follows a sequential series of entries by one or other of the team members, the frequency of which is, in general, a reflection of how acutely ill the patient is. In an intensive care unit, the junior doctors or more senior colleagues may write in the notes several times a day, recording the hour at which they have assessed the patient; as well as the team of doctors responsible for the patient's care, other consultants whose opinion has been sought may write in the notes. On the other hand, the medical records kept in a long-stay ward, in a psychiatric hospital for example, may be written in only a few times a year.

Next will be filed the results of investigations carried out during that hospital admission, which are generally arrayed by sticking them in date sequence on a card, each card representing a different department – histology (the microscopic examination of tissues), biochemistry (blood levels of hormones and drugs, and of compounds the levels of which are indices of the function of the liver and kidneys), haematology (the characteristics of the cells in the blood), or X-ray. If electrocardiograms have been done, these too should be arranged, in a pattern which enables the trace to be interpreted, and kept in the notes.

If an operation is performed while a patient is in hospital, this should be recorded by a junior doctor, but there will also be a separate sheet which has been filled in immediately after the operation by the surgeon and the anaesthetist.

The admission notes are ended by a junior doctor, who should write a list of the drugs which a patient has been given to take at home. There will also be a typed discharge summary, which is usually written to the patient's GP by the specialist registrar or the consultant; this document is often not written until several weeks or even months after the patient has been sent home.

In between hospital admission notes, but occasionally filed separately, there will be handwritten notes made in the out-patient clinic by the consultant, registrar or FY2 doctor who has seen the patient in the clinic; also there will usually be a letter sent to the GP after each clinic visit, and copies of these letters will be kept in sequence in the patient's hospital notes.

Hospital records will contain many records kept by nurses, which may be of medico-legal importance: chief among these is the patient's 'Kardex' record: this is a system of notes kept in a single folder in the sister's office on the ward, each patient having a card which is folded into a specially designed folder which allows the patients' names to be displayed in the same sequence as their beds are arranged on the ward. When the patient leaves the hospital, the card is removed and kept in the patient's hospital records folder. The nursing staff make an entry in the Kardex for each patient every day, noting the basic observations (temperature, pulse rate and blood pressure) and commenting briefly on the patient's progress.

Also filed with the nursing records will be all the charts which have been kept at the end of the patient's bed during the admission. These will include a chart of recordings made of the patient's temperature, pulse rate and blood pressure, which may be measured hourly, four-hourly or daily, according to how acutely ill the patient is. There may also be fluid balance charts which record the volumes of fluid which the patient has been given, orally or intravenously, and the volumes they have excreted.

With these charts will be found a 'treatment card', a new one of which is made out for each hospital admission. This is kept by the patient's bed, and is written on by one of the doctors whenever he wishes to prescribe a drug. The name of the drug should be written clearly, with instructions as to dose and frequency and route of administration, with the doctor's signature. The nurse in charge of the ward, whenever she administers the drug, will sign the card again in a column which gives the date and time.

Most patients require the services of some other professional workers, whether they are social workers, physiotherapists or occupational therapists, while they are in hospital. However, the notes of their activities kept by these other professionals are not usually assembled to be kept with the other records in the patient's hospital record folder, for reasons that are historical rather than logical.

EXAMPLES OF THE FORM AND ABBREVIATION IN MEDICAL RECORDS

Medicine has its own language. In the past, when the knowledge and skill of physicians and surgeons were relatively limited, the dignity of their profession was enhanced and their distance above the patient increased by the use of terms the meaning of which was apparent only to their fellow trained doctors. To what extent that is no longer true today is a moot point.

However, there are other important factors as well as the plethora of 'medical' words – many derived from Latin and Greek – which are still used in notes and make them difficult to understand. NHS doctors making records, whether GPs in the community or junior doctors in hospitals, often work in situations of pressure in which it is inappropriate to spend a high proportion of time in writing. This leads not only to poor legibility,[22] but also to the proliferation of a large number of abbreviations. In using

---

22 In *Prendergast* v *Sam & Dee Ltd* [1989] 1 Med LR 36, MLC 0018, CA, a GP was held 25% liable for injury caused when the pharmacist (held 75% liable) misread his prescription and dispensed Daonil instead of Amoxil.

these abbreviations, doctors assume that their colleagues will be able to interpret them, and they sacrifice the possibility of non-doctors being able to understand. This follows from the prevailing attitude to records throughout the medical profession, which is that they are written for the benefit of other doctors who may be treating the same patient in future; they are certainly not written for the patient to be able to understand them.

In recent decades, advances in diagnostic methods and in treatment have led to a vast proliferation of specialities and of kinds of data that can be assembled about a particular patient. These are often presented using new codes and new words, which are hard to understand unless you have a thorough knowledge of the particular techniques.

To read medical records, one needs a medical dictionary which is up-to-date. Even if the technical words are translated, however, there remains the problem of abbreviations. In the section which follows, one may see what a house surgeon might typically write in the notes when clerking a previously fit woman with acute appendicitis. The purpose is to give an example, not only of commonly used abbreviations, but also of the way in which a doctor's notes are generally laid out and organised in a certain sequence.[23]

Form and abbreviation in hospital records:
an annotated example

	DATE TIME	NAME ADDRESS DATE OF BIRTH
Complains of . . . (Presenting complaint) (duration)	C O	Abdominal pain 3 days
History of presenting complaint RIF = right lower quadrant of the abdomen 1/52 = 1 week (1/12 = 1 month, 1/7 = 1 day)	HPC	Off food with central abdo pain 3 days ago, then pain moved to RIF, and became more severe with nausea and anorexia. Some diarrhoea, 1/52
Previous medical history	PMH	Tonsillectomy age 12
Previous obstetric history P = Parity (number of pregnancies). Figures represent number of births followed by number of miscarriages or abortions (= TOPs) LSCS = caesarean section	POH	P 1 + 1 (TOP 1980) LSCS (elective) 1983 for pre- eclampsia
Social history	S H	Mother and part-time worker Non-smoker Drinks socially
Family history A & W = alive and well Ca = cancer	F H	Mother A & W, age 67 Father died age 68 Ca Lung 2 sibs A & W Daughter age 4 well

---

23   Further hieroglyphs may be found set out in Appendix V.

Systematic enquiry	S E	
Gastro-intestinal system (tract)	GIT	Appetite normal until 3 days ago
B O = bowels open		B O regular
° Diarrhoea = no diarrhoea		° Diarrhoea previous few months
° Melaena = no blood in motions that is black		° Melaena
P R = per rectum		° Fresh blood P R
Weight Ý = weight constant		Weight
Genito-urinary tract	G U	° Haematuria
Dysuria = pain on urinating		° Dysuria
Nocturia = arising from sleep to urinate		° Frequency
		° Nocturia
Gynaecological	Gynae	K 5/27–32
K = menstrual cycle – <u>number of days of bleeding</u> number of days of whole cycle		
Cardiovascular system	CVS	° Palpitations
SOBOE = short of breath on exertion		° SOBOE
Orthopnoea = short of breath on lying flat		° Orthopnoea
PND = paroxysmal nocturnal dyspnoea (attacks of waking up very breathless)		° PND
Oedema = swelling with fluid especially of ankles		° Oedema
Respiratory system	R S	° Cough
° Haemoptysis = coughing blood		° Haemoptysis
		° Wheezing
Neurological system	Neuro	° Headaches – occasional
		° Fits
LOC = episode of loss of consciousness		° LOC
Vision 4 = no problem with visions	Vision 4 Hearing 4	
List of regular medication	Drugs	Nil
List of drugs to which the patient thinks she is allergic	Allergy	Penicillin
ON EXAMINATION	O/E	
General description		Distressed
Not anaemic, cyanosed or jaundiced		°An, °Cy, °J
No clubbing (deformity of nails)		
No palpable lymph nodes		° C I
		° L Ns
		Temp 37.8°C
Cardiovascular system	CVS	
Pulse rate and rhythm		p 90 reg

Blood pressure (arterial)

B P 120/70

JVP = venous pressure estimated by observing jugular vein

JVP

H S = heart sounds (diagram used as visual representation of the sounds)

H S
1   2

R = L = findings same on both sides, ie normal

° Oedema
Pulses R = L

Respiratory system
T • = trachea in centre (normal)

R S

T •

Expansion R = L
P N resonant R = L
B S vesicular, nil added

P N = findings on percussion of chest
B S = breath sounds, heard with stethoscope. (Added sounds may be crackles (= creps, crepitations) or wheezes)

Abdominal examination
LSKK° = liver, spleen and kidneys number palpable (ie not enlarged)
° Masses = no lumps in abdomen

Abdo

LSKK°

° Masses

Guarding = reflex muscle spasm

Tender, with guarding & rebound

Rebound = pain on removal of pressure
B S = bowel sounds
P R = rectal examination
NAD = nothing abnormal detected

P R

B S 4
NAD

P V = per vaginam examination of the pelvis
N/S = normal size (if abnormal, uterine size is often expressed as equivalent of a certain gestational age in pregnancy, eg 14/40 meaning the same as the size of a normal pregnant uterus at 14 weeks after the last period began)
A/V = anteverted (alternative uterine positions are axial or retroverted)
V/V = vulva and vagina
Adnexae = areas at either side of uterus

P V

Uterus N/S A/V
Adnexae NAD

Cervix NAD
V/V – NAD

Central nervous system
Examination (this part of the examination is often highly abbreviated or omitted)
PERLA = pupils are equal and react to light and accommodation
Fundi = contents of the eyeballs are seen by the ophthalmoscope

CNS

Cranial nerves

PERLA

Fundi NAD

Motor = examination of the motor aspect of the nervous system in each limb	Motor	Power Tone R = L Co-ordination NAD Reflexes
Sensory = examination of the different modalities of sensation in the limbs and trunk	Sensory	Pain Light touch R = L Temperature NAD Position sense Vibration
SUMMARY	ANALYSIS	Previously fit mother aged – years with acute abdominal pain and fever
Δ = diagnosis NBM = nil by mouth Hourly obs = instructions to nursing staff to record pulse, temp and bp every hour	Plan	Δ appendicitis NBM hourly obs
IVI = intravenous drip N saline = salt solution of similar concentration to that of plasma. (Other fluids are Dextrose saline, or 5% dextrose, which contain a sugar for energy)	IVI	N saline 1L in 6 hours
FBC = full blood count (haematology) U&E = urea and electrolytes (biochemistry) LFT = liver function tests (biochemistry)	FBC U&E LFTs	

Abbreviations and hieroglyphs

For a list of common abbreviations and hieroglyphs, see Appendix V.

Chapter 20

Experts

Patricia Hitchcock QC

Ein Fachmann ist ein Mann, der einige der grössten Fehler kennt, die man in dem betreffenden Fach machen kann und der sie deshalb zu vermeiden versteht.

[An expert is someone who is aware of a few of the worst mistakes that can be made in his field, and so understands how to avoid them.]

Werner Heisenberg *Der Teil und das Ganze* (1969)

THE EXPERT IS THE BACKBONE OF THE MEDICAL NEGLIGENCE ACTION

The role of the expert in a clinical negligence case is broad and deep, and will vary case by case, but the success or failure of the case will invariably depend in very large part on the intellect, competence and communication skills of the expert witness. Amongst his most crucial functions are:

- to assess the evidence and to advise on breach of duty and/or causation, to enable the lawyers to assess the merits and the litigation risks prior to issue;
- to identify gaps in the medical records and, when vital medical records are missing (as they often seem to be), to reconstruct the chain of events insofar as this is possible;
- to provide practical tips, such as where to look for documents in a hospital filing system, what records should exist, what scans should have been retained, etc;
- to review the medical literature and where possible to provide independent support for his analysis;
- to review the pleadings prior to service, to catch any medical idiocies inadvertently introduced by counsel and to identify at the outset any allegation that he is not prepared to support;
- to support and prove the case, once formulated on the basis of the expert's views – in writing, at the experts' meeting and in the witness box;
- to remain independent throughout, keep an open mind – and tell the lawyers of any change of mind as soon as possible, with reasons.

It is no part of the expert's role to decide factual issues, nor to act as an advocate for one of the parties, tempting though this may be. Usurping either the judge's or the advocate's role in the proceedings will draw trenchant criticism from any judge and is likely to be fatal to the cause of the instructing party.

Expert evidence is needed to prove both breach of duty and causation, and very often causation requires a different specialism from breach. An expert for GP liability, for example, will never be able to give authoritative evidence on causation. In a claim for obstetric injury to the foetus, the obstetrician is seldom used to prove causation, and never without the support of a paediatric neurologist or neonatologist. In some areas, however, and especially in straightforward cases, a single expert may suffice: for example, in a claim for inadequate orthopaedic management, where the orthopaedic consultant may be able to speak to both breach of duty and causation.

In cases in which the injury was long in the past, such as birth brain damage, it may well be necessary to instruct two experts, simply because of the lapse of time: the breach of duty expert will need to have been in practice at the date of the injury and be able to comment in the context of what was standard medical practice at that time, to avoid the use of the 'retrospectoscope' so reviled by judges. The causation expert must, however, be totally up to date and normally will be in current clinical practice; although the wisdom and continuing professional interest of some eminent experts enables them to continue to give authoritative views long after retirement, this is only rarely a good idea. The onward march of medical knowledge can cut both ways, however. In *CJL* v *West Midlands Strategic Health Authority* (2009) MLC 1595, Tugendhat J had to decide the issue of how long it would have taken a reasonably competent obstetrician to deliver the claimant by forceps following onset of foetal bradycardia in 1987, and decided on a total of six minutes; some commentators have queried whether a modern doctor, less used to using forceps, could be expected to achieve delivery that fast.[1]

Experts will also be needed on quantum, as for any personal injury action, both medical (for condition and prognosis, and crucially life expectancy) and from a wide range of related specialisms. The specialisms will vary case by case but also with judicial fashion; 20 years ago employment experts were ubiquitous and financial advisors almost unheard of. The advent first of the Woolf reforms and then of periodical payment orders (and the court's duty to assess the form of damages under CPR 41) have reversed that position. Legal teams should invariably direct their minds at every stage to whether or not a given specialism is really cost-effective and necessary to prove the case and, if so, be prepared to justify and fight for their choices at case management hearings.

Consideration should be given at the outset to the possibility of using a joint expert in any given specialism, so that if the decision is taken to instruct a single party expert, the legal team will be able to explain this at a directions hearing.

---

1   See, for example, the article by Andrew Farkas, consultant obstetrician, *Decision to Delivery Interval* (commentary on CJL case) on *Medical Litigation* website (May 2009).

WHAT THE COURT EXPECTS OF THE EXPERT

The importance in an expert of independence of mind and the ability to rise above the fray has long been identified and emphasised and, even in the bad old days of partisan warhorses and little judicial control, the judges were not slow to comment. In *Loveday* v *Renton* [1990] 1 Med LR 117, Stuart-Smith LJ set out ten attributes of an expert that assist the court in assessing the weight to be attributed to that expert's opinion. The list would not be out of place in today's rules:

- eminence;
- soundness of opinion;
- internal consistency and logic;
- precision and accuracy of thought;
- response to searching and informed cross-examination;
- ability to face up to logic and make concessions;
- flexibility of mind and willingness to modify opinions;
- freedom from bias;
- independence of thought; and
- demeanour.

It is essential for the claimant's advisers thoroughly to explore the profiles of all the experts, on both sides, to cover background, training experience, extent of any original research, qualifications, publications, and clinical and forensic experience, for the purpose of evaluating comparative stature.

In *The Ikarian Reefer* [1993] 2 Lloyd's Rep 68 at 81, Cresswell J said that the expert witness had a duty to give independent evidence, uninfluenced as to form or content by the exigencies of litigation, and to provide objective, unbiased opinion to the court on matters within his expertise, never assuming the role of advocate.

In *Sharpe* v *Southend Health Authority* [1997] 8 Med LR 299, Cresswell J commented further:

> An expert witness should make it clear in his or her report that, although the expert would have adopted a different approach or practice, he or she accepted that the approach or practice adopted by the defendant was in accordance with an approach or practice accepted as proper by a responsible body of practitioners skilled in the relevant fields.

And Thorpe LJ said in *Vernon* v *Bosley* [1997] 1 All ER 577, CA:

> The area of expertise in any case may be likened to a broad street with the plaintiff walking on one pavement and the defendant on the opposite one. Somehow the expert must be ever mindful of the need to walk straight down the middle of the road and to resist the temptation to join the party from whom his instructions come on the pavement.

The judge went on to wonder whether the practising clinician might find it easier to maintain that detachment than the professional expert witness, who has retired and may spend his life doing medico-legal reports. Sadly, the tenets set out by the judges were often honoured in the breach by expert witnesses, many of whom frankly declared themselves to be available to act only for one party – whether defendant or claimant – in every case. The same faces regularly appeared in both the civil and the criminal courts, and many abandoned clinical practice in favour of becoming a full-time expert witness. As Stuart-Smith LJ observed in *Vernon* v *Bosley* (above), the judge had not been assisted, as he should have been, by disinterested evidence from the medical professional witnesses, who were allowed to range unchecked into almost every aspect of the case, and he added, with a degree of prescience:

> In my opinion in this type of case in particular there is much to be said for the practice sometimes adopted in the Family Division of there being a psychiatrist appointed by the court. In the field of psychiatry it may be more difficult for those who have treated the plaintiff to approach the case with true objectivity. That was certainly the case here ... Certain it is that the case would have been much shorter and would have been kept in more manageable bounds. But at present the rules of court do not permit this course. Unless the parties agree on a psychiatrist – these parties never would have – the court has no power to make such an order.

THE CIVIL PROCEDURE RULES (CPR)

The Civil Procedure Rules now enshrine the foregoing jurisprudence into a formal code, providing that it is the duty of an expert to help the court on the matters within his expertise and that that duty overrides any obligation to the person from whom experts have received instructions or by whom they are paid (CPR 35.3). The rules also enable the court to restrict the number of experts instructed by the parties (CPR 35.4), to order that a given issue be dealt with by a single joint expert where appropriate (CPR 35.7), and to appoint an assessor to assist the judge in dealing with an issue in which the assessor has skill and experience (CPR 35.15). (For good reasons, this latter power has yet to be much taken up in the clinical negligence context in the civil courts.) The introduction of the rules has not eliminated old-style partisan experts but it has significantly reduced their number and made them somewhat easier to identify.

It should be noted that 'expert' is defined by CPR 35.2 as an expert 'who has been instructed to give or prepare evidence for the purpose of proceedings'. A preliminary report for a potential claimant at the investigative stage is never intended for disclosure, and so should not be considered to have been prepared for the purpose of court proceedings. The notes to r 35.2 make clear that a distinction is to be drawn between advisory experts (at any stage of the claim) and experts instructed to provide written reports for the court. In practice, this can be a difficult line to draw, especially where, as is commonplace, the expert has advised pre-issue and then has to change roles when proceedings are brought. CPR 35.3 and Practice Direction, paras 2.1, 2.2 and 3.1 make clear that the court expert's overriding duty is to the court: the distinction lies in the presenting of the expert's opinion to the court; if an expert merely advises a party and never advances a view, in person or in writing, to the court then the duty will not arise – but it is a distinction without much of a difference, since the claimant will not be well served by any advice that seeks to please the patient or the family and does not meet the criteria for court evidence. Reliance on such advice is likely merely to delay recognition of the real risks of litigation and to increase the risk of ambush.

By CPR 35.10, the report must contain a declaration that the expert understands his duty to the court and has complied with that duty. The expert is also required to state the substance of all material instructions, written or oral, on the basis of which the report has been written and to verify the report with a statement of truth; a set form of words is provided in para 3.3 of the most recent version of the Practice Direction (effective from October 2009).

The rules also make provision for the content of the report and Practice Direction 35 contains detailed instructions. The report is to be addressed to the court and not to the instructing party, and where there is a range of possible opinion that range must be summarised and reasons given for the expert's preference. The report should contain a summary of all relevant instructions received, both written and oral, and a statement of truth. The Practice Direction is set out in Appendix II (as are the relevant parts of CPR 35).

It should also be remembered that the court expects an expert to take responsibility for his role in the process and to be proactive. There is an under-used power under CPR 35.14 for an expert to ask the court for directions (with copies in advance to the instructing party and to the other side), but under the new rules such requests must be made formally. It is to be hoped that such requests will normally be resolved between the parties when advance notice is given, but in the last resort the expert does not have to put up with unreasonable, unworkable or incomprehensible instructions.

CODES OF GUIDANCE

The first code to guide experts and lawyers working under CPR 35 was produced by the Academy of Experts in 2000. Then a second code was published by the Expert Witness Institute in December 2001, having been prepared by a working party under the chairmanship of Sir Louis Blom-Cooper QC.

The Practice Direction accompanying CPR 35 originally required, at para 1.6, that an expert's report comply with the requirements of any approved experts' protocol. Neither code is or was an approved protocol, but both codes offered guidance that many experts saw as sensible and worth following. They were, moreover, complementary to a considerable extent.

The Civil Justice Council then produced a very detailed authoritative code, drawing on both the EWI and the AoE codes. The CJC Code,[2] together with suggestions and draft guidelines produced by the Clinical Disputes Forum, was used as the basis for a formal Protocol for the instruction of experts to give evidence in civil claims, which has now been approved by the Master of the Rolls and now forms part of CPR 35. It can be found at Appendix II. Its provisions should be carefully studied (and experts should be provided with a copy) as it covers all steps from selection and initial instruction of experts to trial and provides a useful and detailed gloss on CPR 35.

Guidance is also available in the Pre-action Protocol for the Resolution of Clinical Disputes, which was the first major work of the Clinical

---

2   www.civiljusticecouncil.gov.uk/files/Protocol_for_the_Instruction_of_Experts.pdf.

Disputes Forum and appears at Appendix II. The use of experts is dealt with at section 4 of the Protocol, emphasising the need for economy and a less adversarial culture. The CDF have carried out a major consultation on revising the Clinical Negligence Protocol, headed by Tony Allen of CEDR, and submitted their draft revised Protocol to the Civil Justice Council in the summer of 2010, emphasising the need for openness and timeliness by all parties to clinical negligence claims; their proposals have, however, yet to be incorporated.

WHAT THE LAWYER EXPECTS OF THE EXPERT

In essence, lawyers expect medical experts to take their cases as seriously as they do themselves, and to exhibit the same level of courtesy and commitment to the lay client. An expert needs to appreciate that if he accepts instructions, he must review the treatment the patient has received carefully, thoughtfully and in full detail. A quick skim through the records and a short declaration that there was no negligence will not do. He must also beware of the attitude that the expert is doing the patient a favour in agreeing to act. Not so. The expert – like the lawyer – is providing a professional service, and this calls for courtesy to the lay client and high professional standards in written or oral advice. To agree to act is to commit to the case, to undertake to take it seriously and complete work within a reasonable time throughout the currency of the case; only in an emergency is it acceptable to plead supervening clinical commitments to explain late delivery of reports or inadequate preparation for a conference.

What the lawyer does not want is an expert determined to support the claim, regardless of the facts. Not at all. It does the patient no favours if a case initially supported by the expert has to be discontinued at a later stage when the expert is facing cross-examination and resiles from his report. What is needed is a clear, authoritative, well-grounded opinion on the issues on which the expert is instructed to comment, whether or not that provides the patient or relative with a case. If it does not, it should wherever possible provide him with a greater understanding of what happened, the need for which is often the primary motivation for seeking legal advice.

Many reports are inadequate. Some do not address the right questions or provide clear answers, and others are deficient in their presentation. In either case, it is the lawyer's task to explain the shortcomings to the expert and seek amendments prior to service. Some experts are very resistant to making any amendment to a report once written, but there is nothing whatever improper in this, provided that the expert is not being asked to amend his opinion: The Protocol makes this clear at section 15.2/CPR 35.31. It is even possible that the lawyer may raise points or provide references that cause the expert to alter his opinion, in which case it is perfectly proper for the expert to amend the report accordingly, provided that he acknowledges and explains the thought process, if appropriate.

The Practice Direction to CPR 35 provides guidance as to the content of expert reports at para 3 (CPR 35 Practice Direction 3), and see also the Protocol for the Instruction of Experts at section 13 (CPR 35.28). The editors of the *White Book (Civil Procedure)* note at 35.10.2 the family law case of *Oldham MBC* v *GW, PW and KPW* [2007] EWHC 136 (Fam), in which the judge provided a handy five-point summary that the editors recommend as of relevance 'to all contested proceedings where expert opinion is important to the outcome':

- experts need clear instructions and access to all relevant documents, not selected ones;
- the expert's report should set out the expert's analytical process, differentiate between facts, assumptions, deductions and note inconsistent or contradictory features of the case;
- the expert should identify the professional range of opinion and use a 'balance sheet' approach to his own opinion;
- the expert should volunteer where an opinion from other expertise is likely to assist the parties and the court;
- the expert should not stray into the role of decision-maker.

Models for written reports are available from the Academy of Experts and the Expert Witness Institute, and there is plenty of training available, so there is little excuse for an unclear or poorly presented report.

One basic structure can be used for most reports:

1   Expert's qualifications and experience – the level of detail needed will vary with the complexity of the case; often it is sufficient to state the specialism and append a curriculum vitae.

2   Instructions – summary stating when the expert was asked to advise, by whom, on behalf of which party and on what issues.

3   Facts – the history may be as per the medical records or as per the patient's account, as the two are not always consistent. The expert needs to set out the salient extracts from both (with page references – bear in mind questions may be asked about the report months or years after it was written), and must draw attention to any important discrepancies without assuming either source to be right. Exceptionally, an expert may be able to say from clinical experience or medical knowledge that only one version of events is capable of belief; in that case only it is appropriate to express that view, explaining the medical basis for it.

4   The expert's commentary and opinion can take the form of observations appended after each section of the facts has been set out, or it can simply be by way of an opinion section at the end of the report. In either case, it should be clear to what fact (or variant version of the facts) the opinion relates.

5   Medical papers, where appropriate – conclusions need to be supported by appropriate reasoning and, where relevant, texts (NB texts published later than the incident will normally only help on causation, not on liability). Full copies of the sections of relevant texts relied on should be supplied and the significant passages highlighted, to enable the lawyers to explore their own understanding of the background literature and to raise any necessary points with the expert.

It is the expert who has to explain the medical case to the judge, whether in person or on the page, so the ability to communicate clearly is crucial. An expert will be expected to write clearly, grammatically and as succinctly as possible, with sub-headings and numbered paragraphs and pages for ease of reference. The report will be expected to read consistently: the conclusions must tally with the observations and argument in the main body of the report. An expert must also be able to explain his opinion verbally in conference with sufficient clarity and jargon-free English that both the lawyers and the lay client can understand. If this proves a problem, the expert will flounder in the witness box when trying, under considerably greater stress, to explain his opinion to the judge.

SELECTING AN EXPERT

The starting point for the lawyer is to identify the specialism(s) needed to investigate the case and then to set about finding a suitable individual within that specialism. Suitability will depend on the nature, complexity and value of the case: whereas it may be worth waiting six months for the leading expert to advise on a multi-million pound case with a long life expectancy, in a simpler case the criteria may be cost and speed of turnaround. Finding the right expert is not the problem it used to be. The lawyers on both sides will be experienced in the field. They will have their own lists of experts, many of whom they will know personally, and they will know where to seek help if stuck for an expert. An extensive database of medical experts is kept by Action against Medical Accidents (AvMA), which provides a search service for members. Recommendations are made but AvMA emphasise in their expert protocol that the database is not a warranty of expertise nor any form of accreditation – the duty remains on the lawyers to check out anyone they instruct. The Association of Personal Injury Lawyers (APIL) similarly compiles and distributes to members a list of experts but this is in much broader categories and contains fewer names. Professional organisations can also be a useful source: for example, the College of Occupational Therapists Specialist Section (COTSS-IP) publishes a searchable online directory of independent practitioners. Commercial sites abound on the internet. It is important to check the site sponsor before relying on any information provided.

It is important to check that your expert has the right sub-specialism: not every orthopaedic consultant is an expert on hand surgery; not every paediatrician is an expert on meningitis; not every anaesthetist is expert on anaphylactic reactions. Experts commenting on breach of duty will need to be drawn from the same specialism as the clinician whose act or omission is under investigation. In *Hutton* v *East Dyfed Health Authority* [1998] Lloyds Rep Med 335, Bell J criticised the claimant's presentation of specialist evidence to assess the management of a generalist (at 349, 352). See also the Chinese herbalist case of *Shakoor* v *Situ* [2000] 4 All ER 181, where the claimant did not call an expert in Chinese medicine.

Defendants, with all the resources of the NHS Litigation Authority at their disposal, are notorious for identifying, and producing, the top expert for the precise matter in issue (a perfectly proper procedure, of course). It is at that point one glances at the claimant's expert who has brought the case thus far to see if he is showing any sign of strain! Sometimes it may be necessary to look far afield to find an expert with the requisite level of expertise. In one case in which the author was instructed, the allegations were against the leading Welsh practitioner of an esoteric procedure (isolated limb perfusion), who was calling the leading practitioner in England as his expert witness. Those instructing intelligently sought out the leading expert in Holland, where the procedure had first been developed.

It is worth remembering the general rule that there is no property in a witness, particularly where an issue arises about what a treating doctor would have done, had circumstances been different. Either party can see to interview and call the other side's witness, if he wishes. In *Lilly Icos LLC* v *Pfizer Ltd* (17 August 2000, unreported), Ch D, Jacob J held that an alleged contract with a party under which an expert was said to have bound himself not to act for the other party was unenforceable as contrary to public policy.

The Expert Witness Institute and the Academy of Experts

The EWI,[3] set up in 1996 as a direct result of encouragement from Lord Woolf, exists to support, encourage and improve the quality of expert evidence and to act as a voice for experts. It is first and foremost an educational body and its fellows are drawn from a range of disciplines. Its founding funders include both the Medical Defence Union and the Medical Protection Society. It should not be confused with the Academy of Experts, of earlier provenance and originally concerned principally with the construction industry, although it now offers a searchable online database[4] that includes a (rather limited) medical section. There is now a fair degree of amicable interbreeding between the two bodies.

Clinical Disputes Forum

Also distinct from the EWI is the Clinical Disputes Forum,[5] Lord Woolf being again the progenitor of this organisation, whose stated aim is to bring together the 'key people in clinical negligence litigation' to work on practical improvements to procedure and reduce the need for litigation. It was registered as a charity in 2000. As its name suggests, the CDF is concerned with all aspects of clinical disputes. It has produced very detailed Guidelines for Experts' Discussions in the Context of Clinical Disputes. The new Protocol for the Instruction of Experts from the Civil Justice Council incorporates much of the work of the Clinical Disputes Forum in this as in other contexts. The forum is currently composed of 23 individuals including the heads of the NHSLA and of AvMA and representatives of the judiciary, the Law Society, the Bar, the GMC, the LSC, doctors and medical insurers.

INSTRUCTING AN EXPERT

Guidance on the contents of letters of instruction is given at section 8 of the Protocol (CPR 35.23), and experts are enjoined by para 8.2 to refuse

---

3   www.ewi.org.uk.
4   www.academy-experts.org.
5   www.clinical-disputes-forum.org.uk.

to act until instructions have been fully clarified. Basic requirements set out in the Protocol are:

- name, address, date of birth of claimant/injured person;
- date(s) of medical treatment;
- nature and extent of expertise called for;
- purpose of requesting advice or report – matters to be investigated, known issues;
- whether proceedings are contemplated and, if so, whether the expert is asked only for advice;
- outline programme for the completion and delivery of each stage of the expert's work;
- any known or projected court dates or deadlines;
- if issued, the court and claim number and the track to which the case has been allocated.

It is suggested that experts should also be provided with whatever statements of case, relevant disclosed documents and witness statements are available. It will also be necessary to deal with funding – whether public funding is available or is being sought, and whether there are any restrictions on the hourly rate or total fee chargeable. Most experts will also need a brief summary of the relevant law (eg the civil standard of proof; *Bolam* and *Bolitho*; in an oncology causation case, *Gregg* v *Scott*, etc) and of their own duties to the court.

Shrewd solicitors will also include the location of the treatment(s) complained of and the names of treating clinicians, if known. The letter of instruction must provide sufficient detail about the parties for the expert to identify any conflict of interest. Finding out later on can be an expensive mistake. In *Toth* v *Jarman* [2006] EWCA Civ 1028, the Court of Appeal emphasised the need for early disclosure of any interest in the case and recommended that, as a matter of practice, experts should add to their declaration of truth that there is no such conflict. Treating doctors are not infrequently asked to give expert evidence on condition and prognosis, but their involvement with the patient may undermine the weight of, or even render inadmissible, comment on wider issues: see, for example, *Re B (a minor) (sexual abuse: expert's report)* [2000] 1FLR 871A, where a psychiatrist treating a child was held insufficiently independent to provide forensic evidence on issues relating to the father; but compare the treatment of Gill Levett's evidence in *Williams* v *Jervis* [2008] EWHC 2346 (QB).

An integral part of proper instruction in a medical case is to provide a complete set of sorted, paginated medical records. Some solicitors still obtain the medical records and pass them on as received, with no intervening process; this is virtually never cost-effective, as each expert and counsel must then wade through sorting them out from his own perspective, at what is usually a rather higher hourly rate than that of a junior solicitor. If the solicitor does not have the expertise or the time to sort out the records, specialist paginators charge less than medical experts will to do this task, and are likely to be more methodical. Once the records are properly prepared, the paginated set can be used by experts in every discipline and by counsel, and disclosed. Failure to sort the records at an early stage not only creates expensive make-work but also significantly increases the risk that a crucial point will be missed.

DO THE LAWYERS NEED MEDICAL KNOWLEDGE?

The answer is yes, to an extent. That is why the Lord Chancellor set up specialist panels and why one of the criteria for admission to the specialist panels is attendance at medical and medico-legal courses. The lawyer is not expected to be medically trained, but a general understanding of the medical issues in a case is essential. A small number of lawyers in the field are doubly qualified. The medically trained lawyer needs to be careful not to set up by way of challenge to the expert, but rather to use his own medical knowledge to understand, test and explore the expert's opinion. Another potential pitfall for the doctor-lawyer to watch for is allowing one's own understanding to blind one to the need for fuller expert explanation for non-medics, such as the judge.

In March 2010, *Clinical Risk* published a comparative survey of the conduct and outcome of clinical cases conducted by specialist (ie AvMA or SRA panel) and non-specialist solicitors,[6] based on a random sample of 180 cases drawn from one eminent expert's medico-legal practice over 23 years (some 5,800 cases). From this inevitably selective sample, the authors conclude that there is clear evidence that specialist firms perform better in the conduct of cases and have a significantly lower discontinuance rate (after initial assessment) than non-specialist firms. It is less clear whether outcomes are improved, although it is interesting that specialist panel members had a slightly higher settlement rate and that the only cases that went to trial (two!) were panel member cases.

Far more necessary than a general medical training is familiarity with medico-legal litigation. This embraces a number of aspects. The lawyer needs to be familiar with the way this litigation is practised and the way in which different defendants (trusts, health authorities, different firms of solicitors, the medical protection societies) respond to different stimuli, and he needs to be familiar with the various ploys they practise. However, most importantly, he needs to be familiar with the medical focuses of different claims. This is not the same thing as saying that he needs to understand the medicine. Most medical claims fall within one or other of perhaps a dozen types of claim. Within each type, the issues are not very different. The lawyer needs to be familiar with the medical focus of each type of claim and the medical issues and arguments that usually arise. Take one example: if a lawyer is processing a claim for perinatal brain damage leading to cerebral palsy, it is obviously useful to have a general grounding in obstetrics. But it will be enough, and in fact more relevant, if the lawyer understands the terminology and outline concepts relating to likely medical issues in the *forensic* context: antenatal ultrasound scan, estimated date of delivery, absolute and relative disproportion, engagement, cardiotocograph (CTG), early and late deceleration, induction, syntocinon, lie, presentation, descent of head, partogram, foetal distress, relative duties of midwives, SHOs, registrar and consultant, and a lot more besides. After a number of such cases, the lawyer will know what issues to focus on and will understand without further instruction what the obstetric experts are saying, but must be careful not to make assumptions about what this individual case is about; the lawyer must

---

6   Julian Brigstocke, David Shields and John Scurr 'Clinical negligence lawyers: specialists versus non-specialists – the evidence' (*Clinical Risk* Vol 16, No 2).

keep an open mind to all possible issues and encourage the experts to do the same.

When we come to the issue of causation, the situation becomes even more technical. It is not enough for the lawyer to understand that his causation expert is saying that the child would or would not have been uninjured if delivered at a certain time. The lawyer needs to be familiar with the medical arguments on causation and on discussion documents and research in current circulation, and with the general medical consensus as to what factors need to be established if the damage is to be deemed to have been caused by, for example, perinatal asphyxia. A lawyer who is not familiar with the interpretation of CTG traces, Apgar scores, hypoxic ischemic encephalopathy, the different types of cerebral palsy and their possible aetiologies, and alternative causation possibilities, is going to be at a very substantial disadvantage, and therefore so also is the lay client. After doing two or three cases of the same sort (eg cerebral palsy, shoulder dystocia or retinopathy of prematurity) the lawyer is likely to have gathered enough information to ask the right questions, to assess the strength of the proposed case and the direction in which it can proceed. Before that stage, attending medico-legal conferences is an excellent way of achieving a similar type of knowledge, albeit at a less immediate level; such conferences also provide an essential update for experienced practitioners.

INTERLOCUTORY USE OF EXPERTS

Contact with experts is an expensive hobby and a careful cost-conscious eye needs to be kept at all times, but in larger cases it is far more cost-effective to involve the experts as the case progresses rather than saving them up for a pre-trial conference at which all manner of worms emerge from the can. It is good practice where proportionality permits for counsel and the experts to meet in conference before proceedings are drafted, and for the experts to see and approve the proposed Particulars of Claim before service. Conferences on difficult issues, especially where perusal of the medical records during the discussion is necessary, are usually far more productive when all parties attend in person. In the long run, this may well be more cost-effective than telephone conferencing, regarded by some experts as a meeting that can be attended from a moving car, an office not containing the papers, a home with audible children or animals, or a range of other variously unsuitable venues. Video links resolve these problems to a limited extent but can present their own time-wasting technical problems. Sitting across the table from fellow experts, and from the injured person, concentrates the mind and produces answers and agreements at an early stage that may otherwise not emerge till far too late (in serious cases, at court).

Experts are only human and if instructed to write a report in 2005 and then summoned at short notice to court in 2010 are likely to under-perform. Keeping experts in the loop – copying defence evidence to them, keeping them regularly informed of significant developments in the case, giving them prompt and adequate notice of court deadlines for reports, expert joint meetings and hearing dates – is not only courteous, but also likely to ensure optimum support for the lay client. The expert who is thinking about the case will flag up problems before they become insurmountable and retain a lively interest in the issues.

JUDICIAL OVERSIGHT: THE EFFECT OF THE WOOLF AND JACKSON REFORMS

In the early post-Woolf days, there were numerous cases, some of which were cited in the last edition of this work, that demonstrated the court flexing its new case management muscles, sometimes despite agreement between the parties, and by no means always in the interests of justice. One example that leaps to mind is *Oxley* v *Penwarden* [2000] MLC 0250; [2001] Lloyds Rep Med 347: Judge Overend, contrary to the wishes of both parties, ordered a joint single expert report on a highly contentious, fundamental issue of causation of a leg amputation. Fortunately, the Court of Appeal understood what was necessary in such a context. Mantell LJ, having drawn attention to the note attached to CPR 35.7 which stated that 'there is no presumption in favour of the appointment of a single joint expert', said:

> This was eminently a case where it was necessary for the parties to have the opportunity of investigating causation through an expert of their own choice and, further, to have the opportunity of calling that evidence before the court. It is inevitable in a case of this class that parties will find the greatest difficulty in agreeing on the appointment of a single expert. The burden would then be cast upon the court and would, in turn, lead to the judge selecting an expert, if there be more than one school of thought on this issue, from one particular school of thought and that would effectively decide an essential question in the case without the opportunity for challenge.

As the jurisdiction has bedded in, while it is of course still possible to cite some maverick decisions – and case management decisions are notoriously difficult to rectify on appeal – overall the early zeal has come to be tempered by common sense and by the overriding principle, especially in the specialist Masters' corridor of the High Court, and amongst the more experienced (and now specialist) district judges on circuit.

It is still not always easy to get permission from some courts for all the necessary experts for a clinical case to be presented properly, but if the case for a given expert is clearly and forcefully made, and the instruction is proportionate, multiple experts are frequently permitted in complex cases. After all, claimant solicitors are not allowed to act in any legal aid medical negligence cases if they have not proved themselves expert in the field and obtained entry to one of the accredited panels, and they have the expertise to select similarly competent specialist counsel. It is arguably a paradox to create an expert panel and then tell judges, many of them less experienced than the lawyers, to supervise their work. Some district judges, and even on occasion the specialist Masters, still impose impossible deadlines and refuse reasonable requests for necessary experts. The Court of Appeal is unlikely to interfere in a case management decision unless it is very plainly wrong, so the best defence is a well-prepared argument at the initial directions hearing. Co-operative working in case management, recognising the considerable pressures on those managing cases to hold down costs, is more likely to secure a just outcome and one beneficial to the lay client than hostility and confrontation.

CUTTING DOWN ON EXPERTS

20 years ago it was common for parties to call two or even three experts apiece on the main contentious issues, but for many years the trend has been for the number of experts to be reduced. Lord Woolf was highly critical of the over-use and the high expense of experts. Judicial scrutiny of expert-related costs has been growing ever since. Despite the best efforts of defendants, the cost-capping powers under CPR 44.18(5) were rarely exercised in clinical negligence cases, partly because judges perceived this as unjust to injured claimants, and partly because the necessary assessment exercise would tie up a costs judge for almost as long as a final assessment (see eg *Willis* v *Nicolson* [2007] EWCA Civ 199). Prospective cost budgeting, regarded by Lord Woolf as 'artificial and unworkable' in his final report in July 1996, has however been brought back into recent focus. A pilot scheme for cost budgeting in defamation cases came into force in October 2009 under CPR Practice Direction 51D, and this may well be extended to other areas, providing for cost budgeting by the parties, with monthly reviews between the parties' solicitors and the court being able to use the budget as a touchstone on final assessment (very much as with LSC high cost case plans at present). Jackson LJ's Review of Civil Litigation Costs further focuses on reducing expert costs by a number of means, including targeting prolixity, closer case management and increasing the use of single joint experts.

In *Aleyan* v *Northwick Park NHS Trust* [1999] MLC 0150, Buckley J noted that the High Court Masters appeared to have agreed that 'wholly exceptional circumstances are needed in medical negligence situations' before more than one expert in the same discipline would be permitted. Although he was not convinced that in this particular case a second expert was needed, he said that he was not attracted to the words 'wholly exceptional circumstances' and would prefer to say that good reason should be shown why the justice of the case demanded another expert.

E S v *Chesterfield and North Derbyshire Royal NHS Trust* MLC 1051, [2003] EWCA Civ 1284 was a claim for cerebral palsy as a result of perinatal asphyxia – a fairly common claim, unfortunately. A junior doctor (by then a consultant) and a consultant were in the frame, both obstetricians. The claimant wanted two forensic obstetric experts, on the basis that it would not be a level playing field if their single expert was faced not only with a single independent expert for the defence but also with two consultants who would naturally be giving their opinions on the course followed even though they were, strictly speaking, witnesses of fact. The district judge took the unimaginative view, but the appeal succeeded. The court said the case was very important, complex and of high value. The parties would not be on an equal footing if the order of the district judge prevailed. The court said one could not isolate the evidence of the two hospital doctors from the vital question concerning appropriate professional standards. Not only was it not disproportionate to allow the claimant to call two obstetric experts; it was actually necessary for the achievement of justice. Although *E S's case* is still good law, it was distinguished in *Beaumont* v *Ministry of Defence* [2009] EWHC 1258 (QB), in which the court again required to be persuaded of 'exceptional circumstances' before allowing a second expert (and on the facts found there were none). Beaumont's case was itself distinguished in the first instance chancery case of *VTB Capital plc* v *Nutritek* [2011] EWHC 2842, in which two experts were held not to be disproportionate, citing Brooke LJ in E S's case.

WHEN IS AN EXPERT NOT AN EXPERT?

The CPR provides by CPR 35.4 that all expert evidence, written or oral, requires the court's permission, and that the specialty and, if possible, the name of the desired expert should be identified. The court makes a clear distinction these days between permission to put in an expert report and permission to call its maker.

This should be read with CPR 32.1, which gives the court an overriding and comprehensive power with regard to evidence generally and is considerably less draconian: calling witnesses as to fact does not normally require permission from the court. The court may give directions as to the issues on which it requires evidence, the nature of that evidence and its form of presentation. It may also exclude evidence which would otherwise be admissible (and may limit cross-examination). The desire for both strict equality of arms and costs saving that informs case management of experts under CPR 35 runs into difficulties when clinicians with expert-level expertise are called as witnesses of fact, thus ducking that tight control and coming under the lighter rein of CPR 32.

The trite rule that factual witnesses cannot give evidence of opinion is ripe for reconsideration in this context and is, in practice, being stretched to breaking point already. It is commonplace in clinical negligence actions for the defendant to call as factual witnesses one or more consultants in the specialism at issue in the case, (in addition to the forensic experts) allowed under CPR 35. When the treating doctor alleged to have been negligent, or his supervising consultant gives evidence about why he did or did not do the crucial act, this is essentially giving evidence of expert opinion. The problem in which claimants frequently find themselves is that their own experts are governed by the strict rules of CPR 35 while equally august consultants are called by the defence under the rather looser control of CPR 32. This was exactly the problem that the court recognised in *E S* v *Chesterfield* and sought to remedy by allowing the claimant an extra forensic expert (although that still left him 3:2 down).

In *Kirkman* v *Euro Exide Corporation (CMP Batteries) Limited* [2007] EWCA Civ 66, unusually it was the claimant who sought to call a consultant orthopaedic surgeon as a witness of fact: Mr Kirkman had injured his knee in an accident at work and needed surgery; he claimed for the above-knee amputation that followed a perioperative infection. He had a long history of knee problems and D alleged that he would have needed the surgery (and so would have run the risk of infection and amputation) anyway. In addition to forensic experts on both sides, C sought to call his treating surgeon to state, as a matter of fact, whether he would have recommended surgery in the absence of the index accident. The district judge directed that the witness be called at trial, for the trial judge to assess whether his evidence constituted fact or opinion; D appealed and the circuit judge reversed the decision, excluding the evidence. On appeal to the Court of Appeal, Buxton and Smith LJJ held that the statement was one of fact and, should the witness be tempted in cross-examination to stray into giving an opinion, it would be for the trial judge to decide whether or not to permit this.

Outside of the clinical negligence context, there has been a franker admission of expert evidence under the guise of evidence of fact. In *Multiplex Constructions (UK) Limited* v *Cleveland Bridge UK Limited* [2008] EWHC 2220 (TCC), Jackson J sitting in the Technology and Construction Court held that it was perfectly proper for the defendant sub-contractor to call one of his employees, a highly qualified and experienced engineer, as a witness of fact and for that witness to proffer statements of opinion that were reasonably related to the facts within his knowledge, and that, as a matter or practice technical and expert opinions, were frequently expressed by factual witnesses in that court without objection being taken. Similar latitude has been allowed to brain injury case managers in some cases: see for example *C* v *Dixon* [2009] EWHC 708 (QB).

In an article on the *Kirkman* case in the *International Journal of Evidence and Proof*,[7] Deirdre Dwyer (British Academy Postdoctoral Fellow of Law at Oxford) comments that such cases create a legal fiction – that opinion is fact – in order to circumvent the strict operation of the case management rules on experts. Dr Dwyer cites another example, *Gall* v *Chief Constable of the West Midlands* [2006] EWHC 2638 (QB), in which on appeal Tugendhat J allowed the evidence of a police surgeon (ie a GP) to be treated as evidence of fact in a claim based on an alleged assault by the police, despite the fact that the doctor not only described the injuries he had noted on the claimant but also purported to identify what had caused those injuries ('a large boot/ heavy shoe ... which would have a crescent shoe (sic) and a metal stud on the heal (sic)'). The decision is the more surprising as one of D's grounds for objecting to the evidence was that there was no time before trial to enable a medical expert to be called by the defence; Tugendhat J observed that neither party had permission to call an expert and that CPR 35 would have to be complied with if an application were now made to do so. Dr Dwyer proposes that one solution would be to remove the distinction between evidence of facts and of opinions when considering admissibility and to leave to the trial judge the question of what weight to attach to opinion evidence.

JOINT EXPERTS

Section 7 of Practice Direction 35, the latest revision of which came into force on 1 October 2009, sets out the criteria that the court should consider when asked to give permission for the parties to rely on expert evidence. It is arguable (and in a talk to the 2009 JPIL conference, specialist clinical negligence master, Master Roberts considered this a real possibility) that the section creates a presumption in favour of the appointment of joint single experts, at least in smaller cases. It remains open to the parties to rely on the complexity of the issue, the importance to the parties, the existence of a range of expert opinion, the need to discuss the issues in

---

7   Deirdre Dwyer 'The effect of the fact/opinion distinction on CPR 35.2' (IJE&P 2008, 12(2), 141–149).

conference or the fact that one party has already instructed an expert to oppose such a direction. Jointly instructed single experts can undoubtedly save costs and may be able to provide fair and comprehensive evidence in uncontentious areas. In such cases, it is increasingly possible for this simply to be agreed between the parties. It is highly unlikely that joint single experts will ever be appropriate on issues such as complex causation, high-cost care programmes, or breach of duty.

The proposed withdrawal of legal aid for clinical negligence under the Legal Aid, Sentencing and Punishment of Offenders Bill going through parliament at the time of writing will, if enacted, no doubt make it even more difficult for claimants to obtain suitable separate medical evidence and may increase the use of joint experts for all the wrong reasons, especially when coupled with the proposed enactment of Jackson LJ's recommendations to severely limit the use of conditional fee agreements by capping success fees and remove recoverability both of the success fee and the After the Event (ATE) premium from the losing defendant. The withdrawal of public funding is strongly opposed by many, including Lord Justice Jackson himself, who has pointed out that his reform recommendations were put forward in the context of legal aid being available for clinical negligence cases and that maintenance of legal aid for clinical negligence is both sensible and in the public interest. The NHS Litigation Authority has also opposed the withdrawal of legal aid in this area. Nonetheless, the Government appears determined to push the Bill through; it is proposing some exceptions, however, 'to ensure that individual cases continue to receive legal aid where failure to do so would be likely to result in a breach of the individual's rights to legal aid under the Human Rights Act 1998 or EU law';[8] an example of such a case is given as 'obstetric cases, with high disbursement costs, which are currently funded by legal aid but for which it may be difficult to secure a conditional fee agreement' – it remains to be seen whether such cases will in fact be granted exceptional funding if the Bill becomes law. An exception is also proposed to the abolition of recoverability of ATE insurance premiums, to enable claimants in certain circumstances to recover the premiums for policies covering the cost of expert reports only.

The NHSLA is also, at the time of writing, proposing a voluntary Low Value Claims Scheme, currently under discussion with APIL, AvMA and other stakeholders, under which joint experts would be selected and paid for by the NHSLA in smaller cases (up to £25,000) to reduce costs and speed up resolution.

It should be noted that an expert instructed by one party without objection by the other party does not thereby become a joint expert (*Carlson* v *Townsend* [2001] 3 All ER 663). (This case also makes the point that a medical report is privileged from disclosure and that the pre-action protocol for personal injury claims has not affected that privilege, but is now overruled on that point by *Edwards-Tubb* v *JD Wetherspoon plc* [2011] EWCA Civ 136.)

Where a single joint expert's report is unclear (or unhelpful to a party), CPR 35.6 provides that a party may put written questions about his report

---

8   Response to enquiry made via Tessa Jowell MP from Jonathan Djanogly, Parliamentary Under-Secretary of State for Justice, 6 October 2011.

to an expert, whether joint or not (once only, within 28 days of the report, and for the purpose of clarifying the report – unless the court or the other party permits otherwise). In *Mutch v Allen* [2001] PIQR P364, CA, the court said that points not included in the report could be ventilated by this procedure if within the expert's expertise, and that questioning a party's expert in this way rendered him akin to a court expert.

Single joint experts are, like all experts, under a duty to notify those instructing them if they take the view that their expertise is insufficient to cover all the issues on which they are instructed to comment (see, in a different context, *Re W (a child) (non-accidental injury: expert evidence)* [2007] EWHC 136 (Fam)).

Challenging a report from a joint expert

If a topic was thought uncontentious (or the court ordered a single joint expert) but a joint report proves unsatisfactory or damaging and questioning has failed to resolve this, it is open to either party to apply to the court for a new, single party expert. If this is permitted, the other party may and often does retain the expert originally instructed jointly as its own single party expert. This saves costs and provides that party with the tactical advantage that the expert was originally mutually accepted as having the necessary expertise. Careful, and helpful, treatment of the position when a party wishes to reject a jointly instructed expert may be found in Lord Woolf's judgment in *Daniels v Walker* [2000] 1 WLR 1382, CA. In that case, the defendants wanted to instruct their own care expert because they thought that the joint expert had estimated far too much care in the joint report that they had agreed should be obtained. The other side maintained that the defendants were effectively bound by it. Lord Woolf, emphasising that the overriding objective was to deal with cases justly, disagreed. He said that, although in small value cases the objecting party might have to be restricted to asking the joint expert questions, in cases of substantial value it might well be appropriate to permit the objecting party to put his own report in evidence, and even to call the new expert at trial, provided that the issues could not be resolved simply by the experts meeting.

If unopposed, it is unusual for a joint expert to be called and cross-examined at trial – the whole purpose of a joint expert being to avoid calling experts on the issue in question. This was emphasised by Lord Woolf's observations in *Peet v Mid-Kent Healthcare Trust* [2002] 1 WLR 210, suggesting that the evidence of the joint expert should not normally be subject to cross-examination, in the context of ruling that it is not acceptable for one party, without the consent of the other(s), to have access to the single joint expert. In *Popek v Natwest* [2002] EWCA Civ 42, the Court of Appeal said that it was not generally open to parties to cross-examine the single joint expert, particularly where written questions had been asked and answered after the expert's report was made. In *Yorke v Katra* [2003] EWCA Civ 867, the Court of Appeal said that there was no rule that a party should be bound by the instruction given to a joint expert by the other side. Where a defendant's solicitor had communicated with a joint expert without the claimant's consent or knowledge, that expert was tainted and the claimant was entitled to a fresh expert: *Edwards v Bruce & Hyslop (Brucast) Limited* [2009] EWHC 2970 (QB).

MEDICAL LITERATURE

Experts often rely on medical literature to support their arguments but only the most experienced and most carefully instructed collate all the papers on which they propose to rely in good time before trial. This dilatoriness can cause a range of different problems. Any counsel presented with 17 highly technical medical papers the day before the expert is to be called at trial will readily identify the first problem – the lawyers have to have time to understand and assimilate the literature so that it can be admitted, explained to the judge as necessary and used as a basis for cross-examination. The opposing expert is also entitled not to be ambushed and this creates the other potential problem: the evidence may be excluded. In *Wardlaw* v *Farrar* [2004] Lloyds Rep Med 98, the Court of Appeal refused an application to use further medical texts on appeal and gave guidance on the orderly deployment of the literature on which experts sought to rely. The best practice, as found on the standard form of directions used by the specialist Masters of the High Court, should be followed throughout the country.

An eloquent example of the problems caused if this practice is not followed is provided by *Breeze* v *Ahmad* [2005] EWCA Civ 223. The judge decided Mrs Breeze's case on the basis of two medical papers that were not before the court but were summarised for him by the defendant's expert. On that summary, the literature supported D's position and the judge found for him expressly on that basis. On appeal, the two papers were shown by C's counsel to be at worst neutral and at best to support C's position. D's expert had unwittingly summarised the papers inaccurately and/or incompletely and inadvertently misled the trial judge. The judge had placed much emphasis on his belief that, whereas one expert was wholly unsupported by the literature, the other's view was 'compellingly supported' by it. The matter was remitted for retrial.

DISCLOSURE

The secretive nature of litigation has been opened out by the Woolf reforms and the cards-on-the-table approach broadly in use in clinical negligence actions in England and Wales is beginning to trickle into other related areas: new rules for exchange of expert medical and non-medical evidence in clinical negligence cases came into force in Northern Ireland in July 2009.[9] AvMA's long campaign for a statutory duty of candour on medical professionals ('Robbie's Law') is finally attracting government attention, with the Department of Health actively consulting in England and consultation on healthcare standards recently concluded in Wales, although the Government's proposals fall far short of AvMA's. The Government White Paper speaks of 'requiring' hospitals and other healthcare providers to be open and honest when things go wrong but this would be a contractual rather than a statutory duty and would not

---

9   The Rules of the Supreme Court (Northern Ireland) (Amendment No 2) 2009, SI 2009/230.

extend to GPs. There is, however, some prospect of amendments to the Health and Social Care Bill being accepted that would create a legally enforceable duty.

There are, however, still good grounds for retaining legal professional privilege over documents prepared in contemplation of litigation. CPR 35 appears to offer inroads into the principle, specifically stating at CPR 35.10(4) that the material instructions on the basis of which the report was written shall not be privileged. Solicitors on both sides have frequently demanded to see statements of witnesses and any other documents referred to in the expert report but the courts have been slow to ride a coach and horses through established case law on legal privilege, except where there is good reason to think that the instructions were incomplete, inaccurate or misleading. (Lord Woolf had advocated total disclosure of all documents generated by an expert and all instructions, but, wisely, in the final report that was thought a bridge too far).

Toulson J in *General Mediterranean Holding SA* v *Patel* [2000] 1 WLR 272 (where the issue was legal professional privilege) held that if an order for disclosure is made, the court may permit cross-examination on the instructions (para 3 of Practice Direction 35). In *Morris* v *Bank of India* (15 November 2001), Ch D, Hart J ordered disclosure of an expert's instructions on the ground (under CPR 35.10) that the expert report was patently defective in failing to reveal all material instructions.

In *B* v *John Wyeth & Brother Ltd* [1992] 1 WLR 168, a judgment given within the benzodiazepine group litigation, the Court of Appeal said that although each plaintiff's medical history relied on by the medical expert in preparing his report is disclosable, waiver of privilege in respect of documents containing that information should not be inferred; the manner of disclosure lies within each plaintiff's discretion. Two months earlier (October 1991), Tucker J had reached a similar conclusion in *Booth* v *Warrington Health Authority* [1992] PIQR P137. But in *Clough* v *Tameside and Glossop Health Authority* [1998] 1 WLR 1478, Bracewell J, having held that service of a witness statement waives any privilege previously enjoyed by that statement, ordered disclosure by the defendants of a statement by a treating doctor referred to in an expert report served by the defendants. She said that a party should not be forced to meet an expert opinion based on documents he could not see. The decision in *Clough* was doubted in *Bourns* v *Raychem Corporation (No 3)* [1999] 3 All ER 154, where it was held that documents disclosed for a specific purpose (on the facts, taxation of costs) did not constitute waiver of privilege for collateral purposes. See also the report of an interlocutory appeal in *Forbes* v *Wandsworth Health Authority* in [1995] *Clinical Risk* (vol 1, p 153), where it was held that privilege was not lost merely because the pleadings had referred to receipt of a document in support of the argument on limitation. In *Bourns* v *Raychem* , the Court of Appeal held that in order for privilege to be waived, there had to be something more than bare reference to a document in the report, or there had to be reliance by the expert in his report on that document.

One must also bear in mind CPR 31.14, which provides that a party may inspect a document mentioned in a statement of case, a witness statement, a witness summary, an affidavit, or, subject to CPR 35.10(4), an expert's report (CPR 35.10(4), as explained above, relates to the power to order disclosure of instructions given to an expert for the preparation of his report). It is not clear to what extent this rule is intended to go further than the previous RSC, Ord 24, r 10, which gave the court a discretion to order or not to order disclosure.

This rule first came before the Court of Appeal in *Lucas* v *Barking, Havering and Redbridge Hospitals NHS Trust*, MLC 1037, [2003] Lloyds Rep Med 57, CA. The court considered the interplay between the different rules. CPR 31.14, as amended, states a party 'may inspect' a document mentioned in a statement of case, a witness statement or summary, or an affidavit, but, in respect to a document mentioned in an expert report, it says a party 'may apply for an order for inspection' *but* subject to CPR 35.10(4). CPR 35.10(3) requires the expert to 'state the substance of all material instructions, whether written or oral, on the basis of which the report was written, and CPR 35.10(4), having dramatically declared that the instructions shall not be privileged against disclosure, states that the court will not, in relation to those instructions order disclosure of a document unless it is satisfied that the expert's statement of instructions under CPR 35.10(3) is 'inaccurate or incomplete'. The defendants sought sight of documents mentioned in an expert's report on the basis not that the statement of instructions from the expert was inaccurate or incomplete, but on the basis that the documents in question did not form part of his instructions and therefore they had an unfettered right to see them under CPR 31.14(2) – because the words 'subject to rule 35.10(4)' did not apply. The Master acceded to their application, but the Court of Appeal disagreed, holding that the documents did form a part of the instructions and there was no ground for thinking the expert's statement of instructions was inaccurate or incomplete. Waller LJ said the appeal raised a quite fundamental question as to what effect the new CPR were intended to have on the issue of privilege. It is important to note first that there are very strong indications in the judgments, albeit *obiter*, that the judges did not think that CPR 31.14(1) gave an unfettered right to inspect a document mentioned in a statement of case, witness statement or summary, or affidavit. Waller LJ said it was unlikely that the rule had intended to abolish privilege in such cases at a stroke and without saying so. However, the main issue in the case was whether the documents referred to in the expert's report were part of his instructions. As the court found that they were, CPR 31.14(1) was not relevant, only CPR 31.14(2), and as there was no suggestion from the defendants that the expert's statement of instructions was inaccurate or incomplete, they were not entitled to disclosure. Waller LJ made the clear observation that 'material supplied by the instructing party to the expert as the basis on which the expert is being asked to advise should be considered as part of the instructions and thus subject to CPR 35.10(4)'. Further, his lordship said there was no need to set out all the information contained in a statement referred to or all the material that had been supplied to an expert; the only obligation on the expert was to set out '*material instructions*' (the judge's emphasis). Laws LJ said that the purpose of the rule was to ensure that the factual basis on which the expert had prepared his report was patent. In the ordinary way the expert was to be trusted to comply with this obligation.

So we see that the other party does not have an unfettered right to see documents referred to in pleadings, affidavits or witness statements. The other party will be entitled to see documents referred to in an expert report only if the court finds that the statement of his instructions given by the expert is inaccurate or incomplete.

This judgment was echoed the following year in *Jackson* v *Marley Davenport Limited* [2004] EWCA Civ 1225, in which the Court of Appeal held that CPR 35.13 did not empower the courts to order disclosure of draft reports; service of the final report waived privilege in that report only and not in the drafts.

The situation will be otherwise where there is an evidential basis to attack the summary of instruction: In *Morris* v *Bank of India*, Ch D, 15 November 2001, Hart J ordered disclosure of an expert's instructions on the ground (under CPR 35.10) that the expert report was patently defective in failing to reveal all material instructions. Disclosure may also be ordered where a party seeks at a late date to change its expert.

The situation is different when a change of expert is needed, however it will now normally be necessary to disclose the report of the expert originally instructed in order to obtain the Court's permission to rely on the second expert. In *Beck* v *Ministry of Defence* [2004] PIQR P1, CA, the defendant sought to change its psychiatric expert as it had, it said, lost all confidence in its original expert as having proper knowledge of the relevant psychiatric issues in the case. Naturally the claimant's solicitors refused access for a new psychiatric examination. The defendant succeeded in the two lower courts in gaining permission to start again. The single judge then gave leave for a further appeal in this interlocutory matter, a most unusual event. In the Court of Appeal, Simon Brown LJ had some sympathy with the defendant's position, in that this was a high value case, involving allegations against their psychiatric personnel, and without a further report they would be proceeding with an expert in whom they had no confidence. He said that, though it would be unfair to require a defendant upon such an application to argue in detail as to why the original report and the original expert were now deemed to be unsatisfactory because that would give the claimant unfair ammunition for cross-examination of their expert if the application were refused, nevertheless, once it had been decided that the defendant should be permitted to instruct another expert, there were very good reasons why the original report should be disclosed. Ward LJ agreed, saying that expert shopping was to be discouraged and requiring the report to be disclosed was a check against possible abuse. The Master of the Rolls, agreeing, said that a claimant can properly object in any personal injury case to submitting to a second examination without good reason being shown for it. No second examination should be permitted if it appears to be 'a possibility' that the reason a defendant wants a fresh expert is that the first expert has reached a conclusion more favourable to the claimant than the defendant expected. This logic was followed (in the rather different context of restaurant valuation) in *Hajigeorgiou* v *Vassiliou* [2005] EWCA Civ 236, CA and in a personal injury case in *Edwards-Tubb* v *JD Wetherspoon plc* [2011] EWCA Civ 136. In the latter case it was the claimant who wanted to change experts: he had instructed an orthopaedic surgeon (one of three named by him under the protocol, not objected to by the defendant but not jointly instructed); that surgeon examined him and wrote a report, which was never disclosed or relied upon, pre-issue; D admitted liability prior to issue; C served particulars supported by the report of a different expert, who referred in passing to the fact of the earlier examination. D applied for disclosure of the first report, on the basis that the court should require its disclosure as a condition of allowing C to rely on a new expert, relying on CPR 35.4 ('No party may call an expert or put in evidence an expert's report without the court's permission') and the personal injury pre-action protocol (C2-001). The Court confirmed that:

- the first, undisclosed report was subject to legal professional privilege;
- it was not open to the court to infer from C's refusal to waive that privilege that the report was adverse to his case;
- it was however open to the court under CPR 35.4 to require disclosure of the first expert's report as a condition of allowing C to rely on the second expert – this did not override the privilege, but gave C a choice as to whether or not to waive it (although the court accepted that C would realistically be unable to proceed without medical evidence, and so would be forced to waive privilege if he wanted to do so);
- the principle is that, in order to discourage expert shopping, the court should attach a condition of disclosure to permission to change expert, whenever it had power to do so;
- there is no distinction between expert reports acquired pre- and post-issue, or between cases in which the court on case management has identified named experts and those in which it has merely given permission for an expert in a given discipline, in all of which the court should usually exercise its discretion to attach a condition of disclosure;
- expert advice acquired by a party pre-protocol, before the parties have 'engaged with each other in the process of the claim', by contrast, should normally not be subject to disclosure;
- it may be appropriate in some cases to require a party seeking to rely on an opponent's report disclosed in this context to call its author, to enable cross-examination by the original instructing party.

C's counsel had argued that the power under CPR 35.4 existed only in the context of an expert approved by the court post-issue and that pre-issue opinions not relied upon were privileged, and accordingly on these facts there was no such power; Judge Denyer QC (on appeal from the District Judge) had agreed but the Court of Appeal did not, restoring the ruling of the District Judge. Hughes LJ, giving the leading judgment with which Lord Neuberger MR and Richards LJ agreed, reviewed the authorities, including setting out and distinguishing some obiter dicta from *Carlson v Townsend* [2001] EWCA Civ 511 that might appear to support the claimant respondent's position in this case. The Court held that *Beck* was not distinguishable and that the issue of privilege had been fully explored in *Vasiliou*.

It is an unfortunate side-effect of the Edwards-Tubb judgment that parties may now, where there is sufficient time before the limitation period expires, be advised to obtain full medical evidence before entering into the protocol, to ensure that any adverse report will be protected by legal privilege. This, of course, would undermine the spirit of the Woolf reforms and the purpose of the protocols but may be seen as a necessity in what is, after all, still an adversarial system. The alternative of being permitted to cross-examine one's own initial choice of expert is not one that will appeal greatly to either party. It should also be noted that

Hughes LJ specified that pre-protocol advice would fall outside CPR 35.2 (and so CPR 35.4) because the expert had been 'consulted at that time and not instructed to write a report for the court'; so that he could not be said to have 'been instructed to give or prepare expert evidence for the purpose of proceedings'. Given that the pre-protocol privilege is based on evidence being prepared in contemplation of proceedings, this may prove to be a fine distinction where an expert has been instructed to produce a full written report pre-protocol.

JOINT EXPERT DISCUSSIONS

By CPR 35.12 (amended in October 2009), the court may direct experts' discussions for identifying relevant issues and, if possible, reaching agreement, and may direct a written statement of the meeting identifying what was and what was not agreed, and why. The content of the discussion between the experts is not disclosable without agreement (ie is privileged), and any agreement by the experts does not bind a party unless he agrees – although of course the practical reality is otherwise and the rules have been amended expressly to forbid parties from instructing their experts not to make agreements, and experts from accepting any such instruction. The note of the joint discussion, once agreed by the experts, is disclosable and will be put before the court. It was originally intended that lawyers should not be present at these discussions but initial experience suggested that this might be necessary and the Clinical Disputes Forum proposed that lawyers should be present at experts' meetings (unless agreed or ordered otherwise) but not normally intervening, save to answer questions put to them by the experts or to advise them on the law. An explanation for this view is to be found in *Clinical Risk* July 2000, p 149. In practice now, attendance of lawyers at medical expert meetings is vanishingly rare, the case management courts having taken the view that such attendance increases rather than reduces costs. This is not always the case – as when the medics have a cosy chat about the medically interesting points but fail to address the legal issues – but a properly drawn agenda goes a long way to remedying this. There will always be exceptions, too: in *Woodall* v *BUPA Hospitals Ltd*, MLC 0340 Judge Hindley QC, sitting as a High Court judge, allowed an appeal by which he gave permission for lawyers to attend a complex series of expert meetings in a relatively high value case. He said:

> It seems to me that in a complex case such as this involving different specialities it is extremely important for all of the lawyers concerned to have an understanding as to why measures of agreement have been achieved and, more importantly, why there has not been agreement on certain issues, so that the lawyers themselves have an opportunity of considering the cogency of arguments, because only on that basis can they properly advise their clients in terms of either narrowing issues or compromising the case.

He added that the costs of the lawyers' attendance would not be disproportionate to the issues and values of the particular claim.

In *Hubbard* v *Lambeth Southwark and Lewisham Health Authority* MLC 0503, [2002] Lloyds Rep Med 8, claimants unsuccessfully objected to a meeting of experts on the highly original basis that their own experts, overawed by the high standing of the defence expert, would feel unable to contradict him. The Court of Appeal, pointing out that the claimants' experts had already committed their views to paper in the knowledge that they might have to go to court to support those views, dismissed the argument, adding that there was no issue under Art 6 of the Convention. The court also said that lawyers would not normally attend such a meeting: a well-drafted agenda and a recording would suffice.

Agendas

Agendas are problematic. Some experts need little guidance; others, left to their own devices, are perfectly capable of omitting to consider all or most of the issues in the case. The problem arises from the difference in approach of lawyers and doctors presented with the same problem – lawyers seek a legal answer, doctors a clinical solution. Lengthy agendas, however, make things worse rather than better, and some firms undoubtedly run up costs (inadvertently or otherwise) by the sort of to-ing and fro-ing that goes on with commercial agreements before the final draft is agreed. I do not believe that such sanctification of the 'agenda' is necessary. Provided that the experts are clear about the purpose of the meeting, all they need is some tolerably precise guidance as to what they should be looking at, and then let them get on with it. The agenda should not be seen as a means of cross-examining the other expert, and thus requiring many pages of subtly worded questions (and consequent increased expenditure of time and money). Unfortunately, these wise words, written for the last edition, have not been properly heeded, and so it is not unusual to see agendas containing 50 and more questions – sometimes one from each party, because no compromise could be agreed. The effect of this is confusion, often involving inconsistent responses at some point, each side always having tried, by questions sly and subtle, to winkle some useful response out of the opposing expert, and then to put an interpretation on the answers that assists their cause.

The Masters are increasingly unsympathetic to this process and seek to bring agendas in bounds through the Model Direction, now echoed in section 9 of Practice Direction 35, which emphasises:

- expert meetings are not mandatory and should take place only if they are likely to serve a useful purpose;
- the purpose is not for experts to settle cases but to agree and narrow issues and identify what action, if any, may be taken to resolve outstanding points of disagreement;
- if a meeting is to happen, the parties should consider whether an agenda is necessary; and
- if so, an agenda should be agreed if possible, to help the experts focus on the legal issues – *the agenda must not be in the form of leading questions or hostile in tone.*

Lawyers should note that under the new CPR 35.12(2) the court has power to set the agenda itself.

Lengthy agendas often result from (sometimes legitimate) concern on the part of lawyers that the experts will simply carve up the case in their absence. Defendants have often met this by instructing their experts not to agree anything without checking back – this practice is now outlawed by the Rules. A careful, short preamble to the agenda goes a long way to minimising the risk, as does a conference with the expert before the meeting, where costs allow. The points to stress are:

- The purpose of the meeting is to identify the outstanding issues and provide brief reasons for continuing disagreement, to focus the issues for trial.
- The experts are not being asked to reach a compromise settlement.
- No expert should feel pressured to agree or compromise any issue.
- If persuaded to change his mind on any issue, the expert should provide full reasons for this in the joint note.
- Experts should approach factual issues in the alternative – resolution of these is for the judge.
- Experts should approach causation issues on the balance of probabilities, and not apply a medical standard of proof.
- The expert must never sign a joint note that does not completely and accurately reflect his opinion.

When the expert gives the case away

Every experienced clinical negligence lawyer has known that heart-sinking moment when you read the joint expert note and realise that it damages or even apparently finishes the case. This moment is often followed by a telephone call to the expert in which one of the following responses is made:

- 'I didn't think it was important, so I let him have that one';
- 'I didn't really mean that/that's not what I said'; or
- 'I've always thought that – didn't you know?'.

Sometimes (at least in the first two instances) the situation can be rescued by a supplementary report, letter or discussion. Sometimes a speedy recourse to alternative dispute resolution has a great deal to be said for it. Otherwise, application may need to be made for a change of expert. The expert meeting is usually one of the later stages in the case, so this is always going to be difficult, but it is not necessarily always hopeless. Where an expert's view of the case had changed radically, to the detriment of the party instructing him and without any clear reason, following a discussion with his opposite number, a second expert has been allowed: *Stallwood* v *David* [2006] EWHC 2600 (QB). C claimed on the basis that her back and neck injuries prevented her working full-time as a self-employed accountant and claimed about £200,000. An orthopaedic surgeon supported the claim and accepted that she had continuing pain at the four-year point, some of which would be permanent. D's expert stated that full resolution had been achieved by six to 12 months and that C was now malingering. After the joint meeting, C's expert changed his view to recovery at two years post-accident (significantly, D's expert was prepared to agree disadvantage on the labour market up to that point), with all continuing symptoms not accident-related. C lost all confidence in her expert and instructed a new expert, who supported her case. At first instance, the judge refused permission to change experts on the basis that the trial was imminent and the accident was five years ago, without any apparent consideration of the unfairness to the claimant. Teare J noted that case management decisions 'will rarely be the subject of appeal because they are the result of an exercise of discretion', and that 'a party to a claim cannot usually be afforded a second expert merely because his or her first expert has altered his opinion after having discussed it with the opponent's expert', but still allowed the claimant her new expert. After a careful consideration of the matters properly to be considered when seeking to avoid an experts' agreement under CPR 35.12(5), his lordship cited the White Book note – that the agreement could be set aside where an expert has clearly stepped outside his expertise or brief or otherwise shown himself to be incompetent – and the overriding objective and held that the judge had not considered all relevant matters (such as the extent of any delay if the application were to be granted) and had considered irrelevant matters (such as his own backache, despite which he worked full time). The judge had accepted an invitation to recuse himself. Note that no enquiry had been made of the first expert as to his reasons for changing his mind: as Teare J observed, 'they might have been shown to be sound reasons, in which case there could be no ground for seeking additional expert evidence', so the court found that C could not show good reason for needing an additional expert (but then found for her on other grounds).

Much the same point came before Irwin J in *Read* v *Superior Seals Ltd* [2008] QBD (Winchester) CLY 267. C claimed for a back injury at work; C's expert reported five times over four years, consistently concluding that while there was some psychological overlay (ie unconscious exaggeration) there was a genuine, permanent and disabling injury; D alleged malingering; at the experts' meeting C's expert decided for the first time that the damage was merely a two to three-year acceleration. C's lawyers immediately instructed a third expert, who entirely supported the case. Permission to change experts was refused at first instance, but allowed on appeal. Irwin J observed that such cases would be rare but the overriding objective applied and the court should not permit C to be ambushed by his own expert. (It may well be significant that, unusually, this case was at an early stage when the experts' meeting took place.)

The court will be less sympathetic where the expert's change of heart is understandable: compare *Singh* v *CS O'Shea & Co Ltd* [2009] EWHC 1251 (QB), where Macduff J failed to take pity on a claimant whose expert's altered view was based on service of surveillance evidence that showed C walking, jogging, sprinting and driving without any apparent disability.

The more usual approach of the courts is to disallow a change of expert at a later stage (see for example *Jones* v *Kaney* [2011] UKSC 13, a ground-breaking negligence action against an expert (of which more below) following the court's refusal to allow such a late change). Where an expert's late change of heart can be shown to be in breach of duty to the instructing party, this is now actionable.

SPA LITIGATION

The Review of Civil Litigation Costs by Jackson LJ proposes the idea of expert evidence being given in a new forum, now widely referred to as 'in the hot tub' – the judge chairing a discussion between the experts, with counsel having an opportunity to ask questions, in preference to sequential cross-examination. This would be a radical step away from the traditional adversarial approach to clinical cases, and it is by no means clear at this stage how it would work, but it may well be no bad thing. It is to be assumed that 'hot-tubbing' would replace rather than follow a joint expert meeting – otherwise it is just a duplication of costs. Already the parties' lawyers are losing control of the process to the extent that issues are decided in joint expert discussions to which they have no access; lawyers are now expressly forbidden to instruct their experts not to reach agreement on a material issue in the course of the meeting (Protocol 18.7/CPR 35.36) and they are very seldom permitted to be in attendance. Often the outcome of the joint expert meeting determines the outcome of the case.

JUDICIAL PREFERENCE OF EXPERTS

Where there are warring experts, part of the judge's task will inevitably be to choose between them (or, as in some cases, to ignore all of them). The law reports are full of medical (and other) cases decided simply on the ground of the judge 'preferring' one side's expert to the other. The judge may give detailed reasons for such preference, based on the evidence, or may restrict himself to one or two general criticisms, or may simply state that he prefers the evidence of X to Y. This last may be appealable (see Chapter 9). Full, detailed explanations of why a judge considers that an expert has got it wrong and another has got it right are infrequent. More common is the general denigration. In *Hutchinson* v *Leeds Health Authority* [2000] MLC 0287, Bennett J said of an expert haematologist:

> I find Dr R's evidence to be illogical and unsustainable ... Regrettably I did not have the same confidence in Dr R [as in the other experts]. I gained the impression of an expert witness who was clearly allied to Dr C [the impugned doctor] probably because of a shared speciality in medicine ...'

In just one issue of *Medical Litigation* (January 2000), judicial criticisms in no fewer than four different cases appear along the lines of 'spend an undue amount of their time in medico-legal work', 'not entirely detached in their analysis of the evidence', 'a degree of inflexibility which is not entirely becoming', 'unwillingness to make concessions', 'changes in the course of his evidence ... do not give me confidence', 'his evidence starts on a precarious basis', 'forensic considerations had overridden those of objectivity', 'serious allegations placed before the court on a casual and flimsy basis'.

The problem has not gone away, although partisan experts are dwindling in number. More recently, Roderick Evans J observed of a defence neurologist that:

> Although [he] has dealt with the claimant's case voluminously there are clear indications of a lack of thoroughness and a failure to spend adequate time in properly analysing the case. It may be that his heavy workload ... has prevented this. It is equally likely in my judgement that he approached the case with a set view of the claimant and looked at the claimant and her claimed symptomology through the prism of his own disbelief. From that unsatisfactory standpoint he unfortunately lost the focus of an expert witness and sought to argue a case. I am driven to the conclusion that I am unable to place reliance on [his] evidence.[10]

---

10   *Williams* v *Jervis* [2008] EWHC 2346 (QB) at para 119.

Clearly, experts need to bear in mind that anything other than a courteous, moderated and impartial response to questioning in court will damage their credibility.

Perhaps reflecting the occasional shortfalls in expert independence, it is clear that judges are not bound to accept expert evidence, even where it is uncontradicted: see, for example, (in another context) *A County Council v M* [2005] EWHC 31 (Fam). The court, it was said, should be cautious of declining to follow uncontradicted expert evidence but was not bound by it – the approach in *Loveday* v *Renton (No 1)* [1989] 1 Med LR 117 would be followed. Three more recent decisions underline that there are no hard and fast rules governing judicial preference and that the judge has a very broad discretion. In *Huntley* v *Simmons* [2010] EWCA Civ 54, Waller LJ, giving the unanimous judgment of the Court of Appeal, approved the decision of Underhill J to reject the evidence of the care experts on both sides and award an intermediate regime (that coincided with preliminary costings by the claimant's expert) and to prefer the view of one neurospsychiatrist to the joint view of the parties' neuropsychologists as to the likelihood of improvement through rehabilitation. Similarly, in *Masterman-Lister* v *Jewell* [2003] 3 All ER 162, the Court of Appeal had no difficulty with Wright J's preference for the evidence of the defence neuropsychiatrist's view, although it was opposed not only by three eminent experts for the claimant but was not supported by either of the other two defence experts. These are judgments well within the discretion of the trial judge. Similarly, the Court of Appeal of New South Wales upheld a judge's decision to prefer an expert argued on appeal to have less expertise than his opponent, and to form his own view on causation, differing from both the parties' experts.[11] Ipp JA emphasised (citing the court's judgment in the leading NSW case of *Strinic* v *Singh* [2009] NSWCA 15) that a judge should not reach a judgment on findings of fact based on his own knowledge or experience rather than the evidence, but rejected an allegation that this had occurred in the instant case.

Must a judge give reasons for his preference?

This important question, often vital to appeals, is not easy to answer definitively. It is fully treated in Chapter 9 in the section headed 'Must a judge give reasons for his conclusions?'.

AN EXPERT'S IMMUNITY

The position of expert witnesses sued by their own clients was expressly considered in 1992 in *Palmer* v *Durnford Ford* [1992] QB 483, when Simon Tuckey QC, sitting as a deputy High Court judge, ruled that the expert was immune from suit in respect of work done in or in preparation for court. This decision was made in the context of a centuries-long tradition that all those directly taking part in litigation are immune from civil suit, which has since been confirmed in the House of Lords: see *Darker* v *Chief Constable of the West Midlands Police* [2001] 1 AC 435 and *Arthur*

---

11   *Sydney SW Area Health Service* v *Stamoulis* [2009] NSWCA 153.

JS Hall & Co v *Simons* [2002] 1 AC 615. Witnesses could be sued for malicious prosecution or misfeasance in public office, or prosecuted for perjury or contempt of court, but were protected by witness immunity from any action in general negligence. Until very recently, this blanket immunity extended to expert witnesses but the cloak was lifted in *Jones* v *Kaney* [2011] UKSC 13, in which a 5:2 majority of the Supreme Court abolished the immunity and also addressed the concern that to do so would cause a serious expert shortage. In 2006, the Chief Medical Officer, Sir Liam Donaldson, carried out a survey of expert medical evidence in family cases[12] in response to a number of highly publicised cases in which medical experts had been heavily criticised for causing miscarriages of justice (similarly trenchant concerns had also caused review of a large number of criminal cases). Amongst his findings was that there was a shortage of suitable experts, caused in part by a widespread fear that the doctor would be sued or prosecuted for expressing an honest view in cases that, as one respondent put it, 'required the wisdom of Solomon'. Witness immunity was regarded as clearly necessary in appropriate circumstances to keep and increase the pool of experts that AvMA and others have fought so hard to build up. This concern was echoed and underlined by Thorpe LJ in *Meadow* v *General Medical Council* [2007] QB 462. Many commentators argued, however, that there will be circumstances in which it is right that there should be accountability, whether through professional disciplinary proceedings, civil suit or an application for costs and even before the *Jones* case the courts have shown themselves willing to impose costs sanctions, to endorse regulatory controls and where possible to find routes around the blanket ban on civil suit.

In *Landall* v *Dennis Faulkner & Alsop* [1994] 5 Med LR 268, an orthopaedic surgeon was sued in respect of advice given in a personal injury action to the effect that the claimant's condition could be ameliorated by a spinal fusion. The action was settled on that basis. The claimant contended that the advice was negligent and that the operation had damaged him further. Holland J held that the expert was immune from suit, as the report in question had been given for the purpose of assisting the lawyers to conduct the claimant's case, and not for the purpose of advising the claimant about medical treatment. The Court of Appeal expressed a contrary view, however, in the somewhat legally similar case of *Hughes* v *Lloyds Bank plc* [1998] PIQR P98. Following a road traffic accident, the injured party's GP wrote a letter for her detailing her injuries to be sent to the third party's insurers. As the letter was provided before proceedings had been issued and purely for negotiation purposes, the GP was not covered by the immunity of a witness in respect of the allegation that he had not taken reasonable care in describing the injuries.

In *Stanton* v *Callaghan* [2000] 1 QB 75, the Court of Appeal, in a comprehensive review of the ambit of expert witness immunity, held that witness immunity attached not only to oral evidence given at trial but also to preliminary work including the joint statement produced after discussions between experts, so that no claim could be made against an

---

12 *Bearing Good Witness: Proposals for reforming the delivery of medical expert evidence in family law cases* (30 October 2006), Ch 3 'Key issues and challenges'.

expert for negligence in agreeing issues or backtracking on his original report in the experts' meeting.

This principle was necessarily followed by Blake J at first instance in *Jones* v *Kaney* [2010] EWHC 61 (QB), a negligence action arising out of a road traffic case. Mr Jones was stationary on his motorcycle when (in 2001) he was knocked down by a drunk driver, Mr Bennett. Mr Jones sued and Bennett's MIB-appointed insurer admitted liability. Kirwans, solicitors for Mr Jones, instructed an orthopaedic surgeon, who suggested that a clinical psychologist be instructed. Kirwans instructed Dr Kaney, who advised that Mr Jones currently suffered from post-traumatic stress disorder. The quantum case was brought on this basis. The defendant then instructed a consultant psychiatrist, Dr El-Assra, who expressed the view that Mr Jones was exaggerating his symptoms. At their subsequent telephone discussion, Dr Kaney agreed with Dr El-Assra that the injury did not amount to PTSD but only to a short-lived adjustment disorder; that Mr Jones was deceitful and that he was consciously exaggerating his symptoms. She then signed a written joint statement (prepared by D's expert) to the same effect. When challenged by Mr Jones' solicitors to explain her change of heart, Dr Kaney stated that she had not seen Dr El-Assra's reports prior to the experts' meeting; that she had felt that the draft joint statement did not reflect what she had agreed but that she had felt under pressure to sign it; that she believed Mr Jones to be evasive rather than deceptive; that she did believe he had suffered PTSD, although this had now resolved; and that she was content for the joint statement to be amended by the solicitors. Kirwans applied for permission for a change of expert, which was refused. They then settled the case for a sum significantly lower than the claim and sued Dr Kaney in negligence, arguing that the expert witness immunity rule could not stand in the face of the Human Rights Act 1998, in that the expert's actions had precluded a fair trial. Blake J struck out the claim, holding that *Stanton* remained good law, having been cited without criticism in the House of Lords in *Arthur J S Hall & Co* v *Simons* [2002] 1 AC 615 and *Darker* v *Chief Constable of the West Midlands* [2001] 1 AC 435. *Obiter*, however, his lordship observed that so broad and indiscriminate a protection might well be held by a superior court to be disproportionate to the public policy justification for it and granted an application for a certificate under s 12 of the Administration of Justice Act 1969 for the matter to be referred direct to the Supreme Court.

The Supreme Court accepted that this was a point of general public importance and conducted a review of the law in this area, and of the policy considerations driving it. Lord Phillips (with whom Lords Brown, Collins, Kerr and Dyson agreed) put and answered seven central questions (para 38) and then overruled *Stanton* and abolished the immunity from suit previously enjoyed by expert witnesses in respect of their involvement in legal proceedings. The court opined that the principal purpose of the historic immunity was to ensure honest and independent opinion at all stages of litigation (paras 44–45, 55–57), to protect all participants in litigation from 'unjustified and vexatious claims from disgruntled litigants' (paras 15, 58–60) and to ensure a suitable pool of experts would be available (paras 52–54); that any exception to the general rule that every wrong should have a remedy would however need to be justified and kept under review; and that there was no longer any such justification in this context. The court noted that the parallel immunity protecting barristers had been abolished in 2001 (in *Hall* v *Simons*), that there was no evidence that following that decision there had developed either a shortage of barristers or a rash of vexatious litigation; and that removing the immunity would not create any conflict with the expert witness's duty to the court (see para 49 and for example para 99, per Lord Dyson). It was noted that expert witnesses, like barristers, would continue to enjoy an absolute privilege against claims in defamation arising out of statements made in the course of legal proceedings (para 62).

Lord Hope (who had previously considered these issues in Darker's case) and Lady Hale, dissenting, raised concerns that so long-standing a rule of law should be amended without consideration by the Law Commission and the intervention of parliament, Lady Hale expressing the view (at para 190) that it was 'irresponsible to make such a change on an experimental basis'. It was possible that the pool of experts would diminish, and that indemnity insurance premiums – and so expert fees – would rise, but the primary concern for Lady Hale was the risk of what Lord Hope (para 165) described as 'worthless but possibly embarrassing and time-consuming claims' brought by disappointed litigants (para 189). Lord Hope further expressed concern about defining the demarcation line between lay and expert witnesses, where one enjoys immunity and the other does not (para 172). Lord Phillips states that the distinction can be made on the basis of voluntary assumption of risk in entering into a contract for reward, expressly departing from Lord Hoffman's view in *Hall* v *Simons* (at p 698 of that report) that an expert owes no duty to his client once he gets in a witness box (paras 18 and 46). Lord Brown expressly distinguishes expert witnesses from treating doctors or other experts called to give factual evidence, who may be asked for their professional opinions without having been retained by any party, and who retain witness immunity in respect of those opinions (para 64). The expert's contract will normally be with the solicitor rather than the lay client, but it will normally be to the lay client (possibly as well as to the professional client) that a duty of care is owed. It is possible to envisage cases in which a party may be damaged by the negligently formed or expressed view of an expert instructed by another party, or of a medical witness called as a lay witness, in which case the immunity/duty of care boundary will no doubt fall to be tested further. It is interesting in this context that most of the commonwealth cases cited by Lord Collins (para 75) related to claims against adverse or independent experts. Even before *Jones* v *Kaney*, experts have been held responsible for at least part of the costs of a case: *Phillips* v *Symes (a bankrupt) (expert witnesses: costs)* [2004] EWHC 2330 (Ch), in which an expert's 'flagrant reckless disregard of his duties to the court' caused significant expense and he was held to have no immunity against an order for costs. It is also worth bearing in mind that, even while the expert remained immune from civil suit, he was not protected from professional conduct proceedings arising out of evidence given to a court: see *Meadow* v *General Medical Council* [2006] EWCA Civ 1390.

Lawyers who should not have relied on an expert's report or should have known that the case was not strong enough to bring, can also be held liable for wasted costs. A full understanding of this important issue can be obtained by study of the following cases: *Locke* v *Camberwell*

Health Authority [1990] 1 Med LR 253; revsd [1991] 2 Med LR 249, CA; *Scott* v *Bloomsbury Health Authority* [1990] 1 Med LR 214; *Ridehalgh* v *Horsefield* [1994] Ch 205, CA; *Tolstoy-Miloslavsky* v *Aldington* [1996] 1 WLR 736, CA; *Medcalf* v *Mardell* [2001] 05 LS Gaz R 36, CA but note *Jones* v *Chief Constable of Bedfordshire Police* (30 July 1999), where the Court of Appeal said that a hopeless case does not necessarily mean that the lawyers have been negligent, because properly conducted and apparently reasonable cases can turn out to be hopeless. Those using dodgy or incompetent experts, however, may find themselves censured in costs: see *Williams* v *Jervis* [2009] EWHC 1838 (QB), in which costs were awarded on an indemnity basis in respect of the time taken to deal with the evidence of two of the defendant's medical experts, who had unreasonably alleged that the claimant was malingering.

There may be other sanctions available to the disappointed litigant, too. In *Moran* v *Heathcote*, MLC 0344 (2001, unreported elsewhere) a claimant's orthopaedic expert gave a negative opinion which resulted in the discharge of the legal aid certificate. The patient continued on his own and lost at trial. He then told the expert he was going to publish an account of his dealing with the expert on the internet. The expert, fearing he would be defamed, sought an injunction against publication. Eady J declined to grant one, being satisfied that the limited ambit of the patient's commentary, as explained to him by the patient, would not attack the expert's integrity. This issue may be differently approached now in light of some of the extreme and potentially defamatory material appearing on some websites although, unless a 'super-injunction' can be justified, further publicity relating to the application for an injunction may add fuel to the flames.

Chapter 21

Human rights

Hannah Godfrey

INTRODUCTION

It is clearly impossible, and inappropriate, to attempt in this chapter any sort of general overview of the human rights context. Instead this chapter will provide an introduction to the use of human rights arguments, and free-standing and parallel human rights claims, in the context of a clinical negligence practice.

The chapter is in two parts. The first part of the chapter will introduce the mechanics of the domestic human rights statutory framework: the important nuts and bolts you need to know to initiate and successfully run a human rights argument or claim. The second part of the chapter consists of a review of relevant English and European human rights case law, with the emphasis on highlighting where clinical negligence claims are reasonably likely to be assisted by resort to the Human Rights Act 1998.

Although the review of case law will necessarily consider relevant European cases, which must be taken into account by our domestic courts when determining any question relating to the Convention rights, this chapter is specifically focussed on domestic human rights as created by the Human Rights Act 1998. Any wider consideration of international human rights is outside the remit of this chapter. A final note of caution: this chapter should be regarded only as an introduction, and requires to be supplemented where appropriate by reference to one of the many excellent and comprehensive human rights practitioner textbooks.

THE EUROPEAN CONVENTION ON HUMAN RIGHTS AND FUNDAMENTAL FREEDOMS

The Human Rights Act 1998 is based on the European Convention of Human Rights ('the Convention'), opened for signature by the Council of Europe in Rome on 4 November 1950. All new member states of the Council of Europe are required to sign and ratify the Convention. The Convention sets out 'human rights and fundamental freedoms' to be universally recognised by the states signatory to it. Under Art 1, it provides a mechanism by which European states are required to secure legal rules to determine when and how the Convention rights can be recognised and in which circumstances they can be abrogated. It also establishes a supra-national legal institution which citizens can individually petition to have their allegations that a state has violated their rights determined: the European Court of Human Rights (ECtHR) in Strasbourg. Established in 1959, the ECtHR has developed a very substantial body of human rights jurisprudence (over 10,000 judgments delivered) which sets the standards to be expected of the States Parties to the Convention.

The United Kingdom was heavily involved in the drafting of the Convention, and was one of the first signatories. As the citizens of any signatory state could, UK applicants were able to allege directly in the ECtHR that the UK had breached their human rights, and numerous cases against the UK were considered and decided in the ECtHR. However, before the passing of the Human Rights Act 1998, the Convention operated in the sphere of international law, and accordingly it had been held that it did not apply so as to overrule domestic law (*R* v *Secretary of State for the Home Department, ex p Brind* [1991] 1 AC 696). It was not uncommon for the domestic courts to find that they were constrained or that their judgments did not meet with the approval of the ECtHR. By the 1990s, both on the ground in the UK and internationally there was a climate of increasing political pressure to recognise fundamental human rights. There was a growing call for the direct incorporation of the Convention into domestic law, a call that was met by the passage into law of the Human Rights Act 1998 (HRA 1998).

THE HUMAN RIGHTS ACT 1998

HRA 1998 came into force on 2 October 2000. HRA 1998 does not simply incorporate the Convention, but is a domestic statute that creates domestic rights. In *Re McKerr* (2004) 1 WLR 807, Lord Hoffman explained the effect of the Act:

> Although people sometimes speak of the Convention as having been incorporated into domestic law, that is a misleading metaphor. What the Act has done is to create domestic rights expressed in the same terms as those contained in the Convention. But they are domestic rights, not international rights. Their source is the statute, not the Convention. They are available against specific public authorities, not the United Kingdom as a state. And their meaning and application is a matter for domestic courts, not the court in Strasbourg.

The aim of the Act was to comply with the Convention, and it achieves that end by two principal means. First it imposes an interpretative obligation on the courts to read all legislation, so far as it is possible to do so, compatibly with the Convention rights. Insofar as primary legislation is incompatible with Convention rights, the primary legislation is preserved (although the court has the power to make a declaration of incompatibility, s 4 of HRA 1998). Secondly, it imposes an obligation on public authorities to act compatibly with the Convention rights. Directly enforceable rights against public bodies were created, and a ground of illegality is introduced into judicial review (that of acting incompatibly with a Convention right). Finally, it should be noted that even when neither party to proceedings is a public authority, the court is still required so far as possible to read legislation compatibly with the Convention rights, and as a public authority itself, must act compatibly with Convention rights and there is therefore some 'horizontal effect' as between private parties to litigation (even where that litigation is based on the common law and not on statute).

Under s 1 of HRA 1998, certain rights are defined as 'Convention rights', and it is only those rights which are given domestic effect by the Act. The 'Convention rights' (Arts 2–12 and 14 of the Convention, Arts 1–3 of the First Protocol and Art 1 of the Thirteenth Protocol, as read with Arts 16–18 of the Convention) are set out in Sch 1 of the Act.

Interpretation of primary and subordinate legislation

All legislation, whenever enacted, must be read and given effect in a way that is compatible with the Convention rights so far as possible (s 3 of HRA 1998). 'So far as possible' has been held to mean 'unless it is plainly impossible' (*R* v *A (No 2)* [2002] 1 AC 45). This is a very strong interpretative obligation. It amounts to a presumption that Parliament always has, and always will, enact legislation that is compatible with the Convention rights. In this way, respect for Convention rights is made central to any consideration of domestic law. The obligation to read legislation compatibly with HRA 1998 applies not only to the courts, but to all legal persons, natural or corporate, and so this provision has important repercussions for anyone taking decisions by reference to a statutory framework.

Public authorities: the duty to act compatibly with Convention rights

Section 6 of HRA 1998 makes it unlawful in most circumstances for a public authority to act incompatibly with a Convention right (the very limited circumstances where it may act incompatibly are where it is acting under legislation that cannot be read compatibly with the convention). It is important to note that the statutory duty to act compatibly includes not only refraining from interfering with the individual's enjoyment of the right, but also, where appropriate, taking positive steps to protect the enjoyment of that right. These duties are reinforced by the inclusion in s 7 of HRA 1998 of new causes of action through which the new statutory duties can be directly enforced by 'victims' of breaches or anticipated breaches. Even where no free-standing human rights claim per se has been brought, human rights arguments can be relied on in any proceedings, for example as a shield in response to legal proceedings brought against an individual by the state (in respect of which there is no time limitation).

Public authorities: what is a 'public authority'?

The question of what is a 'public authority' is therefore crucial. It is helpful to bear in mind that the underlying logic behind the term 'public authority' is that it is intended to capture *emanations of the state* in its many and varied forms. In the modern state, many functions of government are delegated to private bodies, and the HRA 1998 quite properly attempts to draw within its protection delegated public functions as well as direct acts and omissions of the government.

Parliament is not a 'public body' for the purposes of HRA 1998, and so no domestic claim under s 6 lies in respect of a failure to legislate to give effect to Convention rights (s 6(3) of HRA 1998). Courts and tribunals are public authorities (s 6(3)(a)).

There are some other public bodies which are clearly and obviously public authorities. Often termed 'core public authorities', the relevant members of this group for present purposes include local authorities, government ministers and departments, NHS Trusts, coroners and the General Medical Council. These bodies are subject to the statutory duty under s 6 in respect of all their functions and activities, whether public or private.

There is then a further group of public authorities that are only subject to the s 6 duty in terms of their public functions (for example providing education services) and not in respect of their private functions (for example concluding employment contracts). This group is sometimes referred to as 'mixed function' or 'hybrid' public authorities, or 'functional' public authorities.

The question of whether a private entity like a commercial care home should be considered to be exercising public functions when providing care bought by local authorities in the exercise of its public functions is a much more difficult one. The leading authority on the question of what are 'functions of a public nature' in this context is *YL* v *Birmingham City Council* [2008] 1 AC 95, in which case the House of Lords by a majority of 3:2 (with powerful and detailed dissenting opinions by Lords Bingham and Hale) determined that a privately-owned commercial care home, when providing care to a resident pursuant to agreements made with a local authority under ss 21 and 26 of the National Assistance Act 1948, was not exercising functions of a public nature within the meaning of s 6(3) (b) of the 1998 Act (for public authority test see also *Poplar Housing and Regeneration Community Association Ltd* v *Donoghue* [2001] EWCA Civ 595 and *R (on the application of Heather)* v *Leonard Cheshire Foundation* [2002] EWCA Civ 336). The decision was controversial and the subject of some sustained criticism for allowing organisations which are essentially 'standing in the shoes of the state' to proceed without being subject to responsibility under the Human Rights Act 1998, which, it was argued by some commentators, allowed the state to contract out of its duties under the Human Rights Act so far as recipients of contracted-out state assistance were concerned. It was feared that this could contribute to a serious gap in the protection that the Act was intended to confer, and in respect of some of the most vulnerable members of society – those entitled to care under the National Assistance Act. Parliament took prompt steps to fill this gap to some extent, by enacting s 145 of the Health and Social Care Act 2008, which provides that a care home is to act compatibly with HRA 1998 in respect of a person placed in a care home under s III of the 1948 Act (but, of course, this only protects recipients of care provided under these particular statutory arrangements). A private members bill to address the gap comprehensively by inserting a further definition of public authority into s 6 of HRA 1998 has been introduced several times by Andrew Dismore MP, the Chair of the Commons Joint Human Rights Committee without any lasting success so far. To date, the position remains as set out in *YL*.

The question of whether a particular function is public or private is one to be decided on the facts, and privatised companies or commercial bodies that undertake contracted-out work which would ordinarily have been governmental work (unless caught by the specific exception under s 145 above) are unlikely to be subject to the Human Rights Act in the carrying out of those activities (see also *London & Quadrant Housing Trust* v *R (on the application of Weaver)* [2010] 1 WLR 363, where a social housing trust that had charitable status was exercising public and not purely commercial functions in the allocation of housing resources).

No free-standing claim can be brought under HRA 1998 against a private defendant (or against a mixed body in respect of a private function).

Appropriate forum and procedure: bringing a claim under HRA 1998

There is no special discrete human rights claims procedure: instead human rights claims are to be pursued under the Civil Procedure Rules, with some minor modifications.

A person who claims that a public authority has acted (or proposes to act) in a way that violates a Convention right may bring proceedings against the public authority in the appropriate court or tribunal. In general, claims that a public authority has acted in a way incompatible with a Convention right(s) will be most appropriately progressed in the Administrative Court by way of judicial review (see CPR 54 and para 5.3 of Practice Direction 54). The Act itself does not oblige human rights claimants to proceed by way of judicial review (s 7 of HRA 1998), and proceedings against a public authority may also be brought in the Chancery Division or Queen's Bench, and in the County Court.

Where a human rights claim is limited to seeking damages and no other remedy, the claim cannot be brought as a judicial review (*Andrews* v *Reading Borough Council* [2004] EWHC 937), but where the claim is for damages for maladministration it must be brought as an ordinary claim in the Administrative Court (*Anufrijeva* v *London Borough of Southwark* [2003] EWCA Civ 1406).

For a declaration of incompatibility, proceedings must be issued in the High Court. A claim under s 7(1)(a) of HRA 1998 in respect of a judicial act may only be brought in the High Court, but any other claim under s 7(1)(a) may be brought in any court (CPR 7.11, and see also CPR 19.4A and Practice Direction 19A, para 6.6 for procedure relating to declaration of incompatibility or claims for damages in respect of a judicial act).

Where the claimant seeks to raise any issue under HRA 1998, or seeks a remedy under that Act this must be specified in the claim form and details given in the statement of case (see Practice Direction 54A, para 5.3 and Practice Direction 16, para 15.1).

In *Barclays Bank plc* v *Ellis* (2000) Times, 24 October, CA, the Court of Appeal said that mere reference to the Convention did not help the court; counsel wishing to rely on the Act had a duty to have available decisions of the ECHR which he relied on or which might help the court (see further CPR Practice Direction 39A, para 8 for directions relating to citation of authorities on human rights).

The Court of Appeal has expressed concern about the high and often disproportionate costs of litigating human rights damages claims, and in this respect has given some guidance for the procedures to be followed, see *Anufrijeva* v *London Borough of Southwark* [2003] EWCA Civ 1406.

Limitation

Proceedings against a public authority under s 7(1)(a) of HRA 1998 must be brought 'before the end of the period of one year beginning with the date on which the act complained of took place; or such longer period as the court or tribunal considers equitable having regard to all the circumstances' (s 7(5) of HRA 1998). In practical terms, this means that a claimant wishing to bring a human rights claim for damages against an allegedly negligent NHS hospital will be prudent to issue all claims arising out of the same facts within the one-year basic limitation period set up under HRA 1998. This means being alive to the possibility of an HRA claim at what is usually regarded as a very early stage in the progression of a potential clinical negligence claim.

The one-year basic limitation period is 'subject to any rule imposing a stricter time limit in relation to the procedure in question' which is relevant if, for example, the claim is being brought by way of judicial review – in which case the stricter time limit of bringing the claim within three months of the act complained of will apply.

In fatal cases where there may be significant delays in the coroner's court (particularly if an Art 2, right to life, compliant inquest needs to be held), a sensible way to proceed is to protectively issue all claims and negotiate an extension of time to serve until after the coroner has given his verdict.

There is provision to apply for an equitable extension of time, in respect of which the Court of Appeal has said that the court should examine all the relevant factors in the circumstances of each case and look at the matter broadly and attach such weight as is appropriate (*Dunn* v *Parole Board* [2009] 1 WLR 728; see also *Weir* v *Secretary of State for Transport* [2005] UKHRR 154; *Cameron* v *Network Rail* [2006] EWHC 1133 (QB)).

The Court of Appeal in *Rabone* v *Pennine NHS Trust* [2010] EWCA Civ 698 has given some guidance in respect of human rights claims issued outside the primary limitation period. Jackson LJ said that if the claim was 'doomed to failure' it would not be appropriate to extend time and the burden was on the claimant to show that circumstances exist to make it 'equitable' to extend time. In determining what was 'equitable', the court has a wide discretion and each case will turn on its own circumstances. Proportionality would be taken into account, and in cases involving personal injury or death the court may have regard to s 33 of the Limitation Act 1980-type considerations. An issue of whether the s 7(5) time limit should be extended was decided in the recent Supreme Court appeal of *Rabone* [2012] 2 WLR 381. The extension of time was granted. The required extension was short, P had suffered no prejudice by the delay, R had acted reasonably and, most importantly, they had a good claim for breach of Art 2 (paras 73–79).

Standing: who can bring a claim under HRA 1998?

Only a person who is, or would be, a 'victim' of an act made unlawful by HRA 1998 may bring a claim under s 7 of HRA 1998 against a public authority (s 7(7)). The group includes those who are at risk of being affected by a violation as long as the risk is sufficiently real and immediate. The meaning of 'victim' in HRA is defined by reference to Art 34 of the

Convention, whereby 'any person, non-governmental organisation or group of individuals' can bring proceedings where they can show they have been (or will be) actually directly affected by the act or omission complained of (*Klass* v *Germany* (1978) EHRR 214). A victim can be any legal or natural person, including a company, but a core public authority cannot be a victim for the purposes of the act and an NHS Trust is not a victim for the purposes of the Act (see *Frame* v *Grampian University Hospitals NHS Trust* [2004] HRLR 18).

For present purposes, it is relevant to note that the concept of 'victim' clearly and obviously differs from the familiar concept of claimant in clinical negligence claims as one who has suffered injury and loss caused by a breach of duty by the defendant. One practical effect of this is that persons who have not suffered injury, but have been otherwise directly affected are able to bring claims complaining of human rights violations by, for example, a hospital. An example of this wide application of the victim test is *R (Hooper)* v *Secretary of State for Work and Pensions* [2005] 1 WLR 1681 in which the House of Lords considered (*obiter*) that the applicants were victims for the purposes of the Art 34 test because they could establish they would have claimed the benefits alleged to have breached Art 14 (discrimination) if they had been allowed to. A further example is that potential recipients of information can be 'victims' in relation to claims of Art 10 (freedom of expression) violations (see *Open Door Counselling & Dublin Well Woman* v *Ireland* (1992) 15 EHRR 244)). See also *R (on the application of Holub)* v *Secretary of State for the Home Department* [2001] 1 WLR 1359 in which it was held that a child's parents have standing to bring a claim of breach of Convention rights on the child's behalf.

The ECtHR has held that an individual whose life is put at risk (but survives) can be a victim for Art 2 purposes (*Osman* v *UK* (2000) 29 EHRR 245). It considers relatives of the deceased to be 'victims' in relation to complaints of violations of Art 2 (*Brecknell* v *UK* (App No 324 57/04), 27 November 2007; *Yasa* v *Turkey* (1999) 28 EHRR 408; *McShane* v *UK* (2002) 35 EHRR 23, para 93). Domestically, this point became somewhat confused in the wake of *obiter* comments of Lord Scott in *Savage* to the effect that it was doubtful whether a close family member could claim to be a victim of an omission in breach of the positive Art 2 obligation that had led to death. However, clarity has been restored on this point by the recent decision in *Rabone* v *Pennine NHS Trust* [2010] EWCA Civ 698 in which the point was fully argued and Jackson LJ, after reviewing the ECtHR and domestic authorities, including clear statements of principle on this point by the ECtHR (*Kats* v *Ukraine* (App No. 29971/04), at para 94, and *Micallef* v *Malta* (2010) 50 EHRR 37), confirmed that relatives of a deceased person have standing to claim violation under Art 2. This has recently been upheld by the Supreme Court in *Rabone* [2012] 2 WLR 381.

The availability of alternative remedies and in particular the settlement of a civil law claim for damages can have an impact on standing (*Powell; Cavelli and Ciglio; Hay* v *UK* (App No 41894/98). Also in *Rabone,* Jackson LJ considered the authorities on this point and teased out the following general principles: first that where the applicant brings a claim in his domestic courts in respect of matters which form the basis of his Convention claim and succeeds, that success may deprive him of the status of victim under Art 34; secondly, in order to ascertain whether the settlement or award has that consequence, it is necessary to consider all the circumstances of the domestic litigation and to determine whether it affords effective redress for the Convention breach; finally, it is necessary to consider (a) whether liability for the offending conduct has been accepted by the state authority or found proven by the court, and (b) the adequacy of any compensation awarded by the domestic court. In that case, Jackson LJ said that taking all the factors into account, including the fact that an apology had been given by the defendant, there had been effective redress and therefore the claimants had lost their standing to bring claims. This is a crucial practice point then: practitioners must be aware that any settlement, even one expressed carefully to exclude the human rights claim itself, may result in standing being lost to pursue the human rights claim.

The Supreme Court considered these issues in the *Rabone* appeal [2012] 2 WLR 381. Specifically the court decided that the appellants, who are the deceased's parents, had 'standing', and that they did not lose that status on settlement of a negligence claim brought by the father under the Law Reform (Miscellaneous Provisions) Act 1934 on behalf of his daughter's estate.

Remedies

In relation to any unlawful act (or proposed act) of a public authority, the court or tribunal may grant any relief or remedy or make any order as it considers just and appropriate (s 8(1) of HRA 1998). Damages may be awarded if, taking into account all the circumstances of the case, including any other relief or remedy granted, and the consequences of any decision taken in respect of that act, the court is satisfied that an award of damages is necessary to award 'just satisfaction' to the person in whose favour it is made (s 8(3) of HRA). 'Just satisfaction' is a Convention concept (Art 41 of ECHR), and the domestic court must take into account the principles applied by the ECtHR in relation to the award of compensation under Art 41 (s 8(4)). 'Just satisfaction' can be achieved by means other than compensatory damages, for example by way of a declaration of violation, or by an apology, or by settlement. Indeed damages are to be regarded a remedy of last resort under the HRA, because compensation is of secondary importance to the primary aim of bringing the unlawful interference with the Convention right to an end (*Greenfield* v *Secretary of State for the Home Department* [2005] UKHL 14; [2005] 1 WLR 673).

Damages are not awarded as of right where a claim succeeds: the question of whether to make an award and if so how much, is a matter within the broad discretion of the court. The guiding principle for an award of damages is to place the claimant so far as possible in the same position he would have been in if his convention rights had not been violated. If damages are awarded, the assessment should be informed by the approach of the ECtHR, and damages awarded for breaches in the domestic courts should be roughly comparable to those awarded by the courts in Strasbourg.

The court on assessing damages will take into account a range of factors including the seriousness and manner of the violation (see, for example, *Baiai* v *Secretary of State* [2006] EWHC 1035 (Admin) in which it was said that a 'high threshold of harm was required before a damages award would be made'; *R (application of B) v DPP* [2009] 1 WLR 2072 regarding the specific nature of the harm being a relevant factor). The overall approach is an equitable one, but several recent cases have emphasised the need to establish causation between the violation and the loss and damage caused (see *Re C* [2007] HRLR 14). The decision to award damages needs to strike a balance between the rights of the individual and the rights of the public as a whole.

Damages for non-pecuniary loss (eg distress and anxiety, pain and suffering, humiliation, inconvenience, loss of love and support, invasion of privacy) are available, but the case law does not provide any consistent or coherent approach to their assessment. The levels of damages awarded in respect of torts as set out in the Judicial Studies Board Guidelines, the Criminal Injuries Compensation Board Scheme and the levels of awards made by the Parliamentary Ombudsman and the Local Government Ombudsman may all provide some rough guidance where the consequences of the infringement of human rights are similar to that being considered in the comparator selected (*Anufrijeva v Southwark London Borough Council* [2003] EWCA Civ 1406, Lord Woolf). The ECtHR has awarded pecuniary loss in respect of past and future lost earnings, pension rights, medical expenses, funeral costs and loss of future career prospects.

The ECtHR does not award punitive or exemplary damages and in *R (KB) v Mental Health Review Tribunal* [2003] 3 WLR 185, Burnton J held that 'section 9(3) of the 1998 Act, by prohibiting any award of damages otherwise than by way of compensation, expressly prohibits the award of exemplary damages' at least as regards human rights proceedings in respect of a judicial act done in good faith (see also *Watkins v Secretary of State for Home Department* [2006] UKHL 17).

In *McGlinchey v UK* [2003] Lloyd's Med Rep 264, the ECtHR awarded damages for a breach of Art 3 (torture) in circumstances where no award could have been made under English law as the requirements of injury caused by breach of duty could not be satisfied. The claim was brought by the children of M, a heroin addict, who had died while imprisoned. The applicants were awarded damages of €22,900 in respect of non-pecuniary damage (of which €11,500 was awarded to M's estate, and M's children received €3,800 each) and €7,500 for costs and expenses.

In *Rabone*, where the suicide of a voluntary patient was argued to have been caused by systemic failures by the NHS hospital, the judge said that if actionable breaches of Art 2 had been established, the proper award would have been a modest £1,500 in the case of each claimant (parents of the patient who committed suicide). On appeal to the Court of Appeal, Jackson LJ said that if the case had succeeded in his view the proper level of award would have been £5,000 for each parent (*Rabone v Pennine NHS Trust* [2010] EWCA Civ 698). This figure was upheld by the Supreme Court.

In *Van Colle* (another failed claim for breach of Art 2, in this case, of the police operational duty to prevent murder in *Osman* circumstances) the court said it would have awarded £10,000 to the deceased's estate for the distress suffered by the deceased, and £7,500 to each of the deceased's parents for their own grief and suffering.

The European Court's awards of damages are generally a lot lower than we are accustomed to. General damages are often not awarded at all, on the ground that the finding of the court in favour of the applicant is sufficient compensation. When they are awarded, they rarely exceed £15,000. There are some circumstances where some damages will be available in circumstances where no damages would be available under common law negligence or other available statutory remedies (for example where no physical or psychological injury can be evidenced beyond anxiety, distress and loss of dignity, or for example where relatives do not qualify for bereavement awards), but in the vast majority of clinical negligence cases, the common law continues to provide the most adequate compensation for injury and loss.

Funding

Cases against public authorities which raise significant human rights issues are a priority under the Legal Services Commission's funding code.[1] The usual merits test is modified to allow funding for such cases, even where prospects of success are borderline. The standard costs benefit ratio tests do not apply, but proceedings will still have to be conducted cost effectively: the likely costs must be proportionate to the likely benefits of the proceedings, having regards to the prospects of success and all other factors (see Legal Services Commission Funding Code, Part 1 Criteria, sections 7 and 8; also Ch 6 'The Human Rights Convention' in the guidance to the Funding Code, all published online at www.legalservices.gov.uk).

Taking a case to Strasbourg

As this is a route that will be unlikely to be relevant or indeed useful, to the vast majority of clinical negligence practitioners and clients, it is dealt with only briefly here. However it is important to note at least that such a route is available in the prescribed circumstances. An applicant is able to take a claim to the ECtHR in Strasbourg that his rights have been breached by the state, where he has exhausted all his domestic remedies. The application must be made within six months of the final domestic decision. Some legal aid funding is available from the ECtHR. The conclusion of any settlement is likely to affect the admissibility of an application to the ECtHR.

THE CONVENTION RIGHTS

Interpretation of Convention Rights

Any court or tribunal determining a question which has arisen in relation to a Convention right must take into account any relevant jurisprudence of the ECtHR (s 2 of HRA 1998). Therefore practitioners of domestic human rights need to understand the Strasbourg approach, and have a good working knowledge of the case law.

In order to set the scene for the review of relevant human rights jurisprudence that follows, it is necessary to understand some of the terminology and underlying legal concepts preferred by the ECtHR.

---

1   See further Chapter 24, Funding.

Absolute rights

In ordinary language, a 'right' to something is normally understood as an absolute entitlement. The Convention does include some 'absolute' rights that cannot be derogated from, and in respect of which no interference can ever be justified in the public interest. The Convention supplies an absolute right not to be subjected to torture (Art 3), or to be held in slavery or servitude (Art 4), or to be subjected to a retrospective criminal offence (Art 7(1)). If a claimant can prove a state has acted in violation of an absolute right, the state cannot respond by attempting justification of its conduct. A violation of an absolute right is unjustifiable in all circumstances. In the UK this has proven controversial in the arena of deportation of suspected terror suspects to home regimes that present a risk of torture. The ECtHR has consistently refused to countenance any reduction in the privileged protection afforded to these few absolute rights, despite attempts by states to alter the court's approach (see for a recent example the intervention of the UK Government in *Saadi* v *Italy* (2008) 24 BHRC 123).

Limited rights

The absolute Convention rights are in a clear minority; most of the Convention rights are expressly or impliedly limited. For example, Art 5 (liberty and security) which protects in general the individual's right to liberty, provides expressly in the text of the article for certain circumstances within which a citizen can be lawfully detained without violating his Art 5 rights. Further implied limits on rights can and have been determined by the ECtHR on a case by case basis, however such implied restrictions as have been found are interpreted narrowly by the court, and are subject to the same general principles that govern the qualified rights.

Qualified rights

Interference with a right that is 'qualified' can be justified by proportionate reliance on a legitimate aim. The qualified rights are drafted in two limbs, the first setting out the substantive right, and the second qualifying that right by prescribing circumstances in which that right may lawfully be interfered with (see Arts 8 (privacy), 9 (conscience and religion), 10 (freedom of expression), 11 (association) inclusive, and Art 1, Protocol 1 (property)). A legitimate aim is one that is prescribed or in accordance with the law and necessary in a democratic society. The concept of 'proportionality' is extremely important: an interference with a substantive right can only be justified to the extent that the interference is necessary to achieve the legitimate aim, and no further (see *Silver* v *UK* (1983) 5 EHRR 347; *Handyside* v *UK* (1976) 1 EHRR 737; *Sporrong* v *Sweden* (1982) 5 EHRR 35). There is a balancing act that needs to be carried out between the rights of collective society (the legitimate social aim) and the rights of the individual. A balancing act also frequently needs to be carried out between competing Convention rights, such as when one individual's right to private life needs to be balanced against the need for a free press and freedom of expression.

Margin of appreciation

The 'margin of appreciation' is a European law concept which describes the ambit of discretion given to different sovereign states in terms of how they are allowed to comply with the requirements of an international treaty using different but equally valid means to achieve an appropriate balance of protection of citizen's rights. If a course of action (or inaction) is determined by the court to fall within the state's 'margin of appreciation', this simply means that the state has acted compatibly with the Convention.

Positive obligations

In addition to the specific obligations set out in the body of the text itself (for example Art 5(2) 'everyone who is arrested shall be informed promptly in a language which he understands of the reasons for his arrest and any charge against him'), some of the rights have been interpreted by the ECtHR as impliedly giving rise to further positive and negative obligations on the state. It is generally accepted that the Convention positively obliges the state to adopt sufficient and adequate legal systems to deter and punish individuals guilty of violating the Convention rights of others (for example an obligation to create, maintain and put into practice an effective system of criminal law to deter the commission of offences against the person). Specific arms of the state such as the police or other relevant public bodies have been found to be under positive operational duties to take steps to prevent a violation of individuals rights under Art 2 or 3 (for police see *Osman* v *UK* (2000) 29 EHRR 245; for local authorities see *Z* v *UK* (2002) 34 EHRR 3). Where such obligations have been determined to exist in relation to Convention rights, and are relevant to the present exercise they are set out further below.

Article 2: The right to life

> 1. Everyone's right to life shall be protected by law. No-one shall be deprived of his life intentionally [....]
> 2. Deprivation of life shall not be regarded as inflicted in contravention of this Article when it results from the use of force which is no more than is absolutely necessary
> (a) In defence of any person from unlawful violence;
> (b) In order to effect a lawful arrest or to prevent the escape of a person lawfully detained;
> (c) In action lawfully taken for the purpose of quelling a riot or insurrection.

Article 2 is one of the 'most fundamental provisions in the Convention' which 'together with Article 3 enshrines one of the basic values of the democratic societies making up the Council of Europe' (*McCann* v *UK* (1996) 21 EHRR 97). The right imposes substantive positive and negative obligations on the state (to refrain from taking and to protect life) as well as significant procedural obligations to investigate the taking of life; in particular where the state or its agents are implicated in the loss of life.

How does the Article affect the unborn child?

In the UK, the foetus has no legal rights or interests before birth, however this is not the position across Europe. Some states do recognise a pre-natal right to life (for example Ireland). The vexed philosophical question of when life begins is one to which there is no common or universal answer among the State Parties to the Convention, and for that reason the court in Strasbourg has allowed a generous margin of appreciation to State parties in terms of when they identify Art 2 rights may begin to apply (see *Evans* v *UK* (2007) 22 BHRC 190 in which it was held that the destruction of embryos did not engage Art 2 in the UK).

To date, no Strasbourg case has found a breach of Art 2 in respect of a foetus, however a number of cases have suggested that this may not necessarily remain the case in future. In a case held inadmissible on other grounds, the ECtHR held that in principle a foetus could be a 'victim' under r 34 in relation to a breach of Art 2 (*Boso* v *Italy* (App No 50490/99) 5 September 2002), and in *Vo* v *France* [2004] 2 FCR 577 the Grand Chamber of the ECtHR specifically noted that 'the court has yet to determine the "beginning" of "everyone's right to life" within the meaning of this provision and whether the unborn child has such a right'. The question of when life begins remains firmly within the state's margin of appreciation, as does the balancing of the conflicting interests of the foetus and the mother (see Grand Chamber judgment in *A, B and C* v *Ireland* (App No 25579/05) which concerned three women who were resident in Ireland and travelled to the UK to have lawful abortions for health and social reasons).

Substantive prohibition on taking life – how does this provision affect end of life decisions and clinical decisions that result in death?

It has been held by the Commission that the Article does not require that passive euthanasia, by which a person is allowed to die by not being given treatment, be a crime. In *Widmer* v *Switzerland* (App No 20527/92) 1993, unreported, it was sufficient that Swiss law provided liability for negligent medical treatment causing death.

In the UK there have been several major challenges to the lawfulness of prohibitions on assisted suicide. Diane Pretty brought proceedings seeking an undertaking from the DPP that he would not prosecute her husband if he assisted her suicide. She was terminally ill with Motor Neurone Disease and wished to establish in advance whether her husband would be prosecuted if he assisted her to die with dignity at a time when she judged her mental and physical suffering had become utterly unbearable. Her claim raised issues under Arts 2, 3 and 8. The House of Lords, and the ECtHR held that a 'right to die' could not be read into the Art 2 protection of life (*R (Pretty)* v *DPP* [2001] UKHL 61, *Pretty* v *UK* (2002) 35 EHRR 1) but that the ambit of Art 8 was wide enough to encompass the right to self-determination in terms of life and death issues. In that case, the ECtHR held that while a blanket ban on assisted suicide did engage Art 8, the interference was a legitimate and proportionate one that was 'designed to safeguard life by protecting the weak and vulnerable and especially those who are not in a condition to take informed decisions against acts intended to end life or to assist in ending life'. The interference was reasonable and objectively justified, and there was no violation by the state of Art 8.

In *R (Purdy)* v *DPP* [2009] UKHL 45, the House of Lords revisited this context in the case of a woman terminally ill with multiple sclerosis who sought clarification of the DPP policy in relation to prosecutions for assisted suicide in order to make an informed decision about whether to ask her husband to assist her in travelling to a country where suicide was lawful in order to die. The House of Lords found the Code for Prosecutors was insufficient in this context to meet the requirements under Art 8 of foreseeability and accessibility, and ordered the DPP to promulgate an offence specific policy to identify the facts and circumstances that would be taken into account in deciding whether to prosecute in such a case (since *Purdy*, s 59 of the Coroners and Justice Act 2009 (not yet in force) has been enacted which amends and clarifies to some extent the offence of 'encouraging or assisting suicide', without substantially altering the substance of the offence).

Contrast *Pretty* and *Purdy* with *Ms B* v *An NHS Trust* [2002] All ER 449 (a case about mental capacity in which there is no reference to human rights), in which a competent tetraplegic patient wished to refuse life sustaining artificial ventilation in order to die naturally, but no doctor at her hospital would carry out her wishes. Dame Butler-Sloss PC warned against the 'serious danger exemplified in this case of a benevolent paternalism which does not embrace recognition of the personal autonomy of the severely disabled patient'. Ms B was judged to have capacity to make the decision to refuse treatment that would end her life, and ultimately a doctor was identified outside the defendant NHS trust who was prepared to carry out her wishes.

The domestic courts have also held that where responsible medical professionals take the view that further treatment is not in the patient's best interests, withdrawal of artificial hydration and nutrition will not violate Art 2. In *National Health Service Trust A* v *M* and *National Health Service Trust B* v *H* [2001] 2 WLR 942, [2000] MLC 0272, Butler-Sloss PC held that, if artificial nutrition and hydration were withdrawn from two patients who had been for years in permanent vegetative state, there would not be a breach of the Article. She said that the Article did not impose an absolute obligation to treat if such treatment would be futile. The Article only imposed a positive obligation to give life-sustaining treatment in circumstances where, according to responsible medical opinion, such treatment was in the best interests of the patient (see also *Re J (a minor) (wardship: medical treatment)* [1990] 3 All ER 930). See *Re O T* [2009] EWHC 633 (Fam) for a recent illustration of the balancing exercise the court will undertake to make an assessment of the patient's best interests). The ECtHR has not yet ruled on this point but there is no obvious support in the court's case law for the prolonging of life at all cost, and it is likely the same result would be reached.

In *R (on the application of Burke)* v *General Medical Council* [2005] EWCA Civ 1003, the claimant suffered from the progressively degenerative disease of cerebellar ataxia. He was of full capacity, but there would come a time when he could only survive by artificial nutrition. His cognitive facilities would remain intact, however. He did not want artificial nutrition to be withdrawn until he died of natural causes. He based his arguments on a number of Articles in the Convention. The Court of Appeal confirmed that where a competent patient indicated his wish to be kept alive by the provision of artificial nutrition and hydration (ANH), any doctor who deliberately brought that patient's life to an end by discontinuing the supply of artificial nutrition and hydration would not merely be in breach of duty but would be guilty of murder. However Art 2 did not impose a continuing obligation on health authorities to continue treatment to patients in a permanent vegetative state in all cases. The question of whether or not the withdrawal of ANH would be in his best interests after he had lost capacity was not a question that could be prejudged in advance by application of a simple test. The guidance on withholding and withdrawing life prolonging treatment produced by the GMC did not violate the Convention in the particular way alleged by the claimant. Leave to appeal to the House of Lords has been refused.

In this context, the Mental Capacity Act 2005 provisions for advance directives (previously called 'living wills') should also be considered; see Chapters 10 and 22.

The domestic courts have held that the value of life under Art 2 is not absolute; in appropriate cases a balance has to be struck, as the vexing case of the conjoined twins shows ((2000) 57 BMLR 1, Fam D; affd [2000] 4 All ER 961, CA). The conjoined twins required surgical separation which would inevitably result in the death of the weaker twin, and which the parents understandably could not give their consent for. It was held by the domestic courts both that this was an appropriate case in which to override the parents' decision, and that the operation would not violate the Art 2 prohibition on the taking of life. The ratio was that the doctors *intention* was not to kill the weaker, but to increase the life chances of the stronger twin: a plea of quasi self-defence, modified for the exceptional circumstances, could be available to the doctor acting to save J's life by removing M, who in reality was killing J (*Re A (children)(conjoined twins: surgical separation)* [2001] Fam 147; see also *Re Cox* (1992) 12 BMLR 38).

In summary, an adult with capacity may lawfully: travel to a country where assisted suicide is legal; decide to refuse treatment even where that will certainly result in harm or even death; take active steps to commit suicide; and dictate by way of advance directive (see Mental Capacity Act 2005) that treatment is to be refused when he loses capacity. It remains unlawful to take life by assisting suicide (whether by medicine or by assisting travel abroad for that purpose) unless either the assistance has the primary effect of some form of palliative care and only secondarily hastens death (the doctrine of 'double effect') or the taking of life fulfils the requirements of one of the express exceptions to Art 2 (for example 'self-defence').

Substantive positive obligation to protect life

The Commission has stated that the Article 'enjoins the state not only to refrain from taking life intentionally but, further, to take appropriate steps to safeguard life' (*X v UK* (App No 7154/75), 14 DR 31 (1978)).

Primarily, the substantive positive obligations under Art 2 refer to general or systemic duties to establish and apply an effective criminal law system to deter and punish the taking of life and to take appropriate measures to prevent deaths in custody. The ECtHR has confirmed that the duty on the state to take appropriate steps to protect life applies to public health, in the sense of requiring states to regulate hospitals to adopt appropriately high professional and practice standards (see *Calvelli and Ciglio v Italy* (App No 32967/96) and *Powell v UK* (2000) 30 EHRR CD 362). The House of Lords has recently revisited this general duty under Art 2 in *Savage* v *South Essex Partnership NHS Trust* [2008] UKHL 74, *per* Lord Rodger at 68–69:

> In terms of Article 2, health authorities are under an overarching obligation to protect the lives of patients in their hospitals. In order to fulfil that obligation, and depending on the circumstances, they may require to fulfil a number of complementary obligations. In the first place, the duty to protect the lives of patients requires health authorities to ensure that the hospitals for which they are responsible employ competent staff and that they are trained to a high professional standard. In addition, the authorities must ensure that the hospitals adopt systems of work which will protect the lives of patients. Failure to perform these general obligations may result in a violation of Article 2.'

Where mental health is concerned, the general duty includes putting in place appropriate systems to prevent patients from taking their own lives; see further *Savage*, Lord Rodger at para 69:

> If for example a health authority fails to ensure that a hospital puts in place a proper system for supervising mentally ill patients and as a result a patient is able to commit suicide, the health authority will have violated the patient's right to life under Article 2.

(See also *Herczegfalvy* v *Austria* (1992) 15 EHRR 437.)

There is an important distinction to be drawn between a systemic failure that will engage the state's responsibility under Art 2, and a failure which is the result of the act/omission of an individual(s) which will not. The ECtHR in *Powell* v *UK* (2000) 30 EHRR CD 362 stated that it could not accept that 'matters such as errors of judgment on the part of a health professional or negligent coordination among health professionals in the treatment of a particular patient are sufficient of themselves to call a contracting state to account [under Art 2]'. The logic appears to be that the state must be culpable in some way before it can be held responsible. If the state properly trains, and regulates and provides facilities for healthcare professionals, the fact that a doctor then acts negligently not in accordance with his training is not a matter which should engage the state's liability under Art 2. In such circumstances the individual doctor may be personally liable in negligence for the clinical misjudgement or failure to implement the system in place, and the health authority will probably be vicariously liable but there will be no breach of the state's general duty under Art 2 to have a proper system in place (see *Rabone* v *Pennine NHS Trust* [2009] EWHC 1827, confirmed in [2010] EWCA Civ 698 and by the Supreme Court [2012] 2 WLR 381).

The ECtHR has also held that in certain prescribed circumstances the state will be obliged to take preventive operational measures (distinct from and additional to the general systemic obligations) to protect the lives of specific individuals. In *Osman* v *UK* (2000) EHRR 245, those circumstances were described as where 'the authorities knew or ought to have known at the time of the existence of a real and immediate risk to the life of an identified individual or individuals ... and that they failed to take measures within the scope of their powers which, judged reasonably, might have been expected to avoid that risk'. In *Osman*, the ECtHR rejected the submission made by the UK Government that the failure must amount to gross negligence or wilful disregard of the duty to protect life before it could be said to breach the operational duty.

The 'real and immediate' risk has been described as a high threshold (Lord Carswell, *Re Officer L* [2009] 2 WLR 1667; but see comments by Lord Bingham in *Van Colle* (at para 30) and Baroness Hale in *Savage* (at para 78) warning against treating this as a refinement of the test. In *Van Colle* v *Chief Constable Hertfordshire Police* [2008] UKHL 50, where a prosecution witness had been murdered by a criminal at whose trial he was about to be a witness, the House of Lords reaffirmed and applied the *Osman* test, but found on the facts of that case that, despite evidence of intimidation by the accused, there was no real and immediate risk in circumstances where there had been no actual death threats and the trial was for a relatively minor offence. In *Rabone* in the Supreme Court, the evidence of one of the deceased's treating psychiatrists that there was a 20% risk that she might commit suicide was sufficient to satisfy the 'real and immediate risk' test.

The *Osman* Art 2 operational duty to a specific individual has been extended to the protection of individuals in custody from suicide (*Keenan* v *UK* (2001) 33 EHRR 913) to individuals in immigration detention (*Slimani* v *France* (2004) 43 EHRR 1068) and recently in our domestic courts to detained mental health patients (*Savage* v *South Essex Partnership NHS Trust* [2008] UKHL 74).

In *Osman* (para 116), the court said that the obligation under the Convention to take appropriate steps to safeguard life must be interpreted in a way that does not impose an impossible or disproportionate burden on the authorities. In the healthcare context, this is a necessary position, as it would be impossible to run the NHS if patients were entitled to any life-saving operation or medication without regard to resources. In *Savage*, Baroness Hale also drew attention to the fact that in the case of mental health detention, where the objectives are therapeutic and protective rather than penal, steps taken by the state to protect life must be proportionate and must take into account properly the competing values in the Convention, in particular the liberty and autonomy rights protected by Arts 5 (liberty and security) and 8 (privacy). There was speculation in the wake of *Savage* (inspired in part by *obiter* comments by Baroness Hale at para 101) that the operational duty might also be extended by analogy to circumstances outside detention, such as to voluntary mental health patients, or indeed to non-mental health patients in public hospitals dependent on physical care and assistance. However, the Supreme Court has recently considered and clarified this point in *Rabone* v *Pennine NHS Trust* [2012] 2 WLR 381, holding that health authorities do owe Art 2 operational duties to voluntary patients in hospitals (see also *Mitchell* v *Glasgow City Council* [2009] UKHL 11; *R (Takoushis)* v *Inner North London Coroner* [2005] EWCA Civ 1440).

The state's positive obligations can extend to the provision of information where appropriate, to protect the lives of persons in their jurisdiction. In *Oneryildiz* v *Turkey* (2004) 18 BHRC 145, the state's failure to provide sufficient information about the danger of landslides as well as failure to take appropriate steps to avoid landslides was held by the Grand Chambers to be a breach of the Art 2 rights of slum dwellers killed by landslides. A further line of argument under Art 2 could be a complaint that the state failed to give adequate warnings about life threatening dangers to health, for example from radiation (see *LCB* v

UK (1998) 27 EHRR 212), or contaminated food, or a medical product or medical treatment, such as a vaccination programme; such challenges are likely to fall under the general systemic Art 2 duty.

Procedural obligation

The state's obligation under Art 2 includes the responsibility to establish an effective independent judicial system to promptly and effectively determine responsibility for the death of patients receiving medical treatment. The prompt examination of deaths in hospitals is considered to be important for the safety of all users of health services. A breach of Art 2 was found in *Silih* v *Slovenia* (2009) 49 EHRR 37, where following the death of their son during hospital treatment, resolution of the civil proceedings was still pending 13 years later and the extent of the delays could not be explained by the complexity of the case or other factors. Furthermore, the court was critical of the frequent replacement of the trial judge that had contributed to the delay (see also *Dvoracek* v *Slovakia* (App No 30754/04) in which the ECtHR found violations of Arts 2 and 6 in relation to the length of judicial proceedings to investigate a death in hospital; and *Byrzykowski* v *Poland* (2008) 46 EHRR 32).

In an ordinary clinical negligence case where there is no evidence of any systemic failures, the Art 2 procedural obligation is likely to be met by the availability of internal hospital investigations, with opportunity to pursue a civil negligence suit, as well as disciplinary or regulatory proceedings where appropriate. The inquest system is the principal means for investigating deaths in the UK. The scope of enquiry in an inquest is quite narrowly controlled by coronial rules and law. However, in circumstances where the state or its agents are implicated in a death, the scope of both the nature of the coroner's inquiry and the verdict that may be given is increased to give effect to the Art 2 procedural duty (see further Chapter 17 The inquest).

The inquest system does not have power to investigate cases where death has not in fact occurred, but these circumstances can also invoke the Art 2 duty (See: *R (J L)* v *Secretary of State for Justice* [2008] UKHL 68). In these and other cases where the standard domestic inquest system is unable to fulfil the investigative function adequately, the Art 2 procedural duty may require the state to set up prompt and effective internal or public investigations ('enhanced investigations') with varying degrees of public scrutiny appropriate depending on the circumstances (*R (on the application of Khan (Mohammed Farooq)* v *Secretary of State for Health* [2003] EWCA Civ 1129) and indeed, in a rare case, even to set up a full public inquiry (*Scholes* v *Home Secretary* (2006) HRLR 44, death in custody). Practitioners should also note *R (on the application of Claire Humberstone) (claimant)* v *Legal Services Commission (defendant) & HM Coroner for South Yorkshire (West) (interested party)* (2011) HRLR 12 in which the Court of Appeal dismissed an appeal against a decision of the High Court quashing a decision of the LSC to deny funding for representation at an inquest into the claimant's son's death by asthma attack in which the ambulance service, hospital and GP were interested parties, and where the mother had initially been charged with manslaughter (based on allegations she had failed to appropriately administer asthma medication). It was the view of Mr Justice Hickinbottom that in the circumstances of that case an 'effective investigation' (necessary to meet Art 2 obligations arising in the case) could not be conducted unless the mother was represented. The Court of Appeal commented that the Lord Chancellor's guidance on funding was 'less than satisfactory' and that 'the decision must focus on the effective participation of the family and not on the needs of the Coroner' (paras 73–75, 78–79).

Article 3: Freedom from inhuman treatment

No-one shall be subjected to torture or to inhuman or degrading treatment or punishment.

Although this provision is clearly aimed at quite different contexts than the purely medical (it speaks of torture, degrading treatment and punishment), the ECtHR has held 'the suffering which flows from naturally occurring illness, physical or mental, may be covered by Article 3 where it is, or risks being, exacerbated by treatment, whether flowing from conditions of detention, expulsion or other measures, for which the authorities can be held responsible' (*Pretty* v *UK*). For a recent example finding inadequate medical treatment in detention in breach of Art 3, see *Paladi* v *Moldova* (App No 398061/05) judgment in March 2009).

In one UK case, the ECtHR found that detention conditions for a severely disabled woman breached Art 3 in circumstances where she was dangerously cold, and was unable to use her bed or toilet or wash without great difficulty. Judge Bratza in his opinion held the judicial authorities primarily responsible for the breach, because they had sentenced her to imprisonment without establishing that appropriate and adequate facilities for her care existed in detention. The learned authors of *Blackstone's Guide to the Human Rights Act 1998* (5th edition, OUP) suggest that this idea that Art 3 may be breached through a lack of planning, could be extended to the treatment of those in mental health detention, or perhaps even in relation to inadequate palliative care facilities in open hospitals.

In respect of medical treatment (or lack of) whether in a detained or open setting, the crucial issue under Art 3 will be whether the conduct complained of reaches 'a minimum level of severity' (*Ireland* v *UK* (1978) 2 EHRR 25). Article 3 has a very high threshold before it will be found to be breached. In a case brought by the family of a deceased prisoner who had been handcuffed during his treatment for chemotherapy and who had suffered humiliation and distress throughout his treatment (*R (Faizovas) v Secretary of State for the Home Department* [2009] EWCA 2009), the Court of Appeal held that the threshold for breach of Art 3 had not been crossed (but cf *Mouisel v France* [2004] 38 EHRR 34 in which ECtHR found that Art 3 had been breached when a severely ill man with lymphocytic leukaemia was chained by both feet and wrists during his treatment in hospital). In *R (on the application of MD (Angola)) v Secretary of State for the Home Department* [2011] EWCA Civ 1238, (2011) Times, 13 December, the Court of Appeal held that there was no basis for a human rights claim of breach of Arts 2 or 3 based on the failure of the Home Secretary to adopt the guidance from the British HIV Association, or something equivalent, as a legal standard for the management of the needs of detainees who were HIV positive.

The question of whether the threshold has been breached in a particular case will depend on a number of factors including the type and duration of treatment, and sometimes the individual characteristics (age, sex, health) of the victim of the violation, but it is clear that in all but the most extreme cases, examples of hospital neglect, such as failing to keep a patient clean, warm, fed, appropriately dressed, provided with analgesia, or provided with optimum care, are unlikely to breach the threshold of Art 3. However there is an important overlap here with Art 8, which concerns not only the private and family life of the individual but also extends to such concepts as dignity, autonomy and physical and psychological integrity.

Forcible medical treatment of detainees will not be a breach of the Article where it is reasonably required to preserve physical and mental health, because 'as a general rule, a measure which is a therapeutic necessity cannot be regarded as inhuman or degrading' (*Herczegfalvy* v *Austria* A 244 para 82 (1992)). The court must however be satisfied that the therapeutic need for the treatment exists (see *R (B)* v *Ashworth Hospital Authority* [2005] 2 AC 278, and *B* v *UK* (App No 6870/75) 32 DR 5 (1981) in relation to the psychiatric treatment of a Broadmoor patient). See further the case of *Trust A* v *H (Adult patient)* [2006] EWHC 1230 (Fam) in which the court noted a patient had a right not to be subjected to degrading treatment under Art 3, but held it to be lawful to sedate and reasonably restrain a resisting patient who lacked capacity to consent to an operation if the treatment was in her best interests.

Experimental treatment without full consent could come within the terms of the Article (*X* v *Denmark* (1988) 32 DR 282); but in such a case, there would presumably be a claim in negligence anyway (though the claim under the Act might obviate possible defences, such as the contention that consent would have been given if properly sought, or that the treatment was in fact beneficial).

As well as the obvious negative obligation to not engage in conduct in breach of Art 3, the ECtHR has developed implied positive obligations on the state to prevent conduct that violates Art 3. In *A* v *UK* (1998) 5 BHRC 137, the UK was found to be in breach of Art 3 for failing to adequately protect a child from corporal punishment amounting to conduct in breach of Art 3 by insufficiently defining what constituted 'reasonable' (and therefore legal) punishment of a child by a parent. The ECtHR found breaches of Art 3 in two cases where the UK authorities had failed to take steps that 'could have had a real prospect of mitigating the harm' to children at real risk of abuse or neglect (*Z* v *UK* (2002) 34 EHRR 97; *E* v *UK* (2003) 36 EHRR 519).

However, these positive obligations are not without limit – the terminally ill applicant in *Pretty* v *UK* argued that the state's positive obligation to prevent suffering in breach of Art 3 should extend to allowing lawful assistance with suicide where otherwise she faced significant mental and physical torment before death, but this was rejected by the ECtHR (*Pretty* v *UK* (2002) 35 EHRR 1).

Article 6: The right to a fair trial

> In the determination of his civil rights ... everyone is entitled to a fair and public hearing within a reasonable time by an independent and impartial tribunal ...

The greater part of Art 6 deals with the requirements of a fair criminal trial, but the protections of Art 6(1) apply to the determination of civil rights and obligations as well. There are some significant points to note in relation to civil procedure and substantive access to civil justice.

There are a number of general entitlements that have been held by the ECtHR to be implicit in the notion of a fair trial, for example the right to real and effective access to a court, without unreasonable delay, and a real and effective opportunity to present your case to an impartial and fair court or tribunal, in public, and to receive a decision which is clear and supported by reasons. The ECtHR has held that because the recognition and protection of all human rights depends on a fair and effective judicial process, the right to a fair trial holds a prominent place in a democratic society, and there can be no justification for interpreting Art 6(1) restrictively (*Moreira de Azevedo* v *Portugal* (1990) 13 EHRR 721).

Does Article 6 have any part to play in fair case management?

The basic elements of the right to a fair trial set out above are really no more or less than what is expected by an English litigant. Our civil justice system was reformed in 2000 by the coming into force of the Civil Procedure Rules. The rules are bound together by the 'overriding objective' set out in CPR 1, which is to 'deal with cases justly' which means, *inter alia,* ensuring the parties are on an equal footing, saving expense, dealing with the case in a way proportionate to the amount of money involved, the complexity and importance of the issues and the financial position of each party, as well as expeditiously and fairly in the context of the whole resources of the civil justice system (CPR 1.1). The CPR was obviously drafted with the Convention in mind, and broadly does satisfy the requirements of Art 6.

If the expectation among personal injury lawyers had, not unreasonably, been that the procedural constraints on the proper preparation of cases could be challenged under this Article, it appeared to be rudely dispelled by the trenchant observations of Lord Woolf in *Daniels* v *Walker* [2000] 1 WLR 1382, CA. The claimant had been severely injured in a road traffic accident. A joint care report was obtained by consent. The defendants wanted to challenge it by getting their own expert report, as they considered it recommended far more care than was needed. A careful argument was compiled to the effect that to deny them their request would be a breach of Art 6. Lord Woolf said:

> I will deal with the Human Rights Act point first. It was raised in a supplementary skeleton argument on behalf of the defendant. It relies on Article 6 of the Convention. It refers to *Mantovanelli* v *France* (1996) 24 EHRR 370, and suggests that, having regard to the provisions of Article 6, the order of the judge in this case conflicted with Article 6 because it amounted either to barring the whole claim of the defendant or barring an essential or fundamental part of that claim ... Article 6 has no possible relevance to this appeal. Quite apart from the fact that the Act is not in force, if the court is not going to be taken down blind alleys it is essential that counsel, and those who instruct counsel, take a responsible attitude as to when it is right to raise a Human Rights Act point. The point was raised in this case and was supported by a skeleton argument which referred to different authorities under the Convention. It covered four pages. It resulted in a supplementary skeleton argument ...

Article 6 could not possibly have anything to add to the issue on this appeal. The provisions of the Civil Procedure Rules, to which I have referred, make it clear that the obligation on the court is to deal with cases justly. If, having agreed to a joint expert's report a party subsequently wishes to call evidence, and it would be unjust having regard to the overriding objective of the Civil Procedure Rules not to allow that party to call that evidence, they must be allowed to call it.

...

It would be unfortunate if case management decisions in this jurisdiction involved the need to refer to the learning of the European Court of Human Rights in order for them to be resolved. In my judgment, cases such as this do not require any consideration of human rights issues, certainly not issues under Article 6. It would be highly undesirable if the consideration of case management issues was made more complex by the injection into them of Article 6 style arguments. I hope that judges will be robust in resisting any attempt to introduce those arguments ... When the Act of 1998 becomes law, counsel will need to show self-restraint if it is not to be discredited.

In effect, Lord Woolf was saying that considerations of a fair trial in respect of procedural issues have nothing to do with the right to a fair trial under Art 6 and everything to do with the overriding objective under CPR 1. Justice in this context would be justice under the Rules, not under the Convention. Clearly, he was worried that the restraints placed on the preparation of cases in the interests of cutting costs and delays could be the subject of innumerable challenges under the Act as the Convention does not explicitly recognise that what is the just solution in a procedural context must be heavily affected by considerations of expense and delay (something that CPR 1 makes abundantly clear).

The right to a fair trial includes the 'right to equality of arms'. This has been expressed by saying that a party must have a reasonable opportunity of presenting his case to the court under conditions which do not place him at substantial disadvantage *vis-à-vis* his opponent. In *Dombo Beheer* v *Netherlands* A 274 (1993) para 33, a breach was found where one party was not allowed to call a factual witness relevant to the factual evidence called by the other side. It has been held in other cases that equality of arms requires that the parties be allowed to cross-examine witnesses and be allowed access to facilities on equal terms. This is unlikely in practice to afford any greater protection than that afforded by the overriding objective in CPR 1 (see *Daniels* v *Walker*, above).

A fair hearing also requires a reasoned judgment, albeit only a brief statement of reasons would probably suffice (*Hiro Balani* v *Spain* (1994) 19 EHRR 565; cf *Stefan* v *GMC* [1999] 1 WLR 1293, PC; see also *Hyams* v *Plender* [2000] 1 WLR 32, CA, where the court said that the judge should properly have identified in what way a Practice Direction had not been complied with, rather than leaving it to the claimant to conjecture why his application for permission to appeal had been refused, and *English* v *Emery Reimbold* [2002] EWCA Civ 605, CA, where the Court of Appeal held that the European jurisprudence required that a judge give reasons for his decision but they did not need to be spelt out *in extenso*).

There have been several decisions condemning the failure to allow a party to comment on a report prepared for the court. In *McMichael* v *UK* (1995) 20 EHRR 205, the European Court unanimously held that the refusal at a children's hearing under Scots law (where the mother was seeking to avoid her child going into care), and on appeal at the Sheriff's Court, to disclose to her 'vital' documents, including social reports, was a breach of her right to a fair trial. Compensation of £5,000 was awarded. Meanwhile, her child had been adopted without her consent. The court said that a litigant should have an opportunity to have knowledge of and to comment on observations filed and evinced by another party.

Where a sufficient procedure is provided but not used, there is no breach of Art 6. In *McGinley* v *UK* (1998) 42 BMLR 123, where ex-servicemen complained, in relation to the Christmas Island nuclear tests, that the Ministry of Defence had not disclosed available medical records, the court held that there had been no violation of Art 6. It was not established that the UK had in its possession documents relevant to the questions at issue in the pension appeals of the applicants and, in any case, it was open to them to apply for disclosure of the relevant documents under r 6 of the Pensions Appeals Tribunals (Scotland) Rules 1981. Since this procedure was provided and the applicants had failed to use it, they were not denied a fair hearing or effective access to the Pensions Appeal Tribunal.

In *S* v *Gloucestershire County Council* [2000] 3 All ER 346, CA, the court said that a summary hearing could be a fair hearing within the meaning of the Article. Nevertheless, our courts have already changed their approach to applications for a claim to be struck out as disclosing no cause of action (see *Barrett* v *Enfield London Borough Council* [1999] 3 WLR 79, HL). It is clear that the reluctance now shown by the House of Lords to see a case struck out, where it would have been unlikely some time ago to be so charitable, is largely due to the influence of the 'fair trial' provision in the Convention (see, for example, *Waters* v *Metropolitan Police Commissioner* [2000] 1 WLR 1607, HL).

However, even the most draconian case management sanctions that debar a party from pursuing litigation will not necessarily breach the convention, because a breach of Art 6(1) can be justified where proportionate and necessary for a legitimate purpose. The court's power to impose sanctions on parties exists in order to enable fair trials to be achieved. Therefore, in cases where a party's right to proceed is debarred or made subject to onerous conditions, the court must consider whether the appropriate balance has been struck in the individual case. But assuming it has, the sanction will be convention compliant. To hold otherwise would undermine the ability of the civil justice system to manage cases at all.

It seems that although there has perhaps been some perceptible rise in the threshold for application of the most draconian case management powers (see *Waters* above; *Goode* v *Martin* [2002] PIQR P333, where the Court of Appeal, influenced by Art 6, took a more relaxed view of an application to amend a statement of case after the expiry of the relevant period of limitation; and *Cachia* v *Faluyi* [2001] 1 WLR 1966 in relation to relaxing procedural bar s 2(3) of the Fatal Accidents Act 1976 to comply with Art 6) broadly speaking any matter arising out of case management will be decided in the domestic courts according to the CPR's view of justice.

Overall, the CPR holds firm as a Convention compliant procedural code and it will be an unusual case indeed where facts will support a complaint of breach of Art 6 where the domestic courts have acted in accordance with the CPR. The Court of Appeal in *Woodhouse* v *Consignia plc* [2002] 1 WLR 2558 at para 43 stated that provided judges make their decision within the general framework provided by CPR 1.1 (and in that case specifically CPR 3.9), they are unlikely to fall foul of Art 6 (for further examples see, in relation to relief from debarring sanctions under CPR 3.9, *Momson* v *Azeez* [2009] EWCA Civ 202; and, in relation to default judgment, *Akram* v *Akram* [2004] EWCA Civ 1601).

Article 6 and expert evidence

Under the CPR, the court has power to appoint a single joint expert in circumstances where two or more parties wish to submit expert evidence on a particular issue (CPR 35.7), and the power extends to choosing that expert (from an agreed list) if the parties are unable to agree on an individual. The appointment of experts by the court is not objectionable per se under Art 6, but such experts must be free from actual and apparent bias (*Bradnsletter* v *Austria* (1993) 15 EHRR 378; *Bonisch v Austria* (1987) 9 EHRR 191; *Eggertsdottir v Iceland* (2009) 48 EHRR 32) and the parties must be able to take part in the process of preparation of expert evidence, insofar as is necessary to ensure the parties are on an equal footing and have had opportunity to provide evidence and comment where appropriate to the expert.

In *Mantovanelli* v *France* (1996) 24 EHRR 370, the parents of a 20-year-old woman who died in hospital after contracting jaundice applied for a declaration that the hospital was responsible for her death; they complained that she had been given excessive doses of halothane during anaesthesia. In the course of the proceedings, the parents applied for the appointment of an expert. The appointment was refused. The application was renewed, and an expert was appointed by the court. The applicants complained there had been a breach of Art 6 as the expert prepared his report for the court without the parties having an opportunity to make representations to him. In particular, the expert had interviewed hospital doctors without the parties being present, and without the applicants having an opportunity to examine those witnesses or some of the documents available to the expert. The European Court found that:

> ... while Mr and Mrs Mantovanelli could have made submissions to the Administrative Court on the content and findings of the report after receiving it, the court is not convinced that this afforded them a real opportunity to comment effectively on it. The question that the expert was instructed to answer was identical with the one that the court had to determine ... it pertained to a technical field that was not within the Judge's knowledge. Thus, although the Administrative Court was not bound by the expert's findings, his report was likely to have a preponderant effect on the assessment of the facts by that court. Under such circumstances, and in the light also of the Administrative Court's refusal of their application for a fresh expert report, Mr and Mrs Mantovanelli could only have expressed their views effectively before the expert report was lodged ... they were prevented from participating in the interviews ... As to the documents taken into consideration by the expert, the applicants only became aware of them once the report had been completed and transmitted. Mr and Mrs Mantovanelli were thus not able to comment effectively on the main piece of evidence. The proceedings were therefore not fair as required by Article 6(1) of the Convention.

In *H* v *France* (1989) 12 EHRR 74, the European Court considered whether a court's refusal to allow a party to call an expert should constitute a breach of Art 6. On the facts of that case, it was found that no breach had occurred, as it was reasonable for the administrative court to reject the application for a medical expert's report when the applicant had failed to make out a *prima facie* case on the existence of a causal link between the treatment he received and the alleged damage. The court said:

> ... the Conseil d'Etat's decision not to order an expert's report might at first sight seem open to criticism in a case concerning medical treatment with a controversial drug ... However, having regard to all the circumstances ... the fact that it did not order an expert's report did not infringe the applicant's right to a fair trial.

Therefore it seems there is no right under Art 6(1) to call expert evidence where the court considers that such evidence would serve no useful purpose.

Although a claim would seem to be possible along the lines that, for example, there was a breach of the right to fair trial on the equality of arms principle because the patient was only allowed one expert, whereas the defendants had, in addition, the treating doctors to offer their views, it seems clear that Lord Woolf would not approve. A claim in respect of restrictions imposed on the specialties for expert reports allowed to a party seems equally unlikely to succeed where the civil procedure rules have been appropriately applied.

Does Article 6 create substantive rights?

The right to a fair trial includes the right of access to a court (*Golder* v *UK* A 18 (1975); *Osman* v *UK* [1999] 1 FLR 193, 5 BHRC 293). This is not, however, an absolute right; within the margin of appreciation allowed to the state, restrictions on the right of access may be implied where they can be justified as a proportionate response to a legitimate need (for example the limitation on access to court for persons of unsound mind was considered and found to be justifiable by the ECtHR in *Ashigdane* v *UK* A 93 (1985), para 57). In *Z* v *UK*, the ECtHR recognised that the right to a hearing was concerned with procedural obstacles to a hearing and not situations where the substantive law precluded any basis for a hearing, quietening speculation that Art 6 would catalyse development of new substantive rights to action in UK tort law ([2002] 2 FCR 246; see also *Matthews* v *Ministry of Defence* [2003] 1 AC 1163; *Thompson* v *Arnold* [2007] EWHC 1875 (QB)).

Impartiality of the tribunal

It remains to be seen whether any challenge under the Act will be permitted in respect of alleged dependence or partiality of the court or tribunal. There are several decisions from the European Court in respect of the impartiality of tribunals and the need for a hearing in open court. But as our appeal courts are in any event scrupulous in their application of the bias principle (see, for example, the *Locabail* case [2000] QB 451, CA; *Roylance* v *General Medical Council* (1999) 47 BMLR 63, PC; *Taylor* v *Lawrence* (25 January 2001, unreported), CA), it is probable that reference to European decisions would not add anything to the strength of a claimant's case. *Quaere*: would a judge who was also a member of an NHS Trust Board involve a breach of this right? Would a judge who had gone on record as saying that cerebral palsy awards were bleeding the NHS dry be an acceptable tribunal for assessing quantum? We all know the judges who favour defendants. Medical negligence claims arouse strong and often polarised views. Will we be bolder to challenge the impartiality of a judge in the future?

Article 8: The right to respect for private and family life, home and correspondence

1. Everyone has the right to respect for his private and family life, his home and his correspondence.
2. There shall be no interference by a public authority with the exercise of this right except such as is in accordance with the law and is necessary in a democratic society in the interests of ... public safety, ... for the protection of health or morals, or for the protection of the rights and freedom of others.

The impact of Art 8 on domestic law has been more extensive than many of the Convention rights, and has led to the establishment of a free standing right to privacy under UK law where none existed before. Article 8 encompasses a wide ranging sphere of concerns important to the individual, not only the obvious protection of family life and privacy, but also the protection of identity, dignity, autonomy, self-determination, physical and moral integrity (*Connors* v *UK* (2005) 40 EHRR 9). It is a right expressly qualified by the second limb, as set out above, as interference with Art 8 can be justified in appropriate circumstances. It has been recognised as involving an increasing number of positive, as well as negative obligations on the state.

The ambit of Article 8

In *Pretty* v *UK*, the ECtHR recognised the 'notion of personal autonomy is an important principle underlying the interpretation of its guarantees'. The court held that an individual had a right to choose how and when to die that was protected by Art 8, but that the existence of laws prohibiting assisted suicide were a justified and proportionate interference with that right that was within the state's margin of appreciation.

Threats to physical and psychological integrity can engage Art 8. In *Bensaid* v *UK* (2001) 33 EHRR 205, the ECtHR held that 'treatment which does not reach the severity of Article 3 treatment may none the less breach Article 8 in its private life aspect where there are sufficiently adverse effects on physical and moral integrity'. In *Tysiac* v *Poland* (2007) 22 EHRR 155, the court found an unjustified breach of Art 8 in circumstances where the national law failed to provide an effective mechanism for determining whether the preconditions for a lawful abortion had been met and a visually impaired applicant had been refused a certificate for lawful abortion in circumstances where continuing the pregnancy put her own health at significant risk.

In *R* v *North and East Devon Health Authority, ex p Coughlan* [2000] 2 WLR 622, [1999] MLC 0105, the Court of Appeal set aside a decision by the health authority to close a home for disabled residents, on the ground that, having told the residents at an earlier date that it would be a permanent home for them, there was no sufficient 'over-reaching public interest' which would justify the health authority breaking that 'home for life promise'. The court was also satisfied that to move the elderly applicant from her home, which had been shown to be likely to be 'emotionally devastating and seriously anti-therapeutic' would, in circumstances where the financial benefit to be gained by such a move would be small, be in breach of Art 8(1) and disproportionate and accordingly unable to be justified under Art 8(2). For a recent case where this balance has been considered, see *R (on the application of Elaine McDonald) v Kensington & Chelsea Royal London Borough Council* (2011) PTSR 1266, (2011) All ER 881, in which a local authority's decision to replace an overnight carer who assisted the applicant to a commode with incontinence pads and/or absorbent bedding was found not to breach Art 8.

In the unhappy case of *Glass* v *United Kingdom* [2004] Lloyds Rep Med 76, violent disputes broke out between the family of a seriously ill child and the hospital doctors. The doctors wanted to give morphine as analgesia, but the parents refused consent as this would be likely to hasten his death. The ECtHR held that a claim under Art 2 was manifestly ill-founded and should be declared inadmissible (claims under Arts 6, 13 and 14 met a similar fate) but the claim under Art 8 was not struck out and later succeeded: the failure to seek authorisation from a court in relation to providing treatment that the parents refused consent for, and in respect of which it was known by the hospital there would be significant opposition from the parents, was a breach of Art 8. This case is often cited as support for the proposition that even if there is no legal requirement to do so, it is best practice for doctors to seek a court declaration in relation to proposed treatment where the legality of that treatment is in dispute.

In *Simms* v *A (a child)* [2004] Lloyds Rep Med 236, a case concerning the treatment of variant CJD, Dame Elizabeth Butler-Sloss PC said a reduced enjoyment of life even at quite a low level was to be respected and protected under Arts 2 and 8.

In cases under Art 8, the ECtHR recognises that access to relevant information can help individuals to protect their Convention rights. In a case where the Government was directly engaged in activity likely to be hazardous to health, nuclear testing, the ECtHR held that 'Article 8 requires that an effective and accessible procedure be established which enables persons to seek all relevant and appropriate information' (*McGinley and Egan* v *UK* (1999) 27 EHRR 1). The ECtHR has further held that even where the state is not directly carrying out the activity itself, the state can be under a positive obligation to provide information as to adverse effects arising out of local industrial activity that presents a high risk to health (*Guerra* v *Italy* (1998) 26 EHRR 357), and query whether this principle could in appropriate circumstances be transferred to the provision of adequate information about privately marketed chemical or pharmaceutical products.

Access to treatment

The Convention rights do not create a 'right' to any particular treatment on the NHS at any time, but have had some impact on the scrutiny of state decisions about funding choices for treatment. In *R* v *North West Lancashire Health Authority, ex p A, D and G* [2000] 1 WLR 977, [1999]

MLC 0111, the Court of Appeal invalidated the policy of the health authority in relation to the treatment it was or was not prepared to provide to transsexuals, to the effect that such surgery would be refused unless there were exceptional circumstances over and above the clinical need. But the court was not prepared to find that the refusal of treatment had been in breach of Art 8, because that imposed no positive obligations on the authority to provide treatment and there had been no interference with the applicants' private lives or their sexuality.

Watts v *Primary Care Trust* [2003] EWHC 2228 (Admin), was a claim by a patient to obtain reimbursement for the cost of a replacement hip operation carried out in France. She had been unwilling to wait a few months for the operation under the NHS. Insofar as her claim was based on her Convention rights, she relied on Arts 3 and 8. Munby J held that there was no positive obligation to provide treatment, as decided by the *North West Lancashire* case. Article 3 was not engaged unless the ill-treatment in question attained a minimum level of severity and involved actual bodily injury or intense physical or mental suffering, and in any event did not apply as it was not designed to apply to challenges in relation to policy decisions on the allocation of resources. This case was taken to the European Court of Justice by the applicant, where it was held that a patient could, pursuant to Council Regulation 1408/71, Art 22, go to another member state to receive medical treatment and be reimbursed the cost where there would, on an objective medical assessment of his medical circumstances, be an unacceptable delay before treatment could be provided in the UK by reason of waiting lists intended to enable the supply of hospital care to be planned and managed on the basis of predetermined clinical priorities and where there had been no such objective medical assessment of the patient's decision (*R (on the application of Watts)* v *Bedford Primary Care Trust* [2006] QB 667):

> In order to be entitled to refuse a patient authorisation to receive treatment abroad on the ground of waiting time for hospital treatment in the State of residence, the NHS (United Kingdom National Health Service) must show that that the waiting time does not exceed a medically acceptable period having regard to the patient's condition and clinical needs).

In *R (on the application of Condliff)* v *North Staffordshire Primary Care Trust* [2011] EWCA Civ 910 the Court of Appeal held that a primary care trust's individual funding request policy, which provided that non-clinical, social factors could not be taken into account when determining exceptionality, did not breach Art 8. As a result, the trust was entitled to refuse funding for a morbidly obese individual to have a gastric by-pass.

The claimant's obesity was having a seriously adverse effect on his private and family life in the most basic ways, which, without surgery, would continue and was likely to become worse. However, the court held that the application of the policy did not involve a lack of respect for C's private and family life. The policy of allocating scarce medical resources on a basis of the comparative assessment of clinical needs was intentionally non-discriminatory. Performing the function of allocating limited resources strictly according to the trust's assessment of medical need was to do no more than to apply the resources for the purpose for which they were provided without giving preferential treatment on non-medical grounds. The Court noted that any attempts made to impose a positive obligation on the state to provide support for an individual under Art 8 had been unsuccessful (*R (on the application of McDonald) v Kensington and Chelsea RLBC* (2011) UKSC 33, (2011) PTSR 1266 and *Anufrijeva v Southwark LBC* (2003) EWCA Civ 1406, (2004) QB 1124 considered) and concluded that Art 8 could not be relied on as giving rise to a positive duty to take into account welfare considerations wider than the comparative medical conditions and medical needs of different patients. The trust was entitled to set a policy which reflected what it reasonably considered to be the fairest way of treating patients.

Confidentiality of medical records

What follows should be read with the treatment on confidentiality under domestic law found in Chapter 19.

In *MS v Sweden* (1997) 3 BHRC 248, para 41, the European Court acknowledged that the protection of personal data, particularly medical data, is of fundamental importance to a person's enjoyment of his right to respect for private and family life. Any state measures which compel disclosure of such information without the consent of the patient call for the 'most careful scrutiny'. Article 8 is a qualified right, and whether an interference can be justified will depend upon the reason for disclosure and the safeguards surrounding its use.

The collection of medical data and the maintenance of medical records fall within the sphere of 'private life' (*Chare née Jullien v France* No 14461/88, 71 DR 141, 155 (1991)). Unauthorised collection, and, one would suppose, dissemination of medical information on an individual, is likely to engage Art 8 and can only be justified if the circumstances of the collection and/or dissemination is a proportionate response that serves a legitimate social purpose.

Although parties are only required to disclose evidence which is relevant, a defendant may not be entitled to inspect all of a claimant's medical/personal records, as this may be unjustified and disproportionate. The court indicated that the right to privacy is not automatically waived by the mere fact of commencing proceedings, and observed that the disclosure required was limited to the extent that the evidence was material (see also *Z v Finland* (1997) 25 EHRR 371). Although the Article might seem to permit a claimant to refuse to undergo a medical examination requested by the defendant, in such circumstances the Art 8 rights of the claimant have to be balanced against the fair trial rights of the defendant. In such cases, where the defendant is unable to understand the whole case it has to meet or to prepare its own case without such an examination, it has been held not to be a breach of the Convention to stay the proceedings pending consent to examination (or, where possible, to delimit and strike out the particular claims unable to be fairly assessed without the examination; *James v Baily Gibson* [2002] EWCA Civ 1690). The rationale underlying this is that if a person sues another for damages for personal injuries he must be prepared to submit to such examination of his records and person as is necessary to enable a fair trial of the issues to be achieved (see also *OCS Group Ltd v Wells* [2008] EWHC 919 (QB), application for pre-action disclosure of medical records).

In *Woolgar v Chief Constable of Sussex Police* (1999) 50 BMLR 296, CA, an injunction was unsuccessfully sought by the matron of a nursing home to restrain the Chief Constable of Sussex Police from disclosing, to the United Kingdom Central Council for Nursing, Midwifery and Health Visiting (UKCC), the contents of an interview between her and the police which had taken place at Worthing Police Station. The court said that when someone was arrested and interviewed by the police, the content of the interview was confidential, otherwise than in the course of a criminal trial. Article 8 of the European Convention of Human Rights indicated that, to protect private and family life, where information had been obtained in confidence, there should be no disclosure. However, there were exceptional circumstances, recognised by Art 8, where disclosure was justified as being necessary in a democratic society in the interests of national security, public safety or economic well-being of the country, for the prevention of crime and disorder, for the protection of health and morals, or for the protection of rights and freedoms of others. Where a regulatory body such as the UKCC, operating in the field of public health, sought access to confidential material in the possession of the police, being material which the police were reasonably persuaded was of some relevance to the subject matter of the inquiry being conducted by the regulatory body, the police were entitled to disclose the material on the basis that, save in so far as it may be used by the regulatory body for the purposes of its own inquiry, the confidentiality which already attached to the material would be maintained. Even if there was no request from the regulatory body, if the police came into possession of confidential material, which in their reasonable view, in the interests of public health or safety, should be considered by a professional or regulatory body, then the police were free to pass that information to the relevant regulatory body for its consideration.

In *In the matter of General Dental Council* (2011) (reported in Lawtel, 22 November 2011, AC0130440) Mr Justice Sales held that when investigating allegations by an insurance company of possible fraudulent claims concerning treatment of patients by their dentist, the General Dental Council was entitled to pass on patients' records to its investigating committee and, if necessary, practise committee. Given that there was a strong public interest in allowing disclosure of the records for the GDC's investigation, and there were safeguards in place to ensure that the records were used only for that purpose, the GDC did not need to seek a declaration from the court that it was entitled to disclose patients' records before it did so, even where the patients had refused to consent to the disclosure.

In *R* v *Secretary of State for Home Department, ex p Kingdom of Belgium* [2000] MLC 0271, the Court of Appeal ordered disclosure, limited to four named states who had unsuccessfully sought General Pinochet's extradition, of the medical reports which had led the Home Secretary to refuse extradition. The court, while confirming the basic right to confidentiality, said that in the circumstances, the integrity of the international criminal justice system needed to be demonstrated, and that the governing interest was the public interest in operating a procedure which would be perceived and accepted by the great majority to be fair, an imperative which outweighed any private interest. The disclosure fell within the exceptions of Art 8 of the Convention as being both 'in accordance with the law' and 'necessary in a democratic society ... for the prevention of disorder or crime'.

In *Ashworth Hospital Authority* v *MGN Ltd* [2001] 1 All ER 991, [2000] MLC 0285, the Court of Appeal held that there was no breach of the Convention when they upheld an order requiring a journalist to disclose the source of his information gained from medical records held at Ashworth on one of the Moors murderers. The court said only in exceptional circumstances, where vital public or individual interests were at stake, could an order requiring journalists to disclose their sources be justified (as *per Goodwin* v *UK* (1996) 22 EHRR 123), but this was an exceptional case because the disclosure of confidential medical records to the press was misconduct which was not merely of concern to the individual establishment in which it occurred; it was an attack on an area of confidentiality which should be safeguarded in any democratic society and the protection of patient information was of vital concern to the NHS. This decision was upheld by the House of Lords, who confirmed that only in exceptional circumstances could the disclosure of journalists' sources be justified, but that 'the care of patients at Ashworth is fraught with difficulty and danger. The disclosure of the patients' records increases that difficulty and danger and to deter the same or similar wrongdoing in the future it was essential that the source should be identified and punished. This was what made the orders to disclose necessary and proportionate and justified' ([2002] UKHL 29).

A related area that is of the utmost importance to clinical negligence practitioners in this context is that of the now burgeoning surveillance evidence trade. In *Jones* v *University of Warwick* [2003] 1 WLR 954, the defendant obtained surveillance evidence by instructing an agent to use deception to gain access to the claimant's home and film covertly. The evidence obtained was highly damaging to the claimant's case and was seen by both experts who said it was apparent she had significantly exaggerated her claim. The Court of Appeal said that there were competing public interests to consider, on one hand the public interest in discouraging invasion of privacy and on the other hand public interest in discouraging exaggerated or inflated claims. They concluded that the evidence was admissible. The claimant's Art 8 rights were clearly engaged but on balance the interference was justified in pursuit of a legitimate aim and therefore there was no breach of Art 8 (although the defendant was penalised in costs to mark the court's disapproval of this 'improper and unjustified' conduct). It should be noted that this is not an authority setting a principle that all evidence gained covertly will be admissible, but that in each case a balancing act must be carried out by the court. The existence of features aggravating the breach such as the nature of deception used, the severity of the invasion of privacy (for example if the claimant was naked or semi-dressed or engaged in very private functions), the presence of children in the film, and indeed the probative value of the evidence obtained, will all have to be weighed and in some cases the result must be that the interference cannot be justified and the evidence is not admissible.

Article 10: Freedom of expression

Everyone has the right to freedom of expression. This right shall include freedom to hold opinions and to receive and imprt information and ideas without interference by public authority and regardless of frontiers.

Article 10 encompasses both the right to express opinions, and to receive opinions and information. However, there is no general right to freedom of information established under this Article; a right to free information only arises in consequence of protecting another right (for example, see *Gaskin* v *UK* (1989) 12 EHRR 36, where a right to access social services files was considered in relation to an alleged interference with Art 8).

In domestic law, rights of freedom to information are enshrined in the Freedom of Information Act 2000 (see also the Data Protection Act 1998).

Article 10 has been used to found arguments against holding inquiries in private on a number of occasions. In *R* v *Secretary of State for Health, ex p Wagstaff* [2001] 1 WLR 292, the Divisional Court found a decision by the Secretary of State to hold the Shipman inquiry in private was irrational *inter alia* because there was a breach of Art 10 in that there was a reasonable expectation based on prior practice that when many lives were lost as a consequences of a major public disaster, a public inquiry would be held. Further, the court held that holding the inquiry in private constituted unjustified governmental interference with the reception of information that others wished or might be willing to impart. But in *R (on the application of Howard)* v *Secretary of State for Health* [2003] QB 830, a case concerning ministers' decision to hold inquiries into the serious malpractice and criminal misconduct of a GP and consultant in public rather than in private, Scott Baker J distinguished *Wagstaff* on the basis that it was a special and unusual case which had not established any general principle of law, and held that the minister's decision in *Howard* did not breach the claimants' right to freedom of expression under Art 10. His reasoning was that the claimants in *Howard* were complaining about an interference with their right to receive information, rather than to impart information, and the Convention did not afford a right to receive information that others were not willing to impart (*Leander* v *Sweden* (1987) 9 EHRR 433; *R* v *Bow County Court, ex p Pelling* [2001] 1 UKHRR 165). In those circumstances, therefore, holding an inquiry in private did not breach the claimant's rights under Art 10 (see also *Persey* v *Secretary of State for the Environment* [2003] QB 794 regarding the foot and mouth inquiries).

Article 12: The right to marry and have a family

> Men and women of marriageable age have the right to marry and to found a family, according to the national laws governing the exercise of this right.

In *Briody* v *St Helens and Knowsley Area Health Authority* [2001] MLC 0165, where the claimant, who had been made infertile as a result of negligent hospital treatment, claimed damages for the cost of surrogacy, and Art 12 was prayed in aid, Hale LJ giving the judgment of the Court of Appeal said that while everyone has the right to try to have their own children by natural means, Art 12 does not confer the right to be provided with a child. Damages in respect of surrogacy were not awarded.

In *R* v *SSHD, ex p Gavin Mellor* [2001] EWCA Civ 472, the Court of Appeal held that there was no breach of Art 12 where the Secretary of State had refused a prisoner permission to artificially inseminate his wife. The Court of Appeal held that the consequences of imprisonment on the exercise of human rights were justifiable provided that they were not disproportionate to the aim of maintaining a penal system designed both to punish and deter. The restriction on a prisoner's Art 12 right to found a family was a punitive restriction justifiable in the penal context, and in the absence of exceptional circumstances making the refusal disproportionately unfair, the prison authorities would not infringe Art 12 by declining to provide assistance with artificial insemination. However, the Grand Chamber of the ECtHR has since considered a number of complaints by prisoners relating to refusals of artificial insemination and reached a different conclusion: that the Home Office policy of allowing artificial insemination only in 'exceptional circumstances' did not afford sufficient weight to the prisoner's Arts 12 and 8 rights (*Dickson* v *UK* (2007) 24 BHRC 19). As a direct result, the Home Office policy has been amended: the Secretary of State continues to make decisions based on the individual merits of each case, but with a more inclusive consideration of the prisoner's rights.

CONCLUSION

Clinical negligence claimants are often as concerned with achieving a thorough investigation of incidents and deaths as with damages awards, and the development of the domestic law on Art 2 procedural obligations is particularly to be welcomed.

Domestic human rights law will never supplant the common law in terms of providing an effective remedy for the victims of clinical negligence: damages, *if awarded at all*, are rarely comparable to domestic common law compensatory awards. In many areas, the Convention protection overlaps with existing areas of tort liability and the clinical negligence claimant's most effective and comprehensive remedy is under the common law: indeed, where the common law provides an adequate remedy, no further remedy is likely to be available under the convention principles of 'just satisfaction'. However, there are areas to which tort liability does not extend and it is in these areas that it is necessary to consider whether Convention rights have arguably been, or will be, violated. It is important to note that Convention remedies are directly available under Art 2 to distressed and grieving relatives (without need to fulfil the 'secondary victim' requirements of *Alcock*), and to persons who have suffered consequences that would not sound in damages under the ordinary common law (*Wainwright* v *Home Office* [2004] 2 AC 406; *Wainwright* v *UK* 12350/04 (2006) ECHR 807). The ability to bring a claim under HRA is therefore likely to be useful where there may be issues over establishing a duty of care, or in the absence of a dependency, as well as in forcing an adequate and thorough level of investigation in an appropriate case.

Chapter 22

Court of Protection and issues involving capacity

His Honour Judge Denzil Lush (Senior Judge of the Court of Protection)

MENTAL CAPACITY ACT 2005

The Mental Capacity Act 2005 governs decision-making on behalf of adults who have lost the capacity to make a particular decision at a particular time in their lives or where their incapacity has existed since birth. It implements most of the recommendations of the Law Commission in its report on *Mental incapacity*, which was published in February 1995 after extensive consultation. The Government consulted further and published a policy statement, *Making decisions,* in October 1999, in which it set out proposals to reform the law in order to improve and clarify the decision-making process for people unable to make decisions for themselves.

On 27 June 2003, the Government published a draft Mental Incapacity Bill and accompanying notes (Cm 5859-I & II) which was subject to pre-legislative scrutiny by a Joint Committee of both Houses. The Joint Committee published their report on 28 November 2003 (HL Paper 189-I & HC 1083-I). The Government's response to the Joint Committee report was presented to Parliament in February 2004 (Cm 6121).

The renamed Mental Capacity Bill was introduced in Parliament on 17 June 2004 and the Act received Royal Assent on 7 April 2005. Sections 35 to 41 (on independent mental capacity advocates, or IMCAs), 42 and 43 (on the code of practice), and 44 (on ill-treatment and neglect) came into force on 1 April 2007, and the remainder of the Act came into force on 1 October 2007.

The principles

Section 1 of the Mental Capacity Act 2005 sets out key principles applying to all decisions and actions taken under the Act. The starting point is a presumption of capacity. A person must be assumed to have capacity unless it is established that he lacks capacity (s 1(2)). A person must also be supported to make his own decision, as far it is practicable to do so. The Act provides that a person is not to be treated as unable to make a decision unless 'all practicable steps' to help him do so have been taken without success (s 1(3)). This could include, for example, making sure that the person is in an environment in which he feels comfortable, or involving an expert in helping him express his views. It is expressly provided that a person is not to be treated as lacking capacity to make a decision merely because he makes an unwise decision (s 1(4)). This means that a person who has the necessary ability to make the decision has the right to make irrational or eccentric decisions that others may not consider to be in his best interests. Any act done or decision made under the Act for a person who lacks capacity must be done or made in that person's best interests (s 1(5)). The concept of 'best interests' is described in greater detail in s 4 of the Act. Finally, any substitute decision-maker must have regard to whether the intended objective can be achieved in a way that is less restrictive of the person's rights and freedom of action (s 1(6)).

Lack of capacity

Section 2(1) of the Mental Capacity Act 2005 defines a lack of capacity as follows:

> For the purposes of this Act, a person lacks capacity in relation to a matter if at the material time he is unable to make a decision for himself in relation to the matter because of an impairment of, or a disturbance in the functioning of, the mind or brain.

As can be seen from this definition, there has to be both a diagnostic threshold, and a resultant inability to make a decision. The decision itself is both 'matter specific' and 'time specific'.

Section 3(1) provides that for the purposes of s 2:

> a person is unable to make a decision for himself if he is unable:
> (a)   to understand the information relevant to the decision;
> (b)   to retain that information;
> (c)   to use or weigh that information as part of the process of making the decision; or
> (d)   to communicate his decision (whether by talking, using sign language or any other means).

This definition largely replicates the tests developed at common law before the Act came into force.

Section 3(2) states that a person is not to be regarded as unable to understand the information relevant to a decision if he is able to understand an explanation of it given to him in a way that is appropriate to his circumstances (using simple language, or visual aid, for example). The information relevant to a decision includes information about the reasonably foreseeable consequences of deciding one way or another, or failing to make the decision. Section 3(3) states that the fact that a person is able to retain information relevant to a decision for a short period only does not prevent him from being regarded as able to make the decision.

Best interests

If a person ('P') is incapable of making a decision for himself, whoever makes the decision on his behalf must do so in his best interests (s 1(5)).

The Mental Capacity Act does not actually define 'best interests', but s 4 sets out a non-exhaustive checklist of things that must be done (in other words, it is mandatory, and not discretionary) when determining what is in P's best interests. The checklist is as follows:

- He must not make the determination merely on the basis of P's age or appearance, or a condition of his, or an aspect of his behaviour, which might lead others to make unjustified assumptions about what might be in his best interests (s 4(1)).

- He must consider all the relevant circumstances (s 4(2)). 'Relevant circumstances' are those of which the substitute decision-maker is aware, and which it would be reasonable to regard as relevant (s 4(11)). In particular, he must take the following steps.

- He must consider whether it is likely that P will at some time have capacity in relation to the matter in question, and, if it appears likely that he will, when that is likely to be (s 4(3)). This is in case the decision can be put off until P can make it himself. Even if the decision cannot be put off, the decision is likely to be influenced by whether P will always lack capacity or is likely to regain capacity (Explanatory Notes to Mental Capacity Act 2005, para 29).

- He must, so far as reasonably practicable, permit and encourage P to participate, or to improve his ability to participate, as fully as possible in any act done for him and any decision affecting him (s 4(4)).

- He must not be motivated by a desire to bring about the P's death, where the determination relates to life-sustaining treatment, and the substitute decision-maker is considering whether the treatment is in P's best interests (s 4(5)).

- He must consider, so far as is reasonably practical, P's past and present wishes and feelings, and, in particular, any relevant written statement made by him when he had capacity (s 4(6)(a)).

- He must consider, so far as is reasonably practical, P's beliefs and values that would be likely to influence his decision if he had capacity (s 4(6)(b)). These would include, for example, P's cultural background, religious beliefs, political convictions, and past behaviour and habits (Code of Practice, para 5.46).

- He must consider, so far as is reasonably practical, the other factors that P would be likely to consider if he were able to do so (s 4(6) (c)). This might include the effect of the decision on other people, obligations to dependants, or the duties of a responsible citizen (Code of Practice, para 5.47).

- He must take into account, if it is practicable and appropriate to consult them, the views of anyone named by P as someone to be consulted on the matter in question or on matters of that kind, or anyone engaged in caring for P or who is interested in his welfare, as to what would be in P's best interests, and as to what P's wishes and feelings, and beliefs and values would be (s 4(7)(a) and (b)).

- He must take into account, if it is practicable and appropriate to consult them, the views of any other donee of a lasting power of attorney granted by the donor, as to what would be in P's best interests, and what P's wishes and feelings, and beliefs and values would be (s 4(7)(c)).

Best interests is not a test of 'substituted judgement' (what P wants, or would have wanted), but rather it requires a determination to be made by applying an objective test as to what would be in P's best interests. All the relevant circumstances, including the checklist of factors mentioned in s 4 must be considered, but none carries any more weight or priority than another. They must all be balanced in order to determine what would be in the best interests of the person concerned.

The general authority to act reasonably

Section 5 of the Mental Capacity Act 2005 contains what was originally described by the Law Commission, when it prepared the first draft of the legislation, as a 'general authority to act reasonably'. It is also referred to as 'the general defence'. Its purpose is to offer a statutory defence against liability for acts done in connection with the care or treatment of P, provided that the person doing the act or making the decision:

- has taken reasonable steps to determine whether P lacks capacity in relation to the matter in question;
- reasonably believes that P lacks capacity;
- reasonably believes that it will be in P's best interests for the act to be done.

In such circumstances, provided the person doing the act is not acting negligently, his action is to be treated as if P lacked capacity in relation to the matter and had consented to the act being done. One of the leading commentaries on the Act states that, 'It is with the general defence that the MCA is at its boldest and most innovative' (Peter Bartlett and Ralph Sandland, *Mental health law: policy and practice*, OUP 3rd Edition, p 567).

Lasting powers of attorney

Sections 9 to 13 and Sch 1 of the Mental Capacity Act 2005 make it possible for individuals to create a lasting power of attorney (LPA). There was previously an Enduring Powers of Attorney Act 1985, which allowed for the creation of an enduring power of attorney (EPA), which endured, or remained in force, after the donor of the power had lost the capacity to manage his property and financial affairs. The LPA is intended to be an improved version of the EPA, and enables a donor to appoint an attorney to make any health and welfare decisions that the donor is incapable of making at the material time, as well as decisions relating to his property and financial affairs.

There are two prescribed forms of LPA: one for property and financial affairs, and the other for health and welfare. An attorney cannot act on the authority conferred on him in the LPA until the LPA has been registered by the Public Guardian. A formal application for registration should be made, in respect of which a fee of £130 is payable.

LPAs are mainly, though not exclusively, executed by older people, who are planning for the possibility that they may become mentally incapacitated as a result of some age-related mental disorder. It is questionable whether they are appropriate vehicles for the management of a substantial damages award for personal injury or clinical negligence:

essentially because there is no formal oversight or monitoring of the attorney's actions by an independent third party.

Advance decisions to refuse treatment

Sections 24, 25 and 26 of the Mental Capacity Act 2005 place advance decisions to refuse (medical) treatment on a statutory footing for the first time. They codify and clarify the existing common law rules, and integrate them into the broader scheme of the Act. An 'advance decision' is a decision, made by a person who has capacity now, that specified treatment is not to be carried out or continued if, at some time in the future, he lacks the capacity to consent to that treatment.

An advance decision must specify the treatment that is being refused, though this can be expressed in layman's terms. It may also specify the particular circumstances in which the refusal will apply, again in layman's terms. A person can change or completely withdraw the advance decision if he has capacity to do so, and the withdrawal, including a partial withdrawal, of an advance decision does not need to be in writing and can be by any means.

Section 25 of the Act introduces the two important safeguards in relation to advance decisions to refuse treatment: (1) validity, and (2) applicability. Section 25(2) provides that an advance decision is not valid if the person who made it has:

(a)   withdrawn it;
(b)   subsequently created an LPA, which gives the attorney the authority to consent or refuse consent to the treatment to which the advance decision relates (other LPAs will not override the advance decision); or
(c)   done anything else that is clearly inconsistent with the advance decision remaining his fixed decision.

An example of inconsistent conduct arose in a case in 2003, *HE v A Hospital NHS Trust*, where a former Jehovah's Witness became engaged to a Turkish man, and agreed to convert to Islam. Even though she had forgotten to destroy the Jehovah's Witnesses' standard advance decision refusing blood transfusion, her actions could be taken into account in determining whether that earlier refusal remained her fixed decision.

Section 25(3) and (4) provide that advance decision will not be applicable if:

(a)   the person actually has capacity to make the decision when the treatment concerned is proposed;
(b)   the proposed treatment is not the treatment specified in the advance decision;
(c)   any circumstances specified in the advance decision are absent; or
(d)   there are reasonable grounds for believing that the current circumstances were not anticipated by the person who made the advance decision, and if he had anticipated them, it would have affected the decision he made.

An advance decision will not apply to life-sustaining treatment unless it is in writing, and contains a statement that the decision is to apply to that treatment 'even if life is at risk', and is signed and witnessed (s 25(5) and (6)).

If an advance decision to refuse treatment is both valid and applicable it has the same effect as a contemporaneous refusal of treatment by a person with full capacity (s 26(1)). That means the treatment cannot lawfully be given. If the treatment is given, the person refusing would be able to claim damages for the tort of battery and the treatment-provider might face criminal liability for assault. A treatment-provider may safely treat unless satisfied that there is a valid and applicable qualifying advance refusal; and a treatment-provider may safely withhold or withdraw treatment as long as he has reasonable grounds for believing that there is a valid and applicable qualifying advance decision.

If there is doubt or a dispute about whether an advance decision exists, is valid or is applicable to a treatment, the Court of Protection can determine the issue and make a declaration (s 26(4)). Action may be taken to prevent the death of the person concerned, or a serious deterioration in his condition, whilst any such doubt or dispute is referred to the court.

THE COURT OF PROTECTION

Section 45 of the Mental Capacity Act 2005 provides for a superior court of record, known as the Court of Protection, to make decisions in relation to the property and financial affairs and healthcare and personal welfare of adults (and children in a few cases) who lack capacity to make such decisions themselves. The court also has the power to make declarations about whether someone has the capacity to make a particular decision. The court has the same powers, rights, privileges and authority in relation to mental capacity matters as the High Court. In effect, the current Court of Protection represents an amalgamation of the former office of the same name, which had jurisdiction over the property and financial affairs of persons who were incapable, by reason of mental disorder, of managing and administering their property and affairs, with the health and welfare jurisdiction that had been progressively developed by puisne judges of the Family Division since the late 1980s.

Judges of the Court of Protection

The President of the Court of Protection is currently also the President of the Family Division. The Chancellor of the Chancery Division is the current Vice President. The day-to-day running of the court is the responsibility of the Senior Judge. The President has nominated a number of additional High Court, Circuit and District Judges to hear Court of Protection cases. In addition to the Senior Judge, there are several District Judges who hear cases full time at the court's central registry in the Thomas More Building at the Royal Courts of Justice, Strand, London WC2A 2LL. The other judges hear cases on a part time basis in the courts where they sit across England and Wales. The Court of Protection (Amendment) Rules 2011 (SI 2011/2753 (l.19)) provide for the jurisdiction of the court to be exercised in specified circumstances by authorised court officers.

Appeals lie from the decision of a first instance judge to a prescribed higher judge of the Court of Protection. Any second appeal from a first instance decision of a district judge or circuit judge lies to the Court of Appeal (s 53 of the Mental Capacity Act 2005, and r 182 of the Court of Protection Rules 2007).

Court of Protection Rules

The court's procedures are governed by the Court of Protection Rules 2007 (SI 2007/1744 (L12)) and the accompanying Practice Directions. These Rules were made by the President of the Court of Protection (the judicial office holder nominated by the Lord Chief Justice) with the agreement of the Lord Chancellor, makes the following Rules in exercise of the powers conferred by ss 49(5), 50(2), 51, 53(2) and (4), 55, 56 and 65(1) of the Mental Capacity Act 2005, and in accordance with Part 1 of Sch 1 to the Constitutional Reform Act 2005.

Part 2 of the Rules sets out the overriding objective that is to be applied whenever the court exercises its powers under the Rules, or interprets any rule or practice direction. Part 3 contains provisions for interpreting the Rules and for the Civil Procedure Rules 1998 to be applied insofar as may be necessary to further the overriding objective. Part 4 makes provision as to court documents, including the requirement for certain documents to be verified by a statement of truth. Part 5 sets out the court's general case management powers, and includes the power to dispense with the requirement of any rule. The Rules provide procedures for serving documents (Pt 6), notifying the person who lacks capacity and who is the subject matter of the application of certain documents and events (Pt 7), seeking permission to start proceedings (Pt 8), starting proceedings (Pt 9), making interim applications and applications within proceedings (Pt 10), as to how applications will be dealt with (Pt 12) and as to hearings (Pt 13), including provisions as to publication of information and as to privacy and publicity of proceedings.

The Rules set out procedures to be followed in relation to evidence (Pts 14 and 15), disclosure (Pt 16), appointment of litigation friends (Pt 17), change of solicitor (Pt 18), costs (Pt 19), appeals (Pt 20), the enforcement of orders (Pt 21) and transitory and transitional matters (Pt 22). The detail of the transitional and transitory procedures is provided in the practice directions.

Practice Directions

Practice Directions are directions given by the President of the Court of Protection, with the concurrence of the Lord Chancellor, on the practice and procedure of the court (s 50 of the Mental Capacity Act 2005). The following Practice Directions have been issued, and can be found on the court's website:

4A   Court documents
4B   Statements of truth
6A   Service
7A   Notifying P
8A   Permission

Forms

The following forms can also be downloaded from the court's website:

COP 5	Acknowledgement of service/notification
COP 7	Application to object to the registration of a lasting power of attorney
COP 8	Application relating to the registration of an enduring power or attorney
COP 9	Application notice
COP 10	Application notice for applications to be joined as a party
COP 12	Special undertaking by trustees
COP 14	Proceedings about you in the Court of Protection
COP 14A	Guidance notes on completing form COP14
COP 15	Notice that an application form has been issued
COP 15A	Guidance notes for completing form COP015
COP 20	Certificate of service/non-service; Certificate of notification/non-notification
COP 22	Certificate of suitability of litigation friend
COP 23	Certificate of failure or refusal of witness to attend before an examiner
COP 24	Witness statement
COP 25	Affidavit
COP 29	Notice of hearing for committal order
COP 30	Notice of change of solicitor
COP 31	Notice of intention to file evidence by deposition
COP 35	Appellant's notice
COP 36	Respondent's notice
COP 37	Skeleton argument
COP 44A	Application for a fee exemption or remission

Fees

Section 55 of the Mental Capacity Act 2005 enables the Lord Chancellor to prescribe fees in respect of anything dealt with by the Court of Protection. The relevant order is the Court of Protection Fees Order 2007 (SI 2007/1745 (L13)). There are only five fees, namely:

Application fee	Article 4	£400
Appeal fee	Article 5	£400
Hearing fee	Article 6	£500
Copy of a document fee	Article 7 (1)	£5
Certified copy of a document fee	Article 7(2)	£25

Article 8 of the fees order makes provision for exemptions where a person is in receipt of a qualifying benefit, as defined, and Art 9 makes provision for fee reductions and remissions in exceptional circumstances.

Costs

Section 55(1) of the Mental Capacity Act 2005 provides that, subject to the Court of Protection Rules, the costs of and incidental to all proceedings in the Court of Protection are in its discretion. The rules may in particular make provision for regulating matters relating to the costs of those proceedings, including prescribing scales of costs to be paid to legal or other representatives (s 55(2)), and the court has full power to determine by whom and to what extent the costs are to be paid (s 55(3)).

Rule 156 of the Court of Protection Rules 2007 (SI 2007/1744 (L12)) sets out the following general rule for property and affairs cases:

> Where the proceedings concern P's property and affairs the general rule is that the costs of the proceedings, or of that part of the proceedings that concerns P's property and affairs, shall be paid by P or charged to his estate.

Rule 157 sets out the following general rule for personal welfare cases:

> Where the proceedings concern P's personal welfare the general rule is that there will be no order as to the costs of the proceedings or that part of the proceedings that concerns P's personal welfare.

Rule 158 provides that:

> Where the proceedings concern both property and affairs and personal welfare the court, insofar as practicable, will apportion the costs as between the respective issues.

Rule 159 enables the court to depart from rr 156 to 158 if the circumstances so justify, and in deciding whether departure is justified the court will have regard to all the circumstances. This would include the conduct of the parties; whether a party has succeeded on part of his case, even if he has not been wholly successful; and the role of any public body involved in the proceedings.

Practice Direction 19B sets out the fixed costs which solicitors may claim for various categories of work in order to avoid a detailed assessment of their costs. The Practice Direction also sets out the scale of remuneration that a local authority deputy may receive,

Making an application to the Court of Protection

In a case in which there is likely to be a compensation for clinical negligence or personal injury, the solicitor acting on behalf of the claimant in the proceedings ('P') usually makes an application to the Court of Protection for the appointment of a deputy to manage the compensation award on P's behalf. The court produces a booklet, COP 42 *Making an application to the Court of Protection*.

The application consists of:

- form COP1, the application form itself, which asks the applicant to state what order he is seeking;

- form COP1A, which sets out information regarding P's property and financial affairs, such as an inventory;
- form COP2, a permission form, which is only required if the applicant is seeking an order relating to P's personal welfare;
- form COP3, assessment of capacity, which needs to be completed by a medical practitioner or any other person who specialises in assessing mental capacity;
- form COP4, deputy's declaration, in which the deputy provides important information about himself; and
- the application fee of £400.

P will be notified of the application, and so will his relatives and other persons closely involved in his care, and they can signify their consent or opposition to the application on an acknowledgment of service form (COP5). If there is an objection, a judge will set a date for an oral hearing to consider the application and the objection, but in 97% of applications, there are no objections, and the application is dealt with by paperwork alone.

Appointment of a deputy

Although this is not laid down in the Mental Capacity Act itself, judicial precedent generally recognises an order of preference of persons who might be considered suitable for appointment as a deputy. Generally speaking, this order of preference is:

- P's spouse or partner;
- any other relative who takes a personal interest in P's affairs;
- a close friend;
- a professional adviser, such as P's solicitor or accountant;
- a local authority's Social Services Department; and finally, as a last resort,
- a panel deputy (the panel was reconstituted in April 2011 and consists of 64 members,, mainly solicitors, who have experience of managing cases of this kind).

Adherence to any order of preference would, of course, have the effect of negating the court's discretion in deciding whom or whom not to appoint. Accordingly, the court takes into account a wide range of other relevant factors. These include:

- the applicant's own financial track-record;
- the applicant's criminal record;
- the size and complexity of the estate;
- the degree of contact the applicant has with P;
- any particular ethnic or religious considerations;
- P's own wishes and feelings on the matter, so far as they are ascertainable;
- the ability of the applicant to interact successfully with P and his carers;
- any conflicts of interest;
- any special qualities of the applicant;
- any special features of the case;
- whether there are any matters to be investigated, such as alleged fraud or financial abuse; and
- the expense involved in managing P's property and affairs.

During the 1990s, BABICM (the British Association of Brain Injury Case Managers), questioned the Court of Protection's policy of appointing family members in cases where P has an acquired brain injury, and suggested that, in all but exceptional cases, professionals rather than members of the family should be appointed as deputies for people with an acquired brain injury, and that the deputy – whoever is appointed – should have some basic training in the issues relevant to the long-term effects of brain injury. It has given the following reasons for this suggestion:

- *Amount of compensation.* The amount of compensation awarded can be very substantial, and in some cases it is comparable to a lottery jackpot. The families of the individuals concerned almost always have no experience of handling such large sums of money.
- *Burden.* The burden on families of people with an acquired brain injury increases, rather than decreases, over time. The administrative tasks of being a deputy will also increase that burden and add to the stress levels already experienced by the family.
- *Dependency.* There is a danger of mutual dependency in any family which has a disabled member. The involvement of a relative as deputy increases this risk, making it harder for P to begin to lead a life which is as independent as possible.
- *Inability to refuse.* Some people with a head injury have behavioural problems and can be intimidating and difficult to reason with. Family members often have problems in saying 'no' to P's demands, even though these may be clearly unreasonable and not in P's best interests.
- *Moral conflict.* People with a brain injury have the normal desires of other persons in their peer group. They may wish to spend some of their money on activities which could cause conflict with their parents or family: for example, pornography, prostitutes, alcohol, or illegal drugs. People who have not suffered a head injury may choose to indulge in these activities, but are able to do so not only without their parents' knowledge, but also without the need for family consent or financial support.
- *Financial conflict.* Families may be reluctant to spend money on appropriate items such as care, equipment, adaptations and case management, for fear of running out of money. Other families may regard a compensation award as a source of income or as a 'family fund' to use for the benefit of the entire family as they see fit. This often leads to the family providing substandard care against the advice of experienced professionals, and contrary to P's best interests. Regarding the fund as a family resource may also lead to the conservation of capital for the future beneficiaries of any last will and testament.
- *Personal conflict.* People with brain damage may be inhibited in expressing their own wishes and feelings, especially if they perceive these to conflict with those of their family. It may be much easier for them to express their wishes to an independent deputy.

Orders appointing deputies for property and affairs purposes

The order appointing a deputy to make decisions relating to P's property and affairs:

- names the deputy;
- if there is more than one deputy, it states whether they can act jointly and severally, or whether they must act jointly at all times;
- states whether there is any time limit to the appointment – for example, for three years from the date of the order;
- sets out the scope of the deputy's authority, and any restrictions or conditions;
- may require the deputy to keep within a specified budget by limiting the amount the deputy can spend each year, without the need for further authorisation by the court;
- may provide that the deputy cannot buy, sell, mortgage, lease or dispose of P's residence without the prior approval of the court;
- may require the deputy to take professional advice on the investment of P's funds;
- usually requires the deputy to provide accounts and reports to the Public Guardian, when required;
- sets out the terms on which a professional deputy may be remunerated; and
- usually requires the deputy to give security to cover any defalcations by the deputy of up to a specified sum. The premium for this security guarantee is payable each year and in most cases amounts to 0.2% of the payment guaranteed. So, for example, in the case of a guaranteed payment of up to £200,000, the annual premium would be £400.

Duties of a deputy

A deputy takes on a number of duties and responsibilities. These are set out in the Deputy's Declaration (form COP4) in the form of an undertaking:

- I will have regard to the Mental Capacity Act 2005 Code of Practice and I will apply the principles of the Act when making a decision. In particular I will act in the best interests of the person to whom the application relates and I will only make those decisions that the person cannot make themselves.
- I will act within the scope of the powers conferred on me by the court as set out in the order of appointment and I will apply to the court if I feel additional powers are needed.
- I will act with due care, skill and diligence, as I would in making my own decisions and conducting my own affairs. Where I undertake my duties as a deputy in the course of my professional work (if relevant), I will abide by professional rules and standards.
- I will make decisions on behalf of the person to whom the application relates as required under the court order appointing me. I will not delegate any of my powers as a deputy unless this is expressly permitted in the court order appointing me.
- I will ensure that my personal interests do not conflict with my duties as a deputy, and I will not use my position for any personal benefit.
- I will act with honesty and integrity, and will take any decisions made by the person to whom the application relates while they still had capacity, into account when determining their best interests.
- I will keep the person's financial and personal information confidential (unless there is a good reason that requires me to disclose it).

- I will comply with any directions of the court or reasonable requests made by the Public Guardian, including requests for reports to be submitted.
- I will visit the person to whom the application relates as regularly as is appropriate and take an interest in their welfare.
- I will work with the person to whom the application relates and any carer(s) to achieve the best quality of life for him within the funds available.
- I will co-operate with any representative of the court or the Public Guardian who might wish to meet me or the person to whom the application relates to check that the deputyship arrangements are working.
- I will immediately inform the court and the Public Guardian if I have any reason to believe that the person to whom the application relates no longer lacks capacity and may be able to manage his affairs.

The following further undertakings are required if someone is applying to be appointed as a property and affairs deputy:

- I understand that I may be required to provide security for my actions as deputy. If I am required to purchase insurance, such as a guarantee bond, I undertake to pay premiums promptly from the funds of the person to whom the application relates.
- I will keep accounts of dealings and transactions taken on behalf of the person to whom the application relates.
- I will keep the money and property of the person to whom the applicant relates separate from my own.
- I will ensure so far as is reasonable that the person to whom the application relates receives all benefits and other income to which they are entitled, that their bills are paid and that a tax return is completed for them annually.
- I will take reasonable steps to maintain the property of the person to whom the application relates (if applicable), for example arranging for insurance, repairs or improvements. If necessary, I will arrange and oversee a sale or letting of property with appropriate legal advice.

The Office of the Public Guardian (OPG)

When the Court of Protection has appointed a deputy, the responsibility for monitoring the deputy passes to the Office of the Public Guardian. Section 57 of the Mental Capacity Act 2005 provides that there is to be an officer known as the Public Guardian, and his functions are set out in s 58. These functions include:

- supervising deputies appointed by the court;
- directing visits by a Court of Protection Visitor;
- receiving the security which the court requires a deputy to give for the discharge of his functions;
- receiving accounts and other reports from deputies; and
- investigating complaints about deputies.

The OPG operates four supervision regimes:

- Type 1;
- Type 2A;

- Type 2; and
- Type 3, where the value of the assets the deputy has been appointed to manage is less than a specified sum (£18,000 from 1 October 2011; £19,500 from 1 April 2012; and £21,000 from 1 April 2014) and there are no other factors that indicate that a higher level of supervision would be appropriate.

Types 1, 2 and 2A attract an annual supervision fee of £320 and Type 3 attracts an annual supervision fee of £35.

The OPG generally allocates the following cases to Type 1:

- where there was an objection to the deputy's appointment;
- where concerns have been reported to the OPG about the deputy's management of P's funds, as a result of which the OPG considers that it needs to monitor the deputy's decision-making;
- where there is, or will be, a damages award, and the deputy is a family member, and there is a need to ensure that the financial arrangements are set up satisfactorily, and are operating effectively;
- where the sensitivity or complexity of the issues the deputy is managing mean that, at least in the short term, he may require more support;
- where the deputy has a poor credit history, or outstanding judgment debts, or has in the past been declared bankrupt or has entered into an arrangement with his creditors, and the OPG considers that there is a need to monitor his decision-making;
- where the deputy has financial interests that directly conflict with P's: for example, where he lives rent-free in property that P owns; and
- where a report from a Court of Protection Visitor recommends that, for the time being, close supervision is necessary.

Statutory wills

Since 1970, the Court of Protection has had jurisdiction to authorise the execution of a will on behalf of a person who lacks testamentary capacity. This jurisdiction can now be found in s 18(1)(i), 18(2) and Sch 2 of the Mental Capacity Act 2005

Since the Act came into force, there have been two important decisions on statutory will applications.

In *Re P* [2009] LS Law Med 264, [2009] WTLR 651, Mr Justice Lewison considered the difference between substituted judgment and best interests, and held that the earlier law regarding the making of statutory wills, including the landmark decision of Sir Robert Megarry V-C in *Re D(J)* [1982] 2 All ER 37, is no longer good law because it applied a substituted judgment test.

In *Re M, ITW* v *Z* [2009] WTLR 1791, [2009] EWHC 525 (Fam), Mr Justice Munby considered a statutory will application in a case in which an elderly woman had been the victim of financial abuse by a neighbour. He held that the weight to be attached to P's wishes and feelings will always be case-specific and fact-specific. In some cases, in some situations, they may carry much, even, on occasions, preponderant, weight. In other cases, in other situations, and even where the circumstances may have some superficial similarity, they may carry very little weight. Just as the test of incapacity under the 2005 Act is, as under the common law, 'issue specific', so in a similar way the weight to be attached to P's wishes and feelings will likewise be issue specific. He said that there was no hierarchy of factors in s 4 of the Mental Capacity Act 2005, though there may be a single factor of 'magnetic importance'.

CODE OF PRACTICE

Sections 42 and 43 of the Mental Capacity Act provide for a Code of Practice, the first (and so far only) edition of which was issued on 1 April 2007, six months before the rest of the Act came into force. The purpose of the Code of Practice is to supplement the Mental Capacity Act by considering in depth a number of important issues, which are not in themselves suitable matters for inclusion in primary or secondary legislation. It provides practical guidance on how the provisions of the Mental Capacity Act should be applied in ordinary, everyday situations. For example, when:

- assessing whether someone has capacity in relation to a particular matter;
- helping them to make decisions for themselves;
- deciding whether a particular course of action is in a person's best interests;
- acting as a carer or a treatment provider, and in emergency situations;
- acting as an attorney under a lasting power of attorney or as a court-appointed deputy; or
- carrying out intrusive research on a patient who lacks the capacity to consent to such research.

Although the Mental Capacity Act requires certain people, such as deputies and professional carers, to 'have regard to' the code, it does not impose a legal duty on them to 'comply with' the code, nor does it impose specific penalties if they fail to comply with it. The code should be regarded as guidance rather than instruction. But, if anyone with a duty to have regard to the code fails to follow the relevant guidance contained in it, they may need to explain their reasons for departing from it.

The Code of Practice has the potential – perhaps more than any other feature of the Mental Capacity Act 2005 – to revolutionise the way we treat members of society who are unable to make their own decisions. Over time, the standards laid down in the code should permeate and influence good practice. However, the code will only be a success if people know about it, read it, and study it in detail.

Chapter 23

Wales

Linda Jacobs

COMPLAINTS HANDLING AND LOW VALUE CLINICAL NEGLIGENCE CLAIMS IN WALES

Wales has two alternative compensation systems for low value clinical negligence claims, and both will co-exist with the litigation route for the foreseeable future.[1]

THE NATIONAL HEALTH SERVICE (CONCERNS, COMPLAINTS AND REDRESS ARRANGEMENTS) (WALES) REGULATIONS 2011

The most recent alternative scheme is set out in the National Health Service (Concerns, Complaints and Redress Arrangements) (Wales) Regulations 2011.[2] The Regulations were laid before the National Assembly for Wales on 7 February 2011 for approval by resolution.[3] The majority of the Regulations came into force on 1 April 2011. The Regulations are supplemented by Guidance prepared by the Welsh Assembly Government entitled *Putting Things Right – Guidance on dealing with concerns about the NHS from 1 April 2011*, which will be updated as necessary. Version 1 is available online.[4]

The Regulations provide an integrated approach, combining common arrangements for handling and investigating complaints, and dealing with patient safety issues at a local level. The Regulations apply to Welsh NHS Bodies (the seven Local Health Boards, Velindre NHS Trust, the Welsh Ambulance Services NHS Trust and Public Health Wales NHS Trust); primary care practitioners; and independent providers in Wales (collectively called 'Responsible Bodies' in the Regulations). The Regulations also incorporate redress arrangements, including financial compensation for claims against Welsh NHS Bodies that do not exceed

---

1   Welsh Assembly Government, *Putting Things Right – A better way of dealing with concerns about health services* Consultation Report (2 August 2010), p 12.
2   SI 2011/704(W 108).
3   The Regulations were laid under s 11(6) of the NHS Redress (Wales) Measure 2008.
4   www.wales.nhs.uk/sites3/Documents/932/Guidance%20dealing%20with%20 concerns%20about%20the%20NHS%20-%20Version%201%20April%202011.pdf.

the current limit of £25,000. Redress is not available against primary care practitioners and independent providers.

Redress arrangements will also apply when Welsh NHS Bodies enter into arrangements with NHS organisations in England, Scotland, or Northern Ireland for treatment and care provided on behalf of the NHS in Wales. These regulations will not come into force until 1 April 2012,[5] and it is envisaged that the delay will enable further details to be agreed with the Department of Health.

Background

On 11 January 2010, the Welsh Assembly Government published a consultation document entitled *Putting Things Right – A better way of dealing with concerns about health services*. The consultation followed interim guidance issued to NHS Trusts in Wales in October 2009.[6] The *Putting Things Right* project was established by the Welsh Assembly Government to examine the way that the NHS in Wales handled concerns/complaints. The project suggested common methods of investigation, with an emphasis on resolving concerns in a timely fashion, openly and honestly; and included a philosophy to 'investigate once, investigate well'. The stated aims are to ensure that that the investigation is proportionate to the issue in question, and results in appropriate remedies for patients and service users; 'appropriate remedies' includes financial compensation.[7] The new system envisages an integrated team handling and investigating concerns/complaints, incident reporting, claims management, and patient safety issues. In terms of patient safety, it is hoped that the new system will drive improvements in quality, and reduce adverse events and avoidable harm to patients and service users both locally and on an all-Wales basis.

The new arrangements for Responsible Bodies

The new organisation operates with a single point of entry for handling all concerns, and a single address, telephone number, mailbox, fax or text service must be clearly published for raising a concern.[8] The system is managed by a Responsible Officer (who must be an executive director or officer; chief executive officer; sole proprietor or partner, depending upon the nature of the Responsible Body[9]), taking overall responsibility for the effective day-to-day operation of the arrangements for dealing with concerns in an integrated manner.[10] A Senior Investigations Manager

5   National Health Service (Concerns, Complaints and Redress Arrangement) (Wales) (Amendment) Regulations 2011, reg 2(1).
6   Welsh Assembly Government, *Putting Things Right – Dealing with concerns (Interim Guidance on the handling of concerns in the new NHS Structure)* (October 2009).
7   Welsh Assembly Government, *Putting Things Right – A better way of dealing with concerns about health services* Background Policy Paper (11 January 2010).
8   Welsh Assembly Government, *Putting Things Right – Guidance on dealing with concerns about the NHS from 1 April 2011* (Version 1, April 2011), para 5.1.
9   The NHS (Concerns, Complaints and Redress Arrangements) (Wales) Regulations 2011, reg 7(3).
10 The NHS (Concerns, Complaints and Redress Arrangements) (Wales) Regulations 2011, reg 7(1).

is responsible for handling and investigating concerns.[11] The Senior Investigations Manager should be supported by staff of varied experience and skill sets,[12] collectively called the 'concerns team'.[13] The Regulations state that staff should be appropriately trained in the operation of the arrangements for reporting, handling, and investigating concerns.[14] The Guidance includes examples of relevant training, including Root Cause Analysis training, *Being Open* training; records management, and legal training and awareness.[15] The availability of the new arrangements must be published and advertised in a variety of media, formats, and languages;[16] and examples are available on the Welsh Assembly Government's *Putting Things Right* website,[17] and as part of the Guidance.

The new organisation must include arrangements to act upon and monitor deficiencies indentified in the investigation process.[18] This is part of the ethos of 'learning from concerns' to maximise the opportunities to improve services, thereby avoiding future deficient treatment or care. Responsible Bodies must share any lessons learnt with other service providers to improve the wider provision of services and avoid the recurrence of similar concerns in other areas.[19] Responsible Bodies must also monitor the new arrangements,[20] and prepare an annual report.[21]

Potential drawbacks of the new arrangements

The most significant issue raised in the consultation process was the lack of independence in relation to investigating a potential claim of negligence. Independence is an important aspect in patients and service users having confidence in a system of investigation. Concern was also raised in relation to the wide discretion given to Responsible Bodies resulting in a potential lack of consistency in investigations. The Welsh Assembly Government responded that guidance was to be developed about 'how teams within the organisation will work and their accountability arrangements, to ensure that they can act independently within the organisation'.[22]

11　The NHS (Concerns, Complaints and Redress Arrangements) (Wales) Regulations 2011, reg 8(1).
12　The NHS (Concerns, Complaints and Redress Arrangements) (Wales) Regulations 2011, reg 8(2)
13　Welsh Assembly Government, *Putting Things Right – Guidance on dealing with concerns about the NHS from 1 April 2011* (Version 1, April 2011), para 2.10.
14　The NHS (Concerns, Complaints and Redress Arrangements) (Wales) Regulations 2011, reg 9.
15　Welsh Assembly Government, *Putting Things Right – Guidance on dealing with concerns about the NHS from 1 April 2011* (Version 1, April 2011), para 3.5.
16　The NHS (Concerns, Complaints and Redress Arrangements) (Wales) Regulations 2011, reg 5.
17　www.wales.nhs.uk/sites3/page.cfm?orgid=932&pid=50738.
18　The NHS (Concerns, Complaints and Redress Arrangements) (Wales) Regulations 2011, reg 49(1).
19　Welsh Assembly Government, *Putting Things Right – Guidance on dealing with concerns about the NHS from 1 April 2011* (Version 1, April 2011), para 9.5.
20　The NHS (Concerns, Complaints and Redress Arrangements) (Wales) Regulations 2011, reg 50.
21　The NHS (Concerns, Complaints and Redress Arrangements) (Wales) Regulations 2011, reg 51.
22　Welsh Assembly Government, *Putting Things Right – A better way of dealing with concerns about health services* Consultation Report (2 August 2010), p 4.

The Regulations 2011

The National Health Service (Concerns, Complaints and Redress Arrangements) (Wales) Regulations 2011 are divided into ten parts. The Guidance includes ten templates to standardise some aspects of the process. In addition, there are 13 other appendices setting out guidance on particular issues, such as the grading of concerns and an investigation checklist; a legal fees framework; and a financial tariff for the assessment of claims below £25,000.

The Regulations provide a number of general principles that are to be applied in handling and investigating concerns; and are set out in reg 3 and the Guidance as follows:

(a) there is a single point of entry for the submission of concerns;
(b) concerns are dealt with efficiently and openly;
(c) concerns are properly investigated;
(d) provision should be made to establish the expectations of the person notifying the concern and to seek to secure their involvement in the process;
(e) persons who notify concerns are treated with respect and courtesy;
(f) persons who notify concerns are advised of—
  (i) the availability of assistance to enable them to pursue their concern;
  (ii) advice as to where they may obtain such assistance, if it is required; and
  (iii) the name of the person in the relevant Responsible Body who will act as their contact throughout the handling of their concern;
(g) a Welsh NHS body must give consideration to the making of an offer of redress in accordance with Part 6 where its investigation into the matters raised in a concern reveal that there is a qualifying liability;
(h) persons who notify concerns receive a timely and appropriate response;
(i) persons who notify concerns are advised of the outcome of the investigation;
(j) appropriate action is taken in the light of the outcome of the investigation; and
(k) account is taken of any guidance that may be issued from time to time by the Welsh Ministers.

When do the Regulations apply?

The Regulations apply to concerns, complaints, patient safety incidents, and claims for compensation (redress). A concern is defined as any:

1 complaint (an 'expression of dissatisfaction');
2 notification of an incident concerning patient safety ('any unexpected or unintended incident which did lead to or could have led to harm for a patient'); and
3 a claim for compensation.[23]

---

23 The NHS (Concerns, Complaints and Redress Arrangements) (Wales) Regulations 2011, reg 2.

Complaints and the notification of incidents concerning patient safety, but not a claim for compensation, can be made against a 'Responsible Body', defined as

1   a Welsh NHS body (a Local Health Board, or a NHS Trust managing a hospital or other establishment or facility wholly or mainly in Wales);
2   a primary care provider (GPs, dentists, persons providing ophthalmic services and pharmacists who provide services under arrangements with Local Health Boards); and
3   an independent provider (a person or body who (a) provides health care in Wales under arrangements made with a Welsh NHS body; and (b) is not an NHS body or primary care provider).[24]

Claims for compensation (redress) under Pts 6 and 7 of the Regulations can only be made against Welsh NHS bodies.

If a concern involves more than one Responsible Body, the Responsible Body that received the concern must inform the complainant/representative that another Responsible Body is or may be involved in their concern and seek their consent to notifying the other Responsible Body about the concern. This must be done within two days of receiving the concern.[25] Once consent has been received, the Responsible Body must inform the second Responsible Body about the concern within two working days of receiving the consent.[26] All the Responsible Bodies involved with the concern should cooperate and agree who will lead the investigation, who will communicate with the complainant/representative; to share information; and to issue a joint response to the concern.[27]

Who can raise a concern?

The category of people that can raise a concern is wide. The Responsible Body is under a duty to consider whether the concern can be investigated and to handle a concern in accordance with the provisions set out in the Regulations. Regulation 12 provides that a concern may be raised by:

1   a person who is receiving or has received services from a Responsible Body;
2   any person who is affected or likely to be affected by the actions, omissions, or decisions of a Responsible Body;
3   a member of staff of the Responsible Body;
4   an independent member (non-executive director or non-officer member) of the Responsible Body);

---

24   The NHS (Concerns, Complaints and Redress Arrangements) (Wales) Regulations 2011, reg 2(1).
25   The NHS (Concerns, Complaints and Redress Arrangements) (Wales) Regulations 2011, reg 17(2)(a).
26   The NHS (Concerns, Complaints and Redress Arrangements) (Wales) Regulations 2011, reg 17(2)(b).
27   The NHS (Concerns, Complaints and Redress Arrangements) (Wales) Regulations 2011, reg 17(3), (4); and Welsh Assembly Government, *Putting Things Right – Guidance on dealing with concerns about the NHS from 1 April 2011* (Version 1, April 2011), para 6.4.

5   partners in a Responsible Body (for example a partner in a GP Practice);
6   a third party acting on behalf of a person who is unable to raise a concern, for example, a child, a person who lacks capacity within the meaning of the Mental Capacity Act 2005, or a person who has died; and
7   a third party acting on behalf of a person who wants a representative to act on their behalf.

Members of staff should report incidents concerning patient safety, which in turn should raise a concern with the Responsible Body. The *Putting Things Right* project utilised work by the National Patient Safety Agency entitled *Being Open* that was re-launched on 19 November 2009. *Being Open* encourages staff to report errors and concerns; and involves acknowledging, apologising and explaining when errors occur. The advice is based on research that 'shows that patients are more likely to forgive medical errors when they are discussed in a timely manner; and that being open can decrease the trauma felt by patients following a patient safety incident'.[28]

Although the Regulations introduce an ethos of openness, the Welsh Assembly Government did not go as far as incorporating a duty of candour into the Regulations. This issue was raised in responses to the *Putting Things Right* consultation. The Welsh Assembly Government replied that it was unable to introduce a duty of candour, and stated '[w]e believe that we have addressed this issue as far as we can in the powers available to the Assembly. We are keeping a watching brief on development in England, where we know this matter is being further discussed'.[29]

It is regrettable that a duty of candour (and a duty to report a concern) has not been introduced as research undertaken by the National Audit Office in 2004/05 established that only 24% of Trusts routinely inform patients that they were involved in a patient safety incident and 6% of Trusts did not inform patients at all.[30] This is a significant number given that in the same year there were approximately 974,000 reported adverse incidents and near misses.[31] In 2005, the National Audit Office concluded, 'there is still more to do to achieve a fully open and fair culture with regard to communicating with patients'.[32]

---

28   Research by Vincent, C A and Counter, A 'Patient Safety: what about the patient?' *Qual Saf Health Care* (2003) 11: 76–80; and Vincent, C A, Pincus, T and Schurr, J H 'Patients' experience of surgical accidents' *Qual Saf Health Care* (1993) 2: 77–82. Quoted in The National Patient Safety Agency *Patient Safety Alert: NPSA/ /2009/ PSA003 – Being Open* Supporting Information (November 2009).
29   Welsh Assembly Government, *Putting Things Right – A better way of dealing with concerns about health services* Consultation Report (2 August 2010), p 10.
30   National Audit Office (Department of Health) *A Safer Place for Patients: Learning to improve patient safety* (Report by the Comptroller and Auditor Genial) (3 November 2005), p 15.
31   National Audit Office (Department of Health) *A Safer Place for Patients: Learning to improve patient safety* (Report by the Comptroller and Auditor Genial) (3 November 2005), p 1 (96% response rate).
32   National Audit Office (Department of Health) *A Safer Place for Patients: Learning to improve patient safety* (Report by the Comptroller and Auditor Genial) (3 November 2005), p 15.

Methods for raising a concern

A concern can be raised with the Responsible Body in numerous ways, either in writing, electronically (email, fax or text[33]), or verbally, either by telephone or in person.[34] For concerns that are raised verbally, but are not 'on the spot concerns', that is concerns that are raised and resolved at the point of service delivery, the person to whom the concern is made must make a written record, and provide a copy to the person who raised the concern.[35] The Guidance includes a template for recording verbal concerns that will be handled under the Regulations (see Appendix F of the Guidance).

What can a concern be raised about?

Concerns can be raised about any service, decision, care and treatment provided by a Responsible Body in Wales,[36] provided it is not excluded under reg 14. Concerns that that are specifically excluded include:

1   Concerns that are the subject of court proceedings (ie proceedings have been issued). If court proceedings are issued when a concern is under investigation, the investigation must stop.[37]
2   Concerns that are raised and resolved at the point of service delivery 'on the spot'. The concern must be resolved to the satisfaction of the complainant/representative no later that the next working day after the concern was notified.[38] On the spot concerns must be recorded and Appendix A of the Guidance sets out a template.
3   Where a person attempts to re-open a concern that they have already agreed was dealt with satisfactorily on the spot, unless the Responsible Body considers it needs to look into the issue again.[39]
4   Concerns that have already been considered under either a complaints procedure operating before 1 April 2011 or the new Regulations.[40]
5   A concern about an individual patient funding treatment request.[41] This situation is dealt with under the All-Wales Policy: Making Decisions on Individual Patient Requests.[42]

---

33   Welsh Assembly Government, *Putting Things Right – Guidance on dealing with concerns about the NHS from 1 April 2011* (Version 1, April 2011), para 5.2.
34   The NHS (Concerns, Complaints and Redress Arrangements) (Wales) Regulations 2011, reg 11.
35   The NHS (Concerns, Complaints and Redress Arrangements) (Wales) Regulations 2011, reg 11(2).
36   The NHS (Concerns, Complaints and Redress Arrangements) (Wales) Regulations 2011, reg 13.
37   The NHS (Concerns, Complaints and Redress Arrangements) (Wales) Regulations 2011, reg 14(1)(i) and Welsh Assembly Government, *Putting Things Right – Guidance on dealing with concerns about the NHS from 1 April 2011* (Version 1, April 2011), para 5.13.
38   The NHS (Concerns, Complaints and Redress Arrangements) (Wales) Regulations 2011, reg 14(1)(f).
39   The NHS (Concerns, Complaints and Redress Arrangements) (Wales) Regulations 2011, reg 14 (1)(f) and (g).
40   The NHS (Concerns, Complaints and Redress Arrangements) (Wales) Regulations 2011, reg 14(1)(h).
41   The NHS (Concerns, Complaints and Redress Arrangements) (Wales) Regulations 2011, reg 14(1)(j).
42   The Policy was published in September 2011.

There is no right to legal assistance funded by the Responsible Body at this stage. Some concerns may involve medically complex issues, and be difficult for a person with no legal or medical knowledge to articulate in writing. This may be compounded by the fact that patients and service users may not be provided with all the necessary information, relying on an ethos of openness, rather than being owed a duty of candour.

Time limits for notification of a concern to the Responsible Body

In order for the Regulations to apply, the Responsible Body must be notified of a concern no later than (i) 12 months after the date on which the concern occurred, or (ii) if later, 12 months after the date the person raising the concern realised they had a concern.[43] The Responsible Body has discretion to disapply the time limit if it is satisfied that (i) the person raising the concern had a good reason for not notifying the Responsible Body within the time limit, and (ii) it is still possible to investigate the concern effectively and fairly.[44] In the case of a patient that is being represented under reg 12(2)(d), it is the patient's date of knowledge, not the representative's date of knowledge that is relevant.[45]

There is a time limit longstop of three years. Therefore, a concern cannot be notified three or more years from the date the concern occurred; or three or more years from the date the person realised they had a concern.[46] A period of three years was chosen as it is consistent with the limitation period in clinical negligence claims.[47] However, there are no provisions within the Regulations to disapply the time limits for any reason, including the fact that the person raising the concern is a child, or lacks capacity under the Mental Capacity Act 2005.

Withdrawal of concerns

There is no obligation on the complainant/representative to continue with the investigation process and a concern that has been notified to the Responsible Body may be withdrawn at any time by the complainant/representative. The concern can be withdrawn in writing, electronically or verbally, either by telephone or in person.[48] If the concern is withdrawn verbally, the Responsible Body should write to that person as soon as practicable to confirm the decision.[49] Although a concern may be

---

43 The NHS (Concerns, Complaints and Redress Arrangements) (Wales) Regulations 2011, reg 15(1).
44 The NHS (Concerns, Complaints and Redress Arrangements) (Wales) Regulations 2011, reg 15(2).
45 The NHS (Concerns, Complaints and Redress Arrangements) (Wales) Regulations 2011, reg 15(4).
46 The NHS (Concerns, Complaints and Redress Arrangements) (Wales) Regulations 2011, reg 15(3).
47 Welsh Assembly Government, *Putting Things Right – Guidance on dealing with concerns about the NHS from 1 April 2011* (Version 1, April 2011), para 5.18.
48 The NHS (Concerns, Complaints and Redress Arrangements) (Wales) Regulations 2011, reg 16(1).
49 The NHS (Concerns, Complaints and Redress Arrangements) (Wales) Regulations 2011, reg 16(2).

withdrawn, the Responsible Body can continue to investigate the concern if the Responsible Body considers it necessary.[50]

Initial response by the Responsible Body: additional requirements for children, third party representatives, and staff

Where a child or young person raises a concern, the Responsible Body must provide reasonable support to the child/young person in order for him to pursue the concern.[51] Advocacy support can be arranged by Local Health Boards in accordance with the Welsh Assembly Government's *Model for Delivering Advocacy Services to Children and Young People in Wales*.[52] If the concern is raised on behalf of a child, the Responsible Body must satisfy itself that there are reasonable grounds for the concern being notified by a representative as opposed to the child.[53] If the Responsible Body is not satisfied, the concern must not be investigated, and the Responsible Body must notify the representative giving reasons for its decision.[54]

Where a concern is raised on behalf of a child, young person or person who lacks capacity within the meaning of the Mental Capacity Act 2005, the Responsible Body must consider whether the third party representative is a suitable representative, and is pursuing the concern in the best interests of that person.[55] In circumstances where a determination has been made that the representative is not suitable, the Responsible Body may continue with the investigation if it is satisfied that it is necessary to do so.[56] However, the Reasonable Body is not under an obligation to provide a detailed response to the representative, unless it is reasonable to do so.[57]

Members of staff of Responsible Bodies can raise concerns, including reporting errors in treatment/untoward events as a 'patient safety incident'. An immediate investigation of the circumstances will be carried out in order to determine the extent of the harm caused.[58] If the initial investigation reveals that the patient suffered moderate or severe harm (which is not defined in the Regulations or the Guidance[59]) or death, the

---

50   The NHS (Concerns, Complaints and Redress Arrangements) (Wales) Regulations 2011, reg 16(3).
51   The NHS (Concerns, Complaints and Redress Arrangements) (Wales) Regulations 2011, reg 12(4).
52   Welsh Assembly Government, *Putting Things Right – Guidance on dealing with concerns about the NHS from 1 April 2011* (Version 1, April 2011), paras 4.29 and 5.8.
53   The NHS (Concerns, Complaints and Redress Arrangements) (Wales) Regulations 2011, reg 12(3)(a).
54   The NHS (Concerns, Complaints and Redress Arrangements) (Wales) Regulations 2011, reg 12(3)(a), (b).
55   The NHS (Concerns, Complaints and Redress Arrangements) (Wales) Regulations 2011, reg 12(5).
56   The NHS (Concerns, Complaints and Redress Arrangements) (Wales) Regulations 2011, reg 12(5).
57   The NHS (Concerns, Complaints and Redress Arrangements) (Wales) Regulations 2011, reg 12(6).
58   Welsh Assembly Government, *Putting Things Right – Guidance on dealing with concerns about the NHS from 1 April 2011* (Version 1, April 2011), Appendix J, p 130.
59   The NHS (Concerns, Complaints and Redress Arrangements) (Wales) Regulations 2011, reg 2(1) states that 'moderate or severe harm determined in accordance with guidance issued for the purpose of these regulations by the Welsh Ministers'.

Responsible Body must inform the patient or his representative that a report has been made,[60] unless, in the opinion of the Responsible Body, it is not in the best interests of the patient.[61] The Guidance states that it would not be in the patient's best interests if 'involving them could cause a deterioration in their physical or mental health'.[62] Therefore, it seems that a patient or his representative will not be informed if the harm is judged to be relatively low; which does not accord with the *Being Open* principle. If the patient or his representative is told that a concern has been raised, the Responsible Body must involve the patient/representative in the investigation.[63]

Initial response by the Responsible Body: acknowledgement by the Responsible Body

The Responsible Body must acknowledge receipt of the notification of concerns, except for 'on the spot' concerns, and concerns involving primary care providers. The period for the Responsible Body to acknowledge receipt of a concern is limited, and must be made no later than two working days after the day on which the notification was received.[64] The acknowledgement must be in writing even if the notification was made verbally;[65] but if the notification was received electronically, it may be acknowledged electronically.[66] Appendix I to the Guidance sets out the templates for acknowledgment letters. The date that the Responsible Body receives the notification of the concern is important as it is the date from which the limitation for claims for negligence will be suspended.

As part of its acknowledgement, the Responsible Body must provide the complaint/representative with the name of the contact person who will be handling the concern, and details of how to contact that person.[67] The acknowledgment letter or electronic communication must include an offer for the complainant/representative to discuss the following issues by telephone or at a meeting:

- the manner in which the investigation will be handled, including consent to the use of medical records;
- the availability of advocacy and support services in relation to the concern –

---

60   The NHS (Concerns, Complaints and Redress Arrangements) (Wales) Regulations 2011, reg 12(7).
61   The NHS (Concerns, Complaints and Redress Arrangements) (Wales) Regulations 2011, reg 12(8).
62   Welsh Assembly Government, *Putting Things Right – Guidance on dealing with concerns about the NHS from 1 April 2011* (Version 1, April 2011), para 6.40.
63   The NHS (Concerns, Complaints and Redress Arrangements) (Wales) Regulations 2011, reg 12(7).
64   The NHS (Concerns, Complaints and Redress Arrangements) (Wales) Regulations 2011, reg 22(1).
65   The NHS (Concerns, Complaints and Redress Arrangements) (Wales) Regulations 2011, reg 22(3).
66   The NHS (Concerns, Complaints and Redress Arrangements) (Wales) Regulations 2011, reg 22(2).
67   Welsh Assembly Government, *Putting Things Right – Guidance on dealing with concerns about the NHS from 1 April 2011* (Version 1, April 2011), para 6.24.

> – Advocacy services may be provided by the Community Health Council to anyone over 18 years of age; and for children or young people, advocacy services can be arranged by Local Health Boards in accordance with the Welsh Assembly Governments' *Model for Delivering Advocacy Services to Children and Young People in Wales.*[68]
- how long the investigation is likely to take and when a response can be expected;
- any specific needs that the representative may have which should be taken into account as the investigation proceeds; and
- what the complainant/representative expects as an outcome.[69]

The complainant/representative should be given the opportunity to bring a friend, relative or an advocate to the meeting.[70] If the concern is resolved at the meeting, no further investigation is required. The Responsible Body must write to the complainant/representative after the meeting including a full written response based on the discussions and confirmation that the concern has been resolved.[71] If the offer of a discussion is refused by the complainant/representative, the Responsible Body must determine how to manage the concern and inform the complainant/representative about the proposed action plan, including details about the availability of advocacy and support services.[72]

If a concern has been raised about a primary care provider (by a complainant/representative directly or by the primary care provider forwarding on a concern) to a Local Health Board, the Local Health Board must consider whether it or the primary care provider is in the best position to investigate.[73] Once the Local Health Board has decided that it will conduct the investigation, it will send an acknowledgement letter.[74] If the Local Health Board decides that it is more appropriate for the primary care provider to investigate, it will inform the complainant/representative and the primary care provider.[75]

If it is apparent to the Responsible Body when they receive a concern that the patient has entered into a conditional fee agreement or insurance premium, the Guidance indicates that they must liaise with the Welsh Legal Services for support.[76]

---

68 Welsh Assembly Government, *Putting Things Right – Guidance on dealing with concerns about the NHS from 1 April 2011* (Version 1, April 2011), paras 4.29–4.30.
69 The NHS (Concerns, Complaints and Redress Arrangements) (Wales) Regulations 2011, reg 22(4); and Welsh Assembly Government, *Putting Things Right – Guidance on dealing with concerns about the NHS from 1 April 2011* (Version 1, April 2011), para 6.24.
70 Welsh Assembly Government, *Putting Things Right – Guidance on dealing with concerns about the NHS from 1 April 2011* (Version 1, April 2011), para 6.26.
71 Welsh Assembly Government, *Putting Things Right – Guidance on dealing with concerns about the NHS from 1 April 2011* (Version 1, April 2011), para 6.28.
72 The NHS (Concerns, Complaints and Redress Arrangements) (Wales) Regulations 2011, reg 22(4).
73 The NHS (Concerns, Complaints and Redress Arrangements) (Wales) Regulations 2011, regs 19(1) and 20(1).
74 The NHS (Concerns, Complaints and Redress Arrangements) (Wales) Regulations 2011, reg 22(1).
75 The NHS (Concerns, Complaints and Redress Arrangements) (Wales) Regulations 2011, reg 21(2).
76 Welsh Assembly Government, *Putting Things Right – Guidance on dealing with concerns about the NHS from 1 April 2011* (Version 1, April 2011), para 12.3.

Part 5 of the Regulations: Investigation of concern

Obtaining medical records and consent

In most cases, medical records will be required in order for the concern to be investigated; and Appendix J to the Guidance sets out information about the circumstances in which consent is required. Where a patient raises a concern, he is deemed to have given implied consent to the investigation.[77] This principle applies if a concern is raised by a representative who proves that they are legally entitled to act for the patient/service user.[78] However, the patient/representative may refuse access to their records. If the Responsible Body judges that the concern is of not of sufficient seriousness to merit an investigation without access to the medical records, the concern will not be investigated.[79] The Data Protection Act 1998 is likely to apply in patient safety incidents allowing personal data to be processed without consent. However, the Caldicott Principles will apply; and only information relevant to the investigation of the concern should be accessed by those who have a demonstrable need to have access.[80]

Grading the concern

Once the medical records/other records have been obtained, the concern will be graded by the Responsible Body in terms of severity.[81] This will determine the level and scope of the investigation[82] as all investigations are required to be proportionate to the severity of the concern.[83] In addition, grading determines the number and knowledge/competency of the investigators.[84] The aim of the grading framework is to promote a consistent approach across NHS Wales. Appendix K of the Guidance sets out five grades of concern. It is a framework based on a risk matrix developed by the Patient Safety Agency used to assess and manage risks and incidents.[85]

- *Grade 1* where the potential for qualifying liability and redress is 'highly unlikely'. Examples include delay in an outpatient appointment with no adverse health consequences; and difficulty in parking nearby.

77 Welsh Assembly Government, *Putting Things Right – Guidance on dealing with concerns about the NHS from 1 April 2011* (Version 1, April 2011), para 6.35.
78 Welsh Assembly Government, *Putting Things Right – Guidance on dealing with concerns about the NHS from 1 April 2011* (Version 1, April 2011), para 6.35.
79 Welsh Assembly Government, *Putting Things Right – Guidance on dealing with concerns about the NHS from 1 April 2011* (Version 1, April 2011), para 6.37.
80 Welsh Assembly Government, *Putting Things Right – Guidance on dealing with concerns about the NHS from 1 April 2011* (Version 1, April 2011), para 6.41.
81 Welsh Assembly Government, *Putting Things Right – Guidance on dealing with concerns about the NHS from 1 April 2011* (Version 1, April 2011), para 6.48.
82 Welsh Assembly Government, *Putting Things Right – Guidance on dealing with concerns about the NHS from 1 April 2011* (Version 1, April 2011), para 6.48.
83 Welsh Assembly Government, *Putting Things Right – Guidance on dealing with concerns about the NHS from 1 April 2011* (Version 1, April 2011), para 6.48.
84 Welsh Assembly Government, *Putting Things Right – Guidance on dealing with concerns about the NHS from 1 April 2011* (Version 1, April 2011), paras 6.49 – 6.50.
85 Welsh Assembly Government, *Putting Things Right – Guidance on dealing with concerns about the NHS from 1 April 2011* (Version 1, April 2011), Appendix K.

- *Grade 2* where the potential to qualifying liability/redress is 'unlikely'. Examples include concerns regarding care and treatment which span a number of different aspects/specialities; a patient fall requiring treatment; concerns involving a single failure to meet internal standards with minor implications for patient safety and requiring time off work of three days.
- *Grade 3* where the potential for qualifying liability/redress is 'possible in some cases'. Examples include clinical/process issues that have resulted in avoidable, semi-permanent injury or impairment of health or damage that requires intervention; a RIDDOR reportable incident; moderate patient safety implications and requiring time off work for four to 14 days.
- *Grade 4* where the potential for qualifying liability/redress is 'likely in many cases'. Examples include clinical/process issues that have resulted in avoidable, semi-permanent injury or impairment of health or damage leading to incapacity or disability; concerns outlining non-compliance with national standards with significant risk to patient safety; a RIDDOR reportable incident and requiring time off work of more than 14 days.
- *Grade 5* where the potential for qualifying liability and redress is 'very likely'. Examples include concerns leading to unexpected death, multiple harm or irreversible health effects; concerns outlining gross failure to meet national standards; and clinical/process issues that have resulted in avoidable, irrecoverable injury or impairment of health, having a lifelong adverse effect on lifestyle, quality of life, physical and mental wellbeing.[86]

The grading system can be found online.[87]

Investigation

Regulation 23 is the key provision in terms of investigating a concern. The Regulations provide that concerns must be investigated in the most appropriate, efficient and effective way.[88] Regulation 23 includes a list of matters that Responsible Bodies must have regard during the investigation. The issues include the involvement of the complainant/representative in the investigation; whether independent or other advice is required; and whether the concern can be resolved by ADR. Where the Responsible Body is a Welsh NHS body (but not primary care providers or independent providers) and the concern includes an allegation of harm that has or may have been caused, the Welsh NHS body is under a duty to consider whether there is any qualifying liability in negligence.

Appendix R of the Guidance sets out an 'investigation checklist' for the investigator to follow; including an instruction to copy only records that are relevant to the concern; identifying the healthcare professionals who provided the care and/or treatment; and considering

---

86 Welsh Assembly Government, *Putting Things Right – Guidance on dealing with concerns about the NHS from 1 April 2011* (Version 1, April 2011), pp 131–132.
87 www.nrls.npsa.nhs.uk/resources/?entryid45=59833&q=0%c2%acrisk%c2%ac&p=1.
88 The NHS (Concerns, Complaints and Redress Arrangements) (Wales) Regulations 2011, reg 23(1).

whether there is any merit in obtaining a report on breach of duty and/
or causation and prognosis. The investigators are encouraged to use
various tools such as chronologies; the 'Five Whys'; Root Cause Analysis
and other investigation tools provide by the National Patient Safety
Agency website[89] to investigate the concern, and to fulfil the intention
to 'investigate once, investigate well'.[90] Responsible Bodies must also
consider whether the concern raises issues requiring a referral to other
bodies, including the Welsh Assembly Government (serious incidents);
professional bodies, such as the General Medical Council or Nursing and
Midwifery Council; the Healthcare Inspectorate Wales; the Health and
Safety Executive (RIDDOR); the Medicines Healthcare and Regulatory
Agency; the Information Commissioners Office; the Police; the Coroner;
and the Local Children's Safeguarding Board.[91]

Independent expert advice

Investigators will be able to obtain independent medical or other advice.[92]
At the investigation stage, that advice is limited to:

(a) obtaining a second opinion to aid a patient's understanding of their
own care, or to identify any other issues that should be explored in
terms of the provision of care and treatment; or
(b) where an allegation of harm has been made, and where a Welsh
NHS body is unable to determine if there is a qualifying liability in
negligence, an advice dealing with breach of duty and/or causation.[93]

By this stage, patients and service users are still not entitled to legal
advice paid for by the Responsible Body, or to jointly instruct an expert.
A suggestion raised in the consultation was that legal advice should be
available to the complainant/representative at an early stage. However, the
Welsh Assembly Government replied that this would be disproportionate
and increase costs. Independent medical experts can only be commissioned
from a database held by the Welsh Health Legal Services (redress@wales.
nhs.uk).[94] The Guidance includes general terms and conditions that are
applicable to all independent expert advisors (Appendix L of the Guidance),
although additional terms and conditions may be agreed.[95]

Duty to consider whether there might be any qualifying liability in tort

Where a concern includes an allegation of harm that has or may have
been caused, a Welsh NHS body is under a duty to consider the likelihood

89   www.nrls.npsa.nhs.uk/resources.
90   Welsh Assembly Government, *Putting Things Right – Guidance on dealing with
concerns about the NHS from 1 April 2011* (Version 1, April 2011), paras 6.50–6.51.
91   Welsh Assembly Government, *Putting Things Right – Guidance on dealing with
concerns about the NHS from 1 April 2011* (Version 1, April 2011), para 6.68.
92   The NHS (Concerns, Complaints and Redress Arrangements) (Wales) Regulations
2011, reg 23(1)(e).
93   Welsh Assembly Government, *Putting Things Right – Guidance on dealing with
concerns about the NHS from 1 April 2011* (Version 1, April 2011), para 6.56.
94   Welsh Assembly Government, *Putting Things Right – Guidance on dealing with
concerns about the NHS from 1 April 2011* (Version 1, April 2011), para 7.27.
95   Welsh Assembly Government, *Putting Things Right – Guidance on dealing with
concerns about the NHS from 1 April 2011* (Version 1, April 2011), Appendix L.

of any qualifying liability in negligence,[96] and may obtain expert evidence on breach of duty and causation to assist in this determination. This requirement does not apply to primary care providers or independent providers. The threshold to considering liability is that harm has or may have been caused. It is a low threshold; there is no requirement that no harm was probably caused. The Regulations and Guidance do not provide any definition of 'harm'.

'Qualifying liability' is defined as:

> liability in tort owed in respect of, or consequent upon, personal injury or loss arising out of or in connection with breach of a duty of care owed to any person in connection with the diagnosis of illness, or in the care or treatment of any patient:
> (a)   in consequence of any act or omission by a healthcare professional; and
> (b)   which arises in connection with the provision of qualifying services.[97]

Therefore, qualifying liability is the traditional fault-based system which was criticised in the consultation phase.[98]

In cases where the Welsh NHS body determines that there is no qualifying liability, it must respond to the complainant/representative denying any liability and provide reasons for that decision.[99] In addition, it must provide a Final Response under reg 24.[100]

In cases where there is qualifying liability, but damages exceed the current financial limit of £25,000 under the Regulations, the Welsh NHS body must issue a Final Response under reg 24, explaining that the quantum of any potential claim exceeds the financial threshold under the Regulations and so the redress arrangements do not apply.[101] However, an offer of settlement can be made outside the Regulations.[102] An offer made outside the Regulations must be approached with some caution, as the provisions for paid legal and medical advice do not apply. The Guidelines address this issue as follows:

> Welsh NHS bodies might at this stage, and in the spirit of the Regulations, consider offering to pay the patient's legal costs associated with obtaining advice on any such out of court settlement. However, there is no obligation for them to do so.[103]

In cases where a qualifying liability exists or may exist, and the concern requires further consideration, the Welsh NHS body must issue an

---

96   The NHS (Concerns, Complaints and Redress Arrangements) (Wales) Regulations 2011, reg 23(1)(i).
97   The NHS (Concerns, Complaints and Redress Arrangements) (Wales) Regulations 2011, reg 2(1).
98   AvMA (Response to Welsh Assembly Consultation on Proposed NHS Redress (Wales) Measure September 2007). AvMA proposed an 'Avoidability Test' as opposed to a fault or no-fault based system to determine eligibly for redress.
99   The NHS (Concerns, Complaints and Redress Arrangements) (Wales) Regulations 2011, reg 24(2).
100 The NHS (Concerns, Complaints and Redress Arrangements) (Wales) Regulations 2011, reg 24(1).
101 The NHS (Concerns, Complaints and Redress Arrangements) (Wales) Regulations 2011, reg 24(1).
102 The NHS (Concerns, Complaints and Redress Arrangements) (Wales) Regulations 2011, reg 29(3).
103 Welsh Assembly Government, *Putting Things Right – Guidance on dealing with concerns about the NHS from 1 April 2011* (Version 1, April 2011), para 7.31.

Interim Response under reg 26, and is under a duty to consider redress.[104] Where a qualifying liability exists or may exist and the complainant is seeking redress, he is entitled to legal advice.[105] The legal advice must be obtained from firms of solicitors with recognised expertise in clinical negligence, for example, a partner or employee who is a member of the Law Society Clinical Negligence Panel or the AvMA Panel.[106] The legal advice is funded by the Welsh NHS Trust[107] and may be obtained in relation to the joint instruction of medical experts, including clarification of issues arising in their reports; an offer of redress; the refusal to make an offer of redress; and any settlement agreement that is proposed.[108] Appendix Q of the Guidance provides the legal fees framework, and includes capped hourly rates and fixed fees. Any experts instructed at this stage must be instructed as a joint expert by the complainant/representative and the Welsh NHS Trust.[109] Expert evidence can be obtained on breach of duty, causation, condition and prognosis and/or quantum.[110]

Response from the Responsible Body to the complainant / representative

There are two written reports that can be made in response to a concern: an Interim Response issued under reg 26, which only applies to concerns raised against a Welsh NHS Bodies where there is, or may be, a qualifying liability in tort; and a Final Response, issued under reg 24.

An Interim Response report is issued where a Welsh NHS body considers that there is or may be qualifying liability in tort and the financial compensation would be at or below the current limit of £25,000. The timeframe for issuing an Interim Response report is similar to the timeframe for a final report. An Interim Response report should be issued within 30 working days beginning on the day on which the concern was received.[111] If the Welsh NHS body cannot reply within this timeframe, it must notify the complainant/representative, providing reasons for the delay. It must send the response as soon as reasonably practicable, and within six months beginning on the day on which the concern was received.[112] In exceptional circumstances, the written response report can be issued after six months. However, the complainant/representative must be informed about the reason for the delay and given an expected

---

104 The NHS (Concerns, Complaints and Redress Arrangements) (Wales) Regulations 2011, reg 25(1).
105 The NHS (Concerns, Complaints and Redress Arrangements) (Wales) Regulations 2011, reg 32(1).
106 The NHS (Concerns, Complaints and Redress Arrangements) (Wales) Regulations 2011, reg 32(2).
107 The NHS (Concerns, Complaints and Redress Arrangements) (Wales) Regulations 2011, reg 32(4).
108 The NHS (Concerns, Complaints and Redress Arrangements) (Wales) Regulations 2011, reg 32(3)(a)–(d).
109 The NHS (Concerns, Complaints and Redress Arrangements) (Wales) Regulations 2011, reg 32(1)(b)
110 Welsh Assembly Government, *Putting Things Right – Guidance on dealing with concerns about the NHS from 1 April 2011* (Version 1, April 2011), para 6.56.
111 The NHS (Concerns, Complaints and Redress Arrangements) (Wales) Regulations 2011, reg 26(2).
112 The NHS (Concerns, Complaints and Redress Arrangements) (Wales) Regulations 2011, reg 26(3).

date for the report.[113] Appendix P of the Guidance includes an Interim Report template.[114]

The Interim Response report must include a summary of the nature and substance of the concern; explain the investigation, include relevant medical records (if appropriate), the reasons that there is or might be qualifying liability, an explanation of how to access legal advice without charge, the availability of advocacy and support services, the process for considering liability and redress, and offer to discuss the response to the concerns with the executive officer or his nominated representative.[115] Appendix P of the Guidance includes an Interim Report template.[116]

A Final Response report is issued by all Responsible Bodies, but in the case of Welsh NHS Bodies, a final response will only be issued if there is no qualifying liability in tort to which the redress arrangements could apply. The timeframe is limited, and a Final Response report should be issued within 30 working days, beginning on the day on which the concern was received.[117] If the Responsible Body cannot reply within this timeframe, it must notify the complainant/representative, providing reasons for the delay. It must send the response as soon as reasonably practicable, and within six months beginning on the day in which the concern was received.[118] In exceptional circumstances, the written response report can be issued after six months. However, the complainant/representative must be informed about the reason for the delay and given an expected date for the report.[119] The Final Response report is provided to the complainant/representative, except where the concern was raised by a third party, but only if it is reasonable to do so.[120] When the issue is a patient safety incident that was reported by a member of staff and the patient was not informed, a final written response must be sent to the appropriate committee.[121]

The Final Response report must include a summary of the nature and substance of the concern; explain the investigation; include relevant medical records (if appropriate); identify any actions taken as a result of the investigation; include an apology (if appropriate); and an offer to discuss the response to the concerns with the executive officer or his nominated representative.[122] The report must contain copies of any

---

113 The NHS (Concerns, Complaints and Redress Arrangements) (Wales) Regulations 2011, reg 26(4).
114 Welsh Assembly Government, *Putting Things Right – Guidance on dealing with concerns about the NHS from 1 April 2011* (Version 1, April 2011), page 143
115 The NHS (Concerns, Complaints and Redress Arrangements) (Wales) Regulations 2011, reg 26(1).
116 Welsh Assembly Government, *Putting Things Right – Guidance on dealing with concerns about the NHS from 1 April 2011* (Version 1, April 2011), p 143.
117 The NHS (Concerns, Complaints and Redress Arrangements) (Wales) Regulations 2011, reg 24(3).
118 The NHS (Concerns, Complaints and Redress Arrangements) (Wales) Regulations 2011, reg 24(4).
119 The NHS (Concerns, Complaints and Redress Arrangements) (Wales) Regulations 2011, reg 24(5).
120 Welsh Assembly Government, *Putting Things Right – Guidance on dealing with concerns about the NHS from 1 April 2011* (Version 1, April 2011), para 5.7.
121 Welsh Assembly Government, *Putting Things Right – Guidance on dealing with concerns about the NHS from 1 April 2011* (Version 1, April 2011), para 6.77.
122 The NHS (Concerns, Complaints and Redress Arrangements) (Wales) Regulations 2011, reg 24(1).

expert opinion obtained as part of the investigation;[123] and where there is no qualifying liability, a Welsh NHS body must give its reasons for reaching that conclusion.[124] Appendix O of the Guidance includes a Final Response report template.[125]

Part 6 of the Regulations: Redress

If there is or may be a qualifying liability against a Welsh NHS body, it is under a duty to consider redress.[126] An offer of redress may be made by a Welsh NHS body where there is a qualifying liability in accordance with the Regulations.[127] Redress under the Regulations is wider than financial compensation, and reg 27 provides:

(1)   Redress under this Part comprises—
    (a)   the making of an offer of compensation in satisfaction of any right to bring civil proceedings in respect of a qualifying liability;
    (b)   the giving of an explanation;
    (c)   the making of a written apology; and
    (d)   the giving of a report on the action which has been, or will be, taken to prevent similar cases arising.
(2)   The compensation that may be offered in accordance with regulation 27(1) (a) can take the form of entry into a contract to provide care or treatment or of financial compensation, or both.

There are no further details about a 'contract to provide care or treatment' in the Regulations or Guidance. Therefore the parameters are not known. For example, would it be limited to a short-term care after an operation; or does it include long-term care?

The full Investigation Report

Where a complainant/representative is seeking redress, the findings of the investigation must be recorded in an Investigation Report.[128] Following the Interim Response report, the complainant/representative seeking redress will be provided with a copy of the full Investigation Report, which will include a copy of any medical evidence commissioned to determine liability and/or condition and prognosis, and a reasoned decision by the Welsh NHS body on qualifying liability.[129] However, the full Investigation Report need not be provided before an offer of redress; before a decision not to make an offer of redress is communicated; if the investigation of

---

123 The NHS (Concerns, Complaints and Redress Arrangements) (Wales) Regulations 2011, reg 24(1)(c).
124 The NHS (Concerns, Complaints and Redress Arrangements) (Wales) Regulations 2011, reg 24(2).
125 Welsh Assembly Government, *Putting Things Right – Guidance on dealing with concerns about the NHS from 1 April 2011* (Version 1, April 2011), p 142.
126 The NHS (Concerns, Complaints and Redress Arrangements) (Wales) Regulations 2011, reg 25(1).
127 The NHS (Concerns, Complaints and Redress Arrangements) (Wales) Regulations 2011, reg 25(2).
128 The NHS (Concerns, Complaints and Redress Arrangements) (Wales) Regulations 2011, reg 31(1).
129 The NHS (Concerns, Complaints and Redress Arrangements) (Wales) Regulations 2011, reg 31(1), (2).

redress is terminated; or where the report contains information likely to cause the complainant significant harm or distress.[130]

Communication of a decision about redress

On the conclusion of the investigation, the Welsh NHS body must communicate its decision to either offer redress by way of compensation, care and/or treatment, or, if there is no qualifying liability, its decision not to make an offer.[131] The decision must be communicated to the complainant within 12 months of the date that the Welsh NHS body was notified of the concern.[132] In exceptional circumstances, where the Welsh NHS body is unable to make a decision within 12 months, the complainant/representative should be told in writing the reason for the delay and the expected date for the decision.[133]

The complainant/representative has six months to respond to the decision.[134] However, if the complainant/representative cannot respond within six months, they must write to the Welsh NHS body providing a reason for the delay. The time limit for response can be extended to nine months from the date of the offer/decision.[135] However, if no response is received the limitation period (which is suspended under reg 30) will start again.[136] When an offer of redress is accepted, the complaint/representative must sign a waiver of any right to bring civil proceedings in respect of the qualifying liability to which the settlement relates.[137]

The quantification of damages for redress

The financial limit of £25,000 includes both general and special damages.[138] The assessment of general damages for pain, suffering, and loss of amenity will be calculated on a common law basis,[139] and will be made in accordance with the tariff included at Appendix T of the Guidance.[140] The

---

130 The NHS (Concerns, Complaints and Redress Arrangements) (Wales) Regulations 2011, reg 31(4).

131 The NHS (Concerns, Complaints and Redress Arrangements) (Wales) Regulations 2011, reg 33.

132 The NHS (Concerns, Complaints and Redress Arrangements) (Wales) Regulations 2011, reg 33(a).

133 The NHS (Concerns, Complaints and Redress Arrangements) (Wales) Regulations 2011, reg 33(b).

134 The NHS (Concerns, Complaints and Redress Arrangements) (Wales) Regulations 2011, reg 33(b).

135 The NHS (Concerns, Complaints and Redress Arrangements) (Wales) Regulations 2011, reg 33(d)

136 The NHS (Concerns, Complaints and Redress Arrangements) (Wales) Regulations 2011, reg 30(3), (5).

137 The NHS (Concerns, Complaints and Redress Arrangements) (Wales) Regulations 2011, reg 33(e).

138 The NHS (Concerns, Complaints and Redress Arrangements) (Wales) Regulations 2011, Explanatory note; and Welsh Assembly Government, *Putting Things Right – Guidance on dealing with concerns about the NHS from 1 April 2011* (Version 1, April 2011), para 7.22.

139 The NHS (Concerns, Complaints and Redress Arrangements) (Wales) Regulations 2011, reg 29(1), (4).

140 The NHS (Concerns, Complaints and Redress Arrangements) (Wales) Regulations 2011, reg 29(1), (5).

stated aim is that this approach will lead to appropriate and consistent awards,[141] although it is accepted that individual factors will increase or decrease the awards.[142] Some tariff awards refer to the Joint Studies Board Guidelines and/or the criteria selected for the brackets is the same or similar. However, a comparison of the awards under the JSB Guides and the All-Wales Tariff indicates that on occasions the All-Wales tariff awards are lower.[143]

The tariff also includes summaries of case law reports for some injuries, and the Guidance makes it clear that offers may be made above or below the case law examples.[144] The reported quantum cases include out of court settlements, which may be lower than court awards. The awards have been calculated to take account of inflation. The Guidance states that the awards will need to be updated to take account of inflationary increases,[145] but this has been done before publication of the Guidance in April 2011, and therefore does not represent the up–to-date value of the awards at the date of publication.

Any claim for loss of earnings must be supported with evidence, such as wage slips, P60, etc.[146] A deduction will be made from the loss of earnings award for any relevant recoupable state benefits.[147] There is no mention of a claim for gratuitous care and assistance, but in principle, there is no reason why this cannot be included. However, there is no mention in the Guidance for offsetting any relevant benefits in relation to gratuitous care and assistance.

141 Welsh Assembly Government, *Putting Things Right – Guidance on dealing with concerns about the NHS from 1 April 2011* (Version 1, April 2011), para 7.32.
142 Welsh Assembly Government, *Putting Things Right – Guidance on dealing with concerns about the NHS from 1 April 2011* (Version 1, April 2011), page 152.
143 For example:

JSB Guidelines (10th edition)		*All-Wales Tariff*	
Serious injury to ring or middle finger (fractures or serious injury to tendons casing stiffness, deformity and permanent loss of grip or dexterity):	£9,750–£10,750	Fracture or serious injuries to tendons causing stiffness, deformity, and permanent loss of gip or dexterity of ring or middle fingers. Total loss of middle finger with be at top of bracket:	£8.000–£9,000
Total loss of the middle finger:	In the region of £10,250		

144 Welsh Assembly Government, *Putting Things Right – Guidance on dealing with concerns about the NHS from 1 April 2011* (Version 1, April 2011), page 152.
145 Welsh Assembly Government, *Putting Things Right – Guidance on dealing with concerns about the NHS from 1 April 2011* (Version 1, April 2011), page 152.
146 Welsh Assembly Government, *Putting Things Right – Guidance on dealing with concerns about the NHS from 1 April 2011* (Version 1, April 2011), para 7.23.
147 Welsh Assembly Government, *Putting Things Right – Guidance on dealing with concerns about the NHS from 1 April 2011* (Version 1, April 2011), para 7.21.

Court approval of settlement

Where the settlement agreement has been made on behalf of a child or a person who lacks capacity, the approval of the court will be required.[148] The Welsh NHS body must pay the reasonable legal costs of obtaining the approval of the court.[149]

Limitation

If an application for redress is made, the relevant limitation period under the Limitation Act 1980 for bringing a civil claim is suspended.[150] The start date is that date on which the initial concern which became an application for redress was received by the Welsh NHS body.[151] The date that the limitation period restarts is as follows:

* Where the Welsh NHS Trust considers after an investigation that there is no qualifying liability, the complainant/representative has nine months from the date that the Welsh NHS body communicated its decision.[152] The intention is that the complainant and/or his legal adviser will have time to prepare and issue civil proceedings if they do not agree with the decision of the Welsh NHS body.[153]
* Where an offer of redress is made, the complaint/representative has up to nine months to accept/reject an offer of financial compensation. After that nine months, limitation restarts.[154]
* Where court approval of a settlement is required, limitation is suspended until the date upon which the court approves the settlement.[155]

Cross border arrangements of the handling and investigation concerns including redress

The Regulations provide cross border arrangements for concerns about treatment and care provided on behalf of the NHS in Wales by organisations outside Wales. The concern should be handled in accordance with the relevant complaints procedure that applies to the organisation in question. If, during the investigation, a qualifying liability in tort exists or may exist, then the redress provisions in Pt 7 of the Regulations may apply. These Regulations do not come into effect until 1 April 2012, and

---

148 The NHS (Concerns, Complaints and Redress Arrangements) (Wales) Regulations 2011, reg 33(f).
149 The NHS (Concerns, Complaints and Redress Arrangements) (Wales) Regulations 2011, reg 33(g).
150 The NHS (Concerns, Complaints and Redress Arrangements) (Wales) Regulations 2011, reg 30(1).
151 The NHS (Concerns, Complaints and Redress Arrangements) (Wales) Regulations 2011, reg 30(2)(a).
152 The NHS (Concerns, Complaints and Redress Arrangements) (Wales) Regulations 2011, reg 30(5).
153 Welsh Assembly Government, *Putting Things Right – Guidance on dealing with concerns about the NHS from 1 April 2011* (Version 1, April 2011), para 7.14.
154 The NHS (Concerns, Complaints and Redress Arrangements) (Wales) Regulations 2011, reg 30(3).
155 The NHS (Concerns, Complaints and Redress Arrangements) (Wales) Regulations 2011, reg 30(4).

the Welsh Assembly Government has indicated that separate Guidance will be made available. In the meantime, Welsh NHS Bodies are unable to consider redress for care and treatment provided on behalf of Welsh NHS Bodies by NHS organisations in England, Scotland or Northern Ireland.

THE WELSH PILOT SPEEDY RESOLUTION SCHEME

The Speedy Resolution Scheme (the 'Scheme') is the second alternative route for claimants to bring low value clinical negligence claims in Wales. The rules of the Scheme can be found online.[156] It is a fast-track scheme designed to deal with straightforward cases against NHS Trusts in Wales, where the claim is valued between £5,000 and £15,000.

Background to the Scheme

In February 2001, the Auditor General for Wales published a report entitled *Clinical Negligence in the NHS in Wales*. The report highlighted that the management of clinical negligence claims was an expensive, lengthy, and complex process and that there was scope for improvement. The report also recognised that the best way of reducing costs was to reduce the number of incidents of clinical negligence. Therefore, learning from adverse incidents was essential.

Concerns were also raised about the ability of the Welsh Health Pool, a mutual organisation funded by all Welsh Trusts and Local Health Boards, to finance the ever increasing costs and the delays in clinical negligence claims. This resulted in a request to the National Assembly for Wales' Counsel General to consider alternative dispute resolution as a mechanism for reducing costs. Consequently, two pilot projects were established. One provided a fast-track dispute resolution scheme for low value claims – the Speedy Resolution Scheme. The second was a mediation scheme for higher value claims, although this project has not yet been followed through.

The objectives of the Scheme are set out in a Statement of Principles within the Rules. These are:

1   to provide a structured procedure for the quick, inexpensive, proportionate, and fair resolution of straightforward low value clinical claims against Welsh NHS Trusts (claims against GPs, dentists, pharmacists and opticians, and claims for private treatment are excluded from the Scheme);[157]

2   to encourage Welsh NHS Trusts to apologise where treatment is substandard;

3   to encourage Welsh NHS Trusts to provide explanations to claimants for their current medical condition, even where treatment was not substandard; and

4   to encourage Welsh NHS Trusts to learn from any mistakes and reduce the number of claims by preparing Action Plans.

---

156 www.wales.nhs.uk/sites3/page.cfm?orgid=255&pid=41525.
157 Welsh Health Legal Services, Speedy Resolution Scheme, r 4.

The key features are:

- a set timetable leading to a conclusion of the claim within 61 weeks of admission to the Scheme;
- the joint instruction of medical experts in relation to liability, condition and prognosis;
- the joint instruction of counsel in relation to quantum; and
- fixed fees for solicitors, medical experts, and counsel.

Evaluation of the Speedy Resolution Scheme

In 2008, an evaluation of the Scheme took place. The report is entitled *The Speedy Resolution Scheme: Evaluation for the Welsh Assembly Government's Pilot Scheme for Resolving Low Value Clinical Negligence Claims against NHS Trusts in Wales*. The views of the Welsh Health Legal Services, claims managers, claimants' solicitors, and medical experts were sampled. The views of claimants were not considered, due to confidentiality issues.

The evaluation was encouraging. The researchers concluded that the Scheme was viewed positively by all involved, including claimants; that it was 'fit for purpose', and fulfilled its primary objective. Specifically, the researchers concluded that the Scheme delivered enhanced access to justice for claimants, particularly for those who were not eligible for public funding, or were reluctant to litigate as a result of the unpredictable and potentially expensive costs of litigation. There were difficulties in adhering to the strict timescales, although the objective of resolving claims within 61 weeks was met in 90% of claims. On average, the amount of compensation and the costs incurred in individual claims was less than non-Scheme claims, although clearly a direct comparison between cases is not possible.

Concerns were raised about the level of the fixed fees, particularly for medical reports. This has limited the number of experts willing to provide medical evidence under the Scheme, resulting in delay in obtaining medical reports. Although Welsh NHS Trusts prepared action plans, the researchers concluded that the process of learning from mistakes needed to be enhanced. Overall, no substantive operational recommendations were made. Minor recommendations included consideration by the Welsh Assembly Government to increasing the upper limit of admission to the Scheme (the upper limit was considered arbitrary), making provision for claimants to give feedback, and the development and implementation of procedures by Welsh NHS Trusts to ensure that the claimant is advised of the content of any Action Plan.

Rules of the Scheme

Eligibility criteria

Access to the Scheme is controlled by the eligibility criteria set out in Rules 2–7. The Scheme is only available for so called 'straightforward' claims for clinical negligence against NHS Trusts in Wales.[158] To qualify as a straightforward claim, the claim must:

---

158 Welsh Health Legal Services, Speedy Resolution Scheme, r 4.

(a)   involve medical issues that are capable of resolution by a maximum of two medical experts from different medical specialisms;

(b   involve a single defendant;

(c)   not involve any issue as to limitation; and

(d)   be pre-proceedings.[159]

The claimant must be an adult of full capacity,[160] and represented by a solicitor who is a member of the Law Society Clinical Negligence Panel or the AvMA Panel, or working under the direct supervision of a Panel member.[161] The value of the claim should be between £5,000 and £15,000 and the parties must agree this in writing.[162] However, if a claim has already been admitted to the Scheme and it transpires that the value is lower than £5,000 or higher than £15,000, the claim may continue to be considered within the Scheme, but only if the participants agree in writing.[163] The Welsh NHS Trusts are represented by the Welsh Health Legal Services. The Welsh Health Legal Services participates in the Scheme and may enter into a settlement agreement on behalf of the relevant Welsh NHS Trust as its agent.

Time limits

The procedural time limits within the Scheme are relatively narrow, reflecting the objective of the Scheme to provide speedy resolution. However, the participants may agree to extend or reduce any time limits set out in the Rules, provided they take all reasonable steps to ensure that the process is completed no later than 61 weeks from the start date.[164] All agreements to extend or reduce time limits must be in writing.[165]

Notices and communications

All communications and notices under the Rules must be by first class pre-paid mail (recorded delivery, registered post or airmail), DX, or email.[166] Communications must be addressed to the recipient at his last known address and will be deemed to be communicated upon the date of actual delivery.[167]

Procedure for admission to the Scheme

Entry to the Scheme is by consent of the participants. However, the application is initiated by the claimant's solicitor making a written request to the Welsh Health Legal Services,[168] and Annex II to the Rules provides the standard document that must be used. The solicitor must

---

159 Welsh Health Legal Services, Speedy Resolution Scheme, r 2.
160 Welsh Health Legal Services, Speedy Resolution Scheme, r 5.
161 Welsh Health Legal Services, Speedy Resolution Scheme, r 3.
162 Welsh Health Legal Services, Speedy Resolution Scheme, r 6.
163 Welsh Health Legal Services, Speedy Resolution Scheme, r 7.
164 Welsh Health Legal Services, Speedy Resolution Scheme, r 41.
165 Welsh Health Legal Services, Speedy Resolution Scheme, r 41.
166 Welsh Health Legal Services, Speedy Resolution Scheme, r 60.
167 Welsh Health Legal Services, Speedy Resolution Scheme, r 60.
168 Welsh Health Legal Services, Speedy Resolution Scheme, r 8.

provide reasons that the claim is appropriate for admission into the Scheme, and certify that the claim falls within the financial threshold.[169]

The Welsh Health Legal Services must reply with its decision about admission to the Scheme within two weeks.[170] If admission is refused, the Welsh Health Legal Services must set out the reasons for its decision.[171] If the claim is accepted for resolution within the Scheme, the start date for computing the strict timetable begins on the date of admission to the Scheme, which is the date of receipt by the claimant's solicitor of the written agreement by the Welsh Health Legal Services.[172] The participants may withdraw from the Scheme at any time by giving written notice to the other participants.[173]

Case summaries

The resolution process is started with the sequential exchange of case summaries. The claimant's solicitor must provide the claimant's case summary to the Welsh Health Legal Services within two weeks of the agreement by the Welsh Health Legal Services to admit the claim in the Scheme.[174] Annex III to the Rules sets out the standard form that must be used. The information that must be provided includes a description of the events in question, the consequences, and the claimant's medical history.

The defendant's case summary must be sent by the Welsh Health Legal Services to the claimant's solicitor within two weeks of receipt of the claimant's case summary.[175] Annex IV to the Rules sets out the standard form that must be used. The information that must be provided includes a description of the events in question, the consequences of the events, and identify the clinicians that were involved.

Expert evidence: liability

The next stage is for the claimant's solicitor and the Welsh Health Legal Services to appoint and instruct on a joint basis an expert on breach of duty and causation, or an expert on breach of duty and a different expert on causation. Medical experts should be appointed from an Approved List.[176] However, this rule need not be followed if an expert in the required discipline is not included on the Approved List, or the experts on the Approved List cannot prepare the report within the required timescale.[177] Annex V to the Rules sets out draft standard letters for the instruction of experts, and the letter of instruction must be set out in substantially the same form.[178]

---

169 Welsh Health Legal Services, Speedy Resolution Scheme, r 9.
170 Welsh Health Legal Services, Speedy Resolution Scheme, r 10.
171 Welsh Health Legal Services, Speedy Resolution Scheme, r 10.
172 Welsh Health Legal Services, Speedy Resolution Scheme, r 1.
173 Welsh Health Legal Services, Speedy Resolution Scheme, r 43.
174 Welsh Health Legal Services, Speedy Resolution Scheme, r 11.
175 Welsh Health Legal Services, Speedy Resolution Scheme, r 12.
176 Welsh Health Legal Services, Speedy Resolution Scheme, r 13.
177 Welsh Health Legal Services, Speedy Resolution Scheme, r 14.
178 Welsh Health Legal Services, Speedy Resolution Scheme, r 32.

Expert: breach of duty

If an expert is to be instructed on breach of duty, the participants must agree the appointment of an expert, and the claimant's solicitor prepares the letter of instruction, which is to be agreed by the Welsh Health Legal Services.[179] This must be completed within eight weeks of the start date. The expert has four weeks from the letter of instruction to submit his report in writing.[180] Within two weeks of receiving the report, the claimant's solicitor and the Welsh Health Legal Services can ask the expert questions arising from the report.[181] The expert must reply to all participants within two weeks of the receipt of the question.[182] Therefore, this part of the resolution process should be completed within 16 weeks from the start date.

In some cases, it may be appropriate for the expert to opine on both breach of duty and causation. In such cases, an expert will be jointly instructed by the parties and provide his report on breach and causation, in line with the time scales for the breach of duty report.[183]

Expert: causation

If the parties agreed to instruct an expert limited to breach of duty in the first instance, a decision must be made about expert evidence on causation. Within 17 weeks of the start date, the claimant's solicitor and the Welsh Health Legal Services must agree whether a report on causation is required.[184] The expert will be instructed as a single joint expert. Within 20 weeks of the start date, the participants agree the appointment of the expert, and the claimant's solicitor prepares the letter of instruction, which is to be agreed by the Welsh Health Legal Services.[185] The expert has four weeks from the letter of instruction to submit his report in writing.[186] Within two weeks of receiving the report, the claimant's solicitor and the Welsh Health Legal Services can ask the expert questions arising from his report.[187] The expert must reply to all participants within two weeks of the receipt of the questions.[188]

The defendant's decision on liability

Once the medical evidence on liability is completed, the Welsh Health Legal Services must confirm the defendant's position on breach of duty and causation, and/or whether the claim is suitable for settlement under the Scheme.[189] This must be completed within four weeks of receipt of the report on breach of duty and causation, or the answers to any subsequent

179 Welsh Health Legal Services, Speedy Resolution Scheme, r 16.
180 Welsh Health Legal Services, Speedy Resolution Scheme, r 17.
181 Welsh Health Legal Services, Speedy Resolution Scheme, r 18.
182 Welsh Health Legal Services, Speedy Resolution Scheme, r 19.
183 Welsh Health Legal Services, Speedy Resolution Scheme, r 25.
184 Welsh Health Legal Services, Speedy Resolution Scheme, r 20.
185 Welsh Health Legal Services, Speedy Resolution Scheme, r 21.
186 Welsh Health Legal Services, Speedy Resolution Scheme, r 22.
187 Welsh Health Legal Services, Speedy Resolution Scheme, r 23.
188 Welsh Health Legal Services, Speedy Resolution Scheme, r 24.
189 Welsh Health Legal Services, Speedy Resolution Scheme, r 26.

questions, or within four weeks of receipt of the report on causation, or the answers to any subsequent questions.[190] If liability is denied and/or the claim is not suitable for settlement, the Welsh Health Legal Services must provide a reasoned response.[191]

Expert evidence: condition and prognosis

If liability is admitted and the case is deemed suitable for settlement, the claimant's solicitor and the Welsh Health Legal Services must agree whether a condition and prognosis report is required.[192] The time for completing this step is within one week of the admission or liability and/or acceptance that the claim is suitable for settlement. Annex V to the Rules provides a standard letter of instruction to medical experts on condition and prognosis, and the letter of instruction should be in substantially the same format.[193]

The expert opining on condition and prognosis will be instructed as a single joint expert. Within four weeks of the admission of liability and/or confirmation that the claim is suitable for settlement, the participants must agree the appointment of this expert; the claimant's solicitor prepares the letter of instruction, which is to be agreed by the Welsh Health Legal Services. The expert has six weeks from the letter of instruction to submit his report in writing.[194] Within two weeks of receiving the report, the participants can ask the expert questions arising from the report.[195] The expert must reply to all participants within two weeks of the receipt of the questions.[196]

Offer of settlement

Once the expert evidence (if any) on condition and prognosis is finalised, the next procedural stage in the Scheme is an offer of settlement, to include both general and special damages. This is made by the claimant's solicitor to the Welsh Health Legal Services, and as far as possible should be supported with documentary evidence of the financial losses.[197] The offer is made within four weeks of receipt of confirmation that liability is admitted and/or that the claim is suitable for settlement. Alternatively, if a condition and prognosis report is required, within four weeks of the expert's report and the replies to any questions.[198]

Two weeks after receipt of the offer, the Welsh Health Legal Services must either accept the claimant solicitor's valuation, or make a counter-offer of settlement on behalf of the relevant Welsh NHS Trust.[199] Two weeks after receipt of the counter-offer, the claimant's solicitor must accept or reject the counter-offer, and may make a further counter-

190 Welsh Health Legal Services, Speedy Resolution Scheme, r 26.
191 Welsh Health Legal Services, Speedy Resolution Scheme, r 26.
192 Welsh Health Legal Services, Speedy Resolution Scheme, r 27.
193 Welsh Health Legal Services, Speedy Resolution Scheme, r 32.
194 Welsh Health Legal Services, Speedy Resolution Scheme, r 29.
195 Welsh Health Legal Services, Speedy Resolution Scheme, r 30.
196 Welsh Health Legal Services, Speedy Resolution Scheme, r 31.
197 Welsh Health Legal Services, Speedy Resolution Scheme, r 33.
198 Welsh Health Legal Services, Speedy Resolution Scheme, r 33.
199 Welsh Health Legal Services, Speedy Resolution Scheme, r 34.

offer.[200] There is no limit on the number of offers and counter-offers that can be made up until an agreement on quantum is reached or until the participants withdraw from the Scheme,[201] provided the time limits for settlement are adhered to.[202]

If an agreement on quantum cannot be reached, then one week after the Welsh Health Legal Services rejected the claimant solicitor's first offer, the participants can agree to instruct counsel to advise on quantum.[203] This is a joint instruction and the letter of instruction is drafted by the claimant's solicitor, and must be agreed by the Welsh Health Legal Services.[204] The selection of appropriate counsel and the letter of instruction must be agreed within two weeks of the agreement to seek Counsel's opinion on quantum.[205] Counsel must be selected from an Approved List, set out in Annex VI to the Scheme Rules, unless an agreement is made to instruct alternative counsel.[206] Counsel must agree to provide a written advice on quantum within two weeks of receipt of instructions and for a fixed fee,[207] currently £225, plus VAT.[208] Upon receipt of counsel's opinion on quantum, the claimant's solicitor and the Welsh Health Legal Services have two weeks to decide whether to accept the advice.[209] Counsel's advice on quantum is not binding on the participants, and the Rules do not require them to reach a settlement.[210]

Termination of the Scheme

Participation in the Scheme is terminated in two ways. First, by the withdrawal of any participant from the Scheme, which must be by written notice.[211] Secondly, by the acceptance of an offer of settlement, and payment of the agreed sum and fixed costs.[212]

Costs, fees and expenses

Each participant to the Scheme pays its own fees, costs, expenses,[213] disbursements,[214] an equal share of the costs of any joint expert and for counsel's quantum advice (if any).[215] Some disbursement costs may be shared.[216] However, upon conclusion of a successful claim, the claimant

---

200 Welsh Health Legal Services, Speedy Resolution Scheme, r 35.
201 Welsh Health Legal Services, Speedy Resolution Scheme, r 36.
202 Welsh Health Legal Services, Speedy Resolution Scheme, r 36.
203 Welsh Health Legal Services, Speedy Resolution Scheme, r 37.
204 Welsh Health Legal Services, Speedy Resolution Scheme, r 39.
205 Welsh Health Legal Services, Speedy Resolution Scheme, r 39.
206 Welsh Health Legal Services, Speedy Resolution Scheme, r 38.
207 Welsh Health Legal Services, Speedy Resolution Scheme, rr 38 and 40.
208 Welsh Health Legal Services, Speedy Resolution Scheme, Annex 1.
209 Welsh Health Legal Services, Speedy Resolution Scheme, r 40.
210 Welsh Health Legal Services, Speedy Resolution Scheme, r 42.
211 Welsh Health Legal Services, Speedy Resolution Scheme, r 43.
212 Welsh Health Legal Services, Speedy Resolution Scheme, r 50.
213 Welsh Health Legal Services, Speedy Resolution Scheme, r 46.
214 Welsh Health Legal Services, Speedy Resolution Scheme, r 47.
215 Welsh Health Legal Services, Speedy Resolution Scheme, r 47.
216 *Speedy Resolution Scheme: Evaluation for the Welsh Assembly Government's Pilot Scheme for Resolving Low Value Clinical Negligence Claims against NHS Trusts in Wales*, para 3.15.

solicitors' fees will be paid by the relevant Welsh NHS Trust in accordance with the fix fee regime, and reasonable disbursements can be recovered.[217]

The costs of the professional fees of solicitors, counsel, and experts are fixed by the Rules.[218] The fixed fees are currently set are as follows:[219]

	Fee (excluding VAT)
Solicitor's profit costs upon conclusion of a successful claim	£3,500.00
Medical expert: report	£450.00
Medical expert: reply to questions	£75.00
Counsel: advice on quantum	£225.00

The Legal Services Commission has extended public funding to the pursuit of a claim under the Scheme. The certificate is issued for investigative help with a cost limitation of £3,500 (plus VAT).

Apologies, explanation and action plans

In appropriate circumstances, the Welsh NHS Trusts are encouraged to make an apology to the claimant,[220] which will not be treated as an admission of liability.[221] In all cases, Welsh NHS Trusts should provide patients with an explanation of the reasons for the outcome of their treatment.[222]

A key aspect of the Scheme is that lessons are learnt by Welsh NHS Trusts from incidents resulting in clinical negligence claims. Therefore, in successful claims or cases in which a breach of duty is admitted, the relevant Welsh NHS Trust must prepare an action plan in the format set out in Annex VII to the Rules.[223] In cases which are not successful or there is no breach of duty, the relevant Welsh NHS Trust must consider whether an action plan is indicated.[224] If the action plan would be useful for other Welsh NHS Trusts, it must be circulated on a redacted basis.[225]

Limitation of actions

If the claim is admitted to the Scheme, the defendant is deemed to agree that in any subsequent civil proceedings, it will not rely on the time from the start date to the date of termination to support a limitation defence or against an application by the claimant for the court to exercise its discretion to disapply the limitation period under the Limitation Act 1980, s 33.[226]

---

217 Welsh Health Legal Services, Speedy Resolution Scheme, r 49.
218 Welsh Health Legal Services, Speedy Resolution Scheme, r 48.
219 Welsh Health Legal Services, Speedy Resolution Scheme, Annex 1.
220 Welsh Health Legal Services, Speedy Resolution Scheme, r 51.
221 Welsh Health Legal Services, Speedy Resolution Scheme, r 52.
222 Welsh Health Legal Services, Speedy Resolution Scheme, r 53.
223 Welsh Health Legal Services, Speedy Resolution Scheme, r 54.
224 Welsh Health Legal Services, Speedy Resolution Scheme, r 55.
225 Welsh Health Legal Services, Speedy Resolution Scheme, r 57.
226 Welsh Health Legal Services, Speedy Resolution Scheme, r 59.

Restriction on the use of information in subsequent proceedings

Where the case has not been settled under the Scheme, there are restrictions in any subsequent civil proceedings based on substantially the same facts on the use of documents (expert reports, advice from counsel, written case summaries, written submissions, written concessions or admission of law or fact, or written statements, whether prepared specifically for the purposes of the Scheme or not) and oral communications/admissions used or disclosed for the purposes of the Scheme.[227]

However, where such documents or oral statements are permitted, the parties to the civil action are entitled to draw the attention of the court to the purpose of the Scheme and the intention of the parties when deciding what weight, if any, is to be given to the document.[228] In particular, the court's attention can be drawn to the fact that the Scheme aims to provide a quick, inexpensive and fair means of resolving clinical negligence disputes, and '[t]o that end it is the intention of those taking part in the Scheme that statements, reports and other documents prepared for the purposes of the Scheme should be succinct and briefer than might have been expected if they had been drafted for the purposes of a civil trial'.[229]

Timetable summary

The *Speedy Resolution Scheme: Evaluation for the Welsh Assembly Government's Pilot Scheme for Resolving Low Value Clinical Negligence Claims against NHS Trusts in Wales* summarised the time scales by reference to the start date, although not all timescales within the Rules are given by reference to the start date.[230]

---

227 Welsh Health Legal Services, Speedy Resolution Scheme, r 44.
228 Welsh Health Legal Services, Speedy Resolution Scheme, r 1, Statement of Principle.
229 Welsh Health Legal Services, Speedy Resolution Scheme, r 1, Statement of Principle.
230 Para 1.9.

Stage in procedure	Time allowed for completion (from start date)
Claimant to submit claim summary	2 weeks
Defendant to submit a claim summary	4 weeks
Parties agree appointment of and instruct a joint expert to report on breach of duty or breach of duty and causation	8 weeks
Joint experts' reports on breach of duty or breach of duty and causation	12 weeks
Parties to submit questions to the expert arising from report on breach of duty or breach of duty and causation	14 weeks
Experts reply to questions on breach of duty or breach of duty and causation	16 weeks
Parties agree whether separate report is required on causation	17 weeks
Parties agree appointment of and instruct a joint expert to report on causation	20 weeks
Joint experts' reports on causation	24 weeks
Parties to submit questions to the expert arising from report on causation	26 weeks
Expert to reply on questions on causation	28 weeks
WHLS to confirm its position on liability and suitability for settlement	32 weeks (this is shorted if the initial report is on breach of duty and causation)
Parties to agree if a report is required on condition and prognosis	33 weeks
Parties agree appointment of and instruction of joint expert to report on condition and prognosis	36 weeks
Joint experts' reports on condition and prognosis	42 weeks
Parties to submit questions to the experts arising from report on condition and prognosis	44 weeks
Expert to reply to condition and prognosis	46 weeks
Claimant's solicitor to provide details of the amount of the claim	50 weeks (this is shorter if a condition and prognosis report is not required)
WHLS accept claimant's claim to make an offer to settle	52 weeks
Claimant's solicitor to confirm whether offer accepted or rejected	54 weeks
Where offer is rejected, parties agree to instruct counsel	55 weeks
Joint instructions to counsel	57 weeks
Counsel to advise on quantum	59 weeks
Parties to decide whether to accept counsel's opinion	61 weeks

Part Five

Chapter 24

Funding

Nick Knowles

Without adequate funding there can be no access to justice for the victim of a medical 'accident'. For more than ten years there has been an enormous amount of activity in this crucial area for the clinical negligence practitioner.

Funding and costs go hand in hand. Together they determine the bigger picture, the financial context in which the specialist practitioner must operate.

At the present time, as can be seen below, clinical negligence funding is in yet another period of tumultuous flux and there will undoubtedly be further far-reaching changes for the practitioner to contend with.

Medical 'accidents' generate high emotions. The client has suffered a violation of mind and body and can naturally be demanding, sometimes to the point of obsession. The defendant affects outrage that the integrity of the medical profession is at stake and goes to extreme lengths to defeat the claim. The substantive law leaves it to the medical profession, or those clinicians who are prepared to spend the time in court, to determine whether there is a breach and causation. Experts have to be constantly chased to stick to the timetable and to answer the question. Their views determine the success or failure of the claim but they can always change their mind. The more serious the claim, the harder it will be fought, not only to the doors of the court but later also to the doors of the Senior Court Costs Office, invariably following preparation of a detailed bill of costs.

Although much of the work is necessarily done pro bono and a large amount is legally aided, the practitioner is pilloried in the press as a 'fat cat lawyer' and 'ambulance chaser', a prime beneficiary of the compensation culture which is mistakenly believed to exist in this field.

Unless they or their loved ones have suffered a medical 'accident', members of the public will display surprise, even disgust, that claims should be brought against the NHS, a public body paid to do good. Fanned by the turgid media headlines, the perception is that the larger the compensation paid out, the more the squeeze on NHS resources to provide proper care for the public.

The myriad tensions generated by medical 'accidents', the strong feelings concerned, but more importantly the financial ramifications, the vagaries of the economic climate, and crucially the political agenda of the changing governments (all of them driven to reduce public expenditure), all of these things have accounted for the constant tinkering in recent times with the methods by which clinical negligence funding is provided.

The specialist practice has to keep abreast of all these nuances and upheavals if it is to remain in business so as to be able to pursue justice for the victims of medical 'accidents'.

It is particularly because of this time of great uncertainty and the enormity of the changes in the offing that it will be of some benefit to take a brief look back at what has been happening over the past few years as this may enable some sense to be made out of what the future holds in store.

A LITTLE HISTORY

The previous Conservative Lord Chancellor, Lord Mackay, made some inroads into the legal aid system, making the financial eligibility criteria stricter, but he also introduced the conditional fee system, whereby lawyers were permitted to conduct cases on the basis that they would take an uplift to their fees out of any damages recovered for the client, but if the case was not successful they would get nothing. This was a revolutionary idea and completely contrary to the traditional ethos of the legal profession which did not permit lawyers to be financially interested in the outcome of a case (at least, not openly). The lawyer became under pressure to get a settlement.

However, few people foresaw the vigour with which the legal aid system would be attacked by Lord Mackay's successor, the Labour Lord Irvine. As a result, legal aid for personal injury claims became virtually unobtainable. That would also have been the fate of clinical negligence claims, had he not been forced to accept that to abolish legal aid would deprive medical accident victims of access to justice because such claims require significant expenditure on investigation in order to find out whether there is a viable claim. The risks involved in the new conditional fee system would not provide adequate means of funding for the work concerned in such front-loaded cases. These legal aid reforms introduced by the Access to Justice Act 1999 and its supporting legislation required solicitor firms wishing to undertake such category of work to obtain a 'clinical negligence' franchise. In order to obtain such a franchise each firm had to have a category supervisor who belonged to one of the two specialist panels of clinical negligence solicitors. One panel is run by the Law Society and the other is administered by AvMA (then AVMA), the charity which has done so much to support medical accident victims and to empower them, if need be, to litigate successfully for compensation through the courts.

It has to be said that some form of accreditation was necessary for solicitors (and remains necessary for barristers). History is full of horror stories of cases abandoned, lost or simply left to wither because of the lack of experience, enthusiasm and effort of the lawyers involved. So the need for specialist lawyers alone to handle clinical negligence cases was clear.

What had previously been known as 'medical negligence' thereafter generally became known as 'clinical negligence' even outside of legal aid circles. One story was that the medical profession was irked that doctors should be labelled generally as the tortfeasors in the provision of healthcare when other non-medical providers could also be at fault. Cynics wondered whether the new tag could serve to confuse potential claimants amongst members of the public.

It is something of a coincidence that a lot of these changes were going on at the same time as the Woolf reforms were implemented. These far-reaching procedural changes were intended to ameliorate the expense and delays of litigation. (It is arguable whether the reforms have had a beneficial effect on the reduction of costs and indeed in some areas these have resulted in an increase in the costs involved. How many claims have successfully settled at an advanced stage post-issue despite the initial service of robustly defensive Pre-action Protocol letters of response! Generally, however, greater case management by the courts has appreciably speeded up the litigation process).

Later on, in 2003, the Chief Medical Officer, Professor Sir Liam Donaldson, published his report *Making amends: A consultation paper setting out proposals for reforming the approach to clinical negligence in the NHS*. Practitioners in this field anxiously awaited its publication during the two long years of the consultation period, particularly as one of the proposals was a no-fault compensation scheme. They need not have worried. The suggestion of such a scheme was firmly dismissed. Given that a staggering proportion of medical untoward incidents never see the light of day and, on the basis of a duty to disclose all incidents, the scheme would be massively and prohibitively costly. Furthermore, to be affordable any compensation paid would probably not meet the needs of the injured patient, difficult issues of causation might also arise even with the removal of 'fault' and, finally, such a scheme would not be conducive to the need to learn from past mistakes (a priority for the improvement of patient care).

The report made various recommendations, the most important of which was the NHS Redress Scheme whereby redress was to involve investigation and an explanation of the incident, the provision of a package of care where needed and payments for pain and suffering and expenses and for any care or treatment which the NHS could not provide. Any avoidable harm caused by serious shortcomings in NHS care would be eligible for payments in this way up to a maximum of £30,000. Such a scheme, intended to be closely aligned to changes to the NHS Complaints Procedure, got as far as the enactment of the NHS Redress Act 2006. (As late as July 2009, the House of Commons Select Committee on Health expressed concern about the absence of the regulations which have yet to be drawn up to implement the scheme.)

Also in line with another of Sir Liam's recommendations, the new NHS Complaints Procedure, (dealt with in Chapter 3), has now been altered so that the patient's complaint will still be investigated, notwithstanding that the patient intends also to seek compensation through the courts.

THE FUNDING OPTIONS

One of the most important decisions facing a solicitor in relation to any client is whether to take on the case at all and funding considerations will be pre-eminent.

It is of extreme importance to both solicitor and client that for any given claim the correct method of funding is chosen. Obviously the means of funding have to be affordable and appropriate for the client, but from the solicitor's perspective the professional rules of conduct impose a comprehensive duty to fully advise the client as to the funding options available and as to the nature and extent of the costs involved to the client.

In addition, however, the solicitor has to ensure that any claim is profitably undertaken and in particular that its loss would not have any untoward implications for the firm's practice. Even if a claim is successful, the solicitor may well have to go through a lengthy costs assessment process before the final bill can be reckoned. The defendant will be quick to pounce on any solicitor and own client retainer problems. The paying party's liability is to reimburse the winning party only in respect of the latter's liability for costs, ('the indemnity principle', which is still in force despite increasing objection). If the winning party has no liability for costs then there is nothing for the losing party to indemnify.

The Solicitors Regulation Authority (SRA) issued a new Handbook for solicitors implemented on 6 October 2011. A second edition came into effect on 23 December 2011. The new Code of Conduct contained in the Handbook reflects the SRA's fresh, flexible approach to regulation which is outcomes-focused and risk-based. The emphasis is on solicitors running their businesses properly and in a way that best suits the needs of their particular clients.

There are ten new all-pervasive principles which set out the fundamental ethical and professional standards which are expected of solicitors. There is the novel concept of mandatory outcomes which must be achieved to comply with the principles and for the benefit of the clients and the general public. These outcomes are supplemented by indicative behaviours which, although not mandatory, assist in assessing whether an outcome has been achieved.

The outcomes are expressed in more general terms than the old 'Rules of Conduct'. Those particularly relevant to funding include:

O (1.6)   you only enter into fee agreements with your clients that are legal, and which you consider are suitable for the client's needs and take account of the client's best interests;

O (1.13)   clients receive the best possible information, both at the time of engagement and when appropriate as their matter progresses, about the likely overall cost of their matter.

Relevant indicative behaviours under the following headings include:

Dealing with the client's matter
IB (1.4)   explaining any arrangements, such as fee sharing or referral arrangements, which are relevant to the client's instructions;

IB (1.5)   explaining any limitations or conditions on what you can do for the client, for example, because of the way the client's matter is funded;

Fee arrangements with your client
IB (1.13)   discussing whether the potential outcomes of the client's matter are likely to justify the expense or risk involved, including any risk of having to pay someone else's fees;

IB (1.14)   clearly explaining your fees and if and when they are likely to change;

IB (1.15)   warning about any other payments for which the client may be responsible;

IB (1.16) discussing how the client will pay, including whether public funding may be available, whether the client has insurance that might cover the fees, and whether the fees may be paid by someone else such as a trade union;

IB (1.17) where you are acting for a client under a fee arrangement governed by statute, such as a conditional fee agreement, giving the client all relevant information relating to that arrangement;

IB (1.18) where you are acting for a publicly funded client, explaining how their publicly funded status affects the costs;

IB (1.19) providing the information in a clear and accessible form which is appropriate to the needs and circumstances of the client;

IB (1.20) where you receive a financial benefit as a result of acting for a client, either:

  (a) paying it to the client;
  (b) offsetting it against your fees; or
  (c) keeping it only where you can justify keeping it, you have told the client the amount of the benefit (or an approximation if you do not know the exact amount) and the client has agreed that you can keep it.

The different methods of funding a claim are as follows:

1 private retainer,
2 legal expense insurance (LEI),
3 public funding (legal aid),
4 Conditional Fee Agreement (CFA).

There are some instances where a client has the availability of funding through his employment or as a member of an organisation such as a trade union, but these are not very common.

PRIVATE RETAINER

As even a fairly straightforward clinical negligence claim might cost upwards of something in the order of £50,000 to litigate to trial, this is rarely chosen by clients as a method of funding. Few would choose to take that risk and substantially compound their losses. It is more commonly used in limited aspects of the litigation process, for instance, for costs of investigation, often only for disbursements, where the merits of a claim are very uncertain in the absence of specific expert advice. Sometimes it might be used, where appropriate, for representation at an inquest, which can be a useful vehicle for the investigation of the merits of a claim, but always depending, of course, upon the means of the client.

Additionally there is the liability for the opponents' costs to consider should a claim proceed to court and prove unsuccessful at the end of the day. This is not so much of a problem these days, however, with the availability of after the event insurance (ATE) which will be considered in more detail below regarding conditional fee agreements.

LEGAL EXPENSE INSURANCE

It is now an important regular feature of the initial interview with all clients that every policy of insurance which they own is identified and, if necessary, scrutinised for the availability of legal expenses cover. It is a feature which many clients are unaware of, let alone specifically negotiate, at the time of entering into the before the event (BTE) insurance policy.

Legal expense cover is often to be found in household contents policies, car insurance (though it is rare for the legal costs covered to be more that those of a road traffic accident) and sometimes in banking and credit card agreements.

The period of cover needs to be checked to ensure that the negligence occurred within that time frame, and there is often a stringent time limit for reporting as a precondition of the insurer's liability to indemnify under the policy. BTE policies often provide for periods of reporting of between 90 and 180 days after the insured knew or ought of have known of the incident giving rise to the claim.

Sometimes clinical negligence claims are wholly excluded from legal expense cover. In other policies, however, death or bodily injury only is covered and there may be specifically excluded 'any illness or bodily injury which happens gradually or is not caused by a specific or sudden event'. This wording would exclude from cover many claims of clinical negligence which involve a delay in the diagnosis and treatment of a medical condition which occurs over a period of probably anything longer than 24 hours.

Often there is protracted and circular correspondence with the insurers asking to be convinced of the prospects of success before they will fund the investigation.

Even after the insurers agree to indemnify the client, often the specialist practitioner will be faced with the insistence of the insurer that if the client wishes to have the benefit of their policy the claim will have to be handled by a firm which is a member of their own panel of solicitors. (Some personal injury solicitors pay a not insignificant fee for membership of an insurer's panel as a means of obtaining work in their increasingly competitive market). It is often the case that the firm designated by the insurer does not have specialist clinical negligence expertise, although it does seem to be the case that increasingly specialists are becoming involved in this avenue of referrals.

Confronted with this situation, the specialist practitioner would have to seek to persuade the insurer of the need for special expertise and, previously in the absence of legal ruling in this area, would be driven to quoting from helpful decisions of the relevant Ombudsman concerning the insured's freedom of choice in the instruction of solicitors. In the Insurance Ombudsman's Annual Review of 1993, he expressed the view that the governing Insurance Companies (Legal Expense Insurance) Regulations enabled the insured to choose a solicitor only after the claim had actually been issued in court. Additionally, in 2003 the (then) Financial Services Ombudsman expressed his expectation, in the case of *Mrs A* v *B (a company)*, that insurers 'agree the appointment of the policyholder's preferred solicitors in cases of large personal injury claims that are necessarily complex (such as those involving allegations of clinical negligence)'. Despite this clear pronouncement, it is not uncommon for insurers to insist on use of their panel members even in complex clinical negligence claims. This is a highly unsatisfactory state of affairs, particularly given the front-loaded nature of clinical negligence work and the great importance of the (pre-action) investigation process and where the designated panel member has no specialist expertise.

Help was provided on this common contentious issue, in the form of the recent case decided by the European Court of Justice in September 2009 of *Erhard Eschig* v *UNIQA Sachsversicherung AG* (C-199/08) [2010] 1 All ER (Comm) 576. The decision of the court supported the freedom of choice of lawyer for an insured under an Austrian legal expense policy, despite the existence of an express condition restricting this within the policy. The Financial Services Authority (FSA) wrote a letter recently to all UK legal expense insurers drawing attention to the ruling and pointed out that, 'any provisions of a contract that detract from, or qualify in any way, the freedom to choose a lawyer, will not be compliant with the relevant Council Directive 87/344/EEC of 22 June 1987'. The FSA specifically stated: 'It is important to note that freedom of choice arises before the commencement of any enquiry or proceedings'.

More recent was the High Court decision in *Brown-Quinn and Webster Dixon* v *Equity Syndicate* [2010] EWHC 2661. The case concerned a challenge to the insurers' practice of refusing a policy holder's choice of solicitor on the ground that the solicitor's hourly rate exceeded that prescribed by them for non-panel members. Burton J decided that such a refusal was contrary to European and domestic law. Important as this decision is, it does remain to be seen, however, precisely how much of an impact this will have on the insurance industry in practice.

Assuming that specialist practitioners can be accessed more readily than previously and once the other hurdles mentioned above have been surmounted, the practitioner will find that there will invariably be tight reporting restrictions regarding the progress of the claim, sometimes required as often as once a month. All the costs involved in this work may well prove irrecoverable between the parties and it will not be funded by the insurer.

Often the insurer will discriminate between the panel member and the non-panel- member by imposing upon the latter, in comparison to the former, more stringent requirements in the terms of appointment.

It should never be forgotten, of course, that a contract of insurance is one of 'utmost faith' and as such any matter must be reported which any prudent insurer would wish to take into account in deciding whether or not to assume the risk or to continue covering the risk under the policy or upon what terms. The failure to report any such material matter will entitle the insurer to avoid the policy altogether.

It should also be remembered, however the insurer decides to word the policy, that the retainer for the legal work is still that between a solicitor and client in the usual way and the policy is simply to indemnify the client in respect of liability for the solicitor's costs.

There will also be a maximum indemnity under the policy, frequently of £50,000 but sometimes of £100,000, which is to cover both the practitioner's and the opponent's costs. The insurer will often seek also to impose a much smaller 'authorised costs limit'. This will probably be unrealistic in amount but sometimes the insurer seeks to impose such a limit even if it is not included as a term within the policy.

It will be prudent for the specialist practitioner to seek to agree an appropriate hourly rate of remuneration, hopefully if lucky the 'going rate' allowed by the local courts for the firm in question. At the very least, the practitioner should clarify that any lower rate solely relates to the

BTE indemnification and does not alter the position vis-à-vis the client and hopefully the opponent in the event of a win.

The legal expense insurer expects not to have to pay anything under the policy if the case is won, save where any adverse costs have been ordered (where the risk for these particular costs was explicitly assumed by the insurer beforehand). The policy will not usually provide for the payment of interim profit costs but disbursements authorised beforehand can be met, although this is increasingly rare. Some insurers unrealistically demand that all experts and counsel accept deferred payment and limit themselves to fees recovered.

One of the important uses of a legal expense policy is in conjunction with a CFA so as to enable the funding of disbursements in a clinical negligence case.

One unusual advantage of BTE cover which is rarely encountered is a reverse indemnity provision whereby the insurer agrees to pay any judgment sum and costs awarded to the insured in the proceedings in the event that these are not satisfied by the opponent. It is a peculiar feature of clinical negligence claims that, unlike other litigation, the successful claimant does not on the whole encounter any enforcement problems in obtaining payment of all compensation and costs due in the action. In fortunately rare occasions, however, a sole practitioner defendant may not have professional indemnity cover or the means to satisfy any award obtained by the client.

LEGAL AID (PUBLIC FUNDING)

Before the implementation of the Access to Justice Act 1999 in April 2000, the Legal Aid Board acted pursuant to the provisions of the Legal Aid Act 1988, granting certificates to any solicitor whose client was financially eligible for legal aid and whose proposed claim satisfied the test of reasonableness.

At the same time, the right to conduct clinical negligence claims on legal aid was being restricted to firms that had a solicitor on one of the two specialist clinical negligence panels and had a 'clinical negligence franchise'. The panel run by AvMA[1] had been going a long time. The Law Society Clinical Negligence Panel published a set of criteria, which were originally drafted with the help of AvMA so, not surprisingly, the two sets of criteria are similar. They are not easy to satisfy and many able solicitors have been refused admission on the ground of failure to satisfy the criteria. In short, the total number of solicitors on the panels (there is much duplication) is low – about 185 on the AvMA panel. These solicitors tend to gravitate towards larger firms as it is not easy to run a clinical negligence practice as a sole practitioner or as the only fee earner doing

---

[1]   AVMA is a charitable organisation which from minimal beginnings has campaigned with considerable success since its inception in 1982 to improve the lot of the patient in litigation and generally. It has acquired considerable influence in various important quarters, such as with the legal aid authority and conditional fee insurers (CFIs). It recently changed its name, in line with the mood of the times and the spirit of the age, to Action against Medical Accidents (AvMA).

that sort of work in the firm (assuming the firm has already been able to satisfy the criteria relating to backup).

Under the Access to Justice Act 1999, the previous legal aid scheme was replaced by the Community Legal Service, and the Legal Services Commission (LSC) took the place of the Legal Aid Board. The LSC's role was to plan how the available money was to be spent by setting priorities, given effect through a combination of contracts and the Funding Code. This Code is in three parts: Criteria, Procedures and Decision Making Guidance. All providers must now sign a contract, the Unified Contract (Civil).

To qualify for funding, the client has to show financial eligibility and merit for the claim.

The financial eligibility calculator is readily accessible online on the LSC website.[2] Broadly speaking, the income threshold is low (gross income must be less than £2,677 per month) and capital must not exceed £8,000. The value of the client's home is also taken into account subject to certain concessions.

The financial criteria have been steadily lowered through the years, taking more and more people out of eligibility for legal aid.

Criteria for funding

The Funding Code[3] offers seven levels of service to be funded by the Community Legal Service, two of which are relevant to clinical negligence cases: Legal Help – advice and assistance; and Legal Representation, which can be granted in one of two forms, each with its own criteria. One form is Investigative Help – available where a case needs substantial investigation before its prospects of success can be determined. The other is Full Representation – available only for strong cases.

The General Funding Code sets out the criteria, which apply to all cases, subject to any variation by special criteria for particular subject areas. Clinical negligence has its own special criteria in the Funding Code. The Guidance to the Funding Code explains the position in section 18.

Criteria for Investigative Help

Investigative Help may only be granted where the prospects of success of the claim are uncertain, and substantial investigative work is required before those prospects can be determined. In clinical negligence claims, of course, the investigative stage is of vital importance, and special criteria apply to this level of service.

Although under the general criteria the LSC is entitled to refuse funding for Investigative Help in certain cases on the grounds that a conditional fee agreement should be obtained rather than public funding, the availability of a conditional fee agreement became no longer a ground for refusing aid for clinical negligence cases. This was in in recognition of the difficulties in obtaining funding for the investigative costs involved.

---

2   www.legalservices.gov.uk/civil/guidance/eligibility_calculator.asp.
3   www.legalservices.gov.uk/docs/cls_main/FundingCodeDecisionMakingGuidance-OtherGuidance(Sections15-19_21-26and28)Sept07.pdf

If the claim is primarily for damages and has no significant wider public interest, Investigative Help will be refused unless the damages are likely to exceed £5,000. Note that under the General Funding Code, the £5,000 damages cut-off does not apply to claims, which have a significant wider public interest, or are of overwhelming importance to the client.

The LSC may take the view on an application for Investigative Help that the NHS Complaints Procedure is more appropriate for the client than litigation. This is particularly likely to be the case with small claims although no amount is specified and the LSC now recognise that the complaints procedure is irrelevant to the obtaining of compensation.

Paragraph 4 of the Guidance states that the 'private client test' is to be used in each case. Examples which are given of situations where it would not be appropriate to refuse funding here (instead of pursuing a formal complaint) would include the need to issue protective proceedings, a catastrophic injury claim, where any delay in investigation could jeopardise the claim or where the case does not fall within the NHS Complaints Scheme or the complaint cannot be pursued further.

Criteria for Full Representation

As we have seen, the availability of conditional fees is not a ground for refusal in clinical negligence cases. However, the approach to the prospect of success will be the same as in the General Funding Code in that Full Representation will be refused if:

- prospects of success are unclear (Investigative Help may be appropriate);
- prospects of success are borderline and the case does not appear to have a significant wider public interest or to be of overwhelming importance to the client; or
- prospects of success are poor.

Cost-benefit ratio

When clinical negligence work was restricted to specialist firms in February 1999, the guidance published under the Legal Aid Act 1988 recommended minimum cost-benefit ratios. These ratios of costs to damages were more relaxed than those used for other categories of case within the General Funding Code. However, the requirements for clinical negligence were subsequently tightened up and brought into line with these other cases so that the current cost-benefit thresholds are:

- if prospects of success are very good (80% or more) (usually where liability has been agreed), likely damages must exceed likely costs;
- if prospects of success are good (60%–80%) (this is the bracket into which most clinical negligence cases thought viable by the expert solicitor will fall), likely damages must exceed likely costs by a ratio of 2:1;
- if prospects of success are moderate (50% –60%), likely damages must exceed likely costs by a ratio of 4:1.

The tightening up of these cost-benefit thresholds undoubtedly had a marked impact on clinical negligence claims and would have deprived a lot of these claims, particularly those of lower value, of legal aid funding because of the higher costs of these claims when compared with average costs for claims in other categories.

The strict application of the cost-benefit ratios is to some extent relaxed where the solicitor is able to say that there is a likelihood that the case will settle, in which case the likely amount of costs is to be calculated up to the stage of envisaged settlement.

Very High Cost Civil Cases

Very High Cost Civil Cases will be referred to the Special Cases Unit, where likely or actual costs to disposal exceed £25,000 or if the case proceeded to trial the likely costs might exceed £75,000. Thus the vast majority of clinical negligence cases will fall into this bracket and up until fairly recently they used to need a detailed costed Case Plan,[4] reviewable at every stage. They involved a bureaucratic nightmare of form-filling, a strait-jacket of costs, and the necessary prescience to be able to predict every step that would require to be taken in the conduct of the case. By the time endless enquiries had been answered after protracted correspondence, the practitioner would face the disallowance of a large section of 'future' work on the basis that, as it had by now been carried out (albeit during the lengthy period of negotiations), legal aid could not be granted retrospectively.

With the retention of legal aid in 1999 for clinical negligence work, the requirement was for that work to be undertaken by the specialist practitioner. The LSC subsequently went about ensuring that even in respect of old legal aid certificates, the cases concerned were transferred to specialist franchised firms. The LSC co-operated with the NHS in identifying cases to be targeted in this way, the NHS being concerned to rid their books of very significant long-standing potential liabilities.

The LSC compiled detailed statistics of clinical negligence claims, the number of certificates issued each year, the amount of cases issued following the investigative stage, and the proportion of successful conclusions before and after the trial stages. The LSC began to assess the performance of each specialist firm, using Key Performance Indicators. The more successful 'green flag' firms would have larger cost limitations allowed for the initial investigation stage. The LSC introduced the concept of 'peer review' into the work. The poorer performing firms would simply lose their contracts.

The Special Cases Unit would keep the franchised firms informed of its initiatives, hailing the remaining specialist practitioners as the 'success story' of the legal aid scheme and trumpeting the increasing percentages of successful outcomes shown in its latest figures.

The Unit also worked in co-operation with specialist practitioners to compile a 'template' for a standard Case Plan for the investigation of a cerebral palsy claim,[5] the most costly claim to investigate and to litigate. This sort of claim also made up the most significant proportion of the potentially massive bill facing the NHS in terms of compensation and

---

4   There are helpful specimen plans downloadable at www.legalservices.gov.uk.
5   www.legalservices.gov.uk/docs/civil_contracting/investigative_case_plan.pdf.

costs. The template was consulted on from June 2006 and was said by the LSC to have been derived from detailed survey of the 'highest assessed bills'.

In late 2008 in a country-wide roadshow, the Special Cases Unit unveiled to much fanfare the Clinical Negligence Funding Checklist, an alternative to the detailed costs schedules. The Special Cases Unit in Brighton exhorted all practitioners to apply for new certificates with them and to transfer all existing cases there too.

The idea was that the LSC and the practitioner would work together using simplified procedures, providing key information to the LSC, providing a practical risk assessment at the outset with the cost/benefits firmly in mind and in an effort to reduce the bureaucracy involved.

The Clinical Negligence Checklist is now recommended for the initial application for legal aid. There are potentially six stages of work involved in the progress of each case in respect of which the following costs/broad bands of costs will be allowed:

1	Investigative stage	£5,000–£25,000
2	Issue – mutual exchange/conference	£7,500–£20,000
3	Settlement negotiations	£7,500–£23,000
4	Trial	£7,500–£42,000
5	Quantum investigations	£36,000
6	Quantum trial	£43,000

At each stage, a questionnaire is to be answered and particular risks are to be highlighted. The information is to include, though tailored to each stage, a report on the issues in the case, of breach and causation, risk factors, the number and nature of experts to be used, the likely costs both past and future, the prospects of success, a likely timetable and quantum together with the supply of any relevant documents. (Save for the breakdown of costs, this is pretty much what the old Case Plan required, but now in the form of a letter!)

Based on the idea behind the cerebral palsy template, an amount within a range of costs is allowed in respect of each stage, depending on the number of experts to be used. The cost amounts are cumulative and it can be seen that the most that the LSC will allow is £189,000, for instance, for a cerebral palsy case with a split trial and five liability experts and ten quantum experts. The upper range of costs for the number of experts is said to be agreed apparently if there is no cost benefit problem, but if there is, the lower end is used.

As with the costed Case Plans, the agreed amount will form the cost limitation at each stage under the Contract, which has to be signed for each certificate. As previously, the Contract will provide for the first £25,000 of the costs under the Contract, to be calculated on the usual prescribed rate basis of £79.50 per hour for, say, the London solicitor, subject to the relevant enhancement, and with Leading and Junior Counsel being paid £250 and £125 per hour respectively. Once this £25,000 limit is reached, however, the 'risk rates' apply, being as to £70 per hour for the solicitor and £90 per hour for Senior Counsel (ten years call) and £50 for Junior Counsel.

Unfortunately, despite the introduction of this supposedly simplified procedure, the practitioner may well face lengthy and detailed correspondence with the LSC in trying to extend the financial limits or even the scope at each stage.

Nowadays under the modern legal aid contract, there is very little scope for the solicitor to charge the client in respect of any solicitor and own client costs (previously the 'shortfall' between the amount of the solicitor's costs to the fund and the amount (if less) recovered from the defendants. Any shortfall will be the subject of the 'Statutory Charge' and will attach to all damages and costs. The LSC hope that the solicitor will be satisfied with the monies which the client recovers from the defendant.

However, examples of additional costs which the solicitors will be entitled to be paid under cl 16 of the Contract and which will effectively be deducted from his damages include, in appropriate circumstances, using two experts of the same discipline, costs involved in the failure to beat a Part 36 offer and the costs of successful defendants where the client succeeds against some only.

If there is any risk of the client's damages being reduced by reason of adverse costs, particularly with multiple defendants, although Part 36 is not to be ignored, it would be wise for the solicitor to consider with the client the possible need for taking out ATE insurance cover to guard against the risk and to safeguard the damages. In the current austere financial climate, defendants may be readier to enforce orders for costs in their favour.

It has to be the case that many low value clinical negligence claims, because of cost benefit problems, will not be funded by legal aid at all and the only viable method in the absence of any other source of funds will be the conditional fee agreement.

Additionally, the client's means may be such that he may be required to make monthly contributions towards his costs which will continue through the life of the certificate.

As is clear above, the new Solicitors' Code of Conduct merely requires that the solicitor should include in the discussions with his client as to how the case will be funded the question as to 'whether public funding may be available' (see above IB (1.16)). Providing the client is fully advised as to the funding options, and depending on the circumstances, including the terms of any CFA on offer and the pros and cons of each alternative, the client may well feel better served by funding the claim by CFA rather than under a legal aid certificate.

In *LXM* v *Mid Essex Hospital Services NHS Trust* [2010] EWHC 90185 Master Gordon-Saker weighed up the respective pros and cons to the child claimant of funding her cerebral palsy claim through a legal aid certificate and also via a CFA, in the alternative. He upheld as reasonable the litigation friend's decision to abandon an existing legal aid certificate and to instead enter into a CFA with a substantial ATE insurance premium.

ADR

This is very much encouraged as set out in s 18.8 of the Funding Code Guidance.[6]

---

6   www.legalservices.gov.uk/docs/cls_main/FundingCodeDecisionMakingGuidance-OtherGuidance(Sections15-19_21-26and28)Sept07.pdf.

The public interest advisory panel

Even if a case would otherwise fall outside the scope of legal aid (eg a personal injury case, or one where the costs-benefit ratio cannot be satisfied, or even one where the merits might raise a question mark), it may be possible to qualify for legal aid on the ground that the case has 'significant wider public interest', as assessed for the LSC by a special panel. The opinion given by the panel (which includes representatives of the Consumers Association, the Bar Council, the Law Society, Liberty and JUSTICE) is only advisory, but regional offices will naturally take it into account in reaching any decision. 'Exceptional funding' has been granted for representation at inquests concerning deaths in hospital and for judicial review of medical decisions. The test as to whether an issue of 'public interest' is concerned is difficult to satisfy.

CONDITIONAL FEE AGREEMENTS (CFAs)

The history

At common law, any sort of contingency or conditional fee agreement (CFA) between solicitor and client was anathema. It was said by the courts time and again that it was totally unacceptable for the lawyer to have a financial interest in the outcome of a case. This applied equally to the simple situation where it was agreed or understood that the solicitor would only get paid or would only get his full fee if he won the case as to the obviously more contentious situation where he would get more than his full fee if he won and less or nothing if he lost. The terminology is unclear. Semantically, all these agreements could be called either contingency or conditional fee agreements. However, contingency fee is usually reserved these days for the American system, unknown here (as yet[7]), whereby the lawyer gets a share of the damages if he wins and nothing if he loses

Two points need to be made: first, this prohibition, which has the force of law (*Swain* v *Law Society* [1983] 1 AC 598, HL) applies only to contentious business. Solicitors have long been entitled to arrange a conditional fee in non-contentious business. Secondly, there has never been anything wrong, indeed it has been applauded, where a solicitor agrees to act for an impecunious client, it being well understood that he will not get paid if the case is lost. The sin lies in the subtle distinction that he was not entitled to agree that that should be the basis on which he would act, see the *Thai Trading* case (below). If the losing party could prove that that was the basis of acting, they could avoid payment of the winning opponent's costs under the indemnity principle.

Maintenance and champerty

Maintenance consisted in supporting a case financially when having no proper interest to do so ('improperly stirring up litigation and strife by

---

7   See, for example, a recent article in Legal Week: www.legalweek.com/legal-week/news/1586201/jackson-litigation-review-proposes-overhaul-contingency-fees.

giving aid to one party to bring or defend a claim without just cause or excuse').[8] It was permissible if the person concerned had a legitimate interest in supporting the action, whether financial or social or whatever. Champerty was a form of maintenance whereby the person maintaining the action took as a reward a share in the property recovered (ie it adds to maintenance 'the notion of a division of the spoils').[9]

Both used to be both tortious and criminal until the Criminal Law Act 1967. However, that Act preserved the common law rule that they were contrary to public policy.[10]

Lord Denning more than once expressed his horror of champerty, particularly in respect of the lawyer who charged a fee that would only be payable if his client was successful, whether as a portion of the damages recovered or merely his normal fee payable only if he won, or by way of uplift to his normal fee. It was really extraordinary that the contingency fee, traditionally outlawed to protect the client from the lawyer being tempted to cut corners to achieve success and 'in order to preserve the honour and honesty of the profession'[11] should now, for economic reasons only, be sanctified as the panacea for the problems of litigation with the lawyers being held up as men and women of such virtue that they could never be tempted to act other than in the client's best interests. (The Government sings a very different tune when it wants to inflame the public against lawyers and their fees, as it does from time to time.)[12]

In *R v Secretary of State for Transport, ex p Factortame* [2002] EWCA Civ 22, Lord Phillips MR explored the history of champerty, the court concluding that an arrangement under which accountants provided forensic accountancy services to litigants on a contingent fee basis was not one to which s 58 of the Courts and Legal Services Act 1990 had any application and was not void for champerty.

Cases decided under the old law

Conditional fees were first introduced by the Courts and Legal Services Act 1990, which by s 58 (which came into force in July 1993) provided that a lawyer could agree in writing for fees and expenses to be payable only in specified circumstances (any increase above normal fees, ie any uplift, had to be specified as a percentage). The situations in which a conditional fee agreement was permissible were first specified by regulations in 1995, which were amended to cover all proceedings in 1998.

So there was as yet no statutory authorisation for the agreements found to have been made in the *Thai Trading* case or in *Geraghty v Awwad* (see below). Those agreements therefore fell to be considered at common law.

In *Thai Trading Co v Taylor* [1998] QB 781 the arrangement was that the solicitor would recover his profit costs only if the claim succeeded (this may be called a normal costs conditional agreement). The Court

---

8 *Per* Lord Denning in *Re Trepca Mines Ltd (No 2)* [1963] Ch 199 at 219, CA.
9 *Per* Lord Mustill in *Giles v Thompson* [1994] 1 AC 142 at 161, HL.
10 For the current position see *Giles v Thompson* [1994] 1 AC 142 at 161, HL.
11 *Per* Lord Esher in *Pittman v Prudential Deposit Bank* (1896) 13 TLR 110 at 111, CA.
12 'A legal adviser who acquires a personal financial interest in the outcome of litigation may obviously find himself in a situation in which that interest conflicts with that obligation' (*per* Buckley LJ in *Wallersteiner v Moir (no 2)* [1975] QB 373, CA).

of Appeal reversed the trial judge and held that in the context of the current perception of public policy with regard to conditional fees, the agreement was not unenforceable (in this case, unlike the *Geraghty* case – see below). It was not a question of the solicitor seeking his fees against his client, who was his wife, but of claiming costs against the other side – if his client was not legally bound to pay his costs, the losing party would not be bound to pay them either. However, as the Court of Appeal later pointed out in *Awwad* v *Geraghty & Co* [2000] 3 WLR 1041, an essential plank in the reasoning of the court had been that the prohibition in the Solicitors Practice Rules against any sort of contingency fee did not have the force of law.[13] Unfortunately, the court had not been referred to the House of Lords decision in *Swain* v *Law Society* [1983] 1 AC 598 at 608, which established exactly the opposite.[14]

In *Geraghty*, Schiemann LJ listed powerful arguments for holding that in 1993 when the relevant normal fee conditional agreement was made between Geraghty and Co and their client, Mr Awwad, ie before such an agreement was authorised by the relevant statutory instrument, the agreement, although outlawed by the Solicitors Rules, was not unenforceable. Particularly noticeable is the judge's acknowledgement that:

> It seems odd that an open contractual statement of what is unobjectionably in a solicitor's mind should render unenforceable an agreement which would have been enforceable had the solicitor not shared his thoughts with his client and promised not to change his mind.

The arguments he listed in support of his conclusion that the agreement was unenforceable seem far less cogent. In particular, it seems most surprising that he listed the traditional reason, namely that the lawyer might be tempted to cut corners to achieve success if his fee depended on succeeding, seeing that that is precisely the temptation that practitioners are all now exposed to by the introduction of conditional fees.[15] However, he concluded that in 1993, despite the changing public perception and the clear indications given by the 1990 Act, any sort of conditional fee arrangement, even a normal fee agreement ('I get my normal costs if I win but nothing if I lose') was against public policy and so unenforceable at common law.[16]

In *Geraghty*, May LJ spoke of 'the difficulties and delays surrounding the introduction of conditional fee agreements'.

---

13 The Rules have naturally since been amended to permit a contingency agreement where authorised by statute.

14 As a footnote to *Swain,* reference may be made to *Mohamed* v *Alaga & Co* [2000] 1 WLR 1815, where the Court of Appeal refused to validate a contract in breach of the Solicitors' Practice Rules 1990 for payment to the claimant for introducing clients to the defendant firm (but they allowed a *quantum meruit* claim for services rendered).

15 The reader will not need any reminding that the Government has had no interest at all in 'access to justice' when legislating for conditional fees, merely in reducing the legal aid bill. If some few litigants are enabled to sue who would not have been able to do so under the old legal aid rules, that is an irrelevant by-product of the legislation.

16 The court plainly found it to be not without significance that the solicitor had endeavoured to conceal the fact of the agreement (that she would charge her lower normal rate if she lost (£90 per hour) but her higher normal rate if she won (£150)).

What were the initial problems of CFAs?

Conditional fees were introduced by Lord Mackay, but his reforms to the legal aid system had not gone very far before his Government lost power. The succeeding Labour Government pushed them forward precipitately without full consideration of, or sufficient foresight about, the many difficult issues they raised, particularly in the unpredictable context of medical claims (they are less of a problem in the context of simple personal injury claims where the issues of liability and causation at least are usually much clearer and far less often capable of sensible dispute). Seemingly unaware how complex the situation was that they were creating, that Labour Government would have abolished legal aid by now for clinical negligence claims had they not been forced by persistent lobbying to acknowledge that, although removing legal aid support for clinical negligence claims would certainly have the desired effect of reducing the legal aid bill, it was going to leave many wrongly injured patients without a remedy. The cost of investigating whether there was a viable clinical negligence claim was more than the average client could pay or specialist solicitor could afford to risk. In addition, in the beginning there was no market which could offer affordable insurance products to provide the necessary funding or cover the potential liabilities involved.

At first, the success fee of up to 100% of base costs was capped at a maximum of 25% of the damages recovered and it was not recoverable from the unsuccessful defendant. Premiums for ATE insurance were also non-recoverable.

At this time, very few clinical negligence cases were CFA funded as the risks were perceived as too great for claimants, their legal representatives and their insurers, contrasted with the likely rewards.

The current position – the era of recoverability

There are several different types of CFA, including those with success fees, those without success fees, discounted CFAs (where the solicitor gets paid a lower hourly rate if a specific result is not obtained) and variable rate CFAs (where the success fee is calculated in accordance with the sum recovered).

However, if a CFA is to be enforceable it has to comply with the provisions of ss 58 and 58A of the Courts and Legal Services Act (as amended by s 27 of the Access to Justice Act 1999 on 1 April 2000). A CFA is 'an agreement with a person providing advocacy or litigation services which provides for his fees and expenses, or any part of them, to be payable only in specified circumstances'. Such an agreement 'provides for a success fee if it provides for the amount of any fees to which it applies to be increased, in specified circumstances, above the amount which would be payable if it were not payable only in specified circumstances'. (The last clause, though rather tortuously worded, simply means the solicitor's normal going rate or 'base costs').

The CFA must be in writing and it must comply also with the regulations issued by the Lord Chancellor pursuant to s 58. If the CFA provides for a success fee, it must specify the percentage of the success fee, which must not exceed 100% (see the Conditional Fee Agreements Order 2000). 'Advocacy or litigation services' are defined by s 119(1).

Section 58A sets out supplementary provisions dealing with the sorts of work which cannot be funded by CFA and with enabling the Lord Chancellor to require the provider of the services to give certain information before the CFA is made, depending on the type of CFA. Importantly, the section provided for the recovery of success fees from the unsuccessful opponent.

Implemented at the same time under s 29 of the Access to Justice Act was the provision enabling the court to order the losing party to pay the premium under any ATE policy taken out by the successful party, irrespective of whether the case was funded by a CFA.

There is no requirement for a client with a CFA to obtain ATE insurance cover but it is prudent to protect him from liability for any adverse costs orders and for his own disbursements in the event the case is lost. The solicitor is, of course, required to advise the client on ATE insurance.

Even if a claim is successful overall, there may still be adverse costs ordered against the client particularly if a Part 36 offer is not beaten or if there are multiple defendants and one or more is successful in defending the case. Most ATE policies do cover against this risk.

Whilst there has been much success in personal injury claims in keeping ATE premiums to manageable proportions, those sought by insurers prepared to fund clinical negligence work are very high in comparison to the amount of liability covered because of the high risks and costs of such claims. There are nowadays a significant amount of providers with varying policy terms some with fixed premiums and others providing staged premiums depending upon the point at which the case concludes. The policy virtually always includes cover for its own premium and payment of the premium is deferred unless and until a successful outcome is achieved. Hence, providing the claim has adequate merits, there is no difficulty in arranging ATE insurance cover.

The CFA Regulations

There were a series of regulations from 1995 culminating in the Conditional Fee Regulations 2000 which were effective from 1 April 2000. Amending Regulations in 2003 provided for a simplified CFA.

The Regulations set out requirements concerning the form and contents of CFAs, particular requirements for those with a success fee, for those limited to sums recovered (the simplified CFA or 'CFA Lite') and the information to be given before the CFA was entered into and amendments.

The detailed requirements of the 2000 Regulations provided much ammunition for the attacks upon the validity of the CFA launched in so many cases by the losing defendant. These assaults mushroomed to such an extent that they became known as 'the costs wars', which was just one of the many epithets applied to the vast amount of satellite litigation which sprang up around this method of funding. If the client had no liability for costs to his own solicitor, then under the indemnity principle the losing opponent had nothing to reimburse.

The challenges to the validity of the CFAs in manifold cases ranged throughout all the Regulations. In the 'TAG litigation' or Accident Group Test Cases Tranche 2 it was argued that the legal representatives themselves had not provided the information to the client as required.

The Court of Appeal held that this requirement could be delegated if there was sufficient supervision by a solicitor. There were arguments about what counted as a success and that the client had not succeeded against the particular person named as defendant in the CFA. The failure for both parties to sign the CFA was fatal to its enforceability.

Particularly rich pickings were to be had by losing defendants in the area of reg 4, which governed the information to be given to the client before the CFA is entered into. These concerned explaining when the client's liability for costs would arise and when and how the costs could be assessed and whether the client's liability for adverse costs was already covered by existing insurance. Other methods of funding were to be considered and what was the appropriate method for the client, and whether insurance was appropriate for the client and, if so, which particular contract and why and whether the solicitor had an interest in the product he recommended. Some of this information was to be given orally and some of it both orally and in writing.

The failure to specify the amount of the deferment element of the CFA, to consider the availability of legal aid funding and the failure to properly investigate the existence of BTE policies which might be held by the client were all instances of decisions made against the validity of the CFAs concerned.

Some of the decisions, particularly amongst the lower ranks of the judiciary, were quite harsh. The costs involved in the procedural challenges could outweigh the costs of the substantive proceedings themselves. The Court of Appeal was being asked to intervene rather too often in these challenges.

In *Hollins* v *Russell* [2003] 4 All ER 590, the Court of Appeal stated:

> The court should be watchful when it considers allegations that there have been breaches of the CFA Regulations. The parliamentary purpose is to enhance access to justice, not to impede it, and to create better ways of delivering litigation services, not worse ones. These purposes will be thwarted if those who render good service to their clients under CFAs are at risk of going unremunerated at the culmination of the bitter trench warfare which has been such an unhappy feature of the recent litigation scene.

It held that only those departures from a regulation or requirement in s 58 which had a 'materially adverse effect' upon the protection afforded to the client or upon the 'proper administration of justice' could invalidate a CFA.

Sadly the challenges continued. In its later decision in *Garrett* v *Halton Borough Council, Myatt* v *National Coal Board* [2006] EWCA Civ 1017 CA, the Court of Appeal made clear that the validity of the CFA was to be determined at the date of its inception and subsequent events could not affect its enforceability. The degree of materiality of the breach could not be judged by reference to the consequences of the infringement. *Hollins*, it held, merely ruled that 'trivial and immaterial departures from the statutory requirements did not amount to a failure to satisfy the statutory conditions'. The language of Parliament was 'clear and uncompromising: if one or more of the applicable conditions is not satisfied, then the CFA is unenforceable'.

In *Myatt* it was not enough for the solicitor to ask unsophisticated clients whether they had credit cards, household or motor policies or trade union membership. In order to fulfil her duty (under reg 4(2)(c)) to investigate the existence of litigation expenses insurance, she should have taken reasonable steps to ascertain whether the client's risk to pay costs was already insured and these steps will depend upon a variety of circumstances such as the nature of the client, the circumstances in which the solicitor is instructed and the nature of the claim. The cost of the ATE premium may be a relevant factor and whether a referring body has already investigated the availability of BTE.

Garrett concerned the duty of a solicitor (under reg 4(2)(e)) to disclose to the client any interest he might have in recommending any insurance policy to cover the client's liabilities in the case. The solicitor there belonged to a panel which referred work to its member solicitors, provided they recommended a particular policy. The duty was only discharged by not merely informing the client of the fact of membership of the panel but also by explaining its implications.

Unfortunately for those practitioners still acting under CFAs entered into prior to 1 November 2005, the above regulations and series of decisions in force at the date of the CFA in question, can still be relied upon by their clients' unsuccessful opponents (the paying party) to try to defeat, if they can, any order for costs made against them at the end of the cases.

The position after 1 November 2005

For all CFAs entered into after this date, the position has changed again. It was generally felt that the situation had become intolerable. The Department of Constitutional Affairs looked into the problems and concluded that the regulations were too complicated to understand and too complicated to explain to lay clients. As from 1 November 2005, the regulations were quite simply revoked by the Conditional Fee Agreements (Revocation) Regulations 2005.

The very basic statutory provisions remain, effectively in relation to clinical negligence, that in order to be valid the CFA must be in writing and, if it has a success fee, it must specify the percentage success fee uplift, which must be limited to 100%. However, the current additional requirements for the making of CFAs are now dictated by the SRA's Code of Conduct 2011.

As shown above, the Code's principles and mandatory outcomes in relation to client care and funding are of general application. However, outcome O (1.6) requires solicitors to only enter into fee arrangements that are legal and which cater for the client's needs and best interests. Otherwise the sole reference to a CFA is in the non-mandatory indicative behaviour IB (1.17) which exhorts a solicitor acting under a CFA to give the client 'all relevant information relating to that arrangement'.

In the case of *Garbutt* v *Edwards* [2005] EWCA Civ 1206, the Court of Appeal had to consider the effect of non-compliance with the old Solicitors' Practice Rule 15, concerning the giving of costs estimates to clients. It held that although the Code of Conduct had statutory effect, this rule allowed the solicitor some discretion and therefore the failure to follow it could not render the retainer invalid. Non-compliance was a disciplinary matter only.

A Law Society Model CFA was introduced 'for use in personal injury and clinical negligence cases only' from 1 November 2005, which was to be read in conjunction with the Law Society document *What you need to know about a CFA*. (Both of these documents are published on the Law Society website as Appendices 2 and 3 respectively of the latest Law Society Guidance *Payment by Results*.)[17]

This is still the current Law Society Model CFA. It is very short and sets out what work and associated proceedings are covered and what is not covered. It sets out the circumstances in which the client's liability for any costs might arise, the percentage amount of success fee and the percentage of any deferment element.

The accompanying Law Society leaflet, which was designed specifically to assist the client, is clear and informative in explaining the agreement and how it works.

Since 1 October 2008, the CFA and any retainer will need to include the notice of a right to cancel the agreement within seven days if the retainer or CFA was made or offered at the client's or another person's home or at the client's place of work. (See the Cancellation of Contracts made in a Consumer's Home or Place of Work etc Regulations 2008).

Indeed, the practitioner will need to be aware of all changes in any other areas of the law which may impact upon CFAs.

Practical considerations

Whether or not to take on a case funded by a success fee is an important financial decision for the firm and often a committee of partners would be involved in weighing the merits and participating in the risk assessment process whereby the success fee uplift is fixed.

There is no set formula for the calculation but the risk of losing the case as a percentage is converted into a percentage success fee.

As the solicitor will receive no profit costs and often no disbursements until the successful conclusion of the case, the solicitor can charge for the delay in having to shoulder these costs for the relevant period. Often this is something in the order of 10% or whatever can be justified in terms of the firm's overall on-going operating expenses, but it forms part of the maximum 100% success fee uplift on base costs. As this deferment element will not be recoverable from the defendant in high risk cases, this element will just serve to reduce the defendant's liability.

Counsel's fees can be dealt with as a disbursement under the CFA, but normally counsel would be working under a corresponding CFA. A model CFA for use in personal injury and clinical negligence cases has been prepared jointly by the Association of Personal Injury Lawyers and the Personal Injuries Bar Association.

There has been much satellite litigation concerning the reasonableness of success fees in personal injury cases, particularly in RTA cases. The Court of Appeal decision in the case of *Callery* v *Gray*, in the context of RTA claims, suggested that for those cases which were not expected to settle until a later stage of the litigation, a two-stage success fee might be used. A series of subsequent Court of Appeal authorities encouraged the

---

17 www.lawsociety.org.uk/secure/file/188770/e:/teamsite-deployed/documents/
templatedata/Publications/Practice%20advice%20service%20booklets/Documents/
paymentbyresults.pdf.

use of such a two-stage success fee. It was held that a solicitor who sought a lower success fee if the case settled at an early stage in the process might be better able to justify a higher success fee if the case progressed to a more advanced stage of the litigation. (Indeed the Law Society Model CFA 2005 makes provision for a two-stage success fee).

The merits of a clinical negligence case are particularly much more uncertain and difficult to assess at the outset where often the only material to hand would be the client's statement, which might indeed be of little, if any, assistance.

If there were to be a challenge, the reasons in support of the risk assessment which must be disclosed on assessment will necessarily come under critical scrutiny.

It has been the practice of some specialist clinical negligence practitioners to offer a CFA at an early stage and to apply a 100% success fee on the basis that they are assuming a substantial risk of failure in the absence of the relevant facts which prevents them from properly assessing the merits of the claim.

In the case of *Oliver* v *Whipps Cross University Hospital NHS Trust* [2009] EWCH 1104 (QBD), a claim was brought by an estate in respect of the deceased's death in hospital from septicaemia. The costs judge reduced the 100% success fee sought on the basis that the solicitors, in taking the case on, must have felt that it stood better than 50% chance of success. On appeal from his substitution of a 67% success fee (representing a 60% chance of success), Jack J disagreed with the costs judge's finding. He considered that at the outset the case was indeed uncertain and faced difficulties and, bearing in mind what the solicitors then knew, it could easily have been assessed with prospects of success of less than 50%. Jack J also rejected the argument that, in order to establish a 100% success fee, the solicitors would have to have set a two-stage fee.

Six months later in November 2009, the same solicitors' 100% success fee came under scrutiny again in the unreported case of *McCarthy* v *Essex Rivers Healthcare NHS Trust Authority*.[18] The claim was for delay in treatment of compartment syndrome following a leg fracture. The solicitors appealed the costs Master's reduction of their success fee to 80%. In upholding the Master's decision, MacKay J held that if solicitors did offer an early CFA the court would look closely at reasonableness. He interpreted the Court of Appeal's decision in *Ku* v *Liverpool City Council* [2005] EWCA Civ 475 differently from Jack J in *Oliver*. He felt that that the Court of Appeal considered an early success fee of 100% could not be deemed to be reasonable, whereas a 100% fee could have been reasonable if part of a staged success fee.

MacKay J also commented on the presence of a term of the CFA, standard in these agreements, which enables solicitors to end the CFA at any time if they believe that the client is unlikely to win. MacKay J felt that this was highly relevant in his decision as this ability skewed the financial effect of failure if weak cases could be weeded out earlier on and when costs were still relatively low.

This important aspect of risk assessment in clinical negligence is therefore ripe for consideration by the Court of Appeal.

---

18   (13 November 2009, unreported), QBD HQ06X03686; Lawtel Document No AC0123275.

Another significant potential challenge in clinical negligence cases is the amount of the premium paid for ATE insurance to cover the client's liability for the opponent's costs and own disbursements should the claim fail. It is particularly important to fully use up any BTE cover that might exist before seeking ATE cover. However, the later in the stage of the claim such cover is sought, the higher the premium is likely to be. Some insurers maintain that cover can even be arranged, if necessary, as late as during the trial itself!

There are several companies offering cover but the premiums are high and can amount to very significant proportions of the amount of the liability sought to be insured against. It may be wise sometimes to seek quotes from several companies in order to ensure that there is as little justification for challenge as possible.

It is of advantage if the ATE cover is self-insuring as regards its premium. Increasingly these days, cover is staged so that increased premiums become payable once later stages in the litigation are reached. Beware that 'pre-proceedings' may be just that, so that an increased premium becomes payable immediately upon the issue of the Claim Form whether or not it is actually served.

Make sure, however, wherever possible, that adequate cover is sought in the first place because top-up cover may be prohibitively expensive or may need to be sought from a different provider.

Some firms may have membership of a provider's panel and may have delegated authority to issue cover but full advice as to alternative products needs to be given to the client and the solicitor's particular interests have to be declared. This advice should be recorded.

In some costs assessment proceedings, details might need to be provided by the ATE insurer as to how the premium was calculated in order to justify its reasonableness.

Another trap for the unwary is the Notice of Funding. N251 has to be given to the court on issue and must be served with the Claim Form setting out the date of the CFA. The Notice must also specify the policy number and date of any ATE insurance and provide details of the insurer concerned, of the level of cover and if it is staged, the point at which any increased premium is payable. (It is an anomaly that there is no equivalent requirement for those acting under a BTE policy, whether for claimant or for defendant). A separate Notice of Funding needs to be given in this way if ATE cover is obtained after Notice of Funding as to the CFA is served and a fresh Notice of Funding has to be given if any of the information previously supplied is no longer accurate. (The requirement for details of the level of ATE cover and staging of the premiums was brought in pursuant to amendments to the CPR coming into force on 1 October 2009).

Where a solicitor offers a CFA to a client who previously had a legal aid certificate for the same proceedings, the solicitor must properly terminate the legal aid retainer before the CFA can be entered into.

CFAs can be retrospective, in that the date when it is deemed to have come into effect can be an earlier date, although the CFA itself must not be back-dated. *Forde* v *Birmingham City Council* [2009] EWHC 12 (QB) suggests that the operation of the success fee can even be back-dated with the parties' agreement, but this concept has not been fully argued before the courts. Most paying parties would oppose any claim for a success fee preceding the date upon which they received notice of funding.

In *Hollins* (see above), the Court of Appeal also considered:

> that it should become normal practice for a CFA to be disclosed for the purpose of costs proceedings in which a success fee is claimed. If the CFA contains confidential information relating to other proceedings, it may be suitably redacted before disclosure takes place. Attendance notes and other correspondence should not ordinarily be disclosed, but the judge conducting the assessment may require the disclosure of material of this kind if a genuine issue is raised. A genuine issue is one in which there is a real chance that the CFA is unenforceable as a result of failure to satisfy the applicable conditions.

Under para 40.14 of the Costs Practice Direction, the receiving party could elect to rely on other evidence of compliance rather than to disclose the CFA itself.

This consequently remains a common point of dispute in assessments. Arguably the greater the information now required by the Costs Practice Direction post-October 2009 renders disclosure of the CFA superfluous.

As complex and as time-consuming as funding issues can be, especially in discussing them with the client, unfortunately the costs of arranging the funding of the action are not recoverable against the losing party. In the Court of Appeal decision *Motto* v *Trafigura Limited* [2011] EWCA Civ 1150, in the context of CFA funding, the Master of the Rolls stated that such costs 'are ultimately attributable to the need of a litigant to fund the litigation as opposed to the actual funding of the litigation itself'.

THE FUTURE

The Jackson Report

In December 2008, the then Master of the Rolls, Sir Anthony Clarke, commissioned Lord Justice Jackson to 'review the rules and principles governing the costs of civil litigation and to make recommendations in order to promote access to justice at proportionate cost'. His preliminary report (663 pages long) was published in May 2009 and after very wide consultation with all concerned. His *Review of civil litigation costs: final report* (557 pages long) was published on 14 January 2010.

Jackson looked at the amount of litigation, all the methods of funding, those discussed above, third-party funding, contingency legal aid funds (CLAFs) and supplementary legal aid schemes (SLASs), contingency fees (in other jurisdictions) and fixed costs. He devoted 70 pages to personal injuries litigation and discussed other specific types of litigation, including clinical negligence. He looked at methods of controlling costs and the procedures, including the assessment of costs.

What Jackson termed his 'major' recommendations and those of particular relevance to clinical negligence work are as follows:

Success fees and ATE insurance premiums should cease to be recoverable

CFAs, Jackson said, have been the major contributor to disproportionate costs in civil litigation in England and Wales, the two key drivers being the lawyer's success fee and the ATE insurance premium. Their irrecoverability, he felt, will lead to significant savings, whilst providing access to justice. Clients could still enter into 'no win, no fee' agreements, but they would have to bear the success fees, payable likely out of their damages.

Increase in general damages

To ensure proper compensation and that the damages are not substantially eaten into by the legal fees, Jackson recommended that general damages be increased by 10% and that the maximum amount of damages that lawyers may deduct for success fees be capped at 25% (excluding any damages for future care or future losses). Jackson felt that in the majority of cases, successful claimants should be no worse off than under the current regime.

Referral fees

These should not be permitted for personal injury cases. They add to the costs of litigation without adding any real value to it.

Qualified one way costs shifting

ATE insurance premiums add considerably to the costs of litigation, which can be reduced by taking away the need for insurance. Qualified costs shifting means the claimant will not have to pay the defendant's costs if the claim is unsuccessful but the defendant will have to pay the claimant's costs if it is successful. However, a different costs order may be appropriate where conduct or financial resources justify this.

Enhanced Part 36 rewards

A claimant who recovers more than his Part 36 offer should receive a 10% uplift on total damages.

Jackson also recommended that contingency fee agreements for contentious business should be legitimised. Under such agreements, the lawyer is only be paid where the client's case succeeds and on the basis of a percentage of the sum awarded or agreed. However, Jackson recommended that the losing party should only be responsible for the normal between the parties costs and the balance of the fee should be paid by the winning party (with a similar 25% cap applying in personal injury cases as in CFAs). He further recommended that the terms of contingency fee agreements should be regulated.

Clinical negligence

Jackson made some additional recommendations specific to clinical negligence litigation:

- Time for the letter of response (under the Pre-Action Protocol) is extended to four months.
- Where liability is intended to be denied, independent expert evidence should be sought within this period.
- Defendants should be incentivised to get to grips with the issues during the Protocol period.

- The Protocol should provide for a three-month moratorium on the issue of proceedings, where the defendant wishes to offer terms of settlement without admission of liability.
- A screening fee should be paid by clients who can afford it and, if the claim is successful, it will be recoverable as costs, but if clients cannot afford it they can get legal aid.
- Harmonisation of case management directions throughout England and Wales.
- Docketing is essential (where a case is assigned to one particular judge).
- A third clinical negligence Master should be appointed in QBD in London.
- A two-year pilot of Master Yoxall's proposals for clinical negligence budgeting should be carried out.
- Application of a costs budget of £15,000 for costs up to letter of claim and a further maximum of £15,000 up to issue and the claimant is to apply to the court for authority to exceed those figures.
- Hourly rates are to be reviewed by Jackson's recommended Cost Council.
- The NHS Redress Scheme provided for in the NHS Redress Act 2006 should be implemented by the drawing up of the necessary regulations.
- Financial penalties should be introduced for the failure to provide copy medical records in accordance with the Protocol.

Lord Young and the compensation culture

On 14 June 2010, David Cameron announced the appointment of the Rt Hon Lord Young of Graffham as Adviser to the Prime Minister on health and safety laws and the growth of the compensation culture.

In his report *Common sense, common safety*, published in October 2010, Lord Young stated: 'The problem of the compensation culture prevalent in society today is, however, one of perception rather than reality'. However, he was concerned about the steady increase in claims fuelled by the growth of claims management companies, advertising and the payment of referral fees. Also at the root of the problems was the introduction of CFAs and ATE insurance which incentivised the public to bring claims without fear of financial risk.

Lord Young was critical too of the enormous costs racked up by the lawyers, 'secure in the knowledge they will be charged to the losing party' and disproportionately large compared to the damages obtained. Statistics were quoted from the NHSLA.

He called for the adoption of Jackson's proposals as soon as possible. His recommendations included extending the Road Traffic Accident Personal Injury Scheme for claims less than £10,000 with fixed costs to other personal injury and lower value clinical negligence claims. Lord Young suggested that the limit be increased to £25,000. He felt that the NHS Redress Act 2006 had missed an opportunity to fundamentally improve the way clinical negligence claims are handled (in not focussing on the fact-finding phase prior to the pursuit of a claim).

He warmly welcomed the Ministry of Justice's consultation into the implementation of the Jackson Report's proposals due in the Autumn of 2010.

The Ministry of Justice's Consultation Paper CP 13/10, *Proposals for reform of civil justice funding and costs in England and Wales – implementation of Lord Justice Jackson's recommendations*, was published in November 2010. Responses were sought by 14 February 2011.

The Consultation Questions were put in such a way as to encourage agreement with Jackson's proposals. If his primary recommendations were felt to be too unpalatable, resort was had to responses concerning his secondary recommendations.

At the same time, the Ministry of Justice published its *Proposals for reform of legal aid in England and Wales* (Consultation Paper CP12/10). The Foreword by Kenneth Clarke, the Lord Chancellor and Secretary, made clear the Government's view that the legal aid system was far too expensive and needed to be cut dramatically. Economic recovery required a 23% reduction in the Ministry of Justice's budget, to which the proposals would substantially contribute. Responses to this were also requested by 14 February 2011.

'The radical, wide-ranging and ambitious programme of reform, which aims to ensure that legal aid is targeted to those who need it most' proposed the removal from the scope of legal aid altogether many areas of civil litigation, including clinical negligence.

The proposals, however, included the setting up of a funding scheme for excluded cases, so as to ensure the Government was compliant with its domestic and international legal obligations including those under the European Convention of Human Rights to provide for 'equality of arms'. The Consultation expressly referred to obstetric cases with high disbursement costs which might have difficulty securing CFA funding as likely beneficiaries of such a special scheme.

Implementation

On 29 March 2011, Kenneth Clarke formally announced the Government's intention to undertake the implementation of all of the major proposals of Jackson. The only change announced concerned the allowing of the recovery of ATE insurance premiums to cover the cost of expert reports only in clinical negligence cases.

On 21 June 2011, on the same day that it announced its response to the Legal Aid Consultation confirming its intention to remove clinical negligence from the scope of legal aid, the Government introduced into Parliament the Legal Aid, Sentencing and Punishment of Offenders Bill. This is the vehicle for the implementation of such of the Jackson and the legal aid proposals as require primary legislation.

Opposition to the proposals has been galvanised in the House of Lords where the Bill has been receiving a rough ride and it is currently at the Committee Stage .It remains to be seen in precisely what form it emerges and when.

AvMA is currently applying for a judicial review of the Government's decision to remove clinical negligence from the scope of legal aid.

Some of the more minor reforms not requiring legislative authority have already been implemented including the extension of time to four months for service of the letter of response under the Pre-Action Protocol.

Unhelpfully, the Legal Services Commission implemented a 10% reduction in legal aid prescribed rates as from 3 October 2011.

A better way forward

It is a shame that after all the upheavals and ferocity of the costs wars and just at a time when the idiosyncrasies of the current CFA regime are now better appreciated, further profound and far-reaching changes are to be inflicted upon the civil funding system.

Implementation of the present proposals will involve major departures from well-established legal principles, that the tortfeasor pays and that costs follow the event, and the indemnity principle itself.

Further satellite litigation can only be expected when such great changes are brought in with all the uncertainties necessarily attendant upon new rules and legislation, especially when large sums are at stake.

There is no doubt that CFAs succeeded in providing access to justice when legal aid was abolished for personal injury cases. The idea, however, was that the success fee under the CFA was there to compensate the practitioner for the costs of cases lost. The proposed capping of the success fee cannot assist in the achieving of this goal and can only further restrict the cases which the practitioner will agree to take on. Such a success fee may well offer insufficient incentive for riskier claims where trial is a real prospect, as in virtually all clinical negligence claims.

It further bears repeating that the irrecoverability of the success fee and of the ATE premium will have significant adverse consequences for the more seriously injured clients. Needless to say, those who act on behalf of claimants are concerned that claimants should not have to foot any of the costs bill, which the tortfeasors ought to bear. Jackson understood that in the majority of low value cases the claimant may be even better off than at present. The flipside, however, is that in the higher value cases, those suffering serious injuries, the claimant would be much worse off than currently.

Suppose a claim for tetraplegia could likely involve substantial past losses of £780,000 and general damages of £220,000. The solicitors' basic costs could well approach £250,000 (with liability and then quantum issues fought separately to the doors of the court). As compensation for his success fee liability of £250,000, Jackson awards the claimant a 10% increase in his general damages, a paltry £22,000!

General damages have always been appallingly low, as the Law Commission recognised ten years ago when it recommended an increase of up to 50%.[19]

Fixed success fees in RTA and employer's liability cases have assisted in reducing previous excesses, but at the same time they fairly reward those winning cases which are fought to trial.

A fairer solution in clinical negligence, involving less risk of injustice, uncertainty and the wasted costs of satellite litigation, could well be adapted from an extension to the line of recent Court of Appeal decisions on CFA funding based upon several stage success fees, possibly fixed at each stage.

The earlier the case is settled, the less the costs paid and the success fee in any event is subject to the scrutiny of the court in the detailed assessment proceedings at the end of the case.

---

19   Law Commission Report No 257 *Damages for Non-Pecuniary Loss* (1999).

One way costs shifting would well avoid the need for the hefty element of the ATE insurance premium (and indeed the NHSLA is already offering this in some cases), but proper arrangements for funding for the commonly substantial disbursements involved particularly in prolonged complex cases are essential.

The prospect of a large liability for disbursements following an unsuccessful outcome may well deter worthy claimants from even investigating their claims.

Smaller value clinical negligence claims could well be more cost effectively dealt with along the lines contemplated by the Redress Scheme and in tandem with the investigation of NHS complaints and indeed this is currently being explored by the relevant bodies concerned. However, decisions made within the context of such a scheme must be subject to outside impartial scrutiny and challenge, where appropriate. (See for example the Welsh schemes set out in Chapter 23.)

It is the authors' view that, in order to preserve true equality of arms, some form of legal aid must be retained for the funding of costly claims, particularly of vulnerable claimants, or requiring heavy investigation work, or of uncertain merit or issues of major public interest.

Chapter 25

Costs

Martyn McLeish

There are only two bases upon which lawyers provide their services. They are either paid or they offer their services for free: *pro bono publico*. Legal Services Commission (LSC) funding, Conditional Fee Agreements (CFAs), insurance-funded and private client work, are species of retainer providing for payment under certain agreed terms. Funding itself is the subject of its own chapter in this book.[1] However, the essential point made at the outset of this chapter is as simple as it is complex: litigation costs money. How a case is funded and who pays the costs incurred, are fundamental to clinical negligence practice.[2]

This chapter can only scratch the surface of the issues and at best aspire to provide an introduction rather than a definitive analysis.[3] Discussion is limited to a short summary of the basic principles, the twin pillars of costs jurisprudence: the costs-shifting rule and the indemnity principle. This chapter then considers general rules about costs, including Part 36 and costs capping. Reasons of space prohibit any discussion of either detailed or summary assessment, but there is a section on the principles of assessment and, in particular, proportionality. A final section deals with CFAs.

THE TWIN PILLARS OF COSTS JURISPRUDENCE

The twin pillars of costs jurisprudence provide simplicity and symmetry which in the ordinary case will cause little confusion.

The first pillar is the costs-shifting rule by which the 'loser' pays the winner's costs, ie the costs' burden *shifts* from the unsuccessful party to the successful party.[4] Although a fact of everyday life in the context of

---

1 Chapter 24.
2 This chapter is written after publication of *The review of civil litigation costs: final report* and the Legal Aid, Sentencing, and Punishment of Offenders Bill is currently before Parliament. Discussion of the full effect of these changes would require a book in itself. The aim of this chapter is more modest and simply seeks to provide an introduction to the basic principles.
3 The definitive treatment of these issues is to be found in *Cook on Costs*, reference in this chapter is to the 2011 edition, hereinafter '*Cook*'.
4 See CPR 44.3(2)(a) 'the general rule is that the unsuccessful party will be ordered to pay the costs of the successful party', discussed further below.

clinical negligence, it is important to bear in mind that the costs-shifting rule is a historical artefact of the common law and not a principle of universal application. Many other jurisdictions – the USA in particular – do not have such a system, and in the UK itself there are no costs jurisdictions such as the Employment Tribunal. The existence of the costs-shifting rule is one of the unique features of clinical negligence litigation in England and Wales.[5]

The second pillar of costs jurisprudence is the indemnity principle. The costs the losing party pays have to be based upon and cannot exceed the amount the winning party is obliged to pay his legal representatives. In effect the losing party 'indemnifies' the winning party's legal obligations to pay his solicitor's costs.[6]

Applying these principles, the general position at the end of a case will be that the losing party will pay the winning party's costs and those costs will be assessed on the basis of the fees the winning client is charged by his solicitor. Some moments of reflection will lead us to realise the potential problems with the general position: are there not cases in which it is impossible to say who has 'won'? What happens when a party wins on some issues but not others? What happens when a party 'wins' but his conduct has unnecessarily prolonged the litigation or otherwise made it more expensive? What happens when a party beats or fails to beat a Part 36 offer? There may be cases in which it is unjust to allow the losing party to pay the full scale of the fees the lay client is prepared to incur. The process of assessment must limit *inter partes* recovery to those costs which are reasonable, but how does the court determine what is 'reasonable' and what principles apply to this assessment?

SOME RULES ABOUT COSTS

Historically courts have had a wide discretion relating to costs. CPR 44.3 (1) provides that the court:

has discretion as to –
(a)   whether costs are payable by one party to another;
(b)   the amount of those costs; and
(c)   when they are paid.

The 'general rule' is that 'the unsuccessful party will be ordered to pay the costs of the successful party' (CPR 44.3(2)(a)) but 'the court may make a different order' (CPR 44.3(2) (b)).

The overriding objective of the CPR and its costs provisions allow the court to take a forensic and nuanced view of costs. Costs orders can be subtle enough to take into account the 'measure' of success as well as success itself. A party can be awarded a proportion of its costs where it has achieved only partial success. The order can reflect success or failure on a particular issue.

---

5   This point has added resonance at the time of writing because Sir Rupert Jackson proposes the abolition of the costs-shifting rule for personal injury claims and replacement with 'one way costs shifting'.
6   Michael Cook identifies the first record of the principle being expounded in *Harold* v *Smith* (1860) 5 H & N 381, *Cook* p 256.

In making a costs order the court *must* have regard to *all* the circumstances of the case including:

(a)   the conduct of the parties;
(b)   whether a party has succeeded on part of his case, even if he has not been wholly successful; and
(c)   any payment into court or admissible offer to settle made by a party which is drawn to the court's attention, and which is not an offer to which costs consequences under Part 36 apply. [CPR 44.3(4)]

In considering cases when the general rule does not apply, the most important factors to consider will be the conduct of the parties, the nature of 'success' in the particular case, and the nature and consequences of any offer.

The conduct of parties as set out in CPR 44.3(5) includes conduct before as well as during proceedings (CPR 44.3(5)(a)) and:

(b)   whether it was reasonable for a party to raise, pursue or contest a particular allegation or issue;
(c)   the manner in which a party has pursued or defended his case or a particular allegation or issue;
(d)   whether a claimant who has succeeded in his claim, in whole or in part, exaggerated his claim.

Although the wide discretion of the court allows for no hard and fast rules, it is possible to comment on some of the circumstances in which the general rule will not apply or applies in some modified form.

Multiple defendants

Bringing claims against multiple defendants makes litigation more complicated and expensive. Damages recovered against an unsuccessful defendant may be wiped out by the expense of meeting the costs of other successful defendants.[7] Historically the courts have recognised the injustice that the strict application of the general rule creates in these circumstances and the wide discretion the court enjoys in relation to costs includes the power to order that the unsuccessful defendant bear the burden of the successful defendant's costs. This can be achieved in one of two ways: the unsuccessful party pays the successful defendant's costs directly to him following *Sanderson* v *Blyth Theatre Company* [1903] 2 KB 533, CA; or the claimant pays the successful defendant's costs which he then recovers from the unsuccessful defendant as part of the costs of the action following *Bullock* v *London General Omnibus Co* [1907] 1 KB 264, CA.

The fact that the court *can* make either a *Bullock* or *Sanderson* order does not mean that the court *will* make such an order, and the court will have regard to all the circumstances of the case.

In cases where one defendant blames another potential defendant for the claimant's injury, a *Bullock* or *Sanderson* order may be appropriate. Where the allegations made by a defendant against another potential defendant amount to a complete defence to the claim, it may be reasonable for the claimant to sue both defendants. However, the fact that one

---

7   The case of *Johnson* v *John and Waltham Forest Health Authority* is discussed below.

defendant blames another is only one factor to be taken into account and the court has to consider whether or not it had been reasonable for the claimant to pursue the allegations against the successful defendant; see *Irvine* v *Commissioner of Police for the Metropolis* [2005] EWCA Civ 129, cf *Moon* v *Garrett* [2006] EWCA Civ 1121.

The CPR is a complete procedural code. Active case management is intended to root out unmeritorious causes of action at an early stage, and where such claims are continued they are more likely to result in adverse costs orders. The fact that a party has succeeded at a hearing either in whole or in part is still a powerful indicator of where the costs burden should fall. The courts will not readily accept that it is fair for an unsuccessful party to bear the additional burden of a successful party's costs without good reason. *Bullock* and *Sanderson* orders may have diminishing value as the courts encourage the use of issue-based and percentage-based costs orders.

The ability of the claimant to meet an adverse costs order is an important practical consideration. While the inability of an impecunious claimant to meet the costs of a successful defendant should not of itself provide the successful party with the expectation of an indemnity from the unsuccessful party,[8] there is no practical utility in the successful defendant pursuing an impecunious claimant for its costs. In modern litigation, when a claimant has the benefit of ATE insurance the particular problems with which *Bullock* and *Sanderson* were concerned are not present as the successful party's costs will in theory be met by the ATE insurer. However, CFAs give rise to their own problems. In particular 'success' is usually defined as an order for damages in the claimant's favour. CFAs do not provide the client with protection against issue-based or proportionate costs orders. Where there is a shortfall between what is charged to the client by the legal representative and what is recovered *inter partes*, the legal representative will go unremunerated or the shortfall will come out of the claimant's damages.

The consequences of bringing proceedings against multiple defendants are particularly relevant to clinical negligence practice when claims may proceed against an NHS Trust and a GP or others. In many cases claims against either the GP or the trust will not be brought in the alternative, the trust will not criticise the GP or vice versa. The outcome of the case may depend on issues of fact. Allegations of breach of duty and causation may only succeed in full against some but not all defendants. The last edition of this book illustrated the problem by reference to the case of *Johnson* v *John (1) Waltham Forest Health Authority (2)* (31 July 1998, unreported), CA. The case against the GP was that he did not diagnose the deceased's disease. The hospital failed to diagnose and treat the disease. There was a dispute on the facts as to what had been discussed by the GP in consultation with the deceased. The trial judge preferred the evidence of the GP and the claim against him failed. The judge ordered the claimants to pay all the costs incurred by the GP. The costs of bringing the claim against the GP and the burden of paying the GP's costs would effectively wipe out the damages recovered against the health authority. The Court of Appeal considered the quality of the advice

---

8   *Johnson* v *Ribbins* [1977] 1 WLR 1458, CA.

provided by the claimants' legal representatives. They had been in a position before the trial to assess proceeding against the GP. While it was possible that negligence might be established against the GP, the task of establishing causation was difficult. By contrast the health authority's expert appeared to concede negligence. An offer from the GP had been rejected. The value of the claim had to be taken into account. On a costs/ benefit analysis the risks of proceedings against the GP outweighed the benefits. In the circumstances it was not appropriate to interfere with the trial judge's decision.

Johnson has to be considered on its own facts and was decided before the CPR. The availability of Part 36 offers is one way in which the claimant can protect himself from adverse costs orders. If the parties to litigation are clear why the claim is pursued against them and what the potential costs consequences will be, appropriate Part 36 offers on liability in particular may be of considerable assistance in protecting the claimant's position when proceedings are contemplated against more than one party. Issue-based and percentage costs orders can also accrue to the claimant's benefit in such circumstances.

Ganz v *Childs* [2011] EWHC 13 is a more recent case in which the court had to determine whether or not the claimant or an unsuccessful defendant ought to be liable for the successful defendant's case. In this case, although the claim against the GP succeeded, that against the hospital failed. The trial judge (Foskett J) ordered that the claimant should pay the hospital's costs.

Partial success

Mr Storm Larkins brought a claim against five defendants for the failure to diagnose and treat tuberculosis. His case in negligence against four of the defendants succeeded but failed against one defendant. Mr. Larkins' success on liability was compounded by the fact that the judge found that he was not a credible witness, had exaggerated his losses, and had been dishonest. His claim for substantial loss of earnings was unsustainable and he was awarded only general damages. Although Mr Larkins' claim was successful, it was a pyrrhic victory. The costs of the successful defendant wiped out his award of general damages. He had rejected a substantial payment into court, and had to pay the costs of a trial involving 20 lay and 22 expert witnesses.[9] 'Partial' success does not adequately describe the personal disaster the outcome of this trial was for Mr Larkins.

Partial success in clinical negligence cases is common. The claimant may succeed in proving negligence but only modest damages may be awarded by comparison with the large sums claimed, invariably because the claimant fails in some aspect of the case in relation to causation. In *Oksuzoglu* v *Kay* [1998] Lloyds Rep Med 129, CA, the claimant failed to satisfy the court that the negligence of the defendants caused the loss of his right leg. However, their negligence had resulted in a period of pain and suffering prior to the correct treatment being given, justifying a claim for general damages and some care. The defendants effectively 'won' the case.

---

9   (22 May 1998, unreported), QBD, Dyson J.

In most cases, as in that of Mr Larkins, defendants can protect themselves against the costs consequences of partial success by making appropriate Part 36 offers. However, if no effective offers are made the courts have to consider who the real 'winner' is, and in this respect there are several competing arguments. Applying the general rule, if the claimant is awarded damages, even if he did not recover as much as had been hoped, success has still been achieved. The circumstances may be that the claimant would still have had to come to court to recover even those damages recovered, and the partial success made no or little difference to the costs incurred. If it was reasonable for the claimant to proceed in this way, he should be entitled to his costs. At the other extreme, a claimant may win and recover a substantial amount of damages but certain allegations may have failed or been abandoned at trial. In complex litigation, a successful party may well fail in one or more issues and it would be inappropriate to award only part of the successful party's costs.[10] The successful party's costs should not be reduced simply because he had not recovered as much as had been hoped.[11]

Where a claimant's success is only partial, the court has to have regard to the issues in dispute at trial and to what extent the costs incurred relate to the failure. Where the claimant's failure in respect of some aspects of the claim had little relevance or impact on the defendant's conduct, the usual costs consequences will follow. Where the true nature of the case is that the defendant has essentially won on the main or essential issues, the claimant can expect an adverse costs order. However, in many cases the court will be able to make an issues-based or percentage costs order which more accurately reflects the position.

A recent case illustrates the issues discussed above. In *Medway Primary Care Trust* v *Marcus* [2011] EWCA Civ 750, the claimant lost before the trial judge on his central allegation that the negligence of the defendants had resulted in the amputation of his left leg. However there had been breaches of duty which caused delay during which the claimant suffered pain and injury compensatable by a modest award of £ 2,000 general damages. Having achieved judgment for this sum the judge awarded the claimant 50% of his costs. This decision was reversed on appeal and the defendants recovered 75% of their costs. The award of £ 2,000 was 'insignificant' in the context of the claim itself:

> it was in truth a last minute addition to salvage something (0.25%) from an action which the respondent had lost.

The essential issue in the claim was causation and the defendants had succeeded on that point. Moreover, the defendants had maintained the same defence in relation to causation from the outset of the claim. The fact that no Part 36 or Calderbank offers had been made was not relevant to the issue of who had *won* the case. The decision in the Court of Appeal is notable for the dissenting judgment of Jackson LJ. In characteristically blunt terms at the end of his speech he pointed out that:

---

10   See *HLB Kidsons (a firm)* v *Lloyds Underwriters* [2007] EWHC 2699 (Comm).
11   *Hall* v *Stone* [2007] EWCA Civ 1354. The claimants were awarded about a third of the damages asked for and the trial judge awarded 60% of their costs. This was reversed on appeal because the exaggeration of their claims had no real effect on costs.

The defendants made no Part 36 offer in this case and in my view they should accept the consequences.

Underlying this assertion were important public policy considerations:

> Part 36 ... affords protection for defendants who have a weak case on liability but a strong case on quantum. Such defendants can and should protect their position on costs by making an appropriate Part 36 offer at an early stage. If only defendants and their insurers would take this course, a large amount of unnecessary litigation would be avoided.

Although such considerations did not persuade the other members of the Court of Appeal to follow Jackson LJ, his analysis is a powerful one which may well be persuasive in other circumstances.

Issues-based costs orders

The CPR allows the court to make costs orders that accurately reflect the outcome of the adjudication of distinct issues within the case as well as success in the case itself.[12] The new approach allows for a menu of different potential costs orders at the conclusion of a claim. However, a balance needs to be struck between an unsuccessful argument put forward which is an integral part of the claim and where a wholly separate and distinct but unsuccessful position is pursued. In the latter case, the court will have regard to what extent the unsuccessful arguments took up the court's and the parties' time and resulted in a measureable increase in the costs of the claim.[13]

In some cases costs can be made in relation to a discrete issue. For example, in *Webster* v *Ridgeway Foundation School* [2010] EWHC 318 (QB), Nicol J allowed the defendant the costs of defending a human rights claim to be assessed on an indemnity basis. The judge found that the claim was hopeless. The claim was a discrete issue in the proceedings, and there was sufficient clarity as to which costs were attributable to it to treat it differently from the other costs.

In some cases the court could award a successful claimant a percentage of his costs to reflect the fact that some allegations were unsuccessful or not pursued. In *Devon County Council* v *Clarke* [2005] EWCA Civ 266, the Court of Appeal allowed the claimant 70% of his costs. Although the trial judge had allowed the claimant 100% of his costs, the allegations pursued against different professionals employed by the defendant local authority at different times were distinct claims in their own right and could be considered as discrete aspects of the claim.

It is inappropriate to judge the success or failure of a claim at an interlocutory stage. So where the claimant amended his particulars of claim to plead fresh allegations of negligence, it was inappropriate for the judge to award the defendant its costs of defending the original case up until the amendment, see *Chadwick* v *Hollingsworth* [2010] EWHC 2718 (QB). These were matters that were properly considered after trial.

---

12   *Phonographic Performance Ltd* v *AEI Rediffusion Music Ltd* [1999] 1 WLR 1507, CA.
13   *Kastor Navigation Ltd* v *AGF MAT* (No 2) [2004] EWCA Civ 277.

Exaggeration

Many victims of personal injury or medical negligence exaggerate the extent of their symptoms. Experienced judges are used to witnesses 'swinging the lead' and are sensitive to the difference between individuals who may 'honestly' exaggerate their symptoms and those seeking deliberately to mislead the court.[14]

Active case management under the CPR means that resources are allocated to cases based on their value and complexity. In those cases where the claim is significantly overvalued, it is more likely that costs will have been incurred as a result of such overstatement.

In some cases the fact that the claimant has still beaten the defendant's Part 36 may not protect him from an adverse costs order. In *Painting* v *University of Oxford* [2005] EWCA Civ 161, the defendant obtained video surveillance evidence that prompted it to reduce the payment into court it had paid from £184,000 to £10,000. The claimant was awarded £32,000 and the trial judge awarded her costs. The Court of Appeal reversed this decision, limiting the claimant's recoverable costs until the date of the first payment into court, with the claimant to pay the defendant's costs thereafter.

Where the claimant inflates his claim by acts of dishonesty and not just exaggeration, he is unlikely to receive much sympathy. In *Molloy* v *Shell UK Ltd* [2001] EWCA Civ 1272, the claimant was found to have 'grossly deceived' his GP and medical experts. He failed to beat the payment into court. The Court of Appeal held that the trial judge was wrong in ordering the claimant to pay only 75% of the defendant's costs. The judge was obliged under CPR 44.3(5) to consider the claimant's conduct. He had abused the court's process. He was ordered to pay the defendant's costs in full.

The fact that a judge may assess quantum at a figure much lower that that pleaded is not evidence of exaggeration even if the difference is very substantial.[15] In the absence of an effective Part 36 offer, the court will require some evidence of reprehensible conduct for an adverse costs order to be made. In *Wildlake* v *BAA Limited* [2009] EWCA Civ 1256, the Court of Appeal acknowledged that every case would depend on its own facts but set out some basic principles. In deciding which is the unsuccessful party, the most important thing is to identify the party who is to pay money to the other (para 36). Exaggeration is an 'allegation' relevant to 'the issue' of quantum for the purpose of CPR 44.3(5)(b) (para 37). The relevant question is whether or not it was unreasonable of the claimant to pursue his pleaded case as to the extent of her injury (para 38). The way in which the court is to have regard to that conduct is principally to enquire into its causative effect: to what extent did any lies or gross exaggeration cause the incurring or wasting of costs? (para 39). In an appropriate case the court is entitled to consider whether or not conduct is so egregious that a penalty should be imposed on the offending party. There is a considerable difference between a concocted claim and an exaggerated claim and

---

14 For examples of 'honest' exaggeration, see *Digby* v *Essex CC* [1994] PIQR P53, CA and *Darg* v *Commissioner of Police for the Metropolis* [2009] EWHC 684 (QB) (Sir Robert Nelson) 31 March 2009.

15 See *Hall* v *Stone* [2007] EWCA Civ 1354.

judges must be astute to measure how reprehensible the conduct is (para 41). Defendants have the means of protecting themselves from false or exaggerated claims by Part 36. The basic rule is that the claimant gets his costs if the defendant fails to make a good enough Part 36 offer (para 42).

Mediation

The leading case is *Halsey* v *Milton Keynes General NHS Trust* [2004] 1 WLR 3002, CA. This was a fatal accident claim brought by a widow arising from the death of her husband in hospital. Her solicitors wrote a number of letters, including one to the Secretary of State for Health, asking for mediation. The trust refused to mediate. The Court of Appeal held that there was no presumption that a party will mediate. The failure to mediate would not displace the general costs rule unless the failure to mediate had been unreasonable. In order to show that the failure to mediate was unreasonable, the party would have to show that mediation had reasonable prospects of success. The court will have regard to all the circumstances of the case: the nature of the dispute; the merits in the case; attempts to settle the claim by other means; the value of the claim and the costs incurred by mediation; and any delay caused by mediation. In *Halsey*, the court found that there was reason to believe that mediation would have been successful. The defendant was intent on defending the claim and was entitled to take it to trial with the usual costs consequences.

PART 36

Part 36 provides a complete procedure for facilitating settlement.[16] There is little space here to go into detail about these provisions but some general points can be made:

1   A defective Part 36 offer is not a Part 36 offer. Any defect can make the offer non-compliant. However, under Part 44 the court's discretion is wide enough to allow it to make an order as though Part 46 applied: *Huntley* v *Simmonds* [2009] EWHC 406.
2   All Part 36 offers are capable of acceptance until expressly withdrawn in writing even if they have been specifically rejected or impliedly superseded by subsequent offers: *Gibbon* v *Manchester City Council* [2010] EWCA Civ 726 [2010] PIQR P16.
3   In considering whether or not a Part 36 offer has been beaten, the court has to consider whether or not the result is 'more advantageous'. This is an 'open textured' phrase that allows for all the facts and circumstances of the case to be considered, not simply its monetary worth: *Carver* v *BAA PLC* [2008] EWCA Civ 412, [2009] 1 WLR 113.
4   In most cases, while the court can take into account unrecoverable costs and the stress of going to trial, financial success will be the deciding factor: *Gibbon*.

---

16   *Flynn* v *Scougall* [2004] EWCA Civ 873. Part 36 offers are not contractual but wholly procedural and subject to rules of court; *Gibbon* v *Manchester City Council* [2010] PIQR P16.

Greater certainty has now been achieved by a change to the rule. For settlements achieved after 2 October 2011 the rule is that 'in relation to any money claim, "more advantageous" means better in money terms by any amount, however small, and "at least as advantageous" shall be construed accordingly' (CPR 36.14(1A)). This proposal effectively reverses *Carver*.

COSTS CAPPING

The court has a power to impose a 'cap' on a party's costs under CPR 3.1(2)(m), *King* v *Telegraph Group Ltd* [2005] 1 WLR 2282. From 6 April 2009, this power has been formalised in CPR 44.18 and 44.19. In *Willis* v *Nicolson* [2007] EWCA CIV 199, the Court of Appeal felt unable to issue general guidance in relation to costs capping applications (para 24). In *Smart* v *East Cheshire NHS Trust* [2003] EWHC 2806, Gage J set out a three-stage test for imposing a costs cap:

1   a real and substantial risk that without such an order costs will be disproportionately or unreasonably incurred:
2   the risk that increased costs cannot be managed by detailed assessment and conventional case management; and
3   it is just to make such an order.

The costs capping power is to assist the effective case management of cases where the costs burden on either one or both parties would perpetrate a degree of unfairness or where without some degree of control costs will escalate out of control. As the exercise of the power is intrinsically linked to the case management of the claim in a suitable case it will be exercised at an early stage of the proceedings. Active case management by the court allows the costs position to be reviewed at specific stages of the proceedings and the parties will have a clear timetable to work to, knowing the level of costs being incurred. Such active case management allows a degree of flexibility as well as certainty: budgets can be revisited and the costs implications of prospective steps considered in the course of the court's active management of the case. A costs capping order is, by its nature, concerned with prospective rather than retrospective costs.

In *Smart*, Gage J envisaged that the setting of any cap would be determined on application to a costs judge who would set a budget. Such a step provides the party capped with a degree of protection by setting a budget providing clear direction for the future progress of the action. If circumstances arise which require a prospective costs order to be revisited, an application can be made to the court to vary the order or budget imposed.

In applying a costs capping order, the court must be satisfied that the risk of disproportionate and unreasonable costs has to be such as cannot be dealt with by the normal means of case management and post-trial detailed assessment. In *Knight* v *Beyond Properties PTY Limited* [2006] EWHC 1242, Ch, Mann J said:

> Capping costs in advance does indeed involve a degree of speculation which though it can be carried out when necessary (just as the courts have to assess proper sums for the purposes of security for costs applications) is not easy and has its dangers. The consequences of getting it wrong are in fact more serious

than getting the sum wrong in a security application because costs outside the cap are irrecoverable. Costs outside the amount of the security remain recoverable. It is only a partial answer to say that insufficiencies can be dealt with under a liberty to apply. It is possible to remedy insufficiencies at that stage, but it is likely to increase costs if it has to happen … and to require a party to explain and justify its future conduct in the litigation to the counter-party, which it would not normally wish or be required to do. If such matters can properly, fairly and reliably be left to detailed assessment post-trial then, on the whole, they should be. Retrospective judgments about such things are likely to be more reliable than prospective judgments.

The claimant's solicitors should be allowed a margin of appreciation in preparing for trial. There are real risks in imposing a costs capping order close to trial: *Henry* v *BBC* [2005] EWHC 2503. The issues at trial should already have been effectively case managed so, in effect, in the normal case there should be no need for a costs cap at such a late stage. Costs incurred at the end of proceedings, when the case management process is complete, are capable of retrospective assessment in any event.

PRINCIPLES OF COSTS ASSESSMENT

Indemnity costs

Costs fall to be assessed either on the standard or the indemnity basis. The courts will not allow unreasonable or excessive costs (CPR 44.4(1)). When assessed on a standard basis, the onus will be on the receiving party to show that the costs were reasonably incurred. Where the courts order costs to be paid on an indemnity basis the burden is on the paying party to show that the costs claimed are unreasonable and the court 'will resolve any doubt it may have as to whether costs were reasonably incurred or were reasonable in amount in favour of the receiving party' (CPR 44.4(3)). The obvious advantage of an order for indemnity costs is the burden shifting to the defendant but also that the principle of proportionality does not apply to costs assessed on the indemnity basis.

Standard costs: reasonableness and proportionality

While CPR 44.4(1) emphasises reasonableness to costs assessment, CPR 44.4(2) introduces the concept of proportionality. When costs are assessed on the standard basis, the court will:

(a) only allow costs which are proportionate to the matters in issue; and
(b) resolve any doubt which it may have as to whether costs were reasonably incurred or reasonable or proportionate in amount in favour of the paying party.

The factors to be taken into account in determining the amount of costs include the conduct of the parties before and during the proceedings and efforts made to resolve the dispute between the parties (CPR 44.5(3)(a)) and:

(b) the amount or value of any money or property involved;
(c) the importance or value of any money or property involved;
(d) the particular complexity of the matter or the difficulty or novelty of the question raised;

(e)   the skill, effort, specialised knowledge and responsibility involved;
(f)   the time spent on the case; and
(g)   the place where and the circumstances in which work or any part of it was done.

The leading case on proportionality is *Home Office v Lownds* [2002] EWCA Civ 365, [2002] 1 WLR 2450, [2002] 4 All ER 775, CA. Whether the costs incurred in a case were proportionate should be decided having regard to what it was reasonable for the party in question to believe might be recovered. Therefore (a) the proportionality of costs recovered by the claimant should be determined having regard to the sum that it was reasonable for him or her to believe might be recovered at the time the claim was made; and (b) proportionality of the costs incurred by the defendant should be determined having regard to the sum that it was reasonable for it to believe the claimant might recover should the claim succeed.

In assessing the costs, the Court of Appeal indicated that this required a two-stage approach. The 'global approach' is to consider the total sum and consider whether or not it is disproportionate having regard to the circumstances of the case and in particular those factors in CPR 44.5(3). If the total sum is not disproportionate, each item on the bill of costs should be considered and allowed if reasonably incurred. If costs are disproportionate, the court will have to satisfy itself that work in relation to each individual item was reasonably incurred, and the resultant costs are also reasonable.

CONDITIONAL FEE AGREEMENTS (CFAs)

Historically any arrangement by which a legal representative's entitlement to fees was contingent upon the outcome of litigation was unenforceable and unlawful at common law.[17] Section 58(1) of the Courts and Legal Services Act 1990 (CLSA 1990), as amended by the Access to Justice Act 1999 provides that a CFA shall not be unenforceable 'by reason of its only being a conditional fee agreement' so long as it complies with the conditions contained in ss 58 and 58A of the CLSA 1990.[18]

There is no such thing as 'no win, no fee'. A CFA provides a client with the means to pursue a claim by avoiding any liability to pay his own legal representative's costs in certain circumstances, but if the case is lost the client is likely to have to pay the winning party's costs in the usual way.[19] A client's potential costs liability is avoided in practice by a policy of after the event (ATE) insurance.[20] This application of the costs-shifting rule distinguishes 'conditional' fee agreements in the UK from US style 'contingency' fee agreements. In the UK, a successful client will have his costs, disbursements, and insurance premium paid by the losing

---

17 *Awwad v Geraghty* [2001] QB 570, CA.
18 The nature of these conditions is discussed in 'Regulation and Enforceability' below.
19 Of course the client may also incur costs liabilities as a result of adverse costs orders being made against him during the course of the litigation itself. The effect of the failure to do better than better a Part 36 offer or payment into court is discussed below.
20 ATE insurance stands in contrast to before the event (BTE) insurance. A list of those institutions currently providing such policies is widely available, including in *Cook*.

party subject to assessment by the court. Under a US style contingency fee agreement, these costs would come out of the client's damages.[21] In the UK system, a legal representative is still entitled to those additional costs not recovered *inter partes* from the client unless the CFA specifically limits its entitlement to recovered costs in accordance with CPR 43.2.[22]

The incentive a legal representative has to enter into a CFA is an entitlement to recover under the agreement not only the base costs expended on pursuing the claim but also a 'success fee' if the claim succeeds.[23] In every case where a legal representative asks for such a fee there must be a written assessment of the risk. A ready reckoner is usually used to calculate the appropriate success fee depending on the legal representative's assessment of the percentage prospects of success.[24]

Enforceability

An enforceable CFA must satisfy 'all the conditions applicable to it by virtue of' ss 58 and 58A of the CLSA 1990. The conditions are set out in s 58(3):

(a)   it must be in writing;
(b)   it must not relate to proceedings which cannot be the subject of an enforceable conditional fee agreement; and
(c)   it must comply with such requirements (if any) as may be prescribed by the Lord Chancellor.

In writing

Ordinarily this condition will not pose a problem. Most personal injury and clinical negligence litigation is conducted under agreements that follow the terms of the Law Society Model Agreement (Solicitor-Client),[25] and APIL/PIBA 6 (Solicitor-Counsel).[26]

Proceedings

The Conditional Fee Agreements Order 2000 extended the availability of CFAs to all proceedings other than criminal and family proceedings as specified in s 58A(1) of the CLSA 1990.

---

21   When originally introduced in the UK, the insurance premium and success fees were recovered from the client rather than the losing party under the Conditional Fee Agreements Regulations 1995, which were succeed on 1 April 2000 by the Conditional Fee Agreements Regulations 2000.
22   This is the so-called 'CFA lite'.
23   Section 58(2)(b) does not define success fee but defines an agreement that 'provides for a success fee if it provides for the amount of any fees to which it applies to be increased, in specified circumstances, above the amount which would be payable if it were not payable only in specified circumstances'. Of course the CFA need not include a success fee.
24   There is some conceptual confusion over the basis of the calculation of a success fee. Most counsel using the ready reckoner appended to APIL/PIBA 6 assess the risk of the case and the percentage increase reflecting the risk in that particular case. Solicitors entering into CFAs may be in a more commercially-informed position to base the percentage increase on the generic character of a case or on the basis of what the likely proportion of costs incurred will be.
25   Reprinted in the White Book, Vol 2, 7A-77.
26   Reprinted in the White Book, Vol 2, 7B-16.1 and 7B-17.1.

Success Fees

Under s 58(4) of the CLSA 1990, in order for a CFA which provides for a success fee to be enforceable:

(a) it must relate to proceedings of a description specified by order made by the Lord Chancellor;

(b) it must state the percentage by which the amount of the fees which would be payable if it were not a conditional fee agreement is to be increased;

(c) that percentage must not exceed the percentage specified in relation to the description of proceedings to which the agreement relates by order made by the Lord Chancellor.

The Conditional Fee Agreements Order 2000 deals with (a) and (c). Under para 3 of the order all proceedings which can be the subject of an enforceable CFA can provide for a success fee except proceedings under s 82 of the Environmental Protection Act 1990. Paragraph 4 provides that the percentage increase should not exceed 100%. The requirement that the percentage increase must be expressed in writing is embodied within both the Law Society Model Agreement and APIL/PIBA 6.

Regulation and enforceability

Nothing has done more to undermine a practical and efficient CFA regime than the extensive satellite litigation over the requirements specified by the Lord Chancellor exercising his power under s 58(3)(c). In providing that CFAs had to comply with regulations, Parliament provided a losing party – essentially defendant insurers – with a powerful incentive to challenge the extent to which the receiving party had 'complied' with the act. Being illegal at common law, a CFA could not be enforced if there was a breach of the regulations: the paying party would avoid any liability to pay the victorious party's costs (except perhaps the insurance premium and any disbursements).[27]

The Conditional Fee Regulations 2000 provoked a wave of satellite litigation culminating in the Court of Appeal's decision in *Hollins* v *Russell* [2000] 1 WLR 2142 in March 2003. In *Hollins*, the Court of Appeal attempted to check the tide by establishing a 'materiality' test: had the breach of the regulations had an adverse effect either upon the protection afforded to the client by the regulations or upon the proper administration of justice? In *Garrett* v *Halton Borough Council* [2006] EWCA Civ 1017, the Court of Appeal emphasises that the test in *Hollins* was not dependent upon any actual detriment to the client but only with the extent of compliance. ie if the breach was such that the regulations were not satisfied the CFA was unenforceable in the light of the purposes of the regulations. The enforceability of the agreement is determined at its commencement and is not a question to be addressed at its conclusion.

---

27 The all-or nothing approach is clearly set out by Scheimann LJ in *Awwad* v *Geraghty* (see fn 17 above): 'If the court, for reasons of public policy, refuses to enforce an agreement that a solicitor should be paid, it must follow that he cannot claim on a quantum meruit.'

Post-*Hollins*, the courts remained responsive to well-founded challenges to the enforceability of CFAs,[28] including where the legal representative did not make any or any proper inquiries into the availability of BTE insurance,[29] even when no such policy was available;[30] where there is an existing policy of BTE insurance the decision to take ATE insurance will have to be justified;[31] and when legal aid is available, the case should not be funded by CFA.[32]

The growing awareness of the extent of the challenge facing the courts led to the introduction of a simplified CFA under the Conditional Fee Agreements (Miscellaneous Amendments) Regulations 2003. By abrogating the indemnity principle and modifying the client care provisions in the 2000 regulations, 'CFA Lite' was intended to provide a more 'user friendly' alternative, but failed to inspire much confidence within the professions and, although introduced in June 2003, has not been widely used.[33] Around the same time CFA Lite came into being, the Department for Constitutional Affairs (DeCAf) issued a consultation paper with the intention of 'simplifying' the CFA regime.[34] Although a draft bill was produced the following year,[35] in 2005 Parliament decided that the best way to deal with the continuing struggle to implement a workable system was to abolish the regulations altogether.[36] The Conditional Fee Agreements (Revocation) Regulations 2005 took effect on 1 November 2005.[37]

The post-November 2005 regime

Post-November 2005, the CFA regime is not so much deregulated as disaggregated. The enforceability of CFAs, their interpretation, and

---

28   In *Spencer* v *Wood* [2004] EWCA Civ 532, the Court of Appeal applied the test and found that the failure to specify what percentage of the success fee represented the likely delay in the payment of fees was a material breach of reg 3(1)(b) (specification of the percentage increase). The Court of Appeal also followed *Awwad* and refused to allow the claimant's legal representative to recover costs for work rendered:

    in the context of this statute Parliament decided that unless a CFA satisfied all the conditions applicable to it by virtue of section 58(1), it would not be exempt from the general rules as to the unenforceability of CFAs at common law. [para 15]

29   *Richards* v *Davis* [2005] EWHC 90014 (Costs) (Master Hurst); *Myatt* v *NCB* [2007] 1 WLR 554, CA.
30   *Samonini* v *London General Transport Services* [2005] EWHC 90001 (Costs) (Master Hurst).
31   *Sawar* v *Alam* [2002] PIQR P159.
32   *Bowen* v *Bridgend BC* [2004] EWHC 9010 (Costs) (Master O'Hare).
33   One of the main reasons for this was that while the regulations themselves watered down the client care provisions in the 2000 regulations, the Client Care Code still governed the solicitor's dealings with the client.
34   Department for Constitutional Affairs, *Consultation Paper: Simplifying CFAs* June 2003, available at www.lcd.gov.uk/consult/confees/cfa.htm.
35   Department for Constitutional Affairs, 'Making simple CFAs a reality', CP22/04, 29 June 2004, available at www.dca.gov.uk.
36   As proposed by DeCAf in a final report, *New Regulations for Conditional Fee Agreements (CFAs)* CP(R) 22/04, published on 10 August 2005 and also available at the DeCAf website.
37   Revoking the Conditional Fee Regulations 2000, the Collective Conditional Fee Agreements Regulations 2000, the Conditional Fee Agreements (Miscellaneous Amendments) 2003, and the Conditional Fee Agreements (Miscellaneous Amendments) (No 2) Regulations 2003.

implementation are governed not only by statute, statutory instrument, and the CPR, but the Professional Conduct Rules of both professions. In this context the most important change after 1 November 2005 is that the client care component of the 2000 regulations have been incorporated into the Law Society's *Solicitors Costs Information and Client Care Code 1999* (the Code). The Code has been amended to include a provision that when a client is represented under a CFA, the solicitor should explain:

(i)   the circumstances in which the client may be liable for their own costs and for the other party's costs;

(ii)   the client's right to assessment of costs, wherever the solicitor intends to seek payment of any or all of their costs from the client;

(iii)   any interest a solicitor may have in recommending a particular policy or other funding

Although the new Law Society Model CFA reduces the terms of the agreement between solicitor and client to a single page, before it is signed the client has to read the accompanying publication, *Conditional fee agreements: what you need to know*. This includes information on costs which the client will pay if the case is won or lost, how base costs and success fees are calculated, insurance, and termination. In essence, the obligations upon a solicitor to explain the essential terms of the CFA remain the same under the new arrangements as they were under the old. The essential change is not in the substance of the information provided but in the policing of funding arrangements.

Whether or not the failure of a solicitor to comply with the code will render a CFA unenforceable will depend on the circumstances of the case. In *Garbutt* v *Edwards* [2005] EWCA Civ 1206, the Court of Appeal considered whether or not a paying party's liability to pay costs should be discharged or reduced if the solicitor for the receiving party was in breach of the code.[38] In giving the judgement of the court, Arden LJ held that 'the code is there to protect the legitimate interests of the client, and the administration of justice, rather than to relieve paying parties of their obligation to pay costs which have been reasonably incurred' (para 31). In the case of Mrs Garbutt, the failure to give an estimate of costs in breach of the code did not render the retainer unenforceable. The client's remedy for his solicitor's breach lay in a complaint to the Law Society, not in the paying party avoiding the usual liability to pay the winning party's costs. The question of whether the amount of costs claimed could be reduced in light of this failing was one which the judge could take into account on assessment (para 43). Failure to apply the Code will result in challenges to at least the amount of fees recovered, if not the receiving party's entitlement to fees under the CFA. It follows from *Garbutt* that until the Court of Appeal revisits this issue in the particular case of CFAs, the default position is that such agreements are not rendered unenforceable by such a breach, but they may well be subject to reduction on assessment. For example, where the legal representative has failed to properly investigate the availability of BTE insurance, the CFA may remain enforceable but the insurance premium and success fee may be

---

38   The Solicitor's Practice Rules, r 15 provides that solicitors shall provide information in accordance with the code. These rules have the force of secondary legislation: *Swain* v *Law Society* [1983] AC 598.

disallowed. To this end, the court has a range of sanctions that it can apply in cases when legal representatives have failed to adhere to the code without depriving a victorious party of all its costs.

CFAs in practice

There is no space here to go into any detailed or comprehensive guidance about CFAs. The Bar Council has produced very comprehensive guidance, and authoritative guidance is provided in *Cook on Costs* and the Law Society's Guide. The following paragraphs deal simply with some basic points.

Entering a CFA: risk assessment

The risk assessment is for the legal representative's benefit.[39] It is not only a privileged document but it does not need to be disclosed to the client or by counsel to his solicitor.[40] At an assessment of costs, however, a legal representative may have to rely on the assessment to justify the percentage uplift unless he can prove an entitlement to the success fees claimed by some other means.

The legal representative assesses risk on the basis of the information available to him at the time of entering the agreement. At an assessment of costs the court has to discount the benefit of hindsight. The case has succeeded and the anticipated risks either did not materialise or were not so compelling as to defeat the claim.[41] By the same token when during the course of proceedings unforeseen events make the claim less likely to succeed, a legal representative is unable to amend or otherwise alter the agreement to take into account such a change of circumstances.[42] Where, for example, a legal representative enters into a CFA with a small uplift reflecting an opponent's written admission of liability, he will be unable to increase the risk to reflect the reduced prospects of success following a successful application to resile.

The possibility of the unexpected occurring is one reason why two or three stage agreements allowing for a 100% uplift at trial are attractive. Staged agreements take into account the fact that anything can happen during the course of proceedings.

---

39 It has three functions. First, it represents the legal representative's assessment of the risk. Secondly, it can be used by colleagues either for the purposes of screening or if the case is transferred. Thirdly, it is for use at the assessment of costs. Where a legal representative enters a case where the success fees are fixed in any event there may be only limited use in doing a risk assessment as it will only be required in respect of the first and second points above.

40 Though it is a condition precedent of APIL/PIBA 6 not only that counsel sees the solicitor's risk assessment but any risk assessment by previous counsel (if available). In this context the important point that emerges is that counsel in particular has a choice whether or not to include the risk assessment in the Conditional Fee Agreement. Obviously if it is included it will be disclosed with the CFA agreement. If it is not included it remains possible that it would have to be disclosed at an assessment of costs in order to justify counsel's uplift.

41 This is why 'contributory negligence' is not a risk for the purposes of 'success' under the terms of a CFA.

42 *Ku* v *Liverpool City Council* [2005] 1 WLR 2657, CA.

Scope and duration

The essence of a CFA is that the legal representative is only paid if the case is won. In the model agreements success is defined as an entitlement to damages. For the purposes of the indemnity principle, the legal representative's entitlement to fees only arises once such an entitlement has arisen. The agreement presupposes that a legal representative will pursue the claim until trial. What happens after the entry of judgment is dependent on the terms of the agreement. Termination under the model agreements is limited by the terms of the agreements.

Interlocutory hearings

A client's liability to pay his legal representative's costs is dependent upon 'success'. If the client does not win the case, the legal representative is not entitled to any payment.[43] This also applies to any interlocutory costs orders made in the claimant's favour in the course of proceedings. This practical effect of the indemnity principle is a source of potential unfairness. When, for example, a claimant makes an application for pre-action disclosure, the costs incurred in making such an application will not be recovered from the other side unless the claim eventually succeeds. When a defendant successfully applies to withdraw an admission the payment of any costs awarded the claimant will have to await the outcome of the trial. Some CFAs and CCFAs have been drafted to define 'success' as extending to costs orders made in the claimant's favour to allow for the recovery of interlocutory applications. In some cases 'success' may even be defined as a favourable order at an interlocutory stage, for example, a preliminary issue on limitation or defeating a strike out application. In such cases a legal representative would be entitled to payment at the interlocutory stage and any success fee would be dependent on a particular result rather than an entitlement to damages.

Where a legal representative has entered into a model agreement, the entitlement to payment from the client is essentially all or nothing. A solicitor may avoid some of the potential pitfalls by not entering into a CFA until pre-action disclosure has taken place.

Part 36

Part 36 and CFAs are uneasy bedfellows. In clinical negligence actions worth a comparatively small amount, the claimant's entitlement to costs will very often be greater than the amount of damages recovered. In many instances the practical consequence of a failure to beat such an offer will be that the legal representative will be reduced to seeking payment for his fees against a lay client with limited resources.

In many instances a legal representative may conclude that the reality of the situation is that if the Part 36 offer is not beaten, he is simply not going to get paid. In these circumstances one possible strategy is to define success not as an 'entitlement to damages' but in beating a Part 36 offer.

---

43   See the APIL/PIBA 6; and the Law Society Model Agreement.

Where liability is admitted and there are complicated issues in relation to damages, this would be an understandable course of action.[44]

In *C* v *W* [2008] EWCA Civ 1549 the Court of Appeal considered that a success fee of 20% was appropriate where liability was admitted at the time the CFA was entered into. The real risk the claimant faced was the failure to beat a Part 36 offer.

PRO BONO COSTS ORDERS

From 1 October 2008, the Legal Services Act 2007 allows for the recovery of costs in *pro bono* cases. Section 194 allows the court to make an order against a party who is unsuccessful against a party represented *pro bono*. The costs awarded are not payable to the successful litigant but to the Access to Justice Foundation ('the prescribed charity'). CPR 44.3C sets out the relevant procedure including that the order must specify that payment by the paying party is to be made to the prescribed charity (CPR 44.3C(3)). The Costs Practice Direction provides that the general rule is that the court will make a summary assessment of costs 'that would have been claimed by the party with pro bono representation in respect of that representation had it not been provided free of charge' (para 10A.1). The assisted party must prepare some form of statement setting out the costs that would have been claimed had the legal representative charged for his services.

---

44   The question arises of whether or not a Part 36 offer has to already exist at the time the CFA is entered into. If counsel entered a case at an early stage knowing that quantum was the only issue in dispute, would they be justified in allowing themselves a success fee of up to 100% on the basis of speculation that the client might have to beat an as-yet unknown Part 36 offer?

Appendices

All Statutes, Civil Procedure Rules, Practice Directions and Protocols are published with the kind permission of the Ministry of Justice.

Appendix I

Statutes

Contents

1. DAMAGES

[The sections reproduced below are printed as amended, where appropriate.]

Law Reform (Personal Injuries) Act 1948 (11 & 12 Geo 6 c 41)

2. *Measure of damages* ...
(4) In an action for damages for personal injuries (including any such action arising out of a contract), there shall be disregarded, in determining the reasonableness of any expenses, the possibility of avoiding those expenses or part of them by taking advantage of facilities available under the [the National Health Service Act 2006 or the National Health Service (Wales)Act 2006] National Health Service Act 1977, or the National Health Service (Scotland) Act 1978, or of any corresponding facilities in Northern Ireland.
[NOTE: there is a growing lobby for the repeal of this section. If ever enacted, this would have the effect of substantially reducing compensation in many cases.]

Administration of Justice Act 1982 (1982 c 53)

Abolition of certain claims for damages etc

Abolition of right to damages for loss of expectation of life

1.–(1) In an action under the law of England and Wales or the law of Northern Ireland for damages for personal injuries –
    (a) no damages shall be recoverable in respect of any loss of expectation of life caused to the injured person by the injuries; but
    (b) if the injured person's expectation of life has been reduced by the injuries, the court, in assessing damages in respect of pain and suffering caused by the injuries, shall take account of any suffering caused or likely to be caused to him by awareness that his expectation of life has been so reduced.
(2) The reference in subsection (1)(a) above to damages in respect of loss of expectation of life does not include damages in respect of loss of income.

Abolition of actions for loss of services etc

2. No person shall be liable in tort under the law of England and Wales or the law of Northern Ireland –
    (a) to a husband on the ground only of his having deprived him of the services or society of his wife;
    (b) to a parent (or person standing in the place of a parent) on the ground only of his having deprived him of the services of a child; or
    (c) on the ground only –
        (i) of having deprived another of the services of his menial servant;
        (ii) of having deprived another of the services of his female servant by raping or seducing her; or
        (iii) of enticement of a servant or harbouring a servant.

Fatal Accidents Act 1976

3. The following sections shall be substituted for sections 1 to 4 of the Fatal Accidents Act 1976 –
   '...

Bereavement

1A.–(1) An action under this Act may consist of or include a claim for damages for bereavement.

(2) A claim for damages for bereavement shall only be for the benefit –
  (a) of the wife or husband [or civil partner] of the deceased; and
  (b) where the deceased was a minor who was never married [or civil partner] –
    (i) of his parents, if he was legitimate; and
    (ii) of his mother, if he was illegitimate.

(3) Subject to subsection (5) below, the sum to be awarded as damages under this section shall be [£11,800 for deaths from 1st January 2008]

(4) Where there is a claim for damages under this section for the benefit of both the parents of the deceased the sum awarded shall be divided equally between them (subject to any deduction falling to be made in respect of costs not recovered from the defendant).

(5) The Lord Chancellor may by order made by statutory instrument, subject to annulment in pursuance of a resolution of either House of Parliament, amend this section by varying the sum for the time being specified in subsection (3) above.
...'

Claims not surviving death

Exclusion of Law Reform (Miscellaneous Provisions) Act 1934

4.–(1) The following subsection shall be inserted after section 1(1) of the Law Reform (Miscellaneous Provisions) Act 1934 (actions to survive death) –

  '(1A) The right of a person to claim under section 1A of the Fatal Accidents Act 1976 (bereavement) shall not survive for the benefit of his estate on his death.'.

(2) The following paragraph shall be substituted for subsection (2)(a) –
  '(a) shall not include –
    (i) any exemplary damages;
    (ii) any damages for loss of income in respect of any period after that person's death;'.

Maintenance at public expense

Maintenance at public expense to be taken into account in assessment of damages

5. In an action under the law of England and Wales or the law of Northern Ireland for damages for personal injuries (including any such action arising out of a contract) any saving to the injured person which is attributable to his maintenance wholly or partly at public expense in a hospital, nursing home or other institution shall be set off against any income lost by him as a result of his injuries.

2. LIMITATION

Limitation Act 1980 (1980 c 58)

[The sections reproduced below are printed as amended, where appropriate.]

An Act to consolidate the Limitations Acts 1939 to 1980. [13th November 1980]

PART I

ORDINARY TIME LIMITS FOR DIFFERENT CLASSES OF ACTION

Time limits under Part I subject to extension or exclusion under Part II

Time limits under Part I subject to extension or exclusion under Part II

1.–(1) This Part of this Act gives the ordinary time limits for bringing actions of the various classes mentioned in the following provisions of this Part.

(2) The ordinary time limits given in this Part of this Act are subject to extension or exclusion in accordance with the provisions of Part II of this Act.

Actions founded on tort

Time limit for actions founded on tort

2. An action founded on tort shall not be brought after the expiration of six years from the date on which the cause of action accrued.

Actions founded on simple contract

Time limit for actions founded on simple contract

5. An action founded on simple contract shall not be brought after the expiration of six years from the date on which the cause of action accrued.

Actions in respect of wrongs causing personal injuries or death

Special time limit for actions in respect of personal injuries

11.–(1) This section applies to any action for damages for negligence, nuisance or breach of duty (whether the duty exists by virtue of a contract or of provision made by or under a statute or independently of any contract or any such provision) where the damages claimed by the plaintiff for the negligence, nuisance or breach of duty consist of or include damages in respect of personal injuries to the plaintiff or any other person.

(1A) This section does not apply to any action brought for damages under section 3 of the Protection from Harrassment Act 1997.

(2) None of the time limits given in the preceding provisions of this Act shall apply to an action to which this section applies.

(3) An action to which this section applies shall not be brought after the expiration of the period applicable in accordance with subsection (4) or (5) below.

(4) Except where subsection (5) below applies, the period applicable is three years from –
(a) the date on which the cause of action accrued; or
(b) the date of knowledge (if later) of the person injured.

(5) If the person injured dies before the expiration of the period mentioned in subsection (4) above, the period applicable as respects the cause of action surviving for the benefit of his estate by virtue of section 1 of the Law Reform (Miscellaneous Provisions) Act 1934 shall be three years from –
(a) the date of death; or
(b) the date of the personal representative's knowledge;
whichever is the later.

(6) For the purposes of this section 'personal representative' includes any person who is or has been a personal representative of the deceased, including an

executor who has not proved the will (whether or not he has renounced probate) but not anyone appointed only as a special personal representative in relation to settled land; and regard shall be had to any knowledge acquired by any such person while a personal representative or previously.

(7) If there is more than one personal representative, and their dates of knowledge are different, subsection (5)(b) above shall be read as referring to the earliest of those dates.

Actions in respect of defective products

11A.–(1) This section shall apply to an action for damages by virtue of any provision of Part I of the Consumer Protection Act 1987.

(2) None of the time limits given in the preceding provisions of this Act shall apply to an action to which this section applies.

(3) An action in which this section applies shall not be brought after the expiration of the period of ten years from the relevant time, within the meaning of section 4 of the said Act of 1987; and this subsection shall operate to extinguish a right of action and shall do so whether or not that right of action had accrued, or time under the following provisions of this Act had begun to run, at the end of the said period of ten years.

(4) Subject to subsection (5) below, an action to which this section applies in which the damages claimed by the plaintiff consist of or include damages in respect of personal injuries to the plaintiff or any other person for loss of or damage to any property, shall not be brought after the expiration of the period of three years from whichever is the later of –

    (a)   the date on which the cause of action accrued; and

    (b)   the date of knowledge of the injured person or, in the case of loss of or damage to property, the date of knowledge of the plaintiff or (if earlier) of any person in whom this cause of action was previously vested.

(5) If in a case where the damages claimed by the plaintiff consist of or include damages in respect of personal injuries to the plaintiff or any other person the injured person died before the expiration of the period mentioned in subsection (4) above, that subsection shall have effect as respects the cause of action surviving for the benefit of his estate by virtue of section 1 of the Law Reform (Miscellaneous Provisions) Act 1934 as if for the reference to that period there were substituted a reference to the period of three years from whichever is the later of –

    (a)   the date of death; and

    (b)   the date of the personal representative's knowledge.

(6) For the purposes of this section 'personal representative' includes any person who is or has been a personal representative of the deceased, including an executor who has not proved the will (whether or not he has renounced probate) but not anyone appointed only as a special personal representative in relation to settled land; and regard shall be had to any knowledge acquired by any such person while a personal representative or previously.

(7) If there is more than one personal representative and their dates of knowledge are different, subsection (5)(b) above shall be read as referring to the earliest of those dates.

(8) Expressions used in this section or section 14 of this Act and in Part I of the Consumer Protection Act 1987 have the same meanings in this section or that section as in that Part; and section 1(1) of that Act (Part I to be construed as enacted for the purpose of complying with the product liability Directive) shall apply for the purpose of construing this section and the following provisions of this Act so far as they relate to any action by virtue of any provision of that Part as it applies for the purpose of construing that part.

Special time limit for actions under Fatal Accidents legislation

12.–(1) An action under the Fatal Accidents Act 1976 shall not be brought if the death occurred when the person injured could no longer maintain an action and recover damages in respect of the injury (whether because of a time limit in this Act or in any other Act, or for any other reason).

Where any such action by the injured person would have been barred by the time limit in section 11 or 11A of this Act, no account shall be taken of the possibility of that time limit being overridden under section 33 of this Act.

(2) None of the time limits given in the preceding provisions of this Act shall apply to an action under the Fatal Accidents Act 1976, but no such action shall be brought after the expiration of three years from –

(a)   the date of death; or

(b)   the date of knowledge of the person for whose benefit the action is brought;

whichever is the later.

(3) An action under the Fatal Accidents Act 1976 shall be one to which sections 28, 33, 33A and 35 of this Act apply, and the application to any such action of the time limit under subsection (2) above shall be subject to section 39; but otherwise Parts II and III of this Act shall not apply to any such action.

Operation of time limit under section 12 in relation to different dependants

13.–(1) Where there is more than one person for whose benefit an action under the Fatal Accidents Act 1976 is brought, section 12(2)(b) of this Act shall be applied separately to each of them.

(2) Subject to subsection (3) below, if by virtue of subsection (1) above the action would be outside the time limit given by section 12(2) as regards one or more, but not all, of the persons for whose benefit it is brought, the court shall direct that any person as regards whom the action would be outside that limit shall be excluded from those for whom the action is brought.

(3) The court shall not give such a direction if it is shown that if the action were brought exclusively for the benefit of the person in question it would not be defeated by a defence of limitation (whether in consequence of section 28 of this Act or an agreement between the parties not to raise the defence, or otherwise).

Definition of date of knowledge for purposes of sections 11 and 12

14.–(1) Subject to subsection (1A) below, in sections 11 and 12 of this Act references to a person's date of knowledge are references to the date on which he first had knowledge of the following facts –

(a)   that the injury in question was significant; and

(b)   that the injury was attributable in whole or in part to the act or omission which is alleged to constitute negligence, nuisance or breach of duty; and

(c)   the identity of the defendant; and

(d)   if it is alleged that the act or omission was that of a person other than the defendant, the identity of that person and the additional facts supporting the bringing of an action against the defendant;

and knowledge that any acts or omissions did or did not, as a matter of law, involve negligence, nuisance or breach of duty is irrelevant.

(1A) In section 11A of this Act and in section 12 of this Act so far as that section applies to an action by virtue of section 6(1)(a) of the Consumer Protection Act 1987 (death caused by defective product) references to a person's date of knowledge are references to the date on which he first had knowledge of the following facts –

(a) such facts about the damage caused by the defect as would lead a reasonable person who had suffered such damage to consider it sufficiently serious to justify his instituting proceedings for damages against a defendant who did not dispute liability and was able to satisfy a judgment; and

(b) that the damage was wholly or partly attributable to the facts and circumstances alleged to constitute the defect; and

(c) the identity of the defendant;

but, in determining the date on which a person first had such knowledge there shall be disregarded both the extent (if any) of that person's knowledge on any date of whether particular facts or circumstances would or would not, as a matter of law, constitute a defect and, in a case relating to loss of or damage to property, any knowledge which that person had on a date on which he had no right of action by virtue of Part I of that Act in respect of the loss or damage.

(2) For the purposes of this section an injury is significant if the person whose date of knowledge is in question would reasonably have considered it sufficiently serious to justify his instituting proceedings for damages against a defendant who did not dispute liability and was able to satisfy a judgment.

(3) For the purposes of this section a person's knowledge includes knowledge which he might reasonably have been expected to acquire –

(a) from facts observable or ascertainable by him; or

(b) from facts ascertainable by him with the help of medical or other appropriate expert advice which it is reasonable for him to seek;

but a person shall not be fixed under this subsection with knowledge of a fact ascertainable only with the help of expert advice so long as he has taken all reasonable steps to obtain (and, where appropriate, to act on) that advice.

Actions in respect of latent damage not involving personal injuries

Special time limit for negligence actions where facts relevant to cause of action are not known at date of accrual

14A.–(1) This section applies to any action for damages for negligence, other than one to which section 11 of this Act applies, where the starting date for reckoning the period of limitation under subsection (4)(b) below falls after the date on which the cause of action accrued.

(2) Section 2 of this Act shall not apply to an action to which this section applies.

(3) An action to which this section applies shall not be brought after the expiration of the period applicable in accordance with subsection (4) below.

(4) That period is either –

(a) six years from the date on which the cause of action accrued; or

(b) three years from the starting date as defined by subsection (5) below, if that period expires later than the period mentioned in paragraph (a) above

(5) For the purposes of this section, the starting date for reckoning the period of limitation under subsection (4)(b) above is the earliest date on which the plaintiff or any person in whom the cause of action was vested before him first had both the knowledge required for bringing an action for damages in respect of the relevant damage and a right to bring such an action.

(6) In subsection (5) above 'the knowledge required for bringing an action for damages in respect of the relevant damage' means knowledge both –

(a) of the material facts about the damage in respect of which damages are claimed; and

(b) of the other facts relevant to the current action mentioned in subsection (8) below.

(7) For the purposes of subsection 6(a) above, the material facts about the damage are such facts about the damage as would lead a reasonable person

who had suffered such damage to consider it sufficiently serious to justify his instituting proceedings for damages against a defendant who did not dispute liability and was able to satisfy a judgment.

(8) The other facts referred to in subsection (6)(b) above are –

    (a) that the damage was attributable in whole or in part to the act or omission which is alleged to constitute negligence; and

    (b) the identity of the defendant; and

    (c) if it is alleged that the act or omission was that of a person other than the defendant, the identity of that person and the additional facts supporting the bringing of an action against the defendant.

(9) Knowledge that any acts or omissions did or did not, as a matter of law, involve negligence is irrelevant for the purposes of subsection (5) above.

(10) For the purposes of this section a person's knowledge includes knowledge which he might reasonably have been expected to acquire –

    (a) from facts observable or ascertainable by him; or

    (b) from facts ascertainable by him with the help of appropriate expert advice which it is reasonable for him to seek;

but a person shall not be taken by virtue of this subsection to have knowledge of a fact ascertainable only with the help of expert advice so long as he has taken all reasonable steps to obtain (and, where appropriate, to act on) that advice.

Overriding time limit for negligence actions not involving personal injuries

14B.–(1) An action for damages for negligence, other than one to which section 11 of this Act applies, shall not be brought after the expiration of fifteen years from the date (or, if more than one, from the last of the dates) on which there occurred any act or omission –

    (a) which is alleged to constitute negligence; and

    (b) to which the damage in respect of which damages are claimed is alleged to be attributable (in whole or in part).

(2) This section bars the right of action in a case to which subsection (1) above applies notwithstanding that –

    (a) the cause of action has not yet accrued; or

    (b) where section 14A of this Act applies to the action, the date which is for the purposes of that section the starting date for reckoning the period mentioned in subsection (4)(b) of that section has not yet occurred;

before the end of the period of limitation prescribed by this section.

Part II

Extension or Exclusion of Ordinary Time Limits

Disability

Extension of limitation period in case of disability

28.–(1) Subject to the following provisions of this section, if on the date when any right of action accrued for which a period of limitation is prescribed by this Act, the person to whom it accrued was under a disability, the action may be brought at any time before the expiration of six years from the date when he ceased to be under a disability or died (whichever first occurred) notwithstanding that the period of limitation has expired.

(2) This section shall not affect any case where the right of action first accrued to some person (not under a disability) through whom the person under a disability claims.

(3) When a right of action which has accrued to a person under a disability accrues, on the death of that person while still under a disability, to another person under a disability, no further extension of time shall be allowed by reason of the disability of the second person.

(4) No action to recover land or money charged on land shall be brought by virtue of this section by any person after the expiration of thirty years from the date on which the right of action accrued to that person or some person through whom he claims.

(4A) If the action is one to which section 4A of this Act applies, subsection(1) above shall have effect –

(a)   in the case of an action for libel or slander, as if for the words from 'at any time' to 'occurred' there were substituted the words 'by him at any time before the expiration of one year from the date on which he ceased to be under a disability'; and

(b)   in the case of an action for slander of title, slander of goods or other malicious falsehood, as if for the words 'six years' there were substituted the words 'one year'.

(5) If the action is one to which section 10 of this Act applies, subsection (1) above shall have effect as if for the words 'six years' there were substituted the words 'two years'.

(6) If the action is one to which section 11 or 12(2) of this Act applies, subsection (1) above shall have effect as if for the words 'six years' there were substituted the words 'three years'.

(7) If the action is one to which section 11A of this Act applies or one by virtue of section 6(1)(a) of the Consumer Protection Act 1987 (death caused by defective product), subsection (1) above –

(a)   shall not apply to the time limit prescribed by subsection (3) of the said section 11A or to that time limit as applied by virtue of section 12(1) of this Act; and

(b)   in relation to any other time limit prescribed by this Act shall have effect as if for the words 'six years' there were substituted the words 'three years'.

Extension for cases where the limitation period is the period under section 14A(4)(b)

28A.–(1) Subject to subsection (2) below, if in the case of any action for which a period of limitation is prescribed by section 14A of this Act –

(a)   the period applicable in accordance with subsection (4) of that section is the period mentioned in paragraph (b) of that subsection;

(b)   on the date which is for the purposes of that section the starting date for reckoning that period the person by reference to whose knowledge that date fell to be determined under subsection (5) of that section was under a disability; and

(c)   section 28 of this Act does not apply to the action;

the action may be brought at any time before the expiration of three years from the date when he ceased to be under a disability or died (whichever first occurred) notwithstanding that the period mentioned above has expired.

(2) An action may not be brought by virtue of subsection (1) above after the end of the period of limitation prescribed by section 14B of this Act.

Fraud, concealment and mistake

Postponement of limitation period in case of fraud, concealment or mistake

32.–(1) Subject to subsections (3) and (4A) below, where in the case of any action for which a period of limitation is prescribed by this Act, either –

(a) the action is based upon the fraud of the defendant; or
(b) any fact relevant to the plaintiff's right of action has been deliberately concealed from him by the defendant; or
(c) the action is for relief from the consequences of a mistake;

the period of limitation shall not begin to run until the plaintiff has discovered the fraud, concealment or mistake (as the case may be) or could with reasonable diligence have discovered it.

References in this subsection to the defendant include references to the defendant's agent and to any person through whom the defendant claims and his agent.

(2) For the purposes of subsection (1) above, deliberate commission of a breach of duty in circumstances in which it is unlikely to be discovered for some time amounts to deliberate concealment of the facts involved in that breach of duty.

(3) Nothing in this section shall enable any action –
(a) to recover, or recover the value of, any property; or
(b) to enforce any charge against, or set aside any transaction affecting, any property;

to be brought against the purchaser of the property or any person claiming through him in any case where the property has been purchased for valuable consideration by an innocent third party since the fraud or concealment or (as the case may be) the transaction in which the mistake was made took place.

(4) A purchaser is an innocent third party for the purposes of this section –
(a) in the case of fraud or concealment of any fact relevant to the plaintiff's right of action, if he was not a party to the fraud or (as the case may be) to the concealment of that fact and did not at the time of the purchase know or have reason to believe that the fraud or concealment had taken place; and
(b) in the case of mistake, if he did not at the time of the purchase know or have reason to believe that the mistake had been made.

(4A) Subsection (1) above shall not apply in relation to the time limit prescribed by section 11A(3) of this Act or in relation to that time limit as applied by virtue of section 12(1) of this Act.

(5) Sections 14A and 14B of this Act shall not apply to any action to which subsection (1)(b) above applies (and accordingly to the period of limitation referred to in that subsection, in any case to which either of those sections would otherwise apply, is the period applicable under section 2 of this Act).

Discretionary exclusion of time limit for actions in respect of personal injuries or death

Discretionary exclusion of time limit for actions in respect of personal injuries or death

33.–(1) If it appears to the court that it would be equitable to allow an action to proceed having regard to the degree to which –
(a) the provisions of section 11 or 11A or 12 of this Act prejudice the plaintiff or any person whom he represents; and
(b) any decision of the court under this subsection would prejudice the defendant or any person whom he represents;

the court may direct that those provisions shall not apply to the action, or shall not apply to any specified cause of action to which the action relates.

(1A) The court shall not under this section disapply –
(a) subsection (3) of section 11A; or
(b) where the damages claimed by the plaintiff are confined to damages for loss of or damage to any property, any other provision in its application to an action by virtue of Part I of the Consumer Protection Act 1987.

(2) The court shall not under this section disapply section 12(1) except where the reason why the person injured could no longer maintain an action was because of the time limit in section 11 or subsection (4) of section 11A.

If, for example, the person injured could at his death no longer maintain an action under the Fatal Accidents Act 1976 because of the time limit in Article 29 in Schedule 1 to the Carriage by Air Act 1961, the court has no power to direct that section 12(1) shall not apply.

(3) In acting under this section the court shall have regard to all the circumstances of the case and in particular to –
  (a) the length of, and the reasons for, the delay on the part of the plaintiff;
  (b) the extent to which, having regard to the delay, the evidence adduced or likely to be adduced by the plaintiff or the defendant is or is likely to be less cogent than if the action had been brought within the time allowed by section 11, by section 11A or (as the case may be) by section 12;
  (c) the conduct of the defendant after the cause of action arose, including the extent (if any) to which he responded to requests reasonably made by the plaintiff for information or inspection for the purpose of ascertaining facts which were or might be relevant to the plaintiff's cause of action against the defendant;
  (d) the duration of any disability of the plaintiff arising after the date of the accrual of the cause of action;
  (e) the extent to which the plaintiff acted promptly and reasonably once he knew whether or not the act or omission of the defendant, to which the injury was attributable, might be capable at that time of giving rise to an action for damages;
  (f) the steps, if any, taken by the plaintiff to obtain medical, legal or other expert advice and the nature of any such advice he may have received.

(4) In a case where the person injured died when, because of section 11 or subsection (4) of section 11A, he could no longer maintain an action and recover damages in respect of the injury, the court shall have regard in particular to the length of, and the reasons for, the delay on the part of the deceased.

(5) In a case under subsection (4) above, or any other case where the time limit, or one of the time limits, depends on the date of knowledge of a person other than the plaintiff, subsection (3) above shall have effect with appropriate modifications, and shall have effect in particular as if references to the plaintiff included references to any person whose date of knowledge is or was relevant in determining a time limit.

(6) A direction by the court disapplying the provisions of section 12(1) shall operate to disapply the provisions to the same effect in section 1(1) of the Fatal Accidents Act 1976.

(7) In this section 'the court' means the court in which the action has been brought.

(8) References in this section to section 11 or 11A include references to that section as extended by any of the preceding provisions of this Part of this Act or by any provision of Part III of this Act.

PART III

Miscellaneous and General

New claims in pending actions: rules of court

35.–(1) For the purposes of this Act, any new claim made in the course of any action shall be deemed to be a separate action and to have been commenced –
  (a) in the case of a new claim made in or by way of third party proceedings, on the date on which those proceedings were commenced; and
  (b) in the case of any other new claim, on the same date as the original action.

(2) In this section a new claim means any claim by way of set-off or counterclaim, and any claim involving either –

(a) the addition or substitution of a new cause of action; or

(b) the addition or substitution of a new party;

and 'third party proceedings' means any proceedings brought in the course of any action by any party to the action against a person not previously a party to the action, other than proceedings brought by joining any such person as defendant to any claim already made in the original action by the party bringing the proceedings.

(3) Except as provided by section 33 of this Act or by rules of court, neither the High Court nor any county court shall allow a new claim within subsection (1)(b) above, other than an original set-off or counterclaim, to be made in the course of any action after the expiry of any time limit under this Act which would affect a new action to enforce that claim.

For the purposes of this subsection, a claim is an original set-off or an original counterclaim if it is a claim by way of set-off or (as the case may be) by way of counterclaim by a party who has not previously made any claim in the action.

(4) Rules of court may provide for allowing a new claim to which subsection (3) above applies to be made as there mentioned, but only if the conditions specified in subsection (5) below are satisfied, and subject to any further restrictions the rules may impose.

(5) The conditions referred to in subsection (4) above are the following –

(a) in the case of a claim involving a new cause of action, if the new cause of action arises out of the same facts or substantially the same facts as are already in issue on any claim previously made in the original action; and

(b) in the case of a claim involving a new party, if the addition or substitution of the new party is necessary for the determination of the original action.

(6) The addition or substitution of a new party shall not be regarded for the purposes of subsection (5)(b) above as necessary for the determination of the original action unless either –

(a) the new party is substituted for a party whose name was given in any claim made in the original action in mistake for the new party's name; or

(b) any claim already made in the original action cannot be maintained by or against any existing party unless the new party is joined or substituted as plaintiff or defendant in that action.

(7) Subject to subsection (4) above, rules of court may provide for allowing a party to any action to claim relief in a new capacity in respect of a new cause of action notwithstanding that he had no title to make that claim at the date of the commencement of the action.

This subsection shall not be taken as prejudicing the power of rules of court to provide for allowing a party to claim relief in a new capacity without adding or substituting a new cause of action.

(8) Subsections (3) to (7) above shall apply in relation to a new claim made in the course of third party proceedings as if those proceedings were the original action, and subject to such other modifications as may be prescribed by rules of court in any case or class of case.

(9) [*Repealed*]

Interpretation

38.–(1) In this Act, unless the context otherwise requires –

'action' includes any proceedings in a court of law, including an ecclesiastical court;

'personal injuries' includes any disease and any impairment of a person's physical or mental condition, and 'injury' and cognate expressions shall be construed accordingly;

(2) For the purposes of this Act a person shall be treated as under a disability while he is an infant, or [lacks capacity (within the meaning of the Mental Capacity Act 2005) to conduct legal proceedings].

(5) Subject to subsection (6) below, a person shall be treated as claiming through another person if he became entitled by, through, under, or by the act of that other person to the right claimed, and any person whose estate or interest might have been barred by a person entitled to an entailed interest in possession shall be treated as claiming through the person so entitled.

(9) References in Part II of this Act to a right of action shall include references to –

(a)   a cause of action;

(10) References in Part II to the date of the accrual of a right of action shall be construed –

(a)   in the case of an action upon a judgment, as references to the date on which the judgment became enforceable; and

[Note: Words in italic repealed and words in square brackets substituted by the Care Standards Act 2000, from a date to be appointed.]

3. CONGENITAL DISABILITIES (CIVIL LIABILITY) ACT 1976

(1976 c 28)

An Act to make provision as to civil liability in the case of children born disabled in consequence of some person's fault; and to extend the Nuclear Installations Act 1965, so that children so born in consequence of a breach of duty under that Act may claim compensation.

[22nd July 1976]

Civil liability to child born disabled

1.–(1) If a child is born disabled as a result of such an occurrence before its birth as is mentioned in subsection (2) below, and a person (other than the child's own mother) is under this section answerable to the child in respect of the occurrence, the child's disabilities are to be regarded as damage resulting from the wrongful act of that person and actionable accordingly at the suit of the child.

(2) An occurrence to which this section applies is one which –
  (a) affected either parent of the child in his or her ability to have a normal, healthy child; or
  (b) affected the mother during her pregnancy, or affected her or the child in the course of its birth, so that the child is born with disabilities which would not otherwise have been present.

(3) Subject to the following subsections, a person (here referred to as 'the defendant') is answerable to the child if he was liable in tort to the parent or would, if sued in time, have been so; and it is no answer that there could not have been such liability because the parent suffered no actionable injury, if there was a breach of legal duty which, accompanied by injury would have given rise to the liability.

(4) In the case of an occurrence preceding the time of conception, the defendant is not answerable to the child if at that time either or both of the parents knew the risk of their child being born disabled (that is to say, the particular risk created by the occurrence); but should it be the child's father who is the defendant, this subsection does not apply if he knew of the risk and the mother did not.

[(4A) In the case of a child who has a parent by virtue of section 42 or 43 of the Human Fertilisation and Embryology Act 2008, the reference in subsection (4) to the child's father includes a reference to the woman who is a parent by virtue of that section.]

(5) The defendant is not answerable to the child, for anything he did or omitted to do when responsible in a professional capacity for treating or advising the parent, if he took reasonable care having due regard to then received professional opinion applicable to the particular class of case; but this does not mean that he is answerable only because he departed from received opinion.

(6) Liability to the child under this section may be treated as having been excluded or limited by contract made with the parent affected, to the same extent and subject to the same restrictions as liability in the parent's own case; and a contract term which could have been set up by the defendant in an action by the parent, so as to exclude or limit his liability to him or her, operates in the defendant's favour to the same, but no greater, extent in an action under this section by the child.

(7) If in the child's action under this section it is shown that the parent affected shared the responsibility for the child being born disabled, the damages are to be reduced to such extent as the court thinks just and equitable having regard to the extent of the parent's responsibility.

Extension of section 1 to cover infertility treatments

1A.–(1) In any case where –
  (a) a child carried by a woman as the result of the placing in her of an embryo or of sperm and eggs or her artificial insemination is born disabled,

(b) the disability results from an act or omission in the course of the selection, or the keeping or use outside the body, of the embryo carried by her or of the gametes used to bring about the creation of the embryo, and

(c) a person is under this section answerable to the child in respect of the act or omission,

the child's disabilities are to be regarded as damage resulting from the wrongful act of that person and actionable accordingly at the suit of the child.

(2) Subject to subsection (3) below and the applied provisions of section 1 of this Act, a person (here referred to as 'the defendant') is answerable to the child if he was liable in tort to one or both of the parents (here referred to as 'the parent or parents concerned') or would, if sued in due time, have been so; and it is no answer that there could not have been such liability because the parent or parents concerned suffered no actionable injury, if there was a breach of legal duty which, accompanied by injury, would have given rise to the liability.

(3) The defendant is not under this section answerable to the child if at the time the embryo, or the sperm and eggs, are placed in the woman or at the time of her insemination (as the case may be) either or both of the parents knew the risk of their child being born disabled (that is to say, the particular risk created by the act or omission).

(4) Subsections (5) to (7) of section 1 of this Act apply for the purposes of this section as they apply for the purposes of that but as if references to the parent or the parents affected were references to the parent or parents concerned.

[Note: Section 1A was inserted by s 44(1) of the Human Fertilisation and Embryology Act 1990.]

Liability of woman driving when pregnant

2. A woman driving a motor vehicle when she knows (or ought reasonably to know) herself to be pregnant is to be regarded as being under the same duty to take care for the safety of her unborn child as the law imposes on her with respect to the safety of other people; and if in consequence of her breach of that duty her child is born with disabilities which would not otherwise have been present, those disabilities are to be regarded as damage resulting from her wrongful act and actionable accordingly at the suit of the child.

Disabled birth due to radiation

3.–(1) Section 1 of this Act does not affect the operation of the Nuclear Installations Act 1965 as to liability for, and compensation in respect of, injury or damage caused by occurrences involving nuclear matter or the emission of ionising radiations.

(2) For the avoidance of doubt anything which –

(a) affects a man in his ability to have a normal, healthy child; or

(b) affects a woman in that ability, or so affects her when she is pregnant that her child is born with disabilities which would not otherwise have been present,

is an injury for the purposes of that Act.

(3) If a child is born disabled as the result of an injury to either of its parents caused in breach of a duty imposed by any of sections 7 to 11 of that Act (nuclear site licensees and others to secure that nuclear incidents do not cause injury to persons, etc), the child's disabilities are to be regarded under the subsequent provisions of that Act (compensation and other matters) as injuries caused on the same occasion, and by the same breach of duty, as was the injury to the parent.

(4) As respects compensation to the child, section 13(6) of that Act (contributory fault of person injured by radiation) is to be applied as if the reference there to fault were to the fault of the parent.

(5) Compensation is not payable in the child's case if the injury to the parent preceded the time of the child's conception and at that time either or both of

the parents knew the risk of their child being born disabled (that is to say, the particular risk created by the injury).

Interpretation and other supplementary provisions

4.–(1) References in this Act to a child being born disabled or with disabilities are to its being born with any deformity, disease or abnormality, including predisposition (whether or not susceptible of immediate prognosis) to physical or mental defect in the future.

(2) In this Act –

    (a) 'born' means alive (the moment of a child's birth being when it first has a life separate from its mother), and 'birth' has a corresponding meaning; and

    (b) 'motor vehicle' means a mechanically propelled vehicle intended or adapted for use on roads;

[and references to embryos shall be construed in accordance with section 1 of the Human Fertilisation and Embryology Act 1990.]

(3) Liability to a child under section 1 [or 1A] or 2 of this Act is to be regarded–

    (a) as respects all its incidents and any matters arising or to arise out of it; and

    (b) subject to any contrary context or intention, for the purpose of construing references in enactments and documents to personal or bodily injuries and cognate matters,

as liability for personal injuries sustained by the child immediately after its birth.

(4) No damages shall be recoverable under [any] of those sections in respect of any loss of expectation of life, nor shall any such loss be taken into account in the compensation payable in respect of a child under the Nuclear Installations Act 1965 as extended by section 3, unless (in either case) the child lives for at least 48 hours.

(4A) In any case where a child carried by a woman as the result of the placing in her of an embryo or of sperm and eggs or her artificial insemination is born disabled, any reference in section 1 of this Act to a parent includes a reference to a person who would be a parent but for sections 27 to 29 of the Human Fertilisation and Embryology Act 1990.

(5) This Act applies in respect of births after (but not before) its passing, and in respect of any such birth it replaces any law in force before its passing, whereby a person could be liable to a child in respect of disabilities with which it might be born; but in section 1(3) of this Act the expression 'liable in tort' does not include any reference to liability by virtue of this Act, or to liability by virtue of any such law.

(6) References to the Nuclear Installations Act 1965 are to that Act as amended; and for the purposes of section 28 of that Act (power by Order in Council to extend the Act to territories outside the United Kingdom) section 3 of this Act is to be treated as if it were a provision of that Act.

[Note: Sub-s (4A) was inserted by s 35 of the Human Fertilisation and Embryology Act 1990, and the words in square brackets in sub-ss (2), (3) and (4) were substituted by s 44 of that Act.]

Crown application

5. This Act binds the Crown.

Citation and extent

6.–(1) This Act may be cited as the Congenital Disabilities (Civil Liability) Act 1976.

(2) This Act extends to Northern Ireland but not to Scotland.

Appendix II

Practice Directions and Protocols

Contents

1. PRACTICE DIRECTION – PRE-ACTION CONDUCT

SECTION I – INTRODUCTION

1. Aims

1.1 The aims of this Practice Direction are to –
(1) enable parties to settle the issue between them without the need to start proceedings (that is, a court claim); and
(2) support the efficient management by the court and the parties of proceedings that cannot be avoided.

1.2 These aims are to be achieved by encouraging the parties to –
(1) exchange information about the issue, and
(2) consider using a form of Alternative Dispute Resolution ('ADR').

2. Scope

2.1 This Practice Direction describes the conduct the court will normally expect of the prospective parties prior to the start of proceedings.

2.2 There are some types of application where the principles in this Practice Direction clearly cannot or should not apply. These include, but are not limited to, for example –
(1) applications for an order where the parties have agreed between them the terms of the court order to be sought ('consent orders');
(2) applications for an order where there is no other party for the applicant to engage with;
(3) most applications for directions by a trustee or other fiduciary;
(4) applications where telling the other potential party in advance would defeat the purpose of the application (for example, an application for an order to freeze assets).

2.3 Section II deals with the approach of the court in exercising its powers in relation to pre-action conduct. Subject to paragraph 2.2, it applies in relation to all types of proceedings including those governed by the pre-action protocols that have been approved by the Head of Civil Justice and which are listed in paragraph 5.2 of this Practice Direction.

2.4 Section III deals with principles governing the conduct of the parties in cases which are not subject to a pre-action protocol.

2.5 Section III of this Practice Direction is supplemented by two annexes aimed at different types of claimant.
(1) **Annex A** sets out detailed guidance on a pre-action procedure that is likely to satisfy the court in most circumstances where no pre-action protocol or other formal pre-action procedure applies. It is intended as a guide for parties, particularly those without legal representation, in straightforward claims that are likely to be disputed. It is not intended to apply to debt claims where it is not disputed that the money is owed and where the claimant follows a statutory or other formal pre-action procedure.
(2) **Annex B** sets out some specific requirements that apply where the claimant is a business and the defendant is an individual. The requirements may be complied with at any time between the claimant first intimating the possibility of court proceedings and the claimant's letter before claim.

2.6   Section IV contains requirements that apply to all cases including those subject to the pre-action protocols (unless a relevant pre-action protocol contains a different provision). It is supplemented by **Annex C**, which sets out guidance on instructing experts.

3. Definitions

3.1   In this Practice Direction together with the Annexes –
  (1)   'proceedings' means any proceedings started under Part 7 or Part 8 of the Civil Procedure Rules 1998 ('CPR');
  (2)   'claimant' and 'defendant' refer to the respective parties to potential proceedings;
  (3)   'ADR' means alternative dispute resolution, and is the collective description of methods of resolving disputes otherwise than through the normal trial process; (see paragraph 8.2 for further information); and
  (4)   'compliance' means acting in accordance with, as applicable, the principles set out in Section III of this Practice Direction, the requirements in Section IV and a relevant pre-action protocol. The words 'comply' and 'complied' should be construed accordingly.

SECTION II – THE APPROACH OF THE COURTS

4. Compliance

4.1   The CPR enable the court to take into account the extent of the parties' compliance with this Practice Direction or a relevant pre-action protocol (see paragraph 5.2) when giving directions for the management of claims (see CPR rules 3.1(4) and (5) and 3.9(1)(e)) and when making orders about who should pay costs (see CPR rule 44.3(5)(a)).

4.2   The court will expect the parties to have complied with this Practice Direction or any relevant pre-action protocol. The court may ask the parties to explain what steps were taken to comply prior to the start of the claim. Where there has been a failure of compliance by a party the court may ask that party to provide an explanation.

Assessment of compliance

4.3   When considering compliance the court will –
  (1)   be concerned about whether the parties have complied in substance with the relevant principles and requirements and is not likely to be concerned with minor or technical shortcomings;
  (2)   consider the proportionality of the steps taken compared to the size and importance of the matter;
  (3)   take account of the urgency of the matter. Where a matter is urgent (for example, an application for an injunction) the court will expect the parties to comply only to the extent that it is reasonable to do so. (Paragraph 9.5 and 9.6 of this Practice Direction concern urgency caused by limitation periods.)

Examples of non-compliance

4.4   The court may decide that there has been a failure of compliance by a party because, for example, that party has –
  (1)   not provided sufficient information to enable the other party to understand the issues;
  (2)   not acted within a time limit set out in a relevant pre-action protocol, or, where no specific time limit applies, within a reasonable period;

(3) unreasonably refused to consider ADR (paragraph 8 in Part III of this Practice Direction and the pre-action protocols all contain similar provisions about ADR); or

(4) without good reason, not disclosed documents requested to be disclosed.

Sanctions for non-compliance

4.5 The court will look at the overall effect of non-compliance on the other party when deciding whether to impose sanctions.

4.6 If, in the opinion of the court, there has been non-compliance, the sanctions which the court may impose include –

(1) staying (that is suspending) the proceedings until steps which ought to have been taken have been taken;

(2) an order that the party at fault pays the costs, or part of the costs, of the other party or parties (this may include an order under rule 27.14(2)(g) in cases allocated to the small claims track);

(3) an order that the party at fault pays those costs on an indemnity basis (rule 44.4(3) sets out the definition of the assessment of costs on an indemnity basis);

(4) if the party at fault is the claimant in whose favour an order for the payment of a sum of money is subsequently made, an order that the claimant is deprived of interest on all or part of that sum, and/or that interest is awarded at a lower rate than would otherwise have been awarded;

(5) if the party at fault is a defendant, and an order for the payment of a sum of money is subsequently made in favour of the claimant, an order that the defendant pay interest on all or part of that sum at a higher rate, not exceeding 10% above base rate, than would otherwise have been awarded.

5. Commencement of pre-action protocols

5.1 When considering compliance, the court will take account of a relevant pre-action protocol if the proceedings were started after the relevant pre-action protocol came into force.

5.2 The following table sets out the pre-action protocols currently in force and the dates that they came into force –

Pre-Action Protocol	Came into force
Personal Injury	26 April 1999
Clinical Disputes	26 April 1999

SECTION III – THE PRINCIPLES GOVERNING THE CONDUCT OF THE PARTIES IN CASES NOT SUBJECT TO A PRE-ACTION PROTOCOL

6. Overview of Principles

6.1 The principles that should govern the conduct of the parties are that, unless the circumstances make it inappropriate, before starting proceedings the parties should –

    (1)   exchange sufficient information about the matter to allow them to understand each other's position and make informed decisions about settlement and how to proceed;

    (2)   make appropriate attempts to resolve the matter without starting proceedings, and in particular consider the use of an appropriate form of ADR in order to do so.

6.2   The parties should act in a reasonable and proportionate manner in all dealings with one another. In particular, the costs incurred in complying should be proportionate to the complexity of the matter and any money at stake. The parties must not use this Practice Direction as a tactical device to secure an unfair advantage for one party or to generate unnecessary costs.

7. Exchanging Information before starting proceedings

7.1   Before starting proceedings –

    (1)   the claimant should set out the details of the matter in writing by sending a letter before claim to the defendant. This letter before claim is not the start of proceedings; and

    (2)   the defendant should give a full written response within a reasonable period, preceded, if appropriate, by a written acknowledgment of the letter before claim.

7.2   A 'reasonable period of time' will vary depending on the matter. As a general guide –

    (1)   the defendant should send a letter of acknowledgment within 14 days of receipt of the letter before claim (if a full response has not been sent within that period);

    (2)   where the matter is straightforward, for example an undisputed debt, then a full response should normally be provided within 14 days;

    (3)   where a matter requires the involvement of an insurer or other third party or where there are issues about evidence, then a full response should normally be provided within 30 days;

    (4)   where the matter is particularly complex, for example requiring specialist advice, then a period of longer than 30 days may be appropriate;

    (5)   a period of longer than 90 days in which to provide a full response will only be considered reasonable in exceptional circumstances.

7.3   Annex A sets out detailed guidance on a pre-action procedure that is likely to satisfy the court in most circumstances where no pre-action protocol applies and where the claimant does not follow any statutory or other formal pre-action procedure.

7.4   Annex B sets out the specific information that should be provided in a debt claim by a claimant who is a business against a defendant who is an individual.

8. Alternative Dispute Resolution

8.1   Starting proceedings should usually be a step of last resort, and proceedings should not normally be started when a settlement is still actively being explored. Although ADR is not compulsory, the parties should consider whether some form of ADR procedure might enable them to settle the matter without starting proceedings. The court may require evidence that the parties considered some form of ADR (see paragraph 4.4(3)).

8.2   It is not practicable in this Practice Direction to address in detail how the parties might decide to resolve a matter. However, some of the options for resolving a matter without starting proceedings are –

    (1)   discussion and negotiation;

    (2)   mediation (a form of negotiation with the help of an independent person or body);

    (3)   early neutral evaluation (where an independent person or body, for example a lawyer or an expert in the subject, gives an opinion on the merits of a dispute); or

    (4)   arbitration (where an independent person or body makes a binding decision), many types of business are members of arbitration schemes for resolving disputes with consumers.

8.3   The Legal Services Commission has published a booklet on 'Alternatives to Court', CLS Direct Information Leaflet 23 (www.clsdirect.org.uk) which lists a number of organisations that provide alternative dispute resolution services. The National Mediation Helpline on 0845 603 0809 or at www.nationalmediationhelpline.com can provide information about mediation.

8.4   The parties should continue to consider the possibility of reaching a settlement at all times. This still applies after proceedings have been started, up to and during any trial or final hearing.

SECTION IV – REQUIREMENTS THAT APPLY IN ALL CASES

9. Specific Provisions

9.1   The following requirements (including Annex C) apply in all cases except where a relevant pre-action protocol contains its own provisions about the topic.

Disclosure

9.2   Documents provided by one party to another in the course of complying with this Practice Direction or any relevant pre-action protocol must not be used for any purpose other than resolving the matter, unless the disclosing party agrees in writing.

Information about funding arrangements

9.3   Where a party enters into a funding arrangement within the meaning of rule 43.2(1)(k), that party must inform the other parties about this arrangement as soon as possible and in any event either within 7 days of entering into the funding arrangement concerned or, where a claimant enters into a funding arrangement before sending a letter before claim, in the letter before claim.

(CPR rule 44.3B(1)(c) provides that a party may not recover certain additional costs where information about a funding arrangement was not provided.)

Experts

9.4   Where the evidence of an expert is necessary the parties should consider how best to minimise expense. Guidance on instructing experts can be found in Annex C.

Limitation Periods

9.5   There are statutory time limits for starting proceedings ('the limitation period'). If a claimant starts a claim after the limitation period applicable to that type of claim has expired the defendant will be entitled to use that as a defence to the claim.

9.6   In certain instances compliance may not be possible before the expiry of the limitation period. If, for any reason, proceedings are started before the parties have complied, they should seek to agree to apply to the court for an order to stay (i.e. suspend) the proceedings while the parties take steps to comply.

Notifying the court

9.7   Where proceedings are started the claimant should state in the claim form or the particulars of claim whether they have complied with Sections III and IV of this Practice Direction or any relevant protocol.

Transitional Provision

9.8   The amendments to paragraph 9.3 do not apply to a funding arrangement entered into before the 1st October 2009 and paragraph 9.3 in force immediately before that date will continue to apply to that funding arrangement as if paragraph 9.3 had not been amended.

ANNEX A
Guidance on pre-action procedure where no pre-action protocol or other formal pre-action procedure applies

1. General

1.1   This Annex sets out detailed guidance on a pre-action procedure that is likely to satisfy the court in most circumstances where no pre-action protocol or other formal pre-action procedure applies. It is intended as a guide for parties, particularly those without legal representation, in straightforward claims that are likely to be disputed. It is not intended to apply to debt claims where it is not disputed that the money is owed and where the claimant follows a statutory or other formal pre-action procedure.

2. Claimant's letter before claim

2.1   The claimant's letter should give concise details about the matter. This should enable the defendant to understand and investigate the issues without needing to request further information. The letter should include –
    (1)   the claimant's full name and address;
    (2)   the basis on which the claim is made (i.e. why the claimant says the defendant is liable);
    (3)   a clear summary of the facts on which the claim is based;
    (4)   what the claimant wants from the defendant;
    (5)   if financial loss is claimed, an explanation of how the amount has been calculated; and
    (6)   details of any funding arrangement (within the meaning of rule 43.2(1) (k) of the CPR) that has been entered into by the claimant.

2.2   The letter should also –
    (1)   list the essential documents on which the claimant intends to rely;
    (2)   set out the form of ADR (if any) that the claimant considers the most suitable and invite the defendant to agree to this;
    (3)   state the date by which the claimant considers it reasonable for a full response to be provided by the defendant; and

(4) identify and ask for copies of any relevant documents not in the claimant's possession and which the claimant wishes to see.

2.3 Unless the defendant is known to be legally represented the letter should –
(1) refer the defendant to this Practice Direction and in particular draw attention to paragraph 4 concerning the court's powers to impose sanctions for failure to comply with the Practice Direction; and
(2) inform the defendant that ignoring the letter before claim may lead to the claimant starting proceedings and may increase the defendant's liability for costs.

3. Defendant's acknowledgment of the letter before claim

3.1 Where the defendant is unable to provide a full written response within 14 days of receipt of the letter before claim the defendant should, instead, provide a written acknowledgment within 14 days.

3.2 The acknowledgment –
(1) should state whether an insurer is or may be involved;
(2) should state the date by which the defendant (or insurer) will provide a full written response; and
(3) may request further information to enable the defendant to provide a full response.

3.3 If the date stated under paragraph 3.2(2) of this Annex is longer than the period stated in the letter before claim, the defendant should give reasons why a longer period is needed.

3.4 If the defendant (or insurer) does not provide either a letter of acknowledgment or full response within 14 days, and proceedings are subsequently started, then the court is likely to consider that the claimant has complied.

3.5 Where the defendant is unable to provide a full response within 14 days of receipt of the letter before claim because the defendant intends to seek advice then the written acknowledgment should state –
(1) that the defendant is seeking advice;
(2) from whom the defendant is seeking advice; and
(3) when the defendant expects to have received that advice and be in a position to provide a full response.

3.6 A claimant should allow a reasonable period of time of up to 14 days for a defendant to obtain advice.

4. Defendant's full response

4.1 The defendant's full written response should –
(1) accept the claim in whole or in part; or
(2) state that the claim is not accepted.

4.2 Unless the defendant accepts the whole of the claim, the response should –
(1) give reasons why the claim is not accepted, identifying which facts and which parts of the claim (if any) are accepted and which are disputed, and the basis of that dispute;
(2) state whether the defendant intends to make a counterclaim against the claimant (and, if so, provide information equivalent to a claimant's letter before claim);

(3) state whether the defendant alleges that the claimant was wholly or partly to blame for the problem that led to the dispute and, if so, summarise the facts relied on;

(4) state whether the defendant agrees to the claimant's proposals for ADR and if not, state why not and suggest an alternative form of ADR (or state why none is considered appropriate);

(5) list the essential documents on which the defendant intends to rely;

(6) enclose copies of documents requested by the claimant, or explain why they will not be provided; and

(7) identify and ask for copies of any further relevant documents, not in the defendant's possession and which the defendant wishes to see.

4.3   If the defendant (or insurer) does not provide a full response within the period stated in the claimant's letter before claim (or any longer period stated in the defendant's letter of acknowledgment), and a claim is subsequently started, then the court is likely to consider that the claimant has complied.

4.4   If the claimant starts proceedings before any longer period stated in the defendant's letter of acknowledgment, the court will consider whether or not the longer period requested by the defendant was reasonable.

5. Claimant's reply

5.1   The claimant should provide the documents requested by the defendant within as short a period of time as is practicable or explain in writing why the documents will not be provided.

5.2   If the defendant has made a counterclaim the claimant should provide information equivalent to the defendant's full response (see paragraphs 4.1 to 4.3 above)

6. Taking Stock

6.1   In following the above procedure, the parties will have a genuine opportunity to resolve the matter without needing to start proceedings. At the very least, it should be possible to establish what issues remain outstanding so as to narrow the scope of the proceedings and therefore limit potential costs.

6.2   If having completed the procedure the matter has not been resolved then the parties should undertake a further review of their respective positions to see if proceedings can still be avoided.

ANNEX B
Information to be provided in a debt claim where the claimant is a business and the defendant is an individual

1.   Where paragraph 7.4 of the Practice Direction applies the claimant should –

(1) provide details of how the money can be paid (for example the method of payment and the address to which it can be sent);

(2) state that the defendant can contact the claimant to discuss possible repayment options, and provide the relevant contact details; and

(3) inform the defendant that free independent advice and assistance can be obtained from organisations including those listed in the table below.

INDEPENDENT ADVICE ORGANISATIONS			
Organisation	Address	Telephone Number	e-mail Address
National Debtline	Tricorn House 51–53 Hagley Road Edgbaston Birmingham B16 8TP	FREEPHONE 0808 808 4000	www. nationaldebtline. co.uk
Consumer Credit Counselling Service (CCCS)		FREEPHONE 0800 138 1111	www.cccs.co.uk
Citizens Advice	Check your local Yellow Pages or Thomson local directory for address and telephone numbers		www. citizensadvice. org.uk
Community Legal Advice (formerly Community Legal Services Direct)		0845 345 4345	www.clsdirect. org.uk

2.   The information set out in paragraph 1 of this Annex may be provided at any time between the claimant first intimating the possibility of court proceedings and the claimant's letter before claim.

3.   Where the defendant is unable to provide a full response within the time specified in the letter before claim because the defendant intends to seek debt advice then the written acknowledgment should state –
  (1)   that the defendant is seeking debt advice;
  (2)   who the defendant is seeking advice from; and
  (3)   when the defendant expects to have received that advice and be in a position to provide a full response.

4.   A claimant should allow a reasonable period of time of up to 14 days for a defendant to obtain debt advice.

5.   But the claimant need not allow the defendant time to seek debt advice if the claimant knows that –
  (1)   the defendant has already received relevant debt advice and the defendant's circumstances have not significantly changed; or
  (2)   the defendant has previously asked for time to seek debt advice but has not done so.

ANNEX C
Guidance on instructing experts

1.   The CPR contain extensive provisions which strictly control the use of experts both before and after proceedings are started. These provisions are contained in –
  (1)   CPR Part 35;
  (2)   Practice Direction 35; and
  (3)   the Protocol for the 'Instruction of Experts to give Evidence in Civil Claims' which is annexed to that Practice Direction.

2.   Parties should be aware that once proceedings have been started –
  (1)   expert evidence may not be used in court without the permission of the court;

(2) a party who instructs an expert will not necessarily be able to recover the cost from another party; and

(3) it is the duty of an expert to help the court on the matters within the expert's scope of expertise and this duty overrides any obligation to the person instructing or paying the expert.

3.   Many matters can and should be resolved without the need for advice or evidence from an expert. If an expert is needed, the parties should consider how best to minimise the expense for example by agreeing to instruct –

(1) a single joint expert (i.e. engaged and paid jointly by the parties whether instructed jointly or separately); or

(2) an agreed expert (i.e. the parties agree the identity of the expert but only one party instructs the expert and pays the expert's costs).

4.   If the parties do not agree that the nomination of a single joint expert is appropriate, then the party seeking the expert evidence (the first party) should give the other party (the second party) a list of one or more experts in the relevant field of expertise whom the first party would like to instruct.

5.   Within 14 days of receipt of the list of experts, the second party may indicate in writing an objection to one or more of the experts listed. If there remains on the list one or more experts who are acceptable, then the first party should instruct an expert from the list.

6.   If the second party objects to all the listed experts, the first party may then instruct an expert of the first party's own choice. Both parties should bear in mind that if proceedings are started the court will consider whether a party has acted reasonably when instructing (or rejecting) an expert.

2. PRE-ACTION PROTOCOL FOR THE RESOLUTION OF CLINICAL DISPUTES

Clinical Disputes Forum

Contents

Executive Summary
1   Why This Protocol?
2   The Aims Of The Protocol
3   The Protocol
4   Experts
5   Alternative Dispute Resolution

ANNEXES
A   Illustrative Flowchart
B   Medical Negligence And Personal Injury Claims
C   Templates For Letters Of Claim And Response
D   Lord Woolf's Recommendations
E   How To Contact The Forum

EXECUTIVE SUMMARY

1   The Clinical Disputes Forum is a multi-disciplinary body which was formed in 1997, as a result of Lord Woolf's 'Access to Justice' inquiry. One of the aims of the Forum is to find less adversarial and more cost-effective ways of resolving disputes about healthcare and medical treatment. The names and addresses of the Chairman and Secretary of the Forum can be found at Annex E.

2   This protocol is the Forum's first major initiative. It has been drawn up carefully, including extensive consultations with most of the key stakeholders in the medico-legal system.

3   The protocol –
   •   encourages a climate of openness when something has 'gone wrong' with a patient's treatment or the patient is dissatisfied with that treatment and/or the outcome. This reflects the new and developing requirements for clinical governance within healthcare;
   •   provides general guidance on how this more open culture might be achieved when disputes arise;
   •   recommends a timed sequence of steps for patients and healthcare providers, and their advisers, to follow when a dispute arises. This should facilitate and speed up exchanging relevant information and increase the prospects that disputes can be resolved without resort to legal action.

4   This protocol has been prepared by a working party of the Clinical Disputes Forum. It has the support of the Lord Chancellor's Department, the Department of Health and NHS Executive, the Law Society, the Legal Aid Board and many other key organisations.

1 Why this protocol?

Mistrust in Healthcare Disputes

1.1   The number of complaints and claims against hospitals, GPs, dentists and private healthcare providers is growing as patients become more prepared to question the treatment they are given, to seek explanations of what happened, and to seek appropriate redress. Patients may require further treatment, an apology, assurances about future action, or compensation. These trends are unlikely to change. The Patients' Charter encourages patients to have high expectations, and a revised NHS Complaints Procedure was implemented in 1996. The civil justice reforms and new Rules of Court should make litigation quicker, more user friendly and less expensive.

1.2   It is clearly in the interests of patients, healthcare professionals and providers that patients' concerns, complaints and claims arising from their treatment are resolved as quickly, efficiently and professionally as possible. A climate of mistrust and lack of openness can seriously damage the patient/ clinician relationship, unnecessarily prolong disputes (especially litigation), and reduce the resources available for treating patients. It may also cause additional work for, and lower the morale of, healthcare professionals.

1.3   At present there is often mistrust by both sides. This can mean that patients fail to raise their concerns with the healthcare provider as early as possible. Sometimes patients may pursue a complaint or claim which has little merit, due to a lack of sufficient information and understanding. It can also mean that patients become reluctant, once advice has been taken on a potential claim, to disclose sufficient information to enable the provider to investigate that claim efficiently and, where appropriate, resolve it.

1.4   On the side of the healthcare provider this mistrust can be shown in a reluctance to be honest with patients, a failure to provide prompt clear explanations, especially of adverse outcomes (whether or not there may have been negligence) and a tendency to 'close ranks' once a claim is made.

What needs to change

1.5   If that mistrust is to be removed, and a more co-operative culture is to develop –
- healthcare professionals and providers need to adopt a constructive approach to complaints and claims. They should accept that concerned patients are entitled to an explanation and an apology, if warranted, and to appropriate redress in the event of negligence. An overly defensive approach is not in the long-term interest of their main goal: patient care;
- patients should recognise that unintended and/or unfortunate consequences of medical treatment can only be rectified if they are brought to the attention of the healthcare provider as soon as possible.

1.6   A protocol which sets out 'ground rules' for the handling of disputes at their early stages should, if it is to be subscribed to, and followed –
- encourage greater openness between the parties;
- encourage parties to find the most appropriate way of resolving the particular dispute;
- reduce delay and costs;
- reduce the need for litigation.

Why this protocol now?

1.7   Lord Woolf in his Access to Justice Report in July 1996, concluded that major causes of costs and delay in medical negligence litigation occur at the pre-action stage. He recommended that patients and their advisers, and healthcare providers, should work more closely together to try to resolve disputes co-operatively, rather than proceed to litigation. He specifically recommended a pre-action protocol for medical negligence cases.

1.8   A fuller summary of Lord Woolf's recommendations is at Annex D.

Where the protocol fits in

1.9   Protocols serve the needs of litigation and pre-litigation practice, especially –
- predictability in the time needed for steps pre-proceedings;
- standardisation of relevant information, including records and documents to be disclosed.

1.10   Building upon Lord Woolf's recommendations, the Lord Chancellor's Department is now promoting the adoption of protocols in specific areas, including medical negligence.

1.11   It is recognised that contexts differ significantly. For example: patients tend to have an ongoing relationship with a GP, more so than with a hospital; clinical staff in the National Health Service are often employees, while those in the private sector may be contractors; providing records quickly may be relatively easy for GPs and dentists, but can be a complicated procedure in a large multi-department hospital. The protocol which follows is intended to be sufficiently broadly based, and flexible, to apply to all aspects of the health service: primary and secondary; public and private sectors.

Enforcement of the protocol and sanctions

1.12   The civil justice reforms will be implemented in April 1999. One new set of Court Rules and procedures is replacing the existing rules for both the High Court and county courts. This and the personal injury protocol are being published with the Rules, practice directions and key court forms. The courts will be able to treat the standards set in protocols as the normal reasonable approach to pre-action conduct.

1.13   If proceedings are issued it will be for the court to decide whether non-compliance with a protocol should merit sanctions. Guidance on the court's likely approach will be given from time to time in practice directions.

1.14   If the court has to consider the question of compliance after proceedings have begun it will not be concerned with minor infringements, e.g. failure by a short period to provide relevant information. One minor breach will not entitle the 'innocent' party to abandon following the protocol. The court will look at the effect of non-compliance on the other party when deciding whether to impose sanctions.

2 The aims of the protocol

2.1   The general aims of the protocol are –
- to maintain/restore the patient/healthcare provider relationship;
- to resolve as many disputes as possible without litigation.

2.2   The specific objectives are –
Openness
- to encourage early communication of the perceived problem between patients and healthcare providers;
- to encourage patients to voice any concerns or dissatisfaction with their treatment as soon as practicable;
- to encourage healthcare providers to develop systems of early reporting and investigation for serious adverse treatment outcomes and to provide full and prompt explanations to dissatisfied patients;

- to ensure that sufficient information is disclosed by both parties to enable each to understand the other's perspective and case, and to encourage early resolution;

Timeliness

- to provide an early opportunity for healthcare providers to identify cases where an investigation is required and to carry out that investigation promptly;
- to encourage primary and private healthcare providers to involve their defence organisations or insurers at an early stage;
- to ensure that all relevant medical records are provided to patients or their appointed representatives on request, to a realistic timetable by any healthcare provider;
- to ensure that relevant records which are not in healthcare providers' possession are made available to them by patients and their advisers at an appropriate stage;
- where a resolution is not achievable to lay the ground to enable litigation to proceed on a reasonable timetable, at a reasonable and proportionate cost and to limit the matters in contention;
- to discourage the prolonged pursuit of unmeritorious claims and the prolonged defence of meritorious claims.

Awareness of options

- to ensure that patients and healthcare providers are made aware of the available options to pursue and resolve disputes and what each might involve.

2.3   This protocol does not attempt to be prescriptive about a number of related clinical governance issues which will have a bearing on healthcare providers' ability to meet the standards within the protocol. Good clinical governance requires the following to be considered –

(a) Clinical risk management: the protocol does not provide any detailed guidance to healthcare providers on clinical risk management or the adoption of risk management systems and procedures. This must be a matter for the NHS Executive, the National Health Service Litigation Authority, individual trusts and providers, including GPs, dentists and the private sector. However, effective co-ordinated, focused clinical risk management strategies and procedures can help in managing risk and in the early identification and investigation of adverse outcomes.

(b) Adverse outcome reporting: the protocol does not provide any detailed guidance on which adverse outcomes should trigger an investigation. However, healthcare providers should have in place procedures for such investigations, including recording of statements of key witnesses. These procedures should also cover when and how to inform patients that an adverse outcome has occurred.

(c) The professional's duty to report: the protocol does not recommend changes to the codes of conduct of professionals in healthcare, or attempt to impose a specific duty on those professionals to report known adverse outcomes or untoward incidents. Lord Woolf in his final report suggested that the professional bodies might consider this. The General Medical Council is preparing guidance to doctors about their duty to report adverse incidents and to co-operate with inquiries.

3 The protocol

3.1   This protocol is not a comprehensive code governing all the steps in clinical disputes. Rather it attempts to set out a code of good practice which parties should follow when litigation might be a possibility.

3.2   The commitments section of the protocol summarises the guiding principles which healthcare providers and patients and their advisers are invited to endorse when dealing with patient dissatisfaction with treatment and its outcome, and with potential complaints and claims.

3.3   The steps section sets out in a more prescriptive form, a recommended sequence of actions to be followed if litigation is a prospect.

Good Practice Commitments

3.4   Healthcare providers should –
   (i) ensure that key staff, including claims and litigation managers, are appropriately trained and have some knowledge of healthcare law, and of complaints procedures and civil litigation practice and procedure;
   (ii) develop an approach to clinical governance that ensures that clinical practice is delivered to commonly accepted standards and that this is routinely monitored through a system of clinical audit and clinical risk management (particularly adverse outcome investigation);
   (iii) set up adverse outcome reporting systems in all specialties to record and investigate unexpected serious adverse outcomes as soon as possible. Such systems can enable evidence to be gathered quickly, which makes it easier to provide an accurate explanation of what happened and to defend or settle any subsequent claims;
   (iv) use the results of adverse incidents and complaints positively as a guide to how to improve services to patients in the future;
   (v) ensure that patients receive clear and comprehensible information in an accessible form about how to raise their concerns or complaints;
   (vi) establish efficient and effective systems of recording and storing patient records, notes, diagnostic reports and X-rays, and to retain these in accordance with Department of Health guidance (currently for a minimum of eight years in the case of adults, and all obstetric and paediatric notes for children until they reach the age of 25);
   (vii) advise patients of a serious adverse outcome and provide on request to the patient or the patient's representative an oral or written explanation of what happened, information on further steps open to the patient, including where appropriate an offer of future treatment to rectify the problem, an apology, changes in procedure which will benefit patients and/or compensation.

3.5   Patients and their advisers should –
   (i) report any concerns and dissatisfaction to the healthcare provider as soon as is reasonable to enable that provider to offer clinical advice where possible, to advise the patient if anything has gone wrong and take appropriate action;
   (ii) consider the full range of options available following an adverse outcome with which a patient is dissatisfied, including a request for an explanation, a meeting, a complaint, and other appropriate dispute resolution methods (including mediation) and negotiation, not only litigation;
   (iii) inform the healthcare provider when the patient is satisfied that the matter has been concluded: legal advisers should notify the provider when they are no longer acting for the patient, particularly if proceedings have not started.

Protocol Steps

3.6   The steps of this protocol which follow have been kept deliberately simple. An illustration of the likely sequence of events in a number of healthcare situations is at Annex A.

Obtaining the Health Records

3.7   Any request for records by the patient or their adviser should –

- provide sufficient information to alert the healthcare provider where an adverse outcome has been serious or had serious consequences;
- be as specific as possible about the records which are required.

3.8   Requests for copies of the patient's clinical records should be made using the Law Society and Department of Health approved standard forms (enclosed at Annex B), adapted as necessary.

3.9   The copy records should be provided within 40 days of the request and for a cost not exceeding the charges permissible under the Access to Health Records Act 1990 (currently a maximum of £10 plus photocopying and postage).

3.10   In the rare circumstances that the healthcare provider is in difficulty in complying with the request within 40 days, the problem should be explained quickly and details given of what is being done to resolve it.

3.11   It will not be practicable for healthcare providers to investigate in detail each case when records are requested. But healthcare providers should adopt a policy on which cases will be investigated (see paragraph 3.5 on clinical governance and adverse outcome reporting).

3.12   If the healthcare provider fails to provide the health records within 40 days, the patient or their adviser can then apply to the court for an order for pre-action disclosure. The new Civil Procedure Rules should make pre-action applications to the court easier. The court will also have the power to impose costs sanctions for unreasonable delay in providing records.

3.13   If either the patient or the healthcare provider considers additional health records are required from a third party, in the first instance these should be requested by or through the patient. Third party healthcare providers are expected to co-operate. The Civil Procedure Rules will enable patients and healthcare providers to apply to the court for pre-action disclosure by third parties.

Letter of Claim

3.14   Annex C1 to this protocol provides a template for the recommended contents of a letter of claim: the level of detail will need to be varied to suit the particular circumstances.

3.15   If, following the receipt and analysis of the records, and the receipt of any further advice (including from experts if necessary – see Section 4), the patient/ adviser decides that there are grounds for a claim, they should then send, as soon as practicable, to the healthcare provider/potential defendant, a letter of claim. Any letter of claim sent to an NHS Trust or Independent Sector Treatment Centre should be copied to the National Health Service Litigation Authority.

3.16   This letter should contain a clear summary of the facts on which the claim is based, including the alleged adverse outcome, and the main allegations of negligence. It should also describe the patient's injuries, and present condition and prognosis. The financial loss incurred by the plaintiff should be outlined with an indication of the heads of damage to be claimed and the scale of the loss, unless this is impracticable.

3.17   In more complex cases a chronology of the relevant events should be provided, particularly if the patient has been treated by a number of different healthcare providers.

3.18   The letter of claim should refer to any relevant documents, including health records, and if possible enclose copies of any of those which will not already be in the potential defendant's possession, e.g. any relevant general practitioner records if the plaintiff's claim is against a hospital.

3.19   Sufficient information must be given to enable the healthcare provider defendant to commence investigations and to put an initial valuation on the claim.

3.20   Letters of claim are not intended to have the same formal status as a pleading, nor should any sanctions necessarily apply if the letter of claim and any subsequent statement of claim in the proceedings differ.

3.21   Proceedings should not be issued until after four months from the letter of claim, unless there is a limitation problem and/or the patient's position needs to be protected by early issue.

3.22   The patient or their adviser may want to make an offer to settle the claim at this early stage by putting forward an amount of compensation which would be satisfactory (possibly including any costs incurred to date). If an offer to settle is made, generally this should be supported by a medical report which deals with the injuries, condition and prognosis, and by a schedule of loss and supporting documentation. The level of detail necessary will depend on the value of the claim. Medical reports may not be necessary where there is no significant continuing injury, and a detailed schedule may not be necessary in a low value case. The Civil Procedure Rules are expected to set out the legal and procedural requirements for making offers to settle.

The Response

3.23   Attached at Annex C2 is a template for the suggested contents of the letter of response.

3.24   The healthcare provider should acknowledge the letter of claim within 14 days of receipt and should identify who will be dealing with the matter.

3.25   The healthcare provider should, within four months of the letter of claim, provide a reasoned answer –
- if the claim is admitted the healthcare provider should say so in clear terms;
- if only part of the claim is admitted the healthcare provider should make clear which issues of breach of duty and/or causation are admitted and which are denied and why;
- if it is intended that any admissions will be binding;
- if the claim is denied, this should include specific comments on the allegations of negligence, and if a synopsis or chronology of relevant events has been provided and is disputed, the healthcare provider's version of those events;
- where additional documents are relied upon, e.g. an internal protocol, copies should be provided.

3.26   If the patient has made an offer to settle, the healthcare provider should respond to that offer in the response letter, preferably with reasons. The provider may make its own offer to settle at this stage, either as a counter-offer to the patient's, or of its own accord, but should accompany any offer by any supporting medical evidence, and/or by any other evidence in relation to the value of the claim which is in the healthcare provider's possession.

3.27   If the parties reach agreement on liability, but time is needed to resolve the value of the claim, they should aim to agree a reasonable period.

4 Experts

4.1   In clinical negligence disputes expert opinions may be needed –
*   on breach of duty and causation;
*   on the patient's condition and prognosis;
*   to assist in valuing aspects of the claim.

4.2   The civil justice reforms and the new Civil Procedure Rules will encourage economy in the use of experts and a less adversarial expert culture. It is recognised that in clinical negligence disputes, the parties and their advisers will require flexibility in their approach to expert evidence. Decisions on whether experts might be instructed jointly, and on whether reports might be disclosed sequentially or by exchange, should rest with the parties and their advisers. Sharing expert evidence may be appropriate on issues relating to the value of the claim. However, this protocol does not attempt to be prescriptive on issues in relation to expert evidence.

4.3   Obtaining expert evidence will often be an expensive step and may take time, especially in specialised areas of medicine where there are limited numbers of suitable experts. Patients and healthcare providers, and their advisers, will therefore need to consider carefully how best to obtain any necessary expert help quickly and cost-effectively. Assistance with locating a suitable expert is available from a number of sources.

5 Alternative dispute resolution

5.1   The parties should consider whether some form of alternative dispute resolution procedure would be more suitable than litigation, and if so, endeavour to agree which form to adopt. Both the Claimant and Defendant may be required by the Court to provide evidence that alternative means of resolving their dispute were considered. The Courts take the view that litigation should be a last resort, and that claims should not be issued prematurely when a settlement is still actively being explored. Parties are warned that if the protocol is not followed (including this paragraph) then the Court must have regard to such conduct when determining costs.

5.2   It is not practicable in this protocol to address in detail how the parties might decide which method to adopt to resolve their particular dispute. However, summarised below are some of the options for resolving disputes without litigation:
*   Discussion and negotiation. Parties should bear in mind that carefully planned face-to-face meetings may be particularly helpful in exploring further treatment for the patient, in reaching understandings about what happened, and on both parties' positions, in narrowing the issues in dispute and, if the timing is right, in helping to settle the whole matter especially if the patient wants an apology, explanation, or assurances about how other patients will be affected.
*   Early neutral evaluation by an independent third party (for example, a lawyer experienced in the field of clinical negligence or an individual experienced in the subject matter of the claim).
*   Mediation – a form of facilitated negotiation assisted by an independent neutral party. The Clinical Disputes Forum has published a Guide to Mediation which will assist – available on the Clinical Disputes Forum website at www.clinicaldisputesforum.org.uk.

- The NHS Complaints Procedure is designed to provide patients with an explanation of what happened and an apology if appropriate. It is not designed to provide compensation for cases of negligence. However, patients might choose to use the procedure if their only, or main, goal is to obtain an explanation, or to obtain more information to help them decide what other action might be appropriate.

5.3   The Legal Services Commission has published a booklet on 'Alternatives to Court', CLS Direct Information Leaflet 23 (www.clsdirect.org.uk/legalhelp/leaflet23.jsp), which lists a number of organisations that provide alternative dispute resolution services.

5.4   It is expressly recognised that no party can or should be forced to mediate or enter into any form of ADR.

A ILLUSTRATIVE FLOWCHART
[See Part 3 of this Appendix, below]

B MEDICAL NEGLIGENCE AND PERSONAL INJURY CLAIMS
[See Part 4 of this Appendix, below]

C TEMPLATES FOR LETTERS OF CLAIM AND RESPONSE

C1 Letter of Claim

Essential Contents
1.   Client's name, address, date of birth, etc.
2.   Dates of allegedly negligent treatment
3.   Events giving rise to the claim:
- an outline of what happened, including details of other relevant treatments to the client by other healthcare providers.
4.   Allegation of negligence and causal link with injuries:
- an outline of the allegations or a more detailed list in a complex case;
- an outline of the causal link between allegations and the injuries complained of.
5.   The Client's injuries, condition and future prognosis
6.   Request for clinical records (if not previously provided):
- use the Law Society form if appropriate or adapt;
- specify the records require;
- if other records are held by other providers, and may be relevant, say so;
- state what investigations have been carried out to date, e.g. information from client and witnesses, any complaint and the outcome, if any clinical records have been seen or experts advice obtained.
7.   The likely value of the claim:
- an outline of the main heads of damage, or, in straightforward cases, the details of loss.

Optional information
What investigations have been carried out
An offer to settle without supporting evidence
Suggestions for obtaining expert evidence
Suggestions for meetings, negotiations, discussion or mediation

Possible enclosures
Chronology

Clinical records request form and client's authorisation
Expert report(s)
Schedules of loss and supporting evidence

C2 Letter of Response

Essential Contents
1. Provide requested records and invoice for copying:
   - explain if records are incomplete or extensive records are held and ask for further instructions;
   - request additional records from third parties.
2. Comments on events and/or chronology:
   - if events are disputed or the healthcare provider has further information or documents on which they wish to rely, these should be provided, e.g. internal protocol;
   - details of any further information needed from the patient or a third party should be provided.
3. If breach of duty and causation are accepted:
   - suggestions might be made for resolving the claim and/or requests for further information;
   - a response should be made to any offer to settle.
4. If breach of duty and/or causation are denied:
   - a bare denial will not be sufficient. If the healthcare provider has other explanations for what happened, these should be given at least in outline;
   - suggestions might be made for the next steps, e.g. further investigations, obtaining expert evidence, meetings/negotiations or mediation, or an invitation to issue proceedings.

Optional Matters
An offer to settle if the patient has not made one, or a counter offer to the patient's with supporting evidence
Possible enclosures:
   Clinical records
   Annotated chronology
   Expert reports

D LORD WOOLF'S RECOMMENDATIONS

1. Lord Woolf in his Access to Justice Report in July 1996, following a detailed review of the problems of medical negligence claims, identified that one of the major sources of costs and delay is at the pre-litigation stage because –
   a. Inadequate incident reporting and record keeping in hospitals, and mobility of staff, make it difficult to establish facts, often several years after the event.
   b. Claimants must incur the cost of an expert in order to establish whether they have a viable claim.
   c. There is often a long delay before a claim is made.
   d. Defendants do not have sufficient resources to carry out a full investigation of every incident, and do not consider it worthwhile to start an investigation as soon as they receive a request for records, because many cases do not proceed beyond that stage.
   e. Patients often give the defendant little or no notice of a firm intention to pursue a claim. Consequently, many incidents are not investigated by the defendants until after proceedings have started.
   f. Doctors and other clinical staff are traditionally reluctant to admit negligence or apologise to, or negotiate with, claimants for fear of damage to their professional reputations or career prospects.

2. Lord Woolf acknowledged that under the present arrangements healthcare providers, faced with possible medical negligence claims, have a number of practical problems to contend with –

   a. Difficulties of finding patients' records and tracing former staff, which can be exacerbated by late notification and by the health care provider's own failure to identify adverse incidents.

   b. The healthcare provider may have only treated the patient for a limited time or for a specific complaint: the patient's previous history may be relevant but the records may be in the possession of one of several other healthcare providers.

   c. The large number of potential claims which do not proceed beyond the stage of a request for medical records, or an explanation; and that it is difficult for healthcare providers to investigate fully every case whenever a patient asks to see the records.

E HOW TO CONTACT THE FORUM

The Clinical Disputes Forum
Chairman
Dr Alastair Scotland
Medical Director and Chief Officer
National Clinical Assessment Authority
9th Floor, Market Towers
London
SW8 5NQ
Telephone: 020 7273 0850

Secretary
Sarah Leigh
c/o Margaret Dangoor
3 Clydesdale Gardens
Richmond
Surrey
TW10 5EG
Telephone: 020 8408 1012

Published with the kind permission of the Ministry of Justice

3. PRE-ACTION PROTOCOL FOR THE RESOLUTION OF CLINICAL DISPUTES

ILLUSTRATIVE FLOWCHART

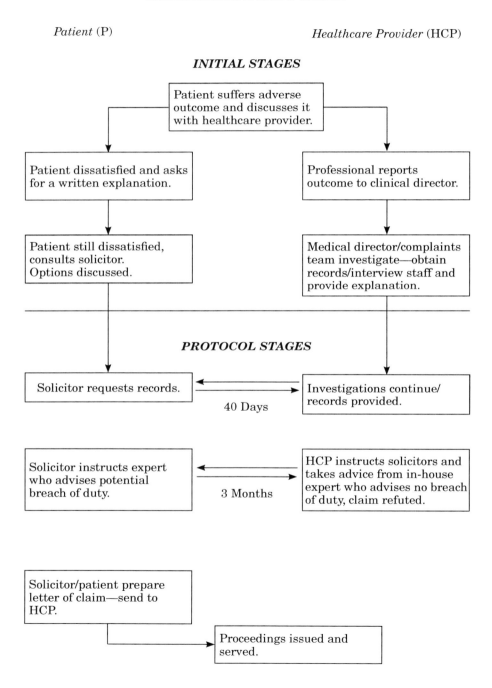

Patient (P)   *Healthcare Provider* (HCP)

INITIAL STAGES

Patient suffers adverse outcome and discusses it with healthcare provider.

Patient dissatisfied and asks for a written explanation.

Professional reports outcome to clinical director.

Patient still dissatisfied, consults solicitor.
Options discussed.

Medical director/complaints team investigate—obtain records/interview staff and provide explanation.

PROTOCOL STAGES

Solicitor requests records.

40 Days

Investigations continue/ records provided.

Solicitor instructs expert who advises potential breach of duty.

3 Months

HCP instructs solicitors and takes advice from in-house expert who advises no breach of duty, claim refuted.

Solicitor/patient prepare letter of claim—send to HCP.

Proceedings issued and served.

4. PRE-ACTION PROTOCOL PROCEDURE FOR OBTAINING MEDICAL RECORDS

CIVIL LITIGATION COMMITTEE
REVISED EDITION JUNE 1998

CIVIL LITIGATION COMMITTEE

REVISED EDITION
JUNE 1998

THE LAW SOCIETY

APPLICATION ON BEHALF OF A PATIENT FOR HOSPITAL MEDICAL RECORDS FOR USE WHEN COURT PROCEEDINGS ARE CONTEMPLATED

Purpose of the forms

This application form and response forms have been prepared by a working party of the Law Society's Civil Litigation Committee and approved by the Department of Health for use in NHS and Trust hospitals.

The purpose of the forms is to standardise and streamline the disclosure of medical records to a patient's solicitors, who are investigating pursuing a personal injury claim against a third party, or a medical negligence claim against the hospital to which the application is addressed and/or other hospitals or general practitioners.

Use of the forms

Use of the forms is entirely voluntary and does not prejudice any party's right under the Access to Health Records Act 1990, the Data Protection Act 1984, or ss. 33 and 34 of the Senior Courts Act 1981. However, it is Department of Health policy that patients be permitted to see what has been written about them, and that healthcare providers should make arrangements to allow patients to see all their records, not only those covered by the Access to Health Records Act 1990. The aim of the forms is to save time and costs for all concerned for the benefit of the patient and the hospital and in the interests of justice. Use of the forms should make it unnecessary in most cases for there to be exchanges of letters or other enquiries. If there is any unusual matter not covered by the form, the patient's solicitor may write a separate letter at the outset.

Charges for records

The Access to Health Records Act 1990 prescribes a maximum fee of £10. Photocopying and postage costs can be charged in addition. No other charges may be made.

The NHS Executive guidance makes it clear to healthcare providers that 'it is a perfectly proper use' of the 1990 Act to request records in that framework for the purpose of potential or actual litigation, whether against a third party or against the hospital or trust.

The 1990 Act does not permit differential rates of charges to be levied if the application is made by the patient, or by a solicitor on his or her behalf, or whether the response to the application is made by the healthcare provider directly (the medical records manager or a claims manager) or by a solicitor.

The NHS Executive guidance recommends that the same practice should be followed with regard to charges when the records are provided under a voluntary agreement as under the 1990 Act, except that in those circumstances the £10 access fee will not be appropriate.

The NHS Executive also advises –
- that the cost of photocopying may include 'the cost of staff time in making copies' and the costs of running the copier (but not costs of locating and sifting records);
- that the common practice of setting a standard rate for an application or charging an administration fee is not acceptable because there will be cases when this fails to comply with the 1990 Act.

Records: what might be included

X-rays and test results form part of the patient's records. Additional charges for copying X-rays are permissible. If there are large numbers of X-rays, the records officer should check with the patient/solicitor before arranging copying.

Reports on an 'adverse incident' and reports on the patient made for risk management and audit purposes may form part of the records and be disclosable: the exception will be any specific record or report made solely or mainly in connection with an actual or potential claim.

Records: quality standards

When copying records healthcare providers should ensure –
1. All documents are legible, and complete, if necessary by photocopying at less than 100% size.
2. Documents larger than A4 in the original, e.g. ITU charts, should be reproduced in A3, or reduced to A4 where this retains readability.
3. Documents are only copied on one side of paper, unless the original is two sided.
4. Documents should not be unnecessarily shuffled or bound and holes should not be made in the copied papers.

Enquiries/further information

Any enquiries about the forms should be made initially to the solicitors making the request. Comments on the use and content of the forms should be made to the Secretary, Civil Litigation Committee, The Law Society, 113 Chancery Lane, London WC2A 1PL, telephone 0171 320 5739, or to the NHS Management Executive, Quarry House, Quarry Hill, Leeds LS2 7UE.

The Law Society

APPLICATION ON BEHALF OF A PATIENT FOR HOSPITAL MEDICAL RECORDS FOR USE WHEN COURT PROCEEDINGS ARE CONTEMPLATED

This should be completed as fully as possible

Insert Hospital Name and Address

TO: Medical Records Officer

Hospital

1	(a)	Full name of patient (including previous surnames)	
	(b)	Address now	
	(c)	Address at start of treatment	
	(d)	Date of birth (and death, if applicable)	
	(e)	Hospital ref. no if available	
	(f)	N.I. number, if available	
2		This application is made because the patient is considering	
	(a)	a claim against your hospital as detailed in para 7 overleaf	YES/NO
	(b)	pursuing an action against someone else	YES/NO

3	Department(s) where treatment was received	
4	Name(s) of consultant(s) at your hospital in charge of the treatment	
5	Whether treatment at your hospital was private or NHS, wholly or in part	
6	A description of the treatment received, with approximate dates	
7	If the answer to Q2(a) is 'Yes' details of	
	(a) the likely nature of the claim,	
	(b) grounds for the claim,	
	(c) approximate dates of the events involved	
8	If the answer to Q2(B) is 'Yes' insert	
	(a) the names of the proposed defendants	
	(b) whether legal proceedings yet begun	YES/NO
	(c) if appropriate, details of the claim and action number	

9	We confirm we will pay reasonable copying charges	
10	We request prior details of (a) photocopying and administration charges for medical records	YES/NO
	(b) number of and cost of copying x-ray and scan films	YES/NO
11	Any other relevant information, particular requirements, or any particular documents <u>not</u> required (eg copies of computerised records)	
	Signature of Solicitor	
	Name	
	Address	
	Ref.	
	Telephone Number	
	Fax number	

Signature of patient	*Please print name beneath each signature.* *Signature by child over 12 but under* *18 years also requires signature by parent.*
Signature of parent or next friend if appropriate	
Signature of personal representative where patient has died	

FIRST RESPONSE TO APPLICATION FOR HOSPITAL RECORDS

NAME OF PATIENT Our ref Your ref		
1	Date of receipt of patients application	
2	We intend that copy medical records will be dispatched within 6 weeks of that date	YES/NO
3	We require pre-payment of photocopying charges	YES/NO
4	If estimate of photocopying charges requested or pre-payment required the amount will be	£ / notified to you
5	The cost of x-ray and scan films will be	£ / notified to you
6	If there is any problem, we shall write to you within those 6 weeks	YES/NO
7	Any other information	
	Please address further correspondence to	
	Signed	
	Direct telephone number	
	Direct fax number	
	Dated	

SECOND RESPONSE ENCLOSING PATIENT'S HOSPITAL MEDICAL RECORDS

Address   Our Ref.

                                                     Your Ref.

1	NAME OF PATIENT: We confirm that the enclosed copy medical records are all those within the control of the hospital, relevant to the application which you have made to the best of our knowledge and belief, subject to paras 2–5 below	YES/NO
2	Details of any other documents which have not yet been located	
3	Date by when it is expected that these will be supplied	
4	Details of any records which we are not producing	
5	The reasons for not doing so	
6	An invoice for copying and administration charges is attached	YES/NO
	Signed	
	Date	

5. PROPOSED – PRE-ACTION PROTOCOL FOR THE RESOLUTION OF CLINICAL DISPUTES

[WARNING: at the time of writing (22 January 2012) this Protocol is not in force. It is anticipated that it will be implemented soon. Before relying upon it, check the Ministry of Justice website to see if it has been implemented: www.justice.gov.uk/guidance/courts-and-tribunals/courts/procedure-rules/civil/contents/protocols/prot_rcd.htm.]

FINAL DRAFT (14) PRODUCED BY THE CDF WORKING GROUP FOR THE LAW SOCIETY

THE CLINICAL NEGLIGENCE PROTOCOL

A. *Introduction*

1 The background to this protocol

1.1   The first Protocol for the Resolution of Clinical Disputes was produced by the Clinical Disputes Forum, a multi-disciplinary body (now a registered charitable company) which was formed in 1997 in response to Lord Woolf's Access to Justice reports. One of the aims of the Forum is to find less adversarial and more cost-effective ways of resolving disputes about healthcare and medical treatment, and the Clinical Disputes Pre-Action Protocol was its first major initiative, drafted after extensive consultation. At the request of the Civil Justice Council and the Law Society, the Forum has again taken the lead in consulting widely to draft this updated Protocol.

1.2   This Protocol (which is set out in Sections 4 to 13 inclusive below)

- encourages a **climate of openness** when something has gone wrong with a claimant's[1] treatment or the claimant is dissatisfied with that treatment and/or the outcome. This reflects the requirements for clinical governance within healthcare;
- provides **general guidance** on how this more open culture might be achieved when disputes arise, in accordance with a 'cards-on-the- table' approach;
- recommends **a timed sequence** of steps for claimants and healthcare providers[2], and their advisers, to follow when a dispute arises. This should facilitate and speed up exchanging relevant information and increase the prospects that disputes can be resolved without resort to legal action.

1.3   This new version of the Protocol also takes into account developments in civil procedure since the Civil Procedure Rules 1998 (the CPR) were implemented, and

---

1   Although no assumption can or should be made that a patient will definitely turn into a claimant, we have chosen to use the word 'claimant' (instead of 'patient') throughout this Protocol, which is after all about behaviour in relation to the bringing of claims. It must be remembered that the claim may be on behalf of a patient without capacity, or be triggered by the death of the 'patient', so that a litigation friend or relative will be the 'claimant'.

2   In this protocol the phrase 'healthcare provider' means those who are registered with or members of the General Medical Council, the Nursing and Midwifery Council, General Dental Council, Health Professions Council and the United Kingdom Public Health Register; and also any body or organisation, public or private, which employs such people or for whom such people work in providing healthcare services in England & Wales. No such definition appeared in the previous protocol. It may be preferred to set out the content of this and the previous footnote in the body of the revised protocol rather than leave these remarks as footnotes.

in particular the terms of the Pre-Action Conduct Practice Direction introduced in April 2009 (the PACPD)[3].

2 The aims of this protocol

2.1   The *general* aims of the Protocol are –
- to maintain and/or restore the claimant/healthcare provider relationship; and
- to resolve as many disputes as possible without litigation.

2.2   Its *specific* objectives are –

Openness
- to encourage early communication of the perceived problem between claimants and healthcare providers;
- to encourage claimants to voice any concerns or dissatisfaction with their treatment as soon as practicable;
- to encourage healthcare providers to develop systems of early reporting and investigation for serious adverse treatment outcomes and to provide full and prompt explanations, including an apology where appropriate, to dissatisfied claimants: such expressions of regret do not constitute an admission of liability in part or in full (the National Health Service Litigation Authority (NHSLA) guidance dated 1 May 2009 on apologies and explanations, as endorsed by other medical organisations, is set out at **Annex C** below);
- to ensure that sufficient information is disclosed by both parties to enable each to understand the other's perspective and case, and to encourage early resolution.

Timeliness
- to provide an early opportunity for healthcare providers to identify cases where an investigation is required and to carry out that investigation promptly;
- to encourage primary and private healthcare providers to involve their defence organisations or insurers at an early stage;
- to ensure that all relevant medical records are provided to claimants or their appointed representatives on request within 40 days as required by the Access to Health records Act 1990 and the Data Protection Act 1998;
- to ensure that relevant records which are not in healthcare providers' possession are made available to them by claimants and their advisers at an appropriate stage;
- to identify a stage before issue of proceedings at which the parties should consider whether settlement discussions, whether by alternative dispute resolution (ADR) or otherwise, are appropriate;
- where a resolution is not achievable, to lay the ground to enable litigation to proceed on a reasonable timetable, at a reasonable and proportionate cost, and to limit the matters in contention;
- to discourage the pursuit of unmeritorious claims and the prolonged defence of meritorious claims.

Awareness of options
- to ensure that claimants and healthcare providers are made aware of the available options to pursue and resolve disputes and what each might involve.

---

3   Jackson recommends repeal of the PACPD. If this happens, references will have to be deleted or amended to refer to any replacement PD.

2.3   This Protocol does not attempt to be prescriptive about a number of related clinical governance issues which will have a bearing on any healthcare provider's ability to meet the standards within the Protocol. Good clinical governance requires the following to be considered:

(1) **Clinical risk management:** the Protocol does not provide any detailed guidance to healthcare providers on clinical risk management or the adoption of risk management systems and procedures. These are matters for the NHSLA, individual trusts and providers, including GPs, dentists and the private sector, including the Medical Defence Organisations. In Wales these are matters for the Welsh Risk Pool, Local Health Boards and Welsh Health Legal Services (WHLS). Effective, co-ordinated and focused clinical risk management strategies and procedures are essential for the management of risk and the early identification and investigation of adverse outcomes.

(2) **Adverse outcome reporting:** the Protocol does not provide any detailed guidance on which adverse outcomes should trigger an investigation. However, healthcare providers should have in place procedures for such investigations, including recording of statements of key witnesses. These procedures should also cover when and how to inform claimants that an adverse outcome has occurred. Providers should also work with the National Patient Safety Agency on data collection on adverse incidents.

(3) **The professional's duty to report:** in his final report, Lord Woolf suggested that the professional bodies might consider changes to their codes of conduct to impose duties to report adverse incidents.. The General Medical Council has published guidance to doctors about their duties to report adverse incidents to the relevant authorities and co-operate with inquiries.

WHERE THE PROTOCOL FITS IN

2.4   Protocols serve the needs of potential litigants in setting out a code of good practice, and assisting with:

- predictability in the time needed for necessary steps early in a dispute;
- standardisation of the requirements for relevant information, including records and documents to be disclosed;
- creating an expectation that steps will be taken before issue of proceedings to facilitate early resolution of cases and/or to minimise the number of issues to be litigated.

2.5   It is recognised that contexts differ significantly. For example:

- claimants tend to have an ongoing relationship with a general practitioner, more so than with a hospital;
- clinical staff in the National Health Service are often employees, while those in the private sector may be contractors;
- providing records quickly may be relatively easy for GPs and dentists, but can be a complicated procedure in a large multi-department hospital.

2.6   This Protocol is intended to be sufficiently broadly based and flexible to apply to all sectors of healthcare, both public and private.

3 Enforcement of the Protocol and Sanctions for non-compliance[4]

3.1   This Protocol – when read with the CPR and the PACPD - is now regarded by the courts as setting the standard of normal reasonable pre-action conduct for clinical disputes.

---

4   Jackson proposes pre-action applications to allege non-compliance. Such a move would apparently need primary legislation. If introduced, this will need amendment.

3.2 If proceedings are issued, it is for the court to decide whether non-compliance with a Protocol merits sanctions. The PACPD explains and supports the Protocols, and sets out a list of sanctions which might be considered for non-compliance with any Protocol (see Section II paragraph 4 of the PACPD).

3.3 If the court has to consider the question of compliance after proceedings have begun, it may be less concerned with minor infringements, e.g. failure by a short period to provide relevant information. One minor breach will not entitle the 'innocent' party to abandon the procedure set out in this Protocol. The court looks at the effect of non-compliance on the other party when deciding whether to impose sanctions. Additionally, the court can itself order a stay of proceedings where **both** parties have failed to observe the requirements of any Protocol, for example by failing unreasonably to consider ADR.

B. The protocol

4 The shape of the protocol

4.1 This Protocol is not a comprehensive code governing all the steps in clinical disputes. Rather it attempts to set out **a code of good practice** which parties should follow when litigation might be a possibility.

4.2 The **commitments** section (Section 5 below) of the Protocol summarises the guiding principles which healthcare providers and claimants and their advisers are invited to endorse when dealing with claimant dissatisfaction with treatment and its outcome, and with potential complaints and claims.

4.3 The **steps** section (Sections 7 to 10 below) sets out a recommended sequence of actions to be followed if litigation is in prospect, in a more prescriptive form.

5 Good practice commitments

5.1 Healthcare providers should –
    (1) ensure that **key staff**, including complaints, claims and risk managers, are adequately trained and have knowledge of healthcare law, complaints procedures, risk management and civil litigation practice and procedure appropriate to their roles;
    (2) develop an approach to **clinical governance** that ensures that clinical practice is delivered to commonly accepted standards and that this is routinely monitored through a system of clinical audit and clinical risk management (particularly adverse outcome investigation);
    (3) set up **adverse outcome reporting systems** in all specialties to record and investigate unexpected serious adverse outcomes as soon as possible. Such systems can enable evidence to be gathered quickly, which makes it easier to provide an accurate explanation of what happened and to defend or settle any subsequent claims;
    (4) use the results of **adverse incidents and complaints positively** as a guide to how to improve services to claimants in the future;
    (5) ensure **that claimants receive clear and comprehensible information** in an accessible form about how to raise their concerns or complaints;
    (6) establish **efficient and effective systems of recording and storing claimant records**, notes, diagnostic reports and X-rays, and to retain these in accordance with Department of Health guidance (currently for a minimum of eight years in the case of adults, all obstetric and paediatric notes for children until they reach the age of 25, and indefinitely for claimants lacking mental capacity);
    (7) **advise claimants** of a serious adverse outcome and provide on request to the claimant or the claimant's representative an oral or written

explanation of what happened, information on further steps open to the claimant, including where appropriate an offer of future treatment to rectify the problem, an apology, changes in procedure which will benefit claimants and/or compensation.

Procedures for handling NHS complaints **in Wales** are under review and may be different.[5]

5.2   Claimants and their advisers should –

(1) **report any concerns and dissatisfaction** to the healthcare provider as soon as is reasonable to enable that provider to offer clinical advice where possible, to advise the claimant if anything has gone wrong and take appropriate action;

(2) consider the **full range of options** available following an adverse outcome with which a claimant is dissatisfied, including a request for an explanation, a meeting, a complaint, and other appropriate dispute resolution methods (including mediation) and negotiation, not only litigation;

(3) **inform the healthcare provider** when the matter will not be pursued further or has been concluded: legal advisers should also notify the provider when they are no longer acting for the claimant, particularly if proceedings have not started.

6 Rehabilitation

6.1   The claimant or the healthcare provider or both shall consider as early as possible whether the claimant has reasonable needs that could be met by rehabilitation treatment or other methods.

6.2   The parties shall consider in such cases how those needs might be addressed. The rehabilitation code (which is attached as **Annex D**) may be helpful in considering how to identify the claimant's needs and how to address the cost of providing for those needs.

6.3   The time limits set out in Sections 7 to 10 of this Protocol shall not be shortened to allow these issues to be addressed, except by consent.

6.4   The provision of any report obtained for the purposes of assessment of provision of a party's rehabilitation needs shall not be used in any litigation arising out of the subject-matter of the claim, save by consent.

7 Obtaining the health records[6]

7.1   Any request for records by the claimant should
- **provide sufficient information** to alert the healthcare provider where an adverse outcome has been serious or had serious consequences;
- be as **specific as possible** about the records which are required.

7.2   Requests for copies of the claimant's clinical records should be made using the Law Society and Department of Health approved **standard forms** (**Annex A** to this Protocol), adapted as necessary.

7.3   The copy records should be provided **within 40 days** of the request and for a cost not exceeding the charges permissible under the Access to Health Records

---

5   Wales currently proposes to introduce the NHS Redress Scheme effectively and its complaints system as from a date to be decided later in 2010. Whether this will indeed come about is still unclear, hence the guarded reference here to complaints systems in Wales.

6   Note that Jackson proposes financial penalties where healthcare providers delay in providing records.

Act 1990 and the Data Protection Act 1998. Payment may be required in advance by the healthcare provider.

7.4   The claimant may also make a request under the Freedom of Information Act 2000.

7.5   Disclosable documents include those created by the healthcare provider in relation to any relevant adverse incident or complaint made by or on behalf of the claimant. They also include any relevant guidelines, protocols or policies. The claimant should make a specific request for all documents reasonably required for the initial investigation of the case. In birth injury cases, it is good practice for the healthcare provider to ensure that a continuous copy of the CTG trace is provided as part of the disclosure of health records. This should not result in any additional charge.

7.6   In the rare circumstances that the healthcare provider is in difficulty in complying with the claimant's request within 40 days, the **problem should be explained** quickly and details given of what is being done to resolve it.

7.7   It will not be practicable for healthcare providers to investigate in detail each case when records are requested, **particularly where insufficient detail is supplied in the request for records.** But healthcare providers should **adopt a policy as to which cases will be investigated** (see paragraph 5.1 above on clinical governance and adverse outcome reporting and note also the provisions regarding commencing investigations in Sections 8 and 9 below).

7.8   If the healthcare provider fails to provide the health records within 40 days, the claimant can then apply to the court under the CPR Part 31.16 for an *order for pre-action disclosure*. The court has the power to impose costs sanctions for unreasonable delay in providing records. The claimant may also refer the matter to the Information Commissioner for a potential breach of the Data Protection Act 1998.

7.9   If either the claimant or the healthcare provider considers that **additional health records are reasonably required from a third party**, in the first instance these should be requested by or through the claimant. Third party healthcare providers are expected to co-operate. The claimant should provide to the defendant, within 40 days of a request, copies of relevant third party records in their possession. CPR Part 31.17 enables claimants and healthcare providers to apply to the court for pre-action disclosure by third parties.

7.10   Legible copies of the claimant's medical records should be placed in an indexed and paginated bundle by the claimant at the earliest opportunity and kept up to date. If the healthcare provider requests copies of the claimant's records including copies of relevant third party records the claimant should where requested provide the healthcare provider with a copy of the indexed and paginated bundle. The healthcare provider should agree to pay a reasonable copying charge in respect of the provision of the bundle.

8 The letter of notification[7]

8.1   This Section of the Protocol introduces a new intermediate stage, which follows on from obtaining the medical records, but is likely to arise before the

---

7   Jackson decided not to recommend a stage like this: see Final Report chapter 23, para 4.10 (p. 240). We had already decided to propose it, and after debate still think that such a step will indeed be a good way for reducing both unnecessary defence investigations while promoting timely responses from the defence where claimants do decide to proceed with a case, even if they cannot yet compile a comprehensive Letter of Claim.

claimant is in a position to send a Letter of Claim in accordance with Section 9 of this Protocol. This Section recognises that a healthcare provider may not be in a position to investigate every potential claim where the records have been requested. The aim of this new intermediate stage is to provide the claimant with an opportunity to send to the healthcare provider a Letter of Notification confirming that the case is one which is proceeding and to enable the provider(s) to consider whether this is a case in which they should now commence their investigations, if they have not done so already.

8.2   **Annex B1** to this Protocol provides **a template for the recommended contents of a Letter of Notification.** The level of detail will need to be varied to suit the particular circumstances.

8.3   Following the receipt and analysis of the records, and the receipt of an initial supportive medical report dealing with breach of duty and/or causation, the claimant should give consideration to sending a Letter of Notification to the healthcare provider as soon as practicable.

8.4   This letter should confirm that the case is one which is still being investigated and that it is premature to send a Letter of Claim in accordance with Section 9 below. It should however advise the healthcare provider that this is a case where the claimant has obtained supportive independent expert evidence about breach of duty and (if this has been obtained) causation and that the case is one which is likely to result in a Letter of Claim being sent in due course in accordance with Section 9. The claimant should at the same time send a copy of the Letter of Notification to the NHSLA, WHLS or other relevant Medical Defence Organisation or indemnity provider (where known).

8.5   The healthcare provider (and any defence organisation sent a copy of the Letter of Notification) should **acknowledge** any Letter of Notification **within 14 days of receipt** and should identify who will be dealing with the matter.

8.6   On receipt of a Letter of Notification the healthcare provider should then consider whether or not to undertake its own investigations into the case and whether or not to obtain its own factual and independent expert evidence, in anticipation of its having to respond to a Letter of Claim in due course[8].

8.7   When subsequently considering whether any request by a healthcare provider for an extension of the time limit for a Letter of Response under Section 9 is reasonable, the claimant should have regard to whether a Letter of Notification was sent to the provider.

8.8   When considering the extent to which either party has complied with its obligations under this Protocol, including the extent to which it is reasonable for a healthcare provider to have an extension of time for its Letter of Response, the court should have regard to whether or not the claimant sent a Letter of Notification and to whether or not the healthcare provider initiated investigations upon receipt of any Letter of Notification. There should be a reasonable lapse of time between a Letter of Notification, which should only be sent where supportive expert evidence as to breach of duty and/or causation has been obtained, and any later Letter of Claim. Attempts to misuse this two-stage process may be met with costs sanctions.

9 The letter of claim

9.1   **Annex B2** to this Protocol provides **a template for the recommended contents of a Letter of Claim**. The level of detail will need to be varied to suit the particular circumstances.

---

8   Jackson suggests that receipt of a Letter of Claim should trigger independent expert advice being sought by the defence. The purpose of a Letter of Notification is to bring the start of defence investigations earlier, for the benefit of both sides.

9.2   If, following the receipt and analysis of the records, and the receipt of any further advice (including from experts if necessary – see Section 12 below), the claimant/adviser decides that there are grounds for a claim, they should then send, as soon as practicable, to the healthcare provider/potential defendant, a **Letter of Claim**. The claimant should at the same time send a copy of the Letter of Claim to the NHSLA, WHLS or other relevant Medical Defence Organisation or indemnity provider (where known)[9].

9.3   This letter should contain a **clear summary of the facts** on which the claim is based, including the alleged adverse outcome, and the **main allegations of breach of duty and causation**. It should also describe the **claimant's injuries**, and **present condition and prognosis**. The **financial loss** incurred by the claimant should be outlined, with an indication of the heads of damage to be claimed and the scale of the loss, unless this is impracticable.

9.4   It is expected that the claimant will have obtained independent expert evidence as to the breach of duty and causation of damage alleged in the Letter of Claim.

9.5   In lower value claims, where total damages are likely to be less than £25,000, particularly where claimants have recovered from their injuries, details of the injuries and losses should be provided as soon as is practicable, including where appropriate an expert's condition and prognosis report.

9.6   In more complex cases, a **chronology** of the relevant events should be provided, particularly if the claimant has been treated by a number of different healthcare providers.

9.7   The Letter of Claim **should refer to any relevant documents**, including health records, and if possible enclose copies of any of those which will not already be in the potential defendant's possession with an index of those records, e.g. any relevant general practitioner records if the claimant's claim is against a hospital.

9.8   Sufficient information must be given to enable the healthcare provider defendant to **commence investigations** (if not already started following a Letter of Notification) and to put an initial valuation on the claim.

9.9   Letters of Claim are **not** intended to have the same formal status as Particulars of Claim, nor should any sanctions necessarily apply if the Letter of Claim and any subsequent statement of case in the proceedings differ.

9.10   **Proceedings should not be started until at least four**[10] **months from the letter of claim**, unless there is a limitation problem and/or the claimant's position needs to be protected by early issue.

9.11   Claimants or their advisers may want to make an **offer to settle** the claim at this early stage by putting forward an amount of compensation which would be satisfactory (possibly including any costs incurred to date). If an offer to settle is made, generally this should be supported by a medical report which deals with the injuries, condition and prognosis, and by a schedule of loss and supporting documentation. The level of detail necessary will depend on the value of the claim. Medical reports may not be necessary where there is no significant continuing injury, and a detailed schedule may not be necessary in a low value case. CPR Part 36 sets out the legal and procedural requirements for making offers to settle.

---

9   Sending copies of any Letter of Notification and Claim to the NHSLA or relevant MDO was something we had already suggested before it was recommended in Jackson.

10   The time limit of four months tallies with the recommendation in the Jackson report for the Letter of Response – see Section 10.3 below. In view of the new Letter of Notification procedure, coupled with the earlier reporting by independent experts, the four month limit may be achievable in appreciably more cases, without an extension being required.

9.12   Every claimant who has Legal Services Commission funding, or has entered into any funding arrangement, should comply with the obligations to serve notices thereof as set out in the CPR and Practice Directions.

10 The response

10.1   **Annex B3** provides a template for the suggested contents of the **Letter of Response**.

10.2   The healthcare provider (and any defence organisation sent a copy of the Letter of Claim) should **acknowledge** any Letter of Claim **within 14 days of receipt** and should identify who will be dealing with the matter.

10.3   The healthcare provider should, **within four[11] months of receipt of the Letter of Claim** (or such other further period as may be agreed with the claimant) provide a reasoned answer. The claimant should generally agree to a reasonable extension of time if the healthcare provider puts forward good reasons for such an extension, particularly in a claim that is of high value and/or of a complex nature.

10.4   It is good practice for the healthcare provider to have obtained independent expert evidence where either breach of duty and/or causation are denied in its Letter of Response.

10.5   If the **claim is admitted** the healthcare provider should say so in clear terms and in particular which alleged breaches of duty and causation are admitted and why.

10.6   If only **part of the claim is admitted** the healthcare provider should make clear which issues of breach of duty and/or causation are admitted and which are denied and why. CPR Part 14.1A applies to the status of admissions made before commencement of proceedings.

10.7   If a healthcare provider wishes to explore **settlement without any admission of liability**, then this should be conveyed to the claimant and/or his/her representatives, who should consider agreeing a reasonable request for a period of time in order to try to resolve the claim without the need for legal proceedings to be issued[12].

10.8   If the **claim is denied**, this should include specific comments on the allegations of negligence, and if a synopsis or chronology of relevant events has been provided and is disputed, the healthcare provider's version of those events.

10.9   The Letter of Response is not intended to have the same formal status as a defence, nor should any sanctions necessarily apply if the Letter of Response and any subsequent defence in the proceedings differ.

10.10   Where additional documents are relied upon, e.g. an internal protocol or documents in relation to an adverse incident or a relevant complaint concerning the same claimant/ incident, copies should be provided.

10.11   If the claimant has made an offer to settle, the healthcare provider should **respond to that offer** at the same time as the Letter of Response, preferably with reasons. The healthcare provider may make its own offer to settle at this stage, either as a counter-offer to the claimant's, or of its own accord, but should accompany the offer with any supporting medical report which deals with the

---

11   The CDF Working Group debated the Jackson recommendation and finally agreed on the Jackson recommendation of four months: see footnote 8 above.

12   We inserted this before Jackson proposed it and agree with his recommendation, though we have not proposed his suggested three month moratorium.

injuries, condition and prognosis, and/or with any counter-schedule of loss and supporting documents which are in the healthcare provider's possession.

10.12   If the parties do not reach agreement on liability, they should discuss whether the claimant should start proceedings and whether the court might be invited to direct an early trial of a preliminary issue or of breach of duty and causation.

10.13   If following receipt of the Letter of Response the claimant and their adviser is aware that there may be a delay of six months or more before the claimant decides if, when and how to proceed, they should keep the healthcare provider generally informed.

10.14   If the parties reach agreement on liability, but time is needed to resolve the value of the claim, they should aim to agree a reasonable period.

10.15   In any event, where comprehensive settlement (as to breach of duty, causation and quantum) does not take place as a result of receipt of the Letter of Response and before the issue of proceedings, the parties should consider the use of ADR.

11 Alternative Dispute Resolution (ADR)

11.1   Starting proceedings should usually be a step of last resort, and proceedings should not normally be started when a settlement is still actively being explored. Although ADR is not compulsory, the parties should consider whether some form of ADR procedure might enable them to settle the matter without starting proceedings. The court may require evidence that the parties considered some form of ADR.

11.2   It would not be practicable for this Protocol to address in any detail how a claimant or their adviser, or healthcare provider, might decide which method to adopt to resolve the particular problem. But the courts increasingly expect parties to try to settle their differences by agreement before issuing proceedings.

11.3   Summarised below are the main alternative processes for resolving clinical disputes:
- **In England**, the **NHS Complaints Procedure**, which is designed to provide claimants with an explanation of what happened and an apology if appropriate. It is not designed to provide compensation for cases of negligence[13]. However, claimants might choose to use the procedure if their only, or main, goal is to obtain an explanation, or to obtain more information to help them decide what other action might be appropriate. A complaint may be pursued at the same time as or in addition to a claim for negligence;
- **In Wales**, its own relevant NHS complaints procedure;
- **Discussion and negotiation,** including **round-table meetings**[14];
- **Mediation,** which is a form of facilitated negotiation assisted by an independent neutral party. It is suitable in many cases, including on occasions pre-action. The CPR give the court the power to stay proceedings for one month for settlement discussions or mediation and sometimes the courts go further at a case management conference and recommend parties to attempt mediation. The CDF has published a Guide to Mediation which will assist: this is generally available on the CDF website at www.clinicaldisputesforum.org.uk.

---

13   Jackson recommends implementation of NHS Redress, and indeed this is due to be introduced in Wales. Future amendment may become necessary to this sentence.

14   Also often called joint settlement meetings, though sometimes they are convened to debate discontinuance rather than settlement.

- Other methods of resolving disputes, which include **arbitration, determination by an expert, and early neutral evaluation** by a medical or legal expert.

11.4   The Legal Services Commission has published a booklet on '**Alternatives to Court**' (LSC August 2000, CLS information leaflet number 23) which lists a number of organisations that provide alternative dispute resolution services. The National Mediation Helpline on 0845 603 0809 or at www. nationalmediationhelpline.com and mediation providers can provide information about mediation.

11.5   The parties should continue to consider the possibility of reaching a settlement at all times. This still applies after proceedings have been started, up to and during any trial or final hearing. Most disputes are resolved by agreement, even after proceedings have been issued. Parties should bear in mind that carefully planned face-to-face meetings, with or without a mediator, may be particularly helpful in exploring further treatment for the claimant, in reaching understandings about what happened and over both parties' positions, in narrowing the issues in dispute, perhaps in involving the relevant clinicians, and, if the timing is right, in helping to settle the whole matter, especially if the claimant wants an apology, explanation, or assurances about how other claimants will be affected.

12 Experts

12.1   In clinical negligence disputes, **expert opinions** may be needed:
- on breach of duty and causation;
- on the claimant's condition and prognosis;
- to assist in valuing aspects of the claim.

12.2   The CPR encourage **economy in the use of experts** and a **less adversarial expert culture**. It is recognised that in clinical negligence disputes, the parties and their advisers will require flexibility in their approach to expert evidence. The parties should cooperate about decisions on whether and which experts might be instructed jointly, and on whether reports might be disclosed sequentially or by exchange and at what stage. The Protocol does not require the claimant to disclose expert evidence with the letter of claim-the claimant and their adviser may choose to do so when they wish to rely upon that evidence, particularly a report on the claimant's condition and prognosis. Sharing expert evidence will often be appropriate on issues relating to the value of the claim.

12.3   Obtaining expert evidence will often be an expensive step and may take time, especially in specialised areas of medicine where there are limited numbers of suitable experts. Claimants and healthcare provider and their advisers, will therefore need to give careful and early consideration as to how best to obtain any necessary expert help quickly and cost-effectively.

12.4   **In Wales**, expert reports may be obtained through the Speedy Resolution Scheme introduced in 2005.

13 Limitation of actions

13.1   If by reason of complying with any part of this Protocol a claimant's claim may be time-barred under any provision of the Limitation Act 1980 or any other legislation which imposes a time limit for bringing an action, the claimant may commence proceedings without complying with this Protocol, but should then apply to the court on notice at the time that proceedings are issued for directions as to the timetable and form of procedure then to be adopted. The court will then consider whether to order a stay of the whole or part of the proceedings pending compliance with the provisions of this Protocol.

ANNEX A: LAW SOCIETY AND DEPARTMENT OF HEALTH STANDARD FORMS FOR OBTAINING HEALTH RECORDS

[The current versions of these documents for both England and (where different, as they currently are) Wales will need to be inserted here in any final published version.]

ANNEX B: TEMPLATES FOR LETTERS OF NOTIFICATION, CLAIM AND RESPONSE

B1 Template for the Letter of Notification

ESSENTIAL CONTENTS

The Letter of Notification should confirm:
1. **The claimant's name**, address, date of birth, etc.;
2. **Dates** of allegedly negligent treatment;
3. **Events giving rise to the claim**, including:
   - a clear summary of the facts on which the claim is based;
   - details of other relevant treatments to the claimant by other healthcare providers.
4. Which **medical records** have been obtained by the claimant. Where possible, details of the medical records obtained should be provided in the form of a document index in accordance with para 6.1 (if not provided previously)
5. Whether a supportive **expert opinion** has been obtained on either or both of breach of duty and causation.
6. That this is a case which is proceeding, but that it is premature for the claimant to send a Letter of Claim at this stage while further investigations remain pending. Where possible the claimant should give an approximate time estimate for provision of the Letter of Claim.
7. That the claimant may have reasonable needs that could be met by **rehabilitation** treatment or other measures. The Rehabilitation Code may be helpful in considering how to identify the claimant's needs and how to address the cost of providing for those needs.
8. An invitation to the healthcare provider to consider commencing investigations into this case at this stage.
9. That failure to do so will be a factor that can be taken into consideration when considering the reasonableness or otherwise of any subsequent application for an extension of time for the Letter of Response.
10. When the claimant has Legal Services Commission funding or has entered into a funding arrangement (a conditional fee agreement within the meaning of CPR43.2(1)), details of this should be provided.

B2 Template for the Letter of Claim

ESSENTIAL CONTENTS

The Letter of Claim should set out:
1. **The claimant's name**, address, date of birth, etc.
2. **Dates of allegedly negligent treatment**
3. **Events giving rise to the claim,** including:
   - a clear summary of the facts on which the claim is based;
   - details of other relevant treatments to the claimant by other healthcare providers.

4. **Allegations of breach of duty and causal link with injuries**, including
   - an outline of the main allegations or a more detailed list in a complex case;
   - an outline of the causal link between the allegations and the injuries complained of;
   - whether a supportive **expert opinion** has been obtained on either or both of breach of duty and causation.
5. **Details of the claimant's injuries, condition and future prognosis** with a condition and prognosis report, if appropriate
6. **Request all clinical records (if not previously provided)**
   - use the Law Society form if appropriate or adapt;
   - specify the records required;
   - if other records are held by other providers, and may be relevant, say so;
   - state what investigations have been carried out to date, e.g. information from the claimant and witnesses, any complaint and the outcome, if any clinical records have been seen or experts advice obtained.
7. **The likely value of the claim**, including
   - an outline of the financial loss incurred by the claimant together with the main heads of damage to be claimed;
   - the scale of the loss, or, in lower value claims likely to be under £25,000 particularly where the claimant has recovered from their injuries, details of the injuries and losses should be provided as soon as practicable to enable the healthcare provider to commence investigations and put an initial valuation on the claim..
8. **Documents relied upon**
   - In more complex cases a chronology of the relevant events should be provided particularly if the claimant has been treated by a number of different healthcare providers.
   - Any relevant documents should be referred to, including health records, and if possible enclose copies of those which will not already be in the healthcare provider's possession.
9. **Funding information**
   When the claimant has Legal Services Commission funding or has entered into a funding arrangement (a conditional fee agreement within the meaning of CPR43.2(1)) details of this should be provided.
10. **Costs incurred**
    An estimate of the claimants costs incurred to the date of the letter of claim should be included.

OPTIONAL INFORMATION
- What investigations have been carried out
- An offer to settle (open for acceptance until the Letter of Response is due to be served) with supporting medical evidence and / or a schedule of loss with supporting evidence if possible
- Suggestions for obtaining expert evidence
- Suggestions for meetings, negotiations, discussion or mediation
- Any reasonable needs not hitherto notified that could be met by rehabilitation treatment or other measures. The Rehabilitation Code may be helpful in considering how to identify the claimant's needs and how to address the cost of providing for those needs.

ADDITIONAL ENCLOSURES
- Clinical records request form and claimant's authorisation

- Expert report(s)
- Schedules of loss and supporting evidence, even where an offer is not being made.

B3 Template for the Letter of Response

ESSENTIAL CONTENTS

The Letter of Response should:

1. **Provide requested records and invoice for copying:**
   - explain if records are incomplete or extensive records are held and ask for further instructions;
   - request additional records from third parties.
2. **Comment on the events alleged and/or chronology:**
   - if events are disputed or the healthcare provider has further information or documents on which they wish to rely, these should be provided, e.g. an internal Protocol;
   - details of any further information needed from the claimant or third party should be provided.
3. **(If this is so) set out that breach of duty and causation are accepted wholly or in part:**
   - this should be set out in clear terms and in particular which alleged breaches of duty and causation are admitted or denied and why:
   - suggestions might be made for resolving the claim and/or requests for further information.
4. **(If this is so) set out that breach of duty and/or causation are denied:**
   - a bare denial will not be sufficient. Specific responses to the allegations of breach of duty and causation should be given. If the healthcare provider has other explanations for what happened, these should be set out as fully as possible:
   - confirm whether any denial is based on receipt of independent expert evidence:
   - suggestions might be made for the next steps, e.g. further investigations, obtaining expert evidence, meetings/negotiations or mediation, or an invitation to issue proceedings.
5. **(If this is so) set out that breach of duty and causation are denied but the healthcare provider nevertheless wishes to explore settlement**, together with any proposals for a time period to be agreed by the parties to try and resolve the claim without the need for the issue of legal proceedings.
6. **The response to any offer to settle** made by the claimant's Letter of Claim should be given.
7. **Costs**
   If the claimant has requested details of the healthcare provider's costs incurred to the date of the letter of response the healthcare provider should provide these details

OPTIONAL MATTERS

- Make an offer to settle if the claimant has not made one, or a counter-offer to the claimant's offer with supporting medical evidence and /or a counter-schedule of loss if appropriate

POSSIBLE ENCLOSURES:

- Clinical records
- Annotated chronology
- Expert reports.

ANNEX C: GUIDANCE OVER APOLOGIES BY DEFENDANTS

May 1st 2009
To: Chief Executives and Finance Directors All NHS Bodies
Dear Colleagues

Apologies and Explanations

I am pleased to report that the Authority's letter of 15 August 2007, on providing apologies and explanations to patients or their relatives, has been updated and endorsed widely by other organisations, so it seemed appropriate to reissue it with those endorsements included. To ensure the widest possible distribution to staff in the NHS and beyond, the co-signatories have all incorporated links to this letter on their own websites. To reduce the possibility of misunderstandings by front-line staff, the original letter has been reworded slightly in places.

Apologies

It is both natural and desirable for clinicians who have provided treatment which produces an adverse result, for whatever reason, to sympathise with the patient or the patient's relatives; to express sorrow or regret at the outcome; and to apologise for shortcomings in treatment. It is most important to patients that they or their relatives receive a meaningful apology. We encourage this, and stress that apologies do not constitute an admission of liability. In addition, it is not our policy to dispute any payment, under any scheme, solely on the grounds of such an apology.

Explanations

Patients and their relatives increasingly ask for detailed explanations of what led to adverse outcomes. Moreover, they frequently say that they derive some consolation from knowing that lessons have been learned for the future. In this area, too, the NHSLA is keen to encourage both clinicians and NHS bodies to supply appropriate information whether informally, formally or through mediation.

Explanations should not contain admissions of liability. For the avoidance of doubt, the NHSLA will not take a point against any NHS body or any clinician seeking NHS indemnity, on the basis of a factual explanation offered in good faith before litigation is in train. We consider that the provision of such information constitutes good clinical and managerial practice. To assist in the provision of apologies and explanations, clinicians and NHS bodies should familiarise themselves with the guidance on Being Open, produced by the National Patient Safety Agency and available at:

www.npsa.nhs.uk/nrls/alerts-and-directives/notices/disclosure/

Formal Admissions

In keeping with our financial and case management responsibilities, the NHSLA will make or agree the terms of formal admissions within or before litigation. This circular is intended to encourage scheme members and their employees to offer the earlier, more informal, apologies and explanations so desired by patients and their families.

Medical Defence Organisations

It is critically important to note that all of the above applies to the provision of NHS indemnity to NHS bodies and employees. Should any individual clinicians wish to adopt a particular policy *vis-à-vis* apologies and explanations, in a matter which might expose them to an action brought against them as an individual, they should seek the advice of their medical defence organisation and/or professional body.

Staff Support

We should not lose sight of the traumatic effect that adverse outcomes, and their aftermath, might have on NHS staff as well as on patients and their relatives. Some may find compliance with these recommendations cathartic or therapeutic; others will not. None will find compliance easy. Recognising this, employers should do whatever is necessary by way of offering training, support, counselling or formal debriefing.

Yours sincerely

Stephen Walker CBE Chief Executive NHSLA

We endorse the NHSLA guidance on apologies and explanations. For many years we have advised our members that, if something goes wrong, patients should receive a prompt, open, sympathetic and above all truthful account of what has happened. Any patient who has had the misfortune to suffer through an error of whatever nature should receive a full explanation and a genuine apology. We encourage members to adopt this approach. There are no legal concerns about taking this course of action: it is quite different from admitting liability.

Dr Michael Saunders
Chief Executive
Medical Defence Union

Dr Stephanie Bown
Director of Policy and Communications
Medical Protection Society

Dr Jim Rodger
Head of Professional Services
Medical and Dental Defence Union of Scotland

Dr Peter Carter
Chief Executive and General Secretary
Royal College of Nursing

Martin Fletcher
Chief Executive
National Patient Safety Agency

Dr Hamish Meldrum
Chairman of Council
British Medical Association

The GMC fully supports this advice from the NHSLA. If something goes wrong, patients deserve an apology and a full explanation. In *Good Medical Practice* we say 'if a patient under your care has suffered harm or distress, you must act immediately to put matters right, if that is possible. You should offer an apology and explain fully and promptly to the patient what has happened and the likely short-term and long-term effects.'

Finlay Scott
Chief Executive
General Medical Council

ANNEX D: THE 2007 REHABILITATION CODE

While the Rehabilitation Code was put together primarily by claimants and insurers in relation to personal injury claims, it still has relevance for clinical disputes of all kinds and is thus reproduced as an Annex to the Clinical Disputes

Protocol. Additions relating specifically to the Clinical Negligence Pre-action Protocol are in italics.

The aim of this code is to promote the use of rehabilitation and early intervention in the compensation process so that the injured person makes the best and quickest possible medical, social and psychological recovery. This objective applies whatever the severity of the injuries sustained by the claimant. The Code is designed to ensure that the claimant's need for rehabilitation is assessed and addressed as a priority, and that the process of so doing is pursued on a collaborative basis by the claimant's lawyer and the compensator. Therefore, in every case, where rehabilitation is likely to be of benefit, the earliest possible notification to the compensator of the claim and of the need for rehabilitation will be expected.

1 Introduction

1.1   The purpose of the personal injury claims process is to put the individual back into the same position as he or she would have been in, had the accident not occurred, insofar as money can achieve that objective. The purpose of the Rehabilitation Code is to provide a framework within which the claimant's health, quality of life and ability to work are restored as far as possible before, or simultaneously with, the process of assessing compensation.

1.2   Although the Code is recognised by the Personal Injury Pre-Action Protocol (*and now also the Clinical Disputes Pre-action Protocol*), its provisions are not mandatory. It is recognised that the aims of the Code can be achieved without strict adherence to the terms of the Code, and therefore it is open to the parties to agree an alternative framework to achieve the early rehabilitation of the claimant.

1.3   However, the Code provides a useful framework within which claimant's lawyers and the compensator can work together to ensure that the needs of injured claimants are assessed at an early stage.

1.4   In any case where agreement on liability is not reached it is open to the parties to agree that the Code will in any event operate, and the question of delay pending resolution of liability should be balanced with the interests of the injured party. However, unless so agreed, the Code does not apply in the absence of liability or prior to agreement on liability being reached.

1.5   In this code the expression 'the compensator' shall include any loss adjuster, solicitor or other person acting on behalf of the compensator (*and any healthcare provider, the NHSLA, WHLS, the Welsh Risks Pool, any MDO or any other indemnifying organisation*).

2 The Claimant's Solicitor

2.1   It should be the duty of every claimant's solicitor to consider, from the earliest practicable stage, and in consultation with the claimant, the claimant's family, and where appropriate the claimant's treating physician(s), whether it is likely or possible that early intervention, rehabilitation or medical treatment would improve their present and/or long term physical and mental well being. This duty is ongoing throughout the life of the case but is of most importance in the early stages.

2.2   The claimant's solicitor will in any event be aware of their responsibilities under section 4 of the Pre-Action Protocol for Personal Injury Claims *and the Pre-Action Protocol for Clinical Negligence*.

2.3   It shall be the duty of a claimant's solicitor to consider, with the claimant and/or the claimant's family, whether there is an immediate need for aids, adaptations, adjustments to employment to enable the claimant to keep his/her existing job, obtain suitable alternative employment with the same employer or retrain for new employment, or other matters that would seek to alleviate problems caused by disability, and then to communicate with the compensators as soon as practicable about any such rehabilitation needs, with a view to putting this Code into effect.

2.4   It shall not be the responsibility of the solicitor to decide on the need for treatment or rehabilitation or to arrange such matters without appropriate medical or professional advice.

2.5   It is the intention of this Code that the claimant's solicitor will work with the compensator to address these rehabilitation needs and that the assessment and delivery of rehabilitation needs shall be a collaborative process.

2.6   It must be recognised that the compensator will need to receive from the claimants' solicitors sufficient information for the compensator to make a proper decision about the need for intervention, rehabilitation or treatment. To this extent the claimant's solicitor must comply with the requirements of the Pre-Action Protocol to provide the compensator with full and adequate details of the injuries sustained by the claimant, the nature and extent of any or any likely continuing disability and any suggestions that may have already have been made concerning the rehabilitation and/or early intervention.

2.7   There is no requirement under the Pre-Action Protocol, or under this code, for the claimant's solicitor to have obtained a full medical report. It is recognised that many cases will be identified for consideration under this Code before medical evidence has actually been commissioned or obtained.

3 The Compensator

3.1   It shall be the duty of the compensator, from the earliest practicable stage in any appropriate case, to consider whether it is likely that the claimant will benefit in the immediate, medium or longer term from further medical treatment, rehabilitation or early intervention. This duty is ongoing throughout the life of the case but is most important in the early stages.

3.2   If the compensator considers that a particular claim might be suitable for intervention, rehabilitation or treatment, the compensator will communicate this to the claimant's solicitor as soon as practicable.

3.3   On receipt of such communication, the claimant's solicitor will immediately discuss these issues with the claimant and/or the claimant's family pursuant to his duty set out above.

3.4   Where a request to consider rehabilitation has been communicated by the claimant's solicitor to the compensator, it will usually be expected that the compensator will respond to such request within 21 days.

3.5   Nothing in this or any other code of practice shall in any way modify the obligations of the compensator under the Protocol to investigate claims rapidly and in any event within 3 months (except where time is extended by the claimant's solicitor) from the date of the formal claim letter. It is recognized that, although the rehabilitation assessment can be done even where liability investigations are outstanding, it is essential that such investigations proceed with the appropriate speed.

4 Assessment

4.1   Unless the need for intervention, rehabilitation or treatment has already been identified by medical reports obtained and disclosed by either side, the need for and extent of such intervention, rehabilitation or treatment will be considered by means of an assessment by an appropriately qualified person.

4.2 An assessment of rehabilitation needs may be carried out by any person or organisation suitably qualified, experienced and skilled to carry out the task. The claimant's solicitor and the compensator should endeavour to agree on the person or organisation to be chosen.

4.3   No solicitor or compensator may insist on the assessment being carried out by a particular person or organisation if (on reasonable grounds) the other party objects, such objection to be raised within 21 days from the date of notification of the suggested assessor.

4.4   The assessment may be carried out by a person or organisation which has a direct business connection with the solicitor or compensator, only if the other party agrees. The solicitor or compensator will be expected to reveal to the other party the existence of and nature of such a business connection.

5 The Assessment Process

5.1   Where possible, the agency to be instructed to provide the assessment should be agreed between the claimant's solicitor and the compensator. The method of providing instructions to that agency will be agreed between the solicitor and the compensator.

5.2   The assessment agency will be asked to carry out the assessment in a way that is appropriate to the needs of the case and, in a simple case, may include, by prior appointment, a telephone interview but in more serious cases will probably involve a face to face discussion with the claimant. The report will normally cover the following headings:-
1.   The injuries sustained by the claimant.
2.   The current disability/incapacity arising from those Injuries. Where relevant to the overall picture of the claimant's needs, any other medical conditions not arising from the accident should also be separately annotated.
3.   The claimant's domestic circumstances (including mobility accommodation and employment) where relevant.
4.   The injuries/disability in respect of which early intervention or early rehabilitation is suggested.
5.   The type of intervention or treatment envisaged.
6.   The likely cost.
7.   The likely outcome of such intervention or treatment.

5.3   The report should not deal with issues relating to legal liability and should therefore not contain a detailed account of the accident circumstances *or the circumstances giving rise to the alleged breach of duty*.

5.4   In most cases it will be expected that the assessment will take place within 14 days from the date of the letter of referral to the assessment agency.

5.5   It must be remembered that the compensator will usually only consider such rehabilitation to deal with the effects of the injuries that have been caused in the relevant accident *or incident* and will normally not be expected to fund treatment for conditions which do not directly relate to the accident *or incident* unless the effect of such conditions has been exacerbated by the injuries sustained in the accident *or incident*.

6 The Assessment Report

6.1   The report agency will, on completion of the report, send copies on to both the claimant's solicitor and compensator simultaneously. Both parties will have the right to raise questions on the report, disclosing such correspondence to the other party.

6.2   It is recognised that for this assessment report to be of benefit to the parties, it should be prepared and used wholly outside the litigation process. Neither side can therefore, unless they agree in writing, rely on its contents in any subsequent litigation.

6.3   The report, any correspondence related to it and any notes created by the assessing agency to prepare it, will be covered by legal privilege and will not be disclosed in any legal proceedings unless the parties agree. Any notes or documents created in connection with the assessment process will not be disclosed in any litigation, and any person involved in the preparation of the report or involved in the assessment process, shall not be a compellable witness at Court. This principle is also set out in paragraph 4.4 of the Pre-Action Protocol *and is agreed also to be applicable to clinical disputes.*

6.4   The provision in paragraph 6.3 above as to treating the report etc as outside the litigation process is limited to the assessment report and any notes relating to it. Any notes and reports created during the subsequent case management process will be covered by the usual principle in relation to disclosure of documents and medical records relating to the claimant.

6.5   The compensator will pay for the report within 28 days of receipt.

6.6   This code intends that the parties will continue to work together to ensure that the rehabilitation which has been recommended proceeds smoothly and that any further rehabilitation needs are also assessed.

7 Recommendations

7.1   When the assessment report is disclosed to the compensator, the compensator will be under a duty to consider the recommendations made and the extent to which funds will be made available to implement all or some of the recommendations. The compensator will not be required to pay for intervention treatment that is unreasonable in nature, content or cost or where adequate and timely provision is otherwise available. The claimant will be under no obligation to undergo intervention, medical or investigation treatment that is unreasonable in all the circumstances of the case.

7.2   The compensator will normally be expected to respond to the claimant's solicitor within 21 days from the date upon which the assessment report is disclosed as to the extent to which the recommendations have been accepted and rehabilitation treatment would be funded and will be expected to justify, within that same timescale, any refusal to meet the cost of recommended rehabilitation.

7.3   If funds are provided by the compensator to the claimant to enable specific intervention, rehabilitation or treatment to occur, the compensator warrants that they will not, in any legal proceedings connected with the claim, dispute the reasonableness of that treatment, nor the agreed costs, provided of course that the claimant has had the recommended treatment. The compensator will not, should the claim fail or be later discontinued, or any element of contributory negligence be assessed or agreed, seek to recover from the claimant any funds that they have made available pursuant to this Code.

6. CPR PART 35 – EXPERTS AND ASSESSORS

Contents of this Part

Rule 35.1   Duty to restrict expert evidence
Rule 35.2   Interpretation and definitions
Rule 35.3   Experts – overriding duty to the court
Rule 35.4   Court's power to restrict expert evidence
Rule 35.5   General requirement for expert evidence to be given in a written report
Rule 35.6   Written questions to experts
Rule 35.7   Court's power to direct that evidence is to be given by a single joint expert
Rule 35.8   Instructions to a single joint expert
Rule 35.9   Power of court to direct a party to provide information
Rule 35.10 Contents of report
Rule 35.11 Use by one party of expert's report disclosed by another
Rule 35.12 Discussions between experts
Rule 35.13 Consequence of failure to disclose expert's report
Rule 35.14 Expert's right to ask court for directions
Rule 35.15 Assessors

35.1 Duty to restrict expert evidence

Expert evidence shall be restricted to that which is reasonably required to resolve the proceedings.

35.2 Interpretation and definitions

(1) A reference to an 'expert' in this Part is a reference to a person who has been instructed to give or prepare expert evidence for the purpose of proceedings.

(2) 'Single joint expert' means an expert instructed to prepare a report for the court on behalf of two or more of the parties (including the claimant) to the proceedings.

35.3 Experts – overriding duty to the court

(1) It is the duty of experts to help the court on matters within their expertise.

(2) This duty overrides any obligation to the person from whom experts have received instructions or by whom they are paid.

35.4 Court's power to restrict expert evidence

(1) No party may call an expert or put in evidence an expert's report without the court's permission.

(2) When parties apply for permission they must identify –
    (a) the field in which expert evidence is required; and
    (b) where practicable, the name of the proposed expert.

(3) If permission is granted it shall be in relation only to the expert named or the field identified under paragraph (2).

(3A) Where a claim has been allocated to the small claims track or the fast track, if permission is given for expert evidence, it will normally be given for evidence from only one expert on a particular issue.

(Paragraph 7 of Practice Direction 35 sets out some of the circumstances the court will consider when deciding whether expert evidence should be given by a single joint expert.)

(4) The court may limit the amount of a party's expert's fees and expenses that may be recovered from any other party.

35.5 General requirement for expert evidence to be given in a written report

(1) Expert evidence is to be given in a written report unless the court directs otherwise.

(2) If a claim is on the small claims track or the fast track, the court will not direct an expert to attend a hearing unless it is necessary to do so in the interests of justice.

35.6 Written questions to experts

(1) A party may put written questions about an expert's report (which must be proportionate) to –

    (a) an expert instructed by another party; or

    (b) a single joint expert appointed under rule 35.7.

(2) Written questions under paragraph (1) –

    (a) may be put once only;

    (b) must be put within 28 days of service of the expert's report; and

    (c) must be for the purpose only of clarification of the report,

unless in any case –

    (i) the court gives permission; or

    (ii) the other party agrees.

(3) An expert's answers to questions put in accordance with paragraph (1) shall be treated as part of the expert's report.

(4) Where –

    (a) a party has put a written question to an expert instructed by another party; and

    (b) the expert does not answer that question,

the court may make one or both of the following orders in relation to the party who instructed the expert –

    (i) that the party may not rely on the evidence of that expert; or

    (ii) that the party may not recover the fees and expenses of that expert from any other party.

35.7 Court's power to direct that evidence is to be given by a single joint expert

(1) Where two or more parties wish to submit expert evidence on a particular issue, the court may direct that the evidence on that issue is to be given by a single joint expert.

(2) Where the parties who wish to submit the evidence ('the relevant parties') cannot agree who should be the single joint expert, the court may –

(a) select the expert from a list prepared or identified by the relevant parties; or

(b) direct that the expert be selected in such other manner as the court may direct.

35.8 Instructions to a single joint expert

(1) Where the court gives a direction under rule 35.7 for a single joint expert to be used, any relevant party may give instructions to the expert.

(2) When a party gives instructions to the expert that party must, at the same time, send a copy to the other relevant parties.

(3) The court may give directions about –

    (a) the payment of the expert's fees and expenses; and

    (b) any inspection, examination or experiments which the expert wishes to carry out.

(4) The court may, before an expert is instructed –

    (a) limit the amount that can be paid by way of fees and expenses to the
        expert; and
    (b) direct that some or all of the relevant parties pay that amount into
        court.
    (5) Unless the court otherwise directs, the relevant parties are jointly and
severally liable (GL) for the payment of the expert's fees and expenses.

35.9 Power of court to direct a party to provide information

    Where a party has access to information which is not reasonably available to
another party, the court may direct the party who has access to the information
to –
    (a) prepare and file a document recording the information; and
    (b) serve a copy of that document on the other party.

35.10 Contents of report

    (1) An expert's report must comply with the requirements set out in Practice
Direction 35.
    (2) At the end of an expert's report there must be a statement that the expert
understands and has complied with their duty to the court.
    (3) The expert's report must state the substance of all material instructions,
whether written or oral, on the basis of which the report was written.
    (4) The instructions referred to in paragraph (3) shall not be privileged(GL)
against disclosure but the court will not, in relation to those instructions –
    (a) order disclosure of any specific document; or
    (b) permit any questioning in court, other than by the party who instructed
        the expert,
unless it is satisfied that there are reasonable grounds to consider the statement
of instructions given under paragraph (3) to be inaccurate or incomplete.

35.11 Use by one party of expert's report disclosed by another

    Where a party has disclosed an expert's report, any party may use that expert's
report as evidence at the trial.

35.12 Discussions between experts

    (1) The court may, at any stage, direct a discussion between experts for the
purpose of requiring the experts to –
    (a) identify and discuss the expert issues in the proceedings; and
    (b) where possible, reach an agreed opinion on those issues.
    (2) The court may specify the issues which the experts must discuss.
    (3) The court may direct that following a discussion between the experts they
must prepare a statement for the court setting out those issues on which –
    (a) they agree; and
    (b) they disagree, with a summary of their reasons for disagreeing.
    (4) The content of the discussion between the experts shall not be referred to at
the trial unless the parties agree.
    (5) Where experts reach agreement on an issue during their discussions, the
agreement shall not bind the parties unless the parties expressly agree to be
bound by the agreement.

35.13 Consequence of failure to disclose expert's report

    A party who fails to disclose an expert's report may not use the report at the
trial or call the expert to give evidence orally unless the court gives permission.

35.14 Expert's right to ask court for directions

(1) Experts may file written requests for directions for the purpose of assisting them in carrying out their functions.

(2) Experts must, unless the court orders otherwise, provide copies of the proposed requests for directions under paragraph (1) –

    (a) to the party instructing them, at least 7 days before they file the requests; and

    (b) to all other parties, at least 4 days before they file them.

(3) The court, when it gives directions, may also direct that a party be served with a copy of the directions.

35.15 Assessors

(1) This rule applies where the court appoints one or more persons under section 70 of the Senior Courts Act 1981 or section 63 of the County Courts Act 1984 as an assessor.

(2) An assessor will assist the court in dealing with a matter in which the assessor has skill and experience.

(3) An assessor will take such part in the proceedings as the court may direct and in particular the

court may direct an assessor to –

    (a) prepare a report for the court on any matter at issue in the proceedings; and

    (b) attend the whole or any part of the trial to advise the court on any such matter.

(4) If an assessor prepares a report for the court before the trial has begun –

    (a) the court will send a copy to each of the parties; and

    (b) the parties may use it at trial.

(5) The remuneration to be paid to an assessor is to be determined by the court and will form part of the costs of the proceedings.

(6) The court may order any party to deposit in the court office a specified sum in respect of an assessor's fees and, where it does so, the assessor will not be asked to act until the sum has been deposited.

(7) Paragraphs (5) and (6) do not apply where the remuneration of the assessor is to be paid out of money provided by Parliament.

7. PRACTICE DIRECTION 35 – EXPERTS AND ASSESSORS

This Practice Direction supplements CPR Part 35

Contents of this Practice Direction

Introduction

1   Part 35 is intended to limit the use of oral expert evidence to that which is reasonably required. In addition, where possible, matters requiring expert evidence should be dealt with by only one expert. Experts and those instructing them are expected to have regard to the guidance contained in the Protocol for the Instruction of Experts to give Evidence in Civil Claims annexed to this practice direction. (Further guidance on experts is contained in Annex C to the Practice Direction (Pre-Action Conduct)).

Expert Evidence – General Requirements

2.1   Expert evidence should be the independent product of the expert uninfluenced by the pressures of litigation.

2.2   Experts should assist the court by providing objective, unbiased opinions on matters within their expertise, and should not assume the role of an advocate.

2.3   Experts should consider all material facts, including those which might detract from their opinions.

2.4   Experts should make it clear –
   (a)   when a question or issue falls outside their expertise; and
   (b)   when they are not able to reach a definite opinion, for example because they have insufficient information.

2.5   If, after producing a report, an expert's view changes on any material matter, such change of view should be communicated to all the parties without delay, and when appropriate to the court.

Form and Content of an Expert's Report

3.1   An expert's report should be addressed to the court and not to the party from whom the expert has received instructions.

3.2   An expert's report must:
   (1)   give details of the expert's qualifications;

(2) give details of any literature or other material which has been relied on in making the report;

(3) contain a statement setting out the substance of all facts and instructions which are material to the opinions expressed in the report or upon which those opinions are based;

(4) make clear which of the facts stated in the report are within the expert's own knowledge;

(5) say who carried out any examination, measurement, test or experiment which the expert has used for the report, give the qualifications of that person, and say whether or not the test or experiment has been carried out under the expert's supervision;

(6) where there is a range of opinion on the matters dealt with in the report –
  (a) summarise the range of opinions; and
  (b) give reasons for the expert's own opinion;

(7) contain a summary of the conclusions reached;

(8) if the expert is not able to give an opinion without qualification, state the qualification; and

(9) contain a statement that the expert –
  (a) understands their duty to the court, and has complied with that duty; and
  (b) is aware of the requirements of Part 35, this practice direction and the Protocol for Instruction of Experts to give Evidence in Civil Claims.

3.3 An expert's report must be verified by a statement of truth in the following form –
I confirm that I have made clear which facts and matters referred to in this report are within my own knowledge and which are not. Those that are within my own knowledge I confirm to be true. The opinions I have expressed represent my true and complete professional opinions on the matters to which they refer.
(Part 22 deals with statements of truth. Rule 32.14 sets out the consequences of verifying a document containing a false statement without an honest belief in its truth.)

Information

4 Under rule 35.9 the court may direct a party with access to information, which is not reasonably available to another party to serve on that other party a document, which records the information. The document served must include sufficient details of all the facts, tests, experiments and assumptions which underlie any part of the information to enable the party on whom it is served to make, or to obtain, a proper interpretation of the information and an assessment of its significance.

Instructions

5 Cross-examination of experts on the contents of their instructions will not be allowed unless the court permits it (or unless the party who gave the instructions consents). Before it gives permission the court must be satisfied that there are reasonable grounds to consider that the statement in the report of the substance of the instructions is inaccurate or incomplete. If the court is so satisfied, it will allow the cross-examination where it appears to be in the interests of justice.

Questions to Experts

6.1 Where a party sends a written question or questions under rule 35.6 direct to an expert, a copy of the questions must, at the same time, be sent to the other party or parties.

6.2   The party or parties instructing the expert must pay any fees charged by that expert for answering questions put under rule 35.6. This does not affect any decision of the court as to the party who is ultimately to bear the expert's fees.

Single joint expert

7   When considering whether to give permission for the parties to rely on expert evidence and whether that evidence should be from a single joint expert the court will take into account all the circumstances in particular, whether:

    (a) it is proportionate to have separate experts for each party on a particular issue with reference to –
        (i)   the amount in dispute;
        (ii) the importance to the parties; and
        (iii) the complexity of the issue;
    (b) the instruction of a single joint expert is likely to assist the parties and the court to resolve the issue more speedily and in a more cost-effective way than separately instructed experts;
    (c) expert evidence is to be given on the issue of liability, causation or quantum;
    (d) the expert evidence falls within a substantially established area of knowledge which is unlikely to be in dispute or there is likely to be a range of expert opinion;
    (e) a party has already instructed an expert on the issue in question and whether or not that was done in compliance with any practice direction or relevant pre-action protocol;
    (f) questions put in accordance with rule 35.6 are likely to remove the need for the other party to instruct an expert if one party has already instructed an expert;
    (g) questions put to a single joint expert may not conclusively deal with all issues that may require testing prior to trial;
    (h) a conference may be required with the legal representatives, experts and other witnesses which may make instruction of a single joint expert impractical; and
    (i) a claim to privilege(GL) makes the instruction of any expert as a single joint expert inappropriate.

Orders

8   Where an order requires an act to be done by an expert, or otherwise affects an expert, the party instructing that expert must serve a copy of the order on the expert. The claimant must serve the order on a single joint expert.

Discussions between experts

9.1   Unless directed by the court discussions between experts are not mandatory. Parties must consider, with their experts, at an early stage, whether there is likely to be any useful purpose in holding an experts' discussion and if so when.

9.2   The purpose of discussions between experts is not for experts to settle cases but to agree and narrow issues and in particular to identify:

    (i)   the extent of the agreement between them;
    (ii) the points of and short reasons for any disagreement;
    (iii) action, if any, which may be taken to resolve any outstanding points of disagreement; and
    (iv) any further material issues not raised and the extent to which these issues are agreed.

9.3   Where the experts are to meet, the parties must discuss and if possible agree whether an agenda is necessary, and if so attempt to agree one that helps the experts to focus on the issues which need to be discussed. The agenda must not be in the form of leading questions or hostile in tone.

9.4   Unless ordered by the court, or agreed by all parties, and the experts, neither the parties nor their legal representatives may attend experts discussions.

9.5   If the legal representatives do attend –
   (i)   they should not normally intervene in the discussion, except to answer questions put to them by the experts or to advise on the law; and
   (ii) the experts may if they so wish hold part of their discussions in the absence of the legal representatives.

9.6   A statement must be prepared by the experts dealing with paragraphs 9.2(i) - (iv) above. Individual copies of the statements must be signed by the experts at the conclusion of the discussion, or as soon thereafter as practicable, and in any event within 7 days. Copies of the statements must be provided to the parties no later than 14 days after signing.

9.7   Experts must give their own opinions to assist the court and do not require the authority of the parties to sign a joint statement.

9.8   If an expert significantly alters an opinion, the joint statement must include a note or addendum by that expert explaining the change of opinion.

Assessors

10.1   An assessor may be appointed to assist the court under rule 35.15. Not less than 21 days before making any such appointment, the court will notify each party in writing of the name of the proposed assessor, of the matter in respect of which the assistance of the assessor will be sought and of the qualifications of the assessor to give that assistance.

10.2   Where any person has been proposed for appointment as an assessor, any party may object to that person either personally or in respect of that person's qualification.

10.3   Any such objection must be made in writing and filed with the court within 7 days of receipt of the notification referred to in paragraph 10.1 and will be taken into account by the court in deciding whether or not to make the appointment.

10.4   Copies of any report prepared by the assessor will be sent to each of the parties but the assessor will not give oral evidence or be open to cross-examination or questioning.

8. PROTOCOL FOR THE INSTRUCTION OF EXPERTS TO GIVE EVIDENCE IN CIVIL CLAIMS

June 2005 amended October 2009

Contents

1. Introduction

Expert witnesses perform a vital role in civil litigation. It is essential that both those who instruct experts and experts themselves are given clear guidance as to what they are expected to do in civil proceedings. The purpose of this Protocol is to provide such guidance. It has been drafted by the Civil Justice Council and reflects the rules and practice directions current [in June 2005], replacing the Code of Guidance on Expert Evidence. The authors of the Protocol wish to acknowledge the valuable assistance they obtained by drawing on earlier documents produced by the Academy of Experts and the Expert Witness Institute, as well as suggestions made by the Clinical Dispute Forum. The Protocol has been approved by the Master of the Rolls.

2. Aims of Protocol

2.1   This Protocol offers guidance to experts and to those instructing them in the interpretation of and compliance with Part 35 of the Civil Procedure Rules (CPR

35) and its associated Practice Direction (PD 35) and to further the objectives of the Civil Procedure Rules in general. It is intended to assist in the interpretation of those provisions in the interests of good practice but it does not replace them. It sets out standards for the use of experts and the conduct of experts and those who instruct them. The existence of this Protocol does not remove the need for experts and those who instruct them to be familiar with CPR35 and PD35.

2.2   Experts and those who instruct them should also bear in mind para 1.4 of the Practice Direction on Protocols which contains the following objectives, namely to:

    (a) encourage the exchange of early and full information about the expert issues involved in a prospective legal claim;

    (b) enable the parties to avoid or reduce the scope of litigation by agreeing the whole or part of an expert issue before commencement of proceedings; and

    (c) support the efficient management of proceedings where litigation cannot be avoided.

3. Application

3.1   This Protocol applies to any steps taken for the purpose of civil proceedings by experts or those who instruct them on or after 5th September 2005.

3.2   It applies to all experts who are, or who may be, governed by CPR Part 35 and to those who instruct them. Experts are governed by Part 35 if they are or have been instructed to give or prepare evidence for the purpose of civil proceedings in a court in England and Wales (CPR 35.2).

3.3   Experts, and those instructing them, should be aware that some cases may be 'specialist proceedings' (CPR 49) where there are modifications to the Civil Procedure Rules. Proceedings may also be governed by other Protocols. Further, some courts have published their own Guides which supplement the Civil Procedure Rules for proceedings in those courts. They contain provisions affecting expert evidence. Expert witnesses and those instructing them should be familiar with them when they are relevant.

3.4   Courts may take into account any failure to comply with this Protocol when making orders in relation to costs, interest, time limits, the stay of proceedings and whether to order a party to pay a sum of money into court.

Limitation

3.5   If, as a result of complying with any part of this Protocol, claims would or might be time barred under any provision in the Limitation Act 1980, or any other legislation that imposes a time limit for the bringing an action, claimants may commence proceedings without complying with this Protocol. In such circumstances, claimants who commence proceedings without complying with all, or any part, of this Protocol must apply, giving notice to all other parties, to the court for directions as to the timetable and form of procedure to be adopted, at the same time as they request the court to issue proceedings. The court may consider whether to order a stay of the whole or part of the proceedings pending compliance with this Protocol and may make orders in relation to costs.

4. Duties of experts

4.1   Experts always owe a duty to exercise reasonable skill and care to those instructing them, and to comply with any relevant professional code of ethics. However when they are instructed to give or prepare evidence for the purpose of civil proceedings in England and Wales they have an overriding duty to help the court on matters within their expertise (CPR 35.3). This duty overrides any obligation to the person instructing or paying them. Experts must not serve the exclusive interest of those who retain them.

4.2   Experts should be aware of the overriding objective that courts deal with cases justly. This includes dealing with cases proportionately, expeditiously and fairly (CPR 1.1). Experts are under an obligation to assist the court so as to enable them to deal with cases in accordance with the overriding objective. However the overriding objective does not impose on experts any duty to act as mediators between the parties or require them to trespass on the role of the court in deciding facts.

4.3   Experts should provide opinions which are independent, regardless of the pressures of litigation. In this context, a useful test of 'independence' is that the expert would express the same opinion if given the same instructions by an opposing party. Experts should not take it upon themselves to promote the point of view of the party instructing them or engage in the role of advocates.

4.4   Experts should confine their opinions to matters which are material to the disputes between the parties and provide opinions only in relation to matters which lie within their expertise. Experts should indicate without delay where particular questions or issues fall outside their expertise.

4.5   Experts should take into account all material facts before them at the time that they give their opinion. Their reports should set out those facts and any literature or any other material on which they have relied in forming their opinions. They should indicate if an opinion is provisional, or qualified, or where they consider that further information is required or if, for any other reason, they are not satisfied that an opinion can be expressed finally and without qualification.

4.6   Experts should inform those instructing them without delay of any change in their opinions on any material matter and the reason for it.

4.7   Experts should be aware that any failure by them to comply with the Civil Procedure Rules or court orders or any excessive delay for which they are responsible may result in the parties who instructed them being penalised in costs and even, in extreme cases, being debarred from placing the experts' evidence before the court. In[1] *Phillips* v *Symes*[1] Peter Smith J held that courts may also make orders for costs (under section 51 of the Supreme Court Act 1981) directly against expert witnesses who by their evidence cause significant expense to be incurred, and do so in flagrant and reckless disregard of their duties to the Court.

5. Conduct of experts instructed only to advise

5.1   Part 35 only applies where experts are instructed to give opinions which are relied on for the purposes of court proceedings. Advice which the parties do not intend to adduce in litigation is likely to be confidential; the Protocol does not apply in these circumstances[2, 3].

5.2   The same applies where, after the commencement of proceedings, experts are instructed only to advise (e.g. to comment upon a single joint expert's report) and not to give or prepare evidence for use in the proceedings.

5.3   However this Protocol does apply if experts who were formerly instructed only to advise are later instructed to give or prepare evidence for the purpose of civil proceedings.

---

1   *Phillips* v *Symes* [2004] EWHC 2330 (Ch).
2   *Carlson* v *Townsend* [2001] 1 WLR 2415.
3   *Jackson* v *Marley Davenport* [2004] 1 WLR 2926.

6. The need for experts

6.1   Those intending to instruct experts to give or prepare evidence for the purpose of civil proceedings should consider whether expert evidence is appropriate, taking account of the principles set out in CPR Parts 1 and 35, and in particular whether:

- (a)   it is relevant to a matter which is in dispute between the parties.
- (b)   it is reasonably required to resolve the proceedings (CPR 35.1);
- (c)   the expert has expertise relevant to the issue on which an opinion is sought;
- (d)   the expert has the experience, expertise and training appropriate to the value, complexity and importance of the case; and whether
- (e)   these objects can be achieved by the appointment of a single joint expert (see section 17 below).

6.2   Although the court's permission is not generally required to instruct an expert, the court's permission is required before experts can be called to give evidence or their evidence can be put in (CPR 35.4).

7. The appointment of experts

7.1   Before experts are formally instructed or the court's permission to appoint named experts is sought, the following should be established:

- (a)   that they have the appropriate expertise and experience;
- (b)   that they are familiar with the general duties of an expert;
- (c)   that they can produce a report, deal with questions and have discussions with other experts within a reasonable time and at a cost proportionate to the matters in issue;
- (d)   a description of the work required;
- (e)   whether they are available to attend the trial, if attendance is required; and
- (f)   there is no potential conflict of interest.

7.2   Terms of appointment should be agreed at the outset and should normally include:

- (a)   the capacity in which the expert is to be appointed (e.g. party appointed expert, single joint expert or expert advisor);
- (b)   the services required of the expert (e.g. provision of expert's report, answering questions in writing, attendance at meetings and attendance at court);
- (c)   time for delivery of the report;
- (d)   the basis of the expert's charges (either daily or hourly rates and an estimate of the time likely to be required, or a total fee for the services);
- (e)   travelling expenses and disbursements;
- (f)   cancellation charges;
- (g)   any fees for attending court;
- (h)   time for making the payment; and
- (i)   whether fees are to be paid by a third party.
- (j)   if a party is publicly funded, whether or not the expert's charges will be subject to assessment by a costs officer.

7.3   As to the appointment of single joint experts, see section 17 below.

7.4   When necessary, arrangements should be made for dealing with questions to experts and discussions between experts, including any directions given by the court, and provision should be made for the cost of this work.

7.5   Experts should be informed regularly about deadlines for all matters concerning them. Those instructing experts should promptly send them copies of all court orders and directions which may affect the preparation of their reports or any other matters concerning their obligations.

Conditional and contingency fees

7.6   Payments contingent upon the nature of the expert evidence given in legal proceedings, or upon the outcome of a case, must not be offered or accepted. To do so would contravene experts' overriding duty to the court and compromise their duty of independence.

7.7   Agreement to delay payment of experts' fees until after the conclusion of cases is permissible as long as the amount of the fee does not depend on the outcome of the case.

8. Instructions

8.1   Those instructing experts should ensure that they give clear instructions, including the following:

    (a) basic information, such as names, addresses, telephone numbers, dates of birth and dates of incidents;

    (b) the nature and extent of the expertise which is called for;

    (c) the purpose of requesting the advice or report, a description of the matter(s) to be investigated, the principal known issues and the identity of all parties;

    (d) the statement(s) of case (if any), those documents which form part of standard disclosure and witness statements which are relevant to the advice or report;

    (e) where proceedings have not been started, whether proceedings are being contemplated and, if so, whether the expert is asked only for advice;

    (f) an outline programme, consistent with good case management and the expert's availability, for the completion and delivery of each stage of the expert's work; and

    (g) where proceedings have been started, the dates of any hearings (including any Case Management Conferences and/or Pre-Trial Reviews), the name of the court, the claim number and the track to which the claim has been allocated.

8.2   Experts who do not receive clear instructions should request clarification and may indicate that they are not prepared to act unless and until such clear instructions are received.

8.3   As to the instruction of single joint experts, see section 17 below.

9. Experts' acceptance of instructions

9.1   Experts should confirm without delay whether or not they accept instructions. They should also inform those instructing them (whether on initial instruction or at any later stage) without delay if:

    (a) instructions are not acceptable because, for example, they require work that falls outside their expertise, impose unrealistic deadlines, or are insufficiently clear;

    (b) they consider that instructions are or have become insufficient to complete the work;

    (c) they become aware that they may not be able to fulfil any of the terms of appointment;

    (d) the instructions and/or work have, for any reason, placed them in conflict with their duties as an expert; or

    (e) they are not satisfied that they can comply with any orders that have been made.

9.2   Experts must neither express an opinion outside the scope of their field of expertise, nor accept any instructions to do so.

10. Withdrawal

10.1   Where experts' instructions remain incompatible with their duties, whether through incompleteness, a conflict between their duty to the court and their instructions, or for any other substantial and significant reason, they may consider withdrawing from the case. However, experts should not withdraw without first discussing the position fully with those who instruct them and considering carefully whether it would be more appropriate to make a written request for directions from the court. If experts do withdraw, they must give formal written notice to those instructing them.

11. Experts' right to ask court for directions

11.1   Experts may request directions from the court to assist them in carrying out their functions as experts. Experts should normally discuss such matters with those who instruct them before making any such request. Unless the court otherwise orders, any proposed request for directions should be copied to the party instructing the expert at least seven days before filing any request to the court, and to all other parties at least four days before filing it. (CPR 35.14).

11.2   Requests to the court for directions should be made by letter, containing.
   (a)   the title of the claim;
   (b)   the claim number of the case;
   (c)   the name of the expert;
   (d)   full details of why directions are sought; and
   (e)   copies of any relevant documentation.

12. Power of the court to direct a party to provide information

12.1   If experts consider that those instructing them have not provided information which they require, they may, after discussion with those instructing them and giving notice, write to the court to seek directions (CPR 35.14).

12.2   Experts and those who instruct them should also be aware of CPR 35.9. This provides that where one party has access to information which is not readily available to the other party, the court may direct the party who has access to the information to prepare, file and copy to the other party a document recording the information. If experts require such information which has not been disclosed, they should discuss the position with those instructing them without delay, so that a request for the information can be made, and, if not forthcoming, an application can be made to the court. Unless a document appears to be essential, experts should assess the cost and time involved in the production of a document and whether its provision would be proportionate in the context of the case.

13. Contents of experts' reports

13.1   The content and extent of experts' reports should be governed by the scope of their instructions and general obligations, the contents of CPR 35 and PD35 and their overriding duty to the court.

13.2   In preparing reports, experts should maintain professional objectivity and impartiality at all times.

13.3   PD 35, para 2 provides that experts' reports should be addressed to the court and gives detailed directions about the form and content of such reports. All experts and those who instruct them should ensure that they are familiar with these requirements.

13.4   Model forms of Experts' Reports are available from bodies such as the Academy of Experts or the Expert Witness Institute.

13.5   Experts' reports must contain statements that they—
(i)   understand their duty to the court and have complied and will continue to comply with it; and
(ii)   are aware of the requirements of Part 35 and Practice Direction 35, this protocol and the practice direction on pre-action conduct.

Experts' reports must also be verified by a statement of truth. The form of the statement of truth is as follows—

'I confirm that I have made clear which facts and matters referred to in this report are within my own knowledge and which are not. Those that are within my own knowledge I confirm to be true. The opinions I have expressed represent my true and complete professional opinions on the matters to which they refer.'

This wording is mandatory and must not be modified.

Qualifications

13.6   The details of experts' qualifications to be given in reports should be commensurate with the nature and complexity of the case. It may be sufficient merely to state academic and professional qualifications. However, where highly specialised expertise is called for, experts should include the detail of particular training and/or experience that qualifies them to provide that highly specialised evidence.

Tests

13.7   Where tests of a scientific or technical nature have been carried out, experts should state:
(a)   the methodology used; and
(b)   by whom the tests were undertaken and under whose supervision, summarising their respective qualifications and experience.

Reliance on the work of others

13.8   Where experts rely in their reports on literature or other material and cite the opinions of others without having verified them, they must give details of those opinions relied on. It is likely to assist the court if the qualifications of the originator(s) are also stated.

Facts

13.9   When addressing questions of fact and opinion, experts should keep the two separate and discrete.

13.10   Experts must state those facts (whether assumed or otherwise) upon which their opinions are based. They must distinguish clearly between those facts which experts know to be true and those facts which they assume.

13.11   Where there are material facts in dispute experts should express separate opinions on each hypothesis put forward. They should not express a view in favour of one or other disputed version of the facts unless, as a result of particular expertise and experience, they consider one set of facts as being improbable or less probable, in which case they may express that view, and should give reasons for holding it.

Range of opinion

13.12   If the mandatory summary of the range of opinion is based on published sources, experts should explain those sources and, where appropriate, state the qualifications of the originator(s) of the opinions from which they differ, particularly if such opinions represent a well-established school of thought.

13.13   Where there is no available source for the range of opinion, experts may need to express opinions on what they believe to be the range which other experts would arrive at if asked. In those circumstances, experts should make it clear that the range that they summarise is based on their own judgement and explain the basis of that judgement.

Conclusions

13.14   A summary of conclusions is mandatory. The summary should be at the end of the report after all the reasoning. There may be cases, however, where the benefit to the court is heightened by placing a short summary at the beginning of the report whilst giving the full conclusions at the end. For example, it can assist with the comprehension of the analysis and with the absorption of the detailed facts if the court is told at the outset of the direction in which the report's logic will flow in cases involving highly complex matters which fall outside the general knowledge of the court.

Basis of report: material instructions

13.15   The mandatory statement of the substance of all material instructions should not be incomplete or otherwise tend to mislead. The imperative is transparency. The term 'instructions' includes all material which solicitors place in front of experts in order to gain advice. The omission from the statement of 'off-the-record' oral instructions is not permitted. Courts may allow cross-examination about the instructions if there are reasonable grounds to consider that the statement may be inaccurate or incomplete.

14. After receipt of experts' reports

14.1   Following the receipt of experts' reports, those instructing them should advise the experts as soon as reasonably practicable whether, and if so when, the report will be disclosed to other parties; and, if so disclosed, the date of actual disclosure.

14.2   If experts' reports are to be relied upon, and if experts are to give oral evidence, those instructing them should give the experts the opportunity to consider and comment upon other reports within their area of expertise and which deal with relevant issues at the earliest opportunity.

14.3   Those instructing experts should keep experts informed of the progress of cases, including amendments to statements of case relevant to experts' opinion.

14.4   If those instructing experts become aware of material changes in circumstances or that relevant information within their control was not previously provided to experts, they should without delay instruct experts to review, and if necessary, update the contents of their reports.

15. Amendment of reports

15.1   It may become necessary for experts to amend their reports:
   (a)   as a result of an exchange of questions and answers;
   (b)   following agreements reached at meetings between experts; or
   (c)   where further evidence or documentation is disclosed.

15.2   Experts should not be asked to, and should not, amend, expand or alter any parts of reports in a manner which distorts their true opinion, but may be invited to amend or expand reports to ensure accuracy, internal consistency, completeness and relevance to the issues and clarity. Although experts should generally follow the recommendations of solicitors with regard to the form of reports, they should form their own independent views as to the opinions and contents expressed in their reports and exclude any suggestions which do not accord with their views.

15.3   Where experts change their opinion following a meeting of experts, a simple signed and dated addendum or memorandum to that effect is generally sufficient. In some cases, however, the benefit to the court of having an amended report may justify the cost of making the amendment.

15.4   Where experts significantly alter their opinion, as a result of new evidence or because evidence on which they relied has become unreliable, or for any other reason, they should amend their reports to reflect that fact. Amended reports should include reasons for amendments. In such circumstances those instructing experts should inform other parties as soon as possible of any change of opinion.

15.5   When experts intend to amend their reports, they should inform those instructing them without delay and give reasons. They should provide the amended version (or an addendum or memorandum) clearly marked as such as quickly as possible.

16. Written questions to experts

16.1   The procedure for putting written questions to experts (CPR 35.6) is intended to facilitate the clarification of opinions and issues after experts' reports have been served. Experts have a duty to provide answers to questions properly put. Where they fail to do so, the court may impose sanctions against the party instructing the expert, and, if, there is continued non-compliance, debar a party from relying on the report. Experts should copy their answers to those instructing them.

16.2   Experts' answers to questions automatically become part of their reports. They are covered by the statement of truth and form part of the expert evidence.

16.3   Where experts believe that questions put are not properly directed to the clarification of the report, or are disproportionate, or have been asked out of time, they should discuss the questions with those instructing them and, if appropriate, those asking the questions. Attempts should be made to resolve such problems without the need for an application to the court for directions.

Written requests for directions in relation to questions

16.4   If those instructing experts do not apply to the court in respect of questions, but experts still believe that questions are improper or out of time, experts may file written requests with the court for directions to assist in carrying out their functions as experts (CPR 35.14). See Section 11 above.

17. Single joint experts

17.1   CPR 35 and PD35 deal extensively with the instruction and use of joint experts by the parties and the powers of the court to order their use (see CPR 35.7 and 35.8, PD35, para 5).

17.2   The Civil Procedure Rules encourage the use of joint experts. Wherever possible a joint report should be obtained. Consideration should therefore be given by all parties to the appointment of single joint experts in all cases where a court might direct such an appointment. Single joint experts are the norm in cases allocated to the small claims track and the fast track.

17.3   Where, in the early stages of a dispute, examinations, investigations, tests, site inspections, experiments, preparation of photographs, plans or other similar preliminary expert tasks are necessary, consideration should be given to the instruction of a single joint expert, especially where such matters are not, at that stage, expected to be contentious as between the parties. The objective of such an appointment should be to agree or to narrow issues.

17.4   Experts who have previously advised a party (whether in the same case or otherwise) should only be proposed as single joint experts if other parties are given all relevant information about the previous involvement.

17.5   The appointment of a single joint expert does not prevent parties from instructing their own experts to advise (but the costs of such expert advisers may not be recoverable in the case).

Joint instructions

17.6   The parties should try to agree joint instructions to single joint experts, but, in default of agreement, each party may give instructions. In particular, all parties should try to agree what documents should be included with instructions and what assumptions single joint experts should make.

17.7   Where the parties fail to agree joint instructions, they should try to agree where the areas of disagreement lie and their instructions should make this clear. If separate instructions are given, they should be copied at the same time to the other instructing parties.

17.8   Where experts are instructed by two or more parties, the terms of appointment should, unless the court has directed otherwise, or the parties have agreed otherwise, include:
   (a)   a statement that all the instructing parties are jointly and severally liable to pay the experts' fees and, accordingly, that experts' invoices should be sent simultaneously to all instructing parties or their solicitors (as appropriate); and
   (b)   a statement as to whether any order has been made limiting the amount of experts' fees and expenses (CPR 35.8(4)(a)).

17.9   Where instructions have not been received by the expert from one or more of the instructing parties the expert should give notice (normally at least 7 days) of a deadline to all instructing parties for the receipt by the expert of such instructions. Unless the instructions are received within the deadline the expert may begin work. In the event that instructions are received after the deadline but before the signing off of the report the expert should consider whether it is practicable to comply with those instructions without adversely affecting the timetable set for delivery of the report and in such a manner as to comply with the proportionality principle. An expert who decides to issue a report without taking into account instructions received after the deadline should inform the parties who may apply to the court for directions. In either event the report must show clearly that the expert did not receive instructions within the deadline, or, as the case may be, at all.

Conduct of the single joint expert

17.10   Single joint experts should keep all instructing parties informed of any material steps that they may be taking by, for example, copying all correspondence to those instructing them.

17.11   Single joint experts are Part 35 experts and so have an overriding duty to the court. They are the parties' appointed experts and therefore owe an equal duty to all parties. They should maintain independence, impartiality and transparency at all times.

17.12   Single joint experts should not attend any meeting or conference which is not a joint one, unless all the parties have agreed in writing or the court has directed that such a meeting may be held[4] and who is to pay the experts' fees for the meeting.

---

4   *Peet* v *Mid Kent Area Healthcare NHS Trust* [2002] 1 WLR 210.

17.13   Single joint experts may request directions from the court - see Section 11 above.

17.14   Single joint experts should serve their reports simultaneously on all instructing parties. They should provide a single report even though they may have received instructions which contain areas of conflicting fact or allegation. If conflicting instructions lead to different opinions (for example, because the instructions require experts to make different assumptions of fact), reports may need to contain more than one set of opinions on any issue. It is for the court to determine the facts.

Cross-examination

17.15   Single joint experts do not normally give oral evidence at trial but if they do, all parties may cross-examine them. In general written questions (CPR 35.6) should be put to single joint experts before requests are made for them to attend court for the purpose of cross-examination[5].

18. Discussions between experts

18.1   The court has powers to direct discussions between experts for the purposes set out in the Rules (CPR 35.12). Parties may also agree that discussions take place between their experts.

18.2   Where single joint experts have been instructed but parties have, with the permission of the court, instructed their own additional Part 35 experts, there may, if the court so orders or the parties agree, be discussions between the single joint experts and the additional Part 35 experts. Such discussions should be confined to those matters within the remit of the additional Part 35 experts or as ordered by the court.

18.3   The purpose of discussions between experts should be, wherever possible, to:
   (a)   identify and discuss the expert issues in the proceedings;
   (b)   reach agreed opinions on those issues, and, if that is not possible, to narrow the issues in the case;
   (c)   identify those issues on which they agree and disagree and summarise their reasons for disagreement on any issue; and
   (d)   identify what action, if any, may be taken to resolve any of the outstanding issues between the parties.

Arrangements for discussions between experts

18.4   Arrangements for discussions between experts should be proportionate to the value of cases. In small claims and fast-track cases there should not normally be meetings between experts. Where discussion is justified in such cases, telephone discussion or an exchange of letters should, in the interests of proportionality, usually suffice. In multi-track cases, discussion may be face to face, but the practicalities or the proportionality principle may require discussions to be by telephone or video conference.

18.5   The parties, their lawyers and experts should co-operate to produce the agenda for any discussion between experts, although primary responsibility for preparation of the agenda should normally lie with the parties' solicitors.

18.6   The agenda should indicate what matters have been agreed and summarise concisely those which are in issue. It is often helpful for it to include questions to be answered by the experts. If agreement cannot be reached promptly or a party

---

5   *Daniels* v *Walker* [2000] 1 WLR 1382.

is unrepresented, the court may give directions for the drawing up of the agenda. The agenda should be circulated to experts and those instructing them to allow sufficient time for the experts to prepare for the discussion.

18.7   Those instructing experts must not instruct experts to avoid reaching agreement (or to defer doing so) on any matter within the experts' competence. Experts are not permitted to accept such instructions.

18.8   The parties' lawyers may only be present at discussions between experts if all the parties agree or the court so orders. If lawyers do attend, they should not normally intervene except to answer questions put to them by the experts or to advise about the law[6].

18.9   The content of discussions between experts should not be referred to at trial unless the parties agree (CPR 35.12(4)). It is good practice for any such agreement to be in writing.

18.10   At the conclusion of any discussion between experts, a statement should be prepared setting out:
  (a)   a list of issues that have been agreed, including, in each instance, the basis of agreement;
  (b)   a list of issues that have not been agreed, including, in each instance, the basis of disagreement;
  (c)   a list of any further issues that have arisen that were not included in the original agenda for discussion;
  (d)   a record of further action, if any, to be taken or recommended, including as appropriate the holding of further discussions between experts.

18.11   The statement should be agreed and signed by all the parties to the discussion as soon as may be practicable.

18.12   Agreements between experts during discussions do not bind the parties unless the parties expressly agree to be bound by the agreement (CPR 35.12(5)). However, in view of the overriding objective, parties should give careful consideration before refusing to be bound by such an agreement and be able to explain their refusal should it become relevant to the issue of costs.

19. Attendance of experts at court

19.1   Experts instructed in cases have an obligation to attend court if called upon to do so and accordingly should ensure that those instructing them are always aware of their dates to be avoided and take all reasonable steps to be available.

19.2   Those instructing experts should:
  (a)   ascertain the availability of experts before trial dates are fixed;
  (b)   keep experts updated with timetables (including the dates and times experts are to attend) and the location of the court;
  (c)   give consideration, where appropriate, to experts giving evidence via a video-link.
  (d)   inform experts immediately if trial dates are vacated.

19.3   Experts should normally attend court without the need for the service of witness summonses, but on occasion they may be served to require attendance (CPR 34). The use of witness summonses does not affect the contractual or other obligations of the parties to pay experts' fees.

---

6   *Hubbard* v *Lambeth, Southwark and Lewisham HA* [2001] EWCA 1455.

Appendix III

Guidelines

EXPERT'S DECLARATION

The expert's declaration can take different forms. The definitive guidance can be found in CPR 35 and the Practice Direction.

At the end of an expert's report there must be a statement that the expert understands and has complied with his or her duty to the court. This is expanded in the Practice Direction accompanying CPR 35.

The Expert Witness Institute

The Expert Witness Institute has suggested the following:

> I understand that my overriding duty is to the court and I have complied with that duty and will continue to comply with it.
>
> I am aware of the requirements of Part 35 and Practice Direction 35 and the CJC Protocol for the Instruction of Experts to give Evidence in Civil Claims.

Statement of truth

In addition, experts' reports must be verified by a statement of truth (PD 35, para. 3.3). The *wording is mandatory and must not be modified* (PD 35 annex, para. 13.5). The new version says: 'I confirm that I have made clear which facts and matters referred to in this report are within my own knowledge and which are not. Those that are within my own knowledge I confirm to be true. The opinions I have expressed represent my true and complete professional opinions on the matters to which they refer.'

Experts Declaration and relevant instructions

The Expert Witness Institute has suggested the following:

> I am aware of the requires of Part 35 & Practice Direction 35, Protocol for the Instruction of Experts to give Evidence in Civil Claims and the Practice Direction on Pre-Action Conduct.
>
> I understand that my overriding duty is to the court, both in preparing reports and in giving oral evidence. I have complied and will continue to comply with that duty
>
> I have set out in my report what I understand from those instructing me to be the questions in respect of which my opinion as an expert are required.
>
> I have done my best, in preparing this report, to be accurate and complete. I have mentioned all matters which I regard as relevant to the opinions I have expressed. All of the matters on which I have expressed an opinion lie within my field of expertise.

I have drawn to the attention of the court all matters, of which I am aware, which might adversely affect my opinion.

Wherever I have no personal knowledge, I have indicated the source of factual information.

I have not included anything in this report which has been suggested to me by anyone, including the lawyers, instructing me, without forming my own independent view of the matter.

Where, in my view, there is a range of reasonable opinion, I have indicated the extent of that range in the report.

At the time of signing the report I consider it to be complete and accurate. I will notify those instructing me if, for any reason, I subsequently consider that the report requires any correction or qualification.

I understand that this report will be the evidence that I will give under oath, subject to any correction or qualification I make before swearing to its veracity.

I have included in this report a statement setting out the substance of all facts and instructions given to me which are material to the opinions expressed in this report or upon which those opinions are based.

That I know of no conflict of interest of any kind, other than any which I have disclosed in my report.

That I do not consider that any interest which I have disclosed affects my suitability as an expert witness on any issues on which I have given evidence.

That I will advise the party by whom I am instructed if, between the date of my report and the trial, there is a change in circumstances which affect my answers to either of the above two points.

The Academy of Experts

Alternatively the Academy of Experts recommends:

Statement of Truth in Civil Proceedings – effective 1 October 2009

I confirm that I have made clear which facts and matters referred to in this report are within my own knowledge and which are not. Those that are within my own knowledge I confirm to be true. The opinions I have expressed represent my true and complete professional opinions on the matters to which they refer.

Appendix IV

Directions

MODEL DIRECTIONS FOR CLINICAL NEGLIGENCE CASES (2012) – BEFORE MASTER YOXALL AND MASTER ROBERTS AND IN MANY OTHER COURTS INSIDE AND OUTSIDE LONDON

Introductory note

These are the Model Directions for use in the first Case Management Conference in clinical negligence cases before the Masters.

A draft order in Word format, adopting the Model Directions as necessary, is to be provided by e-mail to the Master at least 2 days before the hearing.

Although there are no radical changes from the 2007 directions, **parties are requested to use the form of order at the end of this document.**

The e-mail addresses of the Masters are:

master.yoxall@judiciary.gsi.gov.uk

master.roberts@judiciary.gsi.gov.uk

The Model Directions allow the court and the parties to be flexible. For example, sequential exchange of quantum statements (say, with schedule and counter-schedule of loss) may be appropriate. The sequential exchange of expert evidence on breach of duty and causation may sometimes be appropriate.

It would be helpful if dates appeared in **bold** type.

Please note: Solicitors must ensure that the claimant is accurately described in the title to the order: for example, 'JOHN SMITH (a child and protected party by his mother and Litigation Friend, JOAN SMITH). It is never permissible to refer to such a claimant as 'JOHN SMITH'.

The order should make it clear that it is made pursuant to a Case Management Conference or an application or both.

Note the important change to the direction relating to experts and their role in the preparation of Agendas.

The Model Directions

The annotations in italics are to assist the parties and are not part of the Model Directions and need not appear in the order.

A draft order – without the annotations – appears at the end of this document. Parties are requested to adopt this draft.

Allocation

1. The case do remain on the Multi-track.

Allocation: The order states that 'the case do remain on the Multi-track'. Allocation will usually have already been dealt with on allocation questionnaires.

Preservation of Evidence

2.   The defendant do retain and preserve safely the original clinical notes relating to the action pending the trial. The defendant do give facilities for inspection by the claimant, the claimant's legal advisers and experts of the said original notes upon 7 days written notice to do so.

Maintenance of records and reports

3.   Legible copies of the medical (and educational) records of the claimant / deceased / claimant's mother are to be placed in a separate paginated bundle at the earliest opportunity by the claimant's solicitors and kept up to date. All references to medical notes in any report are to be made by reference to the pages in that bundle.

Amendments

The following is suggested:
   Permission to claimant / defendant to amend the Particulars of Claim / Defence in terms of the draft initialed by the Master [or the draft served on / /09]; the defendant to serve an amended defence by / /09. Costs of and occasioned by the amendments to be borne by (usually, the party seeking permission to amend). [Where no draft is available, but the form of the amendments is not contentious] (Party wishing to amend) to serve draft amended [Statement of Case] by / /09. If no objection to the draft amendments, response to be served by / /09, if objection is taken to the draft, permission to restore.

Judgment

The following is suggested:
   There be judgment for the Claimant with damages to be assessed.
   Or
   There be judgment for the Claimant for ...% of the damages as are assessed (or agreed by the parties) as due on a full liability basis.

Split Trial

[An order 'That there be a split trial' is inappropriate. The following is suggested.]

4.   A preliminary issue shall be tried between the claimant and the defendant as to whether or not the defendant is liable to the claimant by reason of the matters alleged in the Particulars of Claim and, if so, whether or not any of the injuries pleaded were caused thereby; if any such injuries were so caused, the extent of the same.

Disclosure

5.   There be standard disclosure [on the preliminary issue] [limited to quantum] by list by 2012. Any initial request for inspection or copy documents is to be made within 7 to 14 days of service of the lists.

Factual Evidence

6.   Signed and dated witness statements of fact in respect of breach of duty and causation [and quantum] shall be simultaneously exchanged by   2012. Civil Evidence Act notices are to be served by the same date. The witness statements of all concerned with the treatment and care of the claimant at the time of the matters alleged against the defendant shall be served under this paragraph.

7.   Signed and dated witness statements of fact in respect of quantum, condition and prognosis shall be served by   2012 (claimant) and   2012 (defendant). Civil Evidence Act notices are to be served by the same date.

Expert Evidence

A. Single Joint Experts.

8.   Each party has permission to rely on the evidence of a single joint expert in the following fields: [state the disciplines]. The experts are to be instructed by   2012 and the joint expert is to provide his report by   2012. In case of difficulty, the parties have permission to restore before the Master.

If the parties are unable to agree on the identity of the expert to be instructed, the parties to restore the CMC before the Master. At such hearing the parties are to provide details of the CVs, availability and the estimated fee of the expert they propose and reasoned objections to any other proposed.

B. Separate Experts.

9.   In respect of breach of duty and causation, each party has permission to rely on the evidence of an expert in the following fields: [state the disciplines]; permission being given to call the said experts on matters remaining in issue.

The reports of the said experts are to be simultaneously exchanged by   2012.

10.   In respect of quantum, condition and prognosis, each party ([where there are several defendants] the defendants acting jointly, unless otherwise directed) has permission to rely on the evidence of an expert in the following fields: [state the disciplines]; permission being given to call the said experts on matters remaining in issue.

The reports of the said experts are to be served by:
Claimant: 2012
Defendant(s):   2012

Literature and CVs

11.   Any unpublished literature upon which any expert witness proposes to rely shall be served at the same time as service of his report together with a list of published literature. Any supplementary literature upon which any expert witness proposes to rely shall be notified to all other parties at least one month before trial. No expert witness shall rely upon any publications that have not been disclosed in accordance with this direction without the permission of the trial judge on such terms as to costs as he deems fit.

12.   Experts shall, at the time of producing their reports, produce a CV giving details of any employment or activity which raises a possible conflict of interest.

Experts' Discussions

13.   **Unless otherwise agreed by all parties' solicitors, after consulting with the experts**, the experts of like discipline for the parties shall discuss the case on a without prejudice basis by   2012. (Usually 8 weeks after the exchange of reports).

Discussions between experts are not mandatory. The parties should consider, with their expert, whether there is likely to be any useful purpose in holding a discussion and should be prepared to agree that no discussion is in fact needed.

> (a)   The purpose of the discussions is to identify:
> > (i)   The extent of the agreement between the experts;
> > (ii)   The points of disagreement and short reasons for disagreement;
> > (iii) Action, if any, which may be taken to resolve the outstanding points of disagreement;
> > (iv) Any further material points not raised in the agenda and the extent to which these issues are agreed;

(b) **Unless otherwise agreed by all parties' solicitors, after consulting with the experts,** a draft agenda which directs the experts to the remaining issues relevant to the experts' discipline, as identified in the statements of case shall be prepared jointly by the claimant's solicitors and experts and sent to the defendant's solicitors for comment at least 35 days before the agreed date for the experts' discussions;

Claimants' solicitors and counsel should note the obligation to prepare the draft agenda jointly with the relevant expert. Experts should note that it is part of their overriding duty to the court to ensure that the agenda complies with the following direction.

The use of agendas is not mandatory. Solicitors should consult with the experts to ensure that agendas are necessary and, if used, are reasonable in scope. The agenda should assist the experts and should not be in the form of leading questions or hostile in tone. An agenda must include a list of the outstanding issues in the preamble.

[Note: The preamble should state: the Standard of proof: the Bolam test: remind the experts not to attempt to determine factual issues: remind them not to stray outside their field of expertise and indicate the form of the joint statement. It will also be helpful to provide a comprehensive list of the materials which each expert has seen, perhaps in the form of an agreed supplementary bundle (it is assumed that experts will have been provided with the medical notes bundle)]

(c) The defendants shall within 21 days of receipt agree the agenda, or propose amendments;

(d) Seven days thereafter all solicitors shall use their best endeavours to agree the agenda. Points of disagreement should be on matters of real substance and not semantics or on matters the experts could resolve of their own accord at the discussion. In default of agreement, both versions shall be considered at the discussions. agendas, when used, shall be provided to the experts not less than 7 days before the date fixed for discussions.

[Where it has been impossible to agree a single agenda, it is of assistance to the experts if the second agenda is consecutively numbered to the first, i.e. if the first agenda has 16 questions in it, the second agenda is numbered from 17 onwards]

14. **Unless otherwise ordered by the court, or unless agreed by all parties, including the experts,** neither the parties nor their legal representatives may attend such discussions. If the legal representatives do attend, they should not normally intervene in the discussion, except to answer questions put to them by the experts or to advise on the law; and the experts may if they so wish hold part of their discussions in the absence of the legal representatives.

15. A signed joint statement shall be prepared by the experts dealing with (a) (i) – (iv) above. Individual copies of such statements shall be signed by the experts at the conclusion of the discussion, or as soon thereafter as practicable and provided to the parties' solicitors within **7 days** of the discussions.

16. Experts give their own opinions to assist the court and should attend discussions on the basis that they have full authority to sign the joint statement. The experts should not require the authorisation of solicitor or counsel before signing a joint statement.

[Note: This does not affect Rule 35.12 which provides that where experts reach agreement on an issue during their discussions, the

agreement shall not bind the parties unless the parties expressly agree to be bound by the agreement]

17.   If an expert radically alters his or her opinion, the joint statement should include a note or addendum by that expert explaining the change of opinion.

18.   Experts instructed by the parties in accordance with this and any subsequent Order shall be provided with a copy of the Order within 7 days after it is sealed, or at the time of instruction, whichever is the later.

Schedules and periodical payments

19.   Claimant do serve a final schedule of loss and damage costed to the date of trial by   2012.

20.   The Defendant do serve a counter-schedule by   2012.

21.   The parties do set out their respective positions on the periodical payment of damages in the schedule and counter-schedule of loss. [or, The periodical payment of damages is not appropriate to this case.]

[Periodical Payments. Parties should, at the first CMC, be prepared to give their provisional view as to whether the case is one in which the periodical payment of damages might be appropriate.

Schedules. Parties are encouraged to exchange schedules in a form which enables the counter schedule to be based on the claimant's schedule i.e. by delivering a disk with the hard copy, or by sending it as an e-mail attachment.]

Trial Directions

22.   The Claimant's Solicitors do by   2012 apply to the Clerk of the Lists in London / [the Listing Officer in the venue] for a listing appointment for a trial period for hearing within the trial window and give notice of the appointment to the defendant. Pre-trial check lists to be filed as directed by the Clerk of the Lists.

   Mode of trial: Judge alone; London [other venue]; Category [Usually] B; time estimate   days.

   Trial window:

   [Certified fit for High Court Judge if available].

Trial Directions

The claimant will usually be directed to apply to the Clerk of the Lists for a listing appointment no later than 6 weeks after the CMC.

   The Clerk of the Lists, in order to maintain the necessary degree of flexibility for listing, will give a 'trial period' rather than a fixed date, but, in order to accommodate the parties' need for certainty as to dates for experts to attend, will, if an approach is made closer to the beginning of the trial period, confirm the date for the trial to begin as the first day of the trial period.

   The trial period will usually be directed to begin at least 2 clear months after the last event besides ADR – this is to allow for ADR.

   In relatively modest claims (in term of quantum), the Master may direct:

   'If the parties reach agreement upon breach of duty and causation, the parties are to immediately restore the case before the Master so that alternative directions on the assessment of damages may be given.'

23.   Parties do agree the contents of the trial bundle and exchange skeleton arguments not less than 7 days before the hearing. Claimant to lodge the skeleton arguments and the Trial bundle under PD 39.3

Trial Bundles

Note: the object is to ensure that all the relevant material is provided at one time to the Clerk of the Lists to pass to the trial judge. The PD sets out both the contents of the bundle and the time when it must be lodged.

Alternative Dispute Resolution

24. The parties shall by   2012 [a date usually about 3 months before the trial window opens] consider whether the case is capable of resolution by ADR. If any party considers that the case is unsuitable for resolution by ADR, that party shall be prepared to justify that decision at the conclusion of the trial, should the trial judge consider that such means of resolution were appropriate, when he is considering the appropriate costs order to make.

25. Such means of ADR as shall be adopted shall be concluded not less than 35 days prior to the trial.

26. The party considering the case unsuitable for ADR shall, not less than 28 days before the commencement of the trial, file with the court a Witness Statement, without prejudice save as to costs, giving the reasons upon which they rely for saying that the case was unsuitable. The Witness Statement shall not be disclosed to the trial Judge until the conclusion of the case.

   ['ADR' includes 'round table' conferences, at which the parties attempt to define and narrow the issues in the case, including those to which expert evidence is directed; early neutral evaluation; mediation; and arbitration. The object is to try to reduce the number of cases settled 'at the door of the Court', which are wasteful both of costs and judicial time.]

Further CMC etc

27. There be a further CMC on   2012 at   am/pm; Room 106/109; time estimate 30 minutes. This hearing may be vacated by consent provided that all directions have been complied with; no further directions are required; and the Master is given reasonable notice.

28. Permission to restore.

   [Note: A party may request the restoration of a CMC or application by letter or e-mail to the assigned Master. If possible the Master should be provided with an agreed list of dates to avoid. Where the application is urgent and the time estimate is no more than 30 minutes, the Master will endeavour to list a hearing at 10.00am as soon as possible. Applications estimated to take more than 30 minutes should be applied for as private room appointments in the usual way.]

   [Both Masters are willing, in appropriate cases, to hear applications by telephone link, provided sufficient notice is given **directly to the Master concerned** and the relevant papers are provided in advance. E-mails are an acceptable means of communication, provided that they are copied to all parties.]

   [Note: The court file in cases proceeding before the Masters will not routinely be placed before the Master. Parties wishing for it to be produced should notify the Case Management Section **five clear days** in advance of the appointment. In all other cases parties should bring with them copies of any filed documents upon which they intend to rely.]

29. Costs in case [Or other costs order sought].

30. Claimant to draw and file the order by   2012 and serve the defendant (or claimant to serve sealed order by   2012).

   Dated the

DRAFT ORDER

IN THE HIGH COURT OF JUSTICE   Claim No. HQ09X0zzzz

QUEEN'S BENCH DIVISION

MASTER [YOXALL / ROBERTS]

B E T W E E N

ABC

Claimant

And

DEF NHS TRUST

Defendant

ORDER

UPON a Case Management Conference

[AND UPON the Claimant's / Defendant's application issued on   2012]

AND UPON hearing solicitor/counsel for the Claimant and solicitor/counsel for the Defendant

IT IS ORDERED that

1.   The case do remain on the Multi-track.

2.   The Defendant do retain and preserve safely the original clinical notes relating to the action pending the trial. The Defendant do give facilities for inspection by the Claimant, the Claimant's legal advisers and experts of the said original notes upon 7 days written notice to do so.

3.   Legible copies of the medical (and educational) records of the Claimant / Deceased / Claimant's Mother are to be placed in a separate paginated bundle at the earliest opportunity by the Claimant's Solicitors and kept up to date. All references to medical notes in any report are to be made by reference to the pages in that bundle.

4.   A preliminary issue shall be tried between the Claimant and the Defendant as to whether or not the Defendant is liable to the Claimant by reason of the matters alleged in the Particulars of Claim and, if so, whether or not any of the injuries pleaded were caused thereby; if any such injuries were so caused, the extent of the same.

5.   There be standard disclosure [on the preliminary issue] [limited to quantum] by list by   2012. Any initial request for inspection or copy documents is to be made within 7/14 days of service of the lists.

6.   Signed and dated witness statements of fact in respect of breach of duty and causation [and quantum] shall be simultaneously exchanged by   2012. Civil Evidence Act notices are to be served by the same date. The witness statements of all concerned with the treatment and care of the Claimant at the time of the matters alleged against the Defendant shall be served under this paragraph.

7.   Signed and dated witness statements of fact in respect of quantum, condition and prognosis shall be served by   2012 (Claimant) and   2012 (Defendant). Civil Evidence Act notices are to be served by the same date.

8.   Each party has permission to rely on the evidence of a single joint expert in the following fields: [state the disciplines]. The experts are to be instructed by   2012 and the joint expert is to provide his report by   2012. In case of difficulty, the parties have permission to restore before the Master.

9.   In respect of breach of duty and causation, each party has permission to rely on the evidence of an expert in the following fields: [state the disciplines]; permission being given to call the said experts on matters remaining in issue. The reports of the said experts are to be simultaneously exchanged by   2012.

10.   In respect of quantum, condition and prognosis, each party ([where there are several defendants] the Defendants acting jointly, unless otherwise directed) has permission to rely on the evidence of an expert in the following fields: [state the disciplines]; permission being given to call the said experts on matters remaining in issue. The reports of the said experts are to be served by:
      Claimant: 2012
      Defendant(s):   2012.

11.   Any unpublished literature upon which any expert witness proposes to rely shall be served at the same time as service of his report together with a list of published literature. Any supplementary literature upon which any expert witness proposes to rely shall be notified to all other parties at least one month before trial. No expert witness shall rely upon any publications that have not been disclosed in accordance with this direction without the permission of the trial judge on such terms as to costs as he deems fit.

12.   Experts shall, at the time of producing their reports, produce a CV giving details of any employment or activity which raises a possible conflict of interest.

13.   **Unless otherwise agreed by all parties' solicitors, after consulting with the experts**, the experts of like discipline for the parties shall discuss the case on a without prejudice basis by   2012.
      Discussions between experts are not mandatory. The parties should consider, with their expert, whether there is likely to be any useful purpose in holding a discussion and should be prepared to agree that no discussion is in fact needed.
      (a)   The purpose of the discussions is to identify:
            (i)   The extent of the agreement between the experts;
            (ii)   The points of disagreement and short reasons for disagreement;
            (iii) Action, if any, which may be taken to resolve the outstanding points of disagreement;
            (iv)   Any further material points not raised in the Agenda and the extent to which these issues are agreed;
      (b)   **Unless otherwise agreed by all parties' solicitors, after consulting with the experts,** a draft Agenda which directs the experts to the remaining issues relevant to the experts' discipline, as identified in the statements of case shall be prepared jointly by the Claimant's solicitors and experts and sent to the Defendant's solicitors for comment at least 35 days before the agreed date for the experts' discussions;
            The use of agendas is not mandatory. Solicitors should consult with the experts to ensure that agendas are necessary and, if used, are reasonable in scope. The agenda should assist the experts and should not be in the form of leading questions or hostile in tone. An agenda must include a list of the outstanding issues in the preamble.
      (c)   The Defendants shall within 21 days of receipt agree the Agenda, or propose amendments;
      (d)   Seven days thereafter all solicitors shall use their best endeavours to agree the Agenda. Points of disagreement should be on matters of real substance and not semantics or on matters the experts could resolve of their own accord at the discussion. In default of agreement, both versions shall be considered at the discussions. Agendas, when used, shall be provided to the experts not less than 7 days before the date fixed for discussions.

14.   **Unless otherwise ordered by the Court, or unless agreed by all parties, including the experts**, neither the parties nor their legal representatives may

attend such discussions. If the legal representatives do attend, they should not normally intervene in the discussion, except to answer questions put to them by the experts or to advise on the law; and the experts may if they so wish hold part of their discussions in the absence of the legal representatives.

15.   A signed joint statement shall be prepared by the experts dealing with (a) (i) – (iv) above. Individual copies of such statements shall be signed by the experts at the conclusion of the discussion, or as soon thereafter as practicable and provided to the parties' solicitors within **7 days** of the discussions.

16.   Experts give their own opinions to assist the court and should attend discussions on the basis that they have full authority to sign the joint statement. The experts should not require the authorisation of solicitor or counsel before signing a joint statement.

17.   If an expert radically alters his or her opinion, the joint statement should include a note or addendum by that expert explaining the change of opinion.

18.   Claimant do serve a final Schedule of loss and damage costed to the date of trial by   2012.

19.   The Defendant do serve a Counter-Schedule by   2012.

20.   The parties do set out their respective positions on the periodical payment of damages in the Schedule and Counter-Schedule of loss.

21.   The Claimant's Solicitors do by   2012 apply to the Clerk of the Lists in London / [the Listing Officer in the venue] for a listing appointment for a trial period for hearing within the trial window and give notice of the appointment to the Defendant. Pre-trial check lists to be filed as directed by the Clerk of the Lists.
    Mode of trial: Judge alone; London[other venue]; Category [Usually] B; time estimate   days.
    Trial window:
    [Certified fit for High Court Judge if available].

22.   Parties do agree the contents of the trial bundle and exchange skeleton arguments not less than 7 days before the hearing. Claimant to lodge the skeleton arguments and the Trial bundle under PD 39.3

23.   The parties shall by   2012 [a date usually about 3 months before the trial window opens] consider whether the case is capable of resolution by ADR. If any party considers that the case is unsuitable for resolution by ADR, that party shall be prepared to justify that decision at the conclusion of the trial, should the trial judge consider that such means of resolution were appropriate, when he is considering the appropriate costs order to make.

24.   Such means of ADR as shall be adopted shall be concluded not less than 35 days prior to the trial.

25.   The party considering the case unsuitable for ADR shall, not less than 28 days before the commencement of the trial, file with the Court a Witness Statement, without prejudice save as to costs, giving the reasons upon which they rely for saying that the case was unsuitable. The Witness Statement shall not be disclosed to the trial Judge until the conclusion of the case.

26.   There be a further CMC on   2012 at   am/pm; Room 106/109; time estimate 30 minutes. This hearing may be vacated by consent provided that all directions have been complied with; no further directions are required; and the Master is given reasonable notice.

27.   Permission to restore.

28.   Costs in case [Or other costs order sought].

29.   Claimant to draw and file the order by   2012 and serve the Defendant
(or Claimant to serve sealed order by   2012).
      Dated the

[*Note: the Court File in cases proceeding before the Masters will not be placed before the Master. Parties wishing for it to be produced should notify the Registry in Room E07 FIVE CLEAR DAYS in advance of the appointment. In all other cases parties should bring with them copies of any filed documents upon which they intend to rely.*]

[The Model Directions may be changed soon. Sir Rupert Jackson has given HHJ Grenfell the task of constructing uniform Model Directions and there has been discussion between Master Yoxall, Master Roberts and various District Judges as to what form the new directions should take. Master Yoxall and Master Roberts expect to agree new Model Directions for use in the RCJ in the next couple of months (from 23 January 2012) or so.]

[*These model directions are reproduced by kind permission of Master Yoxall and Master Roberts.*]

Appendix V

Common hieroglyphs and abbreviations

Here is a list of common abbreviations and hieroglyphs, reproduced by kind permission of Ann Winyard.

COMMON HIEROGLYPHS

+ + +	much/many
#	fracture
Δ	diagnosis
diff. Δ or ΔΔ	differential diagnosis
R	treatment
J° (no jaundice)	nil/nothing/no
↑	up, increasing
N,→	constant, normal or lateral shift (eg of apex of heart)
↓	down, decreasing
⊥	central (of the trachea)
$\frac{1}{7}$	one day
$\frac{2}{52}$	two weeks
$\frac{3}{12}$	three months
T38.6°C	temperature 38.6
T−14	term (ie date baby due) less two weeks
T+7	term plus one week
$\frac{35+4}{40}$	35 weeks and 4 days
$\frac{37+3}{40}$	37 weeks and 3 days

COMMON ABBREVIATIONS

AAL	Anterior axillary line
ATCH	Adrenocorticotrophic hormone
AE	Air entry
AFB	Acid fast bacillus (TB)

AFP	Alpha-fetoprotein (maternal serum and occasionally amniotic fluid levels tested in pregnancy to screen for neural tube defect in foetus).
AJ	Ankle jerk (reflex: see also BJ, KJ, SJ, TJ)
Anti-D	This gamma globulin must be given by injection to Rhesus negative mother who delivers/aborts Rhesus positive child/foetus to prevent mother developing antibodies which could damage a subsequent Rhesus positive baby.
Apgar	Apgar score: means of recording baby's condition at birth by observing and 'scoring' (0, 1 or 2) 5 parameters
A/V	Anteverted
BJ	Biceps jerk (reflex: see AJ)
BNF (plus date)	British National Formulary (prescriber's 'bible' supplied free to all NHS doctors). New edition each year. You can buy one (about £10 from medical bookshops).
BO	Bowels open
BP (plus date)	British pharmacopoeia
BP	Blood pressure
BS	(a) Breath sounds (b) Bowel sounds (c) Blood sugar
c	With (Latin: cum)
C_2H_5OH	Alcohol
Ca	(a) Carcinoma/cancer (b) Calcium
Caps	Capsules
CAT scan	Computed axial tomograph
CNS	Central nervous system
CO	Complaining of
CO_2	Carbon dioxide
COETT	Cuffed oral endotracheal tube (see COT and ETT)
COT	Cuffed oral tube (endotracheal tube used for ventilating a patient who cannot breath unaided)
CPD	Cephalo-pelvic disproportion (baby too big to fit through pelvis)
CSF	Cerebo-spinal fluid
CTG	Cardiotocograph (trace during labour of baby's heart and mum's contractions)
CVA	Cerebo-vascular accident (stroke)
CVS	Cardio-vascular system
Cx	Cervix
CXR	Chest X-ray
DNA	(a) Did not attend (b) Deoxyribonucleic acid
D & V	Diarrhoea and vomiting
DOA	Dead on arrival
DVT	Deep vein thrombosis
Dx	Diagnosis
EGG	Electro-cardiogram/graph (electric heart recording)
ECT	Electro-convulsive therapy
EDC	Expected date of confinement
EDD	Expected date of delivery
EEG	Electroencephalogram/graph (brain scan)
ERCP	Endoscopic retrograde choledochopancreatico/graphy/scopy
ERPC	Evacuation of retained products of conception

ESR	Erythrocyte sedimentation rate (blood)
EtOH	Another code for alcohol
ETT	Endotracheal tube (see COT above)
FB	Finger's breadth
FBC	Full blood count
FBS	Fetal blood sampling (carried out during labour to check baby's condition)
FH	Family history
FHH	Foetal heart heard
FHHR	Foetal heart heard regular
FHR	Foetal heart rate
FLK	(Used by paediatricians) Funny looking kid
FMF	Foetal movements felt
FSE	Foetal scalp electrode
FSH	(a) Family and social history
	(b) Follicle-stimulating hormone (produced in pregnancy)
GA	General anaesthetic
GFR	Glomerular filtration rate
GIT	Gastro-intestinal tract
GTT	Glucose tolerance test (for diabetes)
GUT	Genito-urinary tract
Hb	Haemoglobin (blood)
HPC	History of presenting complaint
HS	Heart sounds
HVS	High vaginal swab
Hx	History
ICS	Intercostal space (usually as xICS, where x = a number from 1 to 11)
IJ	Internal jugular vein
IM	Intramuscular
IVI	Intravenous infusion (drip)
JVP	Jugular vein pressure
K	Potassium
KJ	Knee jerk (reflex: see AJ)
kPa	Kilopascal, approximately 7.5 mmHg
L	Litre
LA	Local anaesthetic
LFTs	Liver function tests
LIH	Left inguinal hernia
LMP	Last menstrual period
LN	Lymph node
LOA	Left occiput anterior (position of baby's head at delivery; see also LOP, ROA, ROP)
LOC	Loss of consciousness
LOL	Left occipitolateral
LOP	Left occiput posterior (see LOA above)
LSCS	Lower segment caesarean section (the 'normal' type of caesarean)
LSKK	Liver, spleen and kidneys
mcg	Microgram
MCL	Mic clavicular line
µg	Microgram
mg	Milligram
mist	Mixture
ml	Mililitre
mmHG	Milimitres of mercury (pressure)

mMOL	Milimol
N & V	Nausea and vomiting
Na	Sodium
NaHCO₃	Sodium bicarbonate (alkaline substance: *inter alia* given to counteract metabolic acidosis following oxygen deprivation)
NAD	Nothing abnormal diagnosed/detected
NBM	Nil by mouth
ng	Nanogram
NG	Carcinoma/cancer (neoplastic growth)
NMCS	No malignant cells seen
NOF	Neck of femur
N/S	Normal size
O₂	Oxygen
OA	Occipito-posterior
P	Pulse
π	Period
Pco₂	Partial pressure of carbon dioxide (normally in blood)
PERLA	Pupils are equal and react to light and accommodation
PE	(a) Pulmonary embolism
	(b) Pre-eclampsia
PET	Pre-eclamptic toxaemia
pg	Pictogram
pH	Negative log of hydrogen icon activity: 'acidity and alkalinity' scale. Low is acidic. High is alkaline. pH7 is about neutral.
PH	Past/previous history
PID	(a) Pelvic inflammatory disease
	(b) Prolapsed intervertebral disc
PMH	Past/previous medical history
PN(R)	Percussion note (resonant)
PO₂	Partial pressure of oxygen (normally in blood)
POH	Past/previous obstetric history
po	Per os (by mouth)
pr	Per rectum (by the rectum)
prn	As required – of, eg, pain killers
pv	Per vaginam (by the vagina)
RBC	Red blood cell (erythrocyte)
Rh	Rhesus (blood type, can cause problems in pregnancy if mother is Rhesus *negative* and father Rhesus *positive*)
RIH	Right inguinal hernia
ROA	Right occiput anterior (see LOA above)
ROL	Right occipito-lateral
ROM	Range of movement
ROP	Right occiput posterior (see LOA above)
RS	Respiratory system
RTI	Respiratory tract infection
s	Without (Latin: sine)
S/B	seen by
S/D	Systolic/diastolic (heart and circulation)
SH	Social history
SJ	Supinator jerk (reflex: see AJ)
SOA	Swelling of ankles
SOB (OE)	Short of breath (on exertion)
SOS	(a) si opus sit (if necessary)
	(b) see other sheet
SROM	Spontaneous rupture of membranes (labour)

SVC	Superior vena cava
SVD	Spontaneous vaginal delivery
SVT	Supraventricular tachycardia
TCI/52	To come in, in 2 weeks' time
TGH	To go home
THR	Total hip replacement
TIA	Transient ischemic attack
TJ	Triceps jerk (reflex: see AJ)
TVF	Tactile vocal fremitus
U & E	Urea and electrolytes (biochemical tests)
URTI	Upper respiratory tract infection
UTI	Urinary tract infection
VE	Vaginal examination
VF	Ventricular fibrillation
VT	Ventricular tachycardia
V/V	Vulva and vagina
WBC	White blood corpuscle/white blood cell count
XR	X-ray

Appendix VI

The Hippocratic oath

This oath, taken at the time of graduation by medical students at some universities, dates back to the 4th century BC. It was handed down as part of the *Hippocratic Collection*, a philosophy developed by the Greeks from the writings of Hippocrates and others, from which the whole of their science grew. One version of the oath states:

> I will look upon him who shall have taught me this Art even as one of my parents. I will share my substance with him, and I will supply his necessities, if he be in need. I will regard his offspring even as my own brethren, and I will teach them this Art, if they would learn it, without fee or covenant. I will impart this Art by precept, by lecture and by every mode of teaching, not only to my own sons, but to the sons of him who taught me, and to disciples bound by covenant and oath, according to the Law of Medicine.

> The regimen I adopt shall be for the benefit of my patients according to my ability and judgment, and not for their hurt or for any wrong. I will give no deadly drug to any, though it be asked of me, nor will I counsel such, and especially I will not aid a woman to procure abortion. Whatsoever house I enter, there will I go for the benefit of the sick, refraining from all wrongdoing or corruption, and especially from any act of seduction of male or female, of bond or free. Whatsoever things I see or hear concerning the life of men, in my attendance on the sick, or even apart therefrom, which ought not to be noised abroad, I will keep silence thereon, counting such things to be as sacred secrets.

Clinical negligence funding checklist (abridged version)

Below are the proposed costs limitations/contract prices to cover all work in a publicly funded clinical negligence case. If the likely final costs exceed £25,000 a High Cost Case contract will be entered into when the certificate is first amended. The VHCC contract terms are unaffected by the Funding Checklist.

If the attached questionnaires are answered in full and the proposed costs limitations agreed there is no need to provide a separate case plan or detailed costs schedule.

These staged sums represent the maximum likely to be authorised and payable by the LSC if the case is unsuccessful. These sums will be revised downwards if necessary to keep cases within the Funding Code cost/benefit ratios: (1:4 for cases with 50–60% prospects, 1:2 for cases with 60–80% prospects, 1:1 for cases with 80%+ prospects).

The proposed stages are:

1 – The Investigative Stage, 2 – Issue of Proceedings to Mutual Exchange, 3 – Settlement, 4 – Trial, 5 – Quantum Investigations, 6 – Quantum Trial

Hourly rates (1st £25,000)

Solicitor – £120 ph (i.e. £75 + 60% enhancement), Leading Counsel – £250 ph, Senior Junior acting alone – £150 ph, Junior Counsel – £125 ph, Medical Experts – £200 ph or less.

Hourly rates (post £25,000)

Solicitor – £70 ph, Senior Counsel – £90 ph, Junior Counsel – £50 ph.

Simplified claims for payment

Where you have agreed costs limits with the Special Cases Unit using the Funding Checklist there is no need to submit a detailed bill. Please submit Claim 1 (omitting detailed schedule on page 4) and attach: (a) this Funding Checklist (b) your time recording sheets for each stage (c) counsel's fee notes (d) disbursement vouchers.

Bills for cases (or stages) funded by a Regional Office should continue to be submitted in the usual way.

INVESTIGATIVE HELP – APP1 (STAGE 1)

Includes attendance on client, medical records, client statement(s), instructing experts, considering reports, supplementary questions to experts, instructing counsel, conference(s) with counsel and experts, protocol letter and response.

- **1 expert – £5,000**
- **2 experts – £7,500**
- **3 experts – £10,000–£15,000**
- **4 experts – £15,000–£20,000**
- **5/6 experts (+ MRI) – £22,500–£25,000**

For authorisation of the above sums please answer the following:

(a) Please provide a brief statement (in addition to any client statement) including date of injury, date of knowledge, nature of injury, prognosis (if known), likely particulars of negligence. **Please ensure you have addressed the funding requirement that the NHS complaints procedure is followed unless clearly inappropriate.**

(b) Are there any additional risk factors e.g. limitation, multiple defendants, client credibility (client evidence conflicts with medical records)?

(c) List all medical experts likely to be instructed before proceedings are issued and in relation to each:
  – Discipline of expert (and name if known)
  – Medical issue the expert will address
  – Proposed order of instruction
  – Approximate timetable for instruction and receipt of report

(d) Have there been any informal or informal admissions (e.g. through the complaints procedure)?

(e) An estimate of costs:
  – To date (if any)
  – To conclude investigative stage (Stage 1)
  – To conclude settlement
  – To conclude trial

(f) Is a split trial likely to be appropriate? Please give brief reason. (In a case where numerous quantum experts are required the assumption will be that funding is provided on the basis of a split trial unless liability/causation is conceded or a realistic offer of settlement has been made)

(g) An estimated date for pre-issue conference with counsel and expert

(h) An estimated date for final hearing

(i) An estimate of general and special damages, specifying likely heads of damage. A broad estimate is acceptable if quantum is complex or the prognosis unclear.

(j) The assumption at this stage is that prospects are unclear. Please confirm.

ISSUE OF PROCEEDINGS – MUTUAL EXCHANGE (STAGE 2)

Includes issue/service, allocation questionnaire, CMC, considering Defence, experts' consideration of defence/revision of reports, exchanging statements and reports, Part 35, conference with counsel and experts.

There is an assumption that Leading Counsel may be involved in a 4/5 expert case.

- **1 expert – £7,500**
- **2 experts – £10,000**
- **3 experts – £12000–£15,000**
- **4 experts – £15,000–£17,500**
- **5 experts – £17,500–£20,000**

For authorisation of the above sums please answer the following:

(a) Please provide a brief updated report on case including particulars of negligence, causation, injury and prognosis, defendant's response to letter of claim, any formal or informal admissions. Are there any additional risk factors e.g. limitation, multiple Defendants, client credibility?

(b) List all medical reports obtained and in relation to each:
  – Discipline of expert and name
  – Medical issue addressed
  – Specific conclusion of each expert
(c) Is a split trial likely to be appropriate? Please give brief reason. (In a case where numerous quantum experts are required the assumption will be that funding is provided on the basis of a split trial unless liability/causation is conceded or a realistic offer of settlement has been made)
(d) An estimate of costs:
  – To date
  – To conclude mutual exchange (Stage 2)
  – To settlement.
  – To trial
(e) An estimate of general and special damages specifying heads of damage. A broad estimate is acceptable if quantum is very complex or the prognosis unclear.
(f) Prospects of success in percentage terms.
(g) Likelihood of settlement
(j) Estimated date of final hearing
(k) Please submit copies of all reports, Notes of Conference or Counsel's Advice and Defendant's letter of response.

SETTLEMENT (STAGE 3)

Includes considering (preliminary?) quantum reports, instructing experts for meetings and revision of reports, making Part 36 offer, considering response, settlement meeting/negotiations.
  • **1 expert – £7,500**
  • **2 experts – £7,500–£10,000**
  • **3 experts – £12,500–£15,000**
  • **4 experts – £20,000**
  • **5 experts – £23,000**

For authorisation of the above sums please answer the following:

(a) Please provide a brief updated report on case including a brief summary of the defence theory, any formal or informal admissions and any other risk factors.
(b) Is the case proceeding by way of a split trial?
(c) Prospects of success (if case does not settle) in percentage terms.
(d) An estimate of costs:
  – To date
  – To settlement (stage 3)
  – To trial
(e) An estimate of general and special damages
(f) Please submit copy of Notes of Conference or Counsel's written Advice

TRIAL – FULL TRIAL OR LIABILITY ONLY (STAGE 4)

Includes PTR, finalising statements, conference, trial bundle, trial preparation, and attendance at trial.
  There is an assumption that in a 4/5 expert case, Leading Counsel may be involved and that a 5-day trial is likely.
  • **1 expert – £7,500–£10,000**
  • **2 experts – £12,500–£15,000**
  • **3 experts – £20,000–£30,000**
  • **4 experts – £37,500**
  • **5 experts – £42,000**

For authorisation of the above sums please answer the following:

(a) Please provide a brief updated report on case including a summary of key issues in dispute, any admissions, outcome of any settlement negotiations including details of offers made/rejected and any other risk factors.
(b) List all medical experts to attend trial and in relation to each:
 – Discipline and name
 – Issue they will address
 – Specific conclusion of each expert
 – Summary of defendant's expert's view.
(c) Prospects of success in percentage terms.
(d) An estimate of costs:
 – To date
 – To conclude trial (stage 4)
 – To conclude quantum trial if appropriate
(e) An estimate of general and special damages.
(f) Defendant's valuation of claim
(g) Prospects of beating any Part 36 offer and advice to client
(h) Please submit copies of joint expert reports and Notes of Conference or written Advice.

QUANTUM INVESTIGATIONS (STAGE 5)

Includes instructing experts, considering reports and defendant's reports, revision of reports, schedule of loss, indexation issues, conference, and settlement negotiations.

 • **8–10 quantum expert case – £36,000**

For authorisation of the above sum please answer the following:

(a) Please specify number and disciplines of experts
(b) Please detail any offers to settle and response
(c) An estimate of costs
 – To date
 – To conclude quantum investigations (stage 5)
 – To conclude the quantum trial

QUANTUM TRIAL (STAGE 6)

Includes PTR, finalising witness statements, conference, trial bundle, trial preparation, attend trial.

 • **8–10 quantum expert case and 5 day trial – £43,000**

For authorisation of the above sum please answer the following:

(a) Please specify number and disciplines of experts attending trial
(b) Please detail any offers to settle and response and likelihood of beating any Part 36 offer
(c) An estimate of costs:
 – To date
 – To conclude quantum trial (stage 6)
(d) Please submit claimant and defendant schedules of loss

Please note that the LSC is likely to authorise a maximum of £189,000 in total for a fully contested cerebral palsy case (split trial) with 5 liability and 10 quantum experts.

[*Published with the kind permission of the Legal Service Commission.*]

Practice Direction 19B
Group Litigation

This Practice Direction supplements Section III of Part 19

INTRODUCTION

1   This practice direction deals with group litigation where the multiple parties are claimants. Section III of Part 19 (group litigation orders) also applies where the multiple parties are defendants. The court will give such directions in such a case as are appropriate.

PRELIMINARY STEPS

2.1   Before applying for a Group Litigation Order ('GLO') the solicitor acting for the proposed applicant should consult the Law Society's Multi Party Action Information Service in order to obtain information about other cases giving rise to the proposed GLO issues.

2.2   It will often be convenient for the claimants' solicitors to form a Solicitors' Group and to choose one of their number to take the lead in applying for the GLO and in litigating the GLO issues. The lead solicitor's role and relationship with the other members of the Solicitors' Group should be carefully defined in writing and will be subject to any directions given by the court under CPR 19.13(c).

2.3   In considering whether to apply for a GLO, the applicant should consider whether any other order would be more appropriate. In particular he should consider whether, in the circumstances of the case, it would be more appropriate for –
    (1)   the claims to be consolidated; or
    (2)   the rules in Section II of Part 19 (representative parties) to be used.

APPLICATION FOR A GLO

3.1   An application for a GLO must be made in accordance with CPR Part 23, may be made at any time before or after any relevant claims have been issued and may be made either by a claimant or by a defendant.

3.2   The following information should be included in the application notice or in written evidence filed in support of the application:
    (1)   a summary of the nature of the litigation;
    (2)   the number and nature of claims already issued;
    (3)   the number of parties likely to be involved;
    (4)   the common issues of fact or law (the 'GLO issues') that are likely to arise in the litigation; and
    (5)   whether there are any matters that distinguish smaller groups of claims within the wider group.

3.3   A GLO may not be made –
   (1)   in the Queen's Bench Division, without the consent of the Lord Chief Justice,
   (2)   in the Chancery Division, without the consent of the Vice-Chancellor, or
   (3)   in a county court, without the consent of the Head of Civil Justice.

3.4   The court to which the application for a GLO is made will, if minded to make the GLO, send to the Lord Chief Justice, the Vice-Chancellor, or the Head of Civil Justice, as appropriate –
   (1)   a copy of the application notice,
   (2)   a copy of any relevant written evidence, and
   (3)   a written statement as to why a GLO is considered to be desirable.
   These steps may be taken either before or after a hearing of the application.

High Court in London

3.5   The application for the GLO should be made to the Senior Master in the Queen's Bench Division or the Chief Chancery Master in the Chancery Division. For claims that are proceeding or are likely to proceed in a specialist list, the application should be made to the senior judge of that list.

High Court outside London

3.6   Outside London, the application should be made to a Presiding Judge or a Chancery Supervising Judge of the Circuit in which the District Registry which has issued the application notice is situated.

County courts

3.7   The application should be made to the Designated Civil Judge for the area in which the county court which has issued the application notice is situated.

3.8   The applicant for a GLO should request the relevant court to refer the application notice to the judge by whom the application will be heard as soon as possible after the application notice has been issued. This is to enable the judge to consider whether to follow the practice set out in paragraph 3.4 above prior to the hearing of the application.

3.9   The directions under paragraphs 3.5, 3.6 and 3.7 above do not prevent the judges referred to from making arrangements for other judges to hear applications for GLOs when they themselves are unavailable.

GLO MADE BY COURT OF ITS OWN INITIATIVE
4   Subject to obtaining the appropriate consent referred to in paragraph 3.3 and the procedure set out in paragraph 3.4, the court may make a GLO of its own initiative. (CPR 3.3 deals with the procedure that applies when a court proposes to make an order of its own initiative)

THE GLO
5   CPR 19.11(2) and (3) set out rules relating to the contents of GLOs.

THE GROUP REGISTER

6.1   Once a GLO has been made a Group Register will be established on which will be entered such details as the court may direct of the cases which are to be subject to the GLO.

6.1A   A claim must be issued before it can be entered on a Group Register.

6.2   An application for details of a case to be entered on a Group Register may be made by any party to the case.

6.3   An order for details of the case to be entered on the Group Register will not be made unless the case gives rise to at least one of the GLO issues. (CPR 19.10 defines GLO issues)

6.4   The court, if it is not satisfied that a case can be conveniently case managed with the other cases on the Group Register, or if it is satisfied that the entry of the case on the Group Register would adversely affect the case management of the other cases, may refuse to allow details of the case to be entered on the Group Register, or order their removal from the Register if already entered, although the case gives rise to one or more of the Group issues.

6.5   The Group Register will normally be maintained by and kept at the court but the court may direct this to be done by the solicitor for one of the parties to a case entered on the Register.

6.6
   (1)   Rules 5.4 (Register of Claims), 5.4B (Supply of documents from court records – a party) and 5.4C (supply of documents from court records – a non-party) apply where the register is maintained by the court. A party to a claim on the group register may request documents relating to any other claim on the group register in accordance with rule 5.4 as if he were a party to those proceedings.
   (2)   Where the register is maintained by a solicitor, any person may inspect the Group Register during normal business hours and upon giving reasonable notice to the solicitor; the solicitor may charge a fee not exceeding the fee prescribed for a search at the court office.

6.7   In this paragraph, 'the court' means the management court specified in the GLO.

ALLOCATION TO TRACK
7   Once a GLO has been made and unless the management court directs otherwise:
   (1)   every claim in a case entered on the Group Register will be automatically allocated, or reallocated (as the case may be), to the multi-track;
   (2)   any case management directions that have already been given in any such case otherwise than by the management court will be set aside; and
   (3)   any hearing date already fixed otherwise than for the purposes of the group litigation will be vacated.

MANAGING JUDGE
8   A judge ('the managing judge') will be appointed for the purpose of the GLO as soon as possible. He will assume overall responsibility fo the management of the claims and will generally hear the GLO issues. A Master or a District Judge may be appointed to deal with procedural matters, which he will do in accordance with any directions given by the managing judge. A costs judge may be appointed and may be invited to attend case management hearings.

CLAIMS TO BE STARTED IN MANAGEMENT COURT
9.1   The management court may order that as from a specified date all claims that raise one or more of the GLO issues shall be started in the management court.

9.2   Failure to comply with an order made under paragraph 9.1 will not invalidate the commencement of the claim but the claim should be transferred to the management court and details entered on the Group Register as soon as possible. Any party to the claim may apply to the management court for an order under CPR 19.14 removing the case from the Register or, as the case may be, for an order that details of the case be not entered on the Register.

TRANSFER

10   Where the management court is a county court and a claim raising one or more of the GLO issues is proceeding in the High Court, an order transferring the case to the management court and directing the details of the case to be entered on the Group Register can only be made in the High Court.

PUBLICISING THE GLO

11   After a GLO has been made, a copy of the GLO should be supplied –
  (1)   to the Law Society, 113 Chancery Lane, London WC2A 1PL; and
  (2)   to the Senior Master, Queen's Bench Division, Royal Courts of Justice, Strand, London WC2A 2LL.

CASE MANAGEMENT

12.1   The management court may give case management directions at the time the GLO is made or subsequently. Directions given at a case management hearing will generally be binding on all claims that are subsequently entered on the Group Register (see CPR 19.12(1)).

12.2   Any application to vary the terms of the GLO must be made to the management court.

12.3   The management court may direct that one or more of the claims are to proceed as test claims.

12.4   The management court may give directions about how the costs of resolving common issues or the costs of claims proceeding as test claims are to be borne or shared as between the claimants on the Group Register.

CUT-OFF DATES

13   The management court may specify a date after which no claim may be added to the Group Register unless the court gives permission. An early cut-off date may be appropriate in the case of 'instant disasters' (such as transport accidents). In the case of consumer claims, and particularly pharmaceutical claims, it may be necessary to delay the ordering of a cut-off date.

STATEMENTS OF CASE

14.1   The management court may direct that the GLO claimants serve 'Group Particulars of Claim' which set out the various claims of all the claimants on the Group Register at the time the particulars are filed. Such particulars of claim will usually contain –
  (1)   general allegations relating to all claims; and
  (2)   a schedule containing entries relating to each individual claim specifying which of the general allegations are relied on and any specific facts relevant to the claimant.

14.2   The directions given under paragraph 14.1 should include directions as to whether the Group Particulars should be verified by a statement or statements of truth and, if so, by whom.

14.3   The specific facts relating to each claimant on the Group Register may be obtained by the use of a questionnaire. Where this is proposed, the management court should be asked to approve the questionnaire. The management court may direct that the questionnaires completed by individual claimants take the place of the schedule referred to in paragraph 14.1(2).

14.4   The management court may also give directions about the form that particulars of claim relating to claims which are to be entered on the Group Register should take.

THE TRIAL

15.1   The management court may give directions –
   (1)   for the trial of common issues; and
   (2)   for the trial of individual issues.

15.2   Common issues and test claims will normally be tried at the management court. Individual issues may be directed to be tried at other courts whose locality is convenient for the parties.

COSTS

16.1   CPR 48 contains rules about costs where a GLO has been made.

16.2   Where the court has made an order about costs in relation to any application or hearing which involved both –
   (1)   one or more of the GLO issues; and
   (2)   an issue or issues relevant only to individual claims;
and the court has not directed the proportion of the costs that is to relate to common costs and the proportion that is to relate to individual costs in accordance with rule 48.6A(5), the costs judge will make a decision as to the relevant proportions at or before the commencement of the detailed assessment of costs.

Appendix IX

Letters of instruction to expert

1 EXAMPLE LETTER OF INSTRUCTION TO CLAIMANT'S EXPERT

Our Ref: XXX/YYY/Z
Your Ref:

[Date] 2012

FIRST CLASS
Dr CCC
[address]

Private and Confidential

Dear Dr CCC,
Mr XXX
ADDRESS:
DOB:

I refer to previous correspondence regarding this matter. You wrote on .... confirming that you could report in this case. I now enclose my instructions to you to prepare a report on [liability and/or causation and/or condition and prognosis].

Accordingly, I now enclose the following documents to assist you in preparing your report(s):-
1 Chronology
2 Medical records
   (a) GP records
   (b) ....
   (c) ....
3 Statement of ....
4 Protocols/Guidelines
5 Draft previous reports obtained (if relevant)
6 Complaint documentation

Some general issues

As I am sure you appreciate, it is partly on the basis of your report that a decision will be taken about the prospects of successful litigation for Mr XXX. Therefore the report needs to address the medical treatment received with reference to the legal tests that we have to meet to pursue a claim successfully. The legal tests require that we establish at least one incident of breach of duty, or substandard treatment, and then that that breach caused an injury to the Claimant. Even if an injury was not wholly the result of substandard care it is possible to argue that it was materially contributed to by the breach. The test is whether the breach's contribution to the Claimant's injuries was more than insignificant.

In order to establish breach we must show that the investigation or treatment in question probably fell below medically acceptable standards of a reasonably competent practitioner in the relevant field practicing at the relevant time. To establish causation we must show that any substandard treatment probably caused or materially contributed to the injury sustained.

You will be aware that it is a defence to an allegation of professional negligence to show that a substantial body of reputable practitioners in the relevant field at the relevant time would have carried out the treatment the same way that the Defendant did in this case. However the Courts look to our experts to provide evidence-based support for their opinions as to why a treatment may be substandard, and so providing academic texts etc as well as your advice on whether a method of treatment adopted was reasonable to use is very helpful.

Thus the test for assessing criticisms of Dr YYY's treatment will be whether the allegations can be justified on the balance of probabilities, ie is it more likely than not that the treatment fell below a medically acceptable standard.

I would be grateful if in your report you could refer to at least one contemporary academic published standard for each main criticism of Dr YYY's technique and where referring to such text(s) please provide a copy of the whole of the chapter(s) from which your reference(s) is extracted along with a copy of the front sheet showing details of the author, publisher and date of publication.

I have provided you with my client's statement. In forming your opinion on issues of liability and causation please consider my client's version of events as accurate. If you find for any reason that you are unable to do so, please advise any specific comments which you have discounted and why this was necessary.

If after your review you are of the opinion that a medical expert in a field other than your own should be asked to report in order to examine further issues of liability or causation, please state so specifically in your report so I can advise my client and consider appropriate next steps.

In terms of expert immunity from being sued, I am sure that you have heard of the case of *Jones* v *Kaney*, where the Supreme Court abolished the immunity from suit for breach of duty by expert witnesses in relation to their participation in legal proceedings. I would like to reassure you that your duty to the client and the Court remains unchanged, to perform your function as an expert with the reasonable skill and care of an expert drawn from the relevant discipline. This includes a duty to perform the overriding duty of assisting the Court. The Court held in *Jones* that:

> If the expert gives an independent and unbiased opinion which is within the range of reasonable expert opinions, he will have discharged his duty both to the court and his client.

(Lord Dyson SCJJ).

The Court went on to find that in this case the expert had no immunity from being sued. As a consequence you need to carry indemnity insurance to cover you for carrying out medico-legal work. It would be appreciated if you could confirm that you do hold such cover.

Finally, this report will not be disclosed to the Defendant. It is a preliminary report intended for myself, my client and counsel if or when instructed as an indication of the evidence you would give if it became necessary to call you as an expert witness.

History of treatment

[Refer expert to relevant documents and highlight here the key aspects of the treatment that you want him to focus on, or that you think are particularly important, making clear why you hold that opinion.]

INSTRUCTIONS
Report on liability

Would you please comment in general on the standard of care of the medical management and treatment given to Mr XXX by Dr YYY, summarising those aspects of his treatment which you feel relevant to this particular claim. It is of course essential for this claim to be successful that I establish causation ie was any failure in the treatment of Mr XXX's condition the probable cause of his pain and suffering. Therefore wherever you identify substandard care can you advise what treatment should have been provided, and what difference that may have made to the patient.

Please also consider the following particular issues [*examples of issues to be raised follow*]:

1   Was any aspect of the treatment provided inappropriate? If yes, would you please describe that treatment and on what grounds you advise that that treatment should not have been provided. What difference would it have made if different treatment had been provided?
2   Was there any omission of treatment, eg should they have ....
     and if they had would that have led to a different outcome?
3   Was there a failure to adequately diagnose or recognise ....?
     If the condition had been diagnosed earlier, what action should have been taken, and what difference would that have made to the Claimant?
4   Do you think there are any consent issues here? Was Mr XXX adequately consented with respect to the treatment that was provided, and were there any known risks of it that he should have been warned of? Also was there any alternative treatment he could have had that carried less risk, and that he was not advised of?
5   Do you think there was any aspect of the aftercare provided to Mr XXX that fell below a medically acceptable standard?

If you are of the opinion that Mr XXX's care was managed negligently in any respect would you also consider the possible arguments that may be raised by the Defendant. For instance, what reason could the other side be expected to use to back up an argument that the treatment carried out in this case was appropriate.

Report on condition and prognosis

I would like you to also arrange to see my client in order to prepare a condition and prognosis report. This should be a stand alone document from the report(s) on liability and causation, as if proceedings are commenced this report will be served on the Defendant with the pleadings.

In considering Mr XXX's condition and prognosis please could you advise on the following:

[Set out questions regarding the impact of the injuries and how severe they are.]

I have raised a number of questions in my instructions to you. However, there may be issues that I have not raised that you feel should be considered. If so please raise these in your report. If there are any aspects of this case that you would like to discuss with me before finalising your report please do not hesitate to contact me.

Finally, I would be grateful if you or your secretary could confirm receipt of these instructions and all the documents so that I know you have received everything

safely. I thank you for accepting instructions and look forward to hearing from you further.
Yours sincerely

2   EXAMPLE LETTER OF INSTRUCTION TO DEFENDANT'S EXPERT
Our Ref:
Your Ref: YYY/ZZZ/1

[Date] 2012

FIRST CLASS
Dr DDD
[address]

Private and Confidential

**REPORT REQUIRED BY [DATE] ON
[BREACH OF DUTY/CAUSATION/CONDITION AND PROGNOSIS]**

Dear Dr DDD,
Mr YYY
ADDRESS:
DOB:
I am instructed by .... to act on behalf of the Defendant, ..., to investigate allegations of clinical negligence by the above named Claimant, ... The Claimant alleges the Trust was negligent in that it ....

I am grateful to you for confirming that you are able to accept instructions on behalf of the trust to consider the allegations and report on by [insert date].

Factual background

....

Procedural background

....

Breach of duty

I refer you to the allegations in the Claimant's witness statement [if Defendant – Letter of Claim/Particulars of Claim] dated .... where the Claimant alleges ....

Causation

It is alleged that but for the Trust's negligence ....

The law

As you are aware, in order to succeed in any clinical negligence claim, the Claimant must show:
(a) the Defendant [clinician/nurse/midwife] breached their duty of care to the Claimant by failing to provide the required standard of care; and
(b) their breach of duty caused injury, loss or damage.

It is a defence to any allegation of professional negligence to show a responsible body of opinion would have treated the Claimant in the same way. The term '*responsible*' means the Court must be satisfied the body of opinion relied upon can demonstrate the opinion has a logical basis. Furthermore, in terms of the standard to be applied, it is the standard of care applicable at the time of the incident [insert year] rather than the standard of care applicable at the time you write your report.

If the Claimant cannot show that on the balance of probabilities (more than 50% likely) that but for the alleged breach of duty he would have avoided injury, the claim will fail as causation will not be established.

Documents

I enclose copies of the following documents for your consideration:

Volume One
Pleadings (if available)
Claim Form dated ....
Particulars of Claim dated ....
Schedule of Loss dated ....
Claimant's expert evidence
Condition and prognosis report of [insert discipline] dated ....
Letter from [insert discipline] dated ....
Defendant's evidence (not disclosed)
Condition and prognosis report of [insert discipline] dated ....
Letter from [insert discipline] dated ....
Miscellaneous
Guidelines for experts
Letter from Tom Fothergill (NHS Litigation Authority's Director of Finance) regarding experts' fees

Volumes Two and Three: medical records
Claimant's GP records
Claimant's medical records from King's College Hospital NHS Foundation Trust medical records
2 × CD-Rom of Radiography

Instructions

I should be grateful if you would please consider the Claimant's medical records and report on [the standard of care the CLaimant received from the Trust and whether, on the balance of probabilities, this has caused the Claimant's current condition]. In particular, I should be grateful if you would provide comments on the following:

It is important your report is supported by medical literature where relevant. I should be grateful if you would attach a list of references, together with copies of any extracts to your report.

As you know, your report may be disclosed to the Claimant [and/or Co-Defendant] and you may need to attend a conference with counsel in due course. More importantly please bear in mind when preparing your evidence that you may be required to give evidence at trial and be cross examined on the contents of your report.

[The documents in enclosure .... are privileged from disclosure to the Claimant's solicitors. Please do not refer to them in your report unless your opinion is based on this document.]

I confirm my client will be responsible for your reasonable fees in preparing your report.

Statement of truth

It is a requirement of the Civil Procedure Rules that your report must be verified by a Statement of Truth in the following form:

> I confirm that I have made clear which facts and matters referred to in this report are within my own knowledge and which are not. Those that are within my own knowledge I confirm to be true. The opinions I have expressed represent my true and complete professional opinions on the matters to which they refer.

I should be grateful to receive your report by .... If this deadline causes difficulty, please advise me at your earliest opportunity. If you require any additional information or documentation, please do not hesitate to contact me.

Please kindly acknowledge safe receipt of these instructions by email.

Thank you again for your assistance and I look forward to receiving your report by ....

Kind regards.

Yours sincerely

....

Enc

Example of an agenda for the experts

IN THE HIGH COURT OF JUSTICE
QUEENS BENCH DIVISION
(IF ANY DISTRICT REGISTERY)

XXX

Claimant

-and-
YYY

Defendant

AGENDA FOR [INSERT] EXPERTS

1   **Objectives**
    The purpose of the discussion is to assist the Parties, their solicitors and the Court to identify:
    (a) the extent of agreement between the experts;
    (b) the points of disagreement and the reasons for disagreement;
    (c) any further material points not raised in the Agenda, and the extent to which there is agreement or disagreement with respect to them;
    (d) the steps, if any, which might usefully be taken by the parties, with a view to resolving the outstanding points of disagreement.
    This Agenda is intended to provide a guide to the experts' discussion. It is not intended to be exhaustive and the experts should feel free to discuss any other issue that they consider to be relevant.

2   **Basic legal principles**
    (a) When considering the answers to the questions relating to the standard of care or management, regard should be had to the standards applicable at the relevant time and not (if different) to the standards of the present day.
    (b) The actions of medical or nursing staff should be judged by the standards of the 'reasonably competent' practitioner; substandard management is therefore management which falls below that to be expected from the 'reasonably' competent practitioner; alternatively it is management which would not be adopted or condoned by a 'responsible body of professional opinion' in the particular field.

(c) A 'material contribution' to injury or damage is a contribution which is not 'de minimis' and is therefore a contribution which is of more than trifling importance.

(d) When an answer depends on facts which are understood to be in dispute, that should be expressly indicated, and it should be explained whether (and, if so, to what extent) the answer would be different, if the facts were different.

(e) When considering causation or questions of hypothetical fact (eg what might the findings or outcome have been if certain steps had been taken) the question should be answered on the balance of probabilities – 'what probably would have been found/happened'. The Court considers an event or outcome to have been a probability if there was a greater than 50% chance that it would have occurred, so the approach should be 'what is more likely than not to have been found/happened'. Certainty is not required nor expected.

(f) No attempt should be made by any expert to deal with matters outside that expert's particular area of expertise.

(g) It should be remembered that the experts' overriding duty is to the Court, and not to the party instructing him or her.

(h) It is not intended that the experts should arrive at a compromised view during the discussion or otherwise attempt to 'settle the case'.

3   Outcome

At the beginning of the discussion one of the experts should be nominated to prepare the experts' joint statement for the Court, recording the conclusion of each part of the discussion. At the end of the discussion the joint statement should be signed by each individual participating in the discussion, setting out in respect of each question (whether arising from the agenda or because it has been separately identified by the experts as being material):

(a) those matters on which there is agreement as to the answer;

(b) those matters on which there is disagreement and a summary of the reasons for disagreement;

(c) a note of any steps which might usefully be taken by the Parties to resolve any areas of disagreement;

(d) any further material points not raised in the Agenda and the extent to which those issues are agreed.

A copy of the joint statement should be signed by both experts and forwarded to their instructing solicitors within seven days of the experts' discussion.

QUESTIONS THAT THE PARTIES WOULD LIKE TO BE ADDRESSED BY THE EXPERTS

1

2

3

4

etc

[dd.mm.yyyy]

Index

All references are to page numbers.